ART
MUSEUMS
OF THE
WORLD

ART MUSEUMS OF THE WORLD

Afghanistan–Nigeria

VIRGINIA JACKSON
Editor-in-Chief

MARLENE A. PALMER and ERIC M. ZAFRAN
Associate Editors

ANN STEPHENS JACKSON
Assistant Editor

INTRODUCTION by JAMES L. CONNELLY
Advisory Editor

GREENWOOD PRESS
NEW YORK • WESTPORT, CONNECTICUT • LONDON

Library of Congress Cataloging-in-Publication Data
Main entry under title:

Art museums of the world.

Bibliography: p.
Includes index.
Contents: v. 1 Afghanistan–Nigeria————v. 2 Norway–Zaire.
1. Art museums.   I. Jackson, Virginia.
N410.A78   1987   708   85-5578
ISBN 0-313-21322-4 (lib. bdg. : set : alk paper)
ISBN 0-313-25876-7 (lib. bdg. : v. 1 : alk paper)
ISBN 0-313-25877-5 (lib. bdg. : v. 2 : alk paper)

R   708
ART

Copyright © 1987 by Virginia Jackson, Marlene A.
Palmer, Eric M. Zafran, and James L. Connelly

Library of Congress Catalog Card Number: 85-5578
ISBN 0-313-21322-4 (lib. bdg. : set : alk paper)
ISBN 0-313-25876-7 (lib. bdg. : v. 1 : alk paper)
ISBN 0-313-25877-5 (lib. bdg. : v. 2 : alk paper)

First published in 1987

Greenwood Press, Inc.
88 Post Road West
Westport, Connecticut 06881

Printed in the United States of America

The paper used in this book complies with the
Permanent Paper Standard issued by the National
Information Standards Organization (Z39.48-1984).

10 9 8 7 6 5 4 3 2 1

Contents

Contributors   vii

Preface   xi

Acknowledgments   xv

Introduction: An Imposing Presence—The Art Museum and Society   1

Entries   26

Glossary of Terms   1505

Selected Bibliography   1517

Index   1543

About the Contributors   1665

Contributors

PHILIP R. ADAMS (Cincinnati, Ohio, USA)
BARBARA C. ANDERSON (Mexico)
GRETCHEN ANDERSON (Austria)
MARTHA SHIPMAN ANDREWS (Philadelphia, Pa., USA)
EMMANUEL N. ARINZE (Nigeria)
JULIA F. BALDWIN (Toledo, Ohio, USA)
ELIZABETH COURTNEY BANKS (Greece)
LEAH TOURKIN BAR-Z'EV (Israel)
MARJORIE HARTH BEEBE (Detroit, Mich., USA)
DANIEL P. BIEBUYCK (Belgium)
ILARIA BIGNAMINI (Italy)
KAREN L. BLANK (Australia)
CAROLINE R. BOYLE-TURNER (France)
CLAUDIA BROWN (Taiwan)
LORRIE BUNKER (San Francisco, Calif., USA)
CHIRA CHONGKOL (Thailand)
TADEUSZ CHRUŚCICKI (Poland)
ELLEN P. CONANT (Japan)
MICHAEL P. CONFORTI (Minneapolis, Minn., USA)
JAMES L. CONNELLY (Introduction; France)
ROBERT E. CONRAD (Brazil)
URSULA E. CONRAD (Brazil; German Democratic Republic)
GLEN COOKE (Australia)
EUSTATHIA P. COSTOPOULOS (France)
SAMUEL P. COWARDIN III (Worcester, Mass., USA)
THOMAS J. DENZLER (New York, N.Y., USA)
FELICITY DEVLIN (Ireland)
CARLOS F. DUARTE (Venezuela)

BURTON L. DUNBAR III (The Netherlands; Kansas City, Mo., USA)
NANCY HATCH DUPREE (Afghanistan)
ANN E. EDWARDS (Cleveland, Ohio, USA)
PATRICIA J. FISTER (Japan)
AGNES ANN FITZGIBBONS (Denmark)
GERALDINE E. FOWLE (France; UK)
ELLEN K. FOX (Italy)
ANN GALONSKA (Hartford, Conn., USA)
SUZANNE GARRIGUES (Colombia; Mexico)
ANDREA GASTEN (The Netherlands)
SUZANNE E. GAYNOR (UK)
DEBORAH A. GRIBBON (Boston, Mass., USA)
MARILYN GRIDLEY (Kansas City, Mo., USA)
ELEANOR GURALNICK (Germany, Federal Republic of; Greece; Italy)
CHURLMO HAHN (Korea)
WILLIAM HAUPTMAN (Switzerland)
MOLLY SIUPING HO (People's Republic of China)
NILS G. HÖKBY (Sweden)
PETER HUGHES (UK)
ALICE R. M. HYLAND (Japan; Kansas City, Mo., USA)
DAVID A JAFFÉ (Australia)
REINHILD G.A.G. JANZEN (Germany, Federal Republic of; German
Democratic Republic)
FLORA S. KAPLAN (Nigeria)
LORRAINE KARAFEL (Austria; Greece; Italy; The Netherlands; Switzerland;
Turkey; UK; Brooklyn, N.Y., USA; New York, N.Y., USA; The Vatican)
VIRGINIA M. KERR (Chicago, Ill., USA)
DUNCAN KINKEAD (Spain)
CHRISTIAN M. KLEMM (Switzerland)
CHRISTOPHER A. KNIGHT (Los Angeles, Calif., USA)
RUTH E. KOLARIK (Yugoslavia)
ELLEN JOHNSTON LAING (People's Republic of China)
JAN MERLIN LANCASTER (Washington, D.C., USA)
ELLEN G. LANDAU (Washington, D.C., USA)
CYNTHIA LAWRENCE (Belgium; The Netherlands)
WILLIAM R. LEVIN (Italy)
FELICIA LEWANDOWSKI (Italy)
BARBARA B. LIPTON (Newark, N.J., USA)
YVONNE A. LUKE (France; UK)
JUDITH A. McCANDLESS (Houston, Tex., USA)
LAWRENCE J. McCRANK (Spain)
WENDY H. McFARLAND (Sarasota, Fla., USA)
JANET MacGAFFEY (Zaire)
LETHA E. McINTIRE (People's Republic of China)

DIANNE SACHKO MACLEOD (San Francisco, Calif., USA)
REKHA MORRIS (India)
FRANCIS D. MURNAGHAN, JR. (Ireland)
SEAN B. MURPHY (Canada)
DIANE M. NEMEC-IGNASHEV (USSR)
ROBERT NEUMAN (Italy)
MARTINA R. NORELLI (USSR)
GREGORY OLSON (Germany, Federal Republic of; Italy)
GABRIELLE G. PALMER (Ecuador)
SAMUEL PAZ (Argentina)
ELINOR L. PEARLSTEIN (People's Republic of China; Cleveland, Ohio, USA)
MARLA F. PRATHER (Fort Worth, Tex., USA)
CARMEN QUINTANA (Spain)
DONALD RABINER (Italy; Pasadena, Calif., USA)
RONALD D. RARICK (UK)
TARA K. REDDI (New York, N.Y., USA)
GEORGINE SZALAY REED (Hungary)
CATHARINE H. ROEHRIG (Egypt)
ERNEST AUGUST ROHDENBURG III (Boston, Mass., USA)
NOVELENE ROSS (St. Louis, Mo., USA)
ANDRZEJ ROTTERMUND (Poland)
RENATA RUTLEDGE (Germany, Federal Republic of; New York, N.Y., USA;
Washington, D.C., USA)
RONNIE J. SCHERER (Italy)
MARILEE SCHMIT (Ecuador)
RAYMOND V. SCHODER (Greece)
GYDE VANIER SHEPHERD (Canada)
RANDI E. SHERMAN (Spain)
ROBERT B. SIMON (Italy)
CAROL HYNNING SMITH (France; Baltimore, Md., USA)
JUDITH BERG SOBRÉ (Spain)
THOMAS W. SOKOLOWSKI (Italy)
ADRIANA SOLDI (Peru)
MARIE SPIRO (Tunisia)
FRAUKE STEENBOCK (Germany, Federal Republic of)
KATE STEINWAY (Hartford, Conn., USA)
ANDREA STONE (Guatemala)
EDWARD J. SULLIVAN (Portugal; Rumania)
MARSHA TAJIMA (Japan; Boston, Mass., USA; Philadelphia, Pa., USA)
RENÉ TAYLOR (Ponce, Puerto Rico, USA)
GERARD C. C. TSANG (Hong Kong)
NNENNAYA SAMUEL UKWU (Nigeria)
PILAR VILADAS (New York, N.Y., USA)
STEPHEN VOLLMER (Argentina)

BRET WALLER (Norway)
STEPHEN H. WHITNEY (France; Switzerland)
MARY LOUISE WOOD (France; Switzerland; UK; Baltimore, Md., USA)
DAVID A. YOUNG (Canada)
PATRICK YOUNGBLOOD (UK)
ERIC M. ZAFRAN (Norfolk, Va., USA; Washington, D.C., USA)
RUTH ZIEGLER (Germany, Federal Republic of)

Preface

Many guides to art museums have appeared within the past two decades. Most of these publications offer brief descriptive entries on the institutions included, and most are confined to museums of a single country. Some of the guides to the museums of a specific nation are valuable and offer a wealth of useful information, but they are not comprehensive in international terms. This work, which is neither a guide nor a directory, was formulated as a response to a need for a serious research source offering scholarly articles on the history and collections of the world's major museums. *Art Museums of the World* is intended as a reference tool for readers seeking information and bibliographic guidance on the most important of the world's museums, as well as in the areas of museum history and museology.

There are many thousands of art museums in the world, and a selection of a few hundred of them for inclusion in this publication constituted one of the editorial board's greatest challenges. Initially, approximately one hundred institutions were included automatically for self-evident reasons: the Louvre, the Metropolitan Museum of Art, and the Vatican Museums are examples. Following them, choices made were based on the museum's international or national importance in terms of the quality, breadth, and depth of its collections. Museums devoted to the work of a single artist were not included. Outstanding and famous museums specializing in the work of a particular period—ancient, medieval, or modern art—have been included. Some libraries contain important collections of manuscripts and other art objects but were considered to fall outside the scope of this publication. Some small and highly specialized museums, admittedly exquisite, were omitted. At this point, a different editorial board might have made different selections, and perhaps no two people would ever produce identical lists of the most important art museums in the world. The selections presented here are the result of careful consideration of many factors, most particularly an effort on the part of the editorial board to include those museums about which readers would be most likely to seek information.

In eighteenth-century Europe, which gave birth to both the concept of the museum and its first realities, the word *art* was generally understood to mean painting and formal sculpture and architecture of the Western world. During the late nineteenth century, and certainly in the twentieth century, the concept of what constitutes "art" was gradually extended. In this context, some of the institutions included in *Art Museums of the World* are officially and technically museums of archaeology or ethnology, but no one would contest the fact that they must also be regarded as art museums of primary significance.

For the purpose of this publication, a *museum* is a building in which art objects are collected, preserved, and displayed. If a museum building is of particular historical or architectural importance, these facts are discussed. Buildings housing works of art in situ, such as the Sistine Chapel, are not included in this reference work. The editors regret the fact that some museums in some parts of the world could not be included because of political and practical circumstances, lack of substantive and reliable information, and the impossibility of finding expert contributors.

Museums are not static institutions and many of them have undergone substantial and substantive changes in recent years. New wings have been built, the presentation of collections has been altered, new collections have been introduced, and new acquisitions are always being added. Some of the information presented in some entries is based on data concerning the institutions as they existed at the beginning of this project and may not include important changes. But the editorial board and contributors have made every effort to revise entries where necessary and to make them as accurate and current as possible.

Some European nations are so rich in art museums that selection for inclusion here was particularly difficult. In such cases, the editors tended to choose the most well-known and internationally recognized museums, although they are not necessarily the largest or most comprehensive institutions. The pattern of collecting and museum development in some European countries has produced a variety of specialized museums of the highest quality (museums of ancient art, galleries of painting only, period museums), and from among these museums the board has made representative selections reflecting the most significant of them.

A majority of the entries are concerned with European and American museums. The reasons for this preponderance are manifold and can best be explained through an understanding of the development of the art museum as a social and cultural entity.

The concept of the art museum was European in origin. Social and educational structures and historical patterns of collecting and funding have produced an almost bewildering wealth of art museums in Europe and the United States. In many parts of the world, the art museum is a relatively new phenomenon. James

L. Connelly traces the history of the museum and of museology in general in the Introduction to this book.

Each article in *Art Museums of the World* is entered alphabetically by country, city, and name of institution, generally in English, since this work is primarily for use by English-speaking readers. Variants of the name of the museum, its official title in the vernacular, and the address are given at the head of the entry. Entries include the history of the museum with development of the collections, the administrative structure and funding of the museum (when known), a selective analysis of its collections, and a select bibliography of museum publications and references from other sources.

Most museums, particularly those in the Western world, have extensive education and exhibition programs. For this reason, materials on these two aspects of the institutions are limited, and the entries focus largely on information about the permanent collections that make each museum unique. For the use of students and scholars, facts about library facilities and the availability of slides and photographs are given.

The Introduction provides a bibliography on the history of museums and collecting, and a general bibliography on museums and museology, arranged by subject, is given at the end of the work. An extensive glossary is included as well.

When practical, diacritical markings have been retained, as in the entries on the Indian museums and those in Poland and Hungary. Transliteration from the Russian follows the Library of Congress system. After careful consideration and consultation with specialists, it was decided to keep the familiar Wade-Giles romanization of Chinese names and words. The official Pinyin is used as well in the names and addresses of each Chinese museum.

Although editors attempted to assure accuracy and consistency within and among the many entries, the challenge of processing so much data was complicated by the fact that much of it was written in other languages and translated or was written in English by persons not fluent in the English language. Furthermore, much of the material was based on primary and in situ sources available to the contributor but not usually to the editors, a circumstance that made clarification extremely difficult. In certain cases, material was rewritten or edited to satisfy stringent space requirements and to attempt to provide some structural balance.

For any errors the editors offer their apologies to the contributors; the museums, galleries, and collections; and, of course, the reader. Corrections sent to us in care of the publisher will be kept on file pending future printings or editions.

Information regarding the many talented and industrious contributors is available in the section About the Contributors. We want to thank all of them for the work they have done, the diligence they have exhibited, the enthusiasm they have shown for the project, and the cooperation and encouragement they have given, particularly to the editor-in-chief. In the continuing effort to keep the articles accurate and current, we have had to go back to many of the authors, who have responded promptly and with patience. When a contributor could not provide this information, the public relations departments of many museums (especially in the United States) replied to our queries with courtesy and interest. Indeed, many museum staff members have aided not only the editors but the authors, and we thank them sincerely.

For the selection process we gratefully acknowledge the suggestions and help of outstanding scholars in their respective specialties: Professors Stephen Addiss, Elizabeth Banks, Pramod Chandra, Robert Engass, Annette Juliano, Edward Masser, Miyeko Murase, Dr. Donald Goodall and Elizabeth Boone. Those who were kind enough to read entries in their areas of expertise include Professors Pomrod Chandra, Annette Juliano, Edward Sullivan and Dr. Robert Simon, to whom we are most grateful. Three people whose contributions to this work cannot be overestimated are Pamela Kingsbury, Patricia M. Young and Gretchen Anderson, all of whom acted as volunteer field editors in suggesting names of art historians who might be interested in contributing to this project.

Without the faith, support, and guidance of our editor at Greenwood Press, Marilyn Brownstein, this work would have floundered mid-stream, and to her we owe our deepest debt of thanks. Virginia Jackson and Marlene Palmer want to recognize the constant help, advice, and support in many ways of their husbands, Ira J. Jackson and Harold D. Palmer.

Acknowledgments

The editors want to acknowledge the generous help and assistance that was given by the following persons to our many contributors: Mrs. J. E. Asselman, Dr. Ellinoor Bergvelt, Mrs. Gertrude Borghero, Mev. Leen de Jong, Dr. Simon de Pury, René De Roo, Dr. Eliane De Wilde, Dr. A. L. den Blaauwen, Janis Ekdahl, Fang Xiaolian, Sarah Fraser, Gao Jinglin, Georgia Herring, Stanley Hess, H. R. Hoetink, Gail Hutchinson, Dr. A. Janssens de Bisthoven, John Kefferstan, Dr. Hannelore Kersting, Professor Alison Kettering, J. B. Kist, Dr. Jan Piet Filedt Kok, Sonia Krug, Sandor Kuthy, Mrs. M. Lammertse-Cats, Sidney Lawrence, Nora Ling-yun Shih Liu, Robert Little, Dr. Richard Marks, Meir Meyer, Dr. Micheline Moisan, Vivian Broman Morales, Léone Nora, Rao Xingyi, Dr. Myra Rosenfeld, Susan Tourkin-Komet, Nicole Schouten, Dr. Pauline Lunsingh Schuerleer, Gary D. Schwartz, Loekie Schwartz-Hendriks, David Scrase, Linda Shearouse, Dr. James Shedel, Dr. Lisbeth Staehlin, Ellen Stanley, Barbara Stephen, Sun Chuanxian, Carol Troyen, Gerard van der Hoek, Mrs. E. van der Vossen-Delbrück, Professor Dr. Evert van Uitert, Mrs. E. H. Verheus, Dr. Christian von Holst, Dr. W. H. Vroom, Katherine Warwick, Wu Bolun, and Xie Suilian.

ART
MUSEUMS
OF THE
WORLD

Introduction: An Imposing Presence—The Art Museum and Society

by James L. Connelly

Museums have become so much a part of the fabric and culture of the modern world that their presence is taken for granted. Museums of every kind are to be found in bewildering numbers and great diversity, especially in the Western world. Historical museums, museums of natural history, anthropological and ethnological museums, art museums, and museums of science are the largest and most complex types of museums, but modern interest in museums has also produced a wide variety of small and highly specialized institutions. Large cities take pride in the number and richness of their museums and use such institutions as a means of attracting flows of visitors. Every national capital regards its national museums—and especially its national museum of art—as essential marks of prestige that reflect the country's heritage, culture, and civilization in a highly public and literally visible manner.

The term *art museum* in itself encompasses an area of great breadth. Art museums range in size and scope of collections from monumental and comprehensive institutions such as the Metropolitan Museum of Art (q.v.) in New York and the Louvre (q.v.) in Paris to small and intimate museums such as the Nissim de Camondo in Paris, an important collection of eighteenth-century French furniture and decorative arts arranged in what was once a private house. Some museums of art display only paintings or prints, or decorative arts, or even a category within the decorative arts, such as glass or ceramics. Other museums confine their acquisitions and exhibitions to a particular period, such as medieval art or the art of antiquity. During the past fifty years there has been a marked increase in the number of museums devoted exclusively to the work of a single artist. The broader definition of the term *art* that has developed in the nineteenth and twentieth centuries has created museums of folk art and requires that large sections of archaeological and ethnological museums must now be considered art museums. This wide range in size and type of art museums reflects both the complexity of civilizations and increasing awareness of that complexity and is also a manifestation of modern response to the concept of the art museum and easy accessibility to art by the general public. Such a concept and such accessibility, however, are relatively new in the cultural history of the world: the idea of the public museum of art is scarcely more than two centuries old, and most museums are far younger.

The proliferation of art museums and the overwhelmingly large and varied collections of many of them has actually produced adverse reactions and some warnings about the value of the museum as a cultural and social institution. The great Spanish philosopher, José Ortega y Gasset, tended to see the art museum as the cold repository of dead civilizations:

> In the museum we find the lacquered corpse of an evolution. Here is the flux of that pictorial anxiety which has budded forth from man century after century. To conserve this evolution, it has had to be undone, broken up, converted into fragments again and congealed as in a refrigerator. Each picture is a crystal with unmistakable and rigid edges, separated from the others, a hermetic island.[1]

André Malraux, one of the most important literary figures of twentieth-century France, also had reservations about art museums. Malraux was always intensely interested in the visual arts and was minister of culture in the de Gaulle government. He readily conceded that "a museum is one of the places that show man at his noblest," but he was acutely aware of the limitations of even the greatest museums: objects are isolated from their original context and meaning; even very large collections are incomplete in terms of the whole and have significant deficiencies; museums can neither acquire nor display important elements of the world's art and can therefore offer only a "mutilated possible."[2] As early as 1798, which is a very early date in the history of museums, the possible distortions created by the dislocation of works of art and their concentration in museums provoked a brooding response from no less a personage than the great Goethe, Germany's pre-eminent philosopher and writer:

> For the education of the artist, for the pleasure of the art patron, where works of art are to be found has never been of great importance. There was a time when, with few exceptions, works of art remained generally in the same location and place. However, now a great change has occurred that, in general as well as specifically, will have important consequences for art. Perhaps there is more cause than ever before to realize that Italy as it existed until recently was a great art entity. Were it possible to give a general survey, it could then be demonstrated what the world has now lost when so many parts have been torn from this immense and ancient totality. What has been destroyed by the removal of these parts will remain forever a secret.[3]

Goethe was reacting specifically to the fact that vast numbers of works of art from all over Europe, but especially from Italy, were being taken to Paris as a result of the conquests of France's triumphant Revolutionary armies; but the concerns expressed by the German philosopher at the end of the eighteenth century are similar to those expressed by France's own Malraux 150 years later. The dislocation of great quantities of varied art and its arbitrary reassemblage elsewhere that Goethe witnessed during the Revolutionary and Napoleonic periods was a new phenomenon, at least on such a scale. Since Goethe's day, however, this kaleidoscopic fragmentation and rearrangement of art in new patterns has intensified enormously, although primarily by purchase rather than by military conquest.

Goethe was also conscious of the intimidating nature of great art collections and the fact that they can fatigue the intellect and stupefy the senses simply by virtue of the prestige and numbers of the objects to be seen. Indeed, Goethe considered the idea that museums might inhibit or even stifle the creativity of artists: "One blames libraries and galleries, which through their imposing presence, through a certain incoherent intrusion upon the human spirit, are more detrimental than beneficial to the pure development of talent."[4] This theme was reiterated recently in a series of six Mellon Lectures by Jacques Barzun that constitute a provocative analysis, by a distinguished cultural historian, of the place and destiny of art in the modern world. Like Goethe, Barzun stated that, "At the same time, advanced civilizations are bound to suffer from their long memory, their piling up of artifacts and ideas—the dreadful clutter that Balzac depicted in the curiosity shop of his *Peau de chagrin*."[5] He also believes that we have "become gluttons for art and have lost all restraints about its uses," and that the modern world, inundated by art of all kinds and from every quarter, produces, collects, and presents so much art that "there is too much to sort out, let alone assimilate."[6] The thousands of art museums that have come into being in the past two hundred years, their richness and astonishing variety, and the enormity of some of them are factors that have indeed created certain kinds of fragmented visual "clutter" and cultural disorientation clearly perceived by Goethe, Malraux, and Barzun but recognized instinctively by anyone who has visited an art museum of even moderate size.

But the doubts of philosophers and the hesitations of critics about art museums have meant little; by the middle of the eighteenth century, the public yearned for museums accessible to it and responded enthusiastically to the few museums and galleries that were established in Europe before 1800. The enthusiasm of that response grew and widened in the nineteenth century and has in no way diminished in the twentieth century. Collecting preceded museums, however, and the holdings of most museums, now greatly augmented by donation and purchase, are based on collections that were originally private or royal. During the Late Middle Ages and the Renaissance, European kings and princes began to assemble large collections of varied objects, including art. A prime example of such a princely collector was Jean, duc de Berry (1340–1416), brother to Charles V of France, whose insatiable appetite for objects could be fed by his wealth and position. The duc collected anything of beauty, interest, rarity, or value or that would enhance the splendor of his castles: tapestries, rich manuscripts, jewels, gold and silver objets d'art, relics, medallions, vases, and enamels. The duc de Berry's extravagant and glittering collection was primarily an assemblage of small, precious objects of the Late Middle Ages.

With the advent of the Renaissance, a more serious kind of royal collecting began to appear. Francis I of France (reigned 1515–47) must be credited with laying the modest but solid foundation of what was to become one of the richest and most extensive royal art collections in Europe. Fascinated by the Italian Renaissance and possessed of a highly developed taste for luxury and beauty, Francis began systematically to assemble a collection of important paintings and other art objects that came to constitute the nucleus of the great French national collections. Francis' interest in art and collecting undoubtedly stemmed from mixed motives. He cannot have been insensitive to the prestige value inherent in the possession of many rich, valuable, rare, or curious articles, and his passion for displaying such items in his residences was surely due in some part to his desire to appear before the world as a cultivated sovereign of refined taste presiding over a brilliant and elegant court. Nevertheless, Francis also surely made many purchases simply because the object intrigued him, titillated his curiosity, or satisfied his personal aesthetic values. He did not confine his collecting to great paintings but also assembled a "cabinet of curiosities" in which there were enshrined oddities such as "dried rare plants, exotic stuffed animals, ancient medals, fragments of antique sculpture, the feet of an Egyptian mummy, and feathered robes of American savages."[7]

This kind of catholic, magpie collecting was entirely within the tradition of the Renaissance prince with his complex of interests and his growing awareness of parts of the world hitherto unknown or known but dimly. Any royal collector of those times would buy with equal eagerness and impressive impartiality a great painting, the horn of a unicorn, a Roman bronze, a dubious holy relic, or an ostrich egg; virtually anything was welcomed into the collection as long as it was singular, beautiful, bizarre, intriguing because of cunning workmanship, exotic, or precious because of the materials of which it was made. Indeed, it was to be a long time before the concept of a gallery of art—as distinct from the cabinet of curiosities, the relic collections, and the natural history specimens—was clearly to emerge in Western culture. But although Francis I bought parts of mummies and Indian feather cloaks, he also bought many other things of greater artistic significance: paintings by great Renaissance masters such as Leonardo da Vinci, Raphael, Andrea del Sarto, Fra Bartolommeo, and Sebastiano del Piombo; and he acquired vases and medallions, antique bronzes, drawings, antique sculptures, and tapestries.

During the sixteenth century, collecting became a passion and the cabinet of curiosities a standard feature at royal and princely courts throughout Europe. Cabinets were also assembled by nobles, newly rich bourgoisie, scholars, and connoisseurs. Many of these lesser cabinets were accessible to the interested and the educated, although none was a public museum in the sense in which that term is used today. These heterogeneous collections—which juxtaposed paintings and mineral specimens, sculpture and astrological instruments, antiquities and coconuts mounted in silver—reflected the period's intellectual restlessness, its new wealth, its burgeoning response to the arts, and its increasing curiosity about the world and the cosmos. Collections of surpassing significance were formed in Austria and in Prague by the Hapsburg archdukes (who were also Holy Roman emperors); in Munich by the dukes of Bavaria; in Madrid and elsewhere in Spain by the Hapsburg sovereigns of Spain; in France by the Valois kings and Queen Catherine de' Medici; in Florence by the Medici grand dukes of Tuscany, who built on earlier collections formed by this famous family; and in Rome by nobles, prelates, and a succession of cultivated popes who had both antiquity and the best of the Renaissance at their disposal. The art objects in these cabinets, eventually sorted out from the natural history specimens and the exotica, later provided the foundation for some of the richest and most extensive public art museums in the world.

The seventeenth century was the era of successful absolute monarchy, a form of government that, in most countries, proved at the time to be the only practical alternative to the disasters of perpetual civil wars caused by religious strife and the ambitions of great nobles. Royal and dynastic powers and splendors foretold in the sixteenth century flowered fully in the seventeenth century. Louis XIV of France (reigned 1643–1715), the Sun King, provided a dazzling model of absolutism for other European sovereigns, a model that other rulers, no matter how petty their holdings, struggled to emulate. Art and architecture were summoned to participate in a glorification and exaltation of monarchy, and art collecting assumed a stately and majestic tone. Cardinal Mazarin, himself an obsessive collector of art, ruled France during most of the king's minority. Colbert, Louis' most important minister of state, envisioned a culturally dominant and politically powerful France symbolized by the crown. Mazarin and Colbert trained the young king to understand what the arts could do for the monarchy, taught him to consider patronage of the arts as a royal duty, and put before him the idea that the development of a great art collection was a royal responsibility. They were successful. When the king came to the throne in 1643 at the age of five, the crown owned about two hundred paintings; at Louis' death in 1715, however, the collection possessed nearly twenty-five hundred paintings. During Louis XIV's long reign the French royal collection grew with astonishing rapidity from its modest beginnings under Francis I to a collection of the first magnitude. The royal collection was developed from many sources during Louis XIV's time. Cardinal de Richelieu, who did so much to make Louis' reign possible, died in 1642 just before Louis' accession to the throne. The cardinal, a tireless and discriminating collector, willed his Palais Royal to the crown together with many items of artistic importance; they included Italian paintings of significance and Michaelangelo's *Slaves*, two of the most important pieces of sculpture in the Louvre today.

The French royal collection was enormously enriched, in an indirect manner, by the political disaster and personal tragedy that befell the Stuarts in England in the 1640s. This impressive increase in Louis XIV's collection took place in two great strokes of acquisition. Charles I of England, who was much interested in art, acquired in 1627 the gallery of the bankrupt duke of Mantua whose collection was justly regarded as one of the most splendid in Italy. Charles added to this core from other sources and by the time of his execution in 1649 owned more than thirteen hundred paintings and about four hundred items of sculpture, as well as a huge collection of drawings by the great masters. Between 1650 and 1653, the Parliamentary government of England gradually put Charles' collections on the sale block. There were in Europe at this time two collectors whose passion for possession amounted almost to obsessive madness. One of them was Cardinal Mazarin; the other was Evrard Jabach, a banker of Cologne who normally resided in Paris. Both men were well able to indulge their tastes, and by virtue of their heavy purchasing, the cream of the unfortunate Charles I's collection came to France. Cardinal Mazarin, who had been collecting all of his life, died in 1661 in possession of a collection that was little short of amazing for its richness, scope, and depth. Moving swiftly and with the king's authority behind him, Colbert acquired the best of Mazarin's hoard from the cardinal's heirs. The French crown thus acquired more than six hundred paintings at one time. Many of them were masterpieces.

The second great windfall occurred in 1671, when Colbert acquired for the king, at a bargain price, some one hundred paintings and fifty-five hundred drawings from the financier Jabach, who was struggling with reverses of fortune. Within a decade, then, Colbert aggrandized the royal collection to the extent of more than seven hundred paintings, thousands of drawings, and hundreds of pieces of sculpture. Nearly all of these items had been in the Mantua and Stuart collections and had reached the crown by way of the Mazarin and Jabach collections. By the time of the king's death in 1715, the crown owned about twenty-five hundred paintings, of which fifteen hundred were regarded as being by masters of the various schools; an impressive collection of thousands of drawings, many of them from the hands of the great; a print cabinet enclosing about a quarter of a million items; hundreds of pieces of sculpture, both ancient and modern; and innumerable objects of decorative art—tapestries, medallions, coins, gems, gold and silver vessels, bronzes, ivories, and furnishings.

During the seventeenth and eighteenth centuries, the accumulation of an art collection came to be a virtual requirement for royal and princely families; such a collection was a mark of prestige and a symbol of power, cultivation, and greatness. Philip IV of Spain (reigned 1621–65) enriched the Spanish royal collection, particularly with Italian Renaissance and Flemish paintings. The imperial collection at Vienna was enhanced by the fact that the international Hapsburg family ruled not only in Austria, Bohemia, and Hungary and in Germany as Holy Roman emperors but also in the Netherlands (Belgium) and Spain. In 1646, for example, Archduke Leopold Wilhelm of Austria became governor of the Netherlands and while there assembled a famous collection of hundreds of paintings by Italian and Flemish masters and many other works of art of the highest quality. When the archduke died in 1662, he left these treasures to his brother, Emperor Ferdinand III, and they entered the Vienna collection. The Bavarian royal family continued to enrich its collection at Munich. King Frederick the Great of Prussia (reigned 1740–86), scion of a house not previously notable for its interest in the arts, was devoted to French culture and collected the works of eighteenth-century French painters. Empress Catherine the Great of Russia (reigned 1762–96), German by birth and French by cultural conviction, had inherited a cabinet of curiosities established by Peter the Great but one that included very little art. As if to make up for lost time, the empress bought lavishly, almost feverishly, and usually in lots: entire libraries, complete collections of drawings, every painting in a collection (sometimes hundreds). By the time of her death, Catherine had acquired nearly four thousand paintings and had built an extension (The Hermitage [q.v.]) onto the Winter Palace in St. Petersburg to house the collection.[8]

A brilliant center of art collecting developed during the first half of the eighteenth century in Dresden, the capital of Saxony. Two successive dukes and electors of Saxony, father and son (who were also kings of Poland as Augustus II and Augustus III), virtually ruined the finances of their country with their extravagant tastes for art, but they assembled one of the finest collections in central Europe. Lesser sovereign dukes and princes throughout Europe felt compelled to imitate greater monarchs and to have their galleries of paintings and collections of art.[9] Several of them did very well. Nor was collecting by any means confined to royal families; significant collections were assembled by nobles and by wealthy amateurs, connoisseurs, and antiquarians. Collecting became highly fashionable, and art became a commercial commodity. Art auctions were great events thronged by competitive buyers, and auction houses were established. Agents crisscrossed Europe with commissions to ferret out masterpieces for their royal and princely employers. The art of Europe came to be concentrated in these various collections, which were to provide the museums of the future.

The concept of the public museum of art came relatively late to Western civilization in the train of the Enlightenment, the egalitarian ideas emerging from the French Revolution, the romanticism and nationalism of the nineteenth century, and the higher level of general education achieved in modern times. In the ancient world, the temples and public monuments served to bring art to the people and performed, at least to some degree, the role that museums have in modern life. The same may be said of the Christian church in all of history but particularly of the medieval church. By the time of the Renaissance, however, art began increasingly to be isolated from the masses. Ordinary people could still see great art in the churches and in obviously public places, but from about 1500 forward much of Europe's most important art—and this was especially true of painting—came to be enclosed in collections that were essentially private: royal collections and the collections of newly wealthy bankers and men of money. "These were private collections, assembled for the glory of their owners and to satisfy their tastes as enlightened lovers of art. Secondarily they could serve for the instruction of artists. They were open to foreigners possessing letters of recommendation and to people of importance, but they were not public museums and they were not for the crowd.''[10]

With the Enlightenment of the eighteenth century came an emphasis upon education and the idea, basically rooted in John Locke's concept of knowledge, that people could improve their education, intellect, and taste by the exposure of their intelligence and senses to works of greatness in every field of cultural endeavor. Indeed, this philosophy went further and insisted that self-improvement was both a personal and a social responsibility; from the betterment of the individual, it was believed, would come superior future generations and the ultimate perfection of a reformed and reconstituted society. This faith of the Enlightenment in the efficacy of education and a refined environment was one of the prime motives of those who began to clamor in the eighteenth century for the establishment of museums and the opening of the royal art collections to the public.

Art museums began to appear in Europe in a limited manner in the eighteenth century. Some were attached to art schools and academies. Some were included in collections that also offered natural history museums and scientific museums. In these latter institutions, paintings, drawings, and objects of art were housed with stuffed fauna and dried flora, collections of seashells and minerals, ethnological exhibitions, natural curiosities, examples of scientific inventions and experiments, and, sometimes, a library. What these museums amounted to was a continuation into the eighteenth century and a projection into the world of the Renaissance prince's ''cabinet of curiosities'' with its jumble of wonders, peculiarities, and art of every kind and a projection of such princely cabinets into the world of the public. They also reflected higher levels of education and the social and scientific interests fostered by the Enlightenment. Nevertheless, the concept of the museum of art as it is understood today did not emerge in a clear and defined manner until the later years of the century.

In Rome, the Capitoline (q.v.) and Pio-Clementino museums were established, both papal institutions; access to both was relatively limited. The British Museum (q.v.) was founded in London in 1753 but was so difficult to get into that it could hardly be considered a public institution, although it was owned and administered by the state. The great Medici bequest of art to the city of Florence was opened to the public about 1790. In 1777 the electoral prince of the Palatinate assumed the rule of Bavaria and created a gallery of art in Munich that was ''accessible to artists and dilettanti.''[11] The important Dresden art collection, the possession of the elector and duke of Saxony, was open to a limited public. ''A catalogue of the Electoral Gallery of Dresden, dated 1765, informs us that the gallery 'serves to conserve the monuments of art which adorn the spirit and form the taste of the nation.' On the other hand, while keeping its character of a private collection, the gallery was widely open in the interest of the 'quality public,' to art lovers and foreigners.''[12] In Vienna the splendid imperial collection of the Hapsburgs was opened in 1781; a catalogue of 1784 reveals that the collection was available gratuitously to the public three days a week. This imperial museum was the creation of Emperor Joseph II, a dedicated disciple of the Enlightenment. Unlike so many of the older galleries, the Vienna museum was carefully and rationally arranged to emphasize, in the best Enlightenment tradition, the idea of education. Just how much this Hapsburg gallery was a product of the Enlightenment and how far museum planning had moved toward modern concepts can be seen in the introduction to the museum's 1783 catalogue:

> The aim of all these endeavors has been so to arrange the gallery that, in its entirety and its detail, it should be, as much as possible, a source of instruction and a visual history of art. A great public collection of this kind, aiming at educational purposes rather than at passing pleasure, can be likened to a rich library, where he who is thirsting for knowledge will be happy to find works of every kind and of all periods, not only things enjoyable and perfect, but varied contrasts, by the study and comparison of which he can become a connoisseur of art.[13]

In the eighteenth century, France was the dominant cultural and intellectual force in Europe. By the middle of the century, French writers, critics, and philosophers of the Enlightenment were publishing demands that at least some part of the famous and fabulously rich royal collection be made available to the public and also began agitating for the establishment of a French national gallery of art based on the royal holdings. These demands were met in a temporary and modest fashion when a small exhibition of royal paintings and drawings was opened in the Luxembourg Palace.[14] This little museum, which was the first of its kind in France and one of the few of its kind anywhere in Europe at the time, was available to the public for two days a week and was a popular attraction that drew many people each day it was open. This exhibition included about one hundred paintings, most of them French and Italian and many of them important, and about a dozen drawings of the great Italian masters. The official catalogue, sold at the entrance, went through multiple editions between 1750 and 1779, at which time the exhibition was closed and dismantled. By 1779, however, the crown was firmly committed to a project for establishing a great French national gallery in the Louvre, a museum of art based on the best of the royal collection and open to all. The royal government worked patiently on this complex and difficult project until the French Revolution of 1789 brought an end to the monarchy and the Old Regime in France.[15] The Revolutionary government confiscated the royal art collection and the royal properties and palaces; in August 1793 the Louvre, formerly the official Paris residence of the kings of France, was opened to the public for the first time as a museum and France's national gallery of art. The Louvre was to develop into one of the greatest, largest, and most comprehensive museums of art in the world. This novel institution became immediately and enormously popular. "The *Décade philosophique* in 1795 called it 'the most visited of our public promenades,' the *Archives littéraires* reported that it had watched 'hosts of people rush' to the museum which they 'look on eagerly, on which they demand explanations and which they appreciate or condemn perspicaciously.' "[16] By the end of the eighteenth century, then, the basic concept of the art museum and the fundamental principles of modern museology had been established. The development had been rapid and had occurred within a period of less than fifty years.

To trace in detail the history of the art museum and of museology in the nineteenth and twentieth centuries is not possible here, nor would any such effort be useful or appropriate. The phenomenal increase in the number and size of art museums of every kind and in every location is a self-evident fact of modern civilization. Several important social and economic reasons lie behind the swelling success of the art museum in the past century and a half. The rapid industrialization of the Western world created vast sources of new wealth that allowed museums to expand and steadily to enhance their collections and acquisitions programs. Existing collections were enriched, and new areas for collecting—in Egyptian or Asian art, for example—were developed. The intensified nationalism of the nineteenth century found a focal point in art museums, which were seen as repositories of a country's national cultural heritage and exhibition places of its international cultural sophistication. Every nation sought to establish a national museum of art housed in an impressive and commanding building; newly independent countries throughout the world came to regard such an institution as a necessary accessory to independence.

The romantic historicism of the nineteenth century also contributed to the importance of the art museum. This pervasive cultural movement fostered a nostalgia for the past and for national "roots" that influenced religion, literature, music, and all of the arts. Romantic interest in the Middle Ages gave birth not only to the novels of Sir Walter Scott, the restoration of the Gothic cathedrals of France, and scholarly works on medieval history but to departments of medieval art in museums and the establishment of museums dedicated entirely to the arts of the Middle Ages. Romantic interest in peasant life led not only to the polonaises in Chopin's music, the Hungarian rhapsodies in Liszt's compositions, and the publication of traditional folk and fairy tales but also to a growing dedication to folk art and the creation of museums of folk art. Some aspects of this intense interest in the past and other aspects of romanticism cannot be separated from nationalism, and all of these manifestations must be seen, at least to some degree, as reactions on the part of a society that was becoming suddenly and overwhelmingly industrialized. But all of these passions served to benefit the art museum, which was seen as the ideal guardian of past greatness and of fragile cultures threatened by urbanization and factories.

Faith in the value of education was a legacy inherited by the nineteenth century from the Enlightenment, a legacy that was taken seriously and treated with sober respect. Literacy gradually increased and higher levels of general education were achieved throughout the Western world. A certain basic level of education came to be established as a right and, indeed, eventually as law in most Western countries. This increasing emphasis on education also enhanced the position of the art museum in society in that the museum was seen as a pre-eminently important educational institution, a resource for self-improvement and cultivation, and a significant factor in an educational construction designed—it was hoped—to elevate and improve society as a whole. Furthermore, education and the art museum have a symbiotic relationship; the museum is an educational institution, but the higher the level of general education, the wider the response to what the museum has to offer.

The social forces set in motion by the French Revolution had displaced the Church, the monarchies, and the aristocracies from the dominant positions they had held before 1789. All of those institutions survived the upheavals of the Revolutionary and Napoleonic years (1789–1815) but never recovered their earlier positions in the social and political structures of society; they ceased to be the major patrons of the arts, which they had been. The nineteenth century witnessed the gradual but inexorable triumph of a prosperous and educated middle class, and it was to this newly powerful middle class that the arts had to look for the patronage that had previously come to them from popes, bishops, sovereigns, and nobles. A prosperous and self-confident middle class had existed in many parts of Europe from the Middle Ages and had become increasingly important by the middle of the eighteenth century, but in the nineteenth century their numbers were enlarged by the widening effects of industrialization, and their economic success was crowned by political and social power. The public in the nineteenth century was extremely interested in contemporary art, flocked to art exhibitions, reacted strongly—in one way or another—to new movements in art, and eagerly read the reporting of all of this activity and the art criticism that appeared regularly in proliferating newspapers and journals. This interest in contemporary art also stimulated interest in museums in that all of the contemporary art made some kind of reference, either of reverence or rejection, to the great art of the past enshrined in the galleries.

During the Revolutionary and Napoleonic wars, triumphal French armies conquered most of Europe. As an aspect of the peace treaties negotiated with defeated nations, the various French governments involved (ultimately that of Napoleon, emperor of the French from 1804 until his defeat in 1814) arranged to bring the best art of Europe to Paris. Famous masterpieces of painting and sculpture from Rome (the Papal States) and the other Italian sovereignties, from the various royal collections in Germany, from Belgium and Holland, and from the imperial collection in Vienna flowed into France. Most of these objects were returned to their original owners and collections after Napoleon's downfall, but for a brief period the Louvre (called the Musée Napoléon then) housed the greatest art collection ever assembled in one place at one time. As these treasures arrived in Paris, they were displayed in a series of spectacular exhibitions that awed and delighted the public. The French intended these artistic rewards of military success to be permanent, but it can well be argued that the celebratory exhibitions arranged for them in the Louvre were the prototypes of the dazzling temporary and loan exhibitions that came to be so much a part of museum policy and with which the public today is so familiar.

The spectacular exhibition became a nineteenth-century tradition, one to which the general public responded with great enthusiasm. This was particularly true after the Great Exhibition of 1851 in London (often called the Crystal Palace Exhibition). The Great Exhibition was the first of the "world fairs" and was organized on a theme of modern industrial technology and the application of technology to the arts and design. Some critics were appalled at the level of Victorian taste displayed in the Crystal Palace, but the public was captivated by this ambitious and impressive undertaking and flocked in hordes to see it. Other such efforts followed in other countries, and art museums obviously benefited from the fact that all such "world fair" exhibitions, regardless of theme, were concerned with art and taste and stimulated interest in museum exhibitions. Furthermore, these events conditioned the public to want and to patronize the special and temporary exhibition and established the tradition and the taste that produced the crowds for touring exhibitions such as "Treasures of the Vatican." The special exhibition, constituting a "one time only" assemblage of specially chosen art objects, became a standard, popular, and expected feature of museum programming. It is a heritage of the nineteenth century and its love for the "great exhibition."

Finally, the advent of photography in the middle of the nineteenth century and the rapid advances in its technological processes revolutionized perceptions of art and contributed to the popularization of it. Photographs of architectural monuments and art objects and photographic reproductions of paintings and graphic works made available to millions of people visual images of things they would probably never see. Photography made art history possible, made a knowledge of the arts of all times and places widely available, provided a new dimension to publicity about the arts, and increased interest in art exhibitions and art museums, the repositories of real objects.

Social, economic, and historical circumstances dictated that the development of the art museum in the United States would have a very different history from the European experience in spite of the fact that America looked to Europe for cultural guidance until well into the twentieth century. The United States had no great royal art collection to provide the foundation for a national gallery and no strongly organized central government to provide the impetus for such an institution. A museum founded in Charleston, South Carolina, in 1773 is usually cited as the first such institution in America; it was essentially a natural history museum and was sponsored by the Charleston Library Society. In the early nineteenth century a museum opened in Salem, Massachusetts, that was organized according to an old tradition that had by then begun to disappear in Europe: it included some paintings but also ethnographic objects and exhibits relating to sailing and maritime science. In the 1780s Charles Wilson Peale, a famous early American artist, established in Philadelphia a museum of art, history, science, and technology, although the art consisted only of portraits of heroes of the American Revolution. Two of Peale's sons operated museums during the first third of the nineteenth century, most notably an art gallery in Baltimore, which opened in 1814. The Peale enterprises, however, were private ventures. The Boston Athenaeum was founded in 1826, the Athenaeum (q.v.) in Hartford, Connecticut, opened in 1844. A few university and college art museums were founded in the first half of the nineteenth century. But the great era of museums in the United States did not even begin until after the Civil War.

In 1832, and in reference to American art galleries, the tart-tongued Mrs. Trollope, an Englishwoman famous for her jaundiced view of contemporary American life, dryly observed: "The Medici of the Republic must exert themselves a little more before these can become even respectable."[17] Mrs. Trollope was right. Until the last half of the nineteenth century, only small and limited art galleries existed in America. They were the products of literary and scientific societies, cultural clubs, and individual effort, and they had little art with which to work. These early museums, however, did establish a tradition that was to continue in America: they were created by the initiative of private groups and persons, not elements of government, and from local organizations, not a centralized source. The enormous size of the nation, constantly expanding westward from coast to coast, was also an influence in shaping the local nature of museums in America; geographical reality determined from the beginning that art museums in the United States would have a regional quality that they have retained despite the international status achieved by some of them in the twentieth century.

"Respectable" art museums cannot come into being without collections of some stature, which is precisely what a young country in the New World did not have. European museums had been able to open their doors to the public with sumptuous ready-made collections, many of them rich in the variety and depth of centuries. The creation of important art museums in America had to wait for collecting activity that was not going to come from government. The industrialization of America and the exploitation of its immense natural resources had begun in earnest by the middle of the nineteenth century. The Civil War accelerated this economic growth, and by 1870 enormous and untaxed fortunes had emerged from mines, timber, steel mills, railroads, shipping, factories, expanded agriculture, and speculation. Wealth demands use, and one thing it can be poured into is art. Newly rich American tycoons began to buy art, although at first they tended to confine their interest in painting to landscapes and contemporary European works from the academies in Düsseldorf and, most particularly, Paris. This *salon* art of the late nineteenth century came to be scorned and repudiated by the twentieth century and relegated to the basements of museums, but since World War II there has been a revival of both scholarly and popular interest in "Victorian art" (a generic term). In the late nineteenth and early twentieth centuries, American collectors, guided by critics and dealers like Bernard Berenson and Lord Duveen of London, began to accumulate Old Master paintings, Italian Primitives, medieval objects, miniatures, illuminated manuscripts, and prime examples of the various decorative arts (tapestries, French and English furniture, silver, porcelain, majolica, glass) from the Late Middle Ages through the eighteenth century. Some collectors were even buying French Impressionist paintings. "The Medici of the Republic" had begun to exert themselves.

While these collections were being formed, the museums that were ultimately to benefit from them were being established. After the Civil War, the United States was beginning to regard itself as a world power, newly unified, immensely rich, with unlimited potential. National pride and an awakened cultural consciousness began to demand museums; indeed, America's lack of great art galleries to compare to those of Europe was considered a national disgrace. The decades between 1870 and 1890 saw the foundation and opening to the public of some of the institutions that were to become the largest and most comprehensive in America: the Boston Museum of Fine Arts (q.v.), the New York Metropolitan Museum of Art, the Philadelphia Museum of Art (q.v.), the Detroit Institute of Arts (q.v.), and the Art Institute of Chicago (q.v.). Important museums continued to be established well into the twentieth century. The Cleveland Museum of Art (q.v.) was founded in 1913 and opened in 1916. The National Gallery of Art (q.v.) in Washington, D.C., was not opened until 1941; both the building and most of the dazzling collection were the donation of Andrew W. Mellon. The exhibitions presented by the newly established museums were usually small in their early days, but their galleries were soon filled by a sudden and impressive showering of whole collections, substantial endowments, and gifts. European art not enclosed in museums began to move to American institutions. The major museums expanded from the collection of traditional European art and antiquities to Asian, Near Eastern, pre-Columbian, and African art. Chapels, cloisters, and rooms were dismantled in their native countries and rebuilt in American institutions. Museums of modern art were founded. The charge has been made that America has plundered the world's art with money. Nevertheless, within a few generations, American museums grew with such astonishing rapidity that they were able to present to the public sophisticated collections of phenomenal scope and quality. Isolated by oceans and distance, few Americans could have traveled to see the art made available in the museums; the art was brought to them.

The number of art museums in the United States is difficult to determine with precision, because some museums of other types—historical museums, for example—include art galleries. There are probably about 350 American art museums as such; of this number, only a few are large and comprehensive institutions with national reputations and international stature, although some of the smaller ones have collections of high quality.[18]

The general developmental history of American museums has been one of local generation, regional importance, and local governance. The Smithsonian complex of museums in Washington, D.C., is owned and operated by the federal government. Some art museums are owned and administered by the municipalities for which they were created. For the most part, however, American art museums are not the possessions of the federal government, the states, or cities and are controlled by boards of trustees, usually self-perpetuating, who hire the professional curatorial staffs. Methods of administration are diverse, but the board-of-trustees pattern is the most common form of organizational structure. The funding of art museums in America is also complex and is based on several sources; private patronage and income from endowments traditionally have been the most important elements in museum funding in the United States. Corporate patronage has become increasingly significant in recent years. Many museums, however, do benefit, either directly or indirectly, from various kinds of assistance derived from different levels of government. This governmental assistance ranges widely from federal grants and tax benefits to maintenance contributions made by municipalities. During the past twenty years, the steadily rising costs of maintenance, staffing, and acquisitions have compelled some museums to charge nominal entrance fees. From their beginning, American art museums espoused the democratic ideal of being totally public institutions, but admission is no longer necessarily entirely free. The administration and funding of American museums, then, is very different from the strongly centralized and state-owned museum systems prevalent in most of the world. American museology, which has its own peculiarities, has evolved from the realities of American life, geography, economics, and social history.

The concept of the art museum was wholly the product of Western society and was in no way native to the cultures of Asia. Western self-consciousness about art and history and egalitarian Western principles of education and public accessibility to art were alien to Asian philosophies, social structures, and modes of thought. Apart from religious art and temple sites, which were always public, the Asian attitude toward art traditionally was one of private contemplation and appreciation on the part of scholars, connoisseurs, collectors, and princes. The art museum open to the general public had no place in this philosophy in which response to art was an essentially private and aristocratic matter nor in societies in which literacy and education were limited until very recent times. André Malraux, who lived in Asia, said:

> The reason the art museum made its appearance in Asia so belatedly (and, even then, only under European influence and patronage) is that, for an Asiatic, and especially the man of the Far East, artistic contemplation and the picture gallery are incompatible. In China, the full enjoyment of works of art necessarily involved ownership, except where religious art was concerned; above all it demanded their isolation. A painting was not exhibited, but unfurled before an art lover in a fitting state of grace; its function was to deepen and enhance his communion with the universe. The practice of confronting works of art with other works of art is an intellectual activity, and diametrically opposed to the mood of relaxation which alone makes contemplation possible. In Asiatic eyes, the museum may be a place of learning and teaching, but considered as anything else it is no more than an

absurd concert in which contradictory themes are mingled and confused in an endless succession.[19]

Public museums of art began to appear in Asia in significant numbers only in the later nineteenth century, about a hundred years after the earliest European museums.[20] Hundreds more were established in the twentieth century. There have been various motivations behind this extremely rapid phenomenon of proliferation. The example of Western museums and Western museology has been a major factor and is simply another manifestation of the strong influence of Western ideas in Asia that began to occur at the beginning of the colonial period and that has been accelerated by modern technology and communications. Conversely, Asian art museums are the product of growing nationalism, intensified in some countries by new independence from Western colonial powers and by heightened awareness of native cultures and determination to preserve native artifacts. This desire to satisfy and assert nationalistic pride by enshrining culture in museums was also an important element in the creation of Western museums.

The governments of Asian countries became aware of the fact that museums could provide economic benefits by stimulating tourism; this economic consideration has been especially important in the years since World War II, an era of mass travel to distant places. Again, this motivation was also present in the earliest museological philosophies formulated in Europe. In 1788 the count d'Angiviller, director general of buildings, wrote a memorandum to Louis XVI concerning the royal project for transforming a portion of the Louvre into a great French national gallery of art; among other points, Angiviller stated that such a gallery would help to bring foreign tourists and their money to France and that this economic benefit would return "a hundredfold" the investment made in the completion of the museum.[21] In the very early nineteenth century, and partly in reference to museums proposed for Munich, Crown Prince Ludwig of Bavaria said that he wanted "to make of Munich a city which would be such an honour to Germany that no traveller would leave Germany without having seen Munich."[22] Finally, the creation of many Asian art museums has been directed by patterns of native collecting and religious traditions. As in Europe, royal and princely collections have been acquired by new governments; the development of archaeological explorations at temples and burial sites, particularly in India and China, have provided almost overwhelmingly rich yields in architecture and artistic treasures.

The oldest museum in India is the Indian Museum (q.v.) in Calcutta; ironically, but not surprisingly, this institution owes its origin to two Englishmen, Sir William Jones and Charles Wilkins, who founded the Asiatic Society of Bengal in 1784. The British colonial government was less than enthusiastic about such societies and was apprehensive that they might encourage national feeling. Nevertheless, the society began to collect Indian artifacts—not confined to art—and established the Indian Museum in 1814, although it was not opened to the general public until 1878. The Madras Museum (q.v.) was founded in 1851 and the

Victoria and Albert Museum in Bombay in 1855. These earlier museums tended to be broad and to include natural history exhibitions and other holdings as well as art collections; they were, in essence, latter-day and Indian versions of the "cabinet of curiosities" formed by European princes during the Renaissance. Museums of this comprehensive type continued to be founded in India until well into the twentieth century. Many of the older museums established under the British raj are regional, a reflection of the size of the subcontinent and the regional diversities of its cultures.

India's national museum is the National Museum (q.v.) of New Delhi, a creation of Indian independence and nationalism. Founded in 1949, but not opened until 1960, the National Museum is one of the largest art museums in India and, as a matter of policy, is comprehensive in its collections. Two different but not necessarily opposed philosophical and museological approaches to the National Museum were stated in the inaugural publication of 1960. Humayun Kabir stated that "in the modern world this museum cannot restrict itself to a representation of national art and culture alone. For one thing, modern science and technology . . . have reduced distances and made a parochial or even a national approach obsolete. . . . " But Vice-President Radhakrishnan of India declared that the National Museum must exhibit "the antiquity, the continuity, the prolific creativeness and outstanding vitality of the people of India."[23]

As in Europe, an important source for museums in modern India has been the private collections of the native princes. These collections, some of which are very rich, remained private property after the establishment of the Republic of India in 1947, but most of the palace collections have now been opened to the public, and some have been donated to the government.

Apart from the National Museum of New Delhi, Calcutta holds the most prominent place among Indian museums. Bombay has been a cultural and artistic center for centuries, and the Prince of Wales Museum (q.v.) there, founded in 1914, is particularly important. The pre-eminent state (regional) museum is probably the Madras Museum. The most important of the private and princely museums is that of the Maharajah of Jaipur; the collection is administered in a trust for the former ruler and occupies several buildings in the royal "City Palace" complex.

There are more than three hundred museums in India, and the nation has become very conscious of museums and museology, especially since independence. The Museums Association of India was founded in 1943. The Central Advisory Board of Museums, which is part of the national government, was established in 1956. Museum training programs appeared in the universities in the 1950s. Indian museums are organized, administered, and funded in a variety of ways. The most important museums are owned by the central government or the governments of the various states (Madras, for example); in some instances, the administration of an institution is shared by the central government and a state government. There are also large and small private museums, university museums, and municipal museums.

A substantial part of the artistic heritage of China has been scattered throughout the Western world. Western interest in Far Eastern art, especially that of China and Japan and especially objects of decorative art, dates from at least the Middle Ages. This interest expanded during the Renaissance, the Age of Explorations, when sea routes to the Far East were established and commerce no longer had to depend on caravans making their way along the old "Silk Routes." Chinese porcelains in particular were extravagantly admired and collected in the West. During the seventeenth and eighteenth centuries, Chinese porcelains, lacquers, and textiles became increasingly popular in Europe and were imported in significant quantity; most of these objects were manufactured by China specifically for export to foreign markets. Newly founded European ceramic and porcelain factories copied Chinese porcelains, and European artists and designers adapted Chinese motifs to Western taste in a highly popular style called chinoiserie or *à la Chinois* (in the Chinese manner). This passion for Chinese themes and styles did not influence Western painting or sculpture, but it became extremely important as an exotic note in interior design and the decorative arts (furniture, ceramics, lacquer panels, fabric, wallpaper). "The Chinese taste" also manifested itself in some of the more playful aspects of European architecture, particularly in garden buildings designed to resemble pagodas and Chinese temples.

Japan was protectively closed to the Western world during the seventeenth and eighteenth centuries, the period of the shoguns, although some Japanese products did reach Western markets. In 1853, however, Japan's self-imposed isolation was terminated by an American naval action, and by the late nineteenth century the Western world was being influenced by Japanese art on two levels. Popular taste responded to the colorful quality of Japanese decorative arts; the Japanese met this demand by producing quantities of goods (especially porcelain) for export, much of it exaggerated to satisfy popular Western expectations. On the other hand, Japanese woodcuts and the more restrained objects of native taste began to influence both Post-Impressionist painting in Europe and movements toward modern design such as Art Nouveau and the "Anglo-Japanese" style.

With this long-established tradition of interest in Chinese and Japanese art in the background, Western museums were predisposed to want to collect Asian art of every kind. The best opportunity for assembling important collections of Chinese bronzes, porcelains, and paintings came in the twentieth century, after the Revolution of 1911 overturned the imperial dynasty and established the Republic of China. In the years of war, internal disintegration, and political confusion that followed the revolution, Westerners were able to purchase Chinese works of art for modest prices and to remove them from the country. Western museums began to develop important Chinese holdings, and most of the larger Western art museums now pride themselves on extensive Asian collections. American museums have some of the best Asian collections in the Western world, and some of the most exquisite art of China is to be seen in the United States.

The art treasures of China were further dispersed by political and historical circumstances during and after World War II. When the Nationalist Chinese government was defeated, it fled to Taiwan and took a substantial part of the old imperial art collection with it. This collection, called the National Palace Collection, is on display in the National Palace Museum (q.v.) in Taipei; it includes early bronzes, more than twenty thousand ceramics, and the most important collection of Chinese painting outside the People's Republic.[24] The People's Republic was founded in 1949, but the Palace Museum (q.v.) in Peking was established in 1914 and includes the remainder of the imperial collection. Efforts have been made to compensate for the removal of so many works to Taiwan. The entire Forbidden City in Peking is a vast museum; it was the old imperial residential complex and includes the Imperial Palace in which many apartment interiors are open to the public and present the decorations and art objects unaltered and in situ. In the past twenty years the Chinese have discovered and excavated several spectacular archaeological sites that have yielded an extraordinarily rich treasure of art objects. In the five years between 1966 and 1971, more than 1 million objects were recovered from archaeological sites in Honan Province alone.[25] These archaeological findings have created art museums with a distinctively nationalistic tone in which displays are arranged for didactic purposes.

The idea of the public art museum is very much a twentieth-century innovation in Chinese society and did not appear until after the Revolution of 1911. The development of this Western institution, so alien to the old China, has been influenced by political, military, and economic circumstances. The Museums Association of China was organized in Peking in 1935, for example, and expressed a desire to westernize and modernize Chinese museums as rapidly as possible; but the Japanese invasion of China, World War II, and the political and military turmoil following the war inhibited the goals of the association. Western museology was originally—and still is to some degree—nationalistic both specifically and in terms of European culture generally. Chinese museology follows this pattern of development; it is strongly nationalistic and concerned with a teaching mission. Western art never penetrated China to any significant degree, and no important collections of Western art were formed there.

Japan, more industrialized and "westernized" than any other country in Asia, is rich in museums of every kind and size. The Tokyo National Museum (q.v.), opened in 1871, is the oldest and most important Japanese museum. The National Museum has more than one hundred thousand items of art and archaeology in its collection; it has a fully developed educational and support system based on European and American prototypes. Japanese and Korean works are included in the Japanese Folk Craft Museum opened in 1936. The National Museum of Modern Art in Tokyo, established in 1952, specializes in modern Japanese art. An important collection of ancient Buddhist art is in the Nara National Museum (q.v.), opened in 1897 in a city famous for its old temples. The Kyoto National Museum (q.v.) in Japan's old capital city also opened in 1897 and presents a particularly significant collection of traditional Japanese art and decorative arts.

Temple sites and treasures are of great importance in the Japanese museum system. The temple treasures of the seventh-century Hōryūji Temple near Nara were opened to the public in 1940. The eighth-century Shoso-in Treasure House, Nara, originally belonged to the Todaiji Temple to house its collection of eighth-century treasures. An additional new building was constructed on the site in 1963 to provide better and more secure housing for the treasure, although the original eighth-century wooden building was carefully preserved. The Japanese temple treasure museums are analogous to the cathedral and sacristy treasuries of Europe; in both cases, these treasuries enclose some of the most important religious art created in their civilizations. Many other museums of Japanese art are to be found throughout the nation, and several of them are institutions of considerable stature with valuable collections.

Unlike collectors in most Asian countries, the Japanese have been interested in Western art and have formed large collections of nineteenth- and twentieth-century French art, including both painting and sculpture and with an emphasis on the Impressionist and Post-Impressionist periods. There are four major European collections open to the public in Japan: the Museum of Western Art in Tokyo based on the collection of Prince Kojiro Matsukata and opened in 1959 in a building designed by Le Corbusier; the Kurashiki Museum of Art created by M. Soichiro Ohara; the Hiroshima Museum of Art, opened in 1978; and the Bridgestone Museum of Art in Tokyo. The Bridgestone, one of only a few privately owned museums in Japan, was opened in 1952 in a new building; the collection was formed and the museum founded by Shojiro Ishibashi, an executive of the Bridgestone Tire Company. The Bridgestone has the largest and best collection of Western art in Japan. The core of the collection is Impressionist and Post-Impressionist painting, the most extensive such collection in Japan, but the Bridgestone also displays objects from Mediterranean antiquity.

Although its history is precipitous, museology in Japan has followed certain established patterns. The earliest public art museums were founded to preserve and to glorify the national cultural heritage by drawing attention to its artistic achievements. Rapid and successful industrialization, especially after World War II, created the wealth to sustain and to enhance museums and to establish new ones. Industrial wealth also allowed private individuals to form extensive and sophisticated collections that have become available to the public. Japanese museology has been strongly influenced by the West but combines museological elements from both Europe and America. As is true of Europe, Japan had a vast body of native art upon which to draw when establishing its museums, a heritage that had not been so scattered as China's. Most Japanese museums are owned by the state, and this is also the case with regard to the most important European museums. In this sense, Japanese museological theory and practice parallels the European concept of the public art museum as a social function of the state. On the other hand, the American tradition of the great private collection created by new wealth but eventually made public is also to be seen in the history of Japanese museums.

In recent years the world of the art museum has been agitated by debates and criticisms. Questions have been raised regarding the role of the art museum in contemporary society. Can the art museum retain its scholarly qualities and also appeal to a mass audience? Can scholarship and showmanship be balanced? Is this really a problem at all? Are some museums becoming too big? Have they been afflicted with institutional "giantism," the urge to undisciplined growth inherent in all social structures and institutions? Have art museums been weakened by internecine rivalries and displays of professional egoism on the part of administrators and curators? Significantly, these issues have been sharpest in the United States where most art museums are not owned by governments and where most funding has to come from a variety of sources. Realizing that they must depend on private patronage and public approval, art museums in America have made determined and successful efforts to extend themselves to their communities and to dispel any lingering image of aloofness and exclusivity. This has been primarily an American problem; the social context of European museums is different and the history of museology in Europe has had a different development from its American counterpart. Since the French Revolution, major European museums have been owned and funded by their governments and, in that sense at least, taken for granted as part of the responsibility of government to society. Public art museums in most Asian societies are still relatively novel and innovative and in experimental states of establishment and development; the most important museums in the Asian world, however, are also state institutions.

American debates about the art museum have in no way diminished the popularity of museums, inhibited their growth, or prevented the establishment of new ones; these controversies and questions have essentially the quality of self-generated dialogues among professionals and critics. Insofar as the public is concerned, and really the museums themselves, the fundamentals of museology have not changed since they were first formulated in late-eighteenth-century Europe. The primary function and social duty of the museum is now what it has always been: to collect, conserve, and exhibit works of art as visual and aesthetic manifestations of cultural heritage and individual talent. Education is still perceived as one of the major aspects of the place of the art museum in society. The Enlightenment's emphasis on the value of personal and communal self-improvement is stronger than it has ever been. Art museums now are no less aware of their traditional educational mission than they have always been; objects are displayed with didactic purpose, and most museums offer programs of public lectures, gallery tours by trained professionals, and active departments of education for both adults and children. "The museum has metamorphosed into a university for the general public—an institution of learning and enjoyment for all men."[26] The element of national and civic prestige surrounding art museums is more pronounced than ever. A national gallery of art is a necessity for countries; art museums are considered landmarks in the landscape of civic pride, essential to the "quality of life" offered by a particular place. Existing institutions are enlarged, and new ones are established by ambitious cities; efforts are made to engage the services of internationally famous architects so that new wings and new buildings attract the attention—admiring or adverse—of critics and the public. Moreover, the art museum is still regarded as a direct and indirect economic asset to a nation or community, a magnet for travelers, a tourist attraction.

Perhaps the most significant element to be added to museology in the nineteenth century—and one that has become even more marked in the twentieth century—was a linking of the concept of pleasure with art museums. The idea of education continued to dominate the philosophy of museums, but eventually it came to be accepted that art museums could also be places of pure enjoyment. The museum-going public had undoubtedly always included people who lightheartedly enjoyed art as well as those bent on serious education, but the pleasure principle was only gradually confronted and admitted. A clear distinction between pleasure and learning in the art museum probably cannot be made; those who go to a museum out of curiosity or to while away a few idle hours in an environment totally different from their daily lives probably learn something; those who go to a museum with serious intellectual intent probably enjoy the process. But it is no longer considered frivolous to go to museums simply because one enjoys them, and museums now present themselves as havens, sanctuaries from the stresses of modern life, places of refuge where the visitor can escape into other times and other worlds.

Museums in the nineteenth century began to cater to the physical needs of visitors and to provide food services. Nineteenth-century British museums began offering teas, and restaurants of various kinds are now an accepted and expected amenity in museums. So are the museum retail stores, some of them elaborate and extensive, a profitable attraction few can resist. But the idea of the museum shop is not new; Baron Vivant Denon, director of the Louvre (Musée Napoléon) during the Napoleonic period, enhanced the revenues of the museum by the brisk sale of souvenir catalogues, engravings of paintings in the collection, and plaster casts of sculpture.[27] The art museum can now provide an excursion for a day, including lunching or dining and exotic shopping. Modern museology encourages such excursions even if they are undertaken solely for diversion and pleasure.

In many external respects, art museums have been drastically transformed during the twentieth century. New concepts about the interior spaces of museums and their lighting have altered their architectural design. Collections have been both edited and enhanced. Modern theories of installation and presentation have dramatically modified the physical appearance of museums. But the essential ideas of what an art museum is and what its relationship to society should be have only expanded from their original inceptions and have not undergone any substantive changes. André Malraux asserted that photography has created a "museum without walls," an "imaginary museum," a museum without limits, and one that could never exist within the confines of an actual institution. "A museum without walls has been opened to us, and it will carry infinitely farther that limited revelation of the world of art which the real museums offer us within their walls. . . . " He referred to this "museum without walls" as "an interrogation," an endless challenge that provides "an enigmatic release from time."[28] For Malraux, the real museum "is governed by history" and is "an affirmation" rather than "an interrogation." Nevertheless, Malraux acknowledged the unique value of real museums and stated that they constitute a kind of "vast resurrection" that offers mortal humanity a glimpse of the immortal. The importance of the "imaginary museum" is obvious and incomparable, but real museums also invite us to transcend self, time, and place. Whether or not they manifest a "vast resurrection"—a poetic term in context—they undeniably present to us with real objects an essential element of that vast continuity of culture, of collective memory, upon which civilization depends.

NOTES

1. José Ortega y Gasset, "Point of View in the Arts," in *The Dehumanization of Art and Other Writings on Art and Culture* (Garden City, N.Y.: Doubleday Anchor Books, 1958), 99.

2. André Malraux, Introduction to *Museum Without Walls* (Garden City, N.Y.: Doubleday & Company, 1967), 10–11. This work was originally published in France in 1965 as *Le Musée Imaginaire*.

3. Johann Wolfgang von Goethe, Introduction to *Propyläen*, 1798. See Elizabeth Gilmore Holt, *The Triumph of Art for the Public* (Garden City, N.Y.: Anchor Press/Doubleday, 1979), 76–77.

4. Johann Wolfgang von Goethe, "A Brief Survey of Art in Germany," first published in *Propyläen*. See Holt, *The Triumph of Art for the Public*, 73. *Propyläen* was an art and literary review that was published between 1798 and 1800 and was founded by Goethe.

5. Jacques Barzun, *The Use and Abuse of Art*, Bollingen Series 35 (Princeton, N.J.: Princeton University Press, 1974), 80. This volume is a series of six lectures (the A. W. Mellon Lectures in the Fine Arts) given in 1973 at the National Gallery of Art, Washington, D.C.

6. Ibid., 144–45.

7. Francis Henry Taylor, *The Taste of Angels* (Boston: Little, Brown and Company, 1948), 190. Quoted from a letter written to Taylor by Jean Adhémar, a French authority on the collection of Francis I.

8. Germain Bazin, *The Museum Age* (New York: Universe Books, 1967), 124–26.

9. The words *cabinet, gallery*, and *museum* have complex histories rooted in the use and display of art objects in certain architectural settings, but in earlier periods the distinctions were not always clear. The terms *gallery* and *museum* are now sometimes used interchangeably, but *gallery* has gradually come to mean institutions devoted exclusively or primarily to the exhibition of paintings; the word *museum* has the definite connotation of an institution with comprehensive collections and exhibitions. See Sir Nikolaus Pevsner, "Museums," in *A History of Building Types*, Bollingen Series 35 (Princeton, N.J.: Princeton University Press, 1976), 111–38, bibliography, and 306–9nn.

10. Edouard Michel, *Musées et conservateurs: Leur rôle dans l'organisation sociale* (Brussels: Office de Publicité, Université Libré de Bruxelles, J. Lebègue et Cie., 1948), 11. Translation from the French by James L. Connelly.

11. Hans Tietze, *Treasures of the Great National Galleries* (London: Phaidon Press Ltd., 1954), 134.

12. Michel, *Musées et conservateurs*, 14.

13. Ernst H. Buschbeck and Erich V. Strohmer, Introduction to *Art Treasures from the Vienna Collections Lent by the Austrian Government* (n.p., 1949–50), 9. This work is the official catalogue of the exhibition of that part of the Hapsburg collection that was shown in the United States in 1949–50.

14. James L. Connelly, "Forerunner of the Louvre," *Apollo Magazine* (London) 95, no. 123 (May 1972): 382–89.

15. James L. Connelly, "The Grand Gallery of the Louvre and the Museum Project," *Journal of the Society of Architectural Historians* 31, no. 2 (May 1972): 120–32.

16. Pevsner, "Museums," 120.

17. Frances Trollope, *Domestic Manners of the Americans*, ed. Donald Smalley (New York: Knopf, 1949), 345.

18. Karl E. Meyer, *The Art Museum: Power, Money, Ethics* (New York: William Morrow and Company, 1979), 59.

19. Malraux, Introduction to *Museum Without Walls*, 10.

20. Information for this section on Asian museums has been derived from a research project undertaken by Ronald A. Rarick, a graduate student in the Department of Art History at the University of Kansas. The author gratefully acknowledges his contribution and the thoroughness of his research. Periodical literature provides the most useful source of information about Asian museums, especially journals such as *Museum News, Museum* (UNESCO), *The Magazine of American Art, Museums Journal, Arts Magazine, Das Kunstwerk, Apollo, The Connoisseur, L'Oeil, Parnassus, Art News, Art in America, Oriental Art, Artibus Asiae,* and *The Japan Architect (International Edition of Shinken-chiku)*. For Japan, see also *The Connoisseur's Guide To Japanese Museums* (Tokyo: John Weatherhill, 1967). The UNESCO publications are particularly important.

21. Archives Nationales de France, 0¹ 1670, 246.

22. Pevsner, "Museums," 123.

23. Grace L. McCann Morley and K. N. Puri, "The National Museum, New Delhi," *Museum* (UNESCO) 14, no. 2 (1961): 69–72.

24. For an account of the hiding and removal of Palace Collection works during and after World War II, see Chu-tsing Li, "Recent History of the Palace Collection," *Archives of the Chinese Art Society of America* 12 (1958).

25. Edmund Capon, "Archaeology in China Today: Principles and Practice," *The Connoisseur*, no. 168 (January 1975): 2–6.

26. Bazin, *The Museum Age*, 261.

27. Pevsner, "Museums," 120.

28. Malraux, *Museum Without Walls*, 12–13, 162, 233–34.

SELECTED BIBLIOGRAPHY

Bazin, Germain. *The Museum Age*. New York: Universe Books, 1967. A general and conceptual work, both factual and philosophical.

Burt, Nathaniel. *Palaces for the People: A Social History of the American Art Museum*. Boston: Little, Brown and Company, 1977.

Lee, Sherman E., ed. *On Understanding Art Museums*. Englewood Cliffs, N.J.: Prentice-Hall, 1975.

Meyer, Karl E. *The Art Museum: Power, Money, Ethics*. New York: William Morrow and Company, 1979.

Michel, Edouard. *Musées et conservateurs: Leur rôle dans l'organisation sociale*. Brussels: Office de Publicité, Université Libré de Bruxelles, J. Lebègue et Cie., 1948.

National Endowment for the Arts. *Museums USA: A Survey Report*. Washington, D.C.: Government Printing Office, 1975.

O'Connor, Francis, ed. *Art for the Millions*. Boston: New York Graphic Society, 1973.

Pevsner, Sir Nikolaus. "Museums." In *A History of Building Types*. Bollingen Series 35. Princeton, N.J.: Princeton University Press, 1976, 111–38, bibliography, and 306–9nn. This chapter is primarily concerned with the museum as an architectural phenomenon and problem but also contains valuable material on the histories of collecting and museums.

Ripley, S. Dillon. *The Sacred Grove: Essays on Museums*. New York: Simon and Schuster, 1969.

Tietze, Hans. *Treasures of the Great National Galleries*. London: Phaidon Press Ltd., 1954. This work contains material concerning the histories of the great museums of Europe.

Wittlin, Alma S. *The Museum: Its History and Its Tasks in Education*. London: 1st ed., 1949; 2nd ed., 1970; 3rd ed., 1974.

———. *Museums: In Search of a Usable Future*. Cambridge, Mass.: MIT Press, 1970. This work is an expanded and revised version of the work cited above.

Afghanistan

—— Kabul ——

NATIONAL MUSEUM OF AFGHANISTAN (formerly KABUL MUSEUM; officially MUZYAM-MILLI-YI AFGHANISTAN), Darulaman, Kabul, Afghanistan.

Amir Habibullah who ruled Afghanistan from 1901 to 1919 collected rare and unusual objects, including weapons and accoutrements inlaid with gold and precious stones. The amir's brother Nasrullah was a discriminating collector of illuminated manuscripts. In 1919 the amir was assassinated, and Nasrullah was consigned to a prison inside the Karul Arg (citadel), where he died.

King Amanullah, third son of Amir Habibullah, seized the throne in 1919 and in that same year transferred both collections to Bagh-i-Bala (High Garden), a graceful nineteenth-century domed and arcuated palace on a hill overlooking Kabul, capital city of Afghanistan. The amir's collection was later returned to the stoutly walled Arg for security reasons and displayed in the Koti Baghcha (Garden Pavilion), which was officially inaugurated as the Kabul Museum by King Amanullah in November 1924. The first museum director, Ghulam Mohayuddin, was assigned at this time.

Nasrullah's manuscripts were placed in the mausoleum of Amir Abdur Rahman (reigned 1880–1901), father of Amir Habibullah, outside the Arg, which was opened to the public as the Kitab Khana-i-Melli (National Library). During the civil war that brought about the downfall of King Amanullah in 1929, the library was looted, and many fine folios were destroyed.

Peace was restored at the end of 1929, and in 1931 the Kabul Museum reopened in the suburb of Darulaman, six miles southwest of Kabul in the same building housing the National Museum today. This International Style building had been built in 1927 as a town hall and has many shortcomings as a museum. No major efforts to improve display facilities were made until 1957–58, when the Begram and Islamic rooms were redesigned. About 1965 the Kabul Museum was renamed the National Museum of Afghanistan. East and west wings were added in December 1977.

A bloody coup in April 1978 established the Democratic Republic of Afghanistan (DRA). In June 1979 the DRA determined to turn Darulaman into a military zone, a last refuge for a leadership beset by revolts. Consequently, the museum collections were boxed and stored. The return of the objects to the former museum building in Darulaman began in April 1980, and the National Museum reopened to the public on October 13. A potsherd study collection for students was prepared in 1981.

The museum is administered and funded by the Ministry of Information and Culture of the central government. It is a supporting institutional member of the International Council of Museums, a nongovernmental organization of UNESCO. The National Museum is also responsible for the small, mostly poorly organized provincial museums at Kandahar (major city in the Southwest), Mazar-i-Sharif (in the North), and Herat (in the Northwest), all founded in 1933. The Ghazni Museum, south of Kabul, was founded in 1935, but in 1966 it was shifted to the restored mausoleum of Sultan Abdur Razaq, a superb example of sixteenth-century A.D. Timurid architecture, and renamed the Museum of Islamic Art. Escalating revolts following the Soviet occupation of Afghanistan in December 1979 has led the DRA to contemplate the transfer of all provincial collections to the National Museum in Kabul.

Site museums at Ghazni and Hadda, near the eastern border, were established during the 1960s. The Hadda Museum was destroyed in 1980 during antigovernment revolts. The Ghazni Museum remained unscathed as of November 1981.

The National Museum of Afghanistan is unique in many ways. The overwhelming majority of its present holdings were scientifically excavated from Afghan soil. The displays record fifty thousand years of Afghanistan's cultural history almost without interruption, from the Middle Palaeolithic period to the ethnographic present. Many specific collections have no parallels elsewhere. In short, the National Museum of Afghanistan ranks among the most opulent cultural depositories in the world.

A transitional Middle Palaeolithic flake-blade industry dating thirty thousand to fifty thousand years ago was excavated in 1966 from sites in the northeastern province of Badakhshan. A human skull fragment with both Neanderthal and *Homo sapien* characteristics was found in association with these tools. These important displays indicate that Afghanistan represents a transitional zone where various modern civilizations developed and, with the advent of the Upper Palaeolithic blade industry, began to revolutionize Stone Age technology.

The twenty thousand Upper Palaeolithic flint implements recovered from northern Afghanistan in 1962 and 1965 are of such high quality and beauty that experts have described the tool makers of Aq Kupruk as the Michelangelos of the Upper Palaeolithic era. Among the unique holdings from this period is a sculptured object representing a human face that is possibly the oldest sculpted piece found in Asia, dating about fifteen thousand years ago.

The appearance of the Neolithic at Aq Kupruk about nine thousand years ago indicates that northern Afghanistan was an early center for the domestication of plants and animals. Guaranteed food supplies permitted the growth of the great Bronze Age urban civilizations in the Nile, Tigris-Euphrates, and Indus river valleys. Between these centers provincial cities grew in response to specialized supply needs, and trade routes flourished. Graceful painted pottery goblets, sculptured human and animal figurines, necklaces of semiprecious stones, copper mirrors, and seals of copper, bone, and steatite excavated at Mundigak near Kandahar from 1951 to 1958 speak of a burgeoning city life during the third to second millennium B.C. Mother Goddess figurines from Mundigak and its nearby village supplier at Deh Morasi Ghundai, excavated in 1951, speak of emerging religious cults.

Fragments of five gold and twelve silver vessels dated about 2500 B.C. were recovered in 1966 from Tepe Fallol near the famous lapis lazuli mines of Badakhshan. They carry artistic motifs relating to India, Iran, Mesopotamia, and Central Asia, attesting to an intensive lapis lazuli trade between these areas during the second half of the third and the end of the second millennium B.C. Evidence for direct contact with the Harappan culture is provided from the site of Shortugai, also in the Northeast. These extensive finds include examples of the famous Indus Valley seals. Excavations began in 1975.

Material excavated since 1965 at Ai Khanoum, the easternmost Greek city yet known and the largest Greek town plan found outside of Greece, date from the fourth to the second century B.C. Evidence points to the possibility that this outpost on Afghanistan's northeastern border was established by order of Alexander the Great, who sojourned in the Afghan area from 330 to 327 B.C. A permanent Ai Khanoum exhibit, opened in 1981, provides striking evidence of the determination with which these Greek colonists maintained their own culture while living five thousand miles away from their homeland. Delphic oracle inscriptions, tombstones inscribed in Greek, mosaic flooring, Greek gods and goddesses, herma, comedy masques, dolphin fountainheads, and Ionic capitals are among the stunning testimonies. They illuminate the development of art styles in this pivotal area.

Greek and Aramaic inscriptions give evidence of the extension of Eastern influences under Mauryan King Ashoka, who ruled northern India from 268 to 233 B.C. The inscriptions found at Kandahar in 1963 and 1967 are the westernmost *Ashokan Edicts* yet discovered, and they represent the only *Ashokan Edicts* written in Greek, indicating the presence of an important Greek-speaking community in Kandahar.

An amazing hoard of more than twenty-one thousand gold ornaments, many studded with semiprecious stones including lapis lazuli, was excavated in 1978 from Tillya-tepe (Golden Hill) near Shibarghan in northern Afghanistan. This hoard dates from the first century B.C. to the first century A.D. soon after the arrival of the Yueh-chih from Central Asia. In addition to being sophisticated masterpieces of ancient art, these pieces will contribute immeasurably to the now hazy understanding of the founding of the Great Kushan Empire during the first to the third century A.D., when the Afghan area sat at the center of an empire stretching from north-central India to the Gobi desert.

Tillya-tepe was a sepulchral mound for early Kushan nobility. A little more than fifty miles east of Tillya-tepe a gigantic fifty-foot-high mound rises above a now starkly barren desert waste. Delbarjin-tepe, excavated since 1969, represents a city founded in the Achaemenid period in the sixth century B.C. that blossomed at its peak under the Kushans, who embellished interior walls with paintings during the fourth to fifth century A.D., using both Buddhist and Hindu motifs. Many of these murals were painstakingly removed and are now displayed in the Bakhtar (Bactrian) room opened in November 1980.

The magnificent Begram collection of incomparable beauty and diversity speaks of Kushan affluence. The approximate 1,772 artifacts excavated at Begram (ancient Kapisa) north of Kabul, in 1937 and 1939, date mostly from the height of Kushan power during the mid-second century, when Kapisa was the Kushan summer capital on the fabled Silk Route between India and China. The collection includes carved ivories in classic Indian styles, Chinese lacquers, and an infinite variety of Roman bronzes, plaster matrixes, and glass from Alexandria, including large painted goblets that had been known only by fragments before the Begram excavations. The museum's ancient glass collection is unequaled.

From the same general periods are scores of schist and limestone relief sculptures in the Gandharan style. They adorned Buddhist complexes established during the Kushan period in the valleys north of Kabul and at Kunduz, on the Turkestan plains north of the Hindu Kush mountains. Sculptured pieces from Surkh Kotal just north of the Hindu Kush, where excavations began in 1952, include statues of the most renowned Kushan king, Kanishka, who ruled about 128, and the first lengthy inscription in the Kushan language ever found. It is written in Greek script. Other important finds from Surkh Kotal are the carved capitals and pilasters with Classical, Iranian, and Central Asian elements that give rise to new interpretations of the development of Gandharan art. It now appears that the Afghan area was the experimental ground from which these Western forms moved to mix with the styles of northern India.

Stucco and clay-molded sculpture also from Buddhist monasteries of this and later periods at Hadda, Tepe Sardar at Ghazni, and in Kabul are so extensive that only a small portion can be displayed. Hadda, although extensively excavated in 1923, during the 1930s, and again from 1965 to 1980, continued to give forth treasure and much more lies untapped. Since 1967, the Tepe Sardar excavations have produced a wealth of material including polychrome wall paintings, mosaic flooring, and some of the finest clay statuary recovered to date. Tepe Sardar's peak period occurred during the seventh-eighth century.

Some 348 elegant, highly refined seventh-century clay sculptures in the museum collection from Fondukistan in the central mountains were excavated in

1937. In addition, 169 examples of the famous frescoes at Bamiyan, also in the central mountains, may also be viewed in the museum. Archaeological investigations at Bamiyan, where two colossal standing Buddhas, thirty-eight and fifty-five meters tall, were carved into a limestone cliff during the third and fourth centuries, began as early as 1922. The frescoes date from the eighth and ninth centuries. The art from these sites exhibits a complex hybrid style strongly permeated with influences from India, Sasanian Iran, and Central Asia that spread along the trade routes of Central Asia and passed into China from where they were disseminated to Japan and Southeast Asia. They illustrate Afghanistan's continued importance as a point of artistic diffusion throughout its early history.

Exciting evidence of Hinduism, which flourished under Hindu Shahi rulers during the sixth to ninth century, is provided by a number of masterful marble sculptures exhibiting styles unique in the history of Indian art. They shed welcome light into the murky corners of this transitional period before Islam was introduced to the Afghan area.

The most brilliant Islamic period unfolded under the Ghaznavids, whose capital was at Ghazni. This period from the tenth to twelfth century is well represented in the museum by high-quality bronzes, marble reliefs, ceramics, and frescoes. Also included in the total of almost five thousand items from the Islamic periods are examples of sixteenth-century miniature painting from the Timurid capital at Herat. The large manuscript collection containing countless miniatures, however, no longer resides in the National Museum. It was removed in 1966 and relocated in the National Archives, which opened in 1980.

A small collection of canvases by the first Afghan artists to experiment with Western techniques exists, but there have been no systematic attempts to develop this collection.

The museum's coin collection of more than thirty thousand items is one of the most extensive in the world, ranging from the pre-Achaemenid period in the eighth century B.C. to the modern periods. The Greek coins found accidentally in Kabul in 1930 offer the first evidence of the spread of Greek coinage into the Afghan area during the Achaemenid period in the sixth century A.D. The Graeco-Bactrian Kunduz hoard found in 1946 is the finest collection of Graeco-Bactrian coins in existence. In addition to containing the largest Greek coins ever discovered, this cache of more than six hundred coins dating from the third to second century B.C. is distinguished for its artistry and consummate craftsmanship.

The ethnographic collection included in the museum's original holdings was not returned to the museum when it reopened in 1980. It remains in storage pending the projected opening of a special ethnographic museum. The most stellar attractions in this collection are twenty unsurpassed Kafir ancestral wooden effigies from Nuristan dating from the days before this area in eastern Afghanistan was converted to Islam in 1895–96.

Selected Bibliography

Museum publications: Dupree, Nancy Hatch, Louis Dupree, A. A. Motamedi, *The National Museum of Afghanistan: An Illustrated Guide*, 1974; *Ai Khanoum*, May 1981.

Other publications: Allchin, F. R., and Norman Hammond (eds.), *Archaeology of Afghanistan* (London 1978); Auboyer, Jeannine, *The Art of Afghanistan* (Middlesex 1968); Carratelli, G. Pugliese, and G. Garboni, "A Bilingual Graeco-Aramaic Edict by Ashoka," *Serie Orientale Roma*, vol. 29 (1964); Dupree, Louis, et al., *Prehistoric Research in Afghanistan* (Philadelphia 1972); Dupree, Louis, et al., "The Khosh Tapa Hoard," *Archaeology*, vol. 24, no. 1 (1971), pp. 28–34; Francfort, Henri-Paul, and M.-H. Pottier, "Sondage préliminaire sur l'établissement protohistorique Harappéen et post-Harappéen de Shortugai," *Arts Asiatiques*, vol. 34 (1978), pp. 29–86; Hallade, Madeleine, *The Gandhara Style* (London 1968); Kruglikova, Irina, *Delbarjin* (Moscow 1974, 1977); *Mémoires de la Délégation archéologique française en Afghanistan*, vols. 1–23 (Paris 1928–79); Rahman, Abdur, *The Last Two Dynasties of the Shahis* (Islamabad 1979); Rice, Frances M., and Benjamin Rowland, *Art in Afghanistan: Objects from the Kabul Museum* (London 1971); Rowland, Benjamin, *Ancient Art from Afghanistan: Treasures of the Kabul Museum* (New York 1966); Sarianidi, Victor, *The Golden Hoard of Bactria* (New York 1985); Taddei, Maurizio, "Tepe Sardar," *East and West*, n.s., vol. 20ff. (1970 to present).

NANCY HATCH DUPREE

Argentina

———— Buenos Aires ————

NATIONAL MUSEUM OF FINE ARTS (officially MUSEO NACIONAL DE BELLAS ARTES), Avenida de Liberatador 1473, Buenos Aires, Argentina.

The creation of the National Museum of Fine Arts was realized through a government decree dated or issued July 16, 1895. The original museum, located on the Mall Bon Marche at 733 Florida Street, was inaugurated toward the end of 1896. The first exhibition of 163 works from the collections of Adriano Rossi and José Prudencio Guerrico were displayed in five galleries. After the founding of the museum the collections grew through the generosity of several patrons, most notably Don Eduardo Schiaffino.

In 1910 the museum was transferred to the Argentine Pavilion, originally erected for the Exposicion Universal de Paris in 1889 by the Republic. The structure, made of iron, ceramic, and glass, was later dismantled and transported to Buenos Aires, where it was to house the national collections until 1931. In that year a government decree was issued on November 23, stating that the Museum of Fine Arts and its collections were to be moved to the buildings formally occupied by facilities run by the National Health Services. The location has since remained the address of the museum, where there have been continual adaptations made to the original structure to improve the functions of the museum, most notably in the years 1941, 1944, and 1960.

During 1960, as part of the sesquicentennial celebrations of Argentina's independence, a new pavilion, or annex, was constructed to display temporary exhibitions. In 1980 the museum opened a new gallery structure that measures sixteen by one hundred meters, with an actual exhibition space of six thousand square meters.

The museum collections include those donated by Mercedes Santa Marina,

José Prudencio Guerrico, and Adriano E. Rossi, who, along with the Argentine government, may be considered as the founders, as was the first director, Don Eduardo Schiaffino (painter, writer, historian, and critic).

Those mentioned above formed the intellectual and artistic elite of Argentina in the later part of the nineteenth century. They were the primary and unifying factors in the literary society El Ateneo and later in the Estimulo de Bellas Artes. It was from those two centers that the campaign to persuade the government that there was a need for a national museum of fine arts began. Later acquisitions by the museum have been supported by the Association of Friends of the Museum and the National Academy of Fine Arts, as well as by artists and other institutions. Regardless of origin or period, the exhibitions sponsored by the museum have stressed quality, and as a result, the museum is the most important cultural center in the country.

The museum is composed of three defined areas of activities: Administration, Museum Studies (curatorial), and Exhibitions. Responsibilities of the Museum Studies include restoration facilities, photographic laboratories and archives, cataloguing and archives, the cultural extension, and the library. The library, open to the public, contains forty-five thousand volumes for students and professionals specializing in the plastic arts, dance, music, and theater. The handling of the permanent collections and the temporary exhibits, as well as the docent programs, fall under the jurisdiction of the Exhibition area.

Exhibitions are held in thirty-four galleries subdivided into two groups, the first into galleries of even numbers, the second into galleries of uneven numbers. This division was adapted to meet the needs of architectural space. The galleries are grouped by chronology and by other criteria due to the diversity of artists, themes, and media.

Among the most prized works in the collection are those by Argentine artists such as Pettoruti (*Arlequin* and *Vino Rosso*), Spilimbergo (*El Rapto*), Berni (*Lili*), Juan del Prete (*Juicio de Paris*), Castagnino (*La Maria*), Polesello (*Lupa, Lente, Prisma*), and Badii (*Torrente*). Others from the nineteenth century are C. Morel (*Retrato dela Senora Macedonia Escardo*), Palliere (*Idilio Criollo*), and P. Pueyrredon (*El Rodeo*).

Non-Argentine works of art are represented most strongly by those of French and Spanish painters. Notable French works are *P. Lescau and La Goulu in the Moulin Rouge* by Toulouse-Lautrec, *Peaches and Cherries* by Renoir, *The Bridge at Argenteuil* by Monet, the *Study for Two Ballerinas on Stage* by Degas, the *Bathers* by Gauguin, and *Eloquence* by Bourdelle. Among the Spanish works are examples by Goya, *Carnaval* and *Seated Woman* by Gutierrez Solana, and *Garden of Aranjuez* by Rusiñol.

Two important examples of academic painting are Lefebvre's *Diana Discovered* and Bouguereau's *The First Duel*. Romanesque sculpture is represented by two notable works, a *Crucifix* and *St. Anne and the Virgin*, both by unknown artists.

Twentieth-century art is well represented, including pieces by Picasso, Ben

Nicholson's *White Column*, Vasarély's *Attika*, Léger's *Marie, the Acrobat*, Torres-Garcia's *El Hombre*, and Jackson Pollock's *Shooting Star*. By Dubuffet is *Texture*; Kandinsky, *Brown Circle*; Fougita, *Self Portrait*; and Klee, *Boats at Rest*. *From One Sector* by Maldonado can be viewed as can *Lovers* by Chagall, *Plaza* by de'Chirico, and *Red House* by Carrà.

The upper floor of the new gallery includes an audiovisual gallery that will hold two hundred adults. Depending on the needs, the museum is able to adapt this gallery to the needs of the activities surrounding lectures or presentations used in instructing young children, students, or adults. Daily films are shown on the theme of art and the lives and works of painters, sculptors, and recognized personalities in the world of art. On occasion, experimental films are shown, and it is not unusual that instructional activities are coordinated with temporary exhibitions brought to Argentina through the help of various foreign embassies located in Buenos Aires.

The museum offers to the public concerts performed by various groups, and it regularly presents short courses and lectures by well-recognized figures in the world of culture. Every Sunday a diverse cultural program is prepared specifically for children. Activities may include theater, music, dance, works by themselves, or amusement such as cartoons.

There is a museum shop that sells cards, catalogues, and books pertaining to the permanent collection and to the eight to ten special exhibitions installed yearly. The museum does not have a printed catalogue of its collection available to the public.

SAMUEL PAZ, translated by STEPHEN VOLLMER

Selected Bibliography

Museum publications: *Nomina de las omas del Museo de Bellas Artes de la Boca: El Museo*, 1956.

MARY LOUISE WOOD

Australia

—— Adelaide ——

ART GALLERY OF SOUTH AUSTRALIA (formerly NATIONAL GALLERY OF SOUTH AUSTRALIA), North Terrace, Adelaide, South Australia 5000.

The National Gallery of South Australia's collection dates from 1875, when gifts were made to the state. In 1880 the House of Assembly voted funds, and the Gallery opened in 1881 in the Public Library building. From 1889 to 1900 the collection was displayed in the Jubilee Exhibition building, and then the collection moved to its present site. In 1967 the name of the Gallery was changed to the Art Gallery of South Australia.

Although principally government funded, substantial gifts from Sir Thomas Elder, Alexander Melrose, and other supporters have significantly added to the acquisition capacity of the Gallery. In 1969 the Friends of the Art Gallery of South Australia was formed, and this body applies annual dues to support the museum as does the Foundation established in 1980. Since 1940 the Gallery has been run by an art gallery board presently consisting of nine members appointed on three-year overlapping terms. It is administered by a director, deputy director, and curatorial departments of Paintings, Prints and Drawings, Decorative Arts, and historical collections. The building was officially opened on June 18, 1881, by Prince Albert Victoria.

The gallery initially bought contemporary English and Continental paintings but has also accumulated some fine Old Master paintings and decorative art objects. Something of the diverse character of the collection can be envisaged by the fact that more than two-thirds of the collection was either donated or purchased from bequest funds. The Master of the Uttenheim altarpiece's *St. Martin of Tours and St. Nicholas of Bari* (c. 1470) and Bonifazio Veronese's

Rest on the Flight into Egypt are the token representatives of the Renaissance. Several Dutch seventeenth-century paintings lead to a group of English late-eighteenth-century portraits. Late-nineteenth-century taste is represented by purchases of G. F. Watts, Henri Fantin-Latour, Emile Claus, Giovanni Segantini, W. Bouguereau, and Lord Leighton. Predictably, the colonial response to modernism was through English artists, and so the collection boasts good examples of Sickert, Gore, and Gilman's work. A 1956 Bacon and Richard Long's *Stone Circle*, 1979, continue the Anglophile flavor, whereas a Duane Hanson *Woman with a Laundry Basket*, 1974, and a Donald Judd Minimalist sculpture of the same year assert the American presence.

The European decorative-arts collection contains some fine examples commencing with the English silver-gilt *Standing Salt* of 1583 and the Thomas Thompson *Bracket Clock* (c. 1678). There is a small collection of Oriental and Indian art, including Thai ceramics with lifesize Sawankhalok stoneware objects. However, the most impressive holdings are undoubtedly in the Prints and Drawings Department. In 1907 the Honorable David Murray left funds and 2,073 engravings to establish the department that now boasts fine Barocci, Guercino, and Tiepolo drawings and good holdings of Piranesi, Goya, Turner, and Rouault prints.

The Art Gallery of South Australia has a comprehensive collection of Australian painting from the late eighteenth century to the present. Australia's late-nineteenth-century Impressionist movement, the Heidelberg school, is particularly well represented, including Tom Roberts' *The Breakaway*.

The museum publishes an annual bulletin and annual report as well as exhibition catalogs and a picture book.

Selected Bibliography

Museum publications: *Picture Book—Selected Works from the Collections of the Art Gallery of South Australia*, 1972; *Catalogue of Drawings*, 1958; *Catalogue of the Unfinished Works of Sir Hans Heysen OBE* (1877–1968): bequest of the artist to the Art Gallery of South Australia, 1975; *Hans Heysen Centenary Retrospective* (1877–1977), 1977; *Special Exhibitions at the Art Gallery of South Australia*; Sixth Adelaide Festival of Arts 1970, 1970; *Thai Ceramics—Banchiang, Khmer, Sukothai, Sawankhalok* (from the) *Art Gallery of South Australia*; Mather, J. B., *Oil and Water Colour Paintings and Pastels, National Gallery of South Australia*, 6th ed., 1960; Thompson, Judith, *South Australian Ceramics 1900–1950, Art Gallery of South Australia*, 1983; Astbury, L., "Tom Roberts' *The Breakaway* Myth and History, *Bulletin of the Art Gallery of South Australia*, vol. 38 (1980); Carroll, A., "Mantegna and the Mantegnesque in the Art Gallery of South Australia," *Bulletin of Art Gallery of South Australia*, vol. 35 (1977), n.p.; idem, "A Study by Sir Edward Burne Jones for the Story of Phyllis and Demphoon," *Bulletin of Art Gallery of South Australia*, vol. 33 (1978), pp. 44–48; Gaston, R., "Bonifazio Veronese's *Rest on the Flight into Egypt*," *Bulletin of Art Gallery of South Australia*, vol. 35 (1977), pp. 36–41; Neylon, J., "Gorgons and Gold Seven *Wonder Book* Drawings by Walter Crane," *Bulletin of Art Gallery of South Australia*, vol. 38 (1980), pp. 2–6; North, I., "Bert Flugelman from Heroism to Reflection," *Bulletin of Art Gallery of South Australia*, vol. 33 (1978), pp. 2–15; Thomas, D., "Frederick McCubbin's *Winter Sunlight*," *Bulletin of Art Gallery of South Australia*, vol. 33 (1978), pp. 34–43; White, C., "Three Etchings by Rembrandt," *Bulletin of Art Gallery of South Australia*, vol. 33 (1978), pp. 16–21.

Other publications: Mountford, Charles Pearcy, *Aboriginal Art from Australia; Bark Paintings and Sculpture Lent by the National Gallery of South Australia, Adelaide* (Worcester, Mass. 1966); Carroll, A., "A Newly Discovered Drawing by Giambattista Tiepolo in Adelaide," *Master Drawings*, vol. 18 (1980), pp. 147–148.

DAVID A. JAFFÉ

—————— Canberra ——————

AUSTRALIAN NATIONAL GALLERY, Canberra, ACT 2600.

The Australian National Gallery was opened on October 12, 1982. Although the Commonwealth Art Advisory Board was established in 1912, it was not until 1969, at the instigation of James Mollison, that substantial government funding was obtained. In 1975 the National Gallery Act was passed, and in 1977 the present director, James Mollison, was appointed.

The Australian National Gallery building and collections were funded by the commonwealth government until the opening in 1982, after which corporate and individual donor appeals and revenues derived from admission charges and commercial activities have been used to supplement the government acquisition allocation. The Australian National Gallery Association, a members' body established in 1982, also applies annual dues to support the Gallery.

The Australian National Gallery is governed by a council consisting of a director and ten members appointed on three-year overlapping terms. It is administered by a director, an administrator, departments of Conservation and Education, and the curatorial departments of International Art (Contemporary Art, International Paintings, Sculpture and Decorative Arts, 1900–1970, European Art before 1900, Theatre Arts and Textiles, South-East Asian Art, Primitive Art), International Prints and Illustrated Books, Photography, and Australian Art.

The building, opened by Queen Elizabeth II on October 12, 1982, was designed by the Sydney architect Colin Madigan. This cement structure was designed in the new brutalism style to harmonize with the adjacent High Court building designed by the same architect.

Successive councils of the Australian National Gallery have been committed to a small collection of European art before 1900 to represent major movements in Western art with a more extensive coverage of modern international art. The international collection is initiated by a Cycladic female figure, c. 2300 B.C. (attributed to the Goulandris Master), followed by Giovanni di Paolo, *Crucifixion*, c. 1450; a Ferraese wooden statue of the *Madonna of Humility*, c. 1470;

Peter Paul Rubens, *Self Portrait*, 1623; and Giambattista Tiepolo, *Marriage Allegory*, c. 1746. The achievements of just one decade of serious collecting are more extensive from the nineteenth century: a fine Ingres drawing, *Portrait of Jean-Pierre Granger* of 1810, heralds Courbet's study for the *Young Ladies on the Banks of the Seine in Summer* done in 1856; Daumier's plaster relief *The Emigrants*; and two Monets representing the *Haystack* and *Waterlilies* series.

Modigliani's life-sized statue *Standing Figure*, c. 1909–15; Kasimir Malevich's *House under Construction*, c. 1914; Miró's *Landscape*, 1927; Matisse's *Europa and the Bull*, 1927; and Brancusi's marble *Birds in Flight*, 1933, are masterpieces of early twentieth-century art. Jackson Pollock's *Blue Poles*, 1952, is the focus of the extensive New York School holdings, which also include good examples of works by Gorky, De Kooning, Rothko, and David Smith. Morris Louis, Andy Warhol, and Guston are the principal representatives of the sixties in American art, whereas some twenty-six Matisse drawings and Léger's large *Trapezists* (1954) are impressive reminders of the continued European contribution. As the recent purchases of Enzo Cucchi and Rainer Fetting pictures illustrate, the Gallery is actively collecting the art of the 1980s.

If the Gallery's holdings of international drawings are little better than token, the situation with nineteenth- and twentieth-century prints and photographs is far more encouraging. In both areas the collection approaches comprehensive representation. There is an outstanding collection of early-twentieth century Russian pamphlets and illustrated books.

The Gallery also has achieved a select display of pre-Columbian and Oceanic art. Particularly fine are the holdings of the art of New Zealand Maoris and Papua New Guinea and the Australian aboriginal people. The African sculpture collection already gives a comprehensive regional picture of their stylistic diversity.

The Australian art collection displays the development of painting, sculpture, and decorative arts from the date of the first European settlement in 1778 to the present. The Gallery's collection differs from the more established Australian public collections, which concentrate on stringing masterpieces together, in that it is concerned with a comprehensive integration of iconography and taste to present a cultural history. Photographs, prints, drawings, and illustrated books add to the displays. Early Australian silver and furniture are well represented. Paintings are displayed in period frames and aboriginal art is introduced to appear beside artists who were responding to it.

The Gallery's policy of displaying prints and watercolors, photographs, and drawings to supplement the painting collection means that the prints and photographic galleries are not the only areas to undergo changes every two months. A similar rapid turnover is experienced in the theater arts and fashion gallery, where the strength is again in early-twentieth-century material.

Although the Gallery rarely accepts traveling exhibits, it has its own modern art gallery space, the Drill Hall on the campus of the Australian National University, where it mounts exhibitions of contemporary Australian and international art from its own considerable reserve collections.

The Australian National Gallery has an art library of more than thirty-five thousand volumes, with an emphasis on sale and exhibition catalogues from the late nineteenth century to the present.

Selected Bibliography

Museum publications: *Australian National Gallery: An Introduction*, 1982; *Annual Report*, 1975; Bonyhady, T., *Australian Colonial Paintings in the Australian National Gallery*, 1984; Gilmore, P., and A. Willsford, *Paperwork*, 1982; Gleeson, J., *William Dobell Drawings*, 1984; McPhee, J., *Australian Decorative Arts in the Australian National Gallery*, 1984; Mollison, J., and N. Bonham, *Albert Tucker*, 1982; *Aspects of Australian Art*, 1978; *Genesis of a Gallery*, 1976; *Genesis of a Gallery*, part 2, 1978; *How Formal Should I Go?* 1982; *Eugene von Guerard*, 1980; *Fred Williams*, 1981.

DAVID A. JAFFÉ

———— Melbourne ————

NATIONAL GALLERY OF VICTORIA, 180 St. Kilda Road, Melbourne, Victoria 3004.

The idea of establishing Australia's first art gallery was put forward at the inaugural meeting of the Victorian Society of Fine Arts in 1856, and with the support of parliamentarian Sir Redmond Barry, land was reserved on the south side of the Melbourne Public Library complex (built in 1856) on Swanston Street. Two thousand pounds were voted toward the purchase of works of art in England, so that when the Museum of Art was opened by Governor Sir Henry Barkly in 1861, a small collection of casts, medals, bas-reliefs, coins, paintings, and objets d'art were on display.

The government gave another two thousand pounds in 1863 to form the nucleus of a museum gallery and art school. Sir Charles Eastlake, president of the Royal Academy, made the first major purchase of thirteen paintings by contemporary British artists; however, the collection remained undistinguished until 1904. At that time, the National Gallery of Victoria (renamed in 1875) became one of the wealthiest galleries in the British Commonwealth, sharing half of the income from the almost fourteen thousand-pound bequest of Alfred Felton. Other major bequests have been those by Everard Stadley Miller (1956), Maude Matilda Nott (1967), and Samuel E. Wills (1967).

The National Gallery Society assists the work of the Gallery with lectures, films, volunteer guides, and fund-raising events. It also sponsors the McCaughey Art Prize and an annual drawing prize for students of the Gallery School.

A main picture gallery was completed in 1869 and extended eastward and north of the original gallery in a long U-shape. The opening was closed with the construction of the drawing school the following year. More galleries extending eastward into the building occupied by the National Museum were added in 1875 (the McArthur and Latrobe galleries), 1925 (the McAllen Gallery with funds willed in 1903), and 1928 (the Murdock Gallery). Soon, however, the Gallery became inadequate for its growing collection, and in 1943 the trustees of the library commissioned architects to report on the potential development of the three institutions. After much discussion and many recommendations, director Eric Westbrook was asked by the government in 1956 to report on the art center. This report was used to enable legislation to proceed, and the National Gallery was given priority in the building program.

The building, designed by Sir Roy Grounds assisted by the director and his staff, was opened on August 20, 1968. It displays a classic severity and palazzo-like proportions in the clerestory windows and impressive arched entrance. The building contains two display areas and administrative and storage floors surrounding three internal courtyards (an oriental water garden, a sculpture court, and an open-air performance area). The clerestory windows provide the painting galleries with natural light (supplemented where necessary with artificial light), as well as the study-storage mezzanine level above. The display cases, designed by Grant and Mary Featherstone, are effective in the Mediterranean Gallery. Nowhere is a white wall used as a background to the paintings. Most walls are surfaced with honey-colored mountain ash, although some of the Old Masters are displayed against panels of green baize. The Great Hall, used for public performances and official banquets, is spanned by a vast stained-glass ceiling designed by Melbourne artist Leonard French.

The first director was appointed in 1882 and, with his staff, was given official grading in the Victorian public service. The government still pays all salaries and maintenance and provides a small purchasing grant. When financing major purchases is considered, additional funds are provided. All funds generated by the small admission charges are directed to acquisitions. The director now heads a professional staff of 22, an administrative staff of 14, and a support staff of 120. There are eight curatorial departments: European Art before 1800, European Art after 1800, Asian Art, Tribal Art, Australian Art, Prints and Drawings, Decorative Arts, and Photography (the first in Australia), as well as a Department of Exhibitions.

The Gallery has recently acquired *Banyule*, a Victorian mansion in the suburb of Heidelberg, which is being used to display nineteenth-century paintings, furniture, and decorative arts. Consideration is being given to the acquisition of an exhibition space in the central-city area of Melbourne to house displays of avant-garde works and temporary exhibits.

The naturalistic, devotional art that flourished in the Netherlands in the fifteenth century is seen in four excellent works—Hans Memling's *Christ in the Arms of the Virgin*, 1475; Simon Marmion's *Virgin and Child*, 1465–75; Jan van Eyck's magnificent *Ince Hall Madonna* (one of the masterpieces of the period); and *Triptych with the Miracles of Christ* from the workshop of Pieter van der Weyden. The Late Gothic style is exemplified by the wooden *St. Barbara* from France. The early Italian Renaissance is represented by a Paolo Veneziano *Crucifixion*, but paintings by Sienese Domenico di Bartolo (*St. George Slaying the Dragon*) and Sassetta (*The Miracle of the Sacrament*) and the Florentine *Profile Portrait of a Lady*, all works of the fifteenth century, are more significant.

Paintings by Fontana, Perino del Vega, Titian, Tintoretto, Bassano, El Greco, and a North Italian *Portrait of a Youth* all are represented in the collection. Bernini is represented by the bust *Cardinal Richelieu*, the gilt-bronze statuette *Countess Matilda of Tuscany* (1633–37), and the *Self Portrait* in oils. The tender *Virgin Annunciate* by the Roman Bernardo Cavallino and more dramatic works by the Neopolitans Mattia Preti and Luca Giordano are shown here. The decorative virtuosity of the Venetian school is seen in the major work in the collection, Tiepolo's *The Banquet of Cleopatra* of 1743–44 (formerly in the Hermitage) and in the works of Veronese and Sebastiano Ricci, and Guardi's fluid touch is seen in two works.

Rubens, the northern Baroque master, is represented by two oil sketches, one of which is the mythological *Hercules and Antaeus*, c. 1625–30. A caravaggesque influence is noticable in Rembrandt's early *Two Philosophers* (1628), but his style comes into its own in his later *Self Portrait* and *Portrait of a Man* (1677). Dutch painting is one of the strongest sections of the collection and includes fine works by de Heem, Kalf, Ter Borch, Mor, Ruysdael, Ruisdael, Hobbema, Steen, Teniers. France at the time is represented by one of Poussin's major works, *The Crossing of the Red Sea*, and his classical vision is continued with Claude Lorraine's *Landscape with River and Rocks*. Court portraiture is shown to excellent effect in Rigaud's *Double Portrait*, Largillierre's *King Frederick Augustus of Poland*, and two works by Pompeo Batoni.

Van Dyck's elegance inspired most of the English eighteenth-century portraitists (Ramsay, Highmore, Reynolds, Gainsborough, Zoffany, Hoppner, and Lawrence), while a more informal note is struck with Romney's *The Leigh Family*, c. 1768. This most comprehensive section also contains an interesting group of Highmore's illustrations to Richardson's *Pamela*. The English affinity for landscape is seen in a group of eight works by Constable, the most impressive of which is *Boulter's Lock*, and several works by J. M. W. Turner, including the late *Val d'Osta*. Also included is a group of watercolors by Cozens, Cotman, De Wint, Varley, Towne, Palmer, and Prout.

Only selections of the post–1800 collections are on display in the small gallery. The French Romantic school is represented by Delacroix and Géricault. The collection includes Corot's *Bent Tree (Morning)*, about 1855–60; works by the Barbizon School, as exemplified in Millet, Daubigny, and Rousseau; and several Boudin seascapes. By Puvis de Chavannes, there are two works in the collection; one of which, the large cartoon *St. Genevieve Provisioning Paris*, is permanently displayed in the Great Hall.

Representing the Impressionists are two Monets; three Pissarros, including the superb *Rue Montmartre* of 1897; two excellent Sisleys; a marvelous Manet, the *House at Rueil* of 1882; a Degas; and a Renoir. A fine Signac (*Gasometers Clichy*) and a Lucien Pissarro represent Neo-Impressionism. There are representative Post-Impressionist works by Cézanne, van Gogh, Rouault, Utrillo, Matisse, and Bonnard. Also, by Vuillard is *Portrait of Mme. Bonnard*, which Bonnard had in his possession at the time of his death. Two works by Ernst and Magritte's *In Praise of Dialectics* are Surrealist. More recent European art in the collection is furnished by Saura, Appel, Tapies, Vasarély, and Soto.

The Gallery houses extensive collections of nineteenth- and twentieth-century British painting, including a very fine group of paintings by the Pre-Raphaelites and their associates, which were acquired largely before 1920. Works by Ford Madox Brown, Holman Hunt, Millais, Hughes, Rossetti, Burne-Jones, Watts, and Alma-Tadema are included. The twentieth century is represented by paintings by Sickert, Steer, Stanley Spencer, Nash, Spear, Wyndham Lewis, Augustus John, Tunnard, and Hitchens and more recent works by Pasmore, Bacon, Michael Andrews (including the frequently illustrated *All Night Long*), Bridget Riley, David Hockney (*Marriage of Styles No. 2*), and John Hoyland. Contemporary American paintings are also being collected. This small group includes works by Sam Francis, Albers, Frankenthaler, Mark Tobey, Noland, Poons, and Jenkins.

To the group of Rodin bronzes has been added the monumental statue *Balzac* (1891–98), which shares space with a Moore bronze, *Large Seated Draped Figure* (1957). Also by Moore is *Half Figure Seated*. Eleven plaster models were recently donated by the widow of Jacob Epstein. More recent European sculpture includes an important Ipousteguy, *Death of the Father*, and works by Phillip King, Caro, and Pomodoro. The United States is represented by works of Cremean, Gallo, a kinetic Royer (*Sun Machine*), and a superb early Gaston Lachaise (*Torso*).

The greatest holdings in the Gallery lie in the more than fifteen hundred works in the prints and drawings collection. There are more than two hundred Rembrandt prints including famous etchings such as the *Hundred Guilder Print, The Three Trees*, and *The Three Crosses*. The purchase of Sir Thomas Barlow's collection in 1956 brought into the Gallery a nearly complete representation of Dürer's graphic oeuvre. Other significant groups are Goya's *Disasters of War* and *The Bullfights*, van Dyck's *Iconography*, Turner's *Liber Studiorum*, Kokoschka's *Odyssey*, and an extensive collection of English eighteenth-century mezzotints. William Blake is represented by a significant number of works as well as a series of thirty-six watercolors for Dante's *Divine Comedy*. The collection also has two of the most famous Renaissance prints: Pollaiuolo's *Battle of the Naked Men*, c. 1470, and Mantegna's *Battle of the Sea Gods*.

Australian artists are also well documented. The department has a complete set of Lionel Lindsay's etchings and woodcuts, Sidney Nolan's *Leda Suite*, and Arthur Boyd's *St. Francis Series*. Modern American prints are also being collected.

Drawings include magnificent works such as Andrea del Sarto's *St. John the Baptist*, Parmigianino's *Staghunt*, Carracci's *Ignudo* for the Farnese Ceiling, Tiepolo's *Scene of Baptism*, and Castiglione's *Tobit Burying the Dead*. Later artists represented are Romney, Boucher (a delicate pastel, *Madame de Pompador*), Ingres, Degas (a marvelous *Dancer*, c. 1880), Rodin, Picasso, and

Modigliani (*Caraytid*). Of note is a group of more than three hundred drawings by the English nineteenth-century artist Charles Keene from the Lionel Lindsay Collection. Apart from the Blake watercolors, the collection has works by Turner (*Red Rigi*, 1842, once owned by John Ruskin), Klee (*Thistle Picture*, 1924), Vuillard, Chagall (*Lion and Rat*, 1926), Dubuffet, Zadkine, Paul Nash, Piper, Moore, Sam Francis, and Gottlieb.

The Department of Decorative Arts possesses the most diverse collection in the Gallery. The collection of silver is principally English and demonstrates the changes in style and taste from a chalice and paten of 1535, the earliest piece in the collection, to the present. Notable items are a toilet service by Anthony Nelme (c. 1695), an elaborate epergne in the Chinese taste by Thomas Pitts (1762–63), and a two-handled cup by Paul Storr (1806–7). There are two important items relating to Australia: a presentation centerpiece by the Castlemaine silversmith Ernest Leviny (c. 1863) and a group of three gilt candelabra presented to the governor of Australia by Queen Victoria. Continental silverware is sparsely represented, although an important sixteenth-century Nuremberg pineapple cup by Peter Vischer and modern works by Jensen and Puiforcat have been added. Displayed with the silver is a collection of Italian Renaissance and Mannerist bronzes, largely from the bequest of Howard Spensley.

It is possible to document the history of English ceramics, from the robust pottery of the fourteenth century to the present. The eighteenth century, with its tin glazed wares and figure groups from the major factories of Chelsea, Bow, Worcester, Derby, and so on, has the richest representation, largely through the Templeton gift of porcelains in 1941. There is a small but choice collection of Italian majolica of the fifteenth century. The minutely decorated istoriato plates by Nicola Pellipario, Francesco Avelli, and from the workshop of Giovanni Maria are, in fact, some of the few pieces in the collection that exemplify the Renaissance. Especially interesting are a pair of grotestque vases from Urbino dated 1580–1600. The collection is rich in French and Dutch faience and also has some important German and Spanish examples. The representation of Continental porcelain is not extensive, but the Gallery does possess some fine German Rococo figure groups.

The William and Margaret Morgan Endowment was formed specifically to acquire the G. Gordon Russell Collection of seventeenth- and eighteenth-century British drinking glasses and pieces to complement the collection. The Gallery now possesses a collection that demonstrates every phase of glassmaking during those centuries and is, in fact, one of the finest collections in the world. Of special interest are the engraved commemorative glasses connected with the Stuart and Jacobite causes. The collection is displayed in the C. R. Roper Gallery and contains a small group of Continental glass; a German *reichsadlerhumper* (beaker) and two magnificent Dutch flute glasses of the seventeenth century are of special note.

The strength of the costume collection is in the eighteenth and nineteenth centuries, although some earlier items are of interest, for example, a Coptic robe of the fourth to seventh century and some ecclesiastical vestments. Because of the interest generated by the purchase and display of the Ann Schofield Collection in 1974 (more than one thousand costumes and accessories), numerous donations have ensured that this is the most rapidly expanding collection in the museum. There is also an important collection of peasant costumes dating around the turn of the century, largely from Eastern Europe. Although the gallery possesses a large collection of textile fragments and embroideries and a rich collection of laces, the most spectacular items are the tapestries *Carlo and Ubaldo at the Fountain of Laughter* (after a painting by Simon Vouet, 1640–50), Jean Lurçat's *Adam before Creation*, and a seventeenth-century Trinitarias carpet from Tabriz.

A magnificent pair of Italian walnut cassoni of the late sixteenth century are displayed in the picture gallery, although the collection again focuses on English furniture from 1600 to the present. Noteworthy are a gilt table in the manner of William Kent and a superb Chippendale breakfront bookcase.

Modern furniture is also collected. An interesting item is a colored chair by the Dutchman Gerrit Reitveld. A particular emphasis has been laid on the work of Australian craftsmen, and the collection contains items such as the Prenzel suite of gumnut Art Nouveau furniture and a shallow chest on a stand, c. 1948, by Schulman Krimper.

The Department of Decorative Arts also encompasses a small but choice collection of Mediterranean antiquities. Notable works include a Sumerian *Head of Gudea*, the Roman portraits *Head of Vespasian* (first century A.D.) and *Septimus Severius* (late second century A.D.), and the funerary bust of a woman from Behnesa, Egypt. There is a small collection of Roman glass, Egyptian jewelry, and Cypriot vases from the excavations at Vounous and Stephanai. The Greek vases, acquired mainly on the advice of A. D. Trendall, are the outstanding parts of the collection. Two black-figure amphora, one attributed to the Inscriptions Master (c. 540 B.C.), the other ascribed to the circle of Exekias (c. 530 B.C.), and a red-figure cup attributed to the Nicosthenes Painter are of the highest quality. The most important acquisition in recent years is a white ground lekythos by the Achilles Painter. A Campanian hydria by the Libation Painter, an Apulian volute krater by the Ganymede Painter, and an Apulian lion-headed rhyton are representative of South Italian art of the fourth century B.C.

The Australian collection covers the history of artistic endeavor on the continent. The first painting to enter the collection, Nicholas Chevalier's *The Buffalo Ranges, Victoria*, was selected from the forty-three competing works at the opening of the first public gallery in 1864. Earlier colonial works have been acquired, including thirteen watercolors by Conrad Martens and John Glovers' *River Nile: Nan Diemens Land*, while Dowling's *Early Effort: Art in Tasmania* is an example of late colonial work. William Gilbee gave a thousand pounds to commission Australian historical paintings from E. Phillips Fox (*The Landing of Captain Cook at Botany Bay*). Also commissioned was Longstaff's *Arrival of Burke, Wills, and King at the Deserted Camp*, the largest oil painting in Australia. The arrival of artists such as Louis Buvelot, who captured for the first time the essential character of Australia's trees as seen in *Winter Morning Near*

Heidelberg, and Eugene von Guerard contributed enormously to the emerging local landscape tradition.

The Australian Impressionists are well represented: Streeton's perhaps most famous work *Purple Noon's Transparent Might*, 1896; Roberts' *Shearing the Rams*, 1889–95; David Davies' masterpiece *Moonlight Templestowe*; and McCubbin's *Lost Child*. McCubbin was to develop a true Impressionist touch in his later *Autumn Morning South Yarra*. The expatriate artists are represented by important works, such as Bunny's *Endormies* and the sculptor Sir Bertram McKennak's most famous work *Circe*. The lack of a work to chart the influence of Art Nouveau was rectified when the Gallery Society presented Syd Long's *Flamingoes*. Some of the well-known paintings in the collection are Frater's *The Red Hat* (1937), Dobell's *Helena Rubenstein*, Drysdale's *The Rabbiters*, Smart's *Cahill Expressway* (1962), Boyd's *Nude with Beast I*, Fred Williams' *Upwey Landscape*, Roger Kemp's *Organized Forms*, John Coburn's *Primordial Garden*, and Sydney Ball's *Sassanian Encounter*. The gallery supports the work of younger artists such as Dale Hickey, Robert Hunter, Dick Havaytt, John Peart, Paul Partos, John Balsatis, Robert Jacks, and Ti Parks. Recent sculptures in the collection are by Norma Redpath, Clement Meadmore, Bob Wilson, and Ron Robertson-Swann.

After the public responded so enthusiastically to the display of their Chinese ceramics and bronzes, Mr. and Mrs. Herbert Wade Kent donated more than 130 works in 1938, and now, supplemented by outstanding pieces from the Felton bequest, the collection charts an almost complete history of Chinese ceramics. There is a good representation of bronze vessels from the Shang-Yin and early Chou periods; the period of the Warring States is shown by bronzes, jades, and domestic pottery. A pair of life-sized Buddhist stone figures from the Northern Ch'i period, a stone relief Maitreya of the sixth century, and a polychromed Sung Kwan Yin are among the most important sculptures. Chinese painting is represented by notable works by Shen Chou, Yuon Yao, and P'ien Wen-chin.

A screen by the sixteenth-century painter Tosatsu and a select group of *ukiyo-e* prints are evidence of the pictorial art of Japan. A wooden figure of Kannon from the Heian period and two figures and a mask of the Kamakura period represent its sculpture. The remainder of Asia has sparser representation. The finest Indian example is the twelfth-century stone *Dancing Figure* from the Hoysala period, and from Tibet there is a significant collection of devotional objects, *tankas*, and a large bronze figure of Avalokiteshvara, Buddhist god of mercy and compassion. A fine Persian lakabi dish, a head from Borodvodur, a good Khmer torso of Uma, a tenth-century standard figure from Cambodia, some sculpture, and a large collection of textiles from Indonesia complete the Asian collection.

The National Gallery of Victoria produces the *Annual Report* and *Quarterly Bulletin*.

Selected Bibliography

Museum publications: National Gallery of Victoria Booklets: *Renaissance Art*; *French Impressionism and Post-Impressionism*; *English Pottery 15th to 19th Century*; *Greek*

Vases; *Early Australian Painting*; *Australian Abstract Art*; *Four Contemporary Australian Landscape Painters*; *18th Century Costumes and Accessories*; Cox, L. B., *The National Gallery of Victoria, 1861–1968*, 1969; Finemore, B., *Freedom from Prejudice*, 1977; Hoff, U., *European Painting before 1800*, 2d ed., 1967; idem, *The National Gallery of Victoria*, 1973; Hoff, U., and M. Plant, *The National Gallery of Victoria Paintings, Drawings, and Sculpture*; Lindsay, D., *The Felton Bequest: An Historical Record, 1904–1959*, 1963; Peng, Mae Anna, *An Album of Chinese Art from the National Gallery of Victoria*, 1983; Topsfield, Andrew, *Paintings from Rajastan in the National Gallery of Victoria*, 1980; Westbrook, Eric, *Birth of a Gallery*, 1968; Whitelaw, Bridget, *Australian Drawings of the Thirties and Forties in the National Gallery of Victoria*, 1980; *Decorative Arts from the Collections of the National Gallery of Victoria*, 1979.

GLEN COOKE

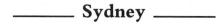

——— Sydney ———

ART GALLERY OF NEW SOUTH WALES (also NATIONAL GALLERY OF NEW SOUTH WALES), Art Gallery Road, Sydney, New South Wales 2000.

The Art Gallery of New South Wales was founded in 1874, when a committee of trustees from the New South Wales Academy of Art was appointed to administer a government grant obtained through the influence of the Honorable Edward Coombes. The National Art Gallery of New South Wales opened to the public in 1876 and in 1899 incorporated under the state government's Library and Art Gallery Act. The Art Gallery of New South Wales Act of 1958 placed it under the aegis of the New South Wales Department of Education. Annual grants from the state government cover the costs of acquisitions and exhibitions, and salaries and maintenance are met by the government public services administration. The director of the gallery, who heads a professional staff of fifteen and a support staff of sixty-eight, is responsible to a board of trustees of thirteen members appointed on the advice of the minister of education. The administration is organized into six curatorial departments: European Art, Contemporary Art, Australian Art, Prints and Drawings, Asian Art, and Photography.

The original collection was housed in the New South Wales Academy for Art. In 1880 it was transferred to the Fine Arts Annex in the Botanical Gardens built for Sydney's International Exhibition in 1879. By 1884 the building was declared unsafe, and the government set aside land for a new gallery to be designed by John Horbury Hunt. The building was opened in 1885 and, although well lighted and fireproof, was considered temporary. It was often referred to as the "art barn" or the "wool store." Hunt produced designs for the exterior but was dismissed by the trustees in 1895 and replaced by W. L. Vernon, the New South Wales colonial architect. By 1897 two galleries were opened. One formed a portion of the ornamental facade and now houses European art from the sixteenth to the eighteenth centuries. The other gallery replaced Hunt's southwest gallery and now houses Australian art of the Edwardian period. By 1901 two more picture galleries supplanted Hunt's original building, and a long watercolor gallery terminating in domed rooms for sculpture was built. In the following year the portico was completed along with Vernon's great masterpiece, the grand oval lobby, which now contains displays of fine marbles quarried in the state. The principal facade was completed in 1909 with the addition of a gallery and boardroom; however, no northern gallery was built to correspond to the watercolor gallery.

Vernon's design included large bronze reliefs on all facades; only four of the six on the front gallery were executed: *Phyrne before Praxiteles* by Percival Ball, *Assur Nassir Pal, King of Assyria* by Gilbert Bayes, *Queen Hatasu of Egypt* by Countess Fedora Giechen, and *Augustus at Nimes* by William Reid Dick. Two large equestrian groups by Gilbert Bayes (*The Offerings of Peace* and *The Offerings of War*), not in Vernon's plan, were installed in the front plaza in 1926.

By the late 1960s, the buildings had deteriorated to such a degree that the New South Wales government decided a rebuilding of much of the site should form part of the Captain Cook bicentennial celebrations. The architects E. H. Farmer and Andrew Anderson were chosen to complete an extension to the building that would add more than twice the exhibition space. The new extension, which opened in 1972, does an excellent job of blending the old Victorian grandeur with modern architecture. The new building provides facilities for a temporary exhibit area, conservation section, storage area, bookshop, library, new curatorial and administrative offices, and restaurant. The cost of the project was shared by the New South Wales state government and the public. It is maintained by the state government, and its trustees are responsible to the minister of cultural activities.

In 1953 the Art Gallery Society of New South Wales was formed to acquire works of art for the gallery and to further art interest within the community. It now has forty-five hundred members.

The character of the collection reflects the 1874 decision to collect contemporary British and Australian works. Old Masters were first collected in the 1930s when two hundred prints, including works by Dürer, Mantegna, and Piranesi, were acquired; however, European paintings have entered the collection only recently. This small group includes a Netherlandish wood carving (once owned by Pugin) and a French limestone Virgin, both dated about 1500. The Sano di Pietro *Madonna and Child* (c. 1480), gift of John Fairfax Pty. Ltd., represents fifteenth-century Siena, and the marble relief *Madonna and Child* (c. 1480) by the Florentine Francesco Ferrucci reflects the humanistic influence of Verrocchio. Strozzi's *The Release of St. Peter* and Matthias Stromer's *Mucius Scaevola in the Presence of Porsenna* are evidence of Caravaggio's influence in Italy and the North.

A portrait of *Dr. Benjamin Hoadley* by Hogarth and a charming landscape by

Orizonte are the first eighteenth-century paintings to enter the collection. Portraits by Raeburn, Reynolds, and Pine; Richard Wilson's *St. Peter and the Janiculum, Rome*; William Hamilton's *Christ and the Woman of Samaria*; and Benjamin West's *Joshua Passing the Jordan with the Ark of the Covenent* are important examples of this period.

The art of Victorian England forms the strength of the collection. The earlier part of the century is represented by watercolors from De Wint, David Cos, John Sell Cotman, Samuel Palmer, and J.M.W. Turner and landscapes by James Baker Pyne and David Roberts. Works by Francis Danby (*The Three Sisters of Phaeton Weeping over the Tomb of Their Brother*), John Glover (*Classical Landscape*), William Etty (*The Golden Age*), and William Westfall (*Landscape Solitude*) can also be seen.

The Gallery's large masterpiece *Chaucer at the Court of Edward III* by Ford Madox Brown is the first European work acquired for the collection. Burne-Jones' *The Fight, St. George Kills the Dragon* is representative of the link between Brown's medievalism and the decorative style of Strudwick and Spencer Stanhope. Edward Poynter is represented by *Helen*, the late portait *Honorable Violet Moncton*, as well as the vast *The Visit of the Queen of Sheba to King Solomon*, the most important of the "Victorian Olympian" works. The Gallery also possesses Long's *A Dorcas Meeting of the Sixth Century* and paintings by the master of the style, Lord Leighton in his *Cymon and Iphigenia*, *Winding the Skein*, and *Wedded* (possibly the most popular of his works). Alma-Tadema's *Head of Cleopatra* and works by Goodall, Waterhouse, Griffenhagen, and Sant reflect this influence into the twentieth century. The Gallery also possesses an interesting group of neoclassical marbles by John Gibson, Harriet Hosmer, Hiram Powers, and Benjamin Spence and a large group of bronzes. The main pieces are Rodin's *Prodigal Son* and Alfred Gilbert's *Comedy and Tragedy*. The largest work is *Retaliation* by C. B. Birch.

A note of social consciousness was introduced in the Gallery's second major purchase in 1883, Luke Fildes' *The Widower* (1876), a theme that continued in the Newlyn school (Napier Hemy, H. S. Tuke, Stanhope Forbes, and Forbes' wife, Elizabeth). Victorian traditions were carried well into the twentieth century by Brangwyn, Cameron, and Munnings.

Walter Sickert's *Second Turn of Katie Lawrence* and works by Wilson Steer and McTaggart are examples of a British para-Impressionism. Post-Impressionist works did not enter the collection until 1933, when works by Dame Ethel Walker, Duncan Grant, Samuel Peploe, Spencer Gore (*Icknield Way*), and James Pryde were acquired. Cubist-Futurist trends are reflected in the three sculptures and thirty drawings of Gaudier-Breszka and Vorticism in an excellent piece by William Roberts, *The Interval before Round Ten*. Works by the primitive artist Christopher Wood and the Surrealist influence in Stanley Spencer, Graham Sutherland (*Welsh Mountains*), Paul Nash (*Sunflower and Sun*), Tristian Hillier, and Albert Burra precede the abstract works of Ben Nicholson (*Still Life*) and Pasmore

(Relief Construction). The paintings are supported by sculpture of the period by Moore, Caro, Hepworth, and others.

Paintings by William Scott, Keith Jones, Prunella Clough, and Jack Smith exemplify styles of the 1950s. Abstract Expressionism is represented by works of Alan Davie *(Flag Dream No. 4: Wheel)* and Jean Paul Riopelle; Op Art is demonstrated through the works of Bridget Riley.

The Gallery has only a small section of fine French painting, since French art was not purchased until 1926, when a Boudin and a Corot were acquired. Later large pictures painted for the Royal Academy or the Paris Salon were obtained. They include *The Sons of Clovis (Les enerves de Jumièges)* by Luminais and the vigorous battle paintings of Detaille and de Neuville *(Rorke's Drift)*. Oriental subjects by Landelle and Dinet were also acquired. The Barbizon School is represented by works of Corot, Diaz, Daubigny, and Mauve. The Gallery owns only one example each of the Impressionist and the Neo-Impressionist periods: *Port-Goulphar, Belle-Ile* by Monet and the brilliant *Peasants Houses Erangy* by Pissarro, respectively. Of the Fauves, Derain, Vlaminck, and Marquet are seen in the works from the 1920s. The influence of later Cubism is reflected in Zadkine's sculpture *Head of a Woman*; Hayden's *The Guitarist*; and Lurçat's *Macedonian Woman*. The most recent European paintings are the moving *Self Portrait* (c. 1940) by Bonnard and a Vasarély.

A group of American abstract paintings of the 1960s and 1970s is frequently displayed with selected British and Australian contemporary paintings and three-dimensional works.

A separate curatorial department for contemporary art was established in 1979. While the Departments of Australian Art, Prints and Drawings, and Photography continue to develop their collections in the contemporary field, the establishment of a separate Department for Contemporary Art was designed to ensure that the Gallery would have some continuing focus on the evolving state of the art.

The historical strength of the Gallery is its collection of Australian art, and it has supported local artists from its inception. The first act of the trustees in 1884 was to commission a watercolor from Conrad Martens, the most eminent and respected artist of the colony. The neglect of earlier periods has recently been rectified by the purchase of several watercolors by J. W. Lewin, O. Brierly, S. T. Gill, and Skinner Prout and the 1972 donation of *A View of Trevallyn* by the colonial artist John Glover. Works by Eugene von Guerard and Louis Buvelot, important Melbourne artists of the 1870s, have entered the collection in recent decades.

Although Charles Condor's *Departure of the S.S. Orient, Circular Quay* and Arthur Streeton's *Still Glides the Stream* were acquired from Melbourne in 1890, most of the Gallery's important collection of "Australian Impressionist" painting, the first national school, was acquired locally. Good examples are Withers' *The Storm*, Davies' *A Summer Evening Templestowe*, and Ashton's *The Prospector*. The celebration of a national identity is portrayed in Tom Roberts' *The*

Golden Fleece and *Bailed Up*, Frederick McCubbin's *On the Wallaby Track*, Streeton's *Fires on Lapstone Tunnel*, and George Lambert's *Across the Black Soil Plains*.

A response to Art Nouveau is seen in Sydney Long's *Pan*, while the artistic climate of France was the inspiration for the expatriate artists, as seen in Rupert Bunny's delightful *A Summer's Morning*, John Peter Russell's impressionistic gouache *Belle-Ile*, E. Phillip Fox's *The Ferry*, and Bertram McKennal's bronze relief *Sarah Bernhardt*. Watercolors by J. J. Hilder, Blamire Young, Hans Heysen, and Norman Lindsay (also a prolific printmaker) are well represented. Hugh Ramsey (*The Sisters*, 1904) and Max Meldrum (*The Lane Pace*) emulate European Old Masters, as do later artists such as William Dobell in his luxuriant portrait of his fellow artist *Margaret Olley* and Lloyd Rees in his serene landscapes. Ronald Wakelin, Grace Cossington Smith, Roy de Maistre, Arnold Shore, and William Frater developed their colorful art from Post-Impressionism; however, Cubist overtones can be seen in the works of Rah Fizelle, Eric Wilson, Grace Crowley, Ralph Balson, and Frank Hinder during the 1930s. In the case of Crowley, Balson, and Hinder, the style evolved into Abstractionism in the 1950s. An Art Deco classicism is evident in the works of Napier Waller, Arthur Murch, and the sculptor Rayner Hoff (*Faun and Nymph*); traditional values remained the concern of the members of the Sydney Charm School—Donald Friend, David Strachan, Sali Herman, and Jean Belette. Surrealism influenced much of the work of the 1940s as seen in Drysdale's desert interiors (*So fala*); Nolan's nationalistic *Pretty Polly Mine*, 1948; and Gleeson's horrific *The Sower*. It was the spark that inspired the new national school, the "Antipodean Expressionists," that includes Arthur Boyd, Albert Tucker, and John Percival. Melbourne was the center for figuration (e.g., the acid edge of Brack's *Nude with Two Chairs* and the nostalgia of Blackman's *Suite V*), while Sydney was more consciously modernist in the Cubist mosaics of Miller's *Unity Blue* and the Abstract Expressionism of Pasmore, Rapotec, Rose, Olsen, Upward, and the younger artists Brett Whitley and Michael Taylor. The Gallery also owns paintings by Johnson Lancley, Earle, Coburn, Hessing, and Lynn.

The Australian collection of sculpture is not strong but includes a significant representation of the works of Robert Klippel and interesting pieces by Margel Hinder, Clement Meadmore, Baldessin, Danko, and Coleing.

The primitive art collection began in 1956 with the gift of aboriginal bark paintings collected by Charles Montford for the commonwealth government, seventeen Melville Island graveposts, and a set of Yirrkala bark paintings, commissioned by Stuart Scogall and presented in 1958 and 1959, along with one hundred other items. The collection, restricted to objects from a small portion of Northwest Australia, has been increased with a group of Milingimbi and Port Keats bark paintings and a collection of totemic emblems from the Reverend E. A. Wills.

Small collections of Melanesian artifacts have been purchased from dealers.

However, the major focus is the art of the Sepik River District collected by the deputy director of the Gallery, Tony Tuckson, in 1965. Artifacts from the Solomon Islands, Long Island, and some objects from Africa and South America are also included.

During recent years S. G. Moriarty, who died in 1978, presented to the Gallery his famous collection of New Guinea Highland art. Containing more than five hundred items, the collection includes wooden figures, basketry figures, examples of costume and decoration of all kinds, wigs, headdresses of feathers and tapa cloth, gourd masks, decorated shields, and headrests, all of which illustrate the variety of styles, decoration, and techniques in differing Highland regions.

The Gallery houses a large collection of artworks on paper by Australian, European, and American artists. It attempts to display the most significant works from the collection at least once every two or three years, with Australian work and the established masters of American and European art intermingled.

The larger part of the collection is Australian, with wide and varied holdings of drawings and of the print media—etchings, woodcuts, lithographs, and screenprints. The collection has a strong Sydney bias, and since it only began to be consciously developed in the early years of this century, the nineteenth century has but a token representation. Australian artists represented by significant groups of drawings include Rupert Bunny, William Dobell, Hans Heysen, Robert Klippel, George Lambert, Lionel Lindsay, Godfrey Miller, Thea Proctor, Lloyd Rees, and Eric Wilson.

Australian printmaking has enjoyed two periods of strong activity, from the end of World War I to the beginning of World War II and again from the late 1950s until the early 1970s. Both periods are widely represented. The etchers of the 1920s and the 1930s include Lionel Lindsay, Sid Long, Ure Smith, and Jessie Traill. The collection has a very fine selection of relief prints (woodcuts, wood engravings, and linocuts), with particular emphasis on the outstanding artists Lionel Lindsay, Margaret Preston, Ethel Spowers, and Eric Thake. In marked contrast, the technique of lithography seems to have been little used in this period; however, the collection has some representative examples.

Australian prints of the past thirty years are equally well represented. Etchings by George Baldessin, Bea Maddock, and Fred Williams are prominent, but screenprints by younger artists also are part of the collection. Art documentation in the form of prints, photographs, photostats, and more unusual media is beginning to be added to the collection.

The British collection includes many etchings of the 1920s and 1930s, as well as an important collection of Turner's *Liber Studiorum* and the full series of William Blake's engraved illustrations to the *Book of Job*. In addition there is a small group of interesting mezzotints, some fine etchings by Seymour Haden, and some outstanding examples by his American-born brother-in-law James Whistler. The print boom in England of the 1960s is also represented.

Among the drawings, the best are by Benjamin West, Thomas Munro, and

Edward Lear, with a moving portrait of the ailing Charles Conder drawn by William Orpen. There is a group of Henri Gaudier-Brzeska's drawings given by Rudy Komon in the 1950s and several good Henry Moore drawings.

European masters are represented chiefly by prints (engravings, etchings, and lithographs), although a small number of drawings is also held. Ranging from Mantegna and Dürer to Cubism, the limited holdings also include some of the greatest masterpieces in the Gallery's entire collection, mostly bought on the advice of Harold Wright between 1937 and 1942. Particularly outstanding are the two Rembrandt etchings and the recently acquired Georges Braque drypoint *Bass* of 1911.

Emphasis has been placed on French prints of the nineteenth and early twentieth centuries, from neoclassicism and Romanticism to Cubism and the bases of modern art. The collection includes major lithographs by Delacroix, Gauguin, Redon, Bonnard, and Vuillard and etchings by Corot, Ensor, and Braque. There are examples by Daumier and some particularly fine works by Meryon and Matisse. A few very interesting drawings by Millet, Boudin, and Tissot give further strength to holdings of this period.

The collection of Asian art presents an excellent display of ceramics and other forms of Asian art from Neolithic times to the twentieth century. On display are several funerary objects that were produced in imperial workshops, including a glazed equestrian figure of the T'ang Dynasty and a rare and attractive pair of court ladies whose elaborate gowns present a glimpse of the fashions of their day. Examples of many Chinese ceramic types are exhibited (e.g., pieces of Lung-ch'uän, Tz'ŭ-chou, and other wares), as well as a good collection of porcelains from the imperial kilns at Ching-tê Chên. Outstanding among the Ming blue-and-white porcelain is a stemcup of the Hsüan-tê period (1426–35). Another interesting and rare piece of Ming porcelain is a dish of the Hung-chih period (1488–1505), decorated in underglaze blue and white with a design of dragon and waterweeds.

The collection includes several examples of Japanese ceramics such as the Ko-Kutani vase from the seventeenth century. The Japanese ceramics collection is strong in the area of contemporary ceramics, with examples of the work of leading potters such as Shoji Hamada, Fujiwara Yu, and Kawai Kanjiro on display.

The collection of East Asian ceramics is another area of acquisition that has been aided by several generous gifts. Thai, Khmer, and Vietnamese ceramics are represented in the collection.

Only occasionally on display is the Gallery's collection of Japanese paintings. This collection includes screens, hanging scrolls, and illustrated books from the Edo period (1615–1867) to the present. A fine example of eighteenth-century Japanese painting is the hanging scroll by Watanabe Nangaku. A skillful composition, this painting exemplifies the popular category of *bijin-ga* (paintings of beautiful women). Artists represented in the Japanese painting collection include Ike no Taigo, Soga Shohaku, and Kubo Shumman. The most significant item in the collection is an important seventeenth-century pair of six-fold screens depicting views in and around Kyoto, purchased recently with funds donated by Kenneth Myer.

Sculpture in the Asian collection comprises mainly Indian and Southeast Asian pieces, including an intricately carved thirteenth-century Hoysala relief and a Khmer twelfth-century relief of two dancing Apsarases.

Photography is the only new field to be added to the Gallery in many years. The first photographs were accessioned into the permanent collection in 1975, when the trustees accepted a gift of some ninety photographs by Harold Cazneaux (1878–1953). Cazneaux was the leading figure of the Pictorial movement in Australian photographs that flourished from the turn of the century to the advent of World War II.

The photography collection is the strongest in the representation of Australian photographers of the period 1900–1960, which covers the Pictorial movement and the rise of a younger generation of photographers allied to the modern movement in the visual arts. Recently, modern prints made from collections of nineteenth-century negatives by Nicholas Caire (1837–1918) and Charles Kerry (1858–1928) have been added to the collection through exhibitions of their work.

Because the Museum of Applied Arts and Sciences in Sydney collects decorative arts, the growth of the Gallery's decorative arts collection depends largely on gifts, notably a group of English pewter given by Agnes Carvic Webster and eighteenth-century ceramics given by Dr. and Mrs. Sinclair Gilles. Australian ceramics are collected, and the Gallery is seeking other Australian decorative arts.

The Gallery has an important resource library for Australian art of more than fifteen thousand volumes and produces exhibitions that travel to smaller centers in the state. The Gallery also has a bookshop that has a selection of postcards, color reproductions, and transparencies of works in the collection. Also on sale are art books, Gallery publications, and exhibition catalogues.

The *Report of the Trustees* (from 1921) and the list *Purchases and Acquisitions* are published annually in addition to the *Art Gallery of New South Wales Quarterly*.

Selected Bibliography

Museum publications: *An Illustrated Catalogue*, 1906; *A Selection of 80 Reproductions*, 1950; *Catalogue of Australian Oil Paintings*, 1953; *Gallery Guide: Art Gallery of New South Wales*; *Artists and Galleries of Australia and New Zealand*, 1979.

Other publications: "The Archibald Prize, 1921–1981," *Art and Australia*, Summer 1982.

GLEN COOKE AND KAREN L. BLANK

Austria

———— Vienna ————

ALBERTINA GRAPHIC ART COLLECTION (officially GRAPHISCHE SAMMLUNG ALBERTINA; also THE ALBERTINA), Augustinerstrasse 1, A 1010 Vienna 1.

The Albertina, one of the foremost graphic arts collections in the world, houses a comprehensive collection of works on paper from the fifteenth through the twentieth century. The collection was founded in the eighteenth century by Duke Albert Casimir August, son of August II, elector of Saxony and king of Poland. Following the lead of his father who had helped the Dresden Art Gallery during its most brilliant period of acquisitions, Duke Albert was a passionate collector, first of prints and then of drawings. There are few secure facts about the origins of Albert's collection, which is today the core of the Albertina's exceptional holdings, but it is known that in 1768–74 Duke Albert was purchasing engravings from Johann Georg Wille, a collector and dealer in Paris. In 1774 Duke Albert commissioned the imperial ambassador in Venice, Count Jacopo Durazzo, to assemble as complete a collection of Italian engravings as possible, and in 1776 when Albert visited Italy to pick up his prints, he was also presented with a complete set of etchings by Piranesi from Pope Pius VI.

Duke Albert began collecting contemporary drawings on a small scale, and today the Albertina's rich collection of sheets by F. H. Füger is a result of Albert's ventures. From 1783 to 1792 the duke spent lavishly on his collection and in 1792 purchased works auctioned at the death of Prince de Ligne. They included drawings by Carpaccio, Liberale da Verona, and Leonardo da Vinci, sheets that may have been from Vasari's five-volume *Libro de' disegni*. Other drawings were acquired from the collections of Crozat, Mariette, d'Argenville, and Julien de Parme. In 1796 Duke Albert made perhaps the most important

purchase of his career when he acquired drawings from the Hapsburg imperial and private collections. Among the works was a block of sheets by Albrecht Dürer. Albert continued collecting assiduously: Italian drawings from the Dresden collection of W. G. Becker were purchased, and in 1820 works were acquired from Count Moriz von Fries. At his death in 1822, Albert's collection included about 15,000 drawings and 166,000 prints.

The collection was inherited by Albert's nephew Archduke Carl, who slowed the acquisition rate considerably. In 1827 Carl appointed a curator, Franz Rechberger, former curator of the Count von Fries Collection. Under Rechberger, a systematic classification of the collection was undertaken, and several important print acquisitions were made (i.e., Italian *chiaroscuro* sheets). Drawings by Netherlandish artists such as Jan Bruegel and Martin Heemskerck were added.

In 1847 the collection passed to Archduke Albrecht, Carl's eldest son. Acquisitions continued to be modest, but early works by Italian and German artists were added, among them heraldic designs for stained glass by Hans Baldung Grien and notebooks by Stefano della Bella. Attention was given to nineteenth-century Austrians, and drawings by these artists were actively acquired.

The name "Albertina" first came into use in 1873, the year that the collection was set up as a museum and opened to the public with a program of changing exhibitions. The first of a series of directors was appointed, Moriz von Thausing, professor of art history at the University of Vienna and a Dürer scholar.

In 1895 the collection was passed on again, this time to Archduke Frederick, nephew of Albrecht. Joseph Meder, another Dürer scholar, was named curator, and under Meder the collection was enlarged and important acquisitions including a Dürer drawing were made.

The Albertina's collection became state property in 1920 and during the next years took on the form it essentially has today. The purchases made by Meder were returned as personal property to Archduke Frederick, but the rest remained. An important merger took place when the Albertina was combined with the Print Room of the National (formerly the Imperial) Library. The Albertina's collection was enormously enriched, and a program of selling duplicates of prints to raise funds for new acquisitions was initiated. Important acquisitions were added in these years, including the Julius Hoffmann Collection of Goyas, Lessing's collection of Menzels, and early Italian drawings from Luigi Grassi (including sheets by Ghiberti, Pisanello, and Paolo Veronese). Drawings by Dürer were added, including preparatory sheets for paintings such as *The Feast of the Rose Garlands*. Austrian Baroque drawings, notably entire blocks by Maulbertsch and Volterrano, were acquired as were twentieth-century sheets by Fauvist, Cubist, and Expressionist (especially Klimt and other Austrian) artists. The Albertina benefited from bequests such as that from Oswald Kutscher-Woborsky, who gave a fine group of Italian drawings.

From 1934 to 1938 the Albertina was under the supervision of the director of the National Library, and during the years of World War II, the nineteenth- and twentieth-century watercolors and drawings by Austrian artists were moved to the Austrian Gallery of Nineteenth and Twentieth Century Art at the Belvedere. In 1947 the Albertina again took up its program of acquisitions adding works by Altdorfer, Wolf Huber, and other masters of the Danube School (from the Liechtenstein collection) and drawings by Burgkmair and Strigel (from former monastic collections). The first drawing by Hans Holbein to enter the Albertina's collection came after 1947 as did three more drawings by Rembrandt. A comprehensive collection of drawings and watercolors by Austrian Expressionist Egon Schiele was established when the Alfred Kubin Foundation was acquired. The Albertina continues today to enrich its exceptional holdings of works on paper.

The Albertina, a state collection since 1920, is administered today by a director, an assistant director, and a staff of curators who oversee the collection and its program of special exhibitions. A conservation department is headed by a chief restorer.

The Albertina is housed in the Silva-Tarouca Palace built in 1745–47 by Manuel Graf Silva-Tarouca, minister under Queen Maria Theresa. The palace was purchased by the queen in 1757 to use as a guesthouse, and in 1796 it was given by Franz II to Duke Albert and his wife, Marie Christine. For his collection, Albert rented and adapted the top floor of the Augustinian monastery next to the palace. He broke down the partitions between the former monks' cells, creating a single long room. Today this space is preserved in its original form as the "Old Albertina." The palace itself was rebuilt at the same time by Albert (1801–4) in a neoclassical style. The work was executed under the architect Louis de Montoyer. Further alterations were made to the palace in 1822–23 by Albert's heir Carl, including the refitting of the Music Room (today the Albertina's Study Room) in the then new Empire style. Other alterations followed in 1873, when an access from the Minerva Hall to the collection in the monastery was constructed (no longer existing). Since 1920 the entire palace has been used to house the collection, and although damaged during World War II and reconstructed, the Albertina's collection remains in the home first provided for it by its eighteenth-century founder.

The drawings collection is organized chronologically by school and medium, that is, fifteenth-century Italian drawings or seventeenth- to eighteenth-century Netherlandish drawings. Various types of drawings are included, among them finished drawings, studies, designs, sketches, preparatory drawings, and cartoons. The collection comprises the following: Italian drawings from the fifteenth to twentieth century, German drawings from the fifteenth to twentieth century, Netherlandish drawings from the fifteenth to twentieth century, French drawings from the sixteenth to twentieth century, Austrian drawings from the seventeenth to twentieth century, English drawings from the seventeenth to twentieth century, Spanish drawings from the seventeenth to twentieth century, and modern drawings from Eastern Europe, Russia, and Scandinavia.

Prints include artists' proofs, early impressions, late impressions, and so on. Works from Italy (fifteenth-twentieth century), Germany (fifteenth-twentieth cen-

tury), Netherlands (sixteenth-twentieth century), France (sixteenth-twentieth century), Austria (sixteenth-twentieth century), England (seventeenth-twentieth century), and Spain (seventeenth-twentieth century) are in the collection as is a group of prints from Japan and China (eighteenth-twentieth century).

Special collections at the Albertina include sketchbooks and sketched maps, architectural drawings, miniatures, historical woodcut sheets, playing cards, illustrated books and maps, a collection of views, posters, and original woodblocks from Dürer's time.

Drawings from fifteenth-century Italy include Pisanello's *Allegory of Luxury* in ink on paper and Domenico Ghirlandaio's *Angel appearing to Zaccharius*, a preparatory sketch for a fresco at St. Maria Novella, Florence. Portraits by Lorenzo di Credi and sheets by Perugino, Jacopo Bellini, Andrea Mantegna, and Antonella da Messina are in the collection. Prints include "tarocchi cards" and sheets by Pollaiuolo and Mantegna.

Sixteenth-century German drawings are rich in works by Albrecht Dürer. Among the master's most famous drawings at the Albertina is the watercolor *Large Piece of Turf* (1503) and his ink drawing *Portrait of the Artist's Wife* (c. 1495). Sheets by Hans Suess von Kulmbach, Hans Burgkmair, Lucas Cranach, Hans Baldung Grien, and Mathis Grünewald are in the collection. Prints include Dürer's series the *Apocalypse*, the *Large Passion*, and the *Life of Mary*. An impression of Dürer's *Adam and Eve* (first state) is at the Albertina as is an impression of the engraving *Melancolia* (1514).

Italian works of the sixteenth century include Michelangelo's drawing in black crayon with white heightening, *A Nude Man Seen from the Rear* (a study for the *Battle of Cascina*), and a sheet with *Three Standing Men* by the same artist. Several important drawings by Raphael include his *Madonna with an Apple* in crayon and an ink sheet with studies for the *Madonna in Green* (a painting in the Vienna Kunsthistorisches Museum [q.v.]). Drawings by Fra Bartolommeo, Andrea del Sarto, Baccio Bandinelli, Rosso Fiorentino, Giorgio Vasari, and Domenico Beccafumi are in the collection as are sheets by Venetian masters Lorenzo Lotto, Andrea Shiavone, Jacopo Tintoretto, Paolo Veronese, and Palma Giovane. Prints from sixteenth-century Italy include Federico Barrocci's etching *The Annunciation* and works by Giovanni Antonio da Brescia and Nicoletto da Modena.

Netherlandish artists of the sixteenth century are well represented. A famous pen-and-ink drawing by Pieter Bruegel the Elder presenting the *Artist and His Critic* is in the collection as is Hieronymus Bosch's ink sheet the *Tree Man*. Engravings by Lucas van Leyden (*The Milkmaid*, 1511) and Hendrick Goltzius (*The Flagbearer*, 1587) are among the many prints by Netherlandish artists.

From sixteenth-century France, Francesco Primaticcio's study for a mural at Fontainebleau, rendered in red and black crayon with white highlights, represents *Venus and Amor with Cupid*. Prints from this period feature sheets by Jean Duvet (the *Apocalypse* series) and Jacques Bellange (*The Three Women at the Tomb*, etching).

Italian works of the seventeenth-eighteenth century include an ink drawing by Guercino, *Christ and the Adultress*, a preparatory sheet for the painting of the same theme at Dulwich. An *Adoration of the Shepherds* by Giovanni Benedetto Castiglione is executed in pencil and red-brown oil color, and Giovanni Battista Piazzetta's charming *Head of a Shepherd Girl* is executed in black crayon on paper. Drawings by Bellotto, Canaletto, Giovanni Battista Tiepolo, and others are at the Albertina. Prints from the seventeenth and eighteenth centuries include a complete set of Piranesi's work presented to Duke Albert by Pope Pius VI and most of the work of Agostino Carracci. Caravaggio's *Denial of Peter*, 1603, is in the collection as are impressions by Bellotto, Giovanni Battista Tiepolo, and so on.

Works on paper from the Netherlands (seventeenth and eighteenth centuries) are exceptionally well represented. Peter Paul Rubens' *Portrait of Isabella* in black crayon, sepia, and white is in the collection as is a *Self Portrait* and the portrait *Helene Fourment*. Anthony van Dyck's *Imprisonment of Christ* is executed in pen and ink. The Albertina is rich in drawings by Rembrandt, among them the *Holy Family*, shown seated in a seventeenth-century Dutch interior, and the *Departure of Tobias*, in ink, dating from about 1647 to 1648. Drawings by Rembrandt's students (i.e., Lambert Doomer, Nicolas Maes, and so on) are numerous. Prints from the seventeenth to eighteenth century include works by Hercules Seghers, among them an impression of the *Three Books*. An etching by Willem Buytewech is titled *Wooded Landscape* (1621), and prints by Rembrandt include the etchings *St. Jerome, Christ before the People* (first state, 1655), and *Christ before the People* (seventh state). Impressions of the famous "Hundred Guilder Print" are also at the Albertina.

French works from the seventeenth to eighteenth century include drawings by Claude Lorraine (*View of a Forest with a Man Drawing*), Honoré Fragonard (*The Large Cypress Grove at the Villa d'Este, Tivoli*), and Jean Pillement (*Study for a Woman's Theatre Costume*). Jacques Callot's etchings at the Albertina number more than fourteen hundred and include the series *Capricci, Varie figure gobbi*, and *Diverse vedute*. An etching by Claude Lorraine from 1636 is titled *A Herd of Cows (Le Bouvier)*, and an etching by Gabriel de Saint-Aubin from 1753, the *Salon of the Louvre*.

German drawings from the seventeenth to eighteenth century include Matthius Günther's *Reception of St. Elizabeth in Heaven*, a study for the artist's fresco in the cupola of the Church of St. Elizabeth's Hospital in Munich (1765). German prints from the period include etchings by Adam Elsheimer, portraits by Jacob van der Heyden, and etchings by the South German artist Johann Georg Bergmüller.

Austrian works on paper from the seventeenth to eighteenth century are exceptionally well represented at the Albertina. Drawings by Johann Spillenberger, Martino Altomonte, and Franz Anton Maulbertsch are included. Ferdinando Galli-Bibena and his son Giuseppe, artists from Bologna who worked in Vienna for Carl VI, are represented by perspective drawings for stage sets and theater designs. A highlight of the Austrian collection is a small group of drawings by royal amateurs, among them sheets executed by Queen Maria Theresa, Franz I, Marie Antoinette, and the collection's founder Duke Albert of Saxony-Teschen and his wife, Marie Christine. Austrian prints include Franz Anton Maulbertsch's etching the *Assumption of Mary*, an artist's proof.

Art from seventeenth- to eighteenth-century England is represented by Sir Peter Lely's drawing in black crayon with white on blue paper, *Two English Heralds*. Sheets by Sir Joshua Reynolds, Thomas Gainsborough, and George Romney are also in the collection. English prints include caricatures by Thomas Rowlandson and James Gillray.

The highlight of the Spanish collection from the seventeenth to eighteenth century is Francisco de Goya's work. The Albertina possesses examples of most of his prints, including the series *Caprichos*, *Proverbios*, *Tauromaquia*, and the *Disasters of War*. Drawings by Goya include a depiction of a *Blind Beggar*. Also in the Spanish collection are drawings by Jusepe de Ribera.

French graphic art of the nineteenth and twentieth century is particularly well represented at the Albertina. Drawings include a pen-and-ink sheet by Jacques Louis David, *Diomedes and Aphrodite*, signed and dated "Rome 1776." Works by Théodore Géricault, Jean Auguste Dominique Ingres, and Eugène Delacroix date from the first part of the century. A drawing by Jean Baptiste Camille Corot was executed during an Italian sojourn. Drawings by the Barbizon painters are also in the collection. Impressionist drawings include two watercolors by Cézanne (*Monte Ste.-Victoire* and the *Aqueduct at Arles*) and sheets by Édouard Manet, Alfred Sisley, Camille Pissarro, and Edgar Degas. A pen-and-ink rendering by Auguste Renoir is titled a *Woman after the Bath*. French drawings of the twentieth century include Pablo Picasso's Cubist *Portrait of a Woman* of 1909 as well as works by Matisse, André Derain, and Fernand Léger. French prints from the early part of the nineteenth century through the present are included in the collection. A lithograph by Eugène Delacroix, *A Wild Horse*, is dated from 1828. Ingres' *Portrait of Gabriel Cortois de Pressigny*, an etching (second state), is in the Albertina. Works by Corot, Daubigny, and others are included, as is a large part of Honoré Daumier's graphic work. Etchings, lithographs, and a woodcut by Édouard Manet total about twenty-eight sheets. Toulouse-Lautrec's work is represented by more than sixty lithographs, including *Elsa, Known as the Viennese*. Etchings by Cézanne, with woodcuts and etchings by Paul Gauguin, are at the Albertina. More than one hundred prints by Picasso span his entire lifetime. Sheets by Braque, Derain, Matisse, Delaunay, and post–World War II artists (e.g., Sergej Poljakoff) are in the collection.

Netherlandish drawings of the nineteenth to twentieth century include landscape sheets from the early nineteenth century. Two ink drawings by Vincent van Gogh are in the collection as are twenty drawings by James Ensor (which came to the museum in 1942). Etchings by both van Gogh and Ensor are in the collection as are woodcuts by Frans Masereel and color lithographs by Raoul Obae.

From nineteenth- and twentieth-century Germany, a fine collection of drawings (much of which was acquired under Alfred Stix) includes early-nineteenth-century landscape sheets, a group of works by the Romantic artists (e.g., Caspar David Friedrich), and several drawings by the Nazarenes (e.g., Carl Philipp Forr's ink *Portrait of a Heidelberg Law Student, Ludwig von Mühlenfels*). A fine collection of Adolf Menzel's drawings are at the Albertina, including a crayon rendering, *Standing Officer*, 1860. Drawings by Max Liebermann, Franz von Stuck, Max Klinger, and Käthe Kollwitz are in the collection. Emil Nolde is represented by several sheets including a watercolor, *The Winter Sun*. Kirchner, Franz Marc, and other German Expressionists are included at the Albertina as well. German prints include a woodcut by Caspar David Friedrich, *Melancholie*, and almost one thousand prints by Adolf Menzel in various techniques acquired in 1924 from the Julius Lessing Collection. Works by Paula Modersohn-Becker and Max Klinger are also at the Albertina, as are prints by Nolde, Kirchner, and other Expressionists. Post–World War II artists such as Hans Hartung and Willy Baumeister are represented.

The collection of Austrian works on paper from the nineteenth century is exceptional. A large group of drawings by Friedrich Heindrich Füger includes an illustration for the *Messiade*. Drawings by the sculptor Josef Klieber and a large group of landscape drawings by various artists are in the collection. A watercolor by Moritz Michael Daffinger is the *Countess Potocka*, and a watercolor by Carl Schindler is the *Landscape with Trees*. Drawings by the Viennese Biedermeier artists include sheets by Ferdinand Georg Waldmüller and Josef Donhauser. Works from the second half of the nineteenth century include Hans Makart's pen drawing *A Woman at a Spinet*, a preparatory sheet for a painting in the Austrian Gallery of Nineteenth and Twentieth Century Art (q.v.). Prints by Austrian artists include etchings by Füger and a lithograph by Jakob Alt. Portraits by Vincenz Georg Kininger, Friedrich Lieder, and others are in the collection, and lithographs from the second half of the nineteenth century feature sheets by August von Pettenkofen. The major part of the Austrian print collection was added to the Albertina in 1920, when the Print Room of the Royal Library merged with the Albertina.

Austrian twentieth-century drawings include Kolo Moser's *The Dancer Loie Fuller*, a preparatory work in watercolor for a poster. An exceptional collection of drawings and watercolors by Egon Schiele is housed at the Albertina. Other Austrian Expressionist works include *Reclining Nude* (watercolor) by Oskar Kokoschka. A large group of drawings by Alfred Kubin was acquired in 1960, among them *Wasted Night* (in tusche and wash). Artists active after 1945 are well represented, and their work is actively acquired. Prints include sheets from the Jugendstil period, particularly works by Kolo Moser, Erst Stöhr, and Maximilian Kurzweil. A large group of color woodcuts by Carl Thiemann is at the Albertina as are lithographs by Alfred Kubin.

Works from Italy (nineteenth-twentieth century) include drawings by Giovanni Segantini and Luigi Sabatelli. The Futurists, among them Carlo Carrà, Gino

Severini, and Giorgio de'Chirico, are represented. Etchings by Carrà and Morandi are in the collection as are twenty sheets from de'Chirico's *Apocalypse* series.

English artists including Sir Edward Burne-Jones and Aubrey Beardsley (*A Snare of Vintage*, preparatory drawing for Lucian's *True History*, London, 1894), are represented. A watercolor by Henry Moore is dated 1940. Prints include classic caricatures by George and Robert Cruikshank. A woodcut by Charles Shannon is titled *Daphnis and Chloe*. More than two hundred sheets are by Frank Brangwyn, and Henry Moore is represented by color lithographs.

A small collection of American and Latin American drawings and prints feature five drawings by Lyonel Feininger (acquired from the Kubin Foundation). The sheets all date from the period 1910–20 and include the pen-and-ink drawing *A Street Scene*. Whistler is represented by etchings and lithographs. Prints by Mary Cassatt and Ben Shahn are also in the collection. Latin American artists, including Rufino Tamayo, are represented by printed works.

From nineteenth- to twentieth-century Scandinavia are etchings, woodcuts, and lithographs by Edvard Munch, including his 1896 lithograph *The Offended Girl*. Other artists represented in the collection include Carl Larsson, Anders Zorn, and Olaf Lange.

Swiss graphic art includes drawings by Ferdinand Hodler and *Self Portrait* by Alberto Giacometti. More than twenty drawings by Paul Klee include his ink drawing from 1911, *Galloping Riders*. Prints by Hodler, Félix Valloton, Cuno Amiet, and Paul Klee are at the Albertina.

Spanish art of the nineteenth to twentieth century includes color etchings by Joan Miró and etchings by the early twentieth-century fashion designer Mariano Fortuny. A small collection of prints by nineteenth- and twentieth-century Russian artists includes work by Alexander Archipenko, Marc Chagall, Alexander Orlowski, and others. Drawings and prints from Poland, Czechoslovakia, Hungary, Yugoslavia, and Bulgaria complete the Albertina's collection of European art.

A small collection of Japanese prints from the eighteenth to twentieth century is housed at the Albertina (about one hundred sheets). The prints, which represent many of the most famous artists, range from the early black and white woodcuts by Nishikawa Sukenobu (1671–1751) to the colored woodcuts of Torii Kiyonaga (1752–1815), Kitagawa Utamaro (1753–1806), Katsushika Hokusai (1760–1849), and Utagawa Kuniyoshi (1798–1861). Modern Japanese graphic artists are represented at the Albertina, and works by Masaji Joshida, Mitsuo Kano, and Fumio Kitacha are included. Japanese drawings include a work in oil color and tusche by Tadeo Ohno, *Saint Mark's Square, Venice*.

Aspects of the various special collections at the Albertina deserve particular notice. The architectural drawings collection is rich in sheets by Italian Baroque architects, especially Carlo Maderno, Lorenzo Bernini, and Borromini (*Perspective for the Facade of the Oratorio of S. Filippo Neri, Rome*). The second part of the collection emphasizes works by Austrian architects; among these sheets is Bernhard Ficher von Erlach's ink *Sketch for Historical Architecture*, from the *Codex Montenuovo*.

The poster collection, a group of about three thousand works, was strengthened when the Print Room of the Royal Library merged with the Albertina. Of particular interest are posters from the Wiener Werkstätte, among them Josef Hoffman's poster for their 1905 competition.

A special group of original woodblocks includes blocks for Dürer's monumental series *The Triumph of Maximilian I*. Other blocks by Dürer, Hans Springenklee, and Altdorfer are also in the collection.

Several archives are available for use by scholars and researchers. They include the Archive for the Architectural Drawings Collection, the Kubin Archive, the Schiele Archive, and the Klimt Archive. Personal documents such as letters as well as exhibition catalogues and other information are kept in these study collections.

The Albertina's library, started by Duke Albert, became state property in 1920 along with the graphic arts collection. The library is rich in reference works related to prints, drawings, and other works on paper and is open to scholars and researchers.

The Albertina maintains an active publishing program and produces various exhibition catalogues to coincide with graphic art shows held at the museum. A comprehensive catalogue of drawings in the Albertina was begun in the 1920s but was never completed. Volumes in this series include catalogues of Italian drawings (Venetian school; Tuscan, Umbrian and Roman schools; and works from Ferrara, Bologna, Parma, Modena, Lombardy, Genoa, Naples, and Sicily), Netherlandish drawings from the fifteenth and sixteenth centuries, and German drawings. The scholarly journal *Albertina-Studien* was published during the 1960s and 1970s (until 1976).

Selected Bibliography

Museum publications: *Beschreibender Katalog der Handzeichnung in der Graphische Sammlung Albertina*: I. *Venezianischen Schule*, Vienna, 1926 (A. Stix and L. Fröhlich-Bum); II. *Die Zeichnungen der Niederländischen Schulen des XV. und XVI. Jahrhunderts*, Vienna, 1928 (O. Benesch); III. *Die Zeichnungen der Toskanischen, Umbrischen, und Römischen Schule*, Vienna, 1932 (A. Stix and L. Fröhlich-Bum); IV. *Die Zeichnungen der Deutschen Schulen bis zum Beginn des Klassizismus*, Vienna, 1933 (H. and E. Tietze, O. Benesch, and K. Garzarolli-Thurnlackh); VI. *Die Schulen von Ferrara, Bologna, Parma und Modena, der Lombardei, Genuas, Neapels, und Siziliens*, Vienna, 1941 (A. Stix and A. Spitzmüller).

Other publications: Benesch, Otto (with Eva Benesch), *Master Drawings in the Albertina: Drawings from the Fifteenth to Eighteenth Centuries* (London 1967); Koschatzky, Walter, and Strobl, Alice, *Die Albertina in Wien* (Salzburg 1969); Meder, Joseph, "Herzog Albert von Sachsen-Teschen. Zu seinem hundertjährigen Todestag," *Die Graphische Künste*, vol. 45 (1922), pp. 73 ff.; Stix, Alfred, "Herzog Albert von Sachsen-Teschen," *Die Zeichnung*, no. 2 (1927); Thausing, Moriz von, "La Collection Albertine à Vienne,

Son histoire, sa composition," *Gazette des Beaux-Arts*, vol. 29, no. 2, series 4 (1870–71), pp. 72 ff. and 147 ff.

LORRAINE KARAFEL

AUSTRIAN GALLERIES AT THE BELVEDERE: MUSEUM OF AUSTRIAN MEDIEVAL ART, AUSTRIAN BAROQUE MUSEUM, AUSTRIAN GALLERY OF 19TH AND 20TH CENTURY ART (officially DIE ÖSTERREICHISCHE GALERIE IM BELVEDERE: MUSEUM MITTELALTERLICHER ÖSTERREICHISCHER KUNST, ÖSTERREICHISCHES BAROCKMUSEUM, ÖSTERREICHISCHES GALERIE DES 19. UND 20. JAHRHUNDERTS; also THE BELVEDERE), Prinz Eugen Strasse 27, 1030 Vienna.

The Belvedere Palace houses three museums: the Museum of Austrian Medieval Art, the Austrian Baroque Museum, and the Austrian Gallery of 19th and 20th Century Art. These three collections, formed by the state in 1918, provide an overview of Austrian painting and sculpture from the thirteenth through the twentieth centuries.

The palace, which exemplifies in its style the golden period of Austrian art known as the "Austrian Baroque," was constructed by Prince Eugene of Savoy. The Lower Belvedere, used as a summer residence by the prince, and the Orangerie were designed by architect Johann Lucas von Hildebrandt and were completed in 1714–16. The Upper Belvedere, designed for receptions and parties, and the Menagerie were constructed from 1721 to 1723. The magnificent gardens composed of parks and terraces were designed about 1700. The relatively sober exterior of the Belvedere contrasts with the flamboyant Baroque style of its interior, with decorations mostly by Altomonte and Rottmayr. In 1752 the Belvedere became imperial property, and from 1781 to 1892 it was used to house the imperial art collection. The Upper Belvedere was used from 1892 to 1914 as the residence of the successor to the throne, Archduke Franz Ferdinand (who was assassinated at Sarajevo in 1914).

In 1918 the Belvedere Palace became state property as did its art collections, and after that the Austrian Galleries were formed under the supervision of the newly created Austrian Administration for Museums. Today, each museum, supported by the government, is administered by its own director and assistant director with a curatorial and restoration staff.

The Museum of Austrian Medieval Art opened to the public in 1952 installed in its present home, the Orangerie. The collection includes more than one hundred paintings and sculptures. The earliest work is an *Enthroned Madonna and Child*, dating from the mid-twelfth century. The sculpture executed in stone was created by an anonymous Austrian artist and features the severe Romanesque style of the period. The sandstone *Madonna and Child* from about 1310, formerly in the Minorite Cloister in Vienna, is marked by a Gothic elegance and grace. A late-fourteenth-century sandstone portrait of Duke Albrecht II (?) is by an anonymous sculptor. A stone representation, *St. Martha*, probably from the Thann Castle near Leoben, is most likely by a Salzburg sculptor (c. 1390). A sandstone image, *St. George*, by Hans von Judenburg was created about 1415 as a console figure for the presbytery of the parish church at Grosslobming. Also by Hans von Judenburg is the wood representation *Christ Blessing* (c. 1425) and the sandstone *Pietà* (formerly in the church at Garsten). The wood representation *St. Peter as Pope* dates from about 1445–50 and is attributed to the workshop of Jakob Kaschauer. The magnificent carved wood *Znaimer Altar* is dated 1440 and was most likely created by a Bavarian sculptor with a Viennese assistant. The triptych represents the *Crucifixion* on its central panel with *Christ Taking the Cross* (left wing) and the *Way to Calvary* (right wing). A Tirol sculptor carved the wood depiction *Magus* (c. 1490), probably for a sculpture group of the *Adoration of the Magi*. Andreas Lachner's wood group *St. Blasius with Saints Rupertus and Virgilius* is dated 1518.

Paintings in the Museum of Austrian Medieval Art include, by the Master of the Viennese Adoration, a representation on panel, the *Birth of Christ* (c. 1410). From the same period is the *Birth of Christ* by an anonymous Salzburg master. The *Presentation in the Temple* by the Master of the Presentation from about 1430 is an altarwing formerly in the cloister at Wiener Neustadt. Works by Hans von Tübingen include an altarwing, the *Way to Calvary* (c. 1430), and, on linden wood, the *Holy Trinity*, which still retains its original painted frame. The Master of the Albrechtsaltar is represented by an altarwing of about 1438, the *Annunciation to Joachim*. A panel with the same subject and dating from about 1435 is attributed to the workshop of the Master of Liechtenstein Castle. The *Crucifixion*, 1449, by Konrad Laib was originally the central panel of a triptych; the wings with the *Annunciation* and *Birth of Christ*, and the *Death of Mary* are today housed in collections at Padua and Venice, respectively. The *Lamentation*, 1469, is by the Master of the Viennese Schottensaltares.

The Austrian painter Michael Pacher is represented by several works at the Belvedere. Among them is an altarwing fragment on panel with the *Marriage of Mary* (recto) and the *Flagellation* (verso) of about 1490. *The Departure of St. Lawrence*, dated about 1465–70, is also an altarwing on panel. The Master of the Uttenheimer Page created the triptych *Madonna and Child with Saints Margaret and Barbara*; until 1722 the work was kept at the Church of St. Margaret at Uttenheim. Rueland Frueauf the Elder is represented by several works, including, from the last quarter of the fifteenth century, the *Portrait of a Young Man* and, from 1490, an altarwing with *Christ on the Mount of Olives* (recto) and the *Assumption of Mary* (verso). The *Ecce Homo*, 1508, is by the Mondsee Master, and another work of the same subject from the same period is by Urban Görtschacher. A panel from 1519 is by Wolf Huber and represents *Christ's Departure from Mary*. An altarwing on panel by Marx Reichlich is titled the *Meeting of Mary and Elizabeth* (c. 1515). A martyrdom scene, the *Beheading of Saints Cantius, Cantianus, Cantianilla, and Probus* by the Master of the Krainburg Altar, includes a self-portrait of the artist. Other artists represented at the Museum of Austrian Medieval Art include the Master of Grosslobming.

The Austrian Baroque Museum, housed in the Lower Belvedere, opened on May 11, 1922, with about two hundred objects. The museum was refurbished, restored, and reopened in 1953. The collection of paintings and sculptures ranging from the late seventeenth through the eighteenth century are presented in a series of rooms that preserve their original stucco and painted decoration from the same period. The rooms of the Baroque Museum include the Blue Room, the Room of the Grotesques, the Marble Gallery, the Hall of Mirrors, the Red Room, the Green Room, and the Great Marble Hall. The spirit of the museum is epitomized in Martino Altomonte's fresco in the Marble Hall, *Prince Eugene's Glorification*, with its dramatic, sweeping style. Much of the decoration at the Lower Belvedere is by Altomonte and Johann Martin Rottmayr. Among the frescoes is the representation *Tarquinius and Lucretia* by Rottmayr. Paintings by Paul Troger include *Christ on the Mount of Olives* and *St. Sebastian Tended by the Holy Women*. Several portraits by Jan Kupetsky include a *Self Portrait* by the artist, and the depiction *Queen Maria Theresa* was executed by Martin van Meytens. The greatest of Austrian Baroque painters, Franz Anton Maulbertsch, is represented by numerous compositions, including *Assumption of the Virgin*, a scene with *St. James of Compostela*, and a *Self Portrait* by the artist. Paintings by Martin Johann Schmidt include a New Testament scene, the *Adoration of the Christ Child*, and a mythological work, *King Midas*. Johann Christian Brand, whose landscapes were executed in a calm and controlled neoclassical style, executed the *View of Laxenburg*. Other portraits in the collection include Christian Seybold's delicate *Portrait of a Young Girl*.

Sculpture at the Austrian Baroque Museum features bronze and stone works by Franz Xaver Messerschmidt, among them the bronze bust *A Laughing Man* and a marble portrait, *Doctor Gerard van Swieten*. The Austrian sculptor Georg Raphael Donner is well represented. Donner's pieces include a personification, *Providence*; a relief, *Hagar in the Wilderness*; and a free-standing depiction, the *Nymph*. Other sculptors represented in the collection include M. Zürn and Johann Meinrad Guggenbichler and Balthasar Permoser's marble masterpiece of the "Austrian Baroque," *Apotheosis of Prince Eugene*. Also in the collection is a fine group of medals by Kayserswerth, Krafft, Widemann, and Mathias Donner.

The Austrian Gallery of 19th and 20th Century Art, housed first in the Lower Belvedere, opened in 1918, when the Belvedere Palace and its royal collections passed to the Austrian state. The Gallery was restored and reopened in the Upper Belvedere on May 15, 1955, where it is located today. The Gallery houses the most comprehensive collection of modern Austrian painting and sculpture in the world and is particularly important for its collection of Austrian Expressionist works.

Paintings from the late eighteenth and nineteenth centuries feature oils by Friedrich Heinrich Füger. *Hortensia*, a portrait of the artist's wife, is in the collection as is Füger's portrait, *Queen Maria Theresa*, signed and dated 1776. A subject from classical history, the *Death of Germanicus*, is dated 1789. Numerous other paintings by Füger include a group of miniatures. Idyllic landscapes of the Austrian countryside by Johann Christian Brand, Ferdinand Georg Waldmüller, Heinrich Reinhold, and Ludwig Ferdinand Schnorr von Carolsfeld are in the collection. Friedrich von Amerling's oeuvre is represented by several canvases, among them the portrait *Rudolf von Arthaber with His Children*, signed and dated 1837. Amerling's *Girl in a Yellow Hat* is in the collection, as is the portrait, signed and dated 1838, *Frau von Striebel*. Also by Amerling is the *Portrait of the Artist's Mother*.

Other works in the collection include Ferdinand Georg Waldmüller's *Self Portrait* and his *Am Fronleichnamsmorgen*. A portrait of the musician, *Ignaz Schuppanzigh*, is by Joseph Danhauser as is a composition, *The Spendthrift* (dated 1836). Hans Makart is represented by several canvases, including the *Portrait of Clothilde Beer* and the oil *Girl at a Spinet*. Works by August von Pettenkofen include a sketch, *After the Battle*, as well as other military scenes. Also by Pettenkofen is the *Painter's Garden in Munich*, rendered in oil on cardboard and dated 1883. Adolf Menzel's *Eszterhazy Bar in Vienna* is an oil on canvas from 1871.

Works from the early twentieth century include Rudolf von Alt's watercolor on paper, *A View from the Artist's Apartment in the Suburb, Alservorstadt*, dated 1910. Another scene of contemporary Vienna by Alt is *St. Stephen's Church*. The "Secession" artist Gustav Klimt is well represented at the Austrian Gallery. The artist's decorative, ornamental style is epitomized in his famous composition *The Kiss*. Among other works by Klimt is his *Austrian Peasants' House*. Works by the Austrian Expressionist artists Egon Schiele and Oskar Kokoschka are included in the museum. Schiele's compositions include the portraits of his wife and family and landscapes such as *Four Trees* and *Häuserwand*. By Kokoschka are *Still Life with a Dead Lamb*, *Portrait of a Child*, and the landscape *Dolce-Bridge*. The following generation of Austrian painters, among them Anton Kolig, Anton Faistauer, Franz Wiegele, Gerhart Frankl, and Herbert Boecke, were influenced by both the Expressionists and the style of the earlier Impressionists. Paintings by these artists are included in the collection.

Sculpture from the late eighteenth and nineteenth century at the Austrian Gallery includes examples by Josef Klieber. A marble bust, *Archduke Carl*, from the early nineteenth century was housed at the Albertina until 1923. Johann Nepomuk Schaller, a sculptor active in the first half of the nineteenth century, created the marble *Cupid*, which was acquired for the imperial collection at the Belvedere in 1842, and a relief sculpture in Carrara marble, *Mars and Venus*. A *Bust of King Franz II* was made by Franz von Zauner for the Mineral Room of the Imperial Library (1796). Other nineteenth-century sculptors in the collection include Hütter, Gasser, Kühnelt, and Tilgner. Austrian twentieth-century sculpture includes Anton Hanak's bronze *Young Sphinx*, a work influenced by the monumental style of Auguste Rodin. Fritz Wotruba was active as a sculptor in the 1930s, and his abstract and archaizing style is exemplified in the *Large Seated Man*. Other twentieth-century sculptors in the collection include Josef Humplick and George Ehrlich.

The Austrian Galleries publishes catalogues of the collection as well as short guides. A current journal produced annually, *Mitteilungen der Österreichische Galerie*, encourages scholarship on Austrian painting and sculpture from the Middle Ages to the present. The journal includes articles on works in the collections, on the history of the Belvedere, on Prince Eugene of Savoy, and on the various activities at the Austrian Galleries.

Selected Bibliography

Museum publications: *Galerie des Neunzehnten Jahrhunderts im oberen Belvedere*, 1924; *Katalog des Museum Mittelalterliches österreichischer Kunst*, 1971; *Katalog des österreichisches Barockmuseum im Unteren Belvedere in Wien*, 1980; *Mitteilungen der Österreichische Galerie*, 1982–83; *Museum Mittelalterlicher österreichischer Kunst in der Orangerie des Belvedere, Katalog*, 1953; *Österreichische Galerie Barock Museum in Unteren Belvedere, Katalog*, 1958; *Die Österreichische Galerie im Belvedere in Wien*, 1967; *Prinz Eugen und sein Belvedere*, 1963; Schroll, Anton, *Das Barockmuseum in Unteren Belvedere*, 1923.

Other publications: Aurenhammer, Hans and Gertrude, *Das Belvedere in Wien: Bauwerk, Menschen, Geschichte* (Vienna 1971); Dunan, Marcel, "Un nouveau musée viennois: Le musée du 'Baroque Autrichien,' " *Gazette des Beaux-Arts*, vol. 8 (1923), pp. 243–50; Ottmann, Franz, "Die neue Moderne galerie in Wien," *Die Kunst für alle*, vol. 44 (1928–29), p. 355.

LORRAINE KARAFEL

VIENNA ART MUSEUM (officially KUNSTHISTORISCHES MUSEUM), Burgring 5, Vienna 1.

The origins of the Kunsthistorisches Museum, Vienna, are intimately linked with the history of the Imperial Hapsburg House. Its rise to prominence in the sixteenth century was reflected in its art collections, beginning with Emperor Maximilian I (ruled 1493–1519), whose portrait by Albrecht Dürer heads an important collection of imperial family portraits. Maximilian's daughter, Margaret of Austria, regent of the Netherlands, assembled at Mecheln a remarkable number of fine paintings, primarily by masters of the Flemish Renaissance. Archduke Ferdinand of Tirol (1529–95), son of Emperor Ferdinand I (ruled 1556–64), built up a rich assemblage of armor and weapons at Schloss Ambras in the Tirol, where the collection remains intact as administered by the Kunsthistorisches Museum.

Emperor Rudolf II, grandson of Ferdinand I, was the first large-scale collector among the Hapsburg monarchs. Ruling from the Hradschin Castle in Prague, Rudolf brought together a superb treasure of valuable works in all media, including antiquities, decorative arts, and paintings by Dürer, Correggio, Parmigianino, and Bruegel. In accordance with contemporary taste, Rudolf displayed his art objects along with curiosities and marvels of nature in his Prague *Kunst-*

kammer or Art Chamber. In Prague Rudolf established the "Imperial Court Workshop," with leading European goldsmiths, engravers, enamelists, and painters, whose works now enhance especially the decorative arts collection and the imperial treasury. Regrettably, Rudolf's collections suffered badly during the Thirty Years War; by 1648 the looting of Prague by Swedish troops resulted in the eventual scattering of as many as five hundred paintings and other objects.

Archduke Leopold William (1614–62), son of Emperor Ferdinand II (ruled 1619–37), is widely regarded as the real founder of the Vienna Picture Gallery. During his regency of the Catholic Netherlands, this ardent connoisseur amassed a brilliant gallery, including important acquisitions from the sale of the two leading seventeenth-century collections of paintings, namely, those magnificent holdings of the duke of Buckingham and the unlucky King Charles I. Before his death Archduke Leopold William brought to Vienna more than fourteen hundred paintings, with the Venetians and Flemish particularly well represented. In the seventeenth century dynastic marriages between the Austrian and Spanish Hapsburgs led to the acquisition of marvelous Velázquez portraits in Vienna.

By the early eighteenth century Emperor Charles VI (ruled 1711–40) displayed the first "modern" gallery of these treasures in the "Stallburg," part of the imperial palace, including important acquisitions by Rubens, van Dyck, and Rembrandt. In the second half of the eighteenth century, under the direction of Empress Maria Theresa and her son Joseph II, the collections from the Stallburg were rehung in the Belvedere Palace, Lucas von Hildebrandt's summer residence designed for Prince Eugene of Savoy (1663–1736), who had saved Vienna from the Turks in 1683. For the first time, the paintings were hung according to periods and schools under the direction of Christian von Mechel, a friend of Winckelmann. The gallery was opened to the public in 1781, twelve years before the Louvre (q.v.). This arrangement in the Upper and Lower Belvedere, catalogued and published by Mechel in 1783, remained largely unchanged for more than a century.

The current Kunsthistorisches Museum, officially opened in the autumn of 1891, was erected between 1872 and 1891, according to plans by Gottfried Semper and Karl Hasenauer; the two architects also collaborated on the corresponding Natural History Museum. The juxtaposition of these two collections reflects Rudolf II's original *Kunstkammer*, with the display of artistic and natural objects. These two symmetrically domed buildings with Renaissance facades frame the Maria Theresien Platz, whose central enthroned sculpture of Empress Maria Theresa commemorates the glory of her reign, including four equestrian monuments and six statues of public servants and musicians.

The Kunsthistorisches Museum is the property of the Republic of Austria and is administered through the government civil service. Its director, Hermann Fillitz, oversees the following curatorial departments: Egyptian-Oriental, Greek and Roman, European Paintings, Sculpture and Decorative Arts, Medals and Coins, Arms and Armor, Imperial Coaches (at Schönbrunn Palace), Antique

Music Instruments, Nineteenth-Century Painting (Neue Galerie), the Imperial Treasury, and Schloss Ambras.

The Oriental and Egyptian Collection, begun in 1821, offers a rich cross-section of statues, reliefs, sarcophagi, and architectural elements from all dynastic periods. Two seated granite figures of the lion-headed war goddess Sechmet (Karnak, c. 900 B.C.) flank the entrance to the seven Egyptian galleries. The Old Kingdom is well represented by numerous objects from Giza, including a limestone male portrait head (fourth dynasty), a restored cult chamber from the mastaba of Prince Kaninisut, with original reliefs depicting the culture of the Nile delta (c. 2700 B.C.), and various limestone and bronze figures dating from 2563 to 2423 B.C. From the Middle Kingdom comes a small hippopotamus of blue faience, painted with a bird and aquatic vines (c. 2000 B.C.); two monolithic red-granite temple columns with later cartouches (eighteenth dynasty); and a nearly life-size black-granite figure, *Sebek-en saf*, a beloved Theban orator (before 1800 B.C.). The widely varied styles of the New Kingdom include a number of mummies, such as the priest Panohemisis (c. 600 B.C.), the sarcophagus of Nes-Schutef-nut (Ptolemaic), and the papyrus and linen *Book of the Dead of Chensu-Mose* (first century B.C.).

The collection of antiquities, comprising a range of Greek, Etruscan, Roman, and Early Christian objects, is highlighted by works of exceptional quality. Among the finest examples of Classical sculpture is the life-size bronze *Youth from Magdalensberg* (Roman copy after the original by Polyclitus of Argos, active 460–420 B.C.). Another bronze statue of an athlete (third to second century B.C.), also preserved in a Roman copy, exemplifies the Baroque Hellenism of the third and second centuries B.C. Hellenistic marbles can be seen in a fine small head of Artemis from Tralles (Asia Minor, fourth to third century B.C.); the portrait *Aristotle* (fourth century B.C.); the statue *Artemis* from Larnaka, in the style of Praxiteles; and the *Fugger Amazon Sarcophagus* (late fourth century B.C.). Gold coins dating from the fifth to third centuries B.C. are Greek and Ptolaemic. Examples of Greek vases include the black figure hephaistoshydria (sixth century B.C.), the red figure brygosskyphos (late sixth century B.C.), the white ground lekythos (mid-fifth century B.C.), as well as early Geometric style vases (c. 900–700 B.C.). An exceptional piece from the third century B.C. is the onyx *Ptolemy Cameo*, depicting Ptolemy II and his wife, Arsinoe II.

Outstanding cameos from Rome are the *Eagle Cameo* (c. 27 B.C.), the *Cornucopia Cameo* (A.D. 49–54), and the *Gemma Augustea* (c. 9 B.C.), an Arabian sardonyx showing Augustus and Roma welcoming the victorious Tiberius. Roman Imperial art is represented by the marble head of Augustus (c. A.D. 1); a mosaic depicting a couple attended by two servants, probably based on a Hellenistic prototype; and Imperial coins. Later Roman art may be seen in the marble battle scene from the Parther Monument (after A.D. 165); the relief from a hunting sarcophagus, mummy portraits from Egypt (first to fourth centuries A.D.); and the portrait bust of Eutropios (Ephesus, fifth-sixth century A.D.), already a fusion of Classicism and Early Christian art. The gold chain with fifty-two charms and a topaz pendant, (part of the gold treasure from Szilágysomlyo (c. A.D. 400), is one of many splendid examples of central European metalwork. The silver hoard of Kuczurmare (seventh century A.D.) indicates the survival of antique Classicism in provincial areas. The Bulgarian gold hoard of Nagy-szentmiklós (ninth century A.D.), the so-called Hoard of Attila, comprises twenty-three vessels of exceptional quality.

The Department of Sculpture and Decorative Arts houses one of the most distinguished collections of its kind in the world, both in the comprehensiveness of styles and media represented and in the outstanding quality of so many individual objects. Medieval ivories are well represented, as in the small panel *St. Gregory with Three Scribes* (Lotharingian, c. 980), probably the central section of a sacramentary cover; the icon *Saints Peter and Andrew* (Constantinople, mid-tenth century); and the *Ascension of Christ* (Metz, c. 980), a sacramentary cover. Further examples of secular ivory work can be seen in the eleventh-century Italian elephant tusks, marvelously carved with hunting scenes and inscriptions.

Romanesque metalwork reaches a high point in the *Bertoldus Chalice* from Wilten (lower Saxony, c. 1160–70), gilded silver and *niello* with engraved biblical scenes and inscriptions. The chalice from St. Peter's, Salzburg (c. 1160–80) combines similar metalwork with high relief carving and the use of semi-precious stones. Fanciful metalwork creations include the bronze aquamanile griffon (Lotharingian, late twelfth century) and the so-called Püsterich, a bronze grotesque (twelfth-century North Italian). Late medieval Italian stonework may be studied in various rock crystal goblets as well as in the onyx cameos *Poseidon as Lord of the Ismus Games* and the *Crucifixion* (both thirteenth century). Precious jewelry cases range from the early twelfth-century wood coffer with engraved panels in bone to the jewelry chests from the workshop of Baldassare Embriachi (Venice, c. 1400) and the intricately carved wood love chest (late fifteenth century) from the Upper Rhine. The state goblet of Emperor Friedrich III is a splendid piece of late-fifteenth-century Burgundian metalwork and enamel. Related examples are the goblet of Hugo von Werdenberg (Burgundian, 1475–1500) and the mid-fifteenth-century Burgundian goblet engraved with wild animals, possibly after designs by the Master of the Playing Cards.

The seven highly individualized *Prophet Busts* from the circle of Pier Paolo and Jacobello dalle Masegne (Venice, c. 1400) are characteristic of Italian Early Renaissance portraiture. Among the finest sculpture from the German Renaissance are the *Krumauer Madonna* (South Bohemian, c. 1400), *Maria and the Christ Child* by Tilman Riemenschneider (c. 1510), and the *Allegory of Vanity* by Gregor Erhart (c. 1500). Exceptionally rare graphics of the Early Renaissance include the *Wiener Musterbuch* (Austrian, c. 1400–1425), a model book of fifty-six red-toned drawings, and the *Ambras Court Playing Cards*, ink-and-wash drawings (c. 1440, Upper Rhine, circle of Konrad Witz).

The museum has rich holdings in Italian Renaissance sculpture. Outstanding fifteenth-century Florentine works can be seen in Desiderio da Settignano's *Laughing Boy*, Antonio Rosselino's marble *Madonna Relief*, Luca della Robbia's terracotta *Madonna and Child*, Benedetto de Maiano's terracotta *Male Portrait Head*, and Bertoldo di Giovanni's bronze *Belerephon Taming Pegasus*. Neapolitan works of the fifteenth century are well represented by the polychrome marble *Bust of Isabella of Aragon* by Francesco Laurana and the anonymous marble *Bust of Alfonso I of Aragon, King of Naples*. The High Renaissance in North Italy can be studied in the marble relief *Bacchus and Ariadne* and bronze *Venus*, both by Tullio Lombardo, as well as in various works by Andrea Riccio: silver relief *Doubting Thomas*, terracotta *Resting Woodsman*, bronze *Boy with a Goose*, bronze *Satyr*, and bronze *Negro Slave*. Antico's work for the Gonzaga in Mantua includes his bronze busts *Ariadne* and *Bacchus* and bronze statues *Mercury* and *Venus*.

The extensive body of German Renaissance sculpture is highlighted by Jörg Muskat's bronze portrait busts *Emperor Maximilian* and *Empress Eleanore*; Hans Daucher's stone reliefs *Emperor Maximilian I as St. George* and the *Judgment of Paris*; and Christoph Weiditz's pearwood *Adam and Eve*. The so-called Dürer goblet is probably the most famous of a series of beautifully worked silver-gilt goblets from Nürnberg, about 1500. Also from this period is Hans Kels' elaborately inlaid backgammon board, with a remarkable decorative program of history and mythology, made for Emperor Charles V and his brother King Ferdinand. The fine display of German clocks and astronomical instruments of the sixteenth and seventeenth centuries comprise many superb specimens from the *Kunstkammer* of Rudolf II in Prague: Jost Burgi's table clock, Christoph Margraf's rolling-ball clock, Michael Sneberger's mantel clock, Georg Roll's planet clock, and Erasmus Habermel's gilt-brass compasses. This collection includes many Augsburg clocks of the period, as well as a series of seventeenth-century mechanical objects: Hans Schlottheim's automated ship and the Augsburg *Triumph of Minerva*.

Among the most famous works of the Italian Late Renaissance is Benvenuto Cellini's *Salt Cellar*, an allegory of the world with Neptune and Tellus made for King Francis I of France. Bronzes by Giovanni da Bologna include the *Rape of a Sabine*, *Hercules and the Centaur*, *Hercules and the Wild Boar*, *Astronomy*, and *Mercury*. Examples of portraiture from this period are Alessandro Vittoria's *Portrait of an Old Woman* and Leone Leoni's bronze busts *Charles V* and his sister *Maria of Hungary*. Virtuoso etched crystal can be seen in the work of Annibale Fontana, Francesco Tortorino, and the Sarrachi workshop. Examples of French Mannerism are primarily Limoges porcelain, as well as dishes of gold and semiprecious stones. From the *Kunstkammer* of Ferdinand of Tirol (sixteenth century) are amber vessels, Tirolean glasswork, and the intricately carved stone sculptures *Abraham's Sacrifice*, the *Crucifixion*, and the *Resurrection of Christ*. Further works from the court of Rudolf II demonstrate the consummate artistry of his *Hofwerkstatt*: bronze bust *Emperor Rudolf II*, bronze relief *Allegory of the Turkish Wars* by Adriaen de Vries, objects in semiprecious stones, *pietre dure* landscapes and religious scenes by Ottavio Miseroni, and silver pieces by Christoph Jamnitzer, Anton Schweinberger, and Wenzel Jamnitzer.

In the area of post-Renaissance decorative arts and sculpture, the museum's strongest holdings are from the Austrian High Baroque and Rococo. Important sculpture of this period can be seen in F. X. Messerschmidt's *Emperor Joseph II* (1767), J. B. Lemoyne's *Marie Antoinette as Sixteen-Year-Old Dauphine of France* (1771), Georg Raphael Donner's marble relief *Charles VI*, and Matthias Steinle's ivory equestrian statuettes *Leopold I* and *Charles VI*. Among the relatively small collection of Roman Baroque sculpture, two fine examples are Alessandro Algardi's seated figure *Pope Innocent X* and Camillo Rusconi's *Portrait Bust of Giulia Albani degli Abati Olivieri*. Throughout the galleries of sculpture and decorative arts are displayed the superb collection of the tapestries: sixteenth-century French series Petrarch's *Triumphs*, sixteenth-century Netherlandish Gobelins with scenes from the *Life of St. Paul*, sixteenth-century Brussels Gobelins with scenes from Ovid's *Metamorphoses*.

The European paintings are unquestionably the most renowned portion of the Kunsthistorisches Museum's collection. The holdings in the Vienna Picture Gallery rank among the finest in the world, with particular strengths in Venetian, Flemish, and Danube school painting. With the exception of the Prado, no other museum can rival Vienna's works by Titian and Velázquez. The canvases by Bruegel and Rubens are unparalleled outside of the Netherlands. The early Italian Renaissance (fifteenth century) is represented by Pisanello's *Portrait of Emperor Sigismund of Luxembourg* (c. 1433), Gentile da Fabriano's *Stoning of St. Stephen*, Benozzo Gozzoli's *Virgin and Child with Saints* (c. 1452), Andrea Mantegna's *St. Sebastian* (c. 1460), Cosimo Tura's *Dead Christ with Two Angels* (c. 1475), and Antonello da Messina's *Virgin and Child with Saints* (1475–76).

The superb collection of sixteenth-century Venetian paintings begins with two important works by Giovanni Bellini: *Presentation in the Temple* (c. 1490–1500) and *Young Woman at Her Toilette* (c. 1515). Significant examples of Giorgione's small oeuvre can be studied in *Laura* (1506), *Three Philosophers* (1508–9), and *Boy with an Arrow* (c. 1505), as well as his workshop's *Adoration of the Shepherds*. Lorenzo Lotto's seven canvases include the *Portrait of a Young Man* (c. 1508), a *Sacra Conversazione* (c. 1533), and *Three Views of a Goldsmith* (c. 1530–35). Titian's entire career is evident in the museum's remarkable group of more than twenty of his paintings. Among the most important Titians are the *Gypsy Madonna* (c. 1510), *Lucretia and Tarquin* (c. 1515), *Violante* (c. 1515–18), *Virgin and Child with Saints Stephen, Jerome, and Maurice* (c. 1520), *Madonna with Cherries* (c. 1516–18), *Woman in a Fur* (c. 1535), *Ecce Homo* (1543), *Danaë* (c. 1554), *Portrait of Jacopo Strada* (1567–68), *Diana and Callisto* (c. 1568), and *Nymph and Shepherd* (after 1570). Further examples of sixteenth-century Venetian painting are Catena's *Portrait of a Man with a Book* (c. 1520) and Paris Bordone's *Young Woman Standing at a Table* (c. 1550), *Allegory with Flora* (c. 1560), and *Allegory with Victory* (c. 1560). Tintoretto may be viewed retrospectively in more than twenty paintings, among which are a series of six Old Testament scenes (1545–47), *Portrait of Lorenzo Soranzo* (1553), *St. Nicholas of Bari* (c. 1550s), *Portrait of a Man in Armor* (c. 1555–60), *Susanna and the Elders* (early 1560s), *Portrait of Sebastiano Venier* (1560s), *St. Jerome* (c. 1571–75), *Portrait of Senator Marco Grimani* (c. 1576–83), and the *Flagellation* (late 1580s).

As with Titian and Tintoretto, Veronese is well exhibited by nearly twenty canvases, among which the following are of particular importance: the *Annointing of David* (c. 1555–60), *Marcus Curtius* (c. 1550s), *Lucretia* (c. 1580–83), *Hagar and Ishmael in the Desert* (c. 1580s), *Esther before Ahasuerus* (c. 1580s), *Christ and the Samaritan Woman* (c. 1580s), *Hercules, Dejanira, and Nessus* (c. 1580s), *Venus and Adonis* (c. 1580s), and *Adam and Eve* (c. 1580s). Among the numerous holdings by the Bassano family are Jacopo Bassano's *Adoration of the Kings* (c. 1565–70) and *Entombment of Christ* (c. 1573–74) and Francesco Bassano's *Hercules and Omphale* (c. 1587).

The High Renaissance in Bergamo, Ferrara, and Brescia can be studied in Savoldo's *Lamentation* (c. 1510–20), Dosso Dossi's *St. Jerome* (c. 1515) and *Jupiter, Mercury, and Virtue* (c. 1529), and Moretto da Brescia's *St. Justina with a Donor* (c. 1530). Central Italian painting of the High Renaissance includes two Madonnas by Perugino, both about 1493, in addition to the *Baptism of Christ* (c. 1498–1500) and *St. Jerome* (c. 1502). Two exceptional works by Raphael are the *Madonna del Prato* (1505) and *St. Margaret* (c. 1520). Important works of the Florentine Late Renaissance are Fra Bartolommeo's *Presentation in the Temple* (1516) and the half-length *Virgin and Child* (c. 1516), Andrea del Sarto's *Archangel Raphael with Tobias, St. Leonard, and a Donor* (c. 1511) and the *Lamentation* (c. 1519–29), and Sodoma's *Holy Family with St. John* (c. 1540s). Florentine Mannerism is represented by Bronzino's *Holy Family with St. Anne and the Infant St. John* (c. 1550), Alessandro Allori's *Christ in the House of Martha and Mary* (1605), and Salviati's *Portrait of a Bearded Man* (c. 1530s). Further examples of Mannerist painting are Nicolò dell' Abbate's *Portrait of a Gentleman with a Parrot* (c. 1552–55), Jacopo dell Empoli's *Susanna and the Elders* (1600), and Arcimboldi's allegorical heads *Summer, Winter, Fire,* and *Water* (all from the 1560s, painted for Ferdinand I and Maximilian II). The High Renaissance in Parma is well displayed by Correggio's *Virgin and Child* (c. 1512–14), *Jupiter and Io* (c. 1530), and the *Abduction of Ganymede* (c. 1530); and Parmigianino's *Self Portrait with a Convex Mirror* (c. 1523–24), *Cupid Carving His Bow* (c. 1533–34), and the *Conversion of St. Paul* (c. late 1530s).

The museum has important holdings in Italian Early Baroque painting, among which are Annibale Carracci's *Venus and Adonis* (c. 1588–89), *Pietà* (c. 1603), and *Christ and the Woman of Samaria* (c. 1604–5); Caravaggio's *David with the Head of Goliath* (c. 1605) and the *Madonna of the Rosary* (c. 1606); and Orazio Gentileschi's *Mary Magdalene* (c. 1626) and *Rest on the Flight into Egypt* (after 1626). Caravaggesque paintings by non-Italians include Simon Vouet's *Mary and Martha* (1625), Johann Liss' *Judith and Holofernes* (c. 1620s), and Jusepe de Ribera's *Jesus in the Temple* (c. 1625). Further examples of the Italian

Baroque can be seen in works by Guido Reni: the *Four Seasons* (c. 1615–20), *Baptism of Christ* (c. 1623), and *St. Jerome* (c. 1635); Bernardo Strozzi: *Lute Player* (c. 1635) and *Salome with the Head of John the Baptist* (c. 1635); and Guercino: *Return of the Prodigal Son* (1619). The museum owns twelve paintings by Domenico Fetti, among the finest of which is *Hero and Leander* (c. 1622–23). Further examples of High and Late Baroque painting in Italy may be seen in Pietro da Cortona's *Return of Hagar* (c. 1637–42), Guido Cagnacci's *Death of Cleopatra* (c. 1660), and Salvator Rosa's *Return of the Goddess Asatraea* (c. 1650s). The extensive collection of Luca Giordano's works is highlighted by his early *Beggar* and the *Archangel Michael* (c. 1650s).

Eighteenth-century Italian painting includes several stunning canvases. Among them are Giambattista Tiepolo's *Death of the Consul Lucius Junius Brutus* and *Hannibal Recognizing the Head of Hasdrubal* (c. 1725–30); Sebastiano Ricci's *Christ on the Mount of Olives* (1730); Canaletto's *View of the Custom House Landing at Venice* (1738–40); and Francesco Guardi's *Miracle of St. Hyacinth* (1763). Of particular historical interest is Francesco Solimena's *Emperor Charles VI and Count Althann* (1728), commemorating the completed installation in Vienna of pictures from the Prague gallery of Ferdinand III and Archduke Leopold William. Further eighteenth-century works are Solimena's *Judith with the Head of Holofernes* (c. 1728–35), Pompeo Batoni's *Emperor Joseph II and Grand Duke Leopold of Tuscany* (1769), and Bernardo Bellotto's thirteen *Views of Vienna* (1759–60), of which the *View of Vienna from the Belvedere* is perhaps most famous.

The museum owns a small but superb collection of Spanish paintings, concentrating largely on dynastic portraiture. A sixteenth-century example is Sanchez Coëllo's *Anne of Austria, Queen of Spain* (1571). Among the nine Velázquez portraits the following are outstanding works: *Infanta Margareta at the Age of Three* (c. 1654), *Infanta Margareta at the Age of Eight* (c. 1659), and *Prince Philip Prosper* (1659). Other seventeenth-century works are Mazo's *Family of the Artist* (c. 1659–60) and Antonio da Pereda's *Allegory of Vanity* (c. 1654).

The holdings in French painting are relatively limited, with notable examples in Poussin's *Conquest of Jerusalem* (1638–39), Rigaud's *Portrait of Count Sinzendorf* (1728), Josèphe Sefrède Duplessis' *Portrait of Gluck* (1775), and J. L. David's *Equestrian Portrait of Napoleon* (1801).

Flemish painting, along with Venetian, forms one of the most distinguished of the museum's collections. An outstanding series of fifteenth-century Netherlandish paintings begins with two portraits by Jan van Eyck: *Cardinal Albergati* (c. 1431–32) and the *Goldsmith Jan de Leeuw* (1436). The stunning portrait *Jester Gonella* from Ferrara is by a follower of van Eyck working in Italy about 1440. Rogier van der Weyden's work can be seen in the diptych *Virgin and Child* and *St. Catherine* (c. 1435) and the *Crucifixion* (c. 1440–45). Later fifteenth-century paintings in the museum are by Hans Memling, *St. John Triptych* (c. 1465); Hugo van der Goes, diptych *Adam and Eve* and the *Lamentation* (c. 1470); Juan de Flandes, *Christ Nailed on the Cross*; and Gerard David, *Night*

Nativity (c. 1495) and *St. Michael Triptych* (c. 1500). Rare examples of fifteenth-century Dutch painting are Bosch's *Carrying of the Cross*, with an *Allegorical Scene* on the verso, and Geertgen tot Sint Jans' *St. John Altar* (1480s) and *Lamentation* (after 1484).

The museum's holdings in sixteenth-century Flemish painting are extensive and of high quality. The following are exceptional examples from the Renaissance in Flanders: Joachim Patinir's *Baptism of Christ* (c. 1515), Jan Gossaert's *St. Luke Painting the Virgin* (c. 1520) and *Portrait of a Man* (c. 1525–30), Bernard van Orley's *Altar of Saints Thomas and Matthew* (c. 1515) and *Circumcision* (c. 1523–30), Joos van Cleve's *Portrait of Queen Eleanor of France* (c. 1530), Frans Floris' *Last Judgment* (1565), and Lucas van Valckenborch's *Four Seasons Landscapes* (1585–87) and *Landscape with an Angler* (1590). The oeuvre of Pieter Bruegel may be surveyed in a dozen splendid canvases, among which are the *Tower of Babel* (1563), *The Procession to Calvary* (1564), *Hunters in the Snow* (1565, from a series of months or seasons, two others in Vienna), *The Conversion of Saul* (1567), the *Peasant Wedding* (c. 1568), the *Peasant Dance* (c. 1568), and the *Storm at Sea* (c. 1568). Sixteenth-century works from the North Netherlands include Maerten van Heemskerck's *Vulcan, Mars, and Venus* (c. 1536), *Vulcan Bringing Thetis the Shield for Achilles* (c. 1536), and two *Altar Wings with Donors* (c. 1540–45); Jan van Scorel's *Presentation in the Temple* (c. 1528–30); Anthonis Mor's *Portrait of Granvella* (1549); Pieter Aertsen's *Vanitas Still Life with Christ, Martha, and Mary in the Background* (1552) and *Market Scene* (c. 1560); and Joachim Bueckelaer's *Market Woman* (1561) and *Cook* (1574).

A special gallery is devoted to the paintings done for Rudolf II in Prague. Of particular interest among this large corpus are Bartholomaeus Spranger's *Hercules and Omphale* (1575–80), *Self Portrait* (c. 1580–85), *Triumph of Wisdom* (c. 1591), and *Venus and Adonis* (c. 1595); Roelandt Savery's *Forest Landscape with Hunters* (1604) and *Paradise* (1628); Hans von Aachen's *Bacchus, Ceres, and Amor* and *Emperor Rudolf II* (c. 1600–1603); and Jan Bruegel's *Adoration of the Magi* (1598), *Ceres and the Four Elements* (1604), and a number of landscapes and floral still-life pieces.

The splendid group of paintings by Peter Paul Rubens constitute the museum's most extensive holdings by a single artist, including thirty-five works by the master as well as ten canvases attributed to Rubens' workshop and school. Early Rubens can be seen in his portraits of *Francesco Gonzaga, Duke of Mantua* (1604–5) and *Isabella d'Este, Duchess of Mantua* (c. 1605–8). Among works from Rubens' middle years are the *Lamentation* (1614), the *Four Quarters of the World* (c. 1617), the oil sketches and altars depicting miracles in *St. Francis Xavier* and *St. Ignatius Loyola* (c. 1617–18), and the *Stormy Landscape* (1620). Mature Rubens is illustrated by *Angelica and the Hermit* (c. 1626–28), the *Ildefonso Altar* (1630–32), the *Park of a Castle* (c. 1635), *Helene Fourment in a Fur* (c. 1638), and the *Self Portrait* (1638–40). Anthony van Dyck is represented by a slightly smaller group than the Rubens corpus, namely, twenty-five paintings. Among the most important van Dyck portraits are the *Young General* (c. 1624), *Chamberlain John of Montfort* (c. 1628), and *Nicholas Lanier* (c. 1630–32). Other genres include the *Lamentation* (c. 1620), *St. Hermann Joseph* (c. 1630), and *Samson and Delilah* (c. 1630). Other seventeenth-century Flemish paintings of note are Jacob Jordaens' the *Daughters of Cecrops Finding Erichthonios* (c. late 1630s) and the *Bean Feast* (c. 1656), Frans Snyders' *Fishmarket* (c. 1618), Gaspard de Crayer's *Equestrian Portrait* (c. 1627–28) and *Lamentation* (1649–56), and David Teniers the Younger's two portraits *Archduke Leopold Wilhelm in His Gallery in Brussels* (c. 1651 and 1653).

The museum's collection of seventeenth-century Dutch paintings is rich in breadth and quality. Dutch landscapes can be seen in the work of Hendrik Avercamp: *Winterlandscape* (before 1610); Esaias van de Velde: *Banquet in a Castle Park* (1624); Jan van Goyen: *Panoramic Landscape* (c. 1630s) and *View of Dordrecht* (1644); Salomon van Ruysdael: *Stormy Landscape* (1631) and *May Festival* (1655); Aert van der Neer: *River Scene with Fishermen* (c. late 1660s); and Jacob van Ruisdael: *Great Forest* (c. 1650s) and *Mountain Landscape with a Waterfall* (c. 1659–65). Portraiture of the period includes Frans Hals' *Young Man* (c. 1640–41) and *Male Portrait* (c. 1645–55), as well as Gerrard Dou's *Portrait of a Physician* (1653). The fine group of eight Rembrandts is exclusively portraiture, with three remarkable self-portraits from the 1650s. Of special interest are family portraits: *Rembrandt's Mother as the Prophetess Hannah* (1639) and *Titus Reading* (c. 1656–57). Examples of Dutch genre pictures are Adriaen van Ostade's *Peasant Cottage Interior* (1647), Gerard Ter Borch's *Woman Peeling an Apple* (1651 or 61), and Jan Steen's *Topsy-Turvy World* (1663?). *The Artist in His Studio* (c. 1665–66) is an exquisite masterpiece from Jan Vermeer's mature period.

Among the earliest German works in the collection is the *Holy Family* (c. 1480s), a rare panel by Martin Schongauer, the engraver who influenced Albrecht Dürer so profoundly. Eight Dürer paintings are highlighted by the *Portrait of a Young Venetian Lady* (1505), *Martyrdom of the Ten Thousand* (1508), the *Adoration of the Trinity* (1522), the *Virgin and Child* (1512), and the *Portrait of Johann Kleberger* (1530). Except for the *Venetian Lady*, all paintings mentioned come from the collection of Rudolf II. Lucas Cranach's work can be seen in seventeen panels, among which are the *Penitent St. Jerome* (1502), *Stag Hunt of Freiderich the Wise* (1529), and *Judith with the Head of Holofernes* (c. 1530). The Danube School is well represented by Albrecht Altdorfer's *Martyrdom of St. Catherine* (c. 1505–10), *Entombment* and *Nativity* wings (c. 1515) and Wolf Huber's *Christ Taking Leave of Mary* (1519) and *Portrait of Jacob Ziegler* (1544–49). Six portraits by Hans Holbein the Younger include the *Portrait of Dirck Tybis* (1533), *Jane Seymour, Queen of England* (1536), and *Dr. John Chambers* (1543). Sixteenth-century portraiture can be seen in Jakob Seisenegger's *Emperor Charles V* and François Clouet's *King Charles IX of France*. A very small group of English eighteenth-century paintings contains portraits by Sir Joshua Reynolds,

Sir Henry Raeburn, and Sir Thomas Lawrence, in addition to Thomas Gainsborough's *Landscape in Suffolk* (c. early 1750s).

The Sekundärgalerie, located directly above the main picture galleries, contains nearly six hundred paintings from the sixteenth through eighteenth centuries.
Some of the most important artists represented in these six galleries are Anthony
van Dyck, David Teniers, Jan Bruegel, Jacob Jordaens, Lucas Cranach, Vivarini,
Paris Bordone, Francesco Bassano, Guido Reni, Luca Giordano, Alessandro
Magnasco, Sebastiano Ricci, Bartolomé Esteban Murillo, Francisco de Zurbarán,
and Bartholomaeus Spranger.

The Neue Galerie in the Stallburg contains the museum's collection of nine-
teenth- and early-twentieth-century art, except for Austrian paintings, which are
in the Österreichischen Galerie (q.v.). French nineteenth-century paintings can
be seen in the works of Jean François Millet: *Plain at Chantilly* (1862); Camille
Corot: *Portrait of Mme. Legois* (1838) and various landscapes; Théodore Géricault: *Hussar Trumpeter*; Eugène Delacroix: *Large Floral Still Life* (c. 1842);
Gustave Courbet: *Portrait of a Young Girl* (1872); and Édouard Manet: *Lady
with a Fur* (c. 1880). French Impressionist paintings include Auguste Renoir's
After the Bath (1876), Claude Monet's *Fishermen on the Seine at Poissy* (1882),
and Camille Pissarro's *Street in Pontoise*. The Neue Galerie has a large collection
of German nineteenth-century paintings. Among the outstanding examples of
German Romanticism are works by Philipp Otto Runge and Caspar David Fried-
rich. German Realism includes works by Adolf Menzel, Hans Thoma, and the
Munich Circle of Haider, Leibl, and Trübner. Biedermeier artists are represented
by Karl Spitzweg and Wilhelm Busch. Later nineteenth-century German painting
can be seen in the works of Fritz von Uhde, Max Slevogt, Max Lieberman, and
Lovis Corinth. Important late works in the collection are Vincent van Gogh's
Plain at Auvers (1890), Edvard Munch's *Summer Night on the Shore* (c. 1902),
Paul Cézanne's *Still Life* (c. 1905), and Ferdinand Hodler's *Distress* (1900).

The Crown Jewels and Ecclesiastical Treasure Chamber are located across the
Ring in the Schweizerhof. As its name implies, this is the *ne plus ultra* of the
museum's collections. Concentrating heavily on decorative objects—jewels, textiles, and imperial regalia—the treasury contains works of rare quality. Among
the exceptional examples of regalia are the imperial crown (West German, 962);
the imperial cross (West German, c. 1024); and the sabre of Charlemagne (Hungary, ninth century). From the renowned fifteenth-century Burgundian treasury
come splendid mass vestments of the Order of the Golden Fleece, the Burgundian
court goblet, the cross of the Order of the Golden Fleece, and a gold brooch
with a pair of lovers in a garden. The treasury has a rich assemblage of sev-
enteenth- and eighteenth-century liturgical vestments, small family altars of precious materials, and religious sculptures. Hapsburg regalia include the crown of
Emperor Rudolf II, the principal achievement of Rudolf's Imperial Court workshop, and artists such as Jan Vermeyen and Paulus van Vianen; and the crown
of Stephan Bocskay (Turkish, seventeenth century). Magnificent objects from

the nineteenth century are the silver gilded cradle of the King of Rome, the Austrian imperial mantle, and the Golden Rose Tree.

The art library of the Kunsthistorisches Museum has more than a hundred thousand volumes. The library is open to visiting scholars and students; it is noncirculating.

Slides and photographs of works in the collection are available through the Photo Dokumentation or the Archiv des Kunsthistorisches Museums. The *Jahrbuch der kunsthistorischen Sammlungen des allerhöchsten Kaiserhauses* was founded in Vienna in 1883 and reflected the very high standard of art historical scholarship in Austria at the time. In 1926 it was renamed the *Jahrbuch der Kunsthistorischen Sammlungen in Wien, Nueu Folge*, which is published annually. The museum publishes catalogues of major exhibitions.

Selected Bibliography

Museum publications: *Verzeichnis der Gemälde, Kunsthistorisches Museum, Wien,* 1973; *Katalog der Sammlung für Plastik und Kunst gewerbe, Kunsthistorisches Museum, Wien,* 1964; *Die Sekundärgalerie des Kunsthistorischen Museums,* 1971; Fillitz, Hermann, *The Crown Jewels and the Ecclesiastical Treasure Chamber* (Schatzkammer), 1963; *Das Kunsthistorisches Museum in Wien,* 1978; *Meisterwerke,* 1968.

Other publications: Glück, Gustav, *The Picture Gallery of the Vienna Art Museum* (Vienna 1931); *Art History Museum Vienna: Picture Gallery* (Milan 1969); Tietze, Hans, "Vienna, the Picture Gallery," *Treasures of the Great National Galleries* (New York 1954).

GRETCHEN ANDERSON

Belgium

——— Antwerp ———

ROYAL MUSEUM OF FINE ARTS (officially KONINKLIJK MUSEUM VOOR SCHONE KUNSTEN), Leopold de Waelplaats, 2000 Antwerp.

The origin of the Royal Museum of Fine Arts dates from 1664, when the Antwerp painters' guild merged with the newly created Academy of Fine Arts and moved to larger quarters that were decorated with works now in the museum's collection. These paintings, with 328 others saved by the intervention of French and Belgian officials during the suppression of the convents in 1797, formed the core of the academy's early holdings. In 1815 approximately forty works that had been removed during the earlier French occupation of the city were returned and added to the academy's collection. Their publication in 1816 was followed in 1817 by the first complete inventory of the entire collection, which was referred to in this period as the Museum of Antwerp. Shortly thereafter, the paintings were moved to larger quarters in the former Convent of the Récollets, formally inaugurated as the Royal Academy of Fine Arts in 1843. The first official catalogue of the collection, listing more than four hundred works, was published in 1849, and subsequent editions document the steady increase in the museum's holdings to 1,556 items in 1890. By this time, the academy's facilities were no longer adequate, and during the term of Mayor Leopold de Wael, after whom the museum's present site is named, a new building was dedicated on August 11, 1890.

The direct acquisition of painting and sculpture from churches and convents in Antwerp and the surrounding area, as well as museum purchases and private donations, has increased the institution's holdings during the past two centuries. The 1841 legacy of Florent van Ertborn, a former mayor of Antwerp, expanded the Renaissance collection by nearly 150 works, and the bequest of François and Charles Franck significantly increased the number of works by nineteenth- and twentieth-century Belgian artists. Other notable donations have been made by the families van den Hecke-Baut de Rasmon, Bouckaert-Linnig, Meer-Huybrechts, Vleeshauwer, Blomme, Huysmans, Nottebohm, and Beernaert. The Artibus Patriae Society and the Society of Friends of Modern Art have made generous contributions of paintings, sculpture, medals, and archival materials.

The state-owned museum is administered by a director who supervises the curatorial staff of thirteen assistants.

The neoclassical museum building, constructed between 1884 and 1890, was designed by the Belgian architects F. van Dijk and J. J. Winders. The main entrance, located on the west side of the building, features an impressive portal of four Corinthian columns flanked by loggias on each side. The attic is decorated with allegorical figures and medallions by Dupuis, de Pleyn, Ducaju, and Fabri. The rear facade contains a bronze group by Mignon erected in honor of the Antwerp painter Anthony van Dyck. The gardens at the side of the museum contain bronzes by the sculptors Meunier, Marin, Mascré, van Deurden, and Dupon. The vestibule is decorated with a series of paintings by Nicaise de Keyser depicting the history of painting and sculpture in Antwerp and stressing the association of Antwerp artists with their contemporaries in both the Low Countries and Europe. Several large rooms with skylights were added to the ground floor in 1927 to house the collections of modern painting and sculpture, and about the same time, a conference room, library, and documentation center were completed.

The museum's holdings span the fifteenth through the twentieth centuries and contain more than a thousand works by Old Masters and fifteen hundred by modern artists. The museum owns an extremely important group of Flemish paintings, with a strong concentration in works by Antwerp artists. Dating from the fifteenth through the seventeenth century, these were originally held in local churches and private collections. Additional acquisitions have provided the collection with an impressive representative group of nineteenth- and twentieth-century canvases by Belgian artists and a small but selective number of works by Dutch, French, German, and Italian painters.

The collection contains outstanding examples of fifteenth-century Flemish painting. Among the most important works are Jan van Eyck's *St. Barbara* (c. 1437) and the *Madonna of the Fountain* (c. 1439) and Rogier van der Weyden's *Seven Sacraments Triptych* (c. 1450) and the portrait *Philippe de Croy* (c. 1460). Other significant examples from this period are Dirk Bouts' *Madonna and Child*, Hans Memling's *Christ Surrounded by Musical Angels* (from the Najera Triptych, c. 1480) and portrait *Jean de Candida* (c. 1480), and Gerard David's *Rest on the Flight into Egypt* and wings from a triptych depicting female saints and Jewish judges and Roman soldiers (c. 1480). The collection also contains two rare works by the Master of St. Veronica as well as *Christ Crowned with Thorns* (c. 1500), attributed to Hieronymus Bosch.

The museum owns a particularly significant group of paintings by sixteenth-century Antwerp artists. Among the most important early works in this group are Quentin Metsys' *St. Mary Magdalene* and *St. Christopher* (c. 1490), a diptych with the risen Christ, and the *Entombment Triptych* (c. 1510); Joachim Patenir's *Landscape with the Flight into Egypt* (c. 1520); and Jan Gossaert's *Ecce Homo* (1527). Examples of Antwerp painting from mid-century are Pieter Aertsen's *Jan Van Der Biest Triptych*, Frans Floris' *Adoration of the Shepherds* and *Fall of the Rebel Angels* (1554), Joachim de Beuckelaer's *Return of the Prodigal Son* (1563), and Lambert van Noort's *Sybil* series (1565). The museum owns more than thirty works by the late-sixteenth-century painter Martin de Vos, notably his *Temptation of St. Anthony* (c. 1590), as well as panels by members of the Francken family: among them are Hieronymus' *St. Eloy Triptych* (1588); nineteen works by Ambrosius, including his *Miracle of the Loaves* (1598); and works by Frans II and Frans III. Artists from Bruges exhibited in this section are Adrian Isenbrandt, Ambrosius Benson, and the portraitists of the Pourbus family: Frans I, Frans II, and Pieter. Brussels is represented by Bernard van Orley's *Triptych of the Last Judgment and the Seven Sorrows* (c. 1530), Pieter Coecke van Aelst's *Pieta* (c. 1535), Michael Coxie's *Martyrdom of St. Sebastian* (1575) and *Triumph of Christ* (originally in the Cathedral, Antwerp), and numerous works by the descendants of Pieter Bruegel, including Pieter II and Pieter III and Jan I, Jan II, and Jan III.

The collection contains more than thirty works by Antwerp's most celebrated painter, Peter Paul Rubens. Among the most important canvases in an exceptionally strong group are the *Doubting Thomas Triptych* (1613–15); the *Virgin with a Parrot* (1614); the *Nativity Triptych* (1618); the *Last Communion of St. Francis* (1619) and the *Coup de Lance* (1620), both formerly in the Church of the Récollets, Antwerp; the *Adoration of the Magi* (1624), formerly in St. Michael's Abbey, Antwerp; two portraits, painter *Nicolas Rockox* and humanist scholar *Gaspard Gevartius*; and the sketch for the *Chariot of Kallo* (c. 1636). Rubens' one-time assistant Anthony van Dyck is represented by two *Crucifixions* (1627 and 1629), the *Pietà*, and numerous portraits. The museum also owns seventeen works by Jacob Jordaens, including his famous *As the Old Sing, so Pipe the Young* (c. 1638). Popular seventeenth-century Flemish subjects are represented by Cornelis Vos' group portraits, Adrian Brouwer's tavern interiors, Sebastien Vranckx's market scenes, and David II Teniers' cityscapes and landscapes.

The collection includes a particularly comprehensive group of works by nineteenth-century Belgian artists. Baron Henri Leys, an Antwerp native, is represented by more than forty canvases, including portraits, genre, and romanticized historical scenes, such as his *Albrecht Dürer in Antwerp* (1855). The collection also contains numerous examples of Henri de Braekeleer's still lifes and landscapes (twenty-one), Jacob Smit's portraits and landscapes (twenty), and James Ensor's landscapes, interiors, and fantasy compositions (twenty-eight), including his *Entry of Christ into Brussels* (1888). Other significant artists represented in the collection include the Romanticists N. de Keyser, L. Gallait, and G. Wappers;

the Realists C. de Groux, P. Pantazis, F. Rops, E. Laermans, and F. Lamonière; the Impressionists L. Artan, H. Boulenger, and W. Vogels; the Post-Impressionist H. Evenepoel; and the Expressionist F. van den Berghe.

The twentieth-century holdings can be considered strong only through the first quarter of the century. The Laethem-St. Martin group (c. 1900–1914) is particularly well represented by the market scenes, landscapes, and seascapes of Constant Permeke, as well as by the canvases of G. de Smet, G. van Woestyne, and R. Wouters. Examples from the second quarter of the century are even more limited. Significant works from this period include I. Opsomer's two portraits, writer *Felix Timmermans* and statesman *Camille Huysmans* (1928); J. Brusselmans' *The Sea* (1928); R. Magritte's watercolor *Revenge*; P. Delvaux's *Pink Parts* (1937); and E. Tijtgat's *Loves of a Sculptor* (1951).

Due to the collection's regional concentration, its European holdings, although of high quality, are somewhat more limited. The museum owns four outstanding works from the Early Italian Renaissance. They include Simone Martini's *Passion of Christ*, four panels from his Avignon period (c. 1340); Bici di Lorenzo's figures *St. Paul* and *St. Nicolas of Bari*; Fra Angelico's *St. Romauld*; and Antonello da Messina's *Crucifixion* (1475). A later work by Titian, *Jacopo Pesaro Presented to St. Peter*, is also in the collection. The Renaissance in France is represented by Jean Fouquet's portrait *Agnes Sorel*, otherwise known as the *Madonna of the Angels* (c. 1455); Jean Clouet's portrait *Dauphin François*; and Corneille de Lyon's male portraits (c. 1530). Barthel Bruyn's portraits and *Resurrection*; Lucas Cranach the Elder's *Adam and Eve* (1521), *Caritas*, and *Eve*; and Hans Hoblein the Younger's male portraits provide a brief survey of early sixteenth-century German painting. Dutch works from this period include Jacob Corneliszoon's *Triptych with the Madonna and Child* (c. 1530) and Jacob de Backer's *Last Judgment* (1571). Seventeenth-century Dutch portraiture is particularly well represented by Rembrandt's *Eleaser Swalmus* (1637) and *Saskia* (1651), Frans Hals' *Fisherboy* (1640) and *Stephanus Geeraerdts*, and Ferdinand Bol's portrait *Man and His Sister* (1661). Other popular Dutch subjects in the collection include landscape, in works by van Goyen, Berchem, Hobbema, and Ruisdael; still lifes, such as those by van Caelraet and de Heem; and city views by Berckheyde and others. David's *Man with a Hat* and Ingres' *Self Portrait* (1865) are among the most important nineteenth-century holdings, and a small number of relatively minor works by Vuillard, Rouault, Chagall, and Dufy are representative of late-nineteenth- and early-twentieth-century French painting.

The museum's sculpture collection contains a small but interesting group emphasizing regional works from the seventeenth through the twentieth century. Important examples from the Baroque period are Artus II Quellien's *St. Sebastian* (1661), H. II Duquesnoy's *Caritas Romana*, M. van Beveren's small ivory *Christ* (c. 1670), and G. Petel's bust *Peter Paul Rubens*. Other Flemish sculptors represented include F. van Bossuit, G. van Opstal, and J. van der Steen. The collection also has a decided concentration in early-twentieth century Belgian sculpture, with works such as G. Minne's *Volders Monument* (1898), C. Meunier's *The Sowers* (1905), and R. Wouters' *Foolish Virgin* (1912), the *Dreamer*, and *Domestic Bliss*. Later works of interest are G. Grand's *Standing Nude* (1948) and C. LePlae's *Agnes as a Dancer* (1945). Among the most important foreign holdings are works by the French sculptors Clodion, Caffieri, and Rodin, especially the latter's *Age of Bronze* (1876), the *Burghers of Calais* (1886), and *Balzac* (1894).

The museum houses a restoration center, two photo archives, and a cafeteria. The library, containing more than forty thousand volumes, is open to the public. Copies of reproductions, guides, and catalogues of the museum's permanent collection as well as of special exhibits may be purchased at the entrance.

Since 1954 the museum has published an annual, *Het Jaarboek van de Koninklijk Museum voor Schone Kunsten van Antwerpen*, which lists new acquisitions.

Selected Bibliography

Museum publications: *Koninklijke Museum voor Schone Kunsten, Beschrijvende Catalogus, Oude Meesters*, 1959; *Koninklijke Museum voor Schone Kunsten, Beschrijvende Catalogus, Moderne Meesters*, 1958 (both of the above appeared in French translations in 1958 and 1950, respectively); *Addendum van de Beschrijvende Catalogue, 1948. Een Verzameling Tekeningen van James Ensor, de Hollandse Reis*, 1969; Buschman-Van Ryswyck, E., *Beschrijvende Catalogue. Koninklijk Museum voor Schone Kunsten, Antwerpen. Moderne Meesters*, 1948.

CYNTHIA LAWRENCE

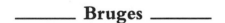

Bruges

MUNICIPAL MUSEUM OF FINE ARTS (officially STEDELIJK MUSEUM VOOR SCHONE KUNSTEN; also GROENINGEMUSEUM, GROENINGE MUSEUM), Dijver 12, 2000 Bruges.

The foundation of the Municipal Museum of Fine Arts, also commonly known as the Groeninge Museum, dates from the addition of a study collection to the Bruges Academy of Drawing, Painting, Sculpture and Architecture shortly after its formation in November 1717. The contents of the collection, which included Italian as well as Flemish works, were destroyed by fire in 1755, and a new collection, created by the contributions of painters active in Bruges at that time, was inaugurated in the following year. This collection grew considerably during the Revolutionary period, when numerous private collections became the property of the municipality, which in turn ceded them to the academy. At the same time, the academy's holdings were significantly enriched by works originally owned by religious institutions from Bruges and the surrounding area. The marked expansion of the collection during this period is recorded in the first formal list of the academy's holdings, which was published in 1824. In 1827–28 the collection was further increased with more than forty works from the Town Hall and the collection of the Central School.

The growing academy holdings demanded larger facilities, and consequently, the collection was moved in 1886 to the Chapel of the Bogaerde School. Continued expansion forced the transfer in 1898 of the eighteenth- and nineteenth-century paintings to the Jesuit College. The city of Bruges became the sole owner of the collection in 1892, thereby transforming it into a municipal museum. In 1910 the city purchased land in the Groeningestraat, the source for the frequently used designation of Groeninge Museum, for a new museum building designed by the architects Delacenserie and Dewulf. These plans were set aside during World War I and the subsequent recovery period, and it was not until 1930 that the current building, designed by M. J. Viérin, was completed. The fourteenth-through seventeenth-century paintings were transfered to the new facility in the same year, and the eighteenth- through twentieth-century works in the following year. The building was remodeled in 1956 to accommodate the installation of modern cooling and ventilation systems.

The Groeninge is one of a group of four Bruges municipal museums (including the Gruuthusemuseum, Arentshuis, and Steinmetzkabinet) administered by a director and his curatorial staff. The collection itself is organized into five sections that include Flemish primitives, works of the sixteenth and seventeenth centuries, works of the eighteenth century, modern painting, and Flemish Expressionism.

During the past two centuries, the museum has been the recipient of generous donations and legacies, which account for the concentrations and quality of its holdings. In 1808 Pieter van Lede presented the famous portrait *Margaret van Eyck* by her husband, Jan, and in 1876 his kinsman Karel van Lede donated an extensive collection of eighteenth- and nineteenth-century works that were augmented in 1898 by the legacy of Desirée van Houtte. The first exhibition of Flemish primitives, which was held at the museum in 1902, inspired contributions that created the collection's considerable strength in this area. Of particular importance are the works presented by or purchased with funds raised by the Amis de Musées de Bruges (founded in 1903) and the Cercle Artistique Brugeois. Other important legacies include those of Anaise Bouvy (1907), Auguste Beernaert (1913), and the baron B. Houtart van Monceau-sur-Sambre (1926). In 1955 the Oudheidkundig Genootschap donated its rich collection to the city, and, in turn, it became part of the museum's collection.

The Groeninge contains a collection of Flemish and Belgian painting dating from the fifteenth through the twentieth century. The first five of its fifteen rooms house the core of its holdings, an outstanding group of fifteenth-century panels by Bruges masters. Foremost among the fifteenth-century panels are two works by Jan van Eyck, the *Madonna with Canon Van Der Paele* (1434–36, originally in the Church of St. Donatus, Bruges) and the aforementioned portrait of the artist's wife, *Margaret van Eyck* (c. 1439). Van Eyck's student and follower Petrus Christus is represented by *St. Elizabeth with a Servant*. The collection also contains several works attributed to the school of Rogier van der Weyden, including *St. Luke Painting The Virgin*, *Mater Dolorosa*, *Christ Crowned with Thorns*, and the portrait *Philip the Good*, which may be by the master himself. Hugo van der Goes' *Death of the Virgin* (c. 1480, originally in the collection of the Abbey of the Dunes, Bruges), is also on display as are eight panels by the Master of the St. Ursula Legend (c. 1480, originally from the Convent of the Black Sisters, Bruges) and several works by the Master of the St. Lucy Legend.

The museum also owns four important works by the late-fifteenth-century Bruges artist Hans Memling. These works include the artist's *Annunciation* (c. 1470) and the *Moreel Triptych* (1484, originally in the Church of St. James, Bruges), which is generally acknowledged as his greatest work. Another Bruges painter, Gerard David, is represented by the panels *Justice of Cambyse* and *Flaying of Sisamnes* (both dated 1498 and originally located in the Town Hall, Bruges), the *Baptism of Christ*, and the *St. Basile Triptych* (c. 1500). The century is brought to a close by Hieronymus Bosch's *Last Judgment Triptych*, part of the Beernaert legacy.

Unlike many Belgian museums, the Groeninge's sixteenth-century collection emphasizes the contributions of Bruges artists over those from Antwerp. The generation of Bruges Mannerists following David is particularly well represented by Jan Provost's *Crucifixion* and *Last Judgment* (1525), Adrien Isenbrandt's triptych the *Madonna and Child with Saints John and Jerome* (originally in the Oudheidkundig Genootschap collection) and portrait *Paulus De Nigro* (acquired in 1956), and several panels by the decorative painter Lancelot Blondeel, including his *St. Luke Painting the Virgin* (c. 1545, originally owned by the Corporation of the Painters and Saddlers, Bruges). The collection also owns an important group of works by the Bruges painter Pieter Pourbus, including *Last Judgment* (1551); the pendant portraits *Jan Fernagut* and his wife *Adriana De Buck* (1551); and a rare grisaille, *Descent from the Cross* (c. 1570, originally included in a triptych in the Church of Our Lady, Damme). Late-sixteenth-century works in the collection are panels by Pieter II Bruegel, Pieter II Claeissens' *Convention of Tournai* (c. 1550), Anton Claeissens' *The Banquet of Esther* (c. 1574), and Jakob van den Coornhuuze's *Last Judgment* (c. 1578, purchased in the Wemaer Sale, 1876).

The museum's seventeenth-century collection, featuring works by artists from Antwerp and Brussels as well as from Bruges, presents a broad range of categories and styles. Earlier traditions are recalled in portraits by J. B. Herregouts and in the religious compositions of J. B. Francken and J. I. van Oost, especially the latter's series of male saints (Martin, Anthony, and Augustine) from various Bruges churches. Contemporary interest in landscape is evidenced in numerous panels including those by J. d'Arthois, L. Achtschellinck, P. van Bredal, P. van den Bogaerde, and B. d'Hooghe. Cityscape painting is represented by the urban scenes of H. van Minderhout, such as his *Commercial Dock at Brugge* (1653), and J. B. van Meuninckhove, especially his scenes the *Grand Place* and the *Burg at Brugge* (c. 1696). Genre painting, somewhat less frequent than in other collections, is best represented by J. II van Oost in works such as *The Artist's Studio* (1666). Jan van Goyen's *Riverscene* and Rachel Ruysch's *Flowers* (1685) are among the rare foreign works in a collection that is primarily devoted to local artists.

Painters from Bruges are especially well represented in the eighteenth-century holdings due to their donations to the academy collection following the fire of 1755. Of particular importance are those works by J. B. Suvée, including his *Invention of Drawing* (c. 1799) and the portrait *Louis Rameau*; those by J. Garemijn, such as the *Construction of the Gent Canal* (1753, a gift of the Société d'Archaeologie de Bruges); the urban and interior scenes of P. LeDoulx and J. Beerblock; and the portraits of J. A. van der Donckt. The majority of the museum's holdings from the seventeenth and eighteenth centuries are not always on exhibition but instead are hung in constant rotation from storage in a documentation center.

The museum also owns an extensive collection of nineteenth-century painting, acquired in large part through the legacies and donations of Bruges artists and collectors. Of particular importance are the landscapes, especially the Hasselt artist Djef Anten's *Autumn Day* (donated by the Cercle Artistique de Bruges). Other landscape artists in the collection include F. Bossuet, J. T. Coosemans, T. Fournois, and E. Beernaert. The collection reflects its regional emphasis in a number of dock and harbor scenes such as A. L. van Sassenbruck's *Harbor at Oostende*, P. J. Claes' *Commercial Dock at Brugge* (1870, from the legacy of Karel van Lede), and A. Asselberg's *Dock of the Menetriers at Brugge* (1895). Early nineteenth-century portraiture appears in representative works such as J. Odevaere's *F. B. de Chauvelin* (1805) and F. J. Kinsoen's *Comte de Viry* (1806). Later portraitists in the collection include E. J. Copman, E. Jans, J. Odevaere, and J. B. Vanacker. Typical of late Romantic Flemish history painting are E. A. Wallays' *Memling Painting the Reliquary of St. Ursula* and E. C. Legencere's *King of England in the Guild of St. George*. Traditional Flemish genre is present in works like J. B. Madou's *Inn Table* (1867), F. Cogen's *Distribution of Bread at Katwijk*, and E. Carpentier's *The Strangers* (1887).

Of particular interest in the early-twentieth-century holdings are the many views of Bruges, such as L. Reckelbus' *The Roman Catholic Convent at Brugge* (1902), F. van Acker's *By the City Walls at Brugge* (1903), E. Viérin's *Begijnhof at Brugge* (1911), J. Middeleer's *Highway at Brugge* (1913), and the numerous canvases of A. Joosten. These works, as well as earlier views of the city dating from the seventeenth through the nineteenth centuries, are displayed together in a separate exhibit. Traditional landscapes, such as those by the Bruges painter G. De Sloovere and the Dutch expatriate D. Baksteen, and genre scenes, such as G. Anthoine's *Art Student's Garret* (c. 1926), are also represented in the collection.

The museum owns a small but comprehensive collection of modern painting emphasizing Belgian Expressionism and Surrealism. Early Expressionist works include J. Delville's *De Godsman* (1901–3); J. Smit's *Christ with Peasants*

(1902); and F. Khnopff's *Secret/Reflect* (1910). Post-war Expressionism is represented by J. Ensor's *Birdpark* (1918), L. Spilliaert's *Bather* (1918) and *Last Rites* (1923), G. van den Woestyne's *Last Supper* (1927), and C. Permeke's *Hay Harvest at Jabbeke* (1929) and *Angelus* (1934). The collection also contains a number of canvases by E. Tijtgat, dating from the *Fair at Watermael* of 1911 through the *Priest and Gulls* of 1947. The museum owns two particularly fine examples of Belgian Surrealism in René Magritte's *Act of Violence* (1932) and Paul Delvaux's *Serenity* (1970).

The museum's modern section contains a growing collection of works by regional artists dating from the decades of the fifties through the present. Of interest among the earlier artists is Luc Peire, who was the subject of a major retrospective exhibition at the museum in 1966. Representative contemporary works in the collection include Pol Mara's *Theme: Stone* (1970), D. van Severen's *Composition* (1970), G. Decock's *Amaterasoe* (1970), A. Visson's *Hymn to the Sea* (1970), and E. Elias' *It Can Be so Nice* (1972). Also on display are R. De Keyser's shaped canvases and R. Slabbinck's portraits, landscapes, and still lifes.

The Groeninge shares the facilities of a library, archive, photograph archive, and restoration laboratory, all located at Dijver 12, with the other Bruges municipal museums. The library is open to scholars upon written application. Color slides and reproductions of works in the collection as well as guides and catalogues published by the museum may be purchased at the entrance.

Selected Bibliography

Museum publications: *The Municipal Museums of Bruges. Summary Catalogue: Paintings* (1973; this work, which includes paintings exhibited in the other municipal museums, is also available in Dutch and French); Hosten, E., and E. I. Stubbe, *Illustrated Catalogue of the Municipal Fine-Art Museum of Bruges* (1948); Pauwels, H., *Catalogue du Musée Communal des Beaux-Arts* (1963).

CYNTHIA LAWRENCE

——— Brussels ———

ROYAL BELGIAN MUSEUMS OF FINE ARTS (officially KONINKLIJKE MUSEA VOOR SCHONE KUNSTEN VAN BELGIE/MUSÉES ROYAUX DES BEAUX-ARTS DE BELGIQUE), Museum Street 9, 1000 Brussels.

The Royal Belgian Museums of Fine Arts include the Museum of Modern Art (Museum van Moderne Kunst/Musée d'Art Moderne, Place Royale 1), its dependency, the Wiertz Museum, Vautier Street 62, 1040 Brussels, and the Museum of Old Masters (Museum van Oude Kunst/Musée d'Art Ancien, Regent Street 3).

The decision to attach a museum to the École des Beaux-Arts in 1797 marked the foundation of the institution and collection that was to become the present Royal Belgian Museums of Fine Arts. Under the direction of its first curator, G.J.J. Bosschaert, nearly fifteen hundred works from the Department of the Dyle were placed in the nearby Hôtel de Nassau, the former court of Charles of Lorraine. This was named the Museum of Brussels and designated as one of fifteen official departmental collections in 1799. Between this date and the fall of the Empire in 1815, many Flemish paintings, including several important works by Rubens, were returned from France, bringing the number of canvases cited in the first official catalogue (1811) to more than three hundred. Ironically, early catalogues omitted the museum's collection of Flemish primitives, which were not admired at this time.

The museum's holdings were purchased from the city by the state in the early 1840s, and to mark the transfer of ownership, it was renamed the Royal Belgian Museum of Painting and Sculpture. Numerous additions to the collection throughout the century required the creation of a separate modern division in 1834, followed by the construction of a new building that was inaugurated on May 26, 1887. The collections of both old and modern masters continued to expand, and in 1919 it was decided to administer the collections separately. The museum was renamed the Royal Belgian Museums of Fine Arts, which today includes the Museum of Modern Art, its dependency the Wiertz Museum, and the Museum of Old Masters. All three institutions are responsible to the same director; however, each museum is separately administered by its own curators and their assistants.

The Museum of Modern Art owns an extremely important collection of more than five thousand paintings, sculptures, and drawings from the nineteenth through the twentieth century with the greatest concentration in Belgian and French painting from the neoclassical through the Symbolist periods. Although designated as an official collection in 1835, the museum was not organized as such until ten years later. It was moved to its present location, the former site of the Hôtel de Nassau, in 1962, pending the construction of a new building in the vicinity. Due to the temporary nature of the current facilities, only a fraction of the holdings is on display at any time. Paintings from the collection are presented annually in four sequential exhibitions that focus on a particular period or theme. The most important items of sculpture are on display in the Great Hall of the Museum of Old Masters (q.v.).

Works by Belgian artists make up a significant portion of the museum's collection. The neoclassical Charleroi portraitist F. J. Navez, a student of Jacques Louis David, is represented by twenty canvases, including his group portrait *Hemptine Family* (1816). H. Leys' *Reestablishment of the Cult in Antwerp Cathedral* (1845) and L. Gallait's *Plague in Tournai* (1882) temporally bracket a survey of mid-century Romantic history painting. The collection also contains numerous examples of nineteenth-century bourgeois Realism in J. Steven's *Dog at the Mirror*; H. De Braekeleer's *Card Party*, *Medlars*, and *Man in a Window* (among twenty-nine of his works in the collection); and H. Evenepoel's *Henrietta in a Large Hat* (1899, among fourteen works on exhibit). Belgian landscape painting from the second half of the nineteenth century is represented by H. Boulenger, G. Vogels, E. Laermans, J. Brusselmans, and L. Artan. Impressionistic artists in the collection include E. Claus, A. Bloch, and I. Verheydan.

The museum has particularly strong holdings in Belgian Expressionism, a regional style encompassing Post-Impressionism through Surrealism. By the Ostend artist James Ensor are twelve canvases and drawings including his *Masks*, *Lamplighter* (1880), *Woman in Blue* (1881), and *Russian Music* (1881). Works such as C. Permeke's *Stranger* (1916), G. De Smet's *Eve or the Apple*, and E. Tijtgat's *Embarkation of Iphigenie* (1950) usher in the more developed Surrealism of Brussels' René Magritte (the *Savior of Tears*, 1948; and the *Empire of Light*, 1959) and Liège's Paul Delvaux (*The Couple*, 1929; and the *Crucifixion*, 1952). Later twentieth-century Belgian works in the collection are by the artists I. Opsomer, A. Bonnet, L. van Lint, and G. Bertrand.

Works by foreign artists are representative of the various stylistic periods from the neoclassicism of the early nineteenth century through the Abstract Expressionism of the twentieth century. Canvases by French painters are predominant in a generally European group. Early works in this section include Jacques Louis David's *Death of Marat* (1793) and Eugène Delacroix's *Apollo, Conqueror of the Python*. Gustave Courbet's portrait of the Belgian artist *Alfred Stevens* is typical of nineteenth-century Realism, and Impressionism is represented by several works by Alfred Sisley. Other Post-Impressionists include Édouard Vuillard's *Two Schoolboys* (1894) and Pierre Bonnard's *Nude* (1908). The collection contains one of Georges Seurat's studies for the *Grande Jatte* and four works by Paul Gauguin, including the portrait *Miss Cambridge* (1891) and *Calvary* (1889). Fauvism appears in works by Henri Matisse, Georges Rouault, and Raoul Dufy, especially the latter's *Harbor At Marseille* (1925). By the Surrealist painter Dali is the *Temptation of St. Anthony*, and there are numerous works by the Abstract Expressionists Hans Hartung and André Manessier among the most important contemporary works.

The Modern Museum's collection of Belgian sculpture includes works by C. Meunier, G. Minne, R. Wouters, O. Jespers, C. LePlae, and P. Caille. Holdings in European sculpture include pieces by A. Rodin, E. A. Bourdelle, A. Maillol, O. Zadkine, G. Richier, H. Moore, L. Chadwick, and M. Marini.

The collection has grown extensively in the past decade due to the generosity of several important donations and bequests. Among them are the Tournay-Solvay legacy, exhibited in 1973; the Paul Maas donation, and the legacy of Dr. Franz Delporte (1973), which provided the collection with works by Wouters, Ensor, Permeke, and Derain. Past contributions have been made by the Société des Amis des Musées royaux de l'Etat; more recently, the Vrienden van de Koninklijke Museum voor Schone Kunsten van België/Les Amis des Musées royaux des beaux-arts de Belgique have been instrumental in planning for the museum's future expansion.

The Museum of Modern Art shares the library and publications of the Museum of Old Masters.

The Wiertz Museum, considered officially a dependency of the Museum of

Modern Art, is the house and studio of the nineteenth-century Romantic painter Anton Wierz (1806–65) and contains a state-owned collection of the Dinant artist's paintings, drawings, and sculptures.

The Museum of Old Masters is located in the Palace of Fine Arts, which was designed by the Belgian architect Alphonse Balat and constructed between 1875 and 1881. Originally intended as an exposition hall, the neoclassic building was soon insufficient for the needs of a modern museum; consequently, surrounding buildings have been periodically incorporated into the structure during the past century. The main facade features four large columns of Scottish granite with bronze socles and capitals. Above the three doors separated by the columns are busts of Peter Paul Rubens, Giovanni da Bologna, and J. van Ruysbroeck, representing painting, sculpture, and architecture, respectively. On the entablature are large allegorical statues of the fine arts by G. de Groot, and above the windows are marble reliefs of the applied arts and music by C. Brunin and T. Vincotte, respectively. Before the two wings are bronze allegorical groups of *The Crowning of Art*, by P. de Vigne, and *The Teaching of Art*, by C. van der Stappen. The south facade is decorated with bronze motifs representing the art of various cultures. The gilded figure of *Genius* atop the cupola is by G. de Groot.

The Museum of Old Masters contains more than fifteen hundred paintings dating from the fifteenth through the eighteenth centuries. Although the collection owns notable works by Dutch, French, German, and Italian artists, the emphasis is on works by Flemish masters, a concentration that reflects the formation of the original collection from regional ecclesiastical art. The museum is particularly rich in examples of fifteenth-century painting. One of the rarest works from this period is a pre-Eyckian retable, *Life Of the Virgin* (c. 1410). Three panels by Robert Campin (the Master of Flémalle), including his *Annunciation*, can be examined beside works of his student Jacques Daret and his probable follower Rogier van der Weyden, who is represented by six panels including the *Pietà* and the portrait *Antoine de Bourgogne*. Other significant holdings in this period include Petrus Christus' *Lamentation*, Hugo van der Goes' *St. Anne, the Virgin and Child with Donors*, and Dirk Bouts' two panels *Justice of the Emperor Otto* (c. 1475, originally in St. Peter's, Louvain). The museum also owns four works by Hans Memling, notably his *Martyrdom of St. Sebastian*; two by Gerard David, *The Adoration of the Magi* and the *Virgin with the Milk Spoon* (c. 1500); and two by Hieronymus Bosch, including his triptych *Temptation of St. Anthony* (c. 1500, formerly in the collection of King Philip II of Spain).

The museum has an impressive sixteenth-century collection containing more than a dozen works by Pieter Bruegel the Elder. They include his *Adoration of the Magi* (1556), the *Fall of Icarus* (1558), the *Fall of the Rebel Angels* (c. 1562), the *Winter Landscape* (1565, obtained from the Delporte legacy), the *Census at Bethlehem* (1566), and a rare series of allegorical representations, the *Seven Deadly Sins*. Other major works from the first half of the sixteenth century are Quentin Metsys' retable *St. Anne* (c. 1509, originally in St. Peter's, Louvain),

Bernard van Orley's *Hanneton Triptych* and the retable *Virtue of Patience* (c. 1521), and Jan Gossaert's *Venus and Cupid* (1521). Representative paintings from the second half of the century include Pieter Aertsen's *Cook with Assistant* (1559) and *Christ With Mary and Martha*; Marc de Vos' *St. Paul at Ephesis* (1568), the portrait *Anselmus Family* (1577), and *Apollo with Muses*; and Antonio Moro's portrait *Hubert Goltzius*. The collection offers a particularly good survey of sixteenth-century Flemish landscape paintings in works by J. Patenier, H. Met de Bles, J. de Momper, and P. Bril.

Extensive holdings of paintings by the Antwerp artists Peter Paul Rubens and Jacob Jordaens has necessitated the creation of separate galleries devoted to their works. Among the dozen canvases in the Rubens' room are his *Assumption of the Virgin* (c. 1614, originally painted for the Church of the Capuchins, Tournai), the *Adoration of the Magi* (1615–20), the *Assumption of the Virgin* (1618–20, originally painted for the Church of the Carmelites, Brussels), *St. Francis Protecting the World* (1633, originally painted for the Church of the Franciscans, Gent), the *Martyrdom of St. Livinius* (1635), the *Ascent to Calvary* (1637), and numerous portraits, including Rubens' second wife, *Helene Fourment*, and the *Archduke and Archduchess Albert and Isabella*. The Jordaens room contains the artist's *Holy Family* (1615), the *Satyr and the Peasant* (1620), the *Allegory of Plenty* (1625), *Susanna and the Elders* (1630), *The King Drinks* (1635–40), and the *Triumph of Frederick Henry* (1652). Another Antwerp-born painter, Anthony van Dyck, is represented by his *Genoese Lady and Her Daughter* (1625) and an important series of male portraits, including the painter *François Duquesnoy, J. K. des Cordes, J. van Caestre*, and *J-Ch. della Faille*, with *Faille* located in the room containing the legacy left to the museum by the Count della Faille de Leverghem in 1946. The seventeenth-century collection also contains examples of Adrian Brouwer's genre scenes; Snyders, de Vos and Fyt's hunting scenes; the Teniers' landscapes and cityscapes; and the Neeffs' church interiors.

Although not as extensive as its Flemish collections, the museum's holdings of Renaissance and Baroque painting from outside Flanders include many important works. Fifteenth-century French painting is represented by two rare works, the Master of the Aix Annunciation's *St. Jerome* (c. 1445) and the Master of Moulins' *Virgin and Child with Angels* (c. 1490). Seventeenth-century French holdings include canvases by Champaigne, Vouet, Lorraine, and Poussin. Two panels by Carlo Crivelli, particularly his *Virgin and Child with St. Francis*, dominate the small collection of Italian paintings, which includes works by Veronese, G. B. Tiepolo, and Guardi. The museum also owns more than a dozen works by German artists, notably Lucas Cranach the Elder; English masters such as Reynolds, Lawrence, and Constable; and of the Spanish school, El Greco, Ribera, and Goya.

By far the most important foreign holdings are those in seventeenth-century Dutch painting. Portraiture is exceptionally well represented with works by Rembrandt (the *Bambeeck* portrait), Hals (the *Hoornebeeck* and *Heythuysen* portraits), Maes, Bol, Vermeer, and van der Helst. The Dutch collection also presents an especially comprehensive survey of landscape painting, with examples by Hobbema, van Goyen, Ruysdael, Cuyp, and van de Velde. Genre scenes by Steen, Metsu, Ostade, and de Hoogh and still lifes by de Heem and van Beveren are also on display.

The museum's collection of painting is paralleled by complementary holdings of nearly four thousand watercolors and drawings. The majority of them were originally in the Grez Collection, which was bequeathed to the museum in 1912. Due to a lack of space, works in this collection are not exhibited and can be seen only by written request.

The museum also owns more than four hundred pieces of sculpture. Primarily of local origin, these examples date from the seventeenth and eighteenth centuries and represent all media. The museum also temporarily houses a portion of the sculpture in the collection of the Museum of Modern Art. The most important of these works are on display in the Great Hall.

The sculpture collection has exceptionally strong holdings in seventeenth-century works from Antwerp and Brussels, with the greatest concentration of them in the last quarter of the century. Particularly well represented are the sculptors Ludovicus Willemssens (eight pieces including his *St. Martin of Tours*, c. 1675), Hendrik Frans Verbrugghen (seven works including the study for the *Church Triumphant*, c. 1699, the completed work, now destroyed, originally in the Cathedral, Antwerp), and three generations of the prolific Quellien family, including Artus I (study for *St. Peter*, c. 1658, the completed work in St. Andrew's, Antwerp), Artus II (seven works including his 1678 studies for an altar in the Cathedral, Antwerp), and Thomas (study for *Prudentia*, c. 1700). The collection also contains a number of works related to important Flemish sepulchral monuments including L. Fayd'herbe's study for the Snyers-Rigauts monument (c. 1675, completed work in St. Gummarus, Lier), M. van Beveren's study for the Turn and Taxis Chapel (c. 1676, completed work in Our Lady of Sablon, Brussels), fragments of an epitaph by J. van Delen, P. II Verbrugghen's study for the van der Cammen monument (c. 1692, completed work in St. Gummarus, Lier), and M. van der Voort's figures for the Coxie monument (c. 1709) and portrait for the Caverson monument (c. 1713), both formerly in the Dominican Church, Brussels. The museum's holdings also include examples from the oeuvres of A. de Nole, H. II Duquesnoy, P. I van Baurscheit, J. C. de Cock, P. Scheemaeckers, and G. Kerricx. Gabriel Grupello, a Flemish expatriate, is represented by a marble wall, *Fountain with Sea Gods* (c. 1675), and by both the studies and completed figures *Diana* and *Narcissus* (c. 1675, originally in the garden of the Turn and Taxis Palace, Brussels).

The library, located at Museumstraat 5/Rue du Musée 5, contains more than a hundred thousand volumes and subscribes to three hundred periodicals. It is open to the public on a noncirculating basis four mornings each week. Slides and reproductions of works in the collection as well as guides, catalogues, and other museum publications may be purchased at the museum's entrance. Between 1938 and 1944, the Royal Belgian Museums of Fine Arts published a yearbook, the *Jaarboek der Koninklijke Museums voor Schone Kunsten van Belgie/Annuaire des Musées Royaux des Beaux-Arts de Belgique*; since 1952, they have published the quarterly *Bulletin* containing articles on works in the collections and on Flemish art in general.

Selected Bibliography

Museum publications: *Chefs-d'oeuvre des Musées royaux des beaux-arts de Belgique*, 1950; Bruxelles, Musées royaux des beaux-arts de Belgique, Musée d'art moderne, *Acquisitions, 1961–1966, Première exposition*, mai 12–août 6, 1967; *Acquisitions récentes*, novembre 26-fevrier 13, 1972; *Chefs-d'oeuvres de la peinture Belge des XIXe et XXe siècles dans les collections au Musée d'art moderne*, 1963; Devigne, M., *Catalogue de la sculpture*, 1922; 1923; idem, *Collection della faille de Leverghem*, 1944; Fierens-Gevaert, P., and Laes, A., *Catalogue de la peinture moderne*, 1928; d'Hulst, R. A., *Musées royaux de Belgique: Le musée de Bruxelles, Art ancien*, 1965; 1984.

CYNTHIA LAWRENCE

ROYAL MUSEUMS OF ART AND HISTORY (officially KONINKLIJKE MUSEA VOOR KUNST EN GESCHIEDENIS / MUSÉES ROYAUX D'ART ET D'HISTOIRE), Jubelpark 10, 1040 Brussels.

In 1406 Anthone de Bourgogne established the Arsenal in Brussels for the purpose of storing and exhibiting the arms, trophies, and ornaments of the royal Burgundian House. This collection, transferred to the library of the Jesuit College in 1773, was formally declared the Museum of Arms, Armaments, Art and Numismatics in 1835. Two years later, it was moved to the Palais d'Industrie, where it joined the artillery collection of the Ministry of War. In 1847 the collection was reorganized as the Museum of Armaments, Antiques and Artillery, with headquarters in the Porte de Hal and additional exhibition space in two nearby buildings. It was moved in 1889 to the Palais du Cinquantenaire, where it was enlarged with casts of Classical sculpture formerly in the collection of the Commission for International Exchanges and was renamed the Royal Museum of Decorative Arts and Crafts. In 1905 the Egyptian, Greek, and Roman collections were reinstalled in the second wing of the palace, the Pavilion of Antiquities, and, in 1921, the sections on crafts and the history of Belgium were moved to new facilities. From 1912 the institution was called the Royal Museums of the Cinquantenaire; in 1929 it was given its present name, the Royal Museums of Art and History.

The Palais du Cinquantenaire was built in 1879–80 by Bordiau as an exposition hall for the celebrations marking the fiftieth anniversary of the creation of Belgium. Its two projecting wings, connected by a semicircular colonnade, were completed in 1905 with the addition of a triumphal arch, forty-five meters tall, designed by C. Girault and donated by King Leopold II. On the attic of the arch is a Roman chariot pulled by four horses, the work of the sculptors T. Vincotte and J. Lagae. Symbolic figures of Belgium and Brabant, the province in which Brussels is located, ride in the chariot, and figures representing the eight other Belgian provinces are placed in pairs above the four pilasters on the obverse and reverse faces. The Royal Museums of Art and History occupy the southern wing; the northern wing houses the Royal Museum of the Army and Military History.

The personnel of the state-owned museum are organized into administrative and technical staffs. The first includes the museum director, the associate directors, and the managerial, accounting, and secretarial departments. The technical staff includes curators, associate curators, assistants, and technicians, as well as the departments responsible for acquisitions, documentation, inventories, research, reproductions, the library, the slide collection, and the various educational services. The museums also administer three smaller collections located outside the Cinquantenaire complex: the Porte de Hal Museum, the Bellevue Museum, and the Chinese Pavilion at Laeken.

The museums' collections are divided into three large departments: antiquity (including ancient Egypt, the ancient Near East, Greece, and Rome) and the early history of Belgium; crafts, primarily western European, from the Middle Ages to the present; and ethnography, folklore, and the art of the Far East. The quality and size of these collections places the museums among Europe's most important.

The Antiquity Department's extensive Egyptian collection, exhibited in thirteen rooms, is representative of all periods of Egyptian civilization from the prehistoric through the Christian. Of particular interest are the works from the end of the eighteenth dynasty, which include a relief portrait of Queen Tiyi, an alabaster head of Amenophis IV, and a granite head of Tutankhamen. The Neferrenpet *Book of the Dead*, from the New Kingdom, is perhaps the collection's most valuable manuscript. The textile holdings contain an especially strong group of funerary palls, cushions, and clothing, as well as examples of dyed, printed, and painted cloth. The cloth is represented by an important Coptic portrait, *Aurelius and His Wife, Pisoia*. The Queen Elisabeth Egyptology Foundation, a research institution, is attached to this section.

The collection of pre-Christian art from the Ancient Near East is arranged by civilization. Particularly significant are the neolithic ceramics from Jericho, the Mesopotamian and Babylonian cuneiform texts and cylinder seals, the Assyrian reliefs, and the Persian prehistoric pottery and Luristan bronzes. The Islamic section contains examples of terracotta, faience, and textiles from Persia, Turkey, and Morocco, dating from the ninth through the nineteenth century.

The Greek, Etruscan, and Roman collections are exhibited together in a hall containing a reconstruction of a colonnade, dating from the second century A.D., excavated in Apamea, Syria, by a Belgian archaeological expedition in the 1930s. The hall also contains original fifth-century A.D. mosaics from Apamea and Syrian glass from the second and third centuries A.D. The museums own a fine collection of Greek ceramics, especially vases, as well as several outstanding examples of Roman sculpture, including a bronze figure of Septimus Severus, a terracotta bust of Hercules, and several torsos of athletes. In addition to sarcophagi and funeral stelae, the Roman collection contains examples of painting from Boscoreale. There is also an interesting model of fourth-century Rome by

P. Bigot and, in a separate room, a documentary explanation of daily life in ancient Greece and Rome.

The museums' second major department, western European crafts, is subdivided into more than twenty sections. The emphasis in each section is on objects of Belgian origin, dating from the Middle Ages to the present. The rooms devoted to wood carving contain an outstanding group of retables and retable fragments from the fifteenth and sixteenth centuries. Among the most important are the *Passion* (Claude de Villa, c. 1470); *St. George* (J. Borreman, c. 1493); the *Kinship of St. Anne* (Brussels, c. 1500–1510); *St. Barbara and St. Leger* (Wannebacq, c. 1530); the *Passion* (associated with Lambert Lombard, from St. Pierre-lez-Libramont); and three later anonymous works of Antwerp origin, from the churches of Pailhe, Herbais-sous-Pietrain, and Oplinter. The division also contains an interesting exhibit tracing the evolution of the eleventh-century *Sedes Sapientiae* into the fourteenth-century seated Virgin, sixteenth-century figures from Mechelen, and wooden figures and reliefs from the seventeenth and eighteenth centuries. The division of stone and marble sculpture features a group of Romanesque and Gothic baptismal fonts in addition to sepulchral and commemorative sculpture, alabaster figures from Mechelen, and an entombment group from Mons (1502). Early seventeenth-century portraiture is represented by the busts *Archduke Albert* (J. and R. de Nole) and *Justus Lipsius*. Another important holding from this period is a gilded bronze flagellation group attributed to Frans Duquesnoy.

The museums own a remarkable collection of ivory sculpture dating from the fifth through the twentieth century. Among the rarest early works are a book cover with St. Peter (sixth-seventh century), the Genoelselderen diptych (eighth century), plaques from Tongeren (eighth century), a Mosan reliquary with a scene of the Crucifixion (eleventh century), and several small coffers of Byzantine origin. Of special interest are works by seventeenth-century Flemish sculptors. They include Frans Duquesnoy's *Sleeping Cupid*, Artus I Quellien's beakers with scenes of the birth of Venus, M. van Beveren's small altar with the dead Christ, and F. van Bossuit's *Calvary*. The division also contains an exhibit of Art Nouveau ivories. The museum's terracotta holdings include an important series of studies by Lucas Fayd'herbe, including his *Rest on the Flight into Egypt* (1675), as well as works by Artus II Quellien and Laurent Delvaux.

A cradle, decorated with the arms of Mary of Burgundy and Maximilian of Austria and said to have belonged to the infant Charles V, is one of the furniture division's most valuable pieces. Although examples of church furniture, such as the pulpit from Alsemberg (c. 1480) and the choir stalls from Köln (c. 1510), appear in the collection, the majority of the pieces, including chests, beds, cabinets, and secretaries, were made for secular use from the sixteenth through the nineteenth century. Also of interest in this division are a period room decorated in the Parisian Regency style and the Wolfers store (c. 1890), designed by Victor Horta, which has been reassembled in the museum to house an exhibit of Art Nouveau objects.

The museums' collection of gold work attests to the skill achieved by the artists of the Mosan school during the twelfth and thirteenth centuries. Of greatest interest are those objects by Godefroy de Huy and his followers. They include a portable altar with scenes of the passion from Stavelot; a reliquary of Pope Alexander, also from Stavelot (c. 1145); and a reliquary triptych from the early thirteenth century. Another master, Hugo d'Oignies, is represented by two reliquaries of unusual design. The division also contains thirteenth-century enamels from Limoges and sixteenth-century enamels curiously worked in polychrome and grisaille. The silver collection presents a comprehensive group of objects, both domestic and foreign, decorated with stamped designs. Other important pieces in this division include an early sixteenth-century collar presented to Charles V by the Nivelles guild of silversmiths, a gilded bowl by Loys van Nieukerke of Bruges, and a bowl and equestrian figure from Augsburg. The collection also contains significant examples of liturgical silver, especially chalices, from the sixteenth and seventeenth centuries and silverware from the eighteenth century. Among the most notable holdings of the division devoted to works in brass, bronze, and copper are a baptismal font from Tienen (c. 1145) and chandeliers from the abbeys of Postel and Parc, dating from the seventeenth century. Also on exhibit are examples of lecterns, standards, bowls, mortars, pestles, and bells. Objects made of pewter, dating from the twelfth through the eighteenth century, are displayed together in a separate room.

The division of textiles, embroidery, and costume is particularly renowned for its collection of historiated liturgical embroideries from the thirteenth through the sixteenth century. Of special interest is a valuable group of antependia. The division also contains comprehensive collections of liturgical vestments and eighteenth-century secular clothing. The textile holdings, including Oriental, Egyptian, Byzantine, Italian, and French examples, is particularly rich, and the Flemish, German, and Italian embroideries are highly regarded. The Isabella Errera Textile Collection, although not on display, is available to scholars.

The museums own one of the most important lace collections in Europe, and the holdings in Brussels lace, from the sixteenth through the eighteenth century, are unparalleled. The collection is comprehensive, including lace of both regional (Antwerp, Bruges, Brussels, Binche, Mechelen, Valenciennes, Lille, and Couvins) and foreign (Italy, France, England, Spain, and Scandinavia) origin. Works of particular importance include a coverlet of the Archdukes Albert and Isabella (c. 1599), a collection of eighteenth-century veils, and a coverlet containing the arms of the Imperial Russian House (early nineteenth-century). Also displayed are examples of nineteenth- and twentieth-century embroidered lace, Art Nouveau lace, infants' clothing decorated with lace and embroidery, and knitting.

The museums' outstanding tapestry collection, containing more than 120 items, traces the history of Western tapestry manufacture from the fifteenth through the eighteenth century, emphasizing the contributions of Belgian artists and craftsmen. Late Gothic works from Tournai include the *Youth of Hercules*, the *Passion*, *Judith and Holofernes*, the *Tonte des Moutons* (1460–75), and the *Battle of*

Roncevaux (c. 1480). The division also contains a particularly comprehensive group of early-sixteenth-century tapestries from Brussels. Among the most significant are the *Glorification of Christ* (1500), the *Invention of the Cross* (Leonard Knoest, 1510), the *Legend of Herkenblad* (1513), the *Legend of Our Lady of Sablon* (1516–18), the *Triumph of Virtue* (1518), and the *Legend of Jacob* (after cartoons by Bernard van Orley, c. 1530). Early seventeenth-century artisans represented include F. Spiering, M. Reynbouts, F. Tons, and F. van Maelsaeck. Additional Baroque holdings include a group of eight tapestries derived from Peter Paul Rubens' *Decius Mus* series; seven tapestries, depicting hunting scenes, after compositions by Rubens and Antonio Tempesta; and two works, *Neptune Creating the Horse* and the *Luteplayer and His Lady*, after sketches by Jacob Jordaens. Among the division's foreign holdings is a rare fourteenth-century French work, the *Presentation in the Temple*.

The ceramics collection includes an important comprehensive group of soft-paste porcelain from Tournai. Other works of Belgian origin are the hard-paste porcelain pieces from the area around Brussels (Etterbeek, Ixelles, and Mont-plaisir). The division also contains examples of French (Saint-Cloud, Chantilly, Mennecy, Sèvres, and Paris), German (Meissen, Höchat, Frankenthal, and Ludwigsburg), English (Chelsea), Dutch (the Hague), and Austrian (Vienna) porcelain. A separate collection of two hundred eighteenth-century porcelain boxes and tobacco holders, of French and German manufacture, were bequeathed to the museum by Mme. L. Solvay. Of additional interest are the Dutch tiles from the seventeenth through the nineteenth century, especially Cornelis Bouwmeester's multiple-tile compositions (Rotterdam).

The museums own what is generally considered to be the world's most complete collection of delftware. The two thousand pieces, many of which were obtained in the Evenepoel legacy, are representative of changing taste in color and design from the seventeenth through the nineteenth century. Important works of Belgian origin in the faience division include five hundred paving stones from Herkenrode Abbey (1532) and a painted jar by Jan van Bogaert (1562). General surveys of later faience from Belgium (Brussels, Bruges, Tournai, Liège, Namur, and Nimy), Luxembourg, France (Strasbourg, Niderviller, Lunéville, Saint-Clément, Rouen, Sceaux, Saint-Amand-les-Eaux, Bailleul, and the famous *terres de Lorraine* of P. L. Cyfflé), and Germany (Winterthur) are on display, along with Italian majolica and Spanish lusterware. The museums' collection of stoneware, spanning the sixteenth through the eighteenth century, contains works from Köln, Siegbourg, Raeren, and Westerwald. Works by Jan Emens and the Mennicken are of special interest. In addition to the terracotta sculpture noted above, the collection also includes interesting examples of tableware and ornaments, especially the glazed terracotta from Torhout. Modern ceramic works dating from the late nineteenth century to the present survey activity in Denmark, England, and France with particular emphasis on the Art Deco period. A special room has been set aside to display the work of contemporary Belgian ceramicists, including de Caille, Strebelle, Vermeersch, Landuyt, Dionyse, and de Vinck.

The history of glass manufacture from antiquity through the nineteenth century is documented by the museums' extensive collection. Pieces of special importance include a Venetian beaker (1500), an engraved glass from Antwerp (1592), examples of Bohemian and Silesian glass (eighteenth century), works in crystal (nineteenth century), and Art Nouveau glass design. A special room has been devoted to the work of the master glassmaker Maurice Marinot (1881–1960). A display tracing the evolution of stained-glass windows in Belgium and western Europe from the twelfth through the sixteenth century draws attention to examples from Leuven and Mechelen. The collection also contains a fine group of Belgian painted-glass medallions from the sixteenth and seventeenth centuries, notably the works by Antwerp's Dirk Vellert (c. 1520), as well as a contemporary group of Swiss painted windows. Valuable small works in ivory and porcelain are from the Godtschalck legacy. The museums' collections of arms, armaments, and artillery, including works from the Titeca Collection, is on display in the Porte de Hal Museum.

The third major department, ethnography and folklore, has geographic concentrations in Belgium, the Far East, Southeast Asia, Oceania, India, and the Americas. There art objects serve primarily to illustrate particular civilizations or periods. Displays of archaeological discoveries in Belgium, dating from the Neolithic period through the Middle Ages, are especially significant. Pre-Christian exhibits include Paleolithic implements; neolithic pottery (Omalion and Vaux-et-Borset); and Bronze Age jewelry (Fauvillers), arms (Court St. Etienne), and sepulchral artifacts (tomb of Eigenbilzen). The museums own a strong collection of bronze objects from the Roman period such as the vases from Bois-et-Borsu and Herstal, figures of Mercury from Tienen and Givry, and weights from Engis. Other Belgo-Roman articles on display include jewelry, pottery, and stone sculpture. Objects found in the necropolises of Anderlecht, Harmignies, Lede, Marilles, and Haillot reflect Belgian civilization during the Merovingian period, as the jewelry of gold and precious stones from Muizen are indicative of the Carolingian period. A comprehensive group of medieval ceramics is also on display. The section devoted to Belgian folklore, primarily of the nineteenth century, includes reconstructions of a Brussels pharmacy, a marionette theater, a cabaret, and a guild hall. Also exhibited are religious images, toys, household implements, playing cards, and popular woodcuts. The museum also owns a notable collection of eighteenth- and nineteenth-century vehicles.

The museums' collection of Chinese art, one of Europe's most important, includes ceramics (Neolithic from Gansu, and T'ang period from Honan), bronzes (Shang through Chou), and an exhibit showing the stylistic evolution of Buddhist statues, reliefs, and frescoes from the T'ang through the Ming periods. The Far Eastern collection also contains a notable group of Korean ceramics from the Three Kingdoms through the Yi periods. Japanese art, dating from the Edo through the Meiji periods, includes painting, porcelain, arms, masks and costumes of the Nō Theater, lacquer ware, inro, and netsuke. A separate collection of Japanese books and prints may be seen by appointment. Other Oriental works from the museums' collections are on display in the Chinese Pavilion at Laeken.

The Southeast Asian collection features a Javanese theater, complete with masks, costumes, and decorations, with displays from Sumatra, Kalimantan, and Nias, including an important group of ikats. Other areas represented in this collection include Indonesia (Buddhist and Hindu art from Java and Bali, as well as a comprehensive display of batiks), Cambodia (important Khmer sculpture from the tenth through the twelfth century); Vietnam (the Clément Huet Collection of neolithic bronzes and ceramics), Thailand, and Nepal and Tibet (a strong group of tangkas). The Oceanic exhibits contain works from Melanesia and Polynesia, including pierced bark and Pascuane figures. Most notable in the collection of Indian art are the stone Buddha figures from the second and sixth centuries and the bronze figure of Siva from the twelfth century.

Important works included in the museums' ethnographic exhibits on the Americas are an Olmec stone figure (c. 1000 B.C.), terracotta figures from Colima (c. 250 B.C.), a Mayan stone relief of a warrior (A.D. 600–750), Totonaque figures (c. A.D. 800), a Toltec-Aztec stone eagle head (c. A.D. 1350), and a coat of red feathers from the Tupinamba tribe in Brazil (c. A.D. 1500). Attached to this section is the L. Siret Collection of prehistoric art and artifacts from Spain.

The museums' library, containing more than one hundred thousand volumes, and slide collection, housing more than fifty thousand slides, are open to the public. Books do not circulate, but slides may be borrowed for a small fee. The cast collection, holding more than five thousand examples of Classical sculpture, is also available for public use. In addition to weekly lectures and guided tours, the museums sponsor thematic lecture series based on concentrations in the collection. Of special interest are the "Dynamuseum," a series of creative workshops arranged in conjunction with current exhibitions or lecture series, and the "Encounters with Artists and Craftsmen," a program demonstrating materials and techniques. The museums also maintain the Museum for the Blind, located at Nervienslaan 10/Avenue des Nerviens 10, that sponsors tours and workshops for the visually handicapped. The museums' store sells more than ten thousand reproductions of art, architecture and crafts, as well as archaeological and historical documents and materials. Also available are catalogues of the collections and museum publications. Since 1901 the museums have published the *Bulletin Van De Koninklijke Musea voor Kunst en Geschiedenis/ Bulletin des Musées royaux d'art et d'histoire*, a scholarly annual devoted to objects in the collection and to Flemish art generally, and the *Artes belgicae*, a monographic series. Two independent research centers, the Georges Dossin Foundation of Assyriology and the Institute for Advanced Chinese Studies, are located in the museum complex.

The Porte de Hal Museum (Museum van de Hallepoort/Musée de la Porte de Hal), Boulevard Waterloo, is located in a fourteenth-century city gate, and contains arms, armaments, and artillery dating from the Middle Ages through the eighteenth century.

The Bellevue Museum, Bellevue Pavilion (Bellevue Museum/Musée Bellevue), Place de Palais 7, was founded in 1978. The collection is devoted to art objects and furnishings from the eighteenth and nineteenth centuries. The museum sponsors monthly seminars, "Les Conferences à Bellevue," on topics related to the collection.

The Chinese Pavilion (Chinees Paviljoen/Pavillon Chinois), Avenue van Praet 44, is located in the Royal Park at Laeken, and renowned for its collection of Chinese and Japanese porcelain and art objects from the seventeenth and eighteenth centuries. It also houses the Vergaeghe de Naeyer Collection, an important group of Far Eastern porcelain and paintings, and European ceramics.

Selected Bibliography

Museum publications: Bauer, Rotraud, and Delmarcel, Guy, *Les tapisseries de Bruxelles au siècle de Rubens*, 1977; Berryer, A.-M., and Lébioles, L. Presse de, *La mesure du temps à travers les âges aux Musées royaux d'art et d'histoire*, 1961; Capart, Jean, *Le temple des muses*, 1932; Derveaux-Van Ussel, Ghislaine, *Exposition de sculpture anglaises et malinoises d'albatre*, 1967; Destrée, Joseph, *Catalogue des ivoires, des objets en nacre, en os gravé, et en cire peinte*, 1902; idem, *Les tapisseries*, 1910; Errera, Isabelle, *Catalogue d'étoffes anciennes et modernes*, 1927; Mariën-Dugarden, A.M., *Faïences fines*, 1961; idem, *La céramique en Belgique de la préhistoire au moyen âge*, 1962; Risselin-Steenebrugen, Marie, *La dentelle de Bruxelles*, 1963; idem, *Les dentelles Belges*, 1963; idem, *Les dentelles étrangères aux Musées royaux d'art et d'histoire*, 1963; Santa, Elisabeth della, *Les collections polynésiennes et micronésiennes des Musées royaux d'art et d'histoire*, 1952.

CYNTHIA LAWRENCE

——— Tervuren ———

ROYAL MUSEUM OF CENTRAL AFRICA (officially KONINKLIJK MUSEUM VOOR MIDDEN-AFRIKA/MUSÉE ROYAL DE L'AFRIQUE CENTRALE; formerly MUSÉE DU CONGO [1897–1910], MUSÉE DU CONGO BELGE [1910–52], MUSÉE ROYAL DU CONGO BELGE [1952–62]), 13, Chaussée de Louvain, B–1980 Tervuren.

The origin of the Royal Museum of Central Africa dates from 1897, when King Léopold II of Belgium decided to create the Section de L'État-Indépendant du Congo in Tervuren as part of the Brussels International Exhibition. Although the basic aim of the exhibition was economic, an important place was given to the arts and crafts of the Congo Free State. Th. Masui, secretary-general of the section, in 1897 and 1899 prepared guides to the peoples, cultures, and economies of the Congo and to the art collections. The ethnographic objects, organized into six large geographical regions, had been secured by agents of the Congo Free State and by the Société Anonyme Belge pour le Commerce du Haut-Congo. The initial success of the display encouraged the organizers to transform the temporary exhibit into a permanent Musée du Congo, which by 1902 included about eight thousand objects from Zaire. The curator E. Coart and the director A. de Hauleville embarked on the publication of systematic inventories, descriptions, illustrations, and classifications of musical instruments (1902); of amulets, figurines, and masks (1906); and of ceramics (1907). Until his death in 1909, King Léopold II was instrumental in securing funds (by passing royal decrees) for the building program of the museum. The plans for the new museum building were drafted after 1902 by the famed French architect Girault following the royal decree of 1902 deciding to replace the Palais de l'Exposition Coloniale de Tervuren with the construction of a large museum building. The work was undertaken (1904–8) by the Brussels firm of Wouters-Dustin, which also was involved in other monumental structures of the era of Léopold II. The museum building has many of the grandiose and sumptuous aspects of palaces and other public buildings erected under Léopold II. Particularly impressive is the huge marble gallery (made with rare marbles from French quarries) in which many of the artworks are displayed. In 1910 the new museum was inaugurated by King Albert I. Later additions to the museum were made in 1958 and 1964, and restorations of existing display areas have continued since 1947.

The museum, called Musée du Congo belge from 1910 and Musée Royal du Congo belge from 1952, depended on the Belgian Ministry of Colonies. After the Belgian Congo became the independent Zaire Republic in 1960, the name of the museum changed to Musée Royal de l'Afrique Centrale (1962). Since then the museum has been dependent on the Division of Scientific Research in the Belgian Ministry of Education. Founded on a tradition of public support, the museum has received many gifts of collections and objects and has acquired others through scientific missions, bequests, and purchases. In 1951 the museum director Olbrechts created the Association des Amis du Congo belge to assist in the expansion of collections, documents, and archives and to contribute to the general enrichment of the museum through the organization of lectures, special exhibitions, performances of ethnic music, the journal *Congo-Tervuren* (called *Africa-Tervuren* after 1960), and other publications. Largely financed by patrons of the arts, the association also purchases collections for the museum.

The museum is administered by a director. It is organized into the departments of Cultural Anthropology, Geology and Mineralogy, Zoology, Agriculture and Economics, and History; an administrative department includes the library and educational services. The Department of Cultural Anthropology comprises four sections: Linguistics and Ethnomusicology, Prehistory and Archaeology, Social Anthropology and Ethnohistory (including the important bureau for ethnographic documentation), and Ethnography. The Ethnography section mainly manages the vast collections from Central Africa, and more recently from sub-Saharan Africa as a whole; Oceania; and the Americas.

The fame of the museum rests on its extensive ethnographic and art collections from Zaire. The most comprehensive and representative collections in the world, they cover diverse aspects of technology, material culture, and art from virtually all ethnic groups in Zaire. The artworks are primarily sculptures in wood, ivory, bone, stone, mud, clay, ceramics, and metals; construction masks in leaves, fibers, cloth, feathers, and other materials; and figurines made in cloth. The range of sculptured forms is unusually large. Outstanding artworks drawn from different ethnic groups may be found in each of the following categories: anthropomorphic and zoomorphic figurines and masks; carved tree branches, house posts, panels, doors, and jambs; neckrests, backrests, and stools; snuffboxes and mortars; pots, vases, jars, cups, beakers, boxes, powder kegs, engraved calabashes, and potlids; ceremonial spoons, dippers, ladles, axes, adzes, spears, arrow stands, knives, swords, and paddles; musical instruments (idiophones, aerophones, cordophones, membranophones); scepters, swatters, batons, staffs, and walking sticks; combs, hairpins, necklaces, pectorals, bracelets, armlets, and anklets; coffins; drumstands; divination devices; miniature sculptured replicas of utensils; and carved bellows. Many sculptures excel because of their beautiful patinations and polychromy, others because of accumulations of sacrificial matter and beads, shells, resins, cloth, hide, feathers, and iron objects with which they are adorned. Many sculptured wooden masks are enhanced by various added constructions of collarets, hoods, costumes, beards, hats in fibers, cloth, and hide. The handles, hafts, and shafts of axes, adzes, scepters, batons, knives, spears, and slit-drums are frequently decorated with heads, busts, and human or animal figurines carved in the round or in relief. Some stools, neckrests, and drums are supported by human or animal caryatids. Many musical instruments are enhanced with colored designs and sculptures in the round or in relief. There are many artistically superb specimens among the pottery, basketry, mats, textiles, regalia, and paraphernalia (e.g., hats, caps, hoods, diadems, belts made in fibers, feathers, shells, beads, scales, pods).

A large part of the Zaire artworks in the museum were collected in situ by colonial administrators, travelers, explorers, missionaries, magistrates, traders, merchants, personnel working for various companies, and settlers, as well as by museum personnel on scientific missions and by scholars not directly attached to the museum. The collections also include important gifts made by chiefs, headmen, and other tribal authorities on the occasions of state visits by Belgian kings and high-ranking officials. Other objects were purchased from dealers and private collectors and obtained through exchange. In recent years the Musées Royaux d'Art et d'Histoire transferred a significant number of artworks to the museum. Large acquisitions of artworks and ethnographic objects were made throughout the existence of the museum, culminating between 1910 and 1926 and 1947 and 1958. In 1910 a royal decree notified the African personnel that objects acquired from the Belgian Congo pertaining to the "political, moral, scientific, and economic history of the colony" and not reserved for particular institutions should be deposited in the museum. By the end of 1947, 45,525 numbers had been assigned to ethnographic holdings and artworks, with several items sometimes registered under a single number. During the period between 1947 and 1958, F. M. Olbrechts, director of the museum, anthropologist, and eminent connoisseur of African art, secured many collections noted not only for their range and quantity but also for their quality. By 1959 there were about 100,000 objects in the museum and in 1967 about 118,000 pieces. Since 1961, mainly through purchase and scientific missions, the Zaire collection has been complemented by the addition of sculptures and ethnographic items from sub-Saharan Africa, Oceania, and the Americas; the number of representative pieces from each of these regions has steadily been increasing.

The artworks from Zaire represent and illustrate virtually the entire spectrum of regional, local, ethnic and subethnic styles and forms, as well as their inherent usages, functions, and meanings. Of great artistic and scholarly significance also are the artworks derived from less commonly known areas and groups. For the rich artistic province of southwestern Zaire, where cultural units overlap with others in the Peoples' Republic of the Congo and Angola, the museum possesses large representative collections from all Kongo subgroups and from Teke, Yaka, Suku, Pende, Mbala, Mbuun, Holo, Hungaan, and Cokwe and from the less frequently mentioned Mfinu, Wuum, Sakata, Sengele, Dia, Buma, Yansi, Dzing, Nkanu, Soonde, Kwese, and Pindi. From the artistically poorer northwestern Zaire province are included sculptures from Bolia, Eleku, Mongo, Ntumba, Ngala, Ngombe, Ngbandi, Sango, Ngbaka, Gobu, Langbwase, Mbanja, and Togbo. The northeastern Zaire province, which extends into the Central African Republic, the Sudan, and Uganda, is represented by works from the Zande, Mangbetu, Bali, Mamvu, Bwa, Lori, and Bari. From eastern Zaire there are specimens from Mitoko, Lengola, Mbole, Yela, Komo, Pere, Lega, and Bembe; and from southeastern Zaire, Hemba, Binja, Bangubangu, Kusu, Tabwa, the riverain populations of Lake Tanganyika, Boyo, and various Luba subdivisions. Objects from south-central Zaire include those by Songye, Nsapo, Tetela, Kanyok, Luntu, Luluwa, Luba-Kasai, Lunda, Cokwe, Ndembu, Kuba, Kete, Binji, Leele, Wongo, Ndengese, Salampasu, Lwalwa, and Mbagani.

Among the outstanding artworks, only some selections can be mentioned: royal statues of the Kuba; mother and child figurines of the Kongo, Yaka, Mbala, Luba, and Luluwa; funerary figurines from the Ndengese; nail and mirror fetishes from Kongo and Songye groups; ancestral and bowl-holding statues from the Luba; initiation masks from the Pende, Yaka, Suku, Cokwe, Kuba, Bembe, and Luba; wooden and ivory masks from the Lega; caryatid and other sculptured stools and neckrests from the Luba, Luluwa, Kusu, Kanyok, Yaka, Pende, Cokwe, Songye, and Mbala; anthropomorphic harps from the Ngbaka and the Mangbetu; anthropomorphic, painted, and decorated drums from the Kongo, Cokwe, Leele, and Kuba; anthropomorphic pots from the Mangbetu, Luba, Kanyok, Cokwe, and Kongo; anthropomorphic adzes and axes from the Luba,

Pende, and Teke; sculptured batons from southwestern Zaire and sculptured ceremonial spears from the Luba; and anthropomorphic pipes from the Kuba, Mangbetu, and Ngbaka.

The museum possesses rare sculptures from the Bari, Bwa, Bali, Pere, Komo, Mbole, Yela, Lengola, Mitoko, Luntu, Mputu, Nsapo, Tetela, Kete, Binji, Lunda, Pindi, Kwese, Nkanu, Eleku, Mongo, Ngala, Togbo, and Langbwase. Among the miniatures and nonfigurative carvings are exquisite combs from the Yaka and Cokwe, cups and boxes from the Kuba, whistles from the Kongo and the Pende, and miniature masks and pectorals from the Pende and the Hungaan. There are unusually large collections from the Kongo, Yaka, Pende, Kuba, Luba, Songye, Luluwa, and Lega.

These and other artworks derived from widely diverging cultural contexts were made essentially in the nineteenth and twentieth centuries, but the formal and stylistic traditions that they reflect and incorporate are often much older. Only relative *ante quem* chronologies can be constructed to assess the age of individual pieces. The usages, functions, and meanings of the artworks illustrate the widest possible patterns. They are part of the rituals, institutions, and ideologies connected with cults of the dead and of the ancestors; worship of the soul, other spiritual principles, and nature spirits; capture of life force; birth and marriage ceremonies; initiation, enthronement, and burial ceremonies; insignia and paraphernalia of rank and status in the social system, in cults, and in associations and exclusive groups; magic of fertility, aggression, protection, and curing; divination and witch finding; oath taking and legal procedures; sociopolitical control and integration.

Only a small fraction of the artworks and the ethnographical objects are permanently displayed. Some of the finest artworks are arranged by ethnic group and by region and exhibited in two large rooms. A huge display area presents artworks and other manufactured items based partly on ethnic and regional grouping and partly on typology and function. Separate exhibition windows illustrate economic, social, religious, and political activities such as hunting, fishing, and blacksmithing; ceramics, woodwork, weaving, and basketry; dress and adornment; marriage, initiation, cult, death, and burial; magic and divination; legal and political authority; music, dance, and games; and communication systems. The museum organizes small changing exhibits of masterpieces and recent acquisitions and contributes artworks to national and international exhibitions.

The museum has an extensive library that covers all scientific fields represented at the museum. It includes broad coverage of the major journals in anthropology, non-Western art, ethnomusicology, linguistics, oral literature, history, political science, and economics. The library is highly specialized in journals and books pertaining to all facets of Central Africa. Of unique relevance for the scientific study of Central African art, technology and material culture, and general ethnography are the museum's archival documents, ethnographic dossiers, and photographic documentation (photographs of the collections, ancient and recent field photographs, and comparative photographic materials from other public and private collections). Especially significant for the scientific study of wood sculptures is the Service d'Anatomie des bois tropicaux, which identifies the types of woods used in carvings and their properties. The library is open to the public, but the holdings do not circulate.

Slides and photographs in the collection may be purchased by application to the Section ethnographique. Publications by the museum are available from the Patrimoine du Musée Royal de l'Afrique Centrale, B–1980 Tervuren, Belgium. Some of the publications are out of print; others are reserved for exchanges or purchases of an entire series. The museum has engaged in an intensive program of scholarly publications involving all represented disciplines (geology, zoology, economics, history, social and cultural anthropology) and, within social and cultural anthropology, the subfields of prehistory and archaeology, ethnomusicology, linguistics, oral literature, ethnohistory, and ethnography. The *Annales, Sciences humaines*, have appeared since 1899. The *in quarto* editions of the *Annales* include many descriptive studies of sculptures, musical instruments, ceramics, mats, and textiles prepared by various museum curators and also early ethnographic monographs relevant for an understanding of the sociocultural contexts in which the arts of many diverse groups are manifested. Three other types of publications (ethnographic monographs, archives of anthropology, bibliography) complete the documentation provided by the *Annales*. Of great research value are the forty-two volumes of systematic annotated bibliographies (called *Bibliographie ethnographique du Congo belge* and, since 1962, *Bibliographique ethnographique de l'Afrique sub-Saharienne*). The museum also publishes separate series in other scientific fields. The quarterly journal *Africa-Tervuren* (called *Congo-Tervuren* before 1960) devotes much attention to the art and other museum collections. In cooperation with the Belgian Radio and Television, since 1968 the museum has produced a series of documented recordings of African music.

Selected Bibliography

Museum publications: Boone, O., *Les tambours du Congo belge et du Ruanda-Urundi*, 1951; Burssens, H., *Yanda-beelden en Mani-sekte bij de Azande (Centraal-Afrika)*, 1962; Coart, E., and de Hauleville, A., *La musique*, 1902; *La religion*, 1906; *La céramique*, 1907; Laurenty, J. S., *Les cordophones du Congo belge et du Ruanda-Urundi*, 1960; *Les sanza du Congo*, 1962; *Les tambours à fente de l'Afrique Centrale*, 1968; *La systématique des aérophones de l'Afrique Centrale*, 1974; Maes, J., *Fetischen of tooverbeelden uit Congo*, 1935; *Kabila-en grafbeelden uit Kongo*, 1938; *Kabila-en grafbeelden uit Kongo: Addenda. Moedereerebeelden uit Kongo*, 1939; Maesen, A., and Van Geluwe, H., *Art d'Afrique dans les collections belges*, 1963; Masui, Th., *Les collections ethnographiques du Musée du Congo*, 1899; Olbrechts, Frans M., *Quelques chefs-d'oeuvre de l'art africain des collections du Musée Royal du Congo belge*, 1952; Torday, E., and Joyce, T. A., *Notes ethnographiques sur les peuples communément appelés Bakuba, ainsi que sur les peuplades apparentées. Les Bushongo*, 1911.

Publications of Amis du Musée Royal de l'Afrique Centrale: *Guide, préhistore et anthropologie* (1959); *Umbangu: Art du Congo au Musée Royal de l'Afrique Centrale*

(1960); *Vingt-cinq sculptures africaines* (1972); journal *Africa-Tervuren* (*Congo-Tervuren* before 1961).

Other publications: Biebuyck, D., *Lega Culture: Art, Initiation, and Moral Philosophy among a Central African People* (Berkeley and Los Angeles 1973); de Sousberghe, L., *L'Art pende* (Brussels, 1958); *Koninklijke Bibliotheek van België . . . Koninklijk Museum voor Midden-Afrika . . .* (Brussels 1969); Maes, J., *Aniota-Kifwebe, les masques des populations du Congo belge et le matérial des rites de circumcision* (Antwerp 1924); *Le musée du Congo belge à Tervuren. Guide illustré du visiteur* (Antwerp 1925); Maesen, A., *Arte del Congo* (Rome 1959); *Art of the Congo* (Minneapolis, 1967); *Arts of Black Africa* (Special Issue of *Sabena Revue* 1974); Olbrechts, Frans M., *Invitation au voyage congolais* (Special Issue of *Sabena Revue* 1954); C.L.L., "Ce que le visiteur ne voit pas," *Belgique d'Outremer*, vol. 15, no. 289 (1959), pp. 215–27; Cahen, L., "Les Amis du Musée," *Belgique d'Outremer*, vol. 15, no. 289 (1959), p. 218; "Le Musée dans le présent et dans l'avenir," *Belgique d'Outremer*, vol. 15, no. 289 (1959), pp. 213–14; Luwel, Marcel, "Histoire du Musée royal du Congo belge à Tervuren," *Belgique d'Outremer*, vol. 15, no. 289 (1959), pp. 209–12; Soupault, Philippe, "L'Art africain du Congo belge," in *Le miroir du Congo belge* (Brussels 1929).

DANIEL P. BIEBUYCK

Brazil

—— São Paulo ——

SÃO PAULO ART MUSEUM ASSIS CHATEAUBRIAND (officially MU-
SEU DE ARTE DE SÃO PAULO ASSIS CHATEAUBRIAND; also MUSEU
DE ARTE DE SÃO PAULO, MUSEU BARDI), 01301 Avenida Paulista 1578,
01000 São Paulo.

Founded by the eminent owner and director of a large chain of Brazilian
newspapers, magazines, and radio and television stations Assis Chateaubriand,
the Museu de Arte de São Paulo was inaugurated on October 2, 1947, as a
privately owned and funded didactic center for the promotion of the arts in
Brazil, although it now receives financial aid from various government ministries.
Directed from its beginnings by the Italian publisher and art historian Pietro
Maria Bardi and associates, this experimental educational institution was first
housed in a newly constructed building of the *Diarios Associados* (Associated
Daily Newspapers), the property of Assis Chateaubriand, located in the heart of
the growing metropolis of São Paulo. From its first days the directors made
serious efforts to assemble an important collection of world art, consisting, as
circumstances would have it, primarily of Western painting. The principal aim
was to achieve high quality, even at the expense of comprehensiveness. The
new institution also quickly promoted a variety of artistic enterprises, including
courses in aesthetics and art history, theatrical and musical performances, and
special exhibits and retrospectives. Some three years after its founding, when
additional space was made available in the original building, the museum greatly
expanded its activities. Schools of industrial design, marketing, gardening, dance,
engraving, and cinema were inaugurated, along with two corps de ballet, one
for children and the other professional, and an orchestra composed of young
people that soon became one of the best in Brazil. Throughout its brief history
the museum has served as a major gathering point for artistic enterprise and
education, aided by a prestigious faculty. Notable in this regard are the many

special exhibitions that the museum has sponsored over the years, of which those dedicated to the work of Le Corbusier, Alexander Calder, Käthe Kollwitz, Toulouse-Lautrec, and Brazilians such as Cândido Portinari, Lasar Segall, and Anita Malfatti are regarded as among the most significant.

On November 7, 1968, Queen Elizabeth II of England inaugurated the imaginative new building that today houses the museum and its various related activities. Designed by the architect Lina Bardi, this multistoried, free-standing structure of glass and concrete has attained international renown. Its two upper floors, which include the main exhibition hall, are contained within one large, glass-encased rectangular block, which is boldly supported on four massive, widely separated concrete pillars, the arrangement resulting in a large, covered, open-air plaza under this structure. Beneath this large open space additional floors were constructed to provide room for a theater, halls for special exhibits, a library, and administrative offices. The entire structure rests on a natural promontory high above a tunnel that is part of an important thoroughfare, the Avenida 9 de Julho. Like the building's architecture, the main exhibition hall contains notable innovations. The paintings are displayed in staggered rows within panels of tempered glass resting on short concrete blocks. Extensive descriptive material concerning each artist, his period, and his work is placed behind each of the paintings, so that the labels do not distract the viewer from the actual work of art. Thus the visitor can view the paintings in a natural light, which enters the hall freely through the surrounding glass walls.

In regard to the collection itself, the museum's organizers were both clever and lucky. Aware of the depressed prices of artworks caused by the ravages of World War II, Bardi was convinced that works of art purchased in Europe and the United States on credit and at low interest rates would greatly increase in value in later years. Thus, unobstructed by cautious trustees, he began a campaign of purchases that in a few years contributed to the gathering of a notable collection of Western painting. The museum's principal financial supporter, Assis Chateaubriand, also used his huge publishing enterprise and personal influence to encourage wealthy Brazilians from all parts of the country to contribute works of art. He rewarded contributors with sumptuous receptions in public buildings or in elegant mansions, and their generosity was prominently publicized in newspapers and on radio and television. Thus it was possible, according to one of the museum's own publications, "to consolidate a large group of friends of the museum, disposed to agree to requests for new acquisitions."

By 1953, through both purchases and contributions, the new museum had brought together an important collection of paintings. Responding to invitations to exhibit the collection in Europe, where interest in the new establishment had grown rapidly, the directors arranged an international tour of one hundred selected works. First shown with great success at the Louvre, the collection was also exhibited at major art museums in Brussels, Utrecht, Bern, London, Düsseldorf, Milan, New York, Toledo, Ohio, and finally in Rio de Janeiro, before its return to São Paulo.

Because of the speed with which the collection was assembled, and because much of it is the result of valuable contributions that could not be rejected, the collection includes in some instances large numbers of works by some artists, whereas others are not represented. Although tapestries, pottery, and some fine works of sculpture can be seen (for example, Degas' bronze sculpture of a ballerina and the Lipchitz bronze sculpture *Pierrot with Mandolin*), the emphasis is decidedly on European paintings, and within that category, Impressionist artists are probably the most heavily represented. Numerous are works of major Brazilian painters, both nineteenth and twentieth century.

Among the museum's earliest paintings are several Italian trecento and quattrocento panels of excellent quality, among them the exquisite *Madonna and Child* by Bernardo Daddi. Highlights of the Italian Renaissance include the *Madonna and Child* by Giovanni Bellini, *Saint Jerome* by Andrea Mantegna, *The Resurrection of Christ* by Raphael, *Portrait of Christopher Madruzzo* by Titian, *Ecce Homo* by Tintoretto, and *Apparition of the Madonna and Child to a Bishop* by Jacopo Palma the Younger. The collection of French paintings is by far the largest, ranging from the Renaissance to the Post-Impressionists to the various art movements of the twentieth century. Outstanding among the early French paintings are François Clouet's *Bath of Diana*; François Le Moine's *Picnic during the Hunt*; Jean-Baptiste Joseph Pater's *Meeting in a Park*; Chardin's *Portrait of Auguste-Gabriel Godefroy*; Fragonard's *Education Is Everything*; Ingres' oval canvas *Angelique Chained*; Corot's *Gypsy with a Mandolin*; Daumier's *Two Heads*, a small canvas depicting a man and a woman; Delacroix' large canvas *Spring; or, Euridice Collecting Flowers*; Manet's large *Portrait of an Artist with a Dog*; Degas' *Four Ballerinas on Stage*; and Cézanne's large canvas *Paul Alexis Reading a Manuscript to Emile Zola*. Included among several Renoirs is one of his most sensuous nudes, *Bather with a Dog*, a work exhibited in 1874 at Chez Nadar, the exhibition that officially initiated the Impressionist movement. *Two Women in a Boat on the Epte* by Monet is another outstanding Impressionist work. The Post-Impressionists are represented by outstanding works such as Gauguin's *Poor Fisherman*, van Gogh's *The Student* and *Evening Walk*, Toulouse-Lautrec's *Portrait of Monsieur Fourcade* and *Portrait of Admiral Viaud*. Other fine canvases are Utrillo's *Sacré-Coeur de Montmarte* and *Château de Brouillards*, one of Bonnard's fine nudes, Vuillard's *Print Dress*, Matisse's *Plaster Torso*, and a seascape by Vlaminck. Also included in the collection are outstanding paintings by Fernand Léger, representatives of Picasso's Blue and Cubist periods, and works by Larionov, Soutine, Modigliani, Max Ernst, Wols, and other German artists.

Outstanding is the collection of Spanish art represented by works such as El Greco's *Annunciation* and the *Stigmatization of St. Francis*, Velázquez' *Portrait of the Count of Olivares*, and Goya's large portraits *Cardinal Luis Marya y Vallabriga* and *Don Juan Antonio Llorente*. Among the important Flemish, Dutch, and German paintings are Memling's *Virgin, St. John, and the Holy Women*, Hans Holbein the Younger's *Portrait of Henry Howard, Earl of Surrey*,

Frans Hals' *Portrait of Maria Pietersdochter Olycan*, Hieronymus Bosch's *Temptation of St. Anthony*, and Rembrandt's *Self Portrait with a New Beard*. An outstanding painting by Lucas Cranach the Elder is the *Portrait of a Young Bridegroom*. Three major representatives of British painting are Sir Joshua Reynolds' *The Children of Edward Holden Cruttenden*, Thomas Lawrence's *The Fluyder Children*, and Turner's *Castle of Caernarvon*.

Several fine landscapes of Brazil by the seventeenth-century Dutch painter Frans Post head the Brazilian collection, of which good examples include Facchinetti's *View of Botafogo Beach* and Benedicto Calixto's *Santos Market Docks* in 1885. The Brazilian Romantic period is represented by Victor Meirelles de Lima's *Moema* and Almeida Junior's *Young Woman*. The important Brazilian painter Elyseu d'Angelo Visconti is represented from his Pre-Raphaelite to his Impressionist phase. Finally, the great Paulista painter Cândido Portinari is represented by remarkable paintings such as *Coffee Plantation Worker* and a large canvas titled *Retirantes (Refugees)*. Also outstanding are works by Emiliano di Cavalcanti, Lasar Segall, Anita Malfatti, and Roberto Sambonet. Finally, the collection includes Brazilian primitive artists, among them José Antonio da Silva, as well as a good collection of Brazilian colonial art and an excellent collection of prints by prominent Brazilian artists.

The museum has a specialized library relating to its holdings, which is open to the public. Photographs and slides of objects in the collection and museum publications such as catalogs can be purchased at the museum shop or by contacting the administration.

Selected Bibliography

Museum publications: Museu de Arte de São Paulo Assis Chateaubriand, *Cem obras primas de Portinari* (Exhibition Catalog), 1970; idem, *Catálogo das pinturas, esculturas e tapeçarias* (Exhibition Catalog), 1963.

Other publications: Bardi, Pietro Maria, *The Arts in Brazil: A New Museum at São Paulo* (Milan 1966); idem, *A Colorslide Tour of the Museum of São Paulo* (New York 1961); idem, *Os museus do mundo: São Paulo* (Buenos Aires 1969); idem, *Museu de Arte de São Paulo* (São Paulo 1978); idem, *Museu de Arte de São Paulo Assis Chateaubriand: Ano 30* (São Paulo 1978); idem, *Coleçao museus brasileiros. Vol. 3: Museu de Arte de São Paulo* (Rio de Janeiro 1981).

ROBERT AND URSULA CONRAD

Canada

——— Montreal ———

MONTREAL MUSEUM OF FINE ARTS, THE (officially also MUSÉE DES BEAUX-ARTS DE MONTRÉAL; alternately MBAM, MMFA), 3400 Museum Avenue, Montreal, Quebec H3G 1K3.

The Montreal Museum of Fine Arts had its origins in 1847 with the formation of The Montreal Society of Artists, the precursor of the Art Association of Montreal, established in 1860. The first home of the Art Association was a building on Phillips Square, completed in 1879. In 1912 the Art Association moved to its present location on Sherbrooke Street. The distinguished neoclassical structure, designed by Edward and W. S. Maxwell, is historically important and architecturally significant. The monumental grand staircase and the Norton staircase, together with the building's facade, are the most important architectural features. In 1976 a new wing, designed by Fred Lebensold, which doubled the size of the museum, was opened.

The Montreal Museum of Fine Arts is owned by its members and is funded by the provincial, federal, and municipal governments together with the private sector. Until 1970 it was almost entirely privately funded.

The museum is governed by the twenty-seven-member Board of Trustees, fifteen of whom are elected by the museum membership and twelve who are appointed by the provincial government. They serve three-year terms. The administration is headed by a director, a director of administration, and a chief curator. There are curatorial departments of European Art, Contemporary Canadian Art, Early Canadian Art, Decorative Art, Prints and Drawings, and Research. Museum services include Education, Library, Slide Library, Diffusion, and Conservation.

The first sizable donation of art to the museum's collection was the Beniah

Gibb bequest of 1877. The museum now houses collections of Canadian art; Inuit and American art; Ancient Near Eastern art; Greek, Etruscan, and Roman art; medieval art; European and American paintings and sculpture from the Renaissance to the twentieth century; prints and drawings; African art; Oceanic art; Asiatic art; Islamic art; pre-Columbian art; and European decorative arts.

The museum has collected objects that span Canadian history from the French regime in the eighteenth century to the present. Since its foundation, the museum has been committed to the encouragement of contemporary Canadian artists. In 1929 F. J. Shepherd created the first fund for the acquisition of Canadian works of art. Recently, Mrs. Samuel Bronfman (OBE) granted the museum a fund for the acquisition of works by Canadian artists age forty and under. Among the most significant donations are those that have been received from the family of the painter James Wilson Morrice, from the architect Ramsay Traquair, and from Mabel Molson. The museum owns an outstanding collection of Quebec furniture and silver of the eighteenth and nineteenth centuries. Most noteworthy are a two-tiered pine buffet from Lotbinière of the late eighteenth century in the Louis XV style and a silver porringer by Paul Lambert, called Saint-Paul (1691–1749), and Samuel Payne (1696–1732) of about 1730. In the field of nineteenth-century art, the Canadian collection comprises key works such as the *Portrait of Madame Ranvoyzé* (1838) by the Quebec painter Jean-Baptiste Roy Audy, a series of the *Stations of the Cross* commissioned for the church of Notre Dame in Montreal in 1837 by Antoine Sebastien Plamondon, and *Montmorency Falls* of 1853 by Cornelius Krieghoff, who was born in Holland. The works of painters active at the end of the nineteenth and the first part of the twentieth century include *L'Heure mauve* (1921) by Ozias Leduc; *Old Holton House, Montreal* (1909), located on the present site of the Montreal Museum, by James Wilson Morrice; and *Cathedral Mountain* (1928) by Arthur Lismer, one of the founders of the Group of Seven and dean of the School of Art of the Montreal Museum of Fine Arts from 1941 until 1969. In the field of contemporary art, the museum's Canadian collection contains paintings by artists such as Paul Emile Borduas, the initiator of the "automatiste" movement; Alex Colville, the Nova Scotia painter; and Charles Gagnon, the exponent of color field painting. The collection of Canadian sculpture is also noteworthy, from an eighteenth-century crucifix from the Gaspé and a group of bronze figures by Marc-Aurele de Foy Suzor-Coté to works by contemporary artists such as Sorel Etog.

The Montreal Museum has one of the oldest collections of Inuit and Amerindian art in Canada. A number of American Indian objects and one artifact of Northwest Coast origin entered the museum in 1917. Today, the collection contains Inuit sculptures, artifacts, and prints dating from the pre-Dorset period (2500 B.C.) to the present. One of the most outstanding sculptures in the collection is the *Migration of Povungnituk* (1964) by Joe Talirunili, depicting a group of Eskimos in a *umiak*, a boat made of animal skins, fleeing from death and starvation. Talirunili was the only survivor of the actual event. Another is the serpentine stone sculpture of a spirit in the form of a sea lion by the Cape Dorset sculptor, Jibybywajita.

The Montreal Museum's collection of Egyptian and Near Eastern art began in 1917 with a gift from F. Cleveland Morgan (1881–1960) of three Coptic textile fragments. It now includes more than a hundred objects. Most important are an Egyptian pottery vase of the Predynastic era (4000–3200 B.C.) and an Assyrian alabaster relief of an eagle-headed winged genie from the Northwest Palace of Ashurnasirpal II, in Nimrod (877 B.C.).

The museum's collection of Greek and Roman art began in 1918 with a purchase of a Greek vase and was enlarged through the donation of the outstanding Harry Norton Collection of Roman glass in 1952. The entire collection extends from Greek works of the Archaic period, such as a black-figure vase representing Dionysius and two satyrs of 500 B.C. to a Roman marble copy of a Republican (50–40 B.C.) bust of a man, made in the second century A.D.

A small collection of medieval art was started at the beginning of the twentieth century and was further enriched by bequests of F. Cleveland Morgan. The earliest object in the collection is a Merovingean fibula in the shape of a bird of the fifth to the seventh century, which was donated by L. V. Randall.

The museum began collecting Renaissance art in 1920, when it acquired two grisaille paintings executed in gold, *Dido* and *Judith* (about 1490), by Andrea Mantegna, through the John W. Tempest bequest. The collection is particularly rich in Italian, Spanish, and Flemish panel paintings of the fifteenth and sixteenth centuries. Important works of this collection are the *Coronation of the Virgin* (about 1390) by Nicolo di Pietro Gerini, the *Portrait of a Young Man* (1480) by Hans Memling, and a lindenwood *St. Sebastian* (1510) by Tilman Riemenschneider, acquired through the Horsley and Annie Townsend bequest. The collection also includes majolica, bronzes, and medals.

The collection of Baroque art is one of the richest in the museum, showing examples of Dutch, French, Italian, and Flemish art of the seventeenth century. It contains the first Old Master painting bought by the museum, *The Woman at the Harpsichord* (1660), by the Dutch painter Emmanuel de Witte, which was acquired in 1894. A key work that is representative of the importance of the Caravaggesque movement in Rome is Valentin de Boullogne's *Sacrifice of Isaac* (1628–30). Dutch painting is represented by Rembrandt's *Portrait of a Woman* (1665) and Jacob van Ruisdael's *Bleaching Grounds at Haarlem* (1670).

The eighteenth-century collection was begun in 1905 with the purchase of Goya's *Portrait of Judge Altamirano of Seville* (1793). The collection now includes Italian and French painting and sculpture of the eighteenth century, as well as the largest collection of eighteenth-century English painting in Canada. The outstanding works of the Rococo era are Canaletto's *Interior View of St. Mark's, Venice* (1760), Augustin Pajou's terracotta *Bust of Jean Philippe du Vidal, Marquis de Montferrier* (1781), and Thomas Gainsborough's *Portrait of Mrs. Georges Drummond* (1780).

The collection of nineteenth-century art was begun in 1909 through a large bequest by William and Agnes Learmont of works by members of the Barbizon School: Corot, Decamps, Fantin-Latour, and Monticelli. The museum also possesses one of the largest collections of the Hague school in North America.

The nineteenth-century collection is particularly noted for its Impressionist paintings, especially Alfred Sisley's *Autumn, Banks of the Oise* (1873). Sculpture is represented by the important bronze *Call to Arms* (1878) of Auguste Rodin.

The collection of contemporary sculpture and painting is small but nonetheless contains several important works. It was begun in 1924 with the acquisition of the bronze *Portrait of Lilian Shelley* (1916) by the British sculptor Sir Jacob Epstein. Lyonel Feininger's *Yellow Street II* was executed in 1918 when the American Expressionists came under the influence of Cubism. Of the most important works is Salvador Dali's realistic *Portrait of Maria Carbona* (1925), which was painted on the back of part of a still life that the artist finished in 1924. This portrait precedes his turn to Surrealism.

The museum acquired its first African work in 1940, when Mabel Molson donated a rare Benin bronze mask. The collection, which comprises a representative selection of works from most parts of Africa, was enlarged in 1975 with the gift of about one hundred sculptures from Everest Gagnon, a Jesuit priest. One of the oldest pieces in the collection is a wood Dogon seated figure of the nineteenth century from Mali.

The Oriental collection includes works of sculpture, pottery, porcelain, bronzes, paintings, and textiles from China, Japan, India, and Korea from the Neolithic period to the present. The collection was begun through donations of F. Cleveland Morgan in 1917. In 1959 Joseph-Arthur Simard gave a group of more than three thousand Japanese incense boxes, or *kogos*, of the eighteenth and nineteenth centuries that belonged to the French statesman Georges Clémenceau. The oldest object in the collection is an earthenware urn from Kansu Province in China of the Neolithic period (2000 B.C.), with a black and red geometric pattern. Another rare piece is a camel tomb figure of earthenware with three-color glaze from North China, executed during the T'ang Dynasty (A.D. 618–906).

The Islamic collection was begun also by donations from F. Cleveland Morgan at the beginning of this century. The collection is varied, combining manuscripts, textiles, ceramics, and carpets. The collection, although small, spans from the eighth to the eighteenth century and includes works from Egypt, Persia, Syria, Turkey, and Moorish Spain. One of the oldest objects in the collection is a ceramic bowl of the Samanid period (A.D. 874–1001) from Nishapur in Persia. The bowl illustrates the use of Arabic script as a decorative and iconographic motif, one of the major characteristics of the early stages of Islamic art. The museum also owns an important collection of fifteenth-century ceramics as well as textiles from Moorish Spain that were donated by Arthur Byne.

The Montreal Museum's collection of pre-Columbian art was begun in 1926 when the Philip Means Collection of Peruvian textiles was donated to the museum. The museum's collection extends from the Olmec (1200–400 B.C.) to the Classic Maya period (A.D. 200–900) and includes ceramics, textiles, and gold objects from the Central Andean region of South America. One of the oldest pieces in the collection is a baby-face figure of terracotta from Veracruz of about 800 B.C. that was acquired in 1973 through the Horsley and Annie Townsend bequest. This figure represents the offspring of a jaguar father and human mother. A tapestry-weave panel of wood and cotton from the Nazea culture (100 B.C.– A.D. 600) of Peru of about 500 B.C., which shows human and animal figures, is a representative piece from the museum's outstanding textile collection.

The decorative arts collection, numbering some fourteen thousand objects, was founded in 1917 by one of the museum's greatest benefactors, F. Cleveland Morgan, considered "one of the most perceptive connoisseurs of his day in North America." Initially, the collection comprised a broad spectrum of primarily European decorative arts. However, Morgan's catholicity of tastes soon embraced ancient, medieval, Islamic, Oriental, and ethnological art, all of which are represented.

There are some 1,250 textiles in the collection, ranging from early Coptic tapestries to twentieth-century Inuit batiks. Notable groupings include the Arthur Byne Collection of twelfth- to eighteenth-century Spanish and Italian textiles and the Parker lace collection. The museum possesses a small but notable group of tapestries, including items from the atelier of Pasquier Grenier of Tournai and the Sheldon atelier in Warwickshire.

In addition to the Harry Norton Collection of ancient glass (about 250 pieces) the museum's glass collection has representation in most major areas, including sixteenth-century Venetian as well as eighteenth-century Bohemian Silesian pieces. The strength of the collection lies in the eighteenth-century English and Irish drinking and related vessels made possible by the acquisition in 1940 of the Smith Collection and the Holt bequest of 1947 and the David R. Morrice bequest of 1981. The gift in 1974 of the Walter Light Collection expanded the Canadian holdings with some 225 examples of nineteenth-century pressed glass. Important gifts from Mrs. Duncan Hodgson and the 1981 bequest of F. Eleanore Morrice gave focus to the museum's silver collection. Outstanding English pieces by Samuel Hood, Robert Cooper, Humphrey Payne, Simon Pantin, and other goldsmiths are highlights of the collection. French goldsmithing is represented by works of renowned Parisian craftsmen such as Jean Fauche Edmé, François Balsac, Nicolas Besnier, and Denys Frankson, in addition to works by provincial craftsmen such as Imlin of Strasbourg. When settlers first came to New France, they initially brought with them their own silver plate. A wine cup in the collection, by Pierre Belleville of Montpellier, France, bears the arms of the marquis de Montcalm. Soon, however, silver artifacts were produced in New France, and the museum's collection includes an extensive range of both ecclesiastical and domestic silver by eminent craftsmen such as Paradis, Amiot, Delezenne, and Lambert. Most of these Canadian examples were either given to the museum by Charles F. Martin in 1947 or bequeathed by Ramsay Traquair in 1952.

European ceramics in the collection range in scope from early Hispano-Moresque wares and Italian majolicas to the modern production of Quebec artists Doucette-Saito. The Baroque styles of the seventeenth and early eighteenth centuries are represented primarily in a selection of Dutch and English delftwares. Eighteenth-century Continental porcelain is represented by wares produced at Meissen, St. Cloud, Doccia, Vienna, Sèvres, and Berlin. In 1964 the museum was the recipient of the Lucile E. Pillow Collection of English porcelain, which includes a cross-section of the finest production of the ceramicist's art from about 1745 to about 1840. Among the earliest items are those from the Chelsea factory, as well as fine Derby vases and figures. This collection includes items from the major factories, such as those at Liverpool, as well as from Bow, Lowestoft, Caughley, Longton Hall, Plymouth, with an extensive representation of the Dr. Wall period Worcester, Chamberlain's Worcester, in addition to wares from Wedgwood and Swansea. Nineteenth-century ceramics are represented by productions of the major French and English factories, along with several examples of Art Nouveau and Arts and Crafts potteries. A large portion of the nineteenth-century ceramic holdings comprise items made in Europe for the Canadian market, as well as examples of every major type of pottery produced in Canada.

The furniture collection comprises some five hundred items of European and North American origins, reflecting the evolution of styles from the Late Gothic period through to the twentieth century. In 1929 the museum purchased a portion of the Arthur Byne Collection of Spanish Renaissance furniture, which rounded out the museum's holdings of Italian and French pieces from the same period. The seventeenth century is represented by a sampling of Dutch and English pieces highlighted by items such as a Grinling Gibbons over-mantle wood carving from Cassiobury Park. The eighteenth-century furniture holdings are the most complete. Examples of French Louis XV and Louis XVI styles are represented by the works of cabinetmakers and chairmakers such as Ohneberg, Mayeux, Brizard, and Gailliard. With regard to the extensive English holdings, one must note the generosity of Mabel Molson and Bartlett Morgan, who provided the museum with furniture after designs by Ince and Mayhew, Hepplewhite and Sheraton, as well as a settee by John Linnell. The museum also possesses a small grouping of American furniture. The first acquisitions of Canadian furniture were made in 1932. Important items made in New France are a rare seventeenth-century gate-leg table in the Louis XIII manner and a contemporary armoire with lozenge carved panel doors.

The Prints and Drawings Department of The Montreal Museum of Fine Arts encompasses works from the most important European schools from the Renaissance to the present. American and Mexican artists are also represented, and the extensive Canadian section includes several hundred works by Inuit artists. In total there are five thousand works in the prints and drawings collection.

The department's earliest major acquisition occurred in 1909 with the purchase of Rembrandt's beautiful *Death of Jacob* (c. 1640), which came to the museum through the William John and Agnes Learmont bequest.

Hendrik Goltzius, another Dutch artist born about fifty years before Rembrandt, is admirably represented by a series of drawings, *The Seven Vices*, executed around 1592, after the artist's return from a stay in Rome. Jacob Matham also treats the same subject in a series of copperplate engravings after earlier lost drawings by Goltzius. A late work by Goltzius—a splendid proof of a burin engraving of the *Adoration of the Magi*—recently came into the collection.

Thanks to the generosity of the family of James Wilson Morrice, this important Canadian artist is well represented by pencil drawings, watercolors, and twenty-four sketchbooks.

Through the Saidye and Samuel Bronfman Fund for the acquisition of contemporary Canadian art, many prints and drawings by young Canadian artists have been added to the department's collections.

The Museum Library is the oldest fine arts library in Canada and one of the most important. It is a research library for the curatorial and educational staff and a reference library open for consultation during museum hours. There are more than 37,151 books and bound catalogues, 17,419 exhibition catalogues, and 37,000 auction catalogues.

Slides and photographs of objects in the collection may be purchased by application to the Registrar's department. In addition to the publications listed below, the museum publishes a monthly bulletin of activities titled *Collage*.

Selected Bibliography

Museum publications: Turner, Brenda B., and Evan H. Turner, *Handbook: The Montreal Museum of Fine Arts*, 1960; Rosenfeld, Myra Nan, *Guide: The Montreal Museum of Fine Arts*, 1977; *Masterpieces from Montreal: Selected Paintings from The Montreal Museum of Fine Arts*, 1965.

SEAN B. MURPHY, WITH ASSISTANCE FROM
MYRA NAN ROSENFELD, ROBERT LITTLE, AND MICHELINE MOISAN

—— Ottawa ——

NATIONAL GALLERY OF CANADA, OTTAWA (officially also GALERIE NATIONALE DU CANADA, OTTAWA; also NATIONAL MUSEUMS OF CANADA, MUSÉES NATIONAUX DU CANADA), Lorne Building, Elgin Street, Ottawa, Ontario K1A OM8.

In 1880, under the patronage of Queen Victoria's son-in-law and representative in her "Dominion of the North," governor-general the marquis of Lorne (1845–1914), the National Gallery of Canada was conceived as one of the major objectives of the newly founded Canadian Academy of Arts. On March 6, 1880, Lorne presided over the opening of the first exhibition of the Canadian Academy of Arts in the Clarendon Hotel, Ottawa. For the Canadian Academy of Arts, soon thereafter to be known as the Royal Academy of Arts, there were two major goals: the institution of a national gallery at the seat of the government and the holding of exhibitions in the principal cities of the dominion.

On March 29, 1880, shortly after the opening of the first Canadian Academy exhibition, a Privy Council decision placed the diploma paintings presented to the National Gallery by the academy under the responsibility of the Ministry of Public Works and the office of the chief architect. Only in 1882, however, was the Gallery given its first curator, John W. H. Watts, an English-born architect and member of the academy, who carried a joint appointment as assistant chief government architect. In the same year the Royal Canadian Academy was incorporated by an act of Parliament and the Gallery moved into its first home in refurbished builders' workshops on Parliament Hill, which it shared with the Supreme Court of Canada. In 1888 the gallery was moved again to a building called Victoria Hall, close to Parliament, which it shared with the Government Fish Hatchery and the Fisheries Exhibit. In 1907 the government initiated annual appropriations for the purchase of works of art by the Gallery. At the same time, to oversee these funds and other administrative matters and to advise the ministry responsible for the Gallery (Public Works), the government established the Advisory Arts Council. Three prominent Canadians, none of whom was a member of the academy and two of whom were collectors active in museum affairs in Toronto and Montreal, were appointed to direct the council's affairs. Eric Brown, an Englishman, was appointed the Gallery's first director in 1911. In 1912 the chairman of the Advisory Arts Council, Sir Edmund Walker (who had helped drive through the provincial legislation incorporating the Art Museum of Toronto—now the Art Gallery of Ontario [q.v.]—in 1900 and who was a major force behind the foundation and early development of the Royal Ontario Museum [q.v.] in Toronto—achieving appropriate buildings for both) succeeded finally in having the National Gallery more suitably housed in the Victoria Memorial Museum in Ottawa, where it shared space with the National Museum of Man, the Geological Survey, and the Department of Mines. In 1913 the government passed the National Gallery of Canada Act, providing the Gallery with an independent board of trustees. Between 1913 and 1968 Canadian governors-general were, appropriately, honorary presidents of the board.

After the destruction by fire of a major section of the Parliament Buildings in 1916, Parliament took over the Victoria Memorial Museum until 1921. Although the collections of the National Gallery were forced to go into storage, a 1913 policy supporting the development of national touring exhibitions was given new impetus. From 1921 to 1959 the Gallery remained in the Victoria Memorial Museum. In the mid–1950s a Canadian architectural competition was held and won by Green, Blankenstein, and Russell of Winnepeg. Problems related to the site selection, however, resulted in the winning architects being asked to build, and adapt for the Gallery's temporary use, a new government office building on Elgin Street near the Parliament Buildings. This ten-story structure, still part of the Gallery's current plant of five buildings and the only one used for exhibition purposes, was opened in 1960 and named after the Gallery's founder, the marquis of Lorne. The cornerstone was laid on May 22, 1959, by Governor-General Vincent Massey, one of the most outstanding Canadians to be involved in the Gallery's history and one of its most generous donors. A second national architectural competition in 1976–77 was won by the Parkin Partnership of Toronto. This competition, like its predecessor, did not result in a new building for the Gallery. In February 1982 the government created the Canada Museums Construction Corporation under the chairmanship of a former director of the Gallery, Jean Sutherland Boggs, to plan and build a new National Gallery of Canada and a new National Museum of Man. One year later, the government appointed Moshe Safdie of Montreal as design architect with the Parkin Partnership to complete plans for the new National Gallery of Canada, located on a picturesque site facing the Parliament Buildings and overlooking the new Museum of Man across the Ottawa River, designed by Douglas Cardinal.

In 1958 the National Gallery Association, now known as Friends of the National Gallery, was founded, with the purpose of stimulating interest in and supporting Gallery programs. Portions of annual dues are applied toward gifts of art and special equipment.

In 1968, impressed by the Washington Smithsonian model of a national museum complex, the Canadian government implemented the 1967–68 National Museums Act, incorporating the National Gallery, the National Museum of Man, the Canadian War Museum, the National Museum of Natural Sciences, and the National Museum of Science and Technology, under a single board of trustees, as the National Museums of Canada, with acquisitions and operations funded by annual government appropriation. The National Museums board now reports to parliament through the minister of communications. Members of the board of trustees (fourteen including the secretary-general as vice-chairman of the board) and the four directors of the Gallery and the three museums are all government appointments. Board members serve from two- to five-year terms for overlapping purposes. Directors are appointed by the government, on recommendation of the board, to serve "during pleasure." In addition, the board has established consultative or advisory committees that advise it on matters related to each institution.

The National Gallery of Canada is presently administered by a director and three assistant directors. Reporting directly to the director are a special advisor for external affairs and a project coordinator for the new building. The three assistant directors are responsible for Collections and Research (curatorial departments, library, registration, conservation), Public Programmes (education, exhibitions, publications, information services), and Administration and Operations. The curatorial departments are as follows: Early Canadian Art; Post-Confederation Canadian Art; Contemporary Canadian Art; European Art; Contemporary Non-Canadian Art; and Prints, Drawings, and Photographs. The Canadian collections in all media, generously enriched by gifts, are understandably the largest in the country, with an emphasis on painting, sculpture, and works of art on paper. The European collection, largely paintings and sculpture from the Middle Ages to the present, is small but distinguished, including important purchases from the collection of the Prince of Liechtenstein, gifts from the Beaverbrook Canadian War Memorials, the unique donation of the Massey Collection of English twentieth-century painting, and a very small collection of European decorative arts. The Prints, Drawings, and Photographs collection, both Canadian and European, are the largest in Canada. The international collection of photographs is one of the most important nineteenth- and twentieth-century art historical collections in the world. There are also several films and video works by Canadian artists in the collection of contemporary Canadian art, which are not for distribution. There are, finally, small but interesting collections of American, Indian, Tibetan, and Chinese art. The total number of works of art in the National Gallery's collection is currently about forty thousand items, of which thirty thousand are prints, drawings, and photographs. Current gallery space in the Lorne Building (only sixty-five thousand square feet) can permit exhibition of only a minute fraction of the permanent collections at one time (an average of 750 works or 2 percent of the total, 7 percent of the total excluding prints, drawings, and photographs).

The Canadian Royal Academy laid the foundation of the Canadian collections with its diploma presentations to the Gallery in the 1880s and 1890s and with its purchases in the 1890s for the Gallery's collections from academy exhibitions. One very popular work in the collection was bought in 1895 following its exhibition in the Paris Salon of 1889 and later in the Chicago World's Columbian Exposition of 1893: Paul Peel's *Venetian Bather* (1889). After two minor purchases in the 1890s of works by artists from the nineteenth-century Hague school, very popular at the time in Montreal, the first Old Master purchase of European painting occurred in 1907 with the acquisition of Gainsborough's portrait *Ignatius Sancho* (1768). The portrait in European art has since become a leitmotif of the Old Master collection of almost eight hundred paintings and sculptures. By 1913 Sir Edmund Walker, the first board chairman, and Eric Brown, the first director, had built on the foundation of the *Sancho* with the purchase of Andrea Sacchi's *Portrait of a Cardinal* (c. 1630), Hogarth's portrait *John Herring* (1740), and Reynolds' portrait *Charles Churchill* (1775). Walker's interest in establishing a broad cultural base for the collections, reaching as far into history as possible, inspired the acquisition of an early Chinese painting and two Assyrian reliefs of Assurnasirpal in 1913 and 1922. Walker's influence and his interest in Italian art were behind the acquisition of three fourteenth-century Florentine planels, and as a print collector, he was crucial in launching the European print collection with Dürer, Rembrandt, and Blake. In this he was helped briefly, between 1921 and 1923, by H. P. Rossiter, a Canadian in the Print Room of the Boston Museum of Fine Arts, whom the Gallery did not succeed in keeping in Ottawa. In 1911 an Old Master drawings collection was begun with purchases from the duke of Rutland's collection, to which was added a group of Barbizon drawings in 1914 and four Goyas in 1923.

In 1921 Lord Beaverbrook's Canadian War Memorials (commissioned paintings by British and Canadian artists of Canadian participation in World War I) were deposited at the Gallery, including a large group of important early-twentieth-century English paintings by Harold Gilman, Wyndham Lewis, Paul Nash,

William Roberts, Edward Wadsworth, and an exceptional mural cartoon by Augustus John. Beaverbrook's War Memorials included, furthermore, one of the most famous of neoclassical history pictures, Benjamin West's *The Death of Wolfe* (1770; given to the Memorials collection by the duke of Westminster in 1918), and Romney's portrait *Joseph Brant* (Chief of the Six Nations Indians; 1776). A similar concept was carried out in World War II under the rubric of the Canadian War Records Collection and with the collaboration of Vincent Massey, then high commissioner for Canada in London. The majority of the works in these two war memorial collections (some five thousand items), except for those referred to above, were transferred to the Canadian War Museum in 1971.

When Sir Edmund Walker died in 1924, the Gallery's collecting had extended into other areas, and the parameters of its acquisitions policy were established. The marquis of Lorne had elicited gifts in the 1880s from three English Royal academicians—Leighton, Millais (a portrait of Lorne himself), and Watts—to which was added, in 1911, Holman Hunt's portrait *Henry Wentworth Monk* (1858). The nineteenth-century French collection of painting was begun with the acquisition of works by Degas, Millet, Monet, Pissarro, and Sisley. Beginning in the years 1912–14, both Walker and Brown nourished the development of Canada's first modern "national" style of landscape painting by a number of artists who became known, in 1920, as the Group of Seven. With an art based on rigorous travel, direct observation, and bold execution in a Post-Impressionist mode, the Group (Franklin Carmichael, Lawren Harris, A. Y. Jackson, Frank Johnston, Arthur Lismer, J.E.H. MacDonald, Tom Thomson, and Frederick Varley) dominated the Canadian art scene in the 1920s. The National Gallery's support of the Group, a matter of great controversy at the time, established a tradition of commitment to modern art that has characterized Gallery acquisition and exhibition programs since.

The Canadian collections of paintings, sculptures, decorative arts, and drawings represent 80 percent of the Gallery's total holdings, if prints and photographs, which number close to twenty-five thousand for all schools, are excluded. The Royal Canadian Academy Collection (works deposited by newly elected academicians, since 1880) is relatively small. The sculpture collection is also modest in number, including religious wood figures of the seventeenth, eighteenth, and nineteenth centuries from Quebec and works by Emanuel Hahn, Louis-Philippe Hébert, Alfred Laliberté, Frances Loring, Robert Tait McKenzie, Elizabeth Wyn Wood, and Florence Wyle. There is an important selection of modern sculpture by artists such as Robert Murray, Royden Rabinowich, and Michael Snow. Until just recently there was only a small collection of furniture and church silver. In 1979, however, the Henry Birks Collection of Canadian Silver, some six thousand pieces, was given to the Gallery, consisting of church and domestic silver, seventeenth to twentieth century, made primarily in Quebec and Nova Scotia. (With this gift a number of American and European pieces also entered the collection.) The extensive collection of Canadian paintings from

1700 to the present, central to the study of the history of Canadian art, includes works by William Berczy, Joseph Légaré, Paul Kane, Cornelius Krieghoff, Antoine Plamondon, Robert Harris, James Wilson Morrice, Tom Thomas and the Group of Seven, Homer Watson, Marc Aurèle Suzor-Coté, Emily Carr, David Milne, Ozias Leduc, LeMoine FitzGerald, Paul-Emile Borduas, Jean-Paul Riopelle, Gordon Rayner, Jack Bush, Guido Molinari, Greg Curnoe, and Michael Snow. Major gifts of Canadian art to the collections have been the J. M. MacCallum bequest of Thomson and the Group of Seven (133 paintings and 1 drawing) in 1943; the Mr. and Mrs. H. R. Jackman gift of the decoration of the MacCallum-Jackman cottage at Georgian Bay, presented during Canada's centennial in 1967; the Vincent Massey bequest of 92 paintings in 1968; the Douglas M. Duncan Collection and the Milne-Duncan bequest of 614 works in 1970, including major collections of the works of Milne and FitzGerald; and 218 of his own drawings presented by the artist A. Y. Jackson in 1974.

In quality and quantity, the European collection of paintings and sculpture is the most important in Canada. It includes a considerable group of medieval capitals, sculptural and architectural fragments, and two murals (French, twelfth-fourteenth century), not on permanent exhibition. The Italian Renaissance and Baroque collections are choice, including Simone Martini's *St. Catherine of Alexandria* (c. 1320) and Filippino Lippi's *Esther at the Palace Gate* and *Triumph of Mordecai* (c. 1474–80), Piero di Cosimo's *Vulcan and Aeolus* (c. 1490), Bartolomeo Veneto's *Portrait of a Young Woman* (1520–30), Lorenzo Lotto's *Madonna and Child with Saints Roch and Sebastian* (c. 1521), Bronzino's *Portrait of a Man* (c. 1540), Orazio Gentileschi's *Lot and His Daughters* (1621–26), and Bernini's bust *Pope Urban VIII* (1632). The Piero and Bronzino were purchased in the 1930s, the Simone and the two Filippinos in the 1950s (three of a splendid group of paintings bought at that time through dealers in New York and London from the Prince of Liechtenstein), the Gentileschi in the 1965 Spencer-Churchill sale, the Bartolomeo Veneto in 1971 and the Lotto in 1976, both from the Contini-Bonacossi Collection, and the Bernini in 1974 from a dealer in New York. A more recent and impressive addition has been Mattia Preti's *The Feast of Absalom* (c. 1665). The Northern European Renaissance and Baroque collection is a small but considerable group of works including Memling's *Virgin and Child with St. Anthony Abbot and a Donor* (1472) and Matsys' *Crucifixion* (c. 1520), both from the Liechtenstein Collection, and Baldung's *Eve, the Serpent and Death* (c. 1510–12). Also from the Liechtenstein Collection, Rubens' *Entombment of Christ* (1613–14), Rembrandt's *Toilet of Esther* (c. 1633), and Maes' *Lacemaker* (1655) enrich the Dutch and Flemish seventeenth-century collection already important for its early van Dyck *Christ Blessing the Children* (c. 1618); two fine oils by Jordaens, in particular the *As the Old Sing, so the Young Twitter* (c. 1640); and paintings by Bloemaert, Lievens, Stomer, Hals, Steen, Cuyp, and Both. There is a small group of Spanish seventeenth-century paintings of which the most well known is Murillo's *Abraham and the Three Angels* (1670–74), originally from the hospital of La Caridad in Seville and later in the duke of Sutherland's collection. The French sixteenth- and seventeeth-century collection is distinguished for oils by Antoine Caron, Vouet (*The Fortune Teller*, c. 1620), Poussin (*Martyrdom of St. Erasmus*, c. 1628, and *Landscape with a Woman Bathing*, c. 1650, gift from H. S. Southam, 1944), Claude (*A Temple of Bacchus*, 1644), Philippe de Champaigne (*Crucifixion*, c. 1660), and Rigaud (*The Le Juge Family*, 1699) and for a marble bust, *King David* (c. 1667–68), by Puget.

One of the more spectacular pieces in the Gallery's small collection of European decorative arts is the marquetry table (c. 1665–70), made by Leonardo Van der Venne for the Medici.

There is also a gallery of British portraits of the sixteenth, seventeenth, and eighteenth centuries in addition to those already mentioned: Hans Eworth's *Lady Dacre* (c. 1558); three portraits by Lely and two others by Mytens the Elder and Cornelius Johnson; a family group by Kneller; good portraits by Hoppner and Lawrence, Raeburn, and Ramsay; a portrait bust by Wilton, *General James Wolfe* (c. 1760, bequest in 1975, of the sixth earl of Rosenbery), and two portraits by Nollekens. The eighteenth-century collections of all schools are most memorable for the two Liechtenstein Chardins (*La gouvernante* and *La pourvoyeuse*, both 1738); a group of Venetian vedute by Canaletto, Bellotto, and Guardi; landscapes by De Loutherbourg, Morland, and Wilson; and an American cityscape by Ouwater.

The nineteenth-century French and English schools are best represented by Corot's *Le pont de Narni* (1827), Daumier's *Third-Class Carriage* (c. 1862), and Turner's *Mercury and Argus* (1836). More recently, a small group of neoclassic works has been acquired, including sculptures by Chinard (bust of *Empress Josephine*, 1805) and Canova (*Dancer*, 1822) and a Girodet portrait *Madame Begon de Misery* (1807). A full-scale landscape sketch in oil by Constable for the well-known composition *Salisbury Cathedral from the Bishop's Grounds* (c. 1820) has enriched a collection previously noted for its relatively conventional Courbets. Millet's *Pig Slaughter* (1867–70), bought in 1978, joined his *Oedipus Taken Down from the Tree* (1847), purchased in 1914. There is a very respectable collection of Impressionist and Post-Impressionist pictures by Degas (a superb *Woman with an Umbrella*, 1886–87), Gauguin, Monet, Pissarro, Renoir, Sisley, and van Gogh (a brilliant *Iris*, 1889) and a group of five Cézannes, some of which came from the Vollard estate sequestered at the National Gallery during World War II. Sculpture is represented by Rodin's *Age of Bronze* (1876) and Gauguin's portrait head in wood, *Meyer de Haan* (1889–90). Simeon Solomon's *First Class Meeting and At First Meeting Loved* (1854) and Rossetti's *Salutatio Beatricis* (1859) form the nucleus of a small group of Victorian pictures.

Vincent Massey's collection of English painting, chiefly twentieth century, came to the gallery in 1946. Numbering more than eighty pictures, the collection includes works by Grant, Greaves, Hillier, Hitchens, Nevinson, Nicholson (Sir William), Piper, Sickert, Smith, Spencer, and Steer and large groups of works by Augustus John and Paul Nash. The twentieth-century sculpture collection is the most representative of the gallery's modest sculpture collections, including bronzes by Bourdelle, Despiau, Epstein, Giacometti, Manzù, and Zadkine; a marble by Arp; and stone sculptures by Lipchitz, Maillol, Hepworth, and Moore. The French school of this period includes Fauve pictures by Braque, Derain, van Dongen, and Vlaminck; two oils by Picasso and Matisse of the 1920s; and an impressive Léger (*The Mechanic*, 1920). The twentieth-century collections as a whole have recently been strengthened by the addition of Klimt's Symbolist *Hope I* (1903), Mondrian's *Composition* (1936–42), and important paintings by Dali, Ensor, Gorky, Klee, and Lissitzky.

Most recently, an outstanding if small twentieth-century American and international collection has been built up on the foundation of Jackson Pollock's *No. 29* (1950), David Smith's *Wagon I* (1963–64), and Clyfford Still's *1949-G* (1949). There are major and monumental works by Flavin (*the nominal three/ to William of Ockham/*, 1964–69), Graves (*Camel VI, Camel VII, Camel VIII*, 1968, and *Variability and Repetition of Variable Forms*, 1971), Kossuth (*The Eighth Investigation A.A.I.A.I. Proposition Five*, 1971), Oldenburg, (*Bedroom Ensemble*, 1st version, 1963), Rosenquist (*Painting for the American Negro*, 1962–63), and Segal (*The Gas Station*, 1963). The Gallery has the most important group of works by Judd in a public collection. A painting and a sculpture by Barnett Newman (*The Way I*, 1951; *Here II*, 1965), with a mobile by Calder (*Jacaranda*, 1949), were added to this collection in 1977–78. There are also works by Aillaud, Albers, André, Beuys, Cornell, Dove, Duchamp, Feininger, Flannagan, Long, Marden, Morris, Noland, Olitski, Richter, Serra, Smith, and Warhol and a related and growing collection of twentieth-century drawings and prints.

The collections of prints, drawings, and photographs are the largest in the country in both Canadian and non-Canadian art, and they include more than thirty thousand works. The Old Master and modern collection of almost a thousand drawings, a stunning memorial to the Gallery's prints and drawings curator of forty years, Kathleen Fenwick, who retired in 1968, is a small but classic one for a gallery of primarily Western art, containing first-class examples of all schools from the Renaissance to the modern. There are impressive holdings of English drawings and watercolors of the eighteenth and nineteenth centuries, and the French nineteenth-century collection is also considerable. The collection is rich in Italian drawings from the sixteenth to eighteenth century. Included in the collections are drawings by Raphael, Jacopo Bassano, Annibale Carracci, Piranesi, Guardi, Giovanni Battista, and Domenico Tiepolo; by Dürer, Bloemaert, Rubens, Jongkind, van Gogh, Nolde, Heckel, and Klee; by Dumonstier, Watteau, Boucher, Ingres, Daumier, Corot, Moreau, Renoir, and Matisse; by Goya and Picasso; and by Romney, Turner, Millais, John, Moore, and Sutherland. In 1973 twenty-seven important drawings of the Italian and French schools were presented by Mrs. Samuel Bronfman in honor of her husband. Fine examples by Rembrandt, van Dyck, Fragonard, and Greuze have recently been purchased. The Old Master and modern collection of more than six thousand prints includes works of all major schools in all graphic techniques, with a special attempt being made now to develop the French nineteenth-century collection. A few of the many major examples from the various schools include Pollaiuolo's *Battle of Naked Men*, a brilliant impression of Dürer's *Madonna with the Monkey*, Bellange's *Adoration of the Magi* (unique first state), Rembrandt's *Jan Lutma, Goldsmith* (first state on parchment), Goya's *Los Caprichos*, Degas' *Serious Client* (monotype), Heckel's *Standing Girl*, Beckmann's *Self Portrait with Hat*, Picasso's *Minotauromachia* (numbered 1/50), and Miró's *Black and Red Series* (3 *bon à tirer* impressions). There is also an interesting collection of Victorian wood engravings. In 1982–83 a fine and representative selection of M. C. Escher's prints was added, given by his son Georges Escher.

The collection of Canadian prints and drawings includes more than six thousand works. This major portion of the National Gallery's permanent collection is a sine qua non for the study of Canadian cultural history and art from the eighteenth century to the present. Major cornerstones of these collections are: the gallery's share (with the Public Archives of Canada) of the government's purchase of the Manoir Richelieu Collection in 1970; the Douglas Duncan bequest of works by David Milne, LeMoine FitzGerald, and many others; the A. Y. Jackson gift of 218 of his drawings; and important holdings in the work of Paul-Emile Borduas, Greg Curnoe, Thomas Davies, Charles Forrest, Clarence Gagnon, Lawren Harris, Lucius O'Brien, Walter Phillips, Carl Schaefer, and Michael Snow.

The nineteenth- and twentieth-century collection of photographs was begun only in 1967. The collection now numbers almost 15,500 prints and is impressive in its representation of David Octavius Hill, Henry Fox Talbot, and a host of other English and Scottish nineteenth-century photographers; of French nineteenth-century photographers and, in particular, of Eugène Atget, Charles Nègre, and Auguste Salzmann; of American photography of the Civil War by George Barnard, Alexander Gardner, and others; and of major twentieth-century American photographers such as Diane Arbus, Walker Evans, Robert Frank, David Heath, Roger Mertin, and Edward Weston. The collection, covering the entire history of the medium, continues to be generously enriched by gifts both collective and individual, from Mrs. E. F. Eidlitz's donation in 1968 to the establishment of a five-year purchase fund by Phyllis Lambert in 1978 and the additional Lambert gift of Walker Evans photographs in 1983. The Canadian portion of the collection features Alexander Henderson, Emile Lacas, and William Notman and the contemporary Canadian photographers Gabor Szilasi, Robert Bourdeau, Lynne Cohen, Sylvain Cousineau, Tom Gibson, and Michael Schreier.

The small collection of American nineteenth- and early twentieth-century paintings includes works by Duncanson, Roesen, Harnett, Bierstadt, Henri, and Prendergast. The small and choice holdings in Oriental art consist of seventeenth- and eighteenth-century Chinese paintings given by R. W. Finlayson, Toronto, and of Indian and Tibetan miniatures, textiles, and sculptures, of the fourth to nineteenth century, from the Heeramaneck Collection of New York, presented by Max Tanenbaum, Toronto.

An important part of the Gallery's Canadian Visual Art Study Centre is a library of more than eighty-two thousand volumes, including complete runs of major art historical art journals. It also has thirty-five thousand catalogues from major auction houses, twenty-five thousand exhibition catalogues, and forty thousand files on Canadian art and artists. The library is open to the public and, with the exception of interlibrary loans, is noncirculating. Its collections, related to the Gallery's acquisitions policies, are strongest in the areas of Canadian and post-medieval Western art. It is considered a national resource collection by the National Library of Canada in these areas, as is the Far Eastern Department Library of the Royal Ontario Museum, Toronto, for Oriental art. The Canadian Visual Art Study Centre also includes a collection of slides and photographs of works of art not in the collections but related to them, used primarily by curators for collections research.

Slides and photographs of objects in the collection may be purchased by application to the Department of Reproduction, Rights and Sales of the gallery. A catalogue is available. A listing of gallery publications with instructions for ordering may be obtained from Order Fulfilment, Publishing Division, National Museums of Canada, Ottawa, Ontario K1A OM8. In addition to publishing the permanent collection catalogues (now out of print and out of date: new editions forthcoming) and the special catalogues, journals, and series listed below, the Gallery publishes catalogues and journals of all major exhibitions in English and French. Publication of the semiannual *National Gallery of Canada Bulletin* began in 1963. An *Annual Report* (called after 1968–69 *Annual Review*) has been published since 1882. In 1979 these publications were combined under the title *Annual Bulletin*. The Gallery has been and continues to be a major publisher of books and studies on Canadian art related to its collections and programs.

The Gallery has an important Restoration and Conservation Laboratory with its own library and archive.

Selected Bibliography

Gallery publications: Hubbard, R. H., *Catalogue of Paintings and Sculpture*, 3 vols., 1959–61; Popham, A. E. and Fenwick, K. M., *Catalogue of European Drawings*, 1965; Wodehouse, R. F., *Check List of the War Collections*, 1968; Hubbard, R. H., *Vincent Massey Bequest/The Canadian Paintings*, 1968; *European Drawings from the National Gallery of Canada/Colnaghi*, 1969; Reid, Dennis, *The Group of Seven*, 1970; Théberge, Pierre, *Gift from the Douglas M. Duncan Collection and the Milne-Duncan Bequest*, 1971; *Masterpieces in the National Gallery of Canada*, nos. 1–12, 1971–78; *Canadian Artists Monographs*, nos. 1–7, 1973–79; Taylor, Mary Cazort, *The Bronfman Gift of Drawings*, 1974; Hubbard, R. H., *Penny Plain, Twopenny Coloured: Vicissitudes in the Collecting of British Art by the National Gallery of Canada* (Journal 21), 1976; Milroy, Elizabeth, *The Evolution of Landscape in Prints and Drawings, 1500–1900* (from the permanent collection: Journal 23), 1977; Stewart, Brian, *Prints of the Impressionists* (from the permanent collection: Journal 33), 1979; Reid, Dennis, "Our Own Country Canada," 1979; Hill, Charles C., *To Found a National Gallery* (Journal 36), 1980; Borcoman, James, *The Magical Eye/Photographs in the National Gallery* (Journal 37), 1980.

Other publications: "The National Gallery of Canada," *artscanada*, vol. 26, no. 1 (special issue: February 1969); *Da Dürer a Picasso/mostra di designi della galleria nazionale del Canada* (Uffizi, Firenze 1969); *De Raphael à Picasso/Dessins de la Galerie Nationale du Canada* (Louvre, Paris: Florence 1969; "La galerie nationale du Canada," *Vie des Arts*, vol. 14, no. 58 (hommage à la galerie nationale du Canada: printemps 1970); Boggs, Jean Sutherland, *The National Gallery of Canada* (London 1971); Reid, Dennis, *A Concise History of Canadian Painting* (Toronto 1973); Bunnell, Peter C., "The National Gallery photographic collection," *artscanada*, vol. 31, nos. 3 and 4 (December 1974), pp. 37–68; Mellen, Peter, *Landmarks of Canadian Art* (Toronto 1978); Kochman, Katharine Jordan, "The Department of Prints and Drawings at the National Gallery: The First Hundred Years," *artmagazine*, vol. 11, no. 48–49 (May-June 1980), pp. 24–28; Thomas, Ann, "13 Years of Collecting Photographs at the National Gallery of Canada," *artmagazine*, vol. 11, no. 48–49 (May–June 1980), pp. 29–33; McNairn, Alan, "American paintings in the National Gallery of Canada, Ottawa," *Antiques*, vol. 118, no. 5 (November 1980), pp. 1010–17; Sisler, Rebecca, *Passionate Spirits: A History of the Royal Canadian Academy of Arts, 1880–1890* (Toronto, Vancouver 1980).

Canadian Heritage Information Network: The National Gallery collections are being recorded with this system, access to which is being made available to participating institutions across Canada.

Library publications, systems recording, and fiches: The card catalogue of the National Gallery of Canada Library has been published in book form by G. K. Hall (Boston 1973). A supplement was published in 1981. In 1978 the library joined the University of Toronto Library Automation Systems (UTLAS) and since 1980 has recorded all acquisitions in UTLAS. National Gallery exhibition catalogues to 1959 have been microfiched by McLauren Micropublishing, Toronto. Data on Canadian artists' files in the library are stored in the National Heritage Information Network and were published by the Gallery in book form as *Artists in Canada*, 1977 (now out of print). In 1980 twenty other Canadian libraries made data on their artists' files available for storage in the Canadian Heritage data base, and *Artists in Canada: a union list*, a list of the artists' files in all the participating libraries, including the National Gallery Library, was published in 1981. Some Canadian artists' files in the National Gallery Library have been microfiched by the Gallery under the rubric Canadian Art Micro Documents and may be purchased by application to the Library.

GYDE VANIER SHEPHERD

———— Toronto ————

ART GALLERY OF ONTARIO (formerly ART MUSEUM OF TORONTO, THE ART GALLERY OF TORONTO; also AGO), 317 Dundas Street, Toronto, Ontario M5T 1G4.

Founded in 1900 as the Art Museum of Toronto, the institution became The Art Gallery of Toronto in 1919 and finally, in 1966—reflecting its expanded role in the province—the Art Gallery of Ontario.

In some ten thousand paintings, sculptures, prints, and drawings of the permanent collection are works from the Old Master traditions, the Impressionists, and the early twentieth-century movements—paintings by masters such as Rembrandt, Hals, Poussin, Chardin, Delacroix, Renoir, and Picasso and sculptures by Rodin, Degas, and Matisse. More than half of the collection is the work of Canadian artists dating from the eighteenth century to the present. The Gallery's Henry Moore Sculpture Centre contains the largest and most comprehensive public collection of Moore works in the world. Traveling exhibitions from other major art museums also offer the public access to important historic and contemporary works of art.

In the Activity Centre, an enormous (10,500 square feet) open, thirty-foot-high, multifunctional space, children and adults enjoy many art-related activities or take classes in the Gallery School.

The original Gallery home, The Grange, a restored Georgian mansion, offers visitors a glimpse of life in the 1830s. The Gallery also provides an art-rental service, the Gallery Book Shop, reproduction and jewelry shops, the Impulse gift shop, a restaurant, and a cafeteria.

Reaching into communities in every corner of Ontario, and across Canada, the extension services offer touring exhibitions, an artists-with-their-work program, and advisory services to community centers, and they contribute to the Ontario Ministry of Citizenship and Culture Festival Ontario Program.

The Gallery's collection, facilities, and programs have attracted a strong membership, which today totals about thirty thousand, the largest per capita in North America.

The Art Gallery of Ontario was founded on July 4, 1900, as the Art Museum of Toronto. In the first decade, it had no home and held only two exhibitions; in 1906 it was located in the Ontario Society of Artists Galleries on King Street; and in 1909, in the Reference Library at College and St. George streets.

In 1911 Mrs. Goldwin Smith donated her historic house, The Grange, and its 3.5-acre parkland to the gallery. By agreement with the city of Toronto, the lands around the house became a public park, maintained by the city as they are today.

The need for more space for exhibitions, conservation, storage, study, administration, and facilities for public activities is reflected in the history of the Gallery. The first building program to create the three South galleries—the F. P. Wood Gallery, the E. R. Wood Gallery, and the Laidlaw Gallery—was completed in 1918. These galleries opened with a joint exhibition under the auspices of the Royal Canadian Academy of Arts and the Ontario Society of Artists. In the words of former Gallery Director Martin Baldwin, the new buildings were an invitation to greater effort by Canadian artists and became "the battleground of the early days of the Group of Seven."

The second expansion, funded by private subscription and the City Council, was completed in 1926, with the addition of the Walker Sculpture Court and two sets of flanking galleries. The Gallery again expanded in 1935. Donations came from the city of Toronto, provincial and federal governments, and the T. Eaton Company.

In 1977 the Gallery completed a major $23 million, two-stage expansion program financed by public and private funds. The first stage, opened in October 1974, featured the Henry Moore Sculpture Centre and the Sam and Ayala Zacks Wing; the second stage, the Canadian Wing. The floor space of the Gallery now totals 120,234 square feet in exhibition and public areas.

In 1966, by an act of the Provincial Legislature, the Gallery's name was changed to the Art Gallery of Ontario, indicating the significance of its role throughout the province. The Gallery is incorporated under the laws of Ontario as a corporation without share capital. The governing body is a board of twenty-seven trustees—ten elected by the membership and five appointed by the College of Founders, two by the Council of the Municipality of Metropolitan Toronto, and ten by the lieutenant-governor-in-council.

The Gallery receives about 70 percent of its annual operating costs from government grants, the large portion of which comes from the province of Ontario, supplemented by grants from federal and municipal governments. The remainder of the budget is earned in various ways: from membership support and program fees, at the gift shop and restaurant, and by private gifts and corporate donations. All works of art in the collection have either been donated or purchased with income from donations.

Since it was incorporated in 1900, the Art Gallery of Ontario has acquired by bequest, gift, and purchase more than ten thousand works of art—paintings, sculpture, watercolors, prints, and drawings. Significantly, no work has ever been acquired with public funds.

The Captive Butterfly by E. A. Hornel was the first acquisition of the Gallery, purchased in 1906 through a subscription for $610. In 1911 the Canadian National Exhibition Association extended a long-term loan of 340 works that, in 1965, became an outright gift.

Since there were no funds to purchase works of art, the Gallery relied on bequests, subscriptions, and donations from generous friends. In 1956 the Art Gallery of Ontario Foundation was created as a result of a bequest to the Gallery by the late Frank P. Wood, a former president and long-time benefactor. The foundation serves as a permanent custodian of the endowment funds. Investment income is used, in part, to acquire works of art for the Gallery collections.

During 1970 the Gallery recorded the largest gifts of art in its history. Included were the bequest from the extensive Charles S. Band Collection of Canadian paintings and sculpture and a substantial gift of more than one hundred works by twentieth-century Canadian artists from the collection of Douglas M. Duncan. The Gallery's Canadian holdings were further strengthened by permanent loans from the J. S. McLean Collection. A highlight was the Sam and Ayala Zacks

Collection of more than three hundred works by nineteenth- and twentieth-century European masters and by a number of contemporary Canadians. Certainly, the most important ensuing gift to the Gallery came from the private collection of British sculptor Henry Moore in 1973 and 1974. The Moore Collection, based on the artist's gift and Gallery purchases and donations, totals approximately seven hundred sculptures, drawings, and prints and is the largest public collection of Moore's work in the world. In 1979 Toronto collectors Mr. and Mrs. Harry Klamer gave to the Gallery a collection of more than six hundred works of Eskimo art.

European masterpieces include works with religious themes, such as Tintoretto's *Christ Washing His Disciples' Feet*, c. 1550, and Rubens' *The Elevation of The Cross*, c. 1638; and outstanding portraits by Rembrandt, Frans Hals, van Dyck, Hogarth, Reynolds, and Augustus John. Major landscape painters include Poussin, with *Venus, Mother of Aeneas, Presenting Him with Arms Forged by Vulcan*, c. 1635; Claude Lorraine's *Carlo and Ubaldo Embarking in Pursuit of Rinaldo*, 1667; and Salomon van Ruysdael's *The Ferry Boat*, 1656. The eighteenth-century Italian collection, which includes Canaletto's *The Bacino di San Marco from the Piazetta*, complements works from the same century in England such as Gainsborough's *The Harvest Waggon*, 1784, and Fuseli's *Lear Banishing Cordelia*, c. 1784–90. Paintings by Delacroix, Puvis de Chavannes, the French Impressionists, Redon, Vuillard, Dufy, and Léger and sculptures by Rodin, Gauguin, Matisse, and Brancusi are other treasures in the European collection.

In the contemporary field, the Gallery has acquired pieces that are considered to be key examples of various artists' work, including Gorky, De Kooning, Rothko, Noland, Morris, LeWitt, Oldenburg, Long, and Smithson.

The Canadian Wing—the Signy Eaton Gallery, the J. S. McLean Gallery, the John Ridley Gallery, and the Georgia Ridley Gallery—provides a permanent exhibition area of about twelve thousand square feet for the Gallery's outstanding collection of Canadian art, reflecting its history from the early nineteenth century to the present.

The Canadian collection now includes about five thousand paintings, sculptures, drawings, and graphics acquired through gifts, purchases, and private donations. In Gallery acquisition policies, aesthetic considerations outweigh the more historical and documentary interests that characterize any public collection of Canadiana. The scope of the collection is extensive and now comprises nearly one-half of the Gallery's permanent holdings. The majority of Canadian works owned by the Gallery date from the twentieth century and are by artists working in Ontario.

The Group of Seven is particularly well represented. Tom Tomson's *The West Wind*, 1917, and Lawren Harris' *Above Lake Superior*, about 1922, are major works of this national landscape movement that first exhibited at the Gallery in 1920. J.E.H. MacDonald's *Mist Fantasy*, 1922, shows the degree of formalism the Group could attain, and Harris' *Lake and Mountains*, 1927–28, demonstrates the increasing tendency toward abstraction. Other important paintings include

Arthur Lismer's *Rock, Pine, and Sunlight*, 1920; A. Y. Jackson's *Barns*, about 1926; MacDonald's *Falls, Montreal River*, 1920; and F. H. Varley's *Portrait of Mrs. E.*, 1921. West Coast artist Emily Carr's *Kispiax Village*, 1929, and L. L. Fitzgerald's *Pritchard's Fence*, about 1928, are excellent examples of tendencies that developed essentially outside the Group of Seven.

The Signy Eaton Gallery represents works produced since 1945. Montreal in the 1950s was particularly active in the development of modern painting in Canada, with artists including Alfred Pellan, Paul-Emile Borduas, and Jean-Paul Riopelle broadening the horizons of Canadian art. Two major works in the collection by Montreal Automatist artists are Borduas' *Black and White Composition*, 1956, and Riopelle's *Blow upon Blow*, 1953.

Toronto during the late fifties and sixties is equally well represented. One of the most important developments was the Painters Eleven, a group of artists who exhibited together because of a common interest in furthering the cause of abstract art. Jock Macdonald in *Slumber Deep*, 1957; Harold Town with *Monument to Hokusai*, 1957; William Ronald with *Exodus II*, 1959; John Meredith in *Frisco*, 1962, and Jack Bush with *Dazzle Red*, 1965, are among those who led Toronto to a greater acceptance of abstract painting.

Subsequent developments in both abstraction and realism are evident in works by individual artists, Kenneth Lochhead's *Dark Green Centre*, 1963 and *Stasis*, 1963, indicate the variety of post-painterly abstraction in Regina. Alex Colville's *Elm Tree at Horton Landing*, 1956, is a masterpiece of symbolic realism. *Spring on the Ridgeway*, 1964, by Greg Curnoe and *Venus Simultaneous*, 1962, by Michael Snow show the Pop Art-related, figurative painting in Ontario during the 1960s. The collection continues to grow with the acquisition of works by young Canadian artists.

Dominating the northeast corner of the exterior of the Art Gallery of Ontario building is a monumental bronze by Henry Moore, *Large Two Forms*, 1966 and 1969. British sculptor Henry Moore first indicated that he would like Toronto to become home for a significant part of his work in 1967. The Gallery was then planning a major expansion. Moore's gift was of such proportions—101 sculptures, 57 drawings, and an almost complete collection of his prints—that it became clear a sculpture gallery would be required. Moore himself assisted in the design of the Sculpture Centre, incorporated into the new building.

The Henry Moore Sculpture Centre, which opened in 1974, contains the large, skylit Henry Moore Gallery, where the major pieces in the collection are displayed. The Irina Moore Gallery, named after the artist's wife, contains the maquettes and smaller pieces, and there are also a 150-seat lecture hall, an Atrium, and educational displays.

The Gallery collection covers over sixty years of the artist's career from the earliest work, the 1921 portrait drawing *Head of an Old Man*, to the recent lithographs and prints of the 1980s. Among the seventy-three drawings documented are a number of life drawings from the 1920s, as well as definitive studies for some of Moore's major early carvings: the Manchester *Mother and Child* of

1924–25, Leeds *Reclining Figure* of 1929, the St. Louis *Reclining Figure* of 1932, and the *Two Forms* of 1934 in the Museum of Modern Art, New York. Moore's wartime drawings include six shelter drawings and three sheets of studies from the Coalmine Sketchbook. Nine pages from a 1970–71 sketchbook are representative of Moore's renewed interest in drawing in the early 1970s.

Of the 126 sculptures in the collection, the earliest work is the beautiful alabaster *Seated Figure* of 1930. The collection is particularly rich in sculpture from the 1950s, 1960s, and 1970s, especially, the unique collection of original plasters. The entire sculpture collection comprises one alabaster carving, seventy-seven original plasters, two plaster casts, one terracotta piece, one clay and wire sculpture, one porcelain cast, three fiberglass casts, and forty bronzes.

The graphic collection, the most complete public collection outside the archives at Moore's home in Much Hadham, Hertfordshire, England, includes rare prints, such as *Spanish Prisoner* of 1939, that were never published commercially.

In 1979 a major gift of Eskimo art was received by the Art Gallery of Ontario from Toronto collectors Mr. and Mrs. Harry Klamer and family. The collection includes 605 pieces of sculpture, prints, drawings, and wall hangings, dating from two thousand years ago to the present. It is the largest gift of Eskimo art ever made to a public museum in Canada. The gift includes early historic material ranging from a black ivory Okvik head (0–500 B.C.) to wooden masks of the nineteenth century. The modern period includes examples by every well-known Eskimo artist. Among more recent works are carvings by Axangayu, Oshooweetook "B," Sheoukjuk, and Joe Talirunili. Among stonecuts, engravings, and drawings from 1961 to the present are works by Kenojuak, Parr, Kiakshuk, Jonniebo, Pitseolak, Oonark, and Anguhadluq.

A major education facility is the Edward P. Taylor Audio-Visual Centre, where 120,000 visual art slides are a comprehensive loan source for scholars and teachers. The department also contains audio and video tapes and films, which are used in-house and circulated throughout the province. The collection covers most periods of the history of art, with particular emphasis on Canadian work.

The Edward P. Taylor Reference Library documents and interprets the works of art in the Gallery's collection. It is an important resource center for museum professionals and other researchers. The library has about 40,000 volumes, 15,000 artist files, and carries about 350 periodicals. It is noncirculating. Special subjects are Canadian, American, and European art from the Renaissance to the present, with a concentration on painting, sculpture, drawing, and engraving.

Selected Bibliography

Museum publications: *Handbook/Catalog illustré*, 1974; *Art Gallery of Ontario: The Canadian Collection*, 1970; Blodgett, Jean, *Grasp Tight the Old Ways: Selections from the Klamer Family Collection of Iniut Art*, 1983; Burnett, David, *Colville* (Toronto 1983); Celant, Germano, *The European Iceberg, Creativity in Germany and Italy Today* (Milan 1985); Hurdalek, Marta, *Humourist Walter Trier: Selections from the Trier-Fodor Foun-*

dation Gift, 1980; Lochnan, Katharine A., *The Etchings of James McNeill Whistler* (New Haven 1984); idem, *Selected Impressions: Recent Acquisitions of Master Prints from the Fifteenth to the Twentieth Century*, 1979; Lownsbrough, John, *The Privileged Few: The Grange and Its People in Nineteenth Century Toronto*, 1980; Nasgaard, Roald, *The Mystic North, Symbolist Landscape Painting in Northern Europe* (Toronto 1984); Wilkinson, Alan G., *The Moore Collection in the Art Gallery of Ontario*, 1979; Yanover, Shirley, *The Gallery School 1930–1980: A Celebration*, 1980.

Museum catalogues: Adamson, Jeremy, *Lawren S. Harris: Urban Scenes and Wilderness Landscapes 1906–1930*, 1978; Burnett, David, *Robert Bourdeau and Philip Pocock*, 1981; Hartman, Ruth Bains, and Sutnik, Maia-Mari, *E. Haanel Cassidy: Photographs 1933–1945*, 1981; Nasgaard, Roald, *Spring Hurlbut/Ron Martin/John Massey/Becky Singleton*, 1981; idem, *Structures for Behaviour: Robert Morris/David Rabinowitch/Richard Serra/George Trakas*, 1978; idem, *Yves Gaucher: A Fifteen Year Perspective/Une Perspective de Quinze Ans*, 1979; Pregrave, Ralph (introduction) and Katharine A. Lochnan (text), *Master Prints from the Pregrave Collection*, 1980; Wattenmaker, Richard, *The Dutch Cityscape in the 17th Century and Its Sources*, 1977; idem, *Puvis de Chavannes and the Modern Tradition*, 1975; Welsh-Ovcharov, Bogomila, *Vincent van Gogh and the Birth of Cloisonism*, 1981; Wilkinson, Alan G. (introduction), and William Fagg (text), *African Majesty: From Grassland and Forest*, 1981; Wilkinson, Alan G., *Gauguin to Moore: Primitivism in Modern Sculpture*, 1981; Zemans, Joyce, *Jock Macdonald: The Inner Landscape*, 1981.

ROYAL ONTARIO MUSEUM (also the ROM), 100 Queen's Park, Toronto, Ontario M5S 2C6; The Sigmund Samuel Canadiana Building, 14 Queen's Park Crescent West, Toronto, Ontario M5S 2C6.

The Royal Ontario Museum in Toronto now has the second largest museum building in North America (seven hundred thousand gross square feet of floor space) and is one of the most modern and best-equipped museums in the world.

By 1909 the efforts of Sir Edmund Walker, then president of the Bank of Commerce, with a small group of other prominent citizens, led to the granting of funds by the Ontario government for a new museum building. On April 16, 1912, the Royal Ontario Museum was established by an act of the Ontario legislature. Archaeological material sent from Egypt by Charles Trick Currelly, the first director of art and archaeology at the ROM; the teaching collections of the University of Toronto, largely in the field of natural history; and other provincial collections were incorporated into five museums to be housed in a single building: archaeology, geology, mineralogy, paleontology, and zoology. The new building, now the west wing, was officially opened in 1914 by the duke of Connaught, governor-general of Canada.

In 1933 new sections were added to the original building, an east wing and a center block. The ROM became the world's largest university museum in 1947, when it was placed under the governance of the University of Toronto by an act of the Ontario legislature. In 1951 the Sigmund Samuel Canadiana Building was completed as a result of a gift from Sigmund Samuel. Four years later, in 1955, Theodore Heinrich was appointed as the first overall director of a single and united ROM, and the museum was reorganized in three divisions of art and archaeology; geology and mineralogy; and zoology and paleontology.

As a result of a gift by Colonel R. S. McLaughlin, the McLaughlin Planetarium was completed and opened in 1968. In the same year, the ROM was separated from the University of Toronto and established as a public corporation funded largely by the Ontario government and controlled by a board of trustees.

In 1978 a $60 million renovation and expansion project was initiated when work began on the complete renovation of the main building and construction of a nine-floor curatorial center building in the south courtyard. Construction of the six-floor terrace gallery building in the north courtyard began in 1980. The two new buildings are linked to the main building by skylighted atria, so that a harmonius integration of the old and the new is achieved. The renovated and expanded main building reopened its doors to the public in September 1982 with a limited selection of the collections on display. New galleries and exhibit areas have been opened since then, and it is anticipated that most of the collections will have been put on display during the ensuing decade.

There are three main organizational streams in the ROM: curatorial, public programs, and operations, headed by two associate directors reporting to a single director.

The collections are now the responsibility of nine art and archaeology departments (Canadiana, Egyptian, Ethnology, European, Far Eastern, Greek and Roman, New World Archaeology, Textile, and West Asian), and nine science departments (Botany, Entomology, Ichthyology and Herpetology, Invertebrate Paleontology, Invertebrate Zoology, Mammalogy, Mineralogy and Geology, Ornithology, and Vertebrate Paleontology). There are five additional departments in the curatorial stream: Conservation, Registration, Preparators, Library and Archives, and Planetarium.

Many of the collections, or individual items within them, are of world significance. The science departments are rich in type specimens, the scientifically accepted specimen from which a new species or mineral has been described. A large percentage of the museum's 6 million artifacts and specimens from research collections are available to visiting scholars from around the world. In addition, these materials are loaned to cultural and educational institutions for study and public display. The work of the curatorial staff in the field and in sophisticated laboratories of the curatorial center provides the solid academic base for all public activities of the museum. Archaeology departments conduct field excavations in many parts of the world such as Belize, Egypt, the Middle East, and Canada. The science departments provide consultations to a variety of international, national, and provincial agencies.

Housed in the Sigmund Samuel Canadiana Building, just south of the ROM's main building, the Canadiana collection consists of European- and American-derived Canadian decorative arts from the seventeenth to the nineteenth century. The size and extent of the present collection of approximately fifteen thousand pieces is due in large measure to the early efforts of Sigmund Samuel, who donated his renowned collection of Canadian material to the ROM and established an acquisitions trust fund.

Changing picture exhibits in the south gallery draw upon an inventory of four hundred oil paintings and four thousand watercolors, drawings, prints, and maps. Included in this collection is a significant collection of twenty-four works of Cornelius Kreighoff. Also included are the *Portrait of General Wolfe*, painted in the 1740s by Joseph Highmore, and the *Portrait of Captain Squire* by John Singleton Copley.

On permanent view in the north gallery are six room settings in which furniture and other examples of decorative arts are arranged to show different periods and cultural traditions. The collection of early Canadian furniture, including four outstanding labeled pieces by New Brunswick cabinetmaker Thomas Nisbet, contains a variety of very fine pieces rarely seen in other collections.

The John and Mary Yaremko Collection of Canadian and American glass (more than a thousand pieces including many outstanding and rare examples of pressed glassware) was donated to the ROM in 1981. This addition more than doubled the ROM's holdings of early Canadian glass, which included the Edith Chown Pierce-Gerald Stevens Collection and the Dominion Glass Research Foundation Collection.

John Langdon's collection of Canadian silver, donated to the museum in 1952 and 1982, and his gift in 1970 of approximately 140 wooden utensils were important additions, along with those of other donors, to the growing collections of high-quality decorative-arts items, including silver, treen, and ceramics.

The Egyptian Department holds the only comprehensive collection of Egyptian material in Canada, numbering more than twenty thousand pieces. Much of the strength of the collection can be attributed to the ROM's first director of archaeology, Charles T. Currelly. His interest in the commonplace objects used by people in their daily lives is clearly reflected in the collection. In addition, there are a variety of mummified remains of animals as well as human beings and exquisitely painted coffins of cartonnage and wood. Among the collection are a painted limestone relief of Metjetjy from Saqqara (c. 2420 B.C.), a gold-handled temple butcher knife of King Djer of the first dynasty, and a painted portrait of the goddess Hathor from the Early Middle Kingdom (c. 2024 B.C.).

The development of the collection of the Ethnology Department is due largely to the early efforts of Charles T. Currelly and T. F. McIlwraith, as well as to the contributions of Canadian missionaries. During the past two decades much of the department's primary research and field investigations have focused on Canada's native peoples, in particular, the Ojibwa and Cree of northern Ontario.

The strength of the ethnographic collection of approximately seventy thousand pieces is demonstrated in the depth and variety of materials from North and South America, Africa, and Oceania. Historic paintings by George Catlin and Paul Kane and contemporary native artworks, including the work of Ojibwa artist Norval Morriseau, are characteristic of the variety of masterpieces that distinguish the collection. Among the variety of materials representing the native

Canadian peoples are four totem poles from the North Pacific Coast, including the *Pole of the Mountain Chief*, which at eighty feet, six inches, is one of the tallest examples known. In addition to the North Pacific Coast, ceremonial and utilitarian objects from the Arctic, Plains, Subarctic, and Eastern Woodlands are also noteworthy.

The African collection is large and representative, with material from tribes such as Baga, Dogon, Bambara, Ashanti, Bakota, Yoruba, and Ekoi. There are, for example, Mende Bundu masks, an Ekoi cap mask, a Baga Nimba mask, and Chi wares from the Bambara.

Among the Oceania collection are materials from Papua New Guinea, Samoa, New Hebrides, Solomon Islands, New Zealand, and Australia. Of particular note, dating from the late nineteenth century, are two Maori ancestral panels, which, holding the spirits of dead ancestors, lined the walls of meeting houses.

The collections of the European Department, more than forty thousand pieces, consist of British and Continental European decorative arts from the Middle Ages to the present: pottery, porcelain, glass, metalwork, sculpture, prints and drawings, clocks and watches, a numismatic collection, and vertu—including icons, architectural paneling, and furniture. The ROM houses the most representative collection of British ceramics in Canada, and the collection of English medieval earthenwares is unique outside Britain. A number of pieces in the ceramics collection, which extends into the twentieth century, offer a unique opportunity to study the influence of Oriental designs. The sculpture collection includes examples in stone, bronze, wood, terracotta, and wax. The collection of portrait miniatures is also worthy of note.

The collections of Worcester, Wedgwood, and English tin glaze are particularly fine, and there are also representative pieces of Derby and Chelsea. Continental ware such as the Meissen pilgrim bottle, 1710–19, by Johann Friedrich Böttger, and other excellent collections of eighteenth- and nineteenth-century porcelain are particularly important. There is also a fine collection of characteristically colorful decorative plates from the sixteenth century, including Hispano-Moresque lusterware and true majolica, many of which were donated to the museum by Sir Edmund Osler. The collection of Italian majolica is one of the few housed in a public institution in Canada.

A student of glass will find the ROM a very rich resource. The European collection consists of Western glass from about A.D. 1500 to the present. The most notable objects among the extensive collection of arms and armor are medieval swords of Continental origin.

The silver collection, which is mostly British, is of the greatest importance in national terms. As a collection in a Canadian museum, it is unique. Most of this collection, including a small grouping representative of the Paul Storr workshop, was donated, with some particularly fine pieces coming from the estate of Gerald Larkin. The earliest silver is found in the Lee Collection, on permanent loan from the Massey Foundation. (The Lee Collection communicates the story of one family's collection and must be displayed as a unit.) The second oldest known steeple cup of 1602–3 is part of the Lee Collection, as is a German silver and parcel gilt table ornament, *Diana on the Stag*, sixteenth century, which would propel itself along a table by means of a clock-work mechanism.

Also found in the Lee Collection are excellent examples of English medieval silver and German and Spanish Renaissance silver and important examples of medieval manuscripts, including the *Giac Book of Hours* of the early fifteenth century. There are also important examples of French medieval metalwork, including a Limoges reliquary chest or chasse of the thirteenth century and an important copper-gilt and enamel pax of the fifteenth century.

The department's collection of medieval sculpture is perhaps the most important of its kind in Canada, containing examples of thirteenth-century and fourteenth-century sculpture in stone and wood, including a number of fine fourteenth-century French and Spanish Madonnas. There are important examples of Romanesque stone capitals, the important Late Gothic stone *Madonna and Child* attributed to Pietro Lamberti (Venetian, early fifteenth century), and important fifteenth- and sixteenth-century Netherlandish, French, and German wood sculptures, including the Brussels reredos of c. 1515, attributed to the atelier of Jan Borman, Jr.

The bronzes are, of their kind, unique in Canada and include statuettes attributed to Severo Calzetta da Ravenna, of the early sixteenth century; a Riccio plaquette; and later bronzes attributed to the workshop of Giovanni Bologna and to some of his northern followers. Notable among them is the bronze *Venus and Cupid* from the workshop of Hubert Gerhard, probably by one of Gerhard's Munich associates or pupils.

There are also important examples of Baroque and later sculpture, including two Neapolitan terracotta tondi of the early eighteenth century, and bronzes, terracottas, and waxes attributed to the Florentine sculptors G. B. Foggini and M. Soldani-Benzi.

The collection of icons is also worthy of mention: Greek, from the sixteenth to nineteenth century; Russian, seventeenth to nineteenth century; and Ukranian, seventeenth to nineteenth century.

The core of the ROM's large collection of European musical instruments is the R. S. Williams Collection, which includes members of the lute family, strange early horns such as the serpent, and various keyboard instruments. Among the Italian instruments are a mandora by Petrus Bulota, 1584, and a unique harpsichord by Johannes Celestini made in Venice in 1596. German instruments include a seventeenth-century trumpet marine and an eighteenth-century tenor viol by Johann Joseph Elsler. Another highlight of the collections is a French hurdy-gurdy made by Cloteaux in the eighteenth century.

Although the collection of paintings is not large, there are a few highlights worthy of note: an oil on canvas by Giovanni Domenico Ferretti of Florence; an oil on canvas, *The Allegory of Music*, attributed to Eustache LeSueur; and a rare fourteenth-century Veneto-Byzantine panel painting.

The graphics collections include drawings by Baccio Bandinelli of Florence,

François Boucher, and Nicholas Maes. There are also prints by Albrecht Dürer, Albrecht Altdorfer, G. B. Piranesi, Jacques Callot, J. Barbault, Rembrandt van Ryn, and Goltzius Hendrick, with sixteenth- and seventeenth-century woodblock playing cards and early eighteenth-century *cuir doré*, gilt and painted leather hangings, probably the only two complete works on the American continent.

The English furniture collections begin with the predominantly oak furniture of the English medieval Tudor period, progressing to about 1600 and proceeding through the "Yorkshire-Derbyshire" furniture characteristic of the early Stuart and Commonwealth, about 1600–1660, continuing with an extensive overview of the history of furniture through the Art Deco.

The Continental furniture collections begin with a few Renaissance pieces, about 1420–1540, and proceed through Mannerism, about 1540–1620; the French, German, and Central European Baroque, about 1620–1730; French Louis XV material, about 1730–70; Louis XVI and Empire; German Biedermeier, French Louis-Philippe, and Second Empire; and Jugendstil and Continental twentieth century.

Early in 1984 the museum purchased five pieces of furniture of outstanding historic and artistic merit for the European department. The furniture, designed by the Scottish architect and designer Charles Rennie Mackintosh, consists of a white painted cabinet made in Glasgow in 1902 and components of a bedroom suite of 1904 consisting of a bed, chest of drawers, wash stand, and mirror. They are among the most important items of furniture ever purchased by the ROM. Their acquisition was made possible by a contribution from the government of Canada under the terms of its Cultural Property Export and Import Act.

The Chinese art and archaeological collections of the ROM's Far Eastern Department, more than fifty thousand pieces, have won international renown. The ROM holds one of the ten best collections, outside of China, of Bronze Age material (c. fifteenth to fifth century B.C.) and the world's largest collection, outside of China, of pottery tomb figurines from the Han to T'ang dynasties (second century B.C. to eighth century A.D.). It is also rich in the Buddhist arts of Asia, especially sculpture and Chinese temple wall paintings.

William Charles White, Canada's first Anglican bishop of Honan Province, and James M. Menzies were mainly responsible for the formation of the ROM's large and diverse collection of Bronze Age material from China.

Bronze vessels are perhaps the most central pieces in the collection and range from ritual vessels of the Shang Dynasty (c. 1600–1028 B.C.) to more secular vessels inlaid with silver and gold dating from the fifth to the third century B.C. In addition to vessels, there are bronze ceremonial and utilitarian weapons, horse and chariot fittings, tools, bells, belt-hooks, and mirrors.

Jade, carved bone, and stone are also well represented in the Chinese Bronze Age collection. Of unique significance are the ROM's oracle bones, one of the largest collections outside China. The inscriptions on the bones are evidence of the earliest Chinese written language and provide invaluable information about Shang Dynasty life.

The ROM collection of jades numbers more than one thousand pieces of widest range and variety: *pi* disks, *tsung* prisms, and other ritual pieces; axes, halberd blades and other weapons; tools; and personal ornament. There are also numerous vessels and sculptures. Best known, perhaps, are the Eastern Chou jades of the fifth to third century B.C. The first pieces of Chinese jade came into the Royal Ontario Museum about 1910 through the generosity of Mrs. H. D. Warren and Sir Robert Mond and later through the collecting activities of George Crofts, Bishop White, and James Menzies.

The ROM has a collection of tomb figurines and models unrivaled in the Western world. These figurines and models date from the Han Dynasty (206 B.C.-A.D. 220) to the Ming Dynasty (A.D. 1368–1644). The most spectacular piece from the Han Dynasty is a marvelous ceramic watchtower four feet in height. The museum has several complete "processions" of figurines as they would have appeared in the tombs; for example, those from the Northern Wei Dynasty (A.D. 386–534), which involve numerous mourners, attendants, animals, and spirit figures. There are also several of such groupings from the T'ang Dynasty (A.D. 618–907) and the Ming Dynasty (A.D. 1368–1514).

The museum also boasts very complete collections of other ceramic types. Chinese ceramic history is well illustrated by vessels from all of the historical periods, and many of them, especially from the T'ang and Sung (A.D. 960–1279) dynasties, are of the highest quality. In addition to housing vessels, the ROM owns a large number of Ming Dynasty temple figures and roof and temple ornaments. A number of them are dated by inscription. Significant for having encouraged George Crofts, Tientsin fur merchant, collector, and connoisseur, to become a buyer for the museum is an over life-size ceramic seated Lohan of the Liao Dynasty (A.D. 936–1125).

Most of the stone sculpture in the Chinese collections shows the influence of Buddhism in China. Noteworthy are a marble Buddha of about A.D. 577 and other Northern Ch'i marbles and a marble work nearly life-size. T'ang Dynasty non-Buddhist stones include the monumental tomb stones of about seventeenth-century date.

The ROM collection also includes three great Chinese wall paintings (c. A.D. 1300), considered among the finest in the Western world. The largest, *Maitreya Paradise* (nineteen by thirty-three feet), was completed about A.D. 1300 in the Hsing-hua Monastery, Shansi Province, and came to the ROM in 1928. It depicts Maitreya or the Future Buddha, accompanied by disciples and celestial attendants. The two slightly smaller Taoist paintings (each ten by thirty-four feet) also come from Shansi Province in northern China and were purchased in 1937. They depict groupings of Daoist deities proceeding through an ethereal world and are estimated to have been executed about A.D. 1325. Both paintings have recently undergone intensive conservation treatment. Among the few Chinese scroll paintings in the collection is a T'ang Yin work, *Scholar in a Summer Landscape*, that is worthy of note.

A museumwide specialization in textiles is well reflected in the Far Eastern collections. Ch'ing Dynasty samples are particularly well represented, including more than a hundred imperial robes. Ming examples include a famous imperial yellow velvet panel with embroidered borders, measuring ten by nine feet. Even Chinese architecture is displayed at the museum, in the form of a Ming tomb and "spirit way."

Although the glory of the Far Eastern Department is the Chinese collection, other Oriental traditions are also represented. From Japan, there is the notable *Taima Mandala* of the Kamakura period (A.D. 1185–1336). This paradise scene, on a rich hanging scroll in colors of gold *kirikane* on silk, is an exceptionally well-preserved example, probably dating from the second half of the thirteenth century. A representative group of more than two thousand eighteenth- and nineteenth-century color woodblock prints are mostly from the Sir Edmund Walker Collection, with additional gifts from J. Clarence Webster. The Sir William Van Horne Collection of Japanese ceramics includes many tea wares. Although the Van Horne Collection is primarily nineteenth century, the ROM has acquired a number of earlier pieces through purchase or donation in recent decades. There is a fairly representative collection of metalwork, particularly sword fittings, and the H. and M. Gustin Collection of Japanese lacquers on loan from the Ontario Heritage Foundation is also of interest. A collection of *kasuri* (ikat) woven textiles and other folk-art textiles is perhaps the most important of its type outside Japan.

In its collection of other Asian art, the ROM boasts a notable collection of Gandhāra stone sculptures and reliefs of the Kushän date, that is, first to fifth century. Indian art is also represented in the form of traditional Hindu arts, notably sculpture.

The ROM has the largest and most representative collection of Greek and Roman material in Canada. Among the approximately fourteen thousand pieces in the collection, apart from about forty-two thousand coins, is an extensive collection of Greek painted pottery. A few of the outstanding pieces in this collection are a krater of the Geometric period depicting a war galley with its crew of (rowers, c. 710;) two Panathenaic amphorae with athletic scenes of the late sixth century; and a Mycenaean alabastron with eight-shaped shield (decoration, c. 1450). The pottery holdings also include Etruscan and Roman ceramics.

A large group of Cypriot artifacts, including a considerable number of Archaic votive sculptures and pottery of all periods, is another strength of the collection. Glass vessels, gold jewelry, and terracotta figurines represent the so-called minor arts, Greek, Roman, and Etruscan.

The fourth-century B.C. Attic tomb relief of Iostrate with her servant girl is a highlight of the collection of sculpture. Other sculpture includes some excellent Roman copies and adaptations of well-known Greek works, for example, an athlete in the style of Doryphorus by Polyclitus. In bronze, a fine Early Classical figurine of Aphrodite (470–460 B.C.) serves as a support in a caryatid mirror. The Roman portrait sculpture is represented by a series of marble busts from the first to the third century A.D., as well as a number of impressive painted mummy portraits from Roman Egypt, about second century A.D. The material from the province of Roman Britain is unique in North America. A major coin collection features the famous silver dekadrachm of Syracuse of the early fourth century B.C. The Greek and Roman Department has participated in the excavations in Crete, England, Tunisia, Italy, and Turkey.

The collections of the New World Archaeology Department include archaeological material from North America, including all major regions of Canada, and from South and Central America. More than 110,000 pieces have been collected for more than a century. From Latin America there are good Mexican collections of every period, including material rarely seen outside of Mexico. These collections are complemented by important Maya material from the ROM's excavations in Belize. The collections from Peru and Ecuador are smaller but also noteworthy. There is also an interesting collection of material from the United States, including the Southwest and Mississippi Valley cultures.The two areas of greatest interest in this department are the exquisite Maya art and architecture created six hundred years ago in Central America and the flint tools made in southern Ontario ten thousand to twelve thousand years ago.

The ROM textile collection of more than forty thousand pieces is one of the most important in North America. It is international in scope, both fine art and ethnographic, and covers a span of approximately sixteen centuries. As might be expected, the collection of Canadian textiles is large and representative, particularly in illustrating the record of early handweaving. The collection of Canadian quilts is equally well balanced, reflecting the different Canadian types and designs.

Printed textiles, including French Jouy and Nantes woodblock prints (eighteenth and nineteenth centuries), are one of the strongest elements in the whole collection, a gift from Mrs. Harry Wearne. Also part of the Harry Wearne Collection is a group of outstanding painted and dyed Indian cottons made for the European trade in the eighteenth century.

The embroidery collection includes a large number of examples from England, Continental Europe, Turkey, Greece, Hungary, and the Far East. A good study collection of lace (Italian, French, Belgian, Irish, and other European) dates from the sixteenth to the twentieth century.

The Far Eastern collection is composed of material from China, Formosa, Japan, Korea, India, Tibet, Bhutan, Burma, Central Asia, and several regions of Southeast Asia. This collection includes an exceptional array of court robes and informal costumes from China. Among them is a notable example of a seventeenth-century dragon robe, as well as several eighteenth- and nineteenth-century twelve-symbol dragon robes. The textiles from Southeast Asia acquired through Canadian missionaries include superb ikats and batiks from Sumatra and Java.

There are also smaller but nevertheless important collections from Central and

South America, Africa, and the South Pacific, as well as a fair representation of American Indian costume from the Plains, Woodlands, and North Pacific Coast.

The collection of the West Asian Department ranges from Bronze Age flint and stone artifacts to Islamic glass and metalwork. Its geographic scope includes the eastern Mediterranean, Mesopotamia, and Iran in ancient times and, for the Islamic period, extends from Spain to Indonesia, that is, all lands touched by the expansion of Islam. Within this broad sweep of responsibility, the department's area of particular expertise is the Iranian world. Many of the artifacts in the collection come from ROM excavations in locations such as Godin Tepe, Seh Gabi, and Mahidasht in Iran and in Jerusalem and Jericho.

Included in the collection of approximately eighteen thousand pieces is one of the neolithic plastered skulls from Jericho. Among a small group of Assyrian royal ivories, one finds the *Winged Male and Papyrus Flowers* inlaid with green paste and lapis lazuli (c. ninth to seventh century B.C.). Of special interest is the large Neo-Babylonian glazed tile *Lion Relief* (c. 600 B.C.) from the Throne Room of the palace of Nebuchadnezzar II. The Islamic collection of pottery, glass, metal ware, and miniature paintings is small but representative.

The main ROM library contains more than seventy thousand books, including copies of all scholarly and popular ROM publications. Its cataloguing and search procedures began to be computerized in the late 1970s. The Far Eastern Library houses twenty thousand volumes and ranks among the leading Far Eastern and archaeology library collections in the world. Both facilities are open to the public on a noncirculating basis.

Reproductions are available in the gift shops. Amateur photography is permitted, but permission for commercial photography or use of special equipment must be requested. The museum has a very active publishing program and publishes an annual report, a quarterly magazine (*Rotunda*), and a catalogue of current publications in print.

Selected Bibliography

Museum publications: Allodi, Mary, *Canadian Watercolours and Drawings in the Royal Ontario Museum*, 2 vols., 1974; Beech, Milo C., *Reflections of India: Paintings from the 16th to the 19th Century*, 1979; Brett, K. B., *English Embroidery—16th to 18th Century*, 1972; Burnham, Dorothy K., *Warp and Weft: A Textile Terminology*, 1980; Burnham, H. B., *Chinese Velvets*, 1959; Chin-hsing, Hsu, *The Menzies Collection of Shang Dynasty Oracle Bones, Vol. I: A Catalogue*, 1972, *Vol. II: The Text*, 1977; idem, *Oracle Bones from the White and Other Collections*, 1979; Cselenyi, L., *Musical Instruments in the Royal Ontario Museum*, 1971; Currelly, C. T., *I Brought the Ages Home*, 1956; Dohrenwend, D., *Chinese Jades in the Royal Ontario Museum*, 1971; Gervers, Veronika, *Studies in Textile History: In Memory of Harold B. Burnham*, 1977; Hayes, J. W., *Roman and Pre-Roman Glass in the Royal Ontario Museum: A Catalogue*, 1975; idem, *Roman Pottery in the Royal Ontario Museum: A Catalogue*, 1976; idem, *Ancient Lamps in the Royal Ontario Museum I: Greek and Roman Clay Lamps*, 1980; idem, *Greek, Roman, and Related Metalware in the Royal Ontario Museum*, 1983; idem, *Greek* and Roman *Black-Gloss Wares and Related Wares in the Royal Ontario Museum*, 1984; Heinrich, T. A., *Art Treasures in the Royal Ontario Museum*, 1963; Hickl-Szabo, H., *Portrait Miniatures in the Royal Ontario Museum*, 1980; Kaellgren, C. Peter, *A Gather of Glass: Glass through the Ages in the Royal Ontario Museum*, 1977; Keeble, K. Corey, *European Bronzes in the Royal Ontario Museum*, 1982; Kenyon, W. A., *The Grimsby Site: A Historic Neutral Cemetery*, 1982; Leipen, N., *Athena Parthenos: A Reconstruction*, 1971; Levine, L. D., ed., *Man in Nature*, 1975; Mino, Y., *Pre-Sung Dynasty Chinese Stonewares in the Royal Ontario Museum*, 1974; Molyneaux, Brian, *The Study of the Prehistoric Sacred Places Evidence from Lower Manitou Lake*, 1983; Needler, W., *Jewellery of the Ancient Near East*, 1966; Pendergast, David M., *Excavations at Altun Ha, Belize, 1964–1970*, Vol. 1, 1979, Vol. 2, 1982; Rogers, E.S., *Forgotten Peoples: A Reference*, 1969; idem, *Big Man Island*, 1970; Staff of the Far Eastern Department, *Chinese Art in the Royal Ontario Museum*, 1972; Storck, Peter L., *Ontario Prehistory*, 1981; Taylor, J. Garth, *The Canadian Eskimos*, 1971; Vollmer, John E., *In the Presence of the Dragon Throne*, 1977; Vollmer, John E., E. J. Keall, and E. Nagai-Berthrong, *Silk Roads—China Ships*, 1983; Waterhouse, D., *Images of Eighteenth-Century Japan: Ukiyoe Prints from the Sir Edmund Walker Collection*, 1975; Webster, D. B., *Canadian Georgian Furniture*, 1981; White, W. C., *Chinese Temple Frescoes*, 1940; Young, T. C., Jr., *Excavations at Godin Tepe: First Progress Report*, 1969; Young, T. C., Jr., and L. D. Levine, *Excavations of the Godin Project: Second Progress Report*, 1974. See also *Rotunda*, a quarterly publication, and *Publications in Print*, an annual publication.

Other publications: Brett, K. B., and John Irwind, *Origins of Chintz* (London 1970); Burnham, H. B., and Dorothy K. Burnham, *Keep Me Warm One Night* (Toronto 1972); Leipen, N., *The Locke Collection of Cypriot Antiquities* (Toronto 1966); Roger, E. S., *The Roundlake Ojibwa* (Toronto 1971); Spendlove, F. St. George, *The Face of Early Canada* (Toronto 1971); Webster, D. B., ed., *Book of Canadian Antiques* (Toronto 1974); White, W. C., *Chinese Jews* (Toronto 1966).

DAVID A. YOUNG

China, People's Republic of

———— Beijing (Peking) ————

MUSEUM OF CHINESE HISTORY (officially ZHONGGUO LISHI BO-WUGUAN [CHUNG-KUO LI-SHIH PO-WU-KUAN]; alternately CHINESE HISTORY MUSEUM, CHINESE HISTORICAL MUSEUM, THE HISTORI-CAL MUSEUM), Tiananmen Square, Beijing.

Located on the east side of T'ian-an Men Square and opposite the Great Hall of the People, the Museum of Chinese History was constructed under government auspices in 1958–59 as part of the expansion and reorganization of T'ien-an Men Square. The building, of gigantic scale (almost one-quarter of a mile long) and massive proportions, reveals Chinese appropriation of the Soviet monolithic architectural style. The right wing houses the Museum of Chinese History; the left wing has the Revolutionary Museum. It was officially opened in 1960 with some eight thousand items in the collection. The extensive archaeological excavation programs undertaken by the Chinese since 1948, as well as the assiduous gathering of memorabilia, continue to amplify the holdings. The museum was closed during the Great Proletarian Cultural Revolution (1966–69) and did not reopen until 1976.

In the Museum of Chinese History, exhibits are arranged chronologically and are divided into four parts corresponding to the Marxist-Leninist interpretation of history and the development of society: Primitive Society, Slave Society, Feudal Society, and Semi-Colonial–Semi-Feudal Society. Since the goals of the museum are not only to demonstrate historical and technological developments but to indicate the contributions of national minority groups as well as cultural contacts with other countries, displays of artifacts and relics are accompanied by individual labels, large information panels (explicating technological or social implications of objects or cultures rather than their artistic import), charts, and maps. In addition, exhibits are further enhanced by photographs and even by modern visualizations of important historical persons or events rendered in sculpture or in painting. Models of machinery and reproductions of unique archaeological finds are also used; the former have sometimes been fabricated on the basis of later textual descriptions (not actual examples found through excavation); for the latter, labels may or may not indicate that the object on display is a reproduction.

The strength of the museum lies in arts and crafts derived from archaeological excavations. From the Paleolithic and Mesolithic periods (500,000–10,000 B.C.) are human and animal bones and remains (teeth, horns, and so on), tools, bone, and shell artifacts. A rich collection of neolithic (10,000–4000 B.C.) stone tools and pottery, and other artifacts, comes from Szechwan, Kiangsu, and Chekiang. Relics of the Yang-shao painted pottery culture are exemplified by agricultural, hunting, and fishing implements of stone and bone; the domestic crafts of this culture, by spinning and weaving accessories, as well as by examples of painted pottery from Pan-p'o in Shensi and related sites in Shansi. The Lung-shan black-pottery culture is represented by the lustrous black wares from Shantung and Chekiang, as well as by grey pottery cooking vessels. There is a display of marks on pottery from Ta-wen-k'ou in Shantung and Miao-ti-k'ou in Honan, which are supposed precursors of Chinese script forms.

Superb bronze vessels highlight the Shang Dynasty (sixteenth to eleventh century B.C.) collection: the Ssu Mu Wu rectangular *ting* (the largest extant bronze vessel, 4 feet high, 875 kilograms), excavated at An-yang in 1939, and a unique square *tsun* vessel composed of four adorsed rams, found in 1938 in Ning-hsiang, Hunan. The collection is enriched by more recent bronze finds from Honan (Cheng-chou and An-yang) and Anhwei. Other Shang materials include clay molds for bronze casting, bronze implements, and bells. Along with pottery vessels are shown the tools to make pottery, clay figures of fish and tortoise, and a clay whistle. There are personal adornments and implements of carved bone and jade, as well as examples of oracle bones and shells. An unusual Shang artifact is the lithophone engraved with a tiger, found in the 1950 excavation at An-yang. It should be noted that included in the Shang exhibits are replicas of stone sculpture now in Taiwan (ox-head, kneeling tiger, owl).

The museum holds a number of Western Chou (eleventh to seventh century B.C.) bronze vessels in various styles, often with lengthy inscriptions recording military victories and other achievements. Outstanding is the *yu* vessel from a hoard of sixteen bronze vessels found in 1955 at Ma-ch'ang-kou, Liaoning, decorated with a rare ornament of a dragon-bird and with an inscription verifying the enfeoffment of the marquis of Yen. Among the Western Chou jades is an unusual eight-inch long curved pendant composed of seven parts held together by a wood-wrapped bronze strip and covered with a surface ornament of carved spirals (from Hui-hsien, Honan, discovered in 1950).

Examples of art from the Warring States and Ch'in periods (475–206 B.C.) include fragments of fabrics and silk from Hunan, painted lacquers from Ch'angsha, Hunan (those exhibited as being from Ma-wang-tui appear to be reproductions), lacquer vessels and stands, as well as bronze bells, from Hsin-yang, Honan. Coins include round, spade, knife, and "ant-nose" types. Further examples of the arts of this period include iron and bronze implements, carved and ornamented jades, and bronze mirrors. Particularly important are the intricately patterned bronzes from the grave of the marquis of Ts'ai in Anhwei and a fourth-century B.C. square bronze vessel ornamented with horizontal and diagonal grid patterns and inlaid with malachite and copper, excavated in Shanhsien, Honan, in 1957. Recent additions to the collection are a few of the more than two hundred life-size clay soldiers and horses from the mausoleum of the first emperor of Ch'in, excavated during 1976–77.

For the Han and Three Kingdoms period (206 B.C.-A.D. 265), the collection has weights, measures, coins, iron implements, and tomb furnishings (such as clay-house models from Canton, jewelry from Canton and Hunan, and bronze mirrors). Clay tiles from Szechwan graves depict genre scenes of salt mining, agriculture, and entertainment. Other burial goods, in abundance, include clay models of houses, animals, vehicles, dancers, and musicians from Szechwan, Hopei, and elsewhere. Along with Han weaponry (crossbows, traps) are bronze mirrors and coins. Some of the finds from the eclectic border culture at Shih-chai Shan in Yünnan include bronze drums with sculptured figural panoramas on the top and lance heads of bronze with two dangling prisoners. The collection is rounded out with examples of pottery and bronzes from the South and Southeast areas of the continent (Fukien, Kwangtung) and from the far West (Sinkiang).

Some of the finest examples of arts during the Northern and Southern dynasties period (265–589) are the clay bricks with line relief depictions of soldiers, processions, or birds from a tomb at Teng-hsien in Honan. Tomb figures of warriors and horsemen come from a Western Chin site, and there are other figures from the Sian and T'ai-yüan areas. Examples of excavated pottery of this era are instrumental in tracing the development of ceramic art.

Crafts from the Sui and T'ang periods (590–906) focus heavily upon the colorful painted or glazed clay tomb figures of camels, horses, foreign grooms, and merchants and court ladies from the Sian area. From the Sui tomb of Li Ching-hsün, excavated in 1957, is a gold necklace inlaid with pearls and jewels, a green glass bottle, a gold stem cup, and a white jade cup with a gold rim. A Sui gilt-bronze Amitabha altar in twenty-three parts is remarkable not only for its complexity and perfection of workmanship, but also because it is signed by the maker, Tung Ch'in, a rare occurrence in Chinese sculpture. One of the best known of recent finds of the T'ang period is the glazed clay tomb figure of a camel carrying a troupe of musicians (from the tomb of Hsiang-yu Ting-hui, 723). T'ang gold and silver-gilt vessels from a hoard discovered in Sian, including silver platters with low-relief, gilt animals in the center, are especially important for the history of Chinese metalwork. Also noteworthy is a round nickel mirror inlaid with mother-of-pearl figures and flowers found in Lo-yang. A rare example of secular stone sculpture is the marble figure of a warrior found in 1958 in a tomb near Sian.

Major examples of later art include pottery from Ta-t'ung in Shansi and objects from a tenth-century Liao tomb in Inner Mongolia discovered in 1954: silks, silverware, and white ceramics.

The galleries devoted to succeeding periods tend to be filled with memorabilia and are of lesser artistic interest.

Selected Bibliography

Museum of Chinese History, Explanatory Notes to Chinese History Exhibition, Peking, 1976.

ELLEN JOHNSTON LAING

PALACE MUSEUM (officially GU GONG BOWUYUAN [KU-KUNG PO-WU-YÜAN]), Beijing.

After the overthrow of the Manchu Ch'ing Dynasty in 1911, the new Nationalist government of the Republic of China assumed responsibility for the Imperial Palace in Peking. In October 1914, under the Ministry of the Interior of the Peking government, the three large ceremonial halls at the front of the palace were closed off from the Inner Palace; they and two halls to the southwest and southeast (the Wu-ying Tien and the Wen-hua Tien) became the "Antiquities Exhibition Center." There were displayed art objects from the Ch'ing hunting lodge in Manchuria, the former Imperial Palace in Shen-yang, and the former Summer Palace at Jehol. In July 1918, the National History Museum (established in 1912 by the Ministry of Education and previously housed in the former Imperial College) was relocated inside the Imperial City in ten large halls between the Tuan-men and the Wu-men (just south of the Imperial Palace proper).

The deposed Emperor P'u-i and his retinue continued to reside in the Inner Palace until November 5, 1924, when they were forced to leave the premises. The government then created the Commission for the Custody of Manchu Household Property, consisting of fifteen members. All important buildings of the palace were sealed, and a full inventory and photographing of the contents was undertaken. The Palace Museum was formally inaugurated on October 10, 1925; it had two departments: Museum and Library. At this time, it was governed by a board of directors assisted by an administrative council of nine members, with the directors and associate directors of the museum and the library as members ex-officio. The museum was open three days a week; because of its vast size, the precinct was divided into three exhibition routes, each one open one day in rotation. In March 1926 political instability forced the museum to suspend operations briefly. In August a new commission was appointed with a view to reorganizing the museum; there was strong opposition to this commission, however, because of its monarchist membership, and it never assumed office.

In December 1926 the nonpartisan Society for Maintenance of the Palace

Museum was established. It consisted of sixty members, among whom the president and two vice-presidents were elected by public vote; the society was headed by an executive council. By 1931 the museum was under the supervision of a commission appointed by the government and composed of five departments: Secretariat, General Administration, Library, Antiquities, and Archives. Its holdings included some 120,000 volumes of rare books, more than 8,000 paintings and calligraphy, more than 6,000 porcelains from Sung to Ch'ing in date, and some 10,000 carved jade and hardstones. The museum was open six days a week, two days being allotted to each of the three sections. A branch of the Palace Museum was established in Nanking in January 1937. After 1945 the museum organization was again revised, and the name changed to The National Peiping Palace Museum. It took over the objects and buildings of the "Antiquities Exhibition Center," and its administration expanded to incorporate other areas of the Imperial City, as well as the former Imperial College and the former Imperial Summer Palace (I-ho Yüan).

When, in 1948, the Nationalist government moved to Taiwan, part of the collection was transferred to the island and is now in the National Palace Museum (q.v.) in Taipei. Now the administration of the museum is guided by one director and several assistant directors. The director is in charge of all affairs relating to the museum. Each assistant director is responsible for the overall affairs of his assigned department and for the construction and renovation of buildings within the museum complex, hiring of personnel, buying of artifacts, and the distribution of funds, which come entirely from the government, to different departments.

There are six major departments at the Palace Museum, each headed by a curator who reports directly to the corresponding assistant director. The restoration department does all restoration work for cultural relics, which include bronzes, ceramics, calligraphy, and paintings. This is also the department where exquisite copies of bronzes, calligraphy, and paintings are made. The research department carries the responsibility of conducting research on architecture, palatial building, calligraphy, paintings, and craft, which include the treatment of lacquer ware. Storage is an important department that provides satisfactory conditions for the artifacts that are not on display. Only personnel working for the storage department have access to the storage area. The exhibition department organizes both the travel exhibitions and the different exhibitions held inside the museum throughout the year. The public service department is of an educational nature. Personnel are trained to lead tour groups visiting the museum. The final department is the library, which keeps all documents concerning the Palace Museum and is closed to the public.

The buildings of the palace, having been the residence of Chinese emperors since 1420, are of great historical and architectural significance. Other imperial palaces in Jehol and Shen-yang (formerly Mukden) are extant, but the palace in Peking is the largest, the oldest, and in the best state of preservation. Construction was carried out between 1406 and 1420 under the Ming emperor Yung-lo. Surrounded by a wall roughly 10 meters high and a moat 52 meters wide, the palace covers 720,000 square meters. Aligned on a north-south axis, it is divided into two main parts: the exterior section of ceremonial halls and the interior portion consisting of living quarters, palaces, gardens, theaters, temples, and service areas. The complex is important for its traditional Chinese architectural preferences (formal north-south alignment of a series of courtyards, gates, and reception halls, with side living areas), for its constructional features (stone platforms, columns topped by intricate bracket systems that support tiled roofs), for its use of bright colors (red columns, white marble balustrades, yellow roof tiles, polychromed beams and brackets), and for its informal gardens. The palace suffered some damage in the seventeenth century when the Ming Dynasty fell to the Manchu Ch'ing conquerors, necessitating reconstruction of damaged buildings. Because of subsequent rebuilding after fires, general renovations, as well as additions, many of the present structures are eighteenth century. Throughout the early years of the twentieth century, the palace was allowed to deteriorate. Between 1927 and 1931, however, many donors, both Chinese and foreign, contributed funds to support museum publications, or to construct storage areas, or to repair various halls or palace structures, or to convert halls into exhibition spaces. These donors included: The China Foundation for the Promotion of Education and Culture, the Sino-French Indemnity Board, General Chiang Kai-shek, the Board of Directors of the Central Park, Peking, Chow Tso-min, Nyi Yu-tan, John D. Rockefeller, Jr., Sir Percival David, the Kailan Mining Administration (Tientsin), Joy Morton, General and Mrs. William Crozier, Robert Allerton, and Sir Miles W. Lampson. A comprehensive restoration program, which continues to the present, was initiated after 1948. Most of the major buildings and many of the lesser ones have been returned to their eighteenth-century appearance (some walls and canopies added to the Imperial Garden in the late Ch'ing period have been removed).

The three ceremonial halls of the outer section of the palace are placed on a single twenty-five-foot-high, three-level marble terrace shaped like the letter I. The rectangular first hall, the T'ai-ho Tien, is the largest and most resplendent of the three: 87 feet high, 210 feet long, and 115 feet wide. On the inside, bright-red lacquer columns support the ceiling; six columns in the center are carved with dragons and gilded. The gilt, carved-wood imperial throne is on a platform six feet high, with a set of four cloisonné incense burners ranged along the front and a gilt, carved multipaneled screen behind the throne. A sculpture of a crane stands on either side of the throne. Beams, ceiling, and bracket supports are all ornamented with gold dragons, colored clouds, and stylized floral patterns. The second hall, the Chung-ho Tien, square in plan, is much smaller than the T'ai-ho Tien, and it has a small throne in the center. The third hall, the Pao-ho Tien, again rectangular and relatively large in size, similarly has a throne in the center, but the remaining space is now sometimes used for special exhibitions. In the western sector of the Inner Palace, private apartments of the emperor Ch'ien-lung (reigned 1736–96) and Empress Dowager Tz'u-hsi (d. 1908) have been refurbished to their former grandeur. These ''period rooms'' clearly reveal the differences between eighteenth- and nineteenth-century imperial taste. The western sector also houses the exhibitions of jade, lacquer, cloisonné, carved wood, and bamboo. In the eastern sector are the exhibition areas for sculpture, painting and calligraphy, bronze, ceramics, textiles, and jeweled treasures.

The growth of the collections until 1911 can best be described as the successive accumulation of applied and decorative arts requisite for household, personal, ceremonial, and religious use of the imperial family, as well as for interior decoration and bibelot: thrones and other furniture, robes and jewels, porcelain dinner and serving ware, religious images and ritual objects, desk paraphernalia, woven tapestries and embroidered wall hangings, rugs, carved jades and other hardstones, lacquer boxes and dishes, carved ivory, cloisonné, fans, snuff bottles, and the like. On the other hand, some groups of items are the result of deliberate collection; this is true of the paintings and calligraphy (some of which were in the Southern Sung and the Yüan dynasties' imperial collections), bronzes, and ceramics. The Ch'ing emperor Ch'ien-lung, in particular, was an avid art collector who made numerous additions to the collections, and, as an art enthusiast, he surrounded himself with carved jades, painted and carved lacquers, and so on, the finest of which were produced in the imperial factories and workshops. Although Ch'ien-lung did have a list of his painting and calligraphy collection compiled in the late eighteenth century, there apparently was no official palace inventory, and so there is no way of knowing how many objects were in the imperial household. Due to imperial prerogative, the "collection" was fluid: numerous art gifts were sent to the emperors by bureaucrats and others; in turn, emperors made presents of art objects to deserving officials or to honor other individuals. The looting and destruction of the Yüan-ming Yüan Summer Palace by Anglo-French troops in 1860 made a small dent in the decorative-arts holdings, as did the theft of objects from the Imperial Palace in Peking by Westerners after the Boxer Rebellion in 1900.

After 1911 P'u-i made serious inroads into the collections, especially that of painting and calligraphy. It is believed he gave away more than one thousand pieces of painting and writing to his brother and to others. He kept several lists of these gifts, which included other antiquities and valuables; these lists were published in 1926 as *The Catalogue of Lost Books, Calligraphy, and Painting in the Palace Collection*. Antiquities, paintings, porcelains, gold and silver objects, were also sold by P'u-i's Household Department to help meet his living expenses or were presented to outsiders as rewards for loyal support. It is suspected that a mysterious fire that destroyed the Chien-fu Hall in 1923 was deliberately set to account for the disappearance of art objects. When P'u-i left the palace in 1924, he took an unknown number of art works with him, some of which were later sold. From 1934 until 1945 P'u-i was puppet emperor of Manchuko (Manchuria) under Japanese occupation. After his capture by the Russians in 1945, he presented some treasures to the Soviet Union (they were eventually returned to China) but still possessed at least one set of Ch'ien-lung carved seals, along with gold and jewels, which, after his repatriation and imprisonment near Peking, he turned over to Chinese authorities in 1950.

Because of Japanese military encroachment into China in early 1931, 63,735 art objects from the palace were moved by the Nationalist government to Shanghai and eventually to Nanking, where the Nanking Branch of the Peiping Palace Museum was established. Between 1934 and 1936, more than eight hundred items were removed from the palace collection as a result of confiscation during legal proceedings investigating claims of malfeasance against a museum administrator.

During the Sino-Japanese conflict of 1937–45, the objects in Nanking, as well as some thirteen thousand crates of art from Peking, were stored in various locations in the provinces of Szechwan and Kweichow. At the conclusion of hostilities in 1945, these objects were returned to Nanking and Peking. In Peking, the museum, upon absorbing the Antiquities Exhibition, the former Imperial College, and the former Imperial Summer Palace (I-ho Yüan), augmented the collection by 354,057 items. On January 22, 1946, Werner Jannings donated his collection of early bronze vessels and more than one hundred Shang and Chou bronze weapons to the Palace Museum; about the same time, the Palace Museum received Kuo Pao-chang's collection of porcelains. In 1948 the Nationalist government of the Republic of China took 231,910 art objects, books, and documents with it to Taiwan, where they now form the nucleus of the National Palace Museum in Taipei.

Since 1949, under the Communist government of the People's Republic of China, the Palace Museum in Peking has tremendously increased its holdings through donations and archaeological excavations; in addition, efforts were made to purchase important Chinese paintings that had left the country. Other areas of the collection that were expanded include those of gems and jewelry, court robes, calligraphy and inscriptions, and weapons and arms. Published statistics give 2 million items on exhibition in 1959. The total number of holdings is unknown. In view of this staggering figure, any survey of the Palace Museum collections can only be tentative; even generalizing about it is difficult and may be misleading.

In the major exhibition areas, a separate, secondary palace (or part thereof) is devoted to works done in a particular medium or works that fall into a general classification of the decorative arts. Once there was a sculpture hall displaying religious images, some of huge size, but this apparently has been closed to the public, at least since the Great Proletarian Cultural Revolution (1966–69).

A recent report is that the number of scroll paintings owned by the Palace Museum runs into the tens of thousands. Of them, only 175 or so are on exhibition at any one time. For reasons of conservation, the finest and oldest works are shown during the autumn, since the weather then is clear and dry, and the Palace Museum has no devices to control humidity or temperature in the exhibition cases or in the galleries.

The works considered pre-T'ang are Ku K'ai-chih's *Virtuous Women* and *Nymph of the Lo River* (of which two other versions exist in the Liao-ning Provincial Museum (q.v.) in Shenyang and in the Freer Gallery of Art (q.v.) in Washington, D.C.) and a landscape, *Traveling in Spring*, attributed to Chan Tzu-ch'ien (a post–1948 purchase). Major T'ang Dynasty (618–906) attributions include *Emperor T'ai-tsung Greeting Tibetan Envoys* (Yen Li-pen), *Six Arhats and Attendants* (Lu Leng-chia), *Four Scholars in a Landscape*, and a rare example of T'ang animal paintings, *Five Oxen*, both attributed to Han Huang. Paintings of the Five Dynasties period (906–60) are highlighted by a post–1948 purchase, *Han Hsi-ts'ai's Night Revels*, a superlative figure painting given to Ku Hung-chung, Huang Ch'üan's *Bird and Insect Sketches*, and Tung Yüan's *Hsiao and Hsiang River* handscroll. Among many Sung Dynasty (960–1280) works are two outstanding representatives of the blue and green landscape style: Chao Po-chü's *Autumn Mountains* and Wang Hsi-meng's *One Thousand Miles of Rivers and Mountains*. Li Kung-lin's *Pasturing Horses* is undoubtedly one of the best and most reliable of works attributed to him, and the *Spring Festival on the River*, attributed to Chang Tse-tuan, is unparalleled in descriptive and narrative scenes. The Southern Sung academic landscape is seen in several examples by or attributed to Ma Yüan, Ma Lin, Hsia Kuei, and Liu Sung-nien. The best of bird, flower, and animal depictions of the period are found in Li Ti's *Hawk Chasing a Pheasant* (1196), in *Two Chicks* and *Dog* (both dated 1197), and in the exquisite, anonymous *One Hundred Flowers* done in monochrome ink, as is Yang Pu-chih's *Four Stages of Blossoming Plum* (1165). The varied stylistic approaches to figure painting are exemplified by Li T'ang's *Po I and Shu Ch'i Gathering Herbs*, Li Sung's *Knick-knack Peddler* handscroll (1211), and his *Skeleton Puppet Master*, along with Ma Ho-chih's *Illustrations to the Odes of Pin*.

The conservative or archaistic trend of Yüan Dynasty (1280–1368) painting is represented by several works in the style of Kuo Hsi, a fine blue and green landscape by Ch'ien Hsüan, and an excellent series of horse or horse and groom depictions by Chao Meng-fu, Chao Yung, Jen Jen-fa, and the little-known Jen Tzu-chao. Major landscapes by the Great Masters of the Yüan include Chao Meng-fu's *Water Village* (1302); Huang Kung-wang's *Stone Cliffs at the Pond of Heaven* (1341), *Rivers and Hills before Rain* (before 1344), *Nine Peaks after Snowfall* (1349); Ni Tsan's *Cold Pines by a Remote Stream*; and Wang Meng's *Dwelling in Seclusion in Summer Mountains* (1365). Superb figure paintings in varying styles are Jen Jen-fa's *Taoist Sorcerer Creating a Horse for T'ang Hsüan-tsung*, Yen Hui's *Li T'ieh-kuai*, and Wang Chen-p'eng's *Po-ya Playing the Ch'in*. Bamboo paintings are well represented with works by Li K'an, Kao K'o-kung, K'o Chiu-ssu, Ni Tsan, and Wang Mien. Landscapes and bird-flower themes by other Yüan painters include scrolls by Shang Ch'i, Fang Ts'ung-i, Sheng Mou, Hsiao Yung, Wang Mien, Chu Te-jun, Ts'ao Chih-po, Wang Yüan, and Yao Yen-ch'ing.

Both major and minor Ming Dynasty (1368–1644) masters are well represented. A number of paintings by artists associated with the early Ming court and the Che school are of exceptionally high quality: bird and flower paintings by Pien Wen-chin, Lü Chi, and Tai Chin and landscapes and figures by Tai Chin, Wu Wei, Chang Lu, and Chu Tuan. Of particular importance in understanding literati attitudes toward painting are the twenty-seven leaves of a forty-leaf album depicting scenes of Mt. Hua by Wang Li (the remaining thirteen leaves are in the Shanghai Museum [q.v]). Examples of works by fifteenth- and sixteenth-century Suchou artists include Shen Chou's *Pine and Rock* (1480), *Temple in the Mountains* (1500), and *Man in Autumn Woods*; Wen Cheng-ming's *Draining the Fields after Floods* (1525), *Scholar and Servant on a Bridge* (1541), and the rare figure subject *The Goddess of the Hsiang River* (1517); figures, flowers, and landscapes by T'ang Yin such as *Court Ladies of Shu*, *A Man Weeping between Two Old Trees*, and *Broken Branch of Plum*; and several colored landscapes by Ch'iu Ying. The museum also owns important works by Ch'ien Ku, Lu Chih, Hsieh Shih-ch'en, Wen Chia, and Wen Po-jen, along with flower and plant paintings in color or in monochrome ink by Ch'en Shun, Chou Chih-mien, Hsü Wei, and Sun K'o-hung.

The diversity of styles prevalent in the seventeenth century is well exemplified in several landscapes by Tung Ch'i-ch'ang, Lan Ying, and members of the Anhwei and Nanking schools (Hsiao Yün-tsung, Mei Ch'ing, Hung-jen, Kung Hsien, Kao Ts'en), as well as early seventeenth-century painters in Suchou (Shao Mi, Li Shih-ta, Sheng Mao-yeh, Chang Hung). There are fine figure paintings by Ch'en Hung-shou, Ting Yün-p'eng, Ts'ui Tzu-chung, and the portraitist Tseng Ch'ing. Representative works by individualist masters Chu Ta, K'un-ts'an, and Tao-chi are also in the collection.

As part of the Ch'ing Dynasty (1644–1911) collection, the museum has paintings by all Six Great Masters of the Ch'ing, as well as scrolls (some unusually large in size) of landscapes and other subjects done by eighteenth-century court artists; both Chinese and foreign. Since very few paintings by the eighteenth-century Yangchou eccentrics were inherited by the museum from the imperial collection, efforts have been made to redress this imbalance, and the museum now owns fine examples of the art of Hua Yen, Li Shan, Chin Nung, and others of this group.

Most of the outstanding Sung, Yüan, Ming, and Ch'ing ceramics were manufactured in the imperial kilns and were among the household effects or in the personal collections of the emperors. The Kuo Pao-chang Collection of porcelain was added to the holdings in the late 1940s. Since 1948 the ceramic collection has been augmented through archaeological excavation, providing examples of pre-Sung wares, and by the acquisition of nonimperial wares of Sung through Ch'ing date, as well as those of twentieth-century manufacture. The total ceramics collection (estimated at three hundred thousand pieces) is probably the most comprehensive in the world. It includes neolithic painted pottery urns, examples from the black pottery of the Lung-shan culture (especially a tripod pitcher); superb Six Dynasties (265–581) stonewares (kneeling ram, an incense holder in the form of a man on an animal) covered with a brownish or greenish glaze, an unusual brown-glazed "chicken" ewer, and a tall funerary vase with high-relief floral and leaf ornament on the body and eight relief medallions of dancers around the neck, glazed in a creamy color. T'ang Dynasty (618–906) three-color and other wares are well represented.

Among outstanding Sung Dynasty (960–1280) wares are *kuan, chün,* and Ting-type vessels, many of the Ting type from the foundations of a Sung pagoda in Ting-hsien, Hopei, including a tall vase with incised fruit blossom motif and a medium-sized bowl with a dragon in clouds done in low relief. There are also Northern Celadon plates and jars. From the Yüan period (1280–1368) is a rare specimen of a bowl with underglaze copper-red peonies and leaves design and an underglaze blue-and-white platter. Other blue-and-white examples include twenty-nine pieces from the former Yüan capital at Ta-tu and from a number of Yüan and Ming tombs in Hopei, Honan, and Nanking. The Ming and Ch'ing (1368–1911) porcelains include primary examples of blue-and-white-ware dishes, vases, jars, pitchers, cups with various designs, monochrome glazed pitchers and bowls; cups and jars decorated with combinations of underglaze blue and overglaze enamel colors; vases and fish jars of the five-color overglaze enamel type; three-color wares and famille rose, famille verte, and famille noire. The collection is also rich in regional wares of later periods: white-glazed blanc de chine figures from Te-hua, Fukien; teapots, cups, and desk objects from I-hsing in Kiangsu; and various ceramic products from the Shekwan kilns near Canton. Twentieth-century and recent ceramic products from the kilns at Ching-te-chen, Shekwan, and elsewhere complete the collection.

The extensive collection of ancient bronze vessels is displayed according to type and function. Methods of bronze casting and bronze technology are also illustrated.

Among the decorative arts, the carvings in jade and related hardstones and the lacquers are perhaps the most important, because in them can be appreciated the increasing freedom, innovativeness, and versatility of craftsmen over the centuries and especially during the Ch'ing Dynasty. It was estimated that at the end of the Ch'ing Dynasty (A.D. 1911) the number of carved jades in the palace ran into the tens of thousands, and, since 1948, they have been augmented through archaeological finds. Outstanding among the carvings from the Shang Dynasty (sixteenth to eleventh centuries B.C.) are a small nephrite pendant with a woman-mask design and a halberd blade of nephrite, 67.6 centimeters long. Chou Dynasty (eleventh to third centuries B.C.) jades include a *ts'ung* 30.9 centimeters high; a *huang* elaborately worked in white jade, tinged with russet terminating in two dragon heads; a white jade *pi* disc covered with incised heart-shaped surface ornament, the center and outer edge of which are shaped as sinuous dragons and phoenixes; and an unusual, relatively realistic, small, standing figure. A handled cup decorated with incised birds, made of creamy white jade with brown streaks, and a lampstand of nephrite ornamented with *lei-wen* pattern all date from the Han Dynasty (206 B.C.-A.D. 221). Important jade carvings from the T'ang Dynasty (A.D. 618–960) include belt plaques showing human figures and a white nephrite cup of lotus petal form. An animal-handled cup of brown-flecked jade comes from the Sung Dynasty (960–1280).

Extremely important is a Yüan Dynasty (1280–1368) *kuei*-shaped, whitish nephrite vessel carved with heavy dragons and clouds. Ming Dynasty (1368–1644) jades include a white jade cup with carved dragon decor, a nephrite ewer with figures in a landscape, and an example of a jade work signed by the maker: a box and lid ornamented with landscape and figures, bearing the name of the famous Suchou jade carver Lu Tzu-keng. Among the hundreds of Ch'ing Dynasty (1644–1911) carvings, the finest of which were produced during the Ch'ien-lung era (1736–96), are jade and nephrite vessels in shape and decor imitating ancient bronze vessels, a white jade censer with intricate open-work floral lid, a white jade bowl inlaid with jewels and gold floral sprays, a malachite miniature mountain with trees and architecture, and at seven feet in height and three feet in width, what was, until recently, the largest nephrite carving extant, *Yü Harnessing the Rivers* (1788).

Among the lacquers, samples of early works, such as eared dishes from the Late Chou and Han periods, are in the collection, but the later lacquers are important because some of them are signed: from the Yüan Dynasty, a red lacquer plate with carved gardenias by the well-known artisan Chang Ch'eng; a red lacquer platter with carved pavilion and terrace scene, as well as a jar with peonies and camellias both by Yang Mao. A Ming Dynasty red lacquer box with a scene of enjoying chrysanthemums in a courtyard is signed Chang Ming-te. Other Ming lacquers include a carved camellia-design red lacquer box of the Yung-lo reign and a number of boxes, round and polygonal, of red or black lacquer, from the Chia-ching reign. Outstanding is an apothocary cabinet of black lacquer painted with gold floral and dragon designs from the Wan-li era. Among the Ch'ing lacquers are a black lacquer censer stand with design of diapers and floral sprays of inlaid mother-of-pearl; a six-legged table with flowers and gold relief designs; a black lacquer box with painted butterfly medallions; boxes shaped like plum blossoms; a black lacquer plate painted with stylized floral and vegetal motifs in gold and colors; a round cinnabar lacquer container, the exterior of which has inlaid mother-of-pearl flowers and the separate dishes of the interior which each have a gold bat; and a lavish four-tier square box in red lacquer ornamented with gourds and melons contained in a gold lacquer cover with relief flowers highlighted by red and blue pigments. Other decorative arts include cloisonné, gold and silver sculpture and vessels, glass sculptures, containers, ewers, and brushholders of bamboo or boxwood.

In the three Treasure Galleries are displayed: (1) musical instruments; (2) replicas of the crowns found in the tomb of The Ming emperor Wan-li and his empress, as well as genuine later jewelry and personal ornaments, along with small-scale religious sculptures, reliquaries, religious symbols, clocks, bowls, cups, washbasins of gold; and (3) jade *ju-i* scepters, vases of artificial flowers fashioned of jade and semiprecious stones, and miniature landscapes.

After the conclusion of World War II, the Palace Museum absorbed the Antiquities Exhibition holdings and became administratively responsible for the former Imperial College (Kuo-tzu Chien) and the former Imperial Summer Palace (I-ho Yüan). At the Imperial College, located in northeast Peking, the sons of high-ranking families were schooled in the Confucian classics under the empire. In 1912 it was converted into the National Historical Museum established by the Ministry of Education. From modest beginnings, the holdings eventually reached 57,127 pieces, including excavated bronze ritual vessels and engraved stones. The collection was transferred in July 1918 to the precincts of the Imperial City. After 1948 the former Imperial College became a Municipal Library.

The I-ho Yüan, about six miles northwest of Peking, covers some 659 acres. The first palace was constructed on this site in 1153. It has long since disappeared in the remodeling of the area under the Ming and, in particular, the Ch'ing rulers. The Ch'ing emperor K'ang-hsi (1661–1722) built here a country villa and gardens. His grandson Ch'ien-lung enlarged the summer retreat by constructing, in the late eighteenth century, the Yüan-ming Yüan, a magnificent set of palaces, gardens, and fountains in European Rococo style erected under the supervision of Jesuit missionaries. The Yüan-ming Yüan and the other Summer Palace buildings were sacked and destroyed in 1860 by Anglo-French troops in the last phases of the Opium Wars. The Yüan-ming Yüan was never reconstructed and lies today in ruins. Other parts of the Summer Palace, however, were rebuilt in 1888 and again after it was damaged in 1900. The garden was opened to the public in 1924, and since 1948 extensive restoration work has been carried out. With its varied topography, it is much more informal and spacious than the palace in Peking. The Summer Palace is noted for its nineteenth-century architecture and interior appointments, theater, garden, and lakes. Especially admired is the covered corridor some nine hundred yards long, which runs along the north shore of K'un-ming Lake, linking together a series of buildings east and west. The beams of this walkway have painted scenes of landscapes of Hang-chou in South China or of historical or mythological subjects. Other attractions are Tz'u-hsi's marble boat, the three-story theater, the seventeen-arch bridge that connects the Island of the Temple of the Dragon King to the lake shore, and the impressive 150-foot-high Fo-hsiang Pagoda.

It should be noted that only portions of the entire palace in Peking are open to the public; many parts are still being restored or for other reasons are inaccessible. Special exhibitions focusing on Communist history or ideology may be displayed in one of the palace buildings. These exhibits may be temporary or permanent and may or may not be open to foreign visitors.

Selected Bibliography

T'ao-tz'u hsüan chi (Selected ceramics), Peking, 1957; *Ku-kung po-wu-yüan ts'ang tz'u hsüan chi* (Selected porcelains from the Palace Museum collection), Peking, 1962, 2 vols.; *Ku-kung po-wu-yüan ts'ang hua* (Paintings in the Palace Museum collection), Peking, 1964. Vol. II only published; *Ku-kung po-wu-yüan ts'ang hua-niao hua hsüan*

(Selected bird and flower paintings in the Palace Museum collection), Peking, 1965; *Ku-kung po-wu-yüan ts'ang kung-i p'in hsüan* (Selected Handicrafts from the Palace Museum collection), Peking, 1974; Fourcade, François, *Art Treasures of the Peking Museum* (New York 1965); Wan go Weng and Yang Boda, *The Palace Museum: Peking* (New York 1984).

ELLEN JOHNSTON LAING

—— Changsha ——

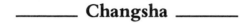

HUNAN PROVINCIAL MUSEUM (officially HUNAN SHENG BOWU-GUAN [HU-NAN-SHENG PO-WU-GUAN]), Lieshi Gongyuan (Park of Revolutionary Martyrs), Changsha, Hunan.

When officially established in February 1956, the Hunan Provincial Museum comprised two buildings documenting the ancient and modern history of this south-central province. Only the second building, beginning with the Opium War and highlighting the Civil War role of Hunan and its native son Mao Tse-tung, remained open during the Cultural Revolution (1966–72). The reopening of the ancient history collection in 1972 coincided with one of the most remarkable discoveries of Chinese archaeology: excavation of a tomb dating from the second century B.C. at a burial mound locally known as Ma-wang-tui. The tomb site, four kilometers east of central Ch'angsha, had been surveyed twenty years earlier and put under museum jurisdiction in 1956 but was not thoroughly investigated until 1971, when projected hospital construction required removal of the mound. Excavation of the underlying shaft pit made medical as well as archaeological history by the extraordinary preservation of the tomb occupant, a female corpse tentatively identified as the wife of a marquis of Tai. She lay shrouded in silks in the innermost of four snugly nested catalpa wood coffins, encased in a tightly sealed chamber of stacked and joined cypress timbers. The entire pit was effectively insulated by surrounding layers of charcoal and limey white clay. Compartments between the outermost coffin and walls of the chamber contained more than one thousand articles of lacquer, silk, and wood, most meticulously packed and inventoried on slips of bamboo. Together, these burial gifts constitute the largest and best-preserved assemblage of perishable art objects from the Western Han Dynasty (206 B.C.-A.D. 9). Subsequent excavations (1973–74) uncovered two adjacent tombs (numbered II and III) containing historical data that verified the identification and dates of all three deceased:

Tomb I: Wife of Li Ts'ang, the marquise of Tai (died after 168 B.C.)

Tomb II: Li Ts'ang, chancellor to the prince of the state of Ch'angsha, the first marquis of Tai (reigned 193–186 B.C.)

Tomb III: Son of Li Ts'ang (buried 168 B.C.)

The ancient state of Ch'angsha was the Han Dynasty successor to the independent state of Ch'u, which dominated the Yangtze River Valley between the eighth and third centuries B.C. (Western and Eastern Chou dynasties). The Ma-wang-tui tomb finds continue the burial techniques and fine arts of the Ch'u people, whose highly literate and cultured civilization has been admired for centuries for their mythology and poetry. However, Ch'u fine arts were totally unknown before the 1930s, when railway and building construction in the modern city of Ch'angsha laid bare a random series of submerged and often flooded tombs. These tombs were most prolific in wood and lacquer objects, whose rich surface decor has since been recognized as hallmark of a "Ch'u" style. Government-sponsored excavations began in the 1950s. Whereas most Ch'u grave goods excavated before 1959 were acquired by the national museums in Peking (Palace Museum and Museum of Chinese History, q.v.), finds since that year are fully represented in the Hunan Provincial Museum. Material attributed to the Ch'u culture remains today the core of its ancient collection.

Of the one hundred thousand objects registered by 1981, approximately 70 percent were scientifically excavated. The museum's own excavation team, composed of graduates of archaeological training classes, is assisted in important field work by members of the national Institute of Archaeology of the Chinese Academy of Science (Academia Sinica). Other museum departments include Administration, Exhibition, and Preservation. The Preservation Department contains two specialized laboratories: one responsible for dehydrating and conserving waterlogged lacquers; the second for analyzing, treating, and mounting delicate textiles for exhibition and storage.

The ancient collection is housed in a two-story brick building that integrates traditional Chinese elements such as the hip-and-gable tile roof and surrounding stone balustrade. Here eleven galleries are arranged chronologically, beginning with Primitive Society (Paleolithic and Neolithic) and progressing through dynastic history. The collection's strong archaeological emphasis is evident in its distribution. The eighth gallery concludes the Han Dynasty (206 B.C.-A.D. 220), the newly unified Chinese empire that absorbed Ch'u. Galleries 9 through 12, spanning the third through eighteenth centuries A.D., are less comprehensive but present a representative selection of ceramics discovered at kiln sites and in tombs in Hunan.

Preceding the general Western Han gallery (7) is a separate gallery (6) devoted to the three tombs at Ma-wang-tui. This gallery provides a brief survey of the more than two thousand objects housed in the adjacent Special Exhibition Hall for Historical Relics from Ma-wang-tui [Ma-wang-tui ch'u-t'u wen-wu ch'en-lieh-kuan], a streamlined edifice of poured concrete opened in July 1974. A frieze above the entrance is abstracted from the painted scrollwork typical of Ma-wang-tui lacquers. Original tomb finds and modern replicas are combined in both this Special Exhibition Hall and in gallery 6. Replicas are used either to duplicate unique material displayed in one location or the other (e.g., replica coffins in gallery 6 duplicate original coffins in the Special Exhibition Hall) or to replace originals deemed too fragile for continuous exposure. All silk paintings and manuscripts are displayed in reproductions, and the originals are preserved in atmospherically controlled storerooms. Painting reproductions are made by museum staff; lacquer reproductions are commissioned from a lacquer factory in Fuchou, Fukien Province.

Hunan's isolation along the southern periphery of the prehistoric and early historic Chinese world gives its earliest artistic finds a strong regional identity. Neolithic pottery vessels from the area of Tung-t'ing Lake represent discoveries since 1974 and styles previously unknown in the Yellow River Valley of northern China, traditionally regarded as the "cradle of Chinese civilization." Artifacts from two major sites—T'ang-chia-kang in An-hsiang district and San-yüan-kung in Li district—are supplemented by photos of excavations, reconstruction of house types, and illustration of hand-built pottery techniques. Earthenware vessels are classified in two successive cultural phases: Ta-hsi (c. 4000 B.C.), named after a type-site in Szechwan Province; and Chü-chia-ling (c. 3000 B.C.), named after a type-site in Hupei Province and widely distributed through the middle Yangtze Valley. They include a finely textured white ware baked almost to stoneware hardness, a softer red ware painted in white or black slip, and a burnished black ware. The predominant form is a wide basin with flaring ring-foot, its surface decorated with stamped, incised, and carved geometric patterns.

Shang Dynasty bronzes include ritual vessels resembling those found at metropolitan sites of the last Shang capital, Anyang (occupied c. 1400-c. 1100 B.C.; Honan Provincial Museum, q.v.) as well as more original forms described by some Western scholars as distinctively provincial products of independent Hunan foundries. (All Shang bronzes listed below, except for the owl *yu*, were unearthed from unknown contexts in Ning-hsiang district.) Within the first group of familiar Anyang styles are three stray finds, each buried as a repository of personal treasures: (1) a covered bowl (*p'ou*) cast with high-relief and three-dimensional animal masks, unearthed in 1959 with 224 miniature bronze axes stored inside; (2) a swing-handle wine bucket (*yu*) cast with high-relief animal masks and inscribed *kuei-ch'uan*, found in 1963 with two strings of 1,172 jade beads; and (3) a larger *yu* cast with high-relief birds and vertical ribbing and inscribed *ko*, found in 1970 with more than 320 assorted jade ornaments. The intricate and hieratic surface decor of these vessels contrasts with a more natural animal style seen in a third *yu* bucket, whose smooth and squat contour is shaped like two addorsed owls (found in Ch'angsha, 1966). This pseudorealistic animal style most closely approaches true sculpture in an elephant-shaped pouring vessel (*ho* or *tsun*), its raised trunk providing a spout and its body teeming with high-relief dragons, birds, and snakes.

Such an inventive and sculptural style was recognized in Hunan as early as 1938, upon discovery of a square wine vase (*fang-tsun*), each of whose four corners is dominated by the projecting head and forelegs of a ram. The now-famous "four ram *fang-tsun*" appears here in a full-scale replica of the black-patined original owned by the Museum of Chinese History in Peking. However, a more startling if still mysterious and controversial example of Shang "realism" was acquired by the Hunan Provincial Museum after its discovery in 1959: a square food cauldron (*fang-ting*) with impassive human faces substituted for the customary animal masks.

As a group, the most imposing Shang bronzes are large, clapperless bells (*nao*), mounted on shanks, mouth-upward, and struck from the outside, which exceed in scale and quantity all similar percussion instruments thus far found in northern China. The gallery features a gradated set of five massive *nao* (height, seventy-one through eighty-nine centimeters), whose convex walls display masks abstracted to ropèlike relief bands under mouthrims cast with elephants and tigers. Their bold surfaces accentuate by contrast a single bell with masks totally dissolved into rows of intaglio scrollwork from which only the eyes protrude. Its smooth jadelike patina enhances this more elegant if less-focused decor.

Bronzes of the subsequent Western Chou Dynasty (eleventh century-771 B.C.) are comparatively few and more interesting historically than artistically. The major "document" of this period is a bronze dagger-axe (*ko*) inlaid with silver ovals and inscribed with the name of a certain "Duke of Ch'u" (Ch'u Kung Wei?). Since the weapon's discovery in a scrap-metal heap in 1959, its authenticity has been debated as the earliest inscriptional record of the state of Ch'u, whose legendary origins have yet to be verified archaeologically.

New and diverse styles of bronze casting are introduced in an array of vessels dating from the Spring and Autumn period (770–476 B.C.), contemporary with the rise of Ch'u. One style, best represented in large shallow basins (*chien*) from Heng-yang and Hsiang-hsiang, is crisply decorative. Small, repeated units, either continuous waffle patterns ("cloud and thunder") or frothy relief curls ("coiled dragons"), seemingly transform the metal into a densely woven textile. A different and more clearly zoomorphic style is exemplified by a wine vase (*tsun*) from Heng-shan, crawling inside and out with snakelike creatures in relief.

The earliest Ch'u burial context exhibited in full is a tomb at Liu-ch'eng-chiao near Ch'angsha, dated fifth century B.C. by museum archaeologists. Photos of its excavation in 1971 illustrate the "vertical pit–wood chamber" structure typical of Ma-wang-tui and other later tomb sites. Noteworthy furnishings are sets of "surrogate" ceramic vessels made exclusively for burial and shown alongside their bronze prototypes; and perishable objects of silk, bamboo basketry, and lacquered wood. The wood includes musical instruments, furniture, and animal sculptures—both realistically reclining deer and goggle-eyed, long-tongued monsters interpreted as tomb guardians (*chen-mu shou*) buried to exorcise evil. Other lacquers, particularly weapon shafts, are remarkable for their painted designs related to those of contemporary inlaid bronzes.

This decorative current is illuminated in the following Warring States (475–221 B.C.) gallery. Bronzes, textiles, lacquers, jades, and painted pottery together illustrate the unity of the so-called "Late Chou decorative style" with its lively zoomorphic and geometric configurations. The bronzes, cast in low relief or inlaid with precious metals, are predominantly personal accessories: belthooks, sword fittings, and mirrors. A sampling of mirrors unearthed from Ch'angsha-area tombs is displayed to show their reverse (nonreflecting) faces cast in typical Ch'u fashion with dragon-arabesques and other fantastically intricate patterns. Analogous decor in lacquer appears on diverse objects such as openwork-carved coffin planks from tombs at Yang-t'ien-hu and painted leather shields from a pre-war find at Wu-li-p'ai.

The simpler beginnings of representational art are seen first in wood tomb figurines of humans—stiffly angular dolls with flat, elongated torsos and flaring robes. Bronze, however, provides the earliest pictorial format. One important pictorial bronze is a fragmentary spouted bowl (*yi*) delicately engraved with scenes of a wine ceremony and archery contest. Its draftsmanship is primitive, with the actors abbreviated to crude silhouettes and their setting indicated by a few trees, birds, and fish. More revealing of true pictorial style are two small figure paintings on silk, each featuring a profile human in fine outline and color: (1) a slender woman juxtaposed with a phoenix and serpent (23.2 by 31.2 centimeters; found in Ch'en-chia ta-shan in 1949); and (2) a man riding a dragon, more fluently painted and partially filled with gold and silver pastels (28.0 by 37.5 centimeters; excavated in Tz'u-t'an-k'u in 1973). Each has been interpreted as a ''portrait'' of the deceased tomb occupant ascending to heaven. Both are significant prototypes for the funerary banners unearthed from Tombs I and III at Ma-wang-tui and, to date, the earliest silk paintings reported in China.

The following gallery provides a sampling of burial objects from Ma-wang-tui, more fully presented in the Special Exhibition Hall. In that hall, ground-floor galleries adjoin a vast hangarlike wing containing the wood coffin chambers from Tombs I and III and the collapsed timbers from Tomb II, damaged by construction of Tomb I and subsequently plundered. Among the few surviving relics from Tomb II are Li Ts'ang's personal seals of jade and bronze, exhibited in the entrance corridor with photos and diagrams of all three excavations. An orientation area beyond these coffin chambers contains a model of the entire site showing relative positions of the three burial pits. (Wall cases, however, show photos of a different Han grave of similar structure: Tomb I at Sha-tz'u-t'ang [excavated 1961], whose furnishings appear in the general Western Han gallery.)

The ground floor of the Special Exhibition Hall features an unparalleled collection of Han decorative arts, primarily from Tomb I. Two galleries and surrounding corridors are arranged typologically and by media. The most important objects may be grouped under four headings:

1. *Coffins.* Three nested wooden chests from Tomb I (excluding the fourth, outermost chest lacquered in plain black) are placed side by side to display their expert carpentry and brilliant surface decoration. The outer two are lacquered with animals and mythical figures amidst winding curves and arabesques, the third in gold and scarlet on a black background, the second in white and gold on a scarlet background. The first, innermost coffin is covered with a rhombic-figured brocade overlaid with colored feathers and bordered with satin-stitch embroidery.

2. *Lacquer ware*. In addition to cylindrical food and cosmetic boxes (*lien*) and oval eared cups (*erh-pei*) familiar from previous Ch'u excavations, there are large vases (average height, fifty centimeters) of unusual square section imitating the bronze *fang-hu*, musical instruments (zither, mouth organ, pitch pipes, flute), and several items of household furniture (armrests, a standing screen, board game, and weapon rack). The majority are wood cored; some are lacquered on a base of laminated hemp or burlap. Almost all retain their original lustrous colors. Surface designs, either painted (usually in lacquer, rarely in oil) or delicately incised, include conventionalized floral and geometric patterns as well as realistic animals, birds, and fish. Some bear inscriptions indicating ownership ("Household of the Marquis of Tai"), function, or unit capacity of the container. Grains, fruits, animal bones, and medicines discovered inside are exhibited in glass vials.

3. *Tomb Figurines*. Wood human images range from crudely scraped talismans to large, skillfully carved manikins (average height, eighty-five centimeters) dressed in linen and silk garments. Clothing of most attendants is simply indicated by carving and painting. Like their Warring States antecedents, these sculptures are stylized with triangular heads and cylindrical trunks. Some can be distinguished as substitutes for specific members of the Li household staff, including musical ensembles from Tombs I and III, whose miniature instruments resemble the full-scale examples in lacquered wood.

4. *Textiles*. As a group, fabrics from Tomb I are most revealing artistically and technologically. Most are of cultivated silk and include garments, pillows, pouches, coffin curtains, and surplus lengths of fabric found rolled up in wicker baskets. Many may be first discoveries in dyeing, printing, spinning, and weaving techniques. The gallery includes all major types: tabby silk, sheer gauze, gauze with painted and block-printed designs, figured lace, monochrome damask, and polychrome brocade, including an unusual "pile loop" brocade resembling velvet. Diaphanous pieces in good condition are mounted between sheets of plexiglass and exhibited upright to display their transparency.

Historically, the most important textiles are silk paintings, maps, and texts from Tombs I and III. Full-scale reproductions are hung in wall cases in the lower level of the Special Exhibition Hall, behind the eviscerated remains of the marquise of Tai, preserved after an autopsy performed by the Hunan Medical College in 1973.

Foremost among the paintings are two similar T-shaped banners, one from each tomb (Tomb I: height, 205 centimeters; top width, 92 centimeters; bottom width, 47.7 centimeters; Tomb III: height, 233 centimeters; top width, 141 centimeters; bottom width, 50 centimeters). Each is fitted with a cord for suspension but when discovered was laying face-down beneath the lid of the innermost coffin. They have been identified as funerary banners (*ming-ching*, or *fei-i*), probably carried aloft in the cortege and buried to escort the deceased to the spirit world. Each painting is a dense but organized composition of human and animal forms, clearly divisible in three horizontal registers depicting ascending stages of the universe: the netherworld populated by aquatic animals and atlantid figures; the human world, by the tomb occupant and attendants; and the celestial or spirit world, by mythological creatures. Although their exact iconography may never be resolved, these banners are eminently valuable documents of early Chinese religion and figure painting. Their neatly descriptive style combines fluent black outline and flat color fill, with modeled areas that demonstrate surprisingly early mastery of shading techniques.

The second painting found in Tomb III is a realistic bird's-eye view of a ceremonial procession crowded with chariots, horses, and officials carrying insignia. The third and fourth paintings are better described as charts or diagrams, one illustrating breath control and body-building exercises, the other consisting of small drawings accompanying a text on astronomical and meteorological prognostications. Also displayed from Tomb III are the earliest maps yet found in China, rendering (1) the southern part of the Han State of Ch'angsha, (2) military garrisons in that area, and (3) other walled cities.

Medicine and divination are prominent themes within more than twenty formerly lost texts from Tomb III, copied on lengths or sections of silk. These oldest-known silk books also include classics of Han and pre-Han literature, some significantly different from previously transmitted versions. Of greatest historical importance are the *I-ching* (*Book of Changes*), the *Lao-tzu* philosophy, and a series of anecdotes related to the *Chan-kuo-tse* (*Intrigues of the Warring States*). Fragments from each of these three texts are exhibited with their transcriptions into modern abbreviated characters. Finally, there are bamboo tablets from Tombs I and III that list their furnishings in neat clerical script. Beyond their value in identifying obscure grave goods, these "inventory slips" (*ch'ients'e*) are primary sources for etymology and calligraphy.

The pristine richness of Ma-wang-tui I and III is evident by contrast with roughly contemporary tomb finds in the Western Han gallery. Most of these tombs have been diminished by looting before excavation, and original lacquers exhibited here have suffered from shrinkage or deterioration of their wood and fabric cores. Prominent examples are displayed in reproductions or scale drawings. The most elaborate drawings replicate lacquered coffin planks from a tomb in the Ch'angsha suburb of Sha-tzu-t'ang (excavated 1961), whose painted arabesque and animal motifs resemble those decorating the second and third coffins of the marquise of Tai. On the lid are depicted thick rings resembling the ritual jade *pi* disc, traditionally identified as a symbol of heaven.

Actual *pi* discs form part of a good collection of ritual and ornamental jades from various cemeteries spanning the Western and Eastern Han regions. Discs and pendants show typically incised or raised spirals ("rice grain pattern"), some bordered by interlaced dragons and phoenixes. More intricately worked stones include narrower rings (*huan*) pierced with stylized felines, sword fittings combining high relief and open-work decor, and small animal sculptures carved fully in the round.

The final phase of the Bronze Age is represented by a heterodox group of bronze vessels and sculptures that show a general decline in casting but an intriguing blend of stylistic influences from areas remote from the Ch'u cultural sphere. Vessel decor is limited to finely chased (chiseled) lozenges, cloudscrolls, sawtooth bands, and "landscape" registers of hills or waves—motifs best known from provinces south and west of Hunan: Kwangsi, Kwangtung, and Kweichow. Two of the most ingenious and functional forms are lamps discovered in Ch'angsha, one cast with an ox-shaped base and the second designed for suspension with a man swinging from chains and holding an oil dish. Bronze figures of horses and grooms excavated in 1976 from an Eastern Han tomb in Heng-yang are exceptional in their large size (average height, fifty centimeters) and exotic features. The grooms are identified as *Hu* people, nomads from the far northern frontier of Han China.

Han ceramics include wares of probable Hunan manufacture, although local kiln sites have yet to be discovered. There are two distinctively southern groups, one of hard earthenware (*ying-t'ao*) that resembles neolithic antecedents, the second of reduction-fired stoneware unevenly coated with a greenish brown iron glaze. Both are decorated with impressed and incised geometric patterns peculiar to this region. The green wares (*ch'ing-tz'u*) are more diverse in shape, ranging from vessels that clearly imitate contemporary bronzes to funerary models of houses and silos that describe daily life with prosaic simplicity.

Subsequent Western Chin (265–317) developments in green-glazed stoneware are exhibited in vessels and in tomb figures that embody a provincial style of whimsical naiveté. Among figures excavated in 1958 at Chin-p'en-ling near Ch'angsha, the most engaging are two pairs from a tomb dated 302: *en-face* musicians playing a lute and reed pipe and a scribe supporting the writing tablet of his mate. Military figures from generally contemporary tombs in the same cemetery are comparatively stiff but closely correspond in squat proportions, tubular modeling, and sharply incised details of costume. The mounted cavalry wear helmets, breastplates, and horse trappings that are valuable records of early Chinese armor.

In 1975 museum-sponsored excavations in the Hsiang-yin district north of Ch'angsha (ancient Yo-chou) recovered the earliest evidence for local green ware production, identified with Yo-chou ware described in the eighth-century *Classic of Tea*. Kiln activity began in the Eastern Chin (317–40) and flourished in the Sui Dynasty (581–618). The Sui kiln finds are precursors to true celadon, all showing a glassy yellowish green glaze that deepens where it pools in simple geometric and floral patterns impressed or carved in the paste. Vessel forms are sturdy and functional: bowls, basins, jars, loop-eared vases, and high-pedestaled trays. That such everyday wares were also used as funerary offerings is evident in the burial hoard of a tomb dated 610, excavated in 1972 in the town of Ch'eng-kuan-chen in Hsiang-yin. This hoard combines vessels of local manufacture with tomb figures of officials, court ladies, and mythological animal symbols of the zodiac (*sheng-hsiao*) dressed in human robes. Similar figures from a later seventh-century tomb at Hsien-chia-hu near Ch'angsha—including pack animals, civil and military officials, and a quartet of female musicians—extend this Yo-chou tradition into the T'ang Dynasty (618–906).

Excavations at the kiln sites of T'ung-kuan-chen and Wa-cha-p'ing north of Ch'angsha have unearthed T'ang ceramics of great diversity and technical innovation. The characteristically pale celadon, a gritty stoneware coated with a transparent or opaque yellow-green alkaline glaze, is distinguished by a variety of applied and underglaze painted designs. One specialty of Wa-cha-p'ing is a spouted ewer decorated under the glaze with applied medallions and patches of iron brown. A selection of these ewers, long recognized as staple exports to Korea and Iran, is displayed together with clay molds used to cast their appliqués: animals, human figures, and heraldic bird and floral motifs of Persian derivation. Historically, the most significant T'ang ceramics from Ch'angsha-area kilns are those decorated with a combination of two or more glazes colored with metallic oxides. In addition to spots and splashes, which constitute a local variation of polychrome or "three color" (san-ts'ai) ware, there are underglaze painted designs ranging from abstract scribbles to carefully outlined flowers, animals, human figures, and landscape motifs. The most unusual example, discovered in 1966, is a ewer painted under the glaze with a seven-story pagoda flanked by two stylized trees. A few vessels are inscribed with poetic couplets. Together, these wares provide some of the earliest-known evidence for underglaze painting and calligraphy, antedating both Sung Dynasty (960–1279), Tz'u-chou type wares, and Yüan Dynasty (1279–1368) blue-and-white.

Ceramics post-dating T'ang are an eclectic group of local kiln products and wares imported from other provinces. Sung Dynasty tomb finds include Lung-ch'üan, ch'ing-pai, and Ting-type wares as well as a celadon resembling northern Chün ware in its blue-green phosphatic glaze. Yüan blue-and-white is exemplified in two refined vessels, both discovered in Ch'ang-te but probably made at Ching-te-chen in Kiangsi Province: (1) a bottle vase (Yü-Hu-Ch'un p'ing) painted with military figures, one identified in cartouche as General Meng-t'ien of the Ch'in Dynasty (second century B.C.); and (2) a large basin (diameter, 45.3 centimeters) painted with fish and water weeds in the center and floral scrolls encircling the cavetto.

Decorative arts of the Ming (1368–1644) and Ch'ing (1644–1911) dynasties are of mixed origins and generally representative of imperial taste. There is a small but select group of blue-and-white, Te-hua (blanc de chine), and overglaze enamel porcelains, as well as molded ink cakes, inkstones, seals, writing brushes, and other scholarly accessories in jade, bamboo, ivory, and lacquer. Local ceramics are well represented by kiln products of Li-ling (southeast of Ch'ang-sha), where traditional and innovative shapes and glazes continue to be produced.

The late painting collection is particularly strong in the calligraphy of Ho Shao-chi (1799-1873) and bold nature studies of Ch'i Pai-shih (1863-1957). Each of these native-born artists has been subject of a special exhibition in recent years.

In 1981 an annual museum journal was scheduled to begin publication at the end of the year. Staff members have regularly contributed field reports to the national archaeology journals: *Wen wu*, *K'ao-ku*, and *K'ao-ku hsüeh-pao*. Major articles and monographs are jointly edited by the museum and the Institute of Archaeology of the Academy of Science. The most significant and beautifully illustrated monograph is *Ch'ang-sha Ma-wang-tui i-hao Han mu (Han Tomb I at Ma-wang-tui, Ch'angsha)*, 1973, which provides a complete report of the excavation and a scholarly catalog of tomb finds.

Selected Bibliography

Museum publications: "Ch'ang-sha Liu-ch'eng-chiao i-hao mu" (Tomb I at Liu-ch'eng-chiao, Ch'angsha), in Chinese, *K'ao-ku hsüeh-pao*, 1972, no. 1, pp. 59–72; "Ch'ang-sha Ma-wang-tui erh, san hao Han mu fa-chüeh chien-pao" (A summary of the excavation of Han tombs II and III at Ma-wang-tui, Ch'angsha), jointly edited with the Institute of Archaeology, Academy of Science, in Chinese, *Wen wu*, 1974, no. 7, pp. 39–48, 63, English translation by Jeffrey K. Reigel, *Chinese Sociology and Anthropology*, vol. 10, no. 2 (Winter 1977–78), pp. 51–103; *Ch'ang-sha Ma-wang-tui i-hao Han mu* (Han Tomb I at Ma-wang-tui, Ch'angsha), jointly edited with the Institute of Archaeology, Academy of Science, 2 vols., in Chinese with English abstract (Peking: Wen-wu ch'u-pan-she, 1973); *Ch'ang-sha Ma-wang-tui i-hao Han mu fa-chüeh chien-pao* (A summary of the excavation of Han tomb I at Ma-wang-tui, Ch'angsha), jointly edited with the Institute of Archaeology, Academy of Science, (n.p., 1972), English translation by Fong Chow, "Ma-wang-tui: A Treasure Trove from the Western Han Dynasty, *Artibus Asiae*, vol. 25, no. 1 (1973), pp. 1–23; *Hu-nan ch'u-t'u t'ung-ching t'u-lu* (Pictorial record of bronze mirrors excavated in Hunan Province), in Chinese (Peking: Wen-wu ch'u-pan she, 1960); *Hu-nan sheng wen-wu t'u-lu* (Pictorial record of cultural relics from Hunan Province), in Chinese (Ch'angsha: Hu-nan jen-min ch'u-pan-she, 1964); "San-shih nien lai Hu-nan wen-wu k'ao-ku kung-tso" (The past thirty years of archaeological work on cultural relics in Hunan Province), in Chinese, *Wen-wu k'ao-ku kung-tso san-shih nien, 1949–1979* (Thirty years of archaeological work on cultural relics, 1949–1979) (Peking: Wen-wu ch'u-pan she, 1979), pp. 310–24.

Other publications: Bush, Mary, "Textile Conservation at Mawangdui," *Museum News*, vol. 59, no. 6 (May-June 1981), pp. 46–49; Ch'angsha Municipal Cultural Bureau, "T'ang-tai Ch'ang-sha T'ung-kuan-yao chih t'iao-ch'a" (An investigation of the T'ung-kuan kiln sites of the T'ang Dynasty in Ch'angsha), in Chinese with English summary, *K'ao-ku hsüeh-pao*, 1980, no. 1, pp. 67–96; Cheng Te-k'un, "T'ang Ceramic Wares of Ch'angsha," *The Journal of the Institute of Chinese Studies*, The Chinese University of Hong Kong, vol. 3, no. 1 (September 1970), pp. 1–53; Chou Shih-yung, "Hu-nan sheng po-wu-kuan hsin fa-hsien ti chi chien t'ung-chi" (Some bronzes recently acquired by the Hunan Provincial Museum), in Chinese, *Wen wu*, 1966, no. 4, pp. 1–6; Hsia Nai, Ch'en Kung-jen and Wang Chung-shu, *Ch'ang-sha fa-chüeh pao-kao* (Report on excavations at Ch'angsha), in Chinese (Peking: Ko-hsüeh ch'u-pan she, 1957); Virginia C. Kane, "The Independent Bronze Industries in the South of China Contemporary with the Shang and Western Chou Dynasties," *Archives of Asian Art*, vol. 28 (1974–75), pp. 77–107; Kao Chih-hsi, "Ch'ang-sha Liang-Chin Nan-Ch'ao Sui mu fa-chüeh pao-kao" (Summary report on the Chin Dynasty, Southern Dynasties, and Sui Dynasty tombs at Ch'angsha), in Chinese with Russian summary, *K'ao-ku hsüeh-pao*, 1959, no. 3, pp. 75–103; *Konan-sho hakubutsukan* (The Hunan Provincial Museum), vol. 2 of *Chūgoku no hakubutsukan*

(Museums of China), in Japanese (Tokyo: Kodansha and Wen-wu ch'u-pan she, 1981); Wen Tao-i, "Ch'ang-sha Ch'u mu" (The Ch'u tombs of Ch'angsha), in Chinese with English summary, *K'ao-ku hsüeh-pao*, 1959, no. 1, pp. 41–60.

ELINOR PEARLSTEIN

———— Chengchou. See Zhengzhou. ————

———— Nanjing (Nanking) ————

NANKING MUSEUM (officially NANJING BOWUGUAN [NANKING PO-WU-YUAN]), 321 Eastern Zhongshan Road, Nanjing, Jiangsu.

The Nanking Museum is one of the three largest museums in the People's Republic of China, equal in scale to the Shanghai Museum of Art and History (q.v.). It is also the largest museum in Kiangsu Province in southeastern China, the last province through which the Yangtze River flows before it empties into the Yellow Sea in the east of the People's Republic. It is located in Nanking City, which is on the inside of the bend made by the Yangtze River, where the Yangtze River changes its course from northeast to east at the southwestern section of Kiangsu before it continues meandering east through the southern part of the province.

Northern China was invaded on several occasions by nomads from the north and west, as during the Northern Wei period (420–534), Liao Dynasty (916–1115), Chin Dynasty (1115–1234), and Ch'ing Dynasty (1644–1911). During these periods, many Chinese of the upper class moved south. Nanking, being a prosperous area, was chosen as an ideal place for settlement. The collection in the Nanking Museum reflects the rich variety of the culture and life of these people.

On the south side of Tzu-chin-shan (also known as Chung-shan), a famous mountain in Chinese literature, the museum complex occupies an area of 90,000 square meters, with an internal exhibition area totaling 3,712 square meters. The major parts of the building are modeled after the palatial building style of the Liao Dynasty (916–1125). The roof is laid with golden yellow-glazed tiles, and the entrance is embellished by seven red-lacquered pillars and latticed doors into which one enters from a three-tiered stone stairway.

The works discovered in different areas of Kiangsu contribute to the museum's collection of nearly four hundred thousand items, which span a period of five thousand years, from the Neolithic period to the T'ai-p'ing t'ien-kuo (1851–64) era. Many of the objects were recovered from recent excavations, and they reflect the importance of Kiangsu in Chinese history.

Evidence of civilization in the Kiangsu area long before the invention of writing is illustrated in the collection of painted pottery of the Neolithic period deposited in the Nanking Museum. They show remarkable achievements in the rendering of clay, the control of fire, and the use of motifs.

Following the Neolithic period, during the Shang (1600–1027 B.C.), Western Chou (1027–771 B.C.), and Eastern Chou (771–221 B.C.) dynasties, the leading centers of civilization developed around the capitals of these dynasties, in what are now the cities of Chengchou, Loyang, and Sian in the Honan and Shensi provinces in central China. During these periods, bronze vessels were the highest art form, and the bronze vessels uncovered from the Kiangsu area show strong similarities with those of central China.

In 222 Nanking was selected to be the capital by Sun Ch'üan, emperor of the Wu Kingdom (222–80). Nanking retained this status during the five succeeding dynasties until the establishment of the Sui Dynasty in 581. It was again chosen as the capital by the Southern T'ang Dynasty (937–58) and later during the Ming Dynasty (1368–1644), Nanking was the capital for the first fifty-three years and considered to be the second capital for the remaining years.

Many emperors, aristocrats, and high officials were buried in the area during the years that Nanking was the capital. Treasures from these tombs were recovered in recent excavations conducted by the Nanking Museum. The richness of the artifacts and their superb quality attest to the glamor of the city in those days. The desire to build a museum to preserve and exhibit the finds seems natural, but efforts to do so have been interrupted several times.

The founding of the museum was interrupted by World War II as well as by internal conflicts. In 1933 a committee was organized to establish a museum called the Central Museum. The construction of the museum building commenced in the fall of 1936 at the same location as the current one. The progress was interrupted by the Sino-Japanese War in 1937, and by the end of the war, the part of the building that was previously constructed was damaged severely. In 1948, when the Nationalist government moved to Taiwan, many treasures were taken along. They are now deposited in the National Palace Museum (q.v.) in Taipei. However, the impetus for founding the museum did not diminish, and on March 9, 1950, the Nanking Museum was officially opened.

Under the supervision of the Kiangsu Cultural Bureau, and with the collective efforts of the staff and citizens, the museum started again to build the collection. Many of the items in the current collection were donated by civilians, and many more were recovered from scientific excavations at archaeological sites in the province. The persistent efforts to establish the museum not only made the founding of the museum possible but also made it into one of the most important museums in China, revealing the continuous achievement of the people of Kiangsu Province.

Since its opening, the museum has been the center for collecting, preserving, exhibiting, and conducting research on the cultural artifacts and art objects of the Kiangsu area. The work is carried out by the departments of archaeology, preservation, exhibition, social education, research, and technology. The basic activities of the museum include hosting a permanent exhibition of "The History of Kiangsu" and other special exhibitions throughout the year.

The Nanking Museum is also the center for archaeological and museological activities in the Kiangsu area. Both the Archaeology Society and the Society of Museology of Kiangsu are headquartered at this museum. Besides organizing meetings for these two societies every year, the museum also organizes symposiums on archaeology, museology, history, and ethnology.

The museum collection is strong in a number of areas but particularly in painted pottery, bronzes, early porcelain, stone reliefs, clay tiles, paintings, and calligraphy.

The painted potteries deposited at the Nanking Museum were recently excavated from the neolithic sites in Kiangsu Province. They are made of fine clay, which was washed several times before use. With the help of scientific tests, scholars have found that they were fired at temperatures of nine hundred to one thousand degrees centigrade. Since they were excavated systematically, the occurrence of certain vessel types and their frequency of occurrence in relation to different strata provided valuable data.

Very few complete vessels and a small number of pottery shards among other artifacts were found in the lowest stratum (3500–3000 B.C.). These vessels are deep or shallow bowls and three-legged pots. Reconstruction of the shards show that they were also parts of bowls or three-legged pots. The application of pigment is confined to the rim, and simple motifs of red or black are painted on the inside of the vessels.

The number of vessel types increased in the middle stage (c. 3000 B.C.), with a greater variety of shallow and deep bowls, urns, and three-legged pots. There are still only a few vessels with ringed feet or handles, but there is a greater variety of pigments and motifs. The motifs are painted on the outside of the vessels. They consist of net, wave, lozenges, and weave-like patterns. They are painted in red, black, purple, brown, and white pigments with great fluidity.

Toward the later stage (2500–2000 B.C.), the proportion of painted potteries increased, and new vessel shapes appeared, such as the three-legged shallow bowls, vessel pedestals, ringed-foot food containers, trumpet-mouth pots, and urns with handles. The motifs are more complicated and are organized in two or more bands. Some motifs are intricate and resemble the animal motifs of the Shang bronzes.

Bronzes deposited at the museum are mostly excavated from the sites of the Shang, Western Chou, and Eastern Chou dynasties in the Kiangsu area. They include ritual and ceremonial vessels, musical instruments, weapons, tools, and some miniatures of animals.

A *kuei* (a grain container made for ritual or ceremonial purposes) excavated from a Western Chou tomb at Yen-tun-shan in southern Kiangsu shows strong similarities to the *kuei* excavated from sites in central China. It bears a lengthy inscription of 126 words, which records the events when K'ang Wang, the third emperor of the Western Chou Dynasty, gave treasures of bronzes, land, weapons, and slaves to Marquis Tse at a place named I. Further investigation is needed to determine whether the I mentioned in the inscription is Yen-tun-shan.

A *kuang* (a vessel in the form of a four-legged animal), one of a pair, from the same site is most unusual in its shape and component parts. The vessel has a relatively realistic animal head and stands on four very short legs. Its back is made into a lid and its belly is flat. A wide band composed of two stylized bird motifs runs across its chest, sides, and rear. The coordination of parts and the soft curves in the profile give an impression of greater freedom than the *kuang* made in central China.

Vessels from the Eastern Chou period show even more freedom in shape and decor. A bronze deer, from Lien-shui in central Kiangsu, is portrayed in a resting pose with ease and affection. The *tsun* (a wine vessel) excavated from Wu-chin, in southern Kiangsu, is decorated with a wide band of spikes on the body, a pattern also not found in the north of China.

The Nanking Museum also contains a collection of Yüeh-kiln ware, a kind of *ch'ing-tz'u* (literally "green porcelain"), that existed from the Wei Dynasty (220–65) to the early Northern Sung Dynasty (960–1127). Yüeh-kiln ware represents an important stage in the development of Chinese porcelain, because it represents the fusion of the glaze with the body, which is the first step toward the manufacture of porcelain in China.

Yüeh-kiln ware was called *piao-ch'ing* ware by the people of that time. In literary sources, we find many examples of praise for the color of *piao-ch'ing* ware, indicating that the color of glaze was a standard for judging the beauty of this type of early porcelain. The *piao-ch'ing* tone is different from the low-temperature green glaze of northern China and is distinctly different from the green glaze of the Sui (581–618) and T'ang (618–907) dynasties that has a bluish tone.

The popularity of Yüeh-kiln ware is reflected by the variety of vessels that were made for daily use and covered all aspects of daily life from tea and wine jars and cups to toilet pots.

One of the distinctive features of the *piao-ch'ing* ware is the frequent use of animal forms. Some vessels are made into animal shapes of bear, goat, fish, and bird, and some urns are laden on top of the vessels with animals, birds, and miniatures of architecture and humans. Other vessels have animals as the legs supporting them.

The stone reliefs and stamped clay tiles in the museum are mostly excavated from tombs of the Eastern Han (25–220) and the Six Dynasties (220–589). The group that belongs to the Eastern Han Dynasty contains vivid representations of the daily activities of the Han people. There are scenes of weaving, ox ploughing, festivals, and myths carved in shallow relief.

On pieces from the Six Dynasties, the scenes change to literary and religious themes. The three sets of *Seven Sages in the Bamboo Grove and Jung Ch'i-ch'i* are the most outstanding finds in recent years. One was recovered from a tomb in Nanking, and the other two were recovered from tombs in T'an-yang, also in southern Kiangsu. Each set is composed of eight scholars, who were respected in literati circles and were known for their unconventional views of life and patterns of behavior. Each figure is depicted in his most representative pose and gesture as recorded in literature. The image is believed to have first been painted on silk, carved into wood, and then pressed onto wet clay. The clay was then sectioned, fired, and assembled again when built into the walls of the tomb. Although it can not be stated conclusively that these tiles were modeled after paintings, the tiles do provide some understanding of the painting tradition of the Six Dynasties.

Another group of stamped clay tiles in the collection are of Buddhist and Taoist origin. They were recovered from the tomb in T'an-yang, which is perhaps the tomb of the emperor of Southern Ch'i Dynasty (479–502). There are images of *apsaras* (heavenly beings), lions, the four cardinal animals (black turtle, red bird, green dragon, white tiger), warriors, attending maids and male servants in procession, and the winged deity playing with the dragon. The presence of different faiths in the same tomb illustrate the rich diversity and tolerance of the period.

The museum has a collection of thirty-four thousand paintings and calligraphy in the form of hanging scrolls, handscrolls, and album leaves. A small number of them are by the famous painters of the Sung (960–1279) and Yüan (1271–1368) dynasties, but the majority consist of paintings of the Ming (1368–1644) and Ch'ing (1644–1911) dynasties. The Nanking Museum's most significant group of paintings are those by the Eight Masters of Nanking and the Eight Masters of Yangchou, who were active in the Kiangsu and Chekiang area.

Besides the works of art already mentioned, there are a few others that are worthy of note. There is a collection of jades intended originally for decorative, ceremonial, and ritual purposes. A collection of inscribed stelae provides historical facts that bridge the gaps in existing literary sources. There are also rare early Buddhist sculptures, well-preserved sculptures of the Sung dynasties, and treasures recovered from the imperial tomb of the Southern T'ang Dynasty (937–58).

Selected Bibliography

Museum publications: *Nan-ching po-wu-yüan* (Nanking Museum) (Nanking n.d.); *Chiang-su li shih ch'en lieh* (A short guide to the exhibition of Jiangsu history) (Nanking 1980); "Chiang-su T'an-yang-hsien Hu-ch'iao, Chien-shan liang tso Nan-ch'ao mu tsang" (Two Southern Dynasty tombs at Hu-ch'iao and Chien-shan in T'an-yang, Kiangsu), *Wen-wu* 2, 1980, pp. 1–17; "Chiang-su T'an-yang Hu-ch'iao Nan-ch'ao ta mu chi chuan k'e pi hua" (The Southern Dynasty tomb at Hu-ch'iao in T'an-yang, Kiangsu, and its engraved pictures on tiles), *Wen-wu* 2, 1974, pp. 49–56; "Chiang-su wen wu k'ao ku kung tso san shih nien" (Archaeological work on the cultural relics of Kiangsu in the past thirty years), *Wen wu k'ao ku san shih nien*, pp. 198–216, edited by the Cultural Relics Editorial Committee (Peking 1979); *Nan-ching po-wu-yüan ts'ang-hua chi* (The painting collection of the Nanking Museum) (Peking 1966); *Nanking Hakubutsukan* (Nanking Museum) (Tokyo 1982), in Japanese; *Nan-T'ang erh ling fa chueh pao kao*

(The excavation report on the two mausoleums of the Southern T'ang Dynasty) (Peking 1957); "Shih t'an 'Chu lin ch'a hsien chi Jung Ch'i-ch'i chuan k'e wen t'i" (Preliminary discussion on the problems of the stamped bricks of the "Seven Sages in the bamboo grove and the Jung Ch'i-ch'i"), *Wen-wu* 2, 1980, pp. 18–23; *Chiang-su liu-ch'ao ch'ing-tz'u* (Six Dynasties porcelain of Kiangsu) (Peking 1980); *Chiang-su ts'ai t'ao* (The painted pottery of Kiangsu) (Peking 1978); *Chuka Jinmin Kyowa-koku Nanking Hakubutsukan ten* (Exhibition of the Nanking Museum, People's Republic of China) (Osaka 1981), in Japanese; *Chiang-su sheng-ch'u t'u wen-wu hsüan-chi* (A selected collection of the cultural relics excavated in the Kiangsu Province) (Peking 1963); Nanking Museum and Nanking Municipal Cultural Relics Preservation Committee, "Nan-ching Hsi-shan-ch'iao Nan-ch'ao mu chi ch'i chuan k'e pi hua" (The Southern Dynasty tomb at the Hsi-shan Bridge in Nanking and its engraved pictures on tiles), *Wen-wu* 8–9, 1960, pp. 37–42; Nanking Museum and Shantung Cultural Relics Administrative Bureau, ed., *I-nan ku hua hsiang shih mu fa chueh pao kao* (Excavation report on the engraved stone tomb ar I-nan) (Shanghai 1956).

Other publications: Ch'en Meng-chia, "I Hou Tse kuei he ti i i" (The kuei of Marquis Tse at I and its meaning), *Wen-wu ts'an-k'ao tzu-liao* 5, 1955, pp. 63–66; Chiang-su wen wu kuan li wei yuan hui (Kiangsu Cultural Relics Administrative Committee), *Nan-ching ch'u t'u liu ch'ao ch'ing tz'u* (Six Dynasties porcelain unearthed in Nanking) (Peking 1957); Hsu Hsin-nung, *Yang-chou pa chia hua chi* (The paintings of the Eight Masters at Yang-chou) (Peking 1959); Laing, Ellen Johnston, "Neo-Taoism and the 'Seven Sages of the bamboo grove' in Chinese painting," *Artibus Asiae* 36, 1974, pp. 5–54; Lin Shu-chung, "Chiang-su T'an-yang Nan-Ch'i mu chuan yin pi hua t'an t'ao" (An investigation of the stamped tile pictures in a Southern Ch'i Dynasty tomb at T'an-yang, Kiangsu), *Wen-wu* 1, 1977, pp. 64–73; Soper, Alexander Coburn, "A new Chinese tomb discovery: The earliest representation of a famous literary theme," *Artibus Asiae* 24, no. 2, 1961, pp. 79–86; Wang Chih-min, *Nan-ching liu-ch'ao t'ao yung* (The Six Dynasties clay figures of Nanking) (Peking 1958).

MOLLY SIUPING HO

——— **Nanking. See Nanjing.** ———

——— **Peking. See Beijing.** ———

——— **Shanghai** ———

SHANGHAI MUSEUM OF ART AND HISTORY (officially SHANGHAI BOWUGUAN), 16 South Henan Road, Shanghai.

The Shanghai Museum of Art and History was established after the revolution through the efforts of the Shanghai Municipal Committee for the Preservation of Cultural Properties. It opened on December 21, 1952, at 325 West Nanjing Road. This first museum lacked adequate storage and exhibition space for further development, so in 1959 the museum was moved to its present location. It reopened on October 1, 1959, the tenth anniversary of the founding of the People's Republic of China. The new building is a remodeled bank building with seven floors; each floor provides about twelve hundred square meters of space. On the ground floor is a special exhibition hall; the first through third floors house permanent exhibitions; and the fourth through seventh floors accommodate laboratories, workshops, storerooms, and offices.

The Shanghai Museum of Art and History is administered by a director, who is assisted by curators and technical staff. Museum activities are divided among a number of departments: Political, Personnel, Preservation, Exhibition and Research, Archaeology, Records, Laboratory of Conservation Technology, Restoration, and Reproductions. These departments have a staff of more than 280 persons. The Exhibitions and Research Department is further subdivided into six sections: Drafting, Metals and Gems Research, Ceramic Research, Calligraphy and Painting Research, Handicrafts Research, and Exhibitions and Planning. The Archaeology Department is subdivided into three sections: Excavations, Research, and Local History.

The outstanding collection of the Shanghai Museum of Art and History was assembled in a relatively short period. From its meager beginning it has grown to a collection of more than 106,000 pieces. Its holdings in Chinese ceramics, ancient bronzes, calligraphy, and painting are recognized internationally. Also its collection of imperial seals, coins, and artistic handicrafts is very comprehensive. The majority of these artworks were acquired through purchase. In this regard the Shanghai Museum is unique among China's museums, in which acquisition through archaeological excavation has been the major avenue for building collections. In Shanghai the fledgling museum enjoyed the patronage of its first post-revolutionary mayor, and generous appropriations enabled museum personnel to purchase antiquities owned by wealthy families. In addition to having purchased works, the Shanghai Museum has received gifts of works of art from citizens of China. The remainder of the collection has been assembled through the museum's own archaeological excavations.

A number of important early bronzes are in the Shanghai Museum. Most are ritual vessels that originally contained wine or food offerings to the ancestors, becoming thereby the featured objects in solemn ceremonies. These ancient bronzes are noted for their handsome shapes and intricate, sharply executed cast designs in relief. They are superb examples of the art of bronze casting; indeed, they are technically unsurpassed. Engraved inscriptions on some of the bronzes provide significant information about the historical period. Key words from the inscription are used to designate individual bronzes. Among the museum's most distinguished bronzes from the Shang Dynasty (sixteenth to eleventh century B.C.) is a wine vessel of the kuang type; from the Western Chou period (eleventh century-771 B.C.) is the Ko Po *kuei*, Pao *yu*, Lu Hou *tsun*, Hsiao Ch'en Tan *chi*, and Ta K'o *ting*. The famous Ta K'o *ting* tripod displays a bold wave pattern, sweeping unbroken around the vessel, and less of the complicated zoomorphic designs of the Shang. From the Spring and Autumn period (770–476 B.C.), the museum holds the Ch'i Hou *i*, Lu P'o Yü Fu *kui* and two important *chung*, or bells. Important Warring States (475–221 B.C.) bronzes include a pedestal vessel, or *tou*, inlaid in red copper with animal and human figures, and a *hu*, exceptional in design and workmanship, enlivened by four horizontal registers filled with animals, birds, and dragons in relief.

The Shanghai Museum's comprehensive collection of painting and calligraphy includes many important works. Wang Hsi-chih (303–79) and his son Wang Hsien-chih, considered the immortals of calligraphy, are represented by Hsi-chih's *Shang Yü T'ieh* and Hsien-chih's *Ya T'ou Wan*. The eccentric Buddhist monk of the T'ang Dynasty (618–906), Huai Su, a genius in the mad-cursive script, is represented by his *K'u Sun T'iech*. Notable paintings include *Seven Sages of the Bamboo Grove* by the T'ang artist Sun Li and *Summer Mountains* by Tung Yüan of the Five Dynasties period (906–60). From the Sung Dynasty (960–1279), the museum holds Kuo Hsi's *Secluded Valleys*, Chü-jan's *Wind in the Pines of Ten Thousand Valleys*, Ma Chü-jan's *Snowy Impressions of Plum Blossoms*, and Li Sung's *West Lake* painting. Shanghai's Yüan Dynasty (1279–1368) paintings include a number of great renown. Chao Meng-fu's *Eastern Mountain of Lake Tung-t'ing* is here as is Ch'ien Hsüan's *Dwelling in the Floating Jade Mountains*. Wang Meng's *Hermit of the Ch'ing-pien Mountains* is a masterpiece of literati textural brushwork. Two works by Ni Tsan, *Autumn Landscape* and *Six Gentlemen*, exemplify his spare, austere style. Of a different sensibility is Wu Chen's *Old Fisherman Landscape*, with its rich, moist ink tones and playful brushwork. From the Ming Dynasty (1368–1644), the museum's fine works by imperial court painters include Tai Chin's *Spring Mountains*, Pien Wen-chin's *Spring Flowering Trees and Birds*, Lin Liang's *White Winged Pheasants in a Mountain Landscape*, Lu Chi's *Swimming Ducks*, and Chou Wen-ching's *Crows in an Old Tree*. Other Ming paintings include examples by the Suchou artists Tiang Yin and Ch'iu Ying. Shanghai also has a good number of fine paintings from the Ch'ing (1644–1911) and modern periods.

Three extensive permanent exhibitions are on view at the Shanghai Museum. These exhibitions reflect the strong points in the museum's holdings and generally introduce the historical development of the arts of bronze, ceramics, and paintings in China. The major divisions are those of medium; within this, objects are arranged by historical period and style in some cases, by other criteria when appropriate.

The selection of Chinese bronzes at the Shanghai Museum includes more than six hundred works and is divided into four parts. The first part presents in general outline the Slave Society period, that is, the Shang and Chou dynasties. In addition, there are rubbings from engraved inscriptions on the bronzes. The second part of the exhibition illuminates the technological development of bronzes: displays cover the opening of mines and smelting, the creation of ceramic molds into which the bronze was poured, and alloy casting. Demonstration models are used along with Shang and Chou dynasties' wine vessels, cooking vessels, weapons, and bronze mirrors from the Han (206 B.C.-A.D. 220) and T'ang dynasties. The exhibition explains differing ratios of metals contained in the alloys of bronzes of differing functions. Also explained is the phenomenon and theory of the reflectivity of the mirror, which represents improved procedures in ancient bronze-casting technology. In the third part of the bronze exhibition the remarkable artistic level of the bronzes is highlighted. Representative pieces from various historical periods are displayed to portray systematically the artistic development. Together they reflect the brilliant cultural achievements of ancient China. The fourth part of the exhibition presents bronzes from China's minority ethnic groups. They demonstrate stages of alternating cultural exchange and subsequent cultural fusion, indicating that the bronze craft was a unifying feature of ancient Chinese civilization.

The Shanghai Museum's permanent ceramics exhibition displays more than six hundred works, ranging from the invention of pottery by the Primitive Society through modern refined ceramics, introducing the most important steps in the historical development of Chinese ceramics. In the first part of the exhibition, "Birth of Pottery and Craft of the Primitive Society Potter," early hand-built painted wares from the neolithic sites at Pan-p'o, Miao-ti-kou, Ma Chia, Pan-shan, and Ma-ch'ang are displayed along with the pottery excavated from Sung-tse in Ch'ing-p'u county, Shanghai.

The second part, "Development of the Art and Technology of Ceramics: Appearance of Primitive Ceramics and Formation of Celadons in the Southeast," connects a natural-color glazed Shang Dynasty *tsun*, or beaker; the Ch'in Dynasty soldiers and horses from the Sian site; a small, black glazed jar from an Eastern Han tomb; and Wei-Chin period celadons.

The third part of the exhibition, "The Rich Colors of Sui, T'ang, and Five Dynasties Ceramic Wares," displays T'ang three-color wares, green glazed celadons from the Yüeh kilns, two-color glazed works from the San-hsien kilns, and underglaze painted wares from Ch'angsha.

The fourth section amply demonstrates the high artistic achievements in ceramics during the Northern and Southern Sung period, renowned for its classical restraint and dignity and for the perfection of shapes and glazes. On exhibition are blue-and-white pieces from the Ching-te-chen kilns, white porcelaneous wares from the T'ing kilns, celadon from the Lung-ch'uan and Yao-chou kilns, and slip-decorated stonewares, usually with white grounds and black or brown designs, from the Tz'u-chou kilns at Teng-feng, Tang-yang-yü, and Pa-ts'un. Other outstanding selections exhibited represent what was known traditionally as the Five Famous Kilns, that is, the exquisite *ko, kuan,* Ju, Chün, and Ting wares.

The exhibition's fifth part is called "New Advances in Ceramic Art and Craft at Ching-te-chen in the Yüan, Ming, and Ch'ing Periods." Here are the high-fired porcelains so well known in the West. They include fine white porcelains with underglaze decoration in cobalt blue or copper red, porcelain with overglaze enamel decoration in rainbow colors, and brilliant monochrome porcelains of which the ox-blood type is perhaps the most famous.

The sixth part of the exhibit displays "Ceramics from Areas Outside Ching-te-chen in the Yüan, Ming, and Ch'ing," and the final section of this impressive collection of ceramics is devoted to export ceramics.

The ceramics exhibition was organized to clarify a number of issues in the study of the art of ceramics. One such issue was the specific time of the invention of ceramics in China, a much-debated problem among scholars in China and abroad. Another area of academic concern has been the scientific difference between pottery and porcelain. The exhibition employs real objects, with photographs and diagrams to explain clearly how to distinguish between pottery and primitive porcelain. Also demonstrated is the fact that as early as the Shang Dynasty a primitive porcelain had been created, and the Warring States to the Han dynasties saw the gradual development and maturity of Chinese celadons. The traditional Chinese classification of white porcelain as a northern achievement and celadon as a southern achievement is challenged by the display of an important early white porcelain excavated from a southern region, Honan Province, and dating from the Eastern Han. Also of note for the art historian specializing in ceramics is the small, black glazed jar excavated from a grave in Chen-chiang on the Yangtze, which is dated 101, from the Eastern Han. At present this is the earliest black glazed ware of absolutely reliable date and thus an important piece for the study of the origin of this genre. It was thought previously that the Eastern Chin (317–420) Te-ch'ing kiln site was the earliest to produce black glazes.

The exhibition of Chinese paintings is a systematic introduction to more than four thousand years of development. Organization in this exhibition is based upon the historical dynasties and the developments within the field of painting. The exhibition gives attention to the influence of period styles and school or academy connections as well as the interplay between these forces.

To explain fully the historical developments, the painting exhibition relies upon copies and tracings of T'ang and pre-T'ang works. On exhibit are the designs painted on the pottery produced by China's Primitive Society, the Neolithic, as well as impressed designs from the wooden crafts of the Slave Society period. From the Warring States and Western Han periods are copies of their painted silks. Copies of representative Han to T'ang wall paintings and scrolls movingly reflect the life-styles of the period as well as the high level of attainment in figurative, landscape, and architectural painting.

Painting after the T'ang period is represented by some 120 original works displayed in three large exhibition rooms. Sung and Yüan paintings are together in one room, Ming and Ch'ing in a second, and modern paintings in a third. Within the historical periods and after chronological considerations, the paintings are assigned to either of the two major affiliations in Chinese painting, the academy or the literati. The arrangement of painting in the Ming-Ch'ing room emphasizes the various regional centers such as Che-chiang, Sung-chiang, Nanking, Anhwei, Yangchou, and so on. This organization reflects traditional Chinese art criticism, which recognized distinctive regional styles and schools of painting: Suchou's painting was called the Wu school; Che-chiang's, the Che school; there was also the Sung-chiang school made famous by Tung Ch'i-ch'ang, a Lu-Shan school from the area of Lu mountain, the Chin-ling school of Nanking, the Hsi-nan school of Anhwei, the Chiang-hsi school, and the Yangchou school. The exhibition's modern painting room features work by the great artists: Chao Chih-chien, Wu Ch'ang-shou, Jen Po-nien, Hsü Ku, Ch'en Heng-k'o, and Ch'i Pai-shih.

The Shanghai Museum on occasion mounts special exhibitions that are not part of the permanent installations. The museum also cooperates with other museums in arranging exhibitions and in sharing collections. A percentage of the works on exhibition at the Shanghai Museum of Art and History are on loan from other institutions. Examples include a Western Chou square pedestal *kui* from the Su-chou Cultural Museum and the Ch'in clay soldiers on loan from the Shensi Cultural Bureau. The Shanghai Museum loaned its Western Chou Ta Meng *ting* and other valuable relics to the National History Museum before its grand opening in 1959. Some of Shanghai's Sung Dynasty paintings were loaned to the Canton Museum, and some jade pieces were sent to an exhibition in Yokohama.

The museum's conservation department is especially noteworthy for its size and sophistication. It is conducting experiments on lacquering bronzes to prevent corrosion and freeze-drying baskets to arrest dehydration.

To strengthen relationships between the museum and the art-loving public, the Shanghai Museum established an association called the Friends of the Shanghai Museum. Its members include scholars, archaeologists, collectors, artists, educators, and designers. They meet at unspecified times to discuss the preservation of artworks within the city, to view new pieces in the museum collection, and to discuss important foreign works of art.

The Shanghai Museum has a reference library with a collection of about two hundred thousand volumes, which, however, does not include any foreign works.

Selected Bibliography

Museum publications: *Shanghai Bowuguan Cang Hua* (Paintings in the Collection of the Shanghai Museum), 1959; *Shanghai Bowuguan Cang Qingtongqi* (Bronzes in the Collection of the Shanghai Museum); 1964; *Songren Huace* (Album Paintings by Song Artists), 1979.

Other publications: *Shanghai bowuguan cang ci xuanji* (A Selection of Ceramics in the Collection of the Shanghai Museum) (Beijing 1979); *Shanghai bowuguan cang lidai fashu xianji* (Calligraphy in the Collection of the Shanghai Museum) (Beijing 1964); *Shanghai bowuguan cang yin* (Seals in the Collection of the Shanghai Museum); *Song ren hua niao* (Birds and Flowers in Sung Dynasty Painting) (Beijing 1966); Lefebvre d'Argencé, René-Yvon, ed., *Treasures from the Shanghai Museum: 6000 Years of Chinese Art* (San Francisco 1983); Shen Zhiyu, ed., *The Shanghai Museum of Art* (New York 1983); Ma Zhengyuan "The Splendor of Ancient Chinese Bronzes," in *The Great Bronze*

Age of China (New York 1980), pp. 1–19; Roberts, Cheryl, "The Curator's Role," *Museum News*, May-June, 1981, pp. 39–40; Zentner, Barbara S., "Registration Methods," *Museum News*, May-June, 1981, pp. 44–45.

LETHA MCINTIRE

—— **Shenyang** ——

LIAONING PROVINCIAL MUSEUM (officially LIAONING SHENG BO-WUGUAN [LIAO-NING-SHENG PO-WU-KUAN]), Shenyang, Liaoning.

In 1933 a Committee for Manchurian-Japanese Culture appointed by the Japanese government of Manchuria authorized the establishment of a National Central Museum. A preparatory office was set up in Mukden (Feng-t'ien, present-day Shenyang) in January 1934, and sorting of the materials already amassed for a museum collection was begun. In the same year, the former residence of T'ang Yü-lin was selected as a museum site, and the three-story neoclassic museum building, fronted by a formal garden, was completed. Known as the National Central Museum-Mukden Branch, it was officially opened on June 1, 1935.

Some of the 1,285 items in the original holdings came from T'ang Yü-lin and his son T'ang Tso-yung; 65 Chinese paintings ranging in date from the Sung Dynasty to the Ch'ing Dynasty (late tenth century-early twentieth century) once belonged to Chang Hsüeh-liang; and a group of Sui-yüan bronzes, as well as 115 Han to Yüan Dynasty (second century B.C. to A.D. 1368) tomb figures had previously been owned by Lo Chen-yü. The Japanese government made additional contributions to the collection, as did Sugimura Yūsō and Kuroda Genji. The collection also had late Buddhist sculptures and religious articles. More than three hundred ceramic pieces of the Liao and Chin dynasties (tenth-thirteenth centuries A.D.), all in perfect condition, constituted the most significant segment of the entire collection. In addition, the collection of Liao ceramic shards was between twenty and thirty thousand pieces. Second in importance were handicrafts of the Ch'ien-lung reign (A.D. 1736–96), formerly kept in the Imperial Palace in Jehol: carved jade and ivory, lacquer, textiles, and cloisonné (including a 2.45-meter-high, three-storied cloisonné pagoda). Among the calligraphy and paintings were an example of writing by Wang Hsien-chih (A.D. 344–88), *Stream and Old Plum* by Wang Mien (A.D. 1335–1407), and *The Cultivating Bamboo Study* by T'ang Yin (A.D. 1470–1523); from the Ch'ing Dynasty (A.D. 1644–1911) were fan paintings by the Four Wangs, Yün Shou-p'ing, and Hua Yen and an album by Chin Nung.

After 1935 this basic collection was expanded by objects from archaeological excavations, such as that at the prehistoric site at Hung-shan-hou in Ch'ih-feng and at the site of the ancient capital of P'o-hai. The collection eventually totaled 37,832 pieces. Of them, 1,833 items were lost during the military occupation of Manchuria by the Soviet Union in 1945–46, when some materials were stolen and dispersed. On January 1, 1947, the museum came under Chinese ownership and was merged with the Shenyang Library. The museum building was renamed the Antiquities Hall and placed under the jurisdiction of the National Shenyang Museum. On September 13, 1947, the National Shenyang Museum was relocated in the former Imperial Palace in Shenyang and, in addition to having administrative responsibility for the Antiquities Hall and the Library, also acquired the Folklore Hall. During this time, museum objects found in the hands of antique dealers were reclaimed. After 1948, under the People's Republic of China, the Shenyang Museum returned to its original quarters under the name of Liaoning Provincial Museum.

In the late 1970s, galleries on the first two floors exhibited archaeological materials from excavations in Manchuria since 1948. Important neolithic items include jades and, of special interest, ceramic vessels (excavated at Ta-tien-tsu, Aohan Banner, in 1974) said to date from 1800–1500 B.C., which are painted with spirals or squared-spirals reminiscent of Shang Dynasty (sixteenth to eleventh century B.C.) bronze decor. Probably dating from the eleventh to early tenth century B.C. is a hoard of six decorated bronze vessels found in 1973 at Pei-tung-ts'un, K'e-tso-hsien (three *ting*, two *lei*, one *kuei*). One of the *ting* vessels, square in shape, exhibits designs normally associated with the Shang Dynasty, whereas a *lei* ornamented with coiled-body dragons is completely Early Chou (late eleventh to early tenth century) in style and concept. Burial goods from the grave of Feng Su-fu of the kingdom of Northern Yen (A.D. 409–36) include gold-covered wooden stirrups, bronze vessels, blown glassware, a gold open-work plaque, and seals. Perhaps the most striking artifacts are furnishings from a tenth-century Liao tomb at Yeh-mao-t'ai in Fa-k'u-hsien excavated in 1974: agate bowls, textiles, and clothing embroidered with animal and floral motifs. Ceramics from this site are mixed; some reflect T'ang Dynasty (A.D. 618–906) traditions, others reveal Sung Dynasty (A.D. 960–1125) forms in white ware and Tz'u-chou type decoration.

The nucleus of the collection of more than five thousand Chinese paintings, rarely on public view, consists of works from the Ch'ing Imperial Palace in Shenyang, as well as those taken from the Imperial Palace collection in Peking to Manchuria by P'u-i, who ruled Manchuria as puppet-emperor under the Japanese from 1934 until 1945. Two of the most important paintings, however, being rare examples of tenth-century landscape and bird, flower, and animal depictions, came from the tenth-century Liao tomb at Yeh-mao-t'ai.

Notable other early paintings are a version of Ku K'ai-chih's (c. 344-c. 406) *Nymph of the Lo River* and the *Ladies with Flowered Headdresses*, attributed to Chou Fang (fl.c. 780–810). The unusual depiction of *A Celestial Steed* is given to Han Kan (mid-eighth century). Five Dynasties and Sung (906–1280) paintings include Tung Yüan's *Awaiting a Crossing at the Foot of Summer Mountains* handscroll; Li Ch'eng's *Wintry Grove*; Emperor Hui-tsung's *Auspicious Cranes Flying over a Palace* and his copy of Chang Hsüan's *Lady Kuo-*

kuo and Her Sisters on an Outing; *Illustrations to Twelve Odes of T'ang*, attributed to Ma Ho-chih; *The White Lotus Society* by Cheng Chi (early twelfth century); and the anonymous *Four Greybeards of Mt. Shang* and *Nine Ancients of Hui-ch'ang* handscrolls. There are also substantial holdings of Sung fan and album leaf paintings. From the Yüan Dynasty (1280–1368) is a rare figure painting by Chao Meng-fu, *Red-robed Monk* (1304), as well as landscapes by him and by Chao Yung, and Wang Meng's *Landscape of Mt. T'ai-po* handscroll. The plant theme is represented by Chao Yung's *Bamboo* handscroll, Li Shih-hsing's *Bamboo and Rock*, Wu Chen's *Plum Blossoms* (1348), and Wu Kuan's *Plum and Bamboo* (1348). Significant Ming Dynasty (1368–1644) works are Wang Fu's *River Landscape*; *The Life of T'ao Yüan-ming* (a series of figure-in-landscape scenes) by Li Tsai, Ma Shih, and Hsia Chia (all early fifteenth century); and Tai Chin's *Six Patriarchs of the Ch'an Sect*. Suchou masters are represented by Shen Chou's *Elegant Gathering in the Wei Garden*, Wen Cheng-ming's *Epidendrum, Bamboo, Pine, and Rock* handscroll, T'ang Yin's *Wu Yang-tzu in Meditation*, and an excellent Ch'iu Ying rendition of *The Red Cliff*. Of exceptional interest is Shen Chou's illustration of Su Shih's poem "Misty River and Layered Peaks" (1507), which is mounted with Wen Cheng-ming's illustration to the same poem (1508), a vivid example of teacher and student working in two different modes.

Some of the other fifteenth- and sixteenth-century paintings are by Yao Shou, Sun Lung, Tu Chin, Hsieh Shih-ch'en, and Chiang Ch'ien. Late Ming works include *White Clouds on the Hsiao and Hsiang Rivers* by Tung Ch'i-ch'ang and a hanging scroll by Lan Ying, *Listening to the Waterfall in a Spring Pavilion*. Ch'ing Dynasty (1644–1911) orthodox painting is represented by, among others, two landscapes after Huang Kung-wang, one by Wang Chien, the other by Wang Hui; and by Wang Yuan-ch'i's album of landscapes after Sung and Yüan masters, Wu Li's *Landscape Inspired by a Ni Tsan Poem*, and Yün Shou-p'ing's *Landscape on a Clear Day*. Other Ch'ing paintings provide samples of the diversity of styles practiced in local schools or by individual masters, such as Hsiao Yün-ts'ung, Cha Shih-piao, Kao Ts'en, Kung Hsien (including his *Spring Streams*, dated 1648), Fa Jo-chen, Mei Ch'ing, Tao-chi, Kao Ch'i-p'ei, Hua Yen, Chin Nung, Ch'eng Hsieh, and Kao Feng-han (including his *Wu-t'ung Tree and Mynah* and *Eagle on a Pine*). Nineteenth-century paintings include examples of Chao Chih-ch'ien's flowers and Jen I's *Lady and Plum Blossoms* (1884).

The third floor of the museum apparently is normally used for special political or historical exhibitions that may have no artistic or archaeological content.

Selected Bibliography

Sung Yüan shan-shui chi-ts'e: Liao-ning-sheng po-wu-kuan ts'ang-hua chi chih i (A collection of Sung and Yüan Dynasty landscape paintings, album leaves, in the Liaoning Provincial Museum), Shenyang, 1960; *Liaoning-sheng po-wu-kuan Liao-tz'u hsüan chi* (Liao Dynasty ceramics in the Liaoning Provincial Museum), Peking, 1962; *Liao-*

ning-sheng po-wu-kuan ts' ang hua chi (A selection of paintings in the Liaoning Provincial Museum), Peking, 1962. *Hsü chi* (Supplement), Peking, 1980.

ELLEN JOHNSTON LAING

———— Sian. See Xian. ————

———— Xian (Sian) ————

SHENSI PROVINCIAL MUSEUM (officially SHAANXI SHENG BO-WUGUAN [SHEN-HSI-SHENG PO-WU-KUAN]; alternately THE SIAN MUSEUM, THE XIAN MUSEUM), Sanxue jieh, Xian, Shaanxi.

The Northwest Administrative Council in 1953 officially designated the Northwest Historical Museum (Hsi-pei li-shih po-wu-kuan) as the Shensi Provincial Historical Museum (Shen-hsi sheng li-shih po-wu-kuan), renamed the Shensi Provincial Museum in 1954. Its early twentieth-century predecessor, generally known in the West as the Shensi Museum at Sian-fu, was administered by the Shensi Bureau of Education as a department of the provincial library. The nucleus of the museum collection, however, originated in 1090 (Sung Dynasty), when stones engraved with the Confucian Classics and writings of famous calligraphers were installed in the area presently occupied by the northern (rear) section of the museum grounds. The museum is traditionally recognized as an enlargement of this nine hundred-year-old "Forest of Stelae" (Pei-lin).

The Shensi Provincial Museum belongs to a government network of provincial museums supervised by the National Bureau of Cultural Relics. The bureau's local subdivision, the Shensi Provincial Commission for the Preservation of Cultural Relics, has offices within the museum compound. This commission, staffed by twenty-six members in 1981, supervises archaeological excavations that have unearthed more than forty-five thousand objects accessioned since 1949. Excavation workers include university graduates and special, government-sponsored, archaeological training classes. Other departments and their Western equivalents include: Administration, Exhibition, Protection (Curatorial), Public Work (Education), Capital Construction (Buildings and Grounds), and Reproduction (Conservation and Replica Making).

The layout and architecture of the museum compound originated in cumulative building projects. An ancestral temple and Confucian temple successively occupied the area south of the Pei-lin, now the entrance courtyard of the museum. The history of these temples is recorded in local registers and in some inscriptions on the Pei-lin stelae chronicling the relocation of individual stones. Among the most important stones are 114 tablets engraved with Confucian texts in the K'ai-ch'eng period of the T'ang Dynasty (837). The so-called *K'ai-ch'eng Stone*

Classics were moved twice. In the early tenth century, following the fall of T'ang, they were moved from their original site immediately south of the T'ang imperial city (Huang-ch'eng) to a Confucian temple in the area of the present Drum Tower. This move was dictated by the rebuilding of a smaller city that left the stones abandoned outside the new city walls. That area, northwest of the Shensi Provincial Museum, is thought to be the original site of the Pei-lin depository. Some stones unearthed near the Drum Tower since 1949 apparently were left behind in 1090, when Lu Ta-chung, an imperial academician, moved the K'ai-ch'eng Classics and other stelae to their present location—the property of a prefectural academy founded in 1035. Galleries for the Pei-lin were constructed in 1094. Directly south of these new galleries, on the site of a T'ang ancestral temple, a Confucian temple (or *wen-miao*, temple of literature) was founded about 1103.

The original layout of the Pei-lin galleries of 1094 and the Confucian temple of about 1103 is preserved along the straight south-to-north axis of the Shensi Provincial Museum. The plan of walled courtyards linked by gateway openings is characteristic of major buildings in dynastic China, religious or secular.

A free-standing screen-wall (*ying-bi*), traditionally built to deflect evil spirits, backs the entrance courtyard at the south end. Aligned directly behind are three structures canonical to Confucian temples and evidently restored, which museum authorities identify as original to the early-twelfth-century temple: a wood tripartite arch (*p'ai-lou*) with decoratively painted lintels, elaborate corbel bracketing, and massive tile roofs; a semicircular pool (*p'an-chih*) bordered by marble balustrades and bridges; and a tripartite gate (*ling-hsing men*) of stone, brick, and tile. The *ling-hsing* gate opens onto the second courtyard, containing the first of seven pavilions erected during the Ch'ien-lung era (1736–95) to protect meritorious (*kung-te*) stelae. The next six pavilions are aligned in two rows in the third courtyard. Each pavilion is an octagonal structure raised on a marble terrace, with thick columns supporting an upcurved tile roof. Wall panels are constructed in decorative lattice wood; horizontal beams are painted with birds, flying deities, and floral rosettes.

The Forest of Stelae immediately south of these pavilions is organized as a separate compound of six halls connected by six open corridors (*pei-lang*). Major repairs to the stones are datable to the thirteenth, fifteenth, and sixteenth centuries; in the late eighteenth century, the scholar-official Pi Yüan had the buildings reconstructed from collapsed ruins. To what extent the present arrangement reflects his rebuilding or the original layout of A.D. 1094 is unknown, although historical records verify that the *Pillar of Filial Piety* long occupied its current position at front and center of the compound. A column-and-beam pavilion with double-hipped roof shelters the pillar and marks entrance to the forest. The halls behind it are brick constructions, housing stelae aligned in narrow parallel rows. Outside walls of the open corridors are lined with tomb epitaphs dating between the Han (206 B.C.-A.D. 220) and Ch'ing (1644–1911) dynasties.

Since the museum's founding, several galleries have been added along the east and west sides of this back-to-back arrangement of temple and stelae halls. They include one gallery for special exhibitions in the second courtyard, two for archaeological finds flanking the third courtyard, and one for stone carving west of the Pei-lin. Two galleries east of the Pei-lin reportedly contain bronzes and ceramics, but they were not open to the public in 1980–81.

The Forest of Stelae, including 1,077 stones on display in 1981, has become the pre-eminent collection of Chinese calligraphy through government acquisition and private donation. For generations of scholar-artists who studied the monuments firsthand or through inked impressions (rubbings), it has provided a library of historical texts and of script styles reproduced in intaglio stone carving. The stelae, dating from the second century B.C. through the nineteenth century A.D., include grave epitaphs, religious texts, and commemorative inscriptions attached to public buildings. Pictorial stones—incised with topographic maps, buildings, figures, landscapes, and bamboo—are less numerous, although some allegedly reproduce paintings by early masters.

In the absence of comprehensive inventories, the following stones have been individually traced to Lu Ta-chung's original assemblage of 1090: (1) The *K'ai-ch'eng Stone Classics* is engraved with twelve Confucian texts under auspices of the T'ang imperial academy in 833–37. This work was commissioned for accurate transmission of standard texts a century before the earliest woodblock printed edition and is of primarily literary interest as the most complete set of stone classics extant. The calligraphers named in the inscriptions are otherwise unknown. (2) The *Pillar of Filial Piety* is the text of the Classic of Filial Piety, with annotations composed and purportedly carved after the clerical and running scripts of Emperor Hsüan-tsung in 743. The capstone and base are embellished with dragons, clouds, and lions. (3) The *Yen Family Stele*, dated 780 consists of a genealogy composed and written by Yen Cheng-ch'ing in "regular" script for his father's ancestral temple. (4) The *Shuo-wen Dictionary* has headings copied in archaistic "seal" script by the Buddhist monk Meng-ying (tenth century).

Among numerous famous calligraphers whose scripts are also preserved in the Pei-lin are Ou-yang Hsün (active 557–64), Ch'u Sui-liang (596–658), the monk Huai-su (737-c.798), Emperor Hui-tsung (reigned 1100–25), and Chao Meng-fu (1254–1322). The most renowned early master, Wang Hsi-chih (321–79), is represented in allegedly faithful engravings after a pastiche of individual characters extracted from his written manuscripts by the monk Huai-jen in the seventh century. Wang's "reassembled" ideographs form the *Ta T'ang san-t'ang sheng chiao hsü*, composed by Emperor T'ai-tsung as a preface to a Buddhist text translated from Sanskrit by Hsüan-tsang, the great monastic pilgrim.

Other stelae in the Pei-lin are important documents of various sects of Buddhism, recording the histories of monasteries and reputed monks. The collection is particularly rich in stelae from T'ang Dynasty temples, most of which were destroyed in mid-ninth-century Buddhist persecutions. The stele of the Hsüan-pi Pagoda in Sian, written by Liu Kung-ch'üan in 841, acquired archaeological interest in 1959, when statues were excavated from the probable site of the An-kuo Temple to which the pagoda belonged. Several of these statues are exhibited in the adjacent Hall of Stone Carving.

A T'ang religious minority is documented in the Nestorian Monument, engraved with Chinese and Syriac texts of Nestorian Christianity and erected in 781 at a Christian shrine in Sian. In the seventeenth century, it was unearthed and translated into Latin and Italian by missionary-priests. Unique in the Pei-lin for its European association, it was moved here in 1907, following a private collector's unsuccessful attempt to purchase it for sale to the British Museum.

Unlike the Pei-lin's prolonged expansion, the museum's archaeological collections have increased from an estimated forty to fifty objects in 1953 to almost eighty-five thousand in 1981. The wealth and importance of these collections follow Shensi's historical prominence as the site of eleven dynastic capitals spanning more than eleven hundred years and consequently prolific excavations of palaces, tombs, temples, kiln sites, and workshops. Except for large stone sculptures exhibited in the Hall of Stone Carving, archaeological materials, limited by space to approximately five hundred, are displayed in two galleries named for and (with few exceptions) restricted to the five major dynasties whose capitals were established in proximity to modern Sian: (Gallery 1) Western Chou (1045–771 B.C.), Ch'in (221–206 B.C.), and Western Han (206 B.C.-A.D. 9); (Gallery 2) Sui (581–618) and T'ang (618–907).

In 1978 some of the museum's earliest material, recently discovered and not yet incorporated into these permanent galleries, appeared in the special exhibition "Finds Excavated Since the Cultural Revolution" (1972–78). Neolithic pottery traditionally designated Yang-shao and Lung-shan represented types once thought to be geographically remote; the Lung-shan site also featured decorative and functional jades. The Bronze Age was introduced by a square cauldron (*fang-ting*) of the Shang Dynasty (c. 1766–1045 B.C.) from Li-ch'üan technically notable for its primitive casting and historically for its resemblance to bronzes made much farther east, in the Honan centers of Shang civilization. Other Shang bronzes, illustrated in museum catalogs (1957 and 1979) but not exhibited, are documented from several districts in northern and central Shensi Province.

Excavation of two Western Chou capital cities (Feng and Hao) southwest of Sian, initiated in the 1930s and intensified since 1955, have yielded abundant bronzes from tombs, chariot burials, and storage pits. Vessels of generally heavy profile and zoomorphic or abstract surface design originate from modern Chang-chia-p'o village and other sites associated with the Chou ancestral homeland. Many are cast with lengthy inscriptions important both as historical texts and as calligraphic art. Recent finds include the so-called Ho *tsun* (wine vase) from Pao-chi, named after the maker cited in its inscription and dating from the eleventh century B.C., and a cache of 103 vessels from Fu-feng, many naming successive kings of a Chou ruling clan. What proportion of this and other large hoards the museum has accessioned or turned over to local museums in Shensi or to the national museums in Peking is unknown. The question is relevant to museum visitors insofar as accurate reproductions are commonly substituted for original objects but not always distinguished in gallery labels. A case in point is a now-famous inlaid bronze rhinocerous urn from Hsing-p'ing (third century B.C.), reportedly unique but displayed in this gallery as well as in the Museum of Chinese History (q.v.) in Peking and at the Huo Ch'ü-ping tomb.

The Shensi Provincial Museum and the Shensi Provincial Commission for the Preservation of Cultural Relics assume joint responsibility for ongoing excavations of trenches surrounding the tumulus of the first Ch'in Dynasty emperor (d. 210 B.C.) near Lin-t'ung county. A life-size terracotta army buried in these trenches, estimated to exceed eight thousand figures in 1980 and more recently augmented by half-scale, gilt-bronze, horse-drawn chariots, is China's most intensive archaeological project. Infantrymen, cavalrymen, charioteers, archers, and horses are individually hand modeled with stylized volumes and naturalistic facial and clothing detail. A representative variety of figures was shown in the museum's 1978 exhibition, and credit lines in subsequent loan shows abroad indicate that many have been accessioned. (A portion of the first and largest burial pit, discovered in 1974, has been roofed over as an on-site exhibition hall and restoration studio.) The permanent gallery, by contrast, shows how scattered were Ch'in relics before this massive discovery: one of five clay figures found near the burial mound between 1932 and 1970 is exhibited with coins, bronze vessels, chariot ornaments, and architectural remains from Ch'in palaces: stamped bricks and eaves-end tiles salvaged from Lin-t'ung and Hsien-yang, the preconquest capital of the Ch'in state.

Ceramic sculpture also predominates in the Han Dynasty section concluding the first gallery. Painted figures from a cavalry of approximately twenty-six hundred, unearthed in 1965 from trenches near the Han imperial tombs at Yang-chia-wan, Hsien-yang, follow the Ch'in concept although they are smaller in scale (average height, twenty inches) and mold produced. Both civilian and military figures wear a variety of costumes depicted with well-preserved painting. Other Han burial figures, including real and imaginary animals of great vitality, are cataloged from San-men Gorge, Fu-feng, and the environs of Hsien-yang.

The second gallery chronicles the Sui and T'ang dynasties, when Sian (then Ch'angan) was rebuilt on unprecedented scale. A wall map of the grid-city locates gates, wards, palaces, markets, temples, and other landmarks. The palace compound ("Great Luminous Palace" and audience halls), surveyed by the Institute of Archaeology since 1957, is reconstructed in plans and elevations shown alongside pillar bases, bricks, and tiles found in situ. The city's international relations are graphically described: layouts of Kyoto and Nara in the eighth and ninth centuries highlight the Ch'angan model for Japanese city planning; maps tracking the Silk Route west from Ch'angan are displayed behind Byzantine and Sassanian coins, textile fragments, and pottery figures with Near Eastern features and clothing styles.

The hall is richest in furnishings from seventh- and eighth-century royal and aristocratic tombs, many datable by the epitaph identifying the occupant. Most tombs have been looted of valuable materials; primarily pottery vessels and figures remain. One major exception is the mausoleum of Li Ching-hsün (d. 608 at nine years), discovered intact in 1957. Her appropriately small-scale mortuary gifts include glass and white-glazed stoneware vessels exemplifying fine craftsmanship of the brief Sui Dynasty. The most precious objects from this tomb (a multijeweled necklace, gold and jade cups) recently have been moved from this gallery to the Museum of Chinese History in Peking. But the outer stone coffin (*kuo*), designed as a miniature gabled building and delicately engraved with architectural details, figures, and floral motifs, is exhibited in the Hall of Stone Carving.

Tombs surrounding the Ch'ien-ling imperial burial ground of Emperor Kao-tsung and Empress Wu have yielded a significant and coherent display of early eighth-century mortuary art. Multichamber tombs of three junior relatives—Princess Yung-t'ai, Prince I-te, and Prince Chang-huai—all deposed but honorably reburied in 706, are most renowned for wall murals that illustrate everyday court life in the "high T'ang" style of rationally descriptive and psychologically expressive figure painting. Fragments of original murals from these three tombs, as well as from the tombs of Li Shou (630), Li Shuang (668), Li Feng (675), and Su Ssu-hsü (745), are kept in museum storage. Full-scale reproductions of wall paintings and rubbings of engraved sarcophagi contributed to the 1981 special exhibition "T'ang Murals and Engravings." Additional reproductions and rubbings are installed in the permanent gallery as backdrops to an impressive array of painted and lead-glazed burial figures of the late seventh through mid-eighth century. Most have been excavated since 1960 from princely tombs at the imperial cemeteries of Chao-ling (Emperor T'ai-tsung) and Ch'ien-ling. Characteristic types are displayed: horses, camels, court ladies, and officials, both civil and military. The earliest polychrome-glazed (*san-ts'ai*) figures come from the tomb of General Cheng Jen-t'ai (d. 663); most striking among the later finds from Ch'ien-ling are painted and gilt cavalry soldiers from Prince I-te's tomb. A unique architectural miniature in *san-ts'ai* pottery comprises courtyard buildings and garden pavilions assembled around a mythical mountain. From the same tomb in Chung-pao village comes a camel bearing a troupe of musicians, one of few recently published examples of this complex sculptural theme.

Luxurious metalwork has been found in isolated pieces as well as collective hoards lost or deliberately buried by the Ch'angan aristocracy during political upheavals in the mid-eighth century. Representing a hoard of more than one thousand artifacts unearthed in Ho-chia village in 1970 are dishes of beaten gold and silver decorated with repoussé, soldered, traced, open-work, inlaid, and parcel-gilt designs. Tentatively identified as the buried treasure of an exiled prince, this hoard exhibits the full diversity of the T'ang decorative style. Other single masterworks include a parcel-gilt silver basin with repoussé lion and flowers found north of Sian in 1956 and a bronze mirror inlaid on lacquer with horses and phoenixes of gold and silver foil, one of the finest examples of this *ping-t'o* technique. More typical Sui and T'ang mirrors are cast with zodiac animals, "lion and grapevine" motifs, jewel-like flowers, and mythological personalities.

Two precisely dated objects of monumental scale are featured in open pavilions outside these archaeological galleries: (1) A stone horse (height, 2.0 meters) is dated by inscription incised under the chest to the Hsing-p'ing reign of the state of Hsia (424). The horse is carved in angular, blocky forms of the early Han Dynasty style current five hundred years earlier (cf. similar Huo Ch'ü-ping horse, below). Presumably placed before a tomb, it was brought to the museum in 1954 from Ch'a-chia-chai, a northern suburb of Sian. (2) A bronze bell (height, 2.7 meters) was cast in the second year of the Ching-yün reign of the T'ang Dynasty (711). Its surface is divided in large, square panels with relief lions, phoenixes, dragons, and cranes, as well as an engraved inscription by Emperor Jui-tsung. It originally hung in the Bell Tower of Chinglung Temple and was moved to the museum in 1953.

The U-shaped Hall of Stone Carving opened in 1963 to house a collection of sculpture that has greatly expanded since publication of an illustrated catalog in 1957. Total holdings are unpublished; sixty-four pieces displayed in 1981 were roughly split between secular and Buddhist material. Unlike the archaeological galleries, this hall contains a number of pre-1949 finds inherited from museums and private collections in Sian.

Secular material comprises almost entirely mortuary monuments: architectural fragments and furnishings of underground tomb chambers as well as sculptures set above ground marking the "spirit road" approach to major burials. The first group includes tomb panels, epitaphs, and coffins notable for carved and incised decoration. Stones aligned near the entrance include free-standing pillars, door leaves, and wall panels carved in low, flat relief with hunting and agricultural scenes, processions, and historical and mythological narratives. Although provenance is not listed on labels, many were documented from the districts of Yü-lin, Mi-chih, and Sui-te in a 1958 museum report. Some can be identified with the tomb of Wang Te-yüan dating from A.D. 100 from an inscribed slab. Their compositions and border designs show a distinctive regional style of early pictorial art, partly influenced by nearby nomadic tribes along the Ordos steppe. Stone epitaphs are identified from the Western Wei tomb of Emperor Wen-ti (d. 552) and the early T'ang tomb of Li Shou (d. 630), a younger cousin of Emperor Kao-tsu. Li Shou's epitaph is shaped like a tortoise; the back shell, inscribed with his official title, forms a cover for the lengthy inscription. His stone coffin, more than twice the scale of Li Ching-hsün's, is delicately incised on the interior with female musicians and dancers and boldly carved on the exteriors with relief silhouettes of military and court officials, female attendants, and animal symbols of the four directions.

True statuary begins with a rearing horse from the reputed tomb of General Huo Ch'ü-ping (d. 117 B.C.) at the Mao-ling imperial necropolis of his commander-in-chief, Emperor Wu of Western Han. Its massive form, hewn roughly as two bas-reliefs from the granite boulder, was considered standard for early monumental sculpture before the discovery of the Ch'in terracotta army. (Exhibition corridors at Mao-ling show a corresponding [original?] horse as part of a set of sixteen statues unearthed near the general's burial mound.) Two striding lions from an unidentified Eastern Han tomb at Hsien-yang strike very different, sinuous, and spirited postures. A series of seated lions from the fifth through the seventh century illustrate subsequent styles in animal sculpture, the earlier being rare examples of Han cultural survival in Northern (foreign-controlled) kingdoms. The seventh-century lion, from the tomb of Li Hu, paternal grandfather of the first T'ang emperor, Kao-tsu, shows powerfully realistic but static qualities common also to a tiger and rhinocerous from Kao-tsu's own spirit road at Hsien-ling.

Perhaps the greatest treasures of early T'ang funerary art are six stone panels depicting in high bas-relief the favorite battle horses of Emperor T'ai-tsung. Traditionally based on designs by the eminent court painter Yen Li-pen, these sculpted portraits are either the originals of A.D. 637 or accurate and early copies set behind the tomb of T'ai-tsung and his empress at the Chao-ling cemetery northwest of Sian. Two panels, owned by the University Museum in Philadelphia, Pennsylvania, are represented in close replicas. The other four (originals) came to the Northwest Historical Museum in 1950. They reportedly were moved from the tombsite to the Sian-fu museum (provincial library) in 1917, shortly after the American acquisition.

Two T'ang stones of unspecified origin warrant mention for the quality and complexity of their carving. One is an uninscribed tombstone head with powerfully arching dragons, a heavier version of many stele capstones in the Pei-lin. Above the blank title cartouche are high-relief birds and winged harpies resembling designs in contemporary metalwork. The second is a columnar "sacrificial lamp" stacked vertically in nine distinctive layers. Its pedestal of intertwined dragons upholds a capital of open lotus leaves, support for the light chamber formed as a roofed pavilion. Whether the provenance listed (West Lake village in Ch'ien district) is the site of a residence, cemetery, or Buddhist temple is unexplained—so also the function of this extravagant piece.

Buddhist stone sculpture begins with votive stelae showing the Buddha and attendant figures carved in shallow niches or against leaf-shaped aureoles. The earliest are dated by incised inscription to the T'o-pa rulers of Northern Wei (late fifth and early sixth centuries), the first great patrons of Buddhism in China. Once considered late and provincial by some Western scholars, the soft and schematic carving of these sandstone stelae is now recognized as a formative regional style related to clay images modeled in cave temples to the far west (Kansu Province). Thereafter a progression of free-standing statues can be followed through the Northern Chou (557–81), Sui, and mid-T'ang dynasties, the T'ang including beautifully proportioned if fragmentary bodhisattva and guardian figures. The eighth-century apex of powerful and refined carving is exemplified in a group of white marbles, including an elaborately armored celestial guardian (*lokapala*). Most unusual are marble and limestone images of wrathful deities seated on rocky thrones, part of an esoteric pantheon unearthed in 1959. Their excavation site east of Sian corresponds with historical records of the An-kuo Temple, a major center of Tantric Buddhism, whose pagoda is memorialized on a stele in the Pei-lin.

Outside corridors surrounding the Hall of Stone Carving also exhibit numerous Buddhist stone sculptures (unlabeled) that appear to date from the Northern Dynasties (386–581), Sui, and T'ang. In 1980 the courtyard in front of the hall was a stockpile of recently found, excavated, and donated stones: spirit road animals, tomb stelae, Buddhist figures, and a huge cigar-shaped boulder (length, 4.9 meters) identified as an artificial fish from the site of Lake T'ai-yeh, originally within the pleasure park of a Western Han imperial palace.

At present, only fragmentary information can be ascertained about the museum's post-T'ang collections: a few examples of later Buddhist sculpture illustrated in the 1957 catalog; Sung (960–1279), Chin (1115–1234), and Yüan Dynasty (1279–1368) ceramics from Yao-chou kiln sites included in the 1978 special exhibition; and an unpublished collection of Yüan, Ming (1368–1644), and Ch'ing (1644–1911) Dynasty scroll paintings reported by museum personnel in 1981.

The museum's scholarly publications include monographs published in cooperation with the Institute of Archaeology and Commission for the Preservation of Cultural Relics, as well as articles in the national archaeology journals: *K'ao-ku, Wen wu,* and *K'ao-ku hsüeh-pao. Wen-p'o ts'ung-k'an,* a museum journal, has been announced for publication at irregular intervals. The museum has loaned generously to exhibitions in the United States, Europe, and Japan; consequently, foreign catalogs have become well-illustrated and up-to-date sources about the collection. However, it should be noted that Shensi Province has an increasing number of municipal, county, and specialized on-site museums that share responsibility for unearthing and preserving the local wealth of archaeological materials. They include the Hsien-yang Municipal Museum, Pao-chi Municipal Museum, T'ung-ch'uan Cultural Center, Fu-feng County Museum, Pan-p'o Neolithic Village Museum, and the Museum of Ch'in Figures at Lin-t'ung. Museums have also been established at the imperial cemeteries of Mao-ling, Chao-ling, and Ch'ien-ling. Relics from extensive excavations often are apportioned between the Shensi Provincial Museum, these local or on-site museums, and the national museums in Peking: the Palace Museum (q.v.) and Museum of Chinese History.

Selected Bibliography

Museum publications: The Northwest Historical Museum, *Ku-tai chuang-shih hua-wen hsüan-chi* (Album of ancient ornaments; rubbings from bronze, ceramic, and stone objects in the museum), in Chinese (Sian 1953). The following are jointly edited by the Shensi Provincial Commission for the Preservation of Cultural Relics and the museum: *Shen-hsi ch'u-t'u Shang Chou ch'ing-t'ung chi* (Bronzes of the Shang and Chou dynasties unearthed in Shensi Province), in Chinese (Peking 1979-); *Shen-pei Tung Han hua hsiang shih-k'e* (Eastern Han brick reliefs in northern Shensi Province), in Chinese (Peking 1958); *Shih-k'e hsüan-chi* (Stone sculpture in the collection of the Shensi Provincial Museum), in Chinese (Peking 1957); *T'ang Li Chung-jun mu pi-hua* (Wall paintings in the tomb of Li Chung-jun, Prince I-te), folio with captions in Chinese (Peking 1974); *T'ang Li Hsien mu pi-hua* (Wall paintings in the tomb of Li Hsien, Prince Chang-huai), folio with captions in Chinese (Peking 1974).

Other publications: *Chūgoku nisenen no bi: China's Beauty of 2000 Years, Exhibition of Ceramics and Rubbings of Inscriptions in the Hsi-an Museum*, in Japanese with English captions, exhibition catalog, Matsuya Department Store and others (Tokyo 1965); *Seian kodai kinseki takuhon to hegiga ten* (Stone and bronze rubbings and mural paintings in the ancient city of Sian), in Japanese, exhibition catalog, Osaka Municipal Museum of Fine Arts and others (Osaka 1980); *Hsi-an wen wu sheng-chi* (Famous historical places and cultural relics of Sian), chapter on the Shensi Provincial Museum, n.p., in Chinese and English (Sian 1959); *Sensei-sho Hakubutsukan* (The Shensi Provincial Museum), vol. 1 of *Chugoku no hakubutsukan* (Museums of China), in Japanese (Tokyo 1981); *Shen-hsi sheng ch'u t'u T'ang yung hsüan-chi* (T'ang tomb figures excavated in Shensi Province), in Chinese (Peking 1958); Fong, Mary H., "T'ang Wall Paintings of the Early Eighth Century," *Oriental Art*, n.s., vol. 24, no. 2 (Summer 1978), pp. 185–94; Lawton, Thomas, "An Introduction to the Sian Pei-lin (Forest of Stelae)" (Paper prepared for the Symposium on Chinese Calligraphy, Yale University, 1977); Shih Hsio-yen, "Han Stone Reliefs from Shensi Province," *Archives of the Chinese Art Society of America*, vol. 14 (1960), pp. 49–63; Wu Po-lun, "Hsi-an Pei-lin chien-shih" (A brief history of the Pei-lin in Sian), in Chinese, *Wen wu*, 1961, no. 8, pp. 17–22; idem, "Hsi-an Pei-lin shu-lüeh" (A summary report on the Pei-lin in Sian), in Chinese, *Wen wu*, 1965, no. 9, pp. 12–21.

ELINOR PEARLSTEIN

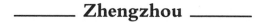

Zhengzhou

HONAN PROVINCIAL MUSEUM (officially HENAN SHENG BOWU-GUAN [HO-NAN-SHENG PO-WU-KUAN]), Zhengzhou, Henan.

The Honan Provincial Museum was established in 1926 in K'aifeng, then capital of the province. Its opening years coincided with the beginning of field archaeology in China and with excavations of the late Shang Dynasty capital (Yin) near modern Anyang (occupied c. 1400–1100 B.C.). The museum's first decade saw important exhibitions of Bronze Age material from Anyang and from an Eastern Chou Dynasty hoard (eighth-sixth century B.C.) accidentally discovered in Hsin-cheng district in 1923. Epitaph stones of the Eastern Wei through Sung dynasties (c. sixth-twelfth century A.D.), gathered from tombs in the Loyang region, constituted a third major collection by 1933, when the most important museum artifacts were published in a catalog of lithographic reproductions and rubbings (*Ho-nan chin-shih-chi t'u* [Illustrated record of bronzes and stones in Honan Province]).

Much of the original Kai'feng collection was dispersed in the 1940s and 1950s: the Anyang and Hsin-cheng material to the national museums in Peking (q.v. Palace Museum and Museum of Chinese History) and to the National Palace Museum (q.v.) now in Taipei. (The Loyang epitaphs, not currently exhibited in the provincial museum galleries, may form part of a huge collection now housed in the Kuan-yu Temple, former site of the Loyang Municipal Museum.) However, the Honan Provincial Museum retains its original strength in prehistoric and early historic material, an emphasis reflecting chronological precedence of northern Honan in China's urban development. Archaeological work in the region of the lower Yellow River Valley, intensified since 1950, has advanced from salvage projects necessitated by road and canal construction to deliberate, problem-oriented, or exploratory excavations.

The museum's sixty-member excavation team conducts major digs under national direction of The Institute of Archaeology, Chinese Academy of Science, which supervises permanent field stations at Anyang and Loyang. Members of the "working team," qualified by a minimum of twenty years of experience, are assisted by graduates of university and special archaeological training classes. Since 1976 some of these senior archaeologists have worked with the Anyang Archaeological Team in excavating the tomb of Fu Hao, the first Shang royal tomb found intact. In 1980 the more than sixteen hundred objects from this tomb were earmarked for classification and apportionment between the national museums and the Honan Provincial Museum.

In addition to its archaeological team, the Honan personnel structure includes the Museum (curatorial) section and departments of Explanation, Exhibition (labels and display), Preservation (storage), and Photography. The scale of the Preservation department can be gauged by the 1980 ratio of approximately twelve hundred objects exhibited to more than one hundred thousand registered. Portions of this reserve collection are on long-term loan to other institutions; for example, a broad selection of ceramics is maintained as a teaching collection at Chengchou University.

In 1960 the museum moved to a two-story Soviet–International-style building (constructed 1958) in Chengchou, the new provincial capital. The Ancient History and Revolutionary History sections occupy separate wings branching off a central vestibule. The Ancient History section of concern here is divided into nine spacious galleries labeled according to the Marxist theory of cultural evolution through class struggle. In 1980 the first (ground) floor covered the periods of Primitive Society (Paleolithic and Neolithic, c. 500,000–2100 B.C.) and Slave Society (Hsia Dynasty, Shang Dynasty, Western Chou Dynasty, Spring and Autumn period, c. 2100–476 B.C.); the second floor, continuing with the Warring States Period (475–221 B.C.) and ending with the Ming Dynasty (1368–1644), is classified under Feudal Society. The transition between these two floors roughly corresponds with the end of the Bronze Age and beginning of the Iron Age.

A comprehensive hall-by-hall reorganization was slated by the director of exhibitions to begin in 1981. Therefore, the following 1980 overview is intended to describe the scope of the holdings rather than specifics of display. Changes observed between 1978 and 1980 suggest a policy of alternating newly unearthed examples within established categories, which are defined in wall and case labels (entirely in Chinese). Dates of excavation since 1949 are usually provided. The installation is strictly chronological: objects from different evolutionary stages or stratigraphic layers at the same site are exhibited in successive cases. The floor plan thus follows a detailed history of human enterprise in Honan Province, with artifacts and accompanying graphics arranged to illustrate settlement patterns, political and economic measures, and technological as well as artistic achievements. Their interpretive combination contrasts the usual Western distribution of comparable material among museums of art, anthropology, history, science, and industry. Historical continuity is facilitated by exact-scale replicas serving for notable objects sent to Peking or otherwise unavailable for exhibition. A few replicas are so labeled, but modern reconstructions based on excavated remnants may not be distinguished from restored originals (e.g., Hsin-yang drum stand, below). The regional history theme is also carried through large photomurals of temples and pagodas in Honan, illustrated as landmarks in themselves rather than as references to artifacts on display.

The exhibition begins with Paleolithic (Old Stone Age) animal fossils and stone implements found during construction of the San-men Gorge Reservoir along the Yellow River and in a cave at Hsiao-nan-hai near Anyang. Diagrams of reconstructed weapons and tools illustrate specialized types of the microlithic industry. Neolithic pottery is classified by cultural category: Yangshao, transitional Yangshao-to-Lungshan, and Lungshan. Painted bowls characteristic of the central plains Yangshao and grey tripod vessels associated with the east coast Lungshan both originate from dwelling sites at Hsia-wang-kang in Hsi-ch'uan. Painted and grey wares from Ta-chang in Lin-ju, including water containers converted to children's burial jars, likewise show confluence of Yangshao and Lungshan types. (Ta-ho-ts'un, conspicuously absent from this display of mixed or transitional neolithic sites, is well represented in the Chengchou Municipal Museum. Lungshan grey and black wares in the following gallery establish clear continuity into the Bronze Age. Here pottery from Hsia-wang-kang precedes bronze fragments from the same site dating from the Hsia Dynasty. The "Hsia" designation, attributed also to white pottery from Kung-hsien and Shang-chieh and (uninscribed) oracle bones from Erh-li-t'ou in Yen-shih, reflects Chinese archaeologists' recent but still problematic verification of the semilegendary Hsia civilization as a historical period with distinctive artifacts. The subsequent "early Shang" (c. 2000–1500 B.C.) phase at these sites is distinguished by pitcher-like tripods and other sophisticated vessel shapes.

A map of Shang Dynasty sites discovered since 1950 in the vicinity of modern Chengchou introduces ceramics and bronzes now identified with a "middle Shang" phase (c. 1500–1300 B.C.), otherwise known as the Erh-li-kang period. The ceramics are predominantly grey earthenware vessels, hand built but some finished on the wheel, with surfaces cord impressed or decorated with appliqué. Most outstanding technologically are proto-stonewares (here termed *tz'u*, ''porcelains'') thinly coated with brownish green glaze, whose discovery revealed the origins of hard glazing almost one thousand years earlier than previously assumed. Primarily, shards are exhibited, the single intact piece being a vase (*tsun*) with flared neck unearthed in 1965 and shown in Europe and America in 1973–75. ''Middle Shang'' ritual bronzes are characteristically thin-walled vessels of awkward shape, decorated with simple bands cast in relief or intaglio. That Chengchou foundrymen of the time cast only such small, lightweight vessels is contradicted by a sturdy, square food cauldron (*fang-ting*), the larger of a pair unearthed in 1974 near the site of the Shang city wall. As the earliest known prototype of the late Shang cooking vessel, it is notable for size, shape, and surface frieze of animal masks cast in thread relief. (The second cauldron is owned by the Museum of Chinese History in Peking.)

Artifacts from the latest occupational phases at Chengchou are shown alongside those of the late Shang, when Anyang was dynastic capital. Two of the most imposing objects from the Anyang site of Wu-kuan-ts'un appear in full-scale replicas: a carved chiming stone (*ch'ing*) excavated from a royal tomb in 1950 and the Ssu-mu-wu *fang-ting*, the largest and heaviest bronze vessel known since its discovery in 1939 in a field near that tomb. There is a comprehensive display of early, middle, and late Anyang-period finds: oracle bones, bronze ritual vessels and weapons, jade sculpture and amulets, stone carvings, grey pottery, and fragments of carved white pottery. The minority of objects identified with specific village sites or tombs include grey pottery from Ta-ssu-kung-ts'un and jades from Kao-lou-chuang. Bronze vessels cast with inscriptions (clan-signs or ancestor dedications) that preface their labels include the Hsi *chia* from Wen-hsien near Loyang, the Mu (Mother) Ya *chia* from Anyang, and the Fu (Father) Ji *fang-ting* from Anyang, all of which have been exhibited abroad.

Bronzes and ceramics of the Western Chou Dynasty (eleventh century-771 B.C.) are comparatively scant. The most impressive vessel is a large bronze *fang-hu* (square vase) discovered in 1968 in Hsin-cheng, which anticipates, albeit in much simpler and heavier form, a pair of now-famous Eastern Chou vessels from the same district attributed to the mid-Spring and Autumn period (seventh to sixth century B.C.). They are the so-called lotus and crane *fang-hu*, the most elaborately cast bronzes from the original 1923 hoard. The pair is split between this museum and the Palace Museum, Peking. ''Lotus and crane'' refers to the lid, formed as a bird poised in flight atop a crown of open-work petals. The vessel body creeps and crawls with real and imaginary animals: birds and dragons interwoven in flat relief bands and horned felines climbing the surface and supporting the base. Its fantastically sculptural silhouette represents only one style of this heterodox and still problematic burial. More austere Hsin-cheng bronzes of the sixth century B.C. include five *ting* cauldrons of graduated size cast with finely textured ''waffle'' patterns.

Painted lacquers unearthed in 1957–58 from two tombs in Hsin-yang county comprise the second major group of Spring and Autumn period grave goods. Most prominent is a laquered wood drumstand sculpted as a pair of tall-necked birds perched back-to-back on crouching tigers. In this gallery reconstruction, the shallow drum is suspended from strings running through the birds' beaks. Original material from the Hsin-yang tombs includes a small lacquer box (submerged in water for preservation) and remnants of silk. Most other lacquers—tables, armrests, a *se* lute, and a frame for suspension bells—are identified as reproductions. Together, all of these works display the expert carpentry, fanciful treatment of animal forms, and geometric painting associated with superior craftsmanship in the ancient kingdom of Ch'u. (Hsin-yang in the Huai River Valley occupied the northern periphery of Ch'u. Similar lacquers, found primarily in Hupei and Hunan centers to the south, are displayed in those provincial museums.)

Increasingly refined and decorative styles of the Warring States period (475–221 B.C.) are exemplified in bronzes and jades embellished with precise linear patterns. Prerevolutionary finds from tombs at Chin-ts'un (well represented in foreign museums) are far outnumbered by those unearthed since 1949 at Hui-hsien, Ch'i-hsien, and Shan-hsien (Shan-ts'un-ling). From the last site, one major tomb (excavated 1975) yielded several vessels cast with intricate interlacery or with depressions inlaid with gold, silver, and semiprecious stones. Among them, a small square basin (*fang chien*) is most distinctive in shape and the jewel-like surface of gold and turquoise panels. More typical cast and inlaid designs appear in mirrors, belthooks, and chariot trappings. Their aristocratic taste is duplicated in jade pendants carved with imaginative animal silhouettes and geometrically textured surfaces.

Early iron technology, introduced with tools and casting molds from Hsin-cheng, is more fully documented in the Western Han (206 B.C.-A.D. 9) section with artifacts from a smithy found in Kung-hsien. The increasing importance of iron during the Han era coincided with the last phase of significant bronze production for ritual and for ornament. Bronze vessels include bulb-necked *hu* vases and other characteristic Western Han shapes from the San-men Gorge region and miniature gilt vessels from Eastern Han (A.D. 9–220) tombs at Yen-shih. The Han galleries otherwise are dominated by ceramic burial objects that present a broader if more prosaic picture of material culture.

There is a very extensive collection of earthenware building models illustrating domestic architecture with varied degrees of realism. With the exception of a Western Han farmstead from Chengchou, the largest and most elaborate structures are dated to Eastern Han. Painted examples include a four-story courtyard dwelling with geometric wall patterns (excavated Chiao-tso, 1972) and a granary complete with windows, exterior stairs, and a figural narrative interpreted to depict a landlord collecting rent (excavated Mi-hsien, 1963). More fanciful lead-glazed "water pavilions" (*shui-hsieh*), their moats populated with a menagerie of humans and animals, originate from tombs in Ling-pao and Che-ch'uan. By far the most unique and enigmatic, a three-story watchtower (*lou*) displays double-tailed nymphs and hermaphrodite figures applied to the corner pillars in caryatid fashion (excavated Huai-yang, 1953).

The large Shao-kou cemetery near Loyang (excavated 1953) is provenance for common but high-quality ceramic vessels and figurines. Vivid examples include unglazed vases encircled by polychrome-painted birds and directional animals (Western Han) and a troupe of dancers abstractly modeled and dynamically posed (Eastern Han). Iridescent green (lead) glazed figures come primarily from Eastern Han tombs in Ling-pao. Higher-fired (iron) glazed stonewares are represented by handsome globular vases with incised birds and cloudscrolls of the type prevalent in southeast China but also found in Loyang.

A small selection of Western Chin (265–317) ceramics from Loyang and Yü-hsien includes celadon-glazed vessels and animal figures of typically stocky proportions. A far scarcer example of contemporary calligraphy appears in the rubbing of a stone stele dated 278. The original stone, whose present whereabouts are not indicated, was unearthed from ruins of the T'ai-hsüeh (Imperial College) founded in Loyang during Han.

The ensuing periods of disunion (Southern and Northern dynasties, 317–589) and reunification (Sui Dynasty, 581–618) are covered more selectively with coherent groups of objects from a few outstanding tombs. Most important for pictorial art is a selection of mold-impressed and polychrome-painted wall tiles from a tomb at Teng-hsien in southern Honan, whose reliefs provide rare evidence for mythology and lost paintings dated about 500. The elegant, animated profiles of flying apsarases, foot soldiers, and other figures exhibited here are generally associated with painting styles originating in south China. Ceramic developments during this formerly obscure "transitional" period are illuminated by tomb finds in northern Honan, which reveal the late sixth century as a period of artistic and technical innovation. The clearest precedent to T'ang Dynasty (618–907) styles is a flat ovoid "pilgrim flask" (*pien-hu*) with foreign musicians molded in relief under amber glaze. Its exotic shape and surface decor were instinctively attributed to T'ang before discovery of this and three similar flasks from the Anyang tomb of Fan Ts'ui (d. 575). Likewise, a glazed stoneware jar from the tomb of Li Yun (d. 576) at P'u-yang prefigures, in its bold green streaks, the T'ang introduction of splashed polychrome glazes. The concurrent refinement of white stoneware is manifest in mortuary gifts for Chang Sheng (buried 595 at Anyang), displayed in three cases with his epitaph and tomb plan. Straw-colored glaze sheaths a variety of sturdy white-bodied vessels as well as a censer, lamp, candlestick, and game board. Chang's well modeled tomb attendants include a small female orchestra, foreigners, and large, alertly postured military officials accented in brown.

T'ang lead-glazed ceramics are well represented but not so precisely documented. A fine and comprehensive group of tomb figures includes camels, horses, grooms, civil and military officials, and mythical beasts (*ch'i-tou*). The majority (reportedly) come from Loyang, in the vicinity of several burial grounds surrounding the adjunct (eastern) T'ang capital. Full-bodied jars with monochrome (blue or green) and splashed polychrome ("three-color") glazes are cataloged from Loyang, Hsin-an, and Kung-hsien. (The last site may refer to place of production rather than burial. Fragments of blue and polychrome-glazed vessels, as well as small figures and molds, have been reported from kiln ruins at Kung-hsien.) By comparison with similar objects from dated tombs near Sian, Shensi, this material generally is attributed to the late seventh and early eighth centuries.

Perhaps the most extraordinary example of three-color ware is an architectural miniature, unusual on the one hand for its finely modeled and stamped detail and on the other for its Northern Sung date. This is a seven-story pagoda, at 98.5 centimeters the tallest and most elaborate of several pottery models excavated in 1966 beneath the pagoda foundation of Fa-hai Temple in Mi-hsien. The continuation or revival of brilliant T'ang-style polychromy is corroborated by the reign-year of 994 incised on the second story.

More typical Sung Dynasty (960–1279) ceramics belong to three categories of stoneware whose production has been firmly, although not exclusively, located at Honan kiln sites listed as provenance on gallery labels: Chün ware from Yü-hsien, Northern Celadon (here designated "Ju ware") from Lin-ju, and Tz'u-chou ware from Hsiu-wu and Tang-yin (Ho-pi-chi). Saggers, molds, and other kiln implements are displayed alongside intact vessels and fragmentary wasters. Most numerous are Tz'u-chou types decorated in black and brown slip, including tiger-shaped and octagonal pillows with headrest surfaces showing floral and landscape motifs related to contemporary painting.

The single scroll painting displayed is a reproduction of Chang Tse-tuan's *Spring Festival on the River*, depicting urban life in Pien-liang (present-day K'aifeng). The original handscroll, owned by the Palace Museum, is generally dated to the late Northern Sung (twelfth century), when Pien-liang was the dynastic capital. The museum has reported, but not published or exhibited, a small collection of Ming Dynasty (1368–1644) painting.

Works of art post-dating Sung comprise primarily ceramic tomb objects. Most lifelike are free-standing figures and carved brick reliefs of officials, attendants, and actors in character from Chin Dynasty (1115–1234) tombs at Chiao-tso and an unidentified Ming retinue aligned before a multiple-courtyard house. This noble compound, carved with gateways, tile roofs, and lattice facades, is the museum's most complex architectural model.

Beginning with the T'ang Dynasty section, an increasing proportion of relics are displayed for political and technological interest. Examples are diverse: inscribed bricks unearthed from T'ang remains of the Han-chia State Granary (treasury to which provinces paid taxes in grain); Sung woodblocks for printing, movable type, and evidence for projectile science; a Yüan bronze seal of the peasant-led Red Turban Army; and the sword of Li Wen-ch'eng, leader of the 1813 T'ien-li-chiao rebellion. This final theme of social uprising links the museum's Ancient History wing with that devoted to the twentieth-century revolution.

In recent years the museum has mounted special exhibitions of bronze mirrors, calligraphy, rubbings, and new archaeological finds. Since 1976, important bronze vessels and ceramics have been shown in national exhibitions sent to Germany, Switzerland, Denmark, Japan, and the United States. The museum has received foreign loans on diverse subjects such as Mexican art and Hans Christian Andersen, the latter brought to Chengchou by Denmark's Queen Margrette II.

Staff members regularly contribute to the national archaeology journals: *Wen wu*, *K'ao-ku*, and *K'ao-ku hsüeh-pao*. Articles about objects in the collection also appear in *Chung-yüan wen wu* (Cultural relics of the Central Plain), a regional quarterly first issued in 1977 under the title *Ho-nan wen-po t'ung-hsün*.

Addendum:

CHENGCHOU CITY MUSEUM (officially ZHENGZHOU SHI BOWUGUAN [CHENG-CHOU-SHIH PO-WU-KUAN]), Laotung gongyuan (Worker's Park), Zhengzhou, Henan.

The smaller and more specialized Chengchou City Museum was established in 1956 to display newly unearthed finds from this archaeologically prolific municipal area. In 1980 the two main galleries focused on the neolithic dwelling site of Ta-ho-ts'un (excavated 1972–75) and the "middle Shang" settlement at Erh-li-kang. The Ta-ho-ts'un exhibit, documented with photo-murals of house foundations and tombs, features representative examples of red, grey, and black pottery from all stratigraphic phases (middle Yangshao through late Lungshan). The Erh-li-kang exhibit of bronzes and ceramics supplements that shown at the Honan Provincial Museum with greater didacticism: for example, the pair of square cauldrons mentioned above is described here in photographs, metallurgical analyses, and a lifelike diorama of slaves casting the vessels.

The museum's tree-lined back yard is the unlikely exhibition space for unrelated groups of recent and significant finds. Stacked against one back wall is a "disassembled" tomb from Hsin-t'ung-ch'iao, dating from the late Western Han (first century B.C.) by excavators who uncovered it in 1970. Hollow tiles used to decorate the single underground chamber are mold impressed, with musicians, dancers, and hunters in landscapes, as well as mythological figures of popular Taoism: Tung Wang-kung (King Father of the East), the nine-tailed fox, and the hare of immortality pounding its elixir. These simple and energetic designs illustrate a regional style of early pictorial art previously recognized from less complete tomb reliefs from the Chengchou area.

Far more unusual is a large collection of Buddhist sculpture, including forty-two stones unearthed in Yung-yang district in 1976. According to a 1980 museum report, the find-site corresponds with literary accounts of the Ta-hai-ssu (Ta-hai Monastery). In the absence of a commemorative tablet, the earliest stone, a votive stele dated 525, points to establishment of the temple before that year and by the T'o-pa reign of Northern Wei. The stele's central image is a pentad with cross-legged Maitreya Buddha flanked by two disciples and two bodhisattvas. All other stones except one Shakyamuni Buddha dated 1081 are attributed to the T'ang Dynasty. (The interval between Wei and T'ang is explained in part by district records that allude to the temple's temporary demise by describing its rebuilding for the medical benefit of Emperor T'ai-tsung [reigned 627–50].) Six T'ang pieces are dated by inscription: an Amitabha of 762 and five bodhisattvas dated between 820 and 824. Among the better-preserved figures are a seated Maitreya and an eleven-headed Kuan-yin, the latter being a rare example of this esoteric deity. Most stones are fragmentary bodhisattvas: sinuous torsos carved in the round, whose *tribhanga* postures and naturalistic modeling are set off with flowing skirts, scarves, and pendant jewelry. Their dynamic grace is retained even while lashed to the trees or propped against the Han tomb tiles together with well-modeled bodhisattva heads coiffed in high chignons. The reconstruction of these figures and of Ta-hai-ssu's history promises a monumental addition to the study of Chinese Buddhist sculpture.

Selected Bibliography

Museum publications: Honan Provincial Museum, *Ho-nan li-shih wen-wu ch'en-lieh chien-chieh* (Brief introduction to the exhibition of historical relics in Honan Province), in Chinese (Chengchou 1978); Chengchou City Museum, "Cheng-chou Hsin-t'ung-ch'iao Han-tai hua-hsiang k'ung-hsin chuan mu" (A Han Dynasty tomb with pictorial hollow tiles at Hsin-t'ung-ch'iao, Chengchou), in Chinese, *Wen wu*, 1972, no. 10, pp. 41–48; idem, "Cheng-chou Ta-ho-ts'un i-chih fa-chüeh pao-kao" (Report on excavations of the Ta-ho-ts'un site near Chengchou), in Chinese, *K'ao-ku hsüeh-pao*, 1979, no. 3, pp. 301–75; idem, "Ho-nan Hsing-yang Ta-hai-ssu ch'u-t'u te shih-k'e tsao-hsiang" (Stone statues unearthed at the Ta-hai Monastery in Hsing-yang, Honan), in Chinese, *Wen wu*, 1980, no. 3, pp. 56–66; Honan Provincial Museum, "Ho-nan wen-wu k'ao-ku kung-tso san-shih nien" (Thirty years of archaeological work on cultural relics in Honan Province), in Chinese, *Wen-wu k'ao-ku kung-tso san-shih nien, 1949–1979* (Thirty years of archaeological work on cultural relics, 1949–1979) (Peking 1979), pp. 271–94; Honan Provincial Museum and Chengchou City Museum, "Cheng-chou Shang-tai ch'eng i-chih fa-chüeh pao-kao" (Report on excavations of Shang Dynasty urban remains at Chengchou), in Chinese, *Wen-wu tzu-liao ts'ung-k'an*, no. 1 (1977), pp. 1–47; Honan Provincial Museum and Chiao-tso City Museum, "Ho-nan Chiao-tso Chin-mu fa-chüeh chien-pao" (Brief report on excavations of Chin Dynasty tombs at Chiao-tso, Honan), *Wen wu*, 1979, no. 8, pp. 1–17.

Other publications: Bishop, Carl W., "The Bronzes of Hsin-chêng Hsien," *The Smithsonian Report for 1926*, Publication 2903 (Washington, D.C. 1927); *Ho-nan chin-shih-chi t'u* (Illustrated record of bronzes and stones in Honan Province), in Chinese, K'aifeng 1933; *Ho-nan Hsin-yang Ch'u mu wen-wu t'u-lu* (An illustrated catalog of cultural relics from the Ch'u tombs at Hsin-yang), in Chinese (K'aifeng 1959); Sickman, Laurence, "Provincial Museums of North China," *The Open Court*, vol. 50, no. 937 (April 1936), esp. pp. 69–70.

ELINOR PEARLSTEIN

China, Republic of (Taiwan)

———— Taipei ————

NATIONAL PALACE MUSEUM (officially KUO LI KU-KUNG PO-WU-YÜAN), Wai-shuang-hsi, Shih-lin, Taipei 111.

The National Palace Museum, which preserves more than 240,000 works of art and archival documents from the Chinese imperial collection, opened the doors of its new permanent building outside Taipei in 1965. The history of the institution, however, dates from 1925, when the Chinese government converted the Imperial Palace in Peking with its vast collections into a public institution called the Palace Museum. By 1931 the Palace Museum had become well established, and special exhibition galleries had been set up to complement the original halls and palaces. Cataloguing and publication projects were well under way when the Japanese invasion prompted a decision to remove part of the museum collections to the South away from the fighting. Some sixty-three thousand objects from the art collections, with an even larger number of books and documents, were packed in crates and, early in 1933, shipped first to Nanking and then to Shanghai. This transportation of objects to the South would ultimately have the effect of splitting the Palace Museum into two branches. During the collection's stay in Shanghai, Palace Museum objects were exhibited abroad for the first time in the International Exhibition of Chinese Art held in 1935 at the Royal Academy of Art in London. A storage building for the objects shipped south from the palace collection was constructed in Nanking in 1936, and the objects were then brought together there. In the following year, however, increasing pressure from the advancing Japanese forces led to a decision to move the Nanking collection to a safer refuge. Once again the objects were packed for shipment, this time bound for Szechwan and Kweichow provinces in southwest China. One portion, primarily objects from the London exhibition, went to Hankow, then to Changsha, and finally to special storerooms built in a cave outside of Anshun, in Kweichow Province. Another shipment went via the Yangtze River to Chungking and ultimately to Loshan in western Szechwan, and a third group of objects was transported overland, first to Paochi in Shensi Province, later to Chengtu, and then to Omei in Szechwan. A relatively small portion of the collection was left behind in Nanking during the war. In 1945, at the end of the war, both the Peking and Nanking branches of the Palace Museum were restored, and the objects that had been removed to western China were shipped back to Nanking. Ironically, the staff and collection of the Peking branch had been preserved largely intact during the Japanese occupation (Palace Museum [q.v.], Peking).

In 1948–49, during the Civil War between Nationalist and Communist forces, most of the collection of the Nanking branch of the Palace Museum was taken to the island of Taiwan together with collections from other public institutions such as the Academia Sinica, the Central Library, and the Central Museum. The National Palace Museum and the National Central Museum collections were stored jointly near Taichung, and the joint administration of these two institutions opened an exhibition hall there in 1957. In 1965, when the new museum building in Taipei was completed, the joint title was dropped, and the collection of the National Central Museum was absorbed into the National Palace Museum. Before the move to Taipei, another major international exhibition, "Chinese Art Treasures," was organized. The exhibition, which included some 250 objects of extraordinary quality and importance, traveled to five major museums in the United States. Another, smaller exhibition was sent to the 1964 World's Fair in New York.

The National Palace Museum, permanently settled in Taipei since 1965, now consists of the following curatorial and administrative units: Department of Antiquities, Department of Painting and Calligraphy, Department of Books and Documents, Exhibition Division, Publications Division, Registration Division, Secretariat, General Affairs Division, Conservation Division, Accounting Division, and Personnel Division. The exterior of the present building, named the Chung-shan Museum in honor of Sun Yat-sen, resembles a traditional Chinese palace with massive walls and a series of monumental stairways leading from the street to the entrance. The interior is divided into spacious, modern exhibition galleries devoted to painting, ceramics, bronzes, and other media as well as areas for special exhibitions.

The collection of the National Palace Museum stems primarily from the eighteenth-century collection of the Ch'ien-lung emperor (reign 1736–96). An avid collector, he inherited some works from his Ch'ing predecessors—some came ultimately from the Ming imperial household—but acquired most of his collection from private owners either by purchase or by gift. With this background, it is not surprising to see that the National Palace Museum collection is characterized by an aristocratic standard of taste. Hence its strong points include paintings from the court academies of various periods, Sung and Ming imperial ceramics, and decorative arts in the Ch'ing court style. But the refined taste of the Ch'ien-lung emperor encompassed a passion for the monochrome ink paintings of China's scholar-painters as well, and the collection has strong holdings in the work of the major Yüan and Ming literati. Of his own contemporaries, the emperor preferred those who worked in the orthodox style; the eccentrics, many of whom were identified with lingering anti-Ch'ing sentiment, are but poorly represented. Many paintings carry the seals of previous emperors and members of the Sung, Yüan, and Ming Dynasty courts, indicating a long history of imperial ownership for these works. The seals of the Ch'ien-lung emperor are numerous and highly visible, and his inscriptions appear frequently on paintings, ceramics, and other objects. So closely is the National Palace Museum collection of painting and calligraphy associated with the eighteenth-century imperial collection that the extensive catalogue *Shih-ch'ü pao-chi*, commissioned under Ch'ien-lung, serves as an important guide to the present collection in Taipei. Indeed, the compilers of the *Ku-kung shu hua lu (Catalogue of Painting and Calligraphy in the National Palace Museum*, 2d ed., Taipei, 1965) quoted extensively from this eighteenth-century source. Many losses to the Imperial collection were incurred during the uncertain times of the nineteenth and early twentieth centuries, notably during the years from 1912 to 1925, when the last Ch'ing emperor, P'u I, still occupied the palace. Allowed to retain the palace collections after the founding of the Republic, he dispersed more than a thousand books and paintings, many of which he awarded as gifts to friends and relatives. Lists of these objects were published in *Ku-kung i i shu chi shu hua mu lu (Catalogue of Lost Books, Calligraphy and Paintings from the Palace Collection*, Peking, 1931). Losses occurred as late as the 1930s, when a group of objects was removed by a court of law after questions of authenticity had been raised during a trial.

The Central Museum, established in 1933 and housed in Nanking, also acquired objects from imperial sources, notably the palaces and hunting lodges of Liaoning and Jehol. During the 1930s and early 1940s, the Central Museum absorbed the collections of several other public institutions and also acquired objects from archaeological excavations in which it participated. More than eleven thousand works of art from the Central Museum were taken to Taiwan in 1948–49 and are now housed in the National Palace Museum.

The National Palace Museum is best known for its extremely important collection of Chinese painting, which spans the thousand-year period from T'ang through Ch'ing. The collection includes several major works that reflect the painting styles of the T'ang Dynasty (618–906) and carry traditional attributions to T'ang masters. Of them, the most important are *Two Horses and a Groom* attributed to Han Kan, *Ten Views from a Thatched Lodge* attributed to Lu Hung, *Envoy Bringing a White Antelope as Tribute* attributed to Chou Fang, and *Emperor Ming-huang's Journey to Shu* associated with Li Ssu-hsün and Li Chao-tao.

One of the great strengths of the National Palace Museum collection is its exceptionally fine and important group of tenth-century paintings and later paintings that preserve tenth-century characteristics. The collection contains works of importance attributed to the famous masters of the Five Dynasties (907–60), including *Mt. K'uang-lu* attributed to Ching Hao, *Travellers in a Mountain Pass* attributed to Kuan T'ung, and several important works attributed to Chü-jan. Other works, mostly of later date, are attributed to Li Ch'eng and Tung Yüan. An important long handscroll, *Early Snow on the River*, is credibly attributed to the tenth-century painter Chao Kan. *Pheasant and Sparrows among Rocks and Shrubs*, a hanging scroll attributed to Huang Chü-ts'ai, stands as an extremely important example of bird-and-flower painting during the Five Dynasties and early Northern Sung periods. Tenth-century figure painting is admirably represented by *Eight Gentlemen on a Spring Outing* attributed to Chao Yen. Important anonymous tenth-century works in the collection include *Deer in an Autumn Forest* and *Deer in Red Maples*, which may reflect the style of north Chinese Liao Dynasty painters.

This spectacular wealth continues into the eleventh century and the fully developed Northern Sung style. Masterpieces such as *Travellers among Streams and Mountains* by Fan K'uan, *Storied Mansions among Streams and Mountains* by Yen Wen-kuei, and *Early Spring* (1072) by Kuo Hsi are of extraordinary importance as authentic signed works by these great masters. Another signed and dated Northern Sung work of monumental importance is T'sui Po's *Hare and Magpie* of 1061. The collection has a large number of unsigned works of excellent quality dating from this period. Among the best known are *Market Village by the River*, *Monkeys in a Loquat Tree*, *Noble Scholar under a Willow*, and *Birds in a Thicket of Plum and Bamboo*.

Paintings of the twelfth and thirteenth centuries constitute one of the most remarkable areas of strength in the collection. The dominant court style is represented in its full chronological range, starting with the artist Li T'ang (*Whispering Pines in the Mountains*, 1124, and the handscroll *Mountains by the River*), who spanned the shift from Northern Sung to Southern Sung court. His contemporary Su Han-ch'en is represented by an extremely fine hanging scroll, *Children at Play*. At the other end of the stylistic spectrum are two monochrome ink album leaves by Ma Ho-chih, *Old Tree by the Water* and *Cranes Crying by the Clear Spring*. The fully developed court style of Hangchou can be seen at its finest in works such as *Cat*, an album leaf by Li Ti, 1174; *Knick-knack Peddler*, an album leaf by Li Sung, 1210; and Ma Yüan's *On a Mountain Path in Spring* and *Banquet by Lantern Light* (inscribed by Yang Mei-tzu). A great many examples, including a large number of album leaves, represent the Ma-Hsia landscape style. Of the paintings given to Hsia Kuei himself, the most important is *Pure and Remote Views of Streams and Mountains*, a long, brilliantly executed handscroll in ink on paper. The collection includes several important signed works by Ma Lin; among them are *Listening to the Wind in the Pines*, which bears a 1246 inscription by Emperor Li-tsung; *Fragrant Spring after Rain*; and *Waiting for Guests by Lamplight*. Three hanging scrolls representing arhats (1207) by Liu Sung-nien and the handscroll *Preparing the Garments* (1240) by

Mou I are also very important. Among unsigned works of this period, some of the more significant are the *Han Palace*, a fan-shaped album leaf once attributed to Chao Po-chü; *Breaking the Balustrade*, a fine example of history painting at the Southern Sung academy; and *Clearing after Snow in the Min Mountains*, a twelfth-thirteenth-century painting that reflects the style of northern painters active under the Chin Dynasty (1115–1234). Also representing Chin painters is the *Red Cliff*, a handscroll securely attributed to Wu Yüan-chih.

The sober and intellectual style of the late thirteenth century, when China came under Mongol rule, can be seen in the museum's *Three Friends of Winter* by Chao Meng-chien and *Squirrel on a Peach Branch* by Ch'ien Hsüan and the important handscroll by Chao Meng-fu, the *Autumn Colors on the Ch'iao and Hua Mountains*. The fourteenth-century artists designated as the Four Great Masters of the Yüan Dynasty (1279–1368) are exceedingly well represented. Two versions of Huang Kung-wang's long landscape scroll *Dwelling in the Fu-ch'un Mountains* (1350) are of utmost importance; they are joined by *Nine Pearl Peaks*, now established as from his hand. Wu Chen is represented by a range of works: *Twin Pines* of 1328, *Fisherman* of 1342, *Manual of Ink Bamboo* of 1350, and others. Ni Tsan's individualistic style is seen in the exquisite *Small Mountain, Bamboo and Tree* of 1371 and the *Jung-hsi Studio* of 1372. The latter has been called by some scholars the most securely authentic of works carrying Ni's signature. *Spring Plowing at the Mouth of a Valley* by Wang Meng probably dates from the early 1360s, and his *Forest Dwelling at Chü-ch'ü* stems from his later period of more expressive brushwork. The collection also includes important works by lesser known Yüan Dynasty artists such as T'ang Ti, Ch'en Lin, Chu Te-jun, and Ts'ao Chih-po.

The Ming academy and the style of the Che school are represented by many excellent paintings. The *Three Friends and Hundred Birds* (inscription dated 1413), by the early Ming court painter Pien Wen-chin, stands out among the several good paintings associated with his name. The Hsüan-te academy and Emperor Hsüan-ts'ung (reigned 1426–35) himself are represented by several works. A large hanging scroll by the great fifteenth-century painter Tai Chin, *Returning Late from a Spring Outing*, admirably reflects the strength and vitality of the Southern Sung-based "Che" style of painting. Wu Wei's *Winter Landscape with Travellers*, Tu Chin's *Enjoying Antiquities*, and several academic bird-and-flower compositions attributed to Lü Chi present a strong picture of the more conservative branches of painting in the early Ming period.

The museum's paintings from the Wu school are numerous and high in quality, partly because this style was favored by the collectors and connoisseurs who had a hand in forming the eighteenth-century imperial collection. The museum's collection boasts a large number of major works by Shen Chou; among them are *Lofty Mt. Lu* (1467), *Walking with a Staff*, *Sitting Up at Night* (1492), and *Album of Sketches from Life* (1494). Several masterful paintings by T'ang Yin are to be found in the collection, including the ink landscape *Whispering Pines on a Mountain Path*, the handscroll *Secluded Fishermen on an Autumn River*, and the figure painting *T'ao Ku Composing a Lyric*. Well-known works by Ch'iu Ying include *Conversation under Wu-t'ung Trees* and *Waiting for the Ferry in Autumn*, along with *Painting for Tung-lin* and *Spring Dawn in the Han Palace*. The collection is extremely rich in paintings by Wen Cheng-ming and his followers. The most famous works by Wen are *Lofty Leisure beneath a Sheer Cliff* (1519), *Spring in Chiang-nan* (1547), and *Old Trees by a Cold Waterfall* (1549), but these works are only a few of the many good examples in the collection. Wen's contemporaries Lu Chih and Ch'en Shun and his followers Wen Chia, Wen Po-jen, and Ch'ien Ku are all represented.

Among the museum's many paintings by Tung Ch'i-ch'ang, the seventeenth-century artist and connoisseur, are *In the Shade of Summer Trees* and *Discussing Antiquity by the River*. Other major late Ming paintings in the collection include works by Lan Ying, Ch'en Hung-shou, Ts'ui Tzu-cheng, and Ting Yun-p'eng.

For Ch'ing Dynasty (1644–1911) paintings of the orthodox school and the court academy, the National Palace Museum is a source of utmost importance. The Four Wangs (Wang Shih-min, Wang Chien, Wang Hui, and Wang Yüan-ch'i) and the other orthodox painters, Yün Shou-p'ing and Wu Li in particular, are survived by an enormous amount of material in the collection. Even the best compositions are too numerous to enumerate here. Ch'ing court painting also constitutes a vast area of the National Palace collection and one that has not yet received much scholarly attention. Paintings by eighteenth-century court artists such as Ting Kuan-p'eng, Tsou I-kuei, and Tung Pang-ta number in the hundreds. The *Ku-kung shu hua lu* lists a hundred paintings by Tung alone. Included, too, are many paintings by Guiseppe Castiglione (Lang Shih-ning), the best known of the Jesuit priests who were active at the Chinese court in the eighteenth century.

The museum has a large and important collection of portrait paintings. They include a few informal works such as a *Gentleman and His Portrait* from the Sung Dynasty (960–1279) and *Portrait of Ni Tsan* of the Yüan period, but most are formal imperial portraits of the various dynasties, many of which entered the collection from the National Central Museum and ultimately the Nan-hsun Hall of the Ch'ing palace. Perhaps best known among them is a set of portraits of Fu Hsi, Yao, Yü, T'ang, and Wu-wang of Chou, traditionally attributed to Ma Lin.

The museum's collection of calligraphy is difficult to separate from its large collection of paintings; together they total considerably more than six thousand items. There is, however, a very large and significant collection of independent calligraphic works aside from the many inscriptions and colophons of importance. Major examples represent Wang Hsi-chih, Huai-su, Su Shih, Huang T'ing-chien, Mi Fei, Emperor Hui-tsung, Chao Meng-fu, Yang Wei-chen, Chu Yün-ming, Tung Ch'i-ch'ang, and many other famous calligraphers.

The museum has an important collection of Shang (c. sixteenth century B.C.– 1028 B.C.) and Chou Dynasty (1027 B.C.–222 B.C.) ritual bronzes, strengthened by the addition of works from the National Central Museum. Many of the

more than four thousand bronzes are important for their historical and epigraphical value as well as their aesthetic interest. The Chou Dynasty Mao-kung *ting*,
for example, has an unusually long inscription of 497 characters. The collection
includes numerous late Shang and early Chou vessels, representing a wide range
of shapes and decorative schemes. The Anyang styles are reflected in several
excellent examples and the transitional style of late Shang-early Chou is also
well represented. Some unusual vessels, including a fluted *li* vessel with a high
flaring neck and a square *tsun* with relief bird motifs at its corners, also appear.
The collection is especially strong in vessels of the tenth to the eighth century
B.C. and in bronzes of the middle years of the Chou Dynasty. Two *hu* vessels,
one with a coiled dragon in relief and the other with meander patterns, are
especially important. The museum's bronzes from the Warring States period
(480–222 B.C.) represent a wide range of styles and techniques; among vessels
of this period are a *hu* with decoration of hunting scenes, a *pien-hu* with panels
of spiral patterns, a *tsun* in the shape of a composite animal, and a *lien* with
inlaid gold and silver.

The museum owns an extremely large collection—nearly twenty-four thousand
pieces—of Chinese ceramics, consisting primarily of wares made for the court
during the Sung (960–1279), Ming (1368–1644), and Ch'ing (1644–1911) dynasties. The high quality and imperial provenance of these works make the
collection of unique importance for the study of Chinese ceramics. From the
Northern Sung (960–1126), there is an important group of Ting ware, and the
museum's twenty-three pieces of Ju ware constitute the largest surviving group
representing this exceedingly rare and controversial type of imperially commissioned celadon ware. The collection also includes a large and important group
of Southern Sung (1127–1279) *kuan* ware. Chün ware, Chi-chou ware, and
Lung-ch'üan ware are also represented. The collection of imperial porcelains of
Ming and Ch'ing is extremely high in quality and comprehensive, with every
important reign period represented in remarkable depth. The collection's early
Ming monochromes—white and red—are especially important, as are the underglaze blue and underglaze copper-red pieces of the late fourteenth and fifteenth
centuries. The Hsüan-te reign (1426–35) is impressively represented, but perhaps
even more significant is the large number of fine pieces from the Ch'eng-hua
reign (1465–87). The underglaze blue or red pieces and enameled *tou-ts'ai*
examples from this reign constitute a group of unusual size and great importance.
The late-fifteenth- to early seventeenth-century reigns of Hung-chih, Cheng-te,
Chia-ching, and Wan-li are represented by a variety of palace wares decorated
in underglaze blue or polychrome overglaze enamels. Ch'ing Dynasty porcelains
include major groups from the K'ang-hsi (1662–1722), Yung-cheng (1723–35),
and Ch'ien-lung (1736–95) reigns. Among them, the enameled porcelains of the
ku-yüeh hsüan type are extremely important.

The museum's large jade collection encompasses ancient jades, including a
Shang Dynasty plaque in the shape of a bird and other ancient ritual jades, but
its great strength lies in the ornamental jades of Han through Ch'ing. They

include sword and belt ornaments of the Han Dynasty (206 B.C.-A.D. 221), jade vessels in archaic bronze shapes attributed to the Sung Dynasty, and brush holders, brush washers, and other paraphernalia of the scholar's desk from the Ming and Ch'ing dynasties. Ch'ing jades, a spectacular area of the collection, range from archaistic vessels to naturalistic sculptures and from jade pebbles carved as mountain landscapes to thin, open-work forms. A marvelous example of the virtuoso jade working of eighteenth-century craftsmen is the Chinese cabbage in green and white jadeite, a piece that also reflects the adoption of this new material by Chinese craftsmen of that period. Other hardstones are also represented.

The Palace Museum collection preserves important examples of embroidery and silk tapestry (k'o-ssu) from Sung through Ch'ing. An embroidered image of Kuan-yin, a k'o-ssu tapestry of *Immortals in a Mountain Palace*, and several Sung Dynasty album leaves of embroidered silk or silk tapestry stand out among the earlier works. Two often published k'o-ssu tapestries, *Landscape* and *Doves on a Flowering Peach Branch*, are of special interest because they bear the signature of the Sung artist Shen Tzu-fan, although they are probably somewhat later in date. Tapestries based on painting and calligraphy by Ming Dynasty artists Shen Chou and Chu Yün-ming reflect an impressive level of skill and technique. Also noteworthy are the many Ch'ing tapestries and embroideries representing Taoist and Buddhist (often Tantric) subjects.

A startling number of Ming and Ch'ing enamels, more than eighteen hundred, are preserved in the National Palace Museum collection. A large proportion of them are eighteenth-century painted enamels on copper, but examples of cloisonné and champlevé enameling of Ming and early Ch'ing are also well represented. The extremely high level of achievement attained by eighteenth-century metalsmiths working under court patronage is seen in a rare group of gold vessels with cloisonné, champlevé, and painted enamels. The eighteenth-century painted enamels in the museum's collection form an important group closely related to the enamel-decorated porcelains of the same period.

The museum's lacquer collection is small compared to its holdings in jades or enamels, but it includes a significant number of carved lacquers of the Ming and Ch'ing dynasties. Among Ming examples are an exquisite mallet-shaped vase from the Yung-lo reign (1403–24), an oval dish with relief patterns of grapes from the Hsüan-te reign, and a dish with designs of dragons and clouds in carved red and yellow lacquer from the Chia-ching reign (1522–66). There are many Ch'ing Dynasty examples of great quality and interest including a group of covered boxes from the Ch'ien-lung reign.

The National Palace Museum has a remarkable collection of eighteenth-century decorative arts including carvings in ivory, rhinocerous horn, wood, and bamboo, as well as objects of gold, silver, enameled copper and glass. There are major groups of inkstones and writing materials, ornaments for the scholar's desk, ritual implements of Tibetan Buddhism, ju-i scepters, snuff bottles, and decorative objects produced for the court.

The Books and Documents section of the museum boasts a very large and extremely important collection of documents from the Ch'ing Dynasty. These Ch'ing archives include a wealth of primary sources vital to the study of Ch'ing history. Rare books in the collection date from as early as the Sung Dynasty. A museum library is maintained and kept current for staff research and extends reading privileges upon application.

The museum has a large research staff and an ambitious publications policy dating from the 1920s, when the first illustrated catalogues and scholarly articles were published. It issues regularly the *National Palace Museum Quarterly*, a journal for scholarly articles in Chinese with English summaries; the *National Palace Museum Bulletin*, a bimonthly publication for scholarly articles in English; and the *National Palace Museum Newsletter*, a monthly leaflet with short, illustrated articles for general interest. Among the museum's educational programs are an active lecture program including English language as well as Chinese speakers, a graduate studies program in Chinese art history developed in cooperation with National Taiwan University, and a Junior Museum established for children.

Requests for photographs and publications should be directed to the Publications Department. Facsimile reproductions of selected paintings and antiquities are available for purchase.

Selected Bibliography

Museum publications: *Chinese Cultural Art Treasures: National Palace Museum Illustrated Handbook*, 12th ed., 1977; *Ku-kung shu hua lu (Catalogue of Painting and Calligraphy in the National Palace Museum)*, 2d ed., 1965; *Ku-kung ming hua san-pai chung (Three Hundred Masterpieces of Chinese Painting in the Palace Museum)*, 1959; *Ku-kung t'ung-ch'i t'u lu (Catalogue of Bronzes in the National Palace Museum)*, 1958; *Ku-kung ts'ang tz'u (Porcelain of the National Palace Museum)*, 33 vols. in 16, 1961–69; *Masterpieces of Chinese Art in the National Palace Museum*, 15 + vols. 1970-; *Wan Ming pien-hsing chu i hua-chia tso-p'in chan (Style Transformed, a Special Exhibition of Works by Five Late Ming Artists)*, 1977; *Wu p'ai hua chiu-shih nien chan (Ninety Years of Wu School Painting)*, 1975; *Yüan ssu ta chia (The Four Great Masters of the Yüan)*, 1975; three short articles, in Chinese with English summaries, on the museum's building, collection and history, in *National Palace Museum Quarterly*, vol. 1, no. 1, July, 1966.

Other publications: *Chinese Art Treasures: A Selected Group of Objects from the Chinese National Palace Museum and the Chinese National Central Museum, Taichung, Taiwan* (Geneva, 1961); Chiang Fu-tsung, "The National Palace Museum and its Collections," *Orientations*, vol. 13, no. 6 (June, 1982); Na Chih-liang, *Ku-kung po-wuyüan san-shih nien chih ching kuo (A Brief History of the Palace Museum: 1925–1955)* (Taipei, 1957); Li Chu-tsing, "Recent History of the Palace Collection," *Archives of the Chinese Art Society of America*, vol. 12 (1958), pp. 61–75.

CLAUDIA BROWN

Colombia

—————— Bogotá ——————

GOLD MUSEUM (officially MUSEO DEL ORO), Bank of the Republic, Bogotá.

The Gold Museum of the Bank of the Republic in Bogotá, Colombia, was founded in 1939 through the joint efforts of Julio Caro, then director of the bank; Luis Angel Arango, then subdirector-secretary of the bank; and the bank's Board of Directors. In an effort to preserve examples of pre-Hispanic Colombian metal-work, the collection was begun by purchasing objects from individuals and treasure hunters and by acquiring well-known private collections such as those of "El Mensajero" in Bogotá, Leocadio María Arango in Medellín, and Santiago Vélez in Manizales. The founding of the museum marked a new consciousness of and appreciation for ancient gold work, which for the first time was being valued for its cultural and artistic importance rather than for its monetary value. Today the collection consists of some twenty thousand pieces and is the finest, both in quality and diversity, in the world.

The design and arrangement of the exhibition spaces reflect the museum's fundamental purpose: to educate the public in Colombia's pre-Hispanic cultural and artistic gold-working past. Exhibitions devoted to each of the ancient metal-working areas present information about the environment, means of subsistence, forms of daily life, scientific and intellectual achievements, religious practices and beliefs, and gold sources and metallurgical techniques. Through the use of maps, charts, photographs, and explanatory notes, with carefully selected examples of sculpture, pottery, tools, and gold objects, the museum provides a logically developed, well-integrated overview of the cultural context within which these gold works were produced as well as excellent visual documentation of regional styles, iconography, and metalworking techniques. This general information prepares the viewer for the display culminating in the last exhibition hall.

Here the majority of the collection is presented in one dramatically lighted room. Thousands of finely worked gold objects cover the walls and, in one powerful impression, attest to the ancient Colombian's brilliant metallurgical and artistic past.

All of the gold pieces in the collection come from pre-Hispanic tombs excavated during this century and date, in many cases, from fifteen hundred years before the Spanish Conquest. Most of the objects are small and were used for personal adornment with nose plugs, pendants, large pectoral plates, earrings, arm bands, and necklaces being the most characteristic forms. In addition, there are tools and implements such as chisels, needles, polishers, scrapers, and fish hooks, as well as status objects such as spoons, bowls, and statuettes.

The museum's gold collection from Nariño, the most recently discovered metalworking region of pre-Hispanic Colombia, is noted for its nose plugs elaborately decorated with dangles and its small paired plaques adorned with repoussé human and feline faces. Other holdings from the area include breastplates, plaques for textile appliqués, bells, and ear discs, each decorated with geometric designs and/or stylized animal forms. They are made of cast and hammered gold and are finished by plating overlay, oxidation gilding, and polishing.

The gold objects in the collection from the Calima region are among the earliest examples of metalwork found in the country and include nose rings, breastplates, bracelets, necklaces, rings, diadems, and masks. The breastplates and funerary masks are of considerable size and extraordinary beauty. Hammered from sheet gold, the masks vary in their degree of naturalism, but the raised human faces on the pectorals, often obscured by large nose and ear ornaments, are more standardized in their realistic depiction of facial features. In addition, the museum has several pin heads decorated with ceremonial figures, birds, monkeys, and bells that are masterpieces of the lost wax process. All of the Calima pieces are made of highly polished, fine-quality gold.

The works in the collection from the Quimbaya region are among the most superb metallurgical accomplishments in pre-Hispanic Colombia. Manufactured variously by the lost wax process, soldering, annealing, and hammering, the characteristic forms, like those found in the Calima region, are masks, breastplates, crowns, nose rings, necklaces, bells, and rings. In addition to containing examples of these forms, the collection features a series of small flasks called *poporos*. They are narrow-necked, gracefully fluted, elegantly proportioned forms that were used to hold lime for ritual coca chewing. Quimbaya pieces, although formally simple, are conceptually among the most complex and sophisticated of all ancient Colombian gold work.

The museum also has a small but fine collection of pieces from the Tolima region. The most characteristic form is a pendant representing either a highly stylized human figure or an animal, probably a bat. Stylistically, these pendants rely on flat, bold, angular shapes that are cast and then stretched by hammering.

The pieces in the museum's Muisca collection are the most stylistically and iconographically distinct of all ancient Colombian gold. Not only do many of the objects have a marked narrative content, but many of the pieces provide specific visual information about dress, ceremony, and a wide variety of life activities. The museum has figures of warriors with trophy heads, coca chewers with *poporos*, large figures carrying smaller ones, and many of the characteristic Muisca *tunjos*, the long, flat, slender, generalized human figures with elaborate decorative elements and genitals. Nearly all of the works are cast in one piece with the surfaces left unpolished.

Besides the fine collection of *tunjos*, ceremonial objects, zoomorphic figures, and objects of personal adornment, the museum has a Muisca gold piece of singular beauty and importance, the well-known depiction of what is thought to be the raft of the legendary El Dorado, The Golden One. Displayed in a separate plexiglass case on a revolving base, the piece is believed to represent the ceremonial voyage of a chief, whose body, covered with gold, went periodically to the middle of the lake to make offerings to the gods by throwing emeralds and pieces of gold into the water. The piece depicts a raft on which an elaborately dressed, prominently placed figure stands surrounded by smaller, presumably, attendant figures. It, too, is cast by the lost wax process and is an extremely intricate, distinctively narrative work.

Gold work from the Sinú region in the northern Colombian lowlands is also well represented in the museum. Globular vessels with bell-shaped feet, tall stemmed goblets, fan-shaped ear ornaments cast in false filigree, necklaces, zoomorphic figures, penis covers, masks, and bird finials are the most characteristic forms. The bird finials are especially well known and are thought to have been used on the tops of staffs, perhaps as indications of office or rank. Sinú gold relies heavily on open geometrical patterns that give much of the work a light, delicate feeling.

There is a particularly large number of pieces in the museum from the Tairona region. They include elaborately headdressed personages, pendants, large pectoral plates, arm ornaments, nose plugs, earrings, *poporos*, and staff finials. These works are most frequently decorated with geometric designs and stylized reptiles and birds and are made of the gold-copper alloy *tumbaga*.

Although gold work from all of the regions is continuously on view, the museum periodically changes its exhibits and installs new ones to keep the exhibitions current and to display new material to regular visitors. One temporary exhibition each year studies in detail some aspect of the museum's collection.

The museum has a specialized library of four thousand volumes on pre-Hispanic archaeology, a card catalogue to the collection, photographs and tapes pertinent to archaeological and ethnographic material, research carrels, and workrooms where artifacts are studied and restored. It also has a Research Department, which is responsible for archaeological studies related to the museum's collection as well as the Department of Museography, which offers study programs to students interested in research methods and procedures for mounting and maintaining temporary and permanent exhibitions.

Selected Bibliography

Museum publications: *Museo del Oro*, 4th ed., 1978; *El Dorado*, Edicion del Cincuentenario, Banco de la Republica, 1973; "Bibliography of Pre-Hispanic Goldwork of Colombia," *El Museo del Oro Estudios*, vol. 1, no. 1, 1971.

Other publications: Jones, Julie, and Warwick Bray, *El Dorado, The Gold of Ancient Colombia* (Greenwich, Conn. 1974); Pérez de Barradas, José, *Los Muiscas antes de la Conquista*, 2 vols. (Madrid 1950–51); idem, *Orfebrería Prehispánica de Colombia, Estilo Calima*, 2 vols. (Madrid 1954); idem, *Orfebrería Prehispánica de Colombia, Estilos Tolima y Muisca*, 2 vols. (Madrid 1958); idem, *Orfebrería Prehispánica de Colombia, Estilos Quimbaya y Otros*, 2 vols. (Madrid 1966); Bray, Warwick, "Ancient American Metal-Smiths," *Proceedings of the Royal Anthropological Institute of Great Britain and Ireland for 1971* (1972), pp. 25–43; Bright, Alec, "A goldsmith's blowpipe from Colombia," *Man*, vol. 7, no. 2 (1972), pp. 311–13; Bruhns, Karen Olsen, "A Quimbaya Gold Furnace?" *American Antiquity*, vol. 35, no. 2 (1970), pp. 202–3; idem, "Two Prehispanic Cire Perdue Casting Moulds from Colombia," *Man*, vol. 7, no. 2 (1972), pp. 308–11; Easby, Dudley T., "Pre-Hispanic Metallurgy and Metalworking in the New World," *Proceedings of The American Philosophical Society*, vol. 109, no. 2 (1965), pp. 89–98; idem, "Early Metallurgy in the New World," *Scientific American*, vol. 214, no. 4 (1966), pp. 73–81; Root, William Campbell, "Metallurgy," *Handbook of South American Indians*, vol. 5 (Washington 1949), pp. 205–25; idem, "Pre-Columbian Metalwork of Colombia and its Neighbors,"*Essays in Pre-Columbian Art and Archaeology* (Cambridge 1964), pp. 242–57.

SUZANNE GARRIGUES

Denmark

──── Copenhagen ────

DANISH ART MUSEUM (officially STATENS MUSEUM FOR KUNST; alternately MUSEUM OF FINE ARTS, THE ROYAL MUSEUM OF FINE ARTS, STATE MUSEUM OF ART, STATES MUSEUM OF ART), Sølvgade, DK–1307 Copenhagen K.

The Statens Museum for Kunst (Danish Art Museum) serves as the national gallery of Denmark and is funded, owned, and administered by the Danish State. For special acquisitions, support is sometimes obtained from private foundations. The museum was built from 1889 to 1896 and has three departments: the Department of Paintings and Sculpture (Danish and foreign), the Department of Prints and Drawings, and the Department for Conservation. Each of these departments has a staff of six to eight persons plus secretarial support. A director is responsible for the administration and operation of the departments and is responsible to the Ministry of Cultural Affairs.

One of the museum's most important tasks is the enlargement and maintenance of the existing collection. This would not have been possible without donations and support from various sources, including the Ny Carlsberg Foundation, the Foundation of 7th January, and Lillian and P. T. Nielsen's Foundation. A distinguished gift of works by Danish abstract painters and sculptors was donated to the museum in 1958 by Elise Johansen.

The origins of the Statens Museum for Kunst may be traced to the development of the Royal Picture Gallery during the reign of Frederik V, 1723–66. He was the first Danish monarch to acquire works from abroad with the specific purpose of establishing an art collection. In 1759 and 1763 the art dealer Gerhard Morell acquired 171 paintings in Amsterdam for the Danish court. Among these works were Rembrandt's *Christ at Emmaus*, 1648, and Mantegna's *Pietà*, which is considered to be the outstanding quattrocento picture in Copenhagen. The latter work was from the collection of Cardinal Silvio Valenti Gonzaga, a portion of which Morell purchased in 1763. Morell was also instrumental in creating an art gallery for the king's friend and adviser A. G. Moltke. The best items of Moltke's collection were purchased by the Statens Museum for Kunst in 1931.

Although the Royal Picture Gallery was housed in the Royal Palace and not properly established until 1824 after the addition of the very important Consul West Collection, it was never closed to serious students. Toward the end of the nineteenth century, the royal collection was moved to its own building and became the State Museum of Art. It was constructed in Sølvgade in 1889–96 after drawings by the architect Vilhelm Dahlerup. Even before it was opened, however, it had been decided to use the ground floor for a collection of plaster casts of antique and European sculpture that Carl Jacobsen, the brewer, wanted to donate to the nation. Thus the museum was too small from the outset, a circumstance that became steadily more apparent as the collections grew.

A thorough conversion of the museum was supervised by architect Nils Koppel between 1966 and 1969. Two inner courtyards were covered with roofs, thereby providing a number of exhibition rooms that receive daylight from above. Below these rooms, three more large rooms are now lit by artificial light. Several extra exhibition rooms, some with daylight and some without, were acquired by the Department of Prints and Drawings.

One of the first important works came into the royal collection in 1763; an altar panel by Petrus Christus, *St. Antony with a Kneeling Donor*, about 1440–45.

Included among the Early Renaissance pictures in the Italian collection of the Statens Museum is a work by the Northern Italian Andrea Mantegna, *Christ the Suffering Redeemer*, about 1475–90.

The famous Venetian painters of the sixteenth century are represented in the museum by a large figure composition, *Christ and the Woman Taken in Adultery* by Tintoretto, and two portraits by Titian. His *Portrait of a Man*, about 1550, represents a bearded man in a fur-trimmed black garment.

Outstanding among the works of Rubens owned by the museum is the *Portrait of Abbot Matthaeus Yrsselius*, 1624–29, originally found in a monastery church in Antwerp. It is a moving portrayal of a frail old man and measures 120.0 by 102.5 centimeters. In the museum's important collection of seventeenth-century Flemish art are five other pictures by Rubens and several by Jordaens.

In 1648 Rembrandt painted two versions of *Christ at Emmaus*. One is now in the Louvre (q.v.) and the other hangs in the Statens Museum. It is one of the most moving of Rembrandt's biblical works. The museum also possesses several portraits by Rembrandt.

One of the highlights among the portraits in the museum's large collection of Dutch paintings of the seventeenth century was purchased with the help of a grant from the Ny Carlsberg Foundation. This is Frans Hals' *Portrait of an Elderly Man*, about 1660.

The landscapes of Jan van Goyen, Salomon van Ruysdael, and Jacob van Ruisdael are well represented in the museum. Also notable is Philips Koninck's *Landscape by the River Waal* of 1654.

The Statens Museum for Kunst possesses a large collection of miniatures. Among many by Danish artists are some by Cornelius Høyer, one of the finest miniature painters in Europe in the latter half of the eighteenth century. Outstanding among the foreign artists represented in the collection are the Italian Rosalba Carriera and the Englishmen Samuel Cooper and John Hoskins.

The excellent collection of French paintings and sculptures of the nineteenth century were to a great extent acquired by private collectors. Outstanding in the field of contemporary French art is the museum's Rump Collection. Beginning in 1912 J. Rump, an engineer from Copenhagen, acquired works by Matisse, Derain, Braque, Rouault, Segonzac, Picasso, and others. In 1928 he presented them to the museum with the understanding that they be exhibited for twenty-five years and then sold. The proceeds would then go to purchase "new, disputed, and stimulating" works not then more than twenty-five years old. Rump believed that the purpose of such a gallery is to bring the best new art from France or elsewhere to Denmark, so that the Danish public will learn to know these works while they are still relatively new. He realized that ideas and tastes change from generation to generation and that those pictures that he would imagine might be the best to dispose of might in later years be regarded as keystones of the collection.

At present the Rump Collection is chiefly comprised of paintings by the Fauves. Among twentieth-century painters admirably represented here are Dufy, Juan Gris, Gromaire, and Modigliani, in addition to the important selection of works by Henri Matisse. The museum has nineteen Matisse paintings (dating from 1898 to 1950). Matisse's *Interior with Violin*, one of the finest, was painted during World War I in a small hotel in Nice. There are also five Matisse sculptures.

The Rump Collection contains statuettes and small sculptures by Aristide Maillol and by Henri Laurens in particular. The specimens of this artist's bronzes owned by the museum are early, excellent casts. Laurens' terracotta figure *Woman Bathing; The Wave*, 1933, is a subtly balanced statuette, 39 centimeters high.

A selection of Maurice Estève's works, with canvases by artists such as Jean Bazaine, Serge Poliakoff, and Pierre Soulages in the Rump Collection, provide an understanding of the younger, lyrical, abstract painters of the Paris school. Estève's *L'Arnon*, 1959, is an abstract composition based on his impressions of nature at a small town on the River Arnon. The Rump Collection also includes works by Jacques Lipchitz and Marc Chagall.

The Statens Museum has a two-room Scandinavian Collection that includes Norwegian, Swedish, Icelandic, and Faroese art. Apart from works dating from the end of the eighteenth century by the Swedes C. G. Pilo, Johan Hørner, and Johan Tobias Sergel, which are to be found in the Danish collections, the oldest part of the Scandinavian Collection consists of a fine group of landscapes painted in Denmark, Italy, Germany, and Norway by the Norwegian J. C. Dahl during the first half of the nineteenth century. From the period after 1880, the museum owns a number of typical works by Norwegian artists Christian Krohg, Edvard Munch (including *Chamber of Death*, 1915), and Ludvig Karsten. A comprehensive collection of Karl Isakson's canvases and a smaller one of Inge Schröler's demonstrate various aspects of Swedish art of the present century. Prominent among the remaining Scandinavian painters are the Icelanders Johannes S. Kjarval and Juliana Sveinsdottir and the Faroe Islander Samuel Joensen-Mikines.

Although the museum possesses portraits and a few figure compositions by the two leading seventeenth-century masters in Denmark, the Dutchmen Karel van Mander the Younger and Abraham Wuchters, and minor works by Late Baroque painters, the display of Danish paintings only acquires breadth from about the middle of the eighteenth century onwards. The core of the older Danish paintings is formed by nineteenth-century Danish Golden Age and Romantic paintings, with landscapes and portraits being the preferred genres. The more recent Danish collections embrace paintings and sculpture dating from the 1870s to the present. Although the work of most of the prominent artists is extensively presented, no attempt has been made to achieve comprehensive historical coverage of individual stylistic periods.

Jens Juel was a distinguished portrait painter and also an inspired landscapist. One of his major works, *The Ryberg Family Picture*, 1796–97, is owned by the museum. The 253- by 336-centimeter painting depicts Niels Ryberg with his son and daughter-in-law in a landscape with a view of the family manor in the distance. Juel, whose style was balanced and harmonious, was both the product of as well as the interpreter of the idyllic age in Danish history before the Napoleonic wars and the battle of Copenhagen in 1801.

The foremost representative of neoclassicism was the painter Nicolai Abraham Abildgaard, who was much inspired by history and literature. The museum owns one of his works painted at the end of the eighteenth century that illustrates Ossian, the old blind Scottish bard, singing the final song of his life.

Three great Danish sculptors, Herman Freund, Herman Bissen, and Jens Jerichau, as young men all frequented Thorvaldsen's studio in Rome and studied the antique under his instruction. They were influenced by his doctrines, but each attempted to free himself of Thorvaldsen's weighty authority. The museum's bronze statuette *Loke* was executed by Freund in 1822. He succeeded in creating a type completely different from the classical in his representation of the demonic Loke, with his mask-like features, bat's wings, and creeping gait. Bissen and Jerichau gradually developed a naturalistic outlook, in deliberate reaction against their youthful style. The museum's bronze group by Jerichau, *The Panther Hunter*, was modeled from 1845–46 and was cast in bronze in 1873.

After having roused attention by his stern and virile realism influenced by Rodin, Kai Nielsen created a number of powerful yet graceful works. The museum possesses two such works—Nielsen's sandstone *Leda with the Swan*, 1919, and his Fakse marble *Leda without the Swan*, 1920.

Einar Utzon-Frank has aimed at a decorative style using sculptural effects in close connection with architecture. The museum's bronze *Aphrodite*, 1915, illustrates Utzon-Frank's sense of ornamental silhouette effects in sculpture.

The bronze *Abyssinian* of 1914–15 by Johannes Bjerg displays this artist's sense of the constructive elements in a work of art. The museum also owns a portrait bust of the Swedish sculptor Nils Möllerberg, created in bronze by Adam Fischer in 1932. Fischer, who was originally influenced by Cubism, freed himself gradually from its doctrines and developed a simple style in his statues and busts.

The earliest group in the nineteenth-century collection is formed by landscapes, marine paintings, and portraits by C. W. Eckersberg and his pupils, foremost among whom were Christen Købke and Constantin Hansen. Views and landscapes painted in Paris and Rome show the young Eckersberg's range. Of his marine paintings, in which he specialized after his return home in 1816, the museum has a number of especially fine pieces. Also there is his picture of the Nathanson family painted in 1818. The Købke group of pictures is significant for the many views of Copenhagen and the surrounding district, such as the large *View of Østerbro in the Early Morning*, dating from 1836.

The selection of Hansen's works emphasizes his talent as a portraitist and architectural painter and includes a number of studies for compositions on themes taken from Greek mythology. His classical *Scene from the Garden of Villa Albani*, 1841, was painted during his residence in Rome, where Danish artists continued to study well into the nineteenth century.

Landscape painting as developed by Johan Th. Lundbye, Dankvart Dreyer, and P. C. Skovgaard until past the middle of the nineteenth century is another major aspect of this collection. Lundbye's oil on paper, *Marling of Vallekilde Rectory Field*, 1846, is a fourteen- by twenty-two-centimeter work that depicts autumn in the open Danish farm landscape in brownish tones and silhouette-like figures.

In the decade before World War I a new generation of Danish painters, inspired by contemporary French art, turned aside from naturalism. In *The Road to Faaborg*, 1920, in the Statens Museum, Harald Giersing created a rhythm and a sense of space by the disposal of areas of green, blue, and yellow behind the vertical black strokes of the telegraph pole and the tree trunks.

The art of Edvard Weie shows clearly how thoroughly Danish painting was renewed in this new attempt to solve the problems of color. Through an intense study of nature, Weie refined his colors and arrived at an imaginative method of abstraction as in his *Arrangement (Still Life)*, 1922.

Danish abstract painting came to the fore in the 1930s and 1940s, and some of the painters in the group included Richard Mortensen, Asger Jorn, and Egill Jacobsen. Jacobsen often uses the green-mask motif inspired by primitive art as in the museum's picture *Green Masks*, 1949, with its wealth of green tones. Richard Mortensen, after his passionately spontaneous painting of the war period, turned to clarity of form and line and pure colors. In his *Collage de Dessin*, 1950, in ink on synthetic fiberboard, he created lines in black and gray, like graphic symbols.

The Royal Print Room, as the Department of Prints and Drawings was formerly called, indicates both the historical background of the collection and its original character. The department functions in two ways. First, it has a study room, where any of the two hundred thousand works can be seen on request. Second, the department has ten rooms in which successive exhibitions are held, particularly of the department's own collections. Since 1970, however, increased financial grants have made it possible to arrange exhibitions based on cooperation with other Danish and foreign museums.

One of the two known drawings by Donato Bramante (1444–1514) is the *St. Christopher* in the Italian collection of the Department of Prints and Drawings. The 30.8- by 19.0-centimeter study in silver point and white color on paper is squared for transfer.

Early Flemish and Dutch art is particularly well represented in the foreign section of the Department of Prints and Drawings. A Rembrandt sheet of ink studies, about 1660, includes a sketch of the *Deposition from the Cross* and two studies of a woman and child. The department is also rich in modern French prints and possesses the largest collection of French books illustrated with original twentieth-century prints outside of Paris and New York. In addition, it has many French drawings, including Picasso's *Bull-Fight*, 1960.

Both the Department of Paintings and Sculpture and the Department of Prints and Drawings have specialized libraries. The Department of Paintings and Sculpture's library has about 60,000 volumes, 150 periodical subscriptions, exhibition and auction catalogs, and newspaper clippings. It is open to the public as a reference library, as is the library of the Department of Prints and Drawings, which owns approximately 40,000 volumes and subscribes to 47 periodicals. The Department of Paintings and Sculpture publishes *Kunstmuseets Arsskrift* (the *Royal Museum of Fine Arts Yearbook*).

There is a cafeteria and a sales shop that sells prints, slides, catalogs, and posters. At the Information Desk one may purchase color postcards reproducing works of art in the collections. Black and white photographs, eighteen by twenty-four centimeters, may be ordered from the museum office on request.

Selected Bibliography

Museum publications: *The Royal Museum of Fine Arts: A Short Guide*; *Aeldre Dansk Malerkunst*, Billedudvalg, 1970; *Aeldre Dansk Skulptur*, 1977; *Catalogue of Old Foreign Paintings*, 1951; Den Kingelige Kobberstiksamling ved Inger Hjorth Nielsen, *Dansk Tegninger: En Oversigt med 181 Illustrationer*, 1979; *Katalog* (Udarb. af Marianne Brøns, Elisabeth Fabritius, og Marianne Marcussen), 1970; *Kunstmuseets Arsskrift*, 1914- (Yearbook); *Moderns Uplenlandsk Kunst, J. Rumps Samling, etc.*, 3d ed., 1958; *Ny Dansk Kunst: Erhvervet, 1963–1973*, 1974.

Other publications: *Albert Marquet, 1875–1947; Malerier, Akvareller, Tegninger, Grafik* (Copenhagen 1950?); Bodelsen, Fru Merete, *Dansk Kunst Historisk Bibliografi* (Copenhagen 1935); Boesen, Gudmund, *Danish Museums* (Copenhagen 1966); Bramsen, Henrik, *Treasures from Danish Museums* (Copenhagen 1956); *Copenhagen* (Copenhagen 1968); *Dansk Tegninger Fra Melchoir Lorck til Fyenboerne* (Copenhagen 1945); *Fem*

Hundrede Dansk og Skandinaviske Malerier (Copenhagen 1954); . . . *Fortegnelse over Billeder Aeldre Malere og Norsk, Svensk, og Finsk Kunst* (Copenhagen 1922); *Fortegnelse over den Danske Samlings Malier og Skulpturer* (Copenhagen 1948); Nørland, Paul, *Danish Art through the Ages* (Copenhagen 1948); Olsen, Harald, *Italian Paintings and Sculpture in Denmark* (Copenhagen 1961); Poulsen, Vagn, *Danish Painting and Sculpture* (Copenhagen 1976); idem, *Illustrated Art Guide to Denmark* (Copenhagen 1959); Garff, Jan, comp., "Maerten van Heemskerck," *Pantheon*, vol. 30 (September 1972), p. 427; "Johan Christian Clausen Dahl," *Parthenon*, vol. 31 (July 1973), p. 311; Siebeneck, Henry King, "Art at Copenhagen: Rump Collection of Modern French Art at the States Museum of Art," *Carnegie Magazine*, vol. 4 (February 1931), p. 277.

AGNES ANN FITZGIBBONS

NEW CARLSBERG GALLERY (officially NY CARLSBERG GLYPTOTEK; also CARLSBERG GALLERY, NEW CARLSBERG GLYPTOTEK, NY CARLSBERG GLYPTOTHEK), Dantes Plads 7, DK 1556 Copenhagen V.

The Ny Carlsberg Glyptotek was founded as an independent institution in 1888 by Carl Jacobsen (1842–1914), proprietor of the Carlsberg Brewery, and his wife, Ottilia. Jacobsen was one of the leading art collectors of the period 1870–1914. He was a firm believer in the inspirational effect of art on the human spirit and wanted to turn his large art collections into a public institution. His father, Jacob Christian Jacobsen (1811–87), was a munificent art patron who had commissioned the Danish sculptor Bertel Thorvaldsen to create works for his villa at Valby, and who had purchased works for the National Antique Collection, the Statens Museum for Kunst, and the Thorvaldsen Museum. In 1871 the elder Jacobsen created the Carlsberg Foundation, financed by the profits of the Carlsberg Brewery. This foundation's original range was artistic, but Carl Jacobsen consolidated it and extended it to cover scientific research.

The Albertina Foundation was created in 1879 by Carl Jacobsen to honor Thorvaldsen through the purchase of sculpture for public gardens and parks. Jacobsen subsequently became one of the most discerning collectors of Classical art in Europe. In 1902 he and his wife established the Ny Carlsberg Foundation, which continues to donate many important additions to the Glyptotek collection. The city of Copenhagen and the Danish government have been generous contributors toward the transformation of the Jacobsen Collection into a public museum. In 1927 Carl and Ottilia's son Helge presented a valuable selection of modern paintings, mainly the works of Paul Gauguin, to the museum. Permanent loans of French paintings from the Statens Museum for Kunst, works by H. E. Freund from the Royal Academy, and Egyptian sculpture from the Episcopal See of Zealand are featured as special collections in the museum.

The Glyptotek is situated in the Dantes Plads. The museum's Modern Department, completed in 1897, faces the square and was designed by Vilhelm Dahlerup. The Glyptotek's Department of Ancient Art was designed by Hack Kampmann and was opened to the public in 1906. The main floor of the Kampmann building contains Egyptian art and portraits. The ground floor of the building contains Etruscan and Palmyrene sculpture. The upper floor of Dahlerup's building houses French painting and bronzes by Degas and Rodin. The ground floor of this building contains French and Danish sculpture, and the mezzanine displays Danish painting and sculpture.

The Glyptotek has no museum organizations and does not have a formal association with any research organization. It is governed by a board of trustees, two members of which are appointed by the state, two by the municipality, three by the Ny Carlsberg Foundation, and one by the Carlsberg Foundation. The administration is run by the director. There is one curator (an art historian) in the Department of Modern Art and two curators (classical archaeologists) in the Department of Ancient Art.

The Ny Carlsberg Glyptotek is one of the most attractive collections of ancient art in existence. The collection shows the development from the ancient Egyptians and Mesopotamians to the fall of the Roman Empire, with the main emphasis on Classical Greek art.

The Glyptotek's Ancient Near Eastern collection is small but contains two important Sumerian stone sculptures that may be regarded as legacies from the oldest civilized people in Mesopotamia. The first sculpture is a standing figure of King Gudea of Lagash (twenty-fourth century B.C.) with a cuneiform inscription. The second sculpture is a Sumerian figure of a man seated on the ground with crossed legs. This forty-three-centimeter-high figure was acquired by Carl Jacobsen in 1912 and is made of green stone. The figure is believed to be from the last part of the early Sumerian period, early Dynastic III period, about 2500 B.C. Since the inscription on the figure's right shoulder and arm does not give any information about the Sumerian's position, his identification is not possible. However, he was evidently not a god but an individual of high rank who was anxious to be remembered.

The Near Eastern collection also contains two great alabaster reliefs representing winged demons wearing horned helmets. These reliefs are believed to have decorated the palace that Assyrian king Assurnasirpal built at Nimrud about 870 B.C. Reliefs that decorated the Ishtar gate and the sacred processional way through Babylon during the reign of King Nebukadnezar (seventh century B.C.) are also part of the Near Eastern collection. They are made of colored glazed brick and depict a lion, a dragon, and a bull.

The provincial style of works from Cyprus may be seen in the three great limestone heads in the Ancient Near Eastern collection. It has been hypothesized that the island's physical location between the Ancient Near Eastern and Greek worlds was an influence on the artistic style of its people.

Some of the Glyptotek's most important holdings are those of ancient Egyptian art. Carl Jacobsen decided to establish an Egyptian collection in 1890 and acquired a number of the most special pieces within five years.

Sculpture from the time of the great pyramids to the era of the Ptolemies is housed within the museum's Great Egyptian Room. In this room one may view a series of wall fragments carved in low relief. Hieroglyphic inscriptions on the fragments list names and titles. A different technique is present in two of the fragments, a type of colored-in outline drawing.

The collection's colossal granite group of Ramesses II (1296–1230 B.C.) and the god Ptah, found at Memphis, exemplifies the monumental size of many Egyptian works. The Great Egyptian Room also contains excellent portraits of distinguished private individuals such as the seated diorite statue of Gebu (c. 1500 B.C.), who held the "Lord Privy Seal" office, and the diorite group of Amosis with his mother, Beket-Re (c. 1500 B.C.).

At Sakkara enormous pyramids of the Pharoahs were surrounded by the more modest burials of the king's relations and courtiers. The Glyptotek's Room of the Mastaba is named after one of its exhibits, the cult chapel of Kaëmrēhu. This chapel is from the upper part of a sepulchre from the time of the fifth dynasty (2560–2420 B.C.) that was found at Sakkara. It was designed for offering gifts to the dead, and the door posts and walls are decorated with artistic masterpieces of low relief. The Room of the Mastaba also contains a wooden coffin, dating from the second dynasty (c. 2800 B.C.), made in the likeness of a house, which affords a glimpse of very early domestic architecture. The most important single artwork in this room dates from about 1400 B.C. It is a beautifully crafted wooden ointment spoon from Sedment, with a handle representing a young slave girl surrounded by papyrus plants.

Smaller sculptures are displayed in the Small Egyptian Room. One of the oldest items in the collection is a prehistoric hippopotamus, which was made in alabaster about 3000 B.C. The great creature of the Nile has been treated in a humorous manner by a master artisan. It is twenty-nine centimeters high and is considered to be the most outstanding piece known from the earliest period of Egyptian sculpture.

The last room in the Egyptian collection is the Egyptian Rotunda, which houses the masterpiece among Egyptian portraits at the Glyptotek. It is called *The Black Head of a King* and is a fragment of an almost life-size statue. Only the head, neck, and crown are partially preserved. Carl Jacobsen acquired it in 1895 with the help of the Danish Orientalist Vlademar Schmidt. *The Black Head of a King* has highly personal facial features, which is unusual in Egyptian art. Furthermore, they change according to the light and point of view. Although the head has neither an inscription nor a royal name, scholars have noted many similarities that it shares with portraits of Amenemhet III (1842–1798 B.C.), the king who reigned toward the end of the twelfth dynasty.

The Egyptian Rotunda also displays a small copper statuette, with silver inlay, which is ascribed to the Dynasty XIX or XX (1350–1090 B.C.). The figure depicts a god with a human body and a ram's head with a double crown. It was originally meant to represent the god Seth but was later transformed into some other god by adding the ram's horns.

The extensive collection of ancient Greek art at the Glyptotek is well represented against blue walls. *The 'Rayet' Head* (c. 530 B.C.) is the most radiant of the five Archaic sculptures from Attica possessed by the Glyptotek. This head of a distinguished-looking young man is a thirty-one-centimeter remnant of a monumental marble statue once placed on a tomb outside the Dipylon, the double gate of Athens. The head, formerly in the Rayet Collection, Paris, is one of the finest pieces of Attic art.

The outstanding specimen in the Glyptotek of Attic marble art dating from the Classical period (c. 420 B.C.) is a votive relief. It reflects a period when the style of the Parthenon marbles still influenced the rendering of reliefs for sepulchral monuments and votive offerings. The relief is seventy-two centimeters high and most likely represents the goddesses Demeter and Persephone between Pluto and Triptolemus, with a small rendering of the donor on the left.

A group of the Glyptotek's most outstanding Greek sculptures may be found in the Room of the Niobids. Two monumental statues were evidently part of a composition depicting the legend of the children of Niobe. The first (c. 430 B.C.) is 1.4 meters high and represents one of Niobe's daughters dressed in a Doric peplos with an overfold and a belt. She is running to the left while looking backwards and naively seeking cover from the arrows of Apollo and Artemis under the fold of her peplos. The second statue (c. 430 B.C.) depicts her brother, who is shown as a young man lying on his left side, mortally wounded. The 1.62-meter-long sculpture is nude, except for the edge of a mantle covering the right thigh. Behind the youth's shoulder is a circular hole that originally held a bronze arrow that the youth is vainly trying to remove.

Both statues are made of fine, white, large-grained marble believed to have come from the island of Paros. Carl Jacobsen bought both of the sculptures in 1888 through his agent Wolfgang Helbig. Helbig acquired them from a German bookseller, Spithoever, on whose land near Rome they had been discovered. In antiquity the Gardens of Sallust were situated on this land. The hypothesis that the two sculptures belonged together and that they had originally been placed in the pediment of a temple has been generally accepted. Although the figures belong to the Classical era of the Parthenon, they were not made in Athens but were probably sculpted by a Greek living in southern Italy.

One of the most recent additions to the Glyptotek's collection of ancient Greek art is a well-preserved black-figure vase. It was acquired in 1980 and dates from the fifth century B.C. Its height is 62.8 centimeters, and because of its form, decoration, and inscription, it may be identified as a Panathenaic prize amphora that, filled with olive oil from the sacred groves of Attica, was given out in Athens every four years. The front of the vase illustrates Athena Promachos moving toward the left. She stands between two Doric columns, the one on the left inscribed: "(I am) one of the prizes from the games at Athens." The other side of the vase is a representation of a wrestling match between two naked, beardless men, with a bearded, cloaked man serving as the judge.

The collection of some five hundred Roman portrait busts in the Glyptotek spans the era of the Republic until A.D. 500. The museum owns a much-damaged head of the goddess Athena, which is considered to be a good reduced-scale rendering of the statue Phidias created for the Parthenon. The oldest Greek portrait in the Glyptotek's collection is a Roman copy of a fifth-century B.C. Greek statue of Anacreon, the great lyric poet. It is an idealized conception of the poet reciting to a lyre, and the prototype is believed to have been a bronze statue executed by Phidias.

The statue of Demosthenes, a Roman copy of a bronze image erected on the Agora of Athens in 280 B.C., is one of the most important among the Glyptotek's early Hellenistic portraits. The statue was a monument to the great patriot and orator who had tried to oppose the Macedonian supremacy over Greece. The marble head of the famous Roman statesman and general, Pompey, is probably a copy of a bronze original dating from about 60 B.C. The twenty-six-centimeter-high head was found on an aristocratic burial place in Rome in 1885 and was acquired by Carl Jacobsen in 1887. Pompey is portrayed in his fiftieth year, and the coarse but intelligent face is an outstanding example of realistic Roman portraiture.

The Glyptotek's portrait bust of Caligula, A.D. 37–41, is fifty-one centimeters high and of white, coarse-grained marble. It was acquired in 1897 and was said to have been discovered in or by the Tiber in the late nineteenth century. Caligula is portrayed as a clean-shaven young man wearing an oak wreath.

The Central Hall of the Glyptotek's Kampmann building has the shape of an ancient courtyard surrounded by colonnades and overlooked by a temple front. In the middle of the floor is a first-century Roman mosaic illustrating the rape of Europa. A staircase from this room leads down to the Etruscan and Palmyrene collections.

The Etruscans immigrated to the Italian peninsula from western Asia Minor in the ninth to eighth century B.C. and settled in the area of the present Tuscany and Latium. The Glyptotek's Etruscan collection was begun in 1891 and is now one of the largest collections of this type of art outside of Italy. With the help of the Ny Carlsberg Foundation, the Glyptotek acquired a group of twenty-seven Etruscan bronze reliefs during 1970–72. These chiseled figure decorations date from the beginning of the sixth century B.C. and include five bronze plaques, which are presumed to have been chariot or wagon decorations. The northern Etruscan city of Chiusi excelled in stone sculpture. A whole series of the cinerary coffins and tomb monuments from Chiusi that are made of the local limestone are part of the Etruscan collections.

Palmyra was an oasis in the desert between Syria and Mesopotamia that enjoyed prosperity during the Roman Empire. The art of Palmyra greatly depended on Greek and Roman sculpture, and practically all Palmyrene sculpture in the Glyptotek was made for funerary use. Most of them are portrait limestone busts of the deceased that were brightly painted and often inscribed with the name and year of death in the Aramaic language.

Although Carl Jacobsen was interested in collecting ancient art, nineteenth-century French sculpture, and paintings by Corot, Delacroix, and Millet, he was not enthusiastic about the Impressionists. However, his son Helge's term of office with the Ny Carlsberg Foundation produced an arrangement whereby the Statens Museum for Kunst permanently loaned the Glyptotek a number of French masterpieces. In 1912 the financial situation of Wilhelm Hansen, a notable collector of Impressionists, made it necessary for him to sell most of his collection. Nineteen of these works were purchased by the Ny Carlsberg Foundation and given to the Glyptotek. Notable among them are works by David, Courbet, Cézanne, van Gogh, and Toulouse-Lautrec.

The earliest French portrait is David's *Comte de Turenne*, 1816, painted by the artist in Brussels. Courbet's *Self Portrait*, about 1853, captures well his independent character. By Manet are three outstanding works, the early *Absinthe Drinkers* (1859), *Execution of Maxmilian* (1867), and the portrait of *Mlle. Lemonier* (1870s). There is also a self-portrait by Cézanne, about 1883–87, as well as his *Still Life* of 1877 and *Bathing Women in a Landscape*. Three important paintings by van Gogh are included in this collection: *Père Tanguy*, 1897; *Saint Remy*, 1889; and *Three Pink Roses*, 1890. By Toulouse-Lautrec is the *Portrait of Suzanne Valadon* and the *Portrait of M. Delaporte in the Jardin de Paris* (1893), a picture of an elegant man-about-town rendered with pungency and humor. Completing the collection of Impressionist paintings are four works by Renoir, including *Young Girls*, 1876; Morisot's *Julie Manet with Her Nerise*, 1880; two Parisian scenes by Pissarro, as well as *The Wood*; Monet's *Shadow on the Sea*, 1882; and three canvases by Sisley.

By Gauguin, who had a Danish wife, the Glyptotek possesses twenty-five paintings and two wood reliefs, one of which is *Eve and the Serpent*, c. 1889. The works represent all periods in his development, from early Parisian works to brilliant late Tahitian pictures, such as *Tahitian Girl with a Flower*, 1891.

Neo-Impressionism is represented by works of Signac, Cross, and Theo van Rysselberghe. Also included are three paintings by Vuillard and his pastel of the *Artist's Mother Reading*. Completing the French painting collection are four paintings by Bonnard, which include *La modiste*, 1907, and his later *The Dining Room*, c. 1925.

The Glyptotek also has a fine collection of nineteenth-century French sculpture. Of particular note are the works by Jean-Baptiste Carpeaux, including the 1869 bust of the Opéra architect *Charles Garnier* and an original plaster cast, *Madame Pelouze*, 1872. In addition to the large selection of works by Carpeaux, there are also major pieces from the early works of Maillol (1900–1910), Rodin, and Barye, with seven by Daumier and the *Seated Woman*, 1906, by Matisse.

The museum has all seventy-three of Degas' bronze statuettes of horses, female models, and ballet girls, in addition to three paintings of ballet scenes, including oils done in 1880 and *Two Dancers* of 1898, and several pastels, including the *Bathing Scene* and a work of two green dancers done in 1890.

The small but choice collection of Danish paintings in the Glyptotek focuses on the first half of the nineteenth century. These works reflect the bourgeois culture that formed the basis of Danish national art. Christen Købke, one of the most talented painters of this era, is well represented in the museum. Among his early works is *The Baker's Yard in the Old Citadel*, c. 1832. Købke caught the dreamy mood of Denmark in the romantic landscape *Autumn Morning by Lake Sortedam. View from Lover's Lane* in Nørrebro, 1838. In 1834 he painted *View Outside the Northern Gate of the Citadel*, his master work. Danish sculpture may also be studied in depth in the Glyptotek. H. W. Bissen, a pupil of Thorvaldsen, created in 1851 a 1.29-meter-high plaster likeness of his wife, Emilie, which was acquired in 1937. She is depicted as an archetype of Danish femininity, sitting demurely with hands and ankles crossed, a rapt expression upon her face. The museum has a rich representation of two outstanding sculptors of the twentieth century, Kai Nielsen and Gerhard Henning. By Kai Nielsen of note are *The Shipwrecked*, 1924, and *The Water Mother*, 1921, which was carved for the central position in the conservatory of the museum. *Seated Girl*, 1938, by Henning is a 1.12-meter-high female nude executed in limestone.

The Glyptotek has a library containing approximately fifty thousand volumes; books may be consulted only on the premises. The Glyptotek has a large selection of photographs of objects in the collection that are available for purchase. Requests may be sent to the museum as such or to the curators.

The Glyptotek publishes the yearbook *Meddelelser fra Ny Carlsberg Glyptotek*, begun in 1944, which includes illustrated scholarly articles on objects in the museum (with English or French summaries) and a summary of information on the previous year's activities, acquisitions, and publications.

Selected Bibliography

Museum publications: Poulsen, Vagn, *A Guide to the Collections*, 17th ed., 1975; *Antik Kunst i dansk privateje*, 1974; *Et hundred fire og tyve fotografier af Gérard Francheschi*, 1969; *From the Collections of the Ny Carlsberg Glyptotek*, vols. I–III, 1931–42; Gjødesen, Mogens, and Flemming Johansen, *Den Etruskiske Samling*, 1966; Heilesen, Simon B., *Nanxuntu, Malerier af Kangxi Kejserens Rejse i Sydkina i 1682: En Introduction*, 1980; Johansen, Flemming, *Reliefs en Bronze d'Etrurie*, 1971; Koefoed-Petersen, Otto, *Catalogue des bas-reliefs et peintures égyptiens*, 1956; idem, *Catalogue des statues et statuettes égyptiennes*, 1950; idem, *Les Stèles égyptiennes*, 1949; Poulsen, Frederik, *Etruscan Tomb Paintings*, 1922; Poulsen, Vagn, *Catalogue des terres cuites grecques et romaines*, 1949; idem, *Ein Führer durch die Sammlungen*, 3d ed., vol. I, 1973; vol. II, 1974; idem, *Vejledning gennem Samlingerne*, 15th ed., 1973; Rostrup, Haavard, *Danske og Franske malerier og tegninger i Ny Carlsberg Glyptotek*, 3d ed., 1966; idem, "Moderne skulptur, dansk og udenlandsk," *Jahrbuch*, vol. 47 (1932), pp. 77–89; Sørensen, Arne Haugen, *Dyr und Damer*, 1981; Rostrup, Haavard, "Excurs," *Meddelelser*, vol. 29 (1972), pp. 107–11; idem, "Hesperia's Doed," *Meddelelser*, vol. 29 (1972), pp. 112–19; idem, "Portraet af en Stoever," *Meddelelser*, vol. 29 (1972), pp. 93–106.

Other publications: Boesen, Gudmund, *Danish Museums* (Copenhagen 1966); Poulsen, Frederik, . . . *Katalog over Antike Skulpturer* (Copenhagen 1940); Vinding, Ole, *I Glyptotekets Have* (Copenhagen 1967); Cabutti, L., "E Per Monumento Fatemi Una Fondazione," *Bolaffiarte* (Italy), vol. 10, no. 87 (March 1979), pp. 41–43, 45–46; Hafner, German, "Das Relief vom Nemisee in Kopenhagen," *Jahrbuch des Deutschen Archäol-*

ogischen Instituts, vol. 82 (1967), pp. 246–74; "Jean-Baptiste Carpeaux: Sculptor of the Second Empire," Apollo, vol. 113, no. 232 (June 1981), p. 377; Krause, Bernd, "Zum Asklepios-Kultbild des Thrasymedes in Epidauros," Archäologischer Anzeiger, no. 2 (1972), pp. 240–57; Muthmann, Fritz, "Bruchstucke einer Panzer statue in Kopenhagen," Deutsches Archäologisches Institut Mitteilungen Römische Abteilung, vol. 51 (1936), pp. 347–52; Nøerregård-Nielsen, Hans Edvard, "The Lyricism of Christen Købke," Apollo, vol. 113, no. 232 (June 1981), pp. 372–73; Poulsen, Frederik, "Ein Neuerworbenes Homerporträt," Antike, vol. 10, no. 3 (1934), pp. 195–208; idem, "Zwei Neuerwerbungen der Antiken Porträtgalerie der Ny Carlsberg Glyptotek," Deutsches Archäologisches Institut Jahrbuch, vol. 47 (1932), pp. 77–89; Poulsen, Vagn, "Note on the Licinian Tomb: Sixteen Portraits," Walters Art Gallery, Baltimore Journal, vol. 11 (1948), pp. 8–13; Vasseur, Pierre, "Paul Gauguin à Copenhague," Revue de l'Art Ancien et Moderne, vol. 67, sup. 2 (March 1935), pp. 117–26.

AGNES ANN FITZGIBBONS

Ecuador

——— Quito ———

MUSEUMS OF THE CENTRAL BANK OF ECUADOR (officially MUSEOS DEL BANCO CENTRAL DEL ECUADOR), Banco Central Building, Avenida 10 de Agosto y Parque Alameda, Quito.

These museums are located on the fifth and sixth floors of the main office building of the Banco Central del Ecuador, a modern building erected in 1967. Facing the historic Alameda Park and situated midway between the old colonial section of Quito and its modern counterpart, this location provides a view of the surrounding green Ecuadorian countryside and the distant snow-capped volcanoes of Cotopaxi, Iliniza, and Cayambe.

The museum complex includes the Gold Museum, the Archaeological Museum, the Spanish Colonial Art Collection, and the Contemporary Art Gallery. It is wholly owned, funded, and supervised by the Banco Central, Ecuador's largest private bank. The museums are administered by a director and an assistant director and are divided into four principal departments: archaeology, Spanish colonial and modern art, archaeological research, and historical research related to the cultural history of Ecuador. The Consejo de Gobierno serves as an advisory council and helps to establish the museum's governing policies. It is comprised of a number of the country's leading citizens, appointed to their terms by the directors of the bank.

Unlike many museums of this type, the museums of the Banco Central did not originate from a large bequest or an important donation of artifacts; rather, holdings were acquired over time and as the result of an official policy not to melt down but to preserve all of the archaeological gold pieces presented to the bank for sale. As this collection grew in size and importance, it was catalogued and studied. In 1959, when a significant holding of six thousand pieces of archaeological ceramics (the Commins Collection) was offered for sale, the bank decided to acquire it. Later, a museum was established for the display of the gold collection as well as for an exhibit of these artifacts. The Luis Cordero Dávila and Luis Felipe Borja collections were later added to the original Commins Collection, and a number of pieces have been acquired through private donations, through purchases, and from archaeological digs. Prompted by a similar desire to preserve and express the historic and aesthetic values of its country, the bank later undertook to assemble an equally important collection of artifacts in the fields of Spanish colonial and modern art. Currently housed on the sixth floor of the bank building, the art museum was opened to the public in 1972.

The museum continues to pursue an active policy of acquiring representative artifacts and important collections: at present, the archaeological holdings number approximately twenty-eight thousand pieces, and those in the colonial and modern ·rt collections total more than ten thousand. Thus from an initial policy of limited preservation, a much broader and more inclusive philosophy has emerged. The museum now supervises archaeological excavations and underwrites research in archaeology and art history; it pursues an active policy in the field of historic preservation, has initiated an innovative educational program for children, has published books in various fields, and is responsible for the presentation of major exhibitions in the United States, France, and Japan.

The artifacts of the Gold Museum represent the Pacific Coastal cultures of La Tolita, Manteño, Jama Coaque, and Milagro during the Regional Development and Integration periods. In addition to ceremonial objects—masks, breastplates, and cups—purely decorative personal items such as earspools, necklaces, facial ornaments, bracelets, and *tupos* are displayed.

The collection's series of masks includes a funerary mask that represents the face of an elderly man. Fine details such as facial wrinkles and a quid of coca leaves in his cheek are vividly and realistically expressed. The single most impressive piece, however, is a mask that represents the Sun God of the La Tolita culture. A halo of rays terminating in serpent heads surrounds the face of the sun; made of finely beaten gold foil, they move at the slightest breeze. This piece, which formerly represented the most venerated Tolita deity, has today become the Ecuadorian national symbol.

The astounding skill with which many of the smaller decorative pieces are made, and the fusing of gold and platinum in single pieces, indicate a remarkable technological ability. The delicacy of several platinum and gold filigree pieces, with the minute details of a series of facial pins, reveals a striking knowledge of advanced metallurgical techniques; solid gold sewing needles, fish hooks, and decorative golden nails for the teeth suggest an opulence and extravagance in the manufacture of even utilitarian wares.

In the Archaeological Museum, the number and variety of artifacts and their display in chronological sequence make it possible to trace the development and interrelation of the principal pre-Columbian cultures that inhabited the coastal and highland regions of Ecuador from 3600 B.C. to the time of the Spanish

Conquest in 1534. In contrast to the objects displayed in the Gold Museum, this collection represents a more mundane reality—artifacts involved in the daily life and environment of the people. Comprised principally of ceramic and metal artifacts, the collection includes cooking vessels, serving bowls, jars for carrying water, and clay cylinders incised with decorative patterns used for printing fabrics.

The Valdivia culture, the earliest of the Ecuadorian ceramic cultures, is represented by a collection of thick-walled, monochromatic clay cookingware and an extensive collection of small clay figurines. Decorated with elaborate coiffures, these female figures have been dubbed the Venuses of Valdivia. Potsherds from this culture have been linked to the Jomon culture of Japan, through the similar incised patterns of the pottery, giving impetus to a theory that South America was colonized by fishermen from the Orient who made their way to Ecuadorian shores by boat.

A series of whistles and whistling stirrup jars incorporate vivid, lively representations of reptiles, birds, and small animals, with an exciting added dimension: when played, each whistle sounds like the animal it represents. This is well illustrated in a working model of a Chorrera stirrup jar in the shape of a small bird that warbles when air is forced through its opening.

The Bahía culture is represented by a remarkable group of hollow clay figures, each about two feet tall. One of the earliest attempts at realism, they represent a man, cheek bulging with a wad of coca; a village elder; and a woman cradling her child. The finer thin-walled vessels of the Panzaleo culture and the distinctive clay stools of the Manteño attest to a growing technical skill and greater decorative ability of the later pre-Columbian cultures.

If a consistent progression in technique can be traced, a parallel development in decorative skill is also apparent. From the earliest motifs of simple incisions or two-toned designs over large areas, there is a gradual advance toward intricate, multicolored designs in which entire surfaces are covered by geometric patterns, often the result of skilled firing techniques. Skill in ceramic construction and decorative complexity combined with utilitarian design reach their highest expression in the artifacts of the Inca culture, which brings to an end the pre-Columbian sequence in Ecuador.

Access to the Spanish Colonial Collection is gained through a small patio, a historical reconstruction of a typical entry to a colonial Quitenian house, and the south windows of the museum provide a view toward the *casco colonial*, providing the visitor with an authentic feeling of the historical ambience. In the galleries, polychrome wood sculptures, oil painting in elaborate carved and gilded frames, various items of furniture, as well as one large, painted wooden altar and another of solid silver, are displayed. These works provide a graphic illustration of the abrupt changes brought to Ecuadorian culture with the Spanish Conquest and the introduction of European artistic canons.

Works of art imported from Spain predominated in the sixteenth and most of the seventeenth centuries. Two examples of Spanish sculpture include a Renaissance carving of Virgin and Child from the school of Jerónimo Hernández, as well as another statue of the Virgin, in a remarkable state of preservation, from the school of Juan Martínez Montañés. By the eighteenth century a school of indigenous Quitenian sculpture had emerged; it is in this field that the museum's holdings are the strongest. A large and varied group of relatively small, Rococo religious statues, among which can be singled out a fine *Virgen de la luz*, a beautifully polychromed San José, and numerous nativity carvings, represent the more important pieces of the school. An important group of crucifixes dates mostly from the eighteenth and nineteenth centuries; a fine small figure of Cristo Yacente and a very delicately carved wooden crucifix represent the apogee of the Quitenian style.

In the eighteenth-century Quitenian paintings, the schools of Rodríguez and Samañiego are the most fully represented. Eighteenth-century Quitenian furniture includes examples of *escritorios, bargueños, arcones*, and *sillones*. The art of the nineteenth century is represented by the emergence of early formal portraits and a blossoming of the minor decorative arts. The paintings of Joaquín Pinto include traditional paintings as well as handsome landscapes and *costumbrista* watercolors. The work of a group of Ecuadorian artists, active in the 1930s, introduces new themes, social repression and sorrow of the Indian, and new stylistic currents from Europe and Mexico. The more contemporary Ecuadorian artists work within the mainstream of modern art, although they maintain a strong, local cultural identity and often incorporate abstract pre-Columbian motifs.

In accordance with their continuing policy for cultural preservation, a number of smaller museums have been established throughout Ecuador and are administered by the Museums of the Central Bank of Ecuador. In early 1980 a typical colonial house in downtown Quito was restored and converted into El Museo Camilo Egas, which exhibits works of contemporary Ecuadorian artists. Additionally, the Church of San Diego in Quito has been extensively restored, and a small museum is being installed in one of its adjacent cloisters to house the convent's collection of Spanish colonial art. A similar facility is under construction in the Convent of La Concepción in Riobamba. There are as well two ethnographic museums: one in Cuenca encompasses the ethnography of the country in general, and another in the coastal town of Monte Cristi is limited to the ethnography of the province of Manabí. A small anthropological museum has been established in Guayaquil.

The museums also administer the archaeological sites of Ingapirca, Rumicucho, and Cotocollao, as well as the on-site museums at the last two locations. The small museum of Cotocollao, located in one of Quito's northern suburbs, demonstrates the techniques used in archaeological excavations and exhibits many of the more important finds from the excavation.

The library's collection includes more than three thousand volumes, various magazines, monographs, articles, and files on different aspects of the art history, archaeology, anthropology, and cultural history of the country. The recent acquisition of the Jijón y Caamaño Collection of rare books, antique photographs, and old maps has enhanced its archives greatly. Both the library and reserves are opened to interested and qualified persons by permission of the museums' director.

The educational department provides slides, videotapes, and movies as well as traveling-suitcase exhibits to local schools. Recently, a children's museum education program was initiated in collaboration with UNESCO to bring the Ecuadorian child closer to his heritage.

The museum publishes a monthly magazine of anthropological research, *Miscelánea antropológica*; a short description of a highlighted piece of the collection, also monthly, *Pieza del mes en el Museo Arqueológico del Banco Central del Ecuador*; and bulletins for schoolchildren on different aspects of Ecuadorian history that are distributed to the local schools.

Selected Bibliography

Museum publications: Stark, Loisa, and Muysken, Pieter, *Diccionario Español-Quichua, Quichua-Español*, 1977.

Other publications: Crespo Toral, Hernán, Samaniego, Filoteo, and Vargas, José Maria, *El arte ecuatoriano* (Barcelona 1976); Lathrap, Donald Ward, *Ancient Ecuador Culture— Culture, Clay and Creativity, 3000–300 B.C. El Ecuador antiguo—cultura, cerámica y creatividad, 3000–300 B.C.* (Chicago 1975); Meggars, Betty Jane, *Ecuador* (New York 1966); Vargas, José Maria, *El arte ecuatoriano* (Quito 1964).

GABRIELLE G. PALMER AND MARILEE SCHMIT

Egypt

——— Cairo ———

EGYPTIAN MUSEUM (officially EL-MATHAF EL-MISRI; alternately CAIRO MUSEUM), Kasr el-Nil, Cairo.

The Egyptian Museum in Cairo was begun under the directorship of Auguste Ferdinand Mariette, who was appointed the first director of Egyptian antiquities (Mamour des Travaux d'Antiquites en Egypte) on June 1, 1858, by the Khedive Saïd Pasha. Mariette had long been concerned about the great exodus of ancient Egyptian artifacts from the country as collectors' items for wealthy treasure hunters and official gifts to foreign consuls and other important political figures. For example, almost all of the pieces in an earlier museum of Egyptian antiquities—the collection of Mohamed Ali the Great, located in the Citadel in old Cairo—had been presented to Archduke Maximilian of Austria by the Khedive Abbas Pasha, Saïd's predecessor. Mariette established the new museum with the express purpose of preserving Egypt's ancient art for Egypt.

He began the new collection with objects from his own excavations throughout Egypt and housed it in the abandoned offices and warehouses of a steamship company beside the Nile in Cairo's Boulaq district. Funding for both the excavation work and the museum was provided through the generosity of the Khedive and was continued by his successor Ishmail Pasha.

When Mariette died in 1881, he had already begun planning for a new museum building to house the growing collection, but it was not to be completed for more than two decades. In 1891 the objects were transferred from Boulaq to a larger building in Giza, and finally, in 1902 the present structure at Kasr el-Nil was ready to house the collection. The transfer of objects was completed in July 1902, and the museum officially opened on November 15 of the same year.

At the front entrance of the museum is a large court with sculpture from various periods. A red granite sarcophagus at the west end honors the founder of the museum. First placed in the courtyard at Boulaq and then transferred to Giza and finally to its present location, it was dedicated on March 17, 1904. The simple inscription in memory of Mariette reads "Egypte Reconnaissante."

For many decades Frenchmen administered the museum and many French Egyptologists such as Mariette and Gaston Maspero held the position of director. Since 1952 Egyptian scholars have directed both the Department of Antiquities and the Egyptian Museum. At present the Department of Antiquities is a division of the Ministry of Culture and oversees all of the museums in Egypt through its Permanent Committee. The director of the Egyptian Museum is a member of this committee. He makes decisions concerning the internal administration of the museum and is assisted by several deputy directors and between twenty and twenty-five curators. The museum also owns a library collection under the direction of a librarian and several assistants. Funding for the museum comes through the Department of Antiquities.

Since its modest beginning at Boulaq, the collection of the Egyptian Museum has grown to huge proportions. The vast majority of objects come from excavations and are therefore of known provenance and date; a small percentage have been obtained through purchase, donation, or confiscation from the illegal antiquities market. They represent styles from all parts of the country and all periods of Egypt's long history from prehistoric through Roman times. One exception is Coptic and early Christian art, which is now housed almost entirely in the Coptic Museum.

The collection is particularly strong in the areas of sculpture-in-the-round, coffins, sarcophagi, wooden tomb furniture, and small objects such as scarabs and jewelry. The more architectural features such as wall paintings and reliefs have been left as much as possible in their original locations, although a few examples from each period may be seen in the museum.

About sixty-five percent of the collection is currently on display, the remaining objects being stored in the museum's basement or in small rooms on the ground floor. Special permission must be obtained from the director of the museum before stored objects may be viewed. To obtain such permission, it is helpful to have a letter of introduction from some person or institution known to the museum's officials.

The collection is divided into seven curatorial departments including: Old Kingdom, Middle Kingdom, New Kingdom, Late Period, Tutankhamen, Papyri and Numismatics, and Scarabs and Sarcophagi. As far as possible the collection is exhibited in chronological order in the galleries around the ground floor, beginning with the Old Kingdom and continuing through the Graeco-Roman Period. The prehistoric material is exhibited on the upper floor as are special collections such as the artifacts from Tutankhamen's tomb or from that of Queen Hetep-heres. Special galleries, mostly on the upper floor, are also set aside for jewelry, coins, scarabs, coffins, mummies, drawings, manuscripts, and other categories of objects.

In general, because of the cumbersome or delicate nature of the objects, the collection on display does not change. There is one exhibition area (on the ground floor, just inside the main entrance) that is used to display the new acquisitions continually being added to the collection as a result of modern excavations by both Egyptian and foreign expeditions. It is also occasionally used for special small exhibits on specific subjects such as mummification or the decipherment of hieroglyphs.

From the Predynastic (prehistoric) Period, the museum's collection contains a large number of flints, beads, clay figurines, stone vessels, and pots, including some painted ware. Unfortunately, due to lack of space, most of this prehistoric material is in storage. The Early Dynastic Period (Dynasties I and II, 3100–2686 B.C.) has somewhat more on display, including pieces of great historical interest. Chief among them is the slate palette of Narmer (c. 3100 B.C.), discovered at Hierakonpolis in Upper Egypt. It is believed to depict the unification of the two kingdoms of Upper and Lower Egypt by King Narmer, whose name appears at the top. The Tjehenu Palette—also of slate but found at Abydos—is probably connected with the unification and may describe military acts of the same king. Another important historical piece, found at Memphis, is the red granite statuette of a kneeling priest, Hetep-dief, upon whose shoulder are inscribed the names of the first three kings of Dynasty II. Two other pieces, both from Hierakonpolis, are from the reign of King Khasekhem of the second dynasty. The first is a stele, the second a well-carved seated statuette of the king in schist, decorated around the base with representations of captives or slain warriors. These pieces are also significant artistically since, although they tend to be stiffer and heavier than later sculpture and relief work, they exhibit the beginning of artistic conventions that became standard in later periods. They also demonstrate the Egyptians' skill, even at this early period, in the use of both hard and soft stone.

The development of both royal and private art in the Old Kingdom (2686–2181 B.C.) may be seen in the many masterpieces displayed in the galleries devoted to this period. The earliest of them is the almost life-size seated limestone statue of King Djoser of Dynasty III from his step pyramid complex at Saqqara. It exhibits many standard attributes of Egyptian royal statuary but also has some unusual elements, such as the lappet wig and the pointed ends of the head scarf, which may be a function of the antiquity of the piece.

An excellent example of nonroyal art coming from Dynasty III (2686–2613 B.C.) is the group of wooden panels of the noble Hesi-re, found in his mastaba tomb at Saqqara. Both the hieroglyphs and the figures of Hesi-re are exquisitely carved with minute detail. The panels depict Hesi-re in different aspects of his career, and although it is impossible to say whether or not the similarity of the figures indicates an attempt at portraiture, it is at least an attempt on the part of the ancient artist (or artists) to represent an individual consistently.

The fourth dynasty (2613–2494 B.C.) is represented by some of the most famous examples of Egyptian art ever discovered. Among them are the painted limestone statues of Prince Re-hetep and his wife, Nefret (reign of Sneferu), from Meidum. The paint on both is in excellent condition and the quartz eyes are almost alive. As in most Old Kingdom statuary, the woman is represented as being the same size as the man instead of on a smaller scale. Another piece from the same period and site is the section of wall painting from the tomb of Neferma'at. It is generally known as the Meidum Geese, because three varieties of geese, both male and female, are depicted with great attention to detail of individual markings. They are fine examples of the comparative realism with which Egyptian artists represented most animals as opposed to humans.

Another important piece of fourth dynasty sculpture is the small seated ivory statuette of King Khufu (Cheops), the only existing piece of sculpture-in-the-round representing this famous king. The life-size seated statue of King Kafre (Chephren) in diorite is a superb example of Old Kingdom sculpture at its height, as are the smaller triads in slate from Giza showing King Menkaure (Mycerenus) with the goddess Hat-hor and a home god or goddess. Among the few examples of private sculpture from this period are several limestone "reserve" or "portrait" heads found in the mastaba tombs surrounding the Giza pyramids.

To give the visitor an idea of the process by which these pieces were sculpted, a set of photographs of Old Kingdom statues in various stages of completion has been assembled and mounted in one of the galleries.

Few pieces of royal statuary are preserved from the later Old Kingdom dynasties. The Egyptian Museum owns several, including the granite head of King Userkaf (Dynasty V, 2494–2345 B.C.) from Saqqara. This fragment is the earliest example of colossal statuary in Egypt. A second, beautifully carved head of a king wearing the red crown of Lower Egypt is probably also Userkaf. It was found in his sanctuary at Abusir and is made of metamorphic limestone. A third piece, made of cast and beaten copper, is a life-size standing statue of Pepi I of the sixth dynasty (2345–2181 B.C.), from Hierakonpolis. It is the oldest extant copper statue on such a large scale, although there is evidence that copper statuary was being made as early as Dynasty II. A smaller copper statue of Pepi's son and successor Merenre is also in the museum's collection.

The fifth and sixth dynasties are well known for the private sculpture that began to appear in the latter half of the Old Kingdom, and many fine pieces can be seen in Cairo. One of the most famous is a painted limestone statue with quartz eyes depicting an unknown man in the cross-legged position of a scribe. A second statue of the same person shown in the standard seated position has a marked facial similarity to the first.

Another pair of statues, belonging to the noble Renefer, also show a striking similarity of feature. Each is of limestone, and each depicts Renefer in a standing position although with different attire. Both of these sets of statues are from the fifth dynasty.

Also from the fifth dynasty is a small statuette of the dwarf Seneb and his family, which shows the willingness on the part of the Egyptian artist to depict human deformity at least occasionally. Another interesting piece is the limestone statue of Ni'ankhre (sixth dynasty). The unusual position of the legs of this statue is a rare example of divergence from the standard art conventions of the period.

The museum has a good collection of Old Kingdom servant figures shown grinding grain, straining beer, slaughtering cattle, and performing other tasks. There is a collection of stone sarcophagi that demonstrate the use of architectural motifs in their decorations. A few examples of stone (and one wooden) false doors and of stelae are also on display as well as fragments of wall reliefs and paintings of the period.

Material from the First Intermediate Period (2181–2060 B.C.) is not as common as that from the Old Kingdom, and few pieces from this period are on display in Cairo. The museum does own two stelae of historical importance in that they belonged to two individuals connected to the pyramid of Merikare, a king of Dynasty X. Since the stelae were found at Saqqara, it is assumed that the king's pyramid was also in this vicinity. Other stelae from this time, including that of Intefi, found at Thebes, are good examples of the provincial styles of art that developed during this period. One may also see, from these and other stelae in the same area, the transition from the style and function of the stele in the Old Kingdom to its new style and function in the Middle Kingdom and later periods.

The Middle Kingdom (2060–1786 B.C.) is well represented by groups of royal and nonroyal sculpture and a fine collection of wooden servant figurines. The earliest of the royal statues is the seated sandstone figure from Thebes of King Nebhepetre Mentuhetep, the founder of the Middle Kingdom. The king is painted black and wears the red crown of Lower Egypt. A second representation of the king, wearing the white crown of Upper Egypt and in the act of subduing an enemy, is on a fragment of limestone relief work from Gebelein. Both of these works demonstrate the continued use of Old Kingdom artistic conventions, although their style is distinctive. The limestone sarcophagus of Princess Kawit (wife of a Mentuhetep of Dynasty XI, 2060–1991 B.C.) shows fine sunk-relief work but is reminiscent of the provincial style of the First Intermediate Period.

The wooden servant figurines, many from the eleventh-dynasty Theban tomb of the noble Meketre, are especially important for what they reveal of Egyptian domestic life; most are in the special galleries on the upper floor that are devoted to this subject. Sometimes entire communities are represented, with people shown attending to their various crafts within small buildings devoted to weaving, baking, butchery, and so on. There are also model houses and gardens.

From the early twelfth dynasty (1991–1786 B.C.) come ten seated statues of of King Senusert I, in limestone, found in his burial chamber at El-Lisht. The similarity between Old Kingdom style and that of these beautiful but expressionless Middle Kingdom statues is unmistakable. They represent the so-called mortuary style of royal sculpture that existed alongside the less idealized official style. This ''official'' style is represented by several statues of Senusert III and Amenemhat III. They are often described as portraits because of the vivid expressions and the similarity among the features of the several statues attributed to each king. A group of photographs of the known portrait sculpture from Dynasty XII is displayed in one of the Middle Kingdom galleries.

Private sculpture from this period is represented by a large number of statues, usually on a small scale, depicting both men and women and sometimes entire family groups. The difference in style between these Middle Kingdom private statues and those of the Old Kingdom is evident. There are several examples of the block-statue that was developed during this period. The museum also owns an entire burial chamber belonging to Horhetep of Thebes (Dynasty XII). The decorated limestone blocks of the chamber walls and the limestone sarcophagus demonstrate the new developments in private tomb decoration of Dynasty XII.

From the Second Intermediate Period (1786–1567 B.C.), as from the First, few works of art have survived. One interesting piece that may be from Dynasty XIII (the date is disputed) is the wooden ka-statue of King Hor.

Of all of the periods in Egyptian history, the New Kingdom (1567–1085 B.C.) is the best represented. This period is perhaps best known for its colossal architecture and wall decorations. Although most of this type of artwork has remained in situ, the museum does own some important examples, including three sections from the temple of Queen Hatshepsut (Dynasty XVIII) at Deir el-Bahri. These fragments depict the famous obese queen of Punt and her retinue. A small barrel-vaulted shrine to Hat-hor, from the same location, but built by Hatshepsut's successor Thutmose III, is painted with typical funerary scenes of the period.

A restored sphinx of Hatshepsut, several beautiful statues of Thutmose III, a kneeling statue of Amenhetep II, one of Thutmose IV and his mother, and a colossal statue of Amenhetep III and Tiy are some of the fine examples of royal sculpture-in-the-round from Dynasty XVIII. Private statuary of this dynasty is represented by a block-statue of Senmut (Hatshepsut's steward) holding Princess Neferure; two seated statues of Amenhetep, son of Hapu (architect of Amenhetep III); and an exquisitely carved wooden statuette of Djey (master of the horses of King Horemhab).

The museum devotes an entire gallery to the art of the Amarna style, which developed during the reign of Akhenaten (son of Amenhetep III). The potential grotesqueness of this style is most strikingly seen in half a dozen colossal standing statues of the king and in an artist's study for the profiles of the king and queen. Fine examples of the more pleasing naturalistic aspect of the style include the limestone head of Nefertiti and the fragments of wall paintings and floor decorations depicting wildlife and plants. The beautiful rich coffin, identified as that of Smenkh-ka-re, successor of Akhenaten, foreshadows the spectacular funerary art of Tutankhamen.

The best examples of royal sculpture from the late New Kingdom (Dynasties XIX and XX, 1320–1085 B.C.) include two small schist statues (one headless) of Ramesses II of Dynasty XIX and a fine head and torso of painted limestone representing a wife or daughter of the same king. Dynasty XX is represented by a much-restored life-size group showing Ramesses III between Horus and a second god whose image is now missing. There is also an unusual statue of Ramesses VI subduing an enemy. Private statuary of good quality from this period includes the seated limestone statue of Djey and Naya (Dynasty XIX) from Saqqara and a scribal figure in granite of the priest Ramesses-Nakht (Dynasty XX, from Karnak), who has a small baboon peering over his head. There are also examples of stelae, wall reliefs, and sarcophagi from this period.

Among the best objects in the Late Period (1085–332 B.C.) collection are a fine granite block-statue of Hor (Dynasty XXIII from Karnak), which is somewhat reminiscent of earlier ages, and the two granite statues (one just the head) of Mentuemhat of Thebes (Dynasty XXV), with their vividly expressive faces. Other statuary as well as some fine sarcophagi and relief work also represent this period. The museum also owns a large group of objects that demonstrate the Graeco-Roman influence on later Egyptian art (332 B.C.–A.D. 200), and there is a collection of coins dating from this period, displayed in a room on the ground floor.

The upper floor of the museum has been dedicated to exhibits of types of objects, tomb groups, and special themes. One of the best-known groups includes the royal mummies of Dynasties XVII–XX. Among them are the famous kings Thutmose III and Ramesses II.

The museum also owns a large collection of wooden coffins from all periods. Other funerary equipment from all periods including canopic jars and chests, cartonnage, funerary boats, ushabtis, and wooden furniture are also well represented in various galleries on the upper floor as are figurines of deities used as votive offerings and cult objects. A large collection of papyri and inscribed ostraca can also be seen.

Most of the jewelry, which dates from Dynasty I through the Graeco-Roman period, is displayed in galleries at the north end of the upper floor. The finest examples of this art include the inlaid pectorals and crowns of Dynasty XII princesses found at Dahshur, the ornaments of Queen Ah-hotep (early Dynasty XVIII) from Thebes, and the jewelry of King Psusennes I (Dynasty XXI) from Tanis.

Related to jewelry are the thousands of seal-amulets and scarabs, dating from their earliest appearance as button-seals in the sixth dynasty and the First Intermediate Period through the Late Period, when large heart scarabs were popular. There is also a large collection of amulets from all periods.

Certain sections of the upper floor are devoted to a series of tomb groups that are of interest because of what they reveal concerning burial customs of various periods. The earliest of them is from the mastaba tomb of Hemaka, found at Saqqara. This group dates from the reign of Den, fifth king of Dynasty I, and includes, among other things, the earliest specimens of papyrus yet discovered.

Another group belonged to Queen Hetep-heres, mother of King Khufu of Dynasty IV, and was found near his pyramid at Giza. The wooden traveling furniture, with its gilding and inlay, has been painstakingly reconstructed, and the resulting display is a tribute to the superb craftsmanship of the ancient artists and the patience of the modern archaeologists who meticulously excavated the remains.

One of the most impressive groups is from the Valley of the Kings tomb of Yuya and Thuya, commoners and parents of Tiy, principal wife of Amenhetep III. At the time of its discovery in 1905, this tomb's set of funerary objects was the most complete ever found but was soon overshadowed by the tomb of Tutankhamun, which was discovered in 1922.

A twentieth-dynasty tomb discovered at Deir el-Medina, belonging to the commoner Sennedjem, is one of the few intact burial chambers ever found. It held twenty mummies in various states of preservation, including Sennedjem, his wife, and other members of their family. Unfortunately, because the tomb was discovered in 1886 before the present laws governing the export of antiquities were enacted, many objects were sold, and the present location of some is unknown.

The royal tombs of Tanis, dating from the Late Period, included three virtually intact royal burials: those of Kings Psusennes I and Amenemopet (Dynasty XXI) and King Sheshonq (Dynasty XXII). They contained many pieces of jewelry; unfortunately, most of the organic material had deteriorated due to the dampness of the region.

Perhaps the most spectacular group of objects anywhere is the one from the tomb of Tutankhamun of Dynasty XVIII. Beginning almost immediately with the discovery of the tomb in 1922, these pieces have been among the chief attractions at the museum. They are important not only for the information they provide about funerary practices of the eighteenth dynasty, but also because they combine the beauty of the classical artistic style with the naturalistic aspects of the Amarna style. Fifty-five pieces of this collection have been on tour outside of Egypt. Funds generated from this tour are being used for the renovation of the museum and particularly for the reinstallation of this exhibit.

The museum's library is located on the ground floor. It was established in 1899 by Gaston Maspero and since then has collected some thirty-five thousand volumes (in all languages) on Egyptology and related subjects. Students and scholars who want to use the library should request permission from the museum's director. Volumes published by the Antiquities Service may be purchased either through the mail or personally. A catalog of the publications is available upon request at the library. Black and white photographs of objects in the collection may be purchased at a nominal fee for study purposes. Interested parties should apply to the director. Color slides of some of the objects are also available through the museum's gift shop.

Selected Bibliography

Antiquities Service Publications: *A Guide to the Egyptian Museum, Cairo*, 1977 (also in Arabic, 1969, and French, 1968); *Champollion et le 150e anniversaire du déchiffrement des hiéroglyphes* (also in Arabic), 1972; *The Egyptian Museum, Cairo, in Ten Years, 1965–1975* (also in Arabic), 1976; *Mummification in Ancient Egypt (Celebrating the*

Hundredth Anniversary of the Discovery (also in Arabic), 1973; *The Treasures of Great Kings and Queens of Ancient Egypt*, 1978; *Catalogue général du Musée du Caire*, 1901– present (including volumes in different languages on various groups and categories of objects in the collection); Englebach, R., *Introduction to Egyptian Archaeology, with Special Reference to the Egyptian Museum*, 3d ed., Cairo, 1979.

Other Publications: *Treasures of Tutankhamun* (New York 1976); Edwards, I.E.S., *The Treasures of Tutankhamun* (London 1972); Maspero, Gaston, *Guide to the Cairo Museum*, trans. J. E. and A. A. Quibell (Cairo 1915); Terrace, Edw. L. B., and Fischer, Henry G., *Treasures of Egyptian Art from the Cairo Museum* (London 1970).

CATHARINE H. ROEHRIG

France

Dijon

DIJON ART MUSEUM (officially MUSÉE DES BEAUX-ARTS DE DIJON; also MUSÉE DE DIJON), Palais des Ducs et des Etats de Bourgogne, 21000 Dijon.

The Dijon Art Museum, like many of the notable art institutions of the French provinces, owes its existence to the wave of enthusiasm for education in the arts that swept through France in the late eighteenth century. A municipal academy of drawing was chartered in 1766 under the directorship of François Devosges, who succeeded in attracting an enormous number of students, including Pierre Paul Prud'hon. Early on, Devosges secured funds from the provincial government to acquire a pedagogical art collection, which at first consisted mostly of prints of High Renaissance paintings. In the mid-1780s the governors of Burgundy voted to establish a fine arts museum to exhibit student works and "the finest productions of art in all genres, in painting as well as in sculpture." From its inception, the museum has been located in the east section of the Palace of the States of Burgundy, which has been the central administrative complex of the province since the period of the Valois dukes. The collections at first occupied two large rooms in the easternmost wing of the palace, added in 1781 for Devosges' drawing school. But since then, with the art school now located under its own roof elsewhere, the museum has taken over the entire east wing and several areas of the palace dating from medieval times.

The museum was separated from the art school administratively during the Revolution, but Devosges remained its director until 1799. During those years, the collections grew substantially, with art confiscated from noble mansions and local chateaux and from abandoned religious establishments. Among the significant acquisitions of the Revolutionary period were the black and white marble tombs of Philippe-le-Hardi and Jean-sans-Peur, with their famous mourning figures, or *pleurants*, that Devosges rescued from certain destruction. Devosges also saved a replica by Jean Marc Nattier of the *Portrait of Marie Leczinska, Queen of Louis XV* (the original is in Versailles). Enough important drawings from the Dijon area were also absorbed into the museum, most notably those of the collection of Jehannin de Chamblanc, that by 1805 a Cabinet of Prints and Drawings was formally established. Devosges was responsible as well for eliciting the first bequest of paintings to Dijon from the national government in Paris. French, Italian, and Flemish pictures, some from the former royal collections, others spoils of the Napoleonic campaigns, reached Dijon in this way. Additional works received from the state in 1812 include many of the museum's most important canvases.

Many of the museum's directors in the nineteenth century were artists under whose care the collections continued to expand. Claude Hoin, a Dijon pastellist and director from 1811 until his death in 1817, left the museum a collection of pastels including two sketches by his master, Maurice Quentin de Latour: the wry *Self Portrait* in bravura style and a portrait of the painter Joseph Vernet. Hoin was succeeded by Charles-Balthazar Févret de Saint-Mémin, the famed silhouettist. As a young man, Saint-Mémin had toured the Eastern Seaboard of the United States, paying his expenses by doing literally thousands of profiles using his *physionotrace* machine. Once resettled in Dijon, where his family's mansion had been emptied of its art collection during the Revolution, Saint-Mémin proved himself one of the museum's most able directors. He was a medieval art enthusiast and had the marble tombs of the dukes restored. In 1827 he expanded the museum into the fifteenth-century Salle des Gardes, a large timbered room with an enormous Late Gothic hearth (c. 1505), where he installed the ducal tombs and other key medieval artworks, many of them from the famous Chartreuse de Champmol. Subsequent directors were able to attract important donations. The son of François Devosges, Anatole, donated a large collection of drawings and some fine paintings in 1850. Antoine-Charles His de la Salle, a Parisian collector, divided his excellent collection of Old Master drawings between Dijon and the Louvre, sending 119 works to Dijon from 1862 to 1865. The Lyon artist Anthelme Trimolet and his wife, Edna, enriched the collections in 1878 with a bequest of paintings, drawings, ceramics, and Louis XV furniture. After thirty-six years as director of the museum, Albert Joliet left a large number of eighteenth-century canvases from the Lowlands, as well as a major collection of designs by the sculptor François Rude.

Two of the most important donations in the museum's history, the Dard and Granville donations, have entered since 1900, but equally significant have been the museum's successful efforts to improve the exhibition of its already-acquired riches.

The interior spaces of the museum present an attractive variety of architectural effects. The Salle des Gardes, with its monumental hearth and carved stone balcony bearing the crest of King Henry II, is grand and imposing; the Tour de

Bar, a tower also dating from the fifteenth century, with a balustered staircase leading up to displays of arms and armor, has an appropriate atmosphere of archaic medievalism. An architectural curiosity, the rib-vaulted kitchen (c. 1445) of the ducal palace is also part of the museum, as is the former fourteenth-century Chapter Room of the Burgundian Sainte-Chapelle, the seat of the Order of the Toison d'Or and, as such, a very important monument of Dijon's era of glory. Today it serves as exhibition space for religious objects from the period of the dukes. Most of the Sainte-Chapelle's treasury was dispersed during the Revolution, but Dijon has managed to recover several important items; for example, a thirteenth-century altar front in repoussé depicting the life of St. Peter and a fine example of sixteenth-century Mannerist metalwork, the gilt-silver *Altarpiece of the Manna*, decorated with the scenes from the story of Moses and the life of Christ.

The exterior facades of the eighteenth-century east wing were erected according to designs drawn up in the seventeenth century by Jules Hardouin-Mansart. The two-story elevation with mansard roof is decorated by masks, scroll brackets, and wrought-iron balconies. The interior is notable for its two large exhibition halls, the Salon Condé and the Salle des Statues, both richly embellished with woodwork by Jerome Marlet. The cove-ceiling décor of the Salle des Statues, the *Allegory in Honor of the Condé Family*, was commissioned in 1786 by the governors of Burgundy from Pierre Paul Prud'hon, who was then in Rome as Dijon's *Prix de Rome* recipient.

The rooms of the Granville Collection, added in 1977, contribute a further element of variety to the museum. Housing a collection of smaller works, mostly from the last two centuries, this area of the museum pleasantly blends effects of traditional Burgundian architecture with current methods of art presentation.

Throughout its two centuries of existence the Dijon Museum has acquired a vast collection of objects from nearly all periods and places, but its strengths lie in its sculptures and paintings of the Late Gothic to Early Renaissance periods of France, Germany, and Switzerland and in its French paintings of the seventeenth and eighteenth centuries.

Most of the sculpture done for the Burgundian court by Claus Sluter, including his famous *Well of Moses*, is still at the site of the former Chartreuse de Champol on the outskirts of the city (and should not be overlooked). However, the sculpture collection in the Dijon Museum provides ample testimony to the impact of Sluter's presence. The marble *Tomb of Philippe-le-Hardi*, on which Sluter worked from 1385 until his death in 1406, consists of an effigy of the duke in repose on a black slab supported by a miniature cloister where hooded monks under its arches mourn the duke's passing. Some of these white-marble *pleurants* figures were lost in the Revolution, but the remaining originals show Sluter's wonderful mastery of realism. By 1411 Sluter's nephew Claus de Werve finished the tomb, which so impressed the Burgundian royalty that its design was imitated in the *Tomb of Jean-sans-Peur and Marguerite de Bavière* (c. 1470), sculpted by Juan de la Huerta of Aragon and Antoine le Moiturier of Avignon. Sluter's influence on local workshops can also be seen in the robust *St. Luke Writing the Gospel* from the *Communauté des soeurs de la charité* in Dijon and the raptly emotional *Virgin and Child* from the Dijon Sainte-Chapelle, both dated about 1450. The advent of more slender, elegant proportions in the later 1400s can be observed in many Burgundian works, such as the *Virgin of Pity*, echoing the style of paintings by Rogier van der Weyden, and in the *Mary Magdalen on Calvary* (c. 1550) from a Dijon church. The sculpted stone altarpiece attributed to Jean Damotte (1500–1562), *Scenes from the Childhood and Passion of Christ*, is a technical tour de force showing Christ's life in illusionistic scenes framed by architecture. This altarpiece originally decorated the church of Sainte-Pierre in Dijon.

In the area of Franco-Burgundian panel painting of the same period the museum has two works of great renown and a high-quality collection of less significant examples. The large *Altarpiece of the Chartreuse de Champmol* (c. 1393–99), a diptych painted in tempera by Melchior Broederlam, shows the transition from International Gothic to the realism of the Netherlandish Renaissance. Passion scenes and figures of saints in niches were intricately carved on the exterior panels by Jacques de Baerze, then polychromed by Broederlam. The museum has a second stunning example of a Broederlam-de Baerze collaboration, the *Altarpiece with Saints and Martyrs*, from Champmol, which, however, has no painted pictures.

The second major work, the Master of Flémalle's *Nativity* (c. 1425), was purchased by Saint-Mémin from a Dijon antique dealer in the mid-1800s. Its vigorous realism is shared by other early fifteenth-century Franco-Flemish panels such as the energetic *St. George Altarpiece* (from Champmol) and the large *Arrest of Christ in the Garden of Gethsemane*, an impressive night scene attributed to the Master of the Beyghem Altarpiece. The collection includes works from later Northern Renaissance masters; for example, Dirk Bouts' poignant *Head of Christ Crowned with Thorns*, Vrancke van der Stockts' large *Annunciation* (c. 1470), and the polished *Crucifixion with the Virgin and St. John* (c. 1500) by an anonymous Flemish master. The more intricate, mannered trends of sixteenth-century art in the Lowlands appears in works such as the Antwerp school triptych *Adoration of the Magi* (c. 1530), the small Adrien Isenbrandt *Magdalen Reading*, and the grotesque *Head of St. John the Baptist* by Jean Mostaert.

Dijon's considerable Franco-Burgundian holdings are complemented by one of the most prominent collections of Swiss and Rhenish Late Gothic pictures in Europe. This unusual group of panels was assembled in the early 1800s by the Baron Pichet-Lamabilais and entered the Dijon Museum in 1916 through the legacy of Dr. Dard, the baron's son-in-law. The Dard legacy also included a few Italian and Spanish works of the same period.

The Swiss and Rhenish works on exhibition number more than forty. Although less technically sophisticated and less appealing than many of their Flemish counterparts, as a group they possess a distinctive intensity of expression with great variety of individual style. Close to Flemish prototypes, the small triptych attributed to Martin Schongauer, *Annunciation between St. Christopher and St. Anthony*, is densely composed and nervously drawn. At the other extreme, the panel of Conrad Witz, *Augustus Caesar and the Tiburtine Sybil* (c. 1435), is softly colored and static but radiant with luminosity. The Witz panel, which probably formed part of a large altarpiece in Basel, is the only work by the artist in a French museum. Of special interest among the Swiss paintings are the large *Altarpiece of Pierre Rup* (c. 1450), done for a Geneva merchant, and the enormous *Altarpiece of the Passion* (late 1400s), decorated on both sides with pictures imitating compositions by Schongauer. Also of interest are two pairs of altar shutters executed by the same Carnation Master from Baden, one of several Swiss primitives of the late 1400s to have used the red carnation as a device. Notable Bavarian panels include the *St. Corbinien and St. Anthony* (c. 1470), with an *Angel of the Annunciation* on the reverse side, and the *Christ and the Two Thieves on the Cross* (late fifteenth century). Examples from lesser-known regional schools are also present, for example, an exquisitely drawn Swabish school diptych showing the *Annunciation* and the *Nativity* (early 1500s).

The museum's holdings of French painting are somewhat thin for the period between the eclipse of the Valois dukes in the early sixteenth century and the rise of Louis XIV in 1643. A delicately executed canvas in the Fontainebleau manner, *Lady at Her Toilet*, was confiscated from the nearby Chateau de Lux during the Revolution, and a portrait believed to be of Jean de Bourbon-Vendôme, probably by Corneille de Lyon, about 1550, came with the Trimolet legacy. The *Portraits of the Four Evangelists* in oval frames by Valentin de Boullogne (c. 1625) once hung in the Chartreuse de Champmol.

By contrast, the second half of the seventeenth century is well covered. The work of Poussin is present in two superb wash drawings; however, the general strength of the academic manner patronized by the Sun King is evidenced by works such as Charles Lebrun's *Christ in Burial Shroud*, which is actually the lower portion of a truncated *Deposition from the Cross*, and the *Fall of the Rebel Angels*, a decorative scheme for the chapel at Versailles. The work of Philippe de Champaigne is seen at its best in the small yet forceful *Study of the Heads of Two Old Men*, bequeathed by Anatole Devosges. Somewhat drier yet impressive is the same artist's large *Presentation in the Temple* (c. 1682), one of six works done for the Carmelite Convent of the Faubourg St.-Jacques in Paris. The tersely sober *Portrait of Cathérine de Montholon* by Jean Tassel vividly characterizes the founder of the Ursuline Convent of Dijon.

The coloristic tendencies that rose to supremacy in the latter half of the *Grand Siècle* can be seen in Charles de la Fosse's sumptuous *Bacchus and Ariadne* (1699), an allegory of autumn executed for the royal Chateau de Marly. The school of noble portraiture that flourished so extravagantly in the *ancien régime* is well represented in Nicolas Largillierre's *Portrait of Antoine-Bernard Bouhier, President of the Parliament of Burgundy* and in Hyacinth Rigaud's portraits of two sculptors, François Girardon (1705) and Antoine Coysevox.

In addition to practitioners of official styles, some interesting artists out of the mainstream are also represented. Among them are the eccentric Monsù Desiderio, *Jereboam in the Temple of the Pagan Gods* (Dard legacy), and Jean-François de Le Motte, *Vanitas and Trompe-l'Oeil* (Anatole Devosges legacy).

Examples of the grand manner of painting in the eighteenth century include Carle van Loo's twin altarpieces *St. George and the Dragon* and *The Condemnation of St. Denis*, which decorated the Chartreuse de Champmol; Antoine Coypel's *Sacrifice of the Daughter of Jephta* (c. 1704), formerly in the collection of Louis XIV; and François Boucher's surprisingly effective *Assumption of the Virgin* (Trimolet legacy). Landscapes and ruin pictures are also exhibited, notably three Hubert Robert views of ruins and a large selection of outdoor scenes by Jean-Baptiste Lallemand. A local painter, Jean-François Gilles, nicknamed Colson, has six canvases in the collection, including a charming genre scene, *The Nap* (1759).

The museum's French neoclassical holdings are highlighted by the work of two artists trained by François Devosges at the Dijon Academy. Twelve canvases by Bénigne Gagneraux are in the collection, of which the best known is the large *Bacchanale*, left unfinished when the artist passed away in Florence in 1795. Better known internationally, Pierre Paul Prud'hon is represented by ten easel paintings—portraits and allegories—in addition to the allegorical decoration of the ceiling in the Salle des Statues.

In Flemish and Dutch art of the Baroque period, the Dijon Museum has had less success in acquisitions, although a few works merit attention. As spoils of the Napoleonic campaigns, two large works by Peter Paul Rubens are now in Dijon: the richly colored *Virgin Presenting the Baby Jesus to St. Francis* (1618), the center panel of a triptych from Saint-Grommaire-de-Lierre, Belgium; and *Jesus Washing the Feet of the Apostles*, an altarpiece taken from the Church of Saint-Rambaud in Malines. Small works by minor Flemish masters—Teniers the Elder, Teniers the Younger, Brouwer, and Jan (Velvet) Bruegel—also figure in the collection. As for Dutch art, only the Frans Hals *Portrait of a Gentleman* deserves to be singled out, but the museum possesses many small eighteenth-century Dutch and Flemish works as a result of the Albert Joliet legacy of 1918.

The Italian pictures offer greater variety and depth, but the collection is still limited. Trecento works include a fine Neri di Bicci *Madonna and Child* and a triptych attributed to Pietro Lorenzetti, with the *Virgin and Child Enthroned* in the center, *St. Christopher* on the left, and the *Crucifixion* on the right. The Dard legacy included two quattrocento altarpieces, one a Florentine triptych, *Virgin with Donor and Four Saints* (c. 1460).

Among the most important Italian canvases that came as state bequests in the early 1800s are Titian's *Virgin, Child, St. Agnes, and St. John the Baptist*; Veronese's *Moses Found in the Nile* and *Assumption of the Virgin*, both formerly in the collection of Louis XIV; and Jacopo Bassano's *Martyrdom of St. Sebastian*, from Leopold William of Austria's collection. From the same Viennese source came the Bernardo Luini *Virgin and Child*. The state also sent important works of the Mannerists, including a Pontormo *St. John the Baptist* (once in the Belvedere Gallery, Vienna) and a Vasari *St. Peter Walking on the Water*.

The collection includes some admirable Baroque canvases as well, such as the delightful *St. Cecilia* by the Milanese painter Bernardo Strozzi, a sensitive Guido Reni *Adam and Eve* (formerly in the collection of Prince Eugene of Savoy), the Giovanni Lanfranco *Repentance of St. Peter*, and the Gaulli *St. John the Baptist* (formerly in the collection of Louis XIV). The splendid Giovanni Battista Tiepolo *Education of the Virgin* and the Gian Antonio Pellegrini *Apostle Writing* were part of the Dard legacy in 1916.

The museum's holdings of French sculpture from the seventeenth century through the nineteenth century are concentrated in a few areas but are of consistently high quality. The crisp realism of the Dijon sculptor Jean Dubois is exemplified in his marble *Kneeling Figure of Joly de Blaisy* (c. 1679) and in the stunning profusion of relief figures on the terracotta models for his altarpiece in Notre-Dame de Dijon, the *Assumption*. From the selection of eighteenth-century portraiture, those of Jean-Jacques Caffieri, Julie Poncet, and Jean-Antoine Houdon deserve note, especially Houdon's *Bust of the Young Emperor Napoleon* (1806). Jean Baptiste Lemoyne's *Detail from the Mausoleum of Crébillon*, destined for Saint-Gervais in Paris, records in marble a profound sense of grief rare in the Rococo period.

The Dijon Museum has a major holding of sculptures by François Rude, who began his art studies under François Devosges in 1800. The collection includes examples of all facets of Rude's style, from the disciplined classicism of *Marius Meditating on the Ruins of Carthage*, a plaster submitted for the *Prix de Rome* competition in 1809, to the emotionalism of *The Dead Napoleon Watched over by the Eagle*, which presages Rodin. Also on exhibit is a model for Rude's famed *Departure of the Volunteers of 1792* (*''La Marseillaise''*), which decorates the Arch of Triumph in Paris. Through the bequest of Albert Joliet, Dijon has an unusual collection of preparatory designs by Rude, most of them dating from his period of exile in Belgium (1814–27). In addition, the museum keeps a large collection of molds in a separate building called the Musée Rude, which is open irregularly to the public.

Rude's student Jean-Baptiste Carpeaux is also represented in the Dijon Museum, largely due to a Carpeaux family gift in 1933. Two notable pieces are the *Young Fisherman with a Shell* and the strikingly handsome *Bust Portrait of Charles Garnier*, both in white plaster.

The collection of French painting acquired by the city during the past hundred years is not of great stature, but the major trends are represented by noteworthy examples. The realist movement is reflected in the nine works by Alphonse Legros, especially his *Ex-voto*, obviously indebted to Courbet. Excellent Barbizon School work can be seen in the landscapes of Charles François Daubigny and Théodore Rousseau, and the academic style is represented in suave, polished works of William Adolphe Bouguereau, especially his copy of Raphael's *Galatea*. The eccentric manner of Gustave Moreau can be seen in overwhelming proportions in *The Canticle of Canticles* (3.0 meters high by 3.19 meters wide), which was exhibited in the Salon of 1853.

Since 1969 any previous insufficiencies in Dijon's holdings of modern art have been amply compensated for by the Pierre and Kathleen Granville donation, a large collection of paintings, sculptures, drawings, and graphics emphasizing French art since 1800. Housed in a specially built wing designed by Pierre Miquel, works such as Eugène Delacroix's oil sketch *The Sultan of Morocco Receiving the French Ambassador* (1832–45), Théodore Géricault's *Study for the Traite des Negres*, Jean François Millet's pastel *Dead Tree Trunk* (1867), and Gustave Courbet's *Cliff at Etrétat* (c. 1870) fill important gaps in the traditional collection. In addition, the Granville donation gives Dijon an excellent selection of paintings of the contemporary School of Paris, which before had been all but totally absent. Works by Georges Braque, Roger de la Fresnaye, and Louis Marcoussis show the later stages of Cubism and its successors. Notable examples by Georges Mathieu, Viereia da Silva, and Wols indicate the vitality of Parisian abstraction during the post–World War II period. The most important modern works are those of Nicolas de Staël, nearly forty in all, which are of particularly high quality. The twenty-seven compositions by the Swiss-born Expressionist Adolphe Péterelle are also very striking. The nineteen pieces by the Rumanian-born sculptor Etienne Hadju likewise deserve special note.

Amidst the wealth of objects in the Dijon Museum, the following additional small collections are well worth attention. The holdings of Old Master drawings contain examples from the Late Gothic period through the nineteenth century, of both Northern and Southern schools. Among those represented are French artists Poussin, Claude Lorraine, Watteau, Ingres, Delacroix, and Manet; Italian artists Fra Bartolommeo, Giulio Romano, Parmigianino, Pellegrino Tibaldi, Guercino, and Salvator Rosa; and Northerners van Dyck and Rembrandt. Many of the museum's rooms are hung with tapestries: sixteenth-century Flemish productions and later French Baroque work. The ceramics collection has some fine Palissy ware, excellent French and Italian faience, and a small collection of Greek vases of all shapes from southern Italy, dating from the sixth to the fourth century B.C. The Egyptian collection consists for the most part of small objects: amulets, scarabs, and figurines.

The Dijon Museum is a *musée classé*, meaning that although it is officially a municipal institution, its director must be approved by national museum authorities.

The museum is staffed by the director and two curators who share the tasks of managing operations. About four temporary exhibitions are put on each year. Operating funds come from both municipal and national sources. A research library primarily for staff use is housed in the museum building and contains general reference works and publications, as well as extensive material pertaining to the art of Burgundy and eastern France. An organization of museum patrons exists, called La Societé des amis du musée de Dijon. In the past the society irregularly published the *Bulletin* and raised funds for the purchase of works to increase the collections. Lectures and tours for local art enthusiasts have also been among their activities. Recent acquisition policy has focused on works from the Dijon region. Catalogues and other museum publications, as well as photographs and slides, may be obtained from the documentation service at the museum's main address.

Selected Bibliography

Museum publications: Quarré, Pierre, *Le Musée de Dijon*, rev. ed., 1966; *Une Ecole provinciale de dessin au XVIIIᵉ Siècle. L'Académie de peinture et de sculpture de Dijon*, 1961; *Catalogue des peintures françaises*, 1968; *Catalogue des pastels-gouaches miniatures*, 1972; *Donation Granville. Tome I: Oeuvres réalisées avant 1900, Tome II: Oeuvres réalisées après 1900* by Serge Lemoine, and *Tome III: Les objets* by Claude Rolley et al.

Other publications: Brookner, Anita, "Masterpieces in the Dijon Museum," *Apollo* (December 1957), pp. 165–69; Réau, Louis, "Primitifs de la collection Dard au Musée de Dijon," *Gazette des Beaux-Arts* (December 1929), pp. 335–56; Fisher, Otto, "Quelques remarques sur les primitifs des écoles suisses et allemandes dans la collection Dard à Dijon," *Gazette des Beaux-Arts* (February 1931), pp. 94–102; Geiger, Monique, and Guillaume, Marguerite, *Dessins du Musée des Beaux-Arts de Dijon*, Musée du Louvre, 1976; *Peintures hollandaises du Musée des Beaux-Arts de Dijon et du Musée Magnin*, Musée Magnin, Dijon, 1968.

STEPHEN H. WHITNEY

Paris

CLUNY MUSEUM (officially MUSÉE DES THERMES ET DE L'HÔTEL DE CLUNY; also MUSÉE DE CLUNY, MUSÉE CLUNY), 6 Place Paul Painlevé, 75006 Paris.

The Cluny Museum, formally called in French the Musée des Thermes et de l'Hôtel de Cluny, is a two-part institution as its French name implies. It is the site of the ruins of a large Gallo-Roman public bath constructed in the late third century and is therefore an important archaeological monument; it is also the location of an important fifteenth-century noble residence, the Hôtel de Cluny, which today houses a national collection of medieval arts and crafts.

The partially underground ruins of the baths were known to exist in medieval times, when private residences were already built against the walls. Shortly after 1485 the Benedictine Order of Cluny, which had owned the baths and the adjacent property since the early 1300s, erected the present Hôtel de Cluny with its west wall abutted against the fabric of the baths. The baths incited little archaeological interest through the years, but the mansion remained continuously inhabited until the mid-eighteenth century, when it too began to suffer neglect. The entire property was confiscated from the religious order in 1789 and then sold to a private citizen.

The baths were reacquired by the state in 1819, with vague plans for their preservation. Believed to be the ruins of Emperor Julian's palace, the ruins were partially excavated and then sold in 1837 to the city of Paris, which intended to make them a museum.

Meanwhile, since 1832 art collector Alexandre du Sommerard had been renting the chapel of the adjacent mansion as a place to exhibit his personal collection of medieval antiquities. Du Sommerard and his collection were both remarkable—he, for his love of a period of art that most connoisseurs of his time disdained; his collection, for its sheer abundance, variety, and eccentricity. Victor Hugo, both amused and impressed, dubbed du Sommerard "le prince du bric-à-brac." The importance of the man's "bric-à-brac," however, was widely enough recognized that upon his death in 1842 the French government purchased the entire collection and acquired the Hôtel de Cluny for its museum. The sale price for the collection was low at 200,000 francs (the English ambassador offered the family three times as much) and came with the provision that Alexandre's son Edmond be named the museum's director. The idea for a joint museum arose naturally, because the state had lately reacquired the Cluny baths from the city and had begun serious work for a museum. On July 24, 1843, the Musée des Thermes et de l'Hôtel de Cluny was created by law, and on May 16 of the following year it opened its doors to the public.

Edmond du Sommerard proved to be perhaps even more significant than his father to the museum's development. He served as director for forty-one years and built up the collection from some fourteen hundred to more than ten thousand objects, including nearly all of Cluny's most precious holdings. While head of the museum he located major pieces such as the *Story of David* tapestries (from a Genoese family), the gold objects from the Basel Cathedral treasury, and the *Unicorn Tapestries* (from the town of Boussac in France). With a collection of such unusual emphasis, the museum also attracted numerous gifts. Viollet-le-Duc, for example, donated a collection of banners and standards.

Since Edmond du Sommerard's death in 1885, the collection has more than doubled again in size and has been expanded in breadth by gifts such as Nathaniel de Rothschild's donation of Jewish objects (1890) and important purchases such as the Victor Gay Collection of bronze, iron, and lead pieces (1909). Particularly since 1945, emphasis has been placed on upgrading the presentation of the holdings. All traces of du Sommerard's picturesque clutter are now gone, and although fewer objects are displayed, the quality of the collection is given its due. New exhibition space has been added; for example, the circular room for the *Unicorn Tapestries* and the tasteful stained-glass display. In addition, a new wing is under construction to increase capacity for the permanent collection and to provide facilities for temporary exhibitions that hitherto have been missing from the museum's program.

The buildings of the Cluny Museum in themselves merit status as architectural treasures independently of the collections housed within. The Gallo-Roman baths originally extended beyond the grounds of the present museum, but the most important parts are accessible to the visitor. They include the vast frigidarium,

14.5 meters high; the tepidarium; and the caldarium. Some of the vaulting has been reconstructed, but most of the thick walls, built of stone alternating with brick courses, can be seen in the original. None of the marble wall revetments remain, however. Archaeological evidence suggests construction occurred in the very early third century A.D. Consoles shaped like the bow of a ship decorate the vaults in the frigidarium, indicating that the baths were in some way subsidized by the corporation of Paris shipbuilders, a seemingly important group in Roman times.

The Hôtel de Cluny was constructed some time between 1485 and 1498 and is one of two secular mansions surviving from Late Gothic Paris. The exterior facades, although much restored in the nineteenth century, retain their original elevation. In plan, the main section of the building and two attached wings form a "U" around an entrance courtyard that is closed off from the street by a crenellated wall. The facades on this entrance courtyard are picturesquely embellished with gargoyles, attic dormers, a flamboyant balustrade, and turrets enclosing spiral staircases. The back of the mansion looks out onto a garden. Except for the flamboyant Gothic chapel, the interior is almost completely modern.

As an important vestige of Parisian Gallo-Roman architecture, the baths of Cluny are an appropriate place to exhibit the fragments of Roman monuments excavated through the years on the Ile-de-la-Cité. The most important objects displayed there are the five stone blocks discovered in 1711 under Notre-Dame Cathedral, which formed part of a monumental pillar dedicated to Jupiter. An inscription dating the pillar to the reign of Tiberius (14 B.C.–A.D. 37) indicates that it was erected by the same group of Paris boatmen that built the baths. Stone slabs with reliefs and three large blocks from a later monument of the second century also belong to the collection.

The medieval collection retains the heterogeneous flavor that it had in the nineteenth century, with objects produced by craftsmen as well as works of artists. Ordinary pieces of tableware, wrought-iron fireplace utensils, and mundane ceramic bowls and goblets remind the spectator of the everyday realities of medieval life; but many of the utilitarian objects are superbly designed and crafted. A boxwood comb (c. 1400) with marquetry decoration, a set of ivory mirror frames gaily decorated with pictures of the hunt and chivalrous scenes, small caskets and chests in carved wood and tooled leather, and literally hundreds of other objects all demonstrate remarkable quality of execution and elegance. The period atmosphere of the small exhibition rooms in the Gothic mansion is enhanced by stained glass fragments in the windows, the presence of hearths (only one of which is original to the building), and the excellent collection of furniture from the Late Middle Ages: chairs, armoires, tables, and so on.

The Cluny Museum's collection of medieval tapestries is one of the most important anywhere. Fine examples decorate nearly every room of the fifteenth-century section of the museum and represent all major centers of manufacture in France and Belgium. The earliest piece, an altar hanging, *The Resurrection*, dates from the early fourteenth century and was probably done in northern France.

Fragments of the *Apocalypse Tapestries* of Angers, woven in 1376, provide a glimpse of the remarkable elegance and fine execution for which the series is famed. The courtly *Gentleman Offering His Heart to a Lady* is the subject of a wool piece done in the early 1400s. More ambitious coloring and layout is evident in the *Delivery of St. Peter*, a section from a large hanging woven in Arras or Tournai in 1480 for the bishop of Beauvais. Mastery of this more involved pictorial approach can be seen in many of the museum's examples dating from the end of the fifteenth century, but most dramatically in the twenty-three-piece series *The Story of St. Stephen* (c. 1490), ordered by the bishop of Auxerre as decoration for the cathedral choir. The range of secular objects favored in the Late Gothic period can also be observed. For example, the *Grape Harvest* (early sixteenth century) presents most of the stages of the gathering and crushing of grapes in a single composition rich with rustic details; and a series of six *mille fleurs* tapestries dating from about 1500, *La Vie Seigneuriale*, shows the pastimes of a noble couple: embroidery, reading, walking, departing for the hunt, and so on. Cluny's most celebrated possessions, its six *Unicorn Tapestries*, are extremely rare *mille fleurs* weavings, with red (now faded to pink) used as the background color rather than the usual blue. These tapestries ostensibly depict the leisure activities of a noble woman accompanied by a friendly unicorn and a lion, but they are also allegories of the five senses. The sixth scene, tantalizingly obscure in meaning, shows the elegant woman putting her jewels away in a casket, perhaps to demonstrate her freedom from vanity. The series bears the arms of the Le Viste family and was probably executed between 1484 and 1500 by a southern Belgium workshop using French designs. The extraordinary early-sixteenth-century group of tapestries, the *Story of David*, long in the Cluny collection, is now in the Renaissance Museum at the Chateau d'Ecouen; however, Cluny's late sixteenth-century Brussels tapestry *Christ on Calvary* is a splendid example of the finest production of the time.

The collection of medieval textiles is very substantial. A fine selection of Coptic and Islamic fragments from the Marcel Guérin legacy of 1948 offers a view of many techniques used throughout Egypt and the Near East from the fourth to the tenth century. Three Byzantine silk pieces, one from the Carolingian treasury at Aix-la-Chapelle, exemplify the brilliance of imperial productions. The extremely busy, yet elegant, patterns of medieval Islamic styles can be seen in superb Spanish and Italian fragments dating mostly from about 1250–1500. The influence of Moorish styles in northern Europe is evidenced by two red velvet panels decorated with stylized lions in gold embroidery, believed to have been done in either England or France about 1425. Embroidery for religious patrons includes an altar hanging of the early fifteenth century, *The Life of St. Mark and St. John*, from the Rhineland (gift of Baron Adolphe de Rothschild) and a colorful French bishop's mitre (1400s) from the treasury of the Sainte-Chapelle of Paris. A thirteenth-century Icelandic embroidery with the legend of St. Martin in rondels demonstrates the persistence of Byzantine influence in medieval fabric production.

Because the Cluny Museum was part of the Commission of Historical Monuments for many years, it acquired an important collection of architectural and sculptural fragments from churches being restored or demolished. From this source the museum received twelve capitals of the eleventh century from the nave of the Paris Church of Saint-Germain-des-Prés and eight pre-Romanesque capitals with floral designs from the Pyrenees. From a Romanesque cloister in Catalonia came six historiated and decorative capitals with figures in high relief retelling Old and New Testament stories. When Viollet-le-Duc restored the *Last Judgment* in the tympanum of the west portal of Notre-Dame in Paris, the museum received fragments of the original work showing an angel sounding the trumpet and souls rising from their graves on the Last Day. Also from Notre-Dame is the life-size figure *Adam* (c. 1250), which shows an influence of classical art. It once stood at the foot of the north tower of the cathedral. The museum also managed to acquire four of the twelve *Apostles* (1243–48) originally mounted on the west facade of the Sainte-Chapelle in Paris. With museum protection, traces of polychrome have survived on these fine examples of royal workshop production. The pleasant harmony of fourteenth-century Parisian stonework may be seen in the four *Apostles* from the Church of Saint-Jacques-l'Hôpital, executed in 1320–25 by Robert de Launoy and Guillaume de Nourriche.

The museum's recent acquisition of 364 sculptural fragments from Notre-Dame is of unsurpassed importance. Discovered in 1977 in the cellar of a Paris mansion, where they were probably hidden by a royalist just after the Revolution, the cache of figural work includes fragments from several of the Gothic portals of the cathedral and twenty-one heads from the Gallery of Kings on the west facade (c. 1215). On most of the heads, which are colossal in scale (twenty-one inches high), traces of paint have been preserved: pink on the cheeks, red on the lips, yellow on the hair and beard, and black on the pupils and eyebrows.

The museum's holdings of smaller freestanding figural sculptures produced for the interiors of churches is a superb complement to its display of statuary for exterior decoration. Of special note is the large group of Madonnas in wood and in stone from France and the Netherlands. They range in date from the twelfth-century wooden *Madonna and Child Enthroned*, typical of Romanesque production in Auvergne, to the early-sixteenth-century marble *Virgin Standing with Child*, carved in northern France with Renaissance composure and naturalism. Additional sculptures of note are the fourteenth-century marble group, the *Presentation in the Temple*, done by a French sculptor with an exceptional talent for drapery, and a poignant *Head of the Dead Christ*, brought from Spain.

Carved and painted wooden altarpieces became a specialty in northern Europe during the Late Middle Ages, and the Cluny Museum possesses some striking examples. A small triptych from the Duchy of Cleves in northern France is the *Lamentation of Christ*, with polychromed wooden figures in the center and six Passion scenes painted in tempera on the inner sides of the shutters. A very unusual altarpiece from the Chapel of Saint Eloi (Eure) presents scenes of Christ's life using clay figurines influenced by the style of fifteenth-century south Flemish painting. The altarpiece by Jean de Molder, 1513, is characteristic of the ornate work of Antwerp shops. Its three crowded and colorful sections are the *Mass of St. Gregory* in the center, the *Meeting of Abraham and Melchizadek* on the left, and the *Last Supper* on the right. A handsomely carved German altarpiece of the early sixteenth century is the *Crucifixion* in boxwood against a colored ground, with low-relief scenes of the Passion cycle on the wings.

Some of the Cluny Museum's most spectacular holdings are objects in precious metals: jewelry, altarpieces, and reliquaries. The oldest pieces date from the periods of the barbarian invasions and are mostly ornaments for dress such as fibulas, rings, bracelets, and two particularly impressive solid gold torques discovered at Montgobert (Aisne), one of which is nearly identical to the torque worn around the subject's neck in the *Dying Gaul* in the Capitoline Museum, Rome (q.v.). Of major importance are the three gold votive crowns excavated by a French officer at the Fuente de Guarrazar near Toledo in 1859 and purchased from Spain by Edmond du Sommerard. Dating from the mid-seventh century, these royal Visigothic emblems, richly studded with precious stones and decorated with pendants, are masterpieces of cloisonné jewelry making. The early eleventh-century gold altarpiece from the Basel Cathedral, considered by many to be the most significant object in the Cluny Museum, was acquired in 1854 after being sold by the Canton of Basel in 1836. The altarpiece is more than six feet wide and has repoussé figures—Christ at center flanked by two saints and two archangels—all framed by arches and floral embellishments. The donors, Holy Roman Emperor Henry II and his wife, Cunegond, are shown prostrate at Christ's feet. The acquisition of the Basel altarpiece was accompanied in 1854 by a gift from Colonel Theubet of the famous *Rose* (also from the Basel Cathedral treasury). The piece consists of a central shaft decorated with filigree that terminates in a five-branched rose bush bearing leaves, buds, and flowers, all in gold. It is believed to have been an Easter gift from Pope Clement V (1305–14) to the bishop of Basel.

Some of the many fine examples of metalwork from the Romanesque period deserve special note, in particular the gilt-copper plaque decorated with the Pascal Lamb at center surrounded by personifications of the four rivers of paradise. The high quality and energy of the incised drawing suggest that this piece is the work of the Mosan master Godefroy de Huy (mid-twelfth century). A portable altar of uncertain origin, perhaps English, and dating from the eleventh or twelfth century, shows the penchant for mixing materials common in medieval times; in this case, a red porphyry slab and ivory panels are joined by a silver band decorated with interlace patterns.

The enormous production of metalwork throughout Europe during the Gothic period is reflected in the wealth of fine pieces at the Cluny Museum. One of the most significant objects is a small reliquary in the form of the Sainte-Chapelle of Paris ordered by Louis IX in 1261 to hold relics of the martyred saints of Beauvais. Three magnificent processional crosses opulently decorated with jewels, filigree, and attached ornaments show how widely fine craftsmanship had spread: one is from Barcelona (1300s), one from Siena (mid–1400s), and one from France (1454). A dazzlingly executed *Daphne* surrounded by red coral bushes is the work of the Nuremburg master Wenzel Jamnitzer (1534–85), and a lavishly decorated monstrance is the work of an Iberian master working in the flamboyant Gothic manner, about 1500.

Enamel work is another area emphasized in the collection. Champlevé and cloisonné examples from the Byzantine period through the fourteenth century show the variety of applications and the exceptional quality attained in this medium. The tiny (two-inch) cloisonné pin, the *Bust of St. Demetrius* (gift of J. Pierpont Morgan), demonstrates Byzantine craftsmanship at its highest level. The twelfth-century *Mosan Altarpiece* from Stavelot Abbey (Belgium) depicts the Pentecost in gilt-copper repoussé, with important details highlighted in colorful enamel. Twelfth-century champlevé work from Germany, central France, and Spain shows the diffusion of the technique throughout Europe. The abundant collection of Limoges pieces from the twelfth through the fourteenth century includes the full range of sacramental objects: reliquaries, sacramental doves, pyxes, and so on.

The ivory collection, although not exceedingly large, is high in quality and variety. The figure *Ariadne*, a voluptuous nude probably executed in Alexandria about 500, is an unusual piece large enough to have served as the leg on a Roman consul's throne. The leaf of the *Nichomachi Marriage Diptych* (c. 390), with a priestess of Ceres in soft Hellenistic robes, is the match to a leaf in the Victoria and Albert Museum (q.v.) in London. The hieratic treatment of figures in the leaf from the *Consular Diptych of Areobindus* (c. 506) presages the approach to figure representation in Ottonian works such as the late tenth-century *St. Paul* and *Christ Crowning the Emperor Otto II and His Wife Theophanu.* Two southern Italian *Oliphants* of the eleventh century are treated with an Islamic taste for profuse decoration, and the Gothic triptych from Saint-Sulpice-du-Tarn shows Parisian artists imitating Byzantine models.

A few very important examples of panel paintings are in the museum. An early-fourteenth-century English altarpiece with painted scenes from the life of the Virgin makes Cluny one of the few museums possessing English painting from that period. A fourteenth-century bishop's mitre, perhaps from the Sainte-Chapelle in Paris, is decorated with pictures in grisaille recalling the famous *Parement of Narbonne* in the Louvre (q.v.). Since the major scene is Christ's resurrection and the colors are black and white, the mitre was probably made for funeral rites.

The panel paintings are primarily works of provincial masters. The most accomplished, the *Pietà of Tarascon* (c. 1450), belonged to Jeanne de Laval, wife of King René of Anjou, and was acquired from the Hospice of Tarascon in Provence. The other examples are predominantly works of Burgundian, Flemish, and northern French schools from the fifteenth and sixteenth centuries.

The art of manuscript illumination, so essential in the development of medieval imagery, can be studied through a selection of leaves from Germany, France,

Spain, and Italy (eleventh through the seventeenth century). These examples attest to the diversity of quality and style. Most notable among them are two leaves by a student of the Boucicault Master (early fifteenth century) depicting the Crucifixion and the Second Coming of Christ.

The stained-glass collection at Cluny is attractive and historically significant. A panel representing two disciples of St. Benoit decorated the Abbey of Saint-Denis (c. 1144), where stained glass first played a major role in Western architecture. Eight circular sections from the Sainte-Chapelle of Paris vividly demonstrate the evolution of stained-glass making from 1200 to 1250, and the four large windows of about 1260 from the royal chateau in Rouen show the increasing range of color and sumptuous effects achieved in later thirteenth-century examples.

Much of the ceramic collection is everyday ware produced in Paris from the twelfth to the sixteenth century; however, the artistic quality of the large glazed platter with relief designs of the instruments of the Passion is considerable. The platter was made in 1511, probably in Beauvais. Highlighting the ceramic collection are the very fine pieces of fifteenth-century Hispano-Mauresque lusterware of the area of Valencia and Seville. A shallow bowl nearly twenty-four inches in diameter is colorfully decorated with geometrical and floral interlace patterns reminiscent of Egyptian motifs, and a magnificent vase with wing-shaped handles is covered with ivy patterns in the same deep blue, ochre, and white color combination. The museum exhibits more than forty pieces in all, one of the most important collections in western Europe.

The Cluny Museum from its beginning has been a state institution. At its founding it was placed under the administration of the Commission des Monuments Historiques, but in 1907 it was made a member of the Réunion des Musées Nationaux, the system of state-administered art museums of which the Louvre is the largest. The director of the Cluny Museum is responsible to the Director des Musées de France. The museum houses a small library of some thirty-five hundred volumes pertaining to the collection; at this time, the library is for staff use only. A photographic inventory is in the process of being made but not systematically. Slides and photographs may be obtained from Service Photographique des Musées Nationaux, 89, Avenue Victor Hugo, 75016 Paris. Museum publications are available from Editions de la Réunion des Musées Nationaux, 10, rue de l'Abbaye, 75006 Paris.

Selected Bibliography

Museum publications: Erlande-Brandenburg, Alain, *The Cluny Museum*, 1971; Verlet, Pierre, and Salet, Francis, *Le Musée de Cluny*, 1965; Du Sommerard, Edmond, *Musée des Thermes et de l'Hôtel de Cluny. Catalogue et Description des Objets de l'Arts de l'Antiquité, du Moyen-Age et de la Renaissance Exposés au Musée*, 1883.

Other publications: *Notices sur l'Hôtel de Cluny et sur le Palais des Thermes* (Paris 1834); Montrémy, François de, "Le lieu dit les Thermes et l'Hôtel de Cluny," *Paris et Ile-de-France*, vol. 7 (1955), pp. 53–147; Erlande-Brandenburg, Alain, "Les sculptures de Notre-Dame de Paris récemment découvertes," *Revue du Louvre*, vol. 27 (1977), pp. 282–83; Lazar, H., "Objets rituels juifs," *Connaissance des Arts*, no. 336 (February 1980), pp. 28–37.

STEPHEN H. WHITNEY

JEU DE PAUME (officially MUSÉE DU JEU DE PAUME, GALERIE DU JEU DE PAUME; also MUSEUM OF IMPRESSIONISM, THE LOUVRE), Place de la Concorde, 75001 Paris.

The Jeu de Paume became the home of the French national collection of Impressionism only in 1947. In the future, these Impressionist paintings will be moved to the Orsay Museum (q.v.). This recently established museum dedicated to late-ninteenth- and early-twentieth-century art will occupy the renovated train station, the Gare d'Orsay, on the Left Bank of the Seine.

The building Jeu de Paume takes its name from its initial use as an indoor tennis court. In 1861 Napoleon III leased this choice site in the Tuileries Gardens near the Place de la Concorde to a man named Delahaye, known as Biboche, to build a tennis court. The architect of the Louvre (q.v.), M. Lefuel, requested that the new structure's facade duplicate that of its neighbor, the Orangerie. Constructed at a cost of 175,000 francs, the Jeu de Paume opened on January 15, 1862. The tennis club enjoyed great success, and a second court was added in 1877. About the turn of the century, however, an English import, lawn tennis, superseded the indoor "jeu de paume," and the building fell into disuse.

The idea to use the building for art exhibitions was first proposed in 1914. Plans were made to expand the building to twice its original size and to mount temporary art exhibitions there. However, with the advent of World War I, these transformations were postponed. Some years after the war, it was once again decided to use the Jeu de Paume to house art. By the 1920s the Luxembourg Museum was overflowing with artworks. To alleviate this problem, it was decided to install modern paintings by foreign artists in the Jeu de Paume. The old tennis court was divided into two stories, with construction beginning in 1931 and completed in 1932. In addition to using the Jeu de Paume to exhibit France's collections of modern foreign paintings, it was also used to mount major loan exhibitions, such as *Cent portraits de femmes des écoles anglaises et françaises du XIXe siècle* (1909), an exhibition of Dutch art in 1921, and an extensive show of contemporary American art in 1938, organized in collaboration with the Museum of Modern Art (q.v.), New York.

During World War II, the Jeu de Paume was taken over by the Nazis to store various artworks they had confiscated. After the liberation of France, the building served as a base for the services responsible for returning the seized works to their rightful owners.

In 1947, under the directorship of René Huyghe, the Louvre's collection of Impressionist paintings was transferred to the Jeu de Paume. In 1954 the Jeu de Paume underwent major renovations to add air-conditioning and greatly improve the lighting and humidity controls. For the period from that time until 1959, when the Jeu de Paume reopened amid much fanfare, the Impressionists were temporarily on display at the Louvre. Since 1959 until the future opening at the Musée d'Orsay, the Jeu de Paume has served as the major French museum of Impressionism.

The first painting of the period to enter the French national collection was Manet's famous *Olympia* of 1863. Monet launched a public subscription to purchase this painting for the Louvre in 1890. The contributors were dealers, collectors, and painters of widely varying styles, including Fantin-Latour, Degas, Toulouse-Lautrec, Pissarro, Rodin, Renoir, Puvis de Chavannes, Ribot, and Carolus-Duran. Shortly after this gift, the museum purchased two fully Impressionist paintings: Renoir's *Young Girl at the Piano* and Berthe Morisot's *Young Girl on the Balcony*. In addition, Fantin's wife donated his *Studio of the Batignolles Quarter*, which showed Manet surrounded by contemporary artists and writers.

It is, however, the generous donations of several private collectors that has created the tremendous wealth of Impressionist paintings now owned by France. In 1894 the Louvre was offered its first major gift of Impressionist paintings, the Caillebotte bequest of sixty-seven paintings. Great controversy surrounded this collection. Due to a very hostile public and official opinion, only thirty-eight of the paintings were accepted. Gustave Caillebotte came from a Parisian bourgeoise family and was financially able to purchase his friends' works. His collection, formed between 1870 and 1888, focused on seven Impressionist painters: Renoir, Cézanne, Degas, Manet, Monet, Pissarro, and Sisley. Caillebotte was a painter himself and participated in the second Impressionist exhibition. The Jeu de Paume owns five paintings by this painter-collector.

By the first decade of the twentieth century, public opposition to Impressionism had lessened, and the private collections of Etienne Moreau-Nélaton and Camondo entered the national domain without incidents, in 1906 and 1911, respectively. Moreau-Nélaton was a biographer of several nineteenth-century painters. His bequest included oils by pre-Impressionist artists such as Corot and Jongkind as well as the Impressionists Monet, Pissarro, Sisley, and especially Manet. The latter's famous *Déjeuner sur l'herbe*, exhibited at the Salon des Refusés in 1863, is a master work of Moreau's selection. Camondo's collection featured works by Cézanne, van Gogh, Toulouse-Lautrec, Manet, and Monet, in addition to numerous Degas.

During the following decades collectors continued to donate their Impressionist pictures to the nation. In the 1920s the dealer Ambroise Vollard left ceramic and wood sculptures by Gauguin to the Département des objets d'art and Le musée des Arts Africains et Océaniens. Subsequently, these works have been transferred to the Jeu de Paume. Pellerin's donation in 1929 increased the Cézanne holdings, and the Perronnaz gift in 1937 added more works by Degas, Monet, Pissarro, Sisley, and Toulouse-Lautrec, as well as paintings by the American Mary Cassatt. During the 1950s, descendants of Dr. Gachet, a close friend of Cézanne and van Gogh among others, contributed paintings by Pissarro,

Renoir, Sisley, Cézanne, and van Gogh. Several of van Gogh's paintings were executed during the last year of his life, when he lived with Gachet in Auvers in 1890. The 1960s saw the donation by Eduardo Mollard of nearly thirty oils of Jongkind, Renoir, Boudin, and Pissarro. His collection also included works by the Barbizon masters Théodore Rousseau, Diaz, and Corot.

During the last decade, the gift of Max and Rosy Kaganovitch of twenty paintings in 1973 further extended the Jeu de Paume's selection of works by Boudin, Cézanne, Monet, Seurat, van Gogh, and Renoir, in addition to earlier paintings by Corot, Courbet, and Daumier. Three years later, Kahn-Sriber donated ten paintings, including van Gogh's *Starry Night*, painted in September 1888 in Arles, and a monumental late Renoir nude, the *Grand Nu* of 1907. However, these two paintings are still in the possession of the family under the provisions of the French "rights of *usufruit.*" At the death of the donors the paintings will be moved to the Musée d'Orsay.

The Jeu de Paume's selection of Manets spans the artist's career from the early 1860s to the late 1870s, a few years before his death. Early examples include *Lola de Valence* of 1862, a Spanish subject that Manet also represented in an etching, and his two major canvases of 1863: *Olympia* and *Déjeuner sur l'herbe*. His portrait of his friend, the author Emile Zola, dates from 1868, as does *The Balcony* (1868–69), in which Manet included a portrait of his only pupil, Eva Gonzalès. Gonzalès' own picture, *A Loge at the Théatre des Italiens* of 1874, also in the Jeu de Paume, follows Manet's earlier composition. Works by Manet from the 1870s include the *Woman with Fans* of 1873, the *Blond Woman with Bare Breasts* of 1878, and *La Serveuse de Bocks* (*Waitress with Beer Glasses*), 1878–79, one of his late café interiors.

Monet is also well represented, from his very early *Farmyard in Normandy* of 1864 to scenes of his gardens at Giverny and depictions of the Houses of Parliament in London, executed in the early twentieth century. Monet's first monumental piece, also a *Déjeuner sur l'herbe* of about 1865–66, remained unfinished, and he later cut the painting into three sections. The Jeu de Paume owns the left fragment of the *Déjeuner*, as well as Monet's subsequent monumental painting, *Women in the Garden* of 1867. The latter canvas was the first large painting that Monet actually executed completely *en plein air*. Other important pictures include his 1868 portrait *Mme. Gaudibert*, his beautiful *Luncheon* of 1873, and *La Gare St. Lazare* (1877), where he was intrigued with representing the rising steam of a railway engine, as well as numerous views of Impressionist haunts, Argenteuil and Vetheuil. The Jeu de Paume is especially fortunate to be able to exhibit five views of *Rouen Cathedral*, painted at different times of the day during 1894.

The collection also contains paintings by Monet's close friends from the 1860s. In Normandy the young Monet learned much from Eugène Boudin and the Dutch artist Jongkind, whom he considered his first teachers. Typically, Boudin portrayed beach scenes, often populated with fashionably dressed promenaders of the Second Empire. *The Beach at Trouville* of 1864, the *Jetty at Deauville* of 1889, and the *Harbor at Bordeaux* of 1874 are characteristic pictures. Jongkind is represented by several seascapes, both in oil and watercolor, executed along the Normandy coast or in Jongkind's native Holland. During the mid–1860s, Monet painted in the Forest of Fontainebleau with Bazille, who posed for the former's *Déjeuner*. Unfortunately, Bazille's career was cut short by his premature death as a soldier during the Franco-Prussian War. The Jeu de Paume, none-theless, owns several of his most important paintings: *The Pink Dress* (also known as the *View of Castelnau*), 1864; the *Family Reunion*, 1867; and the *Artist's Studio*, 1870.

The Degas holdings are extensive. The early works include portraits such as those of the *Bellelli Family* and *Marguerite de Gas*, both of 1858–60, as well as the *Sémiramis Founding Babylon* of 1861, a large painting following the Beaux-Arts tradition of representing a historical scene. *At the Races* and *Musicians in the Orchestra* date from the late 1860s, while numerous oils from the 1870s depict ballet dancers, a favored subject of Degas. An important picture, *At the Café* (also known as *The Absinthe Drinkers*) of 1874, portrays the actress Ellen Andée and Marcellin Desboutin at the Café de la Nouvelle-Athènes and was probably exhibited at the second Impressionist show. From the 1880s are several oils and pastels of nude women bathing, as well as a composition representing laundresses ironing.

Renoir had a very prolific and lengthy career, and the museum's collection contains works from all periods. From the 1860s are early portraits of his friends Sisley and Bazille. Works of the next decade include his *Nude in the Sunlight* of 1876, shown at the second Impressionist exhibition; the colorful *Moulin de la Galette*, also of 1876, a site near a Montmartre windmill, where Renoir's contemporaries danced and socialized; and the *Path through Tall Grass* of 1876–77. Late Renoirs feature bathers, odalisques, and other female figures as well as the sculpture of the *Great Judgment of Paris* of 1914.

The selection of Pissarro and Sisley primarily focuses on landscapes executed in the 1870s. Pissarro portrayed two versions of the *Louveciennes Road* of 1870 and of 1872, the *Entrance to the Village of Voisins* of 1872, the famous *Red Roofs* of 1877, and the *Orchard of Flowering Fruit Trees at Springtime*, painted in Pontoise in 1877. Pissarro painted few self-portraits; only four are known. The Jeu de Paume's *Self Portrait* of 1873 is the earliest example and was painted at Pontoise. Sisley's paintings portray his favorite locales such as the *View of Saint-Martin Canal* (1870), *Saint-Martin Canal* (1872), *Rue de la Chaussée at Argenteuil* (1872), scenes of the flood at Port-Marly in 1876, and *Snow at Louveciennes* (1878).

Berthe Morisot and Armand Guillaumin also exhibited with the Impressionists. Morisot, who married Eugène Manet, Edouard's brother, exhibited the Jeu de Paume's *Cradle* of 1872 at the first Impressionist show. Guillaumin met Cézanne and Pissarro at the Academie Suisse in 1863 and took part in six of the eight

Impressionist exhibitions, although Monet did not think much of Guillaumin's work. The Jeu de Paume owns several of his landscapes, including the *Sunset over Ivry* of 1873, which was shown at the first Impressionist exhibition.

Major works by the four major Post-Impressionists, Cézanne, Seurat, Gauguin, and van Gogh, as well as by Toulouse-Lautrec, are all on view at the Jeu de Paume. Seurat's total oeuvre is limited, due to his short career and the painstaking nature of his pointillist technique. The Jeu de Paume's small selection includes preparatory sketches of each of the three models in Seurat's *Les Poseuses* of 1887, as well as a seascape, the *Outer Harbor at the Port-en-Bessin* (1888), which was exhibited at the Salon des Indépendants of 1890.

The Jeu de Paume's collection of Paul Cézanne follows his career from the late 1860s into the 1890s. Early works include the *Head of Old Man* of 1866 and the *Repentant Magdalen* of 1868–69, which was originally painted on a wall at Cézanne's home, the *Jas de Bouffan*, and later detached. From the 1870s are Impressionist-style works such as *Dr. Gachet's House at Auvers* (1873); the famous *House of the Hanged Man* (1873), shown in the first Impressionist exhibition; *A Modern Olympia*, Cézanne's take-off on Manet; and *The Crossing at the Rue Remy at Auvers* of 1873. By the 1880s Cézanne's style had become more two dimensional and featured richer colors, especially blues, greens, and reds. Characteristic canvases portray *L'Estaque* (1878–79) on the Mediterranean coast and still lifes such as *Still Life with Soup Tureen* (1877) and the well-known *Blue Vase* (1885–87). The 1890s found Cézanne repeating motifs for their compositional variations in subjects such as *Cardplayers* (1890–95) and numerous still lifes with a variety of fruits.

Gauguin, unfortunately, is not represented in great quantity. Most of the Gauguin paintings date from his two stays in Tahiti. Two earlier works are *Les Alyscamps*, painted during Gauguin's brief and tragic stay with van Gogh in 1888, and *La Belle Angèle* (1889), a masterwork from Gauguin's Brittany period. Highlights of the Tahitian subjects include the 1891 *Women from Tahiti* and *Arearea* (1892), executed during his first stay, and *Vaïrumati* (1897) and *The White Horse* (1898), both from his second trip, as well as wood and ceramic sculptures.

The selection of van Gogh is also meager, no doubt reflecting the fact that the artist did not sell well and that much of his work remained in the family, destined ultimately for museums in van Gogh's native Holland. *La Restaurant da la Sirène at Asnières* of 1887 is van Gogh's rendition of Impressionist style. From his Arles period are the *Starry Night* of 1888 (still held by the Kahn-Sriber family), which predated the swirling skies of a painting of the same name owned by the Museum of Modern Art (q.v) in New York, and van Gogh's recording of his *Room at Arles* in 1889. Also painted in 1889 was his famous blue *Self Portrait*. Several paintings date from the last year of his life, 1890, when he lived in Auvers with Gachet: *Dr. Gachet's Garden*, the *Church at Auvers-sur-Oise*, and the portrait *Dr. Paul Gachet*.

In addition, the Jeu de Paume has several works by Henri Toulouse-Lautrec, dating from the 1890s. Characteristic representations of famed Montmartre performers include *Jane Avril Dancing* (1892) and *Cha-U-Kao, the Female Clown* (1895). La Goulue was another popular Montmartre performer. Her popularity at the cafés declined, and she established herself in a booth along the street in 1895, where she wore Egyptian costumes and belly danced. Lautrec executed two panels to decorate La Goulue's booth. These paintings, *La Goulue at the Moulin Rouge* (*La Goulue and Valentin de Désossé*) and one in her Egyptian costume, are now in the Palais de Tokyo, pending transfer to the Orsay Museum. Other Lautrec pictures depict scenes from Paris brothels, such as *In Bed* (1892).

Selected Bibliography

Museum publications: Adhémar, Hélène, and Anne Dayez-Distel, *The Jeu de Paume Museum*, 4th ed., trans. by C. de Chabannes, 1983; idem, *Musée du Jeu de Paume*, 1973; Adhémar, Hélène, "Galerie du Jeu de Paume, dernières acquisitions," *La Revue du Louvre* 17 (1973), pp. 285–98; idem, "La donation Kahn-Sriber," *La Revue du Louvre* 26 (1976), pp. 99–104.

Other publications: de Forges, Marie-Thérèse, *Musée du Jeu de Paume*, vols. 1 and 2 (Lausanne, n.d.); Bazin, Germain, *Impressionist Paintings in the Louvre* (London, 1961, 3d ed., trans. by S. Cunliffe-Owen from the French, *Trésor de l'impressionisme*); idem, "Renovation at the Musée du Jeu de Paume, Paris," *Museum* 14 (1961), pp. 25–44.

CAROL HYNNING SMITH

LOUVRE MUSEUM (officially MUSÉE NATIONAL DU LOUVRE; also THE LOUVRE), Palais du Louvre, 75041 Paris.

The palace of the Louvre is the most important secular architectural monument in France and occupies a unique place in the history of the nation. As a royal fortress and residence, it was a symbol both of French power and of the capital city of Paris; as one of the world's greatest museums of art, it is a symbol both of French culture and of Western civilization.

The first building called the Louvre was a royal castle built by Philip II Augustus between about 1190 and 1204. Primarily a military fortification defending the river access to Paris, the quadrangle of this fortress provided the seed for the future Louvre. Nothing remains of the original medieval castle except some fragments of the foundation and a few thirteenth-century column capitals.

During the fourteenth century, the Louvre came into greater use as a royal residence, although in fact few of the kings of France at any time before the Revolution chose to spend prolonged periods in their capital. The discomforts of the Louvre and the insecurities of the city were such that the sovereigns usually preferred to live in their various châteaux. An exception to this was Charles V (reigned 1364–80), who undertook renovations to transform the Louvre into a sumptuous royal residence. The gloomy old fortress was enlarged, heightened, enriched, and given the appearance of a Gothic fairy-tale castle. Certainly, by the time of Charles V, the Louvre had come to be regarded as a symbol of the

French monarchy, the sovereign's official residence in his capital, in spite of the fact that kings were absent from it more often than not.

The Louvre as it exists today, its various parts dating from the mid-sixteenth through the late nineteenth century, began to take form during the reign of Francis I (reigned 1515–47). Francis had no serious intention of residing in Paris, but he was aware of the value of the Louvre as a visible sign of the royal presence in the capital and of the modern sovereign authority the king proposed to assert as a Renaissance "new monarch." Drastic changes took place in the fabric of the Louvre, and the late medieval château of Charles V began to disappear. Renaissance classicism, of which Francis was enamored and to which the French turned with enthusiasm, was to be the style for the new Louvre. In 1546 Pierre Lescot began building a new Italianate facade on the west wing of the old château courtyard. This elegant facade is considered to be one of the major monuments of French Renaissance architecture.

During the latter half of the sixteenth century and for most of the seventeenth century, work was carried out to complete the destruction of the medieval Louvre and to continue Lescot's projects on an enhanced scale. The original courtyard was quadrupled in size. The new wings were designed by Lemercier and LeVau, architects who were among the creators of the French classical style. The East Facade of the Louvre, the main entrance to the palace, was substantially finished by 1670, and by that date the Cour Carrée (Square Court) had been enclosed. The Cour Carrée at the eastern end of the Louvre complex, a large courtyard enclosed by four wings and based on the site of the courtyard of the original fortification, is the heart of what has come to be known as the "old" Louvre. Apart from the work of Lescot, it dates primarily from about 1625 to about 1670. The famous East Facade (also called the Colonnade), by LeVau, LeBrun, and Perrault is a major example of French Baroque classicism; its magnificent but restrained design has been extremely influential in the history of French architecture.

In the latter half of the sixteenth century and the first decade of the seventeenth century, two important new elements were added to the Louvre complex. A short distance to the west of the Louvre, the palace of the Tuileries was built at the command of Queen Catherine de' Medici. Begun in 1564 as a personal residence for Catherine, the Tuileries' original architect was Philibert de l'Orme, one of the most important architects of the French Renaissance. In the first decade of the seventeenth century, the Louvre and the Tuileries were connected at their southern extremities by a long corridor called the Grande Galerie, or the Grand Gallery. The Grand Gallery, lying parallel to the river, was then approximately thirteen hundred feet in length and thirty feet in width and joined the long, narrow mass of the Tuileries at a right angle. Today the Grand Gallery houses some of the Louvre's most famous works of art.

In the 1660s, even before the East Facade had been brought to completion, Louis XIV (reigned 1643–1715) decided to build Versailles and not to reside in Paris, which he intensely disliked. For all practical purposes, the Louvre was abandoned by the kings of France. Various academies, such as the Royal Academy of Painting and Sculpture, were given space in the palace; it also housed nobles living in "grace and favor" apartments, the Ministry of War, and other government offices. The fabric of the buildings fell into decay, and the entire Louvre area developed a disreputable and even criminal atmosphere. The facades of the palace were disfigured with shantylike buildings and booths erected against them, ramshackle structures housing stables, shops, concessions selling tobacco, old clothes, drinks, and the like. These areas, and the courtyards of the palace, were a constant problem to the Paris police.

By the middle of the eighteenth century, the condition of the Louvre had become a scandal and was considered a disgrace to the city of Paris, to the prestige of the crown, and to the honor of the nation. An outcry for the rehabilitation of the palace was led by the *philosophes*, intellectuals, and pamphleteers. Many ideas for the public use of the Louvre buildings were put forward, and architects designed ambitious projects for the unification of the Louvre and the Tuileries, none of which was realized at the time. Some limited restoration work was undertaken, but no significant progress was made toward the project that had come to be known as "the completion of the Louvre." Indifference to the buildings marked the first half of the eighteenth century. Aroused public opinion engaged the attention of the crown during the last half of the century, but little could be accomplished because of the royal government's often severe financial difficulties.

Among the most prominent ideas put forth for the rehabilitation and use of the Louvre was the suggestion that at least some area of it be set aside for the public display of part of the royal art collection, one of the richest in Europe. By 1775 the crown had committed itself to the transformation of the Grand Gallery into a national museum of art, and during the last years of the ancien régime the royal government worked seriously on the project. But architectural problems involving the lighting of the Grand Gallery and the lack of financial resources repeatedly delayed the achievement of this undertaking. The museum of the Louvre was first opened in 1793 during the course of the French Revolution and by a Revolutionary government that had confiscated the royal art collection.

During the reign of Napoleon I (1804–14), the museum was significantly enhanced and enlarged. The emperor's architects, Percier and Fontaine, directed important projects on both the interior and exterior of the Louvre. Work was begun to enclose the north side of the Louvre area with a long wing that was to lie along the Rue de Rivoli and connect the Tuileries and the Louvre on the north as the Grand Gallery connected the two palaces on the south. About half of this wing was completed by 1825.

After more than three centuries of both effort and neglect, the Louvre was finally brought to completion during the Second Empire, the reign of Emperor Louis Napoleon III (1852–70). The eastern half of the North Wing was built with transverse wings to enclose a sequence of three courtyards extending south. This arrangement was repeated on the south by the construction of three enclosed courtyards extending north from the eastern half of the Grand Gallery (the river wing). The western half of the Grand Gallery was enlarged on the courtyard side and was encased with new facades. The supervising architects for these projects were Louis Visconti, who died in 1853, and Hector-Marie Lefuel, who succeeded Visconti. In the face of some criticism, Lefuel adhered essentially to Visconti's grand design and to Visconti's philosophy of completing the Louvre within the context of the styles of the existing buildings. Lefuel adopted some modification, however, to please Napoleon III and the Empress Eugènie, who preferred a more exuberant style than the reserved Renaissance style of Lescot favored by Visconti. As a result, the extensive Second Empire construction and restoration displays a lavish nineteenth-century interpretation of seventeenth-century French Baroque classicism; rich with sculpture and architectural ornament, it is an important expression of the "imperial" taste of its period and of a style widely used in urban architecture in the latter half of the nineteenth century.

At the end of the Second Empire, then, the Louvre consisted of a complex of buildings with the old Louvre, enclosing the Cour Carrée, at the eastern end. From the old Louvre, two great wings extended west: the North Wing built during the nineteenth century and the Grand Gallery wing on the river. These two wings joined the Tuileries and created a vast enclosed courtyard lying to the west of the old Louvre. Contained within this courtyard on both the North Wing and Grand Gallery sides were buildings enclosing three smaller courtyards; these buildings and their courts, three on each side, adjoined the old Louvre.

The western aspect of the Louvre was changed radically by the disorders in Paris following the Franco-Prussian War of 1870, the fall of the Second Empire, and the siege of the city. The capital fell to the rule of a commune, and in May of 1871, during fighting between government troops and the forces of the commune, the Tuileries was destroyed by fire. The disappearance of the Tuileries opened the west side of the great enclosed courtyard that had been formed by the Tuileries itself, the North Wing, the Grand Gallery, and the old Louvre. The Tuileries was not rebuilt. Lefuel directed necessary restoration work, especially on the North Wing, which was enlarged on the courtyard side of its western terminus. Architectural and sculptural decorations for the Rue de Rivoli facade of the North Wing were also undertaken. Lefuel died in 1880, by which time the Louvre had assumed the appearance it has today.

The Louvre as a museum has existed since 1793. The vast building as it is now seen, majestic and curiously harmonious in its various parts, dates primarily from the seventeenth and nineteenth centuries. But the Louvre as a royal and national symbol of power and culture has had a historical existence of nearly eight centuries, and from the time of the first fortress it has been "our Louvre" to Parisians.

                                                                          JAMES L. CONNELLY

The collections of the Louvre Museum are organized into eight departments that are listed in the order in which they were created: Department of Paintings, Drawings, Chalcography and the Edmund Rothschild Collection of Prints and Drawings; Department of Greek and Roman Antiquities; Department of Egyptian and Coptic Antiquities; Department of Medieval, Renaissance, and Modern Sculpture; Department of Oriental Antiquities; Department of Furniture and Art Objects; Department of Christian Antiquities; and the Section of Islamic Art.

The Department of Paintings, Drawings, Chalcography and the Edmond Rothschild Collection of Prints and Drawings (Département des peintures, des dessins, de la chalcographie et de la collection de gravures et dessins Edmond de Rothschild) holds a collection of paintings that although not the largest in the world is the most comprehensive. Paintings once owned by the French monarchs form its nucleus. Francis I (1494–1547) created the first art collection in France in his newly renovated palace at Fontainebleau. It contained masterpieces of the Italian Renaissance by Leonardo, Andrea del Sarto, and Raphael, among others, and was rich enough for Vasari to call it the "Rome of the North." Moderately expanded by his successors, a keeper was appointed in 1608 by Henry IV, who also used the newly built Grande Galerie and Petite Galerie to exhibit the royal collection of portraits. Marie de' Medici, his widow, entrusted the decoration of the two galleries in the new Palais du Luxembourg to Rubens. Only one of them was completed in 1622, but the cycle of twenty-one historical-mythological scenes of the life of Marie de' Medici has been one of the principal masterpieces of the Louvre since its exhibition there in 1815. During the reign of Louis XIII, the most important addition was Cardinal Richelieu's collection of Italian Renaissance and contemporary paintings, acquired by confiscation (1629) and legacy (1636).

The most magnificent period of expansion came with Louis XIV's reign. Cardinal Mazarin bequeathed to the king 15 Renaissance masterpieces, several of which had once belonged to Charles I of England and before him to the Gonzagas of Mantua. This was also the source of many of the 5,542 drawings and 101 paintings sold under compulsion to the king by the banker Evrard Jabach in 1671. The greatest period of growth coincided with and was caused by the development of Versailles as the main royal court. A comparison of the inventories of 1683 and 1709–10 shows a massive increase from 426 to 2,376 paintings. Of them, 369 were Italian. Louis XIV had a taste for the work of contemporary artists as well as those of the Renaissance; 179 were of the Northern schools, Flemish painters in particular having enjoyed a revival since the mid–1680s; but the largest proportion of French art—930 paintings, with contemporary artists such as Poussin, Claude Lorraine, and Lebrun well represented. It is interesting that the collection today still reflects these proportions.

Under Louis XV a reversal of fortune occurred. The collection suffered from neglect, inaccessibility, and even dispersal, since members of the nobility borrowed paintings for display in their own households. Fortunately, the tradition of personal interest was revived by the next king, Louis XVI. The exhibition in October 1750 of 110 paintings and drawings in the Palais du Luxembourg marked the recognition of a new idea: that the royal collection should be used as an instrument for public edification and artistic study. Although the plans of the Comte d'Angiviller, directeur des bâtiments, to create a museum around the Grande Galerie were thwarted by the Revolution, his methodical acquisition policy, designed to strengthen areas previously under-represented, laid the foundation of future museum policies. Under his direction the holdings in seventeenth-century French art were intelligently amplified, and those of the Northern schools, previously the least well represented, were extensively expanded, with the result that many of the Dutch paintings in the Louvre were acquired during this reign.

The Revolution and Empire periods perpetuated this atmosphere of activity and change. The royal collection, swollen by paintings confiscated from the émigrés and churches and transformed into the Musée central des Arts et de la République in the Grande Galerie on August 10, 1793, grew yet again with requisitioned works from Italy and other countries defeated in battle. From 1804 Baron Vivant-Denon furthered the organization, cataloguing and exhibiting the collection under its new name, the Musée Napoléon. Reflecting the contemporary interest in the primitives, he bought an important series of fourteenth- and fifteenth-century Italian works in 1811. The richness of the collection, combined with its new accessibility, ensured the Louvre a formative influence on French art. This was maintained even after the return of more than five thousand of the requisitioned works to their native lands in 1815.

The next kings, Louis XVIII, Charles X, and Louis Philippe, were eager to rival Napoleon in his patronage of living artists, and these years saw the foundation of the unique collection of French Romantic paintings. They were kept at the Luxembourg from 1818 until 1886, when Ingres and Delacroix were exhibited together at the Louvre.

From the middle of the century the collection was catalogued, reclassified, and exhibited by schools, and a concerted policy of restoration had begun. There were two large additions, the first being the purchase of the collection of the Marquis Campana in 1864. It included 646 paintings, most of mediocre quality, of which the Louvre ultimately kept only 134, mainly to strengthen its holdings in early Italian painting. Five years later it received the most important individual donation ever made to a European museum. Louis La Caze gave to the nation 802 masterpieces of all schools. According to his will, the Louvre retained 500 paintings, of special worth for the seventeenth-century Dutch school and the eighteenth-century French, which filled the last gap in the representation of that tradition. The excess from both collections was distributed among museums in the provinces, a typical event because of the close relationship between the Louvre and other French museums.

Since 1869 the rapid expansion of the collection, brought about mainly by individual donations, has created a large reserve that contains hundreds of fine and historically important canvases. The main changes within the department since the 1930s have been caused by different ideas on how best to display the paintings for an increasingly interested public. During the 1950s the solution was to display only the masterpieces, arranging the galleries on stylistic and aesthetic principles that often split up the works of an artist and immensely reduced the number on show.

The intervention of André Malraux, minister for cultural affairs, reversed this trend starting with the showing of seven hundred paintings previously unexhibited in June 1960. By extensions to the gallery system and a sensitive use of exhibitions, a larger proportion of the collection has been made public. The major extensions and refurbishing have been a suite of twenty-two rooms opened in 1960 on the second floor of the Cour Carrée and the newly partitioned rooms in the Aile and Pavillon de Flore opened ten years later. The part of the Louvre occupied now by the Ministry of Finance will be a future site for expansion. These extensions have been combined with a policy inaugurated in 1968: the rearrangement of the permanent galleries with a new emphasis on national schools and chronology.

Another recent development has been the use of the Musée d'Art et d'Essai at the Palais de Tokyo, a privilege that other departments at the Louvre share. Since March 1968 small temporary exhibitions, such as that on Le Sueur, have been designed to highlight various aspects of the collection. Within the department itself a series of exhibitions since 1971 have explored the collection both in terms of its history (e.g., The Collection of Francis I, 1972) and individual paintings and schools (e.g., *The Fortune Teller* by Caravaggio, 1977). The exhibition facilities in the Salle de l'Orangerie, open since 1878, were used by other departments in the Louvre, as well as other state organizations, and exhibitions drew on material from museums throughout France. With the occupation of the Orangerie by the Walter Guillaume Collection in 1984, the Jeu de Paume (q.v.) is eventually to take over its function, after removal of its holdings to the Orsay Museum (q.v.), planned for 1987.

Two-thirds of paintings in the Louvre are of the French school, and much of the expansion of the last hundred years has been within this field. It begins with what may be the oldest French painting in existence, and certainly the oldest portrait, of *John the Good* by an anonymous Parisian artist (c. 1360). Of two portraits by Jean Fouquet, his *Charles VII* is still in its original frame (c. 1444). The religious spirit of the time is magnificently expressed in a *Pietà* by Jean Malouel but above all in the anonymous *Pietà of Villeneuve-les-Avignon*, one of the masterpieces of Christian art. It was bought by the Société des Amis du Louvre in 1905.

The portrait tradition continues in the sixteenth century in *Francis I* by Jean Clouet. His son François, Corneille de Lyons, and their ateliers are well represented, as is the School of Fontainebleau, which includes *Diana the Huntress* (1550s). *Henry IV* by François Pourbus illustrates the development of more sophisticated and dramatic portraiture.

From the seventeenth century the Le Nain brothers are represented by fifteen paintings including *Peasant Meal* (1642) and *The Disciples at Emmaüs* by Louis. Georges de La Tour, unrepresented in the Louvre before 1926, now has three canvases, including *St. Joseph the Carpenter* (c. 1640), generously given by Percy Moore Turner in 1948. Among the many austere religious works and portraits by Philippe de Champaigne owned by the Louvre are the *Ex-voto* of 1662 and his large *Portrait of Richelieu*. The different interpretations given to these two traditions can be amply followed in works by Vouet, Vignon, Mignard, Lebrun, Jouvenet, Largillierre, and Rigaud.

The splendid group of some forty Poussins includes his own portrait and the masterpieces of mythology *The Triumph of Flora* and *The Shepherds of Arcadia*. His contemporary Claude Lorraine is less generously represented, but the museum owns some of his greatest creations, such as *Seaport at Sunset* (1639), *The Disembarkation of Cleopatra at Tarsus* (1647), and *View from the Campo Vaccino, Rome*.

Before 1869 there was only one Watteau in the Louvre—his Academy reception piece of 1717, *The Embarkation for Cythera*. Eight were bequeathed by La Caze, including the large and solemn *Gilles*, and in 1973 the *Portrait of a Gentleman*, a work exceptional in size and quality, was purchased. Chardin, similarly neglected before 1869, is now magnificently represented by thirty-two paintings from all periods of his career. Most are still-life paintings, but there are some figure pieces such as *The Blessing* (1740). Boucher is represented by some twenty-five works, including *Diana Bathing* (1742), for which Renoir felt a special attraction. The continuation of this female nude tradition in the next generation can be studied in the series of exuberant Fragonards.

The reaction against this type of art, inspired by the remains of classical antiquity and the Poussin tradition of history painting, can be traced in the works of Vien and Greuze but above all in the neoclassical works of David, of which the Louvre owns thirty, including masterpieces such as *Oath of the Horatii* (1784) and *Brutus* (1789). Portraits from his middle years are especially fine and include a *Self Portrait* (1794), the sketch *Bonaparte* (1796), and the unfinished *Madame Récamier* (1800). His contemporary Prud'hon is almost as generously present, a fine portrait being the *Empress Josephine* (1805). Works by David's pupils Girodet, Gérard, and Gros are fewer but include the important *Plague House at Jaffa* (1804) by Gros.

By Ingres, who outlived them all, the Louvre owns almost sixty works. Portraits of special force are those of the Rivière family shown at the 1806 Salon and *Monsieur Bertin* (1832). His nudes can be followed from the early *Bather of Valpinçon* (1808) to *The Turkish Bath*, one of his last works.

The museum is exceptionally rich in Géricaults, among them his most monumental work *The Raft of the Medusa*, exhibited in 1819, and two portraits of mad people. Paintings by his friend Delacroix numerically rival the Ingres. All periods and aspects of his art are covered, with early masterpieces such as *Dante and Virgil* and *Death of Sardanapalus* particularly in evidence. Also of note are examples of his rarer ventures into portraiture and still life, such as the *Portrait of Chopin* and *Still Life with Lobster* (1827).

The flowering of the art of landscape in the eighteenth and nineteenth centuries is brilliantly illustrated as a result of several major bequests. In 1902 M. Thomy-Thierry bequeathed 121 works, and in 1910 M. Chauchard, 140 works by the Barbizon painters and Romantics. From the eighteenth century Joseph Vernet's marine and Hubert Robert's antique landscapes are supplemented by the latter's fascinating series of views of the Louvre. The remarkable gift in 1930 by the Princess Louis de Croy of 127 Italian views by Valenciennes are unusual in being done on cardboard-backed paper. The link between the centuries is maintained by a fine series of landscapes by Michallon.

His pupil Corot is outstandingly represented in more than 120 canvases, many from the great Moreau-Nélaton Collection (1906–27). They include not only his most famous landscapes, such as *The Coliseum from the Farnese Gardens* (1826) and *Bridge at Nantes* (1868–70), but also lesser-known figure pieces such as *Woman in Blue* (1874). Rousseau is represented by 32 works, many being landscapes from the Fontainebleau forest, Daubigny by 28, with most belonging to the last two decades of his life.

Among the twenty-five Millets are the masterpieces *The Gleaners* (1857) and *The Angelus* (1857–59). The many sides of Courbet's genius are shown in portraiture, *Man in a Leather Belt*; in landscapes, *The Shady Stream* (1865); and in his monumental work, *The Atelier of the Painter. Real Allegory* (1855).

The establishment of the Musée d'Orsay with its chronological limits of 1850–1914 will slightly alter the perspective of nineteenth-century art given at the Louvre. Some of the later works of artists mentioned above are to be transferred as are the paintings of Puvis de Chavannes and Gustav Moreau, which the Louvre has housed until now, and Whistler's *Portrait of His Mother* (1872).

The collection of Italian paintings in the Louvre is unique in that from the middle of the thirteenth century to its demise in the eighteenth, there is an uninterrupted display of masterpieces. The large panel *Madonna of the Angels* by Cimabue (c. 1270) illustrates the Byzantine roots of the European religious tradition, which by the time of Bernardo Daddi's *The Annunciation* and Giotto's *St. Francis of Assisi* (1290s) had been permeated by a more Gothic grace. The Sienese school at its most eloquent is exemplified in *Christ Bearing the Cross* by Simone Martini (c. 1339–44), and *Madonna and Child* by Lorenzo Veneziano shows the early Venetian predilection for richness of effect. Among the many early Florentine masterpieces is Fra Angelico's monumental *The Coronation of the Virgin* (1430–35), much admired by Vasari.

Portraiture commences with *Sigismond Malatesta*, one of the few works by Piero di Cosimo outside Italy and only purchased in 1978, and *A Princess of the d'Este Family* by Pisanello. Two vigorous images of the fifteenth century are *The Battle of San Romano* by Paolo Uccello from the Campana Collection (c. 1451) and *The Condottiere* by Antonello da Messina (1475). Within the Venetian religious and allegorical tradition are works by Jacopo and Giovanni Bellini and a magnificent group by Mantegna, including his *St. Sebastian* and

Parnassus. His Florentine contemporary Botticelli is likewise well represented by Madonnas and allegorical subjects. Also of note are several works by Perugino and *St. Etienne Preaching at Jerusalem* by Carpaccio.

The Louvre owns seven Leonardos, amounting to almost half of his existing work. Among them are the universally renowned *Portrait of Mona Lisa*, known as *La Joconde*; the better version of his *Virgin of the Rocks*, the other being in the National Gallery (q.v.) in London; and *The Virgin, Child, and St. Anne*. Raphael is similarly well represented, two sides of his genius being illustrated by one of the most perfect of his Madonnas, *La Belle Jardinière*, and the portrait of his friend, *Balthazar Castiglione*. The Correggios include two masterpieces from his late twenties, *Antiope* and *The Mystic Marriage of St. Catherine*.

Among the schools most magnificently displayed in the Louvre is Venice in the sixteenth century. The collection boasts of one of the most perfect expressions of the Venetian style and ideal, the *Pastoral Concert* attributed to Giorgione. Titian is one of the best represented of the Italian masters. *Man with a Glove* of his portraits, *The Entombment* of his religious paintings, and *Young Woman at her Toilette* of his female beauties are especially unforgettable. Works by Tintoretto include an example of a favorite theme, *Susanna* (c. 1580). Among the different aspects of Veronese's genius captured in the Louvre is his largest canvas, *The Marriage at Cana* (1562–63), an example of the Venetian decorative instinct. His truly religious pictures include the somber *Calvary*.

As a result of the unflagging patronage of Louis XIV, the seventeenth-century collection is important for its size if not for its quality. Works by Annibale Carracci include two early landscapes, *Fishing* and *Hunting*, and pictures by his fellow Bolognese artists Guido Reni, Guercino, and Domenichino are also present. Of greater interest perhaps is the revolution in drama and naturalism of Caravaggio's art, which can be traced from his early *Fortune-Teller* (c. 1589) to the mature *Death of the Virgin* (1605–6).

Within the Venetian eighteenth century the three works by Canaletto are overshadowed by one of the richest groups of Guardis in the world. The Louvre owns eight of the twelve canvases painted in commemoration of the coronation of the Doge Alvise IV Mocenigo. There is an unusual collection of Tiepolos, including his famous *Ecce Homo*, one of the many valuable paintings in the Pereire donation (1949).

A perfectly preserved Jan van Eyck, *The Virgin and Chancellor Rolin* (c. 1435), has headed the collection of Flemish art since the Napoleonic era. Equally important are the *Braque Triptych* by Rogier van der Weyden (1452) and the *Lamentation of Christ* acquired in 1951 and one of only thirty works known by Petrus Christus. The Louvre owns two contrasting works by Hans Memling, *Portrait of an Old Woman* (1470–75) and *The Mystic Marriage of St. Catherine*. The early Flemish school benefited from the Grog donation (1973), with *The Virgin in Majesty* by the Master of the Leaf Embroidery and *The Tax Collector* by Marinus van Reymerswaele. In the same realist tradition of the latter is *The Moneylender and His Wife* by Quentin Metsys (1514). The attraction that Italian art exercised on Flemish painters is again illustrated by the *Diptych of Jean Carondelet* by Mabuse (1517). The only work in the Louvre by Pieter Bruegel the Elder is *The Beggars*, a masterpiece from the very end of his life. Teniers, however, is well represented with a nucleus of nineteen works from the La Caze gift.

The pride of the collection is the series of twenty-one paintings that comprise the *Life of Marie de' Medici* by Rubens. Among the thirty-five other works by this artist are two superb portraits of his wife, Hélène Fourment, one with her children (c. 1636) and one in court costume, purchased in 1977. Jordaens and van Dyck are represented by fine and typical works, especially the latter's *Portrait of James Stuart on Horseback*.

All of the major artists of the Netherlandish school can be seen in the Louvre, although numbers are less extensive than for Italy. The earliest painting distinguishable from Flemish art is the *Resurrection of Lazarus* by Geertgen tot sint Jans (c. 1440). The Dutch tradition of fantastic landscapes is shown in *Ship of Fools* by Hieronymus Bosch (1490s) and *Lot and His Daughters* by Lucas van Leyden (1509–17).

The seventeenth-century Dutch holdings were enriched during the 1920s and 1930s by thirty-nine paintings from the collection of the Princess de Croy. The great landscape artists Hobbema, van der Neer, Potter, Cuyp, Berchem, van der Heyden, and others are all represented. There is a particularly beautiful series of landscapes by Ruisdael, including *The Sunbeam* and *The Storm*. Jan van Goyen is present in three exceptional works from the Lyons gift (1961).

Examples of still lifes and portraits are more modest in number but include several masterpieces by Frans Hals, such as the *Portrait of an Old Woman* and *The Bohemian*, both from the La Caze donation. Honthorst, Ter Borch, Metsu, Steen, Ostade, and Dou can also be seen, and in 1975 the Louvre acquired its third Pieter de Hooch, *The Drinker*. Most important among the Dutch interiors is *The Lacemaker* by Vermeer, one of only two paintings in France by this artist (c. 1664).

The superb series of Rembrandts includes the memorable *Carcass of Beef* (1655); two self-portraits, one in youth and one in old age; a nude *Bethsheba Bathing* (1654); and religious pictures, among them the haunting *Pilgrims of Emmaüs* (1648).

The German, English, and Spanish schools are more thinly represented, although efforts have been made in recent decades to rectify this situation. The Louvre owns several German Renaissance portrait masterpieces, including Dürer's sophisticated *Self Portrait* at the age of twenty-two, painted for his fiancée in 1493; Holbein's powerful and fitting tribute to his friend *Erasmus* (1523); and Lucas Cranach's *Portrait of a Girl*, whose charm and naïveté contrasts markedly with his seductive *Venus* (1529). A new departure was the purchase of a work by the German Romantic Caspar David Friedrich in 1975, his *Tree of Ravens* (c. 1822).

Portraits again dominate the English collection in typical and fine works by

Reynolds, Gainsborough, Hoppner, and Lawrence. Of the latter is one of his most memorable group of children, those of John Angerstein, acquired in 1977. The small but good collection of romantic landscapes by Turner, Constable, and Bonington are of special significance in this museum because of the interest nineteenth-century French artists had in them.

The Louvre offers a brief but intense spectrum of Spanish art, with the main styles being represented by a small number of masterpieces. A recent acquisition is *The Flagellation of Christ* by Jaime Huguet, regarded as important in the evolution of Spanish painting. Another great primitive work is *The Martyrdom of St. George* by Martorelli (1430–35), and the same mysticism pervades *Christ on the Cross* (c. 1580), a typical work by El Greco and one of several pieces owned by the museum. From the seventeenth century are paintings by Ribera, Zurbarán, Murillo, and two Velázquez, which include *Queen Marianne of Austria*, formerly part of an exchange program with the Prado Museum (q.v.) of Madrid. From the eighteenth century Goya's mastery of portraiture is well represented in the marvelous recently purchased *Marquise of Santa Cruz* and *Marquise of Solana* (c. 1791–94). The latter is part of the Beistegui Collection, which also contains fine portraits by David and Ingres. It was given in 1953 on condition that it be exhibited intact on a permanent basis, as was the Picasso donation, a collection of paintings and drawings belonging to that artist given five years after his death. It includes works ranging from Le Nain to his contemporaries and is invaluable for a study of his tastes.

Besides the main painting section there is the collection of drawings (Cabinet des Dessins), the Chalcography Collection, and the collection of drawings and prints that belonged to Edmond de Rothschild, each of which has its own curatorial staff.

The Cabinet des Dessins, housed in the Pavillon de Flore, although not a department in its own right, has a special status because of its long history and size. It contains about one hundred thousand items, which makes it numerically the richest in the world. Its origins lie in the Royal Collection, first documented in 1671 with the drawings from the Jabach sale. Until the nineteenth century more attention was paid to foreign schools, but since then the French section has grown and is now invaluable for the study of most French artists. The Italian school is especially fine, and only the Albertina (q.v.) in Vienna can rival its Flemish collection. Although the English holdings are weak, the German and Dutch collections include fine specimens. The Cabinet des Dessins is only open to students and scholars doing specific research, but there are regular exhibitions for the public. Since 1971 the superb collection of seventeenth- and eighteenth-century pastels has enjoyed a permanent gallery.

The Chalcography Collection began when Louis XIV commissioned artists to celebrate in engravings the events of his reign. Officially organized in 1812 to make use of the material, the collection now contains more than thirteen thousand plates by many famous artists from the seventeenth century onwards. There are both originals, including commissions from modern artists, and interpretations of already conceived images.

The Edmond de Rothschild Collection was given to the Louvre in 1935 by his heirs. It includes three thousand drawings and more than thirty thousand original engravings from the beginning of that art to the end of the eighteenth century. Of special note is the brilliant collection of Rembrandts, which like the other material is featured in the regular temporary exhibitions devoted to this collection.

YVONNE A. LUKE

Almost as old as the museum itself, the Department of Greek and Roman Antiquities (Département des Antiquités Grecques et Romaines), originally designated simply Department of Antiquities, was established in 1800, the first such department to separate itself from the painting collection. The beginnings of the department date from Francis I, who, in addition to acquiring several important ancient works, had a considerable number of molds made from famous works in Italian collections. They were brought to France, cast by Primaticcio in the mid-sixteenth century, and used along with the antique works to decorate the royal parks. Louis XIV continued this policy of acquiring Classical works, sometimes purchasing entire collections, so that by the time of the Revolution, the antique holdings rivaled those of paintings.

In the nineteenth century several major archaeological expeditions were launched in an effort to find some of the famous works mentioned in ancient writings, and although this primary goal was not achieved, many other works were discovered, including one of the Louvre's most celebrated works: the *Winged Victory of Samothrace* (found in 1863). Two other acquisitions—a group of Greek vases from the Campana Collection, bought in 1863, and the Boscoreale Treasure of Roman jewelry, given to the Louvre in 1895 by Baron Rothschild—ensure that the riches of the department's collection are not exclusively sculptural.

The Louvre's collection of Greek vases, thanks to the Campana estate, is one of the most important in the world, with all phases and schools represented, often by major examples. Occupying the entire suite of rooms between the corners of the south side of the Square Court's first floor, they are introduced by a room filled with pre-Hellenic works from the Clarac Collection: large pithoi from Crete (seventeenth to sixteenth century B.C.) and Thera and Rhodes (fourteenth century B.C.) and painted fourteenth century B.C. Minoan and Mycenean ceramics.

The earliest works in the Campana Collection are kraters with funeral scenes found in the Diplyon cemetery (c. eighth century B.C.). From the seventh-century Orientalizing period is the excellent Levy oenochoe. An entire room is devoted to Corinthian and other non-Athenian work of the seventh to sixth century B.C.: small vases with little, finely drawn designs (Protocorinthian); perfume containers; two bowls with scenes from the life of Herakles; the charming kylix of the birdcatcher with its delicately delineated foliage spreading over the surface and a dancing man in the center; plastic vases, one with a grotesque figure of Silenus; the hydriae of Cerveteri, brightly colored vases found in Italy but coming from Asia Minor, one of them the famous *Theft of the Oxen of Apollo*, with the mischievous figure of the child Hermes shown first plotting and then executing his prank.

The dominance of the Attic style for the next centuries shows itself in several rooms, with a large group of works by the best-known masters and many lesser ones. For the black-figured period of about 650–550 B.C., there are works by Amasis, Exekias (*Herakles and Gryon, Return of Hephaistos*), and the Little Masters (kylix with the Dionysiac procession). From the second half of the sixth century B.C. are works by Nikosthenes (oenochoe with Herakles received at Olympus by Athena, kylix with a gallery race) and Andokides (*Herakles and Cerberus*, an amphora in mixed styles, black-figured on one side and red-figured on the other), as well as a series of cups decorated with great staring eyes.

The full flowering of the red-figured style is seen in several works by Euphronios (the *Herakles and Antaeus Krater*), Douris (the *Eos and Memnon Kylix*), Myron (the *Croesus on his Funeral Pyre Amphora*, a rare historical episode on a vase), and the Berlin Painter (a krater with a young man rolling a hoop). All of them reflect the increasing mastery that the major mural painters were attaining over the representation of the human form.

The new importance that lekythi attained in the fifth and fourth centuries B.C. is reflected in a room devoted to this type. The delicacy of their painting style finds its echo in the subjects: small ones of domestic scenes (women seated at their toilet; women and servants at their household duties), larger ones with pastoral scenes (a horseman and pedestrian in a field of reeds), and increasingly decorative ones from the fourth century B.C. (*Athene and Dionysus*, with figures in relief and decorated with gold).

Other decorative arts in the department also span the whole history of Greek art, again thanks in large part to the Campana estate. The earliest of them are four fine Cycladic idols (two of them only heads but one of them a splendidly abstract life-sized work—10.5 inches tall, from Amorgas—that prefigures the work of Lipchitz four millennia later). All of them date from about 2500 to 2000 B.C. Small bronzes and ceramic figurines from Crete and Mycenae date from the fourteenth to twelfth century B.C. (among them a bronze mother goddess holding her breasts). Ceramic figurines of mother goddesses continue into the Geometric period, along with bell-shaped idols from Boetia. Works from the Orientalizing period of the seventh century B.C. include some Daedalian terracotta statuettes. Unusual from the sixth century is a large sarcophagus in baked clay.

By the sixth century genre subjects had begun to appear: many small, baked-clay statues of daily activities from Boetia (a woman kneading bread, a man playing on a lyre, a mourner, men fighting) while traditional subjects continued to be produced there (a statuette of Europa and the bull). Especially famous are those from fourth-century Tanagra in painted terracotta: a dreamer, a young man

(*Il Penseroso*), a woman with draperies holding a fan, and a heavily draped woman. The third-century continuation of this tradition in Myrina is also represented: winged figures (Eros, flying Psyche on a rock) and copies of famous statues (*Venus Genitrix, Crouching Venus*). Of the small bronzes from this century, some (*Aphrodite Fastening her Sandal, Eros and Psyche as Children*—shown as chubby children) make this period seem like a rococo phase of the Late Antique. Finally, the discovery of glass blowing in the first century B.C. has left some evidence in the form of Millefiori bowls, black glass, and painted goblets.

In 1980 the Greek sculpture area was arranged to make a clear distinction between originals and Roman copies, the originals being in rooms laid out in a straight line, with the replicas placed in adjacent rooms, allowing convenient study of specific art historical problems while maintaining the integrity of the display of originals. In addition, two rooms have been set aside for objects, mostly small, related to Graeco-Roman civilization.

All of the works from the Archaic period are originals. Although few, they include some excellent pieces. The statuette of the *Lady of Auxerre* is one of the earliest surviving works known. The most famous, though, are the sixth-century *Hera of Samos* and the *Rampin Head*, the latter shown attached to a plaster cast of its original body, which is now in the Athens Museum (q.v.).

Of the originals from the fifth century, the most celebrated is the *Procession of Marshalls and Maidens* fragment from the frieze of the Parthenon, but there are also several other fragments: a metope (*Centaur Carrying off a Lapith Woman*) and two heads, one of them the *Laborde Head*, of a woman from one of the pediments. From the first half of the century is one of the rare bronzes—surviving because it was lost in the sea for many centuries: the *Piombino Apollo*, four feet tall, found in 1832. In addition, there are two metopes from the Temple of Zeus at Olympia.

The two most celebrated works in the Greek collection belong to the Hellenistic era: the *Victory of Samothrace* and the *Venus de Milo*. The former, well over life-size, is dramatically placed at the top of the first landing leading to the picture galleries, with a case on the right holding the remaining portion of its right hand (discovered in 1950). Dating from about 200 B.C., its left breast and wing are plaster restorations. Controversy still rages about whether the *Venus de Milo* (found by a peasant in 1820) is an original fourth-century variant of Praxiteles' lost *Cnidian Aphrodite*, or a second-century copy of a lost fourth-century original, or a second-century original. The most recent trend is to regard it as an exceptionally beautiful copy. Less famous than these works is the *Borghese Warrior*, a late-Hellenistic original found in Italy in the seventeenth century. Of interest also are the *Sleeping Hermaphrodite* (with a mattress added in the seventeenth century by Bernini) and the colossal *God of the Tiber*, found in the sixteenth century.

The many replicas of lost Greek originals are arranged by century and school. Among the most notable are the *Medici Torso* and *Hermes, Orpheus, and Eu-*

rydice, both inspired by or after Phidias (the latter thought to be a school piece rather than a replica); *Borghese Mars*, after Polycleitos, and *Venus Genitrix*, after a work inspired by that master; *Apollo Sauroktonos* (the *Lizard Killer*), the torso *Cnidian Aphrodite*, and *Diana of Gabii*, after Praxiteles; *Hermes Fastening His Sandal* and portrait of *Alexander the Great*, after Lysippus; *Artemis the Hunter* (*Diana of Versailles*)—one of the first works acquired by Francis I, later taken by Louis XIV to Versailles; *Crouching Venus* (*Venus of Vienna*); *Faun of Vienna*; and *Boy with a Goose*.

Etruscan works in recent years had been unavailable for public viewing, but the 1980 rearrangement of the Graeco-Roman collection made it possible to open three new rooms devoted completely to this collection, which, thanks to the Campana estate purchase, is the richest outside of Italy. A sepulchral vault in Cerveteri has provided a realistic series of mural paintings that illuminate the life of the Etruscans and also the most striking work in the collection: the sarcophagus (c. 500 B.C.—one of two such works in existence, the other being in Rome), with its life-sized terracotta figures of husband and wife, she reclining against his breast, he gently embracing her. Equally fine are the series of *bucchero* vases, the dark lampblack on their clay surface incised with designs (one engaging example shows a marsh bird hopping through a field of spirals) and the concurrent series of painted ceramics. There are, in addition, many small works: statuettes, bronze mirrors, and so on.

Roman sculpture is also extensively represented by a splendid series of portrait busts: Agrippa, Antiochus, Caracalla, and Octavia in black basalt (once thought to be a bust of Livia); and full-length statues: Augusta (the head earlier than the body) and Octavius as Mercury the Orator, a rare example of a Roman portrait in the nude. In addition there is a series of monumental sculpture and reliefs: fragment from the *Ara Pacis*, the *Lion of Miletus*, and the *Mithra and the Bull*.

The small collection of Graeco-Roman paintings are from the Hellenistic period on and generally of two types: fragments of frescoes (*Cupid Gliding on the Waters*, *Dionysian Banquet*, and *Isiac Scenes*, depicting the cult of Isis in Rome) and mosaics (*Mosaic of the Phoenix*, an especially beautiful example of a work created for the mosaic medium, and *Judgment of Paris*). Foremost among the minor arts is the Boscoreale Treasure, found near Pompeii, and composed of more than a hundred pieces of silverware from various times in the Hellenistic era but all before A.D. 79. In this department are barbarian artworks (Gaul, Italy, Romano-Scythian), including the Treasure of Rongéres: bowl, bracelets, and rings with Celtic decorations.

The origins of the Department of Egyptian Antiquities (Département des Antiquités Egyptiennes) lie in the scientific expedition that accompanied Napoleon into Egypt in 1798. The many objects that were collected were unfortunately lost to France when General Menou had to surrender to the allies in 1801, but the curiosity aroused by the mystery of the hieroglyphics stimulated the young Jean-François Champollion to find the clue to their deciphering. In 1826 Champollion accepted the post of curator in the Louvre, and the new department was launched. The Egyptian holdings, which until then had consisted of some sixteen works that had been in the royal collection, expanded considerably during the next few years: the famous Salt Collection of more than four thousand pieces, including some of the most important works now in the Louvre (the *Salt Head*, inscribed *Karnak wall*, contents of the sarcophagus of Rameses III, two large sphinxes, naos from the Temple of Philae); the Drovetti Collection with more famous works in it (the colossus of Sobekhotep IV, the sarcophagus of Lady Tenthapi, a large golden cup given by Thutmos III to his general Thutti); and some two hundred individual works gathered in 1828–29 by the young curator himself during a trip to Egypt (*Seti I and Hathor, Sarcophagus of Taho, Queen Karomana*).

After Champollion's untimely death in 1832 the department had for almost two decades no special curator of its own, and it was virtually reabsorbed into the Department of Antiquities. It was during this period that some insensitive functionary authorized the sawing apart of bas-reliefs that were too long to be conveniently exhibited and the cutting out of the vignettes from funerary papyri. In 1849, though, a new curator was finally appointed, and acquisitions began to increase again (most notably six thousand objects sent by Mariette from the excavations at Serapeum: the great *Apis Bull*, jewels from the funerary chapel of Khaemouas, the god Bes, the Clot-Bey Collection of twenty-five hundred pieces—mainly funerary objects, and the celebrated *Seated Scribe*). By the end of the century, the collection had become unwieldy, and George Benedite, who had been named curator in 1895, reorganized it, eliminating a great deal of bric-a-brac. Objects continued to pour in, however, from a variety of sources, including the entire Egyptian collection of the Musée Guimet, transferred as part of a general exchange after World War II. Thus the Louvre today has the most important collection of Egyptian art outside of Egypt itself.

The earliest groups of works are a large quantity of small utensils, tools, and weapons that helped archaeologists establish a dating system for the Predynastic Period: knives with blades made from flint turned golden with age and ivory handles carved from hippopotomus tusks (of this group the most fascinating is the prehistoric knife of Gebel-el-Arka, about 3400 B.C., its handle decorated with a variety of animals, hunting scenes, and battles); palettes made of schist and similarly decorated (a palette with a bull, a palette with dogs—splendidly imaginative); many figurines of nude women (the *Concubines of the Dead Man*); stone vases and ceramic vases, including the *Gerzean Vase* from the Amratian Period at the end of the fourth millennium B.C., decorated with primitive, stylized, goatlike creatures, ostriches, and women performing a ritual dance. Some larger works belong to this period, most notably the stele of the Serpent King, from Abydos (Dynasty I, c. 3000 B.C.).

With the beginning of the Old Kingdom, large-scale monumental sculpture becomes more abundant: the most famous of these works undoubtedly being the *Seated Scribe*, from Sakkara (Dynasty V, c. 2500 B.C.), with his legs crossed, his hands poised on his papyrus scroll, and his abstractly chiseled face with inset

eyes gazing alertly outward. Among the earliest of these works, however, are
the two life-sized statues, *Sepa* and his wife, *Nesa* (Dynasty III, c. 2750 B.C.).
Of the many other statues from the Old Kingdom, the group of *Raherka and
Mersankh*, from Giza (Dynasty V, c. 2500 B.C.), is an especially fine conception
of a husband-wife relationship. The Dynasty IV holdings are very rich, thanks
to the objects from Abu Roash, including a palace-facade sarcophagus and the
classically serene red sandstone head of King Dedefre, c. 2600 B.C. Noteworthy
among the reliefs are the bas-reliefs from the mastaba of Akhuthotep (Sakkara,
c. 2500 B.C.), with their scenes of daily activities; the small sunken relief of a
girl with a lotus, pulling its blossom close to her head to smell its fragrance; the
little *Stele of Nefertiabet* (Dynasty IV), wearing a leopard skin and seated at a
table offerings. Among the architectural fragments of this period are three columns in pink granite, with lotus-leaf capitals (Dynasty V).

Works from the Middle Kingdom are primarily the fruit of excavation efforts
at Medamoud (many statues of Sesostris III: as a young man, in gray granite;
as an old man, in black granite; a statuette, in green schist; a lintel of Sesostris
III, in limestone, showing the king offering bread to the hawk-headed god
Moutou—all of these works from the first half of the nineteenth century B.C.),
at Tod (many small objects comprising the Treasury of Tod, dating from the
Old Kingdom as well as the New Kingdom, and some cups in pure Aegean
style), and at Assiut (objects from the tomb of Chancellor Nakht: an extraordinarily tall [sixty-nine inches] wooden statue of Nakht complete with inlaid
eyes, funerary furniture, coffin of Nakht with mystical eyes painted on the
outside, stele of Nakht; and *The Trough Bearer* [*La Poteuse d'auge*], a charming,
delicate statuette of a woman bearing offerings on her head). To this period
belong also the colossal statue of Sebekhotep IV (Dynasty XIII); the stele of
Iritisen, chief of the sculptors (twenty-first century B.C.); the stele and offering
table of Senpou in yellow limestone and alabaster (Dynasty XII); a tiny, ivory,
headless female figure, the abstract lines of its robe accentuating the curves of
its body (Dynasty XII); and probably the pink granite sphinx of Tanis (rather
than of the Old or New Kingdom).

All phases of New Kingdom art are represented. From the early part are a
block statue of Hapouseneb, Queen Hatchepsout's vizier, about 1500 B.C. (one
of several like this from different periods—one of the others is *Ou-ab-rah*,
sometimes placed in the Saitic Period); the golden bowl of General Thutti, given
to him by Thutmose II (Dynasty XVIII, 1504–1450 B.C.); an exquisite wooden
cosmetic spoon in the form of a reclining nude girl holding a duck (c. 1400
B.C.); several statues of the lion-headed goddess Sekhmet—one in black granite
from Karnak (Dynasty XVIII, 1405–1379 B.C.) is particularly fine; the *Chamber
of the Ancestors*, from the Festival Hall at Karnak, with its important List of
Royal Names; a remarkable example of the *Book of the Dead* (probably from
Thebes, c. 1400 B.C.), with vignettes showing the funeral of Neb-Qed; a royal
head (Amenophis III?) in red sandstone (1405–1370 B.C.); and many charming,
elegant statuettes of women, stylistically bordering on the Amarna Period: the
Lady Thuya, the Lady Nai, Queen Ahmes Nefertiti, and a young nude girl.

Heading the list of works from the Amarna Period (1370–1352 B.C.) are several portraits of Amenophis IV (Akhenaten) or of members of his family: Akhenaten and Nefertiti in high relief; a statue of Akhenaten as a young man; a bust of Akhenaten, in the idealized Second Amarna style; a royal head, opaque, two-toned blue faience glass formerly inlaid with stone and metal, sometimes thought to represent Tutankhamen; and a statue of Semenkhkare, Akhenaten's son-in-law, in yellow steatite. Among the other notable works are a lovely limestone head of a princess, her thickly braided black hair falling down one side of her head; a red quartzite torso of an Amarnan princess, with her draperies molded to her figure to form a beautifully abstract design on the surface; and a gaunt woman's head, from the top of a harp, in colored wood once inlaid with stone and metal in the eye sockets and eyebrows. To this period probably belongs the famous *Salt Head*, its ears pierced for rings and its features realistic, yet abstractly rendered.

The return to traditional styles in the post-Amarnan Period is also fully represented, beginning appropriately with a gray granite statue of Amun protecting Tutankhamen (the head of the young pharoah knocked off later by Horemheb to sever the link between his predecessor and the god) and continuing with work from Horemheb with scenes of lamentation. Notable among the works from the close of Dynasty XVIII is a limestone bas-relief of Amenmes and his wife, Depet, from Thebes. The beginning of Dynasty XIX is marked by several excellent works from the reign of Seti I (1318–1298 B.C.): bas-relief of Seti I and Hathor gazing at each other in silent communion and the *Stele of the Necklaces*, showing Seti I watching the investiture of one of his officials.

Representing the Ramesseid Period (1298–1166 B.C.) are several bas-reliefs of Rameses II (as a child; as a divinity; offering incense to the sphinx, found between the paws of the Great Sphinx of Giza); the magnificent golden pectoral of Rameses II, inset with stones and glass; the vat from the sarcophagus of Rameses III, showing the nocturnal voyage of the sun; and the *Libyan Captive*, a tiny bronze and silver statuette of a kneeling prisoner.

Several rooms are devoted to work of the late phases of Egyptian art, with small works, especially bronzes, prevalent. From the Pre-Saitic Period the bronze *Ichneumon Worshipper* (with the mongoose reared up on a lotus blossum, front paws raised, while a tiny devotee approaches with offerings, tenth century B.C.) and the ninth-century B.C. *Triad of Osorkon II*, a massive jewel of gold and lapis lazuli, are especially noteworthy as are the damascened bronze statuette of *Queen Karomama*, standing haughtily erect with hands poised in front of her; the *Aegis of Osorkon IV*, also of damascened bronze; and the wooden *Stele of Lady Tent Chenat*. The "Ethiopian" Dynasty XXV brings us the pharoah Taharka offering two wine cups to the Falcon God Hemen, in schist, wood, and bronze, and the wooden Memphite theology group, from Sakkara—both seventh century B.C.

Belonging to the Saitic Period of Dynasty XXVI (late seventh to sixth century B.C.) are the famous statue of Horus pouring out a libation (from the royal collection, remarkably large for an Egyptian work in this medium), a series of small bronze animals (a cat, an ibis, in wood and bronze), several images of the grotesque god Bes, a naos dedicated to Osiris by King Amasis, and two elaborate sarcophagi (of Djedkhonsouioufankh and of the Priest Taho). From the Post-Saitic Period is the large fourth-century *Apis Bull* and several stelae of Apis bulls, discovered at Memphis by Mariette; and a limestone falcon protecting a king, both Dynasty XXX.

The end of the era is marked by increasing evidence first of Greek influence in the arts (a firmly modeled torso of Isis, Ptolemaic Period) and then of Roman influence (a small bas-relief of Horus spearing the crocodile Seth, with Horus dressed in Roman costume, and a female portrait, second century, from Fayum— an extraordinary encaustic with bold application of pigment that anticipates Baroque usage).

Unlike painting, the number of sculptures in the royal collection at the time of the Revolution was relatively few, filling only two rooms and consisting mostly of some ancient statuary and the remains from defunct royal estates and public buildings. Also present in the Palace of the Louvre were works, mostly reception pieces, belonging to the Academy of Painting and Sculpture.

All of these pieces of sculpture were cleared out of the building in 1793 and sent to depositories at Versailles, the Petits-Augustins Convent, and the Hôtel de Nesle, joining objects confiscated from churches, châteaux, and parks. Eventually, most of them were to form the nucleus of the museum's Department of Medieval, Renaissance and Modern Sculpture (Département de la Sculpture du Moyen Age, de la Renaissance et des Temps Modernes) but only after a series of vicissitudes involving the partial dispersal (and subsequent partial repurchase) of these works, as France passed from the Revolutionary era, through the Napoleonic period, to the restoration of the Bourbons.

Since the new national museum was thought of as a collection primarily of paintings and secondarily of Graeco-Roman antiquities, it was not until after Waterloo, when most of the paintings that Napoleon had looted from the rest of Europe were returned to their owners, that anyone thought of exhibiting French sculpture to help fill the void left by the departed masterpieces. It was, however, only post-medieval sculpture that was considered worthy of a place in the building. The museum of French Monuments had been established under the direction of Alexandre Lenoir in one of the depots (the Petits-Augustins, now the home of the Ecole des Beaux-Arts). This was closed and a few select works were sent to the Louvre to join Michelangelo's two *Slaves*, which had gone there in 1794. In June 1818 a listing of these objects totaled just under fifty pieces.

The collection expanded very slowly during the next thirty years, but a period of rapid expansion began in 1848 under the guidance of Léon de Laborde, who was appointed that year and soon received the title Curator of Modern Sculpture. Eager to enlarge and revitalize the collection, Laborde began to gather in some but not all of the works that still remained at the site of the old Museum of French Monuments. After the February Revolution, he also succeeded in bringing back from Versailles some of the academy's works that had been deposited there.

Finally, he recalled other pieces that, unwanted, had been sent to other departments of the Louvre or to the old royal residences. Under his aegis, the first Gothic works became part of the collection. When Laborde left the Louvre in 1854, the collection numbered almost four hundred pieces, Italian as well as French.

Two decades of stagnation followed Laborde's departure, as the Department of Modern Sculpture was reabsorbed by the Department of Antiquities. Not until after the Franco-Prussian War of 1870–71 was it reestablished, but a new spurt of growth did not really begin again until 1874, when Louis Courajod arrived to preside over an expansion that saw the collection more than double, with a noticeable increase in works of the Italian Renaissance and the French Middle Ages as well as a more moderate enlargement of the number of later French pieces. Acquisitions continued during the twentieth century (even during the German occupation in World War II), and by 1970 the department boasted more than three thousand works in its care. This number will be reduced when the new museum of nineteenth-century French art (Orsay Museum) opens in the Gare d'Orsay.

The department is housed in a part of the ground floor underneath the Grande Galerie, beginning at the entranceway to the Cour du Carrousel. During the 1970s this area was reorganized and expanded, enabling the department to display seventeenth- and eighteenth-century French works that had previously been in storage.

By far the largest number of works in the collection are French, but only about a quarter of them are from the Middle Ages. Most of France's great medieval works are still in the places for which they were made, attached to the architecture they were intended to embellish. What the Louvre does have from this early period are primarily works salvaged from buildings now destroyed.

The earliest of these works is a marble capital from the Merovingian Basilica of the Holy Apostles, built by Clovis in the sixth century; the capital was recut when the church was rebuilt and rededicated to St. Genevieve, and the eleventh-century *Daniel in the Lion's Den* now appears on one side and traces of the original acanthus leaf design remain on the other sides. Most noteworthy of the twelfth-century Romanesque sculpture (along with some remains from St.-Denis and Cluny) is the figure *Christ*, which seems to have formed part of a deposition group. Polychromed and gilded, this life-sized wooden figure appears related to the sculpture by Gislebertus at Autun. Also worthy of mention are a head of St. Peter from Autun; a painted and gilded head of Christ from Levaudieu; a fine stone relief of St. Michael and the Dragon from Nevers; a wooden reliquary statue of the Virgin and Child from Auvergne, sculpted in a manner archaic even then; and the statues of Solomon and Sheba from Corbeil, whose more animated style heralds the approach of Gothic naturalism.

The first stages of that new era can be seen in several works from the great cathedrals of the thirteenth century: a youthful St. Matthew writing at the dictation of his angel, from the choir at Chartres; St. Genevieve from the Parisian abbey dedicated to her, carrying on her shoulders an angel who lights his candle and a devil (now mostly destroyed) who puts it out; Childebert from St.-Germaine-des-Près; and two wooden angels from Reims, one with a sober expression, the other a copy of the famous smiling angel from the cathedral. The fourteenth century's turn toward more worldly representations is evident in a series of elegant statues of the Madonna and Child, some painted and gilded, from the Ile de France. Portraiture is more evident, most notably in the statues of Charles V and Jeanne de Bourbon in the guise of St. Louis and Marguerite of Provence. Usually said to be from the Church of Quinze-Vingts, these two works are more probably from the east portal of the old Louvre.

Tomb sculpture is also more frequent during this era: Charles V is seen again in a reclining effigy, attributed to André Beauneveu. The most famous example of this latter type, however, belongs to the late fifteenth century: the six-foot-high *Tomb of Philippe Pot*. The faces of the heavily draped *pleurants* are lost inside the shadows of their deep hoods. The last stages of the Gothic era, extending into the sixteenth century, are highlighted by Michel Colombe's sculpture (including the stone relief *St. George and the Dragon* from Gaillon) and two works by Ligier Richier.

From the Renaissance period there are a greater number of works. The two major French sculptors of the sixteenth century are well represented. By Jean Goujon there are not only the *Caryatids*, built into the wall of a room in another section of the Louvre, but also reliefs from both the Fontaine des Innocents and the rood screens of St.-Germain-l'Auxerrois. By Germain Pilon are the effigies for the tomb of Henri II, the *Three Graces* monument for the heart of Henri II, the terracotta *Mater Dolorosa*, and the sculpture from the chapel of Cardinal Birague. There are also works by Pierre Bontemps (the statue *Charles de Maigny*) and Pilon's follower Barthelemy Prieur (funeral monument and effigies for Constable Anne de Montmorency and his wife). There also is the famous *Diana* of Anet, attributed at various times to either Goujon or Pilon.

The reorganization and expansion of this department in the 1970s has allowed considerably more attention to be paid to the seventeenth and eighteenth centuries. Most of Puget's surviving works are there: among them, *Milo of Crotona*, the *Hercules* executed for Fouquet but owned by Colbert, and the bas-relief *Alexander and Diogenes*. Also from the seventeenth century are the statue *Henri IV* by Tremblay, surrounded by four slaves that used to be around the pedestal of the statue of Henri IV on the Pont Neuf; Guillain's bronze group of *Louis XIII*, *Anne of Austria*, and *Louis XIV* as a child from the entrance to the Pont-au-Change; work by Sarrazin (*Monument of Cardinal de Bérule*, shown kneeling in ardent prayer, and reliefs for the *Heart of Louis XIII Monument*); and work by François Anguier (*Tomb of the Dukes of Longueville*, *Funeral Monument of the Historian de Thou*).

Much of the decorative work for Versailles by Girardon and Coysevox is here—most notably two sculpted marble vases by the former and the latter's

Crouching Venus, modeled on the antique work—in addition to portrait busts by the two. Coysevox's work is particularly numerous (the expressive *Tomb of Mazarin* and many of his portraits that mark the transition to the Rococo of the eighteenth century: the busts the Grand Condé and Charles Lebrun and the Duchess of Burgundy as Diana).

This final century of French sculpture in the Louvre is also richly represented. In addition to a fine number of realistic and intimate portrait busts (Pigalle's *Guérin* and *Self Portrait*), there is a delightful series of playful Rococo subjects: Pigalle's much-imitated *Mercury Putting on His Winged Sandal* and his wistful *Baby Boy with Open Bird Cage* (intended as a pendant to an antique sculpture of the coy *Baby Girl Holding a Bird*); Falconet's *Bather* and *Menacing Cupid* (also widely imitated); Bouchardon's *Cupid Making His Bow from Hercules' Club* (charmingly light-hearted); and Pajou's *Psyche Abandoned*. Visitors to the Graeco-Roman antiquities will find curious parallels between many of these and Late Hellenistic works. Houdon dominates the latter half of the century with many busts (*Diderot, Voltaire, Franklin, Washington, Mirabeau*, the *Brongniart Children*) and full-length statues (*Diana*).

After the French school, the Italian schools of the fourteenth to seventeenth century are most strongly represented. The most famous works are certainly Michelangelo's two *Slaves* from his early project for the tomb of Julius II (among the first sculptural works to enter the Louvre's collection), and Benevenuto Cellini's bronze *Nymph of Fontainebleau*, which had such a profound influence on the development of French sixteenth-century art. Reminders of Bernini's five-month stay in Paris are present in several terracottas by him; in addition, the Louvre has a bronze version of his *Bust of Urban VIII*. The Italian Renaissance is well represented: a *Madonna* by della Quercia; several works by Mino da Fiesole, including the *Bust of the Young Baptist*; two fine reliefs by Agostino di Duccio; the *Bust of Filippo Strozzi* by Benedetto da Maiano; *Beatrice d'Este* by Cristoforo Romano; and works by Desiderio da Settignano, Francesco di Giorgio, and the Della Robbia workshops. Giovanni da Bologna (a version of his bronze *Mercury,* and *Ferdinand I*, grand-duke of Tuscany) joins Cellini in giving the Louvre a sampling of Mannerist sculpture.

Other schools are poorly represented, but mention should be made of two German works, Tilman Riemenschneider's marble statuette *Kneeling Virgin* and the wooden *Magdalene* by Gregor Erhart, and a Spanish work, *Weeping Abbess* by Juan de la Huerta.

Despite its somewhat misleading name, the Department of Oriental Antiquities (Département des Antiquités Orientales) does not have works from China, Japan, India, or the neighboring areas, only from the Near East. There were enough of them early in the Louvre's history to warrant in 1804 the establishment of a special section within the Department of Antiquities, but it was not until 1881 that this unit was elevated to the status of a distinct department of its own. By that time French expeditions in the Near East had unearthed for its care an immense quantity of objects, some of them outstanding masterpieces. These works now occupy the entire northern half of the ground floor of the Square Court and are arranged by geographic location.

The successive civilizations that arose in Mesopotamia are amply represented in all phases, beginning with the Uruk period of Sumerian culture, in the fourth millennium B.C.: a group of ceramics from Susa, made from fine clay and decorated with a variety of geometric shapes, some suggesting animals or hunting scenes, some completely abstract (vase with Saluki hounds, Ibex vase), small stone statues; animal-shaped vases; many seals and cylinders—these last two types continue into the first centuries of the Christian era and are grouped together in chronological sequence.

For the first half of the third millennium B.C. are objects found during the French excavation of the Temple of Ishtar at Mari (the seated figure of the Intendant Ebih-il, found virtually undamaged, its portrait quality enhanced by the inset eyes of shells and lapis lazuli; a head of Ishtar wearing a polos; many stone statuettes of worshippers; a panel of a Mari king with naked prisoners, the figures carved in mother-of-pearl; a tiny warlord carved from a shell) and at Tello, formerly known as Lagash (the votive tablet of Urnanshe, going to lay the foundation stone of a temple; the famous stele of the vultures, celebrating a victory of King Eannadu, with its serried ranks of warriors marching inexorably over the corpses of the enemy; a dedicatory plaque of Dudu, priest of Ningirsu; a fine bull's head, its copper surface contrasting vividly with its shell-and-lapis-lazuli eyes—probably from a harp or a piece of furniture; the vase of Entemena, with its frieze of animals and a lion-headed eagle incised into its silver surface).

The Akkadian interlude (c. 2350–2150 B.C.) is represented primarily by objects that were taken as war plunder to Susa a thousand years later: fragments of the victory stele of Sargon I, who founded the empire, and its masterly presentation of the king ascending triumphantly to the mountain top over his fallen foes.

The Neo-Sumerian period of about 2150–1950 B.C. is richly represented: a large group of objects from Lagash (some fifteen statues of Gudea—about half of them known—standing, seated, a detached head with a turban; Gudea's drinking vessel, in dark green steatite, decorated with serpents and dragons; a headless statuette of Ur-Ningursu, Gudea's son, in alabaster; a head of a youth, in diorite, possibly representing Ur-Ningursu; many squat little statues of worshippers; the statuette of a woman with a scarf in steatite; the dog of Sumu-ilu; a terracotta figurine of a lion-headed demon strangling a bird; a copper figure of a kneeling god, driving a spike into the ground to bind evil spirits), another large group from the palace at Mari (murals in tempera on plaster, one of Ishtar investing King Zimrili, another showing a sacrificial scene—the earliest painting from this area in the Louvre; thousands of tablets from the record office of the kings of Mari, providing historians with a fruitful source of information about the period), and still another group from Susa (a large statue of the goddess Inanna, seated but headless; the bronze Sit-Shamsi, showing a ritual celebration of the sunrise; vases of terracotta with incised decorations encrusted with white paste).

Signaling the beginning of the first Babylonian era in the middle of the second millennium B.C. is the celebrated *Code of Hammurabi* showing the conqueror of Mesopotamia standing before the god Shamash at the top of a 7.5-foot black basalt stone on which are inscribed his 282 laws. Also dating from this period are a bronze and stone lion from the Temple of Dagon; a bronze statuette of the worshipper of Larsa with gold plating on its hands and face; and a head of Hammurabi, bearded, hollow cheeked, and weary, as if he already saw the Hittite invasion that would topple his dynasty.

Remarkable among the Middle Babylonian work of the latter part of the second millennium B.C. are an impressive series of *kudurrus*, milestone-shaped title deeds set up by the Kassites (*Kudurra of King Melishipak*, twelfth century B.C., transferring lands to his daughter); the headless, life-sized statue of Queen Napir-Azu, two tons of solid bronze; and the brick relief of a man-bull and interceding goddess (she has hooves instead of hands), the latter two works from Susa.

With the rise of the Assyrian kingdom in the first millennium, gigantic sculpture, usually relief and secular in theme, becomes more evident. Excavations at three major sites illuminate the reign of three distinctive kings: the Palace of Ashurnasirpal II at Nimrud, ninth century B.C. (eighty-five-inch-long bas-relief of Ashurnasirpal and attendant; and a winged genie sprinkling ceremonial water on a sacred tree—both of these works in gypseous alabaster); the Palace of Sargon II at Khorsabad (Gilgamesh and the lion, the fifteen-foot-tall hero holding a curved sword in one hand while a lion cub waits to be released from the embrace of his left arm; four gigantic winged bulls [three of them originals, the fourth a plaster cast]; a naval expedition to procure and transport wood for Sargon's palace; Sargon and his ministers; and a small bronze lion); and the Palace of Ashurbanipal at Nineveh (hunting scenes, one showing the king with his hand still grasping a spear as he thrusts it into a rearing lion; reliefs depicting scenes and miseries of war). Only a relatively few works come from the Neo-Babylonian era (625–538 B.C.), most notably a series of alabaster vases engraved with Nebuchadnezzar's name.

The invading Persian empire is represented primarily by works from Persepolis (bas-reliefs from the palace) and from Susa: large monumental works (the famous *Archers of the Persian Guard* and a winged bull, both reliefs of enameled bricks, fifth century, from the palace of Darius; a colossal double bull capital, nineteen feet high, in gray marble, from the palace of Ataxerxes II) and smaller ones (the *Charter of Darius*, a terracotta tablet engraved with the story of the building of his palace; a rhyton in the shape of an ibex, of bronze; a graceful and elegant winged ibex, in silver and gold, that was once a vase handle). Belonging to this area also, but coming from the mountainous region of Luristan rather than the cultural centers, is a small group of bronzes, dating from the latter part of the second millennium B.C.: idols, bits in varying shapes such as mountain goats or winged sphinxes, and standard tops.

Compared to the rich treasures unearthed in Mesopotamia and Persia, the collection from Anatolia and neighboring Cyprus is sparse, but it does include the earliest object in the Louvre: a small Anatolian idol, a glazed terracotta fertility image, highly abstract, that appears related to those discovered in 1960 near Hacilar, where one of the oldest-known cultures flourished around 5500 B.C. Much of the early Cypriot works are red lusterware ceramics (among them a goddess of fertility, flat and abstractly conceived, with a slight protrusion to indicate the nose, from the second half of the third millennium B.C.). Later works reflect the tug of different civilizations on the island: the *Hathor Stele*; a statue of a plump woman; an oenochoe with a bird design, seventh century B.C.; a vase of Amanthus, a stone ritual cistern, fifth century B.C.; a gold pectoral with sphinx; the *King of Cyprus*; and a veiled woman's head, perhaps representing Demeter, made of terracotta from the fourth century B.C. The Hittite works come primarily from French excavations at Arslan Tach and at Tell-Ahmar (a stele with the god Teshub, early first millennium B.C.), as well as from other places (a bas-relief of a stag hunt found near Malatya, ninth century B.C.; a stele of Tarnunpiyas, from Marash, c. eighth century B.C.).

Of the work from the Syro-Palestinian coast, Phoenician objects are most prevalent, primarily from the important international trading center of Ras-Shamra (Ugarit), and include a great many precious objects dating mostly from the second millennium B.C. (a patera of Ras-Shamra, with a circle of four ibexes in repoussé gold; a gold pectoral of Byblos; a charming ivory cosmetic box in the shape of a duck; a small bronze goddess—probably Astarte, goddess of fertility; an ivory box-lid showing two goats trying to get some ears of corn from the seated fecundity goddess; a large bas-relief in white limestone of Baal of Ras-Shamra, the storm god holding a bludgeon and a spear; and an impressive beaten gold funerary mask from the first millennium B.C., showing strong Mycenean influence) along with some larger works (a black sarcophagus of Eshmunazar, king of Sidon, fifth century B.C.) and some bronzes, usually small and sometimes plated with gold or silver (statuette of a god, from Ugarit, early second millennium B.C.; and a statuette of Jupiter of Heliopolis, third to second century B.C.).

Finally, there is a small group of objects from Dura-Europos: wall paintings of activities such as a wild ass hunt and statuettes such as a headless Aphrodite. There are also some works relating to the Judaic tradition, most notably a tall jar that contained some of the Dead Sea scrolls, second century B.C.-first century A.D., and the *Moabite Stone*, or stele of King Mesha, with its thirty-four-line inscription telling of his victories over the Israelites.

The decorative-art objects in the Department of Medieval, Renaissance and Modern Art Objects (Département des objets d'art du Moyen Age, de la Renaissance et du Temps Modernes)—precious works, enamels, ivories, pottery and ceramics, small bronzes, armor, tapestries, and furniture—were originally part of the Department of Sculpture before being separated into their own department in 1893. At the time of the Revolution, this collection included all of the objects that had been in the possession of the Crown, as well as objects confiscated from other places—most notably the Order of St.-Esprit, the Royal Abbey of St.-Denis and the Ste.-Chapelle—and from émigrés. Since then, it has been enlarged by donations and purchases and by the transferral, in 1901, of the contents of the National Furniture Museum. Until recently, the department's collection started with the beginnings of the Christian era, but the organization of the Department of Christian Antiquities in 1954 has narrowed the department's scope to Western works from about the Carolingian period on. As now constituted, the collection parallels that of the Musée des Arts Décoratifs, but whereas the latter's purpose is primarily documentary, the Louvre's collection concentrates on works of exceptional artistic merit. The objects are housed primarily around the Square Court, filling the entire east and north sides and half of the west side of the first floor, and spilling over into the Gallery of Apollo on the east face of the Grande Galerie wing.

Probably the most famous part of the department is the collection of precious works, thanks to the royal objects that were in the possession of the Crown or at St.-Denis and that are displayed in the Galerie d'Apollon. Some of the Romanesque works were made earlier but were then given a new setting: the *Eagle of Abbot Suger* (an antique porphyry vase that the abbot had encased in a gilded silver eagle), the rock-crystal *Vase of Eleanor of Acquitaine* and a sardonyx ewer (both given by Eleanor to Louis VII, who then gave them to Suger, who had them mounted in silver) are notable examples.

Belonging to the later Gothic era are the gold *Coronation Sword of the Kings of France* (said to have been Charlemagne's famous sword "Joyeuse" but modified in the fourteenth century); the exquisitely worked *Hand of Justice* (twelfth century but remounted for Napoleon's coronation in 1804); the *Crown of St. Louis* containing relics of the Holy Land (a Parisian work of the thirteenth century); Charles V's sceptre, fourteenth century; the famous *Virgin of Jeanne d'Evreux*, given to St.-Denis in 1339 by Charles le Bel's widow; and the rock-crystal, gilded, and enameled silver *Reliquary Arm of St. Louis of Toulouse*, from fourteenth-century Italy.

The Renaissance works come primarily from the Rothschild donation of 1900 (a Venetian censer, fifteenth century, and numerous other devotional objects—croziers, rosaries, Kisses of Peace—from Italy and Germany as well as France) and the church plate from the Order of St.-Esprit, founded by Henri III in 1578, known as *Kiss of Peace* and made of gilded silver with paintings under crystal, Italy. Of special note is the enameled gold shield and morion of Charles IX.

The core of the Baroque, Rococo, and neoclassic section is the Puiforcat Collection of silver and goldsmiths' work donated by Mr. and Mrs. Stavros S. Niarchos in 1955 (the golden goblet of Anne of Austria, seventeenth century; and silver-gilt trays made for King José of Portugal by Germain and a silver tureen by Joubert, both eighteenth century). The core is enriched primarily by late works from the royal collection (an extravagantly rich sard and onyx ewer shaped like a chalice and mounted on enameled gold, with a lid in the form of

Minerva on whose helmet a fierce dragon crouches—made in Italy and once owned by Louis XIV and the crown of Louis XV), by a superb collection of eighteenth-century snuff boxes, and by works from the Napoleonic era (the crown and coronation ring of Napoleon).

Closely related to the collection of precious objects and overlapping it at times is the enamelware. There are a considerable number of these pieces, both cloisonné and champlevé, ranging from the beginnings of the craft in the eleventh century through the seventeenth century. Noteworthy are the *Reliquary of the Arm of Charlemagne* (Mosan, twelfth century), the *Casket of the St. Louis* (enamel and metal on wood, Limoges, thirteenth century), and champlevé work from Limoges (*Eucharistic Dove* and *Ciborium of Alpais*, both thirteenth century) and Hildesheim (*Reliquary of St. Henry*, mid-twelfth century). The tiny *Self Portrait* by Jean Fouquet, of the mid-fifteenth century, marks the major shift toward fusing the enamel to make it resemble painting more closely. Of the large number of sixteenth-century works by Courteys, the Landins, Nouailher, the Courts, the Reymonds, and so on, the most noteworthy are certainly those by Léonard Limousin (*Portrait of the Constable Anne de Montmorency*) and his school. Seventeenth-century enamels are mainly watches with scenes taken from mythology and often inspired by paintings.

Several fine examples of Carolingian Renaissance begin the ivory collection: works by the accomplished Metz school (*Casket of the Childhood of Christ*, ninth-tenth century—an unusual type for this period; a scene of Samson and the lion on one side of a tenth-century liturgical comb used by priests after vesting) and by the Palatine school (*Dagulfe Psalter* covers, given by Charlemagne to Pope Adrian I) highlight this period.

Ivories of the Romanesque period are relatively scarce, except for a few plaques and some twelfth-century chessmen, but there is an abundance of Gothic work from the Paris workshops and elsewhere. These pieces are usually painted and frequently inspired by large sculpture. They include several particularly fine thirteenth-century examples: the poignant *Descent from the Cross*, part of a series that perhaps came from a reredos; the classically serene *Coronation of the Virgin* group; and the elegant *Virgin of Ste.-Chapelle*.

The collection of pottery commences with the introduction of fine wares in the Renaissance. The department has an extensive collection of richly decorated majolica from Italy; Spanish and French faience, ranging from the fifteenth through the eighteenth century and including several cases filled with the extravagant sixteenth-century work of Bernard Palissy (a faience plate profusely decorated with sea life; a temperance plate, ornamented with designs that Palissy molded onto pewter by François Briot), a case filled with pottery from the St.-Porchaire workshop, and others with the striking blue-white designs of faience from Rouen (sixteenth-eighteenth century).

Bronzes begin with an equestrian statuette traditionally identified as Charlemagne (more likely Charles the Bald), probably a ninth-century reworking of an antique piece. After that there is only a small scattering of this metal (a dramatic French gilt-bronze of Christ on the cross, from the later twelfth century; a candlestick of Hildesheim, featuring Samson riding the lion, from the thirteenth century) until the beginning of the Renaissance, when the number of works increased noticeably: small works by Donatello, or attributed to him (*Flagellation*); works by Riccio (*Poet Arion*); medals by Pisanello and Pilon; a sixteenth-century cast by Fancelli and Sansovino, *Spinario*; a marvelously grotesque *Morgante, Jester of the Medici*, with the subject sitting astride a barrel; and the lacquered bronze Mannerist *Black Venus* from Florence.

The only important complete suit of armor is a ceremonial one, said to have belonged to Henri II, ornamented with battle scenes. The *Helmet of Charles IX*, another ceremonial piece, is of enameled gold and belongs as much in the precious works category as here.

Most of the France's important medieval tapestries are in the Cluny Museum (q.v.), but a few have found their way into the Louvre: the *Virgin in Majesty*, dated 1485 (one of the earliest from the Brussels workshop); the early sixteenth-century *Mille-Fleurs Tapestry*, of French workmanship; a complete set of the *Maximilian's Hunt* (*Beautiful Hunt of the Guises*) tapestries, commissioned about 1535 by Charles V; and the *Noble Pastorale*, three tapestries from the Loire Valley. There are many more from the seventeenth and eighteenth centuries: several fine Gobelins tapestries, a Mortlake tapestry, *La Dance à Deux* from Beauvais (after Huet), and others by Nielson after Boucher.

The furniture collection includes a scattering of works from the Renaissance (the throne of the archbishops of Vienna, a cupboard attributed to Hugues Sambin, and others), but most belong to the seventeenth and eighteenth centuries, coming primarily from the royal properties. Several of the rooms have been arranged as period rooms, representing the styles of Louis XIV, Louis XV, and Louis XVI and fitted with appropriate tapestries and small works. Of special interest from the seventeenth century is the wrought-iron doorway taken from the château of Maisons and now leading into the Gallery of Apollo; a rock-crystal mirror, set in enameled gold and inlaid with stones, said to have belonged to Marie de' Medici; and a fine carved wooden circular table from Vaux-le-Vicomte—one of the many objects confiscated after Nicolas Fouquet's arrest.

The department is especially rich in eighteenth-century furniture, its holdings having been augmented by the donation of the Camondo Collection (kept in three rooms of their own). Most of the famous names of furniture making are represented: André Charles Boulle and sons (including the bureau of the Elector of Bavaria, made of ebony with marquetry in tortoise shell and brass, and a splendid ebony cupboard, inlaid with brass, pewter, tortoise shell, and bronze), Charles Cressent (the famous *Monkey Commode*, and a hanging wall clock from the king's audience chamber), and Martin Carlin (a neoclassic commode in Chinese lacquer).

Organized in 1954 by the gathering together of works that had been scattered around many locations, the Section of Christian Antiquities was formed to display the works from the first millennium of the Christian era in a more coherent fashion. Now elevated to the status of a department (Département des Antiquités Chrétiennes), its purpose is to focus on the new aspects of style and subject that were introduced with the rise of Christianity, rather than presenting the works as the end of three ancient civilizations.

The works are mostly examples of the minor arts—precious objects, ivories, ceramics, and textiles. Paintings mostly take the form of mosaics and encaustics, with some examples also of a tempera and oil mixture. Sculpture is primarily in the form of small marbles and bronzes and architectural fragments. All Byzantine works, even though very late, are included in this section to keep them together. Since the purpose is to show the development of the new style through the intermingling of different traditions, not all of the works in this section have a Christian theme; some are decidedly pagan.

Among the earliest of the precious objects is a small group of cameos (the *Rothschild Cameo*, c. 355; *Christ Crowned by Two Angels*, from the Treasure of Bourges Cathedral, a rare example of a cameo made after the fourth century). Notable among the goldsmith work are a fragment of a gold cup showing Jonah and the whale, set between sheets of glass, from a Roman cemetery, third-fourth century; a tiny silver and gold Sassanid horse head, from Persia but reflecting Greek influence, about fifth century; a Byzantine hunting scene and ornamental appliqué of gilt-bronze with silver inlays, probably part of a piece of furniture, Alexandrian school, fifth-sixth century; a sixth-century bird box; a marble serpentine paten with gold dolphin inlays, from the fifth-sixth century set into a border of the eighth-ninth century; the sumptuous gold and enamel *Maastricht Gospel Case*, inset with stones, illustrating the crucifixion, tenth-eleventh century; and the *Holy Women at the Sepulchre*, a twelfth-century silver repoussé work brought from Constantinople by the Crusaders.

The collection of ivories has a notable number of famous works, primarily from the Byzantine world: the statuette *Good Shepherd*, clad in a Roman tunic (end of the third century); *Rout of Silenus* (the third-century plaque from Alexandria); the *Diptych of the Muses* (sixth century); the *Barberini Ivory*, with its magnificent equestrian figure of an unknown emperor (fifth-sixth century); the *Consular Diptych*, with a sixth-century portrait of Areobindus on one side and a ninth-century *Temptation of Adam and Eve*, carved in Tours, on the other side; the *Harbaville Triptych* (tenth century); and a fine tenth-century wedding chest, found at Volterra, decorated with Homeric as well as biblical scenes.

Sculptural works from this period are all small, and mostly reliefs, with marble or limestone being the most prevalent materials, but also including some metalwork. They come from a variety of places: Italy, Egypt, Syria, Crimea, and Greece. One of the earliest, still strongly antique in style, is a fragment of a sarcophagus cover with Jonah and the whale, a Roman marble of the late third century. Of special interest are two eight-foot-high porphyry columns, with carved capitals from the fourth-century Early Christian Basilica of St. Peter's. Many of the earlier works are from the Crimea (an incised figure of Christ, beardless and extending an arm, fourth-fifth century) or Syria (a head of a man, possibly an emperor, fourth-fifth century; a basalt stele of St. Simon Stylite, late fifth century), along with a few limestone Coptic works, which become more prevalent in succeeding centuries: *Fish and Cross*, fourth-fifth century, from the cemetery of Erment; *Daphne* (?), fifth-sixth century, one of many fragments found in Sheh Abahd; *St. Sisinnios and the Serpent*, in high relief (looking very much like the late Egyptian relief of *Horus Spearing Seth*; a fragment of a cornice with two cherubim, sixth century; and a sixth-century tympanum of two harts drinking from a stream, from Fayum. Greek and Italian Byzantine works become more evident again later in this era: a sculpture of animals in combat, Greek, tenth-eleventh century; and a fragment of a chalice, Pomposa, eleventh-twelfth century.

Bronzes and other metal objects are mostly small works used for liturgical purposes: lamps, incense burners, eucharistic doves, crucifixes (one noteworthy example is an abstract crucifix in cast iron from Syria). A late work is a fourteenth-century door panel from Novgorod, showing St. John the Evangelist. Similarly, most of the ceramics had a liturgical use: lamps, ampules, and so on.

Since all of the Byzantine art has been grouped into this department, mosaics and paintings cover a wide range of centuries, from the third through the seventeenth. The early ones are in encaustic, on wood or cloth: *Portrait of Ammonius*, cloth, from Antinoe, third century; and *Portrait of a Young Girl Lying Down*, a third-century funeral cloth from Gayel. Later, the favorite medium becomes egg tempera and oil on wood: *St. John the Baptist*, Greece, fifth century; *Christ and the Doctors*, Novgorod school, fifteenth century; *St. Simon Stylite*, sixteenth century; and a large *Last Judgment* (height, 6.5 feet), probably from Moscow, seventeenth century. There are also a few mosaics, including one of the Transfiguration, probably from Constantinople, twelfth century.

Finally, there is a fine group of Coptic textiles showing a sea goddess and water games, fifth century, from the von Cledat Collection, and Dionysus, with motifs from the cult of Isis, probably from Antinoe, sixth century.

Joined in 1925 to the Department of Oriental Antiquities, the Muslim Art Section (Section des Arts Musulmans) has expanded considerably since the end of World War II and has begun to assume a semi-independent status with its objects arranged according to art form.

Many of the most famous works are the products of goldsmiths: the *Baptistry of St. Louis*, a fourteenth-century Syrian copper basin inlaid with silver (from St.-Denis via the royal collection); the *Barberini Vase*, a thirteenth-century Syrian bronze inlaid with silver; several richly ornamental aquamaniles (a twelfth-century Hispano-Moorish lion, another lion from Egypt of the tenth-twelfth century, a peacock from either Spain or Sicily); and many bronzes from Persia, Syria, and Egypt of the tenth-twelfth centuries, inlaid with precious metals, including an Egyptian parrot perfume box, about tenth-eleventh century.

Highlighting the glass collection are two fine rock crystals (one a chalice from the royal collection, the other an eagle from St.-Denis); six fine enameled glass mosque lamps—one with the name of Sultan el Hassan on it; an enameled glass goblet featuring three galloping horsemen from fourteenth-century Syria or Egypt; and a splendid tenth-century Egyptian water pitcher ornamented with parrots and spirals.

Included in the extensive collections of ceramics are many fine pieces of lusterware (a Persian cup with a camel suckling its young, ninth-tenth century; a Spanish plate with a pseudo-Arabic inscription forming an abstract blue design on a white ground, fifteenth century; a cup with female busts, faience from Egypt, tenth-eleventh century; and an Egyptian bowl of the eleventh century, featuring a hare and spirals); sixteenth-century Damasware (the *Plate with Floral Design* from the Rothschild donation); sixteenth-century Rhodesware; creamy white ceramics from Persia; green-toned Gabri ceramics; Nishapur ceramics; and a ceramic panel from the wall of the seventeenth-century Persian Pavilion of Forty Columns, showing four people seated in a garden in the manner of miniatures.

Miniatures in the collection also include a great many schools: Baghdad (*Pendulum Composed of Four Peacocks*, from a twelfth-century treatise on hydraulics), Mongolian (*Iskander [Alexander] on the Throne of Persia*, fifteenth century; *Pharamouz Pursuing the King of Kabul*, fifteenth century), Turkey, Hindu, Indo-Persian, Isfahan, Herat, and Tebriz.

The collection of fabrics and carpets are primarily from Persia (the shroud of St. Josse, silk woven with silver featuring an elephant motif, tenth century; a splendid woolen carpet of the twelfth century from the Cathedral of Mantes) and Egypt (a fine silk fragment with winged animals in a red and blue medallion, dated 1056).

Noteworthy among the sculpted works are a richly carved ivory box, dated 967–68, made for the prince of Cordova; and a stone bas-relief from Hamadan, Persia, carved on both sides with abstract images of animals, tenth-twelfth century.

GERALDINE E. FOWLE

Selected Bibliography

Museum publications: *The Louvre Museum, General Guide*, n.d.; *L'Antiquité Chrétienne au Musée du Louvre*, 1958; *Catalogue des Peintures*, vol. 1, *Ecole française*, 1972; *Peinture Ecole Française, XIVe, XVe et XVIe siècles*, 1965; *XVIIe et XVIIIe siècles*, 2 vols., 1974; *XIXe siècle*, 4 vols., 1958–61; *Catalogue raisonné des peintures du moyen-âge, de la renaissance, et des temps modernes. Peinture flamandes du XVe et de XVIe siècles*, 1953; *Département des Antiquités Egyptiennes, Guide-Catalogue Sommaire*, 1932; 1948; *Les Dossiers du Département des Peintures*, 1971-; *Inventaire général des Dessins, Ecole Française*, 1907-; *Ecole Italienne*, 3 vols., 1972-; *Ecoles du Nord: Ecoles Allemande et Suisse*, 2 vols., 1937; *Ecole Hollandaise*, 3 vols., 1929–33; *Ecole Flamande*, 2 vols., 1949; *Maitres des Anciens Pays-Bas Nées avant 1550*, 1968; *Vingt Ans d'Acquisitions au Musée du Louvre*, 1967; Beaulieu, Michele, *Les Sculptures, Moyen Age, Renaissance, Temps Modernes, au Musée du Louvre*, 1957; Charbonneaux, Jean, *La Sculpture Grecque et Romaine au Musée du Louvre*, 1963; Coche de la Ferte, Etienne, *L'Antiquité Chrétienne au Musée du Louvre*, 1958; "Section des Antiquités Chrétiennes," in *Vingt Ans d'Acquisitions au Musée du Louvre*, 1967; David-Weill, Jean, "Section des Arts musulmans," in *Vingt Ans d'Acquisitions au Musée du Louvre*, 1967; Devambez,

Pierre, "Département des Antiquités greco-romaines," in *Vingt Ans d'Acquisitions au Musée du Louvre*, 1967; Gauthier, Maximilien, *The Louvre*, 1962; Parrot, André, *Département des Antiquités Orientales et de la Ceramique*, 1947; Quoniam, P., *Le Louvre*, 1976; Salles, Georges, *Les Collections de l'Orient Musulman*, 1928; Vandier, Jacques, "Département des Antiquités Egyptiennes," in *Vingt Ans d'Acquisitions au Musée du Louvre*, 1967; Vitry, Paul, *Catalogue du Sculpture du Moyen Age, de la Renaissance, et des Temps Modernes*, 1922; Supplement, 1933.

Other publications: Aulanier, Christiane, *Histoire du Palais et du Musée du Louvre*, 11 vols. (Paris 1971); Bazin, Germain, *The Louvre*, translated by M. I. Martin (New York 1958); Blum, André, *Le Louvre, du Palais au Musée* (Paris 1946); Blunt, Anthony, *Art and Architecture in France: 1500–1700*, 2d ed. (1970); Clay, Jean, and Josette Contreras, *The Louvre* (Paris 1980); Hautecoeur, Louis, *Histoire du Louvre, le château— le palais—le musée, des origines à nos jours*, 1200–1940, 2d ed. (Paris n.d.); Hourticq, Louis, *A Guide to the Louvre* (Paris 1923); Huyghe, René, *Art Treasures of the Louvre* . . . *with a Brief History of the Louvre* by Milton S. Fox (New York 1951, London 1960); Levallois, Pierre, *Treasures of the Louvre*, 2 vols. (New York 1966); Prache, Anne, *La Sculpture au Musée du Louvre* (Paris 1967); Regoli, G. et al., *Louvre, Paris* (Great Museums of the World) (New York 1967); Villard, F., "La réorganization du département des antiquités greques et romaines au Musée du Louvre," *Revue Archéologique*, ns. 1: pp. 190–92, 1980.

JAMES L. CONNELLY, YVONNE A. LUKE, AND GERALDINE E. FOWLE

NATIONAL MUSEUM OF MODERN ART (officially MUSÉE NATIONAL D'ART MODERNE; also CENTRE NATIONAL D'ART ET DE CULTURE GEORGES POMPIDOU; alternately THE POMPIDOU CENTER, THE BEAU-BOURG), Plateau Beaubourg, 75191 Paris.

The National Museum of Modern Art (Musée National d'Art Moderne; MNAM) dates from 1818, when during the early Restoration period Louis XVIII decreed the creation of a museum, the Musée des Artists Vivants, to house the works of contemporary artists, and designated for this purpose the former Luxembourg Palace. The new museum was to have only a transitional status, since works entered on a temporary basis before being assigned to either the Louvre or other national and municipal collections. This process was regulated by a flexible chronological criterion, with the original period having been set at ten years and later extended to fifty years after the artist's death. Finally, one hundred years after the artist's birth was chosen as a suitable test date.

In 1886 the growing collection was moved to the renovated Orangerie of the Luxembourg; in 1888 a new room was inaugurated to house the works of living foreign artists; and by the turn of the century an additional annex was added for the Caillebotte bequest. By 1922, due to lack of space, the Fine Arts Commission (Direction des beaux arts) had created an individual section for living foreign artists whose works were then moved to the Musée des Ecoles Etrangères Contemporaines of the Jeu de Paume des Tuileries. From 1922 the Jeu de Paume (q.v.) exhibited works of French-domiciled although not yet French-naturalized artists, such as Picasso, Kupka, Chagall, and Foujita, as well as works by foreign artists such as Permeke and Klee.

While the system of reviewing and transferring the collections was serving the experimental nature of the Luxembourg and its annex, the Jeu de Paume, the state-controlled acquisition policy was focusing on Salon paintings, reflecting the prevailing system based on standard academic values. Therefore, important gaps inevitably became apparent in the historical sequence of nineteenth- and twentieth-century French art as represented at the Luxembourg. Gifts by the Society of Friends of Living Artists of the Luxembourg Museum and its affiliate, the Society of Friends of Living Artists, were unable to fill these gaps, especially those of the Cubist painters. Following a reversal of holdings in 1929, the museum's display policy allowed for supplementing of its collections with a system of loans offered by both collectors and living artists.

In 1936 the decision to create a state museum of modern art (Musée National d'Art Moderne) at the Avenue du President Wilson in the Palais de Tokyo already showed signs of a significant break with the existing concepts of French museology. The foundation stone was laid in 1937, but the outbreak of war slowed construction, and the Musée National d'Art Moderne saw only a partial opening in 1942. (By 1940 the Luxembourg and the Jeu de Paume had seen their doors closed and their treasures evacuated.)

It was finally in 1947 with its official inauguration that the fusion of the two museums took place, thus abolishing the distinction between French-naturalized and nonnaturalized artists (whose work was essentially created in France) and leading the way to the creation of what was to become known as the Ecole de Paris.

The MNAM had benefited at its start from many artists' generosity. In 1947 Picasso gave ten paintings, of which *The Milliner's Workshop* (1925), *The Muse* (1935), *The Aubade*, and a sequence of still lifes were characteristic of his style of the thirties and during the war. Exactly ten years later Brancusi bequeathed to the MNAM his entire workshop, the faithful reconstruction of which, as requested in his will, became the impetus for a series of similar gifts and bequests by sculptors. As a result, the MNAM may boast of being unique in its repository richness of *fonds d'ateliers*.

In Brancusi's case, these studio holdings did comprise a considerable body of works. They have provided the MNAM with the plaster sequences for all of his projects, most of which he used to advance his work simultaneously. Particularly notable are the versions for *Mlle. Pogany* (1913, 1920, 1933), *The Sleeping Muse*, *The Newly Born* (1915, 1920), *Bird in Space*, and *The Kiss*. The MNAM also holds the wooden versions for the *Endless Column*, bronze versions of the marble *Princess X*, stone versions for *The Kiss*, a series of elaborate socles, and his fresco studies and earlier works done in Romania.

Most outstanding in the sequence of important post-war donations to the MNAM has been Rouault's bequest of a group of unfinished works. Among these 888 works that were given to the museum in 1959 by his daughter Isabelle Rouault as "documents," an unusual status, are unpublished projects for all of Rouault's print series, independent and preparatory gouaches, and oils and drawings covering a large thematic range for paintings. Also included are 200 works never displayed but available as a study collection for researchers.

A further step was achieved in support of the Musées Nationaux's purchase policy by establishing a state fund, the Fonds National d'Art Contemporain (administered by the Service de la Création Artistique), whose holdings were to complete the national collections and to facilitate extended loans to provincial museums. The establishment of this fund led to the creation in 1967 of a new experimental organization, the Centre National d'Art Contemporain (CNAC), which played a pivotal role in bringing together modern and contemporary art theories and actual collections.

The final incorporation of the Museum of Modern Art within the Pompidou Center, a many-faceted cultural entity, led to a new partition between the collections of the museum, with the majority of works being transferred to the center and the remainder, currently housed primarily in the Jeu de Paume, the Palais de Tokyo, and the Louvre (q.v.) will be moved to its permanent home, the Orsay Museum (q.v.).

Additional major donations at the MNAM, are Sonia Delaunay's gift of fifty-nine works of her husband as well as fifty-eight of her own, which make the MNAM the richest repository of their works. Delaunay's Divisionist, Cézanne-like, and Cubist phases are followed by landmarks such as *La ville de Paris* and *Manège de cochons*. Delaunay's career is clearly outlined by the *Prose de Trassiberien* and works related to her studies on "simultaneité" (for example, *Electric Prisms*), religious projects (e.g., commissions for churches), and her last series consisting of prisms.

Twenty paintings as well as twenty gouaches and drawings were given to the MNAM from the Dufy bequest covering all of his styles. This was then supplemented by tapestries and the working studies for *La fée électricité*, which were added to the ten paintings already in the museum.

The Claude Laurens gift of two hundred works of his father, Henri Laurens, range from paintings to plasters and terracottas, wood constructions, and Cubist stone sculpture. His bronze series includes state commissions and marine themes such as *Les ondines* and *La nuit*. The purchase of Laurens' *Papiers collés* complete this panorama.

The Jacques Yula Lipchitz Foundation has selected specific holdings of works done while in Paris from the sculptor's *fonds d'atelier*: ten terracottas and one stone relief covering his abstract and Cubist pieces, his portraits, the *Plumanach* variation, as well as late mythological and religious themes. Five bronze purchases complete the series.

Other *fonds d'atelier* are that of Despiau and include a series of works in plaster and wax for his portrait studies, and Duchamp-Villon's sculptural ensemble, including his Puteaux beginnings, relief drawings, and a set of original works in plaster, for example, *Portrait of Professor Gasset*. The Gaudier-Brzeska grouping of gouaches and fifteen representative sculptures was a gift of the Kettl's Yard Foundation (e.g., *Oiseau avalant un poisson*).

The most prestigious acquisition of the MNAM remains thus far the Kandinsky estate, bequeathed by Nina Kandinsky. In her three previous gifts, practically all of his artistic periods (Murnau, Bauhaus Berlin, and Paris) were represented with important groups of related works, including the maquettes for the Jurisfrei exhibition. With the bequest the various periods of his work are fully represented, as are the Kandinskys' personal collections of works.

Other than the major *fonds d'atelier* given by artists and their families, the collection of the museum has representative works relating to major movements of the twentieth century.

Matisse's pointillist *Luxe calme volupté* (1904) precedes the sequence of art movements in the first part of the decade. Braque's port views at Estaque, Derain's *Two Barges*, Vlaminck's *Paysage aux arbres rouges*, Matisse's *Le luxe*, and Dufy's street scenes complete these particularly important Fauve holdings. The early Cubist studies include Picasso's *Tête de femme rouge* (1906), a key piece in his works of figures, as well as Braque's "Cézannian" landscapes, early Cubist compositions (*Les usines du Rio Tinto*), still lifes and papiers collés (*Violon et pipe*). In addition to Delaunay's important contemporary holdings, a group of works by Gleizes, Metzinger, Lhote, and Marcoussis complete the artistic scene in Paris during the Cubist and the "Section d'Or" movement. The Cubist movement is continued chronologically with five works by Juan Gris. Individual figures such as Rousseau, Chagall, and Modigliani are represented with important paintings. De'Chirico's *Portrait prémonitoire* and Matisse's portrait *Auguste Pellerin* are also to be noted.

The presence of works by the Brücke artists is extremely limited. The MNAM owns two Pechsteins, one of which is *Three Nudes in a Landscape*, and only two Kirchners painted in Berlin (including *Le couple*). Nolde's *Nature morte aux danseuses*, two paintings by Macke, and a head by Jawlensky fill the substantial gap in the sequence of avant-garde movements in the first part of the twentieth century. Equally limited is the collection of Futurist works with only Russolo's *Dynamism of an Automobile*, Severini's *La danse de l'ours au Moulin Rouge*, Ballà's *Le planète Mercure passant devant le soleil vue au téléscope*, five paintings by Magnelli, and Cardoso's *Les cavaliers*.

The earliest stages of Russian Rayonism can be seen in Larionov's composition *Portrait of Tatlin* and Gontcharova's *Electric Lamps*. The collection also contains a gift from Pugny, which includes paintings, papiers collés, and counterreliefs by the artist. Often through gifts the MNAM has assembled a unique collection of Malevich's work. It includes the Suprematist painting *La croix noir no.1* (1915), with two other versions in plaster and five unique *Architectones*, which were recently reconstructed (e.g., *Gotha*), and groups of ornamental Suprematist works and late figurative drawings and paintings of symbolic character. Also included in this group are the two *Ptoun* studies by Lissitzky, Sternberg's reconstructed *Spatial appareillage*, and Mansouroff's drawings for the Red Square in Moscow.

The Constructivist holdings came primarily as a gift by Virginia Pevsner and include eight post-war sculptures, maquettes, earlier paintings, and memorabilia of Pevsner. Also included are the *Mask* (1923) and the crystal *Linear Construction in Space* by his brother Gabo.

Among Dada holdings at the MNAM are two major works: Hausmann's assemblage *L'esprit de notre temps* and Picabia's *L'oeil cacodylate*. There are also objects, masks, and plaster reliefs by Janco; paintings and Dada reliefs by Arp (e.g., *Head-Moustach-Bottle*); Tauber-Arp's marionettes; objects and assemblages by Man Ray; and Berlin montages by Baader and Höch.

Also represented in the collections but in limited numbers are the relatively brief post-war movements: German satire and *Sachlichkeit*, and Grosz' collage and photomontage *Remember Uncle August*; portraits by Dix; and Beckmann's *Les bucherons*. Paintings by Morandi and Casorati demonstrate Valori Plastici and Italian realism. Ozenfant's *Nacres*, Le Corbusier's *Nature morte*, and the works of Léonce Ronsemberg are typical examples of French Purism.

Individual personalities of the 1920s running parallel to these movements are also found in the museum's historical sequences. Good examples are Herbin's figurative paintings, Gromaire's *Loterie française*, Soutine's *Le groom*, Sima's *Double paysage*, and Freundlich's *Ascension*.

The early Surrealist holdings at the MNAM include: two works by Miró (*Le Catalan* and *La Siesta*); by Ernst, *frottages* and collage paintings, including later works such as *Loplop présenté à une jeune fille*; Dali's *Partial Hallucination— Six Images of Lenin on Piano*; two major pieces by Magritte (one of which is *Double Secret*); Tanguy's *Le palais aux rochers des fenêtres*; and works by Masson, including a sand painting, *La terre*.

Giacometti is represented in the collection of sculptures by his wood objects, the original plaster cast of *La table*, and three Surrealist assemblages from 1937. Also included are Bellmer's *La poupée*, Miró's *L'Objet du couchant*, Brauner's *Le loup-table*, collages by Eluard and Hugnet, and a series of collaborative drawings *Cadavres exquis* by André Breton and his friends.

The museum also owns sculptures by Zadkine, Gargallo, and a large representational group of about two hundred works by González. Of special note is the *Masque de Moserrat criant*.

With Wols' two oils *La grenade bleue* and *L'Aile de papillon*, France's most important artistic movement of the late forties, the Informel, is introduced. Fautrier's personal impasto technique (*haute pâte*) can be seen in his nude compositions; *La femme douce* and a collection of gouaches, drawings, and a bronze head represent the artist's mature period. Dubuffet's career, which parallels that of Fautrier, can be followed in a sequence of eleven works and a polystyrene architectural environment (*La campagne heureuse*) in which his serial themes and his textural experiments blend together. From this period, the MNAM has a large number of watercolors, gouaches, mescaline drawings, and China-ink paintings by Michaux, a gift from a French foundation (Fonds D.B.C.), as well as drawings and paintings by Chaissac and the *Précambryen* by Bryen.

The MNAM has benefited from a series of generous gifts that were made by many abstract painters of the French tradition who emerged during the Occupation and were active in the fifties and the sixties. These specific holdings now include a series of religious works by Manessier, seven representative compositions by Estève, *Vent de mer* and other works by Bazaine, four oils by Singier, fifteen paintings by Beaudin, works by Lanskoy, and sixteen paintings by Bissière (e.g., *La venus noire*).

The museum has works by Atlan, eleven compositions representative of Poliakoff's work, Vieira da Silva's *La bibliothèque*, and paintings by Szenes. These holdings were further enriched by the purchase of Hartung's most significant early work, *T 1935-I 1935*, and by a group of paintings by de Staël, including his first important piece, *La vie dure*. In addition to these works, a sequence of lyrical and gestural abstract paintings by Soulages, Mathieu (*Les capetiens partout*), and Riopelle (*Chevreuse*) are presented, as well as contemporary abstract compositions by Schnieders, Martensen, Tosimitsu Imai, and Zao-Wou-Ji (*Composition bleue*).

The CoBrA movement is represented at the MNAM by Jorn's *Dovvre Grube* and some of his late canvases. The holdings also include Appel's *Femme et oiseau*, works by Bram and Geer van Velde, and examples of Alechinsky's Expressionist approach in the fifties, as seen in *Au pays de l'encre*. In addition are represented in the collection other individual Expressionist artists of the same period, such as Tamayo and Sutherland. Bacon's *Trois personnages dans une pièce* should also be mentioned.

The second generation of Surrealists has entered the collection with representations by Lam, who worked in the United States (*La réunion*); by Matta, a concave mural work dedicated to Grimau; Delvaux (*L'Acropole*); and also works by Labisse and Roy and holdings by Czechoslovakian artists Toyen, Styrsky, and Zrsavy.

The collection of post-war French and European sculpture shows the variety of materials and methods that were in use. Included among the most important exhibits are Hadju's *Cerf volant*, slate torsos by Ubac and Dodeigne, Lardera's *Spirale rompue*, Stahly' *Big Wood*, Penalba's *Hommage à César Vallejo*, Giacometti's *Large Standing Figure*, and Richier's *L'Ouragan et l'ouragane*. Also in its post-war holdings, abstract geometrical sculpture in France is represented by compositions by Gorin and especially by a group of marbles and yellow bronzes by Giglioli. Among works based on modular systems there is a granite version of Bill's *Endless Ribbon*. The museum's holdings of Swiss concrete art includes paintings by Bill, a study of Lohse on vertical rhythms, Graeser's *Strukter Progression*, works by Honneger, and the *House* by Tuttle.

The important gift by Zoltan Zemeny in 1968 is composed mainly of his six reliefs, which exemplify the progression of his work done in parallel, especially *Pensée traité en forme*; and Calder's pre-war motor experiments, such as *White Disk, Black Disk*, which was further developed into five mobiles and a stabile, partially a gift from the artist.

European work experimenting with different media is exemplified by Burri's

Sacco e Bianco and two burned plastics, Manzoni's *Achroma*, Tapiès' *Grand Blanc Horizontal 19*, and Millares' *Quadro 120*. Teresita Fontana's impressive gift of six punctured canvases experimenting in perforations, accretions, and cuts (forming a chronological grouping that is crowned by three late *Concetti Spaziali*) is also displayed.

The start of a new collection of post-war American art for the MNAM was due essentially to the generosity of the American cultural foundations and individual donors. To the previous Jeu de Paume American holdings are now juxtaposed the two generations of Abstract Expressionists. Masson's *La pythie* (1943), a landmark in the artist's American phase, acts as an introduction to Pollock's *Moon-Woman Cuts the Circle* (1943). Gorky's *Landscape-Table*, two Cornell assemblages, Pollock's last statement, *The Deep*, Reinhart's *Ultimate Painting No. 6*, and Newman's *Shining Forth, to George* are included in this collection. Paintings by Rothko and Still and Tobey's figurative gouaches such as *The Unknown Journey* are to be noted. Sam Francis' "all-over" can be seen in *Otherwhite* and *In Lovely Blueness*. Also included are a relational painting by Stella, *Mas o Menos*, Kelly's geometrical abstraction *Yellow-Red*, Noland's *Air* and works by Frankenthaler and Mitchell. Other contemporary American examples can be seen in Nevelson's *Tropical Garden II* and a collage by Conner (*Screen*). The museum has four paintings by Albers, including *Affectionate*, and a tondo by Glarner.

At the MNAM the sequence of French Nouveau Realisme holdings is preceded by Dewasne's antisculpture *Tombeau d'Antoine Webern*, and the lacerated posters on paper and on sheet-iron by Villeglé and Hains. Klein's *Ci-git l'Espace* and the portrait relief *Arman* resume the protagonist's activities. Of particular importance are: César's *Compression de voiture; Ricard;* Arman's manifesto in gestural aesthetics, *Chopin's Waterloo*; and Etienne Martin's chasuble *Le manteau*, all dating from 1962. Six representative works by Raysse introduce neon and other industrial materials into sculpture (e.g., *America-America*); as do Saint-Phalle's *La mariée* and later sculptures, Spoerri's *Le marché aux puces*, Christo's *Table empaquetée*, Deschamps' *Les chiffons japonais*, and "sculpture-objets animés" by Malaval.

The MNAM has transferred in its entirety the Nice gallery, Magasin de Ben, which had been the center for all of the art activities performed there for more than a decade by Ben Vautier. Fluxus artists Brecht and Vostell are represented with assemblages; Beuys' felt piano *Infiltration Homogen für Konsert Flugel* (1966) represents an excellent summary of German Fluxus attitudes.

Dado's visionary Surrealism is represented with *Le massacre des innocents*; Requichot's wth accumulated shrines such as *Reliquaire de papiers choisis* and Raynaud's assemblage *Psycho Objection*.

As with the American Abstract Expressionists, the MNAM's sequence of Pop artists and their precursors was strengthened by memorial gifts and donations from the Scaler and Menil foundations. Added to Lichtenstein's *Modular Painting* and Rosenquist's *Presidential Election* were Jasper John's early *Figure 5*, heart paintings by Dine, and Warhol's *Electric Chair*; also two soft sculptures by Oldenburg including *Ghost Drum Set*; Rivers' painted construction *I Like Olympia in Black*; and Rauschenberg's *Oracle*, a five-part motorized audio sculpture made of junk pieces. Oppenheim's *Attempt to Raise Hell*, Segal's *La caissière*, and a chamber assemblage by Kienholz are the major examples of American environmental sculpture at the MNAM. The recently purchased primary structure by LeWitt (*Five Cubes*), Judd's *Stacks*, and Bell's *Cube 2* are examples of American minimal sculpture and Los Angeles formalism in the late sixties and early seventies.

The first part of the MNAM's holdings in Optical Art and the Fringe Area was a comprehensive group of early Vasarély oils, collages, an aluminum contruction (*Hommage à Malevitch*), and late "net-paintings" that were offered by the artist himself. Added to this are three of Soto's studies in visual kinetic effects, including *Double écriture*, experiments by Cruz-Diez, Morellet's *Double trames*, and Agam's transformable *Double metamorphoses III*.

A scrap-metal sculpture by Stankiewicz, *Europe on a Cycle*, introduces Tinguely's early *Meta-mechanical Automobile Sculpture* (1954) and his first successful consistent-drawing machine, *Metamatic No.1*, and, finally, a large kinetic construction, *Meta Sculpture*.

The MNAM acquired Malina's mobile painting *Orbits III Lumidynes System* and has other examples of kinetic work associated with the medium of light, such as Schöffer's *Chronos 8*, and the multiple applications of magnetism, such as in Bury's wooden *4057 Cylindres érectiles* and Takis' recent magnetic and light ensemble, *Méduse*.

The MNAM's collection of French and foreign-based artists working with composite or transposed images includes at present only a part of the state's holdings in this specific area, with the rest being gradually assigned a future date: Monory's *Murder 10*, Racillac's *Horloge Indienne*, Fromanger's *En Chine á Hu-Xian*, Stampfli's *Gala*, Rainer's *Gluck*, and *Maijakowsky* by Solbes and Valdes, both members of the Spanish Equipocronica group. Arroyo's narrative figuration *The Four Dictators*; Adami's *Thorwaldsen*; Recalcatti's *Self Portrait*; Pistoletto's *Femme au cimetière*; and two variable game paintings by Fahlstrom, including *The Cold War*, are also to be noted.

The two-sided French movement Support/Surface forms another distinctive group of holdings in which the deconstructive theory of painting and art as an artisan's practice are both exemplified. Included are Barre's two time-displaced canvases, *6OT 545*, and Cane's *Grille*. Among Rouan's various paintings, noteworthy are *Tressage-Papier*, a series of unstretched and reversible paintings by Viallat (*Bache*), Hantai's early experiment *Rosa Tabula*, Meurice's *Penelope*, Jacquard's charred canvas *Trophée*, Saytour's *Trempage*, and Support/Surface materiology, with Page's *Colonne* and Flannagan's parallel experiment *Casb*. In parallel, American works through analytical technique are represented: Hill's *Vitaphore*, Renouf's *New York Sound*, and Reed's method of wet-in-wet working *No. 73–197*.

Within the vast framework of Conceptual Art, various "language-oriented" works by both European and American conceptualists have been acquired gradually by the MNAM: Atkinson's written text *Introduction*, communication pieces by Barry, proposals by Anderson, and a group purchase of schemas and pieces featured at the Wilson-Claura Exhibition and Bochner's *Reading Alternatives*. Also included in this collection are date paintings by On Kawara, Venet's conceptual drawings, and Kosuth's *One and Three Chairs*. Examples of other aspects that use photography instead as a reconstructive method are Dibbet's use of perceptual conflict in his *Big Comet* and Tremlett's *Puglia*. Pure photographic research relating to nonsubjective documentation for the reconstruction of the past can be seen in Boltansky's *Les images modèles*; photography and text in Le Gac's *Le professeur de dessin* as well as various other texts and drawings with photographs by Fulton, Pfeiffer, and Sanejouand; and two works by Buren (*Les couleurs-sculptures* and *Les formes peintures*).

A selection of exhibits relating to both conceptual and environmental art are in the MNAM's collection of contemporary art: Dan Flavin's *Untitled (to Donna)*; Mario Merz's progression series with his *Crocodilus Fibonacci*, a twenty-two-meter-long installation with a fossilized alligator; Acconci's audiotape and neon chamber *The American Gift*; Dan Graham's video piece *Present Continuous Past*; and Nam Paik's *Video-Fish*.

The MNAM's ever-increasing holdings of sculpture of the seventies in various media already include: Panamarenko's metal flying machine *Meganeudon I*, De Andrea's hyper-realist *Couple*, Ruckreim's geometric split piece *Dolomite*, Serra's *5:30*, Steiner's *High and Wide 2*, Andre's carved cedar *Black Creek*, Grand's *Bois ecorcé*, Brown's *Earth Markers*, Mosta-Heirt's oak and pine ensemble *Vicking*, Simond's archaeological tabletop *Abandonned Observatory*, and Reutersward's art and technology assemblage, the conceptual piece *Killroy*, which introduces lasers and holograms. The land artist Richard Long is represented with a wood and flint circle. Also represented are works by Bertholin.

Body and performance art have made their way into the permanent collection, with photographs recording ephemeral artistic actions: Pane's *Corp presentie*, or photographic reports on canvas; Luthi's self-portrait; and the triptych *Pink Depression*, by B. and M. Leisgen.

Italian identity artists activating the cult of poverty in materials within a conceptual framework are also represented by Penone's terracotta *Soffio*, Kounellis' *Untitled*, Paolini's *Caryatid*, and Buraglio's *Fenêtres*.

In the present provisional survey of the recent painting acquisitions at the MNAM, clear-cut divisions cannot be applied. However, specifically represented are the German developments in the last ten years with Penck's pictogram *TM 1974*, Polk's *Cameleonardo da Willich*, Baselitz's expressionistic *Die Mädchen von Olmo*, and Bishop's spacial analysis of the surface in *No-Title*. Ryman's studies on luminosity in *Criterion I* and Charlton's slot painting *Peinture 1971*, have proved the new awareness of monochrome's potential.

The limited holdings of the most recent paintings (1982–83) have also revealed the existence of the New Figuration movement with Szafran's pastel *Imprimerie* and Garouste's *Orthros et le classique*, which runs parallel to the New Subjectivity of Arikha's *Alba*. Present also are strong individualities, such as van Elk, Lindner (*Et Eve*), Klapheck, and Sarkis.

Since its creation the MNAM's Prints and Drawings Department (Cabinet graphique) has grown steadily. Therefore, nearly all important individual holdings have included a selection of graphic works, selections that were carefully chosen by the artists themselves. The recent acquisition policy is oriented toward all the various aspects of contemporary drawings within the abstract and figurative fields. Although artists whose graphic work is most appreciated by the acquisition committee enter the contemporary collections on a preferential basis, recent group purchases of American and Czechoslovakian drawings have enriched the department in different areas and filled the gaps that were missing in the various artistic and historical sequences. Acquisitions of major importance have been Titus Carmel's cycle of 129 drawings (*The Pocket Size Tlingit Coffin*) and a room-sized, five-piece environmental drawing with life-sized figures by Gilbert and George.

In addition to the above-mentioned permanent exhibits, various temporary exhibitions are held on the fifth floor and in the two areas on the ground floor of the center.

Selected Bibliography

Museum publications: *Musée National du Luxembourg. Catalogue-Guide peintures, Mars 1929;* Hautecoeur, Louis, and Pierre Ladoué, *Musée National du Luxembourg. Catalogue des peintures et Sculptures*, 1933; Musée National d'Art Moderne, *Exposition Permanente, Catalogue*, 1942; idem, *Catalogue-Guide*, 1947; 1954; *100 Oeuvres Nouvelles, 1974–76*; *100 Oeuvres Nouvelles, 1977–1981*; Georgel, Pierre, *Acquisitions du Cabinet d'art Graphique, 1971–76*; La Fargue, Jacqueline, *De Burne-Jones à Bonnard: Dessins provenant du Musée national d'art moderne*, 1977; Georgel, Pierre, "Histoire de la Collection" *Dessins du Musée national d'art moderne, 1890–1945*, November 22, 1974–January 20, 1975.

Other publications: Dorival, Bernard, *L'école de Paris au Musée National d'art Moderne* (Paris 1961); idem, *The School of Paris in the Musée d'Art Moderne*, trans. by Cornelia Hart (New York 1962); Lucie-Smith, Edward, *Masterpieces from the Pompidou Center* (London 1983).

EUSTATHIA P. COSTOPOULOS

ORSAY MUSEUM (officially MUSÉE D'ORSAY), 62, rue de Lille, 75007 Paris.

The Musée d'Orsay, a museum dedicated to all of the arts between 1848 and 1914 and housed, appropriately, in the former Gare d'Orsay, is scheduled to open in late 1986. The railroad station and adjacent hotel are being renovated to provide the setting for a museum whose collections will form a link between those of the Louvre (q.v.) and those of the National Museum of Modern Art (q.v.). This ambitious project was conceived as a result of a debate over the fate of the building itself and of the general redevelopment of central Paris. The controversy began in 1961, when the French national railroad company, the SNCF, decided to sell the station that had outlived its usefulness as a railroad terminal. All of the proposed projects to use this property in downtown Paris, on the Quai d'Orsay across the Seine from the Louvre, involved demolishing the building and constructing a modern conference center and hotel facilities that, at that time, Paris sorely lacked. However, in 1971, just before demolition of the station was scheduled to begin, a public debate began over a related question, the recently-completed destruction of the pavilions of the nineteenth-century market of Les Halles.

This controversy ultimately caused the abandonment of the modern hotel project and the initiation of a plan to save the station and its hotel, which was closed by its owners, the Concorde hotel chain, on January 1, 1973. First, the complex was listed in the Historic Monuments registry, a two-part process: on March 8, 1973, the buildings were entered in the supplementary inventory of facades and "grand decors" and, on March 14, 1978, formally classified as historical monuments, at which time the SNCF gave the property to the French government. Then the decision to create a museum in these buildings was reached on October 20, 1977, by a council of ministers, and a public corporation to renovate the buildings and organize the museum was formed on March 20, 1978. The organization, which is responsible for the renovation of the buildings, the hiring of the curatorial staff, and the conception of the future programming, will be replaced by a museum administration when the building opens to the public. The curatorial staff now in place will remain after the opening of the museum to the public.

The actual process of renovating the building began in 1974, when six architects were engaged as consultants to prepare preliminary proposals and cost estimates. On June 14, 1979, the team of Pierre Colboc, Renaud Bardon, and Jean-Paul Philoppon was chosen as project architects; on July 17, 1980, the Italian Gae Aulenti was engaged to renovate the interior and to choose museum furnishings and equipment for installations.

The decision to use the Gare d'Orsay as the home of a museum of nineteenth-century French art enables the designers to evoke the appropriate mood of industrial expansion, hope, and technological innovation, so important to understanding the arts of the period, by actually setting the individual pieces in the shell of a grand railroad station, so evocative of the period. The station, designed by Victor Laloux and built on the ruins of the Palais d'Orsay, which had been burned in 1871, was dedicated for the World's Fair on July 14, 1900. Used solely for passenger service, it was the major station for connections to southwest France, servicing about 150–200 trains a day from 1900 to 1939. The adjacent hotel, in addition to housing passengers, regularly received political visitors, since it was located close to the ministries and the Chamber of Deputies. As electrification made longer trains possible, the short platforms at the Gare d'Orsay became difficult to use. After 1939 the station was used only for suburban trains and, also, successively, as the center for shipping packages to prisoners during World War II and receiving returned prisoners during the Liberation. It has also been the setting for several films, a home for a theater company, and a temporary shelter for an auction house.

As part of the national museum system of France, the Musée d'Orsay is funded solely by the state. In April 1980 the Society of the Friends of the Musée d'Orsay was created to encourage attendance in the museum and to develop its activities and help enrich its collections.

The interior of the building has been organized into exhibit levels for various arts of the period: a sculpture gallery crosses all of the grand hall from east to west; a series of rooms, placed around the central gallery, contains works from 1848 to 1870; a second floor, using natural sunlight, is devoted to the Impressionists, Post-Impressionists, and Nabis; an entre-sol of various size rooms is for arts from 1870 to 1914. The east pavilion has five levels devoted to architecture, urbanism, and world's fairs. Two towers, beginning at the terrace level, are dedicated to Hector Guimard and turn-of-the-century architecture in France and abroad. Glass arcades of the west tympanum are for exhibits concerning the press, books, posters, and sociocultural events of the Second Empire and the Third Republic. The former dining room of the hotel, with the ceiling painted by Gabriel Ferrier, will become the museum restaurant, and the former ballroom, decorated by Pierre Fritel, will serve as a room for chamber music concerts.

Dealing with the arts from 1848 to 1914, the Musée d'Orsay will contain paintings, sculpture, decorative arts, photography, graphic arts, posters, and illustrated books from France and, where possible, other parts of Europe. Special exhibits pertaining to architecture, urbanism, and world's fairs, as well as to the new art of cinema, all so important during the end of the nineteenth century, are also foreseen.

All of the collections to be brought together in the Musée d'Orsay will come from national museums and new acquisitions, either bought or given, since the inception of the project. The paintings will begin with a selection of works by the Romantics, chosen to provide continuity with the canvases exhibited in the Louvre. Since a decree of January 1976 states that all work in national museums executed by artists born before 1870 do not have to be transferred wholesale to the Musée d'Orsay, only a few paintings of the early period will be taken from the Louvre. Also, works that have been dispersed to national museums around the country will be recalled only if needed to fill in gaps. The most significant aspect of the painting collection in the new museum is that space will now be found to display examples of all of the schools and modes of painting to be found in the second half of the nineteenth century, both in France and abroad. This will include well-known masterpieces such as Manet's *Olympia*, Courbet's *Burial at Ornans*, Renoir's *Le moulin de la galette*, van Gogh's *Church at Auvers*, and Seurat's *The Circus*, among the many others from the entire collection of Impressionists of the Jeu de Paume (q.v.) and the Post-Impressionists from the Palais de Toyko. (The Jeu de Paume is to be used for special exhibits only.)

An aggressive acquisitions policy has enabled the museum to fill in some of the gaps in its collection: *The Wheel of Fortune* by Sir Edward Burne-Jones, *Two White Horses* by George-Hendrik Breitner, *The Enigma* by Gustave Doré, and *Roses under the Trees* by Klimt are some examples out of about one hundred excellent canvases added to existing works. The school of Pont-Aven, friends of Gauguin, was not well represented, an error partially remedied by the acquisition of two works by Emile Bernard and six paintings by Paul Serusier. The purchase of the model of the decoration for the cupola of the Théâtre of the Champs-Elysées, by Maurice Denis, is a significant addition to the section of paintings by the Nabis. Paintings by Signac, Luce, and van Rysselberghe have added strength to the Neo-Impressionist collection.

Drawings and watercolors of the period, because of their fragility, will be physically housed in the Cabinet des Dessins of the Louvre, from whose collection they were originally drawn. Pastels, which can be exhibited to the public under certain conditions, will be shown at the Musée d'Orsay for long periods. Of particular note among new acquisitions are those given by descendants of artists, especially the 529 paintings, pastels, and drawings of Odilon Redon left to the museum in 1982 by the artist's daughter-in-law. Caricatures by Carjat, Cham, Léandre, Iribe, and Roubille form another interesting set of new acquisitions. The relationship between book illustration and literature is well represented with a drawing by Doré for *Orlando Furioso* and illustrations by Luc-Oliver Merson for *Macbeth*. Of particular interest for understanding official art of the period are the preparatory sketches by Lehmann and by Ulmann and Ferrier for religious and civil projects.

The Musée d'Orsay has sculptures by more than two hundred artists, mainly works transferred from the Louvre, which range from Carpeaux to Maillol and include sculptures by Rodin, Claudel, Cordier, and Lacombe. The curators have tried to complete the collections by acquiring works by non-French artists, such as a bronze statuette by Bernard Hoetger and another of Robert de Montesquiou by Prince Paul Troubetzkoy, and by French artists, for example, the frieze *The Dance* by Joseph Bernard and sixty-five original models of an animal series by Bugatti (given by a descendant). Another important series is the thirty-six busts by Daumier, *Célébrités du juste milieu*, acquired thanks to the assistance of Michel David-Weil.

In presenting equally all forms of artistic expression of the nineteenth century, the Musée d'Orsay will be giving an important place to architecture and to architectural drawings. In addition to acquiring those works from the Cabinet des Dessins of the Louvre, the museum seeks to collect entire archives of a project: drawings, sketches, correspondence, and so on. The greatest such collection to date is that given by the descendants of Gustave Eiffel, which comprises diverse papers and other documents, both written and visual, concerning his life and principal projects, the Bridge of Bordeaux, the Tower, the Panama Canal, the Statue of Liberty, and others. With the addition of this archive, the collection of the Musée d'Orsay becomes one of the most important in France dedicated to nineteenth-century architecture. The exposition of this archive also makes clear the importance of this engineer during his time and later. Another significant gift comes from the family of Gabriel Ruprich-Robert, professor of drawing and inspecteur des monuments historiques. The largest comprehensive body of work of this important theoretician of the end of the nineteenth century is now available to the public. Some drawings recently acquired are precious records of destroyed monuments, such as those of Max Berthelin of the Palais de l'Industrie des Champs-Elysées, built for the Exposition Universelle of 1855, and one of the first monuments in France to use the new materials of iron, glass, and cast-iron to cover such large spaces.

The purpose of the photographic collection is to represent the broad movements in the field during the nineteenth and early twentieth centuries, both in France and in foreign countries. The nucleus of the collection is formed by materials from various departments and the library of the Louvre, the Institut de France, the library of the National Factory of Sèvres, and the Archives Photographiques. The early French photography section was enriched by a series of works by Charles Nègre and Humbert de Molard, two great primitives of the period (gifts of descendants); four important portraits by Félix Nadar; and a series of genre portraits by Vallou de Velleneuve (gift of Gallery Texbraun). The Crimean War is documented by a remarkable group of works: a panorama of the Battle of Sebastopol and other shots taken from the Tower of Malakoff by Jean-Charles Langlois and an album of scenes of camp life by Roger Fenton. In a different vein are the shots taken by Thomas Annan of the slums of Glasgow, soon to be demolished, and those of Marville executed for the city of Paris. The turn-of-the-century collections, still poor, have been enriched by important acquisitions of two albums by the English photographer P. H. Emerson, father of pictorialism, and a very rare series of complete illustrations by Julia-Margaret Cameron of the poems of Tennyson's *Idylls of the King*. A major acquisition is the complete edition of *Camera Work*, 1903–17, a quarterly created by Alfred Stieglitz, American photographer, as an organ of his group Photo-Secession, which exhibited regularly at his Gallery 291. A sumptuous quarterly whose reproductions could easily be taken for originals, *Camera Work* is an excellent example of the struggle, both in America and in Europe, for the recognition of photography as an art.

The decorative-arts collections of the Musée d'Orsay are not very rich, since the late nineteenth-century portions found in the national museums were not particularly significant to begin with. The reasons for the relative sparseness of this segment of the collection, which should be large and help to express the full flowering of the arts of this period, are many; state commissions either remain in the buildings for which they were designed or were destroyed in the risings of 1870; the keepers of the collections were governed in the selection of pieces by the rules of the Salon and thus did not acquire avant-garde pieces when they were first produced; and the disfavor into which Art Nouveau fell for many years precluded its inclusion in major collections until recently. To remedy the situation, the Musée d'Orsay has been acquiring pieces at a prodigious pace, about two hundred in the years 1980–83, which have concentrated upon various types of objects from the Second Empire and upon Art Nouveau. The latter is best represented by the Frenchman Guimard and the Belgian van de Velde. An especially important acquisition is the dining room paneling commissioned by the banker Adrien Bénard in 1901 from Alexandre Charpentier. Works by foreign artists such as Hoffman and Koloman Moser and a window by Louis Comfort Tiffany after Toulouse-Lautrec add to the collection's depth and breadth.

The Musée d'Orsay will have a library and other documentation open to scholars by appointment. General books, slides, and postcards will be on sale in the bookstore.

Articles concerning the new acquisitions of the museum can be found in *Musée d'Art et d'Essai, présentations temporaires d'oeuvres du musée du Louvre et des collections nationales*. Other publications, in addition to those listed below, will be available as the museum nears completion and after it has opened.

Selected Bibliography

Museum publications: *Orsay 86 un musée nouveau*, 1983; *Catalogue sommaire illustré des nouvelles acquisitions du Musée d'Orsay, 1980–1983*, 1983.

MARY LOUISE WOOD

PETIT PALAIS (officially MUSÉE DU PETIT PALAIS; alternately MUSEUM OF FINE ARTS OF THE CITY OF PARIS; MUSÉE DES BEAUX-ARTS DE LA VILLE DE PARIS; PALAIS DES BEAUX-ARTS DE LA VILLE DE PARIS), Avenue Alexandre III, 75008 Paris.

Although the city of Paris had a special budget to buy works of art and had purchased paintings from the annual Salons since 1875, the municipality did not have a permanent building in which to exhibit its collection until the beginning of this century. The city museum, the Musée du Petit Palais, and its larger neighbor, the Grand Palais, came into existence as new structures created especially for the 1900 Universal Exhibition.

Having such a grand edifice constructed specifically to display art influenced the Rouen collector Auguste Dutuit to bequeath his and his brother's (Eugène, who died in 1866) extensive collection of ancient artifacts, medieval objects, rare books, illuminated manuscripts, prints and drawings, and seventeenth-century Dutch paintings to the capital city. He also provided an endowment for future acquisitions. Following Dutuit's death in Rome in 1902, the Petit Palais officially opened in December 11 that same year with the Dutuit Collection installed for the museum's inauguration.

Architect Charles-Louis Girault designed the beautiful Petit Palais in the Beaux-Arts style. The triangular plot of land between the Champs-Elysées and the new

Avenue Alexandre III on which the museum sits required the structure to be trapezoidal. Construction began on October 10, 1897, and the edifice was completed in April 1900 for the world exposition.

The highly decorated interior contains a peristyle courtyard of pink Vosges granite columns joined by gilt-bronze garlands, marble-lined walls, magnificent stuccoed ceilings, and intricate mosaic flooring. Between 1903 and 1926 several artists were commissioned to execute ceiling paintings. The rotunda displays four allegorical murals by Albert Besnard: *Le plastique*, *La mystique*, *La pensée*, and *La matière*, executed 1906–11. Fernand Cormon, Alfred Roll, and Fernand Humbert painted the ceilings of the large sculpture hall with heroic subjects such as the histories of Paris and France and the triumph of the Republic. Paul Baudouin frescoed the vaults of the garden hemicycle. In 1926 Maurice Denis painted representations of the ages of humanity from medieval times to the nineteenth century on the ceiling over the grand staircase.

The collection of the museum contains samples of Western art from the Egyptian period until the early twentieth century. The three major strengths, however, are the holdings of nineteenth-century French paintings, sculpture, and drawings; eighteenth-century French furnishings, decorative arts, and drawings; and seventeenth-century Dutch and Flemish paintings, drawings, and prints.

Galleries containing art from the ancient eras display Egyptian bronzes, such as the *Stele to Onouris* and a representation of an Egyptian queen such as the deity *Isis*, as well as a selection of vases. The sizable collection of Greek vases includes several notable examples, such as the *Poseidon* vase by the Altamura Painter and an oinoche depicting Artemis petting a fawn by the Dutuit Painter, so named by Beazley for this work. It also includes an array of black- and red-figured pottery from the sixth century B.C. as well as vessels from the Classical period painted on white ground. A fine selection of Greek rhytons with animal or monster heads is also displayed, including the well-known example showing a crocodile capturing a Negro boy. Larger in scale are two Roman copies, the fourth-century *Bacchus* and *Hermes* after the famed High Classical sculptor Polyclitus. Other ancient objects include many Etruscan bronzes with delicate line engravings, the highlight of which is a cistern with two standing figures on the lid found at Palestrina, dating from the third century B.C.

From the medieval period is a group of early block-printed books and illuminated manuscripts from the Dutuit Collection, as well as Byzantine ivories of the tenth and eleventh centuries. Illuminated books dating from the fourteenth through sixteenth century include: Flemish, *Hours of the Virgin* (end of the fifteenth century); several Paris *Books of Hours* (late fifteenth-sixteenth century); and manuscripts from Cologne with colored engravings (c. 1480). Nineteen wood engravings of about 1492 are known as the *Dance of Death*. The *émail champlevé* reliquaries from Meuse date from the second half of the twelfth century, and the Limoges examples are from the thirteenth century. From the fifteenth and sixteenth centuries are carved wooden sculptures from France and Germany, as well as panels from altarpieces such as the *Adoration* by the Master of St.

Bartholomew (Cologne, fifteenth century) and the *St. Sebastian Triptych* by Jan van Hemessen.

The collection of Old Master paintings, with the exception of the seventeenth-century Dutch examples, is limited. Highlights of the small selection are *Christ as Master of the World* attributed to Mantegna, Pieter Breugel the Younger's *Wedding Procession*, Nicolas Poussin's *Massacre of the Innocents*, Rubens' *Proserpina*, Simon Vouet's massive *Bath of Diana*, Lucas Cranach's *Portrait of the Burgermeister's Daughter*, and others by Claude, Bassano, and the Spanish artist Bartolome Bermejo.

The comprehensive array of seventeenth-century Dutch works, built around the collection of Eugène Dutuit, surveys the various genres in which these artists specialized. Exhibited are still-life paintings by Willem Claesz Heda, Jan Weenix, and Pieter Claesz; landscapes and seascapes by Jacob van Ruisdael, Meindert Hobbema, Jan van Goyen, Aelbert Cuyp, Aert van der Neer, Jan Both, and Willem van de Velde; and genre scenes by Nicolaes Maes, Jan Steen, Gerard Ter Borch, Pieter Codde, Gabriel Metsu, Philips Wouvermans, and the van Ostade brothers Issak and Adriaen. Rembrandt's *Self Portrait with Poodle*, an early work of 1631, shows the artist dressed in an Oriental costume.

Eighteenth-century arts, predominantly from France, are exhibited in long, elegant rooms that provide an appropriate setting for the combined display of paintings, sculpture, tapestries, porcelain, furniture, and decorative arts. The 1939 donation from the American Edward Tuck, who lived in Paris on the Champs-Elysées for more than forty years, augmented the Dutuit Collection and greatly enriched the museum's holdings of this epoch. Especially fine are the exquisite Louis XV furniture and eighteenth-century porcelain from Sèvres, Meissen, and Vincennes. The walls are covered with tapestries such as a Tournai representation of the *History of Alexander* (late fifteenth century) and an Aubusson showing hunting and pastoral scenes (mid-eighteenth century). A series of nine Beauvais hangings from the Tuck Collection depict the story of *Psyche*, woven after designs by Boucher, which the Rococo painter exhibited at the 1739 Salon. Six weavings follow compositions by J.-B. Huet, and three are after J.-B. LePrince.

Tuck owned several representations of Benjamin Franklin, including an oil portrait by Greuze, a sculpted bust by Houdon, and a figurine by Caffière (designed as a model for a Sèvres porcelain). Other eighteenth-century paintings are: David's small *Death of Seneca*, Carle van Loo's *Portrait of Louis XV*, and portraits by Elisabeth-Louise Vigée-Lebrun and Jean-Marc Nattier, as well as bucolic scenes by Joseph Vernet, Boucher, and Hubert Robert. Houdon's *Voltaire*, a replica of the sculpture exhibited at the 1779 Salon and Clodion's small Rococo *Bacchante Group* are also on view.

Cases display porcelain from both the Dutuit and Tuck donations, including the very elaborate Saint-Porchaire examples by the school of Bernard Palissy from the second half of the sixteenth century, as well as Italian faience from Gubbio, Faenza, Urbino, and Deruta. The collection also contains Spanish,

Iranian, and Chinese ceramics, as well as Tuck's large collection of enameled watches.

The extensive selection of nineteenth-century French paintings contains works by both Impressionists and Salon painters. Fashionable portraits by several of the popular society painters include representations by Carolus-Duran, Léon Bonnat, Jacques-Emile Blanche, Claude-Marie Dubufe, Paul Baudry, and the American John Singer Sargent. Of special interest are L.-G. Richard's elegant full-length portrait *Mme. La Marquise Landolfo Carcano*; Georges Clairin's striking, larger-than-life *Portrait of Sarah Bernhardt*; Baron François Gérard's refined depiction *Mme. Recamier*, the lady who refused David's more famous portrait of her; and Thomas Couture's painting of the mayor of the ninth arrondisement, *Portrait of M. Ohnet*, which was exhibited in the Salon of 1841.

Landscapes abound by Impressionists such as Alfred Sisley and Camille Pissarro and the Neo-Impressionist Paul Signac, as well as examples by pre-Impressionist painters: Paul Huet, the Dutchman Jongkind, and Eugène Boudin. In addition, several charming landscapes by Armand Guillaumin and Henri Harpignies are on exhibition.

A whole room is devoted to the oils and watercolors of Félix Ziem, who donated some fifty-five paintings and more than a hundred drawings and studies to the museum in 1905. A frequent traveler, Ziem depicted picturesque scenes from Russia, Turkey, and Egypt, as well as dramatic views of Venice, his second home.

A small room is hung with the recent acquisition of more than twenty seascapes by Henry Brokman, which were given to the museum by his relatives. The majority of these paintings, executed during the early years of this century, feature hazy, brilliant blue shore views. By the earlier Romantic painters there is the large oil *Stormy Landscape in Italy* by Théodore Géricault, one of the decorative series he painted before ever visiting Italy and that was rediscovered only in 1953.

Giaour and Pacha, painted by Eugène Delacroix in 1835, was one of several depictions inspired by Lord Byron's poem. Delacroix's rival, the classicist Ingres, is represented by two oils painted during the late teens in the popular troubador type, which depicted historical personalities in genre settings: *Henri IV Playing with His Children* and the *Death of Leonardo in the Arms of François I* were commissioned by the comte de Blacas and exhibited in the 1824 Salon.

The Daumier selection includes several small oils of everyday scenes such as *The Trio of Amateur Musicians*, *The Print Collector*, and *The Checker Players*, as well as the oil sketch *Les émigrants*, a somber scene of nineteenth-century homeless wanderers.

Canvases presenting rural genre scenes painted by the Barbizon artists Millet and Charles Jacque as well as by Jules Breton are also exhibited. Camille Corot is represented by an unusual study of a nude, *La Marietta*.

Gustave Courbet is represented by a comprehensive array of sixteen paintings that survey his oeuvre from early depictions of his sisters *Zélie* and *Juliette*

(1844) and his *Self Portrait with a Black Dog*, his first painting exhibited at the Salon, that of 1844, to a late *Portrait of Regis Courbet*, his father, painted in 1874 just three years before the artist's death in exile. The selection includes several of Courbet's monumental canvases, which stirred critical reaction during his lifetime: the colorful *Young Girls on the Banks of the Seine*, exhibited at the Salon of 1857; the erotic *Sleep*, of 1866, commissioned by Turkish collector Khalil-Bey; the unfinished *Firemen*, painted to honor the urban worker; the *Portrait of Prudhon* (Courbet's friend and a socialist philosopher), exhibited at the 1869 Salon. Several landscapes are also exhibited as well as the *Three Bathers* of 1868.

Figural subjects by artists of the Impressionist circle include: Berthe Morisot's lovely *Dans le Parc*, a gift of Joseph Duveen; Pissarro's *Portrait of His Wife* (c. 1874); and Mary Cassatt's oil *Le Bain* as well as several pastels by the American painter. Manet's small *Portrait of Théodore Duret* depicts the art critic and future biographer of Manet and his Impressionist friends. Other Impressionist paintings are late works by Renoir and the large Degas pastel, *Portrait of Mme. Alexis Rouart and Her Children*.

Of the Post-Impressionist masters there are Gauguin's *Portrait of the Sculptor Aubé and His Son* and *The Old Man with a Staff*. Four tall panels depicting the traditional subject of the four seasons were painted by Paul Cézanne as decorations for his family's house, Jas de Bouffan near Aix-en-Provence. Executed early in his career, these murals are satirically signed "Ingres." Other Cézanne paintings include: *Bathers* (1879–82); the 1899 *Portrait of Vollard*, his dealer and a benefactor of the Petit Palais; and a *Bibemus Landscape* (1904), the site of a quarry near Mont Ste.-Victoire.

The numerous paintings by the Nabi artists include Maurice Denis' *The Sacred Wood*, Pierre Bonnard's brightly colored *Nude in a Tub*, and large individual portraits of fellow Nabis Aristide Maillol, K.-X. Roussel, Denis, and Bonnard painted by Edouard Vuillard. Also by Vuillard are four mural panels executed as interior decoration for the home of Dr. Vaquez in 1896.

Many Symbolist works are exhibited, including four paintings by Eugène Carrière, a dozen by Lucien Levy-Dhurmer, two Gustave Moreaus, and oils by C.-L. Leandre, Emile-René Menard, and Alphonse Osbert, as well as Fantin-Latour's *The Temptation of St. Anthony*. There is an extensive selection of beautiful pastels by Redon.

The sculpture holdings are strongest in the area of nineteenth-century French. The original plaster of the Petit Palais' *Fisherboy* by J.-B. Carpeaux was exhibited in the Salon of 1858 and is now in the Louvre (q.v.). Perhaps Carpeaux's most famous sculpture is *The Dance*, a subject Garnier commissioned him to design for the new Paris Opera. This sculpture was unveiled to the public amid great controversy in 1869. The museum's edition of *La danse des graces* is a later version, which the artist executed in 1874 just one year before his death.

The collection contains many sculptures by Jules Dalou, one of the most sought-after designers of large public and private monuments during the 1890s.

Included are his maquettes for the *Lion* of the Alexandre III Bridge and for his *Monument to Léon Gambetta*, erected at Bordeaux in 1905, three years after his death. Other small pieces include studies by Ernest Barrias, Emile Falguière, Albert Carrier-Belleuse, and F.-A. Bartholdi. In addition, a selection of bronzes by the French *animalier* Barye is displayed.

Life-sized figural sculptures include Rodin's 1877 *Torso* (a study of his *Man Walking*), Antoine Bourdelle's *Penelope* (1907) and *Death of the Last Centaur* (1914), Renoir's *Venus Victorieuse* (1914), and Maillol's 1937 marble *Pomone*.

Reflecting the taste of the Dutuit brothers, the museum's collection of drawings contains seventeenth-century Dutch works by Ferdinand Bol, Hobbema, Adriaen van Ostade, and Rembrandt, as well as eighteenth-century French examples by masters such as Boucher and Watteau. The selection of nineteenth-century works on paper include drawings by Besnard, Daumier, Delacroix, and Rodin, with numerous landscapes by Jongkind and Harpignies, as well as nearly two hundred studies by Pierre Puvis de Chavannes. The museum also owns more than twelve thousand prints, including the array of nearly four hundred etchings by Rembrandt collected by the Dutuits.

The museum organizes major loan exhibitions for which it publishes catalogues.

Selected Bibliography

Museum publications: *Bronzes grecs et romains de la collections Dutuit*, forthcoming; *Catalogue des dessins et peintures de Puvis de Chavannes*, 1979; *Peintures des Collections du Petit Palais*, forthcoming.

Other publications: Gronkowski, Camille, *Catalogue Sommaire des Collections Municipales* (Paris 1927); Lapauze, Henry, *Catalogue sommaire des collection Dutuit* (Paris 1925); Lugt, Frits, *Les Dessins des Ecoles du Nord de la Collection Dutuit au Musée des Beaux-Arts de la ville de Paris* (Paris 1927); Plaoutine, N., *Corpus Vasorum Antiquorum, France, Palais des Beaux-Arts de la ville de Paris (Petit Palais) Collection Dutuit* (Paris 1941); Rahir, Edouard, *La Collection Dutuit, Livres et Manuscrits* (Paris 1899); Adam, Paul, "Le Symbolisme dans l'oeuvre d'Albert Besnard," *Gazette des Beaux-Arts*, s. 4, 6 (1911), pp. 437–54; Cain, Georges, "'Les legs Dutuit," *Gazette des Beaux-Arts*, s. 3, 28 (1902), pp. 441–48; Eitner, Lorenz, "Two Rediscovered Landscapes by Géricault and the Chronology of His Early Work," *Art Bulletin* 36 (June 1954), pp. 131–42; Giraudy, Marguerite, "European Porcelain from the Tuck Bequest," *Connoisseur* 163 (October 1966), pp. 77–82; Gronkowski, Camille, "La Collection Edward Tuck au Petit Palais," *La Revue de l'art ancien et moderne* 58 (1930), pp. 235–46; Worsdale, Derrick, "The Petit Palais des Champs-Elysées: Architecture and Decoration," *Apollo* 107 (March 1978), pp. 207–22.

CAROL HYNNING SMITH

——— Saint-Germain-en-Laye ———

PRIORY MUSEUM (officially MUSÉE DÉPARTEMENTAL DU PRIEURÉ, MUSÉE DE PRIEURÉ), 2, rue Maurice Denis, 78100 Saint-Germain-en-Laye.

The Musée du Prieuré has a dual history, since both the building and the collection of late nineteenth-century works have their own backgrounds. The building was constructed between 1680 and 1686 as a hospital for the poor and aged by Mme. de Montespan in an act of repentance after her dismissal as the mistress of Louis XIV. The chapel was begun in 1698. The hospital remained open until the early nineteenth century, when it was abandoned. It then became, successively, a military hospital, a fabric factory, an artist's studio, a Jesuit retreat house, and finally, in 1913, the studio of the artist Maurice Denis. He named it the Prieuré, after a monastery that once existed down the hill from the present site. Denis restored the chapel and lived in the main building until he died in 1943. In 1973 the site was finally purchased from the Denis family by the Department of Yvelines (the French geographical "county" in which it lies) for the purpose of housing the Denis family art collection.

The Musée du Prieuré is outside the rubric of the French Musées Nationaux, being administered solely by the Departement d'Yvelines. The Board of Trustees (Comité de gestion) consists of fourteen people, half of whom are appointed by the Department of Yvelines and half are elected by the administration. These positions are permanent. The Comité artistique, also appointed and elected by the department, serves to advise the board on matters of acquistions, temporary exhibitions, and conservation. There are no departments within this small museum; a curator is aided by two assistants and a documentalist, as well as temporary and part-time researchers and gallery guides.

Financing for the staff, maintenance, and exhibitions all come from the Department of Yvelines, but acquisitions are helped by the private sector as well as by substantial grants from the French government. Generous gifts have been forthcoming, especially from families of the artists, such as the Ransons, and from various private collections.

The goals of the Musée du Prieuré are twofold: one is to increase the holdings of major works by the artists of the period to which the museum is devoted; and another is to use some of its unique space to display works of the twentieth century. A documentation center for scholars is planned containing letters, books, and publications of the period, such as a newly acquired set of the rare *Ymagier*.

The recent restoration of the Prieuré was done with its eventual use as a museum in mind. The result is a strikingly beautiful museum with superb facilities. First, the building was pared down to its original seventeenth-century simplicity. The large, open galleries (originally hospital wards) were reconstituted as was the monumental double staircase. Nineteenth-century stained-glass windows by Albert Besnard and Jacques Gruber were put in place in the staircase; the juxtaposition of these works of two centuries is not incongruous but harmonious. The large garden around the museum was also restored to provide a setting for sculpture and for walkways and benches. All of the restorations have lived up to their goal: to couple the austerity of the original building with the mystery so prevalent in many of the Symbolist era works of art in the collection. The museum and gardens were opened to the public in October 1980.

The basis for the Prieuré's collection of twenty-five hundred works is a large donation of paintings, sculptures, drawings, cartoons for stained glass, and public commissions by Maurice Denis, given to the Department of Yvelines by the Denis family. Also in the collection are works by other artists collected by Denis himself. In all, there are 950 objects by Denis and 1,250 by his friends and contemporaries.

The focus of the museum's collection is historically narrow, concentrating on the 1890s and the first years of the twentieth century. Maurice Denis was a leading member of the Nabis, a group of young, enthusiastic Parisian painters of the period 1889–95. The Nabis were led by Paul Sérusier and included Denis, Edouard Vuillard, Pierre Bonnard, Paul Ranson, Ker-Xavier Roussel, Henri Ibels, and George Lacombe. The group eagerly pursued the Synthetist ideas begun by Paul Gauguin and Emile Bernard, forging a decorative style based upon abstract ideas of harmony and rhythm. Their work is characterized by flat planes, bold colors, and simple subjects, usually landscapes or interiors. The Nabis saw themselves as a brotherhood and often worked together on projects such as stage sets for Symbolist theater or their own marionette shows. The Prieuré has one of these marionette sets, designed by Denis, Sérusier, Verkade, and Vuillard. Large-scale interior decorations are also represented in the museum, including dining-room panels by Ranson and numerous interior designs by Denis, such as his ceiling painting of *L'échelle dans le feuillage* of 1892.

The Prieuré has a complete survey of the works of Maurice Denis, including the simple *Mystère Catholique* of 1889 and the decorative *Mme. Ranson au chat*, 1892. Stained glass and bedroom decoration designed for Samuel Bing are also on display. Denis' religious works are well represented, as well as designs and maquettes from many of his public works, such as those in the Petit Palais (q.v.) in Paris.

Sérusier is best represented in the Prieuré by his Pont-Aven painting *Louise, la servante bretonne* of 1890 and the striking *La vielle bretonne* of about 1898. Sérusier's life-long concern was for color, clearly illustrated by his two palettes in the museum's collection as well as a hot and cold color chart painted and used by the artist.

A magnificent screen by Bonnard is a recent acquisition, underscoring the Nabis' love of decorative pieces. The other Nabis are represented by drawings, prints, and some small paintings. Major Nabi works are still lacking in the new museum. On the other hand, there is an admirable collection of paintings, sculpture, prints, and decorative art of other French painters of the 1890s and the turn of the century, a collection that creates the artistic context for Denis' works while also providing a thorough survey of the French artistic milieu of this period.

Filiger, a painter associated with some of the Nabis, is represented in the Prieuré through several watercolors and drawings, most notably *La Sainte en prière* of 1893 and *Le Christ au tombeau* of the 1890s. A collection of works and personal souvenirs was given to the museum by his niece Anna Filiger.

Another large gift of drawings came from the daughter of Maurice Marinot. Prints and posters are well represented, including those by Auguste Lepère, Jules Cheret, Henri Ibels, Daniel de Montfried, Jacques Beltrand, Alphonse Mucha, and Henri Rivière.

Sculpture is a great strength of the Prieuré's collection, especially the works of Antoine Bourdelle, some of which can be seen in the garden, including *La force interieur*. Aristide Maillol's work can also be seen, most notably a *Tête de femme* and *La Musique*, the latter sculpted for a monument to Debussy.

Most of the Prieuré's paintings and sculptures are displayed in large, bright galleries on the first and second floors of the museum. On the top floor is a long, narrow room dominated by large beams that create smaller, more intimate spaces. There can be seen smaller objects, decorative arts, and fragile works on paper. The distinction between "fine arts" and "decorative arts" was blurred in the late nineteenth century by various movements, from the Nabi to Art Nouveau. Thus it is important to view the painting and sculpture of this period with the objects that surrounded them in homes and studios. This is done throughout the Prieuré, especially on the third floor. There, ceramics by the brothers Daum and Mogens Ballin, among others, can be seen, as well as furniture, including a magnificent buffet by Devêche. Illustrated books, prints, and woodblocks are also in these exhibition areas.

Museum publications include a handsomely illustrated catalogue of the museum's collection, listing all of the works owned at the time of the opening. There are also catalogues available for the exhibitions held since the opening in 1980: Charles Filiger, Impressionism, the fans of Maurice Denis, and watercolors of the Middle East by Emile Bernard. These publications are available for purchase at the museum entrance as are postcards and new books on artists in the museum's collection. Photographs of the museum's objects can be purchased through the museum's photographer upon request.

Selected Bibliography

Museum publications: *Musée du Prieuré, Symbolistes et Nabis, Maurice Denis et son Temps*, 1980; *Charles Filiger*, 1981; *L'Eclatement d'Impressionisme*, 1892; *Les Evantails de Maurice Denis*, 1983; *Les Aquarelles Orientales d'Emile Bernard, 1893–1904*, 1983.

CAROLINE BOYLE-TURNER

German Democratic Republic

—— Berlin, East ——

STATE MUSEUMS AT BERLIN (officially STAATLICHE MUSEEN ZU BERLIN—HAUPTSTADT DER DDR; alternately BERLIN MUSEUMS, BERLIN EAST; also BERLINER MUSEEN), STATE MUSEUMS, EAST BERLIN, Generaldirektion, Bodestrasse 1–3, 1020 Berlin.

The fourteen state museums of art, architecture, and archaeology in East Berlin, except one in Köpenick, are housed in a complex of five buildings on the Museumsinsel, the world-famous Museum Isle in the river Spree in the heart of the city.

The five buildings on the Museum Isle with their respective entrances are the Old Museum (Altes Museum) on Marx-Engels-Platz; the New Museum (Neues Museum) at Bodestrasse 1–3 (presently closed for reconstruction); the National Gallery (Nationalgalerie) at Bodestrasse 1–3; the Pergamum Museum (Pergamonmuseum) on Kupfergraben; and the Bode Museum (Bodemuseum), formerly the Kaiser-Friedrich Museum) at Kupfergraben and Monbijou Bridge.

The fourteen divisions, the individual collections of which constitute separate museums, and their locations, are as follows:

1. Egyptian Museum and Papyrus Collection (Agyptisches Museum mit Papyrussammlung), Bode Museum

2. Museum of Near Eastern Art (Vorderasiastisches Museum), Pergamum Museum

3. Collection of Far Eastern Art (Ostasiatische Sammlung), Pergamum Museum

4. Museum of Pre- and Protohistory (Museum für Ur- und Frühgeschichte), Bode Museum

5. Collection of Greek and Roman Antiquities (Antikensammlung), Pergamum Museum

6. Collection of Early Christian and Byzantine Art (Frühchristlich-byzantinische Sammlung), Bode Museum
7. Museum of Islamic Art (Islamisches Museum), Pergamum Museum
8. Sculpture Collection (Skulpturensammlung), Bode Museum
9. Picture Gallery (Gemäldegalerie), Bode Museum
10. National Gallery (Nationalgalerie), National Gallery and Old Museum
11. Department of Prints and Drawings and Collection of Drawings (Kupferstichkabinett und Sammlung der Zeichnungen), Old Museum
12. Coin Collection (Münzkabinett), Bode Museum
13. Museum of Arts and Crafts (Kunstgewerbemuseum), Palais Köpenick
14. Ethnological Museum (Museum für Volkskunde), Bode Museum

Other divisions are the Art Library (Zentralbibliothek), Pergamum Museum; Public Relations and Museum Education (Öffentlichkeitsarbeit mit Museumspädagogik) Bodestrasse 1–3; and the Children's Gallery (Kindergalerie), Old Museum.

The history of the Berlin State Museums began in 1797 (for the Hohenzollern collections before this time, see State Museums, West Berlin), when the archaeologist Aloys Hirt proposed that King Frederick II establish a museum in which selected works from the royal art collections should be made accessible to the public. Although Hirt presented actual plans the following year, the project was postponed due to the conflict with France and Napoleon's occupation of Berlin in 1806. Napoleon's subsequent defeat, the return of confiscated artworks to Berlin, perhaps the acquaintance of Frederick William II with the Louvre, and above all, an increasing demand gave new impetus to the idea of a public museum. After an abortive attempt to establish it in the old Art Academy, in 1823 the chief royal architect Karl Friedrich Schinkel presented a new design. His edifice was to be on the narrow island in the Spree on which the royal palace itself was located. A domed classical building with a main facade of eighteen Ionic columns (based on English drawings of the Temple of Apollo at Didyma) was to face the main facade of the palace across a newly created Lustgarten, or formal garden.

The plan was accepted, and in the same year Frederick III gave the order to begin construction. The building, one of Schinkel's major works, and one of the finest examples of German neoclassical architecture, was inaugurated in 1830. Previously, a commission had been appointed to select artworks from the various royal palaces for which the king was, however, compensated by the Prussian State. The important Giustiniani and Solly collections had been purchased already in 1815 and 1821, respectively. In 1829 a Generaldirektion was established, which in turn supervised departments, each headed by its own director. This basic organization was modeled on those of the museums of Paris and London, which Schinkel had visited in 1826. With the establishment of the Generaldirektion the Staatliche Museen zu Berlin officially began to function. Schinkel's new building housed the Picture Gallery, the Collection of Prints and Drawings, the Collection of Ancient Art and Archaeology with its subdivisions, the Coin Collection, the Plaster Cast Studio, and the Museum Library. The Egyptian Collection and Museum of National Antiquities (Pre- and Protohistory) remained in the nearby Palais Monbijou, while part of the Picture Gallery remained in the main palace.

In 1841 Frederick William IV approved a plan to use the island north of Schinkel's edifice for additional museum buildings. The first of them was designed as part of a complex of buildings by Schinkel's pupil August Stüler. Constructed between 1843 and 1847 north of Schinkel's edifice, and opened in 1859, this building furnished a home for the collection that had remained at Monbijou and the Berlin palace, and from Schinkel's "Old Museum," as it was now called to differentiate it henceforth from Stüler's "New Museum," came the Collection of Prints and Drawings and part of the Collection of Ancient Art and Archaeology.

In 1861, ten years before the unification of Germany, the National Gallery was founded. Although the idea had its roots in the Revolution of 1848, the immediate impetus was the bequest in 1861 of a large collection of contemporary, mostly German, paintings by the Berlin merchant Consul Wilhelm Wagener. The building that was to house this collection was a tall, temple-like structure, already part of Stüler's overall plan of 1841, except that at that time it was conceived to house lecture rooms and a large, festive hall and ultimately to be a memorial to Frederick William IV. Adapted as a museum building, it was erected between 1866 and 1876 northeast of the Old Museum under the supervision of another Schinkel pupil, Heinrich Strack.

Between 1871, when Berlin became the capital of the new German Empire, and World War I, the collections grew tremendously, resulting in the construction of two additional huge buildings on the Museum Isle. Generous acquisition budgets, brilliant directors, and excavations in Greece and the Near East supervised by renowned archaeologists enriched the museums with priceless treasures. New departments were founded, such as the Department of Islamic and Far Eastern Art; others were incorporated, like the Museum of Arts and Crafts. In short, the Berlin Museums grew in this period in quality and size to rank among the world's best. Between 1897 and 1903 the architect Ernst Eberhard von Ihne designed and supervised the building of a museum at the northernmost tip of the island, the Kaiser-Friedrich-Museum, renamed after Wilhelm Bode in 1956. It was inaugurated in 1904 and housed the Picture Gallery, the Sculpture Department of the Christian Periods, the Coin Collection, the Museum of Near Eastern Art, and the Museum of Islamic Art.

A separate building, to house only the Great Altar of Pergamum, was constructed in 1902 but was torn down again in 1907 to be superseded by the U-shaped, present-day Pergamum Museum, after plans by Alfred Messel. Its central wing, which contained the altar and other ancient architectural displays, was inaugurated in 1930, the rest of the edifice in 1936. The building's southern wing now accommodates the Museum of Near Eastern and Islamic Art. The northern wing was conceived to house the Deutsches Museum, featuring objects from the Germanic migrations through the Baroque period. Today this wing houses more logically the art and archaeology of Greece and Rome, connecting with the central wing, which displays Greek and Roman architecture.

Between the two world wars the museums did not greatly expand, but this was a period of consolidation, scholarly research, and publications. During World War II the most precious and movable objects were sheltered, either in the museums' basements or in various bunkers in the city. Hundreds of art objects were shipped to underground mines in several parts of Germany. When the war ended, the Old and New Museums were in utter ruins and the other buildings also badly damaged by bombardments. Several large architectural treasures were badly damaged. Some of the finest objects, among them some four hundred precious paintings, were lost in a fire just after the war. The objects that had been sheltered in mines outside Berlin and that were captured by the American and British forces were eventually housed in West Berlin. The objects taken from Berlin by the USSR were returned to East Berlin from Moscow, Leningrad, and Kiev in 1958. The immense task of restoration began on the Museum Isle in 1946, at first financed by the Berlin Magistrate and since 1951 by the German Democratic Republic. All buildings except the New Museum, which is in re-construction, have been repaired. Although the losses resulting from World War II were great, the holdings today of the individual departments, reunited, restored, and enlarged through new acquisitions, still comprise one of the most important art collections of the world.

The State Museums are headed by a director-general (Generaldirektor), each museum having its own director and curatorial staff. The museums have a central restoration facility, headed by a chief restorer. The director-general has two deputies, one of whom is the director of the Office of General Administration (Generalverwaltung) handling employment. There is also a director of the Public Relations Office (Direktionbereich Öffentlichkeitsarbeit). This office handles public information and museum publications and supervises the Department of Museum Education (Abteilung Museumspädagogik).

The origin of the Egyptian Museum and Papyrus Collection dates from the eighteenth-century holdings of the royal family. On the advice of Alexander von Humboldt, Frederick William III purchased the important private collections of Minutoli (1823) and Passalacqua (1827) and the important pieces from the collections of Drovetti and d'Anastasi. The holdings were exhibited from 1823 to 1850 in Monbijou and then in Stüler's New Museum. It was Richard Lepsius, founder of German Egyptology and director of the division from 1865 to 1884, who turned the museum into an exemplary collection. From 1842 to 1845 Lepsius undertook scientific expeditions to Egypt and Nubia, resulting in the acquisition of many important objects. The exhibits in the New Museum, as conceived by Lepsius, aimed to represent Egyptian civilization as a whole by displaying in chronological order only the finest and most representative objects. As a result of German participation at the excavations at Abusir (1901–7), Abusir el-meleq (1913–14), and Tell el-Amarna (1911–14) with the Deutsche Orientgesellschaft, and continuous acquisitions financed in part by F. W. Freiherr von Bissing and above all by James Simon, the museum had almost tripled in size by 1920. Although many of its treasures were lost in World War II, the most important works can be seen again, thanks to the return in 1958 of the evacuated objects from the USSR and the patient restoration work of the museum staff. Restoration of the New Museum has yet to be undertaken, and the exhibition of approximately eight hundred objects, ranging from the Predynastic periods to Roman times, is temporarily shown in ten rooms of the Bode Museum.

Outstanding are Predynastic ceramic vessels with painted navigation scenes of the Negade II culture. A key work is *King Narmer's Baboon*, the first known Egyptian monumental sculpture, about 3000 B.C. The Old Kingdom is represented by some interesting reliefs, such as the *Seasons' Reliefs* and the *Sahure Reliefs*, as well as by the fine wooden statue of an official. The fourth dynasty reliefs from the tomb of Hetepet with hunting and harvesting scenes are also noteworthy. The sandstone statue of *The Steward Kherti-hotep* is considered one of the most significant artworks of the Middle Kingdom, a period that is otherwise represented by fine sculptures, grave stelae, and painted wooden sarcophagi. Outstanding among sculptures of the early New Kingdom are the block statue *Senmut* and the *Sphinx of Queen Hatchepsut* from Deir-el-Bahri. Important also are limestone reliefs from her temple at Deir-el-Bahri (c. 1490 B.C.) and from the time of Amenophis III from Thebes (c. 1380 B.C.). This period is also represented by examples of wall paintings and many small art objects, such as exquisitely carved ointment bowls and spoons. The style of the Amarna Period and the studio of Thutmosis stands out with a model relief of King Akhenaten; with stucco model heads, one of which, the so-called *Seer's Head*, is of Akhenaten; and with beautiful carved stone heads of Queen Nefretiti and her daughter Ankhes-en-pa-Aten, wife of Tutanchamun. The late New Kingdom is represented by fresco paintings from the necropolis at Thebes under Rameses IV, by limestone tomb reliefs, stelae and sculptures, and by many small art objects, among them a collection of scarabs. The Late Period (1085–332 B.C.) is represented by several carved block statues, most of them about 800 B.C., and other fine stone and bronze sculptures, such as the bronze head of an ibex (c. 500 B.C.). There are also some fine granite statues of Ptolemaic and Roman personages. A complex dealing with various aspects of the death cult in Egypt is shown at the end of the exhibition. Displayed there are mummies, canopic jars, small-scale art to accompany the dead, such as representations of the deceased, carved and painted ferry boats to transport the dead into the other world, servant workers for the other world, and books of the dead. There are a number of painted wood coffins, mummy portraits, and painted funerary shrouds, such as the well-preserved shroud of a man from Sakkara (c. A.D. 180), which depicts the deceased as he becomes Osiris.

The Papyrus Collection is a division of the Egyptian Museum. Acquisitions of private collections were made in the 1820s, and since the 1870s the collection was systematically expanded. One exhibition room is devoted to it. The writing materials exhibited include papyri and parchments in the forms of rolls and codices, wax and wood tablets and *ostraka*, which are limestone fragments and potsherds upon which short notes and messages were written. The collection is rich in papyrus scrolls and single leafs of the Middle Kingdom and equally rich in writings from the temple archives and tombs of the New Kingdom. Noteworthy are the many beautifully illustrated *Books of the Dead*. Among the greatest treasures are some unique fables and narratives, for example, *The Story of Sinuhe*.

Important also are the Greek writings that date from the time of Alexander the Great. For example, one of the oldest extant Greek literary papyri of the second half of the fourth century B.C., found in a tomb near Abusir, contains *The Persians* by Timotheus of Miletus. Another key work is the so-called *Gnomon Scroll*, a Roman-Egyptian law collection found in Middle Egypt. Particularly rare items in the collection include writings in Aramaic from the colony on the island of Elephantine. Some Coptic manuscripts are outstanding for their decorations and Arabic writings for their calligraphy.

After the Louvre and British Museum, Berlin has the third largest collection of Ancient Near Eastern art in Europe. Most of its treasures came from German excavations between 1888 and 1939. Major excavations were directed by Jordan, Nöldecke, and Lenzen at Uruk (Warka); Koldewey at Babylon; Andrae at Assur; Lehmann-Haupt at Toprak-Kale; von Oppenheim at Tell Halaf; and Humann, Puchstein, and von Luschan at Sinjirli. On the initiative of Friedrich Delitzsch, an independent museum was founded in 1899 that in 1930 received a permanent home in the Pergamum Museum. This building was partly damaged by direct bomb hits during World War II, but the monumental art treasures fortunately survived. A part of the collection was safeguarded after the war by the USSR, and in 1951 the museum had to reopen in reduced size. However, in 1959, after the return of these artworks, it opened again with its old holdings, exhibiting in fourteen halls and four rooms. The study collection of about sixty thousand objects includes a famous group of about twenty-two thousand cuneiform tablets, ranging from the fourth to the first millennium B.C., and an equally renowned seal collection.

Noteworthy are the collections of polychrome pottery and terracotta figurines from Samarra and Tell Halaf of the fourth millennium B.C., and of major importance are parts of the cone mosaic walls and column from the Temple of Inanna at Uruk (c. 3000 B.C.). Excellent examples of Sumerian art from Uruk, Lagash, Babylon, and Assur can be seen, such as small sculptures, reliefs, carved stone vessels, ceramics, jewelry, and metal tools. The unglazed brick facade of the Kassite Temple of Inanna is an impressive example of architectural ornament in Uruk about 1415 B.C. The Assyrian period is represented by artworks mainly from Assur, Nimrud, and Nineveh, including sculptures, stelae, building ceramics, pottery, bronzes, jewelry, and seals, and above all, outstanding mural reliefs from Nimrud and Nineveh. Leading the way are the large mural reliefs from the palace of Assurnasirpal II (883–859 B.C.) at Nimrud. Other orthostats are from the palaces of Sanherib (704–681 B.C.) and Assurbanipal (668–626) at Nineveh. A gigantic stone basin from Assur (c. 700 B.C.) shows in relief the watergod Ea and his priests. The art of Babylon is represented from Early to Neo-Babylonian times. A key monument is the *Stele of King Mardukapaliddina II* (721–711 B.C.).

The chief attraction of the museum is the Babylonian *Ishtar Gate* of Nebuchadnezzar II, with its processional street and part of the king's throne room facade of about 580 B.C. The reliefed and colorfully glazed brick sheathings of this great architectural conjunct were reconstructed under the direction of W. Andrae, so that the original sections could easily be differentiated from the modern substituted glazed tiles. Among Persian art should be noted a collection of painted pottery from Tepe Giyan (c. 3000–1100 B.C.), a collection of Luristan bronzes, and one small but beautiful glazed relief from the palace of Darius at Susa (c. 500 B.C.). The art of the Hittites is represented with selected major and small art objects. A resonance of Hittite style can be observed in the imposing guardian lions from Sinjirli in southern Anatolia of the tenth and eighth centuries B.C. There are also many remarkable orthostats and stelae from Sinjirli of the Aramaean and Phoenician periods. Best known among them is the *Stele of Barrekub* (c. 730 B.C.). The art of Aramaean and Phoenician Tell Halaf in north Syria is known above all for its carved basalt column figures and column bases. The best example in Berlin is the giant sculpture of a bird of prey (c. 900 B.C.).

On the initiative of Wilhelm Bode, the new division of Far Eastern art was created in 1907. In storage for years, it was moved in 1921 into a building that until then had housed the Museum of Arts and Crafts. About ninety percent of this collection and its outstanding library and photographic archive were destroyed in the war. (The new reference library has thirteen hundred volumes, and four hundred negatives are included in the new holdings.) Some of the finest objects that had been sheltered outside Berlin are now in West Berlin, and a few were returned by the USSR in 1958. The museum had to start practically anew with a small collection of late Chinese porcelain left from the Hohenzollern collections. In 1959, however, on the occasion of the German Democratic Republic's decennial, the People's Republic of China gave the museum a small but comprehensive collection of ceramics and porcelain, ranging from Neolithic times to the Hsuan tung period. This collection is especially valuable, since its objects are securely localized and dated and because of its exquisite beauty.

Imposing are the late neolithic clay vessels of the Ban-shan and Shang-Yin periods; and a group of painted clay objects, such as figurines, representations of houses, stables, and household equipment from graves in Honan Province of the Han period (206 B.C.-A.D. 220), is arresting. The earliest glazed pots date from the Shang-Yin period; others from the Han, East and West Djin, and T'ang periods (A.D. 618–906) have unusually good yellow, green, and brown glazes. Of high quality also are a number of glazed figurines from the T'ang period.

The various stages in the development of porcelain can be observed from the later Han period to the T'ang and Sung periods (A.D. 960–1279). Highlights are porcelain vessels from the Ch'ing Dynasty's Kang Hsi period (1662–1722) and Ch'ien-lung period (1736–95), many of the latter with the mark of Emperor Ch'ien-lung. The museum also possesses a small collection of Japanese pottery, mostly of the Edo period, about 1800; some Chinese and Japanese Buddhist stone, wood, and bronze sculptures; Chinese lacquer and enamel works; jade carvings of the eighteenth century; a collection of Japanese sword-guards; and Chinese textiles, such as silk embroideries from the eighteenth and nineteenth centuries. Recent acquisitions include collections of Chinese and Japanese wood-cuts by well-known masters of the eighteenth and nineteenth centuries, some landscape paintings of the seventeenth to nineteenth century, some reproductions of early paintings in woodcuts, and a collection of the most important contemporary Chinese ink painters. Finally, European seventeenth- and eighteenth-century prints, illustrated travel accounts, and color lithographs with city views taken by the Prussian East Asia expedition in 1869 present outsiders' views of the Far East.

Founded in 1829 as the Museum of National Antiquities, the Museum of Pre- and Protohistory originated in the Kunstkabinett of the Hohenzollerns. Renamed by the mid-nineteenth century the Museum of Northern Antiquities, it got its present name in 1908, because its director Carl Schuchhardt had expanded the areas of collection to all of Europe and the Mediterranean. In 1881, for example, Schliemann's Trojan finds were added to the collection. The museum expanded significantly into the 1930s, especially in the areas of Germanic and Slavic archaeology. After being housed in three locations, in 1921 it was installed in the vacated Museum of Arts and Crafts, where it exhibited in twenty-one halls and where it had an entire floor for its study collection and library. In 1941 complex evacuations to places within and outside the city began, and in 1945 the building was destroyed by bombs. Among the losses must be counted the important precious metal collection, which included Schliemann's Trojan finds. By 1953 part of the collection was reassembled in West Berlin, and in 1960 moved to Charlottenburg. The evacuated objects that had been taken by the USSR from Berlin were returned in 1958, creating the nucleus of the present collection, which is now for the most part in storage. It is available, however, for consultation upon request, and selected objects of its holdings are exhibited in several rooms of the Bode Museum.

The collection includes stone and metal tools and weapons, statuettes, ceramics, glasses, and jewelry of most periods of human development, from about 500,000 to the first century B.C., and from all regions of Europe, the Near East, North Africa, Siberia, and China. Important are fine examples of European and Asian pottery of the Neolithic period and the Bronze Age and many skillfully worked Bronze Age artifacts. A sizable collection of Celtic bronze and iron artifacts includes animal forms, fibulas, belt buckles, torques, armlets, earrings, household and horse gear, tools, and weapons. Another group of artifacts represents the early Germanic tribes of central Europe with typical polychrome metalwork.

The nucleus of the Collection of Greek and Roman Antiquities came from the Kunstkammer of Frederick the Great. In 1830 it was established in Schinkel's New Museum building. It was subdivided into the Antiken-Sammlung, consisting of Greek and Roman large-scale sculpture, and the Antiquarium, with smaller artworks. Because of lack of space, the collection of Greek vases was housed after 1855 in the New Museum. Through German excavations on the west coast of Asia Minor, much significant architectural art was acquired, for which Berlin attained much of its world fame. Theodor Wiegand and Carl Humann, for example, supervised excavations at Didyma, Miletis, Myus, Magnesia, Priene, and Samos; Carl Humann, Alexander Conze, and Wilhelm Dörpfeld led the spectacular excavation at Pergamum; Otto Puchstein excavated Baalbeck; and Olympia was largely excavated by Ernst Curtius, Friedrich Adler, and Wilhelm Dörpfeld. These huge architectural discoveries needed a separate building. The first Pergamum Museum was built in 1902 by the architect Fritz Wolff, in which the Great Altar was reconstructed. But the building soon proved too small and was razed in 1908. In 1930 the new Pergamum Museum by Alfred Messel was inaugurated on the same site. Its central wing housed then as now the architectural displays. Until World War II, therefore, the Greek and Roman collections were scattered in three buildings: the Old Museum, the New Museum, and the Pergamum.

Among irreplaceable war losses were part of the glass collection and the vase collection, as well as miscellaneous objects. About a third of the Antiquarium's holdings ended up in West Berlin. Nevertheless, with the objects returned from the USSR in 1958, the museum reopened again the following year with the paramount part of its original holdings intact. The architectural exhibits had been reopened in 1954. The holdings are now united in one building, occupying twenty-three halls and rooms. Greek and Roman art is now located in the north wing of the Pergamum Museum, logically linked with ancient architecture in the central wing. Following, however, the old internal subdivisions, the central wing is called the Architekturmuseum; the floor of the north wing, which houses large-scale sculpture, the Skulpturensammlung; and the third floor of the north wing, which houses in nine rooms smaller art objects, the Antiquarium. Today the museum is again one of the world's largest and best.

The Architekturmuseum is famous for its *Altar of Zeus and Athena of Pergamum*, erected by Eumenes II between 180 and 159 B.C. The sculptures of the great frieze of this altar depict the battle of the gods and the giants. The sculptures of the smaller Telephos frieze from the altar's inner court rank among the best Hellenistic examples. Almost as prominent is the reconstruction of the *Marketgate of Miletis* (c. A.D. 165), providing an impressive example of Roman monumental architecture of Asia Minor. The museum exhibits an impressive collection of Archaic and Classical Greek architectural fragments and ornaments from Samos, Didyma, Myus, Olympia, Priene, and Pergamum. Truly imposing are about a dozen partial reconstructions of colonnades and facades of Hellenistic temples, courts, and altars from Pergamum, Priene, Magnesia, and Miletis. Reconstructions of part of the Temple of Trajan in Pergamum (A.D. 117) and of two rose granite columns from the altar court of the sanctuary at Baalbeck, and superb carved details from the site, give a good impression of Roman architecture. A key work in the Skulpturensammlung is the Archaic marble statue of the Attic *Maiden with a Pomegranate* from Keratea (c. 580–570 B.C.), and a significant example of the late Archaic style is the *Seated Goddess from Tarentum* (c. 480 B.C.). There are a number of Classical and Hellenistic large sculptures, as well as some large bronzes (e.g., the so-called *Praying Boy*) and various high-quality gravestones and votive reliefs from the sixth to the fourth century B.C. Astonishing is the large collection of Hellenistic, Pergamene, and Roman copies of Classical Greek statues and reliefs, among them a copy of Phidias' *Athena Parthenos* from the library of Pergamum. Important examples of Roman sculpture are the *Medea Sarcophagus* (mid-second century A.D.), and another with Apollo, Athena, and Muses, both from Rome.

Much of Berlin's sculpture is superb Roman portrait sculpture in the form of funerary reliefs, as well as statues and busts. The latter constitutes a large collection, ranging from the first to the fourth century A.D., including almost a complete array of Roman emperors and busts of children, young men, girls, matrons, philosophers, statesmen, soldiers, and foreigners. The Antiquarium has a good collection of bronze figures from Archaic to Hellenistic times, of which a youth from Crete (c. 640–610 B.C.) and bronzes from Samos are noteworthy. A collection of terracottas extends from Archaic to Hellenistic times, of which a Boeotian early fifth-century B.C. group of figurines engaged in various domestic activities and fine figurines from Tanagra are exceptional. Some, like the young woman with blue chiton and pointed hat, are stunning for size and beauty. Another group of such figurines comes from Myrina, dating from the second and first centuries B.C.

Pottery and vase painting include the Greek Geometric period; the Corinthian period, with some fascinating votive plaques, depicting potters working in clay pits and at their kilns; eastern Greek sixth- and fifth-century B.C. sarcophagi frames with painted scenes; black- and red-figured Attic vases in all shapes and sizes, several by well-known painters, such as Exekias and the Penelope Painter. There are a number of beautiful white-background lekythoi of the fifth century B.C. and several fine fourth-century B.C. Apulian and Campanian red-figured vessels. There are also Etruscan ceramics and bronzes and Roman examples of pottery, especially good vessels and lamps of terra sigillata. There are small but fine collections of Roman glass and bronze objects. Finally, several superior mosaics can be found in each of the three subdivisions. A delicate mosaic from the palace of Attalos II in Pergamum (second century B.C.), with the artist's signature "Hephaistion," is laid out in the architectural museum, where a Roman second-century A.D. mosaic from Miletis depicting Orpheus charming the animals can also be found. A well-known mosaic from Hadrian's villa at Tivoli, depicting centaurs and wild beasts, can be seen in the Antiquarium.

The Collection of Early Christian and Byzantine Art was a subdivision of the former Department of Sculpture of the Christian Periods, later the Sculpture Collection, until 1952 when it became independent. Its nucleus consists of the Pajaro Collection of Lombard, Byzantine, and Venetian architectural sculpture purchased in 1840; and many objects, including important ivories, that were added from the Hohenzollern Collection in 1875. Under Wilhelm von Bode and Oskar Wulff, the curator, the collection was systematically enlarged through donations, purchases, and relocations from other departments until World War II. Since 1904 it has been housed in the Bode Museum. The events of World War II resulted in the transferral of many objects to what is now West Berlin, but about three hundred objects are again exhibited in five halls of the Bode Museum, and about five hundred objects make up a study collection of Coptic textiles.

The exhibition covers Late Antique, Early Christian, and Byzantine and post-Byzantine art from Italy, Greece, Asia Minor, Coptic Egypt, and Russia, from the third to the nineteenth century, although the emphasis is on the period from the third to the twelfth century. The Coptic holdings, in part purchased at the beginning of this century by Joseph Strzygowski in Egypt, are outstanding. There are a number of terracottas from Abu Mena from the fourth to the sixth century, ceramics, and painted wooden boxes. Important are several large figurative and ornamental stone carvings from Coptic churches and monasteries, many of them grave stelae, of which an example from Medinet el Fayum, depicting a mother and child, the mother in the type of Isis, is of special interest. Also significant are Coptic textiles with pagan and Christian or decorative motifs and a few encaustic and tempera paintings, of which the icon *Bishop Abraham* from Hermonthis (c. 600) is best known.

Lombard art is represented with an assembly of carved marble ciboria, baptismal fonts, sarcophagi, and architectural sculptures, of eighth-century Northern and Southern Italy. Of great interest are Roman, Etruscan, Jewish, and Christian sarcophagi and fragments from the eastern and western parts of the Roman Empire of the third and fourth centuries. A fourth-century collection of minor art includes metal plaques with Christian scenes and a gold glass from the Roman catacomb from Vigna Randanini with a depiction of the Torah Shrine.

The pride of the museum is the reconstructed Ravennese apse mosaic *San Michele in Affricisco* (545), with the victorious Christ flanked by the archangels Michael and Gabriel. The apse wall depicts Christ at the Last Judgment. Purchased in 1844 by Frederick William IV, it was donated in 1904 by William II when the collection moved into the Bode Museum. Some Early Christian carved stone reliefs from Constantinople are important, since they are among the few extant examples of figure style in the East Roman capital. Principal among them are a large fragment with Christ, flanked by two apostles (c. 400); the portrait head of Fausta Minor (c. 340); and a fragment of St. Peter (fifth century). The life-size, tenth-century, Constantinopolitan marble *Virgin Orans* is exemplary for the Middle Byzantine style. A small but fine group of icons includes a thirteenth-century mosaic from Sicily with a crucifixion, sixteenth-century Russian icons, a Greek seventeenth-century *Anastasis*, and a Russian seventeenth-century icon of the Stroganov school. There is a selection of objects of the Late Middle Ages, including metalwork, ceramics, portable altars, and book covers. Finally, one can see an impressive carved iconostasis wall from Chios (1775) and a proskynitarion, both already in the style known as Turkish Rococo.

In 1903, through negotiations of Joseph Strzygowski, the splendid facade of the Umayyad desert palace Mschatta was presented by the Turkish sultan to the Berlin State Museum. This provided the occasion for the foundation of a separate museum, the Museum of Islamic Art, which in 1904 opened in the Bode Museum. In 1905 valuable carpets from Wilhelm Bode's collection were added, and the important collection of Friedrich Sarre was incorporated in 1922. It also grew through transfers from other divisions but primarily through private contributions that allowed systematic purchases. Finally, excavations in Samarra, Ctesiphon, and Tabgha enriched the museum, so by 1932, when it was moved into the Pergamum Museum, it had become one of the finest in Europe. World War II caused inevitable losses. Treasures that had not been removed, like the Mschatta facade, were badly damaged by bombs. The admirable restoration works on that facade alone took eight years. Valuable carpets were burned. Efforts to shelter the collection resulted in its division, so some fifteen hundred objects are now in West Berlin. In 1954 the museum reopened with the Mschatta Hall and ten rooms, and in 1959, after the safeguarded objects were returned by the USSR, the collection was again exhibited in eighteen rooms. It is again an important collection, providing a survey of Islamic art in Iran, India, Turkey, Syria, Transjordan, Egypt, and Spain.

Mohammedan art was in part indebted to Sassanian. It is, therefore, an advantage to have the stucco art from Ctesiphon (fifth to seventh century) included as a background to Islamic art. Several large stucco wall encasings and stone carvings from Ctesiphon can be seen.

Outstanding is the forty-five-meter-long reconstruction of a segment of the facade of the Umayyad desert palace Mschatta, east of the Dead Sea, built probably by Caliph al-Walid II in 743–44. With its filigree carvings in limestone and monumental scale, it is a truly superior work of art. Excavations led by Ernst Herzfeld in Samarra resulted in further acquisitions of decorated stucco wall encasements, stone carvings, and ceramic vessels, all of the Abbasid period (833–83). The museum is rich in carved-wood panels, doors, and furniture from various regions and periods. For example, Egypt is well represented with woodworks of the Fatimid period (969–1171), some inlaid with ivory. A key work is the Syrian *Aleppo Room* (1600–1603) of the Ottoman period. It is entirely paneled in carved and painted wood, the decoration consisting of arabesques but also of scenes from the life of Christ. The museum has an excellent collection of faience tiles, many displayed in architectural reconstructions. Outstanding among them is an Iranian prayer niche from the Maydan mosque at Kashan, signed by Hasan ben 'Arabshah (1226). Two Isfahan seventeenth-century tile paintings with standing figures closely relate to contemporary Isfahan book paintings, the Riza-i-Abbasi school. There are first-rate Ottoman tiles from Istambul and Isnik. The collection of ceramic vessels covers all of the areas mentioned above. Especially lovely is a faience jug from Rayy (c. 1200) that shows delightful figurative decoration in minai technique. Another outstanding piece is a blue-white Iranian plate with zodiac signs by 'Abd al-Wahid (1563–64) that shows the Chinese influence. Although many of the carpets were burned in the war, the present collection is still impressive, including examples from Asia Minor, Iran, and Egypt from 1400 to 1800.

Important is the collection of Iranian and Indian miniatures from the fourteenth to the eighteenth century. A key work is the Iranian Baisonqur manuscript from Schiras (1420), an anthology of Persian poetry from the tenth to the fifteenth century, with twenty-nine miniatures. Several single-leaf miniatures are in the tradition of Riza 'Abbasi of Isfahan. His own hand can be seen in the *Portrait of the Georgian Prince Muhammad Beg* (first half of the seventeenth century). The Indian miniatures are of the Mogul peroiod (1526–1857), with an emphasis on the seventeenth century. Painted for the imperial house by the imperial workshop, they were assembled in the eighteenth century for a European collector. The museum holds this entire collection of miniatures, which includes portraits of emperors, court officials, and court scenes. Noteworthy are animal studies by the court painter Murad (c. 1630) and many miniatures from the later seventeenth century depicting idyllic scenes and lovers.

In 1830 medieval, Renaissance, and Baroque sculpture was housed in the Old Museum as an appendix to the division of ancient sculpture. Major acquisitions were made in 1828 with the purchase of the Bartholdy Collection and in 1840, the Pajaro Collection. More than one hundred important Italian Renaissance works were purchased by Gustav Friedrich Waagen, followed by more key purchases, especially Italian portrait busts, by Wilhelm Bode. In 1875 sculptures from the royal Kunstkammer were incorporated, and in 1883, under Bode's direction, the collection became independent as the Department of the Christian Periods. In 1904 it moved into the Bode Museum, where it was subdivided into three divisions: Early Christian and Byzantine Sculpture; Medieval, Renaissance and Baroque Sculpture of Italy and Spain; and Medieval, Renaissance and Baroque Sculpture of Germany and the Netherlands. Although they were independent sculpture divisions, their holdings were exhibited with paintings of the same regions and periods, a concept of Bode that is still adhered to today.

The collections were systematically built up into the 1930s, partly through private donations, two alone by James Simon in 1905 and 1918, others through the Kaiser-Friedrich-Museums Verein. In 1930 the German and Netherlandish subdivision was incorporated into the newly founded German Museum, which displayed art from the Germanic migrations to the Baroque period, and which was located from 1930 until the war in the Pergamum Museum, only to be united again after the war. Many large Italian Renaissance sculptures were lost in a fire in the Berlin-Friedrichshain shelter, and many key works are now in West Berlin. Four hundred and fifty objects were returned in 1958 by the USSR. Today the Sculpture Collection consists of an imposing complex of large and small wood, stone, and bronze sculptures from Romanesque through early neoclassicism, with emphasis on the early Italian Renaissance, the Northern Renaissance, and German Baroque, especially works from Berlin.

Italian Gothic is represented with famous works, such as the *Angel, Virgin, and Apostle* by Pisano and the group *Dormition of the Virgin* by Arnolfo di Cambio. Particularly well represented is the Italian Renaissance, with all of its phases of development and characteristic categories, with terracotta works by Ghiberti, Donatello, Benedetto da Maiano, Settignano, Antonio Rosselino, and the della Robbia family. Luca della Robbia is represented by three works, Andrea della Robbia and his workshop by twelve. Desiderio da Settignano's limestone bust of a princess of Urbino (c. 1460) and Antonio Rosselino's bust of a Florentine (c. 1470) are outstanding, as are Francesco da Sangallo's terracotta relief the *Virgin with Reading Child* (c. 1540–50) and Sansovino's *Sacra Conversazione*. Italian Baroque is represented by some good works, of which the marble portrait of *Principe Michele Damasceni Peretti* by Algardi is a fine example. About two-thirds of the former collection of bronze statuettes (donated by Simon in 1905) are now in West Berlin, but fine examples are still left on the Museum Isle, chief among them Pollaiuolo's *Hercules* and works by Giovanni da Bologna.

French sculpture is thinly represented, but two Gothic wood sculptures, a St. Catherine (c.1300) and a St. Michael (late fourteenth century), are noteworthy. Well represented on the other hand is Late Gothic and Renaissance sculpture of the Netherlands. Memorable is the sandstone group *St. Anne, the Virgin, and Child* (c. 1467) by Nicolaus Gerhaert von Leyden. There are many works from Antwerp dating from 1500 to 1520, among which the carved oak *Antwerp Altar* is outstanding. Several works, ranging between 1480 and 1520, are from Brussels. A group of *Prophets* (c. 1520) by Jan Borman is also noteworthy, as is the *Utrecht Passion Altar with Donors* (c. 1520). German Romanesque and Gothic is represented with few but paramount works, such as the famous *Gröningen Gallery* stone carvings with Christ in judgment and seated apostles, from Lower Saxony (c. 1170). Outstanding are the *Naumburg Crucifixion* (c. 1230); four life-size prophets from the Church of Our Lady in Trier (c. 1250); the *Minden High Altar* (1260 and 1425); the stone heads of prophets and a prince (c. 1390) by the Nürnberg Master of the Beautiful Fountain; the small Dangolsheim saint (c. 1480) from the upper Rhine, by the Master of the Dangolsheim Madonna; and Anton Pilgram's sandstone chancel figure (1485–90) from Öhringen. Although most of the Riemenschneider works of the original collection are now in West Berlin, the *Adoration of the Shepherds* (1500–1505) and the *Crucifixion* (1510–15) can be seen. Of high quality is the *Bust of a Young Woman* (before 1518) from the Fugger Chapel in Augsburg by Sebastian Loscher, one of three extant of originally sixteen.

North German Baroque is dominated by the Berlin artist Andreas Schlüter, with eight monumental sandstone figures from the Villa Kamecke, Berlin (c. 1711), and a bronze equestrian statue of Frederick William the Great. Austrian Baroque is represented by the figures *St. Rochus* and *St. Sebastian* by Giovanni Giuliani. Johann Georg Dirr's *Virgin* and *Virgin in Prayer* (c. 1760) are key works of South German Rococo. Of equally high quality is Paul Egell's *Great Mannheim Altar*.

The nucleus of the Picture Gallery, which in 1830 was exhibited in Schinkel's new edifice, consisted of 378 paintings selected from the royal collections in Berlin, Potsdam, and Charlottenburg; the private collections of Giustiniani, with 73 paintings; and those of Solly, with 350 paintings, purchased by Frederick William III in 1815 and 1821, respectively. The accents lay on Early Netherlandish, seventeenth-century Dutch and Flemish, and Italian paintings from the Trecento to the early eighteenth century. From 1872 to 1929 the collection grew remarkably through the activities of Wilhelm Bode and Max J. Friedländer, who was director of the Picture Gallery from 1929 to 1933. In 1904 the collection moved with the corresponding sculptures into the Bode Museum. The German and Netherlandish part was separated from 1930 (the opening of Deutsches Museum) until after the war. The two world wars brought great losses to the Picture Gallery. In 1920 two wings of Jan van Eyck's *Ghent Altar Piece*, which had been acquired in 1818 through Solly, as well as Dieric Bouts' *Louvain Triptych*, purchased in 1834 by von Waagen, had to be returned to Belgium, in accordance with the Versailles Treaty. After World War II, through the various sheltering activities, about twelve hundred paintings that had been seized by the Americans and British were housed in West Berlin. The paintings, which had been taken from Berlin by the USSR, were, however, returned in 1958, and the collection today is still strong in the Florentine Quattrocento, North Italian early sixteenth-century centers, and seventeenth-century Netherlandish paintings. It also possesses a fine collection of miniature paintings. Many paintings are still in storage but can be viewed upon request.

Outstanding among the paintings of the Dugento and Trecento are the *Virgin and Child* (c. 1275) by the school of Cimabue, the *Virgin and Child* (c. 1380) by a follower of Simone Martini, the *Nativity* by the school of Ambrogio Lorenzetti, and a triptych by Starnina with the early *Sacra Conversazione*. The Florentine early Cinquecento is represented by altar panels of the school of Lorenzo Monaco and by the altar panel *Mary Magdalen, St. Lawrence and Donor* by the Maestro del Bambino Vispo. Outstanding among the Italian fifteenth-century works is the *Architectural Perspective* by Francesco di Giorgio Martini (c. 1475). Among the many Florentine fifteenth- and sixteenth-century works are Rosello di Jacopo Franchi's *Garden of Delights* (c. 1450), Paolo Ucello's *Madonna and Child* (c. 1450), Ghirlandaio's *Resurrection of Christ*, the Master of the Gardener Annunciation's *Madonna and Child* (1481), Filippino

Lippi's *Portrait of a Youth*, Fra Bartolommeo's *St. Jerome*, Leonardo da Vinci's and Giovanni Antonio Boltraffio's *Rising Christ, Adored by Saints Leonard and Lucy*, Vasari's portrait of *Bernadetto de Medici* and *Apostles Peter and John*, and the tondo *Virgin, Christ Child, and Little St. John* by Domenico Beccafumi. Lombard and Milanese painters are very well represented. Outstanding examples are Bernardino Fasolo's *Holy Family*; Bernardino Luini's *Girl Accompanying Europa*, one of nine parts of a fresco series; and Francesco Melzi's *Vertumnus and Pomona*. Sixteenth-century masters of other North Italian centers, such as the school of Bergamo, Brescia, Vicenza, Pordenone, Ferrara, and Bologna, are also well represented.

Of the Venetian school from the sixteenth to the eighteenth century are works by Marco Marziale, Catena, Paris Bordone, Bassano, della Vecchia, Marco Ricci, il Dalmatino, Antonio Guardi, Tiepolo, and Canaletto. Roman Baroque is represented by works of Lanfranco, Cerrini, Sassoferrato, Panini, and Batoni; Neapolitan art of the second half of the seventeenth century by works of Luca Giordano and Francesco Mura; sixteenth- and seventeenth-century art of Genoa by works of Sacchi, Cambiaso, and Castiglioni.

The collection of German paintings extends from about 1400 to the early nineteenth century. Outstanding among these works are the *Cologne Crucifixion* (c. 1430), the Housebook Master's *Last Supper*, Hans Leonhard Schäuffelein's *Last Supper*, Georg Pencz' *Portrait of a Young Man* (1534), and Lucas Cranach the Elder's *Last Judgement* after Hieronymus Bosch's altarpiece in Vienna.

Among seventeenth-century works, Adam Elsheimer's *Landscape with Bathing Nymph and Satyr* (c. 1605) is noteworthy. The eighteenth century is represented by works of Christian Wilhelm Ernst Dietrich, Joachim Martin Falbe, Anton Graff, and Anna Dorothea Therbusch. In the collection of Early Netherlandish paintings we find works by Aelbert Bouts, Cornelius van Cleve, Pieter Coecke van Aelst, and Roymerswaele's *St. Jerome*. Of the sixteenth-century artists the Antwerp Mannerist Jan Gossaert stands out with *Neptune and Amphitrite* and *Adam and Eve*. Also noteworthy is *Momus Criticizing the Creation of the Gods* by the Haarlem Romanist Maarten van Heemskerck. An area of concentration is seventeenth-century Dutch and Flemish painting. Of the works of early masters, Savery's *Paradise* (1626) and Uytewael's *Kitchen Still Life* (1605) are outstanding. There are also many fine realistic Dutch landscapes, seascapes, and cityscapes, among which Jan van Goyen's *Seasons* (1621), Salomon van Ruysdael's *Street along a Dutch Canal* (1636), and Hendrik Cornelisz Vroom's *Dutch Ships before the Danish Coast* (1612) are most interesting. There is also a fine selection of genre scenes. Prominent among them are Jan Miense Molenaer's *Artist's Studio* (1631), Honthorst's *Brothel* (1624), and Metsu's *Duet*.

The collection also includes excellent portraits, of which Valckert's *Four Regents of the Merchant's Guild* (1622) and Ter Borch's *Self Portrait* (c. 1676 replica) are but two of many. Although the Rembrandts are now in West Berlin, works by his students and followers abound. The early seventeenth-century Caravaggist Utrecht school is represented by Terbrugghen's *Esau Selling His*

Birth-Rights and Honthorst's *Liberation of St. Peter in Prison*, the later Utrecht style by paintings of Cornelis van Poelenburgh, Dirk van der Lisse, Herman Saftleven the Younger, and landscapists Jan Both and Gysbert Gillisz. Hondecoeter.

Flemish seventeenth-century painting is not as abundantly represented as the Dutch, but several works are noteworthy. Although most of the Rubens are now in West Berlin, two can be seen in the Bode Museum, namely *Christ Handing Peter the Keys to Heaven* (1612–14) and the attributed portrait *Cardinal Infant Ferdinand of Austria* (after 1628). There are works by Willeboirts, Gaspard de Crayer, and Jordaens. Numerous landscapes and seascapes can be seen, among them Paul Bril's *Mountainous Seashore* (after 1624). There are fine portraits by Pieter Franchoys and Pieter Meert and still-life paintings by several artists. Especially notable among them are the floral paintings of wreaths surrounding monochrome scenes by de Heem, Daniel Seghers, and van Verendael.

French painting is not very well represented, but two paintings are outstanding: Poussin's *Self Portrait* (1649) and Rigaud's *Portrait of the Sculptor Desjardins*. Similarly, the English collection is scanty but includes Gainsborough's *Portrait of Sir John Wilkinson* and Raeburn's *Portrait of Sir James Montgomery Bart*.

Finally, the Picture Gallery possesses a fine collection of European minatures, primarily portraits of European nobility. Outstanding are Hans Bol's *Fishermen's Joust* (c. 1550), Cranach the Elder's *Katharina von Bora*, Jean Petitot's *Louis XIV*, Alexander Cooper's portrait-medallions *Frederick V, King of Bohemia, with His Wife and Children*, Richard Cosway's *Caroline Amalie Elisabeth, Queen of Great Britain and Hannover*, Daniel Chodowiecki's *Self Portrait with Wife*, Füger's *Countesses Elisabeth, Christiane, and Marie Karoline Thun*, and a French master's *Portrait of Empress Josephine of France* (c. 1800).

The idea of a National Gallery had its roots in the Revolution of 1848. However, the immediate cause of its foundation was the bequest in 1861 of the collection of 262 recent, primarily German, paintings by the Berlin merchant and former consul to Sweden and Norway, Joachim Heinrich Wilhelm Wagener. The foundation of the National Gallery that would henceforth collect contemporary paintings and sculptures was a condition of Wagener's bequest. At first the collection was installed in the academy, on Unter den Linden, but by 1876 it had its own neoclassical building after plans by August Stüler. Wagener's collection was strongest in artists of the Munich and Düsseldorf schools, and acquisitions in the 1870s concentrated on German Romantic painters and Berlin painters, such as Adolph Menzel, as well as on Romanist painters, such as Böcklin and Feuerbach. In 1877 the Sammlung der Zeichnungen, a subdivision of drawings, watercolors, and oil studies, was founded, which complemented the collection of paintings and sculptures and which in 1969 was joined to the Department of Prints and Drawings. Under Hugo von Tschudi, director from 1896 to 1909, the National Gallery began to purchase French Impressionist paintings, against the growing resistance of nationalistic elements and the inclinations of the emperor. Von Tschudi finally succumbed to these forces and left for Munich. His successor Ludwig Justi was able in 1919 to found the New Division of the National Gallery, installed in the former crown prince's palace, on Unter den Linden.

The Neue Sammlung began with the Impressionists and acquired over the years a significant collection, including the various contemporary trends in Germany, as well as non-German artists, such as Picasso, Braque, Gris, Dufy, de'Chirico, and Carrà. The rapid growth of the National Gallery can be gauged by the fact that two more subdivisions were opened: in 1930 the Rauch Museum in the Orangerie of Charlottenburg and in 1931 the Schinkel Museum in the former princess' palace, also on Unter den Linden. By then the museum had one of the world's finest collections of nineteenth- and twentieth-century art, especially that from Germany. Damaged in the war, the National Gallery's main building was partially reopened in 1949, totally in 1955. Today this building houses the combined pre-war holdings, plus new acquisitions, minus those that are now in West Berlin. Its section of post-war art, primarily of artists of the German Democratic Republic, and its administration are housed in the Old Museum. Although the losses are lamentable, the National Gallery again constitutes an outstanding collection of primarily German paintings and sculpture, from about 1800 to the present, after 1945 almost exclusively the art of the German Democratic Republic. It holds, however, a number of high-quality works by non-German artists. It stages about four yearly special exhibitions and maintains an archive that includes artists' letters and newspaper clippings and documents about nineteenth- and twentieth-century artists.

Sculptures are generally displayed with corresponding paintings, with an impressive concentration of neoclassical works at the beginning of the exhibition. There are a number of excellent works by Johann Gottfried Schadow; some, like the *Tomb of the Young Count of the Mark* (1791), the *Double Statue of Princesses Luise and Friederike of Prussia* (1797), the bust of *Goethe* (1823), and the small relief of *Eros Resting* (1798), are considered key works of German neoclassicism. Works by Canova include *Hebe* (1796), *Paris* (1816), *Venus* (1818), and *Spes* (1830). Thorvaldsen's bust of *Wilhelm von Humboldt* (1808) is also noteworthy. There are a number of works by Schadow's follower Christian Daniel Rauch, among them a fine bust of his daughter *Agnes Rauch-d'Alton* and the bust *Alexander von Humboldt* (1823–50). Other works of this period are by Rudolf Schadow, Emil Wolf, Ludwig von Schwanthaler, and Heinrich Kümmel.

Other noteworthy neoclassical and early Romantic paintings are Anton Graff's 1769 replica of a *Portrait of Gellert*, Ferdinand Kobell's *Neckar Landscape* (1782), Mengs' *Self Portrait* (c. 1774), Tischbein's *Princess Friederike of Prussia* (1790), Füger's *Princess Galitzin* (1782), Weitsch's *Alexander von Humboldt* (1806), Koch's *Death of Oscar* (1804), and Wilhelm von Schadow's *Self Portrait with His Brother Rudolf and Thorvaldsen* (c. 1815–18). There is also Goya's *Maypole* (before 1828). Of major importance are the frescoes of the *Casa Bartholdy* (1816–17) by the Nazarenes Overbeck, Cornelius, Veit, and Wilhelm von Schadow, which can be seen in a separate room. Other interesting works are

Julius Schnorr von Carolsfeld's *Bathsheba* (1821–25), Adolf Senff's *Night with Her Children, Death, and Sleep* (1822) after a relief by Thorvaldsen, Ernst Ferdinand Oehme's *Landscape with Burg Hohenstein* (1827), and Karl Begas the Elder's *Portrait of Thorvaldsen* (1823). Works by Franz Krüger include two of his typical parade paintings, and of a number of works by Karl Blechen, his *In the Park of Villa d'Este* (c. 1830) is outstanding. Several excellent works by Adolph Menzel, such as small landscape paintings and sketches often dealing with Prussian court life, can be seen. Of monumental scale are his *Meeting of Frederick II with Emperor Joseph in Neisse, Aug. 25, 1769* (1857), a gift of the Polish government, and his most important industrial genre work, *Iron Rolling Mill* (1875). The German Neo-Renaissance painters are represented with a number of first-rate works, such as Böcklin's *Angelika* (1873) and *Self Portrait with Wine Glass* (1885), von Marées' *Two Male Nudes*, Feuerbach's *Banquet of Plato* (1870–73), Wilhelm Leibl's *Head of a Girl* (1879), and Hans Thoma's *Mother of the Artist* (1886) and *Portrait of Artist's Wife* (1878–80). Several important works by Liebermann include his *Shoemaker's Shop* (1881) and his monumental *Flax Barn at Laren* (1887).

The museum lost many of its modern French art works, and the works that can be seen today are few but are of high quality. Outstanding among them are Courbet's *Mill Dam* (1866); Fantin-Latour's *Self-Portrait* (1858) and *The Artist's Wife* (1883); Degas' *Conversation* (1884); three beautiful Cézannes: *Still Life with Fruits and Dishes* (1871–72), *Mill at Couleuvre* (c. 1881), and *Still Life with Flowers and Fruits* (1888–90); Dufy's *Harbor* (1908); and Vlaminck's *Still-Life* (c. 1920). There are also several fine bronze sculptures by Meunier, Rodin, and Degas.

The German Impressionists are very well represented, for example, Leistikow's *Grunewaldsee* (1895), Slevogt's early *Self-Portrait* (1888) and *The Singer d'Andrade as Don Giovanni* (1912), Lovis Corinth's *Portrait of Charlotte Berend-Corinth* (1912), and Charlotte Berend-Corinth's *Toledo Landscape* (1915). There are five works by Kokoschka, of which *Herr Hirsch* (1908) and *Pariser Platz Berlin* (1925–26) are most interesting. The German Expressionists are represented by Nolde's *Papuan Youths* (1913–14) and works by Rohlfs, Kirchner (one his fine *Self-Portrait* [1919]), Schmidt-Rottluff, and Pechstein (also with his *Self-Portrait* [1926]). Jawlensky is present with the *Still Life* of his Blaue Reiter period and one of his later characteristic heads, *Desire* (1925). (Kandinsky, Marc, Macke, Klee, and others were among the "degenerate artists" the Gallery lost in 1937.) The Bauhaus school is represented by Feininger's *Teltow* (1918) and Schlemmer's *Mensch* (1919) and *White Boy* (1930). There are also works by Willi Baumeister.

German Verism is represented in its various aspects. Expressionist examples are by Dix, such as *Marianne Vogelsang* (1931) and *Old Lovers* (1923). More surreal are works by Franz Radziwill, such as his *Dunes of Schoorl* (1927). The magic realism of Alexander Kanoldt is represented by two works. There are five paintings by Georg Schrimpf; two by Kurt Günter, among them *The Radio Addict*

(1927); and twelve by Otto Nagel, among which his *Bench in Wedding* (1927) is outstanding. Heinrich Vogeler is represented by thirty-eight paintings, ranging from his Worpswede period and propagandistic works of the twenties (agitation panels) to the many works he painted in the USSR from 1931 to 1942, many of them portraits. Noteworthy among the numerous works of recent and contemporary artists of the German Democratic Republic are those by Max Lingner, Hans Grundig, Willi Sitte, Werner Tübke, Bernhard Heisig, and Wolfgang Mattheuer.

Modern sculpture is represented by works of Adolf von Hildebrand, Karl Begas the Younger, Reinhold Begas, Maillol, Georg Kolbe, Renée Sintenis, Ernst Barlach, Käthe Kollwitz, and Wilhelm Lehmbruck. Noteworthy among sculptors of the German Democratic Republic are Fritz Cremer, Gustav Seitz, Waldemar Grzimek, Walter Arnold, and Wieland Förster.

When in 1831 the Department of Prints and Drawings (founded on recommendation of Wilhelm von Humboldt) moved into the Old Museum, its basic holdings were 480 drawings from the royal collection. Several private collections were purchased, including in 1835 that of Berlin's Postmaster General von Nagler. The department soon grew to international importance as a result of the systematic purchasing policies of its directors. Because of evacuations to places outside Berlin during World War II, about two-thirds of the department's holdings, including many of its finest, ended up in West Berlin. In 1958, however, about 120,000 pieces, taken after 1945 from Berlin to the USSR, were returned to the Museum Isle. In 1969 the Collection of Drawings, which had been founded in 1877 as a subdivision of the National Gallery, was joined to the Department of Prints and Drawings, with holdings of about 30,000 works, mostly of German nineteenth- and twentieth-century artists. Today, again housed in the Old Museum, the combined holdings number about 190,000 items, of which about 150,000 pertain to the Department of Prints and Drawings (including about 1,000 drawings of Old Masters) and some 40,000 to the Collection of Drawings.

Although the more important holdings of the Department of Prints and Drawings are now in West Berlin, a number of important works are in the Old Museum. Chief among them are Botticelli's sixty-one silver-point drawings for Dante's *Divine Comedy* (twenty-seven are in West Berlin), Michelangelo's grand fragmentary sketch for the *Tomb of Pope Julius II*, and drawings by Barocci. Valuable also is a woodcut from seven blocks with a detailed city view of Florence, the so-called *Chain Plan* (c. 1488), the only known example (by an unknown master). Among important German works are Hans Schäufelein's drawing of a *Mercenary* (c. 1507); five drawings by Grünewald, among them a *St. Anthony* (c. 1515) for his Isenheim Altar; Hans Burgkmair's woodcut from eight blocks of *Adam and Eve* (1525); Holbein the Younger's design *Dance of Death*; and Cranach the Younger's *Baptism of Christ*. Also important is the von Derschau Collection of Nürnberg woodblocks (part of it being in West Berlin), of which in 1922 a series of restrikes were made by Max J. Friedländer. They include works by Dürer, Altdorfer, Burgkmair, Pencz, Erhard Schön, and Peter Flötner. There are 250 Netherlandish drawings, and among key works of a collection of French artists are nature studies by Claude Lorraine, and drawings by Watteau, Gabriel de Saint-Aubin, and Hubert Robert.

Since the Collection of Drawings belonged formerly to the National Gallery, its emphasis is also on German works from the late eighteenth century to the present, with emphasis after 1945 on the German Democratic Republic. Noteworthy are drawings by Friedrich, such as his fascinating *Self Portrait* (c. 1810) and Runge's studies for the painting of his parents, now in Hamburg, his brush study *Morning* (1808) and his ink drawings for the *Theatre Almanach* (1809). The Nazarenes are very well represented, as are Berlin artists. Paramount among the latter are forty-five hundred drawings and designs by Karl Friedrich Schinkel, one thousand works by the Biedermeier artist Karl Blechen, and five hundred by Franz Krüger. There are prints and drawings by Böcklin, Feuerbach, and v. Marées and more than six thousand drawings by Adolph Menzel, some studies for his *Iron Mill*, and works by Liebermann, Zille, Kollwitz, and Barlach. In fact, the Collection of Drawings runs by and large parallel to the works in the National Gallery, so the artists mentioned there can also be found here.

Among the important works of the non-German, mostly French, artists are van Gogh's *Sailing Boats* (1888); works by Cézanne, Picasso, Signac, and Rouault; and Munch's extremely rare woodcut *Two People* (1899). There is also a collection of about thirteen-hundred illustrated books and portfolios, which administratively belongs to the Main Library. Furthermore, the department has a collection of about fourteen thousand posters, including eight thousand of the German Democratic Republic. Of interest also is a collection of prints from the USSR. Finally, there are some forty thousand negatives covering original and new holdings, of which more than eighteen thousand pertain to the Department of Prints and Drawings, the others to the Collection of Drawings.

Housed in 1703 as part of the Antiquarium in the Berlin Palace, the Coin Collection originated in the Kunstkammer of the Great Elector. In 1830 it moved into the Old Museum, where in 1868 it became an independent division with about 140,000 items. In 1904 it was housed in the Bode Museum. It survived World War II intact, and after it was returned from the USSR in 1958, the department opened again in the Bode Museum. Its present holdings (at this time in storage) number about five hundred thousand items of coins, medals, and paper money. It is a world-renowned universal collection, aiming to cover all developments chronologically and comprehensively.

The collection holds Greek coins of the seventh century B.C., with fine examples of the Archaic, Classical, and Hellenistic periods, as well as samples of Celtic coins, beginning about 150 B.C., Roman Republican coins beginning with the third century B.C., and Roman Imperial coins to the fifth century. A rich collection of Byzantine coins ranges from A.D. 491 to 1328, and coins of the various Germanic tribes date from about A.D. 500 to 700. There are groups of Merovingian, especially Carolingian, coins (A.D. 534–911), as well as fine examples of the Ottonian, Salian, and Staufer periods from A.D. 936 to 1250.

There are coins of the Holy Roman Empire from A.D. 1300 to the beginning of the Thirty Years War and German coins between A.D. 1618 and the Third Reich. Important is a fine collection of Renaissance medals, the earliest by Antonio Pisano, *Emperor John VIII Palaeologos*. Outstanding among them is a series of portraits by Augsburg master Hans Schwarz, several with their original models. German medals, with emphasis on Berlin, are abundant. Another collection consists of seals, mostly of the Middle Ages. The holdings of paper money range from the first Chinese examples of A.D. 1369 through Danish and Swedish notes of A.D. 1666 and notes of the French Revolution. Beginning with the eighteenth century, emphasis is on German paper money.

Founded in 1867–68 as the German Museum of Industries, the Museum of Arts and Crafts got its present name in 1879 and became a member of the State Museums in 1885. The core of the collection was acquired in 1867 at the Paris World Exhibition, and nine thousand objects were added in 1875 from the royal collections. Through donations and continuous purchases, by 1939 it was an important museum with European arts and crafts from about 1000 to the neo-classical period. It was housed after 1921 in the Berlin Palace, where it remained until World War II, when many of its treasures were lost in a 1945 bombardment. As a result of sequestration by the Western Allies, much of the original collection is now in West Berlin. Despite these losses, the collection quickly began to grow again. What had remained in East Berlin was patiently restored, and objects from Monbijou, also bombed out, were added to the holdings. In 1958 objects taken from Berlin by the USSR were returned. Finally, some new acquisitions were made, bringing the holdings up to the period of the 1930s. Since 1974 a contemporary division has been opened, promoting arts and crafts by artists of the German Democratic Republic. After being housed in several temporary locations, the collection moved in 1963 into the imposing and well-restored Baroque palace, built in 1677–82 for the royal family on an island in Köpenick by the Dutch architect Rutger von Langerfeld.

Gold and silver works from the Middle Ages through the Baroque period are exhibited in a treasury. Most cherished are the late-tenth-century middle-Rhenish Ottonian *Gisela Jewels*, discovered in 1880 in Mainz. Romanesque metalwork is represented by liturgical objects and there are some Mosan and Cologne enamel works. The furniture collection consists of about five hundred fine objects. Among the Gothic examples, a carved Saxon chest (c. 1300) with fabulous animals in roundels is outstanding. The Italian Renaissance is richly represented with Florentine, Sienese, and Venetian furniture, of which a Florentine chest with gilded stucco decoration, the *Four Virtues* (c. 1439), and an inlaid door with the Annunciation (1465–70) by Giuliano da Maiano are outstanding. Among several German Renaissance examples, an Augsburg chest with architectural views (c. 1580) and a Swiss paneled room with perspective inlays by Master H. S. (1548) from Haldenstein Castle, Grison, are most prominent. There are also fine French Renaissance examples, French and Netherlandish works from the eighteenth century, and some Art Nouveau pieces. There are many fine

German examples in the Baroque, Rococo, neoclassical, and Biedermeier styles, the pride of the museum being the writing desk and cabinet of Frederick William II, by David Roentgen (1779).

The glass collection extends from the Gothic period to the present, with emphasis on German Gothic, Spanish and Venetian Renaissance, German Baroque, Biedermeier, and Art Nouveau. The textile collection reaches from the Middle Ages to the nineteenth century, with some masterworks of the Rococo, such as the Gobelin *Diana in the Bath* after a design by Boucher (Paris, 1770–80). In the pewter collection, German Gothic and German and French Renaissance examples predominate. Among the glazed terracotta pieces, those of the Italian Renaissance are most outstanding, whereas the porcelain collection is strongest in eighteenth-century examples from Meissen, Berlin, and France. The seven-meter-high *Berlin Silver Buffet* (Augsburg, 1698) from the Berlin Palace is, with its many seventeenth-century silver and gold vessels, a major work. Finally, the collection of Berlin cast-iron art of the first half of the nineteenth century is impressive. It includes examples of furniture, architectural fittings, jewelry, and small busts. Ceramics, glass, textiles, jewelry, and woodwork by contemporary German Democratic Republic artists are exhibited on the ground floor.

Founded in 1889 on the initiative of the physician and anthropologist Rudolph Virchow, and at first named Museum of German Costumes and Household Crafts, the Ethnological Museum's nucleus was contributed by the collector Ulrich Jahn, who also obtained for the museum the German ethnological objects displayed at the World Exhibition in Chicago in 1893. Through acquisitions and donations, the museum had become before World War II the richest German folklore collection. Seventy percent of its holdings were destroyed in World War II. It has grown again considerably since the war, primarily through donations. In 1953 objects from other museums were incorporated, and in 1958 the objects that had been taken after 1945 from Berlin to the USSR were returned. Since 1957 the collection has been shown in one room in the Pergamum Museum.

The collection is particularly strong in all aspects of weaving and blue-dye fabrics; eighteenth- to twentieth-century folk costumes; embroideries; ceramics, such as middle German Hafner ware; tiled stoves and eighteenth- and nineteenth-century furniture and household equipment; woodcarvings; and wrought-iron objects. Most interesting is a collection of iron votives, mostly from Bavaria.

Most divisions have study collections that can be consulted upon request. The museums also have special libraries, some located in the individual museums, others incorporated into the main library (Zentralbibliothek), but all under the latter's administration. The total holdings are about 130,000 volumes and about 560 periodicals. These noncirculating libraries are open to the public.

The museums also hold photographic archives, with many negatives pertaining to the collections' holdings, often including the pre-war holdings. Photographs from these negatives, as well as slides, can be purchased by writing to the Direktionsbereich Öffentlichkeitsarbeit or to the respective departments. The museum publishes guides, catalogues, and catalogues to special exhibitions, as well as the scholarly journal *Forschungen und Berichte der Staatlichen Museen zu Berlin* and a series of booklets focusing on special areas or subjects within the collections, called *Kleine Schriften*. *Kleine Schriften des Münzkabinetts*, another series, deals with special topics within the coin collection. Bookstands in all buildings offer museum publications, guides and catalogues, posters, plaster-cast reproductions, and some excellent slide sets.

Selected Bibliography

Museum publications: *150 Jahre Staatliche museen zu Berlin*, 1980; Bibliography of museum publications, 1945–78, in *Forschungen und Berichte der Staatlichen Museen zu Berlin*, n. 20, 1979; Müller, W., *Ägyptisches Museum, 1823–1973*, 1973; idem, *Kleiner Führer durch die Ausstellung des Ägyptischen Museums*, 1976; Luft, U., and Poethke, G., *Leben im Ägyptischen Altertum . . . Katalog der ständigen Ausstellung der Papyrus-Sammlung*, 1977; Meyer, G. R., *Was uralte Denkmäler erzählen. Kurze Wegleitung durch das Vorderasiatische Museum*, 1960; Violet, R., *Chinesische Keramik*, 1962; Massow, W. v., *Führer durch das Pergamonmuseum*, 1932; Rohde, E., *Griechische und römische Kunst in den Staatlichen Museen zu Berlin*, 1968; idem, *Pergamon—Burgberg und Altar*, 1961; idem, *Der Altar von Pergamon*, 3d ed. 1980; Bluemel, Carl, *Römische Skulpturen*, 1962; Neugebauer, K. A., *Die griechischen Bronzen der klassischen Zeit und des Hellenismus*, 1951; Wessel, K., *Frühchristlich-byzantinische Sammlung Berlin*, 1953; idem, *Das ravennatische Mosaik in den Staatlichen Museen zu Berlin und seine Wiederherstellung*, 1953; idem, *Rom—Byzanz—Russland*, 1957; Bröker, G., *Koptische Stoffe*, 1966; Dudzus, W., and Enderlein, V., *Islamische Kunstwerke*, 1960; Enderlein, V., *Führer durch das Islamische Museum*, 1980; Maedebach, H., *Deutsche Bildwerke aus sieben Jahrhunderten*, 1, 1958; Fründt, E., *Bildwerke aus sieben Jahrhunderten*, 2, 1972; idem, *Spätgotische niederländische Bildwerke*, 1962; idem, *Italienische Plastik des 15.–17. Jahrhunderts*, n.d.; Sachs, H., *Majolika-Plastik der italienischen Renaissance*, 1964; Geismeier, I., and Nützmann, H., *Malerei/14.–18. Jahrhundert im Bode-Museum, Führer durch die Ausstellung*, 1978; Geismeier, I., *Holländische und flämische Gemälde des siebzehnten Jahrhunderts im Bode-Museum, Katalog*, 1, 1976; Geismeier, W., *Gemälde, Bildwerke und Zeichnungen des 19. Jahrhunderts*, 1978; Janda, A., *Die Nationalgalerie. Wiederaufbau und Entwicklung seit 1945*, 1974; Weidemann, F., and März, R., *National-Galerie. Gemälde des 20. Jahrhunderts. Katalog*, 1977; Timm, W., *Kupferstichkabinett. Kupferstiche, Holzschnitte, Radierungen und Zeichnungen des 16. Jahrhunderts*, 1953; idem, *Zeichnungen alter Meister*, 1962; Janda, K. H., and A., *Zeichnungen deutscher Meister vom Klassizismus zum Expressionismus*, 1951; Geismeier, W., *Zeichnungen deutscher Romantiker*, 1964; Riemann, R., *Deutsche Zeichnungen und Aquarelle des 19. und 20. Jahrhunderts. Neuerwerbungen der Sammlung der Zeichnungen, 1945–1970*, 1971; Ebert, H., and Hinz, S., *Auferstanden aus Ruinen. Druckgraphik und Zeichnungen, 1945–1970*, 1970; Suhle, A., *Geld, Münze, und Medaille, Führer durch die Schausammlung des Münzkabinetts*, 1957; idem, *Petschafte des Münzkabinetts aus dem 13.–16. Jahrhunderts*, 1964; Börner, L., *Italienische Renaissancemedaillen*, 1962; Schultz, S., *Die Münzprägung in Ägypten seit Alexander dem Grossen*, 1975; Kluge, B., *Brakteaten: Deutsche Münzen des Hochmittelalters*, 1976; Fengler, H., *Die Entwicklung der deutschen Geldscheine*, 1976; Schade, G. *Schloss Köpenick. Kunstgewerbemuseum. Europäisches Kunsthandwerk aus zehn Jahrhunder-*

ten, 1976; idem, *Möbel der italienischen Renaissance*, 1964; Krienke, G., *Berliner Porzellan des 18. Jahrhunderts*, 1961; *75 Jahre Museum für Volkskunde zu Berlin. 1889–1964. Festschrift*, 1964.

Other publications: Andrae, W., et al., *Die Berliner Museen* (Berlin 1953); *Staatliche Museen zu Berlin* (in German, English, and French) (Leipzig 1963); Reuther, H., *Die Museumsinsel in Berlin* (Berlin 1977); Klessmann, R., *The Berlin Museum* (New York 1972); Roeder, G., *Ägyptische Bronzefiguren, Mitteilungen aus der Ägyptischen Sammlung*, 6 (Leipzig 1956); Rohde, E., *Griechische Terrakotten* (Tübingen 1970); Effenberger, A., *Koptische Kunst* (Leipzig 1975); idem, *Das Mosaik aus der Kirche San Michele in Affricisco zu Ravenna* (Berlin 1975); Enderlein, V., *Die Minaturen der Berliner Baisonqur-Handschrift* (Leipzig 1969); Suhle, A., *Münzbilder der Hohenstaufenzeit: Meisterwerke romanischer Kleinkunst* (Leipzig 1938).

URSULA E. CONRAD

Dresden

DRESDEN STATE ART COLLECTIONS (officially STAATLICHE KUNST-SAMMLUNGEN DRESDEN; also DRESDENER GALERIEN; alternately DRESDEN ART MUSEUMS, THE DRESDEN GALLERIES), Georg Treu Platz, Albertinum, 801 Dresden.

The state collections of art at Dresden comprise twelve separately administered institutions at six locations in the city. The history of most of them begins with the establishment of the Kunstkammer (cabinet of art) of Prince Elector of Saxony Augustus in 1560. It was a universal museum that embraced all known branches of technology and science. Paintings and sculpture were considered of minor import. It was Elector Frederick Augustus the Strong (1670–1733) who converted provincial Dresden to a modern European royal residence and a center of the arts, especially after his coronation in 1697 as King Augustus II of Poland. As a young man he had seen specialized collections in the old European centers of power and the arts. Compared to them, the concept of Kunstkammer seemed out of date. To develop specialized collections from his stock in the House of Saxony's Kunstkammer corresponded to Augustus the Strong's political goals as well as to his universalist interests. During the years 1723–24, the time of the founding of the Green Vaults as a museum, all of the princely collections were reorganized on a comprehensive scale, and the cabinet of prints, the picture gallery, the porcelain collection, and the natural science collection were instituted. Part of this expansion included the famous exchange of two regiments of dragoons from Saxony that Augustus the Strong sent to Frederick William I of Prussia for part of the latter's collection of antiquities.

On February 13, 1945, all of the museums in Dresden were completely destroyed by massive British-American fire bombing and 206 paintings destroyed. Five of the original eight rooms of the Green Vaults are the only ones of the old Dresden that survived in 1945. Most of the collections themselves had been evacuated from the city for protection. What remained of them after Dresden's capitulation to the Soviet armed forces was recovered by special units of the Soviet army and remained in Soviet custody and care throughout the period of the rebuilding of the Zwinger complex. In 1955 and again in 1958 the Dresden art treasures, approximately 1.5 million pieces, were returned to Dresden into the custody of the German Democratic Republic's government. Since that time, the Dresden State Art Collections have been the property of the people of the German Democratic Republic and are funded by its government. The office of information pertaining to all museums is located in the Old Masters Picture Gallery (Gemäldegalerie Alte Meister) in the Semper building. Additional information services are situated in the Zwinger, in the Albertinum, and at Schloss Pillnitz. They provide guided tours in German, Russian, English, French, Italian, Spanish, Arabic, Polish, Roumanian, Bulgarian, Hungarian, Czech, Slovak, Serbocroatian, Slovene, Swedish, Danish, and Vietnamese. The museums maintain a department of museum education (Museumspädagogik) and youth organization (Jugendclub). The staff of each museum is organized into a collective and works for the receipt of the honorific title ''brigade of socialist work.''

The Dresden State Art Collections at the Zwinger are divided into the Old Masters Gallery in the Semper Gallery; the Historic Museum, also in the Semper Gallery; and the Porcelain Collection. At the Albertinum can be found the Gallery of Modern Masters, the Green Vault, the Numismatics Cabinet, and the Sculpture Collection. The collections located at Güntzstrasse 34 are the Cabinet of Prints and Drawings and the Central Art Library. The Palace of Pillnitz houses the Museum of Arts and Crafts, and at Köpckestrasse 1 is found the Museum of Folk Art; at Leipzigerstrasse 22, the Puppet Collection.

The Old Masters Gallery (Gemäldegalerie Alte Meister) is considered the focal point of the Dresden art collections. It is housed in the so-called Semper Gallery, which is a nineteenth-century addition to the Zwinger complex. The Zwinger is Dresden's most famous architectural monument and an outstanding masterpiece of European Late Baroque court architecture. It was designed by Mathäus Pöppelmann under the patronage of Augustus the Strong and was built of Saxon sandstone between the years 1709 and 1728. The Zwinger's many sculptures were executed by B. Permoser, J. B. Thomae, J. Chr. Kirchner, and P. Heermann. The word *Zwinger* derives from the verb *zwingen*, to force or constrain, and it means the free space between two contiguous fortified walls, referring to its site near the fortifications of the old city of Dresden. Ever since 1728 the Zwinger has accommodated museums. The Zwinger's architecture was completed by a Picture Gallery built between 1847 and 1854 to house the royal collections of paintings. It derives its name from its architect, Gottfried Semper, who designed the Gallery in the Neo-Renaissance style and gave the central entrance a tri-partite porticus to function visually as a counterpart to the Zwinger's Kronentor (coronation gate). The statues and reliefs of the central building were done by E. Rietschel, E. J. Hähnel, and J. Schilling. On February 13, 1945, the Semper Gallery was heavily damaged by fire and bombing. Reconstruction after the original plans began in 1955. In the interior alterations were made to facilitate better lighting, and the original closed rotunda was opened to the exhibition galleries as a connecting link.

The year 1722 is generally acknowledged as the date of the official founding of the Picture Gallery. Augustus the Strong had ordered a general inventory of all of the paintings in his possession, and a selection of the best works were brought together in a gallery in the Stable Block (Stallgebäude) at the Judenhof. This initiated the gradual dissolution of the Kunstkammer and the expansion, diversification, and specialization of its contents into separate collections, a process that was ended in 1831. The Gallery inspector edited the first printed catalogue, which was published in French in 1765 and in German in 1771. The nucleus of the Picture Gallery was paintings by Lucas Cranach, such as the *St. Catherine Altarpiece* (1506), and Hans Krell, both of whom had been court painters for the princes of Saxony. In 1687 Dürer's so-called *Dresden-Altarpiece* (c. 1496) was acquired from the Schlosskirche in Wittenberg. However, the fame and specific character of the Gallery were determined by the Italian and Netherlandish sixteenth- and seventeenth-century masterpieces purchased by diplomats, connoisseurs, and painters in Vienna, Paris, Madrid, Rome, and the Netherlands during the latter part of the seventeenth century until the Seven Year War (1756–63).

During the 1740s the collection of the count of Wallenstein in Dux (Duchcov) was bought for the Dresden Gallery, as well as many paintings from France and Italy and sixty-nine alone from the imperial gallery in Prague. In 1745–46 one hundred of the most important paintings of the collection of the duke of Modena were transferred to Dresden, among them Hans Holbein's *Portrait of Morette* (Charles de Solier, 1534–35); Titian's *Tribute Money* (c. 1514); four altar panels by Correggio, including the *Holy Night* (completed in 1530); three paintings by Veronese from the Casa Grimani in Venice; and paintings by Rubens (e.g., *St. Jerome*, c. 1615); Velázquez, and Andrea del Sarto. Raphael's *Sistine Madonna* (1512–13) came to Dresden in 1754 from the monastery church San Sisto in Piacenza. Then the Seven Year War began and major purchases ceased until the mid-nineteenth century. At that time, however, the emphasis in acquisition policies shifted to contemporary art, now housed in the Gallery of Modern Masters. The Semper Gallery buildings were completed in 1855, and the pictures were transferred from the old Stable Block under the direction of the painter-decorator Schnorr von Carolsfeld.

Today approximately one-third of the Gallery's total holdings, about 650 paintings, are on permanent display on all three levels of the Semper building. The ground floor is reserved for the Italian masters of the sixteenth century and the Flemish and Dutch masters of the seventeenth century. The Gallery comprises paintings from the fourteenth through the eighteenth century, representing Italian, Netherlandish, German, Flemish, French, and Spanish schools, including eighteenth-century Saxon paintings. Key works other than those mentioned above are

Giorgione's *Sleeping Venus* (completed by Titian after 1510), Tintoretto's *Archangel Michael in Combat with Satan* (shortly before 1594), Rubens' *Drunken Hercules* (c. 1611) and *Bathsheba at the Fountain* (c. 1635), and van Dyck's *St. Jerome* (c. 1620). Of twelve paintings by Rembrandt, his *Self Portrait with Saskia* (1635) and *Samson's Wedding Feast* (1638) are of note. Vermeer van Delft's *The Procuress* (1656) and *Girl Reading a Letter* (c. 1657), Jacob Ruisdael's *The Jewish Cemetery*, Jan van Eyck's *Dresden Triptych* (1437), Murillo's *Death of St. Clara* (1645–46), and Poussin's *The Kingdom of Flora* (c. 1630) are important, as are views of Dresden by Canaletto (1747–50) and pastels by Rosalba Carriera (1675–1757) and Anton Raphael Mengs (1728–79). The Picture Gallery maintains a reference library of some sixty-five hundred volumes and a photography archive.

The Historical Museum (Historisches Museum) is located in the East wing of the Semper Gallery. It is not a museum of social or cultural history but an outstanding collection of arms and armor. The exhibitions demonstrate the development of German and foreign-manufactured firearms, edged weapons, hunting weapons and equipment, Oriental weapons, riding equipment, and display costumes from the fifteenth century until the second half of the eighteenth century. These are for the most part decorative, princely arms, show pieces used at official functions such as parades, jousts, hunts, and investiture of office. The collections comprise approximately ten thousand objects, only a fraction of which are on display. The core of the museum is the contents of the former armory and armor rooms of the House of Saxony, of the sixteenth and seventeenth centuries. Between 1586 and 1589 the pieces of show armor and weapons were housed in a building designed for that purpose, the Stallhof (Stable Block) at the Judenhof. After 1876 the collections were installed in the Johanneum. After the return of the Dresden art treasures from the USSR in 1959, the permanent exhibition of the Historical Museum was opened in the East wing of the Semper Gallery. Especially noteworthy are the electoral sword of Frederick the Warrior (Hungarian, pre–1425), which is the earliest piece of Dresden ceremonial armor; the so-called *Hercules Armour* for man and horse made by Eliseus Libaerts (Antwerp, 1562–64); the coronation robes of Augustus the Strong (1697); and a reconstruction of a sixteenth-century jousting tournament with original armor.

The Porcelain Collection (Porzellansammlung) is the largest one of its kind in the world next to the porcelain collection of the Serail in Istanbul. The Dresden porcelain collection was founded between 1710 and 1730, when Augustus the Strong collected Chinese porcelain and the wares of Saxon manufacture in Meissen, which has produced Böttger stoneware and Böttger porcelain since 1710. These pieces were intended to decorate the "Porcelain Palace" of the Zwinger. In about 1730 the Dutch Palace was converted into the Japanese Palace, and although its interior decoration with works of porcelain was not completed, the plans for this project were preserved. In 1876 the porcelain collections were housed on the upper floor of the Johanneum. They were placed into safety outside of Dresden during World War II and after capitulation were kept in the USSR until they were returned to Dresden in 1958. Since 1962 the porcelain collections have been exhibited in three galleries and two rooms of the Zwinger and were partly arranged according to the old plans of the "Porcelain Palace."

The collections comprise early Chinese pottery (from 206 B.C. until the Ming period of the fourteenth to seventeenth century); funerary pottery dating from the Han, Wei, and T'ang dynasties (206 B.C.-A.D. 906); early porcelain from the Sung Dynasty (A.D. 960–1278); and Chinese porcelain from the fifteenth to the eighteenth century. Japanese works are represented by porcelain of the seventeenth to eighteenth century and Japanese Imari porcelain made for export to Europe. Also included in the collections are Meissen tableware and Dresden porcelain, for example, animal figures, portraits, and monumental vases. Of particular note are the so-called *Dragon Vases*, fourteen Chinese monumental urns that, with other porcelain, were exchanged for six hundred Saxon soldiers in 1711; the oldest porcelain carillon; the *Porcelain Temple* by Kändler (c. 1730–60); painted porcelain signed by J. G. Höroldt, Stadtler, and Herold; and the porcelain bouquet from the factory at Vincennes (1749). The entry hall to the galleries is reserved for changing exhibits from the holdings in storage. The museum also maintains a specialized reference library.

The Gallery of Modern Masters (Gemäldegalerie Neue Meister) is located in the Albertinum, a building originally planned as an arsenal (1559–63) and added to the southeastern fortifications on the city, which were known later as "Brühl's Terrace." The original ground plan and the vaulted, pillared ground floor were preserved during alterations made in the eighteenth and nineteenth centuries. Used as a museum since 1887, the Albertinum has housed the Sculpture Collection since 1889–90. The building was severely damaged in the bombing raid of February 13, 1945. Following completed restoration in 1965, the Albertinum became the home of the Gallery of Modern Masters and two other famous Dresden collections whose buildings had been destroyed: the Green Vault and the Numismatics Cabinet.

The Gallery of Modern Masters began as the department for nineteenth-century art of the Picture Gallery. Crucial to its development were the Bernhard August von Lindenau Foundation, instituted in 1843, and the 1848 resolution of the Dresden Art Academy's Academic Council, which presided over the Picture Gallery, to acquire "works of patriotic and of living artists." When the art historian Karl Woermann became director of the Gallery in 1882, the first significant nonprovincial purchases were made of works by Adolph Menzel, Fritz von Uhde, Hans Thoma, Arnold Böcklin, and Carl Spitzweg. After the International Art Show in Dresden in 1897, paintings representative of movements outside of Germany were acquired, such as Gustave Courbet's *Stone Breakers* (1851) and Claude Monet's *Seine near Lavacourt*. The Dresden Museum Association (Dresden Museumsverein) formed in 1911 and the Patron's Association of the State Gallery from 1917 supported acquisitions in the areas of German Romanticism and Impressionism. In 1931 the Old Master Gallery was separated from the Gallery of Modern Masters; however, only since 1955 has the Gallery of Modern Masters had its own director.

The National Socialists confiscated 437 works of twentieth-century artists in 1937, among them paintings by Otto Dix, Emil Nolde, Carl Hofer, Oskar Kokoschka, George Grosz, Conrad Felixmüller, Karl Schmitt-Rottluff, Paul Klee, Erich Heckel, Lyonel Feininger, Ernst Barlach, Lovis Corinth, Max Liebermann, Wilhelm Lehmbruck, and Gerhard Marcks. On February 13, 1945, 149 paintings were destroyed by bombs. Acquisitions made after 1945 attempted to replace these losses. Today the Gallery of Modern Masters comprises the following areas of nineteenth- and twentieth-century art: German Romanticism; nineteenth-century Realism; Impressionism and Expressionism; Proletarian-Revolutionary paintings; and contemporary Socialist Realism of the German Democratic Republic, the USSR, and other socialist countries. The permanent exhibition is organized chronologically and according to countries. The museum maintains a reference library of about fifty-five hundred volumes and a photography archive. It is accountable to the GDR Ministry of Culture.

The Green Vault (Das Grüne Gewölbe) is a collection of thirty-one hundred precious works of art, temporarily housed on the first floor of the Albertinum. There, more than four hundred of the collection's most important items are on display until plans for the rebuilding of the former palace as a museum center and the restoration of the original cabinets of the Green Vault have been completed. The Green Vault is the richest treasury in central Europe, consisting of works in five major categories: goldsmith's work, gems, jewelry, small bronze sculptures, and ivory, all from the fourteenth to the eighteenth century and by German, French, and Italian artists. There are also smaller collections of timepieces, articles made of amber, enamel, mother-of-pearl or rhinocerous horn, and artistically made cupboards.

The collections of the Green Vault originated in the treasury of the princes of Saxony, the so-called Secret Depository underneath the apartments of the elector in the eastern wing of the palace, dating from 1548 to 1554. The original vaulted room was painted green, hence the popular term *Green Vault*. In 1723–24 the Green Vault became a museum, the first of European treasuries conceived of as a museum. When the Kunstkammer was dissolved after 1720, the treasury absorbed everything that was considered precious, rare, and decorative. The treasury's organizer then was the king's First Architect, Raymond Leplat. The architect of the Zwinger, Pöppelmann, was commissioned to design the Green Vault and adjoining rooms for the display of the collections. He had the walls fitted with carved, lacquered, and gilded paneling; consoles for objects arranged in geometric designs in front of mirrored glass; pillars covered with mirrors; and floors and door frames fashioned of polished Saxon marble.

Noteworthy pieces are the cup of Queen Hedwig of Poland, made of rock crystal, silver-gilt, and enamel, from the end of the fourteenth century; a writing case with an allegory of philosophy in silver, parcel-gilt, enamel, velvet, silk, rock crystal, and ebony, which was created by Wenzel Jamnitzer in Nürnberg, in 1562; and the drinking cup *Kovsh* of Tsar Ivan the Terrible, made of gold with niello, sapphires, and pearls, about 1563. This was a present from Tsar Peter the Great to Augustus the Strong. Other important pieces are: a coffee set of gold, gilded silver, enamel, glass, diamonds, peridots, pearls, ivory, lacquer, wood, glass, and iron, which was made between 1697 and 1701 for Augustus the Strong by court jeweller Johann Melchior Dinglinger and his brother Georg Friedrich Dinglinger, and represents the earliest work in Dresden Baroque; *The Four Seasons*, carved in ivory by Balthasar Permoser of Dresden before 1714; and by the Dinglinger brothers, including Georg Christoph, the cabinet piece *The Princely Household at Delhi on the Birthday of the Great Mogul Aurangzeb.* Made in 1701–8 of gold, silver, parcel-gilt, pearls, and enamel, it includes 132 small figures in gold, decorations of 4,909 diamond roses couronnées, 164 emeralds, 160 rubies, 16 pearls, 2 cameos, 1 sapphire, and probably represents the first large piece of chinoiserie in Germany. The Green Vault maintains a reference library and photography archives.

The Numismatics Cabinet (Münzkabinett) has had a permanent exhibition on the first floor of the Albertinum since 1964. It is one of the largest and most diverse collections of its kind in the world and the oldest one in Germany. The collection's origin can be traced to the reign of Duke Georg of Saxony (1500–1539), who not only collected historic coins and medals but also commissioned commemorative medals. At that time the collection was part of the Kunstkammer. It was scientifically classified for the first time under Elector Johann Georg II of Saxony (1656–80). Since the establishment of the institution as an independent museum in about 1728, the collections were considerably expanded by acquisitions and bequests, such as that of the coin collector Benno von Reimer after his death in 1871, which contained twenty-nine thousand mostly medieval coins and fourteen hundred books on numismatics, and the bequest of Johann Georg Geinitz (after 1919), which added thirty-nine thousand to the collection. In 1786 the coin collection was housed with the collection of antiquities in the Japanese Palace; in 1877 it was moved to the royal palace; in 1911 it was moved again, to the Chancellery Building at the Stallhof. There the collections remained until that building was destroyed in 1945. Today the Numismatics Cabinet comprises approximately two hundred thousand coins, medals, dies, signets, banknotes, and a complete collection of all Saxon coins and medals, with more than twenty-five thousand pieces. Outstanding among them are the portrait medals by the artist Tobias Wolf of Breslau (late sixteenth century). The permanent exhibition shows only a very small fraction of the entire holdings. It represents the development of Greek, Roman, and German money and the development of German medals during the Renaissance and Baroque periods. The museum maintains a study collection, an extensive reference library of more than five thousand volumes, and an archive of about twenty-five hundred coins and medals.

The Sculpture Collection (Skulpturensammlung) had its beginning with the acquisition from Frederick William I of Prussia of the so-called Brandenburg

Collection (1723–26) by Augustus the Strong in exchange for Saxon soldiers. Soon other works of ancient sculpture were added with the purchase of the sculpture collections of Prince Chigi and of Cardinal Allessandro Albani in 1728. After August III bought the estate of Prince Eugen (1736) of Savoy containing statues of women from Herkulaneum, as well as bronzes, terracottas, and vases from about the fifth century B.C., the Dresden collection of ancient sculpture was not only the first in Germany but the largest one outside of Italy. It inspired Winckelmann to go to Rome and write the first systematic *History of Ancient Art* (1764). In 1782 the collections were expanded by the purchase of 833 plaster casts of Classical sculptures from the estate of the court painter Anton Raphael Mengs. The Sculpture Collection, which had been housed at various locations in the Zwinger, was installed at the Albertinum between 1890 and 1894 and only then became accessible to the public. Since that time the Sculpture Collection has been systematically expanded, so that today approximately fourteen thousand original works (including vases) and about five hundred plaster casts document the history of European sculpture. Fewer losses were caused by World War II than by the National Socialists' confiscation and removal of many twentieth-century sculptures in 1937.

The Sculpture Collection's permanent exhibit displays only about five hundred original works. Key works among them are Roman marble copies after lost Greek works, such as *Athena Lemnia* by Phidias, the *Boy Victor* by Polyclitus, and *Dancing Maenads* by Scopas, as well as original Greek works in marble. There are signed bronzes by Giovanni Bologna and Adriaen de Vries, the equestrian statuette of *Marcus Aurelius* by Filarete, and works by Balthasar Permoser and Ignaz Günther. Masters of the nineteenth and twentieth centuries are represented by Auguste Rodin, Henri Laurens, Dalou, Dubois, Constantin Meunier, Ernst Barlach, Wilhelm Lehmbruck, Gerhard Marcks, and Georg Kolbe. The Sculpture Collection maintains a plaster cast shop, a reference library and photography archives. Medieval sculptures are on permanent loan at the Albrechtsburg in Meissen, and a number of nineteenth- and twentieth-century sculptures are exhibited in the Gallery of Modern Masters.

The Cabinet of Prints (Kupferstichkabinett) originated as a separate collection of graphic art in 1720. At the same time that Augustus the Strong founded the Picture Gallery he commissioned his personal physician J. H. Heucher to remove all engravings from the Kunstkammer and to create a separate collection of engravings. They were bound into lavish volumes and housed at the Zwinger. In 1746 Carl Heinrich von Heinecken became the collection's curator, and within a decade he developed it into a very significant collection of prints in Europe. Between 1856 and the beginning of World War II, the Print Collection was located on the ground floor of the Semper Gallery and was reorganized and extended, particularly after 1883 under the direction of Max Lehr. Since 1945 the Dresden collections of prints and drawings, which remained essentially unharmed by World War II, have been located at Güntzstrasse 34. Today the Cabinet of Prints in Dresden is one of the largest graphic arts collections in the world, with approximately 180,000 engravings, etchings, woodcuts, lithographs, and silkscreen prints; about 25,000 drawings, watercolors, and pastels; and about 4,000 illustrated books by artists from all of Europe and representing the period from the fifteenth century to the present.

Particularly noteworthy among the drawings are Jan van Eyck's portrait *Cardinal Nicolo Albergati* (silverpoint, c. 1431), a series of drawings by the Master of the Hausbuch, and works by Schongauer, Dürer, Cranach, Holbein, Grünewald, and Hans Baldung Grien. Of the Italian masters, examples are by Lorenzo di Credi, Mantegna, Raphael, Correggio, and Tiepolo. The Netherlands are represented with drawings by masters such as Pieter Bruegel the Elder, Hans Bol, Goltzius, van de Velde, Ostade, Jordaens, Brouwer, Rubens, and van Dyck, with eighty drawings by Rembrandt. Many of them are preliminary studies to paintings in the Picture Gallery, for example, Rembrandt's drawing the *Sacrifice of Manoah* and Holbein's drawing *Morette*. Very well represented are eighteenth- and nineteenth-century French and English graphic arts. Goya ia also well represented by about 270 etchings, including the cycles the *Proverbios*, the *Caprichos*, the *Tauromaquia*, and the *Desastres de la Guerra*, which were purchased between 1906 and 1914. There are lithographs by Delacroix, Daumier, Daubigny, Rodin, and Steinlen. The collection is especially rich in works by nineteenth- and twentieth-century German artists, particularly those who worked in Dresden, such as Schnorr von Carolsfeld and Ludwig Richter. Many prints by German Expressionist artists such as Barlach, Schmidt-Rottluff, Nolde, Heckel, and Kokoschka were confiscated in 1937 by the National Socialists and could only be partially retrieved after 1945. The Cabinet of Prints also contains a collection of posters and early photographs. The works are shown in rotating exhibitions and can be examined upon request in the Study Room; however, pieces of extraordinary rarity may be seen only by special permission. The Cabinet of Prints maintains a reference library and photography archives of more than eight thousand entries.

The Museum of Arts and Crafts (Museum für Kunsthandwerk) has been located in the Palace of Pillnitz (Schloss Pillnitz) since 1962. It had become a part of the Dresden State Art Collection in 1947. The museum originated as an adjunct to the Dresden School of Arts and Crafts, which was founded in 1876. From 1765 until 1918 the Palace of Pillnitz served as summer residence of the House of Saxony. It is situated directly on the east bank of the Elbe upstream from Dresden. The central sections of the Wasserpalais and Bergpalais were built by Pöppelmann between 1720 and 1723 in the Oriental or Indian style, with the characteristic curved roof and the Chinese-style paintings on exterior walls and cornices. Wings in the classicist style were added between 1788 and 1791 after designs by Christian T. Weinlig, who also devised the classicist interior decorations.

Since 1963 a series of permanent exhibitions have disclosed the breadth and the wealth of the collections, which span European arts and crafts from the Middle Ages to the present, including furniture, musical instruments, glass, ceramics, metalwork, textiles, and industrial design. Incorporated into the exhibits are loans from the Picture Gallery, the Gallery of Modern Masters, and the Porcelain Collection, whereas an important part of the furniture collection of the Museum of Arts and Crafts is on loan at the Museum of the Palace at Moritzburg. Key works of the exhibits include a Bohemian antependium (c. 1480); a tiled stove from Erfurt (1470); a Rhenish cupboard (c. 1490); a cabinet by Bernhard van Risenburgh (Paris, c. 1759); a standard clock, rolltop desk, and game table by D. Roentgen (c. 1775); and arm chairs by Mies van der Rohe and Marcel Breuer (c. 1925). Objects in pewter are part of a special pewter collection founded in 1911 under the auspices of the City Council, temporarily in storage at the Palace of Pillnitz.

The Folk Art Museum (Museum für Volkskunst) is located at Köpckestrasse 1, which is the building of the reconstructed Jägerhof (hunting lodge). The Jägerhof is the oldest architectural monument of the Neustadt of Dresden, a remnant of Elector Augustus' hunting lodge built at the site in 1567–68. The Museum of Folk Art was founded toward the close of the nineteenth century and was based upon the collections of the Saxon Ethnological Association. In 1913, under the direction of Professor Seyffert, the museum was opened to the public in the renovated old Jägerhof as the first folk art museum in Germany. The building was destroyed during World War II, but most of its collection remained intact, because it had been evacuated from the city for safety. After the Jägerhof was reconstructed according to the old plans (1950–54), the museum was reopened. Only a small portion of the total holdings are on permanent display. The focus is on old and new Saxon folk art, in particular from Lusatia, the Erzgebirge region, and the Vogtland. Represented are examples of native costume; blue-print linen; peasant furniture; pottery; kitchen utensils of wood, copper, pewter, and iron; and toys. There are also examples of carved and turned woodwork of the home industries of the Erzgebirge area from the eighteenth to the twentieth century. Each year special exhibitions are organized, and since 1968, the museum has maintained a wood-carving school for children. The museum's reference library contained 3,262 entries in 1975.

The State Puppet Collection (Puppentheatersammlung) is located at Leipzigerstrasse 22, which is also the location of the State Puppet Theater. The collection is not yet open to the public but may be seen by appointment.

The Central Art Library (Zentrale Kunstbibliothek) is housed at Güntzstrasse 34. It contains more than forty-four thousand volumes and at least fifty currently published journals dealing with all aspects of the visual arts and including literature on the history of costume and topography. The special collections focus on the literature discussing those works that are in the Dresden State Museum. Special exhibitions can be seen in the library's reading room.

Slides and photographs of the collections may be purchased by application to the Office of Administration of the Dresden State Art Collections, which also can provide a list of museum publications and instructions for ordering. In addition to providing guides to the collections and specialized catalogues such as those listed below, the state museums publish catalogues of all exhibitions; the *Jahrbuch der Staatlichen Kunstsammlungen Dresden*, an annual report of the museum's activities and scholarly articles on objects in the collections; the *Dresdener Kunstblätter* (sometimes the title changes to *Dresdener Galerieblätter*), a periodical published every two months; and information sheets on individual or groups of objects, called *Faltblätter*.

Selected Bibliography

Museum publications: *Inventarium über die Churfürstliche Sächsische Kunst-Cammer im Schloss*, 1595; *Verzeichnis der Gemälde, welche in der Churfürstlichen Galerie zu Dresden befindlich sind*, 1801; *Schätze der Weltkultur: Information on the Dresden Art Museums*, 2d ed., 1976; *Gemäldegalerie Alte Meister*, 19th ed., 1977; *Gemäldegalerie Neue Meister*, 1975; *Einführung in das Grüne Gewölbe*, n.d.; Museum für Kunsthandwerk Schloss Pillnitz: *Kunsthandwerk des 18. und 19. Jahrhunderts*, 1971; Gemäldegalerie Alte Meister: *Der Bauer und seine Befreiung*, 1975; *Werner Tübke*, 1975; *Puppentheater gestern und heute*, n.d.; Haase, Gisela, *Sächsisches Glas vom 17. bis zum Anfang des 19. Jahrhunderts*, 1975.

Other publications: Bachmann, Manfred, *Die Dresdener Gemäldegalerie Alte und Neue Meister* (Leipzig 1978); Menzhausen, Joachim, *The Green Vaults* (Leipzig 1968); Rudloff-Hille, Gertrud, *Dresden Gemäldegalerie* (New York 1961); Schöbel, Johannes, *Fine Arms and Armor, Treasures in the Dresden Collection* (New York 1975); Seydewitz, Ruth and Max, *Die Dresdener Kunstschätze, Zur Geschichte des Grünen Gewölbes und der anderen Dresdener Kunstsammlungen* (Dresden 1960); Seydewitz, Max, *Museen und Menschen* (Berlin 1977); Sponsel, Jean Louis, *Das Grüne Gewölbe zu Dresden*, 4 vols. (Leipzig 1925); *The Splendor of Dresden: Five Centuries of Art Collecting* (New York 1975); Honey, William Bowyer, *Dresden China: An Introduction to the Study of Meissen Porcelain* (New York 1946); de Brun, L., "Johannes Schilling and the Meissen porcelains," *Connoisseur*, vol. 191, pp. 130–32, February 1976.

REINHILD G.A.G. JANZEN

Germany, Federal Republic of

———— Berlin, West ————

STATE MUSEUMS, WEST BERLIN (officially STAATLICHE MUSEEN BERLIN, STIFTUNG PREUSSISCHER KULTURBESITZ; alternately BERLIN DAHLEM, BERLIN MUSEUMS; also STAATLICHE MUSEEN PREUSSISCHER KULTURBESITZ, BERLIN; BERLINER MUSEEN, BERLIN; STAATLICHE MUSEEN), Stauffenbergstrasse 41, 1000 Berlin 30.

The State Museums in West Berlin are housed in three locations. Those at Berlin-Dahlem, 1000 Berlin 33, whose main entrance is on Lansstrasse, include the Picture Gallery, Prints and Drawings Department, Department of Sculpture, Museum of Islamic Art, Museum of Far Eastern Art, Museum of Indian Art, Museum of German Ethnology, and Ethnological Museum. The State Museums at Berlin-Charlottenburg, 1000 Berlin 19, house the Egyptian Museum, the Museum of Greek and Roman Antiquities, Museum of Pre- and Protohistory, Museum of Arts and Crafts, the Plaster Cast House, and the Art Library. The National Gallery is located at Berlin Tiergarten, Potsdamer Strasse 50, 1000 Berlin 30.

The State Museums of West Berlin and of East Berlin are discussed separately because they are administered by the Federal Republic of Germany and by the German Democratic Republic, respectively. However, they did share a common history until Berlin's capitulation in 1945 and the subsequent political division of the city and of Germany. The arbitrary division of the contents of all of the state museums and galleries of Berlin after 1945 depended solely on the locations to which they had been moved during World War II and their reallocation by the occupation forces. To appreciate the historical importance of the Berlin museums, it is necessary to regard the museums on both sides of the political border as complementary.

The history of the former Prussian museums begins with the reign of Frederick William the Great Elector Brandenburg (1640–88). For his picture gallery he acquired mostly Netherlandish paintings, guided in his predilections by his education in Leyden and his marriage to Louise Henrietta of Orange. He also founded the coin cabinet, the ethnological collections, and those of Greek and Roman antiquities. Frederick II of Prussia, also known as Frederick the Great, was the first of the Prussian kings to acquire paintings systematically and make them available to connoisseurs, such as Winckelmann, and artists by placing them in view in the gallery he built at his residence near Berlin, the Palace of Sans Souci in Potsdam (1763–64). In 1798 the architect, urban planner, and painter Karl Friedrich Schinkel was commissioned by Frederick William III (1797–1840) to design a public museum building in the classical style for the royal collections. Its site was close to the royal palace, the cathedral, and the university, an indication of the importance attributed to the museum.

For the first time in museum history, a public picture gallery was planned and implemented by art historians. Baron Karl Friedrich von Rumohr, Gustav Friedrich Waagen, and Franz Kugler worked under the guidance of Wilhelm von Humboldt, minister of state and chairman of the Commission for the Establishment of the Museum, which was in turn responsible to Chancellor Hardenberg. In Humboldt's words, the new museum was to facilitate "the study of the human spirit through contemplation of the greatest masterpieces of all time." Schinkel's building was the first in which architectural form was subordinated to the demands of displaying the collection of works of art from widely different periods and countries, and thus it became exemplary for subsequent museum buildings such as the Alte Pinakothek in Munich and the National Gallery in London. The royal museum, also called the "Old Museum," opened to the public on August 3, 1830. Between then and 1930 the five original departments (Antiquity, Paintings, Print Room, Coin Cabinet, Department of Ethnology) had expanded to nineteen museums, which exhibited their collections in fifteen buildings on the "Museum Isle" near the Hohenzollern royal residences. Two of the most important of these expansions were the Kaiser Friedrich Museum complex and the German Museum (Deutsches Museum) in 1904, planned and completed under the outstanding director Wilhelm von Bode (1845–1929). The destruction and dispersal of the holdings of modern art by the National Socialist regime and the losses caused by World War II brought a halt to this development.

In 1950 the Kaiser-Friedrich-Museum Association, first founded by Wilhelm von Bode in 1897, was reorganized and initiated the return of the former holdings that had been removed to mineshafts in Hessen and Niedersachsen in West Germany. The returned paintings were first accommodated in the Dahlem museum building, since it was the only one in West Berlin to have remained undamaged by the war. In 1957 the Federal Parliament in Bonn decreed by law the formation of a special foundation, the Foundation of Prussian Cultural Property (Stiftung Preussischer Kulturbesitz), whose purpose is to preserve the collections of the former state of Prussia (dissolved by the Allies in 1947) in their original context and to develop the collections insofar as they are located in West Berlin and in the Federal Republic of Germany. Through this federal law of 1957 the Foundation of Prussian Cultural Property became the proprietor of the former Prussian state collections. It has governed the State Museums in West Berlin since 1962, and since 1975 the foundation has been financed by the Federal Republic and all of its Länder, or states. All museum employees are employed by the state.

The administration of the State Museums in West Berlin is headed by a director general, a director of the Office of General Administration, and a director of the Public Relations Office (Aussenamt). The Office of Public Relations, originally founded in 1930 and reinstated in 1961, handles both general information services, such as museum publications, as well as the Department of Museum Education (Museumspädagogik).

After World War II the Dahlem museum became the first home for the state collections in West Berlin. The building had been designed by the architect Bruno Paul and was built between 1912 and 1923 but was never completed. Wilhelm von Bode had intended it to be the museum center for Asiatic art, since the Museum Isle was becoming overcrowded. Before World War II it was used to store the ethnographical collections. After the original Dahlem museum building was considerably expanded in two building periods (1962–64, 1970), it became the permanent location for the Ethnographic Museum and the museums of Asiatic art. All Western European art is to be housed eventually at the new museum complex planned at the Tiergarten area.

On October 2, 1950, Ernst Reuter, mayor of West Berlin at that time, opened the Dahlem museum with an exhibition of 149 paintings from the former Kaiser Friedrich Museum, which had been flown in from Wiesbaden, the Central Art Collecting Point of the American occupation zone. This marked the beginning of the reinstallation of the Picture Gallery (Gemäldegalerie). Today's total holdings consist of about fifteen hundred paintings, nearly half of which are on permanent display. The Gallery provides a comprehensive survey of European painting from the beginnings of panel painting in the thirteenth century to the masters of the Rococo in the eighteenth century.

The following brief historical survey of the Picture Gallery lists only those key acquisitions that are presently in West Berlin. For the other surviving paintings from the pre–World War II era the reader needs to check the Bode Museum (see State Museums) in East Berlin. The nucleus of the collection was paintings by Lucas Cranach, which the Great Elector had inherited from his family. They are *Adam and Eve* (1533), *The Fountain of Youth* (1546), *Venus and Cupid* (c. 1530), and *Venus and Cupid as Honey Thief* (c. 1537). The elector's own collecting efforts were directed mainly toward Netherlandish paintings. He retained Willem van Honthorst as his court painter for nearly two decades, and in 1675 Amalia von Solms, his mother-in-law, bequeathed her important collection to the House of Brandenburg. King Frederick I of Prussia and Frederick II (Frederick the Great) also inherited a number of valuable paintings from the

House of Orange, among them two early Rembrandts, the *Rape of Proserpine* (c. 1630) and the so-called *Minerva* (c. 1631).

Frederick the Great's personal taste favored contemporary French painting, principally the art of Watteau. His purchases included the *French Comedy* (after 1716), the *Italian Comedy* (after 1716), the incomplete *Fête Galante* (c. 1718–20), and the *Dance* (c. 1719). The outstanding works among Frederick the Great's acquisitions of Italian and Flemish Baroque artists are Rubens' *Perseus and Andromeda* (c. 1619–20), Rembrandt's *Moses* (1659), and Correggio's *Leda*, which was part of a cycle painted for Federico II Gonzaga (c. 1530).

After the Napoleonic wars, plans for the public Royal Picture Gallery with a universal collection were carried out. In 1815 the Giustiniani Collection (157 paintings) became the first acquisition by the Prussian State for the public museum in Berlin. This collection's strength was in paintings of the early Roman Baroque in Italy, but many of them were destroyed in the fire at the air-raid shelter in Friedrichshain in 1945. Of the five Caravaggios, only *Love Victorious* (1602) survived.

The next major acquisition followed in 1821 with the purchase of the collection of the English merchant Solly (three thousand paintings), which was to give the Picture Gallery its international reputation. Early Italian, Early Netherlandish, and Early German schools were well represented in the Picture Gallery. Key works among them are Fra Filippo Lippi's *Adoration* (c. 1459), Botticelli's *St. Sebastian* (after 1460), and Hans Holbein's *Merchant Gisze* (1532). The Picture Gallery's director, Wilhelm von Bode, expanded the holdings considerably by significant purchases. In 1874 the Suermondt Collection was acquired, and perhaps its most important work is Jan van Eyck's early *Madonna and Child in a Church* (c. 1425). Later Bode brought to the museum the two monumental altarpieces by Hugo van der Goes, the *Adoration of the Shepherds* (c. 1480), and the earlier Monforte altarpiece, the *Adoration of the Kings* (c. 1470). After 1897 the Kaiser-Friedrich-Museums-Verein supported Bode's collecting activities with important acquisitions such as Schongauer's *Nativity* (c. 1480), Rubens' *Landscape with the Shipwreck of Aeneas* (c. 1620), and, *Man with the Golden Helmet* (c. 1650), formerly attributed to Rembrandt.

The permanent exhibition of paintings is organized in historical sequence according to countries, schools, and individual artists. German, Netherlandish, and Italian painting is represented with nearly equal volume and significance. The section of Italian quattrocento painting remains, despite its severe losses, among the best of its kind outside of Florence and Venice. For example, there are Fra Filippo Lippi's *Madonna in the Woods* from the Palazzo Medici Ricardi in Florence, Giovanni Bellini's *Lamentation* (c. 1480–90), and works by Veneziano and Verrocchio. The section of Early German painting features eight works by Albrecht Dürer, among them the portraits *Hieronymus Holzschuher* (1526), *Jacob Muffel* (1526), and *Frederick the Wise* (c. 1496), as well as the *Madonna of the Siskin* (1506). Also well represented are Albrecht Altdorfer, Lucas Cranach, Hans Baldung Grien, and Martin Schongauer. Outstanding among the Early Netherlandish paintings are four works by Jan van Eyck, such as the portraits *Giovanni Arnolfini* (c. 1438) and *Baudouin of Lannoy* (c. 1431–35); three panels by Robert Campin; two altarpieces by Rogier van der Weyden, the St. John Altarpiece (after 1460) and the Middelburg or Bladelin Altarpiece (c. 1460); the above-mentioned altarpieces by Hugo van der Goes; and works by Bosch, Bouts, Memling, and Pieter Bruegel the Elder.

Highlights of the Italian Renaissance section are Giorgione's *Portrait of a Young Man* (c. 1505–6); five works by Titian, including his late *Self Portrait* (after 1550) and *Venus and the Organ Player* (1550–51); and four portraits by Bronzino, the most notable being *Ugolino Martelli* (c. 1537–38). One room is devoted to five early Madonnas by Raphael, among them the *Madonna Diotalevi* (c. 1502), *Madonna Terranuova* (1505), and *Madonna Colonna* (c. 1508).

Of the seventeenth-century Dutch painters, Rembrandt is the best represented, with twenty-six paintings that reveal all stages of his development, as well as the whole range of his subject matter. Especially noteworthy are two early self-portraits, the portrait of his wife, *Saskia* (1643), and of *Hendrickje Stoffels* (c. 1656–57); the *Mennonite Preacher Anslo and His Wife* (1641); and *Jacob Wrestling with the Angel* (c. 1660). Frans Hals' *Hille Bobbe* (1629–30) and *Nurse with Child* (c. 1616), Jan Vermeer van Delft's *Lady with a Pearl Necklace* (1660–65), and *Man and Lady at Wine* (c. 1660), as well as works by Pieter de Hooch and Gerard Ter Borch, Jacob van Ruisdael, and Hobbema, demonstrate the diversity and the quality of Dutch genre painting.

Dominating the collection of Flemish seventeenth-century masters are nineteen paintings by Rubens. The power of his creative genius is particularly well represented by the *Lamentation* (1608–9), *St. Sebastian* (c. 1619–20), *Child with a Bird* (c. 1616), *Perseus and Andromeda* (1619–20), and *St. Cecilia* (1639–40). Other masterpieces in this section are van Dyck's portraits of a Genoese gentleman and a Genoese lady (c. 1622–26) and two landscapes by Adriaen Brouwer.

Spanish Late Renaissance and Baroque painting is represented by its masters El Greco, Velázquez, and Zurbarán. Key works of the later Italian painters are Annibale Carracci's *Roman River Landscape with Bridge* (c. 1595), six paintings by Tintoretto from his late period (1570–80), seven views of Venice by Canaletto, Guardi's *Balloon-Ascent* (1784), and, of the eight works by Tiepolo, the *Martyrdom of St. Agatha* (c. 1750).

French and German seventeenth- and eighteenth-century painting is represented best by Georges de La Tour's *Finding of the Body of St. Sebastian* (1649), Nicolas Poussin's *Landscape with St. Matthew and the Angel* (1643), Chardin's *Draughtsman* (1737), the Watteaus collected by Frederick the Great, Johann Liss' *St. Paul's Ecstasy* (1737), J. H. Tischbein's *Artist and His First Wife* (1769), and portraits by Antoine Pesne and Anton Graff.

The Picture Gallery maintains a reference library, an archives, and a slide collection.

The Prints and Drawings Department (Kupferstichkabinett) was founded in

1831 by Rumohr at the suggestion of Wilhelm von Humboldt. The department acquired international importance in 1835 through the purchase of the collections of Postmaster General von Nagler, and in 1882 the Duke of Hamilton's collection of illuminated manuscripts was added. In 1937 the National Socialist regime confiscated twentieth-century "degenerate art," notably that of the German Expressionists. Since 1945 this gap has gradually been closed.

Today the holdings consist of 23,000 original drawings and sketchbooks from the fourteenth through the eighteenth century. Those of the Early German school—Dürer, Grünewald, Altdorfer, Cranach, Holbein—are of unique importance. There are 125 drawings by Dürer alone. Equally well represented is the sixteenth- and seventeenth-century Netherlands, with 50 drawings by Pieter Bruegel and 150 drawings by Rembrandt. Indeed, West Berlin's collection of graphic works by Rembrandt is the largest in the world. The Early Italian school is distinguished by Botticelli's twenty-seven silverpoint drawings illustrating Dante's *Divine Comedy*. Drawings by Fouquet and Watteau are outstanding examples of the French school. Among the 350,000 prints are found outstanding examples by Schongauer, Dürer, Rembrandt, Goya, Toulouse-Lautrec, and the German Expressionists.

There are five thousand illustrated books from the fifteenth to the twentieth century. The late fifteenth century is especially well represented with rarities such as the *Ackermann von Böhmen* (1461); Sebastian Brant's *Ship of Fools* (1494); *The Knight of Thurn*, with woodcuts by Dürer (1493); and the Venetian *Hypnerotomachia Poliphili* (1499). Among the most valuable of the more than one hundred illuminated manuscripts from the eleventh to the sixteenth century is *Mary of Burgundy's Prayerbook* (c. 1480). The department also maintains a topographical collection. Changing exhibitions selected from the holdings are on display in five rooms. Visitors may study any item from the collections upon request in a study room, and a reference library may be consulted.

The Department of Sculpture (Skulpturenabteilung) was founded in 1830, before which time it was part of the Department of Antiquities in the Old Museum. Its nucleus is composed of works from the royal Kunstkammer, as well as the acquisition of two private collections of Italian sculptures in 1828 and in 1840. After 1872 Wilhelm von Bode became instrumental in developing the original holdings into a systematic collection of representative masterpieces that demonstrate the development of Western sculpture from late Christian antiquity to the end of the eighteenth century. In 1930 sculptures by German, Netherlandish, French, and English masters were transferred to the German Museum (Deutsches Museum). At the close of World War II the Italian section suffered serious losses from fire and looting.

The Early Christian, Byzantine, and Italian sections of the pre–World War I holdings of the Department of Sculpture can be seen in the Bode Museum in East Berlin. In 1965 the Department of Sculpture was reopened in the Dahlem museum, with approximately two-thirds of its original holdings, or about thirty-five hundred objects, and an active acquisitions policy was resumed.

The Early Christian-Byzantine section comprises icons and jewelry, as well as other works in stone, ivory, wood, bronze, and gold. Major works are *Isis Enthroned with the Horus Child* from central Egypt (fourth century), the *Great Berlin Ivory Pyxis* (Alexandria-Trier, end of fourth century), and the mosaic icon of *Christ as Father of Mercy* (Byzantium, c. 1100).

The collection of medieval German sculpture (the Carolingian, Ottonian, and Romanesque periods) is rivaled only in Vienna and Munich. Key works are the *Angel of the Acension*, made of polychromed wood, from Cologne (c. 1170), and the *Mary of Sorrows* (*Klagende Maria*), also polychromed wood from a Crucifixion in Naumburg (c. 1230).

The most important German works from the fourteenth and fifteenth centuries are a group of works including *Christ and St. John* from Sigmaringen (c. 1320); a terracotta sculpture, the *Bearing of the Cross*, from Lorch-on-the-Rhine (c. 1425); the *Virgin of the Misericord* by Michel Erhart (c. 1480); the *Dangolsheim Madonna* by a master from Strassburg (c. 1470); and the *Four Evangelists* from the Münnerstadt altar by Tilmann Riemenschneider (1490–92). German Baroque sculpture is best represented by Martin Zürn's *Saints Sebastian and Florian* from Wasserburg-am-Inn (1638–39).

The most representative works in the Italian section are Giovanni Pisano's *Lectern* (c. 1310), Donatello's *Pazzi Madonna* (c. 1422), Desiderio da Settignano's *Bust of a Young Girl* (Marietta Strozzi) (1460–64), Bernini's *Putto on a Dolphin* (c. 1620), and Bernardino Cametti's *Diana* (c. 1720) from the Palazzo Orsini. German Rococo sculpture is best illustrated by Ignaz Gunther's *Archangel Michael* (c. 1755–60).

French sculpture of the seventeenth and eighteenth centuries is represented through works by Bouchardon, Pigalle, Falconet, and Houdon. The Department of Sculpture also holds three hundred objects of minor arts, small bronzes, and clay *bozzetti* of the sixteenth to the eighteenth century.

The Ethnographical Museum (Museum für Völkerkunde) consists of nine departments, each with its own division head and curatorial staff. It owes its origin to the seventeenth-century collection of curios of the Great Elector. After the dissolution of the Royal Prussian Kunstkammer, the Ethnographic Collection (Ethnographische Sammlung) was founded in 1829, and in 1873 it became an independent museum. The collections grew so rapidly that a large group of buildings was planned in Dahlem; however, only the present one was actually constructed by 1929. After World War II the entire Ethnographical Museum had to move into this building. The resulting lack of space allows only a small percentage of the museum's approximately 338,000 items to be exhibited, even after the addition of new exhibition halls in 1970. Since the late nineteenth century, the Arthur Baessler Foundation has been instrumental in the financing of publications, research, and collecting in the field.

In the permanent exhibition of the Department of Africa, all cultural areas of West Africa are represented, including terracottas from Ife in western Nigeria, with heads and fragments of larger sculptures of the twelfth to the fourteenth century; bronze commemorative heads and bronze relief plaques of the sixteenth and seventeenth centuries from the Benin kingdom on the lower Niger; and wooden masks and sculptures from the Cameroons, including the bead-covered royal throne, a gift from Sultan Njoya to Emperor Frederick William II.

The collection of the Department of Oceania (Abteilung Südsee) began in 1802 with the purchase of Polynesian objects for the Royal Prussian Kunstkammer, objects that had been brought to Europe by James Cook's expeditions to these newly discovered islands. Since then the collection has grown to more than fifty-one thousand objects and comprises the art and material culture objects from New Guinea, Melanesia, Micronesia, Polynesia, and Australia. Especially noteworthy are cult objects from the Sepik River area, the Papuan Gulf district, and New Ireland; the royal feather cloak of King Kamehamea II of Hawaii from Santa Cruz Island, made in Taumako; the "mourning gown" from Tahiti (which is the oldest piece in the collection, purchased in 1768); and reconstructions of original boats and houses.

In 1956 the former Department of the Americas, consisting then of more than 165,000 objects, was divided into the Department of American Archaeology (Abteilung Amerikanische Archaeologie) and the Department of American Indians (Abteilung Amerikanische Naturvölker). The geographic range of the arts exhibited in a particularly striking, modern installation comprise Central and South America—Mexico, Guatemala, Honduras, El Salvador, Nicaragua, Costa Rica, Colombia, Ecuador, Peru, and Bolivia. The objects date from a timespan of about three thousand years, from the beginning of pre-Classical or formative phases, about 1500 B.C., until the time of the Spanish conquests in the sixteenth century. Especially noteworthy are the collections of ancient pottery from Peru: that of the Paracas culture (300 B.C.-A.D. 200), of the Moche culture (first to seventh century A.D.), from Recuay (first to seventh century A.D.), from Nazka (second to eighth century A.D.), and of the Onca culture (thirteenth-fifteenth century). Other key works are the stone stelae from Lucia Cozumalhuapa, Guatemala; a portrait head of a Mayan prince of painted stucco from Palenque, Mexico (c. A.D. 800); the Aztec stone vessel for the blood of the sacrifice, Mexico (fifteenth century A.D.); and the gold treasury from Colombia, Costa Rica, and Peru.

Due to a lack of space the Department of American Indians does not yet have a permanent exhibition installation. Of its nearly fifty thousand objects, about half are from the North American continent and the remainder from South America. The department's research and acquisition policy focuses on the prehistoric cultures of all of the Americas, including the Eskimos and the Indian aboriginal tribes of the tropical forests of the Amazon. Although the Department of American Archaeology concentrates exclusively on the art of the so-called high civilizations, that of the American Indian holds the material culture objects and the arts of the so-called *Naturvölker*, or "primitive" peoples. As do most other departments of the Berlin museums, this one has its origin in the royal Kunstkammer of the Great Elector. These objects had come from Brazil but are now lost. Today the oldest objects, Nootka masks from before 1778, date from the Cook-Forster voyage to the northwest Coast of North America. The department organizes special exhibitions from its collections.

The Department of West Asia (Westasien) became a separate department from the other Asian collections of the Ethnographic Museum in 1970. The origin of the collections dates from about 1830, after which the museum received numerous private gifts of West Asian arts and crafts. Today its more than five thousand objects comprise the material culture of townspeople, villagers, and nomads from Arab-speaking countries (Saudi Arabia; Yemen; the Persian Gulf states; Iraq; Jordan; Syria; Lebanon; Israel, which was formerly listed as Palestinia; and the Asiatic part of Turkey) and from Persian-language areas such as Persia (Iran), Afghanistan, and parts of Pakistan, such as Baluchistan. There are weapons, jewelry, carpets, saddlebags, precious textiles, and exquisite examples of the crafts of metalworking, enameling, and mosaics. The department does not yet have a permanent exhibition.

Before the Department of South Asia (Südasien) became a separate department in 1963, it was the Indian section of the Ethnographical Museum. Some of its objects derive from the Great Elector's Kunstkammer. The department's domains of research and collecting are ethnographical objects of the autotochthounous peoples and cultures of the following regions: the Indian subcontinent, except for large areas of Pakistan (the Himalayan countries of Nepal, Bhutan, and Sikkim); Ceylon, the Maledives, Lakkadives, Andamanes, Nikobares, and Assam islands; the Southeast Asian continental states of Burma, Thailand, Laos, Cambodia, Vietnam, and Malaysia; and the Indonesian islands from Sumatra in the west to the Aru islands and the Molukkes in the east and the Philippines and Taiwan in the north. Not included are archaeological artifacts, art of the literate cultures of India and Hindu-Buddhist Indonesia, and the Tibetan-Lamaist artifacts in the southern areas of the Himalayan countries. The permanent exhibition displays marionettes and shadowplay puppets from India, Thailand, Java, and Bali and masks from the theater and cults in Ceylon, Thailand, and Indonesia, as well as cult sculptures, textiles, ceremonial weapons, and jewelry.

The nucleus of the collection of the Department of East Asia (Ostasien) is documented in the inventories of 1603 and 1605 of the Great Elector's Kunstkammer. By 1973 it comprised more than 16,105 objects, representing the material culture of China (Han, Manchu, minorities); of Japan (including Ryukyu islanders and Ainu); of Korea, Tibet, and Mongolia; and of twenty-six ethnic groups from northern Asia. In the permanent exhibition objects are organized according to their functional use in all domains of production, with the exception of objects classified as art, and thus the preserve of the Museum of East Asian Art, such as calligraphy, ceramics, and painting. Especially noteworthy are the sculpture of the Kuan-Yin goddess of charity and love (Sung period: 960–1280), T'ang ceramics (618–906), inscriptions on bone and shadowplay figures from China, a reconstruction of an original *yurt*, a Mongolian tent, and lamaistic cult utensils.

The Department of Europe (Europa) has been a separate department within the Ethnographical Museum since 1950, but it does not yet have space for a permanent exhibition based on its approximately fourteen thousand objects. The department defines its area of research and acquisition by the geographical boundaries of the Ural in the north and the Kazakstan with the northern and western shores of the Caspian Sea to the south, and excludes Germany. The collections represent the material culture of European shepherd and peasant peoples and the crafts of preindustrial village and town cultures in their autonomous development and their adaptation to industrial products. Most completely assembled is the material culture of the Lapp from Scandinavia.

Since the reinstitution of the Department of Music Ethnology (Musikethnologie) in 1963, it has become an international center of comparative musicology. In 1973 it held more than 42,500 recordings of European and non-European music, as well as a systematic collection of representative musical instruments from around the world. There is no permanent installation of an exhibit as yet, but the department maintains an audio center for visitors to the Dahlem museums in the main lobby at the Lansstrasse entrance. The collections are accessible to research.

The Museum of Indian Art (Museum für Indische Kunst) is the only museum of Indo-Asian art in West Germany and was created in 1963 by the removal of the Indian art collections from the Ethnographical Museum's East Indian collection. From India's pre- and early history, sculptures, crafts, and miniatures are shown; from Tibet and Nepal, bronze sculptures and scroll paintings; from Indo-China and Indonesia, stone sculptures, bronzes, and tile reliefs; and from Turkistan (Central Asia), the Turfan collection of wall paintings and paintings on textiles dating from the Buddhist periods. They were acquired during four expeditions (1902–14) to Buddhist cave temples in Chinese Turkestan. Turfan art flowered during the fifth to the tenth century in the oases of the Tarim basin, on the northern Silk Route to China, and is considered a link between Gandharan and East Asian art. On exhibit from western Pakistan are Gandhara sculptures from the first to the fifth century, which are Graeco-Buddhist stone reliefs and reveal the influence of Hellenistic art as it spread eastward after the conquests of Alexander the Great.

The Museum of Indian Art also organizes special exhibitions with objects from the museum's study collections, as well as a special exhibition that documents the current excavations at Sonkh Hill in the Mathura district of northern India. A reference library and archives are being developed.

The Museum of Islamic Art (Museum für Islamische Kunst) was founded in 1904 by Wilhelm von Bode. After World War II parts of the collections were placed in the Pergamum Museum in East Berlin. In 1971 a permanent installation of the most important pieces of Parthian and Sassanian art in the Dahlem museum building was completed. It offers a comprehensive introduction to Islamic art, from the beginning of the Islamic epoch in the eighth century until the eighteenth century, ranges in geographic scope from Spain to India and includes specimens of calligraphy, glass of the eighth to fourteenth century, faiences of the second to seventeenth century, and works in bronze. Especially noteworthy are a fragment of a ninth-century Koran and carved ivories from Egypt and lower Italy of the eleventh to twelfth century, such as the carved elephant tusk from Speyer Cathedral, inlaid bronzes, carpets of the fifteenth to the eighteenth century, and a reconstruction of an original prayer niche executed in faience mosaic from an Iranian sixteenth-century mosque.

Before the founding of the Museum of Far Eastern Art (Museum für Ostasiatische Kunst) in 1959, its collection had been known since 1907 as the Collection of East Asian Art. Ninety percent of its holdings were lost during World War II. However, the nucleus of the objects survived, and it is exhibited under the following subdivisions: the early Chinese periods, Far Eastern religious art, arts and crafts from China, Chinese and Japanese painting from the twelfth to the twentieth century, and Korean and Japanese arts and crafts such as a seventy-five-piece set of china for a tea ceremony. The museum's woodblock prints are shown in rotating exhibits. Among the notable new acquisitions is a Chinese ceremonial axe with a human mask in relief, from the twelfth to eleventh century B.C. An extensive specialized library, a study collection, and photography archives are being developed.

The Museum of German Folklore (Museum für Deutsche Volkskunde) was founded in 1889 and defines its purpose today as a museum of cultural history of the middle and lower social classes, that is, of peasants, craftsmen, and workers of the early industrial era. The museum's permanent exhibition presents a selective collection of folklore objects from German-speaking populations in Europe, from the sixteenth century until the present. However, the majority of the objects date from the eighteenth and nineteenth centuries. Particularly noteworthy are the collections of furniture, costumes, and jewelry from north Germany, south Germany, and Austria and the exhibits of the production cycles of a peasant home (cooking, baking, flax-dressing, spinning, weaving, washing, and ironing), with all of the respective tools, crockery, and textiles. Noteworthy also are the collection of toys, ceremonial objects of guilds, votive offerings, popular prints, and native painting.

The State Museums in Berlin-Charlottenburg comprise the Museum of Pre- and Protohistory, the Museum of Greek and Roman Antiquities, the Egyptian Museum, the Museum of Arts and Crafts, the Plaster Cast House, and the Art Library, which is located temporarily near Bahnhof Zoo.

The Museum of Pre- and Protohistory and the Museum of Arts and Crafts are housed in the Charlottenburg Palace itself. It is now the best example of Prussian royal architecture in West Berlin. The palace was begun by Arnold Nehring in 1659 as a country house for Sophie Charlotte, wife of Elector Frederick III. In 1702 the architect Eosander von Göthe converted the main building and wings into a three-sided structure to enclose a court of honor. Three years later the central domed tower (157 feet high) was erected. Frederick the Great then commissioned G. W. Knobelsdorff to add the so-called New Wing on the east side (1740–43) as a counterpart to the Orangerie. Carl Gotthard Langhans built the palace theater in the west wing. In 1943 the palace was badly damaged by high explosives and firebombs. The exterior, the dome, and the historical apartments have been restored. The state apartments are used by the senate of Berlin to host official receptions.

The Museum of Pre- and Protohistory (Museum für Vor- und Frühgeschichte) has been located since 1960 in the west wing (Langhans building) of the Charlottenburg Palace. It was founded in 1829 as the Museum Vaterländischer Altertümer in the palace of Monbijou and had its origin in the Hohenzollern Collections of art and archaeology. Its nucleus was antiquities brought to Berlin from the time of the Great Elector. The museum was destroyed in 1945, and thus vanished the largest collection of its kind in the world. Losses included the great gold treasures, such as Schliemann's finds from Troy (1890), and the Eberswalde treasure. Nevertheless, the return of the pieces that had been evacuated to West Germany, searches among the rubble of the bombed museum, the acquisition of the prehistoric section of the Märkisches Museum of Berlin, and a large number of recent purchases have yielded a representative collection of material culture objects and artifacts from prehistoric and early historic times in Europe and the Near East, displayed in five rooms: the culture of hunters and gatherers of the older and middle Stone Age, peasant cultures of the early Stone Age, the Bronze Age (1700–700 B.C.), the pre-Roman Iron Age (700 B.C. to the beginning of the Christian era), and the cultures of the period of the barbarian invasions (A.D. 400–700), especially that of the Vikings. The museum also maintains a lecture and film room, instructions on prehistoric crafts, and a school museum. The primary intention of the exhibitions is didactic, to show by means of dioramas the chief stages in human civilization. This museum was the first to display, side by side, finds from ancient Europe and the Near East of the same approximate date, so that the visitor can make comparative studies.

The Museum of Greek and Roman Antiquities (Antikenmuseum) was founded as a public museum in 1830. It possessed then about two thousand vases and more than twice as many by 1894. The museum was located then on the principal floor of Schinkel's museum, called the Antiquarium, or Department of Antiquities of the Berlin Museums. Since its reopening in 1960, it has been accommodated in the West Stüler building (1851–58), across from the Charlottenburg Palace. Friedrich Wilhelm IV commissioned the leading architect among Schinkel's followers, Friedrich August Stüler, to build two identical quarters for the officers of the royal Gardes-du-Corps. The king himself was involved in the planning of the square edifices in the classicizing style: the circular colonnaded temple and lectern for the stairwell are his contribution. The twin building houses the Egyptian Museum. In 1973–74 the two main floors were modernized in an unconventional manner by the architects R. Schüler and U. Schüler-Witte to improve lighting conditions and to facilitate a didactic display design. Like most of the Berlin State Museums this one, too, has its beginning in the Kunstkammer of the Great Elector. Between 1696 to 1701 its holdings of antiquities were published in three luxury volumes as *Thesaurus Brandenburgicus*. The stock of about twelve thousand gems and cameos was originated by Frederick the Great's purchase of the Stosch Collection in 1764, which was then published by Winckelmann.

Today the museum's holdings are mostly those pieces of the world-famous Antiquarium that were moved to West Germany, and after 1945 the collections were divided between West Berlin and East Berlin according to where they were during the war. In West Berlin are the masterpieces of red-figured Attic and Italian vases (530–375 B.C.), such as the Sosias cup, two cups by Brygos, the amphora of the so-called Berlin Painter, and the bowl depicting Achilles dressing Patroclos' wounds. Outstanding among the bronzes is the statuette of Zeus from Dodona. The display of gold jewelry and ornaments ranges from 2000 B.C. to A.D. 600; especially noteworthy are the golden Scythian fish from Vettersfelde (sixth century B.C.), a necklace from Assiut, and the Roman silver hoard from Hildesheim, found in 1868. Egyptian mummy portraits from Fayum of the first to the third century A.D. testify to the scope of the Hellenic style.

The Egyptian Museum (Ägyptisches Museum) was first founded in 1823 and reopened in its own building in 1967 in the East Stüler Building, across from the Charlottenburg Palace. World War II had equally disastrous consequences for the former Egyptian Museum on the Museum Isle as on all of the others of the Prussian State Museums. Now about one-third of the pre–World War II collections is in Charlottenburg, and the rest is in East Berlin. The most valuable pieces are from the Amarna Period (1375–1350 B.C.), finds resulting from excavations carried out by the German Orient Society (Deutsche Orient-Gesell-schaft) in 1911–14. Key works of this period in Egyptian art are portrait heads of Queen Tiy and King Akhenaten and the limestone bust of Nefertiti, which is one of the most lifelike portraits in the whole period of Egyptian art. Exemplary of the new court style is the limestone relief of Echnaton and Nefertiti. The permanent installation in seventeen rooms on three floors contains some fifteen hundred objects from all periods of ancient Egypt, from the prehistoric era to the time of Roman domination (500 B.C.-A.D. 300), arranged in chronological sequence. The outstanding work from the Late Period (1085–332 B.C.) is the *Berlin Green Head*, a priest's portrait head in green stone. The collection is rich in sculptures and reliefs from temples and tombs, scarabs, jewelry, objects used in daily life from the pre- and protohistoric period until 2778 B.C., objects from tombs such as mummies and amulets, bronze and terracotta figures, a papyrus collection, and a reconstruction of the mortuary temple of King Sahure (2500 B.C.), with architectural fragments from its site in Egypt.

The Museum of Arts and Crafts (Kunstgewerbemuseum) was founded in 1867 with some sixty-five hundred items from the royal Kunstkammer. From 1921 until 1939 it was housed in the now-demolished city palace called Schlossmuseum. Since 1963 some fifteen hundred pieces, one-eighth of the entire holdings, have been on display in twelve rooms of the Knobelsdorff wing of the Charlottenburg Palace. The exhibition provides a general survey of the religious and the secular arts and crafts of Europe, from the Early Middle Ages until the twentieth century. Key works from the medieval church treasures are the Guelph Treasure (Romanesque), which was acquired in 1935; the treasure of Enger near Herford-Westfalia; the treasure of Basle Cathedral; Barbarossa's baptismal bowl from Cappenberg (c. 1122); and the medallion with the personification of Operatio from the Remaklus Retable in Stavelot-Meuse (c. 1150), acquired in 1978. Goldsmith work of the Renaissance is best represented by the Lüneburg municipal silver (Lüneburger Ratssilber), which is the only surviving large collection of municipal plate and consists of thirty-four cups, dishes, and decanters in the shape of lions (1472–1599).

There are also works by the famous goldsmiths Krug, Jamnitzer, Petzold, Silber, and Lencker. Due to World War II the porcelain collection lost more than two thousand objects, but it is nevertheless excellent, particularly the pieces of Italian majolica, which is the best of its kind in Germany; porcelain from important German manufacturers; and Bauhaus ceramics. The former collections of textiles and glass, which had been unique because of their completeness and quality, suffered the most severe losses during World War II. The textile collection lost many of the European tapestries and fabrics from the Middle Ages to the Rococo, and it lost all of its costume collection. The entire collection of hollow glassware and stained glass perished. What survived World War II is divided between East and West Berlin. The exhibits' sequence is arranged primarily according to chronology and secondarily to material and purpose. The museum's holdings in modern applied arts are not on exhibit at this time due to lack of space. Upon completion of the planned new museum buildings in the Tiergarten area, the Museum of Arts and Crafts will be located there.

The Plaster Cast House (Gipsformerei) was founded in 1840 and is now located near the Charlottenburg Palace. It has show rooms with samples of casts from sculptures of all periods and many cultures. Its main purpose is the sale of casts from about seven thousand molds it owns. They are taken from Egyptian, Near Eastern, Greek, and Roman objects; from Mesoamerican and East Indian sculptures; and from European medieval sculptures until those of the nineteenth century. The casts are produced on order in a great variety of materials, in white or in colors corresponding to those of the originals. Catalogues and prices may be obtained upon request.

The Art Library (Kunstbibliothek) is housed temporarily in a building near Bahnhof Zoo. It, too, is to be part of the new museum complex planned at the Tiergarten area. It has about 120,000 volumes and 630 periodicals that cover all fields of the arts. Special foci are the Lipperheide Costume Library with 13,500 volumes and 46,000 prints; the prints and drawing collection with 9,000 drawings, 40,000 engravings, and 3,300 bound copper engravings on European architectural art and arts and crafts; illustrated books of the nineteenth century; and a collection of graphic designs and posters of the nineteenth and twentieth centuries. Presently, the Art Library has two reading rooms and maintains changing exhibitions.

The first state museum to have been built at Berlin-Tiergarten is the National

Gallery (Nationalgalerie, also called Neue Nationalgalerie). It was reopened at this site in 1968 in a building by Ludwig Mies van der Rohe and was joined with the city's Gallery of the Twentieth Century (Galerie des 20. Jahrhunderts). Its nucleus was Joachim Heinrich Wilhelm Wagener's collection of paintings by German masters of the nineteenth century, which he presented to the king in 1861. The National Gallery was first opened in its own building, designed by August Stüler, on the Museum Isle in 1876. Director Ludwig Justi (1909–33) expanded acquisition policies beyond the national interest and began to buy Picasso, Braque, and Gris. He also founded the association of the Friends of the National Gallery in 1929. As a consequence of the National Socialists' action against so-called degenerate art, 64 paintings, 27 sculptures, and 326 drawings were either sold abroad or destroyed in 1937. Between 1939 and 1945 the National Gallery was closed, its contents were evacuated, and in 1945 those works that had not been destroyed by fire or confiscated by Soviet military were brought to the Western allied art collection points, Celle (British) and Wiesbaden (American).

The inception of the National Gallery is tied to the Romantic movement, specifically to the Düsseldorf artists' petition addressed to the Frankfurt Parliament for a German national gallery. Today the National Gallery sees as its task the completion of its holdings of nineteenth-century art from non-German areas and the establishment of links with the art of the immediate present. In contrast to the traditional organization of works of art according to national and regional schools, the National Gallery exhibits its works in such a way as to demonstrate the scope of technical, aesthetic and thematic problems that artists deal with, such as the exploration of new media. Acquisitions reflect this exhibition goal.

Within the permanent collection, the nineteenth century is best represented in the twelve works by Caspar David Friedrich, of which his *Mondaufgang am Meer* (1861) is notable; the twenty-seven paintings by Karl Blechen, among which his *Schloss Sansouci* (1891) is impressive; and the thirty-nine pieces by Adolf von Menzel, whose *Das Balconzimmer* (1903), *Huldigung der Schlesischen Stände*, and *Theatre du Gymnase* are noteworthy. Works can also be seen by Anselm von Feuerback (*Nanna*, 1861; *Self Portrait*, 1899; and *Ricordo di Tivoli*, 1902), Arnold Böcklin (*Portrait of Karl Wallenreiter*, 1901, and the *Artist and His Wife*), and Hans Thoma (*Still Life of Wild Flowers*). Representative of Hans von Marées work are his *Orangepicker* and *The Rowers*, both done in 1902. An example by Courbet can be found in his *Etrétat*, and examples of French Impressionism are seen in works such as those by Monet (*St. Germain l'Auxerrois in Paris*, 1866) and Renoir (*Evening of the Children in Wargemont*, 1884).

The early twentieth century is best represented by Munch, especially his *Lebensfries* for Max Reinhardt, which constitutes a link between two centuries; Max Liebermann (seven paintings); Lovis Corinth (thirteen); Max Beckmann (ten); Oskar Kokoschka and Paul Klee, as well as other exponents of German Expressionism, the Bauhaus, Surrealism, and contemporary trends.

The National Gallery also maintains a sculpture garden, changing exhibitions in the great glass and steel upper hall, restoration facilities for paintings and drawings, a reference library, and a slide collection.

Entrance to all State Museums is free. Slides and photographs of objects in the collections may be purchased directly at the sales desks of the museums, by applications to the Public Relations Office, or by request to the respective museum or department of the Berlin museums. The museums' libraries are open to the public but are noncirculating. The Public Relations Department (Aussenamt), specifically its division Materialverwaltung, at Stauffenbergstrasse 41, 1000 Berlin 30, furnishes upon request a list of museum publications, as well as a list of all available information sheets (*Führungsblätter*), with corresponding but separate full-page illustrations and slide sets, including instructions for ordering. In addition to providing more comprehensive guides to the collections and catalogs of all exhibitions, the State Museums publish the *Jahrbuck der Berliner Museen, Jahrbuch der Preussischen Kunstsammlungen Neue Folge*, an annual journal begun in 1950, of scholarly articles on objects in the museums. The General Administration Offices (Generaldirektion) of the State Museums publishes acquisition news and reports on the museums' activities, exhibits, and programs in *Berliner Museen, Berichte aus den Staatlichen Museen Preussischer Kulturbesitz*, several issues a year.

Selected Bibliography

Museum publications: *Staatliche Museen Berlin preussischer Kulturbesitz Wegweiser (Itinerary)*, 1976; *Ägyptisches Museum Berlin, Kurzführer*, 1969; *Gemäldegalerie Berlin, Katalog*, 1975; *Neuerwerbungen Gemäldegalerie Berlin*, published irregularly; Gipsformerei: Heft 11—*Deutsche Plastik des 19. Jahrhunderts*, n.d.; Kunstbibliothek: *Mittelalterliche Handschriften*, 1926; *Französische und deutsche Bildillustrationen des 18. Jahrhunderts*, n.d.; *Kunstgewerbemuseum Berlin, Ausgewählte*, Werke Bd. 1, 1963; Kupferstichkabinett, *Vom Späten Mittelalter bis zu David*, 1973; *Museum für Deutsche Volkskunde Wegweiser*, 1977; *Museum für Indische Kunst, Katalog*, 1971; *Beiträge zur Indienforschung*, 1977; *Museum für Islamische Kunst, Katalog*, 1971, 1977; *Museum für Ostasiatische Kunst* (Neuauflage), Katalog, n.d.; *Chinesische und Japanische Holzschnitte*, 1971; *Museum für Völkerkunde: Westafrikanische Plastik I, II, III*, 1965; *Kunst von Sepik I, II, III*, 1977; *Altperuanische Kulturen I*, 1975, *II-III*, 1975–80; *Museum für Vor- und Frühgeschichte; Steinzeit und frühe Stadtkultur*, n.d., and *Frühe Bauern und Schriftkulturen*, 1969; *Nationalgalerie Berlin, Verzeichnis der Gemälde und Skulpturen des 19. Jahrhunderts*, 1976; Skulpturengalerie: *Der Mensch um 1500, Werke aus Kirchen und Kunstkammern*, 1977; *Bildwerke der Christlichen Epochen von der Spätantike bis zum Klassizismus*, 1966; *Catalog of Paintings, Picture Gallery Berlin*, 2d rev. ed., 1978.

Other publications: Furtwängler, Adolf, *Königliche Museen zu Berlin, Beschreibung der Vasensammlung im Antiquarium*, 2 vols. (Berlin 1885); Greifenhagen, Adolf, *Antike Kunstwerke, Ehemals Staatliche Museen Berlin, Antikenabteilung* (Berlin 1960); *Katalog der Ornamentstichsammlung der Staatlichen Kunstbibliothek Berlin*, 2 vols. (new ed., New York 1958); Klessmann, Rüdiger, *The Berlin Museum* (New York 1972); Krieger, K., and Koch, G., eds., *Hundert Jahre Museum für Völkerkunde Berlin*, Baessler Archiv, *Beiträge zu Völkerkunde, Neue Folge* Bd. 21 (Berlin 1973); Luschan, Felix von, *Die Altertümer von Benin* (new ed., New York 1968); Redslob, Erwin, *The Berlin-Dahlem*

Gallery: Great Paintings from the former Kaiser-Friedrich-Museum (New York-London 1967); *Zeichnungen deutscher Meister im Kupferstichkabinett zu Berlin*, 2 vols. (Berlin 1921).

REINHILD G.A.G. JANZEN

——— Cologne ———

SCHNÜTGEN MUSEUM, Cäcilienstrasse 29, D 5000 Cologne.

The Schnütgen Museum owes its existence to the zeal of one individual, Alexander Schnütgen. Schnütgen (1843–1918), a priest at the Cologne Cathedral from 1866, began collecting only after the great enthusiasm for medievalism that swept the Romantic period had subsided. Yet he managed, with luck and perseverance, to save many ecclesiastical treasures from destruction or obscurity. Abiding by his motto "Colligite Fragmenta ne Pereant" (connected fragments will not be lost), he concentrated on finding complete series of iconographically or stylistically interrelated paintings, liturgical objects, and garments, mostly from the Rhineland and Westphalia.

The collection was first introduced to the public and received recognition in 1902 at an exhibition in Düsseldorf. At the suggestion of Otto von Falke, director of the Applied Arts and Crafts Museum, Schnütgen donated his treasures to that museum on the fortieth anniversary of his ordination. They were installed as the Schnütgen Collection in a special, newly erected wing on October 26, 1910, and remained under the donor's care until his death in 1918.

From its inception, Schnütgen was assisted by Fritz Witte (1875–1937), also an ordained priest. He envisioned the museum as a "documentary collection of great style, a showplace of ecclesiastical history." His educator's viewpoint led to the establishment of the Institute of Religious Art, devoted to research of the collection and to the publication of the *Journal of Christian Art*, originally founded in 1851 but discontinued in 1921, a victim of inflation. Of lasting value are Witte's catalogs on sculpture (1912), liturgical objects (1913), and liturgical vestments (1926).

When the Cologne museums were reorganized in 1931, Witte showed great foresight in managing to trade the panel paintings of the Schnütgen Collection for the holdings of church art objects from the Wallraf-Richartz Museum (q.v.) and the Arts and Crafts Museum. Thus the museum gained its unique position as a custodian of church art from the Roman Germanic period through the Baroque era.

Since March 19, 1932, the collection had been housed in the restored Heribert Cloister. The building was destroyed during World War II, but the art objects were kept in safety and, after some adventures, returned to the Rhineland. In May 1956 the museum reopened for a third time under the leadership of Hermann Schnitzler. It is located in the Romanesque Church of St. Cecilia, restored according to plans by the architect Carl Band, which included a new addition for administrative offices. Incorporated in the installation of the collections are both Schnütgen's principle of classification according to type and Witte's emphasis on the art historical aspects of the works. The Society of Friends of the Schnütgen Museum was founded that same year and has been responsible for many new acquisitions.

The museum again underwent structural changes in 1976–77. The new concepts combined aesthetics with education and up-to-date informational media, such as polyvision. The installation of the collections is now based on epochs of style, subjects, historical and liturgical connections, and highlights the significance and function of individual objects within the realm of the church.

Of special importance in all periods of medieval Christianity was the role of the art of Byzantium as a transmitter of antiquity. Byzantine influence is seen in the chasuble of purple silk found in the grave of St. Anno, archbishop of Cologne (1056–75), and in the Romanesque "lion cloth" woven in Regensburg. An example of Byzantine carved ivory is shown in a relief of the *Death of Mary* from the tenth century. Among the Carolingian works, two pieces stand out: an ivory diptych from Aachen (810) and the Heribert comb of the later Metzer school (late ninth century). Ottonian and Romanesque objects are the decorations in ivory or less valuable walrus tooth on book covers, such as the one of Christ with the Apostles (Cologne, late tenth century); panels with evangelist symbols from Northern Italy, early tenth century, or *Christ on the Throne with St. Victor and St. Gereon* in a jewel frame of gilt-copper; and the *Ascension* (1000). Reliquaries such as a small chest (of the Metzer school, early eleventh century) from the Ludwig Collection and the fragment *Three Women at Christ's Grave* (Cologne, 1050) are part of the group.

The so-called stipple-engraved group contains masterpieces such as the patens, with the *Nativity*, the *Crucifixion*, and *Women at the Grave* from the early twelfth century. Two examples of medieval book art are a Carolingian gospel (northern France, 860–70) and the Romanesque *Maiestas Domini*, with embossed work on its cover and an enameled frame (Cologne, 1170). The *Gospel of St. Mary of Lyskirchen*, written and illuminated in Cologne in 1100–1120, depicts a carved ivory crucifixion on the cover (c. 1050). Richly decorated and illuminated are the *Missal of the Steinfeld Abbey* (c. 1180) and a single page from the *Albani Psalter*.

A group of small, bronze crucifixes are from the Romanesque period. Among them are those of the school of Roger van Helmarshausen (1100–1120) and the crucifix by the Maasland master Reiner von Huy (c. 1120). A Modalus crucifix is also attributed to Roger, and from the same school is the embossed copper fragment *Christ with the Shovel*. A cylindrical monstrance made of rock crystal (Westphalia, late twelfth century) is an early example of its type. The great name of Eibertus Coloniensis is linked to a cloisonné cross (c. 1160) whose inlays have unfortunately been lost, but two patens and a disk from the Ludwig Collection demonstrate the intense coloration and masterful cloisonné technique achieved in the Rhine Maas region.

Various altars and shrines originated in the workshops of the Masters of the Three Kings' Shrine, Nikolas of Verdun and his followers. Typical, too, are the masterpieces from Limoges, the center of cloisonné work, such as a bishop's crozier, book cover, and reliquary chest. Examples of the superb bronze casting done in the Rhine and Maas regions and in Westphalia are displayed in crosses, candelabra, incensories, aquamaniles, reliquaries, and door knockers. Early wood carving of the Rhineland can be found in an Ottonian crucifix from the Neuerburg Collection (early eleventh century) and a fragment of the crucifix of St. George (1067).

Among the stone sculptures, the beautiful fragment the *Siegburger Madonna* is particularly effective (Lower Rhine, 1150–60). Monumental in scale, the tympana of St. Cecilia and St. Pantaleon date from the same period. The relief *Fiddler and the Dancer*, classical in concept, is ascribed to the Master of the Cloister Maria Laach. From the same circle originates the *Annunciation Angel* (Cologne, 1210). The finely chiseled scrolls of a stone relief (Cologne, c. 1190) point to the interrelation of the crafts in their resemblance to a goldsmith's work. Such connections also appear in the draped classical garment of the *Aachener Madonna* (c. 1220). This outstanding sculpture introduces a series of Gothic depictions of St. Mary, highlights of the collection. They include: *Madonna with the Rock Crystal* (Cologne, early thirteenth century) and, similar in type, the *Enthroned Mary* and the *Kendenicher Madonna* (c. 1300), both showing Mary stomping the dragon.

A different concept is expressed in the sculpture of the fourteenth century, with the finely colored *Madonna of the Three Kings' Gate* and the more intimate *Maria on the Throne* (Cologne, mid-fourteenth century); the elegant *Madonna on a Wide Throne*; and the delicate *Madonna in the Sun* (Cologne, late fourteenth century), which shows gilding.

Standing madonnas take on an elongated form in the *Ollesheimer Madonna* (Cologne, c. 1290), the full figure of the *Cologne Madonna* (c. 1330) found near the cathedral, the *Friesentor Madonna*, and the *Carthusian Madonna*, of which only a torso survives, typifying the "soft style" of Cologne before 1426. Ranking Gothic works belong to the time of the consecration of the cathedral choir in 1322. Creations such as the marble figures of the *Mensa of the Altar*, the *Apostles of the Dome* (1352–54), and the expressive *Crucifixion Group* (northern France, late thirteenth century); reliquary busts and containers; the so-called pestilence crosses; and a Pietà (late fourteenth century) all date from the same general period. A splendid example of secular art can be found in the bust of a young woman by Heinrich IV Parler (c. 1390).

The intimacy of private worship finds expression in the series of small-scale figurines in polychrome wood: in the seated group, *St. Anna Selbdritt* (Cologne, mid-fifteenth century), and in a later version of the same subject, showing St.

Anna and Mary side by side, from the lower Rhineland, 1480–90. The *Madonna in Full Cloak* (Cologne, c. 1470–80) evokes the close relationship between mother and child reminiscent of Stefan Lochner's approach to the subject. Later Gothic carving distinguishes itself with perfection of plastic detail, such as that seen in the suspended group, *Madonna on a Crescent Moon with St. Anna Selbdritt*, from the workshop of the Masters of Osnabrück (1520). Whereas Cologne sculpture was dominated by the Master of the Dombauhütte, Konrad Kuyn, from whose workshop came the sandstone figure of a prophet (1460), it is Tilman van der Burch who emerged about 1500 to create the elegant *Holy Virgin* and the *Three Wise Men*.

Harsher lines and stronger characterization can be traced to Netherlandish sculpture, with its many-figured altarpieces. A fragment of such a shrine is that of Calvary (Netherlands, 1430–40). Attributed to the famed carved altars of the Kalkar school is the *Passions Altar* (1525), which foreshadows the style of the Renaissance. Various statues of saints bear witness to the manifold production of the workshops of Mechelen and Antwerp. The relief of *Christ on the Mount of Olives* is part of the fragments remaining from the dismantled cathedral choir (1508). Along with the *Resurrection of Lazarus* and the statue *St. Jacobus* (both 1510–20), they represent examples of Gothic stone carving.

Paris was one of the centers of fine ivory carving during the Gothic period, producing artifacts such as a finely finished Madonna (first half, fourteenth century) and the many-figured diptych, with Birth, Adoration, the Crucifixion, and the Last Judgment.

The diversity of forms of the goldsmith's art is reflected in the many liturgical implements, incuding a chalice with rounded cup from about 1300. Besides producing the reliquaries, candelabra, and containers for hosts, the Cologne workshops produced many outstanding monstrances, such as the one from Heimbach-Weis with crucifix reliquary (Cologne, c. 1300). A small silver figure of St. Catherine (Cologne, c. 1380) shows the high quality of artistry. Frequently, monstrances echoed architectural and other figurative and decorative details, such as the elaborate monstrance from the early fifteenth century. The varied techniques and shapes of the goldsmith's skill are combined in a devotional crucifix from Westphalia or the Rhine (late fifteenth century). Other rarities are a rock-crystal cross from Venice (early fourteenth century) and a gold pater noster chain (1500) from Mexico, decorated with typical carved wooden skulls containing miniature scenes from the Bible.

A collection of medieval textiles contains richly ornamented vestments of superb quality from southern Germany, England, Venice, and Lucca. The borders were primarily created in Cologne, based on designs by Cologne master painters, such as the one by Stefan Lochner, *St. Barbara, Dionysius, and Apollonia* (c. 1445). Particularly elaborate is a chasuble of Italian gold brocade, the border of which depicts scenes from the testament in embroidery from Flanders, 1509. Other memorable textiles are wall hangings: one, the *Madonna and Apostles* from Nuremberg; another, from an Erfurt nunnery depicting the Three Wise

Men (1470); and still another, with a basket of flowers from Tournai (c. 1500). A mass cloth of great value was made at the order of Empress Maria Theresa of Austria (Vienna, 1773). In white silk moiré, it has colorful floral, scroll embroidery, and appliqué ornamentation.

The important Cologne tradition of stained glass is well documented with examples from the Romanesque through the Gothic periods. Late Romanesque is represented by the panels of Death and the Coronation of Mary in lively colors, with the pair of donors appearing at the bottom of the panels (Cologne, c. 1250). A fragment from the Cologne Cathedral shows fine Gothic arch forms and delicate bird and flower designs (c. 1320). Against a graphically drawn background of leafy foliage John the Baptist and the kneeling donor, Cuonegundis de Meynwelt, are the subjects of two panels (Cologne, early fourteenth century). In a "soft" style of grisaille are the two panels depicting a vespers picture and Christ carrying the cross. Late Gothic originating from the Church of the Carmelites in Boppard is the *Commandment Window* (Rhineland, 1440–46), showing St. Elisabeth surrounded by angels. A major opus of stained glass from the time between the Gothic and the Renaissance (1500) is the *Crucifixion with St. Lawrence and Donor* from the St. Lawrence Church in Cologne.

The free, bold drawing of the *Virgin with Halo* in a triptych from Freiburg may possibly be based on designs by Hans Baldung Grien but was actually created in the workshop of Hans Gitschmann (1528). Panels with scenes of the life of St. Bernard von Clairvaux originated in Altenberg at the studio of the Masters of St. Severin (early sixteenth century). An important piece is the panel of John the Baptist in a landscape after designs by the Masters of the Book (c. 1480).

Typical of Baroque sculpture is the monumental stone figure *Christ in the Dungeon* from the school of Mauritz Gröninger (c. 1680). A boxwood sculpture, the *Flagellated* (early seventeenth century), is effective in picturing the emaciation of the body. Another expressive boxwood piece is the *Coronation with the Crown of Thorns* by Christoph D. Schenk (1685).

Originating from the house altar of Melchior Paulus are a precious vesper picture of ivory (1703), two saints, and a crucifix. A small bronze statuette, *St. Joseph the Father* (1710), comes from the hand of Gabriel Grupello.

Among the significant masters of South German Baroque sculpture are Egid Quirin Asams with his *St. Bernard of Clairvaux* (mid-eighteenth century) and the *Apostle Paulus* by Ignaz Günther. The expressive *Crucifix* is attributed to Meinrad Guggenbichler, and a richly wrought choir screen comes from the Heisterbach Cloister. Among the precious altar implements are a monstrance by the Cologne master Wilhelm Sittman (1779) and a carved-wood reliquary by Baptist Straub (1757).

At the transfer of the Schnütgen Collection to the city of Cologne, a library was included. It contains works on medieval art, sculpture, goldsmith's art, book illumination, and other Christian artifacts. Catalogs, postcards, and slides are on sale in the foyer of the museum.

Selected Bibliography

Museum publications: *The Schnütgen Museum, A Selection*, 1958; 2d ed., 1961; 3d ed., 1964; 4th ed., 1968; Legner, Anton, *Late Gothic Sculptures of the Schnütgen Museum*, 1970; Westfehling, Uwe, *Schnütgen Museum: Guide to Medieval Art*, 1977; Witte, Fritz, *Liturgical Artifacts of the Schnütgen Collection*, 1913; idem, *The Liturgical Vestments of the Schnütgen Collection*, 1926; idem, *The Schnütgen Collection: Guide with Pictures*, 1910; 2d ed., 1911; idem, *Sculptures of the Schnütgen Collection*, 1912.

FRAUKE STEENBOCK, translated by RENATA RUTLEDGE

WALLRAF-RICHARTZ MUSEUM AND LUDWIG MUSEUM (also WRM), An der Rechtschule, D 5000 Cologne.

In his will in 1816 Ferdinand Franz Wallraf (1748–1824), canon and last rector to be elected at the University of Cologne (since it was suspended by the French in 1798), left his personal collection to his native city of Cologne. In accepting this bequest the city acquired a collection of objects, accumulated over forty years, often through personal sacrifice. It included art, anthropology, and natural history antiquities that were destined to become the nucleus of almost all of the municipal art and cultural history museums of Cologne. Several factors inspired the collector: a reawakened interest in the Middle Ages that characterized the Romantic period, the influence of Friedrich Schlegel's enthusiasm for medievalism, and the suspension of many churches and monasteries as a result of revolution and secularization in addition to the measures taken by the French occupation. All of this gave rise to widespread efforts to save the patrimony of artistic treasures.

The collection of the Boisserée brothers, which went to Munich in 1827, taught Wallraf to appreciate the Cologne school of painting. His high position facilitated his search for and discovery of former ecclesiastical property, but purchases frequently caused great personal deprivation. The legacy of Wallraf, which consisted in paintings alone of more than sixteen hundred pieces, was first housed at the so-called Cologne Court under the supervision of two curators, Matthias Joseph de Noël and Johann Anton Ramboux. After lengthy disputes, it was decided to erect a new building for the collection at the site of an abandoned Minorite cloister. This was made possible through a generous gift from Johann Heinrich Richartz (1795–1861), a local businessman. The architects most prominently involved in the design of the building were Joseph Felton, Ernst Zwirner, and Julius Raschdorff, as well as August Stüler. The cornerstone was laid in July 1855, and the museum opened July 1, 1861, with an exhibit of contemporary art. The museum was named in memory of its chief donors.

From 1892 to 1904 exhibition space was expanded through extensions of the cloister. The neo-Gothic building was destroyed during World War II, but its art treasures were safely stored and therefore only suffered minor damage. The museum was rebuilt according to plans by architects Rudolf Schwarz and Josef Bernard and was reopened in 1957.

With the installation of the Ludwig Collection at the WRM in 1969, a need for a new museum of twentieth-century art arose. A gift from Peter and Irene Ludwig and funds from the city of Cologne created a new and independent museum for modern art, named the Ludwig Museum. This led to a competition for the best design for such a building in 1975; winners were Peter Busman and Gottfried Haberer. The museum is scheduled to open in September 1986 on the banks of the Rhine next to the Dome and the Roman-German Museum.

The director of the WRM automatically bears the title of General Director of the Museums of Cologne. There is also an assistant director and curators of the early, modern, and graphics collections.

The collection of Roman antiquities, originally part of WRM, is now to be found in the Roman-German Museum, and the stained-glass collection of the Boisserée brothers and medieval sculptures are now in the Arts and Crafts Museum.

The Wallraf-Richartz Museum Society was founded by Hans F. Secker in 1928. In 1959 the Friends of WRM, with a membership of leading figures in business, city administration, and finance, formed a committee to support new acquisitions. In contrast with many other German collections of princely origin, the WRM has its roots in the community spirit of the city's municipal cultural life. Numerous donations from local citizens have contributed to making this museum significant beyond the national borders of Germany.

From 1844 until his death in 1866, the curator Johann Anton Ramboux made important contributions by his inventory and his acquisitions, such as Rubens' *Holy Family* and the panels the *Lyversberger Passion*. In the following years Dutch holdings and those of the Düsseldorf school increased. In 1890 Carl Aldhoven, the first art historian to be elected director, initiated a complete reorganization and renovation of the gallery and, in 1902, published the museum's first scholarly catalog. A steady flow of acquisitions and donations enriched the collection, adding works by Dutch masters, as well as Murillo, Ingres, and Leibl, a native of Cologne whose work was featured at the fiftieth anniversary exhibition of the museum in 1911.

The years 1908 to 1914 saw the addition of German and French realists and Impressionists. After an unfortunate phase for the gallery in the 1920s, the acquisition of the Carstanjen Collection in the 1930s greatly complemented the Dutch and Flemish holdings.

At the same time the museum suffered grievous losses with the Nazis' edict against "decadent art." Confiscated were masterworks such as Picasso's *Family Soler*, Juan Gris' *Ash Wednesday*, Franz Marc's *Blue Horse*, Kokoschka's *Dent du Midi*, Gauguin's *Rider on the Beach*, and other important paintings and graphics, especially of the Expressionist school. Fortunately, this section was somewhat restored by the generous gift in 1946 of Josef Haubrich, who, like Wallraf before him, managed to rescue masterworks from destruction and donate them to his city. Acquiring the collections of Wilhelm Strecker and Lilli von Schnitzler Malinkrodt raised the Ludwig Museum's modern art holdings to an international level.

The works of the Cologne school represent the nucleus of the Wallraf Collection. Early examples such as the altar panels of the Virgin Mary and the Crucifixion (c. 1300 and 1425) and paintings of the International Style are all anonymous. The school reached its climax with the Master of St. Veronica (active 1395-1415) with paintings such as the delicate *Madonna of the Vetch-blossoms*. Other Cologne masters are represented by the *Altar of the Holy Family*, *The Martyrdom of St. Ursula at the City of Cologne* (with a view of Cologne in 1411), and the unusually appealing small panel *Maria and Child in the Green*.

Stefan Lochner settled in Cologne in 1440 after study in the Netherlands. His altar panels are now in Munich and Frankfurt, but his last work, the mystical *St. Marie in the Rose Arbor*, is part of the Wallraf collection. Dutch influence is also marked in pieces such as the so-called *Lyversberger Passion* of the Master of St. Marie's Life (1430–80), his *Crucifixion Altar*, and his *Vision of St. Bernard*. Still another Cologne master created the *Altar of the Holy Family* in 1500–1504, as well as the votive picture *Count Gumprecht of Neuenahr*. Schooling in the Netherlands and Lochner's influence are reflected in the works of the Master of St. Severin in his *Mary and the Six Virgins* and *Adoration of the Kings*. The *Portrait of a Woman* is an early example of personalized portraiture.

Unique is the position of the Bartholomew Altar Master, who, although a panel painter, also created the *Book of Hours for Sophia v. Bylant* and *St. Mary with the Nut*. Bartholomew Bruyn the Elder, a sought-after portraitist, painted the *Young Humanist with Carnation* in 1528 and several others in succeeding years. His altar pictures are in the tradition of Gothic Cologne painting.

Significant early German works, other than from Cologne, are from the hand of the Nuremberg Master of the Tucher Altar (1445–50), from the Master of the Karlsruhe Passion, Westphalia, and from the school of the Master of the Housebook (1480).

Portraits of *Barbara and Hans Schellenberg* by Hans Burgkmair the Elder, *St. Magdalen* by Lucas Cranach the Elder (1525), and the *Portrait of a Little Prince* (1529) by the same artist were added to the WRM via the Carstanjen Collection. The *Fife Player* and the *Drummer* by Albrecht Dürer were originally part of the Wittenberger Altar (1504).

Examples of Early Netherlandish painting are by anonymous masters, as well as the *Birth of Christ* by Hans Memling, two Quentin Massys panels, and several others whose origins are not absolutely certain.

The number of sixteenth- to nineteenth-century German masters is limited because of the transfer of some to the Cologne Municipal Museum and sale of others at a time of need. Noteworthy are small seventeenth-century landscapes by Johann König, the *Self Portrait* by Hans von Aachen, and several other portraits, including those of the donor Wallraf by Kaspar Benedickt Beckenkamp.

The gallery offers the opportunity to study German still-life painting. These works include pieces by the classicist Georg Flegel, Gottfried von Wedig, and Johann Michael Hambach and the pastels and watercolors of Cologne artist Anton de Peters, who specialized in genre scenes.

Dutch and Flemish schools from the sixteenth to the nineteenth century constitute another important classification at the WRM, particularly after the acquisition of the Carstanjen Collection in 1936 and other donations, as well as important loans from the Federal Republic. Of Antwerp origin are fantasy landscapes by Paulus Bril and Joos de Momper. Geldorp, known for his portraits, is also noted for his *Christ on the Cross* at the Cologne City Hall. The special quality of the Utrecht school is evidenced in the *Adoration by the Shepherds* by Uytewael, whose signed paintings are rare.

Dutch painting of the seventeenth century, in all of its phases and subject matter, include: seascapes by Jan van de Cappelle and Albert Cuyp and landscapes and nautical scenes by Simon de Vlieger, Hendrick Averkamp, and Esaias van der Velde. Village life is portrayed by Jacob van Ruisdael and Salomon van Ruysdael and peasant life by Isack van Ostade and David Teniers the Younger. Views of Brussels by Hercules Seghers and of Haarlem by Jan van de Meers are topographical. An extensive group of still lifes and genre and interior paintings is also well represented. Noteworthy is Pieter de Hooch's *Couple with a Parrot*.

A predominant subject matter of the seventeenth century was portraiture and is featured at the WRM with many leading masters. Frans Hals' *Portrait of a Man* and *Portrait of a Woman*; Rembrandt's *Portrait of a Scholar*, dated 1644, and his *Self Portrait* from about 1660; Flemish master van Dyck's *Portrait of a Lady*; and others by Jordaens and Rubens are but a few of the extensive holdings in this area.

Themes from mythology and religion dominate in *Jupiter as Satyr with Antiope* by Anthony van Dyck, *Prometheus Bound* by Jacob Jordaens, and *Juno and Argus* by Peter Paul Rubens. Biblical themes are pictured in Jan Steen's *Amnon and Thamar* and *Samson and Delilah*.

Italian, French, and Spanish paintings, some part of the original Wallraf Collection, others added through gift or purchase, such as the Alexander Schnütgen contribution, begin with early Italian paintings, such as the *Madonna* by Simone Martini, purchased in 1961. The earliest is a Lucchesian Madonna from 1260 and the *Martyrdom of St. Reparata* by Bernardo Daddi. Others are by Bicci di Lorenzo, Pietro di Giovanni, and Sano di Pietro. Of Venetian origin, Titian's *Venus at the Mirror*, Tintoretto's *Holy Family* and *Christ's Burial*, and works by Piazzetta and Pellegrini came to the WRM after World War II, but works such as Tiepolo's *Adoration of the Kings* and Canaletto's *Grand Canal* were part of the earlier inventory of the museum.

Among the small selection of earlier French painting, these works are outstanding: two Claude Lorraine landscapes, *Landscape with the Rescue of Psyche* and *Harbor Scene with the Heliads*; Charles Poërson's Poussin-like *Rest on the Flight from Egypt*; and François Boucher's *Sleeping Maiden*.

With the help of fifty-four art lovers of Cologne, Murillo's *St. Francis at the Portiuncula Chapel* was purchased in 1898, and other Murillos such as the *Repentant Magdalen* and *La Vieja* came from the Carstanjen Collection along with Ribera's *St. Paulus*.

Among nineteenth-century holdings, German and French masters dominate. Germans, on the borderline between the classical and the Romantic periods, are represented by Joseph Änton Koch and Johann Christian Reinhart with their magnificent landscapes. In the same tradition is Eduard von Bendeman's famous *Mourning Jews in Exile*. Caspar David Friedrich's *Oaktree in the Snow* and *Trees in Moonlight* are particularly outstanding. Adolf von Menzel's *Thunderstorm at Tempelhof Mountain*, dated 1846, is part of a group of landscapes that also includes works by Blechen and Rottmann depicting Mediterranean themes. Anselm von Feuerback is represented with *Mirjam*.

Classicist French painting is found in Jacques Louis David's *Pericles and the Corpse of his Son* and *Portrait of a Roman Woman*, attributed to Ingres.

In the second half of the century Camille Corot created *La poesie*; Gustave Courbet, *The Hunt Breakfast*; Daubigny, *Valley of Optevoz*; and Eugène Delacroix, *Doubting Thomas*. Leading into Impressionism are Claude Monet's *Rocks at Etrétat*, Sisley's *Bridge at Hampton Court*, Renoir's *The Sisleys*, and Vincent van Gogh's *Drawbridge*, one of his last pictures.

Paintings by Leibl, Liebermann, Slevogt, and Corinth take us into more recent times. Gifts and bequests have expanded the works of Wilhelm Leibl, making the collection complete and affording an all-inclusive overview of this Cologne artist's oeuvre. Max Liebermann's *Jewish Quarter in Amsterdam*, *The Good Samaritan*, and *Self Portrait* are representative of his style, and Max Slevogt is included with four works, among them *The French Curassier*. Lovis Corinth, active in Berlin, presented his large *Still Life* to his wife as a birthday gift. The same year, 1911, brought forth *Emperor's Day in Hamburg*, and the *Walchensee Panorama* is from a later period.

Böcklin's *Attack by Pirates* was donated in 1904, and the same group of Friends of Art of Cologne contributed toward the acquisition of Edvard Munch's *Girls on a Bridge* in 1949.

The revival of the contemporary art collection had already received its first impetus through the gift of Josef Haubrich. This has been expanded, and with the inclusion of the Ludwig Collection, the museum's twentieth-century collection has become very comprehensive.

Beginning with Ernst Ludwig Kirchner's painting as representative of the Die Brücke movement, all trends and manifestations of modern creations, until the present, are included. Josef Haubrich rescued the work of German Expressionists and "Verists" in the Nazi period. He had also acquired works of Ensor, Odilon Redon, Marc Chagall, and Vlaminck. Furthermore, the Schnitzler-Malinkrodt Collection contributed ten splendid Max Beckmann paintings, and with the purchase of the Wilhelm Strecker group, European holdings were expanded with works by Picasso, Braque, Matisse, and Modigliani. Ludwig's collection added American art of the 1960s. The growth of the museum collection continues, constantly expanding to include all new trends such as Conceptual Art and photo, video, and art films. Its highlights are outstanding works by the Expressionists Picasso, Max Ernst, and Léger, as well as Pop Art and the Russian Avant-Garde.

The members of Die Brücke are represented by Ernst Ludwig Kirchner (*Five Women in the Street*), Karl Schmidt-Rottluff (*Still Life with Negro Sculpture*), Otto Müller, and Max Pechstein. Franz Marc lent his own rhythm to *The Deer*, and Emil Nolde offered *Moonlit Night* and flower pieces. Dating from his Berlin days is Oskar Kokoschka's *Tilla Durrieux*; more recent is his *View of Cologne* (1956).

Between realism and abstraction are two important Paul Klee works: *Main Road and Side Road* and *Fool in a Trance*. Linked to the Bauhaus period are the works of Kandinsky, Feininger, and Laszlo Moholy-Nagy—all to be found here along with the Russian Suprematist Kasimir Malevich.

Documents of Russian Constructivism are provided with designs by El Lissitzky, Larionov, Gontcharova, Popova, and Rodchenko. Alexis von Jawlensky displayed a tendency toward the Nabis, with his glowing colors in landscapes, still lifes, and portraits.

Georg Meistermann belongs to the abstract movement of the 1950s and 1960s, with *Birds*, and *Bird Who Wants to Be Fish*. Max Ernst's vision of destruction found expression in *Sauterelles à la lune*, dated 1953. The real and the unreal are linked in René Magritte's *La géante*.

The many phases of Picasso's work can be traced with the Cubist *Woman with Mandolin*, naturalistic *Still Life with Mandolin and Fist*, deformed and many-sided interpretation as in *Reading Woman*, and joyful exuberance in *Musketier and Amor*. Early Cubism is displayed in Fernand Léger's *Pink Tugboat* and *Twins*, whereas *Country Party* depicts his late style. Cubism is also evidenced in Georges Braque's *Still Life*. Fauvism is brought to Matisse's *Jeune fille assise*, whereas the rhythmic paperwork in *Women and Monkeys* is of later origin. Other works on display are by Nicolas de Staël, Hans Hartung, and Jean Dubuffet.

Marcel Duchamp, inspiration to a new generation and the artist who introduced modern European trends to America, is represented with eighty-three miniature reproductions of his work in a red leather case, *Boite en valise*.

The 1950s brought a complete departure in art form. Abstract painting marks the beginning of Ad Reinhardt's series of black paintings. Barnett Newman, Clyfford Still, and Mark Rothko express meditative insight in their abstractions. Color staining serves as a medium of expression for Kenneth Noland in *Provence* and for Morris Louis in *Daleth*. Color experimentation also is the basis of Frank Stella's *Colour Maze*.

A key figure of the 1960s is Jasper Johns, who links object and artistic expression with originality in *Flag on Orange Field*. His influence on Pop Art is felt in Roy Lichtenstein's *Blonde* and *Taka-Taka*, with motifs from newspaper prints. Other exponents of Pop Art are Robert Rauschenberg, James Rosenquist, and Andy Warhol, as well as Robert Indiana with his numbers and geometrics, Tom Wesselman and his use of real objects, and Howard Kanovitz and his social comments. All are represented at the Ludwig Museum with some of their British counterparts such as Richard Hamilton (*My Marylin*), David Hockney (*Sunbathers*), and Allan Jones (*Perfect Match*).

A parallel development is Richard Lindner's dry, bordering on the grotesque, style, leaning toward advertising and consumerism, in *Target No. 1* and *Disneyland*. Realism mixes with surrealism in Jim Dine's *Six Big Saws*; compelling originality marks Claes Oldenburg's style in *Sausage* and *Street Chic*. The artist turned to soft sculpture in 1962 and created *Soft Washstand* and *Giant Swedish Light Switch*. Edward Kienholz displayed realistic environments in *The Portable War Memorial*.

About the same time as the above, Konrad Klapheck painted his machine pictures of somber, everyday objects (*The Dictator*, *The Forefathers*). A departure into another trend is seen in a group of Paris artists of the 1960s, among them Arman (*Accumulation des brocs*), Yves Klein (*Relief eponge bleu*), and Jean Tinguely. Their motives stressed waste products depicted in evocative "natures mortes." Similar in expression are the so-called *Decollage* works of Wolf Vostell. He sought to provoke in his happenings and environments, as in his *Homage to Henry Ford and Jacqueline Kennedy*. Attempting to integrate life and art, Joseph Beuys expressed his concepts with *Sardine Can with Pliers* and *King's Daughter Sees Island*. Group Zero of Dusseldorf, founded 1957, is represented with Otto Piene's *Firepicture* and works by Gunther Uecker and Heinz Mack. Photography is brought to the work of Gerhart Richter in his *Erna-Nude on the Stairs* and to the "naturalism" of Franz Gertsch.

The WRM holdings of sculptures are limited to those dating from 1800. The post-war years saw an increase in the acquisition of sculptures to include many contemporary objects. The earliest sculpture is a bust of J. J. Rousseau by J. A. Houdon, fashioned from the death mask in 1778. Several busts portray personalities connected with the museum, such as the brothers Boisserée, Johann Heinrich Richartz, and Alexander von Humboldt. A noteworthy example of the Romantic period is Rudolf Schadow's *Spinnerin*, acquired only after the war, along with *Ratapoil* by Honoré Daumier and *Salome* by Max Klinger. Various bronzes by Edgar Degas, a female figure by Aristide Maillol, and a portrait head of his son by Renoir, with a variety of copies of the work of Rodin and Bourdelle, complete the nineteenth-century holdings.

Pre-war German sculpture is well represented, with examples of the work of Käthe Kollwitz, Wilhelm Lehmbruck, Georg Kolbe, and many more. Evidence of Cubism is apparent in Jacques Lipchitz's *Reading Woman* and is also seen in Henri Laurens' *Farewell*. The generous gift of Marguerite Arp Aschenbach made the documentation of all phases of Hans Arp's work possible. Original casts, representing steps in the artist's development of an idea, include *Female Torso* and *Relief Nadir*. Italy's leading sculptors are represented with Mario Marini's *Rider*, the *Cardinal* of Giacomo Manzú, and Giacometti's Surrealistic *Nose*.

Abstractions are displayed with the works of Julio Gonzalez, Hans Uhlmann, and the Americans David Smith and Anthony Caro. Caro is represented by his painted constructions. Naum Gabo, exponent of constructivism, brings kinetic rhythm to his *Construction in Space*. Defying gravity is Alexander Calder's mobile *Thirteen Spines*. Harmony of form and space preoccupied Henry Moore in his *Reclining Figure*. Dan Flavin, who pioneered in light sculpture, fashioned *Monument 7 for V. Tatlin* out of neon tubes. Neon tubes also appear in Richard Serra's three-dimensional *God Is a Loving Father*. Geometric forms show trends toward Minimal art in works such as *Timber Piece* and *Lock Piece* by Carl Andre. Art limited by strict concepts also characterizes the pieces of Donald Judd, Sol LeWitt, and Robert Morris. New dimensions of artistic presentation originated with Lucio Fontana and his "concetto spaziale" expressed in *Scultura Spaziale* and *Sposalizio a Venezia*. By painting his sculpture, Eduardo Paolozzi aimed to bridge painting and sculpture in his *Last Idol*. George Segal made his first plaster-cast figure in 1960, shown at the museum as *Woman Washing Her Feet in a Sink*. Out of junk and wood scraps, Louise Nevelson composed her thoughtful box pictures, *World Garden IV*, and Arnoldo Pomodoro organized microcosmic elements into cell-like formation as in *The Tablet of the Mathematician No. 2*. Lacquered autoparts, symbols of the obsolescence of our technological world, are combined by John Chamberlain to create *White Shadow*. Marisol assembled her *Visita* out of masks, figures, and objects that add up to a criticism of the conventional bourgeoisie.

A wide variety of themes motivates the contemporary German sculptor: in the case of Bernard Schultze it is the expansion of space in multi-dimensional collages and objects such as *Migof-Ursula-Ahnentafel*; his wife, Ursula Schultze Blum, expressed alienation through transformation with *The Box of Pandora*. Franz Erhard Walther communicated with *Object as Book*. Land art and earth work are represented by Walter De Maria and Michael Heizer, respectively. Anne and Patrick Poirier's work exemplified the search into the early days of man as in their *Utopian Archaeology Aussee*.

Concepts of movement and time appear in the work of Jan Dibbets, Hanne Darboven, Klaus Rinke, Bernd Becher, and Michael Snow, all artists of the 1970s.

An extensive collection of graphics constituted part of the Wallraf legacy, consisting of forty-five thousand prints. A special room for copper engravings and a library were established in the basement at the time of Ramboux's administration. In the 1880s the collection of a former Jesuit college was added, and in 1900 Oskar Fischel undertook the reorganization and inventory of the prints. In 1911 thirty-one drawings by Leibl and further purchases throughout the years established a nucleus of nineteenth- and twentieth-century prints and drawings. Like the picture gallery, the collection was affected by the Nazi edict against "decadent art." Again, because of Josef Haubrich and his generosity in donating 290 drawings and watercolors by German Expressionists, the collection regained its balance and was further enriched by gifts and purchases. The collection's holdings of earlier works were also increased through high-quality acquisitions.

Of great importance among early holdings are the *Book of Hours of Sophia on Bylant* by the Master of the St. Bartholomew Altar and the only known acknowledged drawing by Bartholomew Bruyn the Elder. *St. Catherine, Maria with Child in a Niche*, and a *Walking Horse* are from the hand of Albrecht Dürer. From the eighteenth century are a group of drawings by the sculptor Paul Egell worth noting and drawings by Anton de Peters.

Many noted artists represent the nineteenth century, such as Joseph Anton Koch, Friedrich Overbeck, Julius Schnorr von Carolsfeld, von Schwind, Feuerbach, von Menzel, Wilhelm Leibl, and Max Liebermann. The architect Jacob Ignaz Hittorf left not only his own sketches but those of other French and German architects to the department. The Netherlands are represented with Goltzius, van de Velde, van Goyen, and Rembrandt. Leonardo da Vinci leads the group of Renaissance artists that includes Raphael, Andrea del Sarto, and Tiepolo. Cirro Ferri, Carlo Maratta, Francesco Guardi Fontebasso, and Piazzetta date from later periods.

Among the French artists, Rigaud, Boucher, Fragonard, and Nattier are worth mentioning; from the nineteenth century there are works by Ingres, Géricault, Millet, Manet, Rodin, Rousseau, and Signac.

Outstanding in quality are the twentieth-century drawings and watercolors by Expressionists such as Kirchner, Schmidt-Rottluff, Nolde, Macke, and Rohlfs, as well as Barlach, Dix, Grosz, Kollwitz, Kokoschka, and Schlemmer.

From the Rhineland hail artists such as Max Ernst, Heinrich Hoerle, Franz Wilhelm Seiwert, Ernst Wilhelm Nay, Josef Fassbender, and Werner Gilles. Internationally known artists are also represented with a specially selected group of prints.

At the completion of the new building in 1957, both the library of the Arts and Crafts (Applied Arts) Museum and the WRM were combined and housed in the new edifice under the name of the Art and Museum Library of the City of Cologne. It is open not only to researchers and scholars at the museum but also to visitors and the public in general. The growth of the library to 130,000 volumes made the planned space inadequate. In conjunction with the Rhineland Picture Archives, a reading room was opened in one of the halls of the Minorite Cloister. The library works in close cooperation with other municipal libraries and has also undertaken special programs in areas of the arts of the Benelux countries and twentieth-century art. Plans are under way to computerize and centralize all of the contents of the Cologne art libraries in a single documentation and information system to facilitate research and availability to the public. Recently a photography and film library was established, drawing from the Ludwig collection and other institutions, that already contains seventy-five hundred volumes.

The Wallraf-Richartz Museum has published a yearbook since 1924, and a regular bulletin is issued by the Museums of Cologne since 1961. The catalogs in the following bibliography are published in German.

Selected Bibliography

Museum publications: *Modern Division, Haubrich Collection*, 1949; *Watercolors and Drawings, Haubrich Collection*, 1958; *The Strecker Collection of the Wallraf-Richartz*

Museum, 1959; *Catalog of Paintings*, 1965; *Catalog of Nineteenth-Century Paintings*, 1964–65; *Catalog of Netherlands Paintings from 1550 to 1800* . . . , 1967; *Catalog of Selected Drawings and Watercolors*, 1967; *Catalog of 20th Century Painting up to 1920 Including Parts of the Ludwig Collection*, 1973; *Catalog of 20th Century Paintings from 1913 on and Parts of the Ludwig Collection*, 1973; *Catalog of German Paintings from 1550 to 1800 at WRM*, 1973; *Art of the Sixties*, 2d ed., 1970, and 5th ed., 1971; *Handbook of the Ludwig Museum*, 1979.

Other Publications: *The Wallraf-Richartz Museum of Cologne, 1861–1911* (1911); *100 Years Wallraf-Richartz Museum, 1861–1961* (1960); Keller, Horst, ed. *Art Culture Cologne*, notes (Cologne 1979); Secker, Hans F., *The Contemporary Gallery at WRM* (Leipzig 1927); Verbeek, Albert, *The First WRM in Cologne* (1961).

FRAUKE STEENBOCK, translated by RENATA RUTLEDGE

Frankfurt

STÄDEL ART INSTITUTE AND MUNICIPAL GALLERY (officially STÄDELSCHES KUNSTINSTITUT UND STÄDTISCHE GALERIE), Schaumainkai 63, 6000 Frankfurt am Main 70.

The Städelsches Kunstinstitut owes its existence to the man after whom it is named, its donor and founder, Johann Friedrich Städel. Born into a patrician Frankfurt family in 1728, he was an independent banker and merchant who never married and so devoted his sizable fortune to collecting paintings, graphics, and books. Typical of a collection of a member of the upper bourgeoisie and of his times, Städel looked upon his assemblage as a cornerstone of a gallery that would be easily accessible to the public and would at the same time serve as a training ground and inspiration for young artists.

After his death in 1816, his bequest clearly outlined the twofold purpose of the Institute: (1) to create an art museum for the enlightenment and enjoyment of the general public, with a provision that encouraged the expansion and improvement of his holdings by means of exchange or sale of present inventories; and (2) to establish an art school offering training to aspiring young artists through instruction aided by scholarships. To this effect Städel donated his house on the Rossmarkt (the original museum), his fortune (about 1 million guilders), and his collection to the community.

The administration was at that time entrusted to five "upstanding citizens of Frankfurt," named by Städel, who were given absolute control, except for a yearly audit and report to the public. This group took on the task of opening the collection to the public on March 10, 1817.

The trustees also began acquiring new works and setting up a school of art. Furthermore, realizing the physical limitations of the Rossmarkt building, they instigated a search for new, larger quarters for the Institute. All of these activities, however, were halted abruptly in that same year, when in September Städel's distant relatives brought suit to fight the terms of his last will and testament. Not until 1828 was the case settled in a compromise that cut deeply into the museum's funds.

By 1833 the trustees had found a new location, and both collections and school were installed in a building on Neue Mainzerstrasse, where the public was invited to the official opening on March 15, 1833. At present the Institute continues to be supported by the Städel trust but also enjoys wide support from the community, its museum association, and municipal and provincial funding. Particularly important, almost vital to its survival, has been the Städelsche Museums Verein (Museum Association), which was founded in 1899 and has been making valuable acquisitions for the museum until the present, except for the period of the Nazi regime. Since its revival in 1959, it has been again actively involved and has made several important purchases.

The museum's activities and prestige received a big boost in 1907, when it was integrated with the Stadtgalerie (Municipal Gallery) and simultaneously became the recipient of the bequest of Ludwig Josef Pfungst of a large collection of local nineteenth-century art. Although the Städtische Galerie was now under the same directorship as the Städel, it retained a certain amount of autonomy, which included the task of establishing a sculpture gallery and the acquisition of contemporary art. In 1907 the city authorities approved this plan and allocated the appropriate funds for its implementation.

The combined institutions are now administered by a director, his associate, and four curators, one of them a city employee. A research library and informational services to the public are also part of the institution.

By the last quarter of the nineteenth century the collection had increasesd so much that the Mainzerstrasse building proved inadequate. A new building was erected on the Schaumainkai after the design of Oskar Sommer in a classical Renaissance style. Its opening took place on November 13, 1878.

The original Städel collection was described in 1797 by Frankfurt's most illustrious son, Johann Wolfgang Goethe. It then consisted of about five hundred paintings, primarily of the seventeenth- and eighteenth-century German, Flemish, and Dutch schools. Very little of other schools and periods was represented. Still present from the original holdings are a Rubens design for an altar and works by Frans Hals, Ruysdael, and the Rhenish school.

This beginning nucleus has been widely expanded to include paintings and altars from the Gothic period to the contemporary, graphics from the fifteenth century to the present, and nineteenth- and twentieth-century sculpture.

An overview reveals German and Flemish paintings from the fourteenth through the nineteenth century that include van Eyck, Dürer, Grünewald, Rembrandt and Holbein, Elsheimer and Hals, Böcklin, Liebermann, Corinth, and German Expressionists of the Brücke. Italian and Spanish artists include Botticelli, Tiepolo, Bellini, and Velázquez. The nineteenth century is represented by the French Impressionists and the twentieth century by modern classics from Picasso to Beckmann, from Klee to Hockney, and from Bacon to Botero. The roster of recent American artists includes Dine, Rivers, Twombly, and Oldenburg.

Both painting and graphic collections were hard hit by Nazi confiscations in 1937, when the whole program of acquisition of modern art, which was built up in the twenties under the inspired leadership of director Georg Swarzenski, came to a halt. No fewer than 77 paintings, among them van Gogh's portrait of Dr. Gachet; 399 graphics; and 3 sculptures became victims of the Nazi "purge of decadent art" and have never been replaced. Director Swarzenski, in office since 1906 and responsible for some of the museum's most outstanding acquisitions, was forced out of office, although the Museum Association retained him in office as long as possible. However, there are few museums that have received as many generous donations as the Städel, and particularly in the post-war years, much effort has gone into making up for the losses caused by the Nazi regime. In 1939 the museum was emptied, and paintings were stored for safety, so after the war only minor paintings were found to have been either lost or stolen.

In the area of Early German and Upper and Middle Rhenish altar painting from the fourteenth to the sixteenth century, the holdings are particularly noteworthy. They include masterworks such as the *Altenberger Altar*, dating from about 1340, with its carved center shrine with Madonna and Child flanked by panel paintings of the life of the Virgin. Several parts of the Frankfurt Dominican Church's altars came to the Städel in the twenties, the highlight being the work of Hans Holbein the Elder. In 1928 the famed Hohenzollern Sigmaringen Collection contributed the *Master of the Pullendorfer Altar* (c. 1500) and the *Torgauer Altar*, depicting the Holy Family in its center panel, is one of Lucas Cranach's masterpieces, painted in 1509. Among the loveliest panels from the brush of the Master of the Upper Rhine is the typical medieval *Garden of Paradise* (c. 1410), depicting the Madonna and Child surrounded by a garden full of symbolic flowers and plants.

Among the Early German masters are Hans Baldung, called Grien, and his *Altar of John the Baptist*, again from the Frankfurt Dominican Church, along with his stark *Two Weather Witches* and the dramatic *Birth of Christ*. Lucas Cranach is further in evidence with several paintings, notably his *Venus* (1532) and his *Mary and Child*.

The work of both Holbeins is seen in portraits: Hans the Elder, with the *Portrait of Herr Weiss*, and Hans the Younger, who chose the circular Roman "Clipeus" form for the elegant *Simon George of Cornwall*. Albrecht Dürer's touching *Portrait of Katharina Fürlegerin* (1497) strongly contrasts in its gentleness with the biting *Mockery of Job by His Wife*, which is part of a many-winged altar (other wings are in the Wallraf-Richartz Museum [q.v.] in Cologne and in the Alte Pinakothek [q.v.] in Munich). Two grisailles, depicting St. Laurentius and St. Cyriakus, are by Mathis Grünewald. The museum's extensive holdings of the work of Adam Elsheimer, a native of Frankfurt, offers a rare opportunity to appreciate this artist's great sensitivity to landscape in work such as his six-paneled *Crucifix Altar*, which reveals the influence of the Italian Baroque.

Early Netherlandish painting, dating from the founder's acquisitions, are still another strong department at the Städel. It boasts masterworks such as Jan van Eyck's *Lucca Madonna* (1425–29), acquired in 1850 from the estate of Wilhelm

II of Holland and named for its previous owner, Karl Ludwig of Bourbon, duke of Lucca, and a small altar by Rogier van der Weyden, *Madonna and Child with St. Peter and John the Baptist*, also known as the *Medici Altar*, presumably because it was commissioned by the Medicis in 1450. The Master of Flémalle is represented by full-length figure panels of *St. Veronica* and a *Madonna and Child* and a detail from an altar with the strongly individualized head of *Gesinas, the Thief*. Hieronymus Bosch's *Ecce Homo* is an example of that artist's biting irony. Fine examples of other early Flemish painting include portraits by Memling and Quentin Massys and the *Annunciation* by Gerard David.

Paintings of the Dutch school extend into the sixteenth and seventeenth centuries. There are several by Rembrandt van Ryn, such as *David and Saul*, acquired in 1817; the large (236 by 302 centimeters) *Triumph of Delilah*; and the portrait *Hendrickje Stoffels* in deep earth tones. Peter Paul Rubens' *Dido and Aeneas* and *The Mystical Marriage of St. Catherine* were part of the original collection, as were the portraits *A Man* and *A Woman* by Frans Hals. Numerous land and seascapes were created by Jan van Goyen and Salomon van Ruysdael and his nephew Jacob van Ruisdael. A charming genre scene, *Lady with a Wine Glass*, is the work of Gerard Ter Borch, and one of the highlights of the Städel is *The Geographer* by Jan Vermeer, which was acquired by the Frankfurt Art Association in 1885. Worth mentioning also are the works by Bruegel the Elder, Brouwer, Teniers, Cuyp, Hobbema, Jordaens, and Janssens.

From 1828 there was a conscious effort to make the collection more comprehensive. Therefore, in the following years several important Italian works were acquired. Some of the earliest are by Florentine masters, such as the almost Byzantine *Mourning St. John* from the late thirteenth century and the *cassone* painting the *Story of Mucius Scaevola*, dated 1480. Also of note are works by Meo da Siena and Ugolino Lorenzetti and the *Madonna and Child* by Andrea del Verrocchio. Other major works are representative of the Renaissance and lead through the Baroque. Of the several madonnas, these works stand out: the particularly fine, faintly Byzantine *Madonna Surrounded by Angels* by Fra Angelico; the *Mary and Child with St. John and St. Elizabeth*, bathed in lovely, soft blues, by Giovanni Bellini; still another *Madonna* by Perugino, and, among the Venetians, the *Madonna and Child with Young John* by Carpaccio.

Superb examples of Renaissance portraits of women abound: the enchanting *Portrait* (Simonetta Vespucci?) by Sandro Botticelli, and the two portraits entitled *A Noble Lady*—one by Jacopo Pontormo of a Florentine lady in a vivid red dress; the other, equally elegant, by Girolamo da Carpi. Noteworthy also is the *Predella* by Raphael Santo.

Works of the Venetian masters run the gamut from Jacopo Tintoretto's *Moses* to paintings by both Tiepolos, notably Giovanni Battista's splendid *Family Grotta*, measuring 195 by 320 centimeters, purchased in 1908 through the Carl Schaub bequest directly from the Calbo Grotta family in Venice. Other eighteenth-century Italian works include an oval view, the *Grand Canal in Venice*, by Canaletto and a portrait and genre scene by Pietro Longhi.

Among the seventeenth- and eighteenth-century Spanish and French artists is Diego Velázquez with his *Portrait of Cardinal Borja*; Esteban Murillo and *The Good Shepherd*; and Francisco Goya depicting horrors in *Scenes of the Spanish War*. An early French picture is the *Portrait of a Widow* by François Clouet, and two splendid examples of landscape painting are Nicolas Poussin's *Stormy Landscape—Pyramus and Thysbe* and Claude Lorraine's *Noli me tangere*. Jean Marc Nattier is represented with some portraits.

A thorough study of nineteenth-century German painting, with all of its diffused, inconsistent, and conflicting trends, can be made at the Städel. There are several reasons for the volume and variety of the holdings of the period. The merger with the Municipal Gallery (Städtische Galerie) brought a large number of works by local artists to the institution; many benefactors, patrons of local artists, contributed their work, and after the Nazi takeover, there was much political pressure to acquire and promote "native" German art. Thus the collection contains examples of all of the different trends of Germany's nineteenth-century art: classicism, Romanticism, luminism, neo-Renaissance, and neo-Gothic trends of the Nazarenes and the Lukasbund. Loyal to the graduates and teachers of its art school and its former directors, they, too, are well represented by the Institute.

German classicism and Romanticism are epitomized in the famed portrait *Goethe in the Roman Campagna* by Goethe's friend Johann Heinrich Wilhelm Tischbein. Another Romantic is Caspar David Friedrich, here seen in his tumultuous *Mountain Landscape*. Poussin's influence is evident in *Noah's Sacrifice* by Joseph Anton Koch, and his associate Karl Phillip Fohr painted the Romantic *Waterfalls at Tivoli*. Franz Pforr favored historical scenes such as the *Count of Hapsburg*, whereas Johann David Passavant, an inspector of the Städel and a noted art historian, did his *Self Portrait in Roman Landscape* in Renaissance style. Otto Franz Scholderer, who specialized in portraits and still lifes, excelled in his *Violinist at the Window*. Some of the other artists on display, several of whom had been students or teachers at the Städel Art School, are Phillip Veit, Steinle, Overbeck, Eysen, Müller, and Rumpf.

Adolf von Menzel, mostly self-taught, points toward Impressionism with his lovely *Old Park*, and so does Hans Thoma with many examples of his work, among them the poetic *Die Ode* and several portraits. Karl Spitzweg, another auto-didact, delights with his small, humorous, genre pictures such as *The Roselover*; Arnold Böcklin found a suitably gloomy subject in *Portrait of the Tragedienne Fanny Janauschek*. Other artists of that era include Wilhelm Leibl, Anselm Feuerbach, Karl Schuch, Ferdinand Waldmüller, and Fritz von Uhde.

The best of German Impressionism is represented here with works such as *Orphanage in Amsterdam*, with its marvelous patterns of light and dark by Max Liebermann, and Max Slevogt and his *Self Portrait*; Lovis Corinth foreshadowed Expressionism in his *Walchensee in Winter* and *Carmencita* (Charlotte Behrend, his wife, in Spanish dress). Exerting a great influence on German Expressionism was the Norwegian Edvard Munch, well represented with paintings such as one that is still another variation of one of his favorite themes, *Jealousy*.

Eugène Delacroix leads us into French nineteenth-century painting with the highly romantic *Fantasie Arabe*, along with Corot and Gustave Courbet, whose *View of Frankfurt* is of special interest. Examples of the masters of French Impressionism are limited to "one of each," but every one is of ranking quality. They were acquired in quick succession between 1906 and 1913 by the Institute's director, Georg Swarzenski. Thus one finds a typical Edgar Degas theater scene, *The Orchestra Musicians*, and a domestic scene, *The Breakfast* by Claude Monet, and another, *Breakfast Outdoors* by Auguste Renoir. Odilon Redon is at his most poetic in *Christ and the Samaritan*. Edouard Manet is seen in *The Croquet Party*; a typical Henri Rousseau is the *Park at St. Cloud*. Mention must be made here of a painting by the Swiss Ferdinand Hodler who in his dream-like *Lake Geneva* comes closer to Impressionism than as is his wont. Van Gogh is represented with *La chaumiére* and Matisse with *Still Life*, a painting that was sold at the famed Luzern auction in 1939 and bought back from American owners with the aid of local banks and donors.

A certain lack of continuity can be found in the collection's holdings of the early part of the twentieth century. The ravages of Nazi confiscation left many gaps that were never filled, since some of the paintings were actually burned, while others were sold overseas. Thus the Städel, once known for its great holdings in the contemporary era, was deprived not only its van Gogh and Matisse, but of its Picassos, Gauguins, and almost all of the paintings of the modern German movements, The Blue Rider and The Bridge (Die Brücke). However, there are few museums that received as much support in efforts to recoup its losses as the Städel. *The Synagogue* by Max Beckmann was actually bought back, after the war, by a public subscription. Other important works by this towering Expressionist seen here are the early *Self Portrait, The Circus Wagon*, and *Still Life with Saxophones*. His *Double Portrait* has an unusual history: given by the artist to the Städel in 1924, he withdrew it in 1938 while in exile. It was returned through the auspices of the Jewish Restitution Successor Organization in 1951. Ernst Ludwig Kirchner, one of the founders of Die Brücke, is much in evidence, primarily through the generosity of the Hagemann Collection, whose principal hid some of the condemned art to save it for posterity. *Two Sisters* and *Portrait of Dr. Carl Hagemann* are among the many examples of his work. Still another repurchased work is *The White Dog* by Franz Marc. The Städel also owns a splendid Paul Klee, *View into the Fruitland*, along with *The Lamb* and *The House of the Thistle*. In a more abstract vein is *The Pond at Gelmeroda* by Lyonel Feininger. Of the many other German Expressionists in the collection, the works of Heckel, Schmidt-Rottluff, Modersohn-Becker, Macke, and Nolde, as well as Baumeister, Schlemmer, Nay, and Dix of later vintage, offer the full range of German pre-war painting.

Of more recent times is the *Portrait of Fernande Olivier* and a *Nude* by Picasso and the Surrealist *Daughters of the Painter* by Max Ernst (1940); the haunting

Blue Maja by Horst Antes is dated 1962, which is also the date of Günther Uecker's organic structure *Nails*. Of other contemporary work, there is Francis Bacon's *Study*, David Hockney's *Jump*, Jesus Rafael Soto's *Vibration*, and Fernando Botero's huge *Nude*, a charcoal drawing on canvas. Furthermore, one must mention works by Carlo Carrà, Morandi, Gino Severini, Miró, Fontana, and Dubuffet.

Many of the Städel Kunstinstitut's and the Städtische Galerie's sculptures are stored at the Liebig House. Frequent exhibitions of them are held in the museum's garden, but there is hope that eventually, an addition to the present building will give them a permanent home. At present some of the sculptures displayed alongside the paintings are Lehmbruck's work, Rodin's *Eva*, Renoir's *Child's Head*, Degas' bronzes, Calder's *Red Lily*, and a Picasso, with figures by Maillol and one by Toni Stadler, a local artist.

The graphics collection is not only extensive but ranges from German drawings, such as the *Girl with a Lily* by the fifteenth-century Master E.S., up to American contemporary works, such as that of Larry Rivers and Claes Oldenburg. Its wide scope includes studies by Raphael, drawings by Dürer and Parmigianino, and other drawings and studies by van Ostade, Rembrandt, Goltzius, and the Germans Fohr and Cornelius. Beckmann, Kirchner, and Käthe Kollwitz are also well represented in the collection, which is frequently exhibited but is not on display continuously.

The Städel Kunstinstitut was enlarged by the addition of two wings in the period 1915 to 1920, but much of the building was destroyed during the heavy bombardments of 1943 to 1944. After the war the restitution proceeded in three slow stages from 1955 to 1963. Many interior improvements regarding installation, lighting and conservation were made in the process of rebuilding the nineteenth-century edifice. The Städel Art School, after many years of struggle, was finally closed in 1923, but the Academy of Fine Art is still associated with the Städel and is located nearby.

The Institute's program includes six major exhibitions annually, guided tours and lectures, evening seminars, and art instruction for children. The Institute's auditorium is used for frequent concerts. The public is also invited to bring works of art for identification on certain designated days.

A library of about forty-one thousand volumes is devoted primarily to history of art. The museum's shop sells catalogs, books, postcards, slides, and prints of the museum's collection.

Selected Bibliography

Städelsches Kunstinstitut, 1971; *Städel Frankfurt am Main*, 1978; *Die Gemälde des 19. Jahrhunderts*, 2 vols., 1972; *Katalog der deutschen Zeichnungen: Alte Meister*, 1973; *Verzeichnis d. Gemälde aus d. Besitz d. Städelschen Kunstinst. u.d. Stadt Frankfurt/ Städelsches Kunstinst.*, 1971; Schmitt, Otto, *Barock Plastic*, 1924; Ziemke, Hans Joachim, *The Städelsche Kunstinstitut: The History of a Legacy*, 1980.

RENATA RUTLEDGE

——— **Munich** ———

ALTE PINAKOTHEK, 2 Barerstrasse 27, 8000 Munich.

The history of the formation of the Alte Pinakothek collections in Munich begins with Duke Wilhelm IV of Bavaria (reigned 1508–50) in his commissioning of works by German artists such as Albrecht Altdorfer, Hans Burgkmair, and Barthel Behan. The first real collection of pictures dates from the time of Albert V (1550–79), with whom the long line of Bavarian patrons of art begins. As a collector he devoted himself to gathering curiosities and some paintings, the most notable of which are by Dürer, Holbein, and Altdorfer. The collections have a rich and varied history of collectors since Albert V, but the greatness of the collection is primarily the result of six outstanding figures. The first of them was Maximilian I of the House of Wittelsbach, who added considerably to the holdings of Duke Wilhelm IV and Albert V. During his long reign from 1598 to 1651, Maximilian, who later became the elector of Bavaria, collected some of the chief works by Dürer. Among them were the *Paumgarten Altar* from the church of St. Catherine at Nuremberg, acquired in 1613; the *Heller Altar* from the church of the Dominicans at Frankfurt, in 1615; and the *Four Apostles*, which he obtained from the Town Hall of Nuremberg. It was also during the reign of Maximilian that Rubens delivered his great *Lion Hunt* in 1618, which was the beginning of the famous Rubens collection in Munich.

The second important figure in the history of the collections was Max Emanuel (1679–1726), who established the Bavarian Gallery as one of the finest in Europe. He built the Palace-Gallery at Schleissheim (1701–26) to hold his new acquisitions. He was stadtholder of the Netherlands, which furthered his opportunities to collect, and in 1698 he bought 105 choice pieces from van Ceulen in Antwerp. Among them were twelve paintings by Rubens, fifteen by van Dyck, and important pieces by Snyders, de Vos, Brouwer, de Heem, Bruegel, Wouwermans, and Murillo.

The third important figure was Johann Wilhelm von der Pfalz, the elector palatine (1690–1716), who resided in Düsseldorf and had one of the finest collections in Europe. He had built a special gallery for it in Düsseldorf, and this collection consisted primarily of Dutch and Italian artists. His marriage to Anna Maria Luisa de' Medici brought several Italian masterpieces to Düsseldorf. This collection included no fewer than forty additional paintings by Rubens, seventeen by van Dyck, three of the finest by Snyders, and works by Jordaens, Rembrandt, and Metsu. Among the Italian paintings then acquired, besides masterpieces by the Carracci, Domenichino, and Reni, were the *Portrait of Vesalius* by Tintoretto, two *Madonnas with Saints and Donors* by Palma Vecchio and Titian, the *Holy Family* by Andrea del Sarto, and the *Holy Family of the House of Canigiani* by Raphael. It also included Rembrandt's *Passion Series* (1633) and other famous works such as *The Lovesick Woman* by Jan Steen and the *The Bean Feast* by Gabriel Metsu. All of the famous seventeenth-century landscape artists are represented in the elector's collection. The collection was moved to Munich in 1805 to avoid the invading Napoleonic forces.

The next important figure in the creation of these collections was Elector Charles Theodore of the Palatinate and Bavaria (1777–99), who established a gallery at Mannheim. This gallery included a large collection of French artists such as Claude Lorraine, Poussin, Lebrun, Lemoine, Desportes, and Boucher and several Dutch and Flemish artists such as Teniers, Ostade, de Heem, Ruysdael, and Metsu. To it belonged the two large Rembrandts, the *Holy Family* and the *Sacrifice of Isaac*. Particularly important were six rare pieces by the German master Adam Elsheimer.

The successor to Elector Charles Theodore was Maximilian Joseph, elector in 1799 and king of Bavaria as Maximilian I in 1806–25. He is important for uniting the collections of Bavaria and the Palatinate and was responsible for moving the collections of Johann Wilhelm from Düsseldorf to Munich.

The last important figure was Ludwig I (1825–68), who directed the purchases to three schools that had formerly been inadequately represented, Early German and Flemish and the Quattro-Cinquecento of Italy. He added magnificent works by Filippo and Filippino Lippi, Botticelli, Ghirlandaio, and Perugino, especially Raphael's two *Madonnas di Tempi and di Tenda*. He also added the old Dutch and old German collections, those of the brothers Boisserée and Prince Wallerstein. The transfer to Munich of the collections of Düsseldorf, Mannheim, and Zweibrücken (Karlstein Castle); the secularization of church art treasures; and a great many extremely important purchases resulted in such a vast accumulation of masterpieces that a very large building was needed. On the orders of King Ludwig I, a building was begun by Leo von Klenze (who also designed the Hermitage Museum in Leningrad) in 1826 and completed ten years later. This is the building that houses the present collections. In 1943 and 1944 the Alte Pinakothek was completely gutted by fire, although all of its treasures were saved. After extensive reconstruction, the museum was reopened in 1957. Today the collections offer an in-depth study of European painting from the early German schools of the fourteenth century culminating in Goya at the beginning of the nineteenth century.

The foundations of the German Gothic section were laid more than four centuries ago. The Dürer and Altdorfer masterpieces were the result of the foresight of Duke Wilhelm IV and Elector Maximilian I. It was through the seizure of monastic property and the incorporation of free imperial cities, Franconian principalities, and convents that the Pinakothek became the most important gallery of German Gothic painting.

The German school can be divided into artists from Cologne, the Lower Rhine, and Westphalia; the Middle Rhine; the Upper Rhine and Switzerland; Swabia; Franconia; Central Germany and Saxony; Tyrol, Salzburg, and Austria; and Bavaria. The collections of the German school are so extensive not only in quantity but also in quality that only a few examples from each area can be mentioned. The collections of the Alte Pinakothek offer a complete survey of Early German painting, perhaps the finest anywhere.

Next to the Wallraf-Richartz Museum (q.v.) in Cologne, the Alte Pinakothek has the most extensive collection of works of the early school of Cologne, built mainly on the Boisserée Collection acquired by Ludwig I. Of the Cologne masters, only Stephan Lochner (*Nativity*, and *Saints Catherine, Hubert, and Querenes*), Bartholomaus Bruyn, and Anton Woensam can be identified. Other painters have names based on their most famous works, such as the Master of the Life of the Virgin, Master of the St. Bartholomew Altarpiece, and Master of St. Severin. The Master of the Aachen Altarpiece's *Virgin and Child with Angels*, purchased in 1940 from the Pölnitz Collection, is considered one of the finest Madonnas of its school.

Cologne's greatest Renaissance master, Bartholomaus Bruyn the Elder, is represented by a series of his earlier works: *Christ Carrying the Cross* and an altarpiece, *Crucifixion*. Representative of the early Westphalian artists is the fine *St. Paul* by Konrad van Soest.

The selection of paintings from the school of the Middle Rhine is not large but is of exceptional quality. The Master of the Darmstadt Passion and the Hausbuchmeister are both represented, but the greatest examples are by Grünewald. His *Mocking of Christ* (1503) is considered among the greatest works of German art. The *Saints Erasmus and Maurice*, painted between 1520 and 1525, is one of the finest individual religious paintings of the German Renaissance and next to Dürer's *Apostles* is one of the finest examples of the early German section in the Alte Pinakothek.

The Upper Rhine and Switzerland are represented by an early work of Martin Schongauer, the *Beheading of St. John the Baptist*, and by six works by Hans Baldung, called Grien, among which is the *Nativity* and some fine portraits.

Next to the school of Cologne, the Swabian school is better represented than any other in the Alte Pinakothek. Examples include the earliest panel, *Man of Sorrows between the Virgin and St. John* (1457), by the Master of Ulm in addition to works of Bartholomaus Zeitblom, Hans Maler, Bernhard Strigel, and Hans Holbein the Elder. Augsburg altar painting during the Renaissance reached its peak with Hans Burgkmair's altarpieces *St. John* and the *Crucifixion*, 1519.

The Franconian school is not represented to the same extent as the schools of Swabia and Cologne, but it is nevertheless given importance by Pleydenwurff and Dürer. Hans Pleydenwurff's wings of the *Hof Altarpiece*, 1465, are characteristic of the Late Gothic Nuremberg school. The selection of works by Albrecht Dürer is one of the greatest treasures of the Alte Pinakothek. The earliest work is the panel *Our Lady of Sorrows*, originally the center piece of the *Seven Scenes of the Passion*, now in the Dresden Gallery (q.v.). The great panel of the *Seven Sorrows of the Virgin* was made in Dürer's workshop for the Schlosskirche in Wittenberg. The *Paumgartner Altar*, the *Self Portrait in a Fur Coat* (1500), and the *Four Apostles* by Dürer are considered to be three of his finest masterpieces in the Alte Pinakothek.

The finest examples of Central Germany and Saxony are from Lucas Cranach, whose *Christ on the Cross* (1503) and several portraits, as well as the *Crucifixion*, exemplify this school. The school of Tyrol, Salzburg, and Austria is best represented by Michael Pacher's solemn *Coronation of the Virgin* and the *Altarpiece of the Church Fathers*, about 1483, which is not only one of the most important works of Tyrolean Late Gothic but of Early German art itself.

Albrecht Altdorfer, the painter *par excellence* of the Danube school, is represented by his *St. George in a Wood*, 1510, one of the first true landscape paintings in Europe. There is also *Birth of the Virgin*, about 1521, and *Danube Landscape near Regensburg*, about 1525, as well as *Susannah at the Bath*, 1526. Considered Altdorfer's masterpiece is the *Battle of Alexander*, 1529, in which fantastic landscape vistas are combined with vast numbers of small figures in combat. This was commissioned by Duke Wilhelm IV of Bavaria.

Of later German masters, the most notable works are Adam Elsheimer's *Sermon of St. John the Baptist, Night Scene of Burning Troy*, and the *Flight into Egypt*, done about 1609 and bought by Elector Palatine Johann Wilhelm, supposedly from Count Werschowitz in Prague.

Although van Eyck, Hugo van der Goes, and Geertgen are not represented, the Alte Pinakothek includes some of the most important examples of early painting in the Netherlands, most of which came from the Boisserée Collection. One of Rogier van der Weyden's masterpieces, the *Adoration of the Kings* from St. Columba in Cologne, is the centerpiece of this collection. Other masterpieces include Dieric Bouts the Younger's *Pearl of Brabant*, Hans Memling's *The Seven Joys of the Virgin*, Gerard David's *Adoration of the Kings*, Quentin Massy's winged altarpiece the *Virgin and Child*, Bernard von Orley's *Sermon of St. Ambrose*, Mabuse's *Danae*, and Lucas van Leyden's *Virgin and Child and St. Barbara*. Cornelis Engelbrechtsz's *Constantine and St. Helena*, about 1520, is an excellent example of Dutch painting of the Late Gothic Mannerist movement. One of the most important and valuable acquisitions is Bruegel's *The Land of Cockayne*, purchased in 1917 at the Richard von Kaufman sale.

It is the Flemish Baroque artists on whom—next to the Early German painters—the Alte Pinakothek's reputation is based. The Rubens collection is unsurpassed not only in quantity but also in quality. Every facet of Rubens' career is represented: religious paintings, history paintings, landscapes, and portraiture. There are more than forty works in all by his hand. There is both the *Large Last Judgment* and the *Small Last Judgment*, the *Fall of the Rebel Angels*, and the famous *Virgin in a Garland of Flowers*, which is a joint work of Rubens and Jan Bruegel. The *Massacre of the Innocents* is illustrative of his late, mature style. Mythological themes include the *Rape of the Daughters of Leucippus* and the *Battle of the Amazons*, which was the first acquisition of Elector Johann Wilhelm, the founder of the famous Düsseldorf Gallery which also has a magnificent Rubens collection. There is a *Pastoral Scene* and the smaller *Two Satyrs*, which represent pastoral themes. The *Drunken Silenius* is the greatest work of the Bacchanalian type. The Alte Pinakothek also possesses the preliminary sketches for the Marie de' Medici cycle, which is now in the Luxemburg Palace in Paris. Four large hunting scenes, of which two are preserved in the Pinakothek, were ordered from Rubens in 1617 by Elector Maximilian for the Alte Schloss, Schleissheim. The *Lion Hunt* is the most famous of them.

Rubens is well represented as a portrait painter in the Alte Pinakothek. The famous *Artist and His First Wife, Isabella Brant, in the Honeysuckle Bower*, 1609, was painted shortly after his marriage and his return from Italy. There are several portraits of Helena Fourment, a frequent model for Rubens, and two very fine examples of Baroque portraiture are *Hendrik van Thulden* and *Jan Brant*, Rubens' father-in-law. Also notable is the portrait *Alathea Talbot, Countess of Shrewsbury*, painted in Antwerp in 1620.

Anthony van Dyck is represented by six full-length portraits, as well as religious works, such as *The Lamentation*, the *Martyrdom of St. Sebastian*, *Susanna and the Elders*, and *Rest on the Flight*.

The Brouwerkabinett, with the largest Brouwer collection in the world, is one of the highlights of the Alte Pinakothek, although it does not include any early works or landscapes. There are seventeen works of such high calibre that it is difficult to name the best. *The Sense of Touch*, about 1630, and *The Brawl* are typical of his peasant scenes. There are three paintings depicting gambling scenes. But the master's latest works are the large *Peasant Quartet* and *Innkeeper and His Wife Sampling Wine*.

The Flemish school is also represented by the landscape painter Paul Bril, by Jan Bruegel (well represented in the Pinakothek), and by Joos de Momper, Teniers, and Frans Snyders.

The Dutch school is not as well represented as the Flemish in the Wittelsbach Collections. There is, however, a comprehensive view of the school, from the works of lesser-known artists such as Terbruggen, Honthorst, and Cornelis van Polenburgh to the works of Rembrandt. Frans Hals is represented by only one small portrait. By Rembrandt there is an early *Self Portrait as a Young Man*, done when he was twenty-three years old. The five scenes of the *Passion*, painted for Prince Frederick Henry, governor of the Netherlands, illustrate Rembrandt's talent at the height of his career. The *Adoration of the Shepherds*, 1646, is a mature work, and a half-length picture, *Christ the Savior*, 1661, is the only example of Rembrandt's late work. There are also examples from the school of Rembrandt, such as *The Jewish Bride* by Aert de Gelder.

The Pinakothek's collection of Dutch interiors and genre scenes is not altogether comprehensive, despite many fine examples, since Pieter de Hooch and Vermeer are not represented. Representations of genre painting include Gerard Dou, Gabriel Metsu, and Jan Steen (particularly outstanding is the *Lovesick Woman*); Frans van Mieris represents the late phase of Dutch genre painting at its best. Represented are only a few works of the "Italianate Dutchmen" Poelenburgh, Berchem, Weenix, and Karel du Jardin.

The Alte Pinakothek presents a very good survey of the development of Dutch landscape painting. Jan van Goyen is represented by five works. Landscapes of

Salomon van Ruysdael, and Jacob van Ruisdael can be studied in all phases from early to late. The *Sandhill Landscape* was bought from Prince Ernst von Sachsen-Meiningen in 1942. Meindert Hobbema is represented by only one work, and there are not many examples of Dutch architectural painting. To complete the survey of landscape painting are works by Paulus Potter, Adriaen van de Velde, and Melchior Hondecoeter. Jan Weenix represents the finest in animal painting; Jan Porcellis and Willem van de Velde illustrate Dutch seascapes; and there is the omnipresent flower piece by Jan Davidsz. de Heem.

The early Italian section was created mainly by Ludwig I, because Italian painting at that time was almost unknown in Munich. Although Giotto's authorship of three predella panels with scenes from the Passion—the *Last Supper*, *Christ on the Cross*, and the *Descent into Limbo*—is not universally accepted, they clearly reflect the master's spirit. The Alte Pinakothek owns no works by Massaccio, but there is the *Virgin and Child* by Masolino. Fra Angelico is represented by four brilliantly preserved predella panels (three scenes from the legend of *Saints Cosmas and Damian*, and the *Entombment*), originally painted for the Monastery Church of San Marco in Florence.

The Florentine painters of the next generation are represented sketchily by Fra Filippo Lippi's *Virgin and Child* and an *Annunciation* and one work by Filippino Lippi. Botticelli's *Lamentation* and Domenico Ghirlandaio's *High Altar*, painted for Santa Maria Novella, Florence, are characteristic of another generation of Florentine painters. The Pinakothek acquired Leonardo's *Virgin and Child* (*Madonna with the Carnation*) in 1889. This is an early work painted in Verocchio's workshop in 1478.

Perugino and Francesco Francia, both of great importance for the transition from Late Gothic to Renaissance, are very well represented in the Alte Pinakothek. Perugino's greatest work, the *Vision of St. Bernard*, is here. Francia's *Madonna in the Rose Garden* is also an example of this phase. Luca Signorelli is represented by a tondo of the *Virgin and Child* and Piero di Cosimo by his *Legend of Prometheus*.

In 1829 Ludwig I succeeded in purchasing Raphael's *Tempi Madonna* (1505), and the *Canigiani Holy Family* came as a wedding present to the Düsseldorf Gallery when Anna Maria Luisa de' Medici married Johann Wilhelm, the elector palatine in 1691. The *Madonna della Tenda* is characteristic of Raphael's Roman middle period.

The Florentine High Renaissance is represented by Albertinelli's *Annunciation*, Andrea del Sarto's *Holy Family*, Franciabigio's *Virgin and Child*, Francesco Granacci's *Four Saints*, and Pontormo's *Virgin and Child*. There are only a very few examples of the fifteenth-century Ferrarese and Sienese schools.

The Alte Pinakothek possesses many works of the Venetian masters of the High Renaissance, but of the Quattrocento, only a few examples are of the highest order, such as Antonello da Messina's *Virgin of the Annunciation* and Cima da Conegliano's *Virgin and Child with Saints Mary Magdalene and Jerome* (1496). Two pictures thought to be by Giorgione, the *Shepherd with a Flute* and the *Portrait of a Man* (although there is some dispute as to their authenticity), represent this rare area of Venetian painting. Lorenzo Lotto and Palma Vecchio are represented by two small but very distinguished examples of their work. The *Mystic Marriage of St. Catherine* belongs to Lotto's early work and dates from about 1506. Palma's *Virgin and Child with Saints Roch and Mary Magdalene* is a late and mature work.

Titian's *Allegory of Vanity* is his earliest work at the Pinakothek, and his *Portrait of a Young Man* was painted not much later. Titian's powerful portrait *Emperor Charles V* was painted at the Augsburg Reichstag in 1548 and is one of the portrait treasures of the Pinakothek. Two religious works are also displayed: the *Virgin and Child in an Evening* dates from shortly after the Charles V portrait, and the *Christ Crowned with Thorns* belongs to his last years and is considered one of the Alte Pinakothek's greatest treasures.

There is hardly a gallery outside Venice where Tintoretto is as well represented as he is in the Alte Pinakothek. It includes the only great historical cycle outside Italy. Tintoretto painted the battles and scenes from the *Life of the Gonzagas* at the request of Duke Guglielmo Gonzaga for the *appartamento maggiore* at Mantua. Considered the finest of Tintoretto's works in Munich is his *Christ in the House of Martha and Mary*. There is also a fine allegory, *Venus, Vulcan, and Cupid*, and two good portraits.

The large *Noli me tangere* (1590) by Federigo Barocci was given to Elector Johann Wilhelm in 1714 by Grand Duke Cosimo III.

The collection is not as strong in Italian Baroque painting, although there are several important examples. The Bolognese school includes Domenichino's *Susanna and the Elders*, Guido Reni's *Punishment of Marsyas*, and Giovanni Lanfranco's *Agony in the Garden*. Also represented are Procaccini, Bernardo Strozzi, Castiglione, Domenico Fetti, Francesco Maffei, and Luca Giordano.

Belonging to the period of transition from the seventeenth to the eighteenth century are Giuseppe Maria Crespi's *Massacre of the Innocents*, Gianantonio Burrini's *Adoration of the Shepherds*, Magnasco's *Coast Scene*, and Sebastiano Ricci's *Temptation of St. Anthony*. The early transitional Venetian painters are represented by Giovanni Battista Pittoni and Jacopo Amigoni and several large historical allegories by Giovanni Antonio Pellegrini that were commissioned for Schloss Bensberg by Elector Johann Wilhelm. Part of the paintings in this cycle are in the Alte Pinakothek, and part are in Schloss Schleissheim. Giovanni Battista Tiepolo's art is the peak of Italian painting, and his *Adoration of the Holy Trinity by Pope Clement* is a fine example of his early work. It was painted in 1735 at the request of Elector Clemens August of Cologne for the former Chorfrauenkirche of the Congregation of Notre-Dame in Nymphenburg (now destroyed). Guardi's *Venetian Gala Concert* in 1782 was acquired in 1911 by the Pinakothek. There are two Venetian views attributed to Bernardo Bellotto and Canaletto.

French painting of the seventeenth century is well represented; that of the eighteenth century, less so. The figure *Diana* of the School of Fontainebleau and a number of small portraits are good examples of sixteenth-century art. The *Duchess Claudia of Lorraine*, daughter of Henry I, was painted by François Clouet. Nicolas Poussin and Claude Lorraine are well represented. Poussin is shown with *Apollo and Daphne*, 1730; *Midas and Bacchus*, 1667; and *Mourning of Christ*, 1628. Claude is represented by four landscapes. Examples by Eustache Le Sueur and Philippe de Champaigne are illustrative of the seventeenth century. Portraits by Hyacinthe Rigaud and Nicolas Largillierre are also on view.

The eighteenth-century collection has good examples of Nattier, Lancret, Pater, and La Tour. By Boucher are his *Madame Pompadour* of 1756; *Louise O'Murphy*, 1752; and *Pastoral Landscape*, 1741. In addition, there are Chardin's *Woman Scraping Vegetables* and Lemoine's *Hunting Party*, which is a good example of the *fête champêtre*.

The Spanish school is the smallest in the Alte Pinakothek. El Greco's final and most famous version of his *Disrobing of Christ* (1583) and his *St. Veronica with the Holy Veil* are fine examples of his genius. The early *Young Spaniard* is the only work shown by Velázquez. There are also works by Sanchez Coello and Alfonso Cano, as well as five very fine examples of Murillo's genre painting, the most universally popular of which is *Beggar Boys Playing Dice*. Zurbarán and Ribera are also represented, and there are three portraits by Goya.

Slides and photographs of objects in the collection may be purchased at the museum, which can also provide a list of museum publications and catalogues. In addition to guides to the collections and special catalogues, a yearly report is published, the *Bayerisches Staatsgemäldesammlungen Jahresbericht*.

Selected Bibliography

Alte Pinakothek München, Katalog I, *Deutsche und Niederländische Malerei zwischen Renaissance und Barock*, 1961; idem, Katalog II, *Altdeutsche Malerei*, 1963; idem, Katalog III, *Holländische Malerei des 17 Jahrhunderts*, 1967; idem, Katalog IV, *Französische und Spanische Malerei*, 1972; idem, Katalog V, *Italianische Malerei*, 1975; Böttger, Peter, *Die Alte Pinakothek in München*, 1972; Buchner, Ernst, *The Munich Pinakothek* (London 1957).

GREGORY OLSON

GLYPTOTHEK (officially MUNICH GLYPTOTHEK; alternately GLYPTO-THEK OF MUNICH, SCULPTURE MUSEUM OF MUNICH, CLASSICAL SCULPTURE MUSEUM OF MUNICH), Königsplatz, Munich.

The Glyptothek of Munich was begun in 1816 and completed in 1830, according to an inscription carved over the main entrance. A Latin inscription over the inner court door documents that "Ludwig I, King of Bavaria, founded this museum and dedicated it as a worthy home for the monuments of ancient sculpture which he collected from everywhere." From the beginning the collection of Greek and Roman sculpture was emphasized. Acquisitions for the museum began as early as 1804. The Aegina pediment groups and subsidiary sculptures were purchased shortly after their excavation in 1812. They are the largest single group of original Late Archaic Greek sculptures outside of Greece itself and are second in importance only to the Parthenon sculptures of the British Museum (q.v.) among original Greek sculpture groups outside of Greece itself. The core of the museum is Greek sculpture from the private collection of Ludwig I. Additionally, there are several important early donations and bequests: a Roman mosaic from Sentinum was given in 1826 by Auguste Herzogin von Leuchtenberg; a Roman relief, *Rustic Scene*, was given in 1858 by Johann Martin von Wagner; the *Portrait of Homer* was given by Paul Arndt in 1892; the *Head of Herakles* was given in 1897 by Franz von Lenbach; the grave relief of Mnesarete and a gladiator relief were given in 1910 by Friedrich Wilhelm Freiherr von Bissing; a banquet relief was given in 1907 by Edward Perry Warren; the Roman *Head of a Boy* was a bequest in 1917 from Anna von Lotzbeck; the statue *Boy*, the *Head of Aphrodite*, a grave lekythos, and the grave stele *Lady and Maid* were given in 1939 by the Bayerischer Verein der Kunstfreunde; and the *Portrait of a Roman* was given in 1971 by Heinz Herzer. A collection of Assyrian sculpture was acquired in 1864 and installed in the covered court. Since 1971 these reliefs and a small Egyptian collection have been housed at the Residenz. The courtyard is now restored to its original open-air state. The modern sculpture of the original collection, chiefly by neoclassic sculptors like Canova and Thorwaldsen, has been housed in the Neue Pinakothek (q.v.) since 1919.

In the early nineteenth century a plan was conceived to create an enormous Königplatz with a propylaeon and with two museums facing each other from opposite sides of the square. Competition for such a plan was held in 1808, and land was allocated for the project in 1812. The first competition for the design of a sculpture museum was held in 1813. No fully satisfactory design was submitted. A second competition in 1816 resulted in Leo von Klenze's appointment as architect and supervisor of construction. The foundation stone was laid in that same year, and in a letter on April 12 Ludwig, writing to Haller von Hallerstein, first used the word *Glyptothek* as the name for the building that would house the ancient and modern sculpture. It is a new word, an analogue with the Greek words *pinakotheke* and *bibliotheke*. The Greek word *glyptic* refers to the art of carving in stone or metal. The main substance of the building was completed in 1820, and the following year the entrance porch was built. Between 1821 and 1830 the interior decoration was completed and the sculptures reconstructed and installed. By 1828 sufficient progress had been made for the court to use the torch-lighted reception rooms for evening functions. The opening of the Glyptothek, the first public art museum in Munich, on October 1, 1830, was not marked by official ceremonies.

A series of Latin inscriptions over various interior doorways document its early history. According to them, the architect Leo von Klenze supervised the construction and the design of both the interior and exterior decoration. The tall central porch has two rows of Ionic columns crowned by a pediment. Johann Martin von Wagner made the models for the pediment sculptures representing Athena as patron of the plastic arts and eight figures of these arts (sculptor, wood carver, and so on). The statues placed in the wall niches flanking the porch were made by different artists. These statues represent mythical and historical patrons and practitioners of the arts: Daedalus, Prometheus, Hadrian, Pericles (destroyed during World War II), Phidias, and Hephaestos. The two exterior side walls of the building have six niches each with Renaissance and modern sculpture, including the statues by Canova and Thorwaldsen. Two of the original works on the east wall were also wartime casualties.

The original interior was magnificent, in contrast with the relatively plain exterior. The lobby, ten exhibition halls, and three reception rooms had ceilings enriched by cupolas; half domes and flat domes on pendentives, both cross-groined; and tunnel vaults further elaborated with diamond-shaped coffers, central rosettes, stars, ornamental motifs, and figure scenes. The walls were once covered with colored stucco painted in imitation of marble wainscot panels, with inset stucco-relief panels painted to resemble white marble. Other stucco-relief panels installed over doorways and into the upper walls and vaulted ceilings were highlighted with brilliant color and gilding; relief subjects ranged from figure groups to arabesques and symbolic, allegorical, and decorative motifs. The three reception rooms had domed painted ceilings by Peter von Cornelius and gleaming marble floors. The interior rooms varied in size and shape, including two that combine a square with a half circle. The ceiling heights also vary, with the entrance lobby considerably higher than the flanking rooms. The wall surfaces have protruding and receding elements, niches of a variety of shapes, sizes, and placements; piers; pilasters; ribbing; and framed fields.

The building has had many changes from its original state. The 1935 paving of the Königsplatz raised its level, and it now conceals the first two steps up to the Glyptothek entrance porch. It is now used as a car parking lot. In 1939, at the beginning of World War II, the building was closed and the sculptures placed in safe storage. Shells destroyed 40 percent of the structure and 90 percent of the interior decoration in 1944. During 1947 to 1953 some temporary reconstruction was done. The museum remained closed to the public while consideration was given to the question of restoring a Glyptothek to Munich. Finally, a decision was made to reject both the idea of restoring it to its pre-war glory and the idea of completely replacing it. In 1964 J. Wiedemann was entrusted with the sensitive job of creating a contemporary setting for sculpture within the reconstructed neoclassical building designed by Klenze. The brickwork (walls and ceilings) was restored to its original configuration and coated with an unobtrusive creamy matte paint. Floors throughout the building were paved with shell-limestone slabs. The courtyard level was raised and glass doors installed in formerly poorly lit rooms overlooking the courtyard. In 1971–72 electric lighting was installed in the galleries to facilitate opening of the museum in the evening. The restored Glyptothek was reopened to the public on April 28, 1972.

In the original Glyptothek the statues were carefully arranged symmetrically to the axis of each room, in a decorative scheme that was often subordinate to the architecture: fixed in niches or placed high on walls or high pedestals without regard for lighting. Emphasis was on the decorative effect of the whole ensemble rather than on the individual pieces. To create these visual effects, mutilated statues were restored to appear complete by the neoclassical sculptors Canova and Thorwaldsen. Post–World War II activities, however, included the cleaning and restoring of the statues to their original state, which in many cases necessitated removal of neoclassical arms and legs. Gallery installations now emphasize the individual sculptures, and the architecture is for background only. The less-crowded presentation means that some items are no longer on public display. These sculptures, in storage, are not included in the current published catalogue. They are, however, the nucleus of the planned study collection. A few new acquisitions are on display but also are not listed in the published guide of 1974. The sculptures are now arranged in accordance with a combination of considerations.

Generally, the sequence is from early Greek toward Late Roman with a tendency to separate certain Greek sculpture from Roman copies and both from essentially Roman sculpture. Exceptions to chronological arrangements include the installation of the Aegina sculptures in the three adjoining former reception rooms along the north wing of the building and the placement of some Hellenistic pieces in Room II, the Room of the Faun, in the southwest corner. There is some typological clustering; for instance, Rooms IV and VI are devoted to Greek grave stelae, and Room XI is devoted mainly to Roman portraits. These exceptions seem to have been determined by architectural considerations so that a number of small-scale pieces might be displayed in enhancing spaces and a large number of large-scale pieces might be displayed in spaces of adequate size to accommodate them without crowding. Thus the original architectural planning continues to retain a significant importance for the presentation of the sculpture.

The Glyptothek collection, now limited to Greek and Roman sculpture, includes examples of each of the major periods from the Archaic Greek to Late Roman, with many outstanding examples of Roman copies of Greek sculpture. All of the sculptures are of marble, except where another material is specifically identified. The exceptional quality of the collection is established by its earliest statues, two almost perfectly preserved Archaic kouroi (figures of young men); the delicately carved, lively, life-size *Tenea kouros* (c. 560–550 B.C.) from near Corinth, acquired in 1853; and the somewhat larger than life-size, athletic, and muscular *Munich kouros* (c. 540–530 B.C.) from Attica, acquired in 1910. An unfinished head (c. 570–560 B.C.) of Parian marble and probably of island workmanship, came in 1896 from the Museum für Völkerkunde of Munich, and a votive relief with a row of women (perhaps the Graces) (c. 570–560 B.C.) from the island of Paros rounds out the small collection of sixth-century B.C. Greek marble sculpture. The one additional figure is the bronze *Zeus Lykaion*, a bearded weathergod or rainmaker, with two thunderbolts, one held, the second being hurled, in which the intense vitality, mastery of form, and fine engraved detail offer a sense of monumentality rarely seen in a statuette.

The pedimental sculptures and other fragments from the Temple of Aphaia,

Aegina, are of such exceptional importance that some attention is directed to
their history. The temple was first noted by an English traveler in Greece in
1675. In 1811 four young scholars, and architects—Charles Robert Cockerell
(English), John Foster (English), Carl Haller von Hallerstein (Bavarian), and
Jacob Linckh (Swabian)—went to measure and draw the temple but remained
to excavate its sculptures. Ludwig I of Bavaria purchased the entire group for
an astounding sum through his agent Johann Martin von Wagner in 1812. He
also arranged for the immediate restoration of the torsos according to models by
the leading Danish sculptor Bertel Thorwaldsen. All missing heads and limbs
were replaced or patched in marble and the figures were provided with bronze
weapons and other attachments. Thus restored, some ten of the original thirteen
figures of the west pediment and five of the eleven of the east pediment were
installed in an Ägineten-Saal on two long bases of equal length, with the pedimental arrangements facing each other. Each group of figures was arranged
in a purely decorative scheme without consideration for the original compositions. The restored parts imitated existing originals even to the weathering of
the surfaces; yet criticism of the reconstruction began soon after the opening of
the Glyptothek and ultimately led to the current reconstruction of the pedimental
figures and their reorganization. This has led to some new confusion, since the
individual figures as they are seen today are not identical with the many older
published photographs, just as the arrangement of the ensembles today differs
from the former. It is a consolation that the current arrangements and figures
include almost exclusively Greek stones and casts of Greek fragments in the
Aegina Museum and the National Archaeological Museum (q.v.) in Athens,
reassembled after careful consideration to the weathering of the surfaces of the
individual fragments, stylistic analysis of the individual fragments, and study
and measurement of the beddings of the figures' plinths in the partially preserved
blocks of the horizontal cornices of the pediments themselves. Information contributing to this new reconstruction has been accumulating as a result of excavations carried out by Furtwangler, Thiersch, and Fiechter in 1902 and the very
substantial excavations in recent years made by the museum.

Today, three rooms of the museum are devoted to the display of Aegina
materials, a room for each pediment and a room for Aeginetan miscellany. There
are two models of the Temple of Aphaia, one showing the exterior complete
with sculptural decoration, the other opening a cross-section through the temple
revealing the interior space. These models are based on the remains, and displayed architectural fragments confirm many details of the models. The Temple
of Aphaia, built between 510 and 480 B.C., was the second temple on its site.
Architectural components displayed in the Glyptothek include: a capital for a
column of the interior colonnade; a fragment of an architrave block; several
elements of the temple roofing system, including marble roof edging tiles, marble
cover tiles with palmette antefix and traces of paint for roof edges, terracotta
pan tile, terracotta cover tile with palmette antefix, and traces of paint that
decorated the roof ridge; the central akroterion of the west facade, two korai

flanking a volute tree carved of a single piece of marble originally two meters high and reconstructed from fragments bearing traces of paint, in the Glyptothek, and casts of fragments, in the Aegina Museum; fragments of a kore and volute tree from the akroterion that crowned the west facade; the torso of the Sphinx that served as akroterion in the northwest corner of the roof; and the exceptionally well-preserved and delicately carved female head for the Sphinx akroterion in the northeast corner. A most unusual artifact is the marble pillar found within the temple with an inscribed inventory of the sanctuary (c. 410 B.C.). Of the cult statue of Athena that stood within the cella, only the right arm has been preserved. A cast is displayed, since the original is in the Athens National Archaeological Museum.

The west pediment (c. 505–500 B.C.) has a miraculously well-preserved Athena standing serenely in a central position presiding over a battle in the second siege of Troy. The participants are both Greeks and Trojans, difficult to identify, yet surely including descendents of Aeacus, first king of Aegina and son of Zeus, particularly his grandson Ajax, son of Telamon; the great archers, Greek Teucer and Trojan Paris; and a warrior in combat, wounded and dying. Many of the nude warriors carry shields, some are restored, but others are original, still carrying their painted devices. Aside from the dressed Athena and armored archers, the life-size warriors battle in heroic nudity, some with helmets and swords; others had these items separately attached in bronze (now lost). Each figure is carved in-the-round of a single piece of marble and completely finished on all sides even to the painted details on the invisible back of the Athena.

The east pediment (c. 485–480 B.C.) likewise has Athena at the center, this time surviving only with its fine head, left arm with aegis, and right foot, presiding over the first campaign against Troy fought by the Greek Telamon, son of Aeacus; his friend Herakles; the sorely wounded King Laomedon of Troy; his surviving son Priam; and battling and fallen Greeks and Trojans. Again heroic nudity prevails, except for Athena and Herakles, an armored archer with a lion-head helmet, two warriors with greaves, and some with helmets or shields. All are carved in-the-round of single blocks of marble and finished on all sides. Heads of two warriors from this pediment and one warrior head from the west pediment are separately displayed at eye level along with the arms of an archer. Also separately displayed are several arms, legs, and fists of warriors from both pediments that could not easily be incorporated into the reconstructions. This pediment has been attributed by some scholars to the Aeginetan sculptor Onatas. There are three additional groups of sculpture that were displayed within the sanctuary peribolos in front of the east facade and that perhaps belonged to early decorative schemes for the temple. One group depicts fighting warriors in the presence of Athena (c. 505–500 B.C.); the other depicts the abduction of the nymph Aegina by Zeus (c. 505–500 B.C.). Both have been attributed to the West Pediment Master; both are extremely fragmentary, with four warrior heads, hands, and so on being housed in the Athens National Archaeological Museum and the Aegina Museum. A central volute tree akroterion originally intended for the eastern facade but on display in the sanctuary, also by the West Pediment Master, is exhibited in the museum.

There are a few pieces of original Greek workmanship from the second half of the fifth century B.C., a small torso of Athena (c. 440 B.C.) acquired in 1900 from the Palazzo Giustiniani-Recanati of Venice, and a votive relief with goddesses, perhaps Demeter and Kore, dating from about 410 and excavated from the Sanctuary of Nemesis at Rhamnous in Attica in 1853. In addition, there are several interesting architectural fragments, including a palmette antefix from the Parthenon in Athens (c. 440 B.C.); an original architrave block from the Erechtheum, including palmette and lotus connnected by spiraling tendrils, leaf and dart, egg and dart, and bead and reel (c. 410 B.C.); and a fragment of a palmette frieze from the Temple of Apollo at Bassae (c. 420 B.C.).

There are a large number of fourth-century B.C. Attic grave markers of a variety of types and a few western and eastern Greek examples. The earliest of the later group is the grave relief *Lyreplayer* (c. 420 B.C.) from southern Italy. The grave relief *Demetrios, Son of Alexes*, a soldier at sea (c. 370 B.C.) from Panderma near Cyzicus on the sea of Marmora, the relief *Mourning Woman* (c. 340 B.C.) from southern Asia Minor, and the relief *Banqueting Couple* (c. 320 B.C.) are all eastern Greek. The Attic pieces, all acquired in Athens in this century, except where noted, include some exceptionally fine examples of the type. The grave markers include the reliefs *Woman with Her Maid* (c. 400 B.C.); *Mnesarete* (c. 380 B.C.), one of the finest to have survived; *Paramythion*, with carved loutrophoros painted with a figure scene (c. 370–360 B.C.); *Youth as Huntsman with Dog* (c. 360 B.C.); the *Lamprokles* fragment (c. 360 B.C.); the monument *Xenocrateia*, a tall, flat pillar, with plant ornament only (c. 350 B.C.); *Artemon* (c. 350 B.C.); the *Head of a Mourning Girl* fragment (c. 340–330 B.C.); and the stele *Plangon* (c. 320–310 B.C.). A fairly commonly shaped grave marker, the marble lekythos (a monument in the shape of an oil flask), is represented by several fine examples, including the lekythos *Eukoline* (c. 400 B.C.); *Philon*, a soldier (c. 400 B.C.); the three-figure relief scene *Woman Showing the Dead Mother Her Child* (c. 390 B.C.); another titled *Husband and Wife Clasping Hands* (c. 375 B.C.), a unique presentation for a lekythos relief and of unequalled quality in the genre; and still another, *Three Women* (c. 350–320 B.C.). Three other Attic funeral sculptures are animals-in-the-round, the *Hunting Hound* (c. 360 B.C.); and a pair of pantheresses (c. 380 B.C.) found guarding the boundaries of the grave of Mnesarete facing her relief. Four other monuments appear to be Greek original work of the fourth century B.C. but have no certain provenance, since three were acquired in Rome and the fourth from the Munich Residenz Antiquarium in 1921. There are the statue *Mourning Maiden* (c. 360 B.C.); the statue *Girl with a Dove*, said to be from a sanctuary in Attica (c. 310 B.C.); the *Head of a Little Girl* (c. 320 B.C.), possibly also from an Attic sanctuary; and the *Torso of a Girl* (c. 300 B.C.). The Attic relief *Young Athlete Gazing at His Spear* (c. 320 B.C.) is from a statue base with athletic scenes.

There is a single example of Attic relief of the third century B.C., a *Hekateion*, or cult pillar, of the household goddess Hekate, shown in triple form with the three Graces dancing around, acquired from the Antiquarium of the Munich Residenz. A fragment of the large votive relief *God or Hero Seated in a Rocky Landscape* (c. 180 B.C.) came in 1898 from the Neue Pinakothek. The votive relief *Sacrifice at a Rustic Shrine* (c. 200 B.C.) and the grave relief *Hiras, Son of Nikanor* (c. 100 B.C.) were excavated at Erythrae in western Asia Minor in 1920.

The Glyptothek collection includes a great many examples of Roman copies of Greek statues of the fifth, fourth, and following centuries B.C., many of which have been identified with no-longer-extant works by outstanding ancient sculptors, some as free variations on Greek themes, some with unidentifiable models, and still others that have sometimes been taken as (and indeed may be) original Greek work. The headless, twisted *Torso of a Kneeling Youth* (c. 300 B.C.) may have been part of a temple pedimental group. It was known in Rome in the sixteenth century, and by the seventeenth century it was in Prague in the collection of Emperor Rudolph II after being in a private collection, from which it came to the Glyptothek in 1814. Three heads have also been considered possible Greek originals: the head of a statue of a woman (c. 300–280 B.C.) of eastern Greek workmanship, the head of a statue of Aphrodite (c. 300–290 B.C.), and still another head of a statue of a woman (c. 310 B.C.), thought to be Attic work, although found at Ostia near Rome and acquired in 1809.

The list of Roman copies of Greek originals is long and includes some outstanding examples of the copyists' art. Dates given refer to original model, not the copy. Works based on fifth-century B.C. models include a torso of *Apollo* (c. 460 B.C.), perhaps by Onatas of Aegina; the so-called *Medusa Rondanini* (c. 440 B.C.), its original attributed to Phidias, associated with the building of the Parthenon in Athens and so named because of its sojourn in the Palazzo Rondanini in Rome before its acquisition by Ludwig I in 1811; the *Diomedes* (c. 430 B.C.), a Trojan war hero, attributed to Kresilas; a bearded god or hero (c. 440 B.C.); the *Apollo* torso (c. 420 B.C.), perhaps also by Polyclitus, from the Villa Ridolfi in Rome in 1812; a youth (c. 410 B.C.) of the school of Polyclitus, acquired in 1939; a head of Ares (c. 430–420 B.C.), thought to be a copy of a cult statue by Alkamenes, acquired in 1812 from the Palazzo Braschi in Rome; a bust of Athena (c. 430–420 B.C.) of very large size, thought to be a copy of a colossal cult statue by Kresilas, found at Tusculum-Frascati near Rome and acquired from the Villa Albani in 1816. Unattributed are the basalt head of a youth (c. 460 B.C.); another head of a youth (c. 460–450); a bronze head of a youth with gilded lips, a first-century A.D. Roman adaptation of the fifth-century B.C. Greek Classical style; another bearded god or hero (c. 440–430 B.C.); a head of Asklepios (c. 420–410 B.C.); a gilded bronze torso, executed about 50 B.C., an eclectic work referring to fifth-century B.C. Classical prototypes, acquired from a private Swiss collection, as the recent gift of the Verein des Freunde und Forderer des Glyptothek; a female head (c. 420–410 B.C.) of Parian marble; and a female torso, a first-century A.D. Roman adaptation from a fifth-century B.C. Classical original (c. 420–400 B.C.), acquired in 1814 from the Palazzo Barberini in Rome. In addition, there are copies of Greek Classical portraits of Homer and Pericles and miscellaneous other heads in storage with fifth-century B.C. antecedents.

Roman copies of fourth-century B.C. Late Classical models are: a torso of *Aphrodite with Goatskin* (c. 380–370 B.C.), a copy of a statue from Epidauros; *Eirene and Ploutos*, personifications of Peace and Plenty (c. 370 B.C.) by Kephisodotos, perhaps the best of several extant copies of the work commissioned by the city of Athens as a cult statue to be set up in the Agora in commemoration of universal peace proclaimed by Athens and Sparta after the Peloponnesian War and acquired in 1816 from the Villa Albani in Rome; a head known as *Winckelmann's Faun* (c. 390 B.C.), once owned by J. J. Winckelmann and probably a copy of a statue of an athlete (the Pan horns are modern); a torso of a woman, a free copy of a model of about 420–400 B.C., acquired in 1814 from the Palazzo Barberini, Rome; a torso of a woman moving forward (c. 410–390 B.C.) from the Palazzo Giustiniani-Recanati, Venice, acquired in 1900, perhaps originally a lyre-playing central akroterion of a temple; a statue of an athlete (c. 360–350 B.C.); a torso of Artemis (c. 360–350 B.C.), perhaps a free copy of a statue by Praxiteles, acquired in 1812 from the Palazzo Braschi, Rome; a nude Aphrodite (c. 350–340 B.C.), a free copy of the *Aphrodite of Knidos* by Praxiteles, found at Fiumicino near Rome and acquired in 1811 from the Palazzo Braschi—two other free copies of the Knidian *Aphrodite* are in storage; a head of a woman (c. 340–330 B.C.), perhaps Sappho or Silanion; a head of Ares (c. 330 B.C.) from a statue modeled on one perhaps by Lysippos; and two copies of the many extant statues of a Satyr (c. 320 B.C.) by Praxiteles—the complete but stiff rendering was acquired in 1812 from the Palazzo Ruspoli, Rome; the more lively torso, perhaps truer to the original, was recorded first in the Palazzo Gaetani and then in the Palazzo Ruspoli from whence it was acquired in 1811.

The *Dead Son of Niobe* (c. 320 B.C.) is the finest of the three surviving copies of this one of the fourteen slain children of Niobe, who was punished by Apollo and Artemis for her overwhelming pride. The original sculptured group was ascribed to either Scopas or Praxiteles in antiquity and stood in Rome. This copy was first recorded in the Casa Maffei, Rome, later in the Palazzo Bevilacqua, Verona, and since 1811 in the Glyptothek. Other Roman copies include the head of a woman (c. 310 B.C.), perhaps of Attic workmanship but found at Ostia near Rome; *Silen Dangling the Child Dionysos* (c. 310–300 B.C.), perhaps a copy of an original by the Peloponnesian sculptor Lysippos of Sicyon, first housed in the Palazzo Gaetani and then in the Palazzo Ruspoli in Rome from whence it was acquired in 1812; head of a youth (c. 310–300 B.C.), acquired in Athens in 1912; a young Dionysos, partially draped, a fine complete copy of a fourth-century B.C. Greek original; a statue of a poet or philosopher (c. 380–360 B.C.), acquired from the Palazzo Rondanini in 1810; and the *Alexander Rondanini* (c. 338–336 B.C.), a copy of a bronze original by Euphranor of Corinth, found in the Mausoleum of Hadrian, Rome, in 1813 and acquired from the Palazzo Rondanini in 1814 (the right leg is a modern restoration). Also included are a head crowned with poplar leaves, perhaps Herakles (c. 330–320 B.C.), a bravura Roman copy of the first century A.D. acquired in 1966; and a head of Hermes, found in Capua in 1821, with a fourth-century B.C. prototype, which was often adapted in Roman times as the idealized figure for a portrait head. One such statue, with portrait head missing, adapted to show the deceased as a huntsman, was acquired in 1811 from the Villa Aldobrandini, Frascati.

Among the third-century B.C. sculptures, two others may be original Greek works judging from their quality alone: a head of a boy, perhaps Eros (c. 280 B.C.), and the head of a woman, perhaps a Muse (c. 180 B.C.). All others are Roman copies, including the *Herm with Portrait Head of Demosthenes* (c. 280 B.C.) after an original bronze statue set up in the Athenian Agora forty-two years after his death, made by Polyeuktos. This copy was found in Rome in the Circus of Maxentius in 1828. Some forty copies of the head but only two of the whole statue are extant. A small copy of the entire portrait statue is on display.

Perhaps the most noteworthy of all of the post-Classical sculptures is the so-called *Barberini Faun* (c. 220 B.C.), discovered in Rome at the Mausoleum of Hadrian during the reign of Pope Urban VIII (Maffeo Barberini, A.D. 1623–44) and housed in the Palazzo Barberini, Rome, until acquired in 1813. The satyr lies sleeping in a drunken sprawl, larger than life, a masterly example of Hellenistic Baroque exaggeration. The *Boy with a Goose* (c. 250–200 B.C.) from a bronze original by Boethos, repeatedly copied in Roman times, was acquired from the Palazzo Braschi, Rome, in 1812. The head and wingtips of the goose are restored. A large head of Aphrodite (c. 250–200 B.C.) was found at Cumae in Italy and acquired in 1821.

The second century B.C. is marked by a number of outstanding Roman copies: *Marsyas Bound Hand and Foot to a Tree* (c. 200–190) is one figure of a group composition with Apollo and Kithara seated on a rock with a slave ready to flay Marsyas; *Drunken Old Woman* (c. 200–180 B.C.), a genre piece attributed by the Romans to a sculptor called Myron, the only extant copy with the head preserved (with the body restorations based on a copy in Rome), was formerly in the collection of the Kurfürst Karl Theodor von der Pfaltz in Mannheim but came from the Antiquarium of the Munich Residenz in 1895; the head of a statue of a woman (c. 180 B.C.), perhaps a Muse; a female torso of eastern Greek origin known as the *Maiden of Cumae* (c. 130 B.C.), perhaps a statue of a Muse adapted to use as a portrait statue, with eighteenth-century restorations by Pacetti replaced in 1812 with restorations by Thorwaldsen; the *Head of Herakles* crowned in oak leaves (second century B.C.), one of many copies of a statue in which he carries a club and apples of the Hesperides and wears thick curly hair and an emphatic attitude; a satyr's head (c. 100 B.C.), known as the *Spotted Faun*, made in the second century A.D., found in the Via Appia, Rome, and acquired from the Villa Albani in 1816; and a bronze satyr's head from a statue (c. 100 B.C.), with a different color alloy for the mocking lips and with lost inlaid eyes, acquired from the Villa Albani, Rome, in 1815.

Another group of copies seems a step farther removed from Greek prototypes, since they were adapted to Roman uses. A leading example of these works is the *Apollo Barberini*, Apollo as Kitharodist, whose original was an early-fourth-century B.C. statue thought by the Romans to be by Scopas and transported by Augustus to the Palatine hill in Rome after his victory at Actium in 31 B.C., with separate bronze eyelashes and inlaid eyes of marble and precious stones, found at Tusculum and acquired from the Palazzo Barberini in 1815; a bronze head of a youth, an adaptation from the Classical style of the first century A.D., found in southern Italy and acquired from the Villa Albani in 1815; and a statue of Diana of the first century A.D., dependent on Greek prototypes, a technically brilliant, eclectic work with rigid pose and billowing drapery, found at Gabii near Rome and acquired in 1811.

There are several Roman portrait statues with some figures carved after Greek prototypes. The latter include a statue of a draped woman, with drapery of a third-century B.C. model, carved after the death of Trajan (c. A.D. 110–130), where the woman appears in the guise of Ceres holding poppies and corn; a statue of a dignified aristocratic draped woman, with a fifth-century B.C. pro-totype, carved during the reign of Marcus Aurelius (c. A.D. 161–180) with a shimmering drapery mantle over her head as if she were a high priestess, perhaps a member of the imperial family, acquired in 1814 from the Palazzo Bevilacqua in Verona; a headless statue of Livia, wife of Augustus (c. A.D. 14 and sub-sequent years), draped in accordance with a fourth-century B.C. prototype, with the inscription AUGUSTAE. IULIAE. DRUSI. E, found at Falerone near Rome and acquired in 1820 from the Palazzo Braschi; and a torso of a headless male nude portrait statue based on a fourth-century B.C. Greek Hermes, found at Frascati and acquired in 1811 from the Villa Aldobrandini. Other Roman portrait statues include a headless Roman imperator in armor (c. 70 B.C.), found at Frascati and acquired in 1930, and a heroic Domitian wearing a sword belt and formerly with a metal garland on his head (c. A.D. 70–80), found at Labricum near Rome and acquired in 1815 from the Villa Albani, Rome.

The collection includes an extraordinary number of Roman portrait heads and busts of members of imperial families and of individuals. Among the busts on display are: the posthumous bust *Augustus* (c. A.D. 40–50), acquired in 1815 from the Palazzo Bevilacqua, Verona; *Tiberius* (c. A.D. 14–37); *Trajan* (c. A.D. 100–110), in unique garb, including an oak leaf crown and aegis with Medusa head and snakes; and *Antinous*, the deified friend of Hadrian (c. A.D. 130–135)—all acquired in 1811 from the Palazzo Bevilacqua; as well as *Appolodorus* of Damascus, architect to Trajan and Hadrian (c. A.D. 140), a posthumous portrait acquired in Rome in 1820; *Antoninus Pius* (c. A.D. 150), in cuirass and cloak, originally acquired by the Casa Crescenzi, later displayed in the Palazzo

Gaetani, and then acquired in 1811 from the Palazzo Ruspoli in Rome; *Lucius Verus*, coregent with Marcus Aurelius, acquired from the Palazzo Bevilacqua; another *Lucius Verus* in his youth (c. A.D. 150), acquired in 1815 from the Villa Albani in Rome; *Commodus*, in cuirass and cloak (c. A.D. 180–192), acquired from the Palazzo Bevilacqua; *Septimius Severus* (c. A.D. 200–210), with cuirass and cloak, an 1815 acquisition from the Palazzo Bevilacqua; and a woman, perhaps Otacilla Severa, wife of Philip the Arab, emperor in A.D. 244–249, with a boldly brutal face. Imperial heads include: *Agrippina*, wife of Claudius, emperor in A.D. 41–54; *Caius Octavius*, father of Augustus (c. 60 B.C.); the colossal head *Titus*, emperor in A.D. 79–81; a woman with a tall diadem, perhaps *Empress Plotina*, wife of Trajan (c. A.D. 100–110); *Empress Faustina*, wife of Marcus Aurelius (c. A.D. 160–170) from Syria; the head *Commodus* (c. A.D. 180–92); *Caracalla as a Boy* (c. A.D. 196), with a family resemblance to the head of his mother, *Julia Domna*, wife of Septimius Severus (c. A.D. 195), found at Porcigliano and acquired in 1816 from the Palazzo Chigi in Rome; *Philip II*, son of Philip the Arab (A.D. 247–49); and a man, perhaps Decius, emperor in A.D. 249–51, acquired in 1967 from the Lenbachhaus in Munich.

In addition, there are nearly forty heads and busts of unknown Romans on display and an almost equal number in storage. They represent Roman portrait styles from about 50 B.C. to A.D. 400. Among them are the so-called *Marius* (c. 50–40 B.C.), and the so-called *Sulla* (c. 50–40 B.C.); woman with high curled coiffure (c. A.D. 80); *T. Caesernius Statianus*, statesman during the reigns of Hadrian and Antoninus Pius, from a statue in armor made about A.D. 130, incorporating two technical innovations, a carved hole to indicate the iris of the eye and use of drill in carving hair; a bust of a man with tunic and cloak (c. A.D. 170), acquired in 1811 from the Palazzo Bevilacqua, Verona; an elderly man with deceitful face wearing tunic and cloak and a second bust of the same individual in storage (c. A.D. 200), also from the Palazzo Bevilacqua; and a magnificent colossal bust of a man with close cropped hair and beard (c. A.D. 220–230).

There are many reliefs, both large and small, that filled a variety of functions originally. The *Honorary Inscription* (A.D. 40), with its pediment crown decorated with plant ornament, tells of the deeds of Saupheios Maker, priest of the Roman emperor cult, from Apollonia-on-the-Rhyndacus in northern Asia Minor; the grave relief *Nikolaos of Miletos, Son of Euodos* (first century A.D.), which came in 1920 from the Antiquarium of the Munich Residenz; the *Priestess Sacrificing at an Altar* (first century A.D.) from the same source at the same date; the grave relief *Eutaktos, Son of Eutaktos* (c. second century A.D.), perhaps from the island of Paros from the same source as the above; an Attic votive relief (second century A.D.), with two figures of Pan, a pine tree, and an altar below a circle of dancing nymphs within a hekateion, acquired in Greece in 1878; and two exquisite first-century A.D. landscape panel reliefs, *Peasant Drives His Cow to Market*, found in Rome in 1858, and the *Herd of Cattle in a Rocky Landscape*, acquired in 1814 from the Palazzo Rondanini in Rome.

Other small reliefs in storage include one with a standing young man and young woman worshipping a Herm, which models the woman on the Nike untying her sandal on the balustrade of the Nike Temple on the Acropolis in Athens (c. 410 B.C.); a low relief with a dancing girl and another with Hercules; a very low relief with a dancing satyr; an archaizing relief with Dionysos, Maenad, and Faun; two very high reliefs with portrait busts of women from the Near East.

On exhibit are three very large and important reliefs. The earliest one consists of two blocks depicting fighting gladiators, probably from a much larger monument. Next is the relief frieze from a large rectangular monument found in Rome, which may have been dedicated by Gellius, a censor of Rome in 70 B.C., as an offering for success in suppressing pirates in the Tyrrenian Sea and that many publications refer to as the *Altar of Domitus Ahenobarbus*. The three blocks depicting the wedding procession of Poseidon and Amphitrite (one long side and two short), acquired in 1816 from the Palazzo Santa Croce in Rome, and the second long side (a cast from the original in the Louvre in Paris), with its scene of censors sacrificing in the Campus Martius, together embody the most extensive sculptural decoration that survives from that period. A section of the frieze of the Basilica Ulpia, built by Emperor Trajan in A.D. 112, excavated and with its famous column of the most admirable sights in Rome, depicts goddesses of victory wreathing with laurel the richly ornamented stands where incense burns. This is one of the many repetitions of this four-figured group that continuously decorated the basilica below its heavy cornice.

A number of impressive Roman sarcophagi are included in the collection: a sarcophagus with a relief depicting Orestes rescuing Ephigenia from the Taurians (c. A.D. 130–140), acquired in 1817 from the Villa Ridolfi in Rome, illustrates the tale of Euripedes, "Iphigenia in Taurus." The small sarcophagus of a girl named Flaminia, dedicated by her father, whose inscription is installed in the wall above the entrance to the small domed room, depicts the childhood of Dionysos (Bacchus) among mountain nymphs and satyrs (c. A.D. 140), acquired in Rome in 1815 from the Villa Albani.

Others are a sarcophagus with the marriage of Dionysos (Bacchus) and Ariadne (c. A.D. 140–150), acquired in 1812 from the Palazzo Braschi in Rome, with a burial cart drawn by a male and a female centaur led by another cart drawn by panthers carrying Semele, led by two satyrs and Silenos; the front panel of a sarcophagus with similar subject material (c. A.D. 150–160), found at Ostia and acquired in 1826, with the bridal pair in a relief-decorated cart drawn by music-making centaurs led by drunken satrys and the Maenads, Eros and Pan; one with the death of the seven sons and seven daughters of Niobe on its front, with the relief lid showing the slain children and a gable portrayal of the grieving mother (c. A.D. 160–170), found in the Via Appia in Rome and acquired in 1828; still another with elements of the myth of Selene and Endymion (c. A.D. 180) depicting Hypnos sprinkling poppy juice from a cornucopia on the sleeping Endymion, watched by Selene riding on a crab, and Latmos, god of the mountain, and Ge, goddess of earth, on the left side of Selene departing, driven by Eos and Eros, found at Ostia and acquired in 1826; one with Apollo, Athena, and the nine Muses (c. A.D. 200) on display in the East Court of the Antikensammlungen; a large, recently acquired (1967) sarcophagus, with a man and his wife holding hands within a shell-shaped aedicula centered on the front, which is otherwise decorated with ripple ornament (c. A.D. 240), with an image of Hymen with a flaming torch at the feet of the couple and at the corners, he as a philosopher (right) and she as a Muse; and fragments acquired in 1969 and 1971 of a sarcophagus with exceptionally fine carving (c. A.D. 250–260), with motifs reconstructed through the help of a similar one in Rome that depicts the dead man in armor, Virtus armed, and the dead man as a lion slayer with companions.

Two fine mosaics are on display; the large (c. A.D. 150–200), 5.25 meters square, from a Roman villa at Sentinum, now Sassoferrato, Umbria, Italy has a central field 2.00 meters square, with depictions of Mithras and the twelve signs of the zodiac and Tellus with the four seasons. A smaller square mosaic consists entirely of geometric design, a trick pattern of cubes conveying a three-dimensional illusion.

Three modern pieces are on exhibit in the inner courtyard of the Glyptothek: a modern bronze cast of the imposing large ancient marble *Head of Hadrian*, found in the Mausoleum of Hadrian in Rome (now the Castel Sant' Angelo) and housed in the Vatican Museums (q.v.), acquired in 1815 from the Palazzo Barberini; an eighteenth-century marble base inscribed "Greek work dug up on the Esquiline Hill to the benefit of the Arts," which once supported a Roman copy of the renowned Diskobolos by Myron; and a column of Untersberg marble from the interior entrance hall of Friedrich von Zieland's neoclassical museum on the south side of the Königplatz facing the Glyptothek, which since 1967 has housed the Antikensammlungen in a rebuilt modern interior.

Today the director, curators, and various staff members of the Glyptothek are employees of the Bayerisches Kultursministerium, which provides support for this public museum. The pre-war Bayerischer Verein der Kunstfreunde has been superceded by the Verein der Freunde und Förderer der Glyptothek und der Antikensammlungen (Society of the Friends and Promoters of the Glyptothek and the Antikensammlungen) as the active supporting membership organization. The Glyptothek and Antikensammlungen share offices for the curatorial staff in the Antikensammlungen and administrative offices at Karolinen Platz 4, Munich 2, Germany. There is a modest reference library for the exclusive use of the joint curatorial staffs in the Antikensammlungen. Photographs of published objects in the collection may be purchased for scholarly purposes. Tourist photographs and slides are for sale in the museum shop for many outstanding items in the collection. The latest guidebook, *The Munich Glyptothek: Greek and Roman Sculpture*, 1974, is published in several languages, with forty-eight plates illustrating outstanding pieces in the collection. It is the most recent in a long series of guides beginning with Adolf Furtwangler's *Beschreibung der Glypto-*

thek, 1830, and continuing with updates by Paul Wolters in 1910 and more recently preceded by Paul Wolters' *Führer durch die Glyptothek*, 1935.

Selected Bibliography

Museum publications: *Katalog Jubilausstellung: Glyptothek München, 1830–1980*, herausgegeben von K. Vierneisel and G. Leinz, 1980; Vierneisel-Schlorb, B., *Katalog der Skulpturen*, Band 2, *Klassische Skulpturen des 5 und 4 Jahrhunderts vor Christ*, 1979; idem, *Katalog der Skulpturen*, Band 3, *Klassische und Hellenistische Grabdenmaler und Votivreliefs* (forthcoming).

Other Publications: Arndt-Amelung, *Photographische Einzelaufnahmen antiker skulpturen* (Munich 1893–1947); Arndt, P., *Grieschische und römische Porträts* (Munich 1891–1942); Beazley, J. D., and B. Ashmole, *Greek Sculpture and Painting to the End of the Hellenistic Period* (New York 1966); Becatti, G., *The Art of Ancient Greece and Rome* (New York 1967); Bieber, M., *Ancient Copies* (New York 1977); idem, *Sculpture of the Hellenistic Age* (New York 1967); Brilliant, R., *Roman Art* (London and New York 1974); Brunn, H., and F. Bruckmann, *Denkmäler grieschischer und römischer Skulptur*, continued by P. Arndt and G. Lippold (Munich 1888–1947); Furtwangler, A., *Masterpieces of Greek Sculpture* (Chicago 1964); Invernizzi, A., *I frontoni del tempio di Aphaia ad Agina* (Torino 1965); Lippold, R., *Kopien und Umbildungen grieschischer Statuen* (1923); Ohly, D., *Die Aeginetan* (Munich 1976); Richter, G.M.A., *Kouroi* (London 1970); idem, *Sculpture and Sculptors of the Greeks* (New Haven 1970); Ridgway, B. S., *The Archaic Style in Greek Sculpture* (Princeton, N.J. 1977); idem, *The Severe Style in Greek Sculpture* (Princeton, N.J. 1970); idem, *Fifth Century Style in Greek Sculpture* (Princeton, N.J. 1981); Strong, E., *Roman Sculpture* (New York 1969); Willers, Dietrich, *Zu den Anfängen der Archaistischen Plastik in Griechenland* (Berlin 1975); Zschietzschmann, W., *Die Hellenistische und römische Kunst* (Potsdam 1939).

ELEANOR GURALNICK

NEUE PINAKOTHEK, Prinzregenterstrasse 1, Munich.

The Neue Pinakothek was officially opened in 1853. While building the Alte Pinakothek (q.v.; 1826–36), King Ludwig I of Bavaria had been contemplating another picture gallery to house his considerable collection of contemporary art. This plan was realized in 1846. The foundation was laid on October 12, the anniversary of the king's wedding. The building was financed privately by the royal family, with the stipulation that it was to contain only works "created not earlier than the nineteenth century." It was Ludwig's third museum building after the Glyptothek (q.v.) and the Alte Pinakothek, both designed by Leo von Klenze and considered architectural masterpieces. Conceived as a counterpart to the Alte Pinakothek, the two rectangular buildings, arranged parallel to each other, formed a cube separated by a tree-lined avenue, the Theresienstrasse. The official architect was August von Voit, primarily known for his cast-iron construction of the glass palace. New research reveals, however, that a considerable contribution was made by his teacher Friedrich von Gärtner, the architect for the lower part of the Ludwigsstrasse, and today is considered of equal importance to von Klenze. Immense outside frescoes, executed by Friedrich Christoph Nilson after oil sketches by Wilhelm von Kaulbach, court painter to Ludwig I and director of the famous Munich Academy, depicted "the latest developments in the arts." The sketches escaped the turmoil of World War II and now are exhibited in Room 12 of the new museum. The original building was not well received; the frescoes and particularly the arrangement of the exhibition areas were strongly criticized.

A decade after its opening, the space had become too limited to house the rapidly expanding collection but plans to enlarge it were not realized. In 1916 the museum changed hands and became the property of the Bavarian State. During World War II, the building was severely damaged and was demolished in 1949, unlike its counterpart the Alte Pinakothek, which was restored and reopened in 1969.

Starting in 1960, attempts were made to find a suitable architect to design a new building and in 1967 Freiherr von Branca was chosen from among more than 280 contestants. The foundation was laid in 1975, and in 1981 the $44.5 million building was reopened. Opinions are sharply divided, but the new Neue Pinakothek is certainly one of the most arresting and remarkable architectural statements made recently. The building consists of two linked parts, the administrative area, for offices and restoration workshops, and the museum itself, all of which encircle eight garden courts. The main building is concrete covered with cream sandstone. The long expanses of walls are broken by mullioned windows, ramparts, and gutter spouts reminiscent of medieval or Gothic buildings. Exterior staircases with timbertrussed roofs add to the eccentric but pleasing view. The entrance is glass with more mullioned windows. Although the exterior received considerable criticism, the galleries are generally praised. The thirty-five rooms are arranged in the form of a figure-eight with filtered, natural ceiling light, a prime consideration in designing the building, and silk wall hangings and parquet floors. The Neue Pinakothek, like all museums owned by the Bavarian State, is governed by the German Ministry of Culture and staffed by a director and several curators.

When the museum originally opened its doors in 1853, the collection consisted of roughly three hundred works; at the king's death in 1868, it had grown to more than four hundred and now is in excess of forty-five hundred, making it one of Europe's most important collections of nineteenth-century art. Its core are paintings from the "Münchener Schule." In 1841 the king purchased Leo von Klenze's collection of more than a hundred works, including paintings by von Koch, Rottman, Catel, and Quaglio. After Ludwig I's abdication in 1848, the museum's collecting activity practically came to a halt; only a few additions were made. Among them were Wilhelm Feuerbach's *Medea* and Moritz von Schwind's *Symphonie*, both acquired from the estate of Otto of Greece. In the late 1880s Spitzweg's *Poor Poet*, Böcklin's *Play of the Waves*, and Leibl's *In der Bauernstube* were given to the museum. In 1891 Hans von Marées' friend Conrad Fiedler donated fifteen of the artist's paintings, two pastels, and two cartoons.

After the formulation of the Secessionist Movement in Munich, the first Symbolist and Art Nouveau works were acquired, among them Khnopff's *I Lock My Door upon Myself* and Stuck's *Sin*. In 1907 the museum purchased its first Impressionist works, and in 1937, after considerable legal difficulties with the estate, six works by Adolf von Menzel were added. The final and most important addition to the collection was the Tschudi bequest. Hugo von Tschudi became director of the State Galleries in Munich in 1909 after resigning as director of the Berlin National Gallery because of acquisition disputes. His appreciation of French painters such as Daumier, Courbet, Manet, and Cézanne had met with little understanding from the emperor or the local artists. Soon similar problems arose in Munich. He acquired Géricault's *Artillery Train Passing a Ravine*, Courbet's *Sluice of Optevoz*, Manet's *Le dejeuner*, and works by Gauguin, van Gogh, the Nabis, Hodler, and Matisse. After his death in 1911, money was raised by his friends, among them Franz Bley, Bernheim-Jeune, Durand-Ruel, Rodin, and Bonnard, for the Tschudi bequest, which included Pissarro's *Street in Upper Norwood*, Gauguin's *Breton Peasant Women*, Daumier's *Drama*, and Manet's *Barge*. In 1914 Friedrich Dornhoffer became the director of the collection and, until his retirement in 1933, concentrated primarily on acquiring works by German Romantic artists such as Friedrich, Catel, Rottmann, Böcklin, Feuerbach, and the Leibl circle.

World War II brought collecting activities to a standstill; however, in the fifties and sixties works by Delacroix, Degas, Klimt, Ensor, Bonnard, Goya, and David were added. Since 1968 the Neue Pinakothek has tried to close the gaps in the neglected area of English painting of the eighteenth and nineteenth centuries, acquiring Germany's finest collection with works by Gainsborough, Romney, Wilson, Raeburn, and Turner.

The collection now roughly embraces two centuries. The earliest work is Gainsborough's *Portrait of Sir Uvedale Tomkins Price*, about 1760; the most recent one, Slevogt's *Sunny Garden Corner*, about 1931. The galleries are arranged chronologically, beginning with international art, about 1800, including Jacques Louis David's *Portrait of the Marquise de Sorcy de Thelusson*, Antonio Canova's statue of *Paris*, a group of English portraits and landscapes, Gainsborough's *Landscape with Shepherd and Flock*, and Goya's *Country Outing*. The next two rooms are devoted to early Romantic painting with Caspar David Friedrich's *Riesengebirge*, Kersting's *Young Woman at Lamp Light*, and Wilhelm von Kobell's *Tegernsee*.

Court art during the time of Ludwig I of Bavaria is represented by Karl Rottmann's *Sikyon and Korinth*, his two landscape cycles, and Josef Karl Stieler's famous *Portrait of Johann Wolfgang von Goethe*. Anton Koch's *Heroic Landscape with Rainbow* exemplifies the ideals of the German classicist painters in Rome. Special among the group of German artists living in Rome were the Nazarenes, a religious brotherhood based on medieval principles. They are represented at the museum with works of Pforr, Cornelius, Veit, Schadow, and Schnorr von Carolsfeld and particularly with Overbeck's famous *Italia and Germanica*.

The romantic tendencies of the Biedermeier and a preference for calm interiors, bourgeois portraits, genre paintings, and gentle landscapes are shown in Moritz von Schwind's *The Visit* and Ferdinand Georg Waldmuller's *The Expected*. Millet's *Le greffeur*, and Géricault's *Heroic Landscape with Fishermen*, Delacroix's *Clorinde Rescues Olindo and Sophronia from the Stake*, and Corot's early Italian *Landscape near Riva at Lake Garda* demonstrate the ideals of the French late Romantic and Realist artists. German late Romantic and Realist painting is represented with Spitzweg's *The Poor Poet* and Adolf von Menzel's *Room with Sister*. Separate exhibition galleries are devoted to the Kaulbach designs, Hans von Marées (*The Golden Age*), Böcklin, Feuerbach, Thoma, and the Leibl circle. Of particular interest are Böcklin's *Pan in the Reeds*, Feuerbach's *Medea*, and Leibl's *Portrait of Mrs. Gedon*. Manet's *Breakfast in the Atelier*, Monet's *Bridge over the Seine*, Degas' *Ironing Woman*, Cézanne's *Railroad Tunnel*, van Gogh's *View of Arles*, and Gauguin's *Birth* represent the French Impressionists and Post-Impressionists. Max Liebermann's *Woman with Goats* and Lovis Corinth's *Portrait of Keyserling* represent German Social Realism, and Max Klinger's sculpture of *Elsa Asenijeff*, Fernand Khnopff's *I Lock My Door upon Myself*, and Gustav Klimt's *Portrait of Margarethe Stonborough-Wittgenstein* represent the Secessionist, Symbolist, and Art Nouveau movements.

In addition to the permanent collections, one large and two small exhibition galleries are available for special and traveling exhibitions as well as print exhibitions.

Two important departments located in the Neue Pinakothek are the Doerner Institut and the Restoration Department. The staff of the Restoration Department consists of six restorers, two doctors of chemistry, two chemotechnical assistants, and a secretary. It is responsible for all paintings belonging to the collections of the Bavarian State and occasionally assists other collections with special problems.

The Doerner Institut, originally an independent private institution, became part of the Bavarian State collections in 1956. Its main concerns are research in art history and painting techniques, as well as chemical analysis. Its laboratory is available to all collections and museums of the Bavarian State, as well as Denkmalpflege and Schlosserverwaltung. Every Tuesday morning free advisory services are available to the public at which information on paintings is given with assistance from the museum's art historians. Technical examinations and authenticity reports for private individuals are provided on paintings, sculpture, and so on for a fee.

The art library is not open to the public, but slides and photographs of the collection may be purchased by application to the Photo Archives. Special tours can be arranged through the museum's Pedagogic Center.

An annual report listing the activities, additions to the collection, personnel changes, and so on is published by the museum.

Selected Bibliography

Museum publications: *Neue Pinakothek München*, a guide to the exhibited collection, 1981; *Die Neue Pinakothek in München*, complete guide to the collection, 1981; Hardtwig,

Barbara, *Nach-Barock und Klassizismus*, 1978; Eschenburg, Barbara et al., *Spatromantik und Realismus*, 1981; Ludwig, Horst, *Malerei der Grunderzeit*, 1977.

RUTH ZIEGLER

Stuttgart

STATE GALLERY, STUTTGART (officially STAATSGALERIE STUTT-GART; alternately STUTTGART STATE GALLERY; also STUTTGARTER GALERIE), Konrad Adenauer Strasse 32, 7000 Stuttgart 1.

Like that of many German museums, the Staatsgalerie Stuttgart's origin can be traced to the collection of a local resident ruler, in this case the House of Württemberg. However, little of the seventeenth-century inventory has survived as part of the museum's present holdings. It consisted chiefly of ancestral portraiture, hunting scenes, and natural science curios, none of which were of great artistic importance.

Not until the erection of the Baroque residential palace in Ludwigsburg in 1704 did the Gallery begin to take shape. With the acquisition of the collection of Count Gustav Adolf von Gotter in 1736, it gained distinction by adding significant paintings such as one by Memling, as well as examples of the Dutch and the German Baroque schools. In 1760 the court painter Nicolas Guibal was appointed director of the Ludwigsburger Collection, establishing a precedent that did not prove to be advantageous to the Gallery. Throughout the nineteenth century, an artist held the post of director, frequently to the detriment of the institution. Lacking historical perspective and totally immersed in the prevailing emphasis on classicism, these directors limited the scope of acquisitions. Thus scarce interest in Early German art as well as false economy led to the museum's failure to acquire the incomparable assemblage of Early German and Netherlandish art by the famed Boisserée brothers, even though it was actually on exhibit at the museum from 1819 to 1827. Stuttgart's loss became Munich's gain.

All of this changed with the erection of the present building in 1843, when certain forces emerged that helped steer the museum in a new direction. The official opening of the museum was on May 1, 1843. The style of the building can best be described as ''Swabian Classicist.'' It was designed by Georg Gottlieb Barth. Among those furthering the cause of the museum was King Wilhelm I of Württemberg, who assured it the acquisition of the Pinacoteca Barbini Breganze Collection in 1852, thus adding Italian paintings to the inventory. These years also saw the expansion of Early German and particularly Swabian art and the purchase of Rembrandt's *Paulus in Prison* in 1867.

Major changes occurred at the turn of the century, when artist-directors made way for directorship by art historians, which led to sweeping reforms in the approach to acquisitions. By complementing and strengthening existing holdings and including contemporary artists, the museum developed its present character. The year 1906 saw the founding of the Stuttgarter Gallery Association, whose primary purpose was to raise funds for the purchase of additional art in the spirit of the new policy.

The existence of the Gallery during the thirties was completely overshadowed by the destructive cultural activities of the Nazi regime. In 1937 almost all of the modern, Post-Impressionist and "non-Aryan" works were confiscated, from Kirchner to Klee, from Baumeister and Schlemmer to Nolde and Beckmann, from Liebermann to Corinth, and from Lehmbruck to Barlach. In 1930 the museum's space was expanded by an annex, the Crown Prince Palace, which was used primarily to house Württemberg art. However, the bombardments of 1944 completely destroyed both buildings (the paintings were safely hidden). After 1945 the Staatsgalerie was slowly rebuilt and reopened with a festive ceremony in the presence of President Theodor Heuss. However, the princely palace fell victim to the modernization of the rebuilt city and thus was never erected again. An expansive new wing, designed by the famed British architect James Stirling, was opened in 1984, contributing considerably to the status of the museum and its function through the extension of facilities such as display of sculptures and graphics, seminar rooms, and an auditorium.

In the post-war years the Gallery emerged from its more regional confines to develop into a museum with international scope. This was particularly true in the area of modern art, where a new beginning had to be made to repair the ravages of Nazism. With the Moltzau Collection, the museum, in 1959, came into possession of important works by Renoir, Gauguin, Cézanne, and Matisse and a series of Cubist compositions by Picasso and Braque. Nor were other, earlier periods neglected: Rubens, Rembrandt, Bouts, and Ruisdael joined the ranks, and certain areas of Italian Baroque, Early German, and Italian art were furthered strengthened.

The full panorama of trends in United States found representation at the Gallery, which was to acquire the first Jackson Pollock in Germany and contains examples of Pop Art, Hard Edge, environments, and Super-Realism. It is a full representation of American and European art trends of our times that has few rivals in Germany.

The museum is state supported under the aegis of the Ministry of Science and Art. The administration is entrusted to a director, his associate, and nine curators, each of whom heads a department. The librarian heads a library devoted mostly to research.

The original collection of the Staatsgalerie has all but disappeared. One of its great strengths lies in its holdings of Early German church art, with emphasis on Swabian art from the fourteenth to the sixteenth century. Others are German classicists and Romantics, with Dutch and Italian art until the eighteenth century. Outstanding are the collections of nineteenth- and twentieth-century paintings of Germany, France, and the United States and international groups of art from after 1945. An extensive collection of graphics spans the last three centuries to the present. Of the four thousand paintings in the Gallery's possession, about six hundred are permanently displayed.

Both artistically and historically, the Early German department is outstanding.

In pieces of highest quality and great rarity it offers a splendid opportunity for the study of the development of German panel painting. It begins with the Swabian *Throne of Solomon* (c. 1335). Its architectural step design is closely linked to the style of the Cloister of Bebenhausen for which it was created. Its spiritual as well as aesthetic approach, with flat figures and gold leaf background, is typical of its period. Greater realism is evident in the so-called *Prague Altar* of 1385, with its wing panels, painted on both sides, where presentation of its donor and family shows individual expression and greater worldliness.

Although the *Ulmer Altar* of 1405 survives only in fragments, it is a fine example of International Gothic, characterized by a softer style. Links to the French bookmasters are suggested in the glowing colors and inventiveness of fine detailing. The Master of the Göttinger Altar depicts in the *Noli me tangere* panel a delightful array of trees, fruit, and flowers (botanically accurate) that dates from the time when such details became popular (see also *Garden of Paradise* from the same period at the Städelsche Kunstinstitut [q.v.], Frankfurt).

Hans Strigel the Younger's *Annunciation* panel (1465) has an interesting history: its companion wing, lost since 1803, surfaced at an auction in London in 1972, so the two wings, thanks to the loan by its present owner, have now been united after 169 years apart.

Trends adapted from Netherlandish paintings appear in the Master of the Darmstädter Passion in the *Sterzinger Altar*, with its dramatic procession of the Three Kings and its new realism, monumental form and bold color. Its proportions are generous (165.5 by 141.9 centimeters).

The school of Ulm is well represented with masters such as Bartholomeus Zeitbolm and his *Eschacher Altar* (1496), which shows elegantly elongated figures and restrained backgrounds. Zeitblom's contemporary portrayal of Bernhard Strigel foreshadows some of Dürer's work in his three panels of *St. Mary's Altar*.

The Master of the Pullendorfer Altar proved himself an artist of extraordinary originality in his vivid portrayal of the prophets, each seemingly peering out of a window, panels that form parts of his *Life of Mary Altar*.

Works by artists such as Martin Schaffner and his *Entombment of Christ* point toward the Renaissance and attest to the influence of Dürer. Among Dürer's followers seen here are Hans Schäufelein, *Adoration of the Kings*, Hans Süss van Kulmbach, *St. Sebastian*, and Hans Baldung called Grien, with his *Christ the Sufferer* and a portrait, *Hans Jakob zu Morsperg*. Out of the same circle emerged the Master of Messkirch, whose *St. Benedict as Hermit* (1540) with its dramatic landscape background symbolizes the three ruling classes with cloister, castle, and town.

The highlight of the department is the work of Jorg Ratgeb. His *Herrenberger Altar*, impressive in size (274 by 147 centimeters), depicts the Passion of Christ in terms mirroring the tempestuous times in which he lived (and was a victim of) with violent and expressive movement. A predella with the *Handkerchief of St. Veronica* flanked by angels shows definite influence by Dürer.

Although altar panels are the focus of the department, one also finds examples of portraiture. They are Lucas Cranach the Younger's *Caspar and Anna von Minkwitz* (1543), Hans Holbein the Younger's *Self Portrait as St. Sebastian*, and Hans Burgkmair's *Portrait of a Nobleman in Golden Helmet*. A recent addition to this group is Bernhard Strigel's *Portrait of an Elderly Man*.

One can trace the close contact of German painters with Netherlandish art in examples such as Albert Bouts' *Christ and Mary* and Dirk Jacobsz's interesting double portrait of donors, with its wing shape and elegant Italianate landscape background. One of the highlights is the Hans Memling *Bathsheba in the Bath* with its elongated proportions (191.5 by 84.6 centimeters). Another important work is by Rembrandt van Ryn, *Paulus in Prison*, as well as his touching *Self Portrait with Red Cap* (1660) and *Tobias Healing His Father*. Other Dutch masters are represented with two Frans Hals portraits (*Portrait of a Young Woman and Man*) and Rubens, Snyders, and Pieter Jansz Pourbus, with landscapes by van Goyen, Ruysdael, and Miron. Among the still lifes, the trompe-l'oeil *Studio Wall* by Hieronymus Hastner is strikingly modern in feeling.

Italian holdings show greatest strength in the Venetian school, but the earliest work is a set of unique panels by a Neapolitan master dated 1340, of the *Apocalypse of St. John*, heavily gilded on a dark background. Florentine in origin is the austere painted *Crucifix* by Orcagna, also about 1340, as well as the *Madonna and Child* by Lorenzo Monaco.

Outstanding among the fifteenth- and sixteenth-century Venetian masters is the monumental (264 by 171 centimeters) *Sacra Conversazione* by Vittore Carpaccio. Others are Jacopo Tintoretto's *Ascension of Christ* and the *Holy Family with Saints* by Veronese. Among the lesser-known artists the *Portrait of a Man* by Francesco Salviati testifies in its elegance to the great popularity of this artist as a portraitist.

Giambattista Tiepolo's visit to Würzburg in 1751 resulted in ceiling and mural designs for the residential palace. One of them, *Apollo Leading Beatrice to Frederic I*, part of a series, provides an illuminating example of the splendor of Venetian Baroque. The same artist also painted the softly romantic *Rest on the Flight to Egypt*.

The lighthearted spirit of Venice is captured in a fine *Veduta* by Antonio Canaletto and in the two gay *Capricci* by Guardi and Marieschi. Rosalba Carriera delights with a female portrait called *Watchfulness*. Italian Baroque holdings have recently increased by the addition of works by Frederico Bencovich, Baldassare Franceschini (Il Volterrano), Pellegrini, and Pittoni.

Giovanni Paolo Pannini's *Roma Antica* is a tour de force of monumental proportions (169 by 227 centimeters), showing an imaginary Roman gallery with deep perspective, full of pictures of famous Roman antiquities. Other Italians displayed are Luca Giordano and Andrea Locatelli along with some of lesser note.

Among the earlier French paintings there is the elegant *Portrait of a Lady* by Jean Marc Nattier. A modest group of nineteenth-century French art includes the outstanding Gustave Courbet *Seascape in an Approaching Storm*, a recent acquisition. Camille Corot points the way toward Impressionism with his *Faggot-Gatherers Around a Big Oak*. Examples of the work of Delacroix and Géricault round out the group, bridging the transition to Impressionism as represented by the Pierre Auguste Renoir *Portrait of Mme. Choquet* (1875) and by Edouard Manet with his *Artist in Studio*, done in light, sketchy brushstrokes. Great sensitivity to nature, the earmark of Impressionism is exemplified with four paintings that offer a good study of various styles and approaches. A delicately conceived snowscape, *Winter in Louveciennes*, by Alfred Sisley contrasts with the joyful *Fields in Spring* by Claude Monet; Camille Pissarro's *Seine at Port Marly* displays poetic realism while Monet's *Coast at Etrétat* borders on the abstract.

A painting by Pissarro, *The Gardener*, has an interesting history: acquired by the Gallery in 1901, the painting was confiscated because the artist was Jewish and exchanged in 1937, it later turned up in Argentina, and was repurchased by the museum in 1962.

Early still lifes like *Apples* by James Ensor afford insight into that artist's beginning style, quite different from what was to follow. Impressionists evolve into the Post-Impressionism of Cézanne (*Bathers*) and Paul Gauguin's Tahitian *Where Are You Going*. The style develops further with interiors by Vallotton and Vuillard. A large genre scene, *Famille Terrasse*, is by Pierre Bonnard.

Moving to the twentieth century, we find the work of Georges Rouault, such as his famed *Ecce Homo*, and a very typical Amadeo Modigliani, *Nude*. Three landscapes are grouped together: *Seine* by Maurice Vlaminck; *Boats* by André Derain and *Le Havre* by Raoul Dufy. Sculptures by Giacometti, Ossip Zadkine, Aristide Maillol, and Wilhelm Lehmbruck are shown along with these paintings.

One of the most comprehensive collections in Germany of the work of Pablo Picasso can be found here. Samples of his Blue Period such as *Crouching Figure* (1902) and *Artistes* (1905) are followed by his Cubist stint as in *Violin* (1912), the classic *Seated Woman* (1921), and the abstract *Buffet of Restaurant* (1943). Others of his era such as Georges Braque and Juan Gris testify to his powerful influence. Fernand Léger is represented by the abstraction *Three Sisters*.

The more recent trends of modern art make up the ever-expanding holdings of the Gallery's collection in contemporary styles. A room devoted to Surrealism displays all of its most famous proponents such as Salvador Dali, Kurt Schwitters, and Man Ray. René Margritte is represented with his mystical *The Apparition*, Max Ernst with *Homage à Violette* and *Bird Wedding*, and Giorgio de'Chirico with *Metaphysical Interior with Factory* (1916). Dadaism and other trends find expression in several small Paul Klees and works by Marcel Duchamp, Dubuffet, the Futurist Italian Giacomo Ballà, and the Russian Constructivist Natalia Gontcharova.

The many facets of American art after 1945 are displayed in depth. The three-dimensional works range from George Segal's white-cast figures to a Calder *Black Mobile*, an Edward Kienholz environment (*The Birthday*), and the Super-Realistic Duane Hanson figure *Cleaning Woman*. Abstractions, soft stain, and

Hard Edge vie with each other in paintings by Rothko, Morris Louis, Jackson Pollock, Mark Tobey, Robert Motherwell, and Franz Kline. Pop Art creations include pieces by Andy Warhol, Rauschenberg, and Lichtenstein. The international gallery runs the gamut from Victor Vasarély, Lucio Fontana, and Jean Tinguely to Yves Klein and packages by Christo. A group of structural designs, all white on white, are noteworthy and include the work of Jesus Rafael Soto, Heinz Mack, Gunther Uecker, and Jan J. Sxhoonhoven.

In tracing the history of earlier German paintings in the gallery, we find a gap of several centuries and take up the thread with eighteenth- and nineteenth-century painters such as Angelica Kauffmann and her *Portrait of Freifrau von Bauer*. It continues with luminist Romantics such as Caspar David Friedrich in his splendid, peaceful *Bohemian Landscape* and Eduard Gärtner's *Bridge in Berlin* (dated 1842). Classicism comes to the fore in a room dominated by the larger-than-life portrait bust *Friedrich Schiller* by his friend Johann Heinrich von Dannecker, whose small sculptures on view also drew inspiration from the classics. The same is true of the large neoclassicist portrait *Frau von Cotta* by Christian Gottlieb Schick and the mournful, expansive (192.5 by 126.5 centimeters) *Iphigenie* of Anselm Feuerbach. Deep gloom prevails around the *Villa by the Sea* by Arnold Böcklin.

In a lighter mood are paintings such as Karl Spitzweg's *The Alchemist* and Adolf Menzl's *Mask Supper*. Rural and peasant genre scenes document the era in the work of Johann Baptist Pflug and Johann Jakob Biedermann, and the Austrian Ferdinand Waldmüller showed a heavy hand in his *Portrait of Mrs. Winiwarth and Son*. Hans Thoma charms with a landscape. Still other artists on view include Wilhelm Leibl, Fritz von Uhde, Karl Schuch, and Josef Anton Koch. Ferdinand Hodler's severe style is softened in his *Genfer Lake*, but in his giant design for the mural *Retreat at Marignano*, he showed his usual heroic mood.

Impressionist tendencies assert themselves in works such as the ones of Max Slevogt, whose dashing *D'Andrade as Don Juan* (1902) is one of his best-known pictures. In his *Old People's Home* Max Liebermann combined an Impressionist style with somber Dutch colors, and Lovis Corinth in one of his numerous *Walchensee* paintings displayed great intensity of color and feeling.

A strong impact leading to Expressionism was exerted by the Norwegian Edvard Munch, among whose works *Four Girls* is particularly noteworthy. Egon Schiele with the somber *City View* and Paula Modersohn Becker with the *Self Portrait* are also significant in setting the trend.

Condemned by the Nazis as decadent, much of this Gallery's pre-war modern holdings were dispersed and had to be reassembled after the war. Expressionism, a particular anathema to Nazism, was an especially strong movement in Germany under the leadership of the group called Die Brücke (founded in 1905), whose prominent member was Ernst Ludwig Kirchner. His *Landscape with Figures* typifies the mood and style. His contemporary, Oskar Kokoschka, created portraits of deep psychological insight such as *Woman in Blue*. Emile Nolde leaned toward Matisse in *Dancers*. Franz Marc with his *Little Yellow Horses* was also a member of Die Brücke.

Without doubt, one of the most important recent gifts to the Gallery is the group of seven full-sized costume mannequins of the *Triadic Ballet* by Oscar Schlemmer, donated by a local bank in 1979 after being reconstructed from the artist's sketches. This extraordinarily versatile artist, a victim of Nazi harassment, whose wide scope included architectural, theater, and ballet design, can be fully appreciated here with examples of masks, constructions, collages, and large panels of a cycle called *Instruction*.

His work is shown along with a magnificent group of ten sculptures by Hans Arp, among which the sensuous *Pyrenaen Torso* (1959) is one of his best works. Here, too, we find examples of the work of Mondrian, Willi Baumeister, Josef Albers, Moholy Nagy, and others associated with the Bauhaus movement.

A large, tumultuous canvas by George Gross fuses Expressionism with Cubism in the emotional *Funeral of the Poet Panizza*, 1917–18. Other modern classics comprising the extensive Lütze Collection are by Emile Nolde, Käthe Kollwitz, and Franz Marc, with sculptures by Lehmbruck and Barlach.

The collection of drawings, watercolors, and graphics is made up of three hundred thousand pieces. They span the Italian Baroque, French eighteenth century, and nineteenth-century Germany. On display to the public only for special exhibits, they can be viewed on certain days in their storage area. The strongest point of the collection lies in the twentieth century, where new acquisitions constantly bring it up to date. The four-to-eight yearly exhibitions at the museum are augmented by several circulating shows throughout the provinces as well as abroad.

Although state supported, the museum is the recipient of considerable donations from various sources. The Stuttgart Galerie Verein (Association) constantly collects funds to be used for the purchase of new works.

Research facilities consist of a library of about forty-five thousand volumes and various archives, notably one of Oscar Schlemmer. The museum also has a restoration and photography studio.

The museum shop has a selection of postcards, posters, prints, and slides on sale. The wide selection of museum catalogues is considered outstanding and has received many prizes for its high quality.

Selected Bibliography

Museum publications: (in German) Arnold, U., *English and American Contemporary Graphics*, 1973; Eichler, Gauss, Geissler, and Thiem, G., *Masterworks of the Stuttgarter Galerie Verein*, 1974; Rau, B., *The Lütze Collection*, 1971; Thiem, G., *Masterworks of Expressionism*, 1972; Wiese, St. v., *Donation Marguerite Arp*, 1975; *From Ingres to Picasso, French 19th and 20th Century Drawings*, 1969.

RENATA RUTLEDGE

Greece

——— Athens ———

ACROPOLIS MUSEUM (officially TO MOUSEION AKROPOLEOS), Athens.

Shortly after the Turks left the Acropolis in 1833, while it was still serving as a fortress for the city, work was initiated by Greek authorities to clear the debris of the Turkish settlement from the ancient monuments. These early efforts at organization, accompanied by some small-scale excavation, yielded antiquities that were housed in various structures on the Acropolis. Larger pieces were kept in the thirteenth-century town of the Frankish dukes of Athens, which had been built into the northwestern wing of the Propylaea, but when the tower, along with other medieval structures on the Acropolis, was demolished in 1836–37, much of the material was transferred into the mosque that stood in the Parthenon. As the collection grew, a large Turkish cistern to the west of the Parthenon and an underground arsenal east of the Erechtheum were used for storage. Vases, bronzes, and small objects from the early excavations were stored in a Turkish house near the Erechtheum to which were brought similar objects from the newly liberated country's first national museum on the island of Aegina in 1837, so that by 1861 this modest structure could be characterized as the major museum for the minor arts in Athens. To make some of the sculpture and architectural fragments accessible to scholars and tourists, smaller pieces were set into wooden frames with plaster and displayed in the Propylaea, and other material was set into a wall at the south side of the Acropolis. When the temple of Athena Nike was extracted from a Turkish bastion in 1835–36 and reerected, it served as a museum for its own architectural elements and the slabs of the parapet frieze.

Although as early as 1844 the archaeologist in charge of the Acropolis, Kyriakos Pittakis, made an appeal for the construction of a museum at the east end of the Acropolis, no official action was taken until 1863, when it was decreed that a museum should be built within the walls of the Acropolis to the east of the Parthenon and that the name of the museum should be the Bernardakion Museum of Antiquities on the Acropolis (Bernardakeion Mouseion en tē Akropolei Archaiotēton) to honor the chief private contributor to the project, Dimitrios Bernardakis, a Greek residing in Russia. The architect was Panayiotis Kalkos, also director of construction for the National Museum in Athens. When the building was completed in 1874, the first exhibition contained not only antiquities but plaster casts of the Parthenon that had been sent from the British Museum (q.v.) at the request of the Greek Archaeological Society. The Archaic sculptures, which are the heart of the present collection, were not uncovered until the excavations conducted by Panayiotis Kavvadias and Georg Kawerau from 1885 to 1890. When the museum's holdings were substantially enlarged by this material, an annex, the so-called Small Museum (Mikro Mouseion) was built to the east of the original structure to house less important material.

Two world wars interfered with plans for the further enlargement of the museum, which was not accomplished until after the antiquities began to be removed from protective storage in 1946–47. The Small Museum was demolished, rooms were built below and in front of the main building for storage and administration, and the museum proper was enlarged and remodeled by Patroklos Karantinos. As it now appears the museum is a long, narrow rectangle of only nine galleries that rise a few feet above the level of the Acropolis rock. With its simple four-pillared facade and exterior of small, rough-hewn local stones, much like those that compose the later walls surrounding the Acropolis, it is unobtrusive and in harmony with its surroundings.

Administratively, the Acropolis, including its ancient buildings and the museum, falls within the jurisdiction of the General Inspectorate of Antiquities and Restoration in the Ministry of Culture and Science. The Ephor (superintendent) of the Acropolis serves as the director of the museum and is assisted by a small administrative and technical staff.

The Acropolis Museum is essentially a museum of sculpture, masterpieces of the Archaic and Classical periods that filled the sanctuary and decorated the buildings honoring Athena, the patroness of the city.

The earliest architectural sculpture, in once brilliantly painted poros stone, comes from pediments of forerunners of the Parthenon and other temples and small buildings whose locations are for the most part unknown. There are two great animal combats of the first half of the sixth century B.C., one with a lioness attacking a bull (height, 1.10 meters), which was flanked by snakes; the other with two lions tearing at a bull (length, 5.35 meters); the latter was possibly flanked by the groups of Herakles wrestling a snaky-bodied monster and the impressive triple-bodied creature, human above, serpentine below, often referred to as "Bluebeard" because of the well-preserved color on the figures. Smaller pediments dating from the early sixth century B.C. represent: Herakles killing the Lernaean Hydra, Herakles in combat with Triton, the ambush of Troilos by Achilles, and the apotheosis of Herakles. From the last quarter of the sixth century comes the fragmentary east pediment in marble of the Old Temple of Athena, which shows Athena and her opponent at the center of a gigantomachy (height, 2.00 meters). With the pedimental sculpture are displayed contemporary architectural elements, such as portions of Doric friezes and sima fragments.

Sculpture from the Parthenon that escaped the ravages of time and the hand of Lord Elgin and his contemporaries gives some idea of the architectural sculpture of the Periclean Age. Most of the pedimental fragments are from the west gable and include Poseidon, the so-called Ilissos, and Kekrops and his daughter; from the east is Selene. Of the metopes, except for half of one of the centauromachy metopes from the south side of the building, only small fragments are preserved in the Acropolis Museum, but considerable portions of the frieze are on display and show all of the major classes of participants in the Pananthenaeic procession, as well as the gods. On one of the best-preserved slabs in any museum are shown Poseidon, Apollo, Artemis, and Aphrodite.

The Erechtheum and Nike parapet reliefs illustrate the tradition of architectural sculpture in the later fifth century. The separate marble figures of the former, apparently representing scenes from Attic legend, are set against a dark ground that simulates the blue-gray Eleusinian stone of the building frieze. The five caryatids of the south porch of the Erechtheum, replaced in 1979 by casts to stop further deterioration from pollution, have been placed in the museum temporarily, pending transfer to a new museum below the Acropolis. The display of the Nike parapet frieze includes not only the famous *Sandal-Binder* but considerable portions of other slabs, with Athenas and Nikes engaged in various activities traditional in the aftermath of victory.

The nonarchitectural sculpture in the museum's collection consists essentially of marble ex-votos set up on the Acropolis by devout worshippers in honor of the city's goddess. Most important is the dazzling display of kore figures that were considered the most appropriate offerings to Athena in the Archaic period. Dating from about 580 B.C. to 480 B.C., the figures range in size from under a meter to over life-size, and there are fragments that must have come from even smaller dedications. Among the more than twenty fairly well-preserved examples on display are: the Pomegranate kore, very early in the series; the lower part of the Lyons kore, with the upper part, which is still in France, represented by a cast; the Peplos kore; the richly draped kore; the bright Chian kore with much of her original color still preserved; the Antenor kore and little "Red Shoes"; and, from the end of the period, the so-called *La Boudeuse*, also known from the name of the dedicator inscribed on the base as the Euthydikos kore.

Although the kore represents the single most numerous class of Archaic offering, other types of votives that were presented to Athena are also included in the collection. Of the seated figures some represent Athena herself, as does the *Endoios Athena*, and the goddess is also represented standing and striding. Among the comparatively few male votives are figures of the kouros type, most notably the *Kritios Boy* and the so-called *Blonde Boy*, both from the time of transition to the Early Classical period, about 480 B.C. Two significant standing draped males are the familiar *Moschophoros* (*Calf-Bearer*) by the sculptor [Rh]ombos and the unusual youth in chiton and himation. Both seated scribes and horsemen are included: among the latter are the distinctive Rampin rider, whose head, shown in a cast, is in the Louvre (q.v.), and the Persian rider or *Miltiades*, who wears the brightly patterned trousers of an eastern horseman. Occasional figures of myth are represented in the collection: Theseus and Herakles or the gods Hermes and Dionysos.

Other marble dedications of the Archaic period are sphinxes and winged victories, and several votive columns, which once supported statues, in some instances preserve the names of sculptors whose works are not extant. Unusual is a large hunting dog (length, 1.25 meters), one of a pair that flanked the entrance to the sanctuary of Brauronian Artemis, which was located on the Acropolis.

Votive reliefs of the Archaic period are also represented in the collection: Athena approached by a family of worshippers, the Graces dancing to the music of a flautist, and Hermes in a broad-brimmed hat, possibly to be related with a figure of a driver (Artemis or Apollo?) mounting a chariot, which is shown on a separate slab. Also included in the exhibition of Archaic material is a limited selection of small terracotta plaques and figurines, typical votive offerings of the less-affluent worshippers of Athena. The plaques show Athena as a warrior goddess or as a patroness of the arts and crafts. The figurines represent an enthroned woman, possibly Athena herself, and standing women reminiscent of the korai. A rare example of larger-scale painting is preserved on a terracotta plaque (height, 0.39 meters), with a running hoplite, which probably served some architectural function.

In the period immediately following the Persian sack of the Acropolis in 480 B.C. there were few dedications to the goddess. Among the more important offerings in the collection are the *Angelitos Athena* (height, 0.895 meters) and the relief *Mourning Athena*. The head of an athlete has been associated with the workshop of Phidias.

The museum has on display only a few fragments of post-Periclean work. A second-century A.D. marble copy of the chryselephantine statue *Athena Parthenos* is interesting for preserving on the Acropolis this type of fifth-century cult statue. The *Prokne* has been associated with the fifth-century sculptor Alkamenes but may be a copy, and a head of Alexander the Great may be from the hand of the fourth-century artist Leochares. A striking portrait of a philosopher, dated by some to the fifth century A.D., is the latest work on display. Thousands of fragments of marble in the museum's storerooms are continuously under study, and joins with well-known works are regularly being made.

A small group of vases, terracottas, and other minor finds dating from the Geometric period into the fourth century B.C. comes from excavations at various locations in Athens, primarily in the environs of the Acropolis.

Official museum publications and transparencies and reproductions of objects in the collection may be secured from the Publications Division of the Archaeological Service, TAP, 1 Tossitsa Street, Athens.

Selected Bibliography

General guides and catalogues: Andronicos, Manolis, "Acropolis Museum," *The Greek Museums*, 1975, pp. 109–16; Brouskari, Maria, *The Acropolis Museum: A Descriptive Catalogue*, The Museums of Greece, Second series, 1974.

Other publications: Boulter, P. N., "The Frieze of the Erechtheion," *Antike Plastik* 10 (1970) pp. 1–28; Brommer, Frank, *Die Metopen des Parthenon* (Mainz 1967); idem, *Die Skulpturen der Parthenongiebel* (Mainz 1963); idem, *Der Parthenonfries* (Mainz 1977); Carpenter, Rhys, *The Sculpture of the Nike Temple Parapet* (Cambridge, Mass. 1929); Heberdey, R., *Altattische Porosskulptur* (Wien 1919); Kokkou, Angeliké, *E merimna gia tis archaiotētes stēn Ellada kai ta prōta mouseia* (Athens 1977); Langlotz, Ernst, and Walter-Herwig Schuchhardt, *Archaische Plastik auf der Akropolis* (Frankfurt 1943); Payne, Humfry, and Gerald Macworth Young, *Archaic Marble Sculpture from the Acropolis* (London 1936); Raubitschek, A. E., and L. H. Jeffery, *Dedications from the Athenian Acropolis* (Cambridge, Mass. 1949); Schrader, Hans, *Die archaischen Marmorbildwerke der Akropolis* (Frankfurt 1939); Wiegand, Th., *Die archaische Poros-Architektur der Akropolis zu Athen* (Cassel and Leipzig 1904).

ELIZABETH COURTNEY BANKS

BENAKI MUSEUM, 1 Koumbari odos, Athens.

The Benaki Museum was founded in 1927, when Anthony Benaki, a cotton merchant from Egypt and an enthusiastic collector of art, decided to create a public museum. He intended to exhibit the numerous objects he had gathered over the years from Egypt, Greece, and western Europe. Today, the Benaki Museum comprises a rich and varied collection with a particular emphasis on the arts of Greece and the Near East.

The museum building was constructed about 1900 as a private residence in the neoclassical style. The turn-of-the-century house with its elegant portico of Doric columns was purchased by Emmanuel Benaki (Anthony's father), who commissioned the architect Anastasios Metaxas to renovate and enlarge the structure. The house was reworked again in 1927–30 by Anthony Benaki, who had decided to use the twenty-four rooms to exhibit his art collection. In 1931 the Benaki Museum was incorporated as an autonomous foundation, and until 1942 the museum was supported solely by Benaki himself. Since that date, the Benaki Museum has been subsidized by the Greek government. A president and director oversee the activities of the museum and its collections, assisted by a small support staff.

The Benaki collection began with a group of Oriental weapons, and over the years treasures of ancient and medieval art were added to this core. After the founding of the public museum, various gifts were presented by both public and private donors, which greatly enhanced the collection and its facilities. Among the gifts was a large group of religious objects brought to Greece in 1923 by refugees from Asia Minor, the Pontos, and Thrace. These works were presented by the Exchange of Populations Foundation. Fine examples of Chinese ceramics were donated by G. Eumorphopoulos along with files and memorabilia of the Greek statesman Eleutherios Venizelos. The St. Dekozis-Vouros Foundation financed the construction of a two-story wing to house lecture halls and exhibition rooms. Damianos Kyriazis also financed an exhibition room (which bears his name) and presented a rich collection of embroideries and ceramics and a group of drawings, watercolors, and lithographs of Greek subjects. Kyriazis gave, in addition, a collection of rare books and historical documents. Carved-wood paneling from the drawing room of an eighteenth-century residence at Kozani was donated by Helen Antonious Stathatos together with icons, embroideries, jewelry, and other objects. Additional gifts came over the years from Marina Lappa-Diomedous, Christian Lampikis, and Loukas Benakis. Various state grants were presented to the Benaki to help maintain the facilities.

The collection of the Benaki Museum features three major areas of concentration: (1) Greek works of art from prehistoric to modern times, with an emphasis on ancient Greek goldsmiths' work and Byzantine and post-Byzantine art; (2) modern Greek art, including folk art, Greek relics, drawings, watercolors, and lithographs of Greek subjects; and (3) minor arts and crafts from the eastern Mediterranean, including embroideries and textiles. The Benaki is particularly noted for its collection of gold objects, which date from the Mycenean period to the present, and for its group of Fayuum portraits (third-fourth century). The collection of Islamic fabrics is one of the largest and most comprehensive in the world.

Ancient Greek art at the Benaki features two gold cups dating from the third millennium B.C., probably from Northern Euboia. A funerary band from Kos is decorated with miniature sphinxes and rosettes. The Thesalian Treasure, originally presented by Mrs. H. A. Strathatos to the National Archaeological Museum (q.v.) in Athens, is rich in examples of ancient jewelry. A diadem, a necklace (decorated with rows of miniature amphorae), and a pair of earrings (which represent a muse playing a lyre) all date from about the third century B.C.

Other examples of Greek metalwork date from the Byzantine period. A group of gold, cloisonné-enamel pieces was created in the sixth and seventh centuries. Post-Byzantine metalwork features a gold buckle inlaid with precious stones. An incense boat from Macedonia dated 1613 is made of gold-plated silver with polychromed enamel. A pendent and crozier from 1738 once belonged to Bishop Parthenos of Cesarea. An elaborate bishop's mitre is a rare work that represents in silver various scenes from the Gospel. A fascinating group of enamel pieces from Greek islands all take the form of miniature ships called "Venetiha" (Venetians). These ships may have been made by Greek goldsmiths working in Venice (seventeenth-eighteenth century). Numerous silver processional crosses, and silver covers for liturgical books are in the collection.

A fine collection of objects from Christian Egypt includes works in bronze, wood, and ceramic. Of particular interest are the portraits executed in the encaustic wax technique, known as Fayuum portraits. A classic portrait of a man dates from the third century and a less formal, more expressive portrait of a woman was created in the fourth century. Egyptian textiles are a highlight of the Benaki and include a fine weaving from the fifth-sixth century with a depiction of the winged horse Pegasus. A group of carved bone pieces, many of which are decorated with figures from classical mythology, features an ivory comb decorated with personifications of the two cities Constantinople and Alexandria, each in the form of a queen wearing a crown made of ramparts.

Small-size Byzantine sculptures, which date mainly from the ninth-thirteenth century, feature an ivory plaque with St. George made in Constantinople (ninth-tenth century). The *Annunciation* (twelfth-thirteenth century), carved in steatite (a soft, porous stone), bears traces of the gold, red, and black pigments with which it was once painted. The collection of Byzantine miniatures at the Benaki is highlighted by two works on parchment once part of the *Mt. Athos Codex*. The illuminations, executed in 1084, represent *Jonah Emerging from the Whale* and the *Three Children in the Fiery Furnace*, both scenes from the Old Testament.

The Benaki houses a fine collection of portable icons from the Paleologian period. The *Hospitality of Abraham* dates from the fourteenth century. A triptych from the same period is painted with scenes related to Mt. Athos (*Virgin Portaëtissa* from the Iviron Monastery, *St. Paul* from the Zeropotamos Monastery, and *St. Eleutherios*). Cretan paintings by both known and unknown artists are numerous in the collection. An early icon of the Cretan school from about 1500 shows *St. Demetrios*. The *Hymn to the Virgin* from the sixteenth century is by the Cretan Theodore Poulakis.

A large and excellent collection of decorative arts includes ceramics from Asia Minor and from the Far East. Rhodian pottery from Nicaea and Kütahya is well represented. Polychromed ceramics from various Greek islands dating from the sixteenth to the eighteenth century include a plate decorated with a lion that was made to be inserted as ornamentation in the outer walls of churches.

Islamic works of art include an entire reception room complete with mosaic floor and decorative fountain from seventeenth-century Egypt. Pottery from Isnik (sixteenth century) and other centers is exhibited. Wood carvings include a door from Bagdad (eighth-ninth century) with ornamental floral motifs. Islamic gold jewelry from Egypt, Syria, Iran, and Spain includes numerous examples from the ninth through the fourteenth century. A selection of finely worked Korans from Persia and Asia Minor includes an illuminated prayerbook from Turkey dated 1785.

The Benaki Museum maintains an active publishing program. Catalogues of the collection and special exhibition catalogues are produced. A series of children's books is aimed at introducing the arts of Greece to young people.

A book and gift shop, located off the museum's entry hall, offers a large number of postcards and slides of works at the Benaki. Catalogues of the collection, exhibition catalogues, and books related to art in the collection are available. The shop also sells reproductions of jewelry and original Greek crafts.

A cafeteria-restaurant with outdoor seating is located on the roof of the Benaki Museum.

Selected Bibliography

Museum publications: *Guide to the Collection*, 1980; Chatzidakis, Nano, *Icons of the Cretan School*, 1983; *Coptic Textiles*; *Epirus and Ionian Islands—Embroideries*; *Islamic Textiles*; *Jewelry*; *Pottery of Asia Minor*; *Silverware*; *Skyros Embroideries*; *Textiles: Crete, Dodecanese, Cyclades*.

Other publications: *The Benaki Museum* (Athens 1975).

LORRAINE KARAFEL

BYZANTINE MUSEUM, 22 Vassillissis Sophias, Athens.

The Byzantine Museum, considered one of the most important museums in Greece, is dedicated to art of the Greek world from the close of antiquity to the establishment of Greece as an independent state (nineteenth century). The museum was first founded in 1914 and the then-small collection was housed in a basement of the Athens Academy. In 1930 the Byzantine Museum was moved to a group of buildings that had until then been used by the Greek army. The complex (present home of the museum) included a country house commissioned in 1840 by a Frenchwoman, the duchesse de Plaisance, and designed by the architect Stamatios Kleantris (a major architect of the period). The house, constructed in the style of a Florentine Renaissance villa, became the center of the new museum.

The villa and its outbuildings were remodeled for the Byzantine Museum by architect Aristoteles Zachos. The ground floor of the house was planned to provide impressions of the three types of churches prevalent in Greece: an Early Christian basilica, a Byzantine cruciform church with dome, and a post-Byzantine, single-space religious structure. This format is kept today. Over the years the Byzantine Museum expanded, and in 1951 a hall in the east wing of the house was reconstructed. In 1963, in one of the outbuildings, the Central Laboratory for Conservation was founded, an organization dedicated to the preservation of wall paintings, mosaics, and icons.

The original collection was formed of objects previously housed by the Greek Archaeological Service in the "Theseion." These pieces had come from various sources and included Early Christian and Byzantine marble sculptures found on the Acropolis, as well as in ruined or demolished churches in the Athens area. Wall paintings from churches in Athens, Delphi, and Atalante, with icons of the Paleologian period and gold-thread embroideries from the area of Thessaloniki, were added. A large collection of icons, manuscripts, and liturgical objects and vestments came from the Christian Archaeological Society. A group of ecclesiastical relics from Asia Minor were shared between the Byzantine Museum and the Benaki Museum (q.v.), and Coptic textiles were presented by art collector Anthony Benaki. Private collections were donated to the museum in their entirety, including those of Christianos Lampikis, John Katsaras, and George Makkas.

Today, as originally, the Byzantine Museum is supported totally by the Greek government. A director oversees the collections and is assisted by a small staff.

The collection is exhibited at the Byzantine Museum in roughly chronological order. From the Early Christian period, a mosaic floor is from a basilica at Ilios. A funerary group with Orpheus seated under an arched frame carved with birds and beasts is from about 400. The Byzantine Museum houses the Mytilene Treasure, a group of gold, silver, and bronze objects and gold coins uncovered in 1951 at Krategos. A rich selection of jewelry features three necklaces with open-work decoration, earrings, belts, bracelets, buckles, and rings. A group of gold coins dates from the period of Emperors Phokas (602–10) and Heraklios (613–29/30). Silver objects, all stamped with the five official seals of the controller of the quality of silver, include a dish decorated with a cross surrounded by a ring of ivy leaves. A *trulla* (hollow vessel with handle) features on its handle an incised decoration with three nude females (seventh century). Also from the Early Christian period is an altar from Thrace (Anchialos) and an ornate iron railing from the basilica at Tegea.

The Middle Byzantine period is represented by a fine group of marble architectural fragments from the post-iconoclastic period. Door frames, lintels, closure panels, and architraves from screens are included. A rare icon of the *Virgin at Prayer* is carved in Pentelic marble. A closure panel represents the *Tree of Life*, with two lions rising to bite the tree. A second closure panel executed in a relatively flat relief presents a lion about to tear his prey to pieces. An image of three Apostles, *James Alphaius, Philip, and Luke*, is from Constantinople and is executed in a champlevé technique.

From the Frankish occupation and the Paleologian period (1204–1435), works include a male figure, possibly St. Stephen, painted on a narrow pilaster formerly in the church at Oropos. A conch from the apse of the church at Lathreno on the island of Naxos depicts a large, painted figure of Christ at the center flanked by the Virgin and St. John the Baptist. From Triglia at Bithynia, a mosaic icon, the *Virgin and Child*, dates from the fourteenth century; this work, in which the Virgin holds the Christ Child in her right arm, is known as the *Glykophilousa*.

The Byzantine Museum houses a large and excellent collection of icons, mainly from the twelfth to fourteenth century and representing the various schools of Greek painting. An icon from northern Greece, the *Crucifixion* (thirteenth century), was painted over an earlier work from the ninth century. From Kastoria in northern Greece is the icon *St. George*, and around this central figure are scenes from the saint's life. The image *Christ* is believed to be from the Church of Hagia Sophia in Constantinople. An aristocratic and formal depiction, the *Madonna and Child*, was painted in Thessaloniki. Later icons, which represent a classical revival in painting style, different from the earlier, more austere compositions, include from the mid-fourteenth century the *Archangel Michael*, known as the *Megas Taxiarches*. The painter, who made use of cast shadows, probably worked in Constantinople. The *Crucifixion* from Thessaloniki (fourteenth century) represents Christ, the Virgin, and St. John the Baptist.

Icons of the Cretan school, characterized by their bright colors, faultless technique, sensitive modeling, and keen rendering of small details, are well represented in the collection. Works that date from the fifteenth-sixteenth century include the *Virgin and Child* by the Cretan painter Angelos. This panel is an unusual type, representing the Virgin affectionately embracing the Christ Child. A triptych from Crete shows the *Transfiguration* with the *Tree of Jesse* and the *Vine* (two corresponding scenes from the Old and New Testament, respectively).

A group of popular paintings from the eighteenth century includes works from the church at Kastri: one dated 1751 shows an old monk in a boat surrounded by large monsters (the "dragons of the sea" described in the Psalter) that rise from the water to expel devoured victims on Judgment Day. A wall painting detached from a ruined church at Atalante is titled *St. James the Persian*, and the *Nursing Madonna* is by Makarios (a painter from Galatista in the Chalcidice). Several works from the nineteenth century include the painting *Blind Eros and the Sirens*, dated 1825, executed by a priest-artist on the island of Siphnos.

The Byzantine Museum has a rich collection of liturgical objects: ecclesiastical plate, including chalices, lamps, and incense burners and numerous crucifixes in both precious and semiprecious metals. A fascinating collection of vestments includes elaborate gold-thread embroideries, among them an *epitaphioi* (an embroidered veil carried in processions on Good Friday). Metalwork gospel covers and a group of exquisite illuminated manuscripts are also at the museum.

The Central Laboratory of Conservation located at the Byzantine Museum is responsible for the preservation and restoration of existing wall paintings and mosaics in hundreds of churches throughout Greece, Cyprus, Palestine, and at the Monastery of St. Catherine on Mt. Sinai (both wall paintings and icons).

A gift shop stocks a number of postcards and slides of works in the museum collection, as well as guides to the collection (available in several languages). Other books related to Byzantine art and architecture are also available.

Selected Bibliography

Museum publications: *Icons in the Byzantine Museum*, n.d.
Other publications: *The Byzantine Museum* (Athens 1975); "Byzantine Museum" in *The Blue Guide-Athens* (London 1981), pp. 133–35.

LORRAINE KARAFEL

NATIONAL ARCHAEOLOGICAL MUSEUM (officially TO ETHNIKON ARCHAIOLOGIKON MOUSEION; alternately THE NATIONAL MUSEUM; also TO ETHNIKON MOUSEION), 1 Tossitsa Street, Athens.

In March 1829, even before the Turks had evacuated Athens, the provisional government of John Kapodistrias had established the first national museum for Greek antiquities in the capital then located on the island of Aegina. To this temporary museum were brought sculptures, inscriptions, vases, and antiquities of all sorts from all over Greece, but particularly from the neighboring islands, and a catalogue of the museum's acquisitions until 1832 was prepared by its director, Leontios Kampanis. When the capital was transferred to Athens in 1834, to so-called Theseion, the temple now generally identified as that of Hephaistos and Athena to the northwest of the Acropolis was designated the Central Archaeological Museum (Kentrikon Archaiologikon Mouseion). Well preserved because it had served as a Christian church, the fifth-century B.C. building soon proved inadequate for the great quantity of material that was accumulating, and parts of the growing collection were housed in other ancient buildings, notably the Library of Hadrian and the Tower of the Winds; material from the Acropolis was kept there in structures both ancient and modern. Other collections were located at various places throughout the city. The most distinguished of them was the collection of the Archaeological Society of Athens (Ē en Athēnais Archaiologikē Etaireia), which was founded in 1837 and by gifts, purchases, and excavation gathered a large and impressive group of antiquities. Housed first in the University of Athens (1858); then in a private school, the Varvakeion (1865); and finally, at the Polytechneion, or School of Fine Arts (1877), the collection was merged with that of the state in 1893. Before the consolidation, the society's collection, open to the public at regular hours, served for many years as the only real museum for the city.

Although distinguished European architects, such as von Klenze and Hansen, went to Athens to plan an architectural setting appropriate to the new capital, the decree of 1834 authorizing the construction of the badly needed Central Public Museum for Antiquities (Kentrikon Dēmosion Mouseion dia tas Archaiotētas) was not implemented immediately because of the limited resources of the new government and the grandiosity of the proposals, like that of von Klenze for a lavish center for all of the arts in the area of the ancient cemetery of the Kerameikos. An international competition likewise failed to produce a satisfactory plan: all fourteen entries were rejected by the panel of judges from the Royal Academy in Munich. Two generous gifts from wealthy Greek philanthropists and a reasonable proposal presented by the philhellene Ludwig Lange, professor of architecture in the Royal Academy at Munich, ultimately made possible the beginning of construction. In 1856 Dimitrios Bernardakis, a merchant residing in Russia, made a substantial contribution to the museum fund, which two years earlier had begun receiving an annual allocation from the state, and in 1866 Eleni Tossitsa, who had already provided land for the Polytechneion, gave the property adjacent to it in the northeastern quarter of the city so that the two establishments for the fine arts in Athens might be together. Construction was officially inaugurated on October 3, 1866, in the presence of King George I.

The plan of Lange, adapted by the Greek architect Panayiotis Kalkos, was one by then standard for the neoclassical museum, with exhibition rooms laid out symmetrically around two interior courts and divided by a central hall. The west wing was completed in 1874, the north by 1881, and the south by 1885.

In 1888 Ernst Ziller, one of a group of German architects who made significant contributions to the development of a neoclassical architectural style in Athens, was commissioned to complete the structure. Ziller's is the simple Ionic facade, which consists of a projecting portico with four columns and flat-roofed attic story decorated with six (now four) terracotta replicas of ancient sculpture and flanking stoas that terminate in slightly projecting rooms with gabled roofs. Transfer of the material from the various collections around Athens began with the completion of the west wing, and in 1888 the name of the museum was changed to the one it still bears, the National Archaeological Museum (Ethnikon Archaiologikon Mouseion).

The museum has been enlarged substantially to meet the needs of the collections and their administration, most notably by a two-story addition around two interior courts that was attached to the east wing between 1932 and 1939. After World War II, before the collections were removed from protective storage, alterations were made both to the original structure and the annex with substantial assistance from the Marshall Plan. There are now fifty-two galleries of varying sizes in which the major collections are exhibited, and additional areas in the administrative wing are used for the Numismatic Collection and for special exhibits.

The museum is state supported and operates as a division of the General Inspectorate of Antiquities and Restorations, which is under the jurisdiction of the Ministry of Culture and Science. The director of the museum serves as curator of sculpture, and there are curators of the Prehistoric Collections, the Department of Vases, and the Collection of Bronzes. The museum maintains its own Department of Conservation and Restoration. Also housed in the National Museum, but administered separately under the General Inspectorate of Antiquities and Restorations, are the Epigraphical Museum and the Numismatic Collection. The Society of Friends of the National Archaeological Museum of Athens was founded in 1933, primarily to provide funds for the purchase of antiquities that appear illicitly on the Greek market.

From the beginning the museum was meant to serve as the national repository of the artistic and archaeological treasures of ancient Greece, a function that it continues to serve today. It has become necessary, however, to limit new acquisitions to objects from Athens and its environs and occasional material of exceptional interest from other sites, for example, the spectacular Bronze Age frescoes from the island of Thera, which require a specially controlled environment. Antiquities from other areas are housed in a growing number of local museums, many of which, like those at Delphi and Olympia (q.v.), were constructed to provide for the display of excavated material close to the locations where it was originally on view.

The museum's holdings fall into two major groups: the Prehistoric Collections and the Collections of Classical Sculpture and Vases. The heart of the Prehistoric Collections is the rich material from the six Late Bronze Age Shaft Graves of Circle A at Mycenae, five of which were excavated by Heinrich Schliemann in

1876. In the great central hall of the museum is displayed a large selection from the inventory of thousands of pieces in the precious metals and bronze, amber and stone, ivory, bone, faience, and terracotta. Among the most noteworthy objects on view are: the gold death masks, including that once thought to be Agamemnon's; bronze daggers inlaid with figured scenes in gold, silver, and niello; ritual vessels of gold and silver in the shape of animals, the fragmentary silver *Siege Rhyton*, with repoussé work depicting warriors defending a beleaguered city, and the *Cup of Nestor*; and hundreds of pieces of gold leaf with raised patterns that served as funerary diadems, pectorals, and clothing ornaments. Also included in the display is a group of objects from the less opulent and slightly earlier finds from Grave Circle B, excavated by John Papadimitriou and George Mylonas between 1952 and 1955; noteworthy pieces are a death mask in electrum, a small rock crystal bowl in the form of a duck, and an amethyst gem bearing the portrait of a bearded Mycenean. Significant items from other areas of Mycenae in the exhibit are the ivory group of three divinities (Demeter, Kore, and Iakhos?), the *Warrior Vase* (c. 1200 B.C.), and the painted limestone head of a sphinx, a rare example of larger sculpture-in-the-round (height, 0.168 meters).

From the neighboring Late Bronze Age citadel of Tiryns there are fragmentary frescoes, including different moments of a boar hunt, as well as the so-called Treasure of Tiryns, a hoard of mixed date with bronzes, gold rings, and a Syro-Hittite cylinder seal. A selection of Linear B tablets, hardened in the fire that destroyed the Mycenean palace at Pylos about 1200 B.C., illustrates the syllabic script employed for the writing of Greek in the Late Bronze Age.

Mycenean tomb finds from a variety of sites make the collection of Late Bronze Age pottery unparalleled; there is material from Attica (e.g., Menidi, Perati, Spata, Thorikos), the Argolid (e.g., Dendra, Prosymna, Nauplion), and the Peloponnese (e.g., Kalamata, Kambos, Pylos, Vapheio). From Vapheio also come the two well-known gold cups with scenes of bull-catching executed in repoussé (height, 0.08 meters).

The Neolithic period (c. 6500–3000 B.C.) and Early and Middle Bronze Ages (c. 3000–1600 B.C.) are also represented in the Prehistoric Collections, primarily by objects of everyday use from settlements and tombs: pottery, figurines, tools and weapons of stone, bone and terracotta, and a few objects of silver, copper, and bronze. A selection of ceramic material from several Thessalian sites shows a fairly complete sequence of styles throughout the Neolithic period, and the type sites of Sesklo and Dimini are well represented. Contemporary wares from central Greece come primarily from Halae in Lokris and Lianokladhi in Phthiotis, and from early neolithic Attica are terracotta and stone vessels from Nea Makri.

The Early Bronze Age material from the mainland is primarily from Orchomenos in central Greece and from the coastal Attic sites of Askitario and Ayios Kosmas, but only a few pieces of Minyan and Matt-painted wares give a restricted picture of the ceramic repertory of the Middle Bronze Age. Small collections from Troy, a gift of Mrs. Schliemann, and from Poliochni on the island of Lemnos represent the Bronze Age of the eastern Aegean.

A separate gallery is devoted to the exhibition of prehistoric material from the Cycladic islands, most of which is from graves of the Early Bronze Age. All distinctive styles of incised and painted pottery are represented, and the exhibit includes several of the so-called frying pans, some incised with the representations of ships. Most characteristic among the grave offerings are the highly schematic figurines of island marble, which range in size from a few centimeters to almost life-size and represent primarily females with their arms tightly folded across their abdomens. Two male musicians are also on display, a seated lyre player and a standing flautist. The British excavations at Phylakopi on the island of Milos are represented by a selection of vases, primarily Middle and Late Bronze Age, and a few fresco fragments, including those of a seascape with flying fish.

The collection of Classical art is distinguished by its unparalleled holdings of original sculptures from the Archaic period into the Hellenistic age. Included are not only free-standing figures and reliefs in stone but important architectural groups and the finest collection of large-scale ancient bronzes to be seen anywhere. The works are displayed in chronological order, the monumental masterpieces accompanied by a judicious selection of works of lesser quality for contrast and by an occasional vase or small bronze that serves to illustrate, in another medium, a theme or a type.

Representative of stylistic tendencies at the end of the Geometric age and the beginning of the Archaic period (725–625 B.C.) are the *Dipylon Goddess* in ivory (height, 0.24 meters); the large marble statue of a woman (Artemis?), dedicated by Nikandre on the island of Delos (height, 1.75 meters); and architectural reliefs from Mycenae.

An impressive series of kouros figures well illustrates the chronological sequence and regional variations of the Archaic style. In the Attic group are included the Dipylon head and over life-size dedications from Sounion (c. 600 B.C.), the youth from Volomandra (c. 550 B.C.), the Anavyssos kouros (c. 530 B.C.), and Aristodikos (c. 500 B.C.). Island workshops are represented by pieces such as the Kea and Milos kouroi, and several dedications from the sanctuary on Mount Ptoan in Boeotia represent yet another facet of the tradition.

The female counterpart of the kouros, the kore, is best seen in Athens in the Acropolis Museum, but there are representative, if fragmentary, examples in the National Museum and one virtually intact figure with well-preserved color found in Attica in 1972, which can be identified from the inscribed base as the maiden Phrasikleia, a work of the sculptor Aristion (c. 540 B.C.). Among the other Archaic sculptures-in-the-round on display are the winged Nike from Delos and an exceptionally fine seated statue of Dionysos.

Architectural sculpture is represented primarily by fragments of the late Archaic pediments of the temple of Aphaia on Aegina (c. 500–480 B.C.), the greater portion of which was sold to Ludwig of Bavaria and can be seen at the Glyptothek (q.v.) in Munich. There is also a fragmentary pedimental group of a lion tearing the hindquarters of a bull of about 500 B.C., the other half of which is in the Metropolitan Museum of Art (q.v.) in New York.

The museum has on display a series of fragmentary funerary reliefs, primarily from Attica, several of which were built into the city walls thrown up at the threat of the Persian attack in the early fifth century B.C. The most common type is the tall, slender stele, topped by sphinx or palmette, such as those of Aristion by Aristokles, that by Alxenor, and that of the unnamed youth whose head is framed by a discus. There is also the rare painted stele of Lyseas, on which the outline of the figure is still visible, and the so-called Marathon runner, a relief, possibly funerary, showing a running hoplite. Among the important bases with relief decoration in the collection are two that once held kouri: one with athletes exercising against a well-preserved red background, the other with the so-called hockey players.

The over life-size Zeus (Poseidon?) brought up from the sea off Cape Artemesion in 1926 and 1928 is the centerpiece of the collection of Early Classical sculpture (480–450 B.C.). Related to it stylistically is an important Roman copy of a bronze original of the period, the *Omphalos Apollo*. A smaller bronze of a bearded male dedicated to Poseidon was found in the sea off the coast of Boeotia. Significant Early Classical reliefs represent a youth crowning himself from Sounion, a boy with a hare from Larissa, and the Melian disc with the head of a woman, possibly a goddess.

The Classical period of the second half of the fifth century B.C. and the beginning of the fourth century B.C. is well represented by a rich series of funerary reliefs on both broad stelae and lekythoi, which reflect the influence of the monumental works of the great masters of the period, such as Phidias, on works designed for private purposes. Among the noteworthy reliefs are those of Mnesagora and her little brother Nikochares; Myrrhine; the unnamed youth with the bird cage and cat; Hegeso; Ktesileos and Theano; and the shipwrecked hoplite Demokleides. An important votive relief of the period is the large slab from Eleusis with Demeter, Persephone, and Triptolemos (height, 2.20 meters); the fragmentary Diotima relief of the end of the century may represent the prophetess from Plato's *Symposium*.

Of original architectural sculpture of the period, there are fragments of the pediments and metopes of the temple of Hera at Argos in the tradition of Polyclitus, as well as a head of Hera from the same site, which may be from a cult statue. From the base of the lost cult statue of Nemesis at Rhamnous by Agorakritos are fragmentary reliefs representing the presentation of Helen to Nemesis by Leda, which were probably executed by students of the master. Another piece probably from the same workshop is the statue of a young man in himation dedicated by Lysikleides.

The Late Classical style of the fourth century B.C. is well represented by both architectural sculpture and original bronzes and a very full series of funerary and votive reliefs. From the early decades of the century come acroteria and significant portions of the pediments of the temple of Asklepios at Epidauros representing the sack of Troy and an Amazonomachy, some of which are the work of Timotheos and Hektoridas. Battered fragments of the pedimental sculpture and acroteria from the temple of Athena Alea at Tegea may be from the hand of Skopas, and from the same site is the fine head of Hygieia.

The large bronzes of the period are exceptional: the ephebe from the sea off Marathon of the Praxitelean school, the youth from the Antikythera wreck, and the head of a boxer from Olympia identified with a portrait of Satyros by Silanion. Praxitelean in style are the reliefs from a statue base found at Mantineia that represent Apollo and six of the Muses, and there are later copies of works in the Praxitelean manner, such as the Hermes of Andros and versions of the tall and small Herculaneum women.

An extensive series of funerary monuments, including stelae, naiskoi, and figures-in-the-round; of votive reliefs, many of which were dedicated to Pan and the nymphs and to Asklepios; and of decrees with relief sculpture gives a comprehensive picture of the major sculptural trends of the fourth century B.C. The Ilissos stele and the monuments of Melitte, Archestrate, Leon, and Leontios; the family of Prokles and that of Alexos; and Aristonautes are representative of the funerary works.

The long Hellenistic period (c. 320–100 B.C.) is unevenly represented in the National Museum, in part because of the reduced importance of mainland Greece in this period, in part because of the plunder of its monuments by the Romans.

Of the more important sculptures-in-the-round by known sculptors are the *Themis of Chairestratos*, the fragmentary cult statues created by Damophon for the sanctuary of Demeter at Lykosura, the colossal head *Zeus* from Aigira by Eukleides, and the head *Athena* by Euboulides. Significant works by unknown artists are the *Poseidon of Milos*; the *Fallen Gaul* from Delos, with Pergamenian affinities; and the so-called head *Ariadne*. Recently set on a massive horse, certainly not his original mount, is the boy jockey from the sea near Artemesion, which dates from the second century B.C.

The growing importance of portraiture in the period is illustrated by several pieces: in bronze, the Antikythera philosopher and the man from Delos, and in marble, a copy of the Demosthenes by Polyclitus; a striking image of a foreign priest, possibly Thracian; and heads tentatively identified as the eastern rulers Mithradates of Pontos and the Cappadocian king Ariarthes. The humorous Aphrodite and Pan in mock conflict illustrate the Late Hellenistic tradition of one-sided groups.

A few stelae show the continuity of the tradition of funerary relief in the islands and the Greek East, and a pair of slabs showing an Ethiopian groom attempting to control a restive horse perhaps decorated a statue base. Two large reliefs (0.95 meters by 0.62 meters) with dancing women from the theater of Dionysos in Athens are representative of the Neo-Attic tradition of the first century B.C.

The collection of Roman sculpture on display is small, with portraits its chief component. Included are a Roman represented as a nude athlete from Delos, a series of Roman emperors beginning with Augustus, Hadrian's favorite Antinous, a Christlike philosopher of about A.D. 200, and a group of portraits of *kosmetai*, officials of the gymnasia, that dates from the first century B.C. to the third century A.D.

The museum's collection of small bronzes is large and important, with a chronological range extending from the Geometric period into the Roman era. A rich variety of objects is represented, including statuettes of men, divinities and animals, caldrons, jugs, mirrors, fibulae of many types, armor and weapons, repoussé plaques for attachment to objects of other materials, and bracelets and other types of jewelry. The nucleus of the collection is the votive material from three great sanctuaries: of Zeus at Dodona, Athena on the Acropolis, and Zeus at Olympia; the first of these three was excavated by the Greek statesman Constantine Karapanos, whose collection is housed in a special gallery that bears his name. All areas of Greece are represented among the bronzes, and hundreds of objects on display illustrate various local styles of metalwork. A hoard of bronzes found in 1959 in the Athenian suburb of Ambelokipi consists of pieces of various sizes and styles, all, however, under life size and of Roman date.

The museum's Collection of Vases fills eight spacious galleries and exhibits a full range of Greek ceramic styles from the Protogeometric into the fourth century B.C. The strength of the collection lies in the vases of the Geometric and Protoattic styles of the tenth to the seventh century B.C. and in white-ground lekythoi of the fifth century B.C. In the Geometric group there are not only masterpieces from Athens, such as the Dipylon vases, but others from a variety of local workshops, such as those of Boeotia and the Argolid. The Analatos hydria represents the beginning of the Orientalizing phase in Athens, and the development of the style can be traced through a series of important vases, including a large group from Vari and noteworthy pieces such as the Peiraeus and Kynosarges amphorae. The work of the Nessos Painter, including his name vase, illustrates the transition to the black-figure style. Orientalizing wares from other areas of Greece are less fully represented, but there are some examples of the most important regional developments, including some of the large amphorae from Milos. Painted terracotta plaques and architectural fragments of the last part of the seventh century B.C. illustrate the Corinthian tradition of large-scale painting.

The most numerous class of vases in the collection dating to the sixth century B.C. is that of the Attic black-figure style, and the work of many of the great masters of the technique is included, if only in fragments, for example, Sophilos, Lydos, Kleitias, Exekias, and Amasis Painter. Scores of black-figure lekythoi from the end of the sixth century and the beginning of the fifth represent the last stages of major production of the ware, and the continuation of the technique in later centuries for specialized vases. Among the few examples of non-Attic black-figure work are Klazomenian sarcophagi, and rare wooden plaques from Pitsas in the Corinthian tradition date to the second half of the sixth century B.C. (copies only on display). Grouped with the vases of the Geometric and Archaic periods is a representative selection of material from the votive deposits of vases, terracottas, bronzes, and other small objects from the sanctuaries of Artemis Orthia at Sparta and of Hera at Perachora and at Argos (Argive Heraeum).

Since much of the best of the production of Attic red-figure vases was exported to other areas, the museum's collection does not equal in quality that of the great museums of western Europe, but the major phases of the development of the style from its beginning in the last decades of the sixth century B.C. to its decline in the fourth can be seen in the works of many of the most celebrated masters. From the late sixth century and early fifth there are fragmentary works by Oltos and Epiktetos; by Phintias, Euphronios, Makron, and Douris; and by the Kleophrades, Berlin, and Brygos Painters. From the middle decades of the fifth century are works by the Niobid and Villa Giulia Painters; Pistoxenos; the Pan, Bowdoin, and Providence Painters; and Polygnotos. From the end of the century are the name vase of the Eretria Painter and other vases by him and the Meidias Painter.

The collection of white-ground vases of the second half of the fifth century is particularly fine, with an exceptional representation of all phases of the work of the master of the style, the Achilles Painter. Other characteristic pieces are by the Timokrates Painter, the Thanatos and Sabouroff Painters, and the Triglyph Painter and the painters of the Reed Workshop, whose production belongs to the end of the century.

The declining standards of artistry in the red-figure tradition in the fourth century are illustrated not only by Attic work but by imitations of the style from Corinth, Boeotia, and Kynouria. There is a small selection of Etruscan pottery, essentially bucchero ware, and a few terracottas, including Tanagra figurines, are displayed with the pottery with which they are contemporary.

In a separate gallery is an exhibit of material from the recent excavations at the Late Bronze Age settlement of Akrotiri on the island of Thera. Most important are the restored frescoes, the best-preserved wall paintings in the Minoan tradition from any site thus far known. On display are the three adjoining walls of the so-called Spring fresco, six meters of the extraordinary miniature frieze depicting a naval expedition, another with a Nilotic scene, and frescoes of a young priestess, the blue monkeys, the antelopes, the boys' boxing match, the fishermen, and others. A small selection of other material from the excavations includes local and imported pottery, bronze vessels and tools, and various stone and bone objects of domestic use.

One gallery is given over to the display of the private collection given to the museum in 1956, along with funds for its installation, by Eleni Stathatou, who continues to make additions to her original gift. Best known for its exceptional holdings of Greek, Roman, and Byzantine jewelry, the collection also includes vases, small sculpture in bronze and terracotta, and other objects small in scale, primarily Classical and Hellenistic, but with a few pieces dating from pre-Classical times.

Official museum publications and transparencies and reproductions of objects in the collections may be secured from the Publications Division of the Archaeological Service, TAP, 1 Tossitsa Street, Athens.

Selected Bibliography

Museum publications: Karouzou, Semni, *Illustrated Guide to the National Museum*, 1977; Kallipolitis, V. G., and Evi Touloupa, *Bronzes of the National Archaeological Museum of Athens*, c. 1971; Karazou, Semni, *National Archaeological Museum: Collection of Sculpture, A Catalogue*, 1968; Papastamos, Dimitrios, *Marble Master Pieces of the National Museum of Athens*, n.d.; Philippaki, Barbara, *Vases of the National Archaeological Museum of Athens*, c. 1975; Sakellarakis, J. A., *The Mycenaean Collection of the National Archaeological Museum of Athens*, 1971; Sakellariou, A., and G. Papathanasopoulos, *National Archaeological Museum: A' Prehistoric Collections—A Brief Guide*, 1965; Sapouna-Sakellarakis, Efi, *Cycladic Civilization and the Cycladic Collection of the National Archaeological Museum of Athens*, 1971.

Other publications: Andronicos, Manolis, "National Archaeological Museum," *The Greek Museums* (Athens 1975), pp. 19–41; Amandry, Pierre et al., *Collection Hélène Stathatou*, 4 t. (Strasbourg et Athènes 1953–1971); Collignon, Maxime et Louis Couve, *Catalogue des vases peints du Musée national d'Athènes*, 3 t. (Paris 1902–4); *Corpus Vasorum Antiquorum, Grèce*: vol. 1. Rhomaios, K. A., and Semni Papaspyridi, *Athènes, Musée national* (Paris c. 1903); vol. 2. Karouzou, Semni, *Athènes, Musée national* (Paris 1954); Kokkou, Angelikē, *Ē merimna gia tis archaiotētes stēn Ellada kai ta prōta Mouseia* (Athens 1977); Lattanzi, Elena, *I ritratti dei cosmeti nel Museo Nazionale di Atene* (Roma 1968); Nicole, George, *Catalogue des vases peints du Musée national d'Athènes*, Supplément, 2 t. (Paris 1911); Sakellariou, Agnes, *Corpus der minoischen und mykenischen Siegel des Nationalmuseums in Athen*, Corpus der minoischen und mykenischen Siegel I (Berlin 1962).

ELIZABETH COURTNEY BANKS

——— Delphi ———

ARCHAEOLOGICAL MUSEUM OF DELPHI (officially MOUSEION ARCHAIOLOGIKON TON DELFON; alternately DELPHI MUSEUM, ARCHAEOLOGICAL MUSEUM), Delphi.

The Archaeological Museum of Delphi was founded in 1902 to provide exhibit and storage space for the many beautiful and important finds from the systematic, scientific excavations at the site of the ancient Sanctuary of Apollo and the surrounding region. Informal explorations began by 1820 and continued sporadically during 1840, 1862, 1880, and 1888. On April 25, 1891, King George of Greece signed a document giving the French School of Athens a ten-year monopoly to excavate in Delphi. The French National Assembly granted a total of 750,000 francs to support this project. As early as 1862, the French government had initiated purchases of property in the sanctuary area. In 1891 this effort accelerated. The modern Greek town, which had grown up within the sanctuary walls, was rebuilt on a site 1.25 miles to the west and the sanctuary land purchased from its former owners and cleared. On October 10, 1892, excavation on the site began under the direction of Théophile Homolle. At present responsibility for excavation is shared by Greek government archaeologists and the archaeologists of the French School of Athens.

The museum collection is limited to the art and artifacts discovered in the ancient sanctuary and the surrounding region and includes nearly everything ever found there. The signal importance of the museum is in no way reduced by this circumscription. In fact, the collection attests to continuous human occupation from Neolithic times to the present. The Sanctuary of Apollo was established probably about 800 to 750 B.C., and from the beginning it was associated with the priestess Pythia, who pronounced oracles that brought international respect. Herodotus, the Greek historian who wrote about 450 B.C., and others attest to this through anecdotal records.

Within the sacred area were the Temple of Apollo, the Theatre of Dionysos, treasury buildings and treasures of many Greek city-states, and a great many other monuments, both sculptural and architectural, votive offerings, commemoratives and dedications, and the gifts of Greeks, Greek city-states, and foreigners. Along the road from the east before reaching the entrance of the Apollo Sanctuary is the Sanctuary of Athena Pronaia, with smaller temples dedicated to Athena, treasuries, and a gymnasium. High on the hill above the sanctuaries is a fine, well-preserved stadium, the home of the Pythian Games, established in 582 B.C., and held quadriennially until the end of the fourth century A.D. The Greek author Pausanias described Delphi's monuments in his *Description of Greece*, written during the second century A.D. Some of these monuments are extant and housed in the museum.

The Ephor for archaeology for the region is the director of the museum. He is appointed to this position by the Ministry of Culture and Science for Greece, under the General Direction of Antiquities and Restoration. The Ephor is assisted by Epimeletes, who are also public employees of the ministry. Other public commissioners serve in museum administration as guards and workmen. The French School of Athens remains very active in local excavation and studies of excavated material and has a special relationship with the Greek government as a result of its very long history of commitment to research at this site. Recent guidelines provide for continued cooperation between Greek archaeologists and foreign archaeologists, specifying an even-handed sharing of responsibility under the direction of a Greek national. Both share the responsibility for the publication of results. The Archaeological Museum of Delphi has no formal relationship with any university or with any other institution other than the Ministry of Culture and the informal, long-term relationship with the French School of Athens. There are no formal or informal supporting organizations.

The original museum building was built in 1902 by the Andreas Singros Foundation. In 1937 it was rebuilt, and after World War II during 1959–61, it was rebuilt and the galleries, storage, and work areas greatly enlarged and modernized. It is located between the Sanctuary of Apollo and the new town of Delphi. There are several major exhibition galleries, each arranged to display artifacts of a single type and period. All exhibits have explanatory labels in three languages, Greek, French, and English. Artifacts are displayed in chronological groups by type and material. In many cases outstanding monuments are displayed in ways that offer impressions of original juxtapositions in the ancient sanctuary. This includes reconstructions of the pediment and frieze of the Siphnian Treasury, the metope frieze of the Sicyonian Treasury, and the pediments of the Archaic Temple of Apollo. *The Naxian Sphinx* still rests on her column and capital.

Several buildings of the sanctuaries have been reconstructed, mainly with surviving ancient materials. In 1903–6 the Treasury of the Athenians was almost entirely rebuilt by J. Replat, architect of the French School of Athens, with funds provided by Athenians, incorporating casts of some of the original sculptured metopes that are housed in the museum. A partial restoration of the "Great Altar" was undertaken by the people of the island of Chios, the original donors of the altar. The French government funded the re-erection of three columns and part of the entablature of the tholos and re-erection of eight columns of the Temple of Apollo during the years 1938–41. The polygonal wall, steps, pavement, and four columns of the Stoa of the Athenians have also been restored.

The museum is a depository for all plans, negatives, diaries, and records relating to all excavation in the region of the Ephorate. All ceramic and other finds from this region are also housed there. The finds on deposit or display come from every part of the Greek world, attesting to the national character of the site in ancient times. Many non-Greek offerings are recorded in the ancient literature, but very few have survived. The earliest artifacts in the collection are neolithic and Early Bronze Age pottery mainly from Kirra and Krissos, where, in 1935 and 1939, some sixty-thousand sherds were excavated from which eighty-eight whole pots were reconstructed. A Cycladic marble figurine was excavated in Delphi itself. Among the Middle Bronze Age sherds are Cycladic wares, evidence of a long-distance sea trade by 1600 B.C. Late Bronze Age remains include vases, terracotta figurines, and a fragmentary marble ceremonial rhyton in the shape of a lioness' head, which has a counterpart from Knossos. Bronzes include an axe head of Minoan type, spearhead, dagger, sword, and pins. There are also a number of glass amulets, beads, and ornaments. The subsequent Dark Age is represented by bronze arms and armor and a very few iron weapons, cremation and burial urns, and pottery of Sub-Mycenean, Protogeometric, and Geometric types attesting to continuous occupation of the site. There are already a number of products of distant Greek workshops in Athens and Corinth that influenced local pottery styles.

Bronzes are important among the artifacts of the Orientalizing and Archaic periods (c. 700–480 B.C.). They include arms and armor, fibulae and pins, and a variety of cauldron attachments including griffin protomes and cast bull's head and sirens. A fine bronze repoussé decorated bowl is Phoenician; a shield is probably Cypriote. Other Phoenician imports include carved tridacna shells, faience scarabs, and a carved stone scaraboid. One splendid ivory figurine using an Orientalizing motif but of Greek workmanship is the so-called *Liontamer* of the late seventh century B.C. Of Greek workmanship, but of the indigenous Daedalic tradition, is a fine bronze statuette, a belted, nude kouros figure approximately contemporary to the above figurine.

Kleobis and *Biton*, two early Archaic kouroi, dating from the early years of the sixth century B.C., are important examples of the earliest period of monumental stone sculpture in Greece. These larger-than-life-size twin figures are stiffly frontal, with left foot forward, clenched fists next to thighs, oval eyes, and hair in three heavy curls on each shoulder. They are identified by an inscription on the base as the work of a sculptor from Argos, probably Polymedes. The figures represent two stalwart brothers rewarded by a peaceful death at the Argive Heraion in return for their services in pulling their mother's cart (in the absence of oxen) to Hera's shrine, as related by Herodotus, who mentioned these specific statues in their honor at Delphi. In the same room are Archaic metope reliefs from the Treasury of Sicyon (c. 560 B.C.): the heroes *Kastor, Polydeukes, and Idas Drive Cattle Stolen in a Raid*, in a composition amusing for its rhythmic arrangement of human and animal legs, one ox of each group looking out toward the spectator, the heroes' spears in neat parallelism over their shoulders. Other metopes from this same treasury are the *Kalydonian Boar*, *Europa and the Bull*, *Helle on her Ram*, and the *Dioskouroi with the Ship Argo*.

An entire room is devoted to striking gold and silver objects, mostly from the sixth century B.C.: decorative plaques with relief (such as griffins), a model flower, a silver head with flowing gold hairbands, a silver bull's head richly gilded, a full-scale metal ox with gold plating, and so on.

A special room displays the admirable Late Archaic reliefs of the Siphnian Treasury. The very high-relief pediment, the *Struggle of Herakles and Apollo for the Delphic Tripod*, shows the major gods and goddesses, who sit below and watch this struggle and those presented on the low-relief frieze that completely encircled the building: the *Trojan War* on the east, the *Combat of Gods and Giants* on the north, the *Ravishing of the Daughters of Leukippos by the Dioskouroi* on the south, and the *Judgment of Paris* (?) on the west. Two korai, statues of young girls, acted as caryatids framing the doorway of the treasury and supporting the porch architrave on their heads. They are elaborately decorated works. All of these sculptures are major testaments to the splendid movement toward Classical grandeur and are marked by a lively vigor. In this same room is the Archaic *Winged Sphinx* squatting on a tall Ionic column, dedicated by the islanders of Naxos about 560 B.C.

Two rooms have remnants of the often-destroyed and rebuilt main Temple of Apollo. The sculptures date from the Alkmaionid period, about 510 B.C. The whole west pediment is displayed, badly fragmented. Its theme is the *Battle of Olympian Gods and the Giants*, and it is thought to be the work of the famous Athenian sculptor Antenor, creator of the signed complete monumental kore in the Acropolis Museum (q.v.), Athens. It has an austere magnificence, a monumental grandeur, and a dynamic sense of movement. Athena is represented at the right extremity, a giant at the left, probably Enkelados. In the other room, the eastern pediment, made of Parian marble, is the *Arrival of Apollo at Delphi*. He is seen in a chariot with his mother, Leto, and sister Artemis, being greeted by the local King Delphos, the sons of Hephaistos, and the daughters of Kekrops. At the left corner of the pediment, a lion is killing a bull; on the right, another lion is attacking a deer whose suffering is reflected in its pathetic eyes. The fine striding *Nike* statue was an akroterion, standing on the temple roof.

Twenty-four metopes, some badly damaged, from the Doric frieze of the Treasury of the Athenians (c. 510–500 B.C.) depict the heroic deeds of Theseus ("founder" of Athens), the labors of Herakles, and a battle between Athenians and Amazons. Of special interest is the inscription from the treasury's front wall preserving a second century B.C. hymn to Apollo and its musical notation for the chorus.

The *Charioteer*, the best-known object in the museum, is a splendid bronze statue, fully life-size, perfectly preserved, a youthful contestant in the chariot race at the Pythian Games. He is standing erect, holding the reins in his front hand (the left arm is not yet recovered). The long garment with rhythmic folds is held in by a belt high above the hips and by criss-crossed thongs across the shoulders and under the arms. The noble head is admirable from all angles, its eyes of inset stone remarkably life-like. The feet are charmingly natural, although invisible in ancient times, when the statue stood in its deep chariot platform. There is a wonderful naturalness, dignified simplicity, and tranquil grandeur about this youth, which ranks it among the major sculptures in the history of art. An inscription indicates that it was dedicated by Polyzalos of Gela in Sicily, about 475 B.C. In a case in the same room is a beautiful kylix vase, recently found, from the same period as the *Charioteer*, depicting a majestic seated Apollo holding his lyre and pouring a libation while a sacred black dove or raven looks on. The room with Funeral Monuments has one excellent Early Classical stele in Parian marble, dating about 465 B.C., showing the deceased as a youthful athlete scraping his body with a metal instrument to remove dirt and oil while a small slave boy holds a bowl of ointment and the youth's dog looks up at his master. The scene is clearly composed and suffused with tenderness.

Several fine free-standing statues in marble remain of the original group of nine members of the family of Daochos II of Pharsala in Thessaly, placed near the Apollo Temple in 335 B.C. The most notable of them is *Agias* as a young athlete; its style refers it to the school of Lysippos. Others represented include *Agelaos*, brother of Agias; *Daochos I*, Agias' son; *Sisyphos I*, his grandson; *Aknonios*, tetrarch of Thessaly; and *Sisyphos II*, son of Daochos II, who dedicated the elaborate monument. An excellent marble statue, a *Philosopher*, of about 275 B.C. stands nearby.

In the same room is a notable and mysterious group of three dancing girls positioned back-to-back around a column sheathed with akanthos leaves. They dance gracefully in their delicate swirling draperies and sacred headgear, the *kalathos*, like fluted columns, evidently in a ritual performance. They stood atop a marble column some thirty-five feet high and carried over their heads a bronze cauldron supported by a tripod whose legs rested on the upper projections of the column. The work is Ionian in style; an inscription says it was dedicated by the Athenians about 330 B.C. The dancers may be the daughters of Kekrops, legendary father of Athens, or they may be the Graces or the Maenads of Dionysos.

There is one splendid marble portrait head of a man in his prime with a close beard, twirled eyebrows, tousled hair, intense look, and partly open lips. It is of the finest quality in the Late Hellenistic manner of the early second century B.C. and is thought by some to be Flamininus, the Roman general who in 197 B.C. defeated Philip V of Macedon at Kynoskephalai. The Roman-era marble, life-sized statue of Antinous, favorite of Emperor Hadrian in the early second century A.D., is perhaps the best of the many extant examples of this portrait, with an air of soft and graceful melancholy.

There are several post-Classical heads. One, a head of Dionysos, has blurred or softened outlines giving a dreamy romantic aura. Another, perhaps the portrait of Plutarch, the Greek man of letters from Boeotia who lived from A.D. 40 to 120, shows a thoughtful, much-idealized rendering of the historian's features.

Many architectural fragments are on display. In particular, parts of the entablature and metopes of the beautiful round Tholos building justify its fame in ancient times for architectural and sculptural elegance. There are also examples of Roman mosaic floors, fine small bronzes, and representative pottery from all periods.

The *Omphalos* is one of the more remarkable objects excavated in Delphi. A Hellenistic or Roman copy of the Archaic omphalos (navel) or center of the world, it is carved as if covered with the agrenon or net. It was originally surmounted by the two golden eagles of Zeus that flew from the two ends of the earth to meet at its center, at Delphi.

The Archaeological Museum of Delphi has a modest reference library reserved for the use of staff archaeologists. Photographs of published objects in the collection may be purchased for scientific purposes only and with the approval of the director of the museum. Tourist photographs and slides are for sale in the museum shop for outstanding items in the collection. Aside from Manolis Andronicos' article on the "Delphi Museum" (M. Andronicos, M. Chatzidakis, and J. Karageorghis, *The Greek Museums* [Athens 1974]), there is no official guide or other museum publication. However, the French School of Athens has been publishing excavated materials since the early explorations of the sanctuaries. Chief among them are the series of volumes *Fouilles de Delphes* (Paris 1902-), with many volumes devoted to the art finds.

Selected Bibliography

Delacoste-Messelière, P., *Au Musée de Delphes* (Paris 1936); Delacoste-Messelière, P., and G. de Miré, *Delphes* (Paris 1948); Ferri, S., "Delphi," *Enciclopedia dell'Arte Antica*, vol. 3 (Rome 1964), pp. 27–44; Hoyle, P., *Delphi* (London 1967); Meletzis, S., and H. Papadakis, *Delphi: Sanctuary and Museum* (Munich 1964); di Neuhoff, S., *Delphi* (Athens 1971); Petracos, B. C., *Delphi* (Athens 1971); Picard, Ch., and P. Delacoste-Messelière, *Les sculptures grecques à Delphes* (Paris 1929); Poulsen, F., *Delphes* (London 1920); Roux, G., *Delphes* (Paris 1970).

ELEANOR GURALNICK AND RAYMOND V. SCHODER

——— Heraclion ———

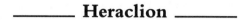

ARCHAEOLOGICAL MUSEUM OF HERAKLEION (officially ARCHAIOLOGIKON MOUSEION, IRAKLION; alternately HERACLION MUSEUM, HERAKLEION ARCHAEOLOGICAL MUSEUM), Xanthoudidou Street, Heraclion, Crete.

The Archaeological Museum of Herakleion was founded in 1883 by the Philekpaideutikes Sylloges (Society for the Promotion of Education) with the function of preserving historical and archaeological monuments and collecting antiquities. Local Turkish authorities had granted the society the rights to carry out these activities along with the authority to halt destruction, collect chance finds of antiquities, undertake excavations, and grant exploration permits to foreign scholars. Concurrently, important antiquities were donated to the new museum by Governor Photiades Pasha, Theodoros Triphyllis, George Mitsotakis, Stephanos Nikolaides, George Kalaitzakis, and others. These gifts, a number of small purchases, and the artifacts from many small early excavations rapidly developed into a rich collection. Initially, the museum was housed in two rooms within the precinct of the Christian metropolis of St. Menas in Herakleion. After 1900, when large-scale excavations began, the collection grew rapidly. The collection was moved to a Turkish barrack after the War for Independence in 1898.

With the support of the Cretan government, the aid of a generous donation from Gaston Arnaud-Jeanti of the Italian Archaeological School and a legacy from the American J. Seager, a two-room museum was built between 1904 and 1908. The formal date given for the official opening of the Archaeological Museum of Herakleion is 1907. Then William Dörpfeld, the German archaeologist and architect, and Panaiotis Kavvadias developed a plan for a museum building in the Classical Greek style, which was partially complete by 1912.

Both the building and the collection were damaged by earthquakes in 1911, 1926, and 1935. Therefore, a new earthquake-proof building was begun in 1937, completed before World War II to plans by the architect Patroklos Karantinos. His goal was to use contemporary architectural style to provide a setting for the display materials. He has succeeded in providing good light and easy circulation for large numbers of visitors. This plan included accommodation for future extensions, which were added in 1950 and 1964. During World War II the collection was stored in air-raid shelters in the basement and miraculously survived, essentially intact with only minor repairable damage to a few large objects. During this period the building was used as a military warehouse, a hospital, a school for chemical warfare, a camp for Italian prisoners, and, finally, a strongpoint with machineguns and barbwire enclosure. These uses made it a target for military assault. It suffered shelling; it received direct hits from aerial bombing and suffered damage from the explosion of a munitions ship in the harbor. The extensive repairs were completed by 1950.

The original museum included artifacts and art of Byzantine and medieval date. Since 1950 this material has been in the care of the Society for Historical Studies in Crete. It is housed along with a mass of other materials of recent historical and popular interest in the new Cretan Historical Museum in the Kalokairinos House. Recently, archaeological museums featuring local finds have been established in Khania, Hagia Nikolaos, Hierapetra, Gortyn, and Rethymno.

The museum is governed by the Ephor of the Archaeological Periphery, who is a commissioner of the Ministry of Culture and Sciences of Greece, under the General Direction of Antiquities and Restoration. The Ephor is assisted by epimeletes (public commissioners) of the Ministry of Culture and Science. The staff also includes commissioners for administration and guards. The Archaeological Museum of Herakleion has no relationship of any kind to a university or to any other institution other than the Ministry of Culture and Science. There are no formal or informal supporting organizations.

The museum is divided into several curatorial departments: Collections, Archives, Laboratory for Pottery, Chemical Laboratory, and Library. The collections are divided into three major units, each containing representative objects from each of the chronological periods represented in the entire collection. These units are: Exhibition of Cretan Antiquities, displayed in twenty rooms; Department of Scientific Collections, research collections well organized in eight rooms; and the Department of Systematic Storage (materials of secondary importance), filling two large storerooms. The official catalogues of the museum itemize some 42,300 objects in the entire collection.

The Archaeological Museum of Herakleion is the only major repository in the world for the art and artifacts of Minoan civilization. Only here may one study its variety and detail throughout its entire development. The collection characterizes the culture and civilization in Crete from the first evidence of human habitation on the island during the Neolithic period (c. 6000 B.C.) to the end of the Roman period (c. A.D. 500), including art and artifacts from the several developmental stages of ancient Minoan civilization, Sub-Minoan, Protogeometric, Geometric, Orientalizing, Archaic, Classical, and Hellenistic periods. A single major private collection of antiquities, that of Stylianos Giamalakis, donated in 1963, is displayed in its own gallery. All other artifacts are displayed by period and in many instances as comprehensive displays of typical or outstanding artifacts from a single site or find circumstance. Most of the artifacts and art in the collection were acquired as a result of large-scale, officially sponsored excavations by the Greek Archaeological Service, Greek Archaeological Society, and foreign archaeological schools in Greece. The foreign schools include the American, British, Italian, French, and German (the Germans were active in Crete only during World War II). Italian explorations began under F. Halbherr in collaboration with the Society for the Promotion of Education in 1884 at the caves of Mt. Ida, from the Minoan, and Eileithyia, where votive figures representing Eileithyia, the goddess protector of mothers in childbirth and of new-born children, were found dating to Minoan times through the Roman period. Excavations have continued intermittently at Gortyn, where the famous Roman Law Code carved on a stone wall is still in situ and, at the Temple of Phythian Apollo, at Geometric-period cemeteries, at Kamares Cave, and at the Messara. Pierre Demargne, a Frenchman, began excavations at Itanos and Lato in the same year. In 1878 the site of the Palace of Knossos was discovered by Minos Kalokairinos, but excavation did not begin until after 1900, when Sir Arthur Evans, an Englishman, purchased the site, devoting the rest of his life to its excavation, study, and restoration. The early commitment of the Americans to archaeological exploration of Crete is exemplified by Harriet Boyd, who led the first American expedition soon after the turn of the century, uncovering an entire Minoan town of the second millennium B.C., Gournia, including temples and votives, a palace, houses, workshops, and utensils, tools, and art; Edith Hall excavated Vrocastro and Kavousi, and Richard Seager excavated Pseira, Mochlos, and Vasiliki. This commitment has continued into the present. The collection of the museum now contains art and artifacts from five major Minoan palaces (Knossos, Phaistos, Hagia Triada, Mallia, and Zakro) and from literally dozens of villas, caves, sanctuaries, cemeteries, and town sites. Almost all of this material represents culture in the well-explored central and eastern portions of the island.

Scientific excavations on Crete have unearthed some important early artifacts from the other established civilizations in the Near East and Egypt that have helped to establish the chronology of Minoan civilization and document its trading relationships. Among the many Babylonian cylinder seals decorated with divinities, demons, mythological animals, and so on is a cylinder seal inscribed with the name of King Hammurabi of Babylon (c. 1750 B.C.). There are also a Hittite sphinx (c. 1450 B.C.) and a substantial number of Sassanian seals or bullas of chalcedony, from Persia of the third through the seventh century A.D.

Egyptian artifacts have turned up in large numbers in the excavations of both Minoan sites and those of later periods, although few of them are on view. Among those that may be seen are: a proto-dynastic mace head; chalices from before the second dynasty (before c. 2800 B.C.); carinated diorite bowls of the fourth dynasty (c. 2590–2470 B.C.); two Old Kingdom porphyry vases and a porphyry bowl (c. 2950–2134 B.C.); a diorite statuette of the seated User, an Egyptian official of the twelfth dynasty (c. 1991–1785 B.C.) from Knossos; an alabaster pyxis lid with the cartouche of the Hyksos Pharoah Kyan (c. 1620 B.C.), of the Second Intermediate Period, from Knossos; an alabaster jar with the cartouche of Thutmose III (c. 1490–1437 B.C.) from a tomb at Katsamba; a large number of alabaster vases, alabastrons, and lamps of Egyptian manufacture from Knossos, Zakro, and Isopata, conical and fluted rhytons made in Crete of imported Egyptian alabaster, polychrome-banded limestone vases and clay vases, all of the eighteenth dynasty (c. 1570–1303 B.C.); glass bottles from Amnissos and Kalyvia of the eighteenth dynasty, as well as bowls and vases of diorite; a series of Egyptian scarabs, including one of Queen Tiy (c. 1437–1410 B.C.); a series of paste and ivory figurines from the Cave of Eileithyia at Inatos (Tsoutouros) from the Sub-Minoan and Early Geometric periods (c. 1100–800 B.C.); faience figurines from Kommos of the Orientalizing and Archaic periods (c. 700–500 B.C.); and a series of Hellenistic and Roman coins from the mints of cities in Egypt and Asia Minor.

The neolithic cultures in Crete (c. 5000–2800 B.C.) are represented by steatopygous burnished terracotta figurines from Apano Khoria near Ierapetra; clay and stone vessels, many in imported Egyptian stones and imitating Egyptian shapes; burnished, hand-made pottery with incised linear patterns; figurines representing animals, birds, and female human beings; miniature votive vases; stone male worshippers; obsidian, bone, and stone tools; and celts and maces.

The pre-palatial period, commonly known as the Early Minoan period (c. 2800–2200 B.C.), is characterized by a greatly diversified selection of artifact types, including several distinctive styles of pottery (some associated with a single or a few sites), fine stonewares, figurines, seals, obsidian, copper weapons and tools, and silver and gold jewelry. Some of the fine stoneware is Cycladic, including marble idols and so-called frying pans. Other fine stoneware is from Mochlos and includes vessels of steatite, serpentine, alabaster, and conglomerate. The natural veining of the banded limestones and other particolored stones is often brilliantly adapted to accent the shape of the vessel. Among the very finest examples of stone carving is the lid of a pyxis from Mochlos, with an incised linear-patterned surface and a handle carved to represent a reclining dog. Simple burnished chalices and ritual kernoi are identified as Pyrgos style. The Hagia Onouphrios-style jugs and cups have linear decorative patterns and are often shaped like huts, animals, boats, barrels, fruits, and pyxides. Vasilike-style vases of the final pre-palatial period have white and red decor on a dark ground, the decoration taking the form of bands, spirals, and schematic fish, and include one pot in the form of a woman holding her breasts in her hands. Terracotta votives have the forms of human beings, horns of consecration, and model sacred boats.

From Palaikastro there are fruitstands, cups with appliqué plastic animals, birds, loaves of bread, a votive dish with a flock of animals, and a herdsman and a four-wheeled cart, all of terracotta. Still other pots are shaped as birds, female deities, bulls, a bull and three men grabbing the horns, a bull with an acrobat leaping over his back, a bull tossing his head, and double and triple kernoi. There are many ivory figurines and many statuettes in marble representing nude women from the Messara, Mochlos, Agia Triada, Lesithi, and the Trapeza Cave. From many of these same sites there are large numbers of seals and amulets of ivory and steatite, modeled in the shapes of animals such as monkeys, and of birds. Also found are those shaped as prisms with schematically incised human beings and with hieroglyphic symbols that remain untranslatable. A great deal of gold jewelry has come to light from graves, including diadems and bands, a small frog, votive breasts, beads, chains, leaves, and rosettes. Other jewelry includes beads of amethyst, carnelian, serpentine, paste, and rock crystal.

The proto-palatial period, commonly known as Middle Minoan I and II, extends from about 2200–1700 B.C. Many of the most important art objects come from Knossos, Mallia, and the Peak Sanctuaries. The faience *Town Mosaic* from Knossos is a series of inlaid representations of multistory Minoan houses. A schist ceremonial axe handle shaped as a leaping panther was excavated at Mallia. The sanctuaries produced numbers of votives, mainly terracotta figurines, including women in bell-shaped skirts; male and female worshippers; animals, especially bulls; fishes, crabs and shells; and model boats. A clay offering table has incised bulls and spirals; another has a pedestal with goddesses holding flowers and surrounded by female dancers. There are many other offering tables, altars, lamps, kernoi, rhyta, libation vessels, and seals decorated with intaglio animals, humans, ships, vases, or hieroglyphs. The pottery of this period includes the finest ''Egg Shell'' ware cups, so called for the fineness of the clay and the thinness of the walls of the ware, and the Kamares ware, named for the cave where examples were first excavated. This ware comes in a wide variety of shapes, painted in red and white on a black fabric with an extraordinary inventiveness combining motifs from the natural world (flowers and fish), symbols from human culture (helmets and double axes), geometric and linear decors, along with pure abstractions. Among the finest of these vases are an octopus vase from Gournia, a krater on a pedestal with plastic lilies, a fruitstand with a crenellated rim, and a pithos with fish and egg sack.

The neo-palatial period includes those periods more commonly referred to as Middle Minoan II and III and Late Minoan I (c. 1700–1400 B.C.). Two outstanding small-scale sculptural monuments are the faience *Snake Goddesses* from the Knossos palace shrine, each a multi-colored triumph of the faience makers' art. From the same shrine and of the same material are votives modeled as dresses, vases, sacral knots, seashells, flowers, and plaques with relief scenes of animals suckling their young, priests with animal masks, and a bull with acrobat. A masterpiece of stone carving is the serpentine, naturalistic *Bull's Head Rhyton*, a libation vessel with incised detail, horns of gilded wood, and inlaid shell, crystal, and jasper eyes. Another rhyton of white limestone is carved in the form of a lioness' head. There are many carved stone vessels, some fragmentary, of two distinctive types. One type is decorated with relief scenes from life: athletic contests, war with archers, an offering bearer at a peak sanctuary, the procession of priests, and a polypod among rocks at sea. Two of the finest in this group are the *Harvester Vase* and the *Young Chieftain's Cup*. The second type of stone vase depends on its classic shape and the integration of shape with the color patterning of the stone for its decorative quality. Most have elegantly graceful or elaborately curvilinear handles. Many vases of this type are from the palace at Zakro (c. 1450 B.C.). The libation vessels include some carved in imitation of seashells and one *Triton Shell* is noteworthy.

The ivories are exceptionally fine with the *Acrobat* or *Bull Jumper* from Knossos being singular for its grace, delicacy, and sense of movement, an encapsulation of the qualities that distinguish Minoan art. Other interesting ivories are sphinxes, each with a plume crest; a gaming board of ivory, inlaid with rock crystal, gold and silver leaf, lapis lazuli, and faience, together with four ivory gaming pieces; helmeted heads; and votive helmets. Much of the gold work is exquisite and preserves unusual motifs. A pendant from Mallia has twin bees and a circular honeycomb executed with granulation accents. A royal sword from Mallia has a pommel of gold-worked repoussé depicting an acrobat circled about the hilt. Another sword has a gold and ivory hilt and rock-crystal pommel.

Among the glories of the Archaeological Museum of Herakleion are the wall paintings from the palaces at Knossos and Hagia Triada and the villas at Tylissos, Psiera, Nirou Khani, and Knossos (c. 1600–1400 B.C.). They encompass three distinct approaches to painting. The so-called Miniature style with large, complex scenes, often with dozens of figures, includes crowd scenes with impressionistic sketches of humans. Examples are *Ladies in Blue*, *Ceremonial at a Pillar Shrine*, and *Dancing Women*, all from Knossos. Of the Large-Figure style, there are the largest number of extant examples, although they are often fragmentary and restored. From the *Procession of Rhyton Bearers*, only one figure is well preserved, of the five hundred once lining the main corridor of Knossos. Perhaps from this same group comes the exquisite head known as *La Parisienne*. From other rooms in the same palace come the *Bull-jumping Fresco*; the frieze *Bull's Hide Figure-of-Eight Shields*; *Saffron Gatherer*; two frescoes from the Queen's Megaron, *Dancer* and *Dolphins, Flying Fish, and Spirals*; and *Wingless Griffins* from the Throne Room. The Knossos House of the Frescoes is the source of *Captain of Blacks*, *Blue Bird in a Landscape*, *Monkey in a Landscape of Iris, Ivy, and Rocks*, and *Monkey in a Landscape of Papyrus and Crocus*. From the Caravanserei are *Partridges and Hoopoe*. From Amnissos come two frescoes, *Lilies Potted* and *Landscape with Lilies and Iris*. Frescoes from the palace at Hagia Triada include: *Lyre Playing Musician Leading Procession, Cat Stalking*

Pheasant, Religious Ceremony, Buck, and other fragments. A shrine in this palace had a painted stucco floor with octopods, dolphins, and flying fish. Perhaps the best-preserved major example of Minoan painting is the *Sarcophagus of Hagia Triada,* from about 1400 B.C. Its long sides each have a religious ceremonial; the short sides have chariot scenes, one with winged griffins. The smallest but most interesting group are the painted stucco relief figures of monumental size. Fine examples survive from Knossos: a bull's head, a priest-king, winged griffins, and limbs of athletes. From Psiera come the seated women figures.

Pottery of the neo-palatial period is finely decorated with vegetation (lilies, grasses, reeds, papyrus), marine life (octopods, seaweed, argonauts, starfish, nautili), and symbols (helmets, sacral knots, double axes, sacral horns, spirals, basketwork), with a few having relief decor (barley, sacral knots, spirals). Vases are often tall and slender; others have bridged spouts. Seals of semiprecious stones are numerous. Scenes engraved on them include: animals in action, animals in combat, and religious scenes with altars, goddesses, dancers, and worshippers. Bronze statuettes of worshippers saluting are numerous. There are quantities of gold objects in addition to those fine works already mentioned, including an exquisite rock-crystal rhyton with gilded faience at the neck and crystal bead handle; fine jewelry including seal rings, necklaces, pendants, and votive offerings of golden double axes, seashells, and bulls. The varied miscellanea include relief decorated stone lamps, lanterns, and altars; lyres; flutes; mirrors; tripod cauldrons; bronze jugs; armor; arms; tools; and weights.

The post-palatial period (c. 1400–1100 B.C.) produced relatively few fine works; nevertheless, there are interesting large terracotta goddesses from shrines at Gazi, Gournia, Kalokhori, Hagia Triada, Prinias, Kannia, Gortyn, Arkannes, and Siteia. There are many votive offerings in the form of human beings, animals, hut-shaped shrines, and boats. Schist molds from Siteia were used for making jewelry and religious objects. Faience jewelry and bronze artifacts are on view, as are Mycenean kraters decorated with birds and wild goat hunts. The Cretan painted pottery includes many stemmed kylikes, stirrup jars, flasks, and rhytons decorated with octopods, birds, concentric circles, and bands. Painted larnaki or sarcophagi use the decor of pottery as well as griffins and religious symbols.

The Sub-Minoan and Geometric periods (c. 1100–800 B.C.) have even fewer examples of fine work. *The Goddesses* from Karphi repeats the earlier types; the votives from the Cave of Eileithyia at Inatos include many types of terracottas: erotic couples, women giving birth, women suckling children, gold rosettes, bronze double axes, jewelry, pins, fibulae, and iron weapons and tools. There are some interesting model sanctuaries and temples, painted funerary urns, and kraters.

The Orientalizing and Archaic periods (c. 800–500 B.C.) see a return to monumental art, particularly bronze and stone sculpture-in-relief and in-the-round. Perhaps the most important of these works is the group of three bronze-on-wood spherelaton cult statues from the temple at Dreros of the first half of the seventh century B.C., probably representing Apollo, Leto, and Artemis. The bronze votive shields, tympanons, cymbals, and bowls from the Idaean cave, decorated repoussé with relief scenes, begin early in the eighth century B.C. The most important stone sculpture is architectural, from the seventh-century B.C. temple at Prinias. This group includes a well-preserved frieze of horsemen (height, 0.84 meter; total preserved length, 3.62 meters), built into the wall of Room XIX; and the lintel of the temple entrance door carved with two identical opposing relief images of a goddess on its lower surface and with friezes of lions and deer on its vertical surfaces, surmounted by two identical statues in-the-round of a seated goddess. The lintel and goddesses are reconstructed in the doorway leading from Room XIX to Room XX. From Gortyn there is a seated goddess, preserved from above the waist to the base, with color exceedingly well preserved to emphasize the elaborate incised floral decor; two high-relief plaques (height, 1.5 meters), each displaying three figures, a central male with a nude female on either side, perhaps Apollo, Leto, and Artemis, all from the mid-seventh century B.C.

From Prinias there are a number of grave stelae with incised figures: a woman with a distaff and many with helmeted warriors with shields and spears, all from the seventh century B.C. Other examples of seventh-century B.C. sculpture are: the *Eleutherna Head* and torso; a relief of a seated goddess from Malles; a goddess from Astritsi, an over life-size torso; a gorgoneion from Dreros; a lion's head from Phaistos; and a poros head from Axos. Fine architectural fragments include a seventh-century B.C. column capital from Arkades formed in the shape of a flower and the sima and waterspout of the Temple of Dictaean Zeus at Palaikastro decorated with a frieze of chariots, charioteers, and warriors, from the sixth century B.C. From this same century are a terracotta seated lion from Praisos and the fragment of a kouros torso. The minor arts of the Archaic period (c. 650–500 B.C.) include: elaborately decorated bronze armor (mithra, corselets, helmets, and shields), with both relief and incision; relief decorated bronze tripods; fibulae; mirrors; stone, bronze, and terracotta statuettes representing Athena, gorgoneion, houses, and shrines; horses, lions, wild goats, oxen, and human beings; Orientalizing pottery including pithoi with relief mythological scenes, Rhodian "Wild Goat" style vases, and Corinthian, Boeotian, and Attic black-figure vases.

The museum's collection of Classical and Hellenistic sculpture is small. The few pieces of any interest are a Classical grave stele with an archer from Hagia Pelagia, work of a fifth-century B.C. Attic sculptor; a grave stele portraying the farewell of a dead man to his wife and son, from Herakleion of the fourth century B.C.; a metope from a fifth-century B.C. temple at Knossos, *Herakles Bringing the Erymanthian Boar to Eurysteus Who Is Hiding in a Pithos*. Of Hellenistic date (c. 330–67 B.C.) are an overlife-size statue of Apollo in a long peplos with inlaid eyes; statues of Pluto and Persephone, Serapis and Isis with Cerberus; the statue of Aphrodite and a series of small heads of Aphrodite; and the life-size bronze statue *Boy in Sandals and Toga* from Ierapetra, from the first century

B.C. The minor arts of this period include mainly Attic red-figure vases, some Gnathian vases, many spouted lamps, votive figurines and plaques from Knossos and Gortyn, and jewelry, including a pair of gold earrings imitative of the Victory of Paionios, from Knossos.

The collection of Graeco-Roman sculpture (c. 67 B.C.-A.D. 323) includes: a portrait head of Emperor Augustus; portraits of other members of the Julio-Claudian imperial families; copies of the *Doryphoros* and *Aphrodite* by Poly-clitus; a Praxitelian torso; a copy of *Pothos* by Scopas; a copy of the *Athena Parthenos*, the chryselephantine cult statue by Phidias; a copy of the *Kneeling Aphrodite* by Diodalsas; a pan with bull's hooves; a philosopher, perhaps a portrait of Heraclitus; Artemis; a large headless statue of emperor Hadrian in full armor; a Dionysos; a marble sarcophagus inscribed Polybos; a cippus; a sarcophagus of Greek type from Mallia of the third century A.D.; a Roman lady from Chersonesos, perhaps Julia Domna; an Archaistic girl from Kisamos; a group depicting Artemis shooting the children of Niobe; and a number of relief-carved fragments of sarcophagi, grave stelae, and miscellanea. A black and white mosaic frames a fine multicolored scene with Poseidon with his trident riding seahorses accompanied by Tritons and dolphins, signed "Apollinaris made it," from Knossos, dating from the second century A.D. The minor arts include many glass vases from Herakleion, Sokara, and Gortyn; bronze figurines; small marble heads; terracotta figurines; coins; gems; and jewelry of gold and silver inlaid with precious stones and including necklaces, pins, and earrings in the form of Nike and birds.

The Giamalakis Collection includes some fine examples of Venetian jewelry of the fifteenth century A.D. and some small Byzantine and Turkish objects.

The Archaeological Museum of Herakleion has an important and extensive library reserved for the use of visiting scholars and archaeologists under the direct supervision of the museum administration. Photographs of published objects in the collection may be purchased only for scientific purposes and with the approval of the museum director. Tourist photographs and slides are for sale in the museum shop for outstanding items in the collection. Aside from the *Guide to the Archaeological Museum of Herakleion*, 1968 and 1979, there are no museum publications. Articles concerned with artifacts and art in the museum collection appear frequently in a large number of American, British, French, German, Italian, and Greek journals concerned with archaeology. *Hesperia*, *Archaeological Reports*, *Annual* of the British School of Archaeology in Athens, *Etudes Crétoises*, Ecole français d'Athènes, *Bulletin de correspondence helle-nique*, *Gnomon*, *Annuario*, *Athenische Mitteilungen*, *Jahrbuch des Instituts*, *Kretika Khronika*, *Archaeologikon Deltion*, *to Ergon tes Archaeologikis Etairias*, *Praktika tes Archaeologikis Etairias*, and *Archaeologiki Ephimeris* are among those journals regularly featuring articles on Cretan antiquities in the museum collection.

Selected Bibliography

Bosanquet, R. C., and Dawkins, W. B., *Unpublished Objects from the Palaikastro Excavations, BSA* 1901–6, *BSA Supplemental Paper* 1 (London 1923), *BSA* 40 (1939–

40); H. Boyd, *Gournia* (Philadelphia 1908); Chazzidakis, J., *The Vaulted Tombs of Messara* (Liverpool 1924); Demargne, Pierre, *Birth of Greek Art* (New York 1964); idem, *La Crete dedalique* (Paris 1947); Evans, Arthur J., *The Palace of Minos* (London 1921– 36); Hawes, H. B., *Gournia, Vasiliki, and Prehistoric Sites on the Isthmus of Hierapetra* (Philadelphia 1908); Kunze, Emil, *Kretische Bronzereliefs* (Stuttgart 1931); Levi, Doro, *Festos e la civilta minoica* (Rome 1976); Marinatos, Spyridon, *Crete and Mycenae* (London 1960); Platon, Nikolaos, *Zakros* (New York 1971); Sakellarakis, J., *Corpus der minoischen und mykenischen Siegel* (Berlin 1969); Seager, R. B., *Explorations in the Islands of Mochlos, Pachyammos, and Pseira, Anthropological Publications* 3 and 7; idem, *Mochlos* (Philadelphia 1912); idem, *Vasiliki* (Philadelphia 1907); Warren, Peter, *Minoan Stone Vases* (Oxford 1969); Xanthoudides, Stephanos, *The Vaulted Tombs of Messara* (Liverpool 1924); Zervos, Christos, *L'art de la Crete Neolithique et Minoenne* (Paris 1956).

ELEANOR GURALNICK

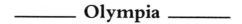

Olympia

ARCHAEOLOGICAL MUSEUM OF OLYMPIA (officially MOUSEION ARCHAEOLOGIKON TIS OLYMPIAS; alternately OLYMPIA MUSEUM, NATIONAL ARCHAEOLOGICAL MUSEUM AT OLYMPIA), Olympia.

The Archaeological Museum of Olympia was founded in 1886 for the purpose of housing the numerous important finds from the systematic, scientific excavations of the site of the ancient sanctuary of Zeus and the complex of surrounding facilities. These excavations were carried out by the German Archaeological Institute beginning on September 22, 1875. The museum collection is limited to the finds from the Sacred Altis and the nearby region and includes nearly everything found there. The geographical limitations on the collection in no way reduce its importance. The district was continuously occupied from Neolithic times and in 776 B.C. became the site of the first of the great international sanctuaries of ancient Greece, continuing in this role until the decline of the Roman Empire in the sixth century. Within the spacious Altis were temples, altars, treasury buildings and treasures of Greek cities, monuments, countless votive offerings, and dedications to and by the winners of the athletic contests of the quadriennial Olympic games. Radiating from the central enclosure were a variety of athletic facilities, hotels, workshops, villas, and civic buildings. In Roman times the very early Temple of Hera was converted into a museum, thus turning Olympia into a repository for an extraordinarily diverse collection of the finest products of more than one thousand years of Classical civilization. Not all of them have survived.

The modest results of the first brief exploration of the site by the French Expédition Scientifique de Morée, under General Maison in 1829, are housed in the Louvre (q.v.), Paris. They comprise fragments of several metopes from the Temple of Zeus. All other finds are housed on the site.

The museum is governed by the Ephor, or commissioner for archaeology of the Ministry of Culture and Sciences for Greece, under the General Direction of Antiquities and Restoration. The Ephor is assisted by public commissioners, or epimeletes, of the Ministry of Culture and Sciences. The staff also includes commissioners for administration and guards. The German Archaeological Institute remains active in excavation and other services under a contractual relationship between the German and Greek governments, which dates from the time of the first German excavations. The Archaeological Museum of Olympia has no formal relationship of any kind to a university or to any other institution other than the Ministry of Culture and Sciences and the German Archaeological Institute. There are no formal or informal supporting organizations.

The museum building of 1886 was designed by the German architects Friedrich Adler and Wilhelm Dörpfeld in a classical style, the entry portico columns being reproductions of those of the Temple of Zeus. The building was funded by Andreas Syngros.

A new museum of efficient contemporary design and expanded capacity was opened in 1972. It displays numerous objects once in the storerooms and many small and monumental sculptures transferred from the old museum; however, the major sculpture exhibits remained in the old building as of 1984. Thus both museum buildings have important displays, but the collection as a whole is treated here as unified.

A fine new model of the Sacred Altis, rendered to scale in plaster, gift of the city of Essen, Germany, to the museum, has been placed in the entrance hall of the new, fully air-conditioned building. The new facility consists of eight major exhibition galleries and two courts, in addition to extensive storage space. All exhibits have explanatory labels in three languages, Greek, German, and English. Artifacts are displayed together in ways that contribute to understanding visual impressions and juxtapositions of the ancient Altis. This includes reconstructions of pediments of the Temple of Zeus and the Treasury of Megara. The finds include the products of workshops everywhere in the Greek world. In contrast, there are few importations from non-Greek sources. The most important of these rare imported artifacts is a fine bronze repoussé plaque of Hittite workmanship. The earliest Greek artifacts, from the Neolithic through the Mycenaean period, consist mainly of sherds, with a few stone, clay, and bronze objects of more archaeological than art historical interest. Among them are the funerary offerings of nearby Sub-Mycenaean chamber tombs that attest to a prospering Mycenaean community.

Artifacts from the Protogeometric and Geometric periods (c. 1050–700 B.C.) include terracotta figurines and a very large number of bronzes, offerings donated by both cities and individuals. The figurines of gods, men, and animals are the products of many Greek cities. One outstanding example of the quality of Geometric bronze work and of the abstract characteristics of this style is a horse cast of solid bronze. Among the many other impressive bronzes from this period are the numerous large tripod stands and cauldrons. The legs of the tripods are generally decorated with cast Geometric or curvilinear designs. The large round cauldron handles stand up from the rim and are decorated in a comparable manner. Eighth-century bronzes have the earliest examples of pictorial illustration of myth. The earliest of such work is a bronze sheet depicting Herakles stealing the Delphic Tripod from Apollo. These bronzes and many from later periods are votive offerings displayed in the Pan-hellenic sanctuary to commemorate victories or answered prayers; many are from workshops in Argos and Laconia.

Bronzes continue among the most important artifacts of the Orientalizing and Archaic periods (c. 700–480 B.C.). They are astonishingly numerous and varied in type and decoration. It is generally agreed that certain of the fine cast-siren attachments found on cauldrons are imports from the Near East, as may be the cone-shaped cauldron stands with repoussé-hammered Near Eastern motifs. The early Orientalizing griffin and lion-head attachments for cauldrons, hammered repoussé, and the somewhat later cast versions are generally accepted as the products of Greek Orientalizing workshops. The examples from Olympia are splendidly fierce and elegant. There are also cast solid-bronze cauldron attachments from Greek workshops in the forms of sirens, bulls' heads, birds, stag heads, and a horse head, as well as some bulls' heads and birds thought to be from the Near East, Anatolia, North Syria, or even Assyria. There are many plaques, hammered repoussé and engraved with scenes illustrating myths. One seventh-century B.C. example shows two Centaurs (in the older manner with full human bodies attached to trunks of horses, instead of a horse with human torso and head) striking a warrior with tree trunks—no doubt the hero Kaineas, who was immortal and could be conquered only by fastening him into the ground. Another depicts a warrior climbing into a chariot, turning back in farewell to his wife holding a child on her shoulder. A long strip with three scenes shows Orestes slaying his mother Clytemnestra, with the help of Athena (or perhaps his sister Electra), while the cowardly Aigistheus runs away; the lower panel is likely Theseus carrying off Antiope. A fine large repoussé hammered-bronze sheet, probably once affixed to a wooden metope, depicts a winged female griffin nursing her young (c. 630–620 B.C.).

There is an unusually fine and varied collection of armor. Shield devices of hammered and incised bronze were centrally mounted on round shields. Gorgon heads were used for some, including a gorgon head with three wings spiraling about it of the early sixth century B.C. Especially noteworthy is a scowling winged gorgon with a large helmet, her body terminating in lion's legs and the tail of a dragon or sea monster. Other motifs used for this purpose are Pegasus, Chimaira, and a cock. Some breastplates are of extraordinary quality. One is beautifully engraved with a scene of Apollo with lyre in the presence of two Hyperborean maidens, Zeus, and two youths, with lions, leopards, bulls, and sphinxes (c. 640 B.C.). An exceptional breastplate from a hoplite's armor (c. 600 B.C.) has simple curvilinear ridges, creating a formal pattern echoing human anatomy. Examples of leg armor (greaves) are shaped to fit closely the legs they protected and likewise are styled to reflect, through the shape and linear ridge decor, the human leg being protected. Many helmets are of both historical as well as artistic interest. An Illyrian bronze helmet is decorated at the forehead with silver appliqués depicting heraldic lions holding a boar at bay with nude youths on horseback on the ear pieces. Two fine helmets are inscribed with dedications to Zeus. One is identified as that of the Athenian General Miltiades, for the victory at Marathon (490 B.C.); the other, a Persian helmet, is Athenian battle spoil from Marathon. There are many other fine helmets of the types made in Corinth, Argos, and Sparta.

There are numerous examples of polychrome terracotta architectural embellishments from several seventh- and sixth-century buildings, including a *sima* from the Treasury of Gela, another from the Bouleterion, the restored monumental disk-shaped acroterion from the Heraion, and a smaller acroterion from one of the treasuries.

The Orientalizing and Archaic sculptures include a great many bronze and terracotta statuettes of the kouros type and athletes illustrating the development of figure style in several local workshops, particularly those of Argos, Corinth, and Sparta, but with examples from as far away as Samos. The large-scale sculpture is fragmentary but includes examples of both architectural pieces and sculpture-in-the-round, in both marble and poros. The colossal marble head is all that remains of the cult statue of Hera from the Heraion (c. 600 B.C.). The marble torso of a kouros (c. 590–570 B.C.) was brought to the Olympia Museum from Phigaleia. It is thought by some to be the victor monument erected to Arrhichion, the pancratiast who won three victories in the pancratian Olympiads 52–54 (572–564 B.C.) and seen and described by Pausanias in Phigaleia in the second century A.D. The remaining fragments of the pediments of the Treasury of the Megarians have been reconstructed. They include a poros group of battling gods and giants, five of each, with the central figure of Zeus triumphing over a fallen giant, of the sixth century B.C. There are also some fine heads in polychrome terracotta, marble, poros, and bronze, including heads of Athena, Hera, and Zeus. There are also bronze fragments, a horn, and an ear of the noteworthy bull dedicated by the Eretrians.

There are two exceptional items from the early years of the fifth century B.C. The Zeus and Ganymede is a large-size polychrome terracotta group, perhaps Corinthian work (c. 470 B.C.). One fine bronze horse remains of a votive offering representing a four-horse chariot (quadriga), possibly the product of an Argive workshop (c. 470–460 B.C.). In addition, there are many bronze statuettes of athletes in action.

The massive Doric *Temple of Zeus* was built between 470 and 456 B.C. Nothing remains of the chryselephantine cult statue of Zeus enthroned, but in the workshop of the sculptor Phidias some of the molds for forming the drapery of the statue were found and are displayed in the museum. Fortunately, much of the exterior decoration of the temple does survive and is a major treasure of the museum. Most notable are the sculptured figures-in-the-round from the two pediments at the eastern and western ends of the building, reconstructed in arrangements close to their original display but at a low height so that the figures may be closely examined. As of 1984 these figures were in the old museum building. The east pediment shows Zeus standing in the middle at the tallest point of the triangular composition, flanked by King Oinomaus and his wife, Sterope, on his left and by Pelops and his bride, Hippodameia, on the right, with chariots, servants, seers, and personifications of rivers, all symbolizing the chariot race that was the mythic first Olympic game. The figures are each one and one-half times life-size, executed in the dignified, restrained, Severe style of the mid-fifth century B.C. Pausanias ascribes these statues to the sculptor Paionios.

The west pediment, attributed by Pausanias to Alkamenes, has for a theme the conflict of Lapiths and Centaurs at the wedding feast of Hippodameia and Pelops—a sequel to the chariot race to win Hippodameia's hand represented by the eastern group. It is dominated by the noble figure of Apollo in the middle towering over the action. The head of Hippodameia is marvelously serene. The reclining Lapith woman at the extreme right corner is of special interest for her fine intense features.

The twelve metopes, six at each end of the cella, high on the exterior east and west walls, depict the twelve labors of Herakles. The very high-relief figures on these panels are nearly life-size. Most are badly damaged; fragments of several are in the Louvre, Paris. Excellent quality casts have been reconstructed along with the original remains in Olympia to offer an idea of the total composition. The best preserved of the metopes are those representing Herakles cleaning the Augean stables, bringing Athena the Stymphalian birds, and holding up, with the help of Athena, the heavens as Atlas fetches the Golden Apples of the Hesperides. Metopes rebuilt in part from casts include the last two, the fight with Geryon, the mares of Diomedes, the Erymanthian boar, the girdle of the Amazon, the Keryneian hind, and the Cretan bull.

Displayed in the museum are large sections of the moldings of the temple including a fine collection of lion-headed water spouts from the sima in styles indicating that they are not all chronological contemporaries.

The Classical marble statue of *Nike of Paionios*, found in 1875, is one of the few unquestionably original Greek sculptures that can be firmly assigned to a particular artist. An inscription on its base records that it was made by Paionios of Mende, as a memorial of victory by the people of Messene and Naupaktos (apparently in 420 B.C.). Although the face, arms, and wings were shattered by its fall from its thirty-foot-high triangular marble pedestal, the body and its wind-blown drapery are outstanding examples of the graceful style, balanced composition, and technical skill of fully Classical work.

Praxiteles' statue of *Hermes* (c. 340 B.C.) was found inside the Temple of Hera, precisely where Pausanias relates having seen it in the second century A.D. As ancient descriptions and imitations show, the god Hermes dangled a bunch of grapes before the infant Dionysos, whom he carries in his left arm. Whether the statue is the original by Praxiteles (or by a follower) or a careful copy replacing the original when it was, perhaps, carried off in Roman times, it is a splendid example of fourth century B.C. Late Classical sculpture. There is a large collection of bronze and marble sculpture and statuettes of Late Classical and Hellenistic times, along with the terracotta sima from the Leonidaion.

The collection of Roman sculpture is large, with many pieces from the Exedra of Herodes Atticus, including a marble bull dedicated by Regilla, the wife of Herodes; six portrait statues of women, perhaps female members of Herodes' family or priestesses; two males wearing togas, perhaps Herodes himself and a male relative; a statue of a young girl and another of a child; the god Apollo; the goddess Kybele; and Antinoos. A series of portrait statues of Roman emperors and their wives includes Hadrian wearing a breastplate decorated with Athena, the owl, the snake, two victories, and the she-wolf suckling Romulus and Remus; Poppea, wife of Nero; Titus wearing a breastplate decorated with Medusa and Nereides overlapping Hippotritons; Claudius; Faustina, wife of Marcus Aurelius; Trajan; and a bust of Augustus.

A very large portion of the small objects in the collection are directly related to the Olympic games and are found for all periods from the inception of the games in 776 B.C. until the final decline of Roman civilization by the sixth century A.D. They include bronze and terracotta statuettes of athletes, horsemen, and charioteers in quadrigas. In addition, there are many implements essential to the games: disks, *stlengides* (scrapers), *halteres* (jumping weights), and the stone of Bybon. Of great importance are the numerous inscriptions identifying dedicants, recipients, occasion, and sculptor. Among such inscriptions are the signatures of the Athenian sculptors Phiathenaios and Hegias and of the sculptor's assistant Preimos, with the base for the statue of Poulydamas, a victor. There are vases from all periods, many showing athletes competing.

The Archaeological Museum of Olympia has a reference library reserved for the use of staff archaeologists, of cooperating members of the German Archaeological Institute, and with prior arrangement, of visiting scholars. Photographs of published objects in the collection may be purchased only for scientific purposes and with the approval of the museum director. Tourist photographs and slides of outstanding items in the collection are for sale in the museum shop. Aside from the illustrated guide by Nikolaos Yalouris, *Olympia: Altis and Museum* (Munich 1980), there is no official guide or other museum publication. However, the German Archaeological Institute has been publishing excavated materials since the earliest explorations of the sanctuary. Of special importance among them are: Ernst Curtius and Friedrich Adler, *Olympia, Die Ergebnisse der vom Deutschen Reich veranstalteten Ausgrabungen*, 5 vols. (Berlin 1890–97); *Berichte über die Ausgrabungen in Olympia*, 8 vols. in print (Berlin 1937–58); *Olympische Forschungen*, 13 vols. in print so far (Berlin 1944–80).

Selected Bibliography

Ashmole, B., and Yalouris, N., *Olympia: The Sculptures of the Temple of Zeus* (London 1967); Curtius, E., *Olympia* (Berlin 1935); Drees, L., *Olympia: Gods, Artists, Athletes*

(London 1968); Gardiner, E. N., *Olympia: Its History and Remains* (Oxford 1925); Karaghiorga, Th., *Ancient Olympia* (Athens 1971); Kreuzer, A., *Der Hermes des Praxiteles von Olympia* (Berlin 1948); Kunze, E., *Neue Meisterwerke aus Olympia* (Munich 1948); Morgan, C. H., "Pheidias and Olympia," *Hesperia* 21 (1952), pp. 259–339, and *Hesperia* 24 (1955), pp. 164–68; Säflund, Maria-Louise, *The East Pediment of the Temple of Zeus at Olympia* (Göteborg 1970).

ELEANOR GURALNICK AND RAYMOND V. SCHODER

Guatemala

——— Guatemala City ———

NATIONAL MUSEUM OF ARCHAEOLOGY AND ETHNOLOGY OF GUATEMALA (officially MUSEO NACIONAL DE ARQUEOLOGÍA Y ETNOLOGÍA DE GUATEMALA; also MUSEO NACIONAL DE ARQUEOLOGÍA Y ETNOLOGÍA), Salón Número 5, Finca La Aurora, Zona 13, Guatemala City.

The origins of the Museo Nacional de Arqueología y Etnología of Guatemala can be traced to early attempts at the formation of a national museum, the first successfully functioning one, between 1866 and 1881. This museum, run by the Sociedad Económica de Amigos del País, included specimens of natural history in addition to archaeological material that was eventually passed on to two leading institutions of Guatemala City: the Museo de Historia Natural of the School of Medicine at the University of San Carlos and the Instituto Nacional Central de Varones. Toward the end of the nineteenth century the latter institution became the focus of a governmental program to organize a strong national museum, but the building was destroyed by the earthquakes of 1917 and 1918. It seems likely that these early collections were destroyed as well.

Accords for a new national archaeological museum were reached in 1922 and 1925, giving rise in 1931 to the Museo de Arqueología, established in Aurora Park, a large tract of public land in southern Guatemala City. From 1931 to 1948 the Museo de Arqueología sheltered archaeological objects in and around a building in Aurora Park known as the "salón de té." Some of the sculpture still remains in this area and can be seen on the grounds of the zoo.

During the latter years of the presidency of General Jorge Ubico (1931–43) a number of exhibit buildings filled the park for the use of the national fair. In September 1948, Building Number 5 was dedicated as the permanent site of the national archaeological museum. This exhibit building, dominated by a colonnaded central courtyard, reflects the Spanish neoclassical style popular at that time. Closed to the public from April 1972 until March 1978, the building received major repairs, and the collections underwent complete museographic revision.

Since 1946 the museum has been under the direction of the Institute of Anthropology and History, a dependency of the Ministry of Education that oversees funds for the maintenance of the museum provided by the annual budget of the national government. In 1948 the museum received its official title, Museo Nacional de Arqueología y Etnología de Guatemala.

The museum is divided into two departments: Archaeology and Ethnology; at present the ethnological section is still in preparation for public viewing. Both departments are administered by the director, appointed by the Ministry of Education.

The Museo Nacional de Arqueología y Etnología owes its present collection in part to government sanctioned excavations of pre-Columbian sites. Donations from private collections are also received. Gifts of small objects, such as ceramics and textiles, are periodically donated by the Tikal Association, a private group that offers nonfinancial support to the museum.

Maya art and culture, as they existed in Guatemala before the Conquest, are comprehensively presented by selected objects ranging from simple utilitarian crafts to monumental sculpture. The exhibits are arranged both chronologically and according to the three major geographical divisions of Guatemala: the Lowlands, the Highlands, and the Pacific Coast.

The museum owns a major collection of Classic period limestone sculpture from the Maya Lowlands, in the center of the state of El Petén (c. 250–900). The Early Classic period (c. 250–550) is represented by a small but important group of sculptures and includes the fragmentary stela from El Zapote (c. 435), an early example of a female figure in Lowland Maya sculpture (not on exhibit); the unusual frontal figure from Uaxactún; a lavishly carved stela from Tres Islas; and an early example of a multifigure composition, from Piedras Negras (c. 534).

The exceptionally large holdings in Lowland sculpture of the Late Classic period (c. 550–900) include one of the most important collections in the museum, an outstanding group of twenty monumental sculptures from Piedras Negras. These works were retrieved from the jungle site in 1931 and 1932 by J. Alden Mason, then curator of the American Section of the University Museum, University of Pennsylvania. Mason shipped the collection to Philadelphia, where it underwent extensive restoration and spent more than a decade on exhibit. Most of the sculptures were returned to Guatemala by 1948, in time for the opening of the new museum.

This distinguished collection illustrates numerous important themes in Classic Maya art: the scattering ceremony, elite bloodletting ceremonies, and obeisance to the ruler, portrayed by no less than three monuments, and two masterpieces of Maya sculpture, the small haute-relief lintel (c. 761) and stela (c. 795). Also on view are an hieroglyphic text displayed by a frontal figure in haute-relief, the fragment of another, and three extensively restored stucco heads. One small stela fragment showing a profile figure in ceremonial garb is on loan to the Museo Nacional de Arte Moderno, Guatemala City. Functional works can be seen in a rare example of a polychrome limestone throne (c. 785), and three large *cauac* monster heads that originally supported a stone slab (the fourth currently on loan to the University Museum, Philadelphia).

Many other Lowland sites are represented by sculptures dating from the middle of the Late Classic period (c. 700–800), with an especially important group of four stelae from Naranjo: the portrait of a noblewoman from Tikal; a seated portrait of the ruler "Smoking Squirrel"; and two showing the ruler in ceremonial costume. Late Classic sculpture also includes: a rhyolite ballcourt marker, from Quiriguá, Izabál; a stela from Tikal, portraying "Ruler B," and a companion piece (c. 751); two works from Tamarindito: the large bound captive in relief from a sculptured ceremonial stairway; and an incomplete fractured stela recently recovered from the site of El Duende, not on exhibit. In addition, the museum displays four small fragments of hieroglyphic stairways from Cancuén, Tamarindito, and Machaquilá.

The collection of Lowland sculpture dating from the Terminal Classic period (c. 800–900) is the finest in any museum. Iconographic innovations can be seen in three stelae from the Central Petén: Ucanal (c. 849), Ixlu (c. 859), and Jimbal (c. 879). Also from the Central Petén are a large pedestal stone from Ucanal and an hieroglyphic text from Ixtutz.

Terminal Classic sculpture from the Pasión River drainage is represented by an incomplete dancing figure from La Amalia, a stela from Seibal, a multiscene stela with extensive non-Mayan influences; and a small ballcourt marker from Cancuén. A set of three well-preserved stelae from Machaquilá [(c. 815), (c. 820), and (c. 830)], demonstrates the progression toward a more geometrical style characteristic of this period.

Also exhibited are examples of two rare media in Classic Maya art: *fresco secco* mural fragments from La Pasadita and an epoxy cast of a large, wooden lintel from Tikal, Temple IV (original in the Museum für Völkerkunde, Basel; c. 741).

Sculpture from the Central Highlands in volcanic and basaltic stone is amply represented by works from Kaminaljuyú, Guatemala. The museum contains the largest collection of Kaminaljuyú sculpture, gradually amassed from twentieth-century explorations. In addition to the pieces on exhibit are numerous fragments and minor works in stone and clay. Stone sculptures in-the-round and in-relief reveal a dynamic succession of styles during the Middle and Late Pre-Classic periods (c. 800 B.C.-A.D. 200).

Sculpture-in-the-round is exemplified by two large, "pot-belly" figures related to the Monte Alto style, with six miniature versions, four of them from Kaminaljuyú. There are also two monumental toad effigies, two finely carved stone drums, and three large, grotesque heads related to masks on Pre-Classic radial pyramids of the Lowlands. Numerous small effigy figures, horizontally tenoned heads, and mushroom stones from Kaminaljuyú and other Highland sites complete this category.

Bas-reliefs sculpted on one plane and multiple planes comprise the most renowned works from Kaminaljuyú exhibited in the museum. Among the latter is the small nude figure found redeposited in a Majadas phase cache (c. 650 B.C.). Relief on complex forms can also be seen in an incomplete monument, an unusual semicylindrical sculpture, and a large vertically tenoned silhouette sculpture that combines stylized serpents on composite geometrical forms.

Among the single-plane reliefs are two famous works of fine-grained basalt, both portraying figures in opulent regalia. Gustavo Espinosa uncovered an altar, which is incomplete, having been broken into three fragments and partially flaked. The stela was discovered in the same pit in 1957 by Edwin M. Shook. Other single-plane reliefs include three stelae: a ring-tailed fish on a plain background; showing a frontal human head; and a fragment of a six-toed dancing figure.

The museum contains a small collection of Central Highland sculpture of the Post-Classic period (c. 900–1550). A ballcourt marker from Mixco Viejo, Chimaltenango, illustrates Toltec influences in the Guatemalan Highlands. Among other Post-Classic Highland sculptures are a stone censer from Ixchimché, Chimaltenango, and a headless, human figure from Chinautla, Guatemala.

Late Pre-Classic sculpture from the Pacific Coast-Piedmont zone (c. 200 B.C.-A.D. 200) can be seen in three monuments from Abaj Takalik, Retalhuleu: the fragmentary stela depicting the lower portion of a profile human figure; a bust-length fragment of a head heavily influenced by Olmec art; and a silhouette sculpture, depicting a bird and a deer.

The collection of Late Classic stone sculpture from the Pacific Coast broadly exemplifies the Cotzumalhuapa style, from the state of Escuintla. Numerous horizontally tenoned heads owned by the museum come from Cotzumalhuapa sites, such as Bilbao (Escuintla) and Palo Gordo (Suchitepéquez), although similar examples come from the Antigua area and the Lowlands (Playítas, Izabál). The museum also houses many human effigy figures, ranging from small to nearly life-size, from Bilbao, Obero (Escuintla), and Sin Cabezas (Escuintla), among others. Four of the horizontally tenoned heads and six large effigy figures are located in a small sculpture garden in the central courtyard.

The powerful rigidity of the Cotzumalhuapa style can best be seen in the ballplayer series, three monuments from Palo Verde, Escuintla, and two from Finca Las Ilusiones, Escuintla, which are ornamented with animal and plant forms (on loan from a private collection). Related to the Cotzumalhuapa style are three monuments from La Nueva, Jutiapa. One circular stone with a frontal skeletal face in relief and the fragment of a stela depicting a seated figure, both from Palo Gordo, complete this category. Holdings in Pacific Coast sculpture also include a small Post-Classic human effigy figure from Tiquisate, Escuintla, and a group of finely carved *hachas*.

The museum's collection of ceramics is vast and occupies approximately half of the exhibition space. Only a portion of this collection is displayed at any time, and exhibits are subject to frequent change. The pieces selected for display give an overall view of pre-Hispanic ceramic production in Guatemala but also include a few examples from North and South America. The ceramics are grouped according to chronology and geographic distribution and additionally to illustrate ceramic technique and vessel shapes.

The collection of ceramic figurines from the Pre-Classic and Late Classic periods is modest but offers some notable examples. A small group of Pre-Classic figurines of a rudimentary, hand-modeled type, as well as more sophisticated figurines from Kaminaljuyú, are displayed, including one hollow, white-slipped "doll" with articulated limbs in the Olmec style.

Late Classic figurines include delicate hand-modeled and molded figurines from the Northern Highlands and Lowlands. A superb example of the mold-impressed technique can be seen in a dancing corn god from Alta Verapaz. The figurine tradition from the Pacific Coast is represented by a group of large, hand-modeled red-ware human figures. Late Classic figurines also include musical instruments: whistle figurines, ocarinas, flutes, and drums.

The museum displays a few Late Pre-Classic ceramic vessels from the Lowlands and a somewhat larger collection dating from the Early Classic period. There are several notable Early Classic polychromes and stunning two-part, polished black-ware effigy vessels from Uaxactún.

Late Classic polychrome cylinders, bowls, and plates derive largely from the Central Petén, although pieces from San Agustín Acasaguastlán, and El Progreso and examples of the Chamá style from Alta Verapaz and Nebaj, El Quiché, are included. Of special note is the collection of large, polychrome plates from Tikal and Uaxactún, as well as a small collection of painted stucco and modeled-carved vessels from the Central Petén. In addition are fine orange modeled-carved vessels and a remarkable ladle censer adorned with a human figure from Altar de Sacrificios, El Petén.

Ceramics from the Central Highlands are extensive. The museum displays a comprehensive collection of Pre-Classic and Early Classic ceramics from Kaminaljuyú. Noteworthy ceramics from the period of Teotihuacán influence (Esperanza phase, c. 400–600) include a superb, although much restored, fine orange human effigy vessel and delicate, painted, stucco cylindrical tripod containers. The museum also houses numerous elaborate censors from Kaminaljuyú and other Highland sites. Late Classic spiked censers from Lake Amatitlán, Guatemala, and Post-Classic Chinautla polychromes form part of the collection of Central Highland ceramics.

The museum displays a varied collection of ceramics from the Northern and Western Highlands, including the largest vessel ever found in Mesoamerica, measuring about six feet in diameter, used for ancient salt production. The Northern Highlands collection is particularly strong in Tohil plumbate effigy jars and elaborate ceremonial censers. Also of note are a group of finely modeled Post-Classic ceramic masks from Alta Verapaz. Ceramic vessels from the Western Highlands can be seen in several examples from Salcajá. Quetzaltenango, such as a Middle Pre-Classic graphite-painted bowl and Post-Classic mold-impressed plates. Pacific Coast ceramics include numerous carved miniature vases and elaborate censers.

Additionally, there is a diverse collection of decorated utilitarian objects, such as metates, mortars, spindle whorls, and Post-Classic copper jewelry. Small ceremonial objects in various media can be seen and include jade, obsidian, flint, alabaster, shell, and bone. Outstanding among them is a carved human skull from Kaminaljuyú and a large collection of eccentric flints. An important corpus of modern indigenous textiles, which are not yet on public display, comes from the Lily de Jonge Osborne Collection and museum acquisitions.

The museum does not have its own library but is adjacent to the library of the Institute of Anthropolgy and History, which is open to the public. The museum provides conference rooms and audiovisual equipment for special meetings and lectures. Requests for slides and photographs may be sent directly to the museum director and are considered on an individual basis.

Selected Bibliography

Civilización Maya de Guatemala (Tokyo 1977); *2000 Años de Cultura Maya: Municipios de San Andrés Sajcabajá y Canillá, El Quiché* (Guatemala 1979); Ichon, Alain, *Rescate Arqueológico en la Cuenca del Río Chixoy: 1. Informe Preliminar* (Guatemala 1979); Graham, Ian, *Corpus of Maya Hieroglyphic Inscriptions: Ixkun, Ucanal, Ixtutz, Naranjo*, vol. 2, pt. 2 (Cambridge 1980); Miles, Suzanna W., "Sculpture of the Guatemala-Chiapas Highlands and the Pacific Slopes," *Handbook of Middle American Indians*, vol. 2 (Austin 1965), pp. 237–75; Morley, Sylvanus G., *The Inscriptions of Peten*, 5 vols. (Washington, D.C. 1937–38); Muñoz, Lujan, *Guía de los Museos de Guatemala* (Guatemala 1971); Parsons, Lee A., "Bilbao, Guatemala: an Archaeological Study of the Pacific Coast Cotzumalhuapa Region," *Publications in Anthropology* 12, vol. 2 (Milwaukee 1969); Satterthwaite, Linton, "Quirigua Altar L (Monument 12)," vol. 2 *Quirigua Reports, I* (Philadelphia 1979).

ANDREA STONE

Hong Kong

—————— Hong Kong ——————

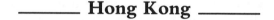

HONG KONG MUSEUM OF ART, City Hall, Edinburgh Place, Hong Kong.

The Hong Kong Museum of Art is housed in the top three floors of the City Hall, which was opened in 1962, replacing the old one established in 1869. The old City Hall already had a museum displaying a collection of valuable exhibits. The City Hall complex is a government-funded project, and the Urban Council of Hong Kong is responsible for the administration of the premises and facilities. Since 1973 the Urban Council has achieved financial autonomy, with most of its revenue coming from government rates. The Urban Council is the policy-making body working through various select committees, one of which is the Cultural Services Select Committee, which makes decisions on major policy concerning the museum. The executive arm of the council is the Urban Services Department, and thus museum staff are civil servants.

The museum is administered by a curator and seven assistant curators; the curatorial departments are Chinese Antiquities, Chinese Fine Arts, Western and Contemporary Art, Historical Paintings, Conservation, Educational and Extension Services, and Administration.

The museum was opened officially on March 2, 1962. The City Hall is a complex of five units—central block, concert block, theater, high block, and enclosed garden—designed by government architects. The high block is a clean and almost starkly utilitarian building, housing on twelve floors the two museum galleries, offices, public libraries, a recital hall, a lecture hall, a marriage registry, an exhibition hall open for public rental, and other facilities. Designs for a new building, about 12,500 square meters of space, were begun late in 1983 and completed in 1985. It is hoped that the new museum will open in 1987.

The nucleus of the collection of Chinese antiquities in the museum can be traced to September 1963, when 166 items of Chinese antiquities, including ceramics, lacquers, and bronzes purchased by the Hong Kong government, were transferred to the then newly established City Museum and Art Gallery, later known as the Hong Kong Museum of Art. The collection of Chinese antiquities is best represented in Chinese ceramics, which number more than six hundred items and represent almost half of the collection. Other items include Chinese textiles, bronzes, snuff bottles, bamboo carvings, jade, lacquer, cloisonné, papercuts, woodblock prints, and other Chinese minor arts and folk craft.

The ceramics collection of the Museum of Art, the strongest one in the Chinese antiquities section both in terms of quality and quantity, demonstrates well the illustrious history of Chinese ceramics, since it includes pieces from the Neolithic period through the twentieth century. Among the earliest wares, the museum possesses a Yang-shao painted pottery jar with swirling, curvilinear designs on the upper half and a Shang Dynasty (sixteenth to eleventh century B.C.) pottery tripod. The Han Dynasty (206 B.C.-A.D. 220) is a period of great strength in the collection, for not only does the museum possess the lead-glazed earthenware in replica of different shapes of bronze vessels, but it also includes examples of Southern Han pottery from Changsha in Hunan. The museum has few vessels dating from the Ch'in (A.D. 265–420) to the Sui (A.D. 581–618) dynasties; however, there is a fine collection of Sui and T'ang dynasties' (A.D. 618–907) *sancai* three-colored wares in an impressive number of shapes—long-necked amphora with dragon handles, tripod, stem-cup, pilgrim flask, and figurines of different sizes.

The famous Ting and Chün wares of the Sung Dynasty (960–1279), celebrated, respectively, for their subtlety of decoration and beauty of glazes, however, are plainly represented in the museum. This also applies to the northern celadon and the black and brown wares. However, there is a relatively good representation of the lustrous blue-tinted celadons of the Southern Sung (1127–1279) to the Ming (1368–1644) Dynasty from Lung-ch'üan of Chen-chiang. The museum houses a lovely and varied collection of Tz'u-chou-type wares, often richly patterned with carved and painted designs in various shapes, and also a good range of the pale blue Yin-ch'ing ware of the Sung and Yüan dynasties.

There is a fine collection of blue-and-white wares dated from the Yüan Dynasty (1279–1368) through the twentieth century, including a small Yüan Dynasty vase, a Hsuante (1426–35) narcissus bowl, and a Chengde (1506–21) brushrest with its typical Arabic inscriptions. The blue-and-white group is best represented in the K'ang-hsi period (1662–1722), with a total of eleven items mostly illustrated with stories from history and popular drama. However, the museum still lacks marked examples of the Ch'eng-hua period (1465–87).

The museum is well endowed with colored wares of the Ming and Ch'ing (1644–1911) dynasties. Outstanding pieces are a large *wucai* five-colored fish bowl of the Wan-li (1573–1620) period, a Kirande bowl, and a few handsome pieces of famille-rose and *doucai* contrasting enamel wares of the Yung-cheng (1723–35) and Ch'ien-lung (1736–95) periods. The museum also has a rich variety of monochrome wares of the Ch'ing Dynasty, including examples of new glazes like iron-rust, tea-dust, and "clair-de-lune."

The most outstanding piece of the ceramics collection is an underglazed red bowl of the fifth century celebrated for its rarity. A group of Guangdong Shiwan wares and Fukien Tehua wares and a few items of Chïangsu Yihsing wares are among the minor items of ceramics owned by the museum. The museum also houses a group of Kraak wares and other export porcelains. There is a group of Southeast Asian wares, mainly from Thailand and Vietnam.

The museum has only a small collection of bronze ritual vessels from the Chou (eleventh century B.C.-A.D. 771) to the Han Dynasty. The recently acquired bronze kuei bowl of early Chou, distinguished by its rare patterned design, is the most outstanding piece of this group. The collection of bronze mirrors is richer in comparison, with a selection of more than twenty-five items dated from the Warring States period (475 B.C.–221 B.C.) to the Sung Dynasty, which illustrates admirably the development of various designs in bronze mirrors over the centuries. The museum also pioneers in collecting a group of later bronzes of the Ming and Ch'ing dynasties in forms of figurines, altar vessels, and scholars' playthings.

The museum owns more than two hundred items of Chinese textiles and costumes, including dragon robes, official robes of various ranks, casual wares of the common folk, and Mandarin squares. The collection of snuff bottles and bamboo carvings has increased substantially to a few dozen, following their respective exhibitions held in 1978. Representative examples of cloisonné, Canton enamels, lacquer, and papercuts, although few, are also among the museum's holdings.

The Chinese fine-arts section is chiefly held responsible for the collection and exhibition of paintings and calligraphy by Chinese artists who are no longer living. The Chinese fine-arts collection has been built up through acquisition and donation from local and foreign sources. By 1980 the museum's collection of Chinese paintings and calligraphy amounted to nine hundred items. Among them were seven hundred paintings and two hundred items of calligraphy.

Owing to Hong Kong's cultural and geographical affinity to Guangdong, a province of great historical significance situated in South China, the museum places its chief emphasis on collecting works by Guangdong artists. The art of Guangdong painting dates from the early Ming period, when Lin Liang served as a court painter. He was most famous for his bird-and-flower painting in a swift and free style. By the end of the Ming Dynasty, when the Manchus invaded China, many patriotic Guangdong artists participated in anti-Ch'ing campaigns. Their works were always imbued with symbolic attributes and nationalistic sentiments. Works by these artists, such as Chang Mu, are represented in the museum's fine-arts collection. In the Ch'ing Dynasty, Guangdong painting continued to flourish as many artists established their reputation through their idiosyncratic styles. Li Chiang, an artist who never left Guangdong, won national recognition through his talent in composing poetry, painting, and calligraphy.

The museum has collected two paintings and two examples of calligraphy by him. A typical work by Su Lupeng, a painter who was most honored for his figure painting in an archaic style, is a painting of an eccentric beggar. Su Jenshan, an eccentric Guangdong landscape and figure painter, is best known for his forceful and ductile brushstrokes. His large painting *The Twelve Celestial Constellations* and a long handscroll, *The Medical Quarter*, in the museum collection can be regarded as two of his masterpieces.

By the nineteenth century, a school of painting known as the Lingnan School gradually emerged in Guangdong, when Sung Kuanpao and Meng Jinyi first introduced in the mid-nineteenth century the "boneless method," a special technique for bird-and-flower paintings achieved by applying color directly without outlining. Chu Lien, Chu Ch'ao, and their followers further exploited the technique through their eclectic experiments. Their works were characterized by a supple, placid, and delicate rhythm. However, the Lingnan School was not yet firmly established until the "Three Masters of the Lingnan School"—Kao Chienfu, Kao Ch'ifeng, and Ch'en Shujen—began to reform Chinese painting. The three masters were all students of Chu Lien and had traveled to Japan to study art theories and techniques. The reform they propagated was the establishment of a personal style through a selection and blending of traditional Chinese painting with Western techniques and theories. Their assiduous efforts and personal achievements brought Chinese painting into a new phase and made a strong impact. The Hong Kong Museum of Art consistently seeks to establish a more complete collection of this significant school of painting through acquisition of works by the Lingnan School. In 1978 the museum acquired an important collection of sixty-nine paintings by Kao Chienfu, which provide an in-depth survey of the artistic achievement of this artist.

In the realm of Guangdong calligraphy, important works by well-known artists in the late Ming and Ch'ing period such as Hsueh Shihheng, Ch'en Tzuchuang, Liang Peilan, Feng Yushan, Song Hsiang, Ch'en Li, and Kang Yu'wei are included.

In addition to collecting Guangdong art, the museum also extends its interest to collecting works by other schools and individual artists. The museum now has a significant collection of more than two hundred fan paintings by late Ch'ing Shanghai masters known for their painting of flowers, birds, landscapes, and figures in a meticulous and delicate manner. Prominent artists among them include the four Jens—Jen Hsun, Jen Hsiung, Jen Yu, Jen Yi—and also Chang Hsiung, Wang Su, and Ch'ien Huian. Works by other famous artists include a landscape painting by Fa Ruozhen and a poem album by Wu Li.

Works by well-known contemporary Chinese artists also fall within the scope of the museum's collection. The contemporary art collection, the largest public collection in Hong Kong, is mainly a collection of works by local artists and was begun at the time of the museum's opening in 1962. Most of the works are collected through acquisition from local sources. In mid–1980 there were more than nine hundred items in the collection, which can be divided into seven categories: oil paintings, watercolors and drawings, Chinese ink paintings, Chinese calligraphy, graphic prints, sculpture, and others. More than one-third of the collection falls into the graphic arts holdings and nearly one-fourth into Chinese ink painting. The increase of Chinese ink paintings in the past fifteen years indicates the chief trend of local artists. A small number of works by contemporary Chinese artists not residing in Hong Kong is also collected by the museum.

The collection of contemporary art reflects the complexity of local art development resulting from the role of Hong Kong as a meeting place of Eastern and Western cultures. Cheung Yee, a leading sculptor of Hong Kong, whose works comprise one-half of the sculpture collection, for example, combined traditional philosophical ideas of ancient China with the techniques and ideas of Western contemporary art. Another example is Lui Shou-kwan, the leading master in contemporary Hong Kong of Chinese ink painting. Besides the works of Cheung and Lui, works by significant Hong Kong artists such as Douglas Bland, Luis Chan, Chao Shao-an, Fung Hong-hou, Hon Chi-fun, and Kwong Yiu-ting are also well represented in the collection of contemporary art.

The historical pictures collection consists of a total of 769 items of which 164 are oil paintings, 270 are watercolors and drawings, and 335 are prints. Among these items, some are paintings executed by Chinese artists that were sold to Europeans as part of the China trade, and others are works of European artists who had either visited or lived in China in the eighteenth and nineteenth centuries. This collection has been mainly built up from the Chater Collection, the Hotung Collection, and the Law and Sayer collections, with new additions through acquisitions in recent years.

The legendary Chater Collection was bequeathed to the Hong Kong government after Sir Catchick Paul Chater died in 1926. Regrettably, three-quarters of the paintings were lost in World War II, and the majority have never been recovered. The remaining pictures that are now being kept in the museum include a number of detailed and attractive oil paintings of Canton, Shanghai, and Macao done by anonymous Chinese artists, which serve as a remarkable historical record of nineteenth-century Anglo-Chinese relations.

The Hotung Collection, which consists of eighty-four paintings, was presented to the Hong Kong government by Sir Robert Hotung in November 1955. This collection was given to the museum when it was opened in 1962.

The Law Collection and the Sayer Collection were purchased by the government in 1951 from two collectors, Wyndham O. Law, formerly chief of the Inspector General of Customs, and G. R. Sayer, formerly director of education in the Hong Kong government. These two collections include oil paintings, drawings, and prints of subjects along the China coast.

The historical painting collection in the museum consists of important works by artists as well as historians. A small watercolor attributed to W. Havell (c. 1816) is possibly the earliest pictorial record of Hong Kong still extant. This watercolor, *The Waterfall at Hong Kong*, depicts a small boat heading toward the water pouring over the cliffs at Waterfall Bay near Aberdeen. Hong Kong as seen in this picture was an island of barren rocks, deep ravines, and mountain torrents. A finely executed oil painting, *City of Victoria*, drawn by an anonymous artist in the early 1950s gives a very detailed representation of the buildings along the coastline.

Most of the paintings claim real artistic merits apart from their historical interest. There are paintings by known artists such as George Chinnery, Auguste Borget, Thomas Allom, William Alexander, William Daniell, Murdoch Bruce, Captain Elliot, and Lamqua. Moreover, the museum owns a significant collection of watercolors by Tinkua, one of the most important Chinese watercolorists executing works in the Western style in the nineteenth century. In general this collection presents a vivid picture of life in the Far East, particularly in the Treaty Ports of Hong Kong and Macao, during the eighteenth and nineteenth centuries.

The museum organizes exhibitions of contemporary Hong Kong art, mainly of local artists, and traveling exhibitions of paintings, prints, and sculpture from overseas in cooperation with foreign cultural institutions. The Contemporary Hong Kong Biennial Exhibition is held every two years and aims to provide an incentive to activate local talent as well as to stimulate the general awareness and interest in the subject. Urban Council Fine Arts Awards are awarded to distinguished artists, with their works exhibited in the exhibition. The exhibition offers an opportunity for those who want to investigate more about an entire new generation of Hong Kong artists.

A Chinese and English bimonthly newsletter includes news on current exhibitions, traveling exhibitions, film programs, lectures, and new acquisitions. It is regularly issued free to educational and cultural institutions, artists, schools, consuls, mass media, and individual readers. Visitors can also obtain the newsletter at the counter of the museum.

The museum has a staff reference library of six hundred volumes that will form the nucleus of an arts library to be included in the planned Cultural Complex. The Hong Kong Cultural Complex being constructed on the other side of the harbor will include the new Museum of Art, ten times larger than the existing one.

Slides and photographs of objects in the collection may be purchased by application to the museum, which can also provide a list of museum publications and instructions for ordering. The museum publishes and sells reproductions and postcards of selected paintings and prints in the collection in addition to providing the exhibition catalogues listed here.

Selected Bibliography

Museum publications: *An Anthology of Chinese Ceramics*, 1980; *The Art of Chen Shuren*, 1980; *The Art of Kao Chien-fu*, 1978; *Chinese Bamboo Carving*, Part 1, 1978; *Chinese Snuff Bottles*, 1977; *Contemporary Hong Kong Art Biennial Exhibition*, 1979; *Fan Paintings by Late Ch'ing Shanghai Masters*, 1977; *Hong Kong Artists: The Early Generation*, 1978; *Hong Kong: The Changing Scene—A Record in Art*, 1980; *Kwangtung*

Painting, 1973; *Monochrome Ceramics of the Ming and Ch'ing Dynasties*, 1977; *Shek-wan Pottery*, 1977; *Snuff Bottles of the Ch'ing Dynasty*, 1978.

Other publications: *Urban Council, Hong Kong City Hall* (Hong Kong 1980); *Urban Council, Annual Report* (Hong Kong 1980).

GERARD C. C. TSANG

Hungary

_____ Budapest _____

FINE ARTS MUSEUM, BUDAPEST (officially SZÉPMÜVÉSZETI MÚ-ZEUM; also MUSEUM D. BILD. KUNSTE), Dózsa György Úf 41, Postf. 463, 1146 Budapest.

The Szépmüvészeti Múzeum, or Fine Arts Museum, in Budapest opened its doors at its present site and under its present name in 1906. It was created by resolution of the millennial Parliament of 1896, in celebration of Hungary's one thousand years of existence as a nation. The building, located at Heroes' Square on the Pest side of the city, presents a great neoclassical facade, with the central pediment copied after that of the Temple of Zeus at Olympia. The architecture of the back side reflects Italian Renaissance influences. The architects Albert Schickendanz and Fulop Hertzog worked in the Beaux-Arts style. Much like their colleagues in the West, they considered themselves heirs to all past styles.

Unlike other great European museums, the Szépmüvészeti Múzeum, or Fine Arts Museum, was not founded on the basis of a single royal or ducal collection. Hungary's unique and turbulent history from the sixteenth century onwards precluded that. Of the many outstanding works of art made in Hungary or sent there, no trace remains. Such was the fate of the *Madonna* by Leonardo and Verrocchio's marble relief *Darius*, well documented as gifts sent to King Matthias Corvinus (1440–90), an early and powerful champion of the Italian Renaissance in Hungary.

These and many other fine medieval and Renaissance works of art, reflecting Hungary's earlier importance in the European community, perished after the country's defeat by the Turks at Mohács in 1526. After that, most of Hungary fell under Turkish rule for 150 years. The liberation from the Turks in 1686 brought to the country a new political system in the form of the "dual monarchy."

The same hereditary Hapsburg ruler acted as emperor of Austria and, separately, as king of Hungary until just after World War I. The imperial seat, however, was maintained in Vienna, and the Hungarian nobles, wanting to be near the royal court, built their palaces and decorated them with their art collections in the Hofburg in Vienna. Unfortunately, some of these collections—with the very notable exception of the Eszterházy Collection—remained in Vienna to form part of the magnificent imperial collection there.

The complicated history of the museum dates from 1802, when Count Ferenc Széchényi deeded his collections to his country, thus establishing the National Museum in Budapest. The first significant works of art, anticipating the future Szépmüvészeti Múzeum, came to the National Museum in 1836 and thereafter.

By the time the second commission for a building for the National Museum based on Count Széchényi's gift was carried out, it required the addition of a wing to house a picture gallery. When this building opened to the public in 1851, the wing contained the real foundation of the future Szépmüvészeti Múzeum: the collection of János László Pyrker, given to the institution in 1836. Pyrker, archbishop of Eger, and former patriarch of Venice, gathered most of these 192 paintings in Northern Italy and in Venice during his stay there.

In 1848 Lajos Kossuth, the leader of Hungary's War of Independence, transferred by decree seventy-eight fine paintings found at Buda Castle from the imperial collection into the National Museum. The most dramatic development, however, in the formation of the future Szépmüvészeti Múzeum took place in 1871 through the purchase of the famous Eszterházy Collection from Prince Pál Eszterházy by the Hungarian State for 1.1 million gold forints. These collections, originally gathered by Prince Miklós the Magnificent and his grandson Prince Miklós Eszterházy during the late eighteenth and early nineteenth centuries, were on view to the public two days a week at their palace in Vienna.

In addition to containing the 636 masterpieces of painting, the Eszterházy Collection included 3,535 drawings and 51,301 prints, all of very high quality. This vast new holding necessitated the establishment of a new museum in Budapest, the Szépmüvészeti Múzeum's direct ancestor, the National Gallery, complete with a department of prints and drawings. This new institution became the recipient of sixty-four paintings, presented as a gift in 1872 by Bishop Arnold Ipolyi. Ipolyi, considered one of Hungary's first professional "art historians," was president of the Society of Fine Arts. His gift of many Early Netherlandish and Italian paintings complemented the Eszterházy Collection of High Renaissance and later works.

The most judicious, intelligent, and careful buying campaigns for works of art were carried out by Károly Pulszky, director of the National Gallery and first director of the Szépmüvészeti Múzeum, during the last decade of the nineteenth century and early years of the twentieth century. His purchases filled certain lacunae, making the collections of European painting and graphic arts comprehensive. Furthermore, his acquisitions included European, mostly Italian, sculpture from the late medieval through the Baroque periods. He also saved a number of frescoes from the fourteenth through the sixteenth century from buildings slated for demolition, mostly in Umbria. These works have been transferred onto canvas and are displayed in the museum's Renaissance Court. Pulszky's example was followed a little later by Elek Petrovics, under whose directorship the Department of Graeco-Roman Antiquities and the Gallery of Modern Art (of mostly nineteenth-century works) were established before World War I.

Thus by the time of World War I, the direction of the Szépmüvészeti Múzeum as a major museum of fine arts, with examples covering all major periods and schools of Europe, was well established. Significant additions followed during the period between the two wars and after World War II, when certain privately owned masterpieces were acquired. One significant change, decided upon in 1957 and finally carried out in 1973, consisted of the removal from the Szépmüvészeti Múzeum of works by Hungarian masters into the then newly restored central section of the war-damaged Royal Palace, or Buda Castle, which was then designated as the Nemzeti Galléria or National Gallery.

From the time the Szépmüvészeti Múzeum was founded, it has always been maintained as a Hungarian State institution, under the auspices of the Ministry of Culture. A governing board is appointed by the state, and a professional staff is divided into six curatorial departments. They are the Old Picture Gallery, the Collection of Prints and Drawings, the Gallery of Modern Art, the Department of Graeco-Roman Antiquities, the Egyptian Department, and the Sculpture Gallery of medieval through Late Baroque European sculpture.

The centerpiece of the Szépmüvészeti Múzeum is its Old Picture Gallery, the gallery of Old Master paintings ranging from the thirteenth through the eighteenth century. The collection comprises some twenty-four hundred paintings on panel or canvas, more than six hundred of which are on permanent display. They are exhibited on the second floor, at the top of two great staircases, in galleries opening off a balcony overlooking the frescoed Renaissance Court. All labels are in Hungarian, but the number of exclamation marks denotes the work's importance.

The pictures are hung in twenty-three galleries and eighteen adjacent small rooms, according to the major national schools and in chronological order, an arrangement devised by director Andor Pigler after the recovery of the collection from various places of safekeeping in Germany after World War II. Thus the galleries on the right contain the Italian and Netherlandish paintings through the Late Renaissance or Mannerist periods, and galleries on the left continue with Flemish, Spanish, German, Austrian, and, to a lesser extent, French and English masters of the Baroque through the early nineteenth century.

A brief survey of the highlights of this collection would commence with two Giottesque paintings of the Florentine Trecento, *A Madonna Enthroned* by Jacopo di Cione (brother of Orcagna) and the *Coronation of the Virgin* by Maso di Banco. These two are followed by the early fifteenth-century Sienese painter Sassetta's predella panel *St. Thomas Aquinas Kneeling before the Altar of the Virgin* (ex-Ranboux Collection, Cologne), and the interesting *Ceres* by the little-known Michele Pannonino (from his name of Hungarian origin), active in Ferrara, 1415–65, both from the Ipolyi bequest. From the Pyrker Collection came two Venetian paintings: Gentile Bellini's *Portrait of Caterina Cornaro* and the *Portrait of Antonio Broccardo* attributed to Giorgione. From among the 121 Old Master paintings bequeathed to the museum by Count János Pálffy in 1912 came the fine *Crucifixion* by the Bolognese Francesco Francia and the justly famous *Portrait of Doge Marcantonio Trevisani* of 1553 by Titian. Among the Pulszky purchases are *St. Stephen Martyr* by Domenico Ghirlandaio, *Madonna with St. Anthony* by Filippino Lippi, and the *Portrait of a Man* by the Venetian Sebastiano del Piombe, painted in Rome between 1515 and 1520. Some of the earlier paintings from the Eszterházy Collection are the signed *Madonna and Child Enthroned*, of about 1476, by the Venetian Carlo Crivelli and an early Raphael, *The Portrait of Pietro Bembo*, of 1506. Also by Raphael is the *Eszterházy Madonna*, formerly in the Kaunitz Collection and of particular interest, since the unfinished state of the small panel throws light on Raphael's working techniques of about 1508. In the *Madonna and Child* by the Milanese Boltraffio, from the last years of the fifteenth century, there may be some touches by his master Leonardo. Correggio's *Madonna del Latte*, of about 1520, and the elegant *Venus, Cupid, and Jealousy* (ex-Kaunitz) by the Florentine Mannerist Bronzino are also from the Eszterházy Collection.

Of the transfers from the imperial collection in 1848, the small *Bust of a Girl* by Palma Vecchio is notable, having come from the Archduke Leopold Wilhelm's famous collection in Brussels. Another is a small Lorenzo Lotto, *Sleeping Apollo*.

David and Abigail by the Bolognese Guido Reni, mentioned in seventeenth- and eighteenth-century sources as one of the sights of Nuremberg when it was still in the Praun Collection there; *St. James of the Compostella Combatting the Moors* by Giovanni Battista Tiepolo; and works by Annibale Carracci, Salvator Rosa, Luca Giordano, Bernardo Strozzi, Sebastiano Ricci, and Bellotto complete the notable Eszterházy pictures from the Italian school.

Among Netherlandish paintings of the fifteenth and sixteenth centuries are the standing *Madonna and Child* by Petrus Christus (d. 1472–73), from the Pálffy bequest; a small triptych by Memling, the central *Crucifixion* panel of which was a gift by Pryker; and the two wings belonging to it, once in the imperial collection in Vienna, acquired by the museum in 1934. The lovely Gerard David *Adoration of the Shepherds* and impressive *Portrait of Emperor Charles V* by Bernard van Orley were purchased by Pulszky during the 1890s. One of the memorable pictures in the entire collection, *St. John the Baptist Preaching* by Pieter von Bruegel the Elder, was acquired by the museum from the Batthyány family in 1951. Among the early German pictures, there is the small but fine *Portrait of a Young Man*, probably by Dürer. This panel, one of the 1848 transfers from Buda Castle, once belonged to Archduke Leopold Wilhelm in Brussels. Another fine painting from the group transferred in 1848 is the *Mystic Marriage of St. Catherine* by Cranach the Elder. The large Hans Holbein the Elder *Death of the Virgin* came as a gift; Hans Baldung Grien's *Adam* and *Eve* and the Altdorfer *Crucifixion* were purchases.

The Szépmüvészeti Múzeum takes special pride in its Spanish collection of about eighty paintings, one of the richest after the Prado. Of the seven El Grecos, six came by gift or purchase from the collections of Marcell Nemes, who, along with his colleague Lipót M. Herzog, was one of the first connoisseurs to rediscover the Spanish master during the very early years of this century. Several important canvases were bought by the Eszterházys before 1820 from Count Edmund Burke, who had been Danish ambassador to Spain. There are also a Murillo and Zurbarán from the other Eszterházy sources. Perhaps the most important Spanish pictures from the Eszterházy Collection came from the Kaunitz Collection in Vienna, namely Ribera's *Martyrdom of St. Andrew* and a famous pair of pictures by Goya—the *Water Seller* and the *Knife-Grinder* of about 1810. Also of note is Velázquez' *Peasant Meal* and Alonso Cano's *Noli me tangere*.

For the Northern Baroque school, again the Eszterházy–ex-Kaunitz paintings head the list, most notably with the Rubens-van Dyck *Mucius Scaevola before Porsenna* of about 1620 and van Dyck's *Portrait of a Married Couple*. Other Eszterházy Collection pictures are Jacob Jordaens' *Satyr and Peasant Family* and Frans Hals' *Portrait of Jan Assely*, as well as works by van Ostade, Steen, Saenredam, and Cuyp. There is also *Portrait of a Woman*, which was once attributed to Vermeer. Ruisdael and van Goyen are represented among the works from the Pálffy bequest, and Pulszky's name is associated with the 1885 purchase of Rembrandt's *Dream of St. Joseph*. Other artists from the Rembrandt circle include Gerard Dou, Nicolaes Maes, and Aert de Gelder.

German and Austrian seventeenth- and eighteenth-century holdings were significantly increased in 1953, when the collection, formed by Count Ödön Zichy during the nineteenth century in Vienna and given to the city of Budapest by Count Jenö Zichy, was transferred to the museum. Johann Kupezky's *The Artist and His Family* came as a gift in 1910 from Marcell Nemes. Angelica Kauffmann's *Portrait of a Woman*, painted in Rome in 1795, is presumed to be that of Princess Eszterházy and came from that collection. There are several religious paintings and mural sketches by the eighteenth-century Austrian master Franz Anton Maulbertsch, a most prolific decorator of churches throughout the predominantly Catholic Austro-Hungarian Empire.

Of the small collection of French paintings, the early Poussin *Rest on the Flight to Egypt* was purchased by the museum in 1957 from a private collection in Budapest. The Eszterházy pictures include the Claude Lorraine *Roman Landscape* and Simon Vouet *Apollo and the Muses*. One of the most ravishing of French seventeenth-century painting is Laurent de la Hyrie's *Theseus and Aethra*. Chardin's *Still Life* was acquired in 1948 from the collection of Lipót M. Herzog.

The collection of English paintings is also small, but there are a number of eighteenth-century portraits, as well as Constable's *Waterloo-Celebration in East Bergholz*, purchased in 1913. Of special interest is the *Portrait of Prince Miklós*

Eszterházy the Magnificent, resplendent in his ambassadorial regalia, painted by Sir Joshua Reynolds in 1786.

The Szépmüvészeti Múzeum has more than 110,000 works on paper, including watercolors. This collection is almost as significant, if not quite as readily visible, as the collection of Old Master paintings. Every major European school is represented by fine examples of drawings from the fifteenth through the twentieth century, more especially in the Italian, German, and Dutch fields, with emphasis on the sixteenth through the nineteenth century.

The largest and most valuable share of prints and drawings came with the 1871 purchase of the Eszterházy Collection. The foundation of the Eszterházy holdings was laid by the acquisition in 1801 (by Prince Miklós Eszterházy) of the Praun Collection in Nuremberg, primarily of Italian and German works of the sixteenth century. In 1803 a number of engravings and a small quantity of drawings, including four by Rembrandt, were added from the collection of Franz Anton Nowohratsky-Kollowrath. The 1811 purchase of A. C. Poggi's collection in Paris increased the works by Italian masters and added significantly to French and Dutch works of the seventeenth century. Eszterházy also made systematic purchases and built up a comprehensive collection of 3,535 drawings and 51,301 prints now in the possession of the museum.

In 1901 the museum was considerably enriched by the legacy of the painter István Delhaes, consisting of 2,683 drawings and 14,453 prints. The majority of them were works by eighteenth- and nineteenth-century masters, thus complementing the Eszterházy material. Systematic and continuing purchases by the museum included a number of Rembrandt etchings in 1904 from Professor Gyula Elischer and the collection of Baron László Podmaniczky in 1914. During the same decade, director Elek Petrovics bought hundreds of drawings, mainly by Dutch seventeenth-century masters and French and German works of the eighteenth and nineteenth centuries; he also acquired an early Picasso drypoint.

Several hundred portrait miniatures were donated to the museum by Béla Procopius, and in 1935 Pál Majovszky left his collection of modern drawings. He started collecting in 1911 and from the beginning intended to donate his collection to the Szépmüvészeti Múzeum. The center of his collection was formed by French masters from Ingres to Picasso, but English, German, and Dutch drawings up through van Gogh are also represented.

The collection of drawings prides itself on the three studies by Leonardo, followed by fine examples from the hands of Raphael, Parmigianino, Veronese, Tintoretto, the Carracci, Guercino, Giovanni Battista Castiglione, Guido Reni, Salvator Rosa, Giovanni Battista, and Domenico Tiepolo, Guardi, and others of the Italian schools. The Northern masters represented include Veit Stoss, Dürer, Altdorfer, Cranach, Hans Baldung Grien, Bruegel, Goltzius, Rembrandt (by fifteen drawings), Rubens, van Dyck, Ruisdael, Ostade, Maulbertsch, Kremser-Schmidt, and others, as well as members of the Austrian Biedermeier movement. From England and France are drawings by Hogarth, Gainsborough,

Rowlandson, Watteau, Boucher, Fragonard, Delacroix, Daumier, Corot, Millet, Courbet, Manet, Monet, Renoir, Pissarro, Sisley, Cézanne, Gauguin, Degas, Rodin, Toulouse-Lautrec, Maillol, and Picasso. Memorable prints, including important series, add to the above list the names of Mantegna, Marcantonio Raimondi, Lucas van Leyden, Goya, and Callot.

The Collection of Prints and Drawings is housed on the right off the Renaissance Court, with a specially selected group of works, centered around a theme or artist, always on view.

The department of modern art came into existence during the directorship of Elek Petrovics in 1912, the year of the Pálffy bequest. In addition to donating the collection of Old Masters, Count János Pálffy also donated fifty-six modern paintings, mostly of the Barbizon School. Petrovics himself made a number of purchases during the second decade of this century, many of them Impressionist and Post-Impressionist works by artists such as Monet, Pissarro, and Toulouse-Lautrec. Among these purchases perhaps the most notable is Manet's early *Lady with a Fan*, depicting Baudelaire's Creole mistress and muse, Jeanne Duval. There are two paintings by Gauguin—a winter scene in Normandy of 1879 and a Tahitian work, *The Black Pigs*, of 1891.

Over the years, the acquisition of the Marcell Nemes and Lipót M. Herzog collections of Impressionist and Post-Impressionist artists augmented the quantity and quality of the museum's holdings from these periods. These paintings include the Cézanne *Still Life*, acquired in 1917, and the stunning *Woman with Daisies* by Corot, purchased in 1946.

The museum collections that came into the Szépmüvészeti Múzeum at the time of its establishment (from the National Museum and the National Gallery) already contained a number of nineteenth-century European and Hungarian paintings, reflecting popular tastes of the second half of the nineteenth century in that part of the world. Since the removal of the works of the Hungarian masters in 1973 into a museum of their own, this part of the collection has been devoted most extensively to German and Austrian works.

The nineteenth-century paintings are exhibited in two large and six small rooms, adjacent to the eighteenth-century galleries on the main floor (second story), as a continuation of the Old Picture Gallery.

Opening off the Renaissance Court on the ground floor, to the right, are the galleries of modern sculpture of the nineteenth and twentieth centuries. This collection is not comprehensive, but it does offer some important highlights, from Thorwaldsen, Carpeaux, Rodin (six works), and the Belgian Meunier—whose monumental *Longshoreman* dominates its space—through Maillol and Despiau to some later artists.

On the left side of the Renaissance Court, opposite the modern sculpture display, there is a small gallery of later twentieth-century art that opened in 1972. Although there are works by Picasso, Kokoschka, Chagall, Sonia Delaunay, Josef Albers, Victor Vasarély, and others, often represented in the graphic medium, this collection shows the Szépmüvészeti Múzeum's efforts to keep up with contemporary trends, as well as its severe budgetary limitations in the world market.

The permanent exhibition galleries of the Department of Graeco-Roman Antiquities link the entrance hall with the Renaissance Court on the ground floor. In its possession are more than four thousand objects, ranging from original Greek and Roman marble statuary, terracotta figurines, Greek vases, bronzes, jewelry, building ornaments, and objects of everyday life. Some of these pieces were already in other museum collections in Hungary and only came into the department during the 1930s, when these various collections were reorganized and consolidated at the Szépmüvészeti Múzeum.

At the time of the museum's founding, only plaster copies represented the masterworks of the Classical period. At first, there was no intention to collect original works. This policy was changed under director Elek Petrovics with the purchase in 1908 of 135 antique marble statues from the collection of Paul Arndt, the Munich archaeologist. In 1913, 650 terracotta pieces were acquired, followed in 1917 by the gift of Marcell Nemes of his collection of vases.

Some of the most important pieces include a Greek Archaic marble torso of a youth; the famous bronze "Grimani" jug from the middle of the fifth century B.C., presumably from a Corinthian workshop; an Athenian tomb stele with three figures from the fourth century B.C., and a Hellenistic marble statuette of a maiden, known as the *Budapest Dancer*. A black-figure amphora by Ezekias and a red-figure kylix by the Andokides Painter (from the Haán Collection, formerly in the museum at Gyula) distinguish the vase collection. One of the best pieces in the Roman collection is the famous marble relief fragment, the *Battle of Actium*, of the Augustan Age.

The Egyptian Collection, composed of some twenty-five hundred pieces, became an independent department in 1962 and opened its permanent exhibition galleries on the ground floor as late as 1972. A major source of this collection consisted of finds from excavations in which Hungarian archaeological teams participated, first during the early years of this century in the Sharuna and Gamhoud regions of Middle Egypt (partially financed by Fülöp Beck) and again in 1964 at Abdallah Nirqui north of Abu Simbel (at the request of UNESCO).

The Egyptian collection was originally established within the Szépmüvészeti Múzeum's Department of Antiquities. It was under the auspices of the Department of Antiquities that, during the 1930s, Egyptian pieces scattered among various Hungarian museums were brought together and classified. Part of this Egyptian collection was then first exhibited in 1939. The collection sustained considerable damage during World War II but was enriched during the post-war years by bequests, such as the one from Boniface Platz, and in 1959 by direct purchases from Egypt.

The collection spans the years of Egypt's complex civilization and cult of the dead from prehistoric times until the Roman conquest in 30 B.C. Among the works of art, the funerary offerings, the artifacts, several wall relief fragments from a temple of the Ptolemaic period, a Theban limestone head of a man from the nineteenth dynasty (New Kingdom), and a mummy case of priestess of Amon of about 1000 B.C. stand out as the most impressive and beautiful objects.

The collection of European decorative and figurative sculpture, from the early medieval through the Late Baroque periods, saw its beginnings with the late-nineteenth-century purchases of Károly Pulszky in Italy. The collection of bronzes, gathered by the Hungarian sculptor István Ferenczy in Rome during the first half of the nineteenth century, was bought for the museum in 1914 during the directorship of Elek Petrovics. The collection of predominantly Italian works became an autonomous department in 1955, when director Andor Pigler gave it its present status. His careful consideration of chronology and geography are reflected in the arrangement of the exhibition rooms of the Sculpture Gallery, similar to the arrangement found in the Old Picture Gallery, although much smaller in scale and far more limited in scope.

The walls of the staircase leading from the main floor of the Old Picture Gallery to the third level of the museum are lined with decorative sculpted pieces from medieval Italy. On the third level, the fifteen small galleries of figurative sculptures, mostly small in scale, start with eleven rooms devoted to Italian schools from the medieval period through the sixteenth century. In the first room is the very important eleventh-century ivory relief plaque from the Salerno cathedral, the *Creation of the Birds and Fishes*. The small *Madonna* by Andrea Pisano of about 1330 is followed by works of the first generation of Florentine Renaissance sculptors (of the schools of Donatello and Ghiberti), and they in turn are followed by works of their successors.

The late Quattrocento is represented by a masterful figure of *Christ* by Verrocchio. Perhaps the most famous work in the collection is the small equestrian bronze figure (from the Ferenczy Collection), executed after drawings by Leonardo for François I of France between 1516 and 1519. On a larger scale is the *Madonna* by Jacopo Sansovino. Works of the Spanish Renaissance are exhibited with the Italians in the last two rooms devoted to southern Europe.

Late Gothic and Renaissance German and Austrian works of the fifteenth and sixteenth centuries are followed by French sculptures from the thirteenth through the sixteenth century. The suite of five rooms between the upper and the main levels house the Baroque and eighteenth-century pieces. Downstairs in the Renaissance Court on the ground floor, there are further examples of decorative sculpture from the Veneto, including a collection of well heads.

The Szépművészeti Múzeum aims to be the center of art historical research in Hungary. Works not on permanent or temporary exhibition may be studied by students or scholars in the storage areas. The Library of more than sixty thousand volumes, source materials, and periodicals in many languages; the Collection of Arts Data and Relics; and the Photographic Archives exist not only in support of the research needs of the curatorial and conservation staff but also in support of the research needs of scholars and students outside the museum.

The museum also maintains an active publication program, dealing with its collections as well as with special aspects of its large holdings, particularly concerning the Old Picture Gallery and the Collection of Prints and Drawings. It publishes a bulletin in Hungarian and French, *Közölmény/Bulletin du musée hongrois des beaux arts* (since 1947), monthly program guides including lectures and tours, guide books to the collections in several languages, slides, postcards, and folios of reproductions of a large selection from its holdings.

The museum's book-form publications are copyrighted and are handled by Hungary's cultural presses, mostly the Corvina Press and occasionally the Akadémiai Kiadó of Budapest.

Selected Bibliography

Museum publications: *Guide du musée hongrois des beaux arts*, 1978; *The Picture Galleries of the Museum of Fine Arts, Budapest: A Guidebook* (Budapest 1977); Agghází, Mária G., *Italian and Spanish Sculpture Collection of Old Sculpture in the Budapest Museum of Fine Arts* (Budapest 1977); Balogh, Jolán, *Katalog der ausländischen Bildwerke des Museums der Bildenden Künszte in Budapest, IV-XVIII Jahrhundert*, 2 vols. (Budapest 1975); Baskovits, Miklós, *Early Italian Panel Paintings: Paintings from the Budapest Museum of Fine Arts and Esztergom Christian Museum* (Budapest 1966); Czobor, Ágnes, *Dutch Landscapes: Paintings in the Budapest Museum of Fine Arts* (Budapest 1967, New York 1968); idem, *Hét évszázad vízfestményei* (exh. cat. 1974); Fenyö, Iván, *North Italian Drawings from the Collection of the Budapest Museum of Fine Arts* (Budapest 1965, New York 1966); Garas, Klára, *Eighteenth-Century Venetian Paintings* (Budapest 1968, New York 1968); idem, *Italian Renaissance Portraits* (Budapest 1965); idem, *Masterpieces from Budapest with 60 Color Plates from the Museum of Fine Arts* (Budapest 1970); idem, *Paintings in the Budapest Museum of Fine Arts* (Budapest 1972; revised by Elizabeth West, Budapest 1977); idem, *Selected Paintings from the Old Picture Gallery, Budapest Museum of Fine Arts* (Budapest 1967); idem, *A Szépmüvészeti Múzeum legszebb rajzai, a XVIII század német és osztrák rajzmüvészete* (Budapest 1980); Genthon, István, *From Romanticism to Post-Impressionism: French Paintings from the Budapest Museum of Fine Arts* (Budapest 1966); Haraszti-Takács, Marianne, *The Masters of Mannerism: Reproductions of Paintings in the Budapest Museum of Fine Arts* (Budapest 1968, New York 1969); idem, *Spanish Masters: Catalogue of Works Selected from the Spanish Collection in the Budapest Museum of Fine Arts* (Budapest 1966, New York 1971); idem, *The Treasures of the Hungarian Museum of Fine Arts* (Budapest 1954); Mojzer, Miklós, *Dutch Genre Paintings in the Museum of Fine Arts, Budapest and István Dobó Museum, Debrecen* (Budapest 1967, New York 1969); Mravik, László, *Felsöiláliai quattrocento festmények, Budapest Szépmüvészeti Múzeum* (Budapest 1979); Pataky, Denés, *Master Drawings from the Collection of the Budapest Museum of Fine Arts, 19th and 20th Centuries* (Budapest 1959, New York 1959); Pigler, Andor, *Catalogue of North Italian Drawings* (Budapest 1967); idem, *Katalog der Galerie alter Meister*, 2 vols. (Budapest 1967); idem, *Válogatott festmények a régi képtárból* (Budapest 1968); Possuth, Krisztina, and Pataky, Denés, *XX századi muvészet* (Budapest 1978); Radocsay, Denés, *Gothic Panel Painting in Hungary in the Collections of the Budapest Museum of Fine Arts and the Esztergom Christian Museum* (Budapest 1963); Szigethi, Ágnes, *French Painting of the Seventeenth and Eighteenth Centuries* (Budapest 1976); Urbach, Zsuzsa, *Early Netherlandish Painting: Reproductions of Paintings from the Collections of the Museum of Fine Arts, Budapest and the Christian Museum, Esztergom* (Budapest 1971); Végh, János,

Fifteenth-Century German and Bohemian Panel Paintings from the Budapest Museum of Fine Arts and the Esztergom Christian Museum (Budapest 1967, New York 1968); idem, *Sixteenth-Century German Panel Paintings in Hungarian Collections* (Budapest 1972). Other publications: Fenyö, Iván, *Meisterzeichnungen aus dem Museum der Schönen Künste in Budapest*, exh. cat. (Vienna 1967); Gerszi, Teréz, *Bruegel and His Age* (New York 1970); idem, *Netherlandish Drawings in the Budapest Museum, Sixteenth Century Drawings: An Illustrated Catalogue*, 2 vols. (Amsterdam and New York 1971–72); Glaras, Klára, intro., *Museum of Fine Arts, Budapest*, Newsweek, *Great Museums of the World* (New York and Milan 1982); Haraszti-Takács, Marianne, "Fine Arts Museum," in *Budapest Museums*, Great Centers of Art Series (Cranbury, N.J., and New York 1970); *Leonardo to Van Gogh: Master Drawings from Budapest*, exh. cat. (Washington, Chicago, Los Angeles 1985); Vayer, Lajos, *Master Drawings from the Collection of the Budapest Museum of Fine Arts, 14th–18th Centuries* (New York 1957).

GEORGINE SZALAY REED

India

—— Allahabad ——

ALLAHABAD MUSEUM (also ALLAHABAD MUNICIPAL MUSEUM), Motilal Nehru Park, Allahabad, Uttar Pradesh.

The Allahabad Museum was established in 1931 through the active support of the local Municipal Board. In 1947 the Prime Minister of India, Pandit Nehru, laid the foundation for the new museum building in Motilal Nehru Park. The entire museum complex was completed by 1965, and the museum's collections, scattered in temporary storage facilities and elsewhere in the city, were consolidated and adequately displayed. The museum is funded and governed by the Municipal Corporation of Allahabad and has from time to time received funds from private and government sources. A director assisted by several officers manages the day-to-day affairs of the museum.

The Allahabad Museum's fine collection of some five hundred stone sculptures provides a comprehensive historical survey of the evolution of sculpture in northern India from about the third century B.C. to the twelfth century A.D. The earliest datable fragment in the museum's collection is the abacus of a pillar assigned to the reign of Asoka (268–231 B.C.), which once constituted part of the pillar in the Allahabad Fort. The pillar is inscribed with several of Asoka's edicts, and this inscriptional evidence, together with the ornamental motif employed on the abacus, the knot and the flower, present in other Mauryan monuments, clearly identifies it as a work of the Mauryan period (322–185 B.C.). Also associated with the Mauryan period are stone discs, often referred to as ring stones. They are divisible into two distinct groups, both represented in the Allahabad Museum. One group usually has a circular opening in the center, with depictions of the mother goddess alternated by a palm tree or honeysuckle along the sloping inner sides of the central opening. These motifs and the sharp and precise workmanship associate this group of ring stones to the Mauryan period and distingush them from the second group. In the latter group of stone discs discovered in a large hoard at Murtaziganj in Patna, the central perforation is absent, and the decorative motifs consist of lotus petals or a stellate pattern in association with a large variety of animals. The workmanship is less refined, and the decorative repertoire is closer to that of the second century B.C. as in monuments such as Sanchi Stupa II.

The museum's collection of fifty-four fragments from the Buddhist stupa at Bharhut of the second century B.C. are second in number and importance to those in the Indian Museum (q.v.) in Calcutta. These fragments were procured for the museum by Pandit Braj Mohan Vyas from villages around Bharhut, where they had been reused as building material and had subsequently suffered mutilation. The pieces consist of fragments of thirty-two pillars, one corner pillar, three crossbars, fourteen coping stones, one fragment of a capital, two blocks, and a part of a stairway. Among them are interesting variants of two types of stone posts, one with large images of Yakṣas and Yakṣīs and the other with a central medallion and lunettes at the top and bottom. The museum's fragmentary posts indicate that on some of the Bharhut posts, the central medallion was replaced by an undulating lotus rhysome that issues from the mouth of a Yakṣa seated in a lunette at the base. Among other interesting fragments of this collection are a relief on a post depicting acrobats forming a human pyramid and another relief depicting the *tri-ratna* symbol in association with Nāgas and a lotus pond, thus presenting a pictographic representation of the complex symbolism of water cosmology centered around the lotus flower. The abstract and hieratic style of this important group of sculptures of the second century B.C. was not an isolated phenomenon. The *makara* capital from Kausambi and the *Prtapgarh Yakṣa*, both in the Allahabad Museum, indicate that the Bharhut idiom extended into eastern Madhyadeśa (eastern Uttar Pradesh).

In the first century B.C. there was a marked stylistic change in sculptures of the various flourishing centers such as Sanchi, Bodhgaya, and Mathurā. In the Allahabad Museum several pieces testify to the relaxation and softening of the abstract and linear style prevalent during the previous century. Among these works, the standing *Yakṣī* and the frieze *Gajalasmī and the Bull* on a fragment of a *toraṇa* architrave, both from Kausambi, embody aspects of the artistic trends of this period.

During the Kuṣāna period (first-third century), Mathurā became the greatest center of northern Indian sculpture, and the Allahabad Museum possesses both works of Mathurā origin and local pieces inspired by the style of Mathurā. In the former category is the headless Bodhisattva image, dedicated in the second year of Kaṇiṣka (A.D. 80) by the nun Buddhamitrā and found at Kausambi. Of local origin are the Buddha torso from nearby Bhita and the *Caturmukha Liṅga* from Kausambi. The taut, energetic rendering of the surfaces and the delicate delineation of drapery are common to both the Mathurā Bodhisattva and the Bhita torso and testify to parallel developments at the two centers. In the *Ca-*

turmukha Liṅga and the large seated *Yakṣa*, both from Kausambi, the strength and firmness is somewhat diluted, and there is a greater surface abstraction, but the underlying aesthetic approach places them squarely within the Kuṣāṇa period. To this group also belong several sculptures from Mathurā that include two male heads, a Jina head, a bust of a Bodhisattva, and the fragmentary bust of a woman whose elaborate headdress is rendered in the precise and delicate manner of the drapery of the Kausambi Bodhisattva discussed earlier.

The variant Kuṣāṇa style of Gandhāra is represented by some dozen pieces that include narrative friezes depicting scenes from the life of the Buddha, two fine examples of the seated Buddha, and a standing Bodhisattva. The distinct Gandhāra facial types, the wide pleatlike patterning of the drapery, and the presence of non-Indian features such as the use of Corinthian pilasters to separate episodes on the reliefs suggest eclectic creative forces at work in this northwestern region of the Kuṣāṇa Empire during the first few centuries of the Christian era.

The next great flowering of creativity is that of the Gupta period (fourth to the end of the fifth century) in major centers such as Mathurā and the Udayagiri-Vidisa region in present-day Madhya Pradesh. It has been supposed that the Gupta style in the eastern part of ancient Madhyadeśa (present-day Kausambi and Sarnath) was the result of influences from Mathurā. However, the museum has three important images of *Viṣṇu* from Bhita, Jhusi and Unchdih rendered in the early Gupta idiom of the late fourth century and early fifth century, which suggest that the Gupta style of this region emerged simultaneously with that of the major centers. These images are characterized by broad, swelling chests; firm, tightly rendered contours of the forms; and decorative motifs such as the thick garlands that marked the early-fifth-century style of Udayagiri. The later evolution of this style is seen in numerous sculptures from the mid to the late fifth century from sites such as Bhumara, Sarnath, Bhita, Khoh, Kausambi, and Mathurā. The sculptures from Bhumara are from a collapsed temple superstructure and include fragments of pilasters, doorway surrounds, relief panels with lotus scrolls, and *candraśālās* (horseshoe arches). They represent some of the most exuberant and assured treatments of decorative details, such as floriated scrolls and lotus rhysomes. The figural representations have the soft and supple rhythms of later Gupta style. The superb *Ekamukha Śiva Liṅga* from Khoh, the standing *Viṣṇu* from Sankargarh, the fragmentary door frame from Nagod, and the various Buddha images from Sarnath testify to the variations in the Gupta style ranging from the confident, reposeful strength of the Khoh image to the attenuated, abstract delicacy of the Sarnath images.

The Allahabad Museum's collection of medieval sculpture from the eighth to the twelfth century is both varied and extensive. However, lack of systematic attempts to study northern Indian sculpture between the sixth and ninth centuries makes this period difficult to analyze. Many of the sculptures in the museum from the sixth to the ninth century reflect dual tendencies, one conservative and looking back to the Gupta idioms and the other more experimental and embodying qualities that would develop more fully in the ninth and tenth centuries. Sculptures such as the *Jaina Tutelary Couple* from Lachhagir and the *Umā-Maheśvara* from Arail, both of the eighth century, reflect these dual tendencies; whereas the treatment of necklaces and coiffure reminds one of the Gupta period, the modeling of shoulders and torso to emphasize solidity and breadth is a forerunner of developments in the ninth century. By the second half of the ninth century there were new forces at work, and sculptures from that time are distinguished by a rich decorativeness and rhythmic movements that had not developed into the hard, schematic patterns of the later medieval style. The magnificent door-frame of a temple from Kausambi in the Allahabad Museum is an example of the grace and elegance of this style. Although the ornamentation is striking, it has not stifled the lively, virtuoso modeling of the forms. Sculptures such as the *Surya* fragment from Lachhagir, the *Hari-Hara* from Manikpur, the *Vāmana* from Phaphamau, and the door-frame fragments from Unchdih indicate the regional character of the sculptures of eastern Madhyadesha in the ninth century.

With the tenth century, sculpture entered a phase where hardness and angularity replaced the swaying elegance of earlier pieces, and it was only infrequently, as in the *Śiva* from Banda, that the verve of the previous century made itself felt. Noteworthy examples of this phase of sculpture in northern India in the museum are the *Saptamātṛkā* panel and the door-frame fragments, all from Gurgi (Rewa District). The many sculptures from Khajuraho in Madhya Pradesh, such as the *Viṣṇu on Garuda*, the *Varāha*, the bust of *Parvati*, and the *Umā-Maheśvara* testify to the general ossification of style where the all-pervasive surface details destroy the softer volumes of figural representation, and the ubiquitous strings of beadwork decorating the images add to the desiccation of forms. These qualities culminate in twelfth-century sculptures, such as the standing *Viṣṇu* from Lachhagir and the five-bracket figures from Jamsot, which mark the final phase of the traditional style of sculpture in northern India, since the Islamic conquests of that century brought artistic activity to an abrupt halt.

An interesting feature of the sculpture collection in the museum is the group of miniature shrines found in the Allahabad region. Although the Islamic invasions destroyed the temples in this area, these miniature shrines from the tenth and eleventh centuries recreate the structural elements of the *latina*-temple type that once enlivened the landscape of this region of northern India.

The painting collection of the Allahabad Museum owes its origins to the generosity of the Municipal Board of Allahabad, which allotted special funds for the acquisition of paintings about 1935. This collection now consists of some fifteen hundred examples that include major schools such as Mughal, Rajasthani, Pahari, and the modern Bengali school of painting. The entire collection is not on permanent display. From this extensive and representative group of paintings, the museum's collection of Rajasthani and Pahari paintings deserve special attention. Of the major Rajasthani schools, miniatures from Malwa and Bundi provide examples that clarify the origins and the later evolution of Rajasthani painting. The conservative tendencies of the Malwa school are to be seen in the *Devī Mahātmya* (c. 1640), where the schematized rendering of landscape, the emphasis on vigorous action, and the use of bold, flat areas of color all have their roots in an indigenous style prevalent in India immediately before the sixteenth century. In the mid-seventeenth-century *Amaru Śataka*, also of the Malwa school, there is evidence of the impact of the Mughal school, since the contours are softer and gestures more restrained. In a *Ragamala* set of approximately the same period, the flat areas of color used to describe the landscape have been replaced by an elaborate landscape of stylized birds, flowers, trees, and shrubs. The Bundi school, emerging as it did from the parent school of Mewar, was less rooted in indigenous traditions, and the museum's fine collection of eighteenth-century works such as *Month of Śrāvaṇa* and *Heroine at Her Toilet* show the evolution of this school away from the flat and abstract representations typical of Malwa. A court scene, *Jogiram Holding Court* (eighteenth century), is obviously inspired by Mughal prototypes, with the ruler seated under a pavilion in a landscape defined by cypresses and the foreground flowerbeds divided in rectangular patches. The most important Bundi miniature is a page from the *Chunar Ragamala* of 1591. Numerous eighteenth-century paintings from Pahari schools, such as *Jahangir Ordering the Poisoning of the Gosāīns* from Basohli, *Lady with Pet Deer* from Kangra, *Raja Govardhan Chand* from Guler, and *Encampment of Travelers*, a line-drawing with color from Jammu, provide a representative survey of this branch of Indian miniature painting. The museum's collection of modern Indian painting includes works by artists such as Roerich and members of the Bengal school, such as Gagendernath Tagore, Nandlal Bose, Shailender Dey, and Yamani Roy.

The Allahabad Museum's collection of terracottas from Kausambi, perhaps the greatest center of terracotta production in ancient India, is especially significant. Some four thousand objects collected between 1931 and 1950 testify to the vigor and variety of this art form in northern India from the third century B.C. to the sixth century A.D. These pieces are made in a soft reddish clay painted red or pink, and a few examples show traces of black and yellowish slip. The thematic range of these religious and secular pieces is very wide and includes plaques and individual figurines representing gods and goddesses, men fighting winged lions, amorous couples, erotic scenes of startling explicitness, dancers and musicians, some in Scythian dress, toy carts, and animals. The stylistic range varies from the archaic, where hand modeling and the use of pinched-out or incised techniques predominate, to the numerous molded pieces predominantly from the first century B.C. to the third century A.D. This collection provides an especially useful adjunct to the collection of stone sculptures in the museum, since they provide supportive material in defining the creative impulses of these early periods and also present a unified picture of the everyday art of the general public as distinct from the stone sculptures that were often produced under powerful religious or secular patrons.

The museum's collections of minor arts include ceramic objects of European origins and indigenous collections of textiles, weapons, and wood and ivory carving. An interesting collection of objects donated by Jawaharlal Nehru include personal memorabilia and objects associated with the independence movement of India such as salt made by Mahatma Gandhi.

Photographs of objects in the collection may be purchased by application to the director of the museum.

Selected Bibliography

Museum publications: Kala, S. C., *Bharhut Vedika*, 1951; idem, *Indian Miniatures in the Allahabad Museum*, 1961; idem, *Terracotta Figurines from Kausambi*, 1950.

Other publications: Chandra, P., *Stone Sculpture in the Allahabad Museum* (Poona 1971).

REKHA MORRIS

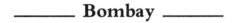

Bombay

PRINCE OF WALES MUSEUM (officially PRINCE OF WALES MUSEUM OF WESTERN INDIA), Mahatma Gandhi Road, Bombay 400 023.

Although the Prince of Wales Museum was established in 1909 by an act of the Bombay government, it did not begin to function as a museum until 1921. The nucleus of the archaeological collection consisted of the sculptures and coins transferred to the Prince of Wales by the Poona branch of the Archaeological Survey and by sculptures loaned to the museum by the Bombay branch of the Royal Asiatic Society. Gifts and museum purchases have continued to enlarge this section of the museum. The museum's collection of paintings and the minor arts originated in 1915, when the museum acquired the collection of Purshottam Vishram Mawji, which included paintings, textiles, weapons, and other miscellaneous objects. Two important bequests of 1922 and 1933 containing important Indian, Oriental, and European objects were made to the museum by the Tata family. Significant purchases of Rajasthani paintings were made between 1948 and 1958, making this an important collection in India.

The museum is governed by a board of trustees established under the 1909 act, and officers of the museum include a director and curators for the various collections. The museum is supported largely by funds from the local and state government, although public contributions and admission fees also provide substantial financial assistance.

The sculpture collection of the Prince of Wales Museum, although not significant, is adequate to illustrate some of the major periods of sculptural development in India with its beginnings in the Indus Valley civilization to its final florescence in medieval India. The Indus Valley civilization (c. 2500–1500 B.C.), which produced magnificent pieces of stone sculpture, a few of which have survived, has left behind a more extensive repertory of a somewhat popular nature, such as masks, toys, and terracotta figurines. The museum has several examples of these works, among them a bull and a horned human mask. Both of them reflect the more abstract tendencies of the seals and limestone heads that have survived and are now largely to be seen in the National Museum (q.v.) in Delhi.

Unfortunately, the singularly brilliant phase of Indian art, that of the Mauryan period (322–185 B.C.), does not find representation in the collections of the Prince of Wales Museum. However, the creativity of the succeeding phase of sculptural development is illustrated by a few sculptures from Bharhut and Pitalkhora of the second century B.C. Remnants from the Buddhist stupa at Bharhut in central India representing rosettes, an elephant head, a damaged Yakṣa figure, and part of a Jataka scene insubstantially reflect the quintessentially abstract idiom of this monument, whose major remains are in the Indian Museum (q.v.) in Calcutta. Although these few pieces from Bharhut do not adequately suggest the finer nuances of the Bharhut style, stylistically, they relate directly to the museum's small group of sculptures from Pitalkhora, a series of Buddhist caves in western India. These caves were created in two major phases of artistic activity associated with the Sātavāhana-Kshahrāta (second to first century B.C.) and Vākātaka (fifth to sixth century A.D.) periods, respectively. The sculptures in the museum representing a *Dvārapāla*, or door guardian; a *Gajalakshmī*; and *mithuna* figures, couples standing arm-in-arm, have been assigned to the second century B.C. Qualities such as the obvious and frontal immobility of some of the figures, the use of sharp contours, and the emphatic linearity of surface details that the Pitalkhora sculptures share with those from Bharhut provide an interesting glimpse of the artistic sensibility of India during the second century B.C.

Sculptures of a later phase, those of the Kuṣānas (first-third century A.D.) in northern India and of the Sātavāhanas and Ikshvakus (first century B.C.-third century A.D.) in the Deccan are well represented in the museum collections. The three important centers of art during this period were Mathurā (Uttar Pradesh), Gandhāra (northwestern India presently in Pakistan), and Amaravati (Deccan). The museum's less than a dozen pieces in red or mottled Mathurā sandstone of the second century A.D. partially illustrate the activities of this prolific center of Kuṣāna art. There is little evidence in these fragments of the dynamic force that radiates from the taut surfaces of the great Mathurā sculptures. However, the four Jina heads do convey some of the assured directness of statement that permeates the Kuṣāna art of Mathurā. Moreover, in the shift from the fuller more voluminous treatment of two of the Jina heads to the marked flat and additive quality of the other two is encapsulated the evolutionary history of Kuṣāna sculpture of Mathurā from the first to the third century A.D.

The museum's holdings of sculptures from the other prolific center of Kuṣāna art, Gandhāra, are more numerous and representative. Gandhāra sculptures were an integral part of the Buddhist sacred area: single statues were placed in chapels and in courtyards, and the relief panels decorated the stupas, staircases, and other areas of worship. On the reliefs are depicted scenes from the life of Buddha Śākyamuni and Jātaka stories; the single figures represent Buddhas and Bodhisattvas. Many of the relief fragments in the museum depict scenes typical of Gandhāra art, such as *Māyā's Dream*, the *Birth of the Buddha*, the *Great Departure*, the *First Sermon and the Turning of the Wheel of the Law*, *Subduing the Elephant Nālāgiri*, the *Dīpaṅkara Jātaka*, and the *Miracle at Śrāvastī*.

These works attest to the variety of narrative reliefs from Gandhāra, which has led some Western scholars to suggest that they are the result of influences from Roman narrative reliefs. Certain aspects of these sculptures, such as the purely decorative use of the nude figure with its back to the audience in the upper register of an unidentified scene, the representation of the standing figure of Hāritī in a chitonlike garment, and the use of the Ganddhāra variation of Corinthian columns used as division points between scenes suggest influences from the Classical art of Rome and its empires. However, these superficial similarities have been both exaggerated and detrimental to an understanding of the eclectic formal qualities of Gandhāra art.

The collection also includes some fine examples of standing figures of the Bodhisattva and two seated Buddhas. For lack of an unanimously agreed-upon, clear chronology for Gandhāra art, these sculptures have been generally placed in the second and third centuries. The artistic activity of Gandhāra lasted well into the fourth century, and because of its strategic location on the great trade route from Pataliputra via Mathurā and Taxila to Afghanistan, its influences were disseminated over a wide area. The museum's collection of stucco heads and figures from Afghanistan of the fourth and fifth centuries attest to the influences by the art of the Gandhāra in these areas.

The art of the Deccan during the first three centuries of the Christian era under the Śātvāhanas and Ikshvakus is seen in the bas-reliefs of the Buddhist stupas at Amaravati, Nagarjunakonda, and Goli. Of the magnificently decorated stupa at Amaravati (probably built in the third century B.C. and enlarged and decorated up to the third century A.D.) the museum possesses a few representative fragments.

Somewhat better represented than the Amaravati pieces are sculptures of the Gupta period, so designated after the dynasty that ruled India from the fourth to the end of the fifth century. The museum's collection of sculptures from this period are from several regions, such as Madhya Pradesh, Maharashtra, and Gujerat. Although none of these sculptures represent the incipient or assured style of the Gupta period, they reflect the late phase and the influence it exerted in these regions. The *Śiva Gaṇa* from Khoh (fifth century) and the *Mithuna* (sixth century), both from Madhya Pradesh, embody the fullness of forms and the graceful, swaying contours that were such characteristic features of the plastic vocabulary of Gupta art. The *Brahmā* and *Kārtikeya* (both of the sixth century) from Elephanta in Maharashtra continue to reflect the Gupta style, but with dry, crisp overtones, where the soft, swaying rhythms have ossified and the decorative elements have begun to reflect the hardness of the medium in which they are created. These qualities become increasingly prominent in figures such as the *Kshetrapāla* (late sixth century) from Shamlaji in Gujerat and the *Sūrya* (seventh century) from Kundhol in Gujerat and anticipate the early medieval forms that retain a few Gupta features but for the most part reflect other and differing qualities at work.

The medieval period is well represented, since the majority of the sculptures in the Prince of Wales Museum are from around the eighth to the twelfth century. This large body of material may be divided into two broad groups, one spanning a period from the seventh to the ninth century and the other from the tenth to the twelfth century. This is not an arbitrary division but is based on the fact that, regardless of regional variations, the first group retains memories of the Gupta idiom, whereas in the second group these latent Gupta features are eliminated and replaced by distinct approaches to anatomical and decorative schema, perhaps partly dictated by the fact that sculpture begins to be increasingly shaped by its ornamental and subsidiary function on the facades and interiors of temples. The emphasis on the corporeality of the human form, so palpable a feature of earlier periods, is destroyed by exigencies of vigorous interest on the decorative surface and the intricate interplay of the sculptural and the architectonic.

As illustration, one need but study the three ceiling slabs, *Umāmaheśvaramūrti*, *Brahmā*, and *Viṣṇu on Śesha* (seventh century), from Aihole in Karnataka; the *Kaumārī* (seventh century), *Dancing Vaishnavī* (seventh-eighth century), and *Ambikā* (ninth century), all from Madhya Pradesh; and the two *Vaikuṇṭha Chaturmūrti* (ninth century) from Kashmir. Although there is a flatness and marked congealing of volumes and the use of sharp, angular contours, the interest in sensitive modeling of the human form remains paramount. The decorative rhythms created by elements such as garlands, scarves, and necklaces are limited and tentative. In contrast, pieces such as the *Chaurī Bearer* (twelfth century) from Gujerat; the *Hari-Hara* (twelfth century) from Maharashtra; the *Salla Fighting the Lion* (1070), the *Bhairava* (twelfth century), the *Woman at Her Toilet* (twelfth century), and the *Sarasvatī* (twelfth century), all from Karnataka, have become elaborate records of decorative intricacy in which the concern with human form is subsumed in a marvelously rhythmic array of surface details carved with a delicacy that dazzles but destroys the solidity and presence of the figures.

If the museum's collection of sculptures is mediocre in some respects, its holdings in medieval miniature paintings are rich and extremely significant. From literary sources it is evident that painting was widely practiced in India as early as the pre-Christian era. Surviving examples of this early tradition are to be seen in some of the caves of Ajanta, where the paintings have been dated from about the second century B.C. to the sixth century A.D. There appear to be few surviving examples of paintings from the early medieval period and none of paintings on wooden panels, cloth, or palm leaf earlier than the twelfth century A.D. From the fourteenth century A.D. paper began to be widely used for illustrated manuscripts. The Prince of Wales Museum has fine illustrated manuscripts of Jain text such as the *Kalpasūtra* and the *Kālakāchārya Katha* of about the end of the fourteenth century A.D. The style of these illustrations is emphatically linear. Forms are flat and delineated with sharp contours. Faces are as a general rule shown in profile but with both eyes depicted, the farther eye projecting into empty space. Colors are primary, bold, and bright, with the background painted a monochrome red. This fixed formula is repeated and makes these illustrations for the most part mechanical and uninspired.

Gradually, this schematic style discarded its more rigid tendencies and adopted certain Persian conventions. Examples of these developments are to be seen in the museum's interesting group of *Laur Chanda* paintings (early sixteenth century A.D.) and the somewhat later but stylistically similar *Gita Govinda* (second half of the sixteenth century). In these paintings, although faces continue to be shown in profile, the projecting farther eye has been eliminated, and the plain, monochromatic background is enlivened by a marked interest in introducing a landscape with trees, vines, and birds.

With the advent of the Mughals a remarkable synthesis of the indigenous Indian idiom with the Persian illustrates the evolution of this school of painting from its inception under Akbar (1556–1605) to its gradual demise in the Aurangzeb and post-Aurangzeb period. Under Akbar's enthusiastic patronage Indian and Persian classics and historical works were illustrated, and examples of them are in the museum, such as the folios from the *Razm Nama* and the *Rāmayāna* and an illustrated manuscript of the *Anwar-i-Suhaili* with 231 illustrations. These works embody dramatic narrations vivid with color and movement captured by quick, energetic brushwork.

In the next phase of painting developed under Akbar's son and successor, Jahangir (1605–28), the expressive brushwork is superceded by a careful and precise finish, less brilliant color schemes, and luxurious border decorations. Portraiture was increasingly prevalent, and the emperor's love for animals and flowers is reflected in exquisite studies of these subjects. The museum has fine examples of Jahangir-period painting such as *Jahangir's Visit to the Mausoleum of Mu'inuddin Chishti at Ajmer*, portraits of courtiers, and a few animal and bird studies.

With Shah Jahan (1628–1658) Mughal painting entered a phase of preciosity, in which colors have a hard, enamel-like quality, and the careful draftsmanship leads to treatment that borders on the mechanical. The museum's several portraits such as *Shah Jahan and His Forefathers* and *Dara Shikoh and Officers* together with the group of *Sufi Saints* reflect the petrification of a style once singularly fresh and vital. With Aurangzeb (1658–1707) Mughal painting begins its swift decline, and the museum's collection of portraits and convivial scenes from this period reflect the sterility of stock types and conventional brushwork.

While Mughal painting flourished in the North, in the Deccan, centers such as Bijapur, Golconda, and Hyderabad produced works allied to Mughal painting but with distinct stylistic variations. The museum's collection of Deccani paintings from Golconda and Bijapur are small but representative and include works such as *The Procession of Abdullah Qutb Shah*, *Chand Bibi and Her Maidens* (both mid-seventeenth century), and the *Rāgamāla* (late seventeenth century), all from Golconda. From Bijapur a few portraits such as *Muhammad Adil Shah* and *Chhatrapati Shivaji* (seventeenth century) suggest the stylistic variations of this Deccani school of painting.

By far the richest group of paintings in the Prince of Wales are those of the Rajasthani schools, such as Malwa, Mewar, Bundi, Bikaner, and Marwar. The origins of this school have been the subject of controversy, although scholarship now strongly inclines to the view that the Rajasthani style evolved about the same time as the Mughal and that it represents a direct evolution from the western Indian style rather than a radical transformation of indigenous tendencies as was the case with the Mughal school. The subject matter of the miniatures is essentially Hindu, drawing upon religious works such as the Bhāgavata Purana and the *Rāmāyana*, love lyrics such as the *Amaruśataka* and the *Rasikapriya*, and themes from *Rāgāmalas* or musical modes. The collection of Rajasthani paintings in the museum includes the important dated *Rāmāyana* of 1649 from Udaipur (Mewar) and the *Gita Govinda* (c. 1640) also from Mewar. From Malwa the museum has the vividly rendered *Amaruśataka* (c. 1680) and from Bundi the well-known painting by Mohan, *Lovers Pointing to the Crescent Moon*, 1689. Also from Bundi are two playful works, *Water Sport of Krishna* (c. 1760) and the *Toilet Scene* (late sixteenth century). The school of Bikaner is represented by illustrations from the *Rasikapriya* series of the last quarter of the seventeenth century. Taken as a group, these paintings reflect two significant general tendencies of Rajasthani paintings. In the two schools that developed early, Malwa and Mewar, the indigenous qualities such as vigorous movement, vivid colors, and an aesthetic that inclines toward direct narrative statement rather than naturalism are pre-eminent and give the miniatures a peculiar sense of sudden revelation otherwise lost in a painstaking accumulation of details. With schools that developed somewhat later, such as Bundi and Bikaner, the incorporation of Mughal features create works of charming delicacy achieved at the expense of vigor and vibrancy.

Pahari paintings allied to the Mughal and Rajasthani schools are also represented by works from Basolhi, Kangra, and Jammu. An interesting adjunct to this collection of paintings is a small but fine collection of European paintings.

Among the minor arts, the museum's collection of ivories is especially important, since it includes fine examples of post-Gupta ivories. Two brilliant examples are *Buddha Meditating on Mount Gridharakuta* and an *Avalokiteśvara with Attendants*. Wood carving is well represented by works from Gujerat from the tenth to the seventeenth century. Among them is a remarkable painted *mandapa*, or shrine (sixteenth-seventeenth century). Jade of the Mughal period and weapons such as the shield of Akbar (1590), the swords of Shah Jahan and Aurangzeb, and the armor of Humayun are a vivid complement to the Mughal miniatures. Metalware of the Mughal period is represented by the remarkable jewel casket of the Akbar period, with elaborate depictions of hunting scenes, and a talismanic cup of the Jahangir period, decorated with signs of the zodiac.

Photographs may be obtained by writing to the curators of the various collections; sculpture, painting, and the minor arts. The museum regularly publishes the *Bulletin of the Prince of Wales Museum*.

Selected Bibliography

Chandra, M., *Stone Sculpture in the Prince of Wales Museum* (Bombay 1974); idem, *Indian Art: Prince of Wales Museum of Western India* (Bombay 1974).

REKHA MORRIS

—————— Calcutta ——————

INDIAN MUSEUM, 27 Jawaharlal Nehru Road, Calcutta 700016.

The Indian Museum is the oldest museum in India and owes its origins to the Asiatic Society founded by Sir William Jones in 1784. Members of the Asiatic Society frequently presented the society with objects of interest, ranging from geological and ethnological specimens to archaeological material such as sculptures, coins, pottery, and other items. These contributions continued to accumulate at a steady pace, so in 1796 the society began to feel the need for a suitable repository. In 1814 Nathanial Wallich, a Danish botanist, offered to serve as an honorary curator were a museum to be set up. In addition, he offered to contribute duplicates from his collection to be included among the society's collection. This proposal, focusing as it did on the society's own desire to create a museum, found ready acceptance. Thus was created the nucleus of what was to become the present collection of the Indian Museum.

The heterogeneous objects were divided into two major categories. One included all of the archaeological and ethnological material, which was placed under the supervision of the librarian of the society. The second group included all of the geological, zoological, and botanical specimens and was under the supervision of Wallich. This museum created by the Asiatic Society was supported and funded privately. Thus matters continued until 1836, when financial difficulties prompted the society to solicit the government for public funds to maintain the museum. In 1839 the Court of Directors in London sanctioned a grant of three hundred rupees a month for the salary of a curator and directed the government of India to make special grants available to the society as the museum's needs required. However, the various collections in the museum continued to be the property of the Asiatic Society until 1866.

By 1862 the society's collections had grown so large that it began negotiating a transfer of its collections to a museum to be created and governed by a board of trustees to be set up by the government. These negotiations culminated in the Indian Museum Act of 1866, which set up the museum as an autonomous body. John Anderson was appointed the first curator on September 29, 1866. However, it was not until 1875 that a separate museum building was ready and the collection consisting mainly of zoological, geological, and archaeological material was moved to the new premises. In 1904, under the government of Lord Curzon, additional funds were provided to extend the already overcrowded facilities of the museum, and so the Chowringee Road extension to the museum was created in which the current collections of the museum are housed on the two lower floors.

The Indian Museum Act of 1866 has been revised from time to time, and at present the administration of the museum is run according to the Indian Museum Act of 1910. According to this act, the number for the Board of Trustees has been fixed and the board holds all of the objects in trust, whether they are received by transfer, exchange, or purchase. The bylaws empower the board to carry on the general administration of the museum through its officebearers. The board is assisted by the Committee of Management, which elects its own chairman. The officebearers of the board are elected annually by the trustees themselves. The six sections of the museum—the Archaeological Section, the Art Section, the Anthropological Section, the Geological Section, the Industrial Section, and the Zoological Section—are each under the care of a curator. The Amended Museum Act of 1960 envisaged coordinating the activities of the various sections by the establishment of a central directorate. Accordingly, a director of the museum was appointed in 1962.

Since the Indian Museum's initial collections included ethnological material, it is not surprising to find a fine representation of objects from the Paleolithic and Neolithic periods. However, it is from the third millennium B.C. that one begins to find objects of interest to the art historian. The earliest sculptures from the prehistoric period are terracotta figurines and pictorial seals from Mohenjo-daro and Harappa. Among these works, a notable example is the figure of a bull. Small as it is, its vigorous modeling prefigures the animal sculptures of the third century B.C. Terracotta figurines representing the mother goddess and pictographic seals depicting indigenous animals such as elephants and rhinoceros, with beads, flint objects, copper implements, and painted pottery, form a small but representative collection of the civilization that existed in northwestern India from about 3000 B.C. to 1500 B.C.

The earliest monumental pieces in the Indian Museum are from about the third century B.C. Two of them are pillar capitals: the *Rampurva Bull* and the *Rampurva Lion*. The Indian artists' interest and skill in representing animals such as the terracotta bull of Mohenjo-daro continues to be reflected in these capitals of the Mauryan period. Free-standing sculpture of this period is represented by two Yakṣas from Patna. Since there is a paucity of extant large-scale sculptures of the Mauryan period, these four pieces in the Indian Museum represent a sizable collection.

The following phase of Indian sculpture is represented by the magnificent remains of the stupa railing and gateway from Bharhut in Madhya Pradesh. These remains are for the Indian Museum what the Elgin Marbles are for the British Museum, a unique group of sculptures that represent the relentlessly abstract style of the second century B.C. The collection in the Indian Museum consists of life-size representations of Yakṣas and Yaksīs and narrative relief depictions from the Jātakas. The emphasis on decorative details and the meticulous linear quality of the renderings exercise a fascination that few other sculptures from India's long and fruitful artistic history can approach. These remains from the Bharhut stupa are also significant for early Buddhist iconography due to the presence of inscriptions that identify the various scenes from the life of the Buddha and the various Jātaka stories. On one of the pillars of the gateway a second century B.C. inscription records the fact that the gateway was erected during the reign of the Suṅgas, and each of the narrative representations is accompanied by Brahmi inscriptions that identify the iconographical content. The presence of inscriptions that refer to the time of its erection and that identify the various scenes make the Bharhut sculptures exceptional examples of early Indian art.

Another example of the artistic life of India in the second century B.C. is provided by a freestanding Yakṣi from Besnagar in Madhya Pradesh. The presence of this sculpture in the Indian Museum is to be especially appreciated, since its two companion pieces are in a small and considerably less accessible museum in Vidisa in Madhya Pradesh. The subsequent development of Indian sculpture in the first century B.C. is represented by a few pieces from the stupa railing from Bodh Gaya and *śālabhanjika*, or tree spirit, from Sānchī.

The extremely creative period of Indian sculpture extending from the first century to about the sixth century finds adequate representation in the collections of the Indian Museum. Among the Kuṣāṇa sculptures from Mathurā are three *Bhutesar Yakṣīs*, a Bacchanalian scene, the well-known representation *Hercules and the Lion*, the inscribed colossal Bodhisattva from Śravasti, and a fine seated Buddha dated in the thirty-ninth year of the Kuṣāṇa King Huvishka. The Indian Museum's collection of Kuṣāṇa sculptures from Gandhāra is next only to that of the Chandigarh Museum in scope and significance. Of the approximately 400 Gandhāra sculptures in the Indian Museum, some 150 or so are on display. Among the numerous Buddhas and Bodhisattvas of various sizes is one of the five dated Buddhas, the image from Loriyan Tangai. Among the narrative scenes displayed, those illustrating the Buddha's life form an interesting series, especially since some of the scenes, such as the *Birth of the Buddha* from the right side of Mayadevi, are absent in indigenous representations. These works, with other miscellaneous pieces, such as the fine group of *Hariti and Pancika*, the votive stupa centrally displayed, and the series of stucco heads, make this collection of Gandhāra sculptures the second most important one in India, the collection in Chandigarh being the most significant.

Sculptures from Amaravati in southern India are of approximately the same period as Kuṣāṇa sculptures from Mathurā and Gandhāra and are represented by some half-dozen fragments that consist of a long coping piece of the Amaravati stupa rail, two crossbars, and a few other fragments. These pieces from Amaravati in the Indian Museum supplement the two major collections of Amaravati sculptures, one in the British Museum (q.v.) and one in the Madras Museum (q.v.). They are thus a small but valuable addition to the museum's sculptural holdings.

Somewhat better represented than the Amaravati pieces are Gupta sculptures (fifth-sixth century) from various sites in India. Of these Gupta pieces, the numerous fragments of the ruined Siva temple in Bhumara in central India form an interesting group. The remains of the temple doorway and the *dvarapalakas*, or door guardians; the figure of Ganesa; a Śurya from a *chaitya*, reminiscent of earlier Kuṣāṇa representations of the deity; and a series of dancing *ganas* typify Gupta qualities in the grace of their postures and the delicacy with which the drapery is rendered. One salient example of this period in the Indian Museum is the standing figure of Buddha from Mathurā, whose intricately carved halo and sinuous flow of drapery lines exemplify the exquisite delicacy of Gupta art. Two pillars from Rajaona in Bihar and other miscellaneous pieces provide an overview of the art of the Guptas.

Medieval (seventh-twelfth century) stone sculpture is represented by numerous pieces, largely from sites in northern India, such as those from Uttar Pradesh, Madhya Pradesh, Bihar, Bengal, and Orissa. Notable examples from Uttar Pradesh are the Uma-Mahesvara group; two unidentified headless, seated figures; an *Ekmukhalinga*; and a large, elaborate depiction of Śurya. The sculptures from Bihar and Bengal form an especially rich and varied collection. From Bihar there are numerous examples of representations of the Buddha, Bodhisattva, Viṣṇu, Hara-Gauri, Varaha, and Śurya. Among them is the large representation *Varāha Lifting Pṛithvi*; two Nāga-Nāginī figures, *Manmatha with Rati and Prīti*; and two inscribed Buddhas. Interesting examples of sculpture from Bengal are a large Viṣṇu image, an inscribed Sadāsiva image, and a mother and child representation that approximates the sharp and incisive qualities of metalwork. There are four female sculptures from Khajuraho in Madhya Pradesh, and the medieval art of Orissa is best represented by a Bodhisattva from Lalitagiri, the *Tara*, the huge broken image *Śurya* from Konarak, the famous *Bhairava* (woman writing a love letter) from Bhubanesvar, and the *Nāginī* from Khiching. These stone sculptures, with bronzes from southern India and those from northern Indian sites such as Nalanda Jhewari and Rangapur, make the medieval galleries of the Indian Museum noteworthy.

The range and quality of the archaeological collection of the Indian Museum is far superior to its collections of Indian painting. This, however, is not to suggest that the museum's holdings in the latter area are insignificant. Prominent among the paintings are the miniatures of the Mughal and Rajasthani schools, although Deccani and Pahari miniatures are also represented. Among the miniatures on permanent exhibit are works by masters such as Aqua Riza, Nanha, and Gholam. Portraits of both Indian and Mughal rulers and their courtiers, innumerable genre scenes, representations of the Indian musical modes (*rāgas*), and depictions of mythological subjects provide a colorful picture of the much textured vitality of Indian life. Of the miniatures, three merit special attention.

They are *A Miserable Horse, Man, and Dog*, attributed to Basawan; *The Emperor Jahangir's Narrow Escape While Shooting a Lion*; and the portrait *Jahangir and His Father, Emperor Akbar*. These miniatures, with several large cartoons of the Rajasthani school of the eighteenth century, originally used as preparatory drawings for wall paintings, suggest the variety of styles and techniques of Indian painting between the sixteenth and nineteenth centuries. Unlike Indian miniatures, which generally used watercolors, Tibetan temple banners were executed in tempera. The Indian Museum's collections of such temple banners from Tibet add significantly to our understanding of the painting techniques of the subcontinent.

The museum's collection of the decorative arts is both extensive and varied. Metal objects from all parts of India, Nepal, and Tibet are supplemented by glassware, pottery, and ivory and wood carvings. The valuable Pearse collection of engraved gems from Greece, Rome, Persia, and India has been loaned to the museum by the director-general of archaeology in India. As part of this collection, various engraved gems of Indian origin can be seen and studied here. The emerald bow-ring and cup of Mughal Emperor Shah Jahan, which were carried off to Persia by Nadir Shah in 1739, have now found a fitting home in the Indian Museum. A significant aspect of the Indian Museum's holdings in the minor arts is its collection of textiles. They offer a full historical coverage of the many-faceted art of weaving from the various textile-producing areas of India, past and present.

The museum's collection of foreign antiquities comprises material from Egypt, Persia, Babylon, and Greece. These works form a small but representative group that includes miniature representations of Osiris and Isis, alabaster vases, necklaces, and scarabs from Egypt; a limestone relief from Persepolis; bricks inscribed with cuniform letters from Babylon; and earthenware lamps and vases from Classical Greece.

The Indian Museum's collection of coins is one of the richest in India, numbering about forty-six thousand. Coins of all of the major dynasties that ruled India are represented. The earliest examples of coins from the subcontinent are punch-marked coins that circulated until the beginning of the Christian era. These and the coins of the Indo-Greeks provide a full account of the cast and die-struck coins of the pre-Christian period in India. Coins of the Pañchalas, Sātavāhanas, and Guptas, with tribal issues like those of Yaudheya, Audumbara, and Mālava, lead up to the Muhammedan coins that are represented from their earliest issues in Delhi to their ultimate demise in the last century. This extremely valuable collection of coins is not on exhibit, but access to them is made available by special permission from the director of the Indian Museum.

A useful adjunct to the museum's rich holdings is a reference library that provides separate study facilities for approximately a dozen research scholars. Photographs for study and research may be obtained from the Photographic Department of the museum.

In addition to publishing the general guides to the collections and specialized

catalogs such as those listed below, the museum also publishes *The Bulletin of
the Indian Museum, Calcutta.* The first issue of this bulletin appeared in 1966.

Selected Bibliography

Museum publications: *Indian Museum: General Guide,* 1959; Kar, C., and Mukerjee,
T., *Art Section, Indian Museum Calcutta: A Short Guide,* 1958; Sivaramamurti, C., *A
Guide to the Archaeological Galleries: Indian Museum, Calcutta,* 1976.

Other publications: Anderson, J., *Catalogue and Hand Book of the Archaeological
Collection in the Indian Museum,* 2 vols. (Calcutta 1883, reprinted 1977); Bloch, T.,
Supplementary Catalogue of the Archaeological Collection of the Indian Museum (Cal-
cutta 1911); Coggin Brown, J., *Catalogue of the Prehistoric Antiquities in the Indian
Museum* (Simla 1917); Majumdar, N. G., *Guide to the Sculptures in the Indian Museum*
(Delhi 1937), Part I: *Early Schools.* Part II: *The Graeco-Buddhist School of Gandhara*;
Smith, V. A., *Catalogue of Coins ... including the Cabinet of the Asiatic Society of
Bengal* (Oxford 1906).

REKHA MORRIS

——— Lucknow ———

LUCKNOW MUSEUM (officially STATE MUSEUM, LUCKNOW), Banarasi
Bagh, Lucknow, Uttar Pradesh.

The State Museum at Lucknow was established in 1863 as the Provincial
Museum, Lucknow. The various collections of the museum are currently housed
in two buildings. In the main building at Banarasi Bagh, consisting of five
galleries, are housed the Natural History Collection, the Decorative Arts, the
Collection of Metal Images and Metal Ware, the Coin Collection, and the Collection of Arms and Weaponry. Temporary exhibitions are also held at this site.
The Archaeological Collection, consisting of sculptures, friezes, terracottas, and
inscriptions, is housed at the museum building in Kaiserbagh, Lucknow. Paintings and other material held in reserve are available for study by prior arrangement
with the director.

The museum is funded by the Cultural Affairs Department of the state government of Uttar Pradesh. The museum staff consists of a director assisted by
curators and assistants for the various collections.

From its inception in the nineteenth century, the museum has had a strong
collection of archaeological material acquired through area excavations carried
out by museum authorities. This special interest in archaeology was fostered by
the fact that in the early years the position of museum curator was held by a
succession of well-known archaeologists such as Dr. Führer, Daya Ram Sahani,
K. N. Dikshit, Hiranand Shastri, and, most recently, V. S. Agrawala. The nucleus of the present archaeological material consists of more than a thousand
objects excavated at Mathurā during the 1880s by Burgess and Führer. Later

excavations and recent purchases and donations have supplemented the initial collections.

The earliest of the stone sculptures in the museum is from about the second century B.C. and is analogous in style to the flat and abstract sculptures from Bharhut. This piece is a fragment of a railing pillar from Mathurā and represents a *makara* in a medallion. The museum has several examples of sculptures from the subsequent century, the most notable being the magnificent headless statue, the *Bodhisattva*, from Ganeshra. The imposing strength of the figure is mitigated by the softness in the rendering of the bare chest and the texture of the girdle and bracelets. From about the same period is a lintel from Mathurā, depicting on the obverse the worship of a stupa by harpies and centaurs and on the reverse a procession involving riders on horses, an elephant, and a horse-drawn carriage. Another lintel from Mathurā of the same stylistic phase is a complex of three registers of processional scenes alternated and bounded by decorative bands of floral motifs. In the spandrel zone are groups of ten male and female worshippers bringing offerings. The figural representations depict human and mythic beings riding fish-tailed animals. Other fragments of lintels and coping stones from railings, a bracket fragment depicting a Yakṣī with an elaborate coiffure, and a fragmentary frieze representing a musical performance with dancers and orchestra present a distinctive and varied sampling of the artistic activity of the first century B.C. in northern India.

Among this collection of early Indian sculpture, the museum has the controversial relief known as the *Āmohinī Tablet*, found at Mathurā and dedicated by Āmohinī, the wife of Pala, and inscribed with a date read variously as the year 42 or 72 B.C. of the era of Mahakshatrapa Śoḍāsa. This piece, representing a royal lady attended by three ladies and a child, has played a crucial role in discussions regarding the evolution of Kuṣāṇa sculpture and has been generally placed within the second half of the first century B.C. and the first quarter of the first century A.D. This transitional dating is supported by stylistic features that retain memories of the softer, more luxuriant style of the first century B.C. anticipating the harder, more static surfaces of the Kuṣāṇa period. Clustered around this piece are various precursors of the fully realized Kuṣāṇa style known as *Āyāgapaṭṭas*, or votive stone tablets found around Mathurā. The representation on these tablets consists of a central medallion with a seated Jina. Around this medallion are carved various sacred symbols such as the wheel, the lotus, the overflowing pot, and the *tri-ratna*. The carving is generally fine and precise, and the decorative scheme, although employing the same basic symbols, is interpreted with imaginative facility.

The museum's collection of Kuṣāṇa sculptures (first-third century A.D.) is extensive and varied; however, it is possible to select a few for closer scrutiny. The innumerable sculptures and friezes from Kankali Tila in Mathurā excavated at various times by Cunningham, Growse, Burgess, and Führer span a period from the first century B.C. to the twelfth century A.D. The Kuṣāṇa pieces are by far the most numerous and are predominantly from Jain monuments, although some sculptures probably belonged to Buddhist or Vaishnava shrines. Various door-frame fragments and railing pillars depict scenes of secular life and in their compositional complexity recall the sculptures of Sanchi Stupa 1 of the first century B.C. These relief scenes and other sculptural panels have been generally assigned to the first half of the first century A.D., whereas railing pillars with depictions of Yakṣīs on crouching dwarfs are generally accepted as examples of Kuṣāṇa work of the second century A.D.

The final phase of Kuṣāṇa sculpture is shown by various seated and standing representations of Jina. Many of them are dated in unknown eras, but on the basis of stylistic comparisons and complex interpretations regarding the Kuṣāṇa era as commencing about 78, they have been assigned dates from the mid-second century to the third century. Noteworthy among them are the two seated Jinas dated in the year 80 (c. 158) and in the year 12 (c. 190). The latter, in its rendering of the hair and the round face and full lips, is seen to be moving toward the stylistic nuances of the Gupta period.

From the second prolific center of Kuṣāṇa art, Gandhāra in present-day Pakistan, the museum has some ninety-four pieces of which twelve are in stucco. The stone sculptures include single figures of the Bodhisattva and Buddha and reliefs depicting scenes from the life of the Buddha and the Jātakas. Most of these sculptures are mediocre in execution, but a few examples are striking for typological and stylistic considerations. Among them is a relief depicting the birth of the Buddha from the right side of his mother, an episode pictographically so depicted almost exclusively in Gandhāra. A fragment depicting an undulating vine with clusters of grapes and a single nude figure with its back to the viewer, an unusual pose in Indian art of this period, directs our attention to the eclectic typological borrowings of Gandhāra art. An early stylistic phase of the style of Gandhāra is marked by the museum's relief of the *First Sermon*, in which the symbolic references to this event, the Wheel of Law and the deer, continue to be represented side by side with the iconic image of the Buddha preaching. The later style of Gandhāra is seen in pieces such as an architectural fragment with several seated Buddhas and the headless Buddha seated on a lotus throne in the pose of the Dharmachakra Mudra. In these depictions of the Buddha, the bare right shoulder, the lotiform throne, and the hard, incised drapery lines suggest the third-century style of Gandhāra.

The museum's collection of sculptures from the Gupta period (late fourth to the end of the fifth century) includes a group of important dated images. With these dated images it is possible to chart the evolution of sculpture during the Gupta period. The earliest Gupta fragment in the Lucknow Museum is a fragment of a Nāga attendant of a lost Jina image. Although undated, the Kuṣāṇa-type headdress and decorative elements of the fragmentary halo have led scholars to place this in the first quarter of the fifth century. Similar to this in style, although much better preserved, is the image of a seated *Tirathankara* in which the modeling of the chest and the *rinceau* on the halo, recalling as they do aspects of early-fifth-century sculptures from Udayagiri, have been contributory factors in this sculpture being selected to mark the early-fifth-century Gupta style in northern India. This view has been reinforced by the dated image of a seated *Tirathankara*, also in the Lucknow Museum. This image dated in the year 113 of Kumaragupta (432–33) and an undated image of the seated *Jina with Attendants* are closer in style to the museum's seated *Mankuvar Buddha* dated in the year 449 and therefore considered to mark the evolution of Gupta style between 425 and 450. The mid-fifth-century style is seen in several pieces that include the *Jina Bust* with a fragmentary halo, the torso and legs of a donor found at Mathurā, two Jina heads, and the Gaḍwa lintel representing a procession with musicians and dancers.

The medieval collection of the Lucknow Museum consists of an important and varied group of stone sculptures from numerous sites, mostly in Uttar Pradesh. These sculptures range from the eighth to the twelfth century.

The Lucknow Museum's collection of some fifteen hundred miniature paintings from the Mughal, Rajasthani, and Pahari schools are held in the reserve collection and are now in the process of being catalogued. The most significant of these miniatures is an Akbar period manuscript of the *Harivamsa*.

The representative collection of coins of the various periods of Indian history include the Paila and Lotapur hoards of punch-marked coins, the Madhuban and Banskhera copperplates of Harsha (seventh century), the copperplates of the Garhwal kings, commemorative portrait medals of Ghaziuddin Haider and Taj Mahal Begum, and a fine collection of coins of Oudh rulers.

The museum's collection of minor arts includes fifty-three Kashmiri shawls from the eighteenth and nineteenth centuries and a representative collection of textile art as seen in *chikan* and *jamdani* work. Representative collections of Indian arms and weapons and ivory and wood carvings make the Lucknow Museum an important center for the study of these aspects of Indian art in Uttar Pradesh.

The many activities of the museum include monthly lectures by members of the staff and annual seminars and special lectures by visiting scholars. The museum also arranges traveling exhibitions on India's cultural history for schools and colleges around the state. The museum has initiated the publication of a series of catalogues that provide much needed documentation of the various collections and since 1968 has published the *Bulletin of Museums and Archaeology in U.P.*

Photographs of objects in the museum collection may be ordered by writing to the director. Periodically, the museum makes available to the public the sale of coins that are superfluous to its collection and not required by other museums in the country.

Selected Bibliography

Museum publications: Brown, C. J. *Catalogue of Coins (Mughal Emperors)*, 2 vols., 1920; Dayal, P., *Catalogue of the Coins of the Sultans of Delhi*, 1926; Joshi, N. P., *Catalogue of the Brahamanical Sculptures in the State Museum, Lucknow*, 1972; Joshi,

N. P., and R. C. Sharma, *Catalogue of the Gandharan Sculptures in the State Museum, Lucknow*, 1969; Srivastava, A. K., *Catalogue of Indo-Greek Coins in the State Museum, Lucknow*, 1969; idem, *Catalogue of Saka-Pahlava Coins of North India*, 1972.

REKHA MORRIS

 **Madras** _____

MADRAS MUSEUM (officially GOVERNMENT MUSEUM AND NA-
TIONAL ART GALLERY; also MADRAS GOVERNMENT MUSEUM), Pantheon Road, Egmore, Madras 600008.

Several of the oldest museums of India, such as the Indian Museum (q.v.) in
Calcutta, owe their inception to the zeal of eccentric scholars and collectors of
the nineteenth century. This was also the case in the formation of the museum
at Madras. In 1846 the Madras Literary Society approached the directors of the
East India Company to establish a museum in Madras. In 1851 the Court of
Directors of the East India Company approved the offer of surgeon Edward
Green Balfour, then the chairman of the Committee of the Madras Literary
Society, to be the honorary officer in charge of the Madras Central Museum.
This museum was created around a nucleus of some eleven hundred geological
objects belonging to the Madras Literary Society.

After the establishment of the Madras Central Museum Balfour launched a
campaign to enlarge the collection by recruiting friends, army engineers, and
medical officers from across India, Burma, Malaya, and England. By 1853 their
overwhelming response increased the museum's holdings to some twenty thousand heterogenous objects. This rapidly increasing collection necessitated a request to the government for more adequate housing. Initially denied, the request
was granted when the weight of the display cases damaged the structure of the
Madras College, where they had been housed. In 1854 the entire collection was
moved to a building known as the Pantheon, which served as offices of the
collector of Madras. The original halls of the Pantheon have been replaced by
recent structures that currently house the vast collection of the Madras Museum.

With its beginnings in the natural sciences (a zoo was briefly added to the
museum in 1853), the museum continued to evolve along the lines established
by Balfour. Under Captain Jesse Mitchell, who succeeded Balfour as superintendent of the museum in 1859, the collections in natural history expanded
significantly, although other areas were not entirely neglected. Under his direction a museum herbarium was created, and the small collection of coins was
enlarged by the addition of medals illustrating the history of the Madras army.
In 1862 a sizable reference library of the museum was opened to the public.
Captain Mitchell continued the efforts first made by Balfour to secure for the
museum the sculptural remains of Amaravati and in 1861 instigated negotiations
to purchase the Foote Collection of prehistoric antiquities.

Under Mitchell's successor, Dr. Bidie, who was part-time superintendent between 1872 and 1884, definite gains were made in areas such as archaeology and numismatics. It was under Bidie that the Amaravati sculptures (of which the Madras Museum's collection is second only to that of the British Museum [q.v.]) were purchased, and the nucleus of the large collection of copper-plate grants, one of the major collections of the museum today, was begun. Bidie was followed by several other able scholars such as J. R. Henderson (1908–19), who instigated systematic cataloguing of the museum collection by himself preparing a catalogue of the coins of Haider Ali and Tipu Sultan. It was under Frederic Henry Gravely (1920–40) that in 1939 the archaeological collection was chronologically organized in a new extension of the museum facilities, and the first regular guide to the archaeological collection was published by the museum. With his encouragement the museum's activities in the realm of scholarship and publication gained a strong impetus, and monographs on various collections such as those of Amaravati sculptures, punch-marked coins, and the Roman and Venetian coins began to be prepared. In recent years the Madras Museum has continued to maintain a high standard in its publication of individual monographs and studies and the *Madras Museum Bulletin*. The museum's primary source of funding is the government of Tamil Nadu.

The Madras Museum is organized into six major sections: Art, Archaeology, Anthropology, Numismatics, Zoology, and Botany and Geology. Conservation and restoration of antiquities is under the direction of an active and well-equipped laboratory. Each of the museum sections and the laboratory are under the charge of curators.

Although the genesis of the museum lay in the natural sciences, in recent years strong effort has been directed in enlarging its holdings in stone sculptures, bronzes, paintings, and coins. In this direct effort at expansion the emphasis has been on collecting material pertinent to the evolution of southern Indian art and culture. Apart from a small group of sculptures and paintings representative of artistic trends in northern India, the Madras Museum's concentration and strength is in its collection of southern Indian objects.

The earliest-known remains of sculptural activity from southern India are the relic caskets from Bhattiprolu, now in the Madras Museum. These three stone relic caskets were found one below the other when the ruined Buddhist stupa at Bhattiprolu was uncovered. Each of them contained crystal caskets, two of which are carved in the shape of a stupa and the third is circular. Based on the southern Brahmi characters inscribed on the stone caskets, they have been assigned to about the third century B.C. Remains of stupas from Jaggayyapeta and Amaravati have yielded sculptures of the first two centuries before Christ. From Jaggayyapeta the representation *Chakravarti Mandhata* and the architectural piece depicting a *punyasala*, an oblong shrine with a barrel-vaulted roof, belong to these early years of southern Indian art. Of the same period are the earliest pieces of sculpture from Amaravati stupa, starting about 200 B.C. These works are undated and few, but on stylistic grounds pieces such as the *Sri on a Lotus* have been attributed to this early period. The majority of sculptures from Amaravati range from the late first century B.C. to the third century A.D., and the Madras Museum's collection of these sculptures is next to that of the British Museum in scope and size. Created in several phases of artistic activity, these remains of railing pillars, crossbars, and marble slabs that encased the stupa, vary in stylistic features such as the treatment of forms, the depth of carving, the relationship of figures to one another, and the space that surrounds them. The scenes depicted range from the life of the Buddha and Jātaka stories to scenes of worship where the presence of the Buddha is indicated by symbols such as the Bodhi tree, the stupa, or the impression of the Buddha's feet. There is a surprising vitality and assurance in treating complex scenes such as the *Division of the Buddha's Relic* and the *Subjugation of Nalagiri*. Not only have dominant events and themes from Buddhist iconography been captured with clarity and sharpness, but the emotional excitement generated by these focal points radiates to encompass subsidiary figures and create a stirring sense of movement.

The next stylistic phase of stone sculptures is represented by works of the Pallava period (fifth-ninth century). Sculptures such as the *Viṣṇu* and a horned *dvārapāla*, or door guardian, are remarkable for the sparse use of decorative details, thus focusing attention on the corporeality of the powerfully molded figures. This sense of strength and force is also present in the magnificent sculpture *Surya*, assigned to the transitional phase between the end of the Pallava and the beginning of the Chola period. Other interesting pieces of this period are *Saptamatrikas* from Satyamangalam (eighth century), the figures *Vayu* and *Agni* from Tirunelveli (c. ninth century), the seated figure *Ardhanarisvara* from Mahabalipuram, and the seated *Shiva* of the late Pallava period.

The Pallavas were followed by the Cholas (ninth-twelfth century), who are responsible for many magnificent temples and the great and prolific creation of bronze sculptures. In the stone sculptures of the early Chola period the emphasis on relatively simple rendering of powerful figures of the Pallava period is still evident as in the *Ardhanarisvara* from Tiruchchinnampundi and the group of *Tripurantaka* and *Tripurasundari* from Kodumbalur of about the tenth century. Toward the end of this period the massive conception of forms began to be destroyed by the elaboration of decorative details and a certain stylization of figural posture. The group of sculptures *Ranganatha with Sridevi and Bhudevi* are typical examples of developments in the eleventh and twelfth centuries.

One important factor that is made clear by the collection of stone sculptures in the Madras Museum is that not all sculptures of the medieval period are Brahamanical. A larger than life-size granite figure of Buddha found in the Sri Kamakshi Amman temple of Kanchipuram has been assigned to the seventh century. Along with Buddhism, Jainism also continued to flourish during this period, as suggested by the relief *Mahavira* found at Deviagaram and assigned to the Pallava period. Another sculpture of the Jain Tirathankar, *Parsvanatha*, from Danavulapadu of the ninth-tenth century, and the large seated Tirathankar from Tuticorn attest to the vigor of Jainism in southern India. However, unlike the Brahamanical sculptures of the Pallavas and the Cholas, these Jain figures lack dynamism and vitality.

The relative simplicity and emphasis on energetic, powerful forms in sculptures from the fifth to the tenth century gives way to an increasing interest in complex and intricate representations perhaps best illustrated at the Madras Museum by fragments of the Hoysala period (twelfth-thirteenth century) such as the *Kubera*, the group of *Saptamatrikas*, and an intricate rendering of a gateway. The last of the great stone sculptures of southern India are those of the Vijaynagar period (fourteenth-sixteenth century) such as the seated *Viṣṇu* and fragments of a temple basement relief.

An interesting feature of the Madras Museum's collection of stone sculptures is an attempt made to arrange some of the architectural fragments to illustrate the evolution of architectural forms such as the *adhisthana* (the socle zone), the *potika* (corbels), and the *Kudu* (horseshoe arches).

Strong as the Madras Museum is in its representative selection of stone sculptures, its pre-eminence lies in its collection of some thousand bronzes of which some four hundred are on permanent display. The majority of these pieces belong to the Chola period, and most of them are from Tamilnad. The casting technique used for these works is the "lost wax" process used in India as early as the Indus Valley civilization, which produced the famous bronze dancing girl of Mohenjo-daro. The bronze collection of the museum has been arranged in terms of iconography, that is, whether the representations are of Buddhas, Jains, or Brahamanical gods.

The earliest group of bronzes are four Buddhist pieces from Amaravati, dated about the fifth and sixth centuries. Some seven Buddhist pieces are from Nagapattinam and range in date from the ninth to the seventeenth century. Of these seven pieces, two large Buddhas of the tenth century and the seated *Avalokitesvara* of the Chola period are of fine quality. Also to be noted are Jain Tirathankaras of the eleventh and twelfth centuries.

The Brahamanical images in bronze are further subdivided into two groups: Saivite and Vaishnavite. From the Saivite group representations of Siva as Nataraja are prominantly displayed. Among numerous splendid examples of them, the *Nataraja* from Velanganni (tenth century), the *Nataraja* from Tiruvelangadu (eleventh century, moved recently to the Art Gallery of the museum), and the *Nataraja* in the reversed leg posture from Poruppumettuppatti (c. 900) are energetic representations that express the passion and effortless movement of Siva's dance. Of the Vaishnavite bronzes, the group *Rama, Laxman, and Sita* from Vadakkuppanaiyur (tenth century) and the group *Rama, Laxman, Sita, and Hanuman* from Tiruvalangadu of the Chola period deserve special attention. Finally, the *Venugopal with Rukmini and Styabhama* from Chimakurti of the Vijayanagar period, rendered with delicate stylization, suggests the altered idiom of the bronzes of the late medieval period of southern India.

Supplementing the collection of stone sculptures and the bronzes are a small group of wooden carvings ranging in date from the late medieval period to the nineteenth century, such as the pillar from Mudibidri with a vase and foliage capital and panel reliefs along its shaft and the temple cars of the last century. A fine group of eighteenth-century wood sculptures from the sixth temple at Kalaiyarkovil may be seen on request in the reserve collection not on display.

Among the collection of the minor arts in various media such as ivory, glazed pottery, and metalwork, perhaps the most interesting objects are various metal lamps for ceremonial use in temples. They are in a variety of forms such as the *dipa-vriksa* in the form of a tree, from which are suspended rows of lamps, or the *dipalaxmi*, which are in the form of women lamp bearers.

The Madras Museum's collection of paintings is both small and insignificant when compared to those of many of the other museums of India. This is partly the result of the fact that the museum's interest in paintings is of recent development. Some seventy paintings that once belonged to the Madras School of Arts were acquired by the museum in 1941–42. This nucleus of works was gradually expanded through the efforts of the South Indian Society of Painters founded in 1946, and in 1951 funds were made available for the creation of the National Gallery of Art, which was formally inaugurated in the same year by the Prime Minister of India Pandit Nehru.

The section devoted to northern Indian schools of painting includes a few miniatures of the Kangra school, four Ragini paintings of the Rajasthani school, and a few examples of Moghul painting. Specimens of Deccani paintings and those of the school of Tanjore complete the collection of premodern Indian paintings. Of the modern artists represented, those of Raja Ravi Varma are prominent in ushering in the sense of disconsonance between Indian subject matter and Western notions of what constitutes the "painterly" style that has continued to make Indian painting a derivative art form in the twentieth century. Among more recent artists represented are D. P. Roy Chowdhuri, Sarada Charan Ukil, Promode Kumar Chatterjee, and others of the Bengal revivalist school created by Abanindranath Tagore.

Unlike its painting collection, the Madras Museum's collection of coins is both extensive and qualitatively superior. There are approximately twenty-five thousand coins of gold, silver, copper, and the alloys billon and *potin*. The majority of these coins are Indian and document the entire history of Indian coinage from the sixth century B.C. to the end of the nineteenth century A.D. The southern Indian coins of this collection were acquired from numerous troves of coins discovered in different parts of southern India. The northern Indian coins, however, were received mainly as gifts donated by northern Indian museums such as the Prince of Wales Museum (q.v.) in Bombay, the Indian Museum in Calcutta, and the Uttar Pradesh Coin Committee. Thus coins of the Indo-Bactrian Greeks, the Kushans, the Guptas, the Muslim sultans of Delhi, and the Moghuls were donated to the Madras Museum under a scheme that provides for the distribution of surplus coins of various Indian museums and allied institutions to fill gaps or supplement the holdings of other museums of India. When necessary, funds have been provided for the purchase of coins from private collectors.

The earliest coins of India are the punch-marked coins of northern India that circulated from about the sixth century B.C. to the beginning of the Christian era. The Madras Museum possesses some three thousand coins of this category that are classified on the basis of the symbols punched on them. The absence of dates and the identity of the issuers of these coins militates against a more precise classification. With the advent of Indo-Greek coinage, use of symbolic devices is replaced by portraiture, and the Madras Museum has in its collection some fine examples of such coins issued by Demetrius, Apollodotus 1, Menander, Strato 1, and Zoilus. Kuṣāṇa coins (first-third century A.D.) created under the eclectic influences that existed in northwestern India during the first three centuries of our era are interesting for their use of Hindu, Buddhist, and Greek images, as well as the use of Greek letters to identify the ruler under whom the coins were issued. The coinage of the Guptas (fourth-sixth century A.D.) eschews foreign influences and uses instead classical Sanskrit for the inscriptions and Hindu iconography for figurative representations. Of this important group of Indian coins, the Madras Museum possesses only twelve. Of the medieval coinage of northern India comprising those of the Rajput states (eighth-eleventh century A.D.), of the Muslim sultans of Delhi (thirteenth century A.D.), and of the Moghuls (sixteenth-eighteenth century A.D.), the Madras Museum's holdings are richest in those of the last. Among them, those of Akbar (A.D. 1556–1605), issued to propogate his syncretic faith; the Din-Ilahi mohurs; and a few of the zodiacal coins issued by Jahangir (A.D. 1605–28) are of special interest.

The earliest southern Indian coins in the Madras Museum are the Pandyan punch-marked coins with symbols of fish on the reverse that circulated between the first and second centuries. They cannot be attributed to specific rulers. The approximately six thousand Andhra coins in the Madras Museum represent the earliest dynastic coins (with secure dynastic names and legends) of the South. The coins of the Chāḷukyas (sixth-ninth century), Cholas (ninth-twelfth century), and of the Vijayanagar empire (fourteenth-sixteenth century) provide rich documentation of the various dynasties that flourished in southern India. The commemorative issues, such as those of the Cholas, are interesting for the fact that they record not only the identity of the rulers but also those of the nations conquered by them. The coins of the two Mysore sultans Haider Ali and Tipu Sultan complete this extremely fine collection of Indian coins.

Of the museum's collection of foreign coins, the Roman gold and silver coins of the first and second centuries; primitive Chinese money of the spade, knife, and key types; and specimens of Swedish plate money of the eighteenth century are of special interest. Some 250 medals ranging in date from those issued by the East India Company to those of the later years of British rule complete the range of numismatic material in the Madras Museum.

In addition to publishing guides to the collections and specialized catalogues such as those listed below, the museum publishes the *Transactions of the Archaeological Society of South India* and the *Madras Museum Bulletin*.

Selected Bibliography

Museum publications: Aiyappan, A., and P. R. Srinivasan, *Guide to the Buddhist Antiquities*, 1952; Gravely, F. H., and T. N. Ramachandran, *Catalogue of the South*

Indian Hindu Metal Images in the Madras Government Museum, 1932; Gravely, F. H., and C. Sivaramamurti, *Guide to the Archaeological Galleries: An Introduction to South Indian Temple Architecture and Sculpture,* 1939; idem, *Illustrations of Indian Sculpture— Mostly Southern.* For use with the *Guide to the Archaeological Galleries,* 1939; Satyamurti, S. T., *Handbook of the Madras Government Museum,* 1964; Sivaramamurti, C., *Amaravati Sculptures in the Madras Government Museum,* 1942; idem, *Early Eastern Chalukyan Sculptures,* 1957; Srinivasan, P. R., *Bronzes of South India,* 1963; *Madras Government Museum Centenary Souvenir (1851–1951),* 1952.

REKHA MORRIS

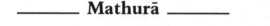

Mathurā

MATHURĀ MUSEUM (officially GOVERNMENT MUSEUM: MATHURĀ), Museum Road, Dampier Park, Mathurā, Uttar Pradesh.

The present Government Museum at Mathurā owes its inception to Mr. Growse, the collector of Mathurā between 1873 and 1874. Since 1836 various sculptures had come to light in the Mathurā region either inadvertently or as a result of archaeological explorations. For lack of a local museum, these objects were distributed to other cities such as Lucknow and Calcutta, and it was to check this flow of antiquities from Mathurā that Growse conceived a plan to house the local finds. An abandoned Victorian building known as "Thornhill's Folly" was selected to house the archaeological finds, and in 1874 funds from the provincial government were obtained to convert the structure to serve as a museum. In 1880 the museum was opened to the public. By 1926 this building proved to be inadequate to house the burgeoning collections of the museum, and the building of the present museum in Dampier Park was initiated. A portion of the new building was completed and opened to the public in 1930; however, the entire spacious, octagonal structure built around a central court was not completed until 1962. Since then the museum's vast collection has been housed and displayed in these facilities, and "Thornhill's Folly" is currently used as the museum's storeroom.

Originally, the museum was under the control and supervision of the Municipal Board, but since 1912 it has been administered and funded by the state government and is directly under the director of the Department of Cultural Affairs of Uttar Pradesh in Lucknow. The staff of the museum consists of a director and an assistant director and a subcurator, gallery assistant, guide, lecturer, photographer, modeler, and chemist.

Of the museum's more than four thousand pieces of stone sculptures, only one-eighth are on permanent display. The sculptures range from about the second century B.C. to the twelfth century A.D. The earliest, and one of the major monuments of Indian art, is a colossal statue, the *Parkham Yakṣa,* found at Parkham near Mathurā. On the base of the pedestal is an inscription in early

Brāhmī letters that identifies the sculptor as Gomitra, a pupil of Kunika. This personal data regarding an artist is extremely unusual in early Indian art. The frontal stance, the flat girdle and chestband, and the hard lines of the bulging stomach clearly associate this sculpture with works of the second century B.C. such as the sculptures of Bharhut. Clustered around this sculpture are a few others at the museum that reflect the second-century B.C. style at Mathurā. Typical examples are the *Nāga* in anthropomorphic form, the *Yakṣi Supporting a Cornice*, and the *Yakṣi with Flywhisk*.

Sculptures of the first century B.C. from Mathurā reflect a marked demise in the depiction of flat, cubistic forms, and a style analogous to that of Sanchi Stupa I emerges. Forms are delineated with graceful, soft contours and with a feeling for the plasticity of volumes. The supreme example of this development in Mathurā is the *Yakṣi Tying Her Waistband*, in which the inimitable tactility of the surfaces belies the hard medium. Other examples of this style in the museum are the railing crossbar with the *Head in a Lotus Medallion*, the *Prince with a Staff*, and the *Mora Torso*. Various miscellaneous pieces such as the railing pillars and *Āyāgapaṭṭas* (votive stone tablets) describe the range of this style, and whether the workmanship is mediocre or superlative, the underlying emphasis on naturalism and plasticity distinguish these sculptures from those of the previous century.

During the Kuṣāṇa period (first-third century) Mathurā became the greatest center of sculptural activity in India, and the museum's holdings from this period are so extensive that only a very small and selective group can be on display. The most famous Kuṣāṇa sculptures are the royal statues from Mān near Mathurā. The powerful, headless statue identified by inscription as *Kaniska* and two others identified as *Wema Kadphises* and *Chaṣṭana* reflect the introduction of foreign, Scythian features into the Indian idiom. They consist not merely of the Scythian costume but of a relentless and unyielding frontality and a knife-edge sharpness of lines that continue to exert their impact, albeit in modified form, on the innumerable reliefs that depict Scythian donors and worshippers found in the Mathurā area. Two interesting examples of Scythian facial types are the *Head with Conical Cap* from Māṭ and the *Male Head with Ram's Horns* from Bhutesvara. Among the numerous Buddha and Bodhisattva images of this period, three deserve special attention. They are the seated *Katra Buddha* (c. 81); the headless, standing *Buddha* dated in the year 35 (112); and the *Maholi Buddha* (c. 110). Sculptures such as the inscribed *Chhargāon Nāga* dated in the year 40 (118), railing pillars with representations of Yakṣīs on crouching dwarfs from Bhutesvara, the colossal Buddha head from Chaubara, the bacchanalian scene from Palikhera, and the image of *Sūrya* in Scythian dress and boots from Kankali Tila testify to the thematic and stylistic range of the Mathurā style during the first three centuries of the Christian era. Recent additions to this compelling group of Kuṣāṇa sculptures are the many pieces excavated at Sonkh. Two of special interest are the *Śalabhanjikā* from a gateway to a Nāga shrine and a lintel with the relief *Nāga King and Queen* flanked by courtiers.

In the museum's Kuṣāṇa collection are several pieces of Gandhāra sculpture that are of interest. A representation of Buddha as an ascetic with gaunt face and emaciated body rendered in a style unusual for its concession to verisimilitude reflects the Gandhāra sculptor's departure from indigenous practices. The standing image *Hāritī*, often referred to as *Kambojika*, found at the Saptarshi mound in Mathurā, is one of the most remarkable images in the Gandhāra style, since it is carved completely in the round.

The Mathurā Museum's collection of Gupta sculptures reflect all the phases of this style with its beginnings in the late fourth century to its demise in the late fifth and early sixth centuries. The early-fifth-century Gupta idiom is seen in sculptures such as the standing *Nāga*, the *Siva Ardhanārī* from Ranivala, the standing *Viṣṇu*, the Buddha head from Bajna, and the fragment *Rishabhanatha with Attendants* from Kankali Tila. In these sculptures the early Gupta idiom of Udayagiri is reflected in the strength and solidity of the figures, the heavy coils of garlands, and the decorative elements of the fragmentary remains of halos. In the assured Gupta style, epitomized by the *Yaśadina Buddha*, the vigorous, massive qualities are replaced by softer nuances reflected in the slender, graceful torsos; the delicate lines of drapery; and the decorative richness of the bands of floral motifs of the halo. Associated with the *Yaśadina Buddha* are the headless standing Buddha and the headless Bodhisattva torso, striking for the intricate precision of the necklaces that adorn the bare chest. The final phase of the Gupta style is best reflected in the colossal Buddha head of the late fifth century, where the definition of features has acquired intense hardness and immobility presaging lines of development in the medieval period. A mid-sixth-century standing Buddha in *abhyamudra*, with its short, squat proportions and schematized drapery rendered by means of incised lines, marks the final phase of the Gupta style in Mathurā. Among these Gupta sculptures is a remarkable dated image excavated recently.

Medieval sculptures in the museum date from the seventh to the twelfth century. The squat proportions and decorative simplicity of the late Gupta period are continued in sculptures such as the *Agni* of the ninth century. With the eleventh century, the massing of brittle decorative details and the hardening of surface modulations signals the arrival of the developed medieval style, as seen in pieces such as the *Viṣṇu in Padamāsan* and the standing *Nāga* from Swami Ghat in Mathurā. The exaggerated torsion of forms such as those of the doorjamb figure *Gaṅgā* (eleventh-twelfth century) and the crowded composition of the relief *Ambikā with Tirthankara Neminatha* (twelfth-thirteenth century) predicate the assured medieval style of northern India.

The museum's extensive collection of some twenty-five hundred terracottas are for the most part in the reserve collection. A representative sampling of terracottas from the fourth century B.C. to the sixth century A.D. are on display. The earliest pieces, those of the fourth century B.C., use a gray clay with black slip and are completely hand modeled with the use of incision and pinching to define features and ornaments. In the Mauryan period (third to second century

B.C.) hand modeling is supplemented by the use of molds that began to be used extensively in the subsequent centuries. The early tradition of concentrating almost exclusively on representations of the mother goddess is widened to include a variety of subjects. Toys, amorous couples, male figures, ladies playing with children or birds, and scenes of dancing and musical performances began to be produced in quantities. In the Gupta period (late fourth-sixth century A.D.) there is a prevalence of plaques for exterior and interior decoration of sacred and secular buildings.

The museum's small collection of paintings, some ten thousand coins, and approximately three hundred bronzes are held in reserve and may be seen by special permission. An exception is made in the case of the two bronzes of the Kuṣāṇa period recently excavated at Sonkh. They are on display with other objects excavated at Sonkh. Photographs may be ordered by writing to the director of the museum.

Selected Bibliography

Museum publications: Joshi, N. P., *Mathurā Sculptures: A Handbook*, 1966; Sharma, R. C., *The Mathurā Museum: Introduction*, 1971; idem, *Mathurā Museum and Art*, 1976.

Other publications: Agrawala, V. S., *A Catalogue of the Brahamanical Images in Mathurā Art* (Lucknow 1951); idem, *Mathurā Museum Catalogue* (Lucknow 1952); Härtel, H., *Excavations at Sonkh*, An Exhibition at the National Museum, New Delhi, and at Museums in Uttar Pradesh, 1977–78; Vogel, J. Ph., *Catalogue of the Archaeological Museum at Mathurā* (Allahabad 1910); idem, "La Sculpture de Mathurā," *Ars Asiatica*, vol. 15 (Paris 1930); Mathurā Museum Centenary Number, *Bulletin of Museums and Archaeology*, nos. 11–12 (1973).

REKHA MORRIS

 New Delhi

NATIONAL MUSEUM, Janpath, New Delhi.

The National Museum in Delhi was formally inaugurated in December 1960 by the vice-president of India, S. Radhakrishnan. However, various collections of the museum were created earlier in 1949, as a result of the successful showing in the Darber Hall of the Rashtrapati Bhavan (the residence of the president of India) of the loans of Indian art to the Burlington House exhibition in London in 1947–48. The cornerstone for the museum building was laid in 1955 by Prime Minister Jawaharlal Nehru. In June 1960 the first unit was completed and handed over to the museum staff. By December of the same year, when the museum was officially opened, all of the departments of the National Museum were functioning with the exception of the Department of Anthropology. This gallery was opened to the public in 1961, and in March 1968 the gallery of pre-Columbian art was inaugurated by the then president, the late Zakir Hussain. The officers of the museum consist of a director, who is assisted by the curators of the various collections.

The holdings of the National Museum appropriately commence with a significant representation of the protohistory of the subcontinent. Sculptures, inscribed seals, pottery, bronze, and jewelry dating from the Harrapan or Indus Valley culture of about 2500–1500 B.C. are extensively displayed. This permanent display is supplemented by rotating displays on loan to the museum by the Archaeological Survey of India. These rotating displays consist of material from recently excavated sites of this ancient culture, originally thought to have been confined to a much smaller geographical area but now seen to extend over an area that includes sites in Rajasthan (Kalibnagan), Gujerat (Lothal), and Uttar Pradesh (Alamgirpur and Hastinapur). The displays are supported by photographs, maps, and explanatory narrative material that are extremely useful both to casual visitors and students. Among the valuable collection of seals are several that merit special attention: the seal with the three-headed animal, another representing a voluminously delineated bull, and the seal representing a seated, ithyphallic image sometimes interpreted as the earliest representation of the god Siva. All three seals are from Mohenjo-daro. Among the terracotta finds of Mohenjo-daro there is an especially fine representation of a bull and a standing female image referred to as a mother goddess. Among the several bearded heads found at Mohenjo-daro, the National Museum possesses the famous male bust carved in limestone and generally interpreted as a votive portrait of a priest. The abstract and conceptual approach to portraiture evident in this piece has led scholars to postulate a relationship between the Indus Valley civilization and Mesopotamia. The most famous pieces of sculpture of this era are two small male torsos in limestone found at Harappa, both in the National Museum. They are extremely sophisticated examples of plastic art, stressing the massive, taut volumes of the body without the exact delineation of musculature. Modeling along these lines is a peculiar feature of Indian sculpture, and it is startling to discover a piece as early as this exemplifying sculptural devices familiar to us through the countless pieces of more recent date. These two male torsos and the bronze dancing girl from Mohenjo-daro, representing a more linear and abstract rendering of the human form, comprise a unique collection of sculptures of the Indus Valley civilization.

There is an inexplicable lacuna of some thousand years in the history of Indian art, for the subsequent phase of creativity seems to occur about the third century B.C. In the National Museum this phase of early Indian sculpture is represented by sculptures of the Mauryan period, 332–185 B.C. Several male heads in Chunar sandstone found in Sārnāth, Uttar Pradesh, reflect the peculiarly Mauryan quality of tensile modeling of broad surfaces seen in the celebrated Mauryan animal capitals.

The subsequent development of early Indian art can be studied in a select group of sculptures from the Śunga, Kuṣāṇa, and Gupta collections of the National Museum. After the breakup of the Mauryan Empire and during the dominance of the Śuṅgas and Sātavāhanas, who ruled in the North and the Deccan, respectively, sculptural activity of the previous age was continued, albeit with stylistic modifications. These stylistic changes are aptly illustrated by sculptures from a variety of artistic centers active during the second and first centuries B.C. A group of fragments from the Śuṅga stupa at Bharhut in central India illustrates a relentlessly abstract style as if this were a result of the utmost distillation of those abstract and linear qualities that were present in the Mauryan age. Softer and more plastic forms are seen in a few sculptures from Pitalkhora (caves in western India), such as the fragment *Prince and His Consort*. These pieces provide a transition from the abstract style of Bharhut to the sensual tactility of sculptures from Sanchi in Central India.

The National Museum has now acquired a fragment of a *torana* architrave from Sāñchī in Central India to illustrate the style of the first century B.C. This fragment depicts a young woman seated on a rock with a toilet box and a pot beside her. An elephant sports in the stream beside which she is seated. The softness in rendering volumes is also to be noted in a fragment of a crossbar from a stupa railing from Mathurā in Uttar Pradesh. This depicts a king and his attendant on an elephant. Similar stylistic features are also to be noted in the head of a Yakṣī from Sārnāth, also in the National Museum. These fragments from different sites of India suggest that stylistic developments tended to be on a pan-Indian basis with regional modifications that created a distinct visual vocabulary for specific sites during each phase of evolution.

Sculptures from the first and second centuries A.D., generally referred to as the Kuṣāṇa period after the dynasty that was predominant at this time, are amply illustrated by reliefs and freestanding sculptures from the great Kuṣāṇa site, Mathurā. The National Museum has a particularly fine example in a *Lakshmī*, goddess of prosperity. The goddess stands on a brimming vessel whose waters are suggested by lotuses. With her left hand she presses her right breast suggesting motherhood, fertility, and abundance. The lingering softness of the late-first-century B.C. style evident in this piece begins to congeal and harden into the typical Kuṣāṇa style. This is reflected in several pieces in the National Museum, among them a Yakṣī under a tree and a group of mother and child watched by a female whose head appears over a screen behind the mother offering a rattle to her child. The sharp, angular contours, the taut rendering of the flesh, and the linear incisiveness of drapery folds and ornaments noticed in these two sculptures heralds a new phase of stylistic evolution. A typical example of the fully developed Kuṣāṇa style is a headless standing Bodhisattva in the speckled red sandstone of Mathurā. The variety and scope of Kuṣāṇa sculptural types may be judged by these pieces and others, such as the fine Scythian head with a conical cap; the corpulent, rotund figure *Kubera*, god of wealth; and the *Bachhanalian Group*, depicting a lady sinking to the ground in a drunken state as her companions try to support her.

The northern counterpart of the Kuṣāṇa school of Mathurā also finds adequate representation in the stone reliefs and stucco heads from Gandhāra. Superficially at variance with stylistic trends noticed in the sculptures from Mathurā, these pieces from Gandhāra nonetheless reflect the eclectic and syncretic art of the Kuṣāṇa period. A Bodhisattva head in schist from Taxila reflects a modification of the indigenous figural tradition modified by the classicizing influences from the West. The various heads depicting extremes of emotional states, such as those in the National Museum of the laughing boy and the man in agony, also suggest an art molded by a variety of creative impulses converging in an area where Indians, Scythians, and the Graeco-Bactrians mingled with assimilative force. Reliefs such as the *Dream of Maya* and the *Hariti and Pāñchika*, with garland bearers and toilet trays, satisfactorily illustrate the art of this region of the Kuṣāṇa Empire.

In the Deccan the art of the first and second centuries is illustrated by the sculptural activity around the Amarāvati area. Although the two major collections of sculptures from Amarāvati are in the British Museum (q.v.) and the Madras Museum (q.v.), the National Museum now has four sculptures from Amarāvati on perpetual loan from the British Museum. Among them is a railing pillar that narrates the visit of Sage Asita to the newborn prince, who is to become the future Buddha. A fragment from a stupa at Nagarjunakonda, which falls within the geographical and stylistic sphere of Amarāvati, is of special significance in recreating the formal aspects of the stupa form, since on this slab is a rich and detailed depiction of a stupa being worshipped. Another slab from the same site depicts in three registers the events from the early days in the Buddha's life: his birth, the casting of his horoscope, and so on. The carving is in low relief, but the elongated, attenuated forms of the style of Nagarjunakonda create a rhythmic movement of peculiar vivacity.

The next major artistic phase in India has often been referred to as the Golden Age of Indian art. After the breakup of the Kuṣāṇa Empire, the Gupta rulers dominated northern India, and to them is credited this florescence of Indian art from the fourth to the sixth century. The National Museum is fortunate in possessing a representative example of Gupta sculptures from several major centers such as Mathurā, Sārnāth, Deogarh, Nāchnā, Ahichchatra, and Unnao. Although the majority of sculptures discussed so far have been primarily Buddhist, those of the Gupta period are both Buddhist and Brahamanical in iconography. Perhaps the most noteworthy of these Gupta sculptures in the National Museum is the torso of the Hindu God *Viṣṇu* in red sandstone from Mathurā. The combination of conceptual idealization with an exquisiteness of technical skill present in this piece becomes, in varying degrees, the characteristic expression of the assured pieces of this style. Another example of approximately the same date is a standing Buddha from Sārnāth, with both hands and feet missing. Of slightly later date than both of these pieces is the figure of Avalokiteśvara standing on a lotus, with a small image of the Amitaba Buddha on his forehead. In this piece the robustness and greater feeling for volumes seen in the two previous pieces begins to give way to a greater delicacy of form that eventually leads to the determined abstraction in the sculptures of the late fifth and sixth centuries. This feature of later Gupta sculpture is to be noticed in the sandstone head of Buddha from Sārnāth. The increased abstraction in rendering surfaces and the emphatic linearity in defining the lips, eyes, and snail-shell curls of the hair make this image an archetypical conceptual rendering of the later phase of Gupta art. Other examples of Gupta sculpture are the two panels from Deogarh depicting events from the *Rāmāyana*; the *dvārapāla*, or door guardian, from Nāchnā; and the two life-size terracotta figures *Ganga* and *Yamuna* rivers, which served as door guardians of a temple in Ahichchatra. Architectural fragments of the Gupta period are exemplified in a pillar and two lintels discovered embedded in a twelfth-century tomb.

The museum has a rich collection of medieval sculptures from all over India, and some deserve special attention. From the early medieval period (sixth-tenth century) are ceiling slabs from Aihole (sixth century) and the *Somāskanda* (panel from the central cell of a Pallava temple), which is the only one of its kind outside a Pallava (fifth-ninth century) monument and in a museum. From the Pala period (eighth-twelfth century) is the early Pala representation *Viṣṇu* which retains characteristics of the Gupta style, and the *Gajalakshmi* bathed by elephants and flanked by *Sankha* and *Padma*, personified treasures. A particularly fine scupture from this period is the *Avalokisteśvara* from Nalanda in Bihar of the ninth century. From Rajasthan is a recent acquisition of the National Museum, *Siva* and *Parvati*, representing their marriage. One is hard pressed to make a selection of sculptures from the numerous pieces from the late medieval period (tenth-fifteenth century). A few memorable examples from Orissa and southern India include two Chola *dvārāpalas* (door guardians) of the tenth and twelfth centuries and an example of the intricate art of the Hoysalas, the *Huntress* from Halebid (twelfth century). Fragments of architectural elements are represented by carved lintels from Hampi and Warangal (twelfth-thirteenth century) and several fragments from the immense Sūrya temple at Konarak (thirteenth century). One of these fragments from Konarak is *Varuṇānī*, the consort of Varuṇa on her *makara* vehicle. An especially grand example from Konarak is the *Sūrya* to whom the temple was dedicated.

Medieval art of India is extremely rich in bronzes, and the National Museum's holdings include some exceptional examples. Perhaps the most significant group of bronzes are those attributed to the Vākāṭakas, who ruled in the Deccan in the fifth and sixth centuries. These pieces are the only bronzes of this period known to date. Among the many Pala pieces from the ninth and tenth centuries, the bronze *Haragauri* from Kurkihār is of special significance. An example of the early idiom of Chola bronzes (tenth-eleventh century), justly famous around the world, is the *Kaliya Krishna*, balanced with incredible equipoise on the hood of a snake on which the personified Nāga is indicated. Other examples of Chola bronzes are the *Somāskanda* and the *Nataraja* from Tiruvaraṅguḷam (tenth century). The latter, in a *chatura* pose, is considered a unique example, since there is no other known example in metal of this specific pose. From Chamba the

National Museum possesses the fine bronze *Devi*, which is inscribed and dated about 1000. Finally, from the Vijayanagar period (fourteenth-sixteenth century) is the bronze *Bharata*, carrying the sandals of his brother Rama, commemorating a poignant moment from the *Rāmāyana*.

The National Museum's vast collection of miniature paintings may be viewed only in part through the museum's well-planned, rotating display, which provides a survey of the variety and sequence of stylistic clusters of regional schools and subschools that include the early western Indian tradition and the Mughal, Rajasthani, and Pahari schools. The western Indian style of painting is represented by a large collection consisting of miniatures and manuscripts. The Mughal school of painting includes the *Ashiqa* of 1568 and the *Babar-nama* of the late sixteenth entury. The National Museum has an especially good collection of miniatures from the late Mughal period.

Of the major schools of Rajasthani painting, the National Museum has some notable examples among its holdings. From Malwa the dated *Rasikapriya* of 1634, the *Rāmāyana* series of about 1650, the *Amaru Sataka* of 1652, and the *Ragamala* of 1680 are of importance. Miniatures from the school of Mewar are amply represented by several series such as the *Dhola Maru* painted at Aghata about 1610, the *Bhramara Gita* series of Suradasa of about 1650, and the brilliant *Ragamala* series often referred to as the "Gem Palace Set" of about 1660. Examples of occasional, isolated miniatures from Mewar are also represented, and one of particular interest in reflecting the increased self-consciousness of Indian artists of this period is the eighteenth-century *Portrait of an Artist at Work*. From Bundi the early unfinished *Ragamala* series of the early seventeenth century and the *Rasikapriya* set of about 1700 clearly suggest the singularly brilliant evolution of the Mewar idiom in the hands of Bundi artists. From the same school we have the delightful *Lovers on a Terrace*, dated 1674, and the *Portrait of Kunwar Anurad Singh*, dated 1680.

The National Museum also has a great collection of Pahari paintings, especially of the Basohli and Kangra schools. An unusual facet of the Pahari collection at the National Museum lies in the museum's holdings of the wall paintings removed from various palaces in the hills. The later evolution of miniature painting is seen in examples from Lucknow and Patna of the late eighteenth and nineteenth centuries, those from Tanjore of the nineteenth century, and the so-called Company Style paintings done by Indian artists to suit the tastes of their European patrons of the nineteenth century.

A separate section of the National Museum is devoted to manuscripts, which include scrolls, volumes, or individual pages of illuminations or fine illustrations and calligraphy, whether on palm leaf, paper, or parchment. These holdings review the historical evolution of writing and book illustration in the several languages of India, such as Sanskrit, Persian, and Arabic. Among them, a significant group consists of richly illuminated copies of the Koran. As with miniature painting, displays in this section are also organized on a rotating basis.

A significant proportion of the National Museum's holdings cover areas such as those of anthropology, the Arms Gallery, and the gallery of wood carvings and decorative arts, which include textiles, metalware, jade, ivory, and jewelry from various periods. The exhibits of the anthropology section emphasize the variety of regional life-styles. An outstanding group of such objects is part of the Verrier Elwin Collection of tribal arts that are illustrative of regions such as Nagaland, Orissa, and Bihar. In the arms section are displayed richly ornamented blades and hilts of jade, ivory, spears, and shields, some of the latter fashioned from rare translucent rhinoceros hide, as well as powder horns of shell, mother-of-pearl, and ivory. Among the numerous examples of wood carving from Nepal, Rajasthan, Gujerat, and South India, fragments of temples from Gujerat and those from Kerala in South India deserve special attention. These works, with the rich and complex tradition of Indian weaving exhibited in the decorative-arts collection, present a full and diverse survey of the artistic traditions of India.

Complementing these areas of Indian art are two fine collections: one of central Asian antiquities and one of pre-Columbian art. The collection of antiquities from central Asia represents three-fifths of the material collected by Sir Aurel Stein during his three expeditions of 1900–1901, 1906–8, and 1913–16. The remaining two-fifths of this major collection of central Asian art is in the British Museum. Among the mural fragments, textiles, ceramics, architectural ornaments, and funerary objects, the murals from Miran (third-fourth century) and Bezeklik (eleventh century) are especially significant. These works and the documents in Kharoshthi script from Niya (second century), painted stucco and wooden figures of animals and humans from Astana (sixth-seventh century), and Buddhist paintings on silk and paper, as well as banners from the Cave of the Thousand Buddhas (sixth-tenth century) have justly made this collection of paramount significance.

The collection of pre-Columbian art, donated to the National Museum by the late Nasli Heeramaneck, an Indian art dealer and collector, consists of discriminating and exceptionally fine examples from Mexico, Central America, Peru, and other centers. Sculptures in stone, terracotta, and bronze and objects in wood, bone, and walrus ivory range from approximately 900 B.C. to A.D. 1300. This unusual collection provides striking contrasts and parallels with objects of Indian origin and thus serves as a refreshing counterpoint to the National Museum as a whole.

Photographs of the objects in the museum may be ordered by writing to the director of the museum.

Selected Bibliography

Museum publications: Morley, G., *A Brief Guide to the National Museum*, 1962; Randhawa, M. S., *Kangra Paintings of the Bhagavata Purana*, 1960; idem, *Kangra Paintings of the Gita Govinda*, 1963; idem, *Kangra Paintings on Love*, 1963; Sivaramamurti, C., *Nataraja in Art, Thought, and Literature*; idem, *Bronzes: Guide to the Gallery of the National Museum of India*, 1956; idem, *Masterpieces of Indian Sculpture in the National Museum*, 1971.

REKHA MORRIS

Ireland

——— Dublin ———

NATIONAL GALLERY OF IRELAND, Leinster Lawn, Merrion Square, Dublin.

First opened to the public on January 31, 1864, the National Gallery of Ireland traces its origins to the Great Exhibition in Dublin of 1853. The interest sparked by the exhibition led to the founding of The Irish Institution, an association dedicated both to holding annual exhibitions and to constructing a permanent gallery. The Gallery was formally established by act of Parliament in 1854. Also that year, a major financial contribution toward the permanent museum was received, the proceeds of subscriptions (some 5,000 pounds) raised to commemorate the generosity of railway magnate William Dargan in connection with the mounting of the Great Exhibition of 1853. The sum of 21,500 pounds received through parliamentary grants further supplemented the building fund during early years. The seventeen-member Board of Governors and Guardians, which under the direction of a chairman and vice-chairman still governs Gallery operations, was incorporated in 1855. The Commission of Public Works owns the Gallery edifice itself.

The Leinster Lawn site chosen for the Gallery was ceded to the Irish Institution by the Royal Dublin Society, which then occupied Leinster House. As a condition to obtaining the property, the society requested that any gallery built be designed to correspond to the style of the Natural History Museum that the society itself planned to build on the south side of the lawn. The painter George Mulvany, who subsequently became the first director of the Gallery, prepared the first Gallery design. His original design was later abandoned in favor of a design submitted by Charles Lanyon. Unfortunately, Lanyon's grand design of 1857, highlighted by a main staircase that would occupy a full one-third of the building's cubic content, promised to cost twelve thousand pounds above the amount originally budgeted for construction.

Thus the board of governors ultimately turned to Captain Francis Fowke to produce a design that would both harmonize architecturally with the museum built by the society and fall financially within the realistic budget of the board. Fowke's modification of the Lanyon design was accepted, dispensing with the grand staircase and shortening overall building length but providing for gas lighting (the Gallery was the first public gallery to be artificially illuminated by gas) and a mezzanine floor for offices.

Today the Gallery is characterized by a main hall on the ground floor, encircled by Corinthian columns embellished with laurel wreaths containing shamrocks and Irish harps. Fowke's split staircase rises directly from the ground floor Sculpture Gallery to a mezzanine landing, which leads to the main Picture Gallery.

Architectural renovations at the turn of the century were precipitated in part by negotiations over the reception of the Milltown Gift, one of the important events in the history of the Gallery. In October 1897 the countess of Milltown offered in memory of her deceased husband the pictures, prints, and furnishings she held at Russborough; the core of this collection came from purchases made in Italy by the first earl of Milltown in the mid-1700s.

Enthusiastic at the prospect of receiving the Milltown Gift, the board immediately requested government assistance for extending the original Gallery building. In October 1898, 20,250 pounds were authorized for the extension, which was first opened to the public in March 1903. The extension provided a much-needed 140 percent increase in hanging space, a new library, offices, and a photography studio. Lady Milltown's personal dissatisfaction notwithstanding (she noticed "the most glaring instances of disorder and incongruity" in the final arrangement of the works), the spatial addition served well the acquisitions of future decades.

Some sixty years later, a second bequest once again was the catalyst for architectural expansion of the Gallery. The bequest was that of George Bernard Shaw, whose will provided that for fifty years after his death, the Gallery was to receive one-third of the royalties derived from his works. Past literary achievements thus supporting the continued vigor of the plastic arts, the Shaw Bequest prompted the government to appropriate 277,000 pounds in 1962 for a second Gallery extension.

One-third of the royalties from Shaw's *Pygmalion* proved a handsome sum, with the success of the musical and movie *My Fair Lady*. By 1968 the Gallery boasted a highly functional addition, including ten exhibition rooms, laboratories, a restaurant, and a library. The 1968 extension also included a grand marble staircase that rises to the full height of the building.

The management and operations of the Gallery are today entrusted to the seventeen-member Board of Governors and Guardians and a director. The Gallery has both a conservation department and an art library. Access to the library is now available to serious students of art history.

Funding for acquisitions comes from three major sources: the Shaw Fund, the Lane Fund, and a grant-in-aid from the government. The funds are used primarily for the acquisition of works of international import, such as Pissarro's *Flowerpiece*, acquired in 1983.

The Lane Fund represents monies derived from the 1915 gift of Sir Hugh Lane, a titan in the world of Irish art appreciation, who served as director of the Gallery between 1914 and 1915. The Lane funds are ordinarily reserved for purchases of particularly outstanding works by Irish artists, with the government's grant-in-aid similarly used to acquire Irish works. Feeling the financial constraints of diminishing returns on the funds, the Board of Governors has sought to maximize the actual purchasing power of its assets by acquiring works primarily at auction, an uncommon practice among most museums.

At the close of 1980, the Gallery held more than twenty-two hundred paintings, excluding watercolors and drawings; the Gallery's strengths lie primarily in works executed before 1870. Seventeenth-century Italian, Dutch, French, and Spanish works are particularly well represented. Today's substantial collection, organized in curatorial departments, including Old Masters, Irish Masters, the National Portrait Gallery, and Prints and Drawings, had its origin in a core of eleven pictures presented to the Gallery by 1855. The first purchase, Koninck's *Portrait of a Burgher*, occurred in 1856. The annual exhibits mounted by the Irish Institution before the Gallery building was completed in 1864 served to spark continuing interest in the arts, and direct solicitation resulted in a holding of more than one hundred pictures by the time the Gallery opened.

A key role in early efforts was played by Lord Chancellor Sir Maziere Brady, who in 1856 arranged for the first major purchase of sixteen pictures in Rome. Of particular interest were the large canvases by Lanfranco from the Basilica of San Paolo fuori le Mure in Rome, *The Last Supper* and *The Miracle of the Loaves and Fishes* (each 229 by 426 centimeters), and works by Boulogne the Elder, *The Call of the Sons of Zebedee*, and Coypel, *Christ Curing One Possessed*. The acquisition by purchase also served to trigger the establishment of an official funding policy on the part of the government. An 1862 appropriation of twenty-five hundred pounds as an "exceptional" measure to reimburse Brady was soon expanded to allow yearly grants to the Gallery. By 1866 the government had adopted the policy of making annual "matching grants," equal to the sum of private donations and presentations up to one thousand pounds.

George F. Mulvany became the first director of the Gallery in 1862. Termed "a competent painter but an indifferent connoisseur," Mulvany distinguished his directorship more by talented administrative dealing than by outstanding acumen in acquisitions. Nonetheless, his attendance at English auctions netted Palmezzano's *Virgin Enthroned* and Jordaens' altarpiece *The Church Triumphant*.

Of the seventy pictures purchased by Mulvany during his tenure as director, many reflect a taste for seventeenth-century painters, Dutch masters, and early German and Netherlandish works. Responding to the board's recognition of the inability to obtain original works of art by the greatest masters, Mulvany was not above purchasing copies. Although the *Catalogue of Oil Pictures in the General Collection* (1932) had once faulted most of the works collected by Mulvany as "remarkable for their area rather than their authenticity," subsequent cleaning has revealed that the purchases constituted a very important collection of Italian seicento paintings. Other major works acquired during the Mulvany years include Rubens' *The Annunciation*, Velázquez' *Torquato Tasso* and *The Infanta Maria Teresa, Later Queen of France*, Jacob van Ruisdael's *A Wooded Landscape*, and Cornelis Bega's *Two Men Singing*.

The Dublin native and artist Henry Doyle was appointed director upon Mulvany's death in 1869 and enjoyed comparative carte blanche in terms of acquisitions; whereas the board had exercised firm control over Mulvany's activities, it chose to accord Doyle great freedom in his pursuit of Dutch and Flemish works. During his twenty-three years as director, Doyle purchased paintings that still number among the Gallery's greatest masterpieces: Fra Angelico's *Martyrdom of Saints Cosmas and Damian*, Rembrandt's *Rest on the Flight into Egypt*, Poussin's *Entombment*, Titian's *Ecce Homo*, and Reynolds' *Charles Coote, 1st Earl of Bellamont*.

Although Doyle possessed a keen eye for works of international scope, he did not ignore the Irish school. Indeed, it was Doyle who initiated a policy of acquiring pictures by Irish artists and who opened one exhibition room as the Irish Gallery. When the government rejected the board's request for a special grant to purchase works for a nascent collection of national portraits, Doyle directed his own efforts to acquiring Irish portraits. As a result of his persistence, the National Portrait Gallery was opened to the public in June 1884. The Portrait Gallery is housed in the Leinster Lawn building.

Walter Armstrong succeeded Doyle as director in 1892. Justly praised as "an Englishman who did good work for Ireland," Armstrong drew upon his training in the arts at Harrow and Exeter to bolster the old Dutch holdings and to begin an impressive publications effort by the Gallery. Between 1895 and 1913 the Gallery produced volumes on Velázquez, Reynolds, and Gainsborough, among others. Dutch acquisitions of the period included Maes' *Vertumnus and Pomona*, Claesz' *A Still Life*, de Witte's *The New Church at Delft*, and Leyster's *An Interior: Woman Serving by Candlelight*.

It was during Armstrong's tenure as director that the Gallery acquired the Milltown Collection, which included about two hundred paintings, some statuary, furniture, and exceptionally fine silver. The most notable pieces presented by Lady Milltown included Batoni's *Joseph Leeson, Afterwards 1st Earl of Milltown* and *Venus and Cupid*, Panini's *The Colosseum* and *The Forum*, and Vernet's *A Coastal Scene*. Reynolds' series of caricatures, including those of Sir William Lowther, Lord Bruce, and Sir Thomas Kennedy, also stand as particularly valuable additions through the Milltown gift. In 1901 Armstrong was able to supplement the Gallery's holdings of Rubens (*Christ in the House of Martha and Mary*) and of Salomon van Ruysdael (*The Halt*) by ten well-considered selections from the estate of Sir Henry Page Turner Barron.

With the untimely death of Sir Hugh Lane in 1915, the Gallery lost its newly appointed director of some fifteen months but gained a most generous bequest. Lane's will provided that, aside from leaving modern works to the Dublin Gallery of Modern Art (now the Hugh Lane Gallery), he left "the remainder of [his] property to the National Gallery of Ireland to be invested and the income spent on buying pictures of deceased painters of established merit." Thus in addition to the value of Lane's Chelsea home and other personal property, the Gallery also received forty-three of Lane's Old Masters, including Titian's *Baldassare Castiglione*, Poussin's *Acis and Galatea* and *Bacchante and Satyr*, van Dyck's *A Boy Standing on a Terrace*, and Gainsborough's *A Landscape with Cattle*.

Wartime Director Robert Langston Douglas was seriously constrained in acquisitions when the government withdrew its one thousand-pounds-a-year grant in 1915. He was able, however, to use the proceeds of the Lane investments to acquire Hobbema's *The Ferry Boat* and a number of fifteenth-century Italian works, including *Scenes from the Life of St. Augustine* by the Master of St. Augustine and the votive picture *The Virgin Invoking God with the Healing of Pope Leo I* by Romano. Douglas also accepted the first works of the Hone Collection, representing the work of Nathaniel Hone the Younger. The initial Hone presentation of almost two hundred works, first exhibited in 1921, was ultimately supplemented by 1951 to include more than 550 oils and 887 watercolors. Having spent his early years in or near Barbizon, Hone represents an Irish artist whose landscapes and seascapes plainly reflect the influence of the open-air painting of the French artists' colonies.

Financial constraints also marked the tenure of Thomas Bodkin as director during the 1920s. In spite of the government's steadfast refusal to provide extra staff or funding, the Gallery has Bodkin to thank for Bruegel's *A Peasant Wedding*, Corot's 1853 *Landscape*, and Delacroix' *Demosthenes on the Seashore*.

With the advent of the war years in the late 1930s, public apathy toward the Gallery manifested itself not only in terms of waning financial support but also in declining attendance. During the first ten months after the building was opened in 1864, 167,698 persons visited the Gallery; by 1941 the annual number of visitors had fallen to a mere 24,723. At the same time, tensions between the board and directorship increased, in no small measure due to the board's policy of rejecting offers of purchase tendered by the director. Works by Gauguin, Monet, and Murillo were all lost to the Gallery as a consequence during the 1940s.

The 1950s were more propitious in terms of acquisitions. Director Thomas McGreevy officiated on the occasion of Sir Alfred Chester Beatty's bequest to the nation of some ninety paintings, primarily of the Barbizon School. The bequest was formally consigned to the Gallery by the state in 1978 and includes Breton's masterpiece *The Gleaners*. Purchases during McGreevy's tenure were most frequently of a religious nature: Dolci's *St. Agnes*, Cranach's *The Virgin and Child with Angels*, and the school of Fra Bartolommeo's *Holy Family*.

In 1958 the first income from the Shaw Fund became available for acquisitions; within the next several years, the income amounted to a most impressive seventy thousand pounds a year. Because of these large funds the Board of Governors and Guardians adopted the policy that only those paintings having a special interest to the nation, or a major artistic or historic value, should be acquired. Early purchases made under that ambitious but well-founded policy included Tintoretto's *Venice*, Ghirlandaio's *Presumed Portrait of Clarice Orsini, Wife of Lorenzo the Magnificent*, Boucher's *A Young Girl in a Park*, and Murillo's *The Holy Family* and *St. Mary Magdalen*.

The substantial income from the Shaw Fund enabled director James White to preside over a virtual "golden age" of the Gallery in terms of acquisitions and architectural expansion. New Gallery rooms boasted not only restored paintings from the extant collection but also important additions made possible by the Shaw Fund. Newly acquired works of international import included Goya's *El Sueno*, Gérard's *Julie Bonaparte, Queen of Naples, with Her Daughters*, and Fragonard's *Venus and Cupid*, or *Day*.

The Irish collection was likewise expanded with important additions of works by Ashford, *A View of Dublin from Clontarf* and *A View of Dublin from Chapelizod*; by Roberts, *A Landscape*; and by Carver, *A Landscape with Peasants and a Dog*. The Irish collection now includes works by seventeenth-century artists, most of whom were trained or studied in the Low Countries, such as Garret Morphey (*Caryll, Third Viscount Molyneux of Maryborough*).

George Barret's *A View of Powerscourt Waterfall* and Thomas Roberts' *A Landscape with a River and Horses* are representative of later landscape work; Royal Academy founding member Nathaniel Hone the Elder focused his talents upon portraiture (*Horace Hone Sketching*).

Representative of the Dublin Society School, which flourished from the middle of the eighteenth century, is Hugh Douglas Hamilton (*Cupid and Psyche in the Nuptial Bower*). James Arthur O'Connor, on the other hand, was attracted by the developing Romantic movement (*A View of the Devil's Glen*). Nineteenth-century Irish work was highlighted by several landscape painters, including William Davis (*A View of the Rye Water Near Leixlip*) and Nathaniel Hone the Younger (*The Coast of County Clare with the Atlantic*). Finally, Roderic O'Conor, who for a time shared a studio with Gauguin and was among the members of the Pont-Aven group, capped Irish art of the turn of the century as a talented exponent of developing Post-Impressionism (*La ferme de Lezaver, Finistère*).

Aside from occasional publications on topics of specific interest (for example, Michael Wynne's 1983 survey *Fifty Irish Painters*), the Gallery makes annual publication of *Recent Acquisitions* pamphlets. As of 1984 Director H. Potterton's *National Gallery of Ireland: Illustrated Summary Catalogue of Paintings* (1981) offered the most comprehensive overview of paintings in the collection, including a detailed introduction to the Gallery's development. Early in 1984 there appeared a catalogue of the five thousand watercolors, drawings, and miniatures in the collection. First established by a bequest of eighty contemporary watercolors from George A. Taylor in 1854, the collection now includes *St. Catherine of Alexandria*, attributed to Dürer; sketches by Raphael; Ruisdael landscapes; and two Degas pastels. Visitors to the Gallery are permitted to photograph works in the collection, provided they use a hand-held camera without flash. Patrons may also purchase photographs of works from the Gallery Bookshop.

Selected Bibliography

Museum publications: *National Gallery of Ireland: Illustrated Summary Catalogue of Drawings, Watercolours, and Miniatures*, 1983; *National Gallery of Ireland's Illustrated Summary Catalogue of Paintings*, 1981; Wynne, Michael, *National Gallery of Ireland: Fifty Irish Painters*, 1983; *National Gallery of Ireland: Exhibition of Acquisitions, 1981– 82*, 1982; idem, *National Gallery of Ireland: Recent Acquisitions, 1980–81*, 1981; *National Gallery of Ireland: Catalogue of the Paintings*, 1971; *Drawings from the National Gallery of Ireland*, 1967; *National Gallery of Ireland: 1864–1964 Centenary Exhibition*, 1964; *National Gallery of Ireland: Illustrations of the Paintings*, 1951; *National Gallery of Ireland: Catalogue of Oil Paintings in the General Collection*, 1932; *Catalogue of Pictures and Other Works of Art in the National Gallery of Ireland and the National Portrait Gallery*, 1928; *Catalogue of Pictures and Other Works of Art in the National Gallery of Ireland and the National Portrait Gallery*, 1920; *Catalogue, Descriptive and Historical, of the Works of Art in the National Gallery of Ireland*, 1878.

FRANCIS D. MURNAGHAN, JR.

NATIONAL MUSEUM OF IRELAND (also ARD-MHÚSAEM NA HÉI-REANN, NATIONAL MUSEUM OF SCIENCE AND ART, SCIENCE AND ART MUSEUM), Kildare Street, Dublin 2.

The history of the National Museum of Ireland is closely linked with that of the Royal Dublin Society. This society was founded in 1731 by a few Dublin gentlemen for the purpose of improving husbandry and manufacture. In 1733 the society opened a museum, which first consisted of agricultural implements but soon broadened in scope to include zoological and botanical specimens.

In 1814 the society purchased Leinster House, a Georgian mansion on Kildare Street, formerly the home of the dukes of Leinster. The society's museum was at first accommodated in Leinster House but due to continued expansion, a special building was erected for the Natural History Museum on the south side of Leinster Lawn in Merrion Square. This was designed by Frederick V. Clarendon and was officially opened on August 31, 1857.

Throughout the years that followed, there was sporadic thinking about the necessity of establishing a national museum. Negotiations took place between the Royal Dublin Society and the British government, which culminated in 1877 with the passing into law of the Science and Art Museum Act on August 25th, the foundation of the National Museum.

It became necessary to erect new buildings to accommodate the museum. Thomas Newenham Deane, the architect, designed two fine and, at the time, commodious buildings to flank Leinster House on its Kildare Street side. The structures (one of which was to accommodate the National Library) were faced with chiseled granite from the Dublin Mountains, and details of the doors, the window surrounds, and the pillars of the colonnades were made from sandstone from Mount Charles, County Donegal. The buildings were formally opened by the lord lieutenant on August 29, 1890.

Following the establishment of the Irish Free State in 1922, Leinster House became the meeting place of the Irish Parliament, which resulted in a decrease in the amount of space available to the museum. For a time the museum was closed to the public, since meetings of the senate were held in the Kildare Street building. However, the Natural History Museum was reopened in June 1924 and the Kildare Street building in June 1925.

The National Museum is financed from government funds through the Department of Education. The director acts in liaison with senior civil servants of the department in planning the overall development of the museum. In addition, a board of visitors of twelve members exists, whose duty it is to make an annual report to the Department of Education on the condition, management, and requirements of the museum and to advise on points affecting its administration. The National Museum is administered by the director; curatorial departments are Irish Antiquities, Art and Industry, Natural History, and Irish Folk Life; administrative sections deal with education and library services.

The collections of the Irish Antiquities Division comprise archaeological and ethnographic material. The nucleus of the collection is that of the Royal Irish Academy, whose museum was transferred to the National Museum in 1890.

The collection is particularly rich in prehistoric gold ornaments. The collection of Bronze Age lunulae, torcs, fibulae, gorgets, and so on is one of the largest in northern Europe, and there is a great variety of examples of the bronze work of the period, including weapons, cauldrons, trumpets, and tools. The gold ornaments are remarkable for their striking beauty, the simplicity of their shapes, and their geometric decoration. The extraordinary richness of this period is best exemplified by what is known as the Great Clare Find of 1854. Although many of the pieces had been melted down when Sir William Wilde, father of Oscar Wilde, made the inventory, it still contained 5 gorgets, 2 neck torcs, 2 unwrought ingots, and 137 rings and armillae. One of the gorgets from this collection is perhaps the most splendid of all of Ireland's prehistoric gold ornaments. It consists of a crescent-shaped sheet of gold with a gold disc at each end. The Ardcroney and Gleninsheen gorgets are also highlights of the Irish Antiquities collection. An intriguing fragment dating from the first century B.C. is the *Petrie Crown*, so-called in honor of the antiquarian George Petrie in whose collection it first appeared. From this period also dates the Broighter hoard, which comprises a collar of hollow sheet gold, a model boat of gold with mast and oars, steering oar and boat hook, two torcs, and two necklets.

It is, however, to the Early Christian era that the most outstanding items in the Irish Antiquities Division belong. They include the *Ardagh Chalice*, a two-handled silver chalice of the early eighth century, regarded as the finest surviving example of Irish metalwork of the Early Christian period. Also dating from this period is the *Tara Brooch*, a magnificent ring-brooch, notable for the delicacy and perfection of its workmanship.

The collection of medieval antiquities is particularly rich in shrines such as the *Shrine of St. Patrick's Bell* and the *Processional Cross of Cong*. Also of interest are the artifacts from excavations conducted by museum archaeologists on the site of the Viking and medieval city of Dublin.

In addition to Irish archaeological material, the Irish Antiquities Division contains a small but representative collection of Egyptian, Babylonian, Greek, and Roman material.

The division also contains an exceptionally fine collection of ethnographic material known as the Trinity College Collection, which was acquired by the National Museum in 1882 and 1885. This comprises material collected by Dr. Patten and Captain King on the second and third voyages of Captain James Cook. Material in the collection illustrates the way of life in many communities in Africa, Asia, Australia, the Americas, and the Pacific Islands and because of the early date of its assembly is of unique importance. At present this collection is not on public display but may be consulted by research workers.

The collections of the Art and Industrial Division fall into three main categories: Industrial and Applied Art; Arms, Military, and Historical Material; and Oriental Material. The Industrial and Applied Art category consists of material from about the sixteenth to the nineteenth century. The main emphasis is on objects of Irish manufacture, but there is a representative selection of material from other countries. There is a large collection of Irish silver not only from Dublin but also from the provincial centers of silver making. This collection gives an idea of the development and variety of goldsmith and silversmith work during the period from about 1500 to 1850. One of the outstanding items is the *De Burgo-O'Malley Chalice*, a Gothic chalice dating from 1494. Also of interest is the collection of two-handled drinking cups, or loving cups, particularly those in the so-called harp-handled style especially associated with Irish silver.

The glass collection traces the development of work in this medium from Egyptian examples to the glass of eighteenth-century Europe. The collection of Irish glass is of particular interest, since it contains examples of items dating from the period 1780 to 1835, during which time glass was produced in a style that was unique to Ireland.

The collection of ceramics is very extensive, containing examples of pottery and porcelain from most European countries and from the Far East. A highlight of this collection is the display of Belleek ware, a hard-paste porcelain manufactured at Belleek, County Fermanagh from 1857 onwards. This porcelain is valued for its light weight, iridescent glaze, and delicate ivory color. The factory was noted for statuary and ornamental objects, including busts of contemporary and literary figures and allegorical types made in Parian ware, a fine unglazed white porcelain. The Industrial and Applied Art Section also has collections of furniture, musical instruments, costume and lace, clocks and watches, coins and medals, stamps, ivories, and seals.

The following collections are included in the category of arms (e.g., edged weapons and firearms from about the sixteenth to the early twentieth century), military (e.g., uniforms, equipment, and medals relating to the modern Irish army and to Irishmen in the armed services of various states), and history (e.g., flags, uniforms, documents, and badges relating to Irish history from about 1691 to 1922).

The Oriental category contains Chinese, Japanese, Indian, Persian, and Burmese material of the following classes: domestic and religious utensils and figures, ornamental and art objects, models, tapestries, arms, armor, costume, games, and textiles. Of particular interest is the Augusta M. Bender Collection of Oriental art presented to the museum in 1935. This includes one of the most extensive collections of Tibetan temple banners in existence.

The aim of the Irish Folk Life Division is to build up a collection of articles from all parts of the country that will fully illustrate various aspects of traditional Irish life. Some examples of the classes of material in the collection are: domestic furniture and appliances; agriculture and dairy equipment; hand tools, equipment, and specimens of handiwork related to traditional trades and crafts; items of dress and footwear; and objects associated with festivals and customs.

The National History Museum is considered part of the National Museum, but description of its important collections is not relevant to this entry.

The National Museum has a library of more than twenty thousand volumes of books and periodicals relating to the subjects covered by the museum collections. It also holds the Dr. J.K.S. St. Joseph Collection of aerial photographs of sites of archaeological or historic interest. Use of the library is confined to museum staff and research workers.

Slides and photographs of objects in the collection may be purchased on application to the Museum Registry, which can also provide a list of museum publications and instructions for ordering.

Selected Bibliography

Museum publications: *Outline Guide to the Principal Collections*, 1977; *Catalogue of Viking and Medieval Dublin Exhibition*, 1973; *Guide to the Indian Exhibition*, 1976; *Irish Silver*, 1980; *Guide to the Collection of Lace*, 1970; *Early Belleek Wares*, 1978; *Guide to the Historical Exhibition Commemorative of the Rising of 1916*, 1966; *Treasures of Munster*, 1977; *Pottery in Ireland through the Ages*, 1977; *Hall-marks on Dublin Silver*, 1968; *Artists and Craftsmen: Irish Art Treasures*, 1980; *The Earliest Irish Coinage*, 1961.

Other publications: Freeman, J., "The Polynesian Collection of Trinity College Dublin," *Journal of the Polynesian Society*, vol. 58 (1949), pp. 1–18; Lucas, A. T., "The National Museum: its place in the cultural life of the Nation," *Oideas*, vol. 1 (1968), pp. 1–12; idem, "The Role of the National Museum in the Study of Irish Social History," *Museums Journal*, vol. 65 (1965), pp. 112–21; MacLeod, C., "Some hitherto unrecorded momentoes of William III," *Studies* (1976), pp. 128–43; *Report of the Board of Visitors, 1880–*.

FELICITY DEVLIN

Israel

——— Jerusalem ———

ISRAEL MUSEUM, THE, Jerusalem.

The Israel Museum is a conglomerate of earlier museums and private collections, with subsequent donations, collections, departments, and services. The establishment of the museum was a result of the decision by the mayor of Jerusalem, Teddy Kollek, in the early 1960s to unite the existing art and archaeology collections in Jerusalem with art that was then being offered for donation and to house it all under one roof.

The museum is privately incorporated. However, 25 percent of its funding comes from government aid, 15 percent is self-generated, and 60 percent is derived from endowments and regular contributions.

The first organization formed to aid The Israel Museum was the American-Israel Cultural Foundation and the British Friends of the Bezalel Museum (1965). Various Friends of The Israel Museum organizations have been established in the United States, Canada, England, France, and other countries throughout Europe and South America. There are various Friends and *Shocharim* (seekers, supporters) groups in Israel as well. These groups help in raising funds, collecting art, directing and channeling art for loans and temporary exhibitions, making acquisitions, and developing a building fund.

The Israel Museum is governed by an international council, a local board of directors, and an executive committee. It is administered by a chief administrator and chief curators for the arts, archaeology, youth wing, and the Shrine of the Book.

The museum was opened officially on May 11, 1965. The building was designed by architects Alfred Mansfeld and Dora Gad; it won both local and international prizes for its design. The plan, based on a system of 1.40-meter-square modules both in the original galleries and subsequent additions, has allowed for the harmonious growth of the multipavilioned museum complex. The museum is situated atop a hill between other notable landmarks of Jerusalem: the Israeli Knesset Parliament Building, the Hebrew University of Jerusalem (Givat Ram Campus), and the Greek Monastery of the Cross.

The museum's concrete and steel structure has a veneer of smooth limestone. The individual pavilions, white rectangular blocks scattered at varying elevations atop a small mountain, are linked by glass-enclosed galleries. The overall effect in Jerusalem's high-intensity daylight is of jewels shimmering under the open sky. Dramatic nighttime lighting repeats this impression. The museum's open-yet-linked plan is not only functional, it is also symbolic, contrasting ancient and modern collections.

The Bezalel National Art Museum, which constitutes a significant part of The Israel Museum's collection was founded in 1906 in conjunction with the Bezalel School of Art. It became an independent entity between 1925 and 1965 and was incorporated into The Israel Museum in 1965. The collection includes Jewish ritual art from throughout the world, manuscripts, paintings by Jewish and non-Jewish artists, and an art library. The museum's Judaica holdings have been expanded through the acquisition of collections donated by the Feuchtwanger and Rappaport families, by Jakob Michael, and by the late Jerusalem artist Anna Ticho.

The extensive Judaica collection is arranged according to the cycle of Jewish holidays, the life cycle of the individual, and the milieu of the object's chief use, home or synagogue. Appropriately, one begins with examples of Menorahs (candelabra), for this lamp in its seven-branched form was chosen to be the symbol of the state of Israel in 1948. One of the oldest objects in the collection is a second-third-century seven-branched Menorah carved out of limestone and with receptacles for oil. It was originally in an ancient synagogue near Tiberias.

Displayed in the Edgar and Libby Fain Torah Gallery are Torah scrolls, the Five Books of Moses, which are written on parchment and embody the basis of Jewish law and tradition. One scroll, housed in a cylindrical case covered with velvet, silver, and gilt, comes from eighteenth-century Iran. Another scroll, covered with an embroidered velvet mantle and surmounted by silver bells atop its two wooden staves, bears a dedicatory inscription stating the cover was made in Germany in 1761. The variation in format and decoration between these two examples of art attest to the range of aesthetic and artistic influences encountered by the Jewish people throughout the world. This diversity of style, media, and technique applies to all examples of Judaica (Jewish ritual art).

Sabbath objects, in a section courtesy of the Ellern family, include ceremonial and large, functional oil lamps necessary for a holy day during which no light is kindled or rekindled during the twenty-four-hour period. Kiddush cups, for the blessing of sanctification inaugurating each sabbath and festival, appear in both gold and silver. The *Havdalah* ceremony separating the holy sabbath from the secular week days is represented by its own ceremonial cup (such as the gold repoussé one of 1765 from Germany), a silver holder for candle and spices (1741, Germany), and a variety of spice boxes in the shape of a windmill, locomotive, flower, and fruit.

The high holidays of autumn are represented by items such as the *shofar* (ram's horn) blown on Rosh Ha-Shana (the Jewish New Year), special garments worn on Yom Kippur (the Day of Atonement), and containers in various shapes for the *etrog* (citron) that is special to the harvest festival of Succoth. The Jew is commanded in the Torah to dwell in a *sukkah* (booth) during the festival to commemorate the nation's wandering in the desert for forty years. The Israel Museum has a painted wood sukkah, courtesy of the Deller family and D. H. Feuchtwanger, complete with hunting scenes and an imaginary Jerusalem, which resembles a European town contemporary to the time that the sukkah was painted in early-nineteenth-century southern Germany.

The wintertime, eight-day festival of lights, or Hanukkah, has an entire wall of the museum dedicated to it, with Hanukkah lamps dating from the fourteenth to the twentieth century. Hanukkah refers to the rededication of the Holy Temple in Jerusalem; hence many of these lamps are decorated with architectural motifs that reflect the local architecture where the particular artist resided. The oldest Hanukkah lamp from southern France has rosettes and fleurs-de-lis. Those from North Africa are Islamic in style; the Italian lamps show Renaissance influences; and the Polish examples depict wooden, shingled structures similar to the local style found in both houses and synagogues. The Hanukkah lamps, used in homes and temples exhibit a wide range of materials: brass, silver, tin, gilt, stone, glass, and, in the twentieth century, chrome and plastic.

For the Purim festival there are *megillahs* (scrolls) of the Book of Esther, ranging from the fourteenth to the twentieth century. One from Amsterdam dates from 1640.

The spring festival of Pessach or Passover is represented by special vessels and the Haggadah read at the Seder table at the start of the holiday. The *Birds' Head Haggadah* is illustrated with Jewish figures, whose heads are birds rather than human, perhaps a strict interpretation of the commandment regarding the making of graven images.

The section devoted to the cycle of Jewish life takes us from cradle to grave. There are the implements used for circumcision and Torah wrappers made by embroidering the swaddling cloth used at the child's circumcision ceremony. Coming of age occurs at the Bar Mitzvah. Marriage brings special rings (a noteworthy collection is from northern Italy, seventeenth to nineteenth century), gifts (a silver box for keys and jewels, with niello engravings of the Jewish wife's chief religious duties is from Ferrara, Italy, fifteenth century), and the *ketuba*, or marriage contract. Although the text is standard, the illustrations vary greatly in style, content, and taste. A ketuba from Yemen has distorted faces, perhaps again a result of the second commandment, whereas an Italian ketuba has female angels influenced by the spirit and style of the Renaissance.

The final stage of the life cycle of the Jew is displayed by alms boxes belonging to the Hevra Kaddisha, the charitable and burial society. A large drinking vessel used at a fraternal order's annual banquet depicts a funeral procession and was made in Prague in 1713.

The Israel Museum's Judaica collection boasts two environments into which the visitor may enter. They are two actual synagogue interiors that were transferred to and reassembled inside the museum. The elegant Italian synagogue from Vittorio Veneto, north of Venice, about 1700, was a gift of Jakob Michael and shows abundant use of gold leaf, many forms of illumination, an Italian Baroque-style Torah ark at its eastern wall, and a niche for the *bimah*, or platform for reading of the Torah, at its opposite wall. The synagogue has a separate gallery upstairs for women who were allowed to observe the service through latticed windows.

The second synagogue interior is from the village of Horb, near Bamberg in southern Germany, and was donated by the Bamberg Municipality and Jakob Michael. An inscription informs us that in 1735 Eliezer Susmann painted the wooden interior with its menagerie of both realistic and mythical animals. The wooden-planked house of worship consisting of one room, without any women's section or gallery, was dismantled and placed in storage during the 1930s, thus saving it from later ravage by the Nazis.

Another major part of The Israel Museum's collection is its archaeology section. All finds excavated in Israel since 1948 belong to the government's Department of Antiquities and are housed in the Samuel Bronfman Biblical and Archaeological Museum on the premises of The Israel Museum. Finds made before 1948 are housed in the Rockefeller Museum located in east Jerusalem, which was placed under The Israel Museum's administration following the reunification of Jerusalem in 1967.

The archaeology collection is most comprehensive and ranges from local to neighboring cultures and includes the Classical world. It begins with prehistory; some objects are so ancient that they were discovered in layers that were geologically tilted after the object, such as a spear or an elephant tusk, had been deposited. The collection is arranged as follows: prehistory; the Chalcolithic period; Early, Middle, and Late Canaanite periods; ancient glass; Times of the Judges; the First Temple period; Persian period; Hebrew script and inscriptions; Second Temple period; Roman period; Byzantine period; Muslim and Crusader periods; and neighboring cultures. Additionally, a future site for Classical archaeology has been laid out.

A glimpse at the vast archaeology display reveals many interesting objects. Found near Beersheba, fourth millennium B.C., is an ivory figure, carved from an elephant tusk and probably brought from Africa via Egypt. It is affectionately known as *Pinocchio* to The Israel Museum visitors because of the figure's distinctive nose. Also from the fourth millennium B.C. and the Chalcolithic-Copper Age is a figure with an urn on its head, as well as a depiction of an ibex, a very important animal in that culture. The Copper Treasure contains 420 objects made about six thousand years ago at the end of the Chalcolithic period. They were discovered near En Gedi and are associated with the Dead Sea Scrolls. Although all of the objects are related to temple rites, no two are alike: incense buckets, spears, mace heads, and ibex heads on standards. Found in a tomb near Ramallah from the fifteenth to early fourteenth century B.C. is a silver cup with a Mesopotamian war inscription. Buried with a soldier, this cup represented war booty.

Several examples from the Late Canaanite period are thirteenth-century B.C. beetle-shaped scarab seals from Egypt, with personal inscriptions on the underside, as well as several delicate Mesopotamian cylinder seals, with cuniform-block-type writing. Found at Chatzor, they represent the first evidence of writing in the thirteenth century B.C. An Assyrian wall relief from Ninevah, Mesopotamia, shows the siege of Lachish of 701 B.C.

Also included in the display of archaeological finds are those from the Jewish quarter of the Old City of Jerusalem during the Roman period, including small stone fragments, a remnant of a mosaic floor, basalt mortars, large stone vessels, rectangular tables from a house of a high priest, and an etched, seven-branched Menorah bearing the Bible's commandments. Also from the first and second centuries A.D. are gold earrings, noserings, and pendants; an iron knife from the Bar-Kokba war period; ancient leather sandals, a linen belt, a ball of wool, and some keys, all dated 135; and a bronze statue of Roman Emperor Hadrian from the second century.

A mosaic floor from a synagogue at Beit Shean (sixth century), slipper-type oil lamps (eighth century), and a rare metal vessel with an inside inscription (twelfth century) are further examples of the wide variety found in this display.

The Joseph and Rebecca Meyerhoff Building houses the Eliyahu Dobkin Pavilion of Ancient Glass. On display are early glass objects from Cyprus, Egypt, Lachish, Persia, and the Eastern Mediterranean and from the Hellenistic and Roman periods. Particularly eye-catching are vases in violet and green (third-fourth century) and perfume bottles found in a burial cave (third century).

The Jacob and Ella Hecht Pavilion is devoted to Hebrew script and inscriptions. This didactic display of various alphabets is illustrated with ancient examples of Hebrew script. One such object is a Hebrew ostracon with a list of numerals, from Kadesh Barnea, seventh to sixth century B.C.

The Numismatics Gallery was donated courtesy of Bank Leumi le-Israel and in memory of Samuel Friedenberg of New York. This collection specializes in Jewish coins and medals. It includes: minting tools, Greek coins, coins of Persian period, coins of Jerusalem, "City Coins" (first-third century), coins of Romans in Judea and Hasmonean coinage, Bar-Kokba (132–35), coins commemorating historical events, and coins of the modern state of Israel whose motifs and symbols, such as the harp and lyre, vineleaf, grape clusters, pomegranates, and palm trees, are derived from ancient sources.

The neighboring cultures collection differs from the museum's archaeology collection in that these artifacts were acquired either as donations to The Israel Museum or were purchased on the antiquities market. These objects provide insight into the culture of Israel's neighbors and their ties, in turn, with the land of the Bible.

In antiquity Persia was a great center for painted pottery, and the museum has several hand-painted rhytons in the form of animals. Also on display from Persia are glazed tiles dating from the thirteenth century B.C. There are fine examples of third to first millennium bronze artifacts, such as horse trappings and bells, standards with human and animal heads, weapons, and pins. Fragments of monumental basalt statues from Pasargadae, built by Cyrus (550–530 B.C.), and silver and gilded vessels of fine quality from the Sassanian period in the third century B.C. are on exhibit.

From Mesopotamia are artifacts dating from the fourth millennium B.C. There are inscribed clay tablets in the Sumerian language; fine examples of the cylinder seal, regarded as a hallmark of their civilization; both naturalistic and mythological figures; and from the Akkadian rule, an inscribed bronze bowl.

From Anatolia there is painted pottery of high quality in the Geometric style from the sixth millennium. Highly developed metalcraft of the second millennium is seen in bronze and silver standards and gold jewelry found in royal tombs. Black and red burnished pottery from the Hittite rule is represented by a clay statuette of a warrior and a clay architectural tile decorated with a painting of a horse and rider.

Hand-made pottery from Cyprus is shown by a variety of tomb finds of the second half of the third millennium, revealing the diversity of their material culture as influenced by the local culture and trade contacts with neighboring countries. Other objects on display show contact with the Mycenean, Syrian, Palestinian, Phoenician, and Greek cultures.

The Israel Museum's collection of Islamic art from Iran is displayed in the Ayoub Rabenou Gallery. This art differs from that of other Moslem countries in that its inscriptions are in Persian Judaeo-Iranian written in Arabic script. Several of the oldest artifacts in this collection (ninth century) have calligraphy for decoration, since figurative art was forbidden. The collection excels in ceramics, famous for rich color and profuse ornamentation. Bronze objects from the twelfth century are on display, such as a perforated incense or perfume holder whose three interlocked animal figures are surmounted by two bulbous forms and a bird.

The display includes a seventeenth-century Isfahan silk carpet, with a garden design and a great prayer niche, or *mihrab*, made of interlocking tiles of the same origin and date, whose decorative inscriptions can be identified as suras forty-eight, eighty-nine, and ninety-six of the Koran.

The museum's section for Jewish ethnography was founded in 1965 at the time of the museum's inauguration. It is based upon two superlative collections: the Zalman Schocken Collection, acquired in Yemen by Carl Rathjens of Hamburg, and the collection of North African jewelry, purchased by Z. Schulmann through the initiative of the late Mordechai Narkiss.

Through systematic collecting of both ceremonial and secular objects, the Jewish Ethnography Section now contains about ten thousand items: costumes, jewelry, tapestries, humble work implements, and household articles. Items have been obtained from the various Jewish ethnic groups now dwelling in Israel but originally from Morocco, Bokhara, Iran, Kurdistan, Turkey, Afghanistan, and European countries.

The Romi and Helene Goldmuntz Gallery and the Lotte and Walter Floersheimer Pavilion display on rotation examples from the museum's collection of European painting—Old Masters, nineteenth-century art, Impressionist, Post-Impressionist, and modern art. Most of the collection consists of nineteenth- and twentieth-century art. A selection of the landscapes includes those by Monet, Sisley, Cézanne (*House by the River*, c. 1882), van Gogh (*Green Ears of Corn* and *Harvest in Provence*, both 1888), Gauguin (*Fire Dance*, 1891, and a *Still Life*, 1899), and Renoir (*Landscape*, 1888).

Representing the next generation of French painters are three paintings by Braque, as well as works by Pascin, Schiele, Soutine, Utrillo, and Feininger. Additionally, the collection features selections by Alechinsky, Appel, Bacon, Chagall, De Kooning, Kokoschka, Matta, Picasso, Soto, Soulages, and Vasarély.

A gallery devoted to works by the Old Masters was donated by Joseph and Madeleine Nash. Included are works by Dutch masters Jacob Gerritsz Cuyp, Aelbert Cuyp (*Portrait of a Family in a Landscape*, 1641), Govaert Flinck (*Venus and Cupid*), Gabriel Metsu (*The Sacrifice of Isaac*), and Jan Victors (*Expulsion of Hagar*).

A special display area, given in memory of Max Goldmuntz, is dedicated to Jewish artists who perished in the Holocaust. Selections from the Caroline and Joseph Gruss Collection and The Israel Museum's own collection are displayed on a rotating basis.

The Israel Museum has four European period rooms. Most impressive is the French Rococo period room donated by the family of Baron and Baroness Edmond de Rothschild, purchased by the baron in 1887 and installed in his own Parisian hôtel. It was formerly the Grand Salon of the Hôtel Samuel-Bernard, designed in 1740–45 by the architect Boffrand and done in the style of Louis XV. Credit for the design of the room itself has been given to the brothers Verbercht (whose design for the Cabinet Intérieur at Versailles was produced five years later). The luxurious French Rococo interior has all surfaces sumptuously decorated: oak paneling with gilded carving in relief; corner panels representing the Four Seasons; the portrait of a lady, *Diana*, by Nattier; the life-size marble *Diana*; four oil paintings representing the Four Continents; gilded paneling; moldings; a great mirror; a *brech violette* marble chimneypiece; ormolu hardware on doors and windows; and the salon's original wood parquet floor. Tapestries made under the direction of Cozette at the Royal Gobelins Manufactory are inscribed with dates of 1771 and 1787. The furniture—ormolu and crystal chandeliers, an ormolu candelabra, fire dogs, a writing table, writing accessories, armchairs, a table and carpet—is for the most part contemporary with the salon.

The three remaining period rooms were acquired through several donations: the Empire period room, courtesy of Henri Samuels (with the John Simons Collection of early-eighteenth-century porcelain on display); the eighteenth-century Venetian period room, the gift of Mr. and Mrs. Renato Bacchi together with the eighteenth-century Italian Art Pavilion donated by Carlo and Gianna Schapira; and the eighteenth-century English period room given by Ida Berg.

The museum's Department of Prints and Drawings is based on a collection that is as old as the Bezalel National Museum. Like the Bezalel collection, it is now part of The Israel Museum's holdings. This collection numbers about sixty thousand works, which come from diverse sources.

Between six to eight exhibits are presented during a calendar year in the Barbara and Isadore M. Cohen Gallery. In addition, the Graphic Study Room is open to the public on a daily basis during specified hours.

The collection's oldest work is a twelfth-century Fatimid drawing. The highlight of the collection of Old Master drawings (mostly Italian and Netherlandish) is one by Rembrandt.

The prints and drawings collection includes works by Rodin, Jongkind, Pissarro, Toulouse-Lautrec, van Gogh, Léger, Chagall, Lipchitz, Miró, Signac, and Feininger. Works by Goya include *The Caprichos*, *The Disasters of War*, and *The Tauromaquia*. There are eleven drawings by Paul Klee. Other contemporary artists such as Rauschenberg, Jasper Johns, Jim Dine, Tilson, Lichtenstein, and Warhol are represented. More than eighty drawings by Jules Pascin were donated by the artist's brother. There are also five hundred prints by Picasso anonymously donated. Works by Israeli artists such as Anna Ticho form part of the collection as well.

The museum's Department of Israeli Art is displayed in galleries donated by George de Menasce and Caroline and Joseph Gruss. The collection has works by more than 130 artists spanning from the start of the century to the present.

Among the earliest works are paintings by Abel Pann, a teacher at Israel's first official art institution, the Bezalel School of Arts and Crafts. Works from the 1920s by Reuven Rubin, Nahum Gutman, Israel Paldi, and Siona Tagger display the first glimpse of modernism. Works by Jacob Steinhardt and Mordechai Ardon in the 1930s demonstrate the important influence brought by immigrants from Germany. Ardon's *The Gates of Jerusalem*, a large triptych dominating the gallery, was painted to commemorate Israel's twentieth anniversary of independence in 1968 and the 1967 reunification of Jerusalem.

Paintings by Pinhas Litvinovsky, Moshe Castel, and Menahem Shemi show influences absorbed in Paris during the 1930s. Joseph Zaritsky, Avigdor Stematsky, Yehezkel Streichman, Marcel Janco, and Avigdor Arikha's works of the 1950s and 1960s reveal the trend toward abstract art. Avant-garde artists, such as Joshua Neustein, Pinhas Cohen-Gan, and Bennie Efrat, are represented by means of annual purchases by the museum. The collection's permanent display is supplemented by periodic temporary exhibitions, both group and one-person shows. The new Pavilion of Israeli Art is in the construction stage at present.

The museum's Design Department was opened in 1973 in the Isadore and Sarah Palevsky Pavilion. The overall approach is educational, concentrating on temporary exhibits devoted to architecture, graphics, industry, and social planning.

Its permanent collection includes a superb selection of European posters from the early part of the twentieth century to the present. The Design Department's modest but continually expanding permanent collection has outstanding examples of products designed in Scandinavia, western Europe, and the United States. The department hopes that its collection and exhibitions will serve for both producers and consumers in Israel as an example for the establishment of a high standard of quality in design and production.

In 1979 The Israel Museum redirected and broadened its approach to artistic creativity throughout the world by establishing the Department of Ethnic Arts. The art, history, and culture of Africa, pre-Columbian Indians, American Indians, and the Pacific Islands will be presented to a public that until the present has had little exposure to or knowledge of these cultures.

The second part of the Maremont Pavilion of Ethnic Arts was opened in 1980. Both ceremonial and utilitarian objects from North American Indian, Australian, Polynesian, New Guinean, Indonesian, and Melanesian tribal societies are on permanent display. The museum owns a large pre-Columbian collection, for which a permanent exhibition area is being planned.

The Israel Museum has had a special section with facilities devoted to youth since its inception. In 1978 the Ruth Rodman Frieman Youth Wing was dedicated. It is one of the most active and largest educational facilities for youth in the world, its ground area comprising 8 percent of the total museum space.

Youth activities concentrate on four main subject areas: guided tours for schoolchildren, publications for children and teachers (chiefly in Hebrew), art classes for children and adults, and didactic exhibitions that, in most cases, have activity corners for participation by museum visitors. Entrance fees are minimal. The Youth Wing possesses an extensive collection of toys and dolls; facilities for their permanent display are being planned.

The Israel Museum's collection of modern sculpture, donated in large part by the late Billy Rose, is situated in an outdoor sculpture garden named after the donor. The Billy Rose Art Garden was designed by Isamu Noguchi, the Japanese-American architect and sculptor. Laid out in 1965, it is situated between The Israel Museum complex and the Shrine of the Book and commands a view of the Hebrew University's Givat Ram campus and the Israeli Knesset building. The sculptures are situated, with large intervals of space between each piece, upon and within undulating terraces whose retaining walls and formations echo the topography of the surrounding Jerusalem hills.

The collection spans the late nineteenth century to the present and includes works by major European and American artists as well as by contemporary Israeli sculptors. Alongside works exhibited in the outdoor garden are works displayed on a rotating basis in indoor pavilions. They include works by Gauguin,

Daumier, Renoir, Degas, Matisse, Rodin, Armitage, Arp, Archipenko, Duchamp Villon, Marcel Duchamp, Giacometti, Nevelson, Pevsner, Stankiewicz, and Segal.

In the outdoor art garden are works by Rodin (*Adam* and a study of *Balzac*), Bourdelle (*La Grande Penelope* and *Warrior of Montauban*), Maillol (*Liberty in Chains* and *L'Harmonie*), Archipenko (*Standing Woman*), and Zadkine (*Orpheus*, or *The Poet*), all done in the late nineteenth or early twentieth century.

Sculptures of more recent vintage include works by Picasso (*Profile*, cast concrete made for and on the site in 1967), Henry Moore (two bronzes: *Reclining Figure*, 1953–54; *Upright Motif No. 7*, 1955–56), Calder (*Mobile—Stabile*, 1966), Vasarély (*Screen*), Lipchitz (*Mother and Child* and *Europa II*), Epstein (*Visitation*, 1926), Chadwick, Butler, David Smith, Tinguely (*Kinetic Sculpture, XK 1965*, operated by electricity), Arman, Volten (*Construction*), and Hepworth.

Works by Israeli sculptors include those by David Palombo (known for his *Gates of the Knesset* nearby), Igael Tumarkin (*Sculpture*, of fire-arm parts, 1967), Yaakov Agam, Shlomo Koren, Menashe Kadishman, Michael Gross, Buky Schwarz, Ivan Schwebel, and Ezra Urion.

A final and vital part of the The Israel Museum's sculpture collection is 140 bronze sketches by Jacques Lipchitz, which are housed in a pavilion named after him. This is one of the most comprehensive collections of his work.

As one approaches The Israel Museum complex to the right, one encounters the Shrine of the Book, the D. Samuel and Jeanne H. Gottesman Center for Biblical Manuscripts, known for its exhibit of the Dead Sea Scrolls. The shrine is a white dome juxtaposed with a black basalt rectangular block designed by Frederick Kiesler and Armand Bartos. It was erected in 1965, concurrent with the construction of The Israel Museum building.

One walks through a tunnel, similar to the experience of descending into a cave, where the Bar-Kokba letters (written in Hebrew, Aramaic, and Greek, on papyrus, c. A.D. 135) and the Bataba letters (in Hebrew, Aramaic, Nabatean, and Greek, turn of the first century A.D.) are on display.

The main hall, under the dome, resembles the interior of a hand-wrought clay pot. It contains the Dead Sea Scrolls, discovered in 1947 at the caves of Qumran. Written in Hebrew on parchment, they are the oldest-known biblical manuscripts in the world. The largest and oldest is the Book of Isaiah, which is more than one thousand years older than any other known biblical manuscript complete in form. Part of the original scroll is on display. Its facsimile is displayed in a raised central platform, which has at its center a sculpted form that resembles an oversized handle for a Torah scroll.

The Shrine of the Book has, in addition to these manuscripts, a display of objects found in the caves with the scrolls. They include glass vessels; bronze jugs; textile fragments; iron keys; a polished bronze mirror; a wooden-handled sickle, which is the only complete sickle from the ancient world; bronze incense shovels; and palm baskets. These artifacts (A.D. 135) are all in an excellent state of preservation due to the arid climatic condition of the caves. They shed valuable light on the everyday life of the people who sought refuge within the caves by the Dead Sea.

The museum periodically changes its exhibitions of objects in the permanent collection, including the recently developed contemporary design collection. It has a library of eighty thousand books and subscribes to 250 periodicals. Its holdings relate to art, archaeology, Judaica, and ethnography. Meant for the museum's curators, it is open also to the public but is noncirculating. Acquisition of titles is made according to the needs of the museum and its various departments.

Photographs of objects in the collection may be ordered from the museum's photographic archives, which are open to the public and publishers alike. Copies of past and current exhibition catalogues are available at the gift shop, as are books dealing with topics parallel to the museum's chief holdings.

The Israel Museum publishes a monthly bulletin, *This Month at the Israel Museum*, in Hebrew and English. It is available to museum members, visitors, schools, and hotels. The museum also publishes *The Israel Museum News*, which has been an annual for the past twelve years and has directed itself to museum friends and donors as a summary of museum events. The museum is now planning to issue this publication three times a year in addition to continuing its annual *News* on a more scholarly and detailed level. A third category of publication is a newsletter; only one issue had come out as of 1985. Finally, the museum publishes catalogues, usually in both Hebrew and English (or a second major European language), that accompany exhibitions and are available for purchase in the museum's gift shop. To date, the museum has published 222 catalogues meant for an adult audience. The Youth Wing has published in Hebrew 25 pamphlets for children.

Selected Bibliography

Museum publications: *The Israel Museum: A brief guide*, 1971, 2d ed. 1975, *Guides' Unedited Notes*, Winter 1981; *The Billy Rose Art Garden*, 1965; *Guide to Ethnographic Collecting*, n.d.; *The Samuel Bronfman Biblical and Archaeological Museum*, provisional guide, 1965; Schwartz-Nardi, Shulamith, *The Shrine of the Book and Its Scrolls*, 1965.

Other publications: Aarhus, Moesgaard Museum, *Exhibition and Ethnic Image: Exhibition of an Immigrant Group's Culture in Israel—Problems and Effects* (Aarhus 1974); Katz, Karl, *From the Beginning, Archeology and Art in the Israel Museum, Jerusalem* (London 1968); Mansfeld, Alfred, "Implemented Design System, 1959—The Israel Museum, Jerusalem," in *Designing for Growth and Change with Open-Ended Cumulative Systems* (Haifa 1976); Pomerantz, Louis, *Restoration and Conservation of Paintings in the Israel Museum* (Paris 1969); Shachar, Isaiah, *The Jewish Year* (Leiden 1975); Benedek, Yvette E., "Letter from Israel: A New Photography Collection Makes a Stunning Debut," *American Photographer*, vol. 6, no. 3 (March 1981), pp. 88–90; Biran, A.; Kahane, P. P.; Broshi, M.; Gordon, A. and Hestrin, R., "The Israel Museum, Jerusalem," *Museum, Paris*, vol 20, no. 1 (1967); Flaxer, Niza, "Der (Youth Wing) des Israel Museums in Jerusalem," *Werk*, vol. 60, no. 1 (January 1973), pp. 82–83; Frackman, Noel, "Is this the world's most unusual museum?" *Arts Magazine*, vol. 52, no. 2 (October

1977), pp. 92–101; Gad, Dora, and Mansfeld, Alfred, "Israel's Museum," *Interiors* (October 1966), pp. 108–20; "The Israel Museum," *Art International*, vol. 9, no. 6 (September 1965), pp. 25–42; Ronnen, Meir, "Preserving the Past, Securing the Future," *Art News, New York*, vol. 70, no. 5 (May 1978), pp. 57–62; Roth, Cecil, "Jewish Ritual Art in the Israel Museum," *Art International*, vol. 9, no. 6 (September 1965), pp. 23–24; Sandberg, W., "The Israel Museum in Jerusalem," *Museum, Paris*, vol. 19, no. 1 (1966), pp. 15–30; Spencer, Charles C., "The Israel National Museum," *Studio International*, vol. 170, no. 868 (August 1965); Weiner, Sheila L., "The Wolf Ladejinsky Collection of Asian Art in the Israel Museum, Jerusalem," *Oriental Art, London*, vol. 26, no. 1 (Spring 1980), pp. 122–26; Weyl, Martin, "The Israel Museum," *Arts of Asia, Hong Kong*, vol. 5, no. 4 (July-August 1975), pp. 25–32; idem, "The Israel Museum: A personal note of the chief curator of the arts," *Arts Magazine, New York*, vol. 52, no. 2 (October 1977), pp. 90–91.

LEAH TOURKIN BAR-Z'EV

Italy

———— Bologna ————

NATIONAL PICTURE GALLERY OF BOLOGNA (officially LA PINA-COTECA NAZIONALE DI BOLOGNA; also LA REGIA PINACOTECA DI BOLOGNA, LA PINACOTECA DELLA PONTIFICIA ACCADEMIA DELLE BELLE ARTI IN BOLOGNA), Via Belle Arti, 56, 40126 Bologna.

The origins of the Pinacoteca Nazionale, Bologna date from 1712, the year of the founding in Bologna of the Instituto delle Scienze e delle Arti. The formation of a permanent picture gallery as part of the academy of fine arts, the Accademia Clementina di Belli Arti, was decreed in 1796 by Napoleon. In 1803 the collection was installed in its present quarters, the former Jesuit novitiate. The holdings grew considerably in 1815, when the Napoleonic spoils taken from the churches of Bologna were returned from Paris. Throughout the nineteenth century the collection increased steadily with the addition of private holdings such as the Zambeccari Collection (1884). More recently, many new acquisitions have been installed, ranging from a trecento cycle of frescoes to canvases executed by the great masters of the Baroque. At present the Pinacoteca is governed by the Soprintendenza per i Beni Artistici e Storici (Superintendency of Artistic and Historic Properties) for the region of Bologna, a subdivision of the Ministero per i Beni Culturali e Ambientali (Ministry of Cultural Properties).

Under the vital leadership of two prominent directors, Cesare Gnudi and Andrea Emiliani, the Pinacoteca was transformed during the last three decades into one of Italy's most attractive and progressive museums. These directors saw as their task the guardianship of an outstanding heritage of Bolognese painting and its use by a diverse public. The most obvious indication of enlightened leadership is the strikingly modern appearance of the gallery, which was reno-vated after 1950 primarily under the sensitive guidance of the architect Leone

Pancaldi. No visitor to the museum can fail to admire the large, simple rooms constructed of marble and concrete, amply lit and well suited to the scale of the pictures.

As is the case with most Italian museums, the collection is intimately related to the art history of the province. The paintings are arranged to emphasize three major phases of artistic activity—proto-Renaissance, Renaissance, and Baroque. Moreover, they are gathered into groups that stress relationships between masters and schools within a chronological framework. The viewer is subtly made aware that the strategic geographical location of Bologna, the capital of Emilia, ensured that its artists were susceptible to influences from both Northern and Central Italy. An essentially conservative climate during the early phases of the Renaissance gradually yielded to the revolutionary efforts of a school of international significance at the end of the sixteenth century.

The Emilian proto-Renaissance first emerged in the late thirteenth century, and it was in Bologna that the reaction against the Byzantine style and the absorption of proto-Renaissance forms developed. The works of the major figure of the early fourteenth century, Vitale da Bologna, are characterized by a tense and dramatic handling of narrative and strikingly daring compositions. These elements appear in his earliest-known painting, the large fresco the *Last Supper with Four Saints* (c. 1340), formerly in the refectory of San Francesco, Bologna, and now in the Pinacoteca, as well as the more mature *St. George Slaying the Dragon* (c. 1355) and the panels *Scenes of the Life of St. Anthony Abbot.*

A similarly dynamic and expressive style may be seen in the numerous altarpieces by other Emilian Primitives that are displayed in the Pinacoteca. For example, the Bolognese painter Simone de' Crocifissi is represented by several works, including the *Madonna and Child with St. Helena*; Tommaso da Modena, whose artistic education took place in Bologna, may be studied in his *Polyptic.* A general dependency on Late Gothic sources for a lively imagery may be seen in both the *Polyptic with Biblical Scenes* and the fresco the *Battle of Clarjo* by Jacopino di Francesco. As a rule, the forms of the Emilian proto-Renaissance contrast considerably with the more composed and grave volumes of contemporary Tuscan painting, a point easily understood by turning to the polyptic the *Virgin with Saints* by Giotto and his followers or Lorenzo Monaco's *Enthroned Madonna and Child.*

The most impressive evidence of fourteenth-century activity in Emilia is the cycle of frescoes from the former church of Sant'Apollonia di Mezzaratta (c. 1350), which were detached in 1949 to forestall further deterioration. The paintings of the altar wall, which include the *Annunciation* and *Nativity*, are probably by Vitale da Bologna, whereas the other scenes are by members of his school, notably Simone de' Crocifissi and Jacopo da Bologna.

The Early Renaissance in Emilia did not match the brilliance of that in Tuscany, but by the mid-fifteenth century the new Florentine ideals were penetrating in the North, first in Ferrara, then Bologna. Various members of the Ferrarese school brought to Bologna an elaborate linear style, by turns harsh and poetic.

Francesco del Cossa was the first to arrive in the 1470s, and his major work, the *Altarpiece of the Merchants* (1474), may be viewed in the Pinacoteca. Ercole di Roberti, who was in Bologna by the late 1470s, is represented by two fragments, *St. George* and a head from the frescoed *Deposition*, formerly in the Garganelli Chapel, San Pietro di Bologna. Lorenzo Costa, who settled in Bologna in 1493 and stayed well into the sixteenth century, had the greatest impact on Bolognese painting, because his soft Peruginesque style was easily accessible (e.g., *St. Petronius with St. Francis and St. Domenic*). Perugino himself supplied works for the churches of the city; his *Madonna in Glory*, originally in San Giovanni in Monte (1494), was a major source of influence. The result of all of this activity was the rise of several Bolognese masters whose art reflected the general tone of late quattrocento classicism current throughout Umbria and Emilia. The greatest of such figures represented in the Pinacoteca is Francesco Francia, with works such as the *Scappi Madonna*, the *Annunciation with St. Jerome and the Baptist*, and the sublime panel from the Pala Felicini, the *Dead Christ Supported by Angels* (1494). An interesting variant of classicism is provided by Amico Aspertini. Although his career spans the High Renaissance, his eccentric bias sets him apart from developments in Central Italy (e.g., the *Tirocinio Altar*, c. 1504).

No single work by an Emilian artist of the High Renaissance period had so profound an effect on Northern Italian painting as Raphael's extraordinary *St. Cecilia* altarpiece (c. 1514), originally in the church of San Giovanni in Monte. The Bolognese school of Raphaelesque imitators is often disconcertingly shallow in its endless variations on the classical formulae provided by the *St. Cecilia* and other altarpieces—there are examples in the Pinacoteca of the work of Bagnacavallo and Innocenzo Francucci da Imola—but Raphael's grace also affected later generations of Mannerist and Baroque artists of greater skill. A painting that occupied a position of authority comparable to the *St. Cecilia* was produced only a little more than a decade later; Parmigianino's *Madonna with St. Margaret* for the church of Santa Margareta (1529) dates from the four-year period of the master's sojourn in Bologna after fleeing the Sack of Rome. In it, the great master of *maniera* acknowledged his debt to Correggio, whose *Madonna of St. Jerome* he had known in his native town of Parma, as well as to Raphael, whose Roman works provided the starting point for Parmigianino's elegant distortions of form. Secular works in the *maniera* style were also carried out in the capital city. The frescoes depicting courtly life painted by the Modenese artist Niccolò dell'Abbate in the Palazzo Torfanini (1548–52) are now installed in the museum.

Venetian painting of the Renaissance, only minimally represented in the gallery, can be viewed in Antonio and Bartolomeo Vivarini's polyptic *Virgin with Saints* (1450), Tintoretto's brilliant *Visitation*, and Jacopo Palma Giovane's *Crucifixion*.

The most memorable section of the Pinacoteca, judged in terms of presentation and museum architecture, is unquestionably that housing the Late Mannerist and

Baroque collection. At its entrance the visitor leaves the sequence of altarpieces, normal in scale and conducive to intimate communication, and enters a suite of large rooms in the *grande galerie* tradition, where paintings of vast dimensions overwhelm his sensibilities. The orchestration of this area, consisting of a sequence of spaces differentiated according to size, lighting, and levels in space, provides an exhilarating experience few other Italian museums can match. The works themselves, in the secularized atmosphere of a picture gallery, are offered up less as religious images (the original function of most) than as supreme works of art rivaling modern painting in terms of scale, brushwork, color, and at times high realism or, alternatively, abstraction. Most of these paintings are by Bolognese artists, offering proof that a school of the first rank was established here by the period of the Early Baroque.

A series of Late Mannerist altarpieces by Bolognese artists is displayed in the company of Giorgio Vasari's *Feast of St. Gregory*: Bartolomeo Passarotti's remarkable *Resurrection* (c. 1570) and *Presentation in the Temple* (c. 1583), Prospero Fontana's *Lamentation*, and Pellegrino Tibaldi's *Mystic Marriage of St. Catherine*. The Flemish Mannerist Denys Calvaert, who opened a studio in Bologna, may be studied in his *Presentation in the Temple* and other works.

It was precisely the Mannerist emphasis on complicated form at the expense of the clear handling of the subject that moved the bishop of Bologna, Gabriele Paleotti, to set down certain rules for religious images in his *Discourse on Sacred and Profane Pictures* (two of five projected volumes were published in 1582). Paleotti stressed the need for accuracy, clarity, decorum, and emotional stimuli to devotion. These very qualities are present in the works of the new generation of the late sixteenth century, such as Bartolomeo Cesi's *St. Anne Adoring the Virgin of the Immaculate Conception* (1600), in which the Immaculata, clothed in the sun, moon, and stars, is surrounded by the symbols of the Ark of the Covenant, the Temple of David, the Spotless Mirror, and the Throne of Wisdom.

Palleotti's call seems to have been answered to the letter by the chief innovative geniuses of the Bolognese school, the three Carracci who around 1585 banded together to create an informal academy. In the large room devoted to the Carracci, Annibale is represented by several pre-Roman works that combine the honesty and vigor of his early "realist" style with the rich color and compositional details of Venice: the *Annunciation* (c. 1587), the *Madonna with Six Saints* (1589–90), and the *Assumption* (1592). Agostino, the chief theoretician of the Carracci school, whose great knowledge of sixteenth-century sources is borne out by the reproductive prints he produced on his extensive travels, is represented by two prime examples, the *Last Communion of St. Jerome* and the *Assumption of the Virgin* (both 1591–93). Ludovico's work surprises the visitor to the Pinacoteca with its powerful effects of light and color and its strongly emotional content. From the early works of the 1580s, such as the *Annunciation* and the *Conversion of St. Paul* with their strong references to Tintoretto, to the late *Martyrdom of St. Angelus* (1608–10), it is clear that Ludovico's style was influential in bringing about the dynamic strain of the Baroque, which many of his followers took to

Rome. Yet Ludovico's art is one of many moods, ranging from the poetic *Bargellini Madonna* and the intimate *Madonna degli Scalzi* to the brutal pendants the *Flagellation* and *Crowning with Thorns* (1594–95).

After leaving the Carracci room, the viewer descends a dramatic flight of stairs into a chamber devoted to the work of Guido Reni, a senior member of the Carracci school, who left the Mannerist studio of Calvaert to enter the more progressive academy in 1595. Directly opposite the stair hangs the huge *Pietà of the Mendicants* (1614–16), wherein the patron saints of Bologna, Petronius, Dominic, Charles Borromeo, Francis, and Procalo, are ranged about a model of the city with its famous leaning towers. Reni's characteristic search for classical beauty led to a personal, often affected exquisiteness, that may be seen in the *Samson* (1620) and the *Plague Ex-Voto* (1630–31). Among other works by the master, the portrait presumed to be of the *Artist's Mother* is particularly well known.

Another of the classicist followers of the Carracci was Domenichino, whose career was chiefly centered in Rome. The Pinacoteca contains examples of his style, such as the *St. Peter Martyr* and the *Portrait of a Cardinal*. Guercino, whose native town of Cento is near Bologna, was not part of the academy, but he took an interest in Venetian painting comparable to that of the Carracci, and he deeply admired the style of Ludovico. His energetic Baroque style may be seen in the *Investiture of St. William of Aquitaine* (1620) and the *St. Sebastian Nursed by St. Irene*. Examples of his soft late style are the *St. Peter Martyr* and the beautiful portrait heads *St. Joseph* and the *Baptist*. Certain lesser members of the Carracci school may also be mentioned here. The followers of Ludovico include Giacomo Cavedoni, represented by the altarpiece *Sant' Alo* (1614), and Alessandro Tiarini, whose dramatic chiaroscuro is best exemplified by his *Deposition* (1617) and *Death of the Virgin*. Two pupils of Reni achieved special merit: G. F. Gessi (*St. Francis*) and Simone Cantarini (several works, among which the touching *Portrait of Reni* is one of the most moving images in the gallery). These paintings by the Carracci successors are installed in the corridor and adjoining rooms leading off the Reni salon. There are in addition examples from other schools, such as Artemesia Gentileschi's *Judith* in a strongly Caravaggesque mode.

A gradual transition in scale and mood may be discerned between Emilian paintings of the seventeenth century and those of the eighteenth century, located in the post-Reni chambers as well as in the corridor displaying drawings. Cabinet pictures by the lesser-known figures Giovan Antonio Burrini and Vittorio Maria Bigari are found here, as well as several portraits and genre scenes such as *Hamlet* (c. 1705) by the great Bolognese genius of the Late Baroque, Giuseppe Maria Crespi. A general lightening of the palette may be observed in the eighteenth-century works of the Gandolfi brothers, Ubaldo and Gaetano. There are superb drawings by both on view, and the latter's dramatic *Wedding at Cana* (1755) from the refectory of San Salvatore, Bologna, astonishes the visitor at the entrance to the museum.

The climax to this perigrination through Emilian painting is the unforgettable spectacle of the great salon at the end of the Baroque section. Although the room serves as an auditorium for lectures, slide presentations, and symposia, it is also the locale housing several huge Baroque altarpieces, each dominating its own facet of the octagonal wall surface. The chief works are Ludovico Carracci's *Transfiguration* (1593), with gigantic Michelangelesque figures in a bluish grey atmosphere, and Federico Barocci's moving *Lamentation*, its sweeping spatial organization unified by a magical palette emphasizing orange and green. Domenichino shows surprising moments of keen realism in two works, the *Institution of the Rosary* and the *Martyrdom of St. Agnes*, while Francesco Albani, another Carracci pupil, is represented by his lyrically classical *Baptism of Christ*. This triumphant conclusion leaves little doubt that whatever the changing fortunes of the Bolognese school, its zenith was reached in the seventeenth century.

The Pinacoteca Nazionale has an art library and a photographic archive. Frequent special exhibitions, which may be held in various locations in Bologna, are the responsibility of the staff. Photographs of holdings may be obtained; according to law, the Gallery may not sell museum publications, but they are available at news kiosks and bookstores in Bologna or may be ordered through a book dealer.

Selected Bibliography

Selected publications: Emiliani, Andrea, *La Pinacoteca nazionale di Bologna* (Bologna 1968); Freedberg, Sydney J., *Painting in Italy, 1500–1600* (Baltimore 1975); Emiliani, Andrea, *La Pinacoteca nazionale di Bologna* (Bologna 1968); Giordani, Gaetano, *Catalogo dei quadri che si conservano nella Pinacoteca della Pontificia Accademia di Belle Arti in Bologna* (Bologna 1826; succ. ed. 1827, 1829, 1835, 1839, 1844); Guadagnini, Anacleto, *R. Pinacoteca di Bologna, Catalogo dei quadri* (Bologna 1899; rev. ed. 1903); Masini, Cesare, *Storia della Pinacoteca di Bologna* (Bologna 1888); Mauceri, Enrico, *La R. Pinacoteca di Bologna* (Rome 1935); Panzacchi, Enrico, *Brevi cenni storici intorno alla Pinacoteca della R. Accademia di Belle Arti in Bologna* (Bologna 1872).

ROBERT NEUMAN

———— Florence ————

ACADEMY GALLERY (officially GALLERIA DELL'ACCADEMIA; also ACCADEMIA DI BELLE ARTI, REAL GALLERIA D'ARTE ANTICA E MODERNA), Via Ricasoli 30, Florence.

Although now part of the national museum system of the Italian state and under the administration of the Florentine Soprintendenza (q.v. Uffizi Gallery), the Galleria dell'Accademia, founded in 1784, originally served as the study collection for the still-adjacent Accademia di Belle Arti, the principal art school and academy of the city. The Accademia itself can trace its origins as an institution to the early fourteenth century, when its forerunner, the Compagnia di San Luca, was established as a guildlike semireligious society of Florentine artists. Reorganized in the mid-sixteenth century under Medici patronage as the Accademia delle Arti del Disegno (Academy of the Drawing Arts), the organization functioned for more than two centuries as the city's principal professional institution of the visual arts.

In 1784 Grand Duke Leopold gave added direction to the Accademia by ordering the merging of the miscellaneous drawing schools in the city into a central institution, now called the Accademia di Belle Arti, with governmental support and authority, for the teaching of art in Florence. As part of this reorganization, a gallery was established within the new (and present) home of the Academy—the deconsecrated church, monastery, and hospital of San Matteo and the adjacent convent of San Niccolò.

The Accademia had already assembled a small group of works of art; to this numerous paintings, chiefly of the Tuscan schools, were added—many in 1786 and in the years 1808–10. Almost all of these works came to the Gallery from local churches and religious institutions, usually as state property from these suppressed organizations. Although subsequent transfers and exchanges among the Accademia, Palatine Gallery, Pitti Palace (q.v.), and Uffizi Gallery have altered the profile of the collection, the ecclesiastic provenance of so many of the pictures evidences itself today in the preponderance of altarpieces and smaller devotional panels.

For many years the Gallery was known as the Real Galleria d'Arte Antica e Moderna, the appellation "Modern" deriving from the collection of contemporary paintings that were exhibited at the Accademia beginning in 1859. They were the pictures that formed the nucleus of the Galleria d'Arte Moderna (q.v.) upon the establishment of that institution in the Palazzo Pitti in 1913.

The single most imposing and important addition to the Accademia's collections occurred in 1873, when Michelangelo's colossal *David* was transferred there from its position in front of the Palazzo Vecchio (a copy by the Florentine sculptor Pio Fedi replaced the original outside). Since its creation in 1504, the sculpture had remained exposed to the elements in its al fresco location; it was moved to protect it from further weathering. A special building, the Tribuna, was built in 1882 to house the gigantic marble (which measures, without its base, about thirteen and a half feet); other works by Michelangelo transferred to the Accademia were placed on exhibit in the long hall preceding the *David*.

The four unfinished *Slaves* (or *Prisoners*) were brought from their positions as decorative elements in the grotto of the Boboli Gardens, adjacent to the Pitti Palace, in 1909. They had been carved by Michelangelo probably in the early 1520s (the dating ranges from 1519 to 1536) as part of the projected tomb of Pope Julius II. An earlier addition to the Accademia had been Michelangelo's *St. Matthew*, an unfinished marble of 1505 and the only surviving work from a planned series of the twelve apostles for the Cathedral of Florence; it was transferred from the cathedral's Opera del Duomo in 1834.

From the Accademia del Disegno's collection comes the terracotta *River God*, perhaps a study for a figure in the Medici chapel; this work had been sold after Michelangelo's death by the artist's nephew Lionardo to Cosimo I de' Medici, from whom it passed to the sculptor Bartolomeo Ammanati, who later gave it to the Academy. Here as well is the *Palestrina Pietà*—purchased for the Accademia by the Italian government in 1939—a work by either Michelangelo in old age or, more likely, a seventeenth-century follower.

Also on exhibit in the left "transept" of the Tribuna are two life-size plaster groups of Giambologna; they are the original models for the marble statues *The Rape of the Sabines* in the Loggia dei Lanzi and *Virtue Dominating Vice* (or *Florence Vanquishing Pisa*), now in the Bargello (q.v.).

The picture collection today concentrates on Florentine works of the thirteenth through the sixteenth century; it serves to supplement and complement works of the same period on exhibit in the Galleria degli Uffizi, where many of the most notable pictures from the Accademia were transferred in 1913. Of special interest among the early paintings remaining in the Accademia are the following: the thirteenth-century panel *Magdalene with Eight Scenes from Her Life* by the eponymous Master of the Magdalene (also by this artist are the two fragments *Scenes from the Life of St. John the Evangelist*); the polyptych *Crucifixion with Saints*, signed and indistinctly dated in the 1310s by Pacino di Buonaguida; the allegorical *Tree of the Cross* and the *Madonna and Child*, attributed to the same artist; the *Madonna and Child with Two Angels and Four Saints* by Andrea di Cione, called Orcagna; the *Trinity with Saints*, 1365, by his elder brother, Nardo di Cione; the *Coronation of the Virgin with Saints*, one of several works in the collection by Orcagna's younger brother, Jacopo di Cione; the triptych *Vision of St. Bernard* by the Master of the Rinuccini Chapel; fourteen *Scenes from the Life of Christ* and ten *Scenes from the Life of St. Francis*, which with four panels in Berlin and Munich comprise Taddeo Gaddi's painted cupboard doors from the sacristy of the church of Santa Croce in Florence; the *Coronation of the Virgin with Saints* by Niccolò di Tommaso; several pictures by Bernardo Daddi and his followers; the unique signed polyptych of Puccio di Simone Fiorentino; two triptychs by Giovanni del Biondo; the *Pietà* by Giovanni da Milano; and *Two Saints* and the attributed *Annunciation* by Andrea Bonaiuti da Firenze.

Fifteenth-century works include several pictures by Lorenzo Monaco, most important of which is the *Annunciation* triptych from the Badia; two works by unknown painters that have served as starting points in the reconstruction of their identities, *The Wedding of Boccaccio Adimari and Lisa Ricasoli* by the Master of the Adimari Cassone and the *Nativity* by the Master of the Castello Nativity (the painting comes from the Medici Villa at Castello); the *Trinity with Saints* by Alessio Baldovinetti; the *Madonna and Child with Saints* by Cosimo Rosselli; and works attributed to or from the workshops of Sandro Botticelli, Domenico di Michelino, Lorenzo di Credi, Francesco Botticini, and Domenico Ghirlandaio.

A series of large altarpieces from the sixteenth century are exhibited together, including Mariotto Albertinelli's *Annunciation* of 1510 and *Madonna and Child with Four Saints*; Pietro Perugino's *Assumption of the Virgin*; the *Deposition of Christ*, begun by Perugino and completed by Filippino Lippi, and the latter's *St. John the Baptist* and *Mary Magdalene*; the *Dispute of the Doctors of the Church* by Giovantonio Sogliani; the *Vision of St. Bernard* and the prophets *Job* and *Isaiah* by Fra Bartolomeo; the *Penitent St. Jerome* by Bartolomeo di Giovanni; the *Madonna and Child with Saints* by Ridolfo del Ghirlandaio; and the *Madonna della Cintola* and *Assumption with Saints* by Francesco Granacci. Other works from the period include Agnolo Bronzino's *Deposition of Christ*; Girolamo del Pacchia's tondo the *Madonna and Child with the Infant St. John*; Santi di Tito's *Entry of Christ into Jerusalem*; and altarpieces by Alessandro Allori, the *Annunciation* (two versions), the *Coronation of the Virgin*, and the *Madonna and Child with Saints*.

With the exception of the entry rooms, there are only eight active galleries in the Accademia besides the Tribuna. A process of restoration and reorganization has been in progress for several years, with the goals of providing appropriate viewing conditions for the many works in the collection, while seeking to provide for the huge crowds of visitors who come to see the *David* and the other works by Michelangelo. The Gallery does not sponsor any temporary or changing exhibitions; ancillary research, education, and conservation services are handled by the local Soprintendenza, which provides similar resources for the other state museums in Florence.

Selected Bibliography

Museum publications: Biagi, L., *L'Accademia di Belle Arti a Firenze* (1941); Marcucci, Luisa, *Gallerie Nazionali di Firenze; I Dipinti Toscani del Secolo XIV* (Rome 1958–65); Procacci, Ugo, *La R. Galleria dell'Accademia di Firenze* (Rome 1936).

Other publications: De Tolnay, Charles, *Michelangelo* (Princeton, N.J. 1969–71); Pieraccini, Eugenio, *Guida della R. Galleria Antica e Moderna e Tribuna del David* (Prato n.d.).

ROBERT B. SIMON

BARGELLO (officially MUSEO NAZIONALE DEL BARGELLO; also IL BARGELLO, IL MUSEO NAZIONALE), Via del Proconsolo, 4, 50122 Florence.

Since it first opened its doors in 1865 for an exhibition of objects of the minor arts from the Middle Ages through the mid-nineteenth century, in celebration of the six-hundredth birthday of Dante Alighieri, the Museo Nazionale del Bargello has been universally recognized as one of the principal repositories for works of Italian, and indeed European, sculpture in a variety of media. Considerably altering the decision made by the Tuscan Provisional Government six years earlier to create a museum demonstrating the history of Tuscany through exhibits showing its institutions, customs, and art, the success of the Dante show was such that on June 15, 1865, a royal decree determined the future of the museum as a showcase for Italian medieval and Renaissance art of both public and private origin, exclusive of paintings and large sculptures that were to be exhibited in the Uffizi Gallery (q.v.).

The basis for the vast art collections of the Bargello, as for the paintings and ancient sculptures in the Uffizi, was the huge Medici family collection. Although only four pieces of sculpture are traceable as far back as the inventory made in 1492 at the death of Lorenzo the Magnificent, many more pieces of the present collections, mostly sculpture but also some medals and armaments, are referred to in Duke Cosimo I's inventory of 1553. Most of the arms collection and many pieces of majolica entered into Medici possession through the marriage of Vittoria della Rovere of Urbino to Grandduke Ferdinando II in the seventeenth century, when that noble family died out, and the number of arms was further augmented by the private collection of their younger son Prince Ferdinando at his death in 1713.

A tremendous source of objects, especially marble sculptures, majolica, and medals, was the collection of the Cardinal Leopoldo de' Medici (died 1675). The accumulated Medici collections became the property of the Tuscan State, immovable and in perpetuity, upon the death of the last Medici grandduke, Gian Gastone, in 1737, through a pact made between Anna Maria Luisa de' Medici and Francesco III of Lorraine, who succeeded Gian Gastone. Francesco and his successor Pietro Leopoldo continued the grandducal tradition of collecting, but, successively, bad judgment prevailed. Ostensibly, for reasons of space within the Uffizi, where the collections were then kept (later to pass to the Bargello), many pieces of arms and armor were sold in 1773 and in 1775 or were assigned to various other governmental agencies that usually mutilated them or denuded them of precious metals and stones. Similarly, the great majolica collection, which had already been reduced by half in the early eighteenth century by Cosimo III's gift to the Englishman Sir Andrew Fountaine, was further decimated by the sale of many of the oldest and most valuable pieces during the last quarter of the century.

Once the fundamental decision had been made concerning the direction the museum's collections were to take, several sources were tapped to procure the objects. From the Uffizi Gallery as well as from Palazzo Vecchio came the numerous objects of arms and armor. The stupendous group of ivories, as well as objects of carved amber, many originally in the possession of the royal family, also came from the Uffizi (those from the royal collection were transferred to the Museo degli Argenti at the Palatine Gallery, Pitti Palace [q.v.] in 1919). The Uffizi additionally provided the bases for the extensive collections of majolica and small-scale bronze statuary. In 1874 the momentous decision was made to transfer from the terrace, corridors, and tribuna of the Uffizi to the Bargello all of the large sculptures of medieval date and later. The Florentine Mint gave its historic collection of coins; seals, both lead and wax, were claimed from the State Archives and augmented early on by select purchases with government funds. A large group of medals, perhaps the most significant collection of this sort in Italy (although presently closed to the public), arrived from the

Uffizi at the end of the century. Many works of sculpture in terracotta, glazed and unglazed, were placed in the Bargello following the monarchy's official suppression of the religious orders and its subsequent appropriation of their patrimony. Similarly, the Hospital of Santa Maria Nuova, the most powerful of the city's charitable institutions, provided terracottas, eight illuminated manuscripts, four decorated linen chests, and a silver altar platform, all produced during the fifteenth century.

The first several decades of the museum's existence also saw the acquisition and display of objects from several other important sources. Perhaps the most unique of them was also the first: in 1887, on the occasion of the fifth centenary of the birth of Donatello, all of his available works were brought together in the large hall on the second floor, as well as plaster casts of his other statues. This display remained until well into the twentieth century, when the casts were removed and replaced by original works of other sculptors. The first great private collection was added to the museum's earliest holdings in 1888 through the generosity of the French antiquarian Louis Carrand, who had long resided in Florence, when his artistic holdings were turned over to the city of Florence by testamentary bequest on condition that they be exhibited in the Bargello. His collection included works of both Italian and foreign origin, in a number of media and materials: painting, bronze sculpture and relief plaquettes, gold, ivory, iron, leather, textiles, armaments, and church furnishings. Carrand's example was a fruitful one, since other private collectors followed suit, although usually their collections were more focused: the 1899 bequest of armaments made by Carrand's friend from Trieste, Costantino Ressman; Giulio Franchetti's gift of his choice selection of textiles in 1906; a group of coins from the Ciabatti Collection that added to the Bargello's already extensive holdings in that area; the Guastalla gift of seals, likewise increasing the museum's previously acquired examples; and majolica donated by the heirs of Luigi Pisa. Gifts to the Bargello continue to augment and refine the various collections, so that today the total number of objects in the museum's possession numbers about thirty thousand.

Certainly, one of the most interesting aspects of the museum is the building itself. Documents establish that construction of the oldest surviving public secular structure in Florence was planned from the year 1250, that the land on which the edifice stands was purchased from private individuals during the next half-decade, and that construction actually began in 1255. Although originally intended as the residence for an official who has served as a public defender, by 1261 the building had become the seat of the *podestà*, a non-Florentine lord employed to maintain civil peace by the city's wealthiest and most powerful citizens. So it remained until 1502, when it became the office of the Council of Justice (known as "The Wheel"). In 1574, early in the grandducal period of Florentine history, it was turned over to the captain of justice, or the chief of police, who was called the *bargello*, thus giving to the building its common name.

The building history is complex, pieced together on the basis of both documentation and structural evidence, about which the few architectural historians who have studied the structure in depth are not in total agreement. What follows is a synthesis of their analyses. The oldest section of the building is the taller part, bounded by the Via Ghibellina, del Proconsolo, and della Vigna Vecchia. It includes the corner tower known as the Volognana, which probably predates the Bargello proper, and which was raised and crowned with machicolations and battlements when it was integrated with the Bargello in the late 1250s. This original structure, probably completed by 1260, is architecturally akin to the block-like castle architecture of German imperial derivation, of which other, older examples in Italy exist (e.g., the Palazzo del Popolo in Orvieto). Although it originally rose to perhaps only two-thirds of its present height, many of the basic structural features of this section remain as they were when it was erected. The whole appears like a fortress in its mass and sobriety, but its simplicity may be more than merely that of a defensive bastion; very likely, it is a conscious attempt to present a business-like appearance to the residence and offices of the individual charged with preserving the rule of law.

Construction of the rear sections, which encompass the remainder of the city block back to the Via dell'Acqua, apparently began very soon after the completion of the first portion, judging by the surviving documentation and from several architectural details. The intention must have been present from the start to create a courtyard enclosed by a vaulted, cloisterlike arcade, thus elaborating on the basic Germanic scheme of a simple architectural block. This arcade, which surrounds the courtyard on three sides, with the massive walls isolating it from the adjacent streets laterally, as well as the rear section of the complex, which closes off the side of the arcade farthest to the rear, may be dated as early as about 1260–85, since several documents from shortly thereafter imply its finished state. One even refers to the arcade as a *claustrum*, thus suggesting a monastic inspiration for this architectural feature. Probably this period also saw the erection of the majestic courtyard open stairway (although the masonry doorframe with an iron gate halfway up dates only from 1503, the work of Giuliano da San Gallo); these steps likely replaced the presumably wooden exterior stairway and two wooden walkways that were once on all four sides of the oldest section of the Bargello, whose former existence is established not only by documents and by the words of the early chronicler Giovanni Villani but also by the rows of square holes and projecting consoles beneath the windows on the outer walls of both the second and third floors.

The temporary residency in the Bargello of Count Guido di Battifolle, vicar of Florence's great ally King Robert d'Anjou of Naples, in the year 1316, provided occasion for construction of the two upper floors of rooms above the portions of the arcade along the Via Ghibellina and the Via dell'Acqua. Upon completion of this work in 1320, the architect Tone di Giovanni (who may have been employed already in 1316) was commissioned to construct a second-floor arcade plus rooms on the story above this, all atop the ground-floor archway along the Via della Vigna Vecchia, thus rounding out the building complex.

This second-story arcade, known as the *verone*, is in its formal details similar to the cloister below it, except that the individual arches span a shorter distance, and hence there are more of them.

A fire on February 28, 1332, destroyed the original trabeated wooden ceilings that covered all of the rooms on the upper two stories throughout the building (excepting possibly the chapel and its sacristy), and the decision was made subsequently to vault some of the second-story rooms and the *verone*. This catastrophe may also have provided the stimulus for the decision to raise the height of the original section of the building, to reestablish its pre-eminence over the surrounding domestic structures of more recent date, which, built taller and grander than the houses of earlier vintage they had replaced, had in the process greatly reduced the prominence of the early civic structure. The admirable, slightly ogival, ribbed groin vaulting, which covers the great hall on the second and third floors of the original section in two bays defined by powerful octagonal-section pilasters, is the work of the architect Neri di Fioravante and took five years, 1340–45, to complete. The two-light lancet window piercing one of the end walls of the great hall is the work of Benci di Cione, from the year 1346. He is mentioned in Bargello documents of the preceding year on several occasions, and it is not unlikely that Benci and Neri were the persons in charge of vaulting or repairing all of the rooms on the upper stories following the great fire.

This early building history was complemented by wall decorations beyond the usual, purely ornamental, sculptural, and painted adornments articulating various elements of the architecture. Little remains, but it suffices along with certain literary references to indicate that the wall decor was consonant with the building's function, as a city office building, as home of the *podestà*, and as the site of various judicial functions. According to Vasari, in the great hall Giotto painted an allegory of the city, enthroned and bearing a scepter like a judge, robbed by an ungrateful citizenry. Another partially extant fresco, this one in the ground-floor hall, issuing from the circle of Taddeo Gaddi perhaps in the 1340s, shows the enthroned *Madonna and Child* as the focus of veneration for representatives from the various sections of the city.

In the chapel is a much-damaged series of frescoes recorded and attributed to Giotto since the fourteenth century but only rediscovered beneath layers of surface paint in 1839–40. Today they are given to his school, although the possibility remains that Giotto himself designed the compositions. On the altar wall is *Paradise* (where a presumed portrait of Dante is included). On the right wall are scenes from the *Lives of St. Mary Magdalen and St. Mary of Egypt* in two registers. On the left wall, punctuated by tall windows, are *St. Venanzio*, the *Feast of Herod* (a reference to John the Baptist, patron of Florence), and the posthumous *Miracle of the Magdalen*. Below the *Paradise* and flanking the altar recess are two small frescoes painted in 1490: Sebastiano Mainardi's *Madonna and Child* and Bartolomeo di Giovanni's *St. Jerome in the Desert*. The concentration of ascetic and penitent saints illustrates an important function performed by the chapel. It was here that condemned criminals, informed of their punishment, prayed through their last night before being led to execution. The *Hell* scene on the exit wall of the chapel, visible as one turns to leave, is part of the original fourteenth-century program; it served as a warning to these desperate souls of the punishment in store for them should they not repent. The *podestà*, who, along with his counselors, was responsible for such judgments, was entitled to erect his coat-of-arms in relief upon the walls of the Bargello courtyard, and this custom was continued in the sixteenth century among the judges of the Council of Justice. Many of these shields are present today, although some are modern copies. In fact, Florentine executions were performed in the courtyard from 1502, when the council was instituted, until 1778, when capital punishment was banned in Tuscany.

Restorations and changes were already being made in the Bargello during the early sixteenth century and continued thereafter, fundamentally altering the original appearance of the structure. The cloister and *verone* arches were walled in, new windows were created, many rooms were subdivided, and even the large hall on the second floor was adapted to house four levels of superimposed jail cells. Only in 1857 did Grand Duke Leopoldo II order the building's restoration; work commenced under the direction of the architect Francesco Mazzei, who oversaw the reversal of these post-fourteenth-century structural changes while also restoring or replacing decorative particulars such as doorframes and handrails. The job was complete by the time the Dante commemorative show opened in 1865.

Like the collections of the Uffizi Gallery, those of the Bargello constitute a history of Italian sculpture and decorative arts primarily of the Renaissance and the Florentine school. A small room on the ground floor known as the "Sala del Trecento" contains the meager holdings of the museum of pre-Renaissance stone sculpture. Amid a number of small pieces of diverse provenance are several important works. The huge statues of the *Madonna and Child Flanked by Saints Peter and Paul* was made for the Porta Romana, about 1328, by Paolo di Giovanni. Of the late thirteenth century, possibly by Arnolfo di Cambio, are the guardian angel with a kneeling boy (a tomb fragment?) and one of the caryatidlike supporting columns from the tomb of St. Dominick in Bologna. Tino di Camaino is represented by the Madonna and Child "Sedes Sapientiae," two warrior caryatids, and a saint representing a kneeling devotee, all fragments from tombs. Two nonfigurated tombs are here as well: that of Cione Pollini (1313) and that of Lapo dei Bardi di Vernio (1342). There is also a Madonna and Child relief by Alberto Arnoldi.

Beneath the arcade surrounding the courtyard on three sides are sculptures principally of the sixteenth century, including four fountain figures (Giambologna's *Ocean* of 1576 from the Boboli Gardens; *Earth, Florence*, and the *Arno River* of 1555–60, all intended for a fountain in Palazzo Vecchio but erected at the Pitti Palace, by Bartolomeo Ammanati), an idealized statue of *Grandduke Cosimo I* dressed as a Roman emperor by Vincenzo Danti, and a figure of *Fiesole* by Niccolò Tribolo. The marble *St. Luke* by Niccolò di Pietro Lamberti (1403–6), made for the Judges and Notaries Guild niche on Or San Michele and later replaced by a bronze figure, is also here. There are two bronze cannons made for the grandducal armies by Cosimo Cenni, the *Falcon* (1620) and the *Cannon of St. Paul* (1638), both with superb relief work.

The vaulted ground floor hall continues the exhibit of Florentine sculpture of the sixteenth century. Most notable are the four works by Michelangelo: the *Bacchus* (1497–99), made for a Roman antiquities enthusiast to resemble a piece of ancient sculpture and in the Medici Collection in 1572; the *Pitti Tondo*, with the Madonna and Child and St. John (c. 1503–4), one of the works marking his transition to his later style; the enigmatic *Apollo-David* (c. 1531), in the Medici Collection by 1553, and the *Bust of Brutus* (c. 1540), also part of the Medici Collection and an idealized portrait of Lorenzino de' Medici, who had killed his cousin Alessandro, as Brutus had killed Caesar. Certain small-scale works in the room are influenced by Michelangelo, including the marble *Leda and the Swan* and the bronze *Moses* attributed to Ammanati, and terracotta figures reproducing Medici Chapel sculptures by Tribolo. Other masterpieces here are Jacopo Sansovino's *Bacchus* (c. 1515–20), in Medici hands by 1553; Danti's marble *Honor Overcoming Deceit* (1570; the Bargello also possesses the earlier terracotta model); Giambologna's *Virtue Overcoming Vice* (1570; also called *Florence Triumphant over Pisa*) from the Palazzo Vecchio; *Adam and Eve* (1551) by Baccio Bandinelli from the cathedral high altar; Vincenzo de' Rossi's languid *Dying Adonis* (for a small fountain); Ammanati's reclining effigy and *Victory* group from the Nari Tomb; and Giovanni Francesco Rustici's round marble relief, the *Madonna and Child with St. John.* The strong personality of Benvenuto Cellini is felt in his marble statues of *Narcissus* from the Boboli Gardens and the group *Apollo and Hyacinth* and even more in his great bronze *Bust of Cosimo I* (1546, 1555–57), in which the subject is strongly characterized but idealized to present the image of an invincible ruler. Cellini is also represented by the dreamlike bronze relief of the *Liberation of Andromeda* and the four accompanying bronze statuettes from the base of the *Perseus* under the Loggia dei Lanzi, as well as the small preparatory models in wax and bronze for the *Perseus* itself.

One enters the second-floor arcade, the *verone*, after ascending the courtyard stairs. Once more, sixteenth-century sculpture is featured, primarily that of Giambologna. His famous series of bronze animals, cast about 1570 for the grotto at the Medici villa at Castello, reveals a close observation of varied surface textures in nature. There, too, is his famous *Mercury* (c. 1564). Carefully balanced on one foot in a graceful and effortless pose, this statue is a paragon of the Mannerist style. Also by Giambologna and others are various bronze statues with marine themes, intended for fountains.

The adjacent great hall, once used for meetings of the Florentine General Council, is now known as the "Salone di Donatello." In it is the largest aggregate collection of works by the fifteenth-century master. One of his earliest efforts, the marble *David* (1408, recut in 1416), was purchased from the cathedral by the Florentine Republic to stand as its symbol. The lion known as *Marzocco* (1420), holding the emblem of Florence, was an older symbol of the city; Donatello's version once stood near the papal apartments at St. Maria Novella before being relocated outside Palazzo Vecchio. The marble *St. George* (c. 1416), set in a niche duplicating its original setting on Or San Michele as patron of the Guild of Armorers and Sword-Makers, was one of the important works of art of its time, as is the famous bronze *David*. Perhaps the first large-scale nude statue of the Renaissance, and a demonstration piece of perfectly proportioned anatomy, this statue once stood in the Medici Palace courtyard and was transferred from there to Palazzo Vecchio in 1495. Although usually dated about 1430–35, a recent reexamination has plausibly proposed a date of about 1460. Other works generally attributed to Donatello include the colored terracotta *Bust of Niccolò da Uzzano* (c. 1430), the bronze *Bust of a Youth*, the *Head of a Bearded Man*, the bronze *Attis-Cupid* (c. 1430–40), the gold-highlighted bronze *Crucifixion* relief, and the *Young St. John the Baptist* (c. 1455). Traditionally given to Donatello, but probably a work of the first half of the sixteenth century, is another marble, *Young St. John the Baptist*.

Works by other sculptors, contemporaries of Donatello, are displayed in the same room. By Lorenzo Ghiberti and Filippo Brunelleschi are two gilded bronze *Sacrifice of Isaac* reliefs for the Baptistry Doors Competition of 1401. Ghiberti is also represented by the *Reliquary Casket of Saints Protius, Hyacinth, and Nemesius* (1428), executed on commission of the Medici. Another artist working in a manner akin to Ghiberti's was Luca della Robbia. Among his works are the *Madonna of the Apple* (c. 1450–60), the *Madonna of the Rose Arbor* (c. 1460), and the *Madonna and Child with Angels* lunette (c. 1470). Two other artists represented are Agostino di Duccio (two reliefs of the *Madonna and Child with Angels*, c. 1465) and Desiderio da Settignano (the busts *Young Woman* and *Boy* and reliefs *St. John the Baptist* and *Madonna and Child*). Other artists include Michelozzo (three reliefs of the *Madonna and Child*, in glazed terracotta, marble, and simple baked terracotta); Bertoldo di Giovanni, a student of Donatello and teacher to Michelangelo (several reliefs, including the *Crucifixion* and the classicizing *Battle between the Romans and the Barbarians* from the collection of Lorenzo the Magnificent); and the Sienese Vecchietta (the life-size, life-like *San Bernardino of Siena*, in polychromed wood, c. 1460).

In the great hall, too, are several *cassoni*, or marriage chests of which there are others elsewhere in the Bargello. Three here are decorated with paintings from the early fifteenth century, the *Procession for the Feast of St. John the Baptist* (attributed to Rossello di Jacopo Franchi), the *Story of Saladino and Torello d'Ischia* from Boccaccio's *Decameron*, and the *Voyage of the Argonauts*.

The other rooms on this floor are devoted to the decorative arts. The Sala delle Oreficerie contains gold and silver implements primarily of church origin. Of special note are: the enameled chalice by Goro di ser Neroccio of Siena (early fifteenth century), the stepped predella with enameled figures from the Baptistry by Andrea Pucci of Empoli (1313), the Florentine late-fifteenth-century reliquary bust of St. Ignatius of Constantinople, and the contemporary reliquary cross attributed to Antonio Pollaiuolo. Of particular interest, too, are the church vestments used by Pope Nicholas V for the canonization of San Bernardino of Siena in 1450.

The Sala delle Majoliche offers examples of ceramic dinnerware of the fifteenth and sixteenth centuries in a host of shapes and sizes from all of the Central Italian centers: Florence, Montelupo, Siena, Faenza, Gubbio, Deruta, Pesaro, Cafaggiolo. However, the collection is dominated by the selection of historiated majolica from Urbino, some illustrated with scenes that reproduce well-known works by painters (one featuring Raphael's *Fire in the Borgo*) or by engravers (another with Agostino Veneziano's *Continence of Scipio*). Especially noteworthy are the fine pieces from the Urbino-Hannibal service, which have plastic as well as painted decoration, and the remaining pieces from the service of Guidobaldo II della Rovere, duke of Urbino, made in the shop of Orazio Fontana, which entered the Medici Collection in the seventeenth century, only to be decimated early in the following century through Cosimo III's gift to the Englishman Fountaine.

The Sala degli Avori displays the museum's collection of ivory carvings, many from the Carrand bequest. From the Early Christian and Byzantine world are the diptych *Adam and the Animals in Eden* and *Scenes of the Life of St. Paul*, the half-diptychs *Empress Arianna* and *Two Men and a Chariot Race*, three small cylindrical boxes, and various rectangular boxes of both ecclesiastical and secular provenance. Medieval works of Islamic origin include six plaquettes with hunters, farmers, dancers, and musicians. Medieval works from the West include a number of chess pieces, several pastoral staff hilts, notably that of St. Ives of Chartres (c. 1100), and the liturgical fan made by Joel in the ninth century for the Abbey of St. Filibert at Tournus. The majority of these Western pieces, however, are fourteenth-century French works. Fifteenth century in date are the Burgundian chess board, two bone saddles (both probably German), and the small bone triptych set in an intarsia frame by the Embriachi shop in Venice. Also represented is the Byzantine eleventh-century miniature mosaic of *Christ Blessing*, one of the few such panels in the world. Around the walls are various late medieval sculptures from Central Italy, notably the Umbrian *Madonna of Mercy*.

The Salone del Podestà is full of a variety of small objects in many media. There is a group of enamels, including works of Rhenish-Mosan origin, although the majority were produced in Limoges. Some examples are the eleventh-century pastoral staff hilt signed by "frater Wilhelmus"; several thirteenth-century chest reliquaries; and various pieces produced in the sixteenth century of both religious and secular origin. There are ancient through seventeenth-century pieces of jewelry, cameos, and gems from Europe and glass objects of Middle Eastern origin (e.g., a fifteenth-century Syrian hanging lamp), Venetian (e.g., the Murano goblet with the *Triumph of Justice* scene, c. 1480), Florentine (e.g., a group of chalices with the Medici coat-of-arms), and French provenance. The collection of late antique, Byzantine, Merovingian, and Langobard morses and fibulae, many filigreed and decorated with colored glass and stones, is outstanding.

There is a wide variety of metal objects, especially in iron, bronze, and silver, and often gilded, from throughout the European and Mediterranean worlds: mundane objects such as locks, keys, dishes, aquamanili, tableware, clocks, and candelabras and relatively rare things such as an Italian astrolabe (c. 1500) and a German fifteenth-century drinking horn with gilded bronze mounts. The majority of the museum's panel paintings (many from the Carrand Collection) are exhibited in this room, of both Italian and Northern schools, including the *Noli me tangere* and *Coronation of the Virgin* by the Master of the St. George Codex (fourteenth century), the Orcagnesque *Coronation of the Virgin* (c. 1350–60), Agnolo Gaddi's *Nursing Madonna* (late fourteenth century), the German *Enthroned Madonna and Child* (late thirteenth century), Dieric Bouts' *Madonna and Child* (fifteenth century), Hans Baldung Grien's *Death and a Young Woman* (early sixteenth century), and Marino van Roymerswaele's *Money Changer and His Wife* (1540). Of special importance is the fourteenth-century polychromed wood group *Madonna and Child with St. Anne* from Or San Michele.

The chapel, whose frescoes were mentioned above, features fine wooden choir stalls with intarsia inlay and a wooden lectern, all carved in the last decade of the fifteenth century and brought here from various churches. The altarpiece triptych is from the mid–1400s, attributed to Giovanni di Francesco of Rimini. The altar is covered by a superb Late Gothic embroidery. Two cases along the walls flanking the door display illuminated manuscripts from the Hospital of Santa Maria Nuova, most notably the late-fifteenth-century missal painted by Gherardo and Monte di Giovanni. Other codices are from the beginning of the century, one illuminated by Lorenzo Monaco and his shop.

The upper story is largely devoted to a continuation of the display of Italian, particularly Florentine, sculpture of the fifteenth and sixteenth centuries. The Sala dei Bronzetti is also called the Sala del Camino after the elaborately carved early sixteenth-century fireplace by Benedetto da Rovezzano at one end. The collection of small bronze statuettes is one of the best in the world. Among the earliest sculptors represented are Andrea Briosco "il Riccio" of Trent (*Shepherd Milking a Goat*, c. 1507) and Pier Jacopo Bonacolsi "l'Antico" of Mantua (*Eros with Raised Arms*). The bronzes of Giambologna and his school (the *Labors of Hercules* series, the *Dwarf Morgante*, the model for the *Equestrian Statue of Cosimo I*) and Bandinelli and his school (the busts of *Cosimo I* and *Eleanora of Toledo* and two *Venuses*) are of paramount importance. Among the other masters represented are Jacopo Sansovino, Benvenuto Cellini (*Ganymede upon the Eagle*), Pietro da Barga, Guglielmo Fiammingo, Niccolò Roccatagliata, and Massimo Soldani. From the Baroque period are several choice objects: two bronze models for a never-executed monument to Louis XIII of France by Pietro

Tacca, the terracotta *Bust of a Young Moor* by Alessandro Algardi, and a small masterpiece by Gianlorenzo Bernini, the marble *Bust of Costanza Bonarelli*, his mistress.

The adjacent small Sala di Andrea della Robbia features a selection of the glazed terracotta works by the nephew of Luca della Robbia. Among his creations are: the *Madonna of the Architects* (1475), made for the Guild of Stone and Wood Carvers, to which the artist belonged (this is his earliest-known work), the tender *Madonna of the Cushion*, the round *Portrait of a Woman* relief, and the three-dimensional *Bust of a Child* (c. 1470–80). Two colored stucco *Madonna* reliefs are attributed to Antonio Rossellino and the school of Benedetto da Maiano.

The Sala di Giovanni della Robbia, son of Andrea and last of this artistically fecund family, presents many of his glazed terracottas. Among the giant altarpieces there are those figuring the *Pietà*, two with the *Noli me tangere* and the 1521 *Epiphany*, with smaller works such as the busts *St. Ursula* and *Bacchus*, the *St. Dominick Tabernacle*, and the *Madonna and Child with St. John* roundel from the Church of Ognissanti, which some attribute to Andrea del Verrocchio. A contemporary, Giovanni Francesco Rustici, is also present because of a group of his works done while under the influence of the della Robbia, in their preferred material, including another large *Noli me tangere* altarpiece from St. Croce.

The Sala del Verrocchio is the showcase for the works of the end of the fifteenth century. The centerpiece by Andrea del Verrocchio is his early *David*, made for the Medici villa at Careggi but sold and transferred to Palazzo Vecchio in 1476 by Lorenzo the Magnificent and his brother Giuliano. Other works by Verrocchio include the unusually full marble *Bust of a Young Woman*; the polychromed terracotta *Resurrection*, made as an overdoor for the chapel in the villa at Careggi following the Palazzi Conspiracy of 1478 (Lorenzo de' Medici is seen as one of the sleeping soldiers); the terracotta relief *Madonna and Child* (c. 1480); and the famous marble relief *Death of Francesca Tornabuoni*, inspired by funeral scenes on ancient sarcophagi. Three other marble reliefs of the *Madonna and Child* have been variously attributed to the master; one is almost unquestionably that recorded by Vasari as in the Medici household. By Verrocchio's contemporary, Antonio del Pollaiuolo, who also was in the forefront of those sculptors seeking a naturalistic portrayal of the human figure, is the *Bust of a Young Warrior*, whose breastplate displays two events from the legend of Hercules. Possibly this represents Lorenzo de' Medici's brother Giuliano at age fifteen, therefore dating the work to 1469. Thematically reminiscent of this bust is the small bronze *Hercules and Antaeus* group, one of those few works known to be in the Medici Collection in the fifteenth century. The group, about 1475, heralds the sixteenth-century taste for small-scale bronzes. Also by Pollaiuolo is the marble *Bust of a Man*, 1495, formerly but incorrectly thought to be an uncompromisingly frank portrait of Machiavelli.

Mino da Fiesole has numerous works there, principally busts (*Piero di Cosimo de' Medici* and his brother *Giovanni*, both from 1456, and the pensive *Rinaldo della Luna* of 1461) and small reliefs (two *Madonnas*, one rectangular, c. 1470, and one round, c. 1481; the *Bust of a Young Woman*; the *Bust of Marcus Aurelius*; and a tabernacle for the Eucharist). Antonio Rossellino is the sculptor of the *Busts of Francesco Sassetti* (1464) and the vigorous *Matteo Palmieri* (1468), both executed in a manner recalling ancient Roman Republican portraits. Also by Rossellino are the statue *Young St. John the Baptist* (1477), the colored stucco relief *Madonna and Child with Three Cherubs*, and the complex marble *Adoration of the Child* (c. 1470). By Benedetto da Maiano is the adroitly characterized *Bust of Piero Mellini* (1474), as well as the unfinished marble group the *Coronation of Ferdinand I of Aragon*, intended for the Porta Capuana in Naples. Among the non-Florentine objects displayed are several works by Matteo Civitale of Lucca; two *Madonnas* by Tommaso Fiamberti, a Lombard follower of Mino; and the *Bust of Battista Sforza*, duchess of Urbino, an idealization of the sitter made perhaps from a death mask, by the Dalmatian Francesco Laurana (c. 1474–77).

The Sala delle Armi presents the finest pieces of the museum's collection of arms, of both ceremonial and battle variety. Pieces originally in the Medici Collection include the Roman-style armor of Cosimo I (c. 1543), the ceremonial suit of his son Francesco I, gilded pieces belonging to Cosimo II's ceremonial armor (1608), the armor of Cosimo III when he was a boy, with a few pieces of Oriental and Orientalizing arms acquired by the Medici and a more numerous group of hunting firearms from their collection and that of their successors, the House of Lorraine. The armor of Duke Francesco Maria della Rovere, the breastplate of which is etched with the Madonna and Child and flanking saints, is the choicest of the many pieces that entered the Medici Collection from the court at Urbino. Pieces from the Carrand and Ressman bequests from the Middle Ages through the Baroque, including a number of Milanese examples, round out the collection. Displayed there, too, are several works of important sculpture: the gilt-copper plaque of the Langobard king Agilulf (reigned 590–616) seated amid his retinue, a pair of fifteenth-century ivory saddles, Francesco da San Gallo's marble *Bust of Giovanni de' Medici "delle Bande Nere,"* and the bronze *Bust of Ferdinando I* by Pietro Tacca.

The Museo Nazionale del Bargello is under the general direction of the Soprintendenza per i Beni Artistici e Storici di Firenze (Superintendency of Artistic and Historic Properties of Florence), an agency of the government of the Republic of Italy. Funding for the museum comes exclusively from the national government. Administration of the museum is in the hands of a director. Restoration work for objects in the collections is entrusted to the Opificio delle Pietre Dure. Photographs of the various objects may be requested from the Gabinetto Fotografico della Soprintendenza per i Beni Artistici e Storici di Firenze, Piazzale degli Uffizi, 1, 50122 Firenze, Italy. There is a documentary archive for the collections in the museum and a library as well, within the building, although the various state and institutional libraries around the city are more readily available to the scholar. A series of booklets on the individual collections, together known as *Lo specchio del Bargello*, edited by Giovanna Gaeta Bertelà, analyzes many of the museum's objects (including certain ones held in storage), with accompanying photographic reproductions in both color and black and white. The series is published by Studio per Edizioni Scelte (SPES), Lungarno Guicciardini, 9 r., 50125 Firenze, Italy.

Selected Bibliography

Museum publications: *Il Palazzo del Bargello e il Museo Nazionale: Album-Itinerario* (Collezione "Mirabilia") (Florence 1960); Martini, G., *Mostra documentaria e iconografica del Palazzo del Podestà* (Florence 1963); Rossi, Filippo, *Il Museo del Bargello a Firenze* (Collezione "Il Fiore dei Musei e Monumenti d'Italia") (Milan 1952); idem, *Il Museo Nazionale di Firenze (Palazzo del Bargello)* (Itinerari dei Musei, Gallerie e Monumenti d'Italia, no. 9), 4th ed. (Rome 1964); Supino, I. B., *Catalogo del R. Museo Nazionale di Firenze* (Rome 1898).

Other publications: Avery, Charles, and Anthony Radcliffe, eds., *Giambologna, 1529–1608: Sculptor to the Medici*, exhibition catalogue (Edinburgh, London, and Vienna 1978); Bucci, Mario, and Raffaello Benci, *Palazzi di Firenze: Quartiere di Santa Croce* (Florence 1971); Davidsohn, Robert, *Forschungen zur Geschichte von Florenz*, vol. 4 (Berlin, 1908); De Tolnay, Charles, *Michelangelo*, 5 vols. (Princeton, N.J. 1943–60); Frey, Karl, *Die Loggia de' Lanzi zu Florenz: Ein Quellenkritische Untersuchung* (Berlin 1885); Gaye, Johann Wilhelm, *Carteggio inedito d'artisti dei secoli XIV. XV. XVI.*, vol. 1 (Florence 1839); Janson, H. W., *The Sculpture of Donatello*, 2 vols. (Princeton, N.J. 1957); Marquand, Allan, series of 7 volumes on the Della Robbia family and their shop (Princeton, N.J. 1912–28); Passavant, G., *Verrocchio: Sculptures, Paintings, and Drawings: Complete Edition* (translated by K. Watson) (London and New York 1969); Passerini, Luigi, *Del Pretorio di Firenze* (Florence 1865); Pope-Hennessy, John, *Luca della Robbia* (Ithaca, N.Y. 1980); Rodolico, Niccolò and Giuseppe Marchini, *I Palazzi del Popolo nei comuni toscani del medio evo* (Milan 1962); Seymour, Charles, Jr., *Sculpture in Italy: 1400 to 1500* (The Pelican History of Art) (Baltimore 1966); idem, *The Sculpture of Verrocchio* (Greenwich, Conn. 1971); Uccelli, Giovanni Battista, *Il Palazzo del Podestà* (Florence 1865); Weinberger, Martin, *Michelangelo the Sculptor*, 2 vols. (London and New York 1967); Ames-Lewis, Francis, "Art History or *Stilkritik*? Donatello's Bronze *David* Reconsidered," *Art History*, vol. 2 (1979), 139–55; Bush, Virginia L., "Notes on the New Installation of Cinquecento Sculpture at the Bargello," *The Burlington Magazine*, vol. 119 (1977), 367–71; Paatz, Walter, "Zur Baugeschichte des Palazzo del Podestà (Bargello) in Florenz," *Mitteilungen des Kunsthistorischen Institutes in Florenz*, vol. 3 (1931), 287–321.

WILLIAM R. LEVIN

PALATINE GALLERY, PITTI PALACE (officially GALLERIA PALATINA, PALAZZO PITTI; also GALLERIA PITTI, MUSEO DEGLI ARGENTI, GALLERIA D'ARTE MODERNA, MUSEO DELLE CARROZZE, MUSEO DELLE PORCELLANE), Palazzo Pitti, Piazza Pitti, Florence.

The Galleria Palatina in the Pitti Palace was first opened to the public in 1833, but like many of the other Florentine galleries, its origins are far older. The original palace was built between 1457 and 1466 for the Florentine merchant Luca Pitti. Although its architectural design has traditionally been attributed to Filippo Brunelleschi, the only name documented in association with the construction of the palazzo is that of Luca Fancelli, a follower of the great architect. As then constructed, the palace formed only the nucleus of the present structure, occupying the central forward section. It was three stories high (as it is today) but only seven windows wide (as compared to the current twenty-three). Eleanora di Toledo, wife of Cosimo I de' Medici, purchased the site in 1549 from the Pitti family, and a series of extensions and renovations to the new principal Medici residence was begun thereafter.

Chief architect of the first modernization campaign was Bartolomeo Ammanati, who, from 1558 to 1577, built the courtyard and modified the facade by converting the subsidiary doors into large windows articulated by classical ornament. In 1620 Giulio Parigi extended the palace laterally by adding three window bays on either side; in 1640 that architect's son Alfonso continued the building to its present width. Two flanking terrace wings, called *rondò*'s, were added in 1746 and 1783–1819, and an adjacent small summer palace, the Meridiana, was brought to completion in the early nineteenth century. A staircase on the north end of the building (still in Renaissance style) was the last addition (in 1896).

In 1620 Cosimo II de' Medici founded the Galleria Palatina as a separate entity within the Pitti Palace. Paintings dispersed throughout the ducal residence, as well as works in storage in the Medici *guardaroba* (literally, wardrobe room), were brought together in rooms on the second floor (*primo piano*) of the palace. Cosimo's death the following year brought to the dukedom his son Ferdinando II, who sponsored the decoration of these rooms with frescoes by Pietro da Cortona and Ciro Ferri (1637–65). In 1631 Ferdinando's wife, Vittoria della Rovere, inherited the ducal collection of Urbino, many paintings from which soon entered the Gallery (others are now in the Uffizi [q.v.]); the bequest of Cardinal Leopoldo de' Medici in 1675 also added several important works. The collection grew, albeit less dramatically, under the later Medici and the dukes of the House of Lorraine. The French occupation of Florence in 1799 brought about the expropriation of many paintings from the Pitti, not all of which were returned from France pursuant to the Congress of Vienna in 1815. Following the restoration, Ferdinand III of Lorraine ordered the continuation of the painted decoration of the Gallery (as well as other rooms in the palace). His son Leopold II opened the Gallery to the public in 1828 (it was visitable only with special permission before that time). Fifteen rooms were then on view; by 1833 twenty rooms were open.

In 1860 the entire palace passed to the newly established kingdom of Italy. In 1911 Vittorio Emmanuele III ceded the Gallery to the Ministero della Pubblica Istruzione, thus placing it under the same state administration as the Uffizi and Accademia galleries (q.v.). The rest of the palazzo, together with the adjacent

Boboli Gardens, was given to the Italian State in 1919. However, the royal family retained for visits the series of rooms known as the Quartiere del Volterrano; they were subsequently ceded to the Gallery in 1928.

Unlike the Uffizi (which is, in effect, a modern museum in a historic structure), the Galleria Palatina conscientiously retains the appearance and ambiance of a princely, "palatine," picture gallery. The marble-floored rooms are richly adorned with furniture, decorations, objets d'art, and ceiling frescoes (the subjects or authors of which give the rooms their names: Sala di Venere, Sala di Giove, Galleria Poccetti, and so on), and the paintings, in elaborate gilt frames, are skied—hung in rows one above the other. Pictures are ordered neither by school, chronology, subject matter, nor historical importance; their arrangement follows the dictates of tasteful appearance and coloristic balance within the constraints imposed by the dimensions of the paintings and a seeming passion to leave no wall space unoccupied. Although it may prove disconcerting to the modern visitor to find masterworks of international renown displayed as part of an overall decorative scheme, the appearance of the sumptuous rooms can evoke, as in no other public institution today, the aura of the great picture galleries of the seventeenth and eighteenth centuries.

The Gallery is extraordinarily rich in its holdings of paintings by some of the greatest masters of the sixteenth century. Raphael is represented by no fewer than eleven paintings: the portraits *Angelo and Maddalena Doni, Tommaso Inghirami, Cardinal Bibbiena*, and the unknown women *La Gravida (The Pregnant One)* and *La Donna Velata (The Veiled Lady)*; the *Vision of Ezekiel*; and the two intimate pictures and two altarpieces, the *Madonnas* of the *"Sedia," "Granduca," "Baldacchino,"* and *"Impannata."*

Paintings by Titian include *The Concert* (a work long held to be by Giorgione); *The Penitent Magdalene*; and the portraits *Pietro Aretino, Ippolito de' Medici, Vincenzo Mosti, Pope Julius II* (after Raphael), *Andrea Vesalius, Diego de Mendoza, Philip II of Spain*, and the unknown sitters *La Bella (The Beautiful One)* and *The Englishman* (or *Man with the Green Eyes*). Several altarpieces, as well as smaller pictures, by Andrea del Sarto are exhibited in the Gallery, among which are two versions of the *Assumption of the Virgin*; the *Disputa*, or *Disputation on the Trinity*; the *Pietà with Saints*; a small *Madonna* and a *Holy Family*; three versions of *The Annunciation*, one of which is, however, largely a studio work; two large representations of the *Madonna and Child with Saints*; *The Youthful St. John*; and two scenes of *The Story of Joseph*, from the celebrated series known as the Borgherini panels.

Although the Gallery's collection concentrates on pictures of the sixteenth and seventeenth centuries, some earlier works are displayed. They include Botticelli's *Portrait of a Young Man* and profile *Portrait of a Lady*, formerly thought to represent Simonetta Vespucci; Filippo Lippi's tondo *Madonna and Child with Scenes from the Life of Mary*; the *St. Jerome* attributed to Piero del Pollaiuolo; Filippino Lippi's *Death of Lucretia*; *Madonna and Child* tondos by Luca Signorelli, Francesco Botticini, and Jacopo del Sellaio; Pietro Perugino's small *Magdalene*, as well as his altarpieces *Madonna del Sacco* and the *Deposition of Christ* (signed and dated 1495).

Among Florentine paintings of the sixteenth century are Rosso Fiorentino's *Virgin and Child with Saints* (1522); Fra Bartolommeo's *The Risen Christ* (1516), *St. Mark*, *Holy Family*, and *Deposition* (completed by Bugiardini); Pontormo's *Adoration of the Magi*, *Martyrdom of the Ten Thousand*, and portrait *Francesco da Castiglione*; Bacchiacca's *Magdalene*; Agnolo Bronzino's portraits *Guido-baldo II de' Montefeltro* and *Luca Martini*; Ridolfo del Ghirlandaio's *Portrait of a Man* (called *The Goldsmith*) and *Portrait of a Lady* (1508); Francesco Salviati's *Three Fates* (once attributed to Michelangelo); the tondo *Holy Family* by Mariotto Albertinelli; Giorgio Vasari's *Holy Family* and *Vision of Count Ugo*; two paintings by the little-known Andrea del Minga, based on designs of Baccio Bandinelli; Domenico Puligo's *Holy Family* and portrait *Piero Carnesecchi*.

Other sixteenth-century works include Paolo Veronese's portrait *Daniele Barbaro*, *Baptism of Christ*, and *Portrait of a Man*; Tintoretto's portraits *Luigi Cornaro*, *Vincenzo Zeno*, and an *Unknown Man*, as well as his *Venus, Vulcan, and Cupid* and *Madonna della Concezione*; Sodoma's two-sided banner *St. Sebastian* (1525); Sebastiano del Piombo's *Martyrdom of St. Agatha* (1520) and portrait *Baccio Valori*; and paintings by Dosso Dossi, Bonifazio de' Pitati, Baldassare Peruzzi, Paris Bordone, Marco Palmezzano, Domenico Beccafumi, Girolamo da Carpi, Jacopo del Conte, and Federico Barocci.

There are several major works by Florentine Baroque painters: Cristofano Allori's *Judith and Holofernes*, *Hospitality of St. Julian*, *Mary Magdalene*, and *Adoration of the Magi*; Ludovico Cigoli's *Ecce Homo*, *St. Francis in Adoration*, *Mary Magdalene*, *Martyrdom of St. Stephen* (1597), *Deposition* (1607), and *Sacrifice of Abraham*; Carlo Dolci's *Virgin Appearing to St. Louis of Toulouse*, *Martyrdom of St. Andrew* (1646), and *St. John the Evangelist*; Matteo Rosselli's *Triumph of David* (1621) and *Shadrach, Meshach, and Abednego in the Furnace* (the same artist also frescoed the ceiling of one of the galleries, the Sala della Stufa, in 1622); Francesco Furini's *Hylas and the Nymphs*; pictures by Gregorio Pagani, Giovanni Bilivert, Orazio Riminaldi, Jacopo dell'Empoli, Giovanni da San Giovanni, and Jacopo Vignali; and numerous portraits by Justus Sustermans, for many years court painter to the Medici.

The Pitti's holdings in non-Florentine pictures from the Baroque period include perhaps the finest collection of paintings by the Neapolitan Salvator Rosa (1615–73), among which are *La Menzogna* (*Falsehood*), *The Temptation of St. Anthony*, *The Philosopher's Grove*, two grand *Battles*, and several *Landscapes* and *Harbor Scenes*. Guido Reni (1575–1642) is represented by his *Suicide of Cleopatra*, *Charity*, and the traditionally, if doubtfully, ascribed *Youthful Bacchus*; Guercino, by his *Madonna della Rondinella*, *St. Peter Raising Tabitha* (1618), *St. Sebastian*, and *Apollo and Marsyas*. Other pictures of note include Caravaggio's *Sleeping Cupid* and portrait *Alof de Wignacourt*, Giovanni Lanfranco's *Ecstasy of St. Margaret of Cortona*, Carlo Maratta's *Vision of St. Philip Neri*, Luca Giordano's *Triumph of Galatea* and *Immaculate Conception*, Artemisia Gentileschi's *Judith* and *Mary Magdalene*, and Volterrano's *Jest of Piovano Arlotto*.

There are several important non-Italian pictures in the Palatina, the earliest of which is the sixteenth-century English portrait *Queen Elizabeth*. Other works include Peter Lely's portrait *Oliver Cromwell*; van Dyck's bust portraits *Charles I* and *Henrietta Maria*, and the large portrait *Cardinal Guido Bentivoglio* (c. 1623); several pictures by Rubens, among which are *The Four Philosophers*, *The Consequences of War*, *Peasants Returning from Work*, and *Ulysses on the Island of the Phoenicians*; Murillo's *Madonna and Child* and *Madonna of the Rosary*; Ribera's *Martyrdom of St. Bartholomew* and *St. Francis*; Velázquez' equestrian portrait *Philip IV*; Jan van Scorel's *Ecstasy of St. Francis*; more than twenty cabinet pictures by Cornelis Poelenburgh (1586–1667); and other small works by Pieter Bruegel the Younger, Jan Bruegel, Paul Bril, Rachel Ruysch, Jan van Kessel, and Godfried Schalken.

There are a few ancient sculptures on exhibition, including a Roman replica, the *Cnidian Aphrodite*. Classically inspired, but from the nineteenth century, is Antonio Canova's *Italic Venus*, a work sculpted as a replacement for the *Medici Venus*, which had been taken from the Uffizi by the French (it was returned in 1815). Of like spirit is the marble *Charity* by the neoclassical Lorenzo Bartolini (1777–1850). Among earlier sculptures are Baccio Bandinelli's *Bacchus* and Piero Francavilla's *Mercury Slaying Argus*. A small *Putto with a Goose* by Niccolò Tribolo is exhibited as sculptural ornament to a massive marble fountain base attributed to Francesco di Simone Ferrucci; the fountain came from the Medici Villa at Castello, where it was originally surmounted by another basin and Verrocchio's *Putto with a Dolphin*, now in the Palazzo Vecchio.

Adjacent to the Galleria Palatina are the former Royal Apartments. These chambers are maintained somewhat as period rooms with an abundance of tapestries, furniture, decorative pieces, and works of art. Irregularly open to the public, the rooms are sometimes used to house temporary exhibitions organized by the local Soprintendenza per i Beni Artistici e Storici (Superintendency of Artistic and Historic Properties). The Meridiana quarter of the palace currently contains the Contini-Bonacossi donation, a group of works of art recently bequeathed to the state and intended for eventual exhibition in the Galleria degli Uffizi. Among the works shown in the eleven rooms there are paintings by Sassetta, Giovanni Bellini, Cima da Conegliano, Savoldo, Zenale, Bramantino, Veronese, Zurburán, Velázquez, El Greco, and Goya; sculptures by Bernini, Bambaja, and Amadeo; and furniture and ceramics.

The Galleria Palatina, operating under the aegis of the Soprintendenza, has its own director, who is responsible as well for the former Royal Apartments. The other museums that share the Pitti Palace with the Palatina are separately administered; research and service facilities are handled centrally by the Soprintendenza.

The Galleria d'Arte Moderna is located in several rooms of the third and fourth stories of the palace. Founded in 1859 as part of the Galleria dell'Accademia (then the Real Galleria d'Arte Antica e Moderna), the Gallery was transferred to the palace in 1913. The collection includes some works of the eighteenth century, as well as several important examples of neoclassical painting and sculpture. Its particular strength lies in its collections of nineteenth-century Italian schools, particularly those flourishing in Tuscany. The Macchiaiuoli are well represented by major examples, as are the varied Romantic movements of the time. There are some twentieth-century works, again principally by Italian painters.

The Museo degli Argenti (Silver Museum) was organized in 1919 in rooms on the ground floor of the palace. The collection brought together objects from the granducal treasury that had been dispersed among the specialized museums in Florence; the Gabinetto delle Gemme (Gem Cabinet) from the Uffizi; the scattered collections of ivories, cameos, vases, porcelain, amber, and glass; the treasury of the bishop-princes of Salzburg and that sent by Catherine de' Medici as dowry for Christine of Lorraine in 1589; the jewelry collection of Anna Ludovici, the last of the Medici (this had been expropriated by the House of Lorraine and only returned, by treaty, in 1919); and various objets d'art executed in gold, silver, rock crystal, and *pietre dure*. Susequent additions include notable collections of lace, textiles, majolica, and clocks. The collection of porcelain has been recently removed from the museum to a new Museo delle Porcellane, housed in the Casino del Cavaliere across the Boboli Gardens from the Pitti.

A museum of carriages (Museo delle Carrozze) is located in the right *rondò* of the palace; it contains sedan-chairs, *berlinas*, and carriages, mostly of the eighteenth and nineteenth centuries.

Selected Bibliography

Museum publications: *Arazzi e Tessuti Antichi a Palazzo Pitti* (1977–78); Chiarini, Marco, and Kirsten Aschengreen Piacenti, *Artisti alla Corte Granducale* (1969); *Collezioni della Galleria d'Arte Moderna di Palazzo Pitti. Ottocento: I* (1972); *Cultura Neoclassica nella Toscana Granducale* (1972); *Curiosità di una Reggia; Vicende della Guardaroba di Palazzo Vecchio* (1979); Eriksen, Svend, and Kirsten Aschengreen Piacenti, *Le Porcellane Francesi a Palazzo Pitti* (1973); *Romanticismo Storico* (1973–74); Rusconi, Arturo Jahn, *Il Museo degli Argenti in Firenze* (Rome 1935); idem, *La Galleria d'Arte Moderna a Firenze* (Rome 1949); idem, *La Galleria Pitti in Firenze* (Rome 1937).

Other publications: Bardi, L., *L'Imperiale e Reale Galleria Pitti* (Florence 1840–42); Campbell, Malcolm, *Pietro da Cortona at the Pitti Palace* (Princeton, N.J. 1977); Chiarini, Marco, *Pitti Palace: Art and History* (Florence 1977); Chiavacci, Egisto, *Guida dell Imperiale e Reale Galleria del Palazzo Pitti* (Florence 1859); Ciaranfi, Anna Maria Francini, *The Pitti Gallery (Galleria Palatina)* (Florence 1967); Cipriani, N., *La Galleria Palatina nel Palazzo Pitti a Firenze* (Florence 1966); Conti, Cosimo, *Il Palazzo Pitti, la sua Primitiva Costruzione e Successivi Ingrandimenti (Florence 1887);* Inghirami, F., *L'Imperiale e Reale Palazzo de' Pitti Descritto* (Fiesole 1828); Morandini, F., *Mostra Documentaria e Iconografica di Palazzo Pitti e Giardino di Boboli* (Florence 1960); Piacenti, Kirsten Aschengreen, *Il Museo degli Argenti* (Milan 1968); Tabakoff, Sheila, "The European Porcelain in Palazzo Pitti: A Historical Survey," *Keramos*, 65 (1974), 3–16.

ROBERT B. SIMON

UFFIZI GALLERY (officially GALLERIA DEGLI UFFIZI; also GLI UFFIZI), Loggiato degli Uffizi, 6, Florence.

As perhaps the oldest gallery in the world, the Galleria degli Uffizi seems almost as venerated as the works of art it contains. Although its formal establishment dates from the late 1500s, the Gallery may be said to originate some two centuries earlier, when the nucleus of the Medici family collection was formed by Cosimo the Elder, called Pater Patriae (1389–1464). His descendents amassed through patronage and purchase an unrivalled collection of works of art, ancient and modern. Cosimo's grandson Lorenzo, called il Magnifico (1449–92), became the most legendary of these Florentine Maecenases, but the later Medici Grand Dukes—Cosimo I (1519–74) and, especially, his son Francesco I (1541–87)—must be considered the founders of the Uffizi.

On July 3, 1559, Cosimo I commissioned the painter, artists' biographer, and architect Giorgio Vasari to erect a building between the Piazza della Signoria and the River Arno to house the diverse offices (*Uffizi*) of the administration of the then Duchy of Tuscany. The structure was referred to at the time as the Magistrati—from the thirteen principal magistracies that comprised the bureaucratic organization under Cosimo. Work on clearing the site had been underway since 1546, when a street was driven through to the river; construction of the building began in 1560.

Stretching in two connecting branches from the seat of government, the Palazzo Vecchio, and the open-air Loggia dei Lanzi, the palace was conceived by Vasari with three stories (the upper two open loggias) elegantly articulated by a harmonious and sophisticated facade. The Uffizi, which incorporated the Romanesque church of San Pier Scheraggio on the east and the old custom house (the Zecca) on the west, was not completed until 1580. By 1565, however, enough work had been undertaken on the eastern wing of the building to allow Vasari's construction of the unique elevated corridor that runs from the Palazzo Vecchio and the Uffizi across the Ponte Vecchio over the Arno and along the Via Guicciardini to the Pitti Palace.

In the early 1580s Francesco I decided to convert the top floor of the Uffizi into a repository for the artistic treasures of his family. (Until this time works of art not exhibited in occupied rooms were stored in the *Guardaroba*, or wardrobe room, of the Palazzo Vecchio.) The architect Bernardo Buontalenti was entrusted with the alterations, which included the enclosing of the open loggia (or *galleria*, from which comes the word *gallery*) with windows, the creation of a roof garden atop the adjacent Loggia dei Lanzi, and the construction of new rooms behind the eastern wing of the building. Most notable among the latter is the octagonal Tribuna, a fantastic room decorated along arcane cosmological lines that formed the central gallery of the germinal museum. The room was filled with a disparate array of objects, including medals, knives, natural history specimens, and trinkets, in addition to bronzes by Giambologna and some thirty paintings—among them, works by Raphael, Andrea del Sarto, Piero di Cosimo, and Pontormo.

In 1581 work commenced on the decoration of the eastern gallery with the painting of grotesques on the ceiling by a team of artists under the supervision of Alessandro Allori. Shortly thereafter (1585–86) a theater was built on the second story (*primo piano*) of the building, also to the design of Buontalenti. This was the renowned Teatro Mediceo, where what is generally acknowledged to be the first opera, Jacopo Peri's *Euridice*, premiered in 1600.

Ferdinando I succeeded his brother Francesco in 1587, and the years of his reign saw the presence in the Uffizi of workshops for armorers, goldsmiths, watchmakers, workers in precious stones (*pietre dure*), glassblowers, and fabricators of perfumes, medicines, poisons, and antidotes. Ferdinando expanded the Gallery as well, installing his collection of scientific instruments in the small room preceding the Tribuna, the arms and armor collection in the galleries following it, and a group of ancient bronzes in the last room facing the Arno, the Galleria della Madama. To this eclectic amalgam Ferdinando's son Cosimo II (1590–1621) added his father's collection of printing presses and type.

Under the reign of Ferdinando II, who succeeded his father Cosimo in 1621, the collections were greatly expanded. Through his wife, Vittoria della Rovere, the Medici inherited, in 1631, the remnants of the rich ducal collection of Urbino (these pictures now being divided between the Uffizi and Pitti collections, Palantine Gallery, Pitti Palace [q.v.]). The demise of various Medici family members added to the Gallery's holdings as works of art were acquired from the estates of Don Antonio de' Medici (1632), Cardinal Carlo de' Medici (1633), and, most notably, Cardinal Leopoldo de' Medici (1675). In addition to the many important pictures in Leopoldo's legacy, two of the Uffizi's special collections arose from his bequest: the series of artist self-portraits and the drawing cabinet; a separate gallery was established to exhibit the former in 1681, and the art historian Filippo Baldinucci organized Leopoldo's vast drawing collection in 1700 into what was to become the present Gabinetto di Disegni e delle Stampe (q.v.).

Under Cosimo III and his son Prince Ferdinando the Gallery's collections grew further through purchase and assimilation of Medici properties. With the death of Gian Gastone de' Medici in 1737 Tuscany passed into the house of Francis of Lorraine, husband to Maria Theresa. The last surviving Medici, Anna Maria Lodovici, entered into a treaty with Francis that ceded to the House of Lorraine essentially all of Florence's works of art with the stipulation that they be maintained forever in the city for public edification. The Uffizi, as well as all artistic properties in Florence, were thus saved from expropriation and exportation.

Under Pietro Leopoldo the Gallery received its first director, Giuseppe Querici (1769); in the following year many works of art from Medici properties and public Florentine buildings were transferred to the Gallery. Acquisitions were made of entire private collections of antiquities, medals, and drawings, and the Uffizi's holdings were organized into chronological arrangements of like media. Renovation of the galleries created the neoclassical Sala di Niobe in the western branch of the building but also saw the destruction of the original decoration of the Tribuna. Ferdinand III (Pietro Leopoldo's son) arranged for an advantageous exchange of pictures with the imperial collections in Vienna and supervised other exchanges among the Pitti, Academy (q.v.), and Uffizi galleries.

In 1795 the Gallery began the then-revolutionary practice of providing labels identifying the artist next to each picture on exhibition. This innovation strikingly reflected the change in the Uffizi from an essentially private gallery (although interested visitors had been admitted for some time) to a museum open to the general public. The advances in the internal organization of the Uffizi were unfortunately overshadowed by the losses the Gallery fell victim to during the Napoleonic occupation. Although only the *Medici Venus* was expropriated from the permanent collection (later to be restored), many pictures gathered from churches and suppressed monasteries found their way to France, never to be returned.

Nineteenth-century alterations to the Uffizi included the renovation and eventual destruction of the Medici Theater, transformed first into a criminal court, then into the Chamber of Deputies, later into the Senate of the Italian nation, and finally into a space currently occupied by the Gabinetto di Disegni and the Uffizi Library. The Gallery lost potential space when the state archive (Archivio di Stato) moved into several rooms of the Uffizi in 1852, expanding gradually into its current area, and when the Post Office occupied part of the old structure of the Zecca in the western branch of the building (it remained until 1917).

Few paintings have ever been sold or otherwise disposed of from the Uffizi (a notable exception were two of Paolo Uccello's *Battle of San Romano* pictures, sold in the late eighteenth century and now in the Louvre [q.v.] and London's National Gallery [q.v.]), but the abundance of artistic treasures in the Uffizi has generated the establishment of many now-autonomous museums. The Gallery's collection of scientific instruments, for example, was transferred in 1775 to the Museo di Fisica e Storia Naturale (now Museo Zoologico) "La Specola" and later (1930) to the new Museo di Storia della Scienza. The workshops and products of the Opificio delle Pietre Dure were transferred to their own building in 1796. Medieval, Renaissance, and modern sculpture, as well as works in the minor arts, went to the Bargello (q.v.) upon the founding of that museum in 1864. Paintings by Fra Angelico were placed in the Museo di San Marco, opened in 1869. The Egyptian and Etruscan collections were established as separate entities at the Cenacolo di Foligno before their transfer to the Museo Archeologico in 1880. At the same museum were deposited portions of the former Uffizi collections of numismatics (the medals went to the Bargello) and gems (most later transferred to the Museo degli Argenti). Those pictures later to comprise the Gallery of Modern Art were moved to the Galleria dell'Accademia in 1859 and subsequently (1913) to the Pitti Palace. Other museums in and about Florence have received works of art from the Uffizi (either as part of their collections or on long-term deposit), including the Museo Horne, Museo dell'Antica Casa Fiorentina (Palazzo Davanzati), Casa Buonarroti, Museo Mediceo (recently closed), the Museo di Casa Vasari at Arezzo, and the picture galleries of Urbino, Pistoia, Lucca, Arezzo, Parma, and Prato. The Uffizi's collection of pictures was, at the same time, increased and refined through exchanges and acquisitions from the Galleria di Santa Maria Nuova (1909), the Galleria dell'Accademia (1919), and the Galleria Palatina (1922).

Following World War II (during which time the collections had been evacuated from the city), the Uffizi was reorganized with a reduced but more effectively presented display of paintings. The renovation of galleries began in the 1950s and continues today. Recent work includes the restoration of the Tribuna to its original form, the renovation of the galleries surrounding it (the rooms of Botticelli, Leonardo, Lippi, and the *Hermaphrodite*), the establishment of a gallery of detached frescoes in the restored remains of the church of San Pier Scheraggio, and the reopening of the Vasari corridor to the Pitti Palace. These recent activities are part of a master plan for the Gallery that would involve the expansion of the art collections into other parts of the Uffizi Palace (the Archivio di Stato intends to move from its cramped quarters into a new building) and the execution of other architectural alterations designed to improve the quality of the Gallery's exhibition spaces, as well as provide sensibly for the nearly 1 million viewers who visit annually.

The Uffizi's fame and distinction rest in the extraordinary collection of masterworks of the Italian Renassiance, with special concentration among pictures of the Florentine school. The earliest major painting on exhibit is an imposing *Crucifix*, the noted "Academy Cross," executed by a Tuscan artist of the second half of the twelfth century. What follows include the three majestic altarpieces of the *Maestà* (the Madonna and Child enthroned with attendant saints and angels), by Cimabue (c. 1285), Duccio (1285), and Giotto (c. 1310)—all transferred from Florentine churches; the polyptych *Madonna and Child with Saints* by Giotto from the Badia; the *Annunciation* of 1333 by Simone Martini, painted for the Duomo of Siena; the *Presentation at the Temple* by Ambrogio Lorenzetti (1342); the polyptych *Blessed Humility* and *Madonna and Child with Saints* by his brother Pietro; the altarpiece *St. Cecilia with Scenes from Her Life* by the eponymous Master of St. Cecilia; the San Remigio *Pietà* given to the mysterious Giotto di Maestro Stefano, called Giottino; the *Madonna in Glory* by Taddeo Gaddi (1355); the large polyptych *Madonna and Child with Saints* by Bernardo Daddi; the *Crucifixion* by Nardo di Cione; the altarpiece *St. Matthew* by his brothers Jacopo di Cione and Orcagna; the *Coronation of the Virgin* (1413) and *Adoration of the Magi* by Lorenzo Monaco; the *Thebaid*, given to Gherardo Starnina; the *Adoration of the Magi* (1423) and *Quaratesi Altarpiece* (four panels) by Gentile da Fabriano; the *Madonna and Child with Saints*, dated 1445, by Giovanni di Paolo; the *Madonna and Child* by Jacopo Bellini; and the painting *Madonna and Child with St. Anne*, of the early 1420s, by Masaccio and Masolino.

Among Florentine paintings of the second half of the fifteenth century, the Gallery exhibits Paolo Uccello's *Battle of San Romano* (c. 1456); Domenico Veneziano's *Sacra Conversazione* from the church of Santa Lucia de' Magnoli

(c. 1445); Piero della Francesca's double portraits *Federico da Montefeltro* and his wife, *Battista Sforza* (c. 1465); Fra Angelico's *Coronation of the Virgin*; several works by Fra Filippo Lippi, among which are the altarpieces *Madonna and Child Enthroned with Saints*, *Coronation of the Virgin*, and *Adoration of the Magi*, as well as the smaller *Madonna and Child with Two Angels*; Alessio Baldovinetti's *Annunciation* and *Madonna and Child with Saints*; Antonio del Pollaiuolo's two small panels, the *Feats of Hercules* and the profile *Portrait of a Lady*; his brother Piero's six *Virtues* (a seventh picture in the series is by Botticelli), the portrait *Galeazzo Maria Sforza*, and the altarpiece *Three Saints* (from San Miniato al Monte); Filippino Lippi's *Madonna degli Otto* of 1486 (possibly based on a design by Leonardo), *Adoration of the Magi* (1496), *Portrait of an Old Man*, and *St. Jerome*; Andrea del Verrocchio's *Baptism* (one angel painted by the young Leonardo); Domenico Ghirlandaio's two large altarpieces of the *Madonna and Child with Saints*, and a tondo *Adoration of the Magi*; Piero di Cosimo's *Immaculate Conception*; Leonardo da Vinci's *Annunciation* from Monteoliveto and the unfinished *Adoration of the Magi*; Lorenzo di Credi's *Annunciation, Venus*, and *Adoration of the Shepherds*; and the extraordinary collections of works by Sandro Botticelli, among which are the *Birth of Venus, Primavera, Adoration of the Magi, Madonna of the Magnificat, Madonna of the Pomegranate, Annunciation, Calumny of Apelles, St. Barnabas Altar*, and *Pallas and the Centaur*.

Quattrocento Italian works from outside of Florence include Luca Signorelli's *Holy Trinity, Crucifixion with Mary Magdalene, Holy Family*, and the allegorical *Madonna and Child*; Melozzo da Forli's two-panel *Annunciation*; Piero Perugino's portrait *Francesco delle Opere* (1494), *Madonna and Child with Saints* of 1493, *Pietà*, and *Portrait of a Young Man* (a portrait of the artist of debated authorship has been attributed to Raphael, Lorenzo di Credi, Verrocchio, and Perugino himself); Marco Palmezzano's *Crucifixion*; Andrea Mantegna's triptych *Ascension, Circumcision*, and *Adoration of the Magi*; *Madonna of the Stonecutters* and the portrait *Carlo de' Medici*; Giovanni Bellini's *Sacred Allegory* and the grisaille *Lamentation of Christ*; Giorgione's *Judgment of Solomon* and *Moses before Pharaoh* (the *Warrior* traditionally ascribed to Giorgione is now attributed to Cavazzola); and pictures by Cosmè Tura, Cima da Conegliano, Carpaccio, Costa, Antoniazzo Romano, Boccati, Genga, Bartolomeo Vivarini, and Francia.

Among sixteenth-century pictures are Michelangelo's unique easel work, the *Doni Tondo* (a Holy Family); Raphael's portraits *Leo X with His Cardinals, Elisabetta Gonzaga, A Young Man*, the attributed *Guidobaldo de' Montefeltro*, and *Self-Portrait*, as well as the *Madonna del Cardellino* and the part-workshop *St. John in the Wilderness* (transferred from the Accademia in 1970 and rehung in the Tribuna); Giulio Romano's *Madonna and Child*; Andrea del Sarto's *Madonna of the Harpies* (1517), *Four Saints* (1528), and *Girl with a Petrarchino*; Correggio's *Adoration of the Child* and *Rest on the Flight into Egypt*; Mariotto Albertinelli's *Visitation*; Vasari's posthumous *Lorenzo de' Medici*; Jacopo Pontormo's companion *Cosimo de' Medici*, as well as his *Supper at Emmaus* (1525), the birthplate of *Birth of St. John, Madonna and Child with St. John, Expulsion of Adam and Eve, Madonna and Child Enthroned with Saints and Angels* (partially by the young Bronzino), *St. Anthony Abbot*, and the portraits *A Musician* and *A Lady with a Basket*; Rosso Fiorentino's *Moses and the Daughters of Jethro, Madonna and Child Enthroned with Saints*, and *Lute-Playing Angel*; Agnolo Bronzino's *Panciatichi Holy Family* and *Lamentation of Christ* and the portraits *Lucrezia* and *Bartolomeo Panciatichi, Eleanora di Toledo* (with her son), *Cosimo I de' Medici*, and his children *Bia, Maria, Giovanni*, and *Francesco*; Francesco Salviati's *Charity, Christ Carrying the Cross*, and *Portrait of a Man*; Daniele da Volterra's *Massacre of the Innocents*; Parmigianino's *Madonna of St. Zaccharias*, and *Portrait of a Man*; and pictures by Franciabigio, Sodoma, Bugiardini, Granacci, Jacopino del Conte, Bacchiacca, Beccafumi, Garofalo, and Mazzolino.

The collection is rich as well in sixteenth-century paintings from North Italy, Venice, and the Veneto: Titian's *Venus of Urbino, Flora, Venus and Cupid* (with workshop), and the portraits *Francesco Maria della Rovere* and his wife, *Eleanora Gonzaga, Ludovico Beccadelli*, and the unknown men *Knight of Malta* and *L'Uomo Malato* (*The Sick Man*, dated 1514, and formerly given to Sebastiano del Piombo); Palma Vecchio's *Judith, Resurrection of Lazarus*, and *Holy Family*; Sebastiano's *Death of Adonis* and *Portrait of a Lady*; Lorenzo Lotto's *Holy Family with Saints* (1534), *Head of a Youth*, and *Chastity of Susanna* (signed and dated 1517; the picture acquired in 1975); Dosso Dossi's *Allegory of Hercules* (or *Witchcraft*), the *Virgin Appearing to Saints John the Baptist and John the Evangelist*, and *Rest on the Flight into Egypt*; Veronese's *Holy Family with St. Barbara* and *Annunciation*; Savoldo's *Transfiguration*; Moroni's portraits *Giovanni Antonio Pantera, Pietro Secco Suardo* (1563), and *Unknown Man*; Tintoretto's *Christ and the Samaritan Woman* (two pictures), *Leda and the Swan* (part workshop), and the portraits *Jacopo Sansovino* and several unknown men; Licinio's *Madonna and Child with St. Francis*; portraits of men by Paris Bordonne, Guilio Campi, Girolamo Romanino, Alessandro Oliverio, Girolamo Muziano, Domenico Campagnola, Tiberia Tinelli, Francesco Beccaruzzi, Sebastiano Florigerio, and Paolo Pino; and other works by Caroto, Jacopo Bassano, and Domenico Tintoretto.

Later Italian pictures include Caravaggio's *Sacrifice of Abraham, Bacchus*, and the painted shield *Medusa*; Annibale Carracci's *Bacchanale* and *Man with a Monkey*; Federico Barocci's *Madonna del Popolo, Noli me tangere, Francesco II Della Rovere*, and *Ippolito Della Rovere*; Guercino's *Concert, Endymion*, and *Samian Sibyl*; Salvator Rosa's *Job*; Bernardo Strozzi's *Tribute Money* and *Parable of the Wedding Guest*; Giambattista Tiepolo's *Erection of a Statue of an Emperor*; the *Madonna della Neve* of Guido Reni; Baciccio's portrait *Leopoldo de' Medici*; Sustermans' portrait *Galileo*; and paintings by Domenichino, Albani, Piazzetta, Pietro Longhi, Canaletto, Guardi, Domenico Fetti, Giuseppe Maria Crespi, Giovanni Domenico Ferretti, Magnasco, Caracciolo, Mattia Preti, Cavallino, Alessandro Allori, Carlo

Dolci, L'Empoli, Pietro da Cortona, Andrea Sacchi, Trevisani, Artemisia Gentileschi, Luca Giordano, Forabosco, Manfredi, Giovanni da San Giovanni, Francesco Rustici, and Cesare Dandini, among others.

Among non-Italian artists the Gallery possesses Hugo van der Goes' *Portinari Altarpiece* (c. 1475); Rogier van der Weyden's *Deposition* (c. 1450); several small panels by Memling; works by the Master of the Baroncelli Portraits, Nicolas Froment (the triptych *Raising of Lazarus*), François Clouet, Cranach, Joos van Cleve, Gerard David; Dürer's *Adoration of the Magi* (1504), the Apostles *Philip* and *James* (1516), *Madonna and Child* (1526), and *Portrait of the Artist's Father* (1490); Altdorfer's two *Stories of St. Florian*; Hans Süss von Kulmbach's *Peter and Paul Altarpiece*; Hans Holbein's portrait *Richard Southwell* (1536); Rubens' portrait *Isabella Brant* and two large canvasses, *Scenes from the Life of Henry IV*; van Dyck's equestrian portrait *Charles V*; two Rembrandt *Self Portraits* and the *Portrait of an Old Man*; Hercules Seghers' *Landscape*, identifiable with a painting owned by Rembrandt and perhaps repainted by him; Jacob van Ruisdael's two *Landscapes*; several tenebrist works of Gerrit van Honthorst, including his *Adoration of the Magi* of 1617 and *Supper with a Lute Player*; Claude Lorraine's *Port with the Villa Medici* (1637); El Greco's *Saints John the Evangelist and Francis* and Goya's portrait *Countess of Chinchòn* (both recent acquisitions); and paintings by Quentin Massys, Georg Pencz, Bernart van Orley, Anthonis Mor, Johann Liss, Jan Steen, Nattier, Chardin, Liotard, Boucher, and others.

Specialized painting collections are organized as separate entities within the gallery. The series of artists' self-portraits, originating from Cardinal Leopoldo de' Medici's Collection but still growing, now includes more than seven hundred examples; the Giovio Collection of nearly five hundred portraits of famous men, exhibited above the windows in the long galleries, has doubled in size from the series of pictures originally copied for Cosimo I from works in the sixteenth-century museum of Paolo Giovio; and the Iconographic Collection remains a further resource of portraits assembled more for their subjects than their authors. More than thirteen hundred examples make up the collection of miniatures, exhibited in the Galleria di Madama and along part of the Vasari corridor; among artists represented are Giulio Clovio, Buontalenti, Bronzino, Pieter Breugel the Elder, Guercino, Dolci, and Rosalba Carriera. The small collection of detached frescoes exhibited in the former church of San Pier Scheraggio includes Botticelli's *Annunciation* from the hospital of San Martino alla Scala and Andrea del Castagno's nine *Famous Men and Women* from the Villa Carducci at Legnaia, recently transferred from the Cenacolo di San Apollonia.

Other media represented in the Uffizi include tapestries of Flemish and Florentine origin, including series such as *The Life of Jacob*, woven by Willem de Pannemaker on designs of Bernart van Orley; *The Months*, a set woven by Rost and Karcher in Florence from cartoons of Bacchiacca; and the *Valois Festivities*, a series of sixteenth-century Brussels tapestries after designs by Lucas de Heere.

The collection of ancient statuary is extensive and includes many important works, the most notable of which are exhibited in the Tribuna: the *Medici Venus* (an ancient replica after a Praxitelean model of the fourth century B.C.); the *Wrestlers* (with added heads taken from the *Niobid Group*); the *Apollino* (based on a Praxitelean model); the *Arrotino*, or *Scythian Sharpening His Knife* (the unique replica of a Pergamene work of the third century B.C.); and the so-called *Dancing Faun* (actually the *Satyr* that formed part of the *Invitation to Dance* group with the seated *Nymph*, a version of which is also in the Uffizi). Exhibited elsewhere in the galleries are the marble *Porcellino* (or Wild Boar), the multi-figured group *Niobe and the Niobides*, the *Sleeping Hermaphrodite*, and the *Molossian Hounds* (all ancient replicas of Hellenistic works); versions of the *Farnese Hercules*, the *Pothos* (Desire) of Skopas, the *Crouching Venus* of Doidalsis, the *Discobolus* of Myron (torso only), two examples of the suspended *Marsyas* (each originally paired with an executing *Scythian* of the type in the Tribuna), and numerous other works. Many of the old restorations of these pieces were carried out by notable sculptors of the day, such as Alessandro Algardi, Giovanni Caccini, Benvenuto Cellini, and, according to Vasari, Donatello, and Verrocchio.

The collections of furniture and ceramics are small and relatively undistinguished, since the Bargello is now the caretaker of works of art in those media; such objects retained by the Uffizi are either integral to the Gallery's design (e.g., the seventeenth-century *pietre dure* grand cabinet and octagonal table in the Tribuna) or are part of the multimedia Contini-Bonacossi bequest of 1969 (those works, however, are provisionally exhibited in the Meridiana section of the Pitti Palace). Similarly, modern sculpture not transferred to the Bargello consists primarily of portrait busts of members of the Medici family (including Giambologna's *Cosimo I*) and a small collection of Renaissance works from the same bequest, including Bernini's marble *St. Lawrence*. One interesting exception is Baccio Bandinelli's vigorous replica of the ancient sculptural group of the *Laocoon*, exhibited at the end of the west gallery. Not officially part of the Uffizi's collection (rather, part of the building's exterior decoration) are Vincenzo Danti's marble figures of *Aequitas* and *Rigor* and, standing between them, Giambologna's marble *Cosimo I*.

The Gabinetto dei Disegni e delle Stampe houses the collection of nearly 110,000 drawings and prints; the drawing collection of the Uffizi Gallery is, both in quantity and quality, among the greatest in the world along with those of London, Paris, and Vienna. Cardinal Leopold de' Medici (1617–75), the brother of Grand Duke Ferdinando III, founded the collection of drawings, and it was Filippo Baldinucci who gave it its present form by devising a new classification system in which, instead of organizing by school, he organized it chronologically by decade. This was done to illustrate the immediate differences and similarities among various Italian and foreign artists, decade by decade.

After the death of Leopold in 1675, Baldinucci continued to work for Cosimo III (1642–1723), who added more to the collection. Between 1690 and 1696 Baldinucci, shortly before his death, was able to add a collection of twelve hundred drawings from the Pandolfini and Strozzi collections. Leopold's collection itself had originally been in the Pitti Palace, but about 1700 it was transferred to the Uffizi. At this time, about forty-seven hundred drawings were eliminated, and a general inventory was done a few years later in 1714; at that time the collection consisted of about twelve thousand drawings. Cosimo III added much to the general collection between 1714 and 1717. Later important additions include the Gaddi-Michelozzi Collection (1778) and the Ignazio Hugford Collection (1798).

Today there are about 50,000 figure, landscape, and ornamental drawings from the fifteenth to the nineteenth century. At the core of the collection are the Florentine drawings, with about 2,000 drawings from the Trecento and Quattrocentro, 10,000 drawings from the Cinquecento, and 6,000 drawings from the Seicento and Settecento. There are about 2,000 Venetian drawings, 5,000 North Italian drawings, and 2,000 Central Italian drawings (exclusive of Tuscany).

The foreign schools are relatively well represented also, with about 1,300 Dutch and Flemish drawings, 1,800 French works, and about 600 Spanish and 450 German drawings. There are about 8,000 architectural drawings. The Ottocento and modern periods are represented by only a few works.

It is impossible to discuss the entire collection in detail, and the following examples serve as highlights of the collection and to give an indication of its breadth and depth. There is a large body of drawings by Jacques Callot, the French etcher who was famous for his scenes depicting the horrors of the Thirty Years War. There are some of the finest drawings by Claude Lorraine, Poussin, and Watteau; a refined selection of Lucas van Leyden and Rubens; and a good selection of Mannerists and landscapists of the sixteenth and seventeenth centuries from Mabuse to Paul Bril, Breenburgh, and Poelenburgh. There is a small group of Dürers and a few drawings by Baldung Grien.

There are rare drawings by Andrea del Castagno, Filippo Lippi, Francesco di Giorgio, Bennozo Gozzoli, Pollaiuolo, and Botticelli and good examples of Carpaccio, as well as fine examples of rare drawings by Pisanello and Bellini and perspective drawings by Uccello. Some outstanding examples from the Cinquecento include Leonardo's drawing for the *Adoration of the Magi*, Michelangelo's *Battle of Cascina* and Raphael's *Esterhazy Madonna*, the *Vatican Stanze*, and *St. George*. Other outstanding artists represented include Giulo Romano, Polidoro da Caravaggio, Parmagianino, Pontormo, Bronzino, Salviati, and Vasari.

The Emilian Mannerists are represented by, among others, Tibaldi, Lelio Orsi, Niccolò dell'Abbate, Primaticcio, Cambiaso, Zuccaro, and Barrocci. The Venetians are represented by Titian and Tintoretto but no works by Veronese. Also included are works by Bassano, Lotto, Romanino, and Savoldo.

As well as scenographic and ornamental drawings, there are more than eight thousand architectural drawings, with outstanding examples by Sangallo, Peruzzi, Vasari, Ammanati, Buontalenti, Pietro da Cortona, Bramante, Scamozzi, and Maderna. The drawing collection is vast and well balanced, so that study of the history of drawings either by decade, as arranged in this particular collection, or by country or school and in some cases by individual artist is readily available.

Cardinal Leopold was also the founder of the considerable collection of more than twenty thousand prints that also offers a relatively complete history of the development of printmaking. The collection is catalogued into twenty divisions as follows: (1) antique Italian prints, chiaroscuro, and woodcuts; (2) Marcantonio Raimondi, Agostino Veneziano, and Marco da Ravenna; (3) school and followers of Raimondi; (4) Cornelius Cort and his school; (5) Roman prints from the middle of the Cinquecento to the middle of the Settecento; (6) Tuscan prints of the Cinquecento to the middle of the Settecento; (7) Venetian prints; (8) Bolognese and Lombard prints; (9) minor German masters; (10) Albrecht Dürer; (11) selected German prints from the middle of the Cinquecento to the middle of the Ottocento; (12) Lucas van Leyden and the Wierix brothers; (13) prints after Rubens and his school; (14) Rembrandt and his followers; (15) Dutch and Flemish prints; (16) selected English prints; (17) Van der Meulen prints; (18) modern Italian prints; (19) miscellaneous prints; and (20) selected French prints.

With these various divisions it is possible to study virtually any area of printmaking as well as outstanding works by individual masters. Some of the weaker areas are the seventeenth-century English school, from which there is a great scarcity of names and works. This is not a fault of the collection but that the famous printmakers of this time were in France and the Low Countries. The eighteenth-century English school is represented by James Gillray and Thomas Watson, but Hogarth and Rowlandson, two of the landmark figures of this school, are absent as are the major aquatintists. Goya is represented by only two or three prints, and the eighteenth-century German school is represented primarily by the Kilian family.

The great periods of printmaking in the sixteenth, seventeenth and eighteenth centuries, however, are well represented. Most of the great Italians are present: Mantegna, Pollaiuolo, Beccafumi, the Carracci, Parmagianino, Raimondi, Guercino, Stefano della Bella, Guido Reni, Antonio Tempesta, and Pietro Testa.

The sixteenth-century German school is well represented by Schongauer, Altdorfer, Lucas van Leyden, Cranach, and Dürer. The sixteenth-century French school is sparse, but there are some good examples. The seventeenth-century German school is seen mostly through examples by Wenzel Hollar. The seventeenth-century Dutch and Flemish schools are best seen through works by Cornelius Bloemart, prints after Rubens and van Dyke, and with Rembrandt particularly well represented by 175 prints. The seventeenth-century French school is rich in examples by the Audran family, Sebastian Le Clerc, Claude Mellan, and Jacques Callot, one of the most famous and well represented. The eighteenth-century French school is rich in representatives by Saint-Aubin, with prints by Madame Pompadour (who was taught by François Boucher).

The eighteenth-century Italian school contains examples by Cipriani and Kauffman and works after Zocchi and Guercino. It is strong in portrait prints and a complete set of the works of Bartolozzi, acquired in 1865 in the Carlo Torrigiani Collection. Canaletto is represented, and there are good examples of Giovanni Battista Piranesi and Marco Ricci.

There are a few examples of eighteenth-century Japanese prints and of nineteenth-century French printmakers such as Daumier and Fantin-Latour.

As with most large print and drawing collections, the Print and Drawing Collection of the Uffizi Gallery has small changing exhibitions of selected works. The available space for display is small, and therefore only a tiny fragment of this extensive collection can be shown at one time. But exhibitions are arranged to show the strengths of the collection and to illustrate a specifically chosen theme such as sixteenth-century Florentine drawings, sevententh-century Venetian drawings, or selected works of a specific artist. To use the collection for study purposes, application can be made to the curator of prints and drawings. There are study areas available for this purpose. Photographs have been made of only the most outstanding examples and can be purchased, but the selection is by necessity limited.

Restoration and conservation work for the Uffizi is handled by separately administered laboratories in the Fortezza di Basso, a sixteenth-century Florentine bastion. These facilities, which serve other Tuscan institutions as well, had been located at the Uffizi before the devastating flood of 1966. Although situated next to the rampaging river, the Uffizi escaped catastrophe since nearly all of the works of art were kept high in the top-floor galleries. However, several works not on exhibit were damaged by the waters; these paintings had ironically been undergoing conservation treatment in the basement restoration studios or had been kept in the ground-floor storeroom of the ex-church of San Pier Scheraggio.

The gallery is headed by a director, who is assisted by several departmental chiefs. A recently established office (Ufficio di Ricerche) supervises the study, documentation, and cataloguing of works of art in the gallery's collection. As with the adjacent library, it is open to members of the public upon application. Similarly accessible is a photographic library, the Gabinetto Fotografico, which serves the documentary needs not only of the Uffizi but of other galleries, museums, churches, and collections throughout Tuscany. As such, this facility (although located within the Uffizi) is properly under the direct authority of the Soprintendenzo per i Beni Artistici e Storici (Superintendency of Artistic and Historic Properties) for the provinces of Florence and Pistoia—the bureaucratic entity that administers the local state museums under the aegis of the Italian government's Ministry of Cultural Properties. The Soprintendenza is responsible as well for organizing special exhibitions as cooperative efforts from among its component institutions. Except for a changing display of drawings, the Uffizi, as an historic permanent collection, does not devote any of its space to temporary or special exhibitions; rather, rooms in the Pitti Palace are often used for such purposes.

Selected Bibliography

Museum publications: *Gli Uffizi: Catalogo Generale*, 1979; Bartolini, Roberto, *Uffizi Gallery*; Borea, Evelina, *Caravaggio e Caraveggeschi nelle Gallerie Statali di Firenze*,

1977; idem, *Pittori Bolognesi del Seicento nelle Gallerie di Firenze*, n.d.; Fasola, Cesare, *The Uffizi Gallery of Florence*, 1961; Giglioli, Oboardo H., *The Drawings of the Royal Gallery of the Uffizi in Florence*, 1922; Mansuelli, G.A., *Galleria degli Uffizi: Le Sculpture*, Rome 1958–61; Marcucci, Luisa, *Gallerie Nazionali di Firenze: I Dipinti Toscani del Secolo XIV*, Rome 1958–65; Pacchioni, G., *The Uffizi Gallery*; Pieraccini, Eugenio, *Catalogo della Galleria degli Uffizi in Firenze*, n.d.; Poggi, Giovanni, R. *Galleria degli Uffizi*, 1926; Rosenberg, Pierre, *Pittura Francese nelle Collezioni Pubbliche Fiorentine*, 1977; *Rubens e la Pittura Fiamminga del Seicento*, 1977; Santarelli, Emilio, *Catalogo della Raccolta di Disegni Autografi*, 1870; Tempesti, Anna Forlani, *I Grand disegni italiani degli Uffizi di Firenze*.

Other publications: Amelung, W., *Führer durch die Antiken in Florenz* (Munich 1897); Bencivenni-Pelli, G., *Saggio Istorico della R. Galleria di Firenze* (Florence 1779); Berti, Luciano, *The Uffizi* (Florence 1971); Bianchi, G., *Ragguaglio delle Antichità e Rarità che si Conservano nella R. Galleria Medicea Imperiale di Firenze* (Florence 1759); "Consistenza e Valore dei Dipinti della Galleria degli Uffizi," *Critica d'Arte*, vol. 12, no. 72 (June 1965), pp. 16–71; Gori, A. F., *Museum Florentinum* (Florence 1732–62); Lanzi, Luigi, *La Real Galleria di Firenze* (Florence 1782); Negrini, Sergio, *The Uffizi of Florence and its Paintings* (New York 1972); Prinz, Wolfram, *Die Sammlung der Selbstbildnisse in den Uffizien; I, Geschichte der Sammlung* (Berlin 1971); Salvini, Roberto, *The Uffizi Gallery* (Florence 1966); Zacchirolli, F., *Description de la Galerie Royale de Florence* (Florence 1783–92).

ROBERT B. SIMON and GREGORY OLSON

——— **Milan** ———

AMBROSIANA GALLERY (officially PINACOTECA AMBROSIANA; alternately THE AMBROSIANA; also IL AMBROSIANA, PINACOTHECA, BIBLIOTHECA AMBROSIANA), Piazzo Pio XI 2, Milan.

The Ambrosiana was founded in 1618 by Cardinal Federico Borromeo as the first public art museum and library in Milan. The collection began as Federico's private holdings. These first works are discussed in his book *Musaeum*, published in 1625, and are also listed in his act of donation of 1618, which is reprinted at the back of the present catalogue of the museum. The collection grew by acquisitions and donations, and in many cases the donations complemented those of the original founder. Twelve manuscripts of Leonardo da Vinci, including the *Codex Atlanticus*, were given in 1637. Some of the other donations are nineteenth-century bronzes by Giovanni Edoardo de Pecis and his sister in 1827 and 1830; curiosities and books and manuscripts from the early-seventeenth-century Settala Museum; twenty-two thousand books, including eight hundred published before 1525, and twenty thousand prints and drawings by the Marchese Fagnani; and twenty thousand volumes in 1829 by Baron Custodi. Further donations were made in 1939, 1959, and 1962.

The physical structure grew along with the collection. The first structure was begun in June 1603, through the initiative of Cardinal Borromeo, and was designed either by Richini or Lelio Buzzi. This building was mostly destroyed in 1943 and has been rebuilt, but many seventeenth-century printed books were lost at that time. In 1613 Cardinal Federico started a building for an art academy like that of the Carracci Academy in Bologna. The new construction, now the Gallery, was built from 1611 to 1630 and separated on the north side from the library by a small garden. The art gallery had a new front added in 1831–36 by Maraglia. The Fagnani and Custodi rooms were built to house the collections of their donors.

The present collection of the museum is arranged chronologically by country and region in fourteen rooms. The most important works in the museum are the *Portrait of a Musician* by Leonardo, the cartoon for the *School of Athens* by Raphael, the *Adoration of the Magi* by Titian, and the *Bowl of Fruit* by Caravaggio. Other very well-represented areas are Lombard painting of all periods and paintings by Jan Bruegel, who was a special favorite of Cardinal Borromeo. The most important manuscript in the library is undoubtedly Leonardo's *Codex Atlanticus*, although the wealth of material in the library is only now gradually being catalogued in the Fontes Ambrosianae series.

In the museum the first room contains paintings of the Trecento and Quattrocento. The earliest painting is a diptych with the *Pietà* by the Sienese painter Lippo Vanni. From Venice there is the polytych *Madonna and Child and Saints* by Bartolomeo Vivarini, signed and dated 1486, and the painting *Christ Risen* by Marco Basaiti. There are important paintings from Central Italy, including the *Madonna of the Baldacchino* by Botticelli, the *Adoration of the Child* by Ghirlandaio, the *Madonna and Child and a Devotee* by Pinturicchio, and the *Eternal Father* by Timeteo Viti. There are two panels of saints by an anonymous master from the Marches region. From Lombardy is the *Flight into Egypt* by an anonymous master of the beginning of the sixteenth century, the *Assumption* attributed to Pseudo-Boccaccino, two panels of saints by Bernardo Zenale, the large and splendid panel *Madonna Enthroned* by Borgognone, and two panels with saints by the same artist. There is also a small portable ancona of the *Virgin and Child* by Geertgen tot Sint Jans in the first room.

The second room contains some early sculpture, including a fourth-century Christian inscription and three pre-Romanesque female figures in high relief, two from the eleventh century and one perhaps from the tenth century. A Lombard Romanesque relief from the second half of the eleventh century is also there.

In the third room is Lombard Renaissance sculpture, mostly by Bambaja, the Milanese sculptor of the first half of the sixteenth century. These works include twelve sculptures from the tomb of Gaston di Foix, a marble with scenes from the *Passion of Christ* from San Francesco Grande in Milan, two candelabra, six pilasters with mythological scenes, and trophies, one with candelabra and one pilaster with a figure, possibly a prophet, in high relief. There are also an anonymous Lombard marble tondo and a niche with Plato in high relief by Piatti from the end of the fifteenth century.

Next is a room mostly devoted to Renaissance German and Flemish works, except for detached frescoes of saints by an early-sixteenth-century Lombard master and some ancient pieces. The oldest object in the museum is a red-figure patera with mythological scenes from the third century B.C. Early Christian and Roman fragments from sarcophagi were found in the portico adjacent to the courtyard of the Ambrosiana. There is also a Roman Lares figure. The Flemish works are the triptych *Adoration of the Magi* attributed to the Master of the Holy Blood, the *Virgin at the Fountain* by Barent van Orley, the *Magdalene* by the Master of the Half Figures, and the *Devotee with a Friar*, possibly by a Flemish master. The German works are the *Madonna with Child* by the Master of the Tucher Altar, the *Portrait of a Man* by the Monogrammist H.L.F., and two portraits by Hans Muelich. In the glass case are three globes showing the epicycle of the moon according to the Ptolemaic system, a gilded clock of about 1550, three Lombard daggers with cases, and a small Flemish Mannerist bronze. There is also a German saddle with stirrups from the fifteenth century.

Most of the fifth room is devoted to small objects. In the glass case is a holy water dish that belonged to Cardinal Federico, with miniatures on ivory with scenes by Jan Bruegel. In the same case are some cameos and gems from the Settala Collection. There is an early Byzantine cross, a *Crucified Christ* from Limoges, and a liturgical purse in red velvet of the antipope John XXIII. There is an ornamented nautilus shell from the turn of the seventeenth century and a table trophy of *Diana on the Stag*, with automated moving figures by Joachim Friess of the early seventeenth century. A stained-glass window by Bertini with scenes from Dante has been at the Ambrosiana since 1867. In addition, there are a few small paintings: two flower pieces (one very fine) by Jan Bruegel and assistants and a fruit and flower piece attributed to Jan Soreau.

In the sixth room are small paintings by Flemish painters of the seventeenth century, including the collection of works by Jan Bruegel, called "Velvet Bruegel." He was a favorite of Cardinal Federico, and these paintings were donated in 1618 at the opening of the Ambrosiana. They include *Daniel in the Lions' Den*; the signed *Garden of Eden*; *Allegories of Air and Fire* from a series of the four elements, of which the other two are in the Louvre (q.v.); the extremely beautiful *Vase of Flowers with Jewels; Coins and Shells*; the signed *Original Sin*; the painting *Madonna and Child in a Garland of Flowers*; and a study of a mouse and a rose. There are also two sets of six paintings each on copper. In Federico's inventory they are called "six pieces of the countryside" and "six other pieces of the countryside." They are among the most important works in the museum.

Other paintings in the sixth room are *Ducks and Geese at a Pond* by Jan van Kessel and a landscape by David Vinckboons. There is a painting of angels by Johann Rottenhammer, with flowers added by Jan Bruegel, and an interior of a cathedral by Hendrik van Steenwijk the Elder, with figures added by Jan Bruegel. Also there is a winter scene attributed to Avercamp.

The seventh room is devoted to Lombard painters of the High Renaissance. Two monochromes on panel, the *Adoration of the Shepherds* and *Presentation in the Temple*, are by Luini, as are *Young Christ, Madonna of the Milk*, and the *Young St. John with an Angel*. Two versions of the *Head of St. John the Baptist* and the *St. Jerome* are by Andrea Solario. Two paintings are by Bramantino, the *Adoration of the Child* and the *Pietà*. There is the *Head of Christ* attributed to Cesare da Sesto, an antique copy of a Giorgione, a monochrome by Cima da Conegliano, and the canvas *Madonna and Child*, signed and dated 1530 by Caesare Magni.

In the eighth room are paintings by Leonardo and the Leonardeschi. The *Portrait of a Musician* is by Leonardo, and the fine *Portrait of a Woman*, possibly Beatrice d'Este, was for a long time attributed to Leonardo but is now considered to be by Ambrogio de' Predis. In the same room is Luini's beautiful interpretation of Leonardo's *Madonna and Child and St. Anne*. There are also versions of the *Adoration of the Shepherds* by Martino Piazza and Giampietrino. An anonymous Flemish painting, *Madonna and Child and Young St. John*, is very Leonardesque. There is the painting by Bramantino *Virgin Enthroned* and a portrait by Bartolomeo Veneto. *St. John the Baptist* by Salai shows the direct influence of Leonardo. Also there is a triptych by Marco d'Oggiono.

Cinquecento paintings of various Italian schools fill the ninth room. The Central Italian ones are a Bugiardini, *Madonna and Child and Young St. John*, and a fine Bronzino portrait and the *Holy Family* by Bacchiacca. By Sodoma is a tondo with the *Holy Family*. From Parma is the painting *Judith with the Head of Holofernes*, possibly by Andrea Fabrizi, and from Ferrara is *Washing of the Feet* by an anonymous early-sixteenth-century master. From Northern Italy is a fine signed and dated portrait by Fede Galiza. The rest of the paintings are from Lombardy: by Altobello Melone of Cremona is the *Madonna*; the bust-length *Portrait of St. Charles Borromeo*, one of two of him in the Ambrosiana, is by Figino; and of the two versions of *Christ in the Garden*, one is by Lomazzo and one by Guilio Campi.

The tenth room contains the Raphael cartoon for the *School of Athens*, other cartoons, and one painting. There is a fragment of Guilio Romano's cartoon for the *Battle of Constantine* in the Vatican. There are also ten cartoons for stained-glass windows, mostly for the Duomo of Milan, by Pellegrino Tibaldi. In addition, there are two cartoons for the frieze of the Palazzo Milesi by Polidoro da Caravaggio and a cartoon by the nineteenth-century painter Giuseppe Bossi for a painting now in the Academy of the Brera (q.v.). The one painting is the fine *Annunciation* by Gerolamo Mazzola-Bedoli.

In the eleventh room are paintings of the Seicento and Settecento, including the famous *Bowl of Fruit* by Caravaggio. The other well-known painting in this room is the *Nativity* by Barocci. From the early seventeenth century are also *Lot and His Daughters* attributed to Spranger, a *Magdalene* by Guido Reni and another by Procaccini. There are also two paintings by Palma il Giovane, the *Crucifixion*, not presently on display, and the canvas *Paradise*. Also there is the *Allegorical Female Figure* by Serodine, *Susanna at the Bath* by Nuvolone, *Adoration of the Magi* by Morazzone, and *St. Michael the Archangel* by Procaccini. There are two still-life paintings, one by Fede Galiza and one by Evaristo Baschenis, as well as the painting *Sower* attributed to Domenico Fetti. From the later seventeenth century is a portrait by Mazzoni, a mythological scene by Luca Giordano, a pastoral scene by G. B. Castiglione, the *Allegory* by Salvator Rosa, and the *Mercury and Argus* from Genoa. From the eighteenth century are paintings from Venice and elsewhere. From the shop of Magnasco is the *Interior of a Hostelry*. There is also the painting *Old Woman with Poultry* by the Monogrammist V.H. of the beginning of the eighteenth century. A portrait of Emperor Leopold II is by Mengs. There is a history painting by the Roman Giuseppe Cades and the painting *Moses and the Bronze Serpent* by Cesare Ligari from the Valtellina. There is also a fine portrait of a youth by Fra Galgario. Finally, there are paintings by the Venetian Giandomenico Tiepolo, including his fine *Presentation at the Temple* and the painting *Bishop Saint*.

In the twelfth room are paintings of the eighteenth and nineteenth centuries and gilded bronzes from the De Pecis Collection. However, there are also fine marble self-portrait busts by Thorwaldsen and Canova. There are four portraits by Andrea Appiani, the first director of the Brera. One of them, although not the best, is of Napoleon. Other paintings are *Youth with a Dove* by Natale Schiavone, *Mercury and the Graces* by Trabellesi, the neoclassical *Young Woman with a Funerary Urn* by Gaspare Landi, and the *Portrait of Felice Bellotti* by Giuseppe Bossi. There are also two scenes by the Milanese Giovanni Migliara, one of the Certosa of Pavia and one of the Arch of Peace at Milan, signed and dated 1814.

The rest of the objects in this room are from the De Pecis Collection. There are five miniatures on ivory with gilded bronze frames by the Milanese painter Gigola. One of the important pieces is a bronze model of the triumphal arch erected for the entrance of Francis I of Austria into Milan. Others are wax lunette models and copies of them in gilded bronze for that arch and also for the Arch of Peace in Milan. There are two nineteenth-century centerpieces and a sugar bowl, a gilded bronze of Hebe by Canova, and a bronze lion also of the nineteenth century. Finally, there is a gilded bronze copy of the monument to Andrea Appiani by Thorwaldsen now in the Brera.

The thirteenth and fourteenth rooms contain Venetian paintings of the sixteenth century and Lombard paintings mostly of the seventeenth century. The latter are downstairs, and between the floors is a stairway with two landscapes by Paul Bril and the cenotaph of the Milanese painter Giuseppe Bossi.

The thirteenth room has paintings both from Venice and from the provinces. Most prominent are those by Titian. The following paintings in the Ambrosiana are by Titian or his assistants: the *Ecce Homo*; the *Deposition into the Tomb*, which is signed; the painting with assistants of the *Madonna and Child*; *St. Cecilia and St. John the Baptist*; the famous and beautiful *Adoration of the Magi*, formerly in the collection of St. Charles Borromeo; the portrait *Old Man in Armor*; and the *Magdalene*, which is from his shop. Also from Venice itself are the *Adoration of the Magi* by Schiavone; two paintings by Cariani, a *Way to*

Calvary and a *Christ and the Pious Women*; and the painting *Sacred Family with Tobias and the Angel* by Bonifacio de' Pitati. By Jacopo Bassano are the *Annunciation to the Shepherds* and the superb *Rest on the Flight into Egypt*. From Brescia is the signed *Martyrdom of St. Peter of Verona* by Moretto, and from Bergamo is the *Portrait of a Man* by Moroni. This room contains the finest paintings in the museum.

In the last room are paintings from Lombardy and predominantly from the Seicento. The earliest are the half-length portrait *St. Charles Borromeo* by Figino and the painting *St. Ambrogio Enthroned* by Simon Peterzano. The rest are from the seventeenth century. They include *Lucretia* by Gherardini, the *Christian Martyrs* by Borgianni, a fine male portrait by Tanzio da Varallo, and three paintings by Nuvolone: the *Magdalene*, the *Virgin and Child with St. Charles Borromeo and St. Francis*, and the *Holy Family*. There is also a picture by Daniele Crespi of *St. Philip Benizzo* and the famous painting by Cerano, *St. Ambrogio*. *Jesus among the Doctors* is by Morazzone. Finally, from the Lombard school of about 1618 is the *Baptism of St. Augustine*, which is a partial derivation from one by Cerano in St. Marco in Milan.

The second part of the Ambrosiana is the library, of which the drawings and manuscripts are gradually being published by the museum. They are listed in the bibliography. The room for the public has reproductions of the most famous manuscripts, including the *Codex Atlanticus* of Leonardo and changing exhibits from the holdings of the library. Slides and photographs may be purchased from the Ambrosiana.

Selected Bibliography

Arrigoni, Paolo, *Mostra di incisioni italaine del Rinascinmento conservate all'Ambrosiana* (Milan 1967); Bora, Giulio, *Disegni di manieristi lombardi* (Vicenza 1971); Barigozzi-Brini, A., and R. Bossaglia, *Disegni del settecento lombardo* (Vicenza 1974); Bromberg, R., *Incisioni di Goltzius* (Vicenza 1969); Cipriani, Renata, *Codici miniati dell'Ambrosiana* (Vicenza 1968); *Disegni e Acquerelli di Albrecht Dürer e di Maestri tedeschi* (Vicenza 1968); Gengaro, A.M.L., F. Leoni, and G. Villa, *Codici decorati e miniati dell'Ambrosiana Ebraici e greci* (Milan 1959); Gengaro, M. L., *Inventario dei codici decorati e miniati (sec. VII-XIII) della Biblioteca Ambrosiana* (Florence 1968); *Guida della Pinacoteca Ambrosiana* (Vicenza 1969); Luzzatto, A., *Hebraica Ambrosiana* (Milan 1972); Oberhuber, K., and L. Vitali, *Il cartone di Raffaello*, 1972; Pacioli, Fra Luca, *De Divina Proportione* (Milan 1956); *Rubens, Peter Paul: I disegni dell'Ambrosiana* (Milan 1975); Ruggeri, U., *Disegni Veneti del Settecento nella Biblioteca Ambrosiana* (Vicenza 1976); Schmitt, Annegrit, *Disegni del Pisanello e di Maestri del suo tempo* (Vicenza 1966); Valsecchi, M., *I grandi disegni italiani del '600 lombardo all'Ambrosiana*, 1976; Valsecchi, F., *Incunaboli dell'Ambrosiana (A)* (Vicenza 1972); Vitali, L., *Incisioni lombarde dell '800* (Vicenza 1970); Diamond, A., "Cardinal Federico Borromeo as Patron and a Critic and his Musaeum of 1625" (Ph.D. dissertation, University of Michigan, 1974); Pedretti, Carlo, *Fragments at Windsor Castle from the Codex Atlanticus* (London 1957); Pischel-Fraschini, Gina, *Pinacoteca Ambrosiana* (Bergamo n.d.).

ELLEN K. FOX

BRERA (officially PINACOTECA DI BRERA; alternately THE BRERA PIC-
TURE GALLERY), Via Brera 28, Milan.

The Brera was established by statute in 1803 following a directive from
Napoleon, who wanted the formation of great national galleries as instruments
of popular education. The neoclassical building, completed in 1784, is the site
of a suppressed Renaissance religious order. The first director of the Brera was
the painter Andrea Appiani.

The major holdings are Renaissance, Baroque, and Rococo paintings of the
Venetian and Lombard schools. There is, as well, a fine collection of Ferrarese
and Bolognese works. However, the three paintings most commonly associated
with the Brera are Central Italian: the *Montefeltro Altarpiece* by Piero della
Francesca, the *Marriage of the Virgin* by Raphael, and the *Supper at Emmaus*
by Caravaggio. In addition to the Italian works, the Dutch and Flemish schools
are well represented.

The earliest paintings in the collection are Venetian, Lombard, and Central
Italian. First there is a *Madonna and Child* by Ambrogio Lorenzetti. From Rimini
is a mid-fourteenth-century painting showing scenes from the life of St. Colomba.
This is the name work of the Master of St. Colomba and was perhaps part of a
dossal painted for the cathedral of Rimini. The *Chapel of Saints Ambrogio and
Catherine* by Mocchirolo is a Lombard work of the second half of the fourteenth
century. Fully restored in 1950, it includes prominent details such as the *Crucifixion* on the altar wall, the *Marriage of St. Catherine*, and the *St. Ambrogio*.
From Venice is a small, five-paneled polytych of the last quarter of the fourteenth
century by Lorenzo Veneziano, with the *Madonna and Child* in the center and
full-length saints in four compartments on each side.

From the fifteenth century in Venice and Central Italy are futher works. There
is the *Polyptych of Valle Romita*, a splendid work by Gentile da Fabriano, and
the *Polyptych of Praglia* by Antonio Vivarini and Giovanni d'Alemagna, as well
as works by Alvise Vivarini, Nicolo di Pietro, and Francesco di Gentile da
Fabriano.

The works of the Venetian school of the Renaissance are among the best in
the collection. Among them are seven paintings by Carlo Crivelli, including a
triptych of the *Madonna and Child*, signed and dated 1482; the large *Coronation
of the Virgin*, signed and dated 1493, from the Church of St. Francesco in
Fabriano; the famous *Madonna della Candeletta*; and the *Dead Christ*. There
are also two works by his supposed kinsman Vittore Crivelli. Two works by
Bartolomeo Montagna include a panel signed and dated 1499. Several famous
paintings by Andrea Mantegna, including the *Polyptych of St. Luke*, the *Dead
Christ*, and the *Madonna with Child and Cherubs*, are also exhibited. All of
these works were acquired during the first years of the nineteenth century. There
is also the magnificent *Preaching of St. Mark* by Giovanni and Gentile Bellini
and three superb paintings by Giovanni Bellini, two *Madonnas*, one signed and
dated 1510, and the *Pietà*. There are as well three paintings by Carpaccio,
including two from the Scuola Albanesis in St. Maurizio in Venice, the *Marriage*

of the Virgin and the *Presentation of the Virgin at the Temple*, and one from the Scuola St. Stefano in Venice, *The Disputation of St. Stephen*.

From the sixteenth century in Venice are more notable pictures. The *Portrait of Antonio Porcia* and the *St. Jerome* are by Titian. The large *Christ at Emmaus* and the *Finding of Moses* are by Bonifazio de' Pitati. The paintings by Bordone are the *Holy Family with St. Ambrose and a Donor* of about 1523 and the *Baptism of Christ*. By Cariani is the *Pala of St. Gottardo*. Palma Vecchio's *Adoration of the Magi* is executed largely by assistants.

Works by Lotto, Veronese, and Tintoretto are among the high points of the museum. The portraits *Laura da Pola* and *Febo da Brescia* by Lotto have a superb elegance. There are also two other portraits and the *Pietà* by Lotto in the Brera. Of the five Veroneses in the collection, the *Christ in the Garden* is most similar to the late Titian. Also by Veronese are a *Last Supper* and the *Supper in the House of the Pharisee*. Tintoretto's *Finding the Body of St. Mark* was commissioned in 1562 to complement the earlier *Miracle of the Slave* in the Scuola San Marco in Venice.

Venetian paintings of the seventeenth and eighteenth centuries in the collection include works by the most notable masters of the period. There are two paintings by Ricci, a landscape and the *Scene from the Life of St. Gaetano*. By Pittoni is the painting *Hannibal Swearing Hatred for the Romans* and the *Venus and Adonis*. The famous *Rebecca at the Well* by Piazzetta is also in the Brera. There are two domestic scenes by Pietro Longhi. Two well-known paintings by Tiepolo are the *Temptation of St. Anthony* and the *Madonna of Mount Carmel and the Souls in Purgatory* from the Church of St. Apollinare in Venice. By his son Giandomenico are two paintings that include a battle scene.

The Lombard school is the one best represented in the museum. The major works are by Vincenzo Foppa, founder of the Lombard Renaissance, and comprise both panels and frescoes. The best-known work *Polyptych of St. Mary of the Mercies*, was not fully reassembled until 1912, although the entire altarpiece except for the predella and the top panel of the *Redeemer* had been in the Brera since the early nineteenth century. The frescoes *Madonna and Child with the Two St. Johns* and *Martyrdom of St. Sebastian* are from the sacristy of St. Mary in Brera in Milan, the old church on the site of the present museum. There is also a triptych and a *Madonna* from the fifteenth century by Butinone. Cremonese works of the fifteenth and early sixteenth centuries include playing cards and other works by Bonifacio Bembo, a painting by Vincenzo Civerchio of Crema, and several works by the Cremonese artists Boccaccio and Camillo Boccaccino. There are also eleven works by Borgognone, including the *Virgin with the Apostles and Saints Ambrogio, Agostino, Gervasio, and Protasio*, the *Madonna and Child with the Beatified Stephen Maconi*, and the *Christ on the Sarcophagus*.

Of the High Renaissance are works by Bramante and the followers of Leonardo. The *Christ at the Column* and fragments of frescoes from the Casa Prinetti are by Bramante. Works by the followers of Leonardo include the name work of the Master of the Pala Sforzesca. The painting *Madonna and Child* by Giampietrino is after one of the drawings of Leonardo for the *Madonna and Child and St. Anne*, in the Church of San Francesco Grande in Milan in the sixteenth century, now in the Louvre (q.v.). There is also the *Madonna and Child with St. John* by Bernardino dei Conti. Drawings, a portrait of a youth, the *Madonna with Saints*, and the *Madonna* based on Leonardo's *Madonna of the Yarn-Winder* are by Andrea Solario. There is also a portrait by Boltraffio and fine paintings by Cesare da Sesto, Marco d'Oggiono, Ambrogio de' Predis, Salai, Francesco Napoletano, and Cesare Magni.

Besides the works of Leonardo's followers, other early sixteenth-century paintings are displayed. Among them is a series of frescoes by Bernardino Luini from the life of Moses, as well as other works, including the beautiful *Madonna of the Rose Garden*. There are also very important paintings by Gaudenzio Ferrari, including detached frescoes *Adoration of the Magi* and *Stories of Joachim and Anna* and the panel *Martyrdom of St. Catherine of Alexandria*.

Paintings from the later sixteenth century in Lombardy include those from Milan, Cremona, Brescia, and Bergamo. There are two works by Lanino, *St. Francis* and *Madonna and Child with Saints Joseph and James and a Donor*. By Lomazzo is a *Self Portrait*, and by his pupil Figino are the *Portrait of Lucio Foppa* and the *Madonna and Child with Saints John the Evangelist and Michael*. From Brescia are the *Madonna and Child* and *Presentation at the Temple* by Romanino and three paintings by Moretto. They include the fine *Triptych of the Assumption*, the *Virgin in Glory with Saints Jerome, Francis, and Anthony Abbot*, and the painting *Madonna and Child with an Angel*. By his pupil Moroni from Bergamo are the *Assumption of the Virgin*, the *Portrait of a Gentleman*, and the very fine *Portrait of Antonio Navagero*. From Cremona are works of the Campi family, which include the *Madonna and Child with Saints Biagio and Anthony* by the father, Galeazzo Campi, and the beautiful *Madonna and Child with Saints Catherine of Alexandria and Francis and a Donor* by his son Giulio. Other works by the Campi are the *Madonna and Child with the Magdalene and Saints Joseph and Agnes* by Antonio Campi, two genre pieces by Vincenzo Campi, and the *Pietà* by Bernardino Campi.

From the Lombard Seicento are many important works. Cerano is represented by seven works that include the *Madonna of the Rosary* and the *Madonna with Saints Francis and Charles*. The *Marriage of St. Catherine* and *St. Charles in Glory* are by Procaccini. There are two portraits by Tanzio da Varallo, as well as the *Martyrdom of the Franciscans at Nagasaki*. The *Martyrdom of Saints Ruffina and Seconda* is a collaboration between Morazzone, Procaccini, and Cerano. There are also works by Nuvolone, Morazzone, and Fra Galgario and seven paintings by Daniele Crespi. Nineteenth-century paintings of the Lombard school include those by Andrea Appiani, the first director of the Brera. The most outstanding are those by Francesco Hayez, including the portrait of an Italian writer, *Manzoni*.

Most of the paintings from the other regions of Italy are from the Baroque era, but there are some from earlier periods. From the sixteenth century, for instance, are two fine works by Correggio, an early painting, the *Nativity*, and a later one, *Adoration of the Magi*. Also from Parma are paintings by Pomponio Allegri and Michelangelo Anselmi.

There is an important collection of Ferrarese paintings, which includes two panels by Francesco del Cossa, *St. John the Baptist* and *St. Peter*; the fragment *St. Francis Receiving the Stigmata* by Cosimo Tura; and the *Madonna and Child with Saints Anna, Elizabeth, and Augustine* by Roberti di' Ercole. Later paintings are the *Adoration of the Magi* by Lorenzo Costa and three paintings by Garofalo, the *Madonna and Child, Lamentation*, and *Crucifixion with a Saint*.

Paintings from other Italian schools include several fine early paintings from Verona, including the *Adoration of the Magi* by Stefano da Verona. From Naples are works by the Caravaggisti Caracciolo and Solimena. From Florence are two paintings by Benozzo Gozzoli, the *Miracle of St. Dominic* and *Christ at the Tomb*. Also, there are four paintings by Signorelli, the *Madonna and Child with Cherubim*, the *Flagellation of Christ*, the *Madonna and Child with Saints James, John, Jerome, and Francis*, and *Stories from the Martyrdom of St. Christina*, which is the predella of a painting now in the National Gallery (q.v.) of London. The portrait *Andrea Doria* is by Bronzino.

From sixteenth-century Bologna are the *Marriage of St. Catherine* by Bagnacavallo, the *St. Cassian Enthroned* by Aspertini, and the *Beheading of John the Baptist* by Pellegrino Tibaldi. However, the Bolognese school is represented primarily by Baroque artists. There are many fine works by the Carracci, including the *Adoration of the Magi* and *Christ and the Woman of Canaan* by Ludovico, the *Adulteress* by Agostino, and the *Samaritan at the Well* and the *Self Portrait with His Father and Nephew Antonio* by Annibale Carracci. Other Bolognese artists represented are Cagnacci (the *Dying Cleopatra*), Guercino (*Abram and Hagar*), and Reni (*Staints Peter and Paul*).

Of the non-Italian schools, the Dutch and the Flemish are the most important. Sixteenth-century paintings are by the Master of the Half-Figures and the Master of 1518, as well as a fine triptych by Jan de Beer and the *Village Scene* by Jan Bruegel the Elder. Seventeenth-century Flemish artists include Rubens, with a *Last Supper*; two paintings by Anthony van Dyck, *Madonna and Child* and a portrait; and work by Jan Fyt. From the early Dutch school is the *Adoration of the Magi* by the Master of the Virgo inter Virginis. Later paintings include landscapes by Jacob Savery the Younger and Jan van Goyen. There is also an oval *Portrait of a Youth* by Rembrandt. Other countries represented are England, France, Germany, and Spain, the latter by four works by Ribera and *St. Francis Meditating* by El Greco.

The Fine Arts Academy, founded by Maria Theresa in 1776, is associated with the Brera. It comprises eighteen schools of art. There is also an important archive and a library with more than eleven thousand volumes. Slides and photographs may be purchased from the collection.

Selected Bibliography

Catalogue of the Royal Brera Gallery, 1933; Matalon, Stella, Preface, *Milan, Pinacoteca di Brera: Catalog*, 1977; Ottina della Chiesa, Angela, ed., *Dipinti della Pinacoteca di Brera in Deposito nelle Chiesa della Lombardia I,* 1969; De Vecchi, Pierluigi, *Lo sposalizaio della Vergine di Raffaello* (Florence 1973); Meiss, Millard, "Ovum Struthionis, Symbol and Allusion in Piero della Francesca's Montefeltro Altarpiece," *Studies in Art and Literature for Bella da Costa Greene,* ed. D. Miner (Princeton, N.J. 1974), pp. 92–101.

ELLEN K. FOX

 **Naples**

NATIONAL ARCHAEOLOGICAL MUSEUM (formerly MUSEO REALE BORBONICO; officially MUSEO ARCHEOLOGICO NAZIONALE; also MUSEO NAZIONALE), Piazza Museo, Naples.

The National Archaeological Museum of Naples, formerly the Museo Reale Borbonico, houses one of the most important collections of Classical art in the world. The Museo Reale Borbonico was established in 1816 to consolidate the growing collections of antiquities amassed by the Bourbons of Naples. In 1860, when Garibaldi became dictator and Naples was incorporated into the kingdom of Italy, the Museo Reale Borbonico was converted into a national museum. Today the museum is administered by the Soprintendenza alle Antichità di Napoli e Caserta.

Construction of the building, which houses the Naples Museum, was initiated in 1585, when the viceroy duke of Ossuna ordered a new barracks for the Cavalry Corps to be built on the deserted hill of St. Teresa not far from the Royal Palace. Found to be unsuitable for its original purpose, the building was subsequently modified under the viceroy count of Lemos to house a university; the architect Giulio Cesare Fontana and the sculptors Finelli and Fanzago collaborated on the project. The building was inaugurated as the Palazzo dei Regi Studi in 1616, and despite some vicissitudes, it remained a university until 1777. Commissioned by Ferdinand IV, the architects Fuga and Schianterelli began work on the building's transformation into a museum in the late eighteenth century. In 1816 the Palazzo degli Studi was renamed the Museo Reale Borbonico. By 1822 the Bourbon collections were installed in the new museum.

The museum's holdings, which are extraordinarily rich and of exceptionally high quality, have a long history of growth. The splendid Farnese Collection of antiquities upon which the Bourbon Collection was built was started in the sixteenth century by the Farnese Pope Paul III. In the eighteenth century, Charles of Bourbon, king of Naples and the Two Sicilies, inherited the collection from his mother, Elisabetta (the last descendant of the Farnese family's Parma branch). The collection comprised, among other things, sculpture excavated from the Baths of Caracalla and the Palatine in Rome, as well as gems that the Farnese family inherited from Lorenzo de' Medici. Charles had the collection transported from Rome and Parma with difficulty, and it was installed in the Palace of Capodimonte in Naples and the royal villa at Portici near Herculaneum.

A major additional source of material for the Bourbon Collection was provided by the excavations of Herculaneum and Pompeii, which Charles of Bourbon promoted. A great volume of archaeological treasures was placed in the museum at Portici, but the finds continued to be so numerous that as a result of the growing scarcity of space, the Palazzo degli Studi in Naples was remodeled as a new museum for the entire Bourbon Collection. By 1822, when everything had been transferred to the Museo Reale Borbonico, the museum's holdings comprised the Farnese Collection; archaeological finds from Pompeii, Herculaneum, Stabiae, and other Campanian sites; and acquisitions including the Borgia Collection of Velletri. The collection was subsequently enriched by new archaeological discoveries and purchases and donations acquired first by the Bourbons and from 1860 onward by the Italian government.

Because of the Naples Museum's great age, the size and character of its collection, and changing museological notions, it has undergone a number of alterations and rearrangements over the years. The transfer of the National Library to the Royal Palace in 1927, the construction of a new wing in the northern courtyard, the interruption and subsequent reorganization caused by World War II, and the transfer of the Picture Gallery to the Palace of Capodimonte in 1956 have resulted in the still incomplete present arrangement of exhibits and space.

Remarkable for their variety, quality, and chronological scope, the Naples Museum's large holdings provide valuable and comprehensive documentation of ancient Mediterranean and particularly Roman civilization. Of relatively recent formation is the collection of stone, bone, bronze, iron, and ceramic artifacts of prehistoric southern Italy, especially Campania and Lucania. Stone, Bronze, and Iron Age sites that have yielded the largest number of finds include the Grotta delle Felci on Capri, Mirabella Eclano, Ariano Irpino, the Gaudo district near Paestum, the village and cemeteries of Murgia Timone, the caves of Zachito and Pertosa, the cemeteries of the Sarno valley, and pre-Hellenic Cumae. Tools, weapons, fibulae, rings, bracelets, razors, and vases provide direct evidence of the conditions of prehistoric life.

The museum possesses a small but important collection of Egyptian antiquities acquired in 1817 as part of the Borgia Collection of Velletri. The holdings range from the Old Kingdom through the Roman period and include stelae, reliefs, portraits, statues of divinities, canopic urns, and mummy coffins.

The extraordinarily large and varied Graeco-Roman collection for which the Naples Museum is world famous provides unique documentation of Classical art and civilization. The Greek colonization of southern Italy in the eighth century B.C. and the subsequent dissemination of Greek culture are reflected in the rich collection of materials unearthed from southern Italian tombs. Particularly noteworthy is the Cumaean collection of the count of Syracuse consisting of tomb furnishings from the necropolis at Cumae (discovered in 1856) donated by Prince Carignano of Savoy and afterwards augmented by the Stevens Collection (1878–95) and subsequent finds. The collection of vases is exceptionally comprehensive and includes Greek imports, imitations of local manufacture, and Italiote creations. The Geometric and Orientalizing periods are well represented by a group of mostly locally produced vases from the site of Cumae as well as from nearby Pithecusae on the island of Ischia. Archaic period holdings provide full documentation of the different currents of vase production both in Greece and Magna Graecia.

There are Etruscan and Campanian bucchero wares, Etruscan black-figure vases, Chalcidian ware probably produced in Italy, a rich series of Attic black-figure vases, and Attic red-figure examples of the Severe style. Among the many masterpieces of Attic vase painting are a black-figure lekanis (c. 560 B.C.) by the C Painter, from Cumae, with a representation of the fall of Troy on its lid, and a red-figure hydria (c. 480 B.C.) by the Kleophrades Painter, from Nola, with the fall of Troy on its shoulder. Among the masterpieces of Attic vase painting of the Classical period are an Early Classical column krater (c. 460 B.C.) by the Pan Painter, depicting a sacrifice to Hermes; a hydria (c. 430 B.C.) by Polygnotos, from Nola, with a representation of girls dancing and tumbling; a fragment of a calyx krater (c. 410 B.C.) from the workshop of the Pronomos Painter, found at Ruvo, depicting a gigantomachy scene evocative of lost large-scale painting; a large volute krater (c. 410 B.C.) by the Pronomos Painter, found at Ruvo, depicting Dionysos and Ariadne with their thiasos and the cast of a satyr play; and a stamnos (c. 420–410 B.C.) by the Dinos Painter, from Nocera, representing maenads at the image of Dionysos.

The many masterpieces among the museum's rich holdings of Italiote vases include a large Lucanian volute krater (first quarter of the fourth century B.C.) by the Brooklyn-Budapest Painter, from Anzi, with the madness of Lycurgus on one side and Dionysus, Ariadne, and sileni on the other; a large Apulian volute krater (c. 370–360 B.C.) from Ruvo, depicting Orestes at Delphi pursued by the Erinyes, and with a polychrome representation of a seated muse on the lid; a large Apulian volute krater (c. 360–350 B.C.) by the Lycurgus Painter, from Ruvo, with Ajax and Cassandra on one side and Dionysos and his thiasos on the other; an Apulian pelike (mid-fourth century B.C.) from Canosa, with the dispute of Aphrodite and Persephone over Adonis; a large Lucanian volute krater (c. 350–340 B.C.) by the Primato Painter, with Elektra, Orestes, and Pylades at the tomb of Agamemnon on one side and Herakles and a woman on the other; two large Apulian volute kraters (c. 340–330 B.C.) by the Darius Painter, one with scenes from the Trojan War and the other with Darius and the Persian court; a Lucanian volute krater (third quarter of the fourth century B.C.) by the Primato Painter, with Apollo, Herakles, and the tripod; a Campanian bell krater (c. 340 B.C.) by the C. A. Painter, from Cumae, depicting a banquet scene; a Campanian hydria (c. 330 B.C.) by the Ixion Painter, from Cumae, with Telephos threatening to kill the infant Orestes; and several Paestan vases (third quarter of the fourth century B.C.) by Assteas and Python. Hellenistic and Roman relief ware includes Calene, Arretine, and terrasigillata vases.

The museum's exceptionally rich holdings in Graeco-Roman sculpture comprise materials from the Farnese Collection of finds from Rome and discoveries from Pompeii, Herculaneum, and other southern Italian sites, as well as acquisitions by purchase or donation. The collection is distinguished by an extraordinary abundance of bronze statuary whose rare preservation is due to the cataclysm that destroyed Pompeii and Herculaneum in A.D. 79. More than sixty bronze statues and busts contained in Herculaneum's Villa dei Papiri alone (excavated between 1750 and 1761) are displayed with other finds from the same villa; the papyri however are in the National Library, Naples.

The Severe style in Greek sculpture is represented by Roman replicas of lost originals, including *Harmodios and Aristogeiton* (the *Tyrannicides*) by Kritios and Nesiotes (477 B.C.) and the *Aphrodite Sosandra* and an *Apollo* by Kalamis. Replicas of sculpture of the Classical period include works identified as Alkamenes' *Hera*; Pyrrhos' *Athena*; Kresilas' *Diomedes*; an adaptation of Phidias' *Athena Parthenos* and the famous bronze ephebus with Phidian overtones from a house on the Via dell'Abbondanza; the *Doryphoros* from Pompeii, considered the best replica of Polykleitos' lost bronze original; and a bronze herm by Apollonios from the Villa dei Papiri, Herculaneum, with the most faithful representation of the Doryphoros' head.

The work of the great sculptors and major artistic currents of the fourth century B.C. and the Hellenistic period is reflected in many replicas including the *Pothos* by Skopas and perhaps also his *Aphrodite* (*Venus of Capua*?), the statue *Adonis* and the *Farnese Eros* associated with Praxiteles, the colossal *Farnese Harakles*, the *Herakles Epitrapezios* (in a larger adaptation, from Pompeii), and the bronze seated *Hermes* from Herculaneum associated with Lysippos. Other noteworthy replicas or adaptations of Greek works are the dead Persian, dying Gaul, dead Giant, and dead Amazon—the originals of which were dedicated on the Athenian Acropolis by Attalos I of Pergamon; several Aphrodites, including the crouching type by Doidalsas, the *Venus Pudens* (similar to the Medici type), the *Venus Kallipygos*, the *Aphrodite of Sinuessa*, and a bronze Aphrodite removing her sandal; an Apollo Citharoedus in green basalt; luxurious Roman imperial adaptations of Greek prototypes, including a seated Apollo in porphyry and marble, and the alabaster and bronze *Artemis of Ephesus*; a head of Jupiter from Pompeii; a statute of Aesculapius found on the island in the Tiber; several satyrs, including a bronze statuette of a satyr playing a flute, from Herculaneum, a bronze statuette of a dancing satyr with a thyrsus, from Herculaneum, a bronze sleeping satyr, bronze satyr holding a wineskin, and the *Dancing Faun* from Pompeii; a bronze drunken silenus; a bronze nymph with shell from Pompeii; the bronze Herculaneum *Dancers*; a group of Pan and Olympus; the colossal *Farnese Bull* group (the *Punishment of Dirce*) from the Baths of Caracalla, Rome; and the group of Orestes and Elektra.

Notable among the many replicas of famous Greek portraits are the bronze statuette presumed to depict Alexander the Great on horseback and a portrait herm of Socrates, related to Lysippos; portraits of Homer, Sophocles, Euripedes, and Aeschylus; the bronze head of Aristotle from Herculaneum; the bronze *Pseudo-Seneca* from Herculaneum; a bronze bust of Sappho from Herculaneum;

the statue of Aeschines; a small inscribed bust of Demosthenes based on Polyeuktos' early third-century B.C. statue; an inscribed bust of the late Hellenistic
scholar Poseidonios; a portrait of Pausanias, king of Sparta; a bronze portrait of
Seleucus Nicator, after an original by Bryaxis; a portrait of Pyrrhus, king of
Epirus; a bust of Philetairos, from Herculaneum; a bust of Ptolemy III (Euer-
getes); and a bronze statuette of a ruler as Hermes, from Pompeii.

The museum has important holdings in the field of Roman portraiture, including many examples from Pompeii and Herculaneum. There is a colossal bust
of Julius Caesar. Representations of emperors include a bronze seminude statue
of Augustus from Herculaneum; a bronze statue of Tiberius sacrificing; a colossal
bust of Tiberius, from Pozzuoli; a bronze statue of Claudius in heroic nudity; a
silver bust of Galba; a colossal bust of Vespasian; a colossal portrait herm of
Titus; a recently discovered fragmentary bronze equestrian statue of Nerva, from
Miseno; portraits of Hadrian, Antoninus Pius, Marcus Aurelius, Lucius Verus,
and Commodus; and a colossal statue of Alexander Severus. Among the emperors' wives are the statue identified as Livia, from the Macellum at Pompeii;
a bust of Plotina; and a statue of Faustina. Among the portraits of distinguished
citizens are a statue of Marcus Holconius Rufus in armor; a bronze portrait head
and herm of the banker Lucius Caecilius Jucundus, from Pompeii; a bronze
portrait of Norbanus Sorex from the temple of Isis at Pompeii; an equestrian
statue of M. N. Balbus and a statue of his daughter, both from Herculaneum; a
statue of the priestess Eumachia; a bronze togate statue of L. Mammius Maximus:
and two statues of Antinous, Hadrian's favorite.

The collection of relief sculpture includes the Greek Borgia stele; a relief with
Orpheus, Eurydice, and Hermes from the collection of the duke of Nola, the
finest among three known replicas of a lost Greek prototype of the late fifth
century B.C.; Hellenistic reliefs, including the couple on horseback from Capri,
Helen and Paris/Alexandros, the youth with courtesans, and a version of the
visit to Ikarios by Dionysos; and Roman reliefs from houses, tombs, and public
buildings, as well as altars and sarcophagi. The subject matter of the sarcophagus
reliefs includes mythology, for example, Selene and Endymion, the story of
Prometheus; Dionysiac subjects; putti engaged in various activities; and the
Muses.

Apart from vases, the collection of terracottas includes architectural revetments
from pre-Roman Campania and Magna Graecia, small-scale votive and decorative sculpture, and larger pieces, including statues of an actor and actress from
Pompeii, the colossal statues of Jupiter and Juno, and a bust of Minerva from
the temple of Zeus Meilichios at Pompeii.

The museum's collection of mural paintings, which is the largest and most
important in the world, comprises the funerary decoration of the pre-Roman
tombs of Ruvo, Paestum, and Cumae and the abundant Roman household decoration of the buried Campanian cities. Although these paintings were primarily
intended as sepulchral and interior decoration, they are derivative of the major
art of Greek and Roman panel painting, which, unfortunately, has not survived

the ravages of time. Therefore, the Naples Museum's collection of mural paintings (made possible by the old-fashioned practice of removing the paintings from
their original context) is crucial to an understanding of the history and development of Graeco-Roman painting. Notable among the pre-Roman tomb paintings are six fragments with the representation of veiled women doing a funeral
dance, from a fourth-century B.C. tomb at Ruvo. The huge and precious collection of detached paintings from the walls of Pompeii, Herculaneum, Stabiae,
and Boscoreale (first century B.C. to A.D. 79) is organized according to chronological style and subject. The enormous repertory of subjects includes mythological panels, still lifes, architectural landscapes, animal landscapes, portraits,
and popular art. Some notable examples are the centaur Chiron and the young
Achilles, the finding of Telephos, the punishment of Dirce, the sacrifice of
Iphigeneia, Perseus and Andromeda, Mars and Venus, Daedalus and Pasiphae,
Theseus and the Athenian children, the abandonment of Ariadne, the epiphany
of Dionysos on Naxos, the infant Herakles strangling snakes, the three Graces,
the portrait of Paquius Proculus (?) and his wife, the riot in the amphitheater,
and the megalographic and architectural paintings from Boscoreale. Also noteworthy is a group of six monochrome paintings on marble (five from Herculaneum
and one from Pompeii) that are closely dependent on lost Greek prototypes, for
example, the knucklebone players signed by Alexandros of Athens and the battle
of the centaur and Lapiths.

The museum's rich collection of mosaics comprises detached pavements, and
some nymphaeum wall decorations and mosaic columns from the houses of
Pompeii and Herculaneum. Among the many masterpieces of mosaic art are the
magnificent *Battle of Alexander and Darius* from the House of the Faun at
Pompeii, a replica of a lost Hellenistic painted prototype; the *Lion Rider* from
the same house; the little scenes of everyday life signed by Dioskurides of Samos;
the *Academy of Plato*; the mosaic portrait of a woman; and the fish mosaic.

The Naples Museum's important and unique collection of household furnishings unearthed for the most part from Pompeii and Herculaneum provides valuable documentation of daily life in Roman times. Apart from small decorative
statuettes, there are lamps, mirrors, vases, braziers, strongboxes, scales, steel-
yards, and surgical instruments. In addition to holding a wealth of objects in
bronze produced in the major metalworking centers of Italy, the museum possesses silver tableware, for example, the treasure from the House of Menander
at Pompeii; glassware; carved cameo-glass vessels; and ivory and bone implements. There is, as well, a collection of remarkably preserved carbonized organic
materials from Pompeii and Herculaneum, including loaves of bread, eggshells,
hazelnuts, almonds, dates, cloth, sandal soles, and wooden objects.

The impressive collection of Greek, Etruscan, Italiote, and Roman gold jewelry ranges from Orientalizing examples of the eighth century B.C. found in
southern Italian tombs to the abundant Roman materials discovered at Pompeii
and Herculaneum. The superb collection of engraved gems, which for the most
part comprises objects the Farnese family inherited from Lorenzo de' Medici,

includes among its masterpieces the Hellenistic *Tazza Farnese*, a large sardonyx cameo in the form of a flat cup, with the mask of Medusa on one side and an elaborate Ptolemaic allegory of the Nile and its blessings on the other, and a sardonyx cameo depicting Zeus in his chariot defeating Giants, signed by Athenion.

The collection of Greek, Roman, medieval, and modern coins and medallions is enormous. To the original Farnese nucleus have been added the Borgia, Carafa, Monteoliveto, and Arditi materials; the important Santangelo Collection, comprising 42,730 pieces acquired in 1865; the numismatic materials from Pompeii and Herculaneum; and the various hoards and treasures discovered in southern Italy.

The museum's rich epigraphical holdings constitute a valuable supplement to the study of Graeco-Roman antiquity. To the inscriptions from Rome and Latium included in the Farnese and Borgia collections were added materials from Campania and the abundant painted and engraved inscriptions from Pompeii and Herculaneum. The religious, historical, political, literary, amorous, and insulting graffiti from Pompeii add colorful detail to our knowledge of Roman life in the first century.

The Pornography Collection (Raccolta Pornografica), which has its own long history, comprises more than 250 erotic artworks that provide unique insight into classical myths, religion, philosophy, superstition, and society. There are statuary, wall paintings, mosaics, and household and funerary objects in the collection; however, access to it is restricted.

The museum possesses an interesting collection of ancient arms and armor, including elaborately decorated pieces of Roman gladiators' parade armor from Pompeii and Herculaneum, as well as bronze horns once used to herald the contests in the amphitheater at Pompeii. There is also a section of the museum where authentic ancient technological materials from Pompeii and Herculaneum are exhibited along with some modern reconstructions that serve as didactic aids.

Requests regarding special access to the collections should be addressed to the Soprintendente alle Antichità di Napoli e Caserta, who is also the director of the museum.

Selected Bibliography

Museum publications: De Franciscis, Alfonso, *Il Museo Nazionale di Napoli* (Naples 1963); Breglia, Laura, *Catalogo delle oreficerie del Museo Nazionale di Napoli* (Rome 1941); Elia, Olga, *Pitture murali e mosaici nel Museo nazionale di Napoli* (Rome 1932); De Franciscis, Alfonso, *Antichi musaici al Museo di Napoli* (Naples 1962); Levi, Alda, *Le terrecotte figurate del Museo Nazionale di Napoli* (Florence 1926); Maiuri, Bianca, *Museo nazionale di Napoli* (Novara 1957); Marini, G. L., *Il Gabinetto Segreto del Museo Nazionale di Napoli* (Turin 1971); Pesce, Gennaro, *Il Museo nazionale di Napoli: Oreficeria, toreutica, gliptica, vitriaria, ceramica* (Rome 1932); Siviero, Rodolfo, *Jewelry and Amber of Italy: A Collection in the National Museum of Naples* (New York 1959); Spinazzola, Vittorio, *Le arti decorative in Pompei e nel Museo nazionale di Napoli* (Milan 1928).

Other publications: *Corpus Vasorum Antiquorum*, Italia, fasc. 20, Napoli, Museo

Nazionale, fasc. 1 (A. Adriani, 1950); Italia, fasc. 22 and 24, Napoli, Museo Nazionale, fasc. 2 and 3 (A. Rocco, 1953 and 1954); De Franciscis, Alfonso, *Il ritratto romano a Pompei* (Naples 1951); Grant, Michael, *Eros in Pompeii: The Secret Rooms of the National Museum of Naples* (New York 1975); Säflund, Gösta, *Aphrodite Kallipygos* (Stockholm 1963); Ward-Perkins, John, and Claridge, Amanda, *Pompeii A.D. 79* (Boston 1978); Gàbrici, Ettore, "Monete inedite o rare del Museo nazionale di Napoli," in *Corolla numismatica* (London 1906), pp. 98–103; Maiuri, Amedeo, in *Enciclopedia dell'arte antica, classica e orientale*, vol. 5 (Rome 1963), pp. 334–39.

RONNIE J. SCHERER

NATIONAL MUSEUM AND GALLERY OF NAPLES (officially MUSEO E GALLERIE NAZIONALI DI CAPODIMONTE; alternately CAPODI-MONTE), Palazzo di Capodimonte, Naples 80100.

The royal villa of Capodimonte, situated on a hilltop overlooking the Bay of Naples, has been the site of one of the principal museums of southern Italy since the mid-eighteenth century. The building itself, begun in 1738 by the architect Giovanni Antonio Medrano as a hunting lodge for the new Bourbon king of Naples, Charles III, is an imposing structure three stories high, consisting of a massive rectangle enclosing two large, square courtyards. By 1758, in addition to serving as a suburban retreat for the royal family, the villa had come to house the Museo Farnesiano, that rich collection of antique sculpture and Renaissance and Baroque art that had descended from Parma to Naples with the Bourbons as part of their Farnese patrimony. In the following decades, and until 1806, when Ferdinand IV fled to Parma in the wake of the Napoleonic occupation, the museum was greatly enriched by the addition of literally thousands of works of art newly unearthed at nearby sites such as Pompeii, Herculaneum, and Stabia. After years of inattention in the first half of the nineteenth century, the collections of antiquities and modern pictures were removed in 1860 to the former university (the present site of the Archaeological Museum of Naples), and the Capodimonte came to house little more than the Royal Armory and a small collection of porcelain and decorative arts. In 1947 and 1948 the museum acquired its present appearance as the renowned collection of Renaissance and Baroque paintings found its permanent residence in newly installed, sky-lit galleries on the top floor of the villa, and the collections of arms and armor, small bronzes, and decorative arts were arranged on the floor below.

Unfortunately for the visitor, works of art that even recently have been cat-alogued as part of the Capodimonte's collection are not necessarily to be seen there today. The Capodimonte is but one of several museums around Naples under the jurisdiction of the Soprintendenza delle Gallerie della Campagna, a branch of the national art ministry responsible for overseeing works of art in the region of Naples. Although the core of the Capodimonte's collection remains fairly stable, individual works of art have been known to shift location with little advance notice to one of the Soprintendenza's other museums. (They include, in Naples, the Palazzo Reale, the Museo Duca di Martina in the Villa Floridiana, the Museo di San Martino, and the Museo della Villa Pignatelli.) Plans for the near future include transforming the second-floor galleries of the Capodimonte into a museum of nineteenth-century Italian art, while the Villa Floridiana recently has been reinstalled as a museum devoted exclusively to the decorative arts and Baroque oil sketches.

The chief glory of the Capodimonte is a picture gallery noted for the breadth and quality of its collection, as well as the spaciousness and ideal lighting conditions of its installation. To the Farnese pictures that arrived in Naples in the eighteenth century have been added in recent years, through donation or purchase, a large number of other paintings that are especially important for documenting the history of Neapolitan painting from the fifteenth to the eighteenth century. In addition, the museum houses the small but important collection of pictures of the Banco di Napoli and, for safekeeping, a number of important paintings (such as the *Flagellation* by Caravaggio and an *Annunciation* by Titian, with studio assistance) from churches in Naples.

The museum's small collection of trecento paintings (including works by the Florentines Bernardo Daddi and Taddeo di Bartolo) is highlighted by one of Simone Martini's masterpieces, *St. Louis of Toulouse Crowning His Brother, Robert of Anjou, King of Naples*, which was painted in 1317 for the Neapolitan church of San Lorenzo Maggiore. Painting of the early Quattrocento is best represented by another well-known work, Masaccio's *Crucifixion* from the dismembered Pisa polyptych (1426), other elements of which are in Berlin, London, Pisa, and Vienna. The dramatic power of this small panel forms a striking contrast to a pair of works by Masolino (Masaccio's collaborator in the Brancacci Chapel) painted for Santa Maria Maggiore in Rome, *Pope Liberius Founding the Basilica*, and the *Assumption of the Virgin*. The first of these works, gently modeled and graceful in composition, records a miracle that occurred in 352, when the pattern of falling snow in Rome marked precisely the plan of the future basilica of Santa Maria Maggiore.

Central Italian painting of the later Quattrocento is well represented with works by Botticelli, Pintoricchio, Signorelli, Perugino, and Filippino Lippi. Although more important works by each of these artists can be found in other Italian collections, a *Massacre of the Innocents* by Matteo di Giovanni stands at the summit of this Sienese artist's production. The collection also contains Raphael's fragmentary *God the Father with a Diadem* and *Bust of the Virgin*, which together with the head of an angel now in Brescia are all that remain of the painter's first documented commission (1500–1501). Venetian paintings of the fifteenth century are highlighted by signed works of Alvise and Bartolomeo Vivarini and by Giovanni Bellini's magnificent *Transfiguration*. Less well known than the above works are the Capodimonte's Neapolitan paintings of the Quattrocento. Colantonio's *St. Jerome in His Study with a Lion* is in the tradition of Antonello da Messina's version of the theme now in London and like the Sicilian master's work points to the strong artistic contacts between Southern Italy and Flanders in the second half of the fifteenth century. An even more striking work in a related style is the portrait of the famed mathematician Luca Pacioli dated 1495 and signed by the still unidentified "Jaco. Bar."

Although the Capodimonte's collection of early sixteenth-century painting lacks any works by Raphael, paintings by two of his chief assistants—Giulio Romano and Francesco Penni—give an indication of the style that flourished in Rome about the time of Raphael's death. Similarly, although the collection has no painting by Michelangelo, it contains two important pictures by Sebastiano del Piombo, who translated many of the great master's ideas into paint. Sebastiano's *Portrait of Clement VII* and *Madonna of the Veil*, with their solid forms bathed in a shimmering silver light, bear witness to the accommodations made by this Venetian painter to the stylistic idiom of Rome and Central Italy. Venetian painting in a "purer" form can be found in the museum's renowned collection of Titians, some ten paintings including several of the greatest importance. With the exception of the *Annunciation* from San Domenico Maggiore in Naples, all are Farnese pictures that have been in Naples since the eighteenth century. *Danae*, a sensual nude about to receive the embrace of Jupiter in the form of a shower of gold, was painted for Cardinal Ottavio Farnese during Titian's Roman sojourn of 1545–46. Seven of the Farnese pictures are portraits, of which the best known is *Paul III with His Grandsons*, an unfinished marvel of Titian's psychological insight and mastery of brush and color. The other portraits are scarcely less important; the seated *Paul III without Cap* and bust-length *Cardinal Alessandro Farnese* likewise stand at the pinnacle of Titian's achievement in this genre. The portraits are complemented by others of great quality by Lorenzo Lotto and Parmigianino, whose *Galeazzo Sanvitale* (1524) is a highly successful example of early Mannerist portraiture.

Among the other important Italian paintings of the early sixteenth century are two small works by Antonio Allegri, called Correggio—the *Mystical Marriage of St. Catherine* and the *Madonna and Child* known as *La Zingara*. The Cinquecento is rounded out by a large number of pictures from virtually all Italian schools, of which perhaps the most important are an *Assumption* by Fra Bartolommeo, *Presentation in the Temple* by Vasari, and several works by Girolamo Mazzola Bedoli. A picture of great documentary value is Marcello Venusti's copy after Michelangelo's *Last Judgment*, executed in 1549 before modifications that covered the nudity of figures in the great fresco.

In addition to its strong collection of Italian paintings of the sixteenth century, the Capodimonte houses a small but important collection of Northern paintings from the same period. Perhaps the best known of them is Pieter Bruegel the Elder's *Parable of the Blind Leading the Blind* (1568), which together with his *Misanthrope* (also 1568), a small tondo, formed part of the Farnese Collection by the early seventeenth century. Four small landscapes by Herri Met de Bles reveal this Flemish Mannerist's exquisite technique in the rendering of cool panoramic views. Other highlights of this collection include triptychs by Konrad Witz, Joos van Cleve, and Jean Bourdichon.

Although the Capodimonte's collection of Baroque paintings includes works from all Italian schools, its particular strengths lie in Neapolitan paintings and in Roman and Emilian works collected by the Farnese. Bolognese classicism is especially well represented with works by the three Carracci: Annibale, Ludovico, and Agostino. Annibale's *Hercules at the Crossroads*, painted in 1595–97 for the Camerino of the Farnese palace in Rome, is among the most important examples of the reforming style that he fostered in the quarter-century before his death in 1609. Its symmetrical composition, broad areas of local color, and highly idealized figure types were to have a profound impact upon other Italian painters of the early Baroque. His dramatic *Pietà* approaches in its brooding light the style of his cousin Ludovico, as exemplified in Ludovico's well-known *Fall of Simon Magus*. Chief among the followers of Annibale Carracci in Rome was Guido Reni, whose *Atalanta and Hippomenes* of about 1620 is a work of the most refined color harmonies and graceful linear movement. Another Carracci pupil, Giovanni Lanfranco, is present with eight works, including his early *Mary Magdalen Transported to Heaven* of about 1605. The little-known Parmesan painter of the early seventeenth century Bartolomeo Schedoni is represented with several works. The most striking of them is the *Allegory of Charity*, delicately colored and bathed in a diffuse light that softens and abstracts the forms. In strong contrast to the works of these Emilian painters is Caravaggio's *Flagellation* (on extended loan from the Neapolitan church of San Domenico Maggiore.) The realistic handling of Christ and his tormenters, and the dramatic light that casts some forms into prominent highlight and others into obscurity, are hallmarks of Caravaggio's influential style. The diffusion of this style can be studied in Simon Vouet's two early *Angels with Symbols of the Passion* and Matthias Stomer's *Christ at Emmaus* and *Holy Family*.

The single greatest strength of the Capodimonte's collection lies in the area of Neapolitan pictures of the seventeenth and eighteenth centuries. They permit the visitor to trace the development of the Neapolitan school from its strictly Caravaggesque origins through the works of Mattia Preti, Luca Giordano, Francesco Solimena, and the major figures of the eighteenth century. The collection is rich in still-life and genre painting, in addition to its wide range of "history" paintings.

Flight into Egypt and *Christ at the Column* document the style of Giovanni Battista Caracciolo (nicknamed "Battistello"), Caravaggio's closest and most profound follower in Naples. The works of Jusepe Ribera—above all, his well-known *Drunken Silenus* of 1626—are powerful in their unabashed realism and dramatic lighting, elements that reflect as much the painter's Spanish origins as his debt to Caravaggio. The development of Neapolitan painting from the 1620s through the 1650s is reflected in major works by Massimo Stanzione (*Madonna of the Rosary*, *St. Agnes in Prison*), Andrea Vaccaro (*The Triumph of David*), and Francesco Guarino (*St. Agatha*). Also in this group are several pictures by the elusive Bernardo Cavallino, who worked almost exclusively on private commission and rarely signed or dated his paintings. The exquisite attenuation of his figures can be studied in key works such as *St. Cecilia* and *Erminia among the Shepherds*.

Although Mattia Preti's sojourn in Naples was limited to 1656–60, he left there many of his finest works. During the plague of 1656 he was commissioned to paint on the seven gates of Naples frescoes showing the intervention of the Virgin and Saints on behalf of the city; the frescoes have been lost, but their appearance can be determined from the two oil sketches at the Capodimonte. They, with other works such as the *Banquet of Absalom* and *Christ Casting Down Satan*, are among the finest works of Preti's career. The work of Luca Giordano, a versatile painter who dominated Neapolitan art in the second half of the seventeenth century, is even better represented. Giordano's *Tarquin and Lucretia* strongly recalls Titian, and his more personal works, such as *St. Francis Baptizing the Neophites* and *St. Catherine of Alexandria Led to Her Martyrdom* (1659), display the fluidity of his brushwork and a chromatic range dominated by pale blues and golds.

The collection of eighteenth-century Neapolitan painting begins with several fine works by Francesco Solimena, including his *Massacre of the Giustiniani at Scio*, the oil sketch for a fresco commissioned in 1715 for the Senate in Genoa. Paintings by Giacomo del Po, Francesco De Mura (notably his *St. Benedict and Totila* of 1740), and Gaspare Traversi help round out this collection of Neapolitan pictures of the eighteenth century. The Settecento elsewhere in Italy is represented in pictures including two views by Panini documenting the visit of Charles III to Rome in 1745, two landscapes by Magnasco, and works by Giuseppe Maria Crespi, Michele Marieschi, and Pompeo Batoni.

Only a small fraction of the Capodimonte's important collection of drawings is on view at any given time, although the two most impressive works—a fragmentary cartoon by Michelangelo of *Three Soldiers* and Raphael's cartoon of *Moses* for the vault of the Stanza di Eliodoro in the Vatican—are almost always on display. In addition to having these well-known drawings, the collection contains works by Pontormo, Luca Cambiaso, Tintoretto, and many others.

Although its sky-lit picture galleries undoubtedly are the Capodimonte's chief attraction, the second-floor galleries also merit the visitor's attention; as noted above, however, they are scheduled for conversion in the near future to a museum devoted exclusively to Italian art of the nineteenth century. The rich collections of arms and armor, small bronzes, and porcelain and majolica will be reinstalled in other museums under the jurisdiction of the Soprintendenza. Many works now on view, however, will remain. The nineteenth-century painting collection, including works by neoclassical artists such as Vincenzo Camuccini and Francesco Hayez and by later landscape painters like Giacinto Gigante, Giuseppe De Nittis, and the Palizzi brothers, will be greatly expanded. The historical apartments, with neoclassical decorations and paintings by Philipp Hackert and Angelica Kauffmann, will be retained, as will the famous *Salottino di Porcellana*, a small and sumptuous room with walls encased by Capodimonte porcelain chinoiseries, executed in 1757–59 and originally at the Bourbon villa in nearby Portici.

The offices of the Soprintendenza are housed in the southeast corner of the Capodimonte. Qualified visitors are welcome to consult its library and extensive photographic archive, research tools essential to the study of the history of art in Naples and throughout Southern Italy.

Selected Bibliography

Museum publications: *La donazione Alfonso Marino*, 1957; *La donazione Mario de Ciccio*, 1958; *Disegni napoletani del Sei e del Settecento nel Museo di Capodimonte*, 1966; *La collezione Angelo Astarita al Museo di Capodimonte*, 1972; *Acquisizioni, 1960–1975*, 1975.

Other publications: Molajoli, Bruno, *Treasures of the Capodimonte* (Milan 1963); idem, *Notizie su Capodimonte*, 5th ed. (Naples 1964); Touring Club Italian, *Napoli e dintorni* (Milan 1976), pp. 269–84.

DONALD RABINER

Palermo

NATIONAL GALLERY OF SICILY (officially GALLERIA NAZIONALE DELLA SICILIA; also PINACOTECA DI PALERMO, MUSEO DI PALERMO, MUSEO DI PALAZZO ABATELLIS), Palazzo Abatellis, Via Alloro, Palermo.

The National Gallery of Sicily was created in 1954, after the old National Museum of Palermo had been divided into two museums: the Archaeological Museum (q.v.) and the National Gallery, whose holdings cover medieval and modern painting, sculpture, and applied arts (thirteenth-eighteenth century). The marvelous collection of medieval and modern art that forms the National Gallery of Sicily originated with gifts from private collectors, mostly Sicilian. In 1814 Giuseppe Emanuele Ventimiglia, prince of Belmonte, presented the University of Palermo with fifty-three paintings and a remarkable group of drawings and engravings, which later entered the museum. During the first decades of the nineteenth century, the collection was enriched by gifts from the Frenchman Bressac, from collections of the prince of Castelnuovo and from Giuseppe Haus (Ferdinando II's preceptor).

After the fall of the Bourbons, the collection became a museum independent from the university. During the 1860s the collection was supplemented by the works confiscated from suppressed religious orders and the works from the museum that had been founded by the Jesuit Ignazio Salnitro at the Collegio Massimo in 1730. In 1869 the collection belonging to the Benedictine abbey of San Martino alle Scale, near Palermo, was purchased. Gifts from private collectors continued to enter the museum during the second half of the nineteenth century. The most important works were from the collections of the prince of Malvagna, Prince Lanza of Ventimiglia, and the duchess of Serradifalco. Under the directorship of Antonio Salinas (1873–1913), the museum became an institution whose aim was "a comprehensive image of the history of arts, manufacturing production, and life in Sicily from the most ancient until contemporary times." The fulfillment of such an ambitious program had to face many difficulties, first the narrow space at the Oratory of the Olivella, seat of the museum since 1866. In 1916 the Council of Palermo decreed that the archaeological collection had to be separated from the collection of medieval and modern art. The decree was fulfilled in 1954, when the restoration work at Palazzo Abatellis, home of the newly created National Gallery, was completed.

The museum was officially opened on June 23, 1954. It is a state museum administered by a regional office called Assessorato Regionale per i Beni Culturali and the Ministry of Education (Ministero della Pubblica Istruzione). As are all Italian state museums, it is governed by a national office called the Soprintendenza.

The building is one of the most remarkable examples of Gothic-Catalan architecture in western Sicily. A commission from Francesco Abatellis (*portolano* and magistrate of Palermo), it was designed by the Sicilian architect Matteo Carnelivari from Noto and built in 1490–95. Decorations, capitals, gateways, and windows are by Giovanni Casada from Majorca and the Sardinian Antioco Cara. The staircase in the courtyard is by the Sicilian Antonio Amato. Francesco Abatellis died without heirs, and the building became the seat of monasteries until World War II. In 1943 it was seriously damaged by bombings but later was restored by the architects Mario Guitto and Armando Dillon, who did not modify the original design. This task was carried on by the architect Carlo Scarpa, whose professional abilities, sensitivity, and taste transformed the interior of the antique palace into one of the most remarkable Italian museums. Giorgio Vigni, with the collaboration of Scarpa himself, is the author of the perfect arrangement of the collection within the building. The arrangement mirrors the content of the National Gallery of Sicily, an unforgettable collection of masterpieces in one of the most beautiful Italian towns, a unique and fascinating mixture of different cultures and styles.

The collection occupies the ground and first floors of the building. On the ground floor there are six rooms, a hall, and a loggia. On the first floor there are ten rooms, which house the painting collection arranged in chronological order. The ground floor is devoted almost completely to sculpture from the ninth-eighteenth century. In the hall, works of sculpture of the ninth century are exhibited with works of the sixteenth century. The most remarkable piece in the hall is a *Madonna with Child*, attributed to a Lombard master of the fifteenth century influenced by Domenico Gagini, the founder of a family of sculptors working in Sicily for more than a century. Among works exhibited in the loggia is a capital representing the Three Ages (thirteenth century) by an unknown artist educated at Pisa.

The first room (Sala I) includes wooden fragments of a door from the demolished house of the Marturano family by an Arabian craftsman of the twelfth century, a wooden polychrome fragment representing St. John from a Crucifixion of the fourteenth century, and a Madonna enthroned (second half of the fifteenth century) painted on wood by an unknown artist influenced by Tommaso De Vigilia, one of the most important artists of the Sicilian Renaissance. The second room (Sala II) is a chapel the architect Antonio Belguardo designed for the Dominican enclosed nuns in 1535–41. The chapel includes sculptures showing the influences on Palermitan art during the fourteenth and fifteenth centuries. Artists from different Italian regions arrived in Palermo from Naples during the fifteenth century, and their contribution to the Sicilian Renaissance was highly important. Antonello da Messina went to Naples during the 1450s, and Domenico Gagini and Riccardo Quartararo (the great Sicilian master of the fifteenth century) stayed in Naples in 1459 and 1491, respectively. Moreover, it has been suggested that the relationships with the international artistic environment in Naples at that time could partially explain some features of the large and famous fresco, the *Triumph of Death*, from the Palazzo Sclafani (Palermo), now in the chapel of the National Gallery of Sicily (since 1954). This masterpiece of the fifteenth century had been attributed to many artists, but the precise identities of the two masters who painted the *Triumph of Death* are still under discussion.

In the third room (Sala III) there are objects significant to the history of the artistic craftsmanship in Sicily during the Middle Ages and Renaissance: a fragment of a wooden carved ceiling of the twelfth century (Sicilian-Arabian art) from Palazzo dei Normanni (Palermo), three Spanish-Arabian dishes of the fifteenth century from workshops of Manises (Valencia), and a vase from the church of the Madonna del Paradiso (Mazzara del Vallo) that is an example of the sophisticated production of Malaga's workshops during the thirteenth-fourteenth century. A bust and a head of two marvelous gentlewomen capture the eyes of the visitor entering the fourth room (Sala IV). They are two celebrated masterpieces by the sculptor Francesco Laurana. The bust is generally said to be the portrait *Eleanora d'Aragona*, daughter of Giovanni, duke of Athens, and wife of Guglielmo Peralta, seigneur of Sciacca and vicar of the kingdom of Sicily. Others suggest that it could be the portrait of Isabella d'Aragona, daughter of Alfonso II, king of Naples, and wife of Gian Galeazzo Sforza, duke of Milan. The female head is possibly a portrait of a sister or nephew of Alfonso II.

The fifth room (Sala V) is devoted to Antonio Gagini (son of Domenico Gagini), who was the dominant figure of Sicilian sculpture during the first four decades of the sixteenth century. The earliest piece by him is a *Madonna and Child* from the monastary of the Maddalena (Corleone). Remarkable is the *Portrait of a Young Man* and the *Madonna del Riposo* (1528) from the chapel of Scipione degli Anzaloni, Church of St. Maria dello Spasimo in Palermo. The sixth room (Sala VI) includes two Madonnas with Child by Antonello Gagini, works by a Lombard master, and the bust *Piero Speciale* by Domenico Gagini. Speciale was an outstanding Palermitan figure of the fifteenth century. Son of

Viceroy Niccolò Speciale, seigneur of Alcamo and Calatafimi, Piero Speciale was a man of humanistic culture and patron of Domenico Gagini and Francesco Laurana. The collection of paintings (rooms VII-XVI) of the National Gallery is a significant starting point in the study of the history of art in western Sicily during the thirteenth to the eighteenth century.

The seventh room (Sala VII) includes mosaics, paintings, and enamels of the twelfth-fourteenth century: a fragment of a mosaic *Madonna with Child* by a Greek master of the fourteenth century; two little paintings on wood, the *Anastasis* and the *Resurrection of Lazarus* (late thirteenth century), which possibly are copies from Venetian mosaics; a *Madonna with Child* by Antonio Veneziano; the *Madonna dell'Umiltà* (1346) by the Ligurian Bartolomeo da Camogli; and a very important cross by the Master of the Cross of Castelfiorentino (thirteenth century), a Pisan painter. The presence of works by painters from Pisa and Siena or educated there was important in Sicily during the fourteenth century: *St. Nicholas*, from the church of St. Nicholas at Sciacca, by Giovanni di Pietro; the *Madonna Enthroned* by Turino Vanni; and the *Madonna Enthroned with St. Catherine of Alessandria* (fragment of a triptych, 1402) by Niccolò di Magio. The National Gallery recently bought an important Valencian-Catalan painting, which testifies to the presence of Spanish masters in western Sicily: the *Last Supper* (c. 1360–70) by Jaime Serra. The eighth room (Sala VIII) is devoted to works by Italian masters in western Sicily during the fifteenth century (*Triptych* by the Master of Coronations), but it also includes a few paintings by primitive Sicilian painters of the same period, such as the *Triptych* by the Master of Galatina.

The ninth room (Sala IX) includes three principal groups of works of the second half of the fifteenth century. To the first group belong works by Italian masters who escaped from Naples to Palermo as a consequence of the profound social and political crisis that followed the death of Alfonso il Magnanimo (1458). Among the international masters who arrived in Palermo during the 1460s were the Master of the Triptych of Monreale (*Triptych* from the church of San Vito, Monreale) and the Master of the Polyptych of Corleone (*Polyptych* from the monastery of San Salvatore, Corleone). The second group includes works by the Palermitan painter Tommaso De Vigilia; seven fragments of a fresco from the chapel of the Teutonic Order at Risalaimi, near Marineo (1480–94); and the so-called *Triptych of the Duke della Verdura* (1486). The third group is represented by the Palermitan painter Pietro Rozzolone, whose production, with the exception of the Cross exhibited in this room, belongs to the sixteenth century. The tenth room (Sala X) is unforgettable. In includes four masterpieces by Antonello da Messina: the *Annunziata* and three saints from a lost polyptych, *St. Augustine*, *St. Gregory*, and *St. Jerome*. The eleventh room (Sala XI) is devoted to the Palermitan painter Riccardo Quartararo and his followers. Quartararo, a great master whose complex personality has not fully been studied, worked in Palermo in 1484–92, went to Naples in 1491–92, and returned to Palermo in 1494, where he died in 1506. His work had been as influential in

Sicily as that of Antonello da Messina. The high quality of Quartararo's paintings can be studied at the National Gallery, which owns important works such as *The Saints Peter and Paul* (1494), a *Coronation of the Virgin*, and a *St. Rosalia*, from a possibly lost altarpiece. The sixteenth century in Sicily is dominated by painters from other Italian regions, whose works are exhibited in the twelfth room (Sala XII). The Master of the Pentecost, a painter possibly from Umbria, is well documented with three paintings: the large *Pentecost*, the *Virgin Mary and Elizabeth*, and a *Pietà*.

The thirteenth room (Sala XIII) includes important Flemish paintings such as the so-called *Triptych Malvagna* by Jean Gossaert, the *Deposition* by Jean Provost, and a *Madonna Enthroned* by Adriaen Isenbrandt. The fourteenth room (Sala XIV) includes paintings by minor Flemish, Dutch, and Italian masters of the sixteenth century. The fifteenth room (Sala XV) is devoted to Vincenzo da Pavia, who worked in Palermo in 1518–20 and 1529–57: *Nativity, Flight to Egypt, Deposition,* and *St. Conrad the Hermit.* After Vincenzo da Pavia's death in 1557, the artistic scene in Sicily was dominated by the Dutch artist Simon of Wobreck (*Holy Trinity*) and Giovan Paolo Fonduli, a pupil of Antonio Campi at Cremona (the attribution to him of the *Annunciation* from the Serradifalco Collection has been debated). The sixteenth room (Sala XVI) includes, besides works by Wobreck and Fonduli, paintings by Pietro Novelli, the most gifted Sicilian painter of the seventeenth century. The collection of the National Gallery of Sicily closes with a group of the Italian paintings from the first decades of the eighteenth century, which include works by Cavalier d'Arpino, Palma il Giovane, Mattia Preti, Corrado Ginquinto, and Francesco Albani.

A new wing of the museum will contain paintings from the seventeenth and eighteenth centuries, as well as a department of applied arts. Every two years the National Gallery organizes exhibitions of recently restored works.

Selected Bibliography

Meli, G., *Catalogo degli oggetti d'arte dell'ex-Monastero e Museo di San Martino alle Scale presso Palermo* (Palermo 1870); Salinas, A., *Catalogo del Museo dell'ex-Monastero di San Martino alle Scale presso Palermo* (Palermo 1870); Meli, G., *La Pinacoteca del Museo di Palermo* (Palermo 1873); Salinas, A., *Del Regio Museo di Palermo e del suo avvenire* (Palermo 1874); idem, *Breve guida del Museo di Palermo* (Palermo 1875, 1882, 1901); idem, *Guida popolare del Museo di Palermo* (Palermo 1882); Delogu, R., *La Galleria Nazionale della Sicilia* (Roma 1977); Fazio Allmayer, V., *La Pinacoteca del Museo di Palermo* (Palermo 1908); Accasciana, M., "L'ordinamento delle oreficerie del Museo Nazionale di Palermo," *Boll. d'Arte*, 23 (1929); idem, "Il riordinamento della Galleria del Museo Nazionale di Palermo," in *Boll. d'Arte*, 23 (1930); Vigni, G., "La Galleria Nazionale della Sicilia a Palermo," *Boll. d'Arte*, 40 (1954).

ILARIA BIGNAMINI

REGIONAL ARCHAEOLOGICAL MUSEUM OF PALERMO (formerly MUSEO NAZIONALE DI PALERMO; officially MUSEO REGIONALE AR-

CHAEOLOGICO DI PALERMO PER LE PROVINCIE PALERMO E TRA-
PANI; alternately PALERMO MUSEUM; also MUSEO ARCHAEOLOGICO
DI PALERMO), Piazza Olivella, Palermo.

The Regional Archaeological Museum of Palermo was established as the
Museo Nazionale di Palermo by 1866, when several local collections of antiquities and art were consolidated under the direction of the Commissione di
Antichità e Belle Arti and housed in the Oratorio di St. Filippo Neri all'Olivella,
where the antiquities remain to this day. During the early years it was greatly
augmented by a major purchase, gifts, and artifacts excavated in Sicily. Annual
funding for the project began in 1863 and not long thereafter public exhibition
of the collection was initiated. Today the museum is administered by the Soprintendenza Archaeologica per le Provincie Palermo e Trapani, Palermo. It is
supported by the government of the Sicilian region. The museum director is also
the executive director of the Soprintendenza Archaeologica, and since 1873 this
person has been simultaneously a professor of archaeology at the University of
Palermo. The museum, however, is not affiliated with the University of Palermo
or with its Institute for Archaeology.

The building housing the museum is important architecturally and historically.
It was begun in 1567 as the Convento dei Padri Filippini. It includes two cloisters,
a gallery, two salons, and a small but important chapel at the focus of a decorative
vista. The principal reconstruction of the building was undertaken after World
War II to repair bomb damage sustained in 1943. One entire wing was rebuilt.

The earliest formal statement of a mission for the museum, in 1873, led to
the collection of art and artifacts representative of the entire history of art of all
Sicily. This mission and the nature of the museum was redefined in the late
1940s, when it was decided to rehouse the post-antique collections in the Palazzo
Abatellis. This transformed the Museo Nazionale into the Museo Nazionale
Archaeologico (1954). A recent decision further limits the scope of future ar-
chaeological acquisition. As a consequence, the museum has been renamed
Museo Regionale di Palermo per le Provincie Palermo e Trapani.

The several founding collections have important histories that strongly influence the character of the collections today. By 1730 Father Ignazio Salnitro had
established the Museo dei PP. Gesuiti di Palermo, known as the Salnitriano. In
1767 this museum, with its collection of sculpture, vases, coins, and epigraphic
materials, was incorporated into the Regia Accademia degli Studi di Palermo.
Earlier, in 1744, the Museo di St. Martino delle Scale was opened with a
collection of seventh-century B.C. vases, fifth-century B.C. coins, medieval
objects, and Renaissance medals, acquired in Rome by PP. Giuseppe Antonio
Requesens and Salvatore Maria di Blasi. By 1809 still another museum of
antiquities had been created, by Antonio Astuto, barone di Fargione, including
inscriptions, ancient sculpture, and Renaissance copies purchased in Rome. They
were installed in the Gabinetto di Storia Naturale with a biblioteca. In 1823 two
young Englishmen, William Harris and Samuel Angell, excavated the Temple
C at Selinus. A sculptured metope was discovered, in fragmentary condition.

After reconstruction by the barone Pietro Pisani, who published the first report on it in 1825, it became the nucleus of the collection of the Museo dell'Università. New excavations in 1827, led by the duca di Serradifalco and Domenico lo Faso, unearthed five metopes from Temple E, two others from Temple C, and a large statue of a seated deity. All were added to the University Museum collection, with gifts from the Bourbon kings: the large bronze statue of *Youth with a Stag* from Pompeii from Francesco I, a *Satyr* from Torre del Greco, and small gold objects from Tindari from Ferdinand II. Another noteworthy gift of this period is five exceptional vases from a sepulcher in Agrigento.

In 1863 a series of activities were begun to bring together the various collections. A collection of paintings begun early in the nineteenth century by Giuseppi Emmanuel Ventimiglia was annexed to the University Museum as a Pinacoteca, or Public Art Gallery, along with miscellaneous works of conventual art, some from the Museo Salnitriano; medieval and modern medals from the Museo St. Martino delle Scale; a triptych, the bequest of Alesandro Migliaccio e Galletti, principe di Malvagna; gifts from collections of majolica vases, intaglio, repoussé metalwork, and Arabic and medieval coins; a sixteenth-century altarpiece, *St. George*, from the Convento di St. Francesco d'Assisi; the *Madonna and Child with St. Dominick* of Antonello Gagni from the Convent of St. Cita; and objects from other convents in Sicily dating from before the year 1600. Most of them were acquired as a result of the abolition of religious corporations in 1866.

In 1863 the University Museum was separated from the university and placed under the management of the Commissione di Antichità e Belle Arti along with the Museo Astutodi Fargione di Nota. By 1866 the two were united with the Museo Salnitriano as the Museo Nazionale di Palermo, and their collections were transferred to the building in which the antiquities remain to this day. In 1869 the collection of the Museo di St. Martino delle Scale merged with them. In 1865 the collection of Etruscan antiquities from Chiusi of Count Bonci-Casuccini, including sculpture, bronzes, bucchero, and Greek vases acquired by the minister Michele Amari, was added to the collection, with another series of gifts received between 1866 and 1868: a Hellenistic bronze ram of the third century B.C. from Emmanuele II, two Punic anthropoid sarcophagi from Cannita from the principe di Niscemi e di Catolica, Egyptian artifacts from abato Paternostro, vases from Magna Graecia and bronze helmets from the duca di Verdura, terracottas and vases from Signore Campolo of Terranova, and four thousand valuable books, coins, incised rocks, and stamps given by Girolamo Valenza, president of the Commissione di Antichità.

Beginning in 1863 a series of archaeological excavations were undertaken in the four provinces of Sicily, Palermo, Trapani, Caltanissetta, and Girgenti; artifacts from these excavations have swelled the collections. Only recently have excavations and acquisitions been limited to artifacts from Palermo and Trapani. Among these major acquisitions are metopes from Selinus; Roman mosaic pavements; architectural revetments from Selinus and Himera; and six thousand coins and objects in 1873 given by Antonio Salinas, then museum director. Underwater archaeological discoveries have been increasing in recent years as a result of amateur explorations.

Today the collection of the Regional Archaeological Museum of Palermo is broadly representative of the ancient art history and archaeology of Sicily and retains major collections of ancient art from mainland Italy. These collections include the Greek vases and Etruscan artifacts from Chiusi of the Bonci-Casuccini Collection, only a few of which are on display. The major Sicilian exhibits are: prehistoric art and artifacts; Punic sculpture; several sets of metopes from Selinus; sculpture decorated architectural revetments from the Temple of Victory, Himera; terracotta figurines from Selinus; artifact groups from tombs excavated in many localities; numismatics; Greek vases; Roman mosaics; and inscriptions. There are also many examples of Greek and Roman stone and bronze sculpture, bronze statuettes, and miscellany.

The paleolithic materials, mainly from northwest Sicily, feature casts of fine incised drawings from three caves at Addaura and others from the island of Levanzo, including exceptionally interesting, fine hooded figures and animals from Cave B at Addaura. The upper paleolithic incised drawing of human beings and animals may be seen at their original sites only with special permission from the Soprintendenza alle Antichità, whereas the casts in the museum are always on public display. Flint implements and paleontological materials from several sites including Addaura and Levanzo are on exhibit.

There are noteworthy collections of artifacts representing a series of early cultures in Sicily, including Neolithic, Copper, Early Bronze, Late Bronze, and Iron ages: beakers from Torrebigini and Villafrati; Capo Graziano-type pottery from Grotta di Moarda (Alcofonte); pottery from Conca d'Oro and the Sant'Isidro tombs at Boccadifalco; artifacts from Serra Ferlichio, Malpasso, Castellucio, and other Copper and Early Bronze Age sites; a huge painted pot from Petralia; painted pottery from Thapsos and Castellucio culture sites at Naro and Partanna; and artifacts from Sant-Angelo Muxaro.

The museum holdings include a small but interesting collection of Egyptian sculpture. The most important of them is a seventh-century B.C. small male torso. The lower part of this portrait of the Bes-Prince of Mendes is in the Cairo Museum (q.v.) in Egypt. There is also a porphry Egyptian Bes of the fourth century B.C., which has the kind of naturalism seen in contemporary Greek art. In addition there is a fourth-century male torso and bronze statuettes representing Isis (two), Osiris (two), Bes, Ptah, Uraeus (two), and Horus falcon (Saitic Period or later), with a kneeling worshipper of the Sait Period (663–525 B.C.). There is a single Ugaritic bronze statuette representing the god Hadad, also known as Baal or Reschef, of the fourteenth to twelfth century B.C., which was recovered from under the sea near Sciacca by a fisherman.

The Punic collection includes some exceptionally fine pieces of sculpture: two huge anthropoid sarcophagi of Sicilian workmanship of a type otherwise known only from Sidon and Carthage of the fifth century B.C.; a limestone torso of a dignitary or priest with a roll in one hand, in an Egyptianizing style of the second half of the sixth century B.C., excavated at Motya; a monumental enthroned Baal of the second century B.C. from Solunto; a sarcophagus from the necropolis at Cannita; a series of twin-headed stelae from the Sanctuary of Demeter Malophoros at Selinus, each depicting a god and a goddess, work of the sixth through the fourth century B.C.; a series of small stelae from the Sanctuary of Zeus Meilichios, of limestone, with the head of the deity carved and painted in single, twin, and quadruple types, of local workmanship of the sixth through the third century B.C., providing an interesting contrast to the Greek architectural sculpture on the same site; and an inscription to Baal-Ammon from Lilybaeum.

The Greek art is the single most important component of the museum holdings. It is the most dramatically displayed of the exhibits. Of these works, the architectural sculpture is of outstanding significance to our knowledge of the evolution of Sicilian Doric style and chronology, for both the sculpture and the buildings it adorned, from the Early Archaic until the Classical period (c. 560–460 B.C.). Fine examples of pediments, metopes, moldings, cornices, and water spouts from several buildings and sites are on display. The metopes from Temple Y at Selinus (c. 560–550 B.C.) are the earliest of the architectural sculptures. Five essentially whole metopes survive with a variety of subjects: a *Sphinx*; *Apollo, Leto, and Artemis*; *Demeter and Persephone in a Quadriga*; *Rape of Europa*; and *Three Goddesses with an Offering Bearer*. Fragments remain of the metope *Herakles and the Cretan Bull* and from still another with a delicately carved head. The three recovered metopes from Temple C (c. 550–530 B.C.) are displayed within a massive reconstruction of the entablature, including the triglyph frieze. These works are reconstructed from many fragments, along with some restoration; yet they remain dominant examples of Archaic Greek art. Their subjects derive from Greek mythology, including: *Athena Aiding Perseus Slay the Gorgon Medusa from Whose Blood Pegasus Is Born*; *Apollo, Leto, and Artemis in a Quadriga*; and *Herakles Punishing the Twin Kerkopes*. Fragments survive of three others, including four heads and a composition, perhaps *Orestes Slaying Clytemnestra*.

From Temple F only two metopes survive in ruinous condition but with some well-preserved details illustrating aspects of Greek art in Sicily just after the beginning of the fifth century (C. 500–490 B.C.). Their subject is gigantomachia: one is *Dionysos Killing a Giant*; the other is *Athena Killing Another Giant*. The last of the sets of metopes comes from Temple E at Selinus, sculpture that immediately precedes the Classical period (c. 480–460 B.C.). This group comprises three delicately carved female heads and four well-preserved metopes of the original set of twelve. They were all carved from the local limestone, with heads and arms separately carved of Parian marble and doweled into the high-relief figures. There are remains of color on the figures. The subjects are the *Mystic Wedding of Zeus and Hera*; *Punishment of Actaeon*; *Herakles Killing an Amazon*; and *Athena Killing a Titan*.

Other fine examples of sculpture include metopes and altar decor from unidentified temples and some well-known reliefs. Outstanding among this group is the metope depicting Eos and Kephalos from the first half of the fifth century B.C., with fine pleated drapery enfolding both figures from an unidentified temple; a series of frieze slabs from a sanctuary at Gaggera with battles between Greeks and Amazons; a relief from an arula with a dancing man and woman, from the Sanctuary of Demeter Malophoros at Selinus (c. 510–490 B.C.); and another partially preserved relief depicting two impressive walking male legs.

Architectural revetments include lion-headed water spouts from the temple at Agrigento, fifth century B.C., and a splendid cornice with lion-headed water spouts from the Temple of Victory at Himera with the colors well preserved. More than fifty of these spouts have been recovered by excavation and are housed in the museum (c. 475–450 B.C.). The reconstructed cornice is one of the more dazzling exhibits. Another is the colorful terracotta gorgon, reconstructed by Ettore Gabrici, which once dominated the central portion of the pediment of Temple C in Selinus, the same temple whose entablature and metope frieze have been described. A single massive reminder of later Greek architecture in Sicily is provided by a reproduction of an enormous Hellenistic capital from Temple G at Selinus, late fourth century B.C.

The interesting variety of other types of Greek sculpture include: an Orientalizing *Lion Attacking a Bull* from Halaera, of the seventh century B.C.; a bronze *Ephebe* (height, 84 centimeters) from a tomb at Selinus, of the early fifth century B.C., only recently acquired from the museum at Castelvetrano, where it had been since 1882, an example of Sicilian rather than pure Greek style; a fragment of the Parthenon frieze, a mid-nineteenth-century gift of Robert Faghan, the English consul; a marble statuette of the fourth century B.C., inspired by the work of the sculptor Timotheos; and miscellany of the fifth century B.C., reliefs and sculptured stelae.

The 408 bronze statuettes include many examples of Greek work representing every period beginning with seventh-century B.C. Daedalic and including fine examples of Archaic, Classical, and Hellenistic works. Among the statuettes as a whole, an enormous variety of types are represented, including gods, goddesses, heroes, kouroi, athletes, warriors, children, ladies both nude and draped, herms, animals, handles, water spouts, pendants, protomes, pins, and astragaloids. Among the Greek objects of particular interest are a Daedalic kouros of unknown origin (c. 650–625 B.C.); an Athena from Temple A, Himera, of the second quarter of the sixth century B.C., wearing a garment comparable to contemporary Samian and a helmet; the *Dancing Maenade* from the Salnitriano Collection (c. 540–530 B.C.), of a type familiar among Laconian bronzes and with an iconographic scheme similar to that found on several metopes from the Temple of Hera at Foce delle Sele; and a fine Laconian hoplite, nude but helmeted, bursting with energy from the Astuto Collection (c. 525–500 B.C.).

The terracottas are mainly statuettes, the largest group being the twelve thousand votives excavated from the Sanctuary of Demeter Malophoros at Selinus. The votive takes the form of a goddess carrying a pomegranate. They were found in stratified deposits dating from the seventh to the fifth century B.C., which enables them to be used as a demonstration exhibition for the chronology and the evolution of style in Greek sculpture from the Daedalic to the Classical. Another important group are the terracottas of Tanagra style excavated at Centuripe and Solunto, dating from the Hellenistic period (late fourth and third centuries B.C.). There are also a large number of terracottas from Himera.

The collection of Greek vases is outstanding, particularly those of the eighth through the fourth century B.C., mainly excavated in Sicily but including a few from Etruscan tombs. Especially noteworthy are the Corinthian vases, eighth and seventh centuries B.C.; the splendid Attic black-figure vases, sixth century B.C.; and the remarkable Attic red-figure vases, fifth century B.C. Also included are superb examples of Greek vase painting of the Classical style; a krater from Gela, *Battle of the Amazons*, in the manner of Polygnotos; a hydria, *Judgment of Paris*; and a fine krater from Agrigento with an unusual scene, *The Departure of Triptolemos*. Vases in the collection have been attributed to Andokides, Oltos, Epiktetos, Brygos, and the Berlin Painter. There are also local imitations of Greek vases, Italiote vases of both Lucanian and Campanian types, mainly with painted decoration; and some other Sicilian types with relief decoration from Centuripe and Solunto.

The collection of Greek inscriptions is important mainly for its many examples from Selinus. The most interesting is the dedicatory inscription to Apollo, excavated in Temple G, Selinus.

The collection of Roman art includes sculpture, mosaics, wall paintings, bronzes, and some interesting and unusual archaeological finds. The finds include a solar clock and sections of lead waterpipe, with junction points and stop-cocks, from the Cornelian Aqueduct at Termini Imeresee. Two of the sculptures have the distinction of being restored by Villareale: a Zeus enthroned, derived from a Greek type of the fourth century B.C., and a colossal statue of Emperor Claudius. Among the Roman funeral stelae is an interesting one with three portrait busts (c. 40–30 B.C.). The holdings include a few imperial portrait busts and sarcophagi, one from the second century A.D. The bronzes are among the founding early gifts. Other major examples of Roman sculpture include a *Matron*, a *Priestess of Isis* from Taormina, a *Mithras Killing the Bull* (all first or second century B.C.), an *Astarte* seated flanked by winged sphinxes from a sanctuary, reliefs of the Vestal Virgins, and a seated god of the second to first century B.C. Roman copies of Greek sculpture are represented by *Herm of a Bearded Dionysos*; *Portrait of Aristotle*, after an original of about 330 B.C.; *Satyr Filling a Cup*, after a Praxitelian original, from Torre del Greco; and a marble copy of a fourth-century B.C. Greek original, chief among the underwater discoveries from near Cape Boco. In addition, there are many small bronze statuettes, including a fine priest, togatus, a gift of Ferdinand I and Ferdinand II (the base and the vine) by way of the University Museum; a Mercury from the Museo di St. Martino delle Scale; a Harpocrates in a Praxitelian stance, with tree stump from Solunto, from the first century A.D.; and many others deriving from both excavation and the founding collections.

The mosaics include types representative of the arts of the first through the fourth century A.D. Several were excavated in the Piazza Vittoria, Palermo; another is from Marsala. The wall paintings include five frescoes from Soluntum and a fragment from Pompeii, all from the first century B.C. Most unusual are the funeral stelae from Marsala, with aedicula containing painted portraits of the dead (mid-first century A.D.).

The Etruscan collection, an early purchase acquisition, includes panels delicately carved in low relief of the Tarquinian type, with traces of paint remaining; both funerary urns and sarcophagi carved in high relief with mythological scenes; a great many bucchero vases, including an oinochoe, with a relief portrayal of the story of Perseus and Medusa, perhaps the finest relief-decorated bucchero piece in existence; bronzes, including mirrors, patera, and statuettes; and other artifacts typical of Etruscan work from Chiusi.

A substantial number of the smaller objects are arranged as a topographical collection, displaying together the finds from single tombs or sets of typical finds from archaeological sites and illustrating the local and chronological evolution of style and cultures in Sicily from the prehistoric through the Bronze and Iron ages, referring to the Punic, Italic, Greek, Hellenistic, and Roman civilizations. Included are typical selections of artifacts from Selinus, Himera, Lilyaeum, Randazzo, Marsala, the Lipari Islands, and other sites. The artifacts include vases, terracottas, bronzes, coins, inscriptions, glass, small works in precious metals, altars, stelae, votives of many kinds, Egyptianizing faience, masks from Selinus, and recent finds, especially those from Palermo.

The library is limited to books and pamphlets on Classical and Punic archaeology and art. It consists of six thousand books and pamphlets of the Soprintendenza Archaeologica (mainly from early gifts) and an additional thirteen thousand books and pamphlets, the bequest of Girolamo Valenza. The library is open to the public.

Usually, the Soprintendenza Archaeologica has photographs of the museum collection and of the related archaeological zones. Special photographs may be made whenever personnel are available. Market prices are charged for all photographs.

Neither the museum nor the Soprintendenza Archaeologica produces its own publications. For the publication *B C A-Bolletina dei Beni Culturali e Ambientali*, apply to the Assessorato per i Beni Culturali, Ambientali e per la Pubblica Istruzione of the Regione Siciliana. This journal began publication in 1980 and contains articles on art, artifacts, museums, and excavations. Distribution is free.

Selected Bibliography

Ashmole, Bernard, *Late Archaic and Early Classical Sculpture in Sicily and Southern Italy: Proceedings of the British Academy*, vol. 20 (1934); Bendorf, Otto, *Die Metopen von Selinunt* (Berlin 1873); Bonacasa, N., *Ritratti greci e romani della Sicilia* (Palermo 1964); Bovio, J. Marconi, *Corpus Vasorum Antiquorum*, Italy, Vol. 14, Museo Nazionale di Palermo, fasc. 1 (Rome 1938); idem, *Museo Nazionale Archeologico di Palermo*

(Rome 1969); Darsow, Wolfgang, *Sizilische Dachterrakotten* (Berlin 1938); Di Stefano, C. A., *Bronzetti figurati del Museo Nazionale di Palermo* (Rome 1975); Di Vita, A., "Le Stele Puniche del recinto di Zeus Meilichios a Selinunte," *Atti del Convegno di Studi Annibalici* (1964), pp. 238 ff.; Giuliani, Luca, *Die Archaischen Metopen von Selinunt* (Mainz-am-Rhein 1979); Holloway, R. Ross, *Influences and Styles in the Late Archaic and Early Classical Sculpture of Sicily and Magna Graecia* (1975); Trendall, A. D., *Red Figured Vases of Lucania, Campania and Sicily* (Oxford 1967); Tusa, V., "Due nuove metope arcaiche de Selinunte," *Archeologica Classica*, vol. 21 (1969), pp. 153 ff.; and various articles on the materials in the museum in *Notizie degli Scavi*, *Kokalos*, and *Sicilia Archaeologica*.

ELEANOR GURALNICK

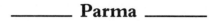 Parma _____

NATIONAL PICTURE GALLERY OF PARMA, THE (officially LA GAL-
LERIA NAZIONALE DI PARMA; also LA REGIA GALLERIA DI PARMA,
LA PUBBLICA PINACOTECA DI PARMA), Palazzo della Pilotta, Via della
Pilotta, 4, 43100 Parma.

The Galleria Nazionale of Parma is housed in one of the most impressive Renaissance ducal seats, the Palazzo della Pilotta, so called because the game of fives (*pelota*) was played within its courtyards. The Farnese dukes had the building erected between 1583 and 1628. Various wings were constructed by a succession of architects, none of whom saw the palace to completion. In its unfinished state the building resembles an ancient Roman ruin, an appropriate symbol of the pretensions of the Farnese dynasty.

Aside from the spectacular entry, little of the original interior is left, except the Teatro Farnese (1618–28) designed by Giovan Battista Aleotti. The theater was constructed at the initiative of Ranuccio I Farnese in the former Hall of Arms and inaugurated in 1628 with the wedding of Odoardo Farnese and Margherita de' Medici. The theater is important as a synthesis of the antique investigations of Palladio, with modern innovations such as the wide, open stage framed by a proscenium arch and U-shaped auditorium with box seats at the perimeter. Considerably ruined during World War II, the theater has been restored.

The Palazzo della Pilotta shelters two other museums in addition to the Galleria Nazionale. The Biblioteca Palatina originated in 1769 with the donation of the collection of one of Parma's early Bourbon dukes, Philip, and was enlarged by the generous gifts of his successors. The Museo Nazionale d'Antichità was founded by Philip in 1760 with objects from the archeological excavations of ancient Roman Velleia. The collection grew with the addition of remains from the Roman theater in Parma (excavated 1844), with prehistoric objects from the region of Parma (excavated 1850), and with a large group of Classical and medieval pieces acquired during the directorship of Giovanni Mariotti (1875–1933).

The origins of the Pinacoteca date from the original *guardaroba ducale*, or picture cabinet, installed in the nearby Palazzo del Giardino by the Farnese dukes—Ottavio, Alessandro, and, particularly, Ranuccio I. However, the collection was transferred to Naples in 1732 by the Bourbon inheritor of the duchy, Charles III, son of Philip V of Spain, who became king of Naples and Sicily. Immediately, Charles' brother Philip began a new collection, which he presented to the Accademia ducale di Belle Arte in 1752. His son Ferdinando added further works, such as the important collection of Tuscan Primitives acquired from Marchese Alfonso Tacoli Canacci in 1787.

Following the fall of the Napoleonic Empire, paintings taken to Paris from Parmese churches and convents were restored to the city and deposited in the Gallery (1816). Duchess Maria-Louise of Austria, who ruled Parma after the period of French governorship, continued the work of enlarging the museum. She brought paintings from the ducal villa of Colorno and oversaw the acquisition of major private collections, such as the Sanvitale, Callani, and Boiardi collections (1834–39). The Galleria became the province of the Italian State in 1882, and today it is under the jurisdiction of the Soprintendenza per i Beni Artistici e Storici per le Provincie de Parma e Piacenza, a peripheral office of the Ministero per i Beni Culturali e Ambientali.

In 1939 gallery director Armando Quintavalle took the first steps toward the organization of the museum along modern criteria. The collection escaped destruction during the bombardments of 1944, although the Pilotta was partially ruined. Newly designed sections were then inaugurated in 1948 and 1951. The current disposition of paintings is provisional.

The Galleria offers an unrivaled opportunity to study the art of the Emilian province and in particular the history of painting in Parma. The visitor will easily perceive the cross-currents between Emilian centers such as Bologna, Ferrara, and Parma, in addition to the contacts they had with the art of the Veneto, Lombardy, and Tuscany. Until the early sixteenth century Parma had no vital tradition of its own but was dependent on other artistic locales for the production of works. That position was suddenly reversed during the Late Renaissance, when two great masters of the local school came to the fore—Correggio and Parmigianino.

During the thirteenth century, the media of fresco and tempera painting did not flourish in the region of Parma in a manner comparable to architecture and sculpture, which witnessed rapid developments in style and were immensely popular in the ecclesiastical realm. Thus the late-thirteenth-century fragment of the fresco *St. Peter and a Bishop*, originally in the ambulatory of Parma Cathedral and now in the Galleria, is a document of exceptional importance. In using bold outline and brilliant flat color, the anonymous artist injected a certain energy into the Byzantine style, which relates his work to frescoes extant in northern Emilia and Lombardy. The Italo-Byzantine style is much in evidence in the

Trecento panel paintings installed in the museum, with examples from Emilia, Tuscany, and the Veneto. The latter province is represented by Paolo Veneziano's triptych with the *Enthroned Madonna and Saints* dating from the early Trecento.

Fourteenth-century painting in Parma was based in large measure on the proto-Renaissance innovations of Giotto. Thus it is appropriate that the Gallery should house several fine examples of the Florentine school, in particular, Bernardo Daddi's *Enthroned Madonna with St. Peter and St. Paul* from San Vitale in Parma and the *Madonna and Child with Saints* from the workshop of Agnolo Daddi. There are also three predella panels by Spinello Aretino, possibly from his St. Ponziano altar (c. 1384), the *Feast of Herod*, the *Adoration of the Magi*, and *St. Benedict Instituting the Rule of the Order*. Altarpieces by lesser-known artists of the fourteenth century may also be studied in the Galleria: Nicolò di Pietro Gerini's *Dormition of the Virgin*, his son Lorenzo Gerini's *Madonna and Child*, and Bicci di Lorenzo's *Enthroned Madonna*.

Tuscany remained a source for stylistic developments in Emilia during the Early Renaissance. The new naturalism sought by Florentine masters was tempered in Parma by a provincialism evident in bold narratives and surprising spatial effects that gives great charm to paintings such as the *Works of Mercy* by an unknown artist (early fifteenth century), the *Enthroned Madonna* by Jacopo Loschi, and the *Doctor of the Church* by Bernardo Butinone (late Quattrocento). The *St. Peter Martyr Altarpiece* for St. Domenico, Modena, by the little-known Simone Lamberti is equally charged with delightful details of formal inventiveness. None of these works possesses the naturalistic subtleties of those Tuscan works hanging in the museum, for example, the religious paintings by Neri di Bicci and Giovanni da Paolo or Fra Angelico's remarkable *Madonna and Child with Saints* (c. 1430; in collaboration with Zanobi Strozzi).

Toward the later fifteenth and into the sixteenth century, waves of influence penetrated Emilia from Northern Italy, especially Venice. A new sensitivity to light and color was introduced to Parma by the Venetian Cima da Conegliano in two large altarpieces, the *Madonna and Child with St. Michael and St. Andrew*, originally in the Annunziata, and the *Enthroned Madonna with Saints*, from the Montini Chapel in the Duomo. In addition, two small tondi by Cima in the collection contain strong Giorgionesque overtones—*The Judgment of Midas* and the *Sleeping Endymion*. Members of the Parmese family of the Mazzola were all trained in the mode of Bellini and his circle. Filippo Mazzola is represented by a *Baptism of Christ* (1493) and *Portrait of a Musician*. His brothers Michele and Pier Ilario, who trained Filippo's son Francesco—better known as Parmigianino—may be studied in their collaborative effort, the *Madonna with Saints* (1499).

Parmese painting in the High Renaissance was still a synthesis of Venetian, Lombardian, and Umbrian styles, as may be seen in Alessandro Araldi's *Annunciation* and the *Annunciation with St. Catherine and St. Sebastian*. Foreigners were still often brought in for important commissions, as is the case with the Bolognese painter Francesco Francia (*Madonna and Child with Saints*, 1515;

Deposition) and one of the greatest figures to reside temporarily in the city, Leonardo da Vinci. Scholars are still attempting to determine the nature of Leonardo's work in Parma and the degree of his impact on the following generation. A single work acts as a reminder of Leonardo's presence, the monochrome sketch of the *Head of a Young Woman*, which probably dates from either the artist's late Florentine or early Milanese period.

Inevitably, a chief goal of a pilgrimage to the Galleria Nazionale is the series of paintings by the greatest of Parma's native artists, Antonio Allegri, called Correggio after his nearby birthplace, who was active during the second and third decades of the sixteenth century. His work combines a soft Leonardesque mode with Venetian coloristic traits, producing a style of translucent richness, overwhelming in its emotional intensity. The viewer may already have seen in various Parmese structures the great vaults frescoed by Correggio—the Camera di San Paolo (overseen by the Galleria), the *Vision of St. John on Mt. Patmos* in the dome of San Giovanni Evangelistica, and the *Assumption of the Virgin* in the dome of the Duomo. Detached frescoes by the master may be studied at close range in the museum: the fragment of the *Coronation of the Virgin* (1522) removed from the apse of San Giovanni Evangelistica in 1587, when the tribune was enlarged; the *Madonna della Scala* (Parma city wall, 1523); and the *Annunciation* (from the Annunziata, 1524–26). The pair of canvases from the del Bono chapel in San Giovanni Evangelistica, the *Pietà* and *Martyrdom of St. Placidus and St. Flavia* (1524–26), now restored to their original color, demonstrate Correggio's pictorial method, which is often termed proto-Baroque on the basis of its influence on the succeeding period. The large altarpieces *Madonna of St. Jerome ("Day")* and *Madonna of the Bowl* show how subtle was the master's synthesis of the divine and the sensual.

Few Emilian artists of the sixteenth century, whether Mannerist or Baroque, escaped the spell of Correggio. His great rival in the history of Parmese art, the slightly younger Parmigianino, borrowed motifs for his early paintings such as the *Nativity* and *Mystic Marriage of St. Catherine*, both in the Gallery. But Parmigianino's work took the direction of the "stylish style," Mannerism, epitomized by his portrait of the so-called *Turkish Slave* (1530–40). Aesthetic abstraction likewise characterizes his *Self Portrait* and the *Madonna and Child with Saints*.

The local school of *maniera* painters whose style was formed on that of Parmigianino and Correggio is represented by several paintings of Michelangelo Anselmi, particularly his *Madonna with St. Sebastian and St. Roch* (c. 1530) and *Holy Family with St. Barbara*, and by numerous works of Girolamo Mazzola Bedoli, including the large *Immaculate Conception* (commissioned 1533) and the *Marriage of St. Catherine* (1556). Other sixteenth-century artists who had contact with the two major Parmese painters may also be studied here: Bronzino, *Madonna and Child with St. John the Baptist*; Sebastiano del Piombo, *Clement VII and a Cleric*; Dosso Dossi, *Gypsy*; and Giulio Romano, *Christ with Four*

Saints (in collaboration with Luca Penni?). There is also El Greco's *Healing of the Blind Man* (from his Italian period, c. 1570).

Toward the end of the sixteenth century, when members of the Carracci family sought to oust from Bologna a feeble Late Mannerist style and introduce the new Baroque manner, they, too, turned to Correggio for inspiration. Annibale Carracci's *Parma Pietà* (1585) is based directly on Correggio's *Pietà* for the del Bono chapel, and Agostino Carracci's *Madonna with Saints* (1586) reflects the Parmese master's *Madonna of St. George* (Dresden [q.v.]). Ludovico Carracci's large pendents, the *Funeral of the Virgin* and the *Apostles at the Virgin's Tomb*, demonstrate his synthesis of Correggesque elements with Michelangelesque power and Venetian coloring.

A comparable artist, Leonello Spada, was trained in Bologna but spent his final years in Parma, where he, too, fell under the sway of Correggio. In works such as the *Judith with the Head of Holofernes*, realism is held in check by the more classicizing mode of the Carracci Academy. The works of the Bolognese painter Guercino possess a similar interest in decorum. One of the major artists of the Roman Baroque, Giovanni Lanfranco, was born in Parma, where he worked under Agostino Carracci and then traveled to Rome to assist Annibale. As may be seen in Lanfranco's *St. Agatha in Prison*, Correggesque elements persisted in both his palette and brushstroke.

The Galleria Nazionale possesses little in the area of non-Italian painting of the Renaissance and Baroque, but reminders of the former Hispano-Flemish connections of the Farnese court are provided by works such as Murillo's *Job* (which entered the museum in 1842); by various small landscapes of Paul Bril, Sebastian Vranx, and Jan Bruegel; and by the two *Alessandro Farnese* portraits by Franz Pourbus the Younger and Anthonis Mor. One of the numerous versions of Hans Holbein the Younger's *Erasmus of Rotterdam* hangs in the Gallery, and van Dyke's portrait *Archduchess Isabella* and an early *Madonna and Child* may also be seen.

Representative examples of Emilian art of the eighteenth century include Guiseppe Maria Crespi's *Madonna and Child with St. Luigi Gonzaga and St. Stanislao Kostzka* (after 1726). The real glory of the Gallery's Rococo collection is a suite of canvases by Venetian masters: Piazetta's *Immaculate Conception*, originally for the Parmese Capuchin church (1744); Sebastiano Ricci's trio of Old Testament heroines—*Rebecca*, *Susanna*, and *Bathsheba*; Tiepolo's *St. Guiseppe de Leonesse and St. Fidele de Signavinga*; and Pittoni's *Magdalene*. In addition, there are architectural caprices by Canaletto and Bellotto. The eighteenth-century rule of the Bourbons witnessed the ascendancy of French culture, apparent in Laurent Pecheux's portrait *Philip Bourbon, Duke of Parma* (1765). Even Giovanni Baldrighi's *Philip Bourbon and His Family*, with its genre-like presentation of the subject and its use of costume and decor, betrays the submission of Italian style to French taste.

The present arrangement of the museum offers little opportunity to see modern painting, but the viewer cannot fail to be charmed by small pictures such as Guido Carmignani's *Orangery of the Giardino Ducale*, with its echoes of nineteenth-century French realism.

The Galleria Nazionale has a library open to the public, a photographic archive, a photographic laboratory, and an Educational Department. Usually, the curatorial staff is responsible for the organization of special exhibitions, which are financed by the Italian government, as are all of the museum's activities, with additional contributions from the Public Body and the Credit Agency. It is possible to obtain photographs of objects in the collection, but the museum is prohibited by law from selling publications. They may be found at local booksellers or art bookstores in major Italian cities.

Selected Bibliography

Ceruti, C., *Il riordimento della R. Pinacoteca di Parma* (Parma 1892); Freedberg, Sydney J., *Painting in Italy, 1500–1600* (Baltimore 1975); Ghidiglia Quintavalle, Augusta, *La Galleria Nazionale di Parma* (Milan 1956; rev. ed. Milan 1964); Martini, Pietro, *La pubblica Pinacoteca di Parma* (Parma 1872); Pigorini, Luigi, *Catalogo della R. Pinacoteca di Parma* (Parma 1887); Ricci, Corrado, *La R. Pinacoteca di Parma* (Parma 1894); Quintavalle, Armando Ottaviano, *La R. Galleria di Parma* (Rome 1939); Quintavalle, Arturo Carlo, "La Pilotta: Segno di una città," *Casabella*, vol. 44 (January 1980), pp. 12–23.

ROBERT NEUMAN

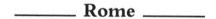

Rome

BORGHESE GALLERY (officially GALLERIA BORGHESE), Villa Borghese, Porta Pinciana, Via Veneto, Rome.

The Borghese Gallery in Rome owes its inception to Cardinal Scipione Borghese (1576–1633), the nephew of Pope Paul V. The collection, of all of the princely collections in Rome, is the only one that can boast such an outstanding homogeneous group of seventeenth-century works. Cardinal Scipione was the leading patron of the arts during the Pauline era (1605–21) and invested much of his immense wealth in buildings, collections, and the patronage of living artists, such as Cavaliere d'Arpino, Cigoli, Caravaggio, Bernini, Domenichino, and Lanfranco. In his patronage, Cardinal Scipione showed preference to the Bolognese painters, particularly to Guido Reni, who belonged to his household from 1608 onwards, and later to Lanfranco. But in his own collection he wanted to represent, as well, the great sixteenth-century artists, Raphael, Titian, and Correggio. In 1633, when Cardinal Scipione died, the Villa and Borghese collections had already acquired that special character that has remained typical of them. Subsequent acquisitions made during the seventeenth century have not detracted from the unity of the collection, which is made up almost entirely of sixteenth-

and seventeenth-century paintings with special emphasis on the Venetian, Tuscan, Emilian, and Roman schools. The sculpture collection is centered around the exceptional group of works by Bernini.

The present Villa Borghese was built by Cardinal Scipione, on the Pincio Hill, 1613–15, and was designed by the Dutchman Giovanni Vasanzio (Jan van Santen). It follows the plan of the Roman *villa suburbana*, established a hundred years before in Peruzzi's Farnesina. Vasanzio covered the whole U-shaped front with niches, recesses, Classical statuary, and reliefs, although much of the decoration was stripped away in the nineteenth century. Nothing remains today of the ornamentation done during Scipione's time, with the exception of four small rooms on the top floor. It was in this villa that Cardinal Scipione displayed his collection.

Another very important period in the villa's history dates from 1763, when Marcantonio Borghese inherited his father's title, and lasts until his death in 1800. Like Cardinal Scipione, Marcantonio was a great patron of the arts, and it was he who commissioned the architect Antonio Asprucci and the painter Mariano Rossi, with a large group of decorators (among which were Pacetti, Righi, Laboureur, Unterbergher, Gagneraux, Giuseppe Cades, and Conca), to decorate the interior. Asprucci placed the most important piece of sculpture in each room so that it dominated the Room and then took the subject of the pictorial decoration from it. For example, in the Apollo and Daphne Room, Pietro Angeletti decorated around the *Metamorphosis of Apollo and Daphne*. This scheme was continued throughout.

The collection suffered considerably between 1802 and 1809, when Prince Camillo, the husband of Pauline Bonaparte, started to break it up by selling several of the pictures in Paris. The *Supper at Emmaus* by Caravaggio and *St. Catherine* by Raphael were among them. Also, in exchange for the fief of Leucadio in the Piedmont, he gave France more than two hundred pieces of Classical sculpture, including the *Mars*, the *Gladiator*, the *Hermaphrodites*, the *Altar of the Twelve Gods*, the *Wild Boar*, and other important works of art that are still exhibited under the Borghese name at the Louvre (q.v.). But it was also Prince Camillo who commissioned the building of the Propylea in Ionic style at the entrance of the Porte del Popolo. The inscription of Camillo Borghese's name and the date of 1830 on the top of the new entrance marked the end of the history of the Villa Borghese. In 1833 Francesco Borghese (whose brother Camillo had died without heirs) created the Fidecommisso Borghese, the foundation that kept the Borghese collections intact. It was so acquired in 1902 by the state, although the objects not covered by the fidecommisso had to be sold in 1892, when the family fortunes collapsed.

The Bernini sculpture collection is outstanding. Bernini first came to the attention of Cardinal Scipione at the early age of nineteen, and it is from this early period (1615–24) that all of the sculptures in the Villa Borghese date. The *Aeneas, Anchises, and Ascanius* of 1618–19 is an early work that still shows some of the Mannerist tendencies from the previous century. Shortly after, however, the first great sculptural group, *The Rape of Proserpina*, 1621, was commissioned by Cardinal Scipione. Then followed successively the *David*, 1623, and the *Apollo and Daphne*, 1622–25. There are also portrait busts, including *Pope Paul V*, Cardinal Scipione's uncle (1618), and one of the cardinal himself, dated 1632. Bernini had left the circle of the cardinal by 1624 to pursue other commissions. The only other great sculptural work in the Villa Borghese is by Antonio Canova. It is *Paolina Borghese Bonaparte as Venus*, 1808, the wife of Camillo Borghese and the sister of Napoleon. Some consider this work Canova's masterpiece.

In addition to the Bernini sculptures, the Borghese collection is famous primarily for its seventeenth-century paintings. Cardinal Scipione, however, was also interested in assembling works by the great sixteenth-century masters. Although the Borghese collection is not large, the individual examples are not only representative of the various Italian schools of painting but of such fine quality that each period can be studied through the few excellent works of the most important sixteenth- and seventeenth-century Italian painters.

The collection emphasizes the Tuscan, Venetian, Emilian, and Roman schools, but there are also a few important examples from the Umbrian, Neapolitan, Lombardian, and Genovese schools.

The Umbrian school is represented by two of its finest masters. There is the *Crucifix between Saints Girolamo and Cristoforo* by Pinturicchio, who was active in Perugia about 1481 and who assisted Perugino with the frescoes in the Sistine Chapel. He is best known for the fresco cycles in the Borgia Apartments in the Vatican (1492–95) and the Piccolomini Library of the Cathedral of Siena (1503–8). The other great Umbrian master, Perugino, the teacher of Raphael, is represented by a *Madonna and Child* and a *St. Sebastian* attributed to him.

The Neapolitan school examples are few but are best illustrated by the seventeenth-century landscape artist Salvator Rosa and by the eighteenth-century artist Sebastiano Conca. The Lombardian school representation is weak, except for the *Sacra Famiglia* by Sodoma, one of the best-known Sienese painters of Lombard origin who had worked in Rome in the Villa Farnesina in the first quarter of the sixteenth century. Three minor Lombardian artists are also represented—Sofonisba Anguiscola, Giovanni Antonio Boltraffio, and Cesare da Sesto. The Genovese school is represented by its greatest sixteenth-century figure, Luca Cambiaso (1527–85), and by its best-known seventeenth-century artist, Giovanni Battista Castiglione (1610–65).

The largest collections that illustrate the other Italian schools—Tuscan, Venetian, Emilian, and Roman—are rich in characteristic examples. The Tuscan school, although not broadly represented, is illustrated by a few excellent examples of sixteenth-century painting. One of the oldest paintings in the collection is the *Adoration of the Christ Child*, about 1505, by Fra Bartolommeo. There is an *Adoration of the Infant Christ* by Piero Cosimo, a Franciabigio *Madonna and Child with St. John*, a Rosso Fiorentino *Madonna and Child with the Little St. John*. There is the fine portrait *Cardinal Marcello Cervnin degli Spannocchi* by Francesco Salviati and a *St. John the Baptist in the Desert* by Bronzino. There are two fine works by Frederico Barocci—*St. Jerome in Meditation* and *Aeneas' Flight from Troy* (1598). There are two portraits by Raphael, the *Portrait of an Unknown Man* of about 1504 and the *Portrait of a Young Woman with the Unicorn*. The *Deposition* by Raphael was removed from the Baglione Chapel in Perugia by the cardinal's agents and thus acquired for his own collection. The major follower of Raphael—Giulio Romano—is also represented. As an example of the extreme range of Cardinal Scipione's taste, there is the *Venus and Cupid with the Honeycomb* by Lucas Cranach the Elder.

The wide range of the Venetian school is well represented by several of the finest Venetian masters from the sixteenth century. There is a *Madonna and Child* of 1510 by Giovanni Bellini, *The Passionate Singer* by Giorgione, the *Courtesan* by Vittore Carpaccio, and the *Sacra Conversazione with a Worshipper* by Palma Vecchio.

One of the most important pieces, which was also part of the initial nucleus of the Gallery, is Titian's *Venus Blindfolding Cupid* (1565). Another of Titian's masterpieces, *Sacred and Profane Love*, dates from a much earlier period, 1515. There is also the fine *St. Dominic*. There are no examples of Tintoretto but Paolo Veronese's *The Baptist Preaching* was sent as a gift to Cardinal Scipione in 1607 by the patriarch of Aquileia. There is the Dürer-influenced *Sacra Conversazione* of 1508 by Lorenzo Lotto, as well as the fine *Self Portrait* of about 1530. Pordenone's *Judith* and Savoldo's *Tobias and the Angel* (c. 1520) are representative of the northern Italian provincial painters. The Savoldo work is one of the finest examples of his entire oeuvre. Representative of the naturalist tendencies in Venetian painting is the *Last Supper* (c. 1550) by Jacopo Bassano. There are three excellent examples of mythological works by Dosso Dossi: *Circe*, *Melissa*, and *Apollo and Daphne*.

There is an extremely fine Correggio, the *Danae*, which belongs to the same group as the *Jupiter and Io* and the *Leda* (now both in Vienna [q.v.]) acquired for the Borghese collection in 1827. These three paintings had been given by Frederico Gonzaga to Charles V on the occasion of his coronation in Bologna. Parmigianino's *Portrait of an Unknown Man* (1524–27) is a fine example of this Mannerist's work.

The collection of six works by Caravaggio formed part of the original nucleus of the Borghese collection. Cardinal Scipione was one of the first patrons of Caravaggio when he was in Rome. (Probably this was about 1589–96, but the dates are uncertain.)

The *Sick Little Bacchus*, considered a self-portrait, and done about 1589, formed part of the Borghese collection from its inception and was presented to Scipione by his uncle, Pope Paul V. It had been confiscated from the estate of the Cavaliere d'Arpino in 1607 by Paul V's tax collectors and is considered one of Caravaggio's first works. Caravaggio had been a member of the household of the Cavaliere d'Arpino, and the *Youth with a Basket of Fruit* (c. 1589) is an example of an early work during his stay in Rome and while he was a part of this household. The *Palafrenieri Madonna* (1605–6) is considered Caravaggio's most serious commission and was destined for the Palace Groom's Altar in the Basilica of St. Peter's, but it met with disapproval because the Virgin was thought to be vulgar. It was then given to Cardinal Scipione. The other three paintings were commissioned by Scipione himself. They are the *David with the Head of Goliath*, which dates from 1605; the *St. Jerome Writing*, from 1605 also; and the *St. John the Baptist in the Desert*, done about 1603.

Of the Caravaggisti works, there is the fine *Concert* by Gerard Honthorst, who was born in Utrecht but went to Rome in 1610, and there is one work by Rubens, *Lamentation Over the Dead Christ*, an early work painted during his stay in Italy (1600–1608).

In addition to the Titians, the Berninis, and the Caravaggios, the Domenichino *Hunt* has always been considered one of the most important items in the Borghese collections, to which it belonged from the beginning. Domenichino was one of the leading Bolognese painters active in Rome (1602–19), and it is his *Hunt of Diana*, about 1617, that was originally done for Cardinal Pietro Aldobrandini but acquired by force by Scipione Borghese. There is also a *Sibyl* acquired in 1617 especially for Scipione's gallery.

The last of the great seventeeth-century Emilian painters to be represented in this collection is Francesco Albani, whose *Triumph of Diana* is a group of four paintings representing the story of the rivalry between Venus and Diana, acquired by Cardinal Scipione in 1622. Other great artists of the period include Guido Reni, Andrea Sacchi, and Pietro da Cortona, who are represented in this collection mostly by portraits.

Photographs and slides of selected works in the collection as well as of the Villa Borghese itself are available. An illustrated guide is also available.

Selected Bibliography

Ferrara, L., *Galleria Borghese* (Novara 1956); Friedlaender, W., *Caravaggio Studies* (New York 1955); Guisti, G., *The Borghese Gallery*, 2 vols. (Citta di Castello 1935); Haskell, F., *Patrons and Painters* (New York 1963); Hibbard, H., *Bernini* (Harmondsworth 1965); della Pergola, P., *Galleria Borghese*, 2 vols. (Rome 1955); Venturi, A., *Il Museo e La Galleria Borghese* (Rome 1893); Wittkower, R., *Art and Architecture in Italy, 1600–1750* (Harmondsworth 1973).

GREGORY OLSON

CAPITOLINE MUSEUMS (officially MUSEI CAPITOLINI), Piazza del Campidoglio, Rome.

The Musei Capitolini, encompassing four collections, is the oldest public art collection in the world. The first collection was initiated in 1471 by Pope Sixtus IV della Rovere as a gift to the Roman people. In the words of an inscription that proclaims the event, Pope Sixtus speaks of restoring the glories of the antique grandeur of the city. The four pieces of sculpture that comprised the original decoration are still revered today not only as fine works of art but as personifications of the Roman State. The most famous is the *Capitoline Wolf* cast in bronze, probably in the fifth or sixth century B.C. The twin figures of Romulus and Remus shown suckling beneath the she-wolf were probably added about A.D. 1500 for the Jubilee year by the Milanese sculptor Cristoforo Solari, called Il Gobbo (The Hunchback). The other well-known first-century A.D. bronze figure is the *Spinario* (*Thorn Puller*), which had been commonly known as the *Capitoline Believer*, because it was thought to represent Marzio, a Roman messenger who refused to halt his journey even though he was hobbled by a thorn embedded in his foot. Two marble pieces are *Camillus*, a statue of a young temple assistant, dating from the Augustan period, and a colossal head of the Emperor Constantine, which today stands in the courtyard of the palace surrounded by other colossal fragments. The head probably was part of a large composite statue whose arms, feet, and head were carved in marble while the remainder of the body was a bronze reveted wooden structure; the statue stood at the western apse of the Basilica of Constantine in the Forum. Sixtus IV also donated a gilt-bronze statue of Hercules, which once stood in the Forum Boarium (cattle market).

A description of the collection, written in 1550 by Ulisse Aldrovandi, records that the museum was by that time already very rich in its sculptural holdings. In 1566 Pope Pius V Ghislieri gave a group of antique statues that had previously adorned the walls of the Belvedere Gardens and Amphitheater attached to the Vatican Palace. By the mid-sixteenth century, this statuary collection formed the major part of the public collection. Overcrowding forced a large part of the sculpture to be moved across the Piazza del Campidoglio into the Braccio Nuovo or Museo Capitolino itself.

Pope Clement XII Corsini officially opened the Museo Capitolino in 1734 after the extraordinary collection of antiques of Cardinal Alessandro Albani had been donated to the museum; Cardinal Albani was the foremost exponent of the neoclassical movement during the eighteenth century and the mentor of the art historian and archaeologist Johann Winckelmann.

After the bequest of two large collections of paintings from the Sacchetti and Pio di Savoia families, Pope Benedict XIV added a picture gallery and thus transformed what had been exclusively an antique statuary collection into a more catholic museum. With the creation of the Museo Pio-Clementino in the Vatican, named after its successive founders Clement XIV Gaganelli and Pius VI Braschi, many of the newer archaeological discoveries were transferred from the Museo Capitolino. It should be noted, however, that the Museo Capitolino, located on the Campidoglio, the seat of civic authority, was the only public museum of painting and sculpture in the Papal State.

Although a number of the finest antique pieces were carried off as spoils of war during the Napoleonic campaign, they were returned in 1816. The busts and herm figures that had previously been housed in the Pantheon were moved to the first floor of the Palazzo dei Conservatori by Pope Pius VII Chiaramonte. The same papal patron donated the altarpiece *St. Petronilla* (1621) by Guercino, which had previously hung in St. Peter's; in the nineteenth century, all of the paintings in the basilica were replaced by mosaic copies.

In 1838 the regulation and upkeep of the Musei Capitolini were given over to the state. At this time, the Egyptiana was transferred to the Vatican Museum (q.v.). More works were donated to the museum complex in 1870 as the result of the new excavations within the city, and in 1876 the Museo del Palazzo dei Conservatori was introduced. In 1925 the Museo Nuovo Capitolino was added to house the overflow of recent archaeological discoveries; this collection is housed in the Palazzo Caffarelli. Finally, the Braccio Nuovo was organized in 1950, and 1957 brought the creation of the Raccolta Lapidaria.

The Campidoglio (Capitoline Hill), the site of the Musei Capitolini, has since Roman times been the seat of civic authority. This most sacred hill, whose name is probably of Sabine origin, was originally composed of two wooded mounds. On the right peak—the Capitolum proper—stood the Temple of Jove; around it stood porticos, public buildings, and honorific monuments. On the left peak, or the Arx, stood the public acropolis; this peak is now the site of the church of Santa Maria in Aracoeli. The area between the two peaks was called the Asylum. At the base of the Asylum was the Tabularium, or public archive, which also provided a splendid lookout point over the area of the Forum.

In the twelfth century a senate house (Palazzo dei Senatori) was placed in the site of the Tabularium, and in the following century, a second palace, Palazzo dei Conservatori, was added to the summit. With the transfer of the bronze statue of Marcus Aurelius from the Lateran Palace to the Campidoglio, there was need for a totally new plan of the land and extant buildings on the hill. (In 1981 the statue of Marcus Aurelius was removed for a lengthy process of restoration. When the conservation process is complete, the statue will probably be housed inside one of the museums on the hill.) At the head of the stairs, as one enters the piazza, are placed the so-called *Dioscuri*, figures of Castor and Pollox, which originally stood near the Theater of Pompey; they were moved to the Campidoglio by Pius IX in the sixteenth century. According to popular legend, as long as the *Disocuri* remain standing, so will Rome stand. Michelangelo added the staircase in front of the Palazzo dei Senatori before his death in 1564, and the work on the Palazzo dei Conservatori had already been started. After Michelangelo's death, several architects, including Martino Longhi the Elder (1578) and Giacomo della Porta (1582), completed the work. The third palace, the so-called Palazzo Nuovo, although begun in 1603, was not completed until the pontificate of Innocent X Pamphili at mid-century.

In the courtyard of the Museo Capitolino (Palazzo Nuovo) sits the colossal personification of *Oceanus* dating from the first century. This figure, known colloquially as "Marforio," was one of the nine "Speaking Statues," so called because of the sarcastic political comments that would be tacked onto their pedestals during the sixteenth and seventeenth centuries.

Although the Egyptiana was moved to the Vatican Museum, a collection of Oriental cult images is still housed in the Capitoline. Notable in this area is a collection of sculpture pertinent to the cult of Jove Dolichenus (Baal), which was popular in Syria, discovered in excavations in 1935 on the Aventine. The *Amendola Sarcophagus* depicting the battle of the Greeks and the Galatians is a fine example of the Pergamon school in the second century. The huge so-called *Sarcophagus of Alexander Severus*, carrying reliefs of the story of Achilles, represents a work of the following century. The colossal statue *Mars* probably is a copy of the cult image that stood in the Temple of Mars Ultor.

A portrait head of Emperor Probius, dating from the third century, is probably the best-known image of this ruler. A Roman copy of the Lysippan original, *Cupid Bending His Bow*, may be seen opposite *Hercules Killing the Hydra*, dating from the second century; the latter work was restored in the seventeenth century by the sculptor Alessandro Algardi.

In the Hall of the Doves, there is a fine example of a mosaic taken from Hadrian's Villa, *Four Doves Drinking from a Basin*, the design of which was copied from the original painting by Sosius of Pergamon. A superb Roman copy of the Hellenistic original of Parius' *The Capitoline Venus* may be viewed in the next room. The chronological installation of sixty busts of Roman emperors allows the visitor to study the changing iconographic conceptions employed in imperial portraiture; unfortunately, not all of the identifications are secure. A similar collection of philosopher busts contains two notable works: a bust *Homer* of the Hellenistic period and a second-century B.C. bust *Cicero*.

Two figures of centaurs, the so-called *Young Centaur* and *Old Centaur* found at Hadrian's Villa, are the work of Aristius and Papius of Aphrodisia; these works are marble copies of bronze originals. The *Wounded Amazon*, a copy of a fifth-century B.C. original, was probably part of the group of Ephesian Amazons executed in a competition between the sculptors Phidias, Polyclitus, and Cresilas. The *Sleeping Satyr*, copied after Praxiteles, is one of the most famous works of antiquity. The *Dying Gaul* (formerly the *Dying Gladiator*) was originally found in the Gardens of Sallust in the fifteenth century A.D. It was originally part of a dedication group to King Attalus I of Pergamon after his victory over the Galatians.

The collection continues across the piazza in the Palazzo dei Conservatori. In the Sala degli Orazi e Curiazi, decorated in fresco by Cavaliere d'Arpino with illusionistic tapestries representing the founding of Rome, can be found papal portraits by the two leading rivals in seventeenth-century sculpture: *Urban VIII* by Gian Lorenzo Bernini, done 1635–39, and *Innocent X* by Alessandro Algardi, in 1645. Another work by Bernini, *The Medusa* (1630), contrasts sharply with Daniele da Volterra's portrait bust *Michelangelo*. The elaborate bust *Emperor Commodus* (172–96) with the attributes of Hercules has had a potent influence on later sculptors.

An entire gallery is given over to sculpture, which was originally found in the gardens of Mecenatus, friend and counselor to Augustus, which stood on the Esquiline Hill. The *Hanging Marsyas*, a copy after the Rhodian original of the first century B.C., is most important.

The Braccio Nuovo contains for the most part sculpture that has been excavated from the areas of the temples of Jove, Juno, and Minerva on the Capitoline. *Apollo Throwing a Spear*, a Greek original of the fifth century B.C., which has been attributed to Pythagorus of Reggio, probably stood in the Temple of Apollo Sosianus. The figure *Aristogiton*, one of the two figures in the *Tyrandiades Group*, which commemorated the murder of the Athenian tyrant Hypparchos in 514 B.C., is an especially good copy.

The Museo Nuovo is particularly notable for its collection of epigraphic stones. A cube of marble said to contain the ashes of Agrippina, wife of the Claudian hero Germanicus, was used during the Middle Ages as a measure of weight by grain merchants. A votive relief with the image of Asclepius, a Greek original, is particularly important. Reliefs from the so-called Arch of Portugal, which was demolished by Alexander VII in 1665, represent scenes from the Apotheosis of Sabina.

The Pinacoteca Capitolina contains a wide range of painting styles and genres. A *Holy Family* by the Ferrarese painter Dosso Dossi is a good example of this eccentric master, as is the *Portrait of a Lady*, with the attributes of St. Margaret by Girolamo Savoldo of Brescia. Titian's early work, *The Baptism of Christ*, still shows elements of the work of his senior, Giorgione. The signed *Magdalen* by Tintoretto represents that Venetian master in a more intimate composition than is usual for him.

Three great Baroque works are Caravaggio's *St. John the Baptist*, an alternate version of the painting in the Galleria Doria Pamphili (q.v.), and two early works by Pietro da Cortona, *The Sacrifice of Polyxena* and *The Triumph of Bacchus*, both dated 1620. The Galleria Cini contains numerous examples of the eighteenth-century porcelain manufactory of Capodimonte in Naples.

Selected Bibliography

Jones, H. Stuart, *A Catalogue of the Ancient Sculptures Preserved in the Municipal Collection of Rome* (Oxford 1912).

THOMAS W. SOKOLOWSKI

COLONNA GALLERY (officially GALLERIA COLONNA), Palazzo Colonna, via della Pilotta, 17, Rome.

The Galleria Colonna was founded in the latter half of the seventeenth century by Cardinal Girolamo I Colonna, son of Contestabile Filippo Colonna and Lucrezia Tomacelli. The Gallery itself, which the late Anthony Blunt called "the most splendid complete baroque room in any Roman palace," was begun in 1654 on the designs of the Roman architect Antonio del Grande. Left unfinished at his death in 1671, the work was completed in 1703 by the Ticinese architect Girolamo Fontana. It was inaugurated in that same year by Filippo Colonna.

Although the dating of the earliest section of the palace falls in the first year of Pope Martin V's papacy in 1417, members of the Colonna family have lived in the vicinity of the church of Santi Apostoli (Saints Filippo and Giacomo) since the Late Middle Ages; the church itself was probably established in the sixth century by Pelagius I after the sack of the Goths. The most important additions to the palace itself were designed by Antonio del Grande at mid-century. This design included an arcaded facade on the main facade of the main court; this arcade has since been blocked up. In 1731 a wing flanking the facade of Santi Apostoli was added after a design by Niccolo Michetti; this building project was later altered by a nineteenth-century building campaign that left only the two end pavilions to reflect Michetti's intentions. At the rear of the palace stretching up the Quirinale hill are located the gardens of the Villa Colonna, laid out in 1713.

Passing through a vestibule hung with canvases by Giulio Romano, Francesco Trevisani, and others, one enters the Hall of the Martial Column (Colonna Bellica), so named for the spiral column of antique red marble that stands in the center of the room. This heraldic emblem of the Colonna family, a facsimile of the Bellica column discovered in the Campus Martius, carries bas-reliefs relating the eventful moments in Roman military history; the column is surmounted by a statue of the Palladium, a figure of Pallas Athena that was believed to have been given by Zeus to Aeneas.

The ceiling vault is decorated with the *Apotheosis of Marcantonio II Colonna*, the victor of the Battle of Lepanto against the Turks on October 8, 1571. The admiral is shown being conducted by Hercules into heaven as he is presented to the Virgin Mary. The central scene as well as the subsidiary allegories of the River Tiber, Glory, the Papacy, and the Church was painted in fresco by Giuseppe Chiari, a follower of Carlo Maratta. The walls of the gallery are hung with portraits of members of the Colonna family. Notable among them are Scipione Pulzone's portrait *Marcantonio Colonna*; Girolamo Muziano's portrait *Vittoria Colonna*, poetess, leader of the Roman circle of Neoplatonists, and mentor of Michelangelo Buonarroti during the sixteenth century; Lorenzo Lotto's portrait *Cardinal Pompeo Colonna*, viceroy of Naples; Anthony van Dyck's portrait *Lucrezia Tomacelli Colonna*; and Pietro Novelli's double portrait *Isabella Colonna and Her Son*. The *Sacra Conversazione* by the Veronese artist Bonafazio di Pitati, a beautiful rendering of the mythological legend of *Narcissus* attributed to Paolo Veronese, and a signed canvas *Venus, Cupid, and a Satyr* by Bronzino make the complement to the range of family portraits.

This first hall is only a preamble to the visual cacophony of the Gran Salone. With the entrance gallery and another small gallery at the opposite end, the militaristic exploits and ambitions of the Colonna family are strung along seventy-six meters of frescoed surface. Legend and reality blend together in this room as evidenced by the cannon-ball that has been left embedded in one of the seven steps leading up to the Salone, a remnant of the bombardment of the city during the siege by French forces in 1849.

The vast decorative cycle focuses on the operatic retelling of the siege, in the *Battle of Lepanto* painted in 1675–78. This central scene and four others are the work of the Roman illusionist ceiling painters Giovanni Coli and Filippo Gherardi; the ceiling ensemble may be seen as a sort of foretaste to Padre Pozzo's work in the church of San Ignazio. Episodes of the historic victory that are picked for narration include: Marcantonio's entrance into Rome, Pope Pius V presenting the admiral with the command of the fleet, the erection of a victory column to Marcantonio on the Campidoglio, and the doge in the Council of War plotting to destroy the Turks.

Subsidiary painted decoration is the work of the German artist Johann Paulus Schor (Giovanni Paolo Tedesco) assisted by his son Philip and the Roman painter Laura Bernasconi. All of the fictive work is framed by a lavishly embellished architectonic setting, inlaid with colored marbles and gilt stucco. Large Venetian mirrors hung along the walls display the collaborative efforts of the noted academician Carlo Maratta and Mario de' Fiori, whose very name proclaims his special talent for floral compositions.

In addition to the luxurious staffage, works spanning the sixteenth and seventeenth centuries cover the walls. *The Assumption of the Virgin*, an early work of Peter Paul Rubens, may be compared with Giovanni Lanfranco's *Magdalene in Glory*. The iconoclastic Salvator Rosa is represented by two works, *St. John the Baptist Preaching* and a *Self Portrait* in the guise of the Baptist. Mid-century classicism is well represented by *Rebecca at the Well* and *Hagar and Ishmael* by Pier Francesco Mola.

The last in the suite of rooms is the Hall of Writing Desks, so named for two opulently carved and inlaid masterpieces of Roman cabinetry. One desk, carved in ebony on a design of Carlo Fontana, is inlaid with twenty-eight intaglio cut ivories reproducing vignettes from Michelangelo's fresco of the Last Judgment on the altar wall of the Sistine Chapel; the ivory carving is the work of the Steinhard brothers and was executed between 1678 and 1709. The ceiling holds the *Allegory of the Battle of Lepanto* by the Venetian master Sebastiano Ricci, dated 1698. On the surrounding walls is represented a microcosmic array of landscape painting, the quintessential part of every proper seventeenth-century art collection. Gaspar Dughet is shown to marvelous advantage with twelve small cabinet pictures as are Paul Bril, the bambocciantist Michelangelo Cerquozzi, Philip Wouwermans, and four landscapes painted by Franck van Bloemen, with figures by Placido Costanzi. On the ground floor of the palace may be found rooms frescoed with landscape scenes dating from 1667 to 1668 by Gaspar Dughet and Pietro Mulier, called Il Tempesta; the *quadratura* (illustionistic architectural staffage) is painted by Giovanni Battista Magno, called Il Modanino.

Although the Hall of the Apotheosis of Martin V (depicted on the vault) claims several fine portraits by the sixteenth-century Venetian school (*Onofrio Panvinio* by Titian, *Portrait of a Gentleman* by Paolo Veronese), it is to the paintings of the soffit that one turns to see the pre-eminent painter of the Roman eighteenth century, Pompeo Batoni. His *Time Unveiling Truth*, a hallmark of the Roman Rococo, makes a nice stylistic foil to the more classicizing *Fame Crowning Merit* by the Florentine Benedetto Luti.

The Throne Room contains documents presented to the Colonna family after the Battle of Lepanto, as well as a permanent throne used only by the pontiff during a visit to the palace.

The last public gallery is named after Maria Mancini, niece of Cardinal Mazzarin, advisor to Louis XIV. Within the context of the late seventeenth century in Rome, Maria Mancini's notoriety resulted not from her marriage to a scion of the Colonna family but from her rivalry with Queen Christina of Sweden. Bartolommeo Vivarini's *Madonna and Child Enthroned* is a hallmark of fifteenth-century Venetian colorism. Jacopo Avanzi's signed *Crucifixion with the Virgin and Saints Mary Magdalen and John* represents the Bolognese school. The portrait *Guidobaldo della Rovere, Duke of Urbino* attributed to Melozzo da Forli marks a calm hiatus in the midst of the overall Baroque panoply.

Selected Bibliography

Museum publications: *Galleria Colonna*, Catalogo, 1907, available in French, Italian, and English.

Other publications: Bandes, S. J., "Gaspard Dughet's Frescoes in Palazzo Colonna, Rome," *The Burlington Magazine* 123 (1981), p. 77; Golzio, V., *Palazzo romani della Rinascita al neo-classicismo* (Bologna 1970); Lavagnino, E., "Palazzo Colonna e l'architteto romano Niccolo Michetti," *Capitolium* 20 (1942), p. 139.

THOMAS W. SOKOLOWSKI

CORSINI GALLERY (officially GALLERIA CORSINI; also GALLERIA D'ARTE ANTICA), Palazzo Corsini, via della Lungara, 10, Rome.

Cardinal Neri Corsini, nephew of Pope Clement XII, was the first patron to systematize both the structure of the pre-existing palace and the various collections that had come to be housed within it. Using the expertise of Monsignor Giovanni Bottari, himself a noted scholar and connoisseur, Cardinal Neri Corsini assembled an immense collection of paintings and sculpture and coordinated the acquisitions of a library, known even today for its rich holdings. Enriched by a succession of art patrons and connoisseurs in the Corsini family, the painting collection was donated in 1883 to the state by Prince Tommaso Corsini. Before this date the government had acquired the use of the palace as a site for the Accademia dei Lincei, a cultural foundation that still functions.

From 1892 to 1895 the content and title of the Galleria Corsini remained unchanged. Then in 1895 the collection was included with other formerly private art collections under the heading Galleria Nazionale d'Arte Antica. By the last years of the nineteenth century even the vast corridors of the Palazzo Corsini were unable to contain the vast number of artworks donated to the National Gallery. One of the most impressive bequests was the contents of the Torlonia Palace, given in 1892 to the state by Duke Giovanni Torlonia. The various art collections, incuding that of Cardinal Silvio Valenti Gonzaga, once housed within the confines of the Torlonia Palace were moved when that structure was demolished to make way for the reconstruction of the Piazza Venezia.

Again in 1892, 187 paintings were added to the national collections; these works were once held under the auspices of the Sacro Monte di Pieta. A sizable group of pictures was donated to the Gallery by the discontinued Fidecommissaria Colonna di Sciarra Gallery in 1896. Finally, in 1918 the government purchased a cache of paintings from the Chigi family.

Encouraged in part by the enthusiastic response to a retrospective exhibition of the National Gallery's holdings at the Castel Sant'Angelo in 1911, pictures antedating the seventeenth century were sent to the newly refurbished galleries in the Palazzo Venezia. Although this most recent addition to Roman museums had originally been planned as a gallery for the applied arts, the bequest by Enrichetta Harris of a major collection of earlier artworks that were housed at the Palazzo Venezia occasioned the transfer of the medieval and Renaissance holdings. At a slightly later date, many of these same fourteenth-century pictures were moved to the gallery of the Palazzo Barberini, which today serves as the administrative seat of the Galleria Nazionale d'Arte Antica; the true heart of the collection, the paintings of the seventeenth and eighteenth centuries, remains in the Palazzo Corsini.

The collection of prints and drawings, which had also been donated in 1848 by Princes Tommaso and Andrea Corsini, was given to the Galleria Nazionale delle Stampe, now housed in the Villa Farnesina across the via Lungara from the Palazzo Corsini.

The first palace built in 1473 on the present site was that of Cardinal Cristoforo Riario, nephew of Pope Sixtus IV della Rovere. The site of the palace abuts the base of the Janiculum hill; in the fifteenth century, this area across the Tiber River was decidedly suburban.

The most famous inhabitant of the palace was Queen Christina of Sweden, daughter of King Gustavus Adolphus, who fled both her crown and religion for Rome and settled in 1659 at the palace, where she remained until her death in 1689. Although Christina was a voracious patron of arts and letters whose collection included important works by Correggio, Raphael, Titian, and Veronese, none of her possessions remains in the Galleria Corsini, having been dispersed after her death.

The present palace was begun for the Corsini in 1736 by Ferdinando Fuga. The form of the palace is atypical of eighteenth-century palace architecture, having a three-aisled vestibule that leads to a passage that crosses the rear garden flanked by two flights of stairs. This double staircase arrangement unites at the landing to deliver the visitor to the *piano nobile* (first floor), the site of the picture gallery.

The sheer range and scale of the Galleria Corsini distinguish it from the Roman patrician collections of the Spada, Borghese, Colonna, and Doria-Pamphili families. The entrance vestibule offers a range of neoclassical sculpture, with works by Pietro Teverani, Camillo Pistrucci, and Cesare Benaglia, all students of Antonio Canova and Thorwaldsen.

Foreign schools are amply represented by the works of Frans Francken, Christian Berentz, and David de Coninck. Frans Snyders, a pupil of Anthony van

Dyck, is represented by a *Catch of the Hunt*, as is Philip Wouwermans by *Hunters*. Willem Kalf's *Kitchen Interior* and Joos de Momper's *Landscape* complement the works of those Northern artists, who adopted Italy as their home. The *Bambocciati* (so named after their leader Pieter van Laer, called Il Bamboccio) are represented by Lingelbach's *Woman Rider* and Jan Miel's *Masquerade*. A particularly sensuous *Madonna and Child* of Murillo is hung in the third hall of the gallery.

The remainder of the Galleria Corsini is arranged according to regional Italian schools. The Late Baroque, Genoese-born master Giovanni Battista Gaulli, called Il Baciccia, is represented by a portrait of his mentor and friend *Gian Lorenzo Bernini*; *bozzetti* (models) for two of the pendentive paintings under the dome of the church of St. Agnese in Agone look more toward Rome and away from his home city. The *Charity of St. Lawrence* by Bernardo Strozzi pays homage to the artist's long career in the Venetian capital. Two landscapes by Alessandro Magnasco lead into the eighteenth century.

Venice is present in the form of its favorite *vedutisti* (scene painters) Luca Carlevaris and Canaletto, whose four Venetian scenes are particularly important. Examples of eighteenth-century figural painting in Venice include Giovanni Battista Tiepolo's *Faun and Young Satyr* and Giovanni Battista Piazzetta's *Judith*.

The seventeenth-century Bolognese and Florentine schools pre-eminently focus on the works of the Carracci Academy. Guido Reni, the prime colorist of his century, is represented by four works, especially the famous (presumed) portrait of Beatrice Cenci, which was to be copied by numerous artists during the nineteenth century and romanticized by Nathaniel Hawthorne. Giovanni Lanfranco and Guercino, the most baroque of the Carracci followers, are seen, respectively, in the altarpiece *Saints Peter, Agatha, and Magdalen Transported to Heaven* and in *Ecce Homo*. The *St. Francis* by Ludovico Cigoli points to the Late Mannerist style that was still popular in Florence during the early years of the seventeenth century.

The other major force in Roman painting, Michelangelo Merisi da Caravaggio, is represented by a brooding image of St. John the Baptist. His Italian followers in the collection include: *St. Francis* by Orazio Gentileschi; *Death of Abel* painted on copper by Michelangelo Cerquozzi; *Bacchus* by Bartolommeo Manfredi, and the altarpiece *St. Gregory the Great* by Carlo Saraceni. Simon Vouet's *Herodias* and Valentin's *Justice of Solomon* depict the encroachment of the tenebrist style among the French artists who traveled to Rome.

Although Gian Lorenzo Bernini dominated the middle years of the century, the works of a school of painters who worked under him at St. Peter's are also included in the Gallery: *Adoration of the Shepherds* and *Adoration of the Magi* by Giovanni Francesco Romanelli and *Guardian Angel* by Pietro da Cortona. The strong vein of Late Baroque style that flourished in Naples far longer than in any other city on the Italian peninsula is included: *St. Onofrius* by Giovanni Battista Caracciolo, the marvelous *Christ Disputing among the Doctors* by Luca Giordano, and the monumental *Heliodorus Expelled from the Temple* by Francesco Solimena. Both exact and caprice views are included in an impressive collection of landscape painting. Examples are *Roman Views of Fantasy* by Giovanni Paolo Pannini, *Portico of Octavia* by Antonio Gaspari, and two topographical views by Gaspare van Wittel (Vanvitelli).

The Odescalchi Collection of Arms acquired by the state in 1959 is one of the most important of its type in Europe. The second floor of the palace houses the Library of the Accademia Nazionale dei Lincei (so called for the lynx that figures in its coat-of-arms). Founded in 1848, its holdings number about one hundred thousand volumes and fascicules. The Bibliotheca Corsiniana founded by Lorenzo Corsini in 1754 contains a noteworthy collection of manuscripts. The Accademia dei Lincei publishes two journals, *Monumenti Antichi* and *Notizie degli Scavi di antichita*.

Selected Bibliography

Museum publications: Hermanin, Federico, *Catalogo della R. Galleria d'Arte Antica* (Bologna 1924).

                                                                      THOMAS W. SOKOLOWSKI

DORIA PAMPHILI GALLERY (officially GALLERIA DORIA PAMPHILI), Palazzo Doria Pamphili, Piazza del Collegio Romano, 1a, Rome.

The Galleria Doria Pamphili was initiated by a Papal Brief of 1651. Issued during the pontificate of Pope Innocent X Pamphili, this document hereditarily entailed all of the artworks and furnishings within the Palazzo Pamphili on Piazza Navona. This collection, which was established under the stewardship of the pope's sister Donna Olimpia Maidalchini, was further enhanced and enlarged by the marriage in 1647 of Camillo Pamphili to Olimpia Aldobrandini, princess of Rossano and widow of Paolo Borghese. Due to the immensity of the family holdings and to the ascent of Giovanni Pamphili to the papal throne, the collection was moved to the Pamphili Palace in the Piazza del Collegio Romano. Three palaces on the via del Corso were combined to form the immense structure of the present palace. The earliest section of this structure, dating from 1435, which is preserved in the courtyard of the present complex, was owned by Cardinal Fazio Santorio, titular head of the adjacent church of Santa Maria in via Lata. Ownership successively passed through the hands of the Della Rovere, Aldobrandini, and Pamphili families, finally coming into the possession in 1760 of the Genoese Doria family, who annexed the name of Pamphili as well as the palace structure itself. Flanking the via del Plebescito on the south is the facade built in 1643 after the design by Paolo Ameli; the northern facade, designed by Antonio del Grande, was constructed in 1660 and faces on the Piazza del Collegio Romano. In 1731–34 Giovanni Valvassori erected a facade along the via del Corso and enclosed the upper loggia of the fifteenth-century courtyard, thus creating three wings to house pictures and turning the fourth wing into the Gallery of Mirrors.

For most of the nineteenth century, the Galleria Doria Pamphili was included among those *Fidecomessi*, or settled private properties, that came under communal jurisdiction. This regulation was changed by law in 1871, returning the property to its private owners. The Sala Aldobrandini was organized in 1838 by Filippo Andrea V. The last major period of acquisitions ended with the purchase of some Italian Primitives by Prince Alfonso in the closing years of the last century.

During the first half of the twentieth century, the palace was variously refurbished and reorganized by the family to separate the private apartments from the public art gallery. In 1960 the private apartments were opened for public viewing after a massive campaign of architectural restoration had been completed.

The entrance to the Gallery, found on the *piano nobile* (second floor), leads into a vaulted vestibule with frescoed decorations by G. Angeloni and Barnarbo; the central panel of the ceiling with *Cadmus and the Dragon* was painted by Luigi Agricola. The selection of landscape paintings hung in this entryway serves as a leitmotif for the entire collection and pays homage to the taste of the original patrons, Camillo Pamphili and his son Cardinal Benedetto Pamphili. Works done by Gaspar Dughet and Jan Frans van Bloemen hint that the only truly international genre of painting in the seventeenth painting was landscape, a genre that was dominated by the studio of the French painter Claude Gellée, called Le Lorraine; the artist is represented by five canvases, among them, *Mercury Stealing the Cattle of Apollo* and *Diana, Goddess of the Hunt*. The very origin of the seventeenth-century classical landscape can be traced to the commission by Camillio Pamphili to the Bolognese master Annibale Carracci and his school for six lunette landscapes with biblical subjects; particularly of note are *The Visitation*, a collaboration between Annibale Carracci and his pupil Sisto Baldalocchio; *Assumption of the Virgin*, painted by Annibale and Francesco Albani; and the *Flight into Egypt* by Annibale. Agostino Tassi's *Tobias and the Angel* and Herman van Swanevelt's *Christ Served by Angels*, both executed near the turn of the century, help to usher in the masterworks of mid-century. Salvator Rosa's *Cliffs along the Seashore* serves as the picturesque antipode to the Claudian classical landscape tradition. Bartolomeus Breenbergh's scenes of the Roman countryside and Paul Bril's urban views of the Campo Vaccino (seventeenth-century name for the grazing pasture that covered the area of the forum) reflect the presence of Northern artists in the city in the first years of the Baroque era. The tradition of the Italian journey was to continue into the eighteenth century as represented in the two scenes by Gaspar van Wittel (Vanvitelli): *The Piazzetta in Venice* and *St. Maria della Salute*.

However, the holdings of the Galleria Doria Pamphili are not confined to works in the landscape tradition. In fact, its very heterogeneous nature not only is a hallmark of its richness but also serves as an archetype for all important seventeenth-century art collections. The works of the classicizing Bolognese school are well represented by Francesco Barbieri, called Il Guercino's *Erminia and Tancred*, Guido Reni's *Madonna Adoring the Sleeping Christ Child*, Giovanni Lanfranco's *Galatea and Polyphemus*, Domenico Zampiere, called Il Domenichino's *St. Francis in Prayer*, and Giovanni Salvi, called Il Sassoferrato's *Holy Family*, but the works by the Caravaggesque movement are equally strong.

Three early works by Michelangel Merisi da Caravaggio, *The Penitent Magdalene*, *Rest on the Flight into Egypt*, and the more darkly sensuous *St. John the Baptist* (an alternate version to the work in the Capitoline Museum [q.v.]) form the nucleus of the international tenebrist works that are represented.

The Italian followers of Caravaggio are represented by Bartolommeo Schedoni (*Madonna and Child with the Infant St. John the Baptist*), Antiveduto Grammatica (*Nativity*), and Massimo Stanzione (*Sybil*); Matthias Stomer (*Supper at Emmaus*) and Trophime Bigot (*Singing Girl with Candle*) represent the Northern exponents of the tenebrist school. The Neapolitan school is well represented by works of Luca Giordano, Francesco Solimena, and Matteo Preti, notable among which is the latter's *The Tribute Money*.

Pope Innocent X is brilliantly preserved in a pair of extraordinary portraits executed by two unsurpassed geniuses of the century, the Gian Lorenzo Bernini marble bust and the Diego Valázquez painted portrait executed during a diplomatic trip to Rome in 1650. The classicist-Baroque split in sculpture can also be seen by comparing Bernini's papal portrait with Alessandro Algardi's bust of the familial matriarch, *Donna Olimpia Maidalchini*.

On the death of his mother, Cardinal Benedetto inherited a large cache of Renaissance pictures that can also be found in the Gallery. Among them are Raphael's *Double Portrait*, Titian's *Herodias*, Parmigianino's *Little Madonna* and *Nativity*, and Sebastiano del Piombo's two monumental portraits of Andrea Doria, the titular head of the Genoese branch of the family.

A series of small rooms displays an admirable collection of Flemish panel pictures, the most notable of which is Pieter Bruegel the Elder's *Battle in the Bay of Naples*, perhaps painted during the artist's trip through southern Italy, and Quentin Massys's *The Money Lenders*. The Sala Aldobrandini contains an array of ancient and seventeenth-century marbles.

The Hall of Mirrors, with painted ceiling and overdoors by Stefano Pozzi, houses one of the pre-eminent collections of eighteenth-century furniture and silvermaking in Rome. The private apartments, which include a chapel, have been exquisitely and authentically restored to provide an exact portrait of an eighteenth-century interior. Works by Pietro Longhi and Domenico Corvi adorn the walls, with prime examples of Gobelin tapestries and Chinese Ming porcelain. The apartments may be visited on separate tours.

Selected Bibliography

Museum publications: *Catalogo sommario della Galleria Doria Pamphili in Roma*, rev. 1975.

Other publications: Bodmer, H., "The Aldobrandini Landscapes in the Doria Pamphili Gallery," *The Art Bulletin* 16 (1934), 260–71; Carandente, Giovanni, *Il Palazzo Doria Pamphili* (Milan 1975); Faldi, Italo, *Palazzo Pamphili al Collegio Romano* (Rome 1957);

Torselli, Giorgio, *La Galleria Doria* (Rome 1969); Vertova, Luisa, "La Galleria Doria Pamphili a Roma," *Tesori d'arte della grandi famiglie* (1966), 47–74.

THOMAS W. SOKOLOWSKI

NATIONAL GALLERY OF ROME (formerly GALLERIA NAZIONALE D'ARTE ANTICA; officially GALLERIA NAZIONALE DI ROMA; alternately THE BARBERINI), Palazzo Barberini, Via della Quattro Fontane, 13, Rome.

The Galleria Nazionale di Roma is the revised name for the Galleria Nazionale d'Arte Antica, which was formerly housed in the Palazzo Corsini in the Trastevere section of Rome from its inauguration in 1895 until 1940. The impetus for the original Galleria Nazionale d'Arte Antica was the gift in 1883 of the private collections of Princes Tommaso and Andrea Corsini to the government, as well as the site of their palace on the via Lungara for the seat of the prestigious Accademia dei Lincei.

The original Corsini Collection, which numbered 600 works at its height during the eighteenth century, was augmented by additional bequests in the last decade of the century: in 1892 the Torloni Collection was donated to the state museum; again in 1892 some 187 paintings from the collection of the Sacro Monte di Pieta gallery were added; subsequent works from the Sciarra (1896), Odescalchi, Chigi (1918), and Barberini Collections were either donated or purchased for the Galleria Nazionale d'Arte Antica.

In 1940 the more than seventeen hundred works acquired by the Galleria Nazionale greatly exceeded the spatial capabilities of the Corsini Palace, and so the first floor of the Barberini Palace was allocated for use by the Galleria Nazionale. A museum of eighteenth-century art is being planned for rooms in the second floor of the South Wing of the palace, rooms that were refurbished in 1728 for the nuptial festivities of Cornelia Costanza Barberini to Giulio Cesare Colonna di Sciarra, prince of Carbognano. A private officers' club housed in the first floor of the South Wing also has a fine collection of seventeenth-century Italian pictures.

The Barberini Palace is an important starting point for all students of seventeenth-century Roman architecture, especially since it incorporates elements of the work of four major practitioners of the craft during the century: Carlo Maderno, Francesco Borromini, Gian Lorenzo Bernini, and Pietro da Cortona. The building itself not only is a rare example of successful collaboration but also serves as a pattern book for subsequent projects by the respective architects later in the century.

Home of Maffeo Barberini, later Urban VIII, the Barberini Palace served as the setting for the lavish theatrical and musical performances written and coordinated by this great papal patron of the arts. In 1625 Urban VIII purchased a palace and a vineyard between the Piazza Grimani and the via Pia from Duke Alessandro Sforza. The newly acquired status of the Barberini family necessitated a lavish familial residence, and various architects, including Michelangelo Buonarroti the Younger, were asked to submit plans. The design of the Lombard

Carlo Maderno was chosen, and work commenced in 1627. However, the actual building campaign did not begin until two months before his death in 1628. Architectural historians agree that the general plan of the building is the work of Maderno. The plan of the palace differs from most of the important Roman palaces due to the absence of a central court, having instead a solid block with projecting wings. Since the palace was set in the midst of a sizable vineyard, the choice of a villa plan rather than an urban palace plan seems appropriate.

At Maderno's death, Gian Lorenzo Bernini was chosen to succeed him. The elegant facade on the via Quattro Fontane, with the large windows and loggia over the wide portico, must be given to Bernini's hand. The lack of disjunction between Maderno's solid forms and Bernini's more lyrical classicism may be due to the presence of Francesco Borromini, the assistant to both Maderno and Bernini. It may be assumed that since Bernini had little experience in the principles of architecture, Borromini played a large role in revised designs; Borromini had assisted Bernini with the construction of the Baldacchino in St. Peter's Basilica. The false perspective windows in the top floor of the loggia and oval staircase in the right wing of the palace predict the fantastic designs that were to evolve into the church of San Carlino in later years.

Athough the structural work had been completed by mid–1635, the interior decoration was to continue for the next several decades. The death of Urban VIII and the subsequent election of his hated rival Innocent X Pamphili occasioned the flight of Taddeo and Cardinal Francesco Barberini, then resident in the palace, from Rome and the halt of all work on the palace; a reconciliation between the two papal families in 1648 brought about a new building campaign. Subsequent additions in the eighteenth and nineteenth centuries dictated a reorientation of the approach to the palace, as well as an irreparable alteration of the carriage way.

Although Pietro da Cortona's submitted plans for the palace had been rejected in favor of Maderno's, evidence for his work may seen in the north door of the facade, as well as in some auxiliary buildings connected to the main building. Some of the garden-side pedimental windows and interior stucco work may also be attributed to Cortona. The artist's most profound contribution to the palace ensemble is the series of frescoed rooms executed between 1623 and 1639.

The earliest frescoes (1632) were decorations for a room on an upper floor of the palace depicting allegorical figures of *Peace* and *Abundance* and *Scenes from the Old Testament*, all rendered in trompe l'oeil panels simulating white and gold stucco. The small chapel is decorated by Cortona with scenes from the life of the Virgin, both along the walls and in the cupola. Stylistically, these works fall midway between the early cycle in the church of Santa Bibiana and the later work in the nave of the Chiesa Nuova.

Cortona's magnum opus is the glorious ceiling of the Gran Salone, with the *Triumph of Divine Providence*, executed between 1633 and 1639. This work advanced the state of illusionistic ceiling painting in Rome and provided the necessary median step for the virtiginous whimseys of the eighteenth century.

Cortona cleverly combined the tradition of sixteenth-century *quadratura* (architectural staffage painting) with the new Baroque conceit of thrusting foreshortened elements into the space of the viewer. Figures seem to be on, over, and under the painted architectonic frame. The visual melée centers around an allegorical recipe conceived by the humanist-poet Francesco Bracciolini. Seen against the mythological legend of the founding of Rome, the papacy in the hands of the Barberini family once again brings order out of chaos as did their forebearers, Romulus and Remus. The flying cartouche of gilt bees in the center of a laurel garland makes certain that the message is clear.

Andrea Sacchi's fresco of *Divina Sapienza* (*Divine Wisdom*) (1629–33) provides a classical response to Cortona's Baroque bombast. However, although the tonality of the palette has been considerably diminished and the activity of the painted participants is far less feverish than in Cortona's work, the daring foreshortening of the ceiling is nothing less than Baroque in conception. Recent scholarship has suggested that the allegorical figures represent planetary bodies and are placed in the exact astrological arrangement as was noted at the moment of Urban VIII's birth; Urban VIII, it has been noted, consulted astrologers to ascertain favorable dates on which to implement his civic and sacred actions. Rooms in the so-called Summer Apartment of Prince Taddeo Barberini on the first floor are decorated with frescoes depicting mythological subjects by Giacinto Camassei and Giuseppe Passeri.

Expanded from its earliest parameters, the contents of the Galleria Nazionale now encompass works ranging from the thirteenth through the eighteenth centuries. An early *Madonna and Child* has been attributed variously to Simone Martini or his school. A *Triptych* by Fra Angelico depicting scenes of the Ascension, Pentecost, and Last Judgment represents that artist in a form unlike those frescoes known in Florence. One may also contrast the works of the Tuscan school with the frenetic decorative quality of Piero di Cosimo's *Magdalene*.

Andrea del Sarto's *Madonna and Child* of 1509, seen in the company of Fra Bartolommeo's late *Holy Family*, gives a fine picture of Florentine High Renaissance painting. Raphael's famous portrait *La Fornarina* (*The Baker's Daughter*) can be viewed as a preamble to the picture by his pupil Giulio Romano, *Madonna and Child*. Three works by Marco Venusti bring the viewer through the art of mid-century and up to Federigo Zuccari's *Portrait of a Gentleman*.

The Venetian school is well represented by Tintoretto's *Christ and the Adultress*, about 1546; Titian's *Venus and Adonis*; and Jacopo Bassano's *Adoration of the Shepherds*, 1565.

Hans Holbein's *Portrait of Henry VIII*, 1540, depicts the monarch in matrimonial garb before his wedding to Anne of Cleves, his fourth wife. A *Deposition*, attributed to Marten van Heemskerck, reflects that artist's interest in the Roman scene during his stay during the middle years of the century. A portrait by Joos van Cleve, that most Italianate of Northern artists, depicts the bishop of Trent, Bernardo Clesio.

In the Gran Salone, displayed beneath Cortona's fresco, are cartoons executed for the pendentives of the minor domes in St. Peter's: *St. Bernardo* by Carlo Pellegrini on a design by Bernini, *St Thomas Acquinas* and *St. Leo the Great* by Andrea Sacchi, and *St. Bonaventure* by Giovanni Lanfranco.

Selected Bibliography

Museum publications: *Catalogo*, 1954.

Other publications: Blunt, Anthony. "The Palazzo Barberini: The Contributions of Maderno, Bernini, and Pietro da Cortona," *Journal of the Warburg and Courtauld Institutes*, 21 (1958), pp. 256–87; Lavin, Marilyn Aronberg, *Seventeenth-Century Barberini Documents and Inventories of Art* (New York 1975); Lechner, G., "Tomasso Campanella and Andrea Sacchi's Fresco of *Divina Sapienza* in the Palazzo Barberini," *Art Bulletin*, 58 (1976), pp. 97–108; Magnanimi, Giuseppina, *Il Palazzo Barberini* (Rome, 1975); Vitzthum, W., "A Comment on the Iconography of Pietro da Cortona's Barberini Ceiling," *The Burlington Magazine*, 103 (1961), pp. 476 ff.; Waddy, Patricia, "The Designs and Designers of Palazzo Barberini," *Journal of the Society of Architectural Historians*, 35 (October 1976), pp. 151–85; idem, "Michelangelo Buonarroti the Younger, *sprezzatura* and Palazzo Barberini," *Architettura* 5, no. 2 (1975), pp. 101–2.

THOMAS W. SOKOLOWSKI

NATIONAL MUSEUM OF VILLA GIULIA (officially IL MUSEO NAZIONALE DI VILLA GIULIA; also, VILLA GIULIA, MUSEO DI VILLA GIULIA, MUSEO DI NAZIONALE ETRUSCO DI VILLA GIULIA), Piazza di Villa Giulia, 9, Viale della d'Arti, Rome.

The National Museum of Villa Giulia in Rome was established by the Italian government in 1889 as a regional archaeological museum for the pre-Roman materials excavated in Latium, the Faliscan territory, and southern Etruria. It is administered by the Soprintendenza alle Antichità per L'Etruria Meridionale.

The museum occupies the former suburban villa of Pope Julius III (Villa di Papa Giulio, or Villa Giulia), a sixteenth-century building of considerable architectural distinction. Most of the building activity of Pope Julius III's brief pontificate (1550–55) was devoted to the embellishment of this villa, which formerly comprised a much more extensive scheme of garden architecture celebrated for its splendid pergolas, belvederes, fountains, pavilions, and walks. Some of the greatest sixteenth-century masters were employed in the construction and decoration of the Villa Giulia, among them Michelangelo, Vasari, Vignola, and Ammanati. The main building is attributed to Vignola, although Michelangelo is generally regarded as having helped with the conception of the villa's plan.

The design of the two-story facade influenced later buildings. Through the large entrance door with its extruded rusticated frame is a pillared atrium in the Corinthian order, flanked by rooms with ceiling frescoes attributed to Taddeo Zucchero and stucco decoration presumably by Romolo Fiammingo, Francesco Castillo, and Federico da Urbino. Beyond is a semicircular portico with Ionic columns and frescoes painted in imitation Roman style by Giovanni da Udine. The portico opens into a courtyard screened at its far end by a loggia that bears

Ammanati's signature. Two curved staircases descend from the loggia to a nymphaeum decorated with statues, grottoes, and fountains. The plan of the nymphaeum is attributed to Vasari, although Ammanati, Vignola, and Baronino are credited with its realization. Noteworthy among the sculptures of the nymphaeum are colossal personifications of the Tiber and Arno rivers and elegant caryatid figures.

The beauty and architectural integrity of the Renaissance villa were adversely affected by the vicissitudes the building later suffered. In the mid-eighteenth century it became a hospital; in 1825 it housed a veterinary school; and in 1870 the Italian government transformed it into a military engineering depot. In 1887 urgent repairs were undertaken, and it was then that Felice Barnabei obtained government funds for the future museum. Finally, in 1889 the villa was transferred into and founded as a national Etruscan museum housing archaeological finds from excavations in the Etrusco-Faliscana territory.

The original core of the collection was at first disposed throughout the various rooms of the villa. But the collection was growing as a result of new archaeological discoveries and acquisitions, including the Barberini and Castellani private collections. A desire for additional space led to the construction of two new longitudinal wings in imitation antique style. The first, on the south side, was built at the end of the nineteenth century; later about 1925, a northern wing was added. The additions were conceived of as independent units, with no link either to each other or to the central block of the Renaissance villa; the visitor was forced to exit and reenter the museum at least five times during the complete visit.

The museum had become a vast, overcowded, and confusing storehouse of archaeological material arranged on the basis of topographical association and chronology. No attempt was made to distinguish between outstanding items and purely documentary material. In the general reorganization of Italian archaeological museums necessitated by World War II, a solution was sought to the problem of enlarging and rearranging the Villa Giulia in accordance with modern museographic concepts. The museum was remodeled between 1950 and 1960 under the direction of Renato Bartoccini and according to Franco Minissi's audacious architectural design. Superfluous material was moved to other newly established regional archaeological museums; for example, the curious warrior from Capestrano was transferred to the National Museum in Chieti.

The new Museum of Villa Giulia is considered a fine example of the modern archaeological museum. Although the systematic chronological classification of materials associated by provenance has been retained, only selected examples of each series are exhibited. The more important objects have been given greater prominence, and didactic materials—labels, maps, and diagrams—are effectively presented; the exhibits and showcases are well lit; and visitors are given close access and can easily follow a logical and unbroken itinerary. More complete collections of less-spectacular materials have been relegated to well-arranged storerooms accessible to scholars.

Today the museum's holdings are large and selectively comprehensive, providing practically uninterrupted documentation of reciprocal artistic influences among neighboring regions of southern Etruria from the ninth to the first century B.C. The old core collection of finds from the area of Latium between the right bank of the Tiber, Umbria, and Tuscany has been considerably enlarged by the transfer of materials from the former Museo Kircheriano, acquisitions and donations including the Barberini Collection (1903) and the Castellani Collection (1919), and the continual influx of archaeological finds from excavations at Civita Castellana, Satricum, Alatri, Segni, Cerveteri, Pyrgi, Vulci, and Veii. Although materials in the collection are generally associated by provenance and exhibited in chronological order, the integrity of special collections like that of the Antiquarium and the Castellani Collection of Greek and Etrusco-Italic vases has been maintained.

The vast assortment of objects in the Antiquarium collection comprises material dispersed from the former Museo Kircheriano, as well as items acquired by purchase or donation. Among the large selection of bronzes manufactured in Etruscan or Italic workshops are important statuettes, armor, fibulae, candelabra, engraved mirrors, and other domestic implements. The terracottas include vases, votive offerings, architectural fragments, oil lamps, theatrical masks, small Hellenistic urns of the Chiusine type, and sarcophagi with the deceased recumbent on the lid. Notable among the vases are an Athenian Geometric amphora (c. 700 B.C.), whose neck and handles are decorated with little serpents in relief; a small bucchero amphora with an Etruscan inscription, found near Veii; the remarkable Protocorinthian polychrome Chigi olpe (c. 640 B.C.), whose miniaturistic scenes presumably derive from large-scale painting; and a fragment of a Paestan calyx krater (mid-fourth century B.C.) signed by Assteas, with a humorous representation of Ajax and Cassandra.

Although comprised in part of very fine jewelry, the Castellani Collection (presented to the state in 1919) is particularly rich in Greek, Etruscan, and Italiote vases. Among the many interesting examples are a Caeretan hydria with Europa on the bull and another with Herakles, Cerberus, and Eurystheus (both c. 530 B.C.); a vase fragment with a procession of warships inside the rim, signed by Exekias; two Athenian red-figure hydriae by the Kleophrades Painter, with Herakles and the Nemean lion on one and two men with a hare on the other; an Athenian red-figure vase with the departure of Odysseus and his companions from Polyphemus' cave; and a pelike, with orgiastic Dionysiac scenes, by Hermonax.

The remainder of the museum's extensive collection comprises materials arranged on the basis of shared provenance. The finds from Vulci tombs range from the eighth to the first century B.C. An eighth-century, bronze, Villanovan hut-type cinerary urn provides valuable evidence for contemporary domestic architecture. The final phase of the Orientalizing period is represented by the furnishings from the Tomb of the Bearded Sphinx Painter (Tomba del Pittore della Sfinge Barbata, c. 630–580 B.C.), which contained imported Corinthian vases, Etruscan imitations of local manufacture, and bucchero pottery. Among the furnishings from the Tomb of the Warrior (Tomba del Guerriero, second half of the sixth century B.C.) is a complete set of bronze armor; two bronze plaques decorated with the legend of Achilles and Troilus; and bucchero, bronze, and Athenian black-figure vases, including a Panathenaic amphora decorated with a boxing scene. The number, variety, and quality of the Greek vases found in the Etruscan tombs at Vulci have added immeasurably to the study of the development of Greek vase painting. Among the stone sculptures in local tufa (nenfro), which probably served as tomb guardians, are a centaur (c. 590 B.C.), a youth riding a sea monster (c. 550–549 B.C.), and a sphinx (second half of the sixth century B.C.). A large tufa sarcophagus (c. 300 B.C.) has reliefs of the battle of Greeks and Amazons on all four sides.

Tomb furnishings from the cemetery of Olmo Bello at Bisenzio (eighth to sixth century B.C.) include a bronze incense burner on wheels and a bronze situla, both richly decorated with human and animal figures-in-the-round. Geometric-style pottery of local manufacture is also noteworthy.

The remarkable Late Archaic terracotta sculptures from the sanctuary of Portonaccio outside of Veii include a Gorgon-head antefix and colossal statues attributed to Vulca or his school depicting Apollo, Herakles with the hind, Hermes, and a goddess and child. Also from Veii is the famous late-fifth-century B.C. Malavolta head, originally part of a votive statue.

Noteworthy among the finds from Cerveteri (seventh to second or first century B.C.) are the architectural terracottas and the terracotta sarcophagi. *The Lions Sarcophagus* (*Sarcofago dei Leoni*) from Procoio di Ceri, which resembles a house with pitched roof, is at present the oldest, preserved, decorated Etruscan sarcophagus (mid-sixth century B.C.). The later sarcophagus with reclining couple (*Sarcofago degli Sposi*, c. 520 B.C.) represents the specifically Etruscan sepulchral subject matter of a couple dining on a banqueting couch. Among the other tomb furnishings from the cemeteries of Cerveteri is an important collection of vases with mythological scenes, for example, a fine East Greek hydria with the entrance of Herakles into Olympus; two Laconian cups with Achilles and Troilus, and the Harpies; one Caeretan hydria with the blinding of Polyphemus and Herakles and Nessus; another Caeretan hydria with satyrs harvesting grapes; an Athenian black-figure amphora depicting Herakles and Triton, by Exekias or his school; a large Athenian red-figure krater with warriors, by the Berlin Painter; and an Athenian red-figure pelike representing Herakles in old age.

The collection of finds from the sanctuary of ancient Pyrgi (Santa Severa) is noteworthy for its painted terracotta architectural decorations, particularly the interesting Late Archaic mythological relief now identified as a column plaque from the front gable of Temple A. Also important are the electrotypes of three inscribed gold tablets discovered in 1964, of which two are rendered in Etruscan and the third in Phoenician.

Ceramics from the cemeteries in the Faliscan territory include an enormous Faliscan red-figure volute krater (mid-fourth century B.C.) from Falerii Veteres

(Civita Castellana), with a representation of the abduction of Cephalus, by the Aurora Painter and the important Gnathian-style dish (first half of the third century B.C.) from Capena, with war elephant decorations that relate to Pyrrhus' presence in Italy. The exhibition of finds from Falerii Veteres spans the sixth to the first century B.C. Remarkable among the terracotta architectural decorations are the Late Archaic fragments from the temple at I Sassi Caduti, including the duelling warriors acroterion (c. 480 B.C.). From the two temples on Colle del Vignale there are terracottas in the shape of maenad and silenus heads. An Archaic female figure in tufa from the temple on Colle di Celle may represent the Sabine goddess Juno Curitis. A fine bearded, polychrome, terracotta head from a temple at Lo Scasato reflects the influence of a Phidian model. Perhaps from another temple on the same site comes a series of terracotta figures that are among the most important examples of Hellenistic Italic sculptures. Of particular note is a fragmentary figure of Apollo that recalls the Lysippean iconography of Alexander the Great.

The museum has extensive holdings in Etruscan and Etrusco-Italic materials from the territory of ancient Latium around or south of Rome. The materials from the temple of Diana at Nemi include a small terracotta model of the roof of an Etrusco-Italic temple clearly showing all of the structural elements. From the important shrine of the enigmatic Latin goddess Mater Matuta at ancient Satricum (modern Conca), the large deposit of Late Archaic architectural terracottas includes heads of warriors and antefixes depicting amorous silenus-maenad couples.

The important holdings from Palestrina include the Barberini Collection, as well as other acquisitions. Among the rich furnishings from the large Orientalizing Barberini and Bernardini tombs are imports from Greece and the East, as well as precious objects of Etruscan manufacture, including a bronze tripod with lebes, exquisite gold jewelry, and little ivory fan handles decorated with real and fantastic animals. Tomb furnishings of the fourth to second century B.C. include the large, richly decorated bronze Ficoroni cist (late fourth century B.C.), formerly in the Museo Kircheriano. The museum possesses a number of fine Praenestine cists.

A hypothetical nineteenth-century architectural reconstruction of the ancient Etrusco-Italic temple of Alatri is maintained in the courtyard of the Villa Giulia. The actual fragments of the temple's polychrome decorations are on display inside the museum.

The library of the Museum of Villa Giulia is accessible upon application to the Soprintendenza alle Antichità per L'Etruria Meridionale, who is also director of the museum.

Selected Bibliography

Museum publications: Bafile, Mario, *Villa Giulia: l'architettura, il giardino*, 1948; Bartoccini, Renata and Alfredo De Agostino, *Museo di Villa Giulia: Antiquarium e collezione dei Vasi Castellani*, 1961; Cultrera, Giuseppe, *Hydria a figure rosse del Museo di Villa Giulia*, 1938; Della Seta, Alessandro, *Museo di Villa Giulia*, 1918; Mingazzini, Paolo, *Vasi della Collezione Castellani*, 1930; Moretti, Mario, *Il Museo Nazionale di Villa Giulia*, 1963; idem, *Nuove scoperte e acquisizioni nell' Etruria meridionale*, 1975; Stefani, Enrico, *The National Museum of Villa Giulia at Rome*, 1949; Vighi, Roberto, *The New Museum of Villa Giulia*, 1958.

Other publications: *Corpus Vasorum Antiquorum*, Italia, fasc. 1–3, Museo Nazionale di Villa Giulia, fasc. 1–3 (G. Q. Giglioli); Curtis, C. D., "The Barberini Tomb," *Memoirs of the American Academy in Rome*, vol. 5 (1925), pp. 9–52; Dohrn, Tobias, *Die Ficoronische Ciste in der Villa Giulia in Rom* (Berlin 1972); Helbig, Wolfgang, *Führer durch die öffentlichen Sammlungen klassischer Altertümer in Rom*, vol. 3, 4th ed. (Tübingen 1969), pp. 467–862; Scichilone, G., in *Enciclopedia dell'arte antica, classica e orientale*, vol. 6 (Rome 1965), pp. 930–31.

RONNIE J. SCHERER

ROMAN NATIONAL MUSEUM (officially MUSEO NAZIONALE RO-MANO; alternately MUSEUM OF THE THERMAE; also MUSEO DELLE TERME, MUSEO NAZIONALE DELLA TERME), Via delle Terme di Diocleziano, Rome.

A decree issued in 1889 established two branches of the National Museum in Rome. Graeco-Roman antiquities discovered or purchased in Rome during the years following the uniting of the kingdom of Italy in 1870 were allocated to the Roman National Museum (or Museum of the Thermae); Etrusco-Italic archaeological materials were assigned to the National Museum of Villa Giulia (q.v.). Administered by the Soprintendenza alle Antichità di Roma, the Roman National Museum houses one of the most distinguished collections of classical art in the world.

The museum was originally installed in the former Carthusian Monastery of the Church of St. Maria degli Angeli in Rome, which in turn occupies part of the vast ruins of the Baths (Thermae) of Diocletian. Maximian, Diocletian's co-emperor, initiated construction of these baths upon his return from Africa in 298. The monumental imperial complex, which according to ancient sources could accommodate three thousand bathers at one time, was dedicated in both Maximian and Diocletian's names between 305 and 306, after both emperors had already abdicated. The well-preserved parts of the ancient structures were put to use during the Renaissance. In 1561 the surrounding land was given to the Carthusian monks of St. Croce in Jerusalem by Pius IV. From 1563 to 1566 Michelangelo converted the central hall of the Baths into the Church of St. Maria degli Angeli. Granaries (Horrea Ecclesiae) were first constructed in the northwestern part of the complex by Gregory XIII; they were extended during the seventeenth century by Paul V, Urban VIII and in the eighteenth century by Clement XI. As a result of excavations to rescue the ancient structure, the granaries were demolished in 1936.

The Baths have been affected as well by centuries of vandalism. Between 1586 and 1589, Sixtus V used explosive charges to demolish about one-fifth of the Baths. The building materials thus obtained were used in the construction of the Villa Peretti Montalto and the Chapel of the Crib in the Church of St. Maria Maggiore. More recently, damage was caused by the opening of the Via Cernaia, the construction of the Massimi Palace, the Ministry of Finance, the Grand Hotel, and the Termini Railway Station. However, in spite of these vicissitudes, the Baths remain one of the largest preserved ancient Roman constructions.

The original nucleus of the Roman National Museum's collection included among its treasures Classical and Early Christian antiquities from the former Museo Kircheriano; the frescoes, stuccoes, and sculpture from the Farnesina garden in Rome (transferred from the former Museo Tiberino); the head of the *Dying Persian* and other sculptures from the Palatine Antiquarium; the *Hermaphrodite* (discovered in Rome); the Subiaco *Youth* (from Nero's Villa, Subiaco); the bronze *Hellenistic Ruler* and the seated *Boxer* (discovered together in Rome); the *Bacchus of the Tiber*; and the *Dionysos* from Hadrian's Villa, Tivoli.

The rapid growth of the museum's holdings necessitated the enlargement of its facilities in 1891 and again in 1895. Important new acquisitions and discoveries—including fragments of the *Ara Pacis*; the famous Ludovisi Collection assembled by Cardinal Ludovico Ludovisi in the seventeeth century and acquired in 1901; the Lake Nemi bronzes; the *Niobid* from the Gardens of Sallust; and the *Discobolos* of Castel Porziano—again resulted in a scarcity of space. At the same time the public began to appreciate the historical and architectural significance of the impressive Roman Thermae. Consequently, a parliamentary act approving the restoration of the Baths was passed in 1907. Between 1908 and 1911 a considerable portion of the ancient structure was isolated and restored; the facilities of the reconstructed rooms were temporarily used for the Archaeological Exhibition of 1911, which celebrated the fiftieth anniversary of the proclamation of the kingdom of Italy. Because the museum's holdings increased steadily over the years, new rooms, halls, and wings have been and continue to be constructed or adapted to provide additional exhibition space. Alterations have also involved the transfer of certain materials, for example: the marbles of the *Ara Pacis Augustae* were removed from the museum and reconstructed near the Mausoleum of Augustus in 1938, and the Nemi bronzes were permanently transferred to the Museum of the Roman Ships at Nemi in 1953.

The expansion and rearrangement of the Roman National Museum is an ongoing process. The application of modern museographic principles to the museum's arrangement is restricted by the desire to preserve the historic integrity not only of its ancient architectural environment but also of its major collections— like the Ludovisi. Nevertheless, in the post–World War II reorganization of the museum, certain discreet alterations were made involving improvements in lighting, pedestals, the arrangement of exhibits, and the color of walls. There was, in addition, a careful reevaluation of earlier restoration work. Due to the ongoing nature of the museum's construction and expansion, as well as to the enormity of its collection, access to the many parts of this huge museum is restricted and variable. Therefore, the following distillation of the many important objects in the collection cannot possibly take into account their actual availability to the public.

The Roman National Museum's rich collection is mainly comprised of Graeco-Roman monuments of unusually high quality that range from the beginning of the fifth century B.C. to the Early Christian era. In the important collection of Greek sculpture, most of the major artistic currents are represented. Among the few precious originals of the fifth century B.C. (probably of Magna Graecian origin) are three pieces discovered in Rome in the area of the Gardens of Sallust: the *Ludovisi Throne*, the *Niobid*, and possibly the akrolithic head of the *Ludovisi Goddess* (also identified as a Neo-Attic work of the first century B.C.). Roman copies or adaptations of lost fifth-century B.C. originals include the *Ludovisi Peplophoros* (Candia type), one of several replicas of a Severe-style work; two replicas of Myron's *Discobolos*—the Castel Porziano and the well-preserved Lancelotti versions; the *Torso Valentini* (now freed of its restorations), which is related to the work of Myron; the *Ludovisi Hermes Logios* (restored by Algardi in the seventeenth century); the heavily restored replica of Phidias' *Athena Parthenos* from the Ludovisi Collection; the *Tiber Apollo*, after a bronze original by Phidias; and the *Artemis of Ariccia*, after an original by Alkamenes or Kresilas.

Although Roman replicas of fourth-century B.C. sculpture are fewer, the period's diverse currents and dominant schools are represented, with particularly strong holdings in Attic work, for example: several replicas of works by Praxiteles, including a version of the *Cnidian Aphrodite* (inferior to the one in the Vatican), the *Satyr Pouring Wine*, the *Youth of Sutri*, and a bronze head formerly in the Museo Kircheriano—adaptations of the *Apollo Lykeios*; and works with Praxitelean traits, including the *Apollo of Anzio* and an Arezzo-type *Athena* from Hadrian's Villa, Tivoli. Replicas of the work of Skopas of Paros include a head of Meleager and a torso of Pothos. Notable among reflections of work by Lysippos of Sikyon are the seated *Ares Ludovisi*, a portrait of Socrates, and a *Dancer* from Hadrian's Villa, Tivoli, identified as the *Drunken Flute Player*.

The museum's holdings in Hellenistic sculpture are exceptionally strong. The schools of Athens, Pergamon, and Asia Minor are particularly well represented. Notable are the Anzio girl, possibly a copy of the lost bronze *Sacrificing Woman* by Phanis, Lysippos' pupil; a version of the *Crouching Aphrodite* by Doidalsas (known in many replicas), from Hadrian's Villa, Tivoli; the *Youth* from Subiaco (sometimes associated with the Niobids), variously identified as a Hellenistic original or a Roman replica; the *Penthesilea* from Sette Bagni, a fragmentary replica of a group with Achilles supporting the Amazon; the famous *Ludovisi Group*—a Gaul killing himself over the dead body of his wife—a replica of a part of a victory monument of Attalos I of Pergamon; the group of an Amazon on horseback striking a fallen Gaul; the head of the *Dying Persian*; the *Aphrodite* of Cyrene, a Roman copy; the head of Asklepios, recognized as a replica of a cult statue by Phyromachos; the head of the sleeping Erinys (or Maenad); the head of a sleeping girl (or nymph), from Subiaco; the sleeping hermaphrodite, a popular Late Hellenistic type; the *Slave Boy with Lantern*; the *Boy Strangling a Goose*, after an original by Boethos of Chalcedon; the head of a young smiling satyr; the group of *Pan and Daphnis*, the best among many known replicas; the bronze *Hellenistic Ruler*; the bronze seated *Boxer*, signed by Apollonios, son of Nestor; *Orestes and Elektra*, a Neo-Attic work signed by Menelaos, student of Stephanos; a Neo-Attic krater with Hermes and the infant Dionysos, signed by Salpion; and a Neo-Attic marble fountain basin decorated with sea creatures.

The collection of Roman sculpture is large and comprehensive. Apart from the many Roman replicas and adaptations of Greek statues just discussed, portraits and sarcophagi are particularly numerous. The collection of portraits presents all of the major tendencies in Roman portraiture from the second century B.C. to the fifth century A.D. Among the many noteworthy examples of portraits of emperors are: the statue of Augustus as Pontifex Maximus, from the Via Labicana; a very fine head of Nero; a head of Vespasian, from Ostia; a head of Nerva; a bust of Hadrian; a bust and a heroic statue of Antoninus Pius; a head of Lucius Verus in high relief; a bust of Commodus; and a head of Gallienus. Notable among the portraits of emperors' wives is a very fine head of Sabina. The portraits of distinguished citizens include the statue of a Republican general, from Tivoli; the head of an elderly lady, from Palombara Sabina; a bust of the High Priestess of the Vestals; and a colossal bust of Antinous, Hadrian's favorite. Portraits of individuals in mythological guise include a statue of a young girl portrayed as Diana, from Ostia; a couple (Commodus and Crispina?) as Mars and Venus; and possibly also, because of its coiffure, the colossal Juno Ludovisi head, identified as Antonia Augusta(?).

The museum's collection of Roman sarcophagi, which includes Attic, Asiatic, and Roman (or Western) types, is the richest in the world. The major classes of subject matter are selectively represented: mythological, Dionysiac, seasons, battle, biographical, philosopher, and the Muses. In addition, there are important Early Christian sarcophagi and a unique Jewish sarcophagus fragment whose decoration surprisingly includes the representation of human beings. Some notable examples are the Acilia Sarcophagus, the sarcophagus of an official responsible for the Annona, the grandiose Ludovisi and Portonaccio Battle sarcophagi, and an oval sarcophagus with pastoral scenes found on the Via Imperiale in Rome.

The collection of Roman sculpture also contains important examples of funerary stelae, urns, altars, cult reliefs, historical reliefs, architectural elements and decorations, and Campana plaques. A Hadrianic altar from Ostia, with representations of Roman legends, is particularly noteworthy. There are, in addition, a series of interesting objects relating to Oriental cults practiced in Rome and a remarkable seated statuette of the young Christ.

The museum's rich holdings in wall paintings are of particular importance for the study of ancient painting. In size and quality, the collection is second only to that of the National Archaeological Museum (q.v.) in Naples. Included are the sophisticated paintings from the House near the Farnesina in Rome (discovered in 1879), the garden frescoes from Livia's Villa at Primaporta (discovered 1863), the historical paintings from the Tomb of the Statilii on the Esquiline, and the mural decoration from the tomb on the Via Portuense. The stuccoes from the vaulted ceilings of the House near the Farnesina are also noteworthy.

The museum possesses an important and varied collection of polychrome and black-and-white mosaic pavements and panels decorated with geometric designs, patterns with complex optical effects, vegetal motives, and figured scenes drawn from mythology and daily life. Noteworthy are the whirling wheel mosaic from the Via Tiburtina at Settecamini; the mosaic with Nilotic scenes, from Collemancio; the large mosaic with wild animal hunts and fantastic sea creatures, from Castelporziano; and the mosaic panels with the four factions of the circus, from the Villa of Septimii at Baccano. The famous Praeneste (Palestrina) mosaic with Nilotic scenes once possessed by the museum has been transferred to the Museo Prenestino Barberiniano at Palestrina.

Among the diverse decorative and utilitarian materials contained in the collection of minor arts there are: Italic and Graeco-Roman bronze statuettes; Tanagra-type figurines; ceramic vases, including Arretine ware; lamps; weights; scales; and household and tomb furnishings in terracotta, bronze, ivory, bone, and colored glass.

The museum's epigraphical holdings are enormous. Among the noteworthy examples are fragments of inscriptions commemorating the inauguration of the Baths of Diocletian; numerous marble tablets with the *Acta* of the *Fratres Arvales*, running from the first century B.C. to the third century A.D.; and two large pilasters with accounts of the *ludi saeculares* celebrated under Augustus and Septimius Severus.

The numismatic collection is exceptionally rich, with particularly strong holdings in Roman materials, including the important Gnecchi Collection of more than 20,400 Roman coins acquired in 1923, as well as some rare late Roman gold medallions. Most famous among the collection of gems is the blood red jasper Aspasios gem with the head of Phidias' *Athena Parthenos*.

Finally, the collection contains some important Egyptian antiquities, for example, a black granite bust in the Ludovisi Collection, identified as a pharaoh of the twelfth dynasty (formerly thought to represent a Hyksos shepherd king), and a large fragment of a granite slab with figures in sunken relief, from the temple of Isis and Serapis in the Campo Marzio in Rome (where it was brought in antiquity from Lower Egypt).

Requests for special access to the collections should be addressed to the director of the museum.

Selected Bibliography

Museum publications: Aurigemma, Salvatore, *The Baths of Diocletian and the Museo Nazionale Romano*, rev. ed., 1974; Felletti Maj, Bianca Maria, *I ritratti*, 1953; Paribeni, Enrico, *Sculture greche del V secolo: originali e repliche*, 1953; Paribeni, Roberto, *Le Terme di Diocleziano e il Museo nazionale romano*, 1928.

Other publications: Felletti Maj, Bianca Maria, in *Enciclopedia dell'arte antica, classica, e orientale*, vol 6, 1965 (Rome), pp. 931–33; Gabriel, Mabel M., *Livia's Garden Room at Prima Porta* (New York 1955); Helbig, Wolfgang, *Führer durch die öffentlichen Sammlungen klassischer Altertümer in Rom*, vol. 3, 4th ed. (Tübingen 1969), pp. 1–465; Porten Palange, Francesca Paolo, *La ceramica arretina a rilievo nell'Antiquarium del Museo nazionale in Roma* (Florence 1966).

RONNIE J. SCHERER

——— Siena ———

MUNICIPAL MUSEUM OF SIENA (officially PALAZZO PUBBLICO, MUSEO CIVICO), Piazzo del Campo, Siena.

The Palazzo Pubblico of Siena is situated on the piazzo del Campo, the main square of the city. Constructed in 1297–1310 with succeeding campaigns, the palace was formerly the home of the Signoria, governing body of Siena, and is now that of the Commune. The Palazzo houses the Museo Civico, supported by the city and containing important works of art commissioned for the Signoria.

The various rooms of the Palazzo display several significant examples of Sienese art. In the Sala del Mappamondo are three major works: Guido da Siena's signed panel, the *Madonna and Child Enthroned*, is dated 1221 but more likely was executed about 1280; Simone Martini's fresco of 1315, the *Maestà* (restored by that artist in 1321), is highly important; and on the opposite wall is the artist's *Guidoriccio da Folignano, Captain of the Sienese*, a fresco executed in 1328 with a view of the city of Siena.

Ambrogio Lorenzetti's frescoes *Good and Bad Government*, executed between 1338 and 1340, are located in the Sala della Pace. Also by Ambrogio are the remains of his fresco the *Maestà* of 1340, located in the vestibule of the museum. Frescoes by Taddeo di Bartolo decorate the Anticapella (1407–14), and numerous panels of the Sienese school are exhibited throughout the palace.

In the loggia of the Palazzo, an exterior terrace at the top of the building, are deposited pieces of the *Fonte Gaia*, a major work by Jacopo della Quercia sculpted between 1409 and 1419. The work was intended as a public fountain and was commissioned by the city in 1409.

A sales desk is located in the Museo Civico, with guides to the Palazzo Pubblico, slides, reproductions, and books relevant to works of art housed in the Palazzo.

Selected Bibliography

Cairola, A., *Il Palazzo Pubblico di Siena* (Rome 1963); Milanesi, G., *Documenti per la storia dell'arte senese*, vols. 1–3 (Siena 1854–56).

LORRAINE KARAFEL

MUSEUM OF THE CATHEDRAL OF SIENA (officially MUSEO DELL'OPERA DEL DUOMO, SIENA), Siena.

The Museo dell'Opera del Duomo houses works of art almost exclusively from the Cathedral of Siena, including several key paintings in the history of Sienese art. The museum was constructed in 1870 in a section to the right of the Duomo (which had served in the past, among other functions, as Jacopo della Quercia's workshop for the Gaia fountain, a masterpiece of quattrocento Sienese sculpture). A variety of works are in the collection, including sculpture in wood, marble, terracotta, and bronze; objects in precious metals; and a number of important paintings.

Among the most noted examples of Sienese sculpture are the figures from the facade of the cathedral. These life-size statues, executed by Giovanni Pisano between 1284 and 1296, represent figures from biblical and classical texts, including Moses, Simeon, Plato, and others. Copies replace the originals on the facade today. Examples by Niccolò Pisano, father of Giovanni, and a major master of Italian Gothic sculpture, are in the collection, as are works by the fifteenth-century Sienese sculptor Jacopo della Quercia (of particular note is his last work, the bas-relief *Madonna with Cardinal Antonio Casini*, executed before 1483).

A work of major importance in the history of Italian painting is the *Maestà* by Duccio di Buoninsegna, completed 1311. The altarpiece was commissioned in 1308 for the high altar of the Cathedral of Siena, and the now-separated panels originally formed a two-sided altarpiece. The original arrangement of the panels is unknown (although reconstructions have been suggested), and after the paintings were separated in 1506 and again in 1771 to be arranged in two chapels of the cathedral, the panels were transferred in 1878 to the museum. Eight panels are now dispersed in various collections throughout the world, and one panel is lost. The work is the *Madonna and Child Enthroned with Saints and Angels*, and fifty-three panels depict scenes from the life of Christ and the life of the Virgin.

The museum also houses an important early work by Duccio, the *Madonna di Crevole*, dating from about 1283. The panel, executed in an archaic Byzantine style typical of the Duecento, is titled the *Madonna and Child*. Other notable works include Pietro Lorenzetti's major *Birth of the Virgin*, signed and dated 1342. The painting was commissioned for the altar of San Savino in the cathedral and is the last known work of the artist. Lippo Vanni, follower of Pietro Lorenzetti, executed five miniatures now in the collection, dating from 1345, and the archaic style of Sienese painting is exemplified by the important *Madonna degli Occhi Grossi*, so called because of the built-up, three-dimensional eyes of the votive figure. Simone Martini's altarpiece *Beato Agostino Novello* and *Four of the Saint's Miracles* dates from 1330 and was formerly in the Church of St. Augustine, Siena. Panels by Ambrogio Lorenzetti, *St. Francis of Assisi* and *St. Mary Magdalene*, originally formed lateral panels of a triptych. Numerous other works, including Matteo di Giovanni's *Madonna and Child*, complete the collection.

The Museo dell'Opera maintains a convenient sales desk near the room housing the *Maestà*, with books, slides, reproductions, and some scholarly material relevant to works of art in the collection.

Selected Bibliography

Carli, Enzo, *Il Duomo di Siena e Museo dell'Opera del Duomo*, n.d. (also English edition); idem, *Il Museo dell'Opera e la Libreria Piccolomini di Siena* (Siena 1945); Lusini, V., *Il Duomo di Siena* (Siena, vol. 1, 1911, and vol. 2, 1939).

LORRAINE KARAFEL

NATIONAL PICTURE GALLERY OF SIENA (officially PINACOTECA NAZIONALE, SIENA; also PINACOTECA), 20 Via S. Pietro, Siena.

The Pinacoteca Nazionale (National Picture Gallery of Siena) is housed in the Palazzo Buonsignori at 29 via S. Pietro. The collection, an outstanding group of Sienese paintings from the twelfth through the early seventeenth century (as well as examples of other schools), is particularly strong in works by Sienese painters such as Guido da Siena, Duccio di Buoninsegna, the Lorenzetti, Paolo di Giovanni Fei, Giovanni di Paolo, Sassetta, Sano di Pietro, Sodoma, and Beccafumi. The nucleus of the present collection was formed by Abbot Giuseppi Ciacheri at the end of the eighteenth century. This group was enriched with works from local churches, convents, and so on, as well as through acquisitions, gifts, and deposits. In 1930 the collection passed to the state and was installed in the Palazzo Buonsignori. Today, the collection is operated under the jurisdiction of the Italian State and the National Museums.

The Palazzo Buonsignori (formerly Tagliacci) dates from the first half of the Quattrocento and is designed of brick and stone in the Late Gothic style. The atrium and courtyard on the ground floor house works of sculpture: Roman sarcophagi and, in the courtyard, Sienese sculptures, mostly from the Trecento. Also on the ground floor is the Sala dei Cartoni, where nine cartoons of biblical scenes by Beccafumi, the sixteenth-century Sienese painter, are exhibited; these cartoons were preparatory drawings for sections of the inlaid pavement in the Cathedral of Siena.

The Pinacoteca is located on the upper floors of the palace; paintings are arranged chronologically by artist. The third floor, reached by a staircase in the entryway of the palace, begins with works of the Late Middle Ages and continues through paintings of the Quattrocento. The Sienese school was exceptionally active during the Duecento and Trecento, and the gallery is strong in major works of these periods. A panel with the *Savior and Symbols of the Evangelists* and the side panels *Stories of the Cross* and *Stories of St. Helen* is the first securely dated Sienese painting, 1215. An anonymous painted *Crucifix* from the late twelfth century was formerly in the Church of St. Peter in Villore at St. Giovanni d'Asso.

Guido da Siena, the traditional "father" of the Sienese school, active in the second half of the thirteenth century, is represented by several works. They include his signed altarpiece *Transfiguration, Entrance of Christ into Jerusalem, and the Resurrection of Lazarus*. The work *St. Peter Enthroned* with *Holy Stories* of about 1270–80 is attributed to Guido or his school. The panels with the *Massacre of the Innocents, The Betrayal of Christ, the Crucifixion, the Deposition, and the Entombment* may have been lateral panels of Guido's *Madonna and Child Enthroned*, now in Siena's Palazzo Pubblico (q.v.). A *Madonna and Child* dated 1262 is by Guido and a *Crucifixion with St. Francis* is by Ugolino di Nerio.

Duccio di Buoninsegna (c. 1255-60–c. 1315-18), the first great Sienese painter and a major influence on succeeding artists, executed several paintings now in the collection. A polyptych by Duccio and his school is titled the *Madonna and Child with St. Agnes, John the Evangelist, John the Baptist, and Mary Magdalene*. Another important altarpiece is the *Madonna and Child with Saints Augustine, Paul, Peter, and Dominic*, and a major work, miniaturelike in execution, is Duccio's *Madonna of the Franciscans*.

The generation following Duccio included Simone Martini (c. 1284–1344) and the Lorenzetti brothers, Pietro (active c. 1308–47) and Ambrogio (active 1319–47). Simone Martini's important *Madonna and Child* from the Church of Lucignano d'Arbia is in the Pinacoteca. A *Madonna and Child* by Lippo Memmi, brother-in-law of and collaborator with Simone, is typical of that artist's style. Several important works by Ambrogio Lorenzetti are housed in the Pinacoteca. The altarpiece with the *Madonna and Child* has the lateral panels *Mary Magdalene* and *St. Dorothy*, important for their monumental quality. The *Madonna of Serre di Rapolano* is noteworthy, and the altarpiece the *Madonna and Child with Saints, Doctors of the Church, and Angels* is a major work. A mature work of 1344 is the *Annunciation*, which uses one-point perspective. Two *Landscape* panels by Ambrogio, which have elicited much discussion, may be the first examples of "pure" landscape in Western art before the fifteenth century, or they may be, as more recent theories have suggested, pieces of a lost larger work, perhaps Ambrogio's documented *Mappadelmondo*. Pietro Lorenzetti, elder brother of Ambrogio, is represented by his *Madonna and Child with St. Nicholas of Bari and the Prophet Elijah*, central panel of his 1328–29 altarpiece commissioned for the Church of the Carmine, and by the predella *Stories of the Carmelite Order* and the panels *Saints Theodore, Bartholomew, Thomas, and Jacob*.

Other Trecento works include the *Adoration of the Magi* by Bartolo di Fredi of about 1370–80 and the *Nativity of the Virgin with Saints Jacob, Catherine, Bartholomew, and Elizabeth of Hungary* by Paolo di Giovanni Fei of about 1380–90. Several other panels by Paolo di Giovanni Fei are also in the collection, including his only signed work, the *Madonna and Child with Three Saints and the Prophet Daniel*, of about 1390. Michelino da Besozzo, the Lombard miniaturist, is represented by his *Marriage of St. Catherine of Alexandria with St.*

John the Baptist and St. Anthony Abbot. This work of about 1400 is executed in the Late Gothic International Style and is the only signed work by that master. Works by Niccolò di Segna include the *Madonna of the Misericordia*, formerly in the Church of the Vertine near Giaole in Chianti, and the *Crucifixion*, signed and dated 1345.

Sienese painting of the Quattrocento is represented by important examples. Works by Giovanni di Paolo include his noteworthy *Last Judgment with Heaven and Hell* and his *Madonna of the Humility*, about 1445. A *Madonna and Child with Angels*, signed and dated 1433, is by Domenico di Bartolo. The Sienese painter Sassetta (Stefano di Giovanni, 1392–1450) executed several paintings, including a *Last Supper* and a *Temptation of St. Anthony*. Sano di Pietro (1460–81) produced the *Madonna with Pope Callisto III*, a panel of 1456, and the polyptych, signed and dated 1444, the *Madonna and Child with Beato Giovanni Colombini*, the first work securely dated by that artist. A number of other pictures by Sano di Pietro include the *Madonna and Child with Saints Margaret, Catherine of Alexandria, Bernardino, and Francis* (c. 1470) and the *Madonna and Child with Eight Angels* of about 1450. Other quattrocento works include Matteo di Giovanni's *Madonna and Child with Angels* of 1470 and paintings by Francesco di Giorgio: the *Annunciation*, the *Coronation of the Virgin*, and the *Madonna and Child with Angels* of about 1472. Neroccio is represented by important paintings: the *Madonna and Child with Saints Jerome and Bernardino* (signed and dated 1476) and a panel from the front of a *cassone*, the *Triumph of David* (executed with an assistant). An important tondo is the *Holy Family with St. John the Baptist* by Pinturicchio, the Umbrian painter, who worked in Siena and also at Fontainebleau, France.

Cinquecento Sienese paintings are found on the second floor of the Palazzo. Sodoma (Giovanni Antonio Bazzi, 1477–1549), a Lombard follower of Leonardo da Vinci, worked in Siena and executed a number of paintings now in the Pinacoteca. Early works include the *Nativity* of 1503 and a *Crucifixion*. A fresco fragment of about 1511–14 is the *Christ at the Column*, and the *Deposition*, a major work by Sodoma, has a predella executed by the artist's shop. An important fresco work is the *Descent of Christ into Limbo*, as well as the *Prayer in the Garden* of about 1554. The Sienese painter Beccafumi (Domenico di Pace, 1484–1551) is represented by a number of works. The important *St. Catherine Receiving the Stigmata* dates from about 1515, with predella scenes of *Stories from the Life of St. Catherine*. The *Nativity of the Virgin*, a mature work, is dated 1543, and the masterpiece *Descent into Limbo* by the artist is placed about 1530–35.

A number of other works from the Cinquecento are also housed in the Pinacoteca. They include Andrea di Niccolo's signed and dated, 1500, altarpiece *Madonna and Child with Saints Catherine of Alexandria, Augustine, Sebastian, and Monica* and Girolamo da Cremona's *Annunciation*. Several fresco works are also exhibited: Benvenuto di Giovanni's *Noli me tangere*, of about 1510, and his *Scenes of Hospital Life*, a monochromatic work formerly in the Ospedale della Scale in Siena. Frescoes by Girolamo Genga, formerly in the Palazzo del Magnifico, are *Aeneas Fleeing Troy* and the *Redemption of the Prisoners*. Also included are the *Resurrection* by Giorgio Vasari of 1550; *Charity, Hope, and Faith*, an early work by Andrea del Brescianino, of about 1507–10; a *Madonna and Child with St. John the Baptist* of the school of Andrea del Sarto; and the important *Nativity* by Lorenzo Lotto of about 1527.

Several portrait paintings are in the collection, works of various schools: Francesco Vanni's *Self Portrait*, Moroni's *Portrait of a Man* (c. 1555–60), and the *Portrait of Elizabeth of England*, traditionally attributed to Federico Zuccaro (c. 1542–1609). Also included are examples of Northern painting: a *Portrait of Charles V* by an anonymous German master (perhaps Christopher Amberger) and the *Holy Family with St. Elizabeth and St. John* by Rubens (perhaps an autograph copy after a panel in the Wallace Collection, London [q.v.]). From the German school are Lucas Cranach's *Lucrezia* and the panel *Herod Receiving the Head of John the Baptist*, attributed to the circle of Altdorfer. Seventeenth-century paintings include works by Rutilio Manetti, notably the signed and dated (1613) *Martyrdom of St. Ansano* and *St. Eligio and the Apostate* of 1631.

Detailed catalogs of the collection are available, and numerous monographs discuss the works of art in the context of the oeuvre of the individual artist. No sales desk is maintained by the Pinacoteca.

Selected Bibliography

La Pinacoteca Nazionale di Siena: i dipinti dal XI al XV, catalog of the collection (Siena 1977); Carli, Enzo, *Guide to the Pinacoteca of Siena* (Milan 1958); Touring Club d'Italia, "Siena," *Toscana* (Milan 1974), pp. 479–547.

LORRAINE KARAFEL

——— Turin ———

EGYPTIAN MUSEUM OF TURIN (officially MUSEO EGIZIO DI TORINO; also MUSEO EGIZIO, MUSEO DELL'ACCADEMIA DELLE SCIENZE, MUSEO D'ANTICHITÀ, MUSEO ARCHEOLOGICO), Palazzo dell'Accademia delle Scienze, Via Accademia delle Scienze 6, Turin.

The Egyptian Museum of Turin was created by Carlo Felice, king of Sardinia, in 1824. It was one of the first major Egyptian collections in the world. Until 1940 Egyptian and Graeco-Roman antiquities were exhibited together. Since that date they have been separated and now occupy different rooms in the same building, the Palazzo dell'Accademia delle Scienze. About 1882 the Egyptian Museum became a state museum administered by the Ministry of Education (Ministero della Pubblica Istruzione) and, since 1976, by the newly created Ministry for the Environment and Cultural Affairs (Ministero per i Beni Culturali e Ambientali). The Association of Friends and Collaborators of the Egyptian

Museum of Turin was founded in 1974, with its principal aim the encouragement of didactic activities such as lectures, seminars, and conferences. The museum is governed by a director and two associate directors.

The Egyptian Museum of Turin was opened to the public in 1831 and is still one of the major collections of Egyptian antiquities in the world. Before 1831 it had been visited only by famous archaeologists and scholars, including Jean François Champollion, who, in 1826, collaborated on the creation of the Egyptian department at the Louvre (q.v.).

The building was designed by the architect Guarino Guarini in 1679 as a College of Nobles (Collegio dei Nobili), directed by the Jesuits. In 1783 it became the official seat of the Academy of Sciences of Turin, founded in 1757, and since that date, the building has been called Palazzo dell'Accademia delle Scienze. In 1824 the government of Carlo Felice bought the wonderful collection of Egyptian antiquities offered by the Piedmontese Bernardino Drovetti and chose Guarini's building as the location for the museum. The architect Giuseppe Maria Talucchi was charged with the remodeling of the interior, which had been modified many times. A congress on Guarino Guarini was organized by Vittorio Viale in 1969, and since then every attempt has been made to restore the building to its original design. A new location for the museum of Graeco-Roman antiquities was found at the Arancere (Parco Reale of Turin) in 1970. As soon as the restoration work at the Arancere is completed, the Egyptian Museum will occupy all of the rooms on the ground floor of the Palazzo dell'Accademia delle Scienze. Serious problems of space arose in 1966, when the *Temple of Ellesija* arrived from Egypt. The arrival of this Nubian temple and the increasing number of visitors (on the average, 250 a day) required a better solution. The separation of the two museums will certainly entail a new arrangement of the Egyptian collection within the building.

The original bequest to the museum included Egyptian antiquities from the Savoy and Donati collections. During the second half of the nineteenth century the very important Drovetti Collection was purchased, as were many objects from minor private collections. From 1898 to 1937 the museum holdings were increased by two of its directors, Ernesto Schiaparelli and Giulio Farina, who organized archaeological expeditions to Egypt. In 1965 the Egyptian government presented the Italian government (which had collaborated on the building of the Aswan dam) and the Egyptian Museum of Turin with a small Nubian temple. Archaeological expeditions organized by the museum itself in 1960–70 made possible the creation of a special Nubian room.

The Savoy Collection was originally a mere "Closet of Curiosities" (*Gabinetto delle Curiosita*). There were about 270 Egyptian objects. Among them, the most famous was the *Isis Table* (*Mensa Isiaca*), then believed to be Egyptian but later identified as a Roman sculpture in the Egyptian style (c. A.D. 600) showing cabalistic signs.

The Donati Collection originated from the Savoy's patronage. In 1753 Vitaliano Donati, professor of botany at the University of Turin, was ordered by

Carlo Emanuele III to form an expedition to Egypt and the Levant to bring back "antiquities or rare manuscripts." In this way, Turin acquired some mummies of animals, a gigantic statue representing Rameses II standing, a statue of the goddess Sekhmet sitting, and a statue believed to represent Tiyi, Amenophis III's wife. Bernardino Drovetti was a follower of Napoleon Bonaparte, and in 1803 he was elected general consul of France in Egypt. Drovetti's archaeological expeditions at Karnak and in the Theban area date from 1811 to 1827. Among the most important objects and documents the Savoys bought from Drovetti are the famous statue of Rameses II sitting and the *Royal Papyrus*.

Before Ernest Schiaparelli became director, the Egyptian collection of Turin was incomplete, because all of the objects were of the New Kingdom. Schiaparelli's directorship was mainly concerned with the historical completeness of the museum. In 1898 he bought, among many other objects, some Coptic textiles and, in 1900–1901, objects belonging to the Predynastic period. From 1903 to 1920 Schiaparelli organized archaeological expeditions to Egypt that brought back to Turin monuments from tombs of the Ancient and Middle Kingdoms; sculpture of the early dynasties; the untouched furniture of the tomb of the architect Kha, and a wooden statuette representing the architect himself; the so-called *Tomb of the Unknown*; and a wall painting from the tomb of the Prince Iti. In 1904 the English traveler Heywood Walter Seton-Karr presented the museum with paleolithic objects made of flintstone. From 1930 to 1937 Giulio Farina directed archaeological excavations at el-Gebelein and brought to Turin Predynastic vases and a precious painted canvas showing ships and human figures, which is the oldest surviving Egyptian painting in the world. In 1920–40 the collection was enriched by a stele of Herbes, the so-called *Mask Garre* (from the giver's name) representing a follower of Isis who lived during the Roman period, and a scarab of Amenophis III from the series of lion hunts. The Nubian *Temple of Ellesija* had been rebuilt in the museum in 1969–70.

The museum at present occupies four rooms on the ground floor, eleven rooms on the first floor, and a few rooms in the basement. (The second floor of the Palazzo dell'Accademia delle Scienze belongs to the Sabauda Gallery [q.v.] [Galleria Sabauda], the major public collection of paintings in Turin.) At the entrance of the museum, visitors are welcomed by two sphinxes of Amenophis III, the Egyptian sovereign who created the town of Thebes about 1400 B.C. On the ground floor are a gallery of plaster casts (Gipsoteca), two galleries of statues (Statuario I and II), and the Nubian room.

In the first gallery of statues (Statuario I) are the two funerary aedicules found by Schiaparelli at el Giza and a series of Egyptian kings and queens. Among the finest statues exhibited in this room are Rameses II sitting between the Theban gods Amon-Re and Mut, Horemheb and his wife, the well-known Rameses II sitting, and a Tuthmosis sovereign. In the second gallery (Statuario II) are statues and sarcophagi. Among the best work exhibited in this room are the goddess Sekhmet and Tuthmosis III. In the Nubian room are the *Temple of Ellesija* commissioned by Tuthmosis III and later restored under Rameses II, with two memorial stelae. In the gallery or room III (Galeria or Sala III) there are a wooden imitation of the wall of an Egyptian tomb; a copy from the Campensis obelisk, the most important cast belonging to the museum; and a whole wall showing stelae in chronological order. From the gallery visitors enter two small rooms where the *Tomb of the Unknown* (Old Kingdom) and the tomb of the architect Kha (New Kingdom) are exhibited with pottery. In the basement are repositories and an architectural models room. Restoration works of the cellars of the antique palace were carried out with the financial support of the Pininfarina and Rotary Club of Turin in 1966–72. Models of Nubian temples and the pyramid of Cheops, gifts of the architect F. Ch. Gau, are exhibited in the architectural models room (Sala di Studio).

A new general catalog of the museum was planned in 1965. Since then five volumes have been published, with the financial support of the Italian Fund for Research (Consiglio Nazionale della Ricerche), edited respectively by Giuseppe Botti, Alessandro Roccati, Mario Tosi, Joseph Omlin, and Lahih Hahachi. The new catalog will assemble single groups of objects and monuments in the different volumes.

The Egyptian Museum of Turin has a library specializing in Egyptian art, history, and culture and is the only major library for Egyptian studies in Italy. The museum publishes essays, theses, and the *Quaderni del Museo Egizio*, a review of information for a wide public.

Selected Bibliography

Curto, Silvio, *Storia del Museo Egizio di Torino*, Centro Studi Piemontesi (Torino 1976); Museo Egizio di Torino, *Atti del Centocinquantenario, 1824–1974* (Torino 1974); Roccati, A., *Museo Egizio di Torino* (Torino 1974); Scamuzzi, E., *Museo Egizio di Torino*, Pozzo ed. (Torino 1964); English ed.: *Egyptian Art in the Egyptian Museum of Turin*.

ILARIA BIGNAMINI

MUNICIPAL MUSEUM OF ANCIENT ART (officially MUSEO CIVICO D'ARTE ANTICA; also MUSEO CIVICO, MUSEO DI PALAZZO MADAMA), Palazzo Madama, Piazza Castello, Turin.

The Municipal Museum of Ancient Art of Turin was established in 1860 as a museum of arts applied to the manufacturing process. Since then new departments have been created, and a lively acquisition policy has, as a consequence, created one of the major Italian public collections of ancient arts. Since 1934 the Palazzo Madama has been the center of the museum, which, with the Municipal Gallery of Modern Art (Galleria Civica d'Arte Moderna) and three other municipal museums, is administered by the Council of Turin (Comune di Torino) and governed by three directors and fourteen officers.

The Palazzo Madama, which since 1934 has housed the Municipal Museum of Ancient Art, has a long history. Before being transformed into one of Juvarra's architectural masterpieces, it had been a Roman gate and later a medieval castle serving as a fortress. The old castle was enlarged and remodeled in 1402–18, when Prince Ludovico d'Acaja was seigneur of Turin. At the end of the fifteenth century, it was revived by Amedeo IX of Savoy and his wife, Yollant of France, who gave it the same importance the building had had, since 1497, under Bianca di Monferrato, Duke Carlo I's wife. In 1537 Turin and Piedmont fell to France, and the old castle was neglected by the new seigneurs. In 1637, after Vittorio Amedeo I's death, Cristina of France became regent in the name of her son Carlo Emanuele (II, after 1648). From 1638 until 1642, she commissioned alterations and decorations of the building, which possibly at that time began to be called Palazzo Madama (the Madam's Palace). During the following decades, the building was decorated by Innocento Guicciardi (closet of the Northern Roman tower, 1639) and later by Domenico Guidobono (Spring room or Guidobono's room, 1710–15). In 1718–21 the architect Filippo Juvarra remodeled the front and the staircase. Juvarra, with the sculptor Giovanni Baratta, transformed the old building into one of the best Turinese palaces, a celebrated masterpiece of European architecture of the eighteenth century.

The museum is divided into fifteen departments: mosaics, illuminated books, paintings, sculptures and carvings, enamels, ivory works, majolicas, chinaware, glassware and stained glass, furniture, tapestries, gold and silver works, bronzes, leather works, and coins and medals. The collection of mosaics includes a few very important works: fragments of the mosaics from the floor of Acqui's cathedral (fourth-fifth century, and 1067) and a mosaic from the church of San Salvatore (Turin, c. 1105) influenced by Lombard and Emilian mosaics of the eleventh-twelfth century. The collection of illuminated books includes some of the most famous European books of the Late Gothic period and Renaissance. The *Milan-Turin Hours* (first half of the fifteenth century) is one of the most admired parts of the *Très Belles Heures de Notre Dame de Jean de France, Duc de Berry*. This codex, a commission from Jean de France (brother of King Charles V), includes a range of dates of execution from the end of the fourteenth century into the following century. The highest artistic quality and most sophisticated scenes were painted by Jan van Eyck, who had a profound influence on other masters of book illumination. Another precious illuminated book of the collection is the *Missal della Rovere*, a commission from Cardinal Domenico della Rovere.

The collection of paintings begins with a *Last Supper* (1325–30) by an unknown Riminese master influenced by Giotto, a *Madonna with Child* (c. 1370) by Barnaba da Modena, a *Madonna Crowned* (c. 1450) by Antonio Vivarini, a *Crucifixion* by Giacomo Jaquerio, and a marvelous *Portrait of an Unknown Man* (1476) by Antonello da Messina. Piedmontese painting of the fifteenth and sixteenth centuries can be studied in the rooms the Municipal Museum of Ancient Art devotes to it. The rich collection includes very important works by Martino Spanzotti from Casale, Defendente Ferrari from Chivasso, Gerolamo Giovenone from Vercelli, Macrino d'Alba, Pietro Grammorseo (of Flemish origin but educated and active in Piedmont), and Giovanni Antonio Bazzi, called Il Sodoma, from Vercelli. Representative of early Tuscan Mannerism is one of the most important paintings of the museum, *St. Michael the Archangel and the Devil* (1525–28), by Jacopo Pontormo.

The collection of paintings of the seventeenth century includes a few well-selected works such as the *Penitent St. Jerome* (1611) by Orazio Gentileschi; the *St. Jerome Meditating* (c. 1620) by Giovanni Serodine from Ascona; the *St. Francis in Ecstasy* by Giovanni Battista Cressi, called Il Cerano; a painting on the same subject by Francesco del Cairo; the *St. Peter* (c. 1620) by Giulio Cesare Procaccini; and the *Nativity Adored by San Carlo* by Tanzio da Varallo. Ten large canvases by Jan Miel are among the best Flemish paintings of the seventeenth century in the museum. Miel was born in Antwerp and later worked in Rome and Turin (1658–63) for the Savoia family. Miel's ten paintings on hunting subjects are from the Castello della Venaria, and they were commissioned to celebrate the wedding of Carlo Emanuele II of Savoy with his first wife Françoise d'Orléans. Among genre paintings, the most remarkable is the *Evening on the Piazza of the Village* (1735–40) by Giacomo Ceruti from Brescia.

Venetian painting of the eighteenth century is well represented by Rosalba Carriera's *Portrait of Clement Augustus von Wittelsbach, Prince of Bavaria* (c. 1727) and Alessandro Longhi's *Portrait of Rev. Sante Bonelli* (1788). Neapolitan painting of the eighteenth century is represented by Francesco Solimena's *Madonna and St. Philip* (c. 1733), a sketch for the altarpiece of St. Philip and Sebastiano Conca's sketch for the altarpiece for the oratory of the Philippan order in Turin (c. 1730). Representative of Piedmontese genre painting of the eighteenth century are eleven paintings by Piero Domenico Olivero and thirty-two by his pupil Giovanni Michele Graneri. *The Prodigal Son* (1740) by Pier Francesco Guala from Casale testifies to the high quality of provincial Piedmontese painting during the eighteenth century.

The collection of sculptures and carvings includes fragments of plutei and chancel-screens (ninth century) by Comacine masters working in Piedmont, capitals from Piemontese churches (eleventh-fifteenth century), and wooden statues (thirteenth-fourteenth century). Sculptures from the valley of Aosta are well documented from the Paleolithic period until the fifteenth century. Sculpture in Savoy is well represented by *St. John the Evangelist* (c. 1470) from Annecy. The bust *Madonna* (c. 1420), made of colored stucco, is from Jacopo della Quercia's workshop. The collection of southern Germany and Tyrolese sculpture includes works from about 1480 until about 1520. Piedmontese "popular" sculpture of the fifteenth century is shown by the *Lamentation over the Dead Christ* from the church of Santa Maria Maggiore, Val Vigezzo. Remarkable examples of the Lombard Renaissance are six marble high reliefs by Agostino Busti, called Il Bambaja, from the tomb of Gaston de Foix (Church of the Agostiniane di Santa Maria, Milan).

The collection of enamels includes a large selection of remarkable works, such as various Limoges objects of the thirteenth-seventeenth century and objects produced in Piedmont (Vercelli), Venice, and northern Italy of the fifteenth-sixteenth century. The collection of ivory works opens with razors and combs of the late Roman period from Egypt or Syria and includes Romanesque, Sicilian-Arabian, and Spanish-Arabian objects, as well as French, German, and Flemish diptychs of the fourteenth century. The Italian production of the fourteenth-fifteenth century is represented by little altars, small cases, and combs. An important ivory piece is the Portuguese *Crucified Christ* of the seventeenth century, and there is a significant group of neoclassical ivories, especially those by Francesco Tanadei, wood and ivory carver to King Vittorio Emanuele I. The collection of majolicas includes objects from various Italian factories, such as those of Faenze (*Adoration*, end of the fifteenth century), Ca' Pirota (a blue cup, 1531), Gubbio (a dish depicting the Miracle of St. Clara, 1526, by the famous craftsman Giorgio Andreoli), Casteldurante (bust of Marta Bella, 1520–30, by Niccolò Pellipario), Urbino (a dish, *The Rape of Helen*, 1548), Castelli in Abruzzo (works of the seventeenth century from the Grues and Gentilis workshops), Milan (works of the eighteenth century from Felice Clerici and Pasquale Rubati's factories), Lodi (works by Giacinto Rossetti), and Piedmont (majolicas of the sixteenth-eighteenth century).

The collection of chinaware is smaller than that of majolicas, but it includes remarkable and well-selected objects such as a rare vase from the factory of Francesco I de' Medici (second half of the sixteenth century). The collection also includes chinaware of the eighteenth century from the workshops of Francesco Vessi in Venice, N. F. Hewelcke (from Meissen) in Udine and later in Venice, Marquis Carlo Ginori at Doccia (Florence), and Du Paquier (Vienna) and from the factories of Capodimonte, Meissen, Frankenthal, Bow, Chelsea, and Giovanni Antonio Brodel at Vinovo (Turin).

The collection of glassware includes two hundred gilded and colored objects from various Italian regions. Among the stained-glass collection, the most remarkable piece is *The Flight to Egypt* (c. 1510) from a cartoon by Martino Spanzotti. The collection of furniture includes pieces of the fifteenth-eighteenth century, especially from Piedmont and France. The collection of tapestries includes a wonderful piece with a hunting scene (1560–70) from Frans Geubel's workshop in Brussels, as well as an important group of Piedmontese tapestries commissioned for the Savoias during the eighteenth century. The most important group of gold and silver works in the museum is the Treasure of Desana, discovered at Desana Vercellese in 1940. It consists of forty-four Early Christian and Longobard pieces from the third and fourth centuries.

The collection of bronzes is large but does not include any remarkable work. Leather bindings of the fifteenth-eighteenth century form the principal group of the collection of leather works. The collection of medals and coins is very important. In 1958 three Turinese numismatic collections were gathered in the museum: from the Museum of Graeco-Roman Antiquities came twenty-four thousand Greek, Roman, and Byzantine coins; the *Medagliere* of King Carlo Alberto, including more than twenty-eight thousand coins of Classical antiquity, as well as medieval Italian and modern coins, medals, and seals; and the collection of the Municipal Museum itself, including more than thirty thousand pieces.

The library of the Municipal Museum of Ancient Art of Turin is among the major art libraries in Italy, and it has a special department for numismatic, Oriental, and ethnological studies.

Since the early 1950s, the Municipal Museum of Ancient Art has organized special exhibitions in Turinese public buildings. Catalogues can be bought at the museum itself, and they include: *Tanzio da Varallo*, ed. G. Testori, 1959; *L'Italia vista dai pittori francesi del XVIII e XIX secolo*, ed. G. Bazin, 1961; *Mostra del Barocco piemontese*, ed. V. Viale, 1963, 3 vols.; *Giacomo Ceruti e la ritrattistica del suo tempo nell'Italia settentrionale*, ed. L. Mallè and G. Testori, 1967; *L'incisione europea dal XV al XX secolo*, ed. L. Mallè and F. Salamon, 1968; *Pelagio Pelagi artista e collezionista*, organized in collaboration with the Municipal Museum of Bologna, 1976; *Valle Susa: arte e storia dall'XI al XVIII secolo*, ed. G. Romano, 1977; *Jaquerio e il gotico internazionale*, ed. E. Castelnuovo and G. Romano, 1979.

Selected Bibliography

Museum publications: Cabutti, L., *Palazzo Madama: Museo Civico d'Arte Antica*, 1976; Viale, V., *Il Museo Civico di Torino*, 1960; Mallè, L., *I dipinti del Museo Civico d'Arte Antica*, 1963; idem, *Le sculture del Museo Civico d'Arte Antica*, 1965; idem, *Museo Civico d'Arte Antica: gli smalti, gli avori*, 1969; idem, *Museo Civico d'Arte Antica: i vetri soffiati e incisi, le vetrate, giade, cristalli di rocca e pietre dure*, 1971; idem, *Museo Civico d'Arte Antica: I mobili e arredi lignei, gli arazzi*, 1972; idem, *I Musei Civici di Torino: acquisti e doni, 1966–1970*, 1970.

ILARIA BIGNAMINI

SABAUDA GALLERY (officially PINACOTECA NAZIONALE DI TORINO; alternately NATIONAL PICTURE GALLERY OF TURIN; also GALLERIA SABAUDA, REALE GALLERIA DI TORINO, REGIA PINACOTECA, PINACOTECA NAZIONALE), Palazzo dell'Accademia delle Scienze, Via Accademia delle Scienze 6, Turin.

The Sabauda Gallery of Turin was founded with paintings primarily from the collections of the House of Savoy. The oldest group of paintings are purchases made by Carlo Emanuele I, and the first inventory is dated 1631. The collection was later increased by Vittorio Amadeo II and Carlo Emanuele II. In 1741 Carlo Emanuele II bought an important group of Flemish and Dutch paintings from Prince Eugenio of Savoy. In 1832 King Carlo Alberto took a step that was very important to the future development of artistic culture in Piedmont: 420 paintings belonging to the Savoy collections were exhibited at Palazzo Madama. In 1860 Carlo Alberto's son Vittorio Emanuele II presented the newly created Italian State with the entire collection, which in 1865 moved to the present site, the Palazzo dell'Accademia delle Scienze.

The Sabauda Gallery is a state museum administered by the Ministry for Environment and Cultural Affairs (Ministero per i Beni Culturali e Ambientali) through a national office called Soprintendenza. The museum is governed by six Soprintendenti (members of the Soprintendenza).

The Sabauda Gallery was opened to the public in 1865, and it is today one of the major Italian collections of paintings. In 1952 the General Directorship for Antiquities and Fine Arts (Direzione Generale per le Antichità e Belle Arti) decided that the Sabauda Gallery, together with the most important Italian museums belonging to the state, had to be restored. In the following years, this task was carried on by a Municipal Committee supported by Turinese public and private institutions such as the Provincia, Comune, Camera di Commercio, Unione Industriale, and Fiat and three banks (Cassa di Risparmio, Istituto San Paolo, and Banca Anonima di Credito).

The building was designed by the architect Guarino Guarini in 1679 as a College of Nobles (Collegio dei Nobili), directed by Jesuits. In 1783 it became the official seat of the Academy of Sciences of Turin, founded in 1757, and since that date the building has been called Palazzo dell'Accademia delle Scienze. Since 1831 the ground and first floors of the building have housed the Egyptian and Graeco-Roman museums. In 1865 the second floor was chosen as a definitive location for the Sabauda Gallery. In 1952 the second floor was completely remodeled by the architect Piero Sanpaolesi: since the original height of the rooms was 11.85 meters, two floors were designed doubling the original space. Consequently, the Sabauda Gallery occupies two floors on the original second floor of the building. On the first floor of the Sabauda Gallery there are twenty-four rooms and three repositories. On the second floor are twenty-three rooms for the display of paintings, a room for engravings and drawings, and six rooms for the Gualino Collection. The holdings of the museum are subdivided into rooms by schools. On the first floor are Piedmontese and Italian painting of the fourteenth-nineteenth century (rooms 24–27 and 1–14); on the second floor, Venetian painting of the sixteenth and eighteenth centuries (rooms 15 and 18), Emilian painting (room 16), Caravaggesques (room 17), Flemish painting (room 19), van Dyck and his pupils (room 20), and Dutch, French, German, and Spanish painting (rooms 21–23). The group of Flemish and Dutch paintings in the Sabauda Gallery forms the richest and most important collection of masters from the Low Countries in Italy, and it represents a very interesting chapter in the history of the Italian patronage.

The variety of styles, influences, and subjects that characterizes the Piedmontese painting can be studied in the rooms the Sabauda Gallery devotes to it. The Piedmontese current that was influenced by the Lombard painting of the fourteenth century is well represented in the Gallery by two fragments of frescoes showing apostles, two wooden statues having deacons as their subjects, and a triptych on high relief, the *Holy Trinity*. The Gothic-Lombard influence on Piedmontese painting of the fifteenth century is seen in a fragment of a fresco with the apostles by Giorgio Turcotto di Cavallermaggiore and the *Madonna Enthroned* by Francesco Filiberto d'Allesandria.

The display of Piedmontese masters also includes works by Macrino d'Alba, influenced by the Lombard painting at the beginning of the sixteenth century; Gaudenzio Ferrari, the most remarkable figure of the Piedmontese movement during the sixteenth century; Bartolomeo Garavoglia, influenced by Guercino; and Niccolò Musso da Casale, Antonio d'Errico, called Tanzio, and Giovanni Antonio Molineri, called Caraccino, all under the spell of the Bolognese school and Caravaggio. The collection of Piedmontese painting ends with *vedute* by Giovanni Migliara, scene designer and landscape painter of the nineteenth century. The museum collection of Italian paintings also includes Tuscan, Lombard, Venetian, Emilian, Bolognese, and Genoese masters (fourteenth-eighteenth century). Tuscan painting of the fourteenth century is well represented by Bernardo Daddi's *Madonna Crowned*; the fifteenth century by the delightful *Triumph of Chastity*, a *Madonna with Child* by Beato Angelico, the famous *Tobias and the Archangel Raphael* by Antonio and Piero Pollaiuolo, *Archangels* by Filippino Lippi, and *Virgins* by Lorenzo di Credi; and the sixteenth century by Bronzino's *Portrait of Eleanora da Toledo* and Sodoma's *Holy Family* and *Madonna Enthroned*. Among Lombard paintings are a rare polyptych (1462) by Paolo da Brescia and Borgognone's *Stories of St. Ambrose*, as well as paintings by Gerolamo Savoldo and Guilio Campi.

Venetian painting is represented by the badly damaged *Holy Conversation* by Andrea Mantegna; the *Trinity* by the young Tintoretto; two large canvases from Veronese's studio, *The Queen of Sheba* and *The Finding of Moses*, which were bought by Carlo Emanuele I in Venice; and Veronese's *Banquet at Simeon's House* (1560). Barnaba da Modena's *Madonna*, Garofalo's *Disputation at the Temple*, and Lodovico Mazzolino's *Holy Conversation* are representative of the collection of Emilian paintings at the Sabauda Gallery. Bolognese paintings of the seventeenth century are the *Four Elements* by Francesco Albani (a commission from Cardinal Maurizio of Savoy) and a series of canvases by Guercino. Among Genoese paintings are a beautiful *Female Portrait* by Bernardo Carbone, a *Holy Family* by Valerio Castello, a *Satyr* by Francesco Castiglione, and the *Portrait of a Prelate* by Bernardo Strozzi. A masterpiece of the Italian seventeenth century is the *Annunciation*, which Orazio Gentileschi presented to Carlo Emanuele I. Among the eighteenth century masters are Pompeo Batoni, Sebastiano Conca, Tiepolo (*Triumph of Aurelianus*), Sebastiano Ricci (*Susan and Daniel* and *Moses*, decorations originally executed for the Royal Palace in Turin, and an interior scene at Hampton Court Palace), Bernardo Bellotto (two *vedute* of Turin painted in 1745), and Francesco Guardi (two *capricci*).

The majority of Flemish and Dutch paintings are from the collection of Prince Eugenio of Savoy, a sophisticated collector and a famous *condottiere*. The collection of Netherlandish masters has different origins. Petrus Christus's *Madonna with Child* and Rogier van der Weyden's *Visitation* and *Portrait of a Donor* are from Carlo Emanuele I's collection and are catalogued in the inventory of 1631. Jan van Eyck's *St. Francis Receiving the Stigmata* was bought at Casale Monferrato by a Mr. Fassio in the nineteenth century and later given to the

Sabauda Gallery. Hans Memling's *The Passion*, a commission from the Florentine banker Portinari, was given by Cosimo de' Medici to Pope Pius V for the church of Santa Croce at Boscomarengo. During the Napoleonic period it was bought by a monk, who later gave it to the Savoys. Finally, Vittorio Emanuele II presented the Sabauda Gallery with it. Particularly important is a group of paintings by Sir Anthony van Dyck: *Children of Charles I*, *Princess Clara Eugenia*, *Prince Tommaso di Carignano*, and *Infanta Isabella of Spain*. The collection of Flemish and Dutch painting also includes landscapes by Paulus Bril, Isaac Soreau, Joost de Momper, Hermann Saftleven, and Jacob van Ruisdael; genre scenes by David Teniers and Adriaen van Ostade; and portraits by Frans van Mieris, Rembrandt, and many others. The collection of French painting includes the *Triptych of Iverny*, a commission from the Ceva family; portraits by Jean Clouet (*Carlo of Savoy*) and François Clouet (*Marguerite de Valois*); *St. Margaret* by Poussin; *Adoration* by Claude Vignon; a still life by Pierre Benoit; two pastel portraits of the painter Carle van Loo and his wife by Antoine Coypel; and the portrait *Daughter of the Engraver Porporati* by Elisabeth Vigée-Lebrun.

The six rooms given to the Gualino Collection were arranged by lawyer Riccardo Gualino himself in 1958. The extensive collection includes Western and Eastern paintings and sculptures, as well as furniture (fourteenth-sixteenth century). Among the finest paintings collected by Riccardo Gualino are a *Madonna Enthroned* by a pre-Giottoesque Tuscan master, an *Ascension* by a Riminese master (pupil or follower of Giotto), two paintings on wood by Lorenzo Veneziano, *Angels* by Spinello Aretino, *Apostles* by Giovanni da Milano, a lunette by Matteo di Gualdo, a *Nativity* by Luca Signorelli, and a *Madonna* by Borgognone. Among the most famous paintings of the collection are Titian's late *Self Portrait*, Lorenzo di Credi's *Portrait of a Young Man*, Liberale da Verona's *Madonna*, an early work by Veronese (*Venus and Mars*), Ferdinand Bol's *Girl at the Window*, and van Dyck's sketch for the portrait of *Sofonisba Anguissola*.

Selected Bibliography

Baudi di Vesme, Alessandro, *Catalogo della Regia Pinacoteca di Torino* (Torino 1899); Bernardi, Maurizio, *La Galleria Sabauda di Torino* (Roma 1968); Gabrielli, Noemi, *La Galleria Sabauda di Torino* (Roma 1968); Mazzini, Franco, *Torino, la Galleria Sabauda* (Torino 1968).

ILARIA BIGNAMINI

———— Urbino ————

NATIONAL GALLERY OF THE MARCHES (officially GALLERIA NAZIONALE DELLA MARCHE; alternately the DUCAL PALACE; also IL PALAZZO DUCALE DI URBINO), Piazza Duca Federico, Urbino.

The National Gallery of the Marches is housed in the Ducal Palace at Urbino and comprises a collection of highly important paintings and works of art of the Renaissance period. The original collection amassed by Federico di Montefeltro, duke of Urbino (1444–82), and his successors was dispersed when the palace passed to the della Rovere and then in 1631 to the Church. Restoration of the palace began in 1756. This activity continued and intensified in 1874 and again in 1912–19, at which time the National Gallery was instituted with a governmental provision. The nucleus of the collection had already been gathered in the Institute of Fine Arts, Urbino (established by 1861), by Lorenzo Valerio, commissioner of the Marches. In 1881 the collection was installed in the palace.

From 1912 the Gallery continued to increment its collection through deposits, acquisitions, and loans, gradually enlarging until it occupied the entire first and part of the second floors of the palace. The works, arranged in the various rooms of the palace, do not follow a rigorous historical sequence but are instead compatible with the ambiance of the surroundings. Together the palace and the collection constitute a harmonious artistic blend of art and architecture evoking the Renaissance period. Today the National Gallery of the Marches is operated under the jurisdiction of the National Museums of Italy.

The Ducal Palace was constructed by Federico di Montefeltro, known for his brilliant humanistic court, which drew artistic and literary talent from throughout Italy and Europe. Life at the urbinate court under Guidobaldo, Federico's son, was described by Baldassare Castiglione in his perceptive record of the period, *Il Cortegiano* (*The Courtier*), begun in 1508 and published in 1528. In 1465 the architect Luciano Laurana, a Dalmatian, was appointed by Federico. Construction of the palace began in 1472, and in 1474, when Laurana departed Urbino, direction of the building was taken over by Francesco di Giorgio, a Sienese architect. The interior decoration was developed by Ambrogio Barocci and Francesco di Giorgio. The top floor of the palace was not added until 1563 by Girolamo Genga. The Renaissance principles governing the style of the building are admirably demonstrated in the courtyard designed by Laurana, its rising and falling arcades an exercise in balance and harmony running along the four sides of the rectangular space.

Papal paintings of the Trecento, particularly of the Riminese school as well as other groups, are well represented. The *Crucifix* attributed to Pietro da Rimini or a follower demonstrates the impact of Giotto's influence on the provincial schools and is comparable to the master's early *Crucifix* in St. Maria Novella, Florence. Several depictions of this subject by anonymous masters further emphasize this point, and in a polyptych, *Madonna and Child*, with *Scenes of the Life of Christ*, by Giovanni Baronzio, Giotto's plasticity is intensified. This masterpiece of the Riminese school is the only signed and dated (1345) work by this artist. A triptych, the *Coronation of the Virgin*, assigned to an anonymous artist, is also in the Riminese mood. The artist, known as the Master of the Urbino Coronation after this painting, is also associated with a wooden *Crucifix* and a *Crucifixion* panel, formerly part of a polyptych (not extant). The *Madonna del Latte* signed by Maestro Antonio, dating from the second half of the fourteenth century, is the only known work by this artist.

The International Gothic style was a significant current in the region, as evidenced by the elaborate fresco decoration of the Oratorio of San Giovanni in Urbino by the Salimbeni brothers (first half of the fifteenth century), and is represented by several panel works. The *Madonna and Child with St. Rose* is attributed to Gentile da Fabriano, and a work of the Fabriano school (*Madonna and Child*, with *Scenes of the Life of St. Bartholomew*, and predella represen- tations *Circumcision*, *Crucifixion*, and *Pentecost*) of the mid-fifteenth century also shows some Sienese and Central Italian influence. The important *Madonna and Child* by Allegretto Nuzi da Fabriano, signed and dated 1372, is the last- known work of the school of Gentile da Fabriano and was formerly in the Fornari Collection. Work of the Salimbeni brothers is represented by the panel *Santa Chiara* by Lorenzo Salimbeni, and wings from the polyptych *Saints John the Baptist and Michael* are executed in his brother Jacopo's style.

Fragments of a panel by the Sienese painter Andrea di Bartolo is also in the collection. Other fifteenth century examples of local trends include a polyptych from the Church of St. Donato in Urbino: the *Madonna and Child with Saints*, signed and dated 1439, is by Antonio Alberti, a Ferrarese artist who worked at Urbino toward the beginning of the fifteenth century in the provincial Gothic mode. Also by Alberti is a *Crucifixion*, as well as the panels *St. Anthony Abbot* and *St. Giacomo Compostella*. Several fresco fragments attributed to this same artist are from the Paltroni Chapel of the Church of St. Francis, Urbino. A triptych in three divided panels by Nicola di Maestro Antonio of Ancona is probably a late work of the artist, who usually worked in the Padovan-Ferrarese style but here shows a marked Umbrian-Marchegian influence and a knowledge of Crivelli. Works by or attributed to Marino Angeli and Antonio Allegri da Ferrara, as well as the *Crucifixion* panel by Girolamo di Giovanni, a noted artist of the Camerino school, are also exhibited.

The Venetian school is well represented, and holdings include the *Altarpiece of Montefiorentino* by Alvise Vivarini, signed and dated 1476. This important work is fundamental for an understanding of the artist's oeuvre and for the development of Venetian painting, here demonstrating the heritage of the artist's uncle, Bartolommeo, and father, Antonio. The *Sacra Conversazione* by Marco Basaiti, a Venetian follower of Giovanni Bellini, is exhibited, and the panel *St. Bernardino of Siena* is attributed to either Carlo Crivelli or his brother Vittore. A Marchegian artist, Lorenzo d'Alessandro of Sanseverino, reflects the influence of Umbrian art as well as the Venetian style of Crivelli in his *Baptism of Christ*. By Giovanni Bellini is the important *Sacra Conversazione* of about 1490. Two works by Titian were executed for the Confraternity of the Corpus Domini in Urbino: the *Last Supper* (with an admirable still life) and the *Resurrection*.

The National Gallery boasts important examples of the Florentine school of the Quattrocento. A *Madonna and Child*, believed to be by Verrocchio, is a rare example of panel painting assigned to that artist, an attribution supported by stylistic and iconographic kinships with known works. Paolo Uccello's predella panel, the *Miracle of the Profanation of the Host* of about 1468, was commissioned by Federico di Montefeltro and was intended as part of the altarpiece with a central panel later executed by Joos van Ghent. Among the Gallery's most important works are two panels by Piero della Francesco: the *Madonna and Child*, called the *Madonna di Sanigallia*, a mature work of after 1465, and the *Flagellation*, a fundamental painting for the study of the artist and one that has elicited much study and discussion. The quality of Piero's penetrating light and abstract geometry is evident in both of these paintings. Also attributed to Piero is a detailed perspective view, the *City of Urbino*, which has also been assigned to Laurana and to Francesco di Giorgio. Luca di Signorelli is represented by his *Crucifixion and Pentecost* panels, and the fresco fragment *Christ as Redeemer* by Melozzo da Forli is in the collection. Raphael Sanzio, a native of Urbino, is represented by his *Portrait of a Gentlewoman*, called *La Muta* (*The Silent One*), dating from his Florentine period and linked to works by Leonardo da Vinci with the same three-quarter formula and sense of the figure emerging from the dark ground as is found in *La Gioconda*. The panel entered the collection from the Uffizi Gallery (q.v.) in Florence in 1927. The tapestries in the Throne Room of the palace are later versions of the famous set in the Vatican, Rome, executed after the designs by Raphael. The original designs were commissioned by Pope Leo X, and these seven tapestries were originally in the Palazzo Royale, Milan.

An integral aspect of the National Gallery is the palace itself; decoration includes work by major artists such as Francesco di Giorgio and Sandro Botticelli. In the Room of the Angels, the elaborate mantelpiece is decorated with stucco, polychromed putti, and, on the wall above, angels bearing a laurel wreath, all by Rosselli and reminiscent of Donatello's work. The exquisite intarsiated doors leading to various rooms of the palace were executed after designs by Francesco di Giorgio (1477–99), Baccio Pontelli (1479–82), and Sandro Botticelli. In the same Room of the Angels, Botticelli is believed responsible for designing several representations, including the figures of Apollo and Hercules. The perspective views and representations of musical instruments are exceptional in their craftsmanship.

The *studiolo* built by Federico is a small room lined with intarsiated panels (executed under the direction of Baccio Pontelli, with designs by Botticelli and other artists); representations include books, musical instruments, and a portrait of the duke as a humanist. The elaborate ceiling in gold and azure is dated 1476. A portrait of Federico and his son Guidobaldo, executed by a Spanish artist working at Urbino, Pedro Berruguete, originally hung in this chamber and is now in another room. The painting reflects the balance of Piero della Francesco, who was in residence at Urbino at the time. Portrait panels of "famous men" executed by Joos van Ghent (perhaps with the collaborative effort of Pedro Berruguete), a Flemish painter who worked at the urbinate court, originally hung in two rows above the intarsiated panels. The twenty-eight portraits that include Cicero, Hippocrates, Homer, Moses, and Petrarch were removed from the *studiolo* in the seventeenth century, and today fourteen panels are displayed in other rooms of the Ducal Palace, and fourteen are in the Louvre (q.v.), Paris. Another work by Joos van Ghent is the monumental altar, the *Institution of the Eucharist*, originally commissioned from Paolo Uccello by Federico. The panel was executed in 1473–74. In the background of the painting are the figures of Federico di Montefeltro and two courtiers conversing with the ambassador of Persia.

Another native of Urbino, Federico Barocci, who worked in the Florentine Mannerist style, is represented by several panels exhibited in two rooms of the palace. Included are an *Annunciation*, the *Madonna of St. Simon*, the *Madonna of St. Augustine*, the *Stigmatization of St. Francis*, the *Crucifixion*, and the *Madonna and Child with St. John the Evangelist*.

Also notable in the collection are the cartoon the *Triumph of Bacchus* by Annibale Carracci and a cartoon by Domenichino for the frescoes executed in the chapel of St. Gennaro, in Naples Cathedral (*Martyrdom of St. Gennaro*). Works by Timoteo Viti (an artist who influenced Raphael's early work), Alessandro Viteli, Simone De Magistris (*Madonna and Child in Glory with Saints John the Evangelist and Francis*, signed and dated 1608 and executed in collaboration with his son Solezio), and various paintings in the eighteenth-century Venetian style are also in the collection. The palace houses a remarkable collection of majolica, a local craft produced in Urbino, Castelli, Faenza, Pesaro, Castel Durante, and elsewhere, as well as examples of Renaissance furnishings.

Bas-reliefs representing machines of war, hydraulics, and so on by Ambrogio Barocci formerly decorated the base of the palace facade. In 1756 the reliefs were removed and installed in the palace, where they are now exhibited. An important relief sculpture by Luca della Robbia, the polychromed terracotta *Madonna and Child with Saints Peter, Dominick, Thomas, and Beato Alberto*, is now in the Gallery. The sculpture was until recently installed in the lunette over the entrance to the Church of St. Dominick (constructed 1365) located opposite the Ducal Palace.

A small shop at the entrance offers postcards and slides of works in the collection. An official guide detailing the collection and the Ducal Palace is published by the government in the series detailing the National Museums of Italy.

Selected Bibliography

Zampetti, Pietro, *Il Palazzo Ducale di Urbino e la Galleria Nazionale delle Marche*, 1963; Rotondi, Pasquale, *Il Palazzo ducale di Urbino* (2 vols., 1950–51); Dennistoun, James, *Memoirs of the Dukes of Urbino, 1440–1630* (London 1909); Lavin, Marilyn Aronberg, *Piero della Francesco: The Flagellation* (London 1972); idem, "Studies in Urbinate Painting, 1458–1476: Piero della Francesco, Paolo Uccello, and Joos van Ghent" (Ph.D. thesis); Mennella, Giovanni, *Il museo lapidario del Palazzo ducale di Urbino: Saggio storico su documenti inediti* (Genoa 1973); Rotondo, Pasquale, *Francesco di*

Giorgio (Martini) nel Palazzo ducale di Urbino (Milan 1970); Salmi, Mario, *Piero della Francesca e il Palazzo ducale di Urbino* (Florence 1945); "Urbino" in *Le Marche: Guida d'Italia del Touring Club Italiano* (Milan 1936).

LORRAINE KARAFEL

—————— Venice ——————

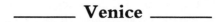

ACADEMY GALLERIES (officially GALLERIE DELL'ACCADEMIA; alternately GALLERIES OF THE ACADEMY OF VENICE; also L'ACCADEMIA), Campo della Carità, Venice; Office of the Director, c/o Soprintendenza ai Beni Artistici e Storici di Venzia, Piazza San Marco 63, 20100 Venice.

The Academy Galleries house the largest and most complete survey of Venetian painting assembled anywhere. Masterpieces of five centuries fill the history-laden buildings of the former Church and Scuola of the Carità and the Monastery of the Lateranensi. Although the Academy dates from the eighteenth century, the edifices themselves are much older. The Church of the Carità was built in the mid-fifteenth century under the direction of Bartolomeo Bon (d. 1508) and his workshop. Its unusual design consisted of a single nave, without transepts, ending in three polygonal apses. The peaked facade boasted a rose window flanked by lancets and a marble lunette. After its suppression in 1807, G. A. Selva sectioned the nave into two floors; the lower story contained the classrooms of the Academy of Fine Arts, and the upper story became part of the Gallery. Little remains of the Lateran monastery built by Palladio in the mid-sixteenth century. Because the monastery suffered severe damage from a fire in 1630, only one wing could be salvaged by G. A. Selva when he undertook restorations in 1807–11. The Gothic courtyard, however, is still preserved.

The entry to the Galleries is via the Scuola della Carità, the oldest (1260) of the six major guilds of Venice. The eighteenth-century facade was executed by Bernardino Maccaruzzi (d. 1799) after a design of Giorgio Massari. At the beginning of the nineteenth century, a new facade was added to the Scuola by Francesco Lazzari. Also at this time the ground floor was given over to classrooms for the Academy of Fine Arts, and the rooms upstairs were adapted as gallery space by G. A. Selva to make the paintings and plaster casts of Classical sculpture (ex-Abbot Filippo Fursetti Collection) available for student instruction in keeping with the academy charter issued on February 12, 1807. The double staircase at the entrance was constructed in 1765 and provides a setting for the two sculptures *Faith* and *Charity* by Gianmaria Morleiter (d. 1782).

The Academy of Painters and Sculptors was founded in 1750 under the directorship of the Venetian painter Giambattista Piazzetta. Official recognition was bestowed upon the academy in 1756, and Giambattista Tiepolo was selected as the first president. At this time, the organization established itself in the Fonteghetto della Farina, or "Little Flour Market"; after the fall of the Venetian

Republic in 1797, the academy was transferred to its present site. The Gallery was formulated by decree of Eugene Napoleon in 1807, but already many of the art treasures of the city had been dispersed across Europe, not a few of which Emperor Napoleon himself had confiscated for the Louvre (q.v.). With the Austrian occupation of 1814, some of these art objects were recovered, but by no means did the number approach the quantity of paintings and altarpieces appropriated from the churches, guilds, and monasteries of the lagoon. Leopoldo Cicognara, the first president of the Academy Gallery, and Peter Edwards, the first inspector of fine arts of Venice, worked diligently to recover as many major works as possible. Cicognara compiled a list of paintings still in the churches of Venice that were in danger of severe deterioration if not removed to the academy; he thereby managed to save a great many pieces through this program of transferral. The initial group included Paolo Veronese's grandiose masterpiece the *Feast in the House of Levi*; Tintoretto's *St. Mark Freeing the Slave*; Leandro Bassano's *Resurrection of Lazarus*; and Paris Bordone's *Presentation of the Ring to the Doge*.

The generous bequest of Girolamo Ascanio Molin, the first private donation to the Gallery, brought a fine group of fourteenth- and fifteenth-century Venetian paintings to the Accademia in 1816. Among the 118 paintings, 2 bronzes, and 5 marbles were 2 pastels by Rosalba Carriera, a triptych by Jacobello del Fiore, and a *Saint Lawrence* by Nicolò di Pietro. To accommodate the growing number of acquisitions, two rooms were added to the Accademia's south side between 1820 and 1834.

The patrimony of Count Girolamo Contarini, numbering 188 paintings, further increased the richness of the collection in 1838. The new acquisitions included Giovanni Bellini's *Madonna degli Alberetti* and the *Allegories*, Cima da Conegliano's *Madonna with Two Saints*, and a group of Venetian scenes by Pietro Longhi. The furniture and sculpture by Brustolon, which was also a part of the Contarini bequest, was consigned in 1902 to the Civil Museums and displayed at Ca' Rezzonico (q.v.).

Countess Felicita Renier Bertrand Hellman's donation in 1850 included notable works such as the *Madonna and Child with Saints* by Giovanni Bellini, the *St. Jerome* by Piero della Francesca, the *Deposition* by Cima da Conegliano, the *Christ before Pilate* by Andrea Schiavone, and the *Adulteress* attributed to Tintoretto. A portion of the Manfrin Collection was purchased in 1856, and among the new paintings were a *Madonna* by Nicolò di Pietro, a small portrait by Hans Memling, the *Washing of the Feet* by Boccaccino, and *Two Saints* by Moretto. During these years the Palladian gallery was refurbished, rooms to the right of the neoclassic vestibule were added in 1841, and in 1858 a new series of salons was constructed to link the existing wings.

Beginning under the directorship of Giulio Cantalamessa in 1894, the galleries were given a rational structural arrangement. It was at this time that the precious core of Venetian paintings was singled out from the other Italian and European works and was hailed as the principal attraction of the Gallery. The sculpture in the collection was removed for a time to the Ducal Palace before its placement in the Ca' d'Oro. Valuable acquisitions during Cantalamessa's tenure as director were Cosimo Tura's *Madonna of the Zodiac*, Palma Vecchio's *Sacra Conversazione*, Jacopo Bassano's *St. Jerome*, Carlo Crivelli's *Saints Peter and Paul*, Lorenzo Veneziano's *Mystical Marriage of St. Catherine*, and Giovanni Battista Tiepolo's *Rape of Europa* and *Diana and Acteon* (also attributed to Sebastiano Ricci).

Gino Fogolari assumed the directorship of the Academy Galleries in 1906 and worked assiduously on their expansion until 1941. His single greatest accomplishment was the acquisition of a crown jewel in Venetian art, the *Tempest* by Giorgione. He also brought into the collection major paintings by Giovanni Bellini and his father, Jacopo; by Cima da Conegliano; and by Bartolommeo Vivarini. The director consistently expanded the museum's holdings, acquiring in 1908 a *Landscape* by Marieschi, in 1910 the *Crucifixion of St. Peter* by Luca Giordano, in the following year a *Last Supper* by Strozzi, and in 1913 a *Madonna* by Paolo Veneziano. Fogolari undertook the reorganization of the galleries in 1920; this arrangement was amended after World War II by the new director, Vittorio Moschini, who served in that capacity until 1961. Architect Paolo Scarpa assisted him in restructuring the limited gallery space to present the collection to the public in the most effective way.

The current director of the Academy Galleries is Giovanna Nepi Scirè. Since the museum is under the jurisdiction of the Italian State, other executives, curators, conservators, and so on are employed by the Soprintendenza ai Beni Artistici e Storici of Venice, which oversees, along with the Accademia, the other state museums in the city: the Galleria Giorgio Franchetti at the Ca' d'Oro and the Museo d'Arte Orientale. Apart from these officials, the director supervises thirty-nine Gallery custodians. The Academy Galleries consist of two departments: the Pinacoteca (Picture Gallery) and the Gabinetto dei Disegni e Stampe (Department of Prints and Drawings); both are under the administration of the director. The museum receives no private contributions and is entirely dependent upon the state for its support.

Of the art objects in the galleries, 95 percent are on permanent display, and the remaining works are subject to minor periodic rotation. The collection as a whole numbers 3,357 items. Because space in the building is at a premium, it is encouraging to learn from the director of the plans to enlarge the Gallery and the adjacent Academy of Fine Arts.

The collection of fourteenth- and early fifteenth-century altarpieces and panel paintings shows Venice's dependence on its Byzantine heritage. Rich, vivid colors on gold backgrounds recall the early mosaic work found throughout the city. Important works include the signed polyptych the *Coronation of the Virgin* (1333–38) and the *Madonna Enthroned* by Paolo Veneziano and, from the hand of Lorenzo Veneziano, the *Mystical Marriage of St. Catherine* and the *Annunciation with Saints* (1356–72), which was commissioned by Domenico Lion, a member of the Venetian Senate, for the Church of Sant'Antonio di Castello.

Several panels display the grace and elegance of the International Gothic style, such as Michele Giambono's polyptych, perhaps from the Church of San Giacomo dei Serviti on the Giudecca; the *Madonna della Misericordia and Saints* by Jacobello del Fiore; and the altarpiece *Madonna and Saints and the Finding of the True Cross* by the Bolognese Michele di Matteo. Presaging the Early Renaissance is a work by Antonio Vivarini, the *Marriage of St. Monica*, one in a series on the life of the saint done for the church of Santo Stefano. Nicolò di Pietro's *Madonna and Child with Angels*, dated 1394–1416, is one of the finest Venetian paintings of the late Trecento. From this general period there is an exquisite cross in rock crystal, silver, and silver-gilt, with modeled figures, that was formerly in the Scuola Grande di San Teodoro.

Giovanni Bellini's eminent position in Venetian art is secure. His genius comes forth clearly in a series of Madonnas, including the *Madonna with Cherubs* from the Scuola della Carità, the *Madonna degli Alberetti*, a *Madonna and Child Blessing*, and a *Madonna and Saints*. Dating from his maturity are the *Pietà* and the *Madonna with John the Baptist*. Several paintings by Cima da Conegliano are the *Doubting Thomas*, a mature work done for the Scuola dei Mureri; the *Madonna and Child with Saints*, from the Church of the Orange Tree, signed by the artist and intended for the former Church of Santa Chiara at Murano. By Marco Basaiti are the *Christ in the Garden of Gethsemane* (1510), done for the Foscari family, and the *Sons of Zebedee*. Two dated paintings are by Vittore Carpaccio—the *Presentation in the Temple* (1510) and the *Ararat Crucifixions* (1515). The *Life of St. Ursula* is a narrative cycle of the utmost significance. It consists of eight canvases painted by Carpaccio at the close of the fifteenth century for the Scuola di Sant'Orsola, which occupied a site near the Church of Santi Giovanni e Paolo. The paintings, which depict scenes of the legend of Ursula and Ereus, have been given a setting in Venice. Lesser-known masters of the late fifteenth and early sixteenth centuries who are represented in the Academy Galleries are Andrea Busati, Vincenzo Catena, Giovanni Cariani, and Bernardino Licinio.

Rivaling the excellence of the works of the Venetian school is the painting by the great Paduan Andrea Mantegna. His admirable *St. George* is an outstanding treasure of the collection. Equally magnificent among the non-Venetian works is Piero della Francesca's *St. Jerome and the Donor*, dating from the mid-fifteenth century.

Because of the rarity of paintings by Giorgione, the *Tempest* is one of the most prized paintings in European collections. There is another work here attributed to the artist, the *Old Woman*, that is displayed in its original frame. Although only a fragment of a fresco, Giorgione's *Nude* should not be overlooked. It was part of his great decorative scheme on the facade of the Fondaco dei Turchi, of which nothing more survives.

One of a series of paintings depicting the life of St. Mark done for the great hall of the Scuola di San Marco is Paris Bordone's *Giving of the Ring* (1534). It depicts a fisherman presenting to the doge the ring that was given him by St.

Mark as a sign of the miracle by which the city of Venice was saved. A masterpiece by Bonifacio Pitati of Verona is here along with three other pieces that he executed for the offices in the Camerlenghi Palace at the Rialto. This piece, admired for its beautiful landscape, depicts the parable of *Dives and the Beggar*. Also from the Camerlenghi is the *Madonna of the Treasures* (1566), *Saints Jerome and Andrew*, and *Saints Louis, George, and the Princess* by Tintoretto. Other remarkable works by this most important of the Venetian artists are several from the Scuola di San Marco—*Miracle of St. Mark*, *Recovery of the Body of St. Mark*, and *Dream of St. Mark*, which was completed by Domenico Tintoretto; from the cycle for the Scuola della Trinità are the *Creation of the Animals*, *Adam and Eve*, and *Cain and Abel*; the *Deposition*; the *Presentation of Christ in the Temple*; the large *Crucifixion*; and the *Portrait of Procurator Jacopo Soranzo*.

Not to be slighted in the face of these masterworks is the much-acclaimed *Portrait of a Gentleman in His Study* by Lorenzo Lotto, the *Saints Anthony Abbot and Paul the Hermit* by Girolamo Savoldo, and the *Sacra Conversazione* and the *Assumption* by Palma Vecchio.

Referred to by many as the greatest of all Venetian colorists, Paolo Veronese is well represented in the Academy Galleries. Along with the *Feast in the House of Levi* are the brilliant canvases of his early years, such as the *Madonna Enthroned with Saints*, the *Annunciation*, the *Mystical Marriage of St. Catherine*, *St. Nicholas Greeted by the People of Myra*, *St. Francis Receiving the Stigmata*, an *Allegory of Venice*, *The Battle of Lepanto*, and, a late piece, the *Crucifixion*.

The *Presentation of the Virgin* is a major work by Titian of 1534–38 and a prize of the collection. It hangs in its original location in the Hall of the Scuola, a room that dazzles one with its rich Renaissance decor. There cannot be found in the Academy collection a more moving, and at the same time more powerful, painting than Titian's *Pietà*. He intended it to be placed at his tomb in the Church of the Frari, but the canvas was left unfinished at his death, only to be completed by his devoted follower Palma Giovane. A late work in grisaille by this pupil is the *Crucifixion of St. Peter*.

Significant works by non-Venetians of the sixteenth and early seventeenth centuries include *Apollo and Marsyas* and the *Sacrifice of Isaac* by Johann Liss of Germany, a *Good Samaritan* by the Roman Domenico Feti, *St. Francis* by Annibale Carraci, and *St. Jerome* by Bernardo Strozzi of Genoa. Other works are by Sebastiano Mazzoni of Tuscany, Francesco Maffei of Vicenza, and an impressive *Pietà* by the Neapolitan Luca Giordano.

Venetian landscape painting became a popular genre in the eighteenth century. Admired by the citizens and collected widely by foreigners, especially the English, many of these works can be found at the Academy Galleries. Chief among them are the *Landscape with Waterfall* and several quixotic scenes by Marco Ricci, two *Landscapes with Biblical Scenes* by Giuseppe Zias, and, in a more Arcadian spirit, pastorales and mythologies in landscape settings by the Tuscan Francesco Zuccarelli. They include a *Bacchanal*, the *Bull Hunt*, and the *Rape of Europa*.

The last outstanding figure in the history of Venetian art of the eighteenth century was Giovanni Battista Tiepolo. Dating from his early career is the *Miracle of the Bronze Serpent*, formerly in the Church of Saints Cosmos and Damian on the Giudecca. Other pieces worthy of esteem are *St. Helen Discovering the True Cross*, a ceiling tondo that at one time was in the Church of the Capuchin nuns at Castello; two *Praying Figures*, which are all that remain of the ceiling frescoes done by Tiepolo for the Church of Santa Maria degli Scalzi, which was destroyed by an enemy bombardment in 1915; the small altarpiece *St. Joseph with the Christ Child and Saints*; the *Glory of St. Dominic*; and a series of four mythologies generally accepted as by the master, *Diana and Acteon*, the *Rape of Europa*, *Diana and Callisto*, and *Apollo and Marsyas*.

Another major figure painter of the Veneto is Giambattista Piazzetta. One of his best and most famous paintings, the *Soothsayer*, is in this collection. Important as well are the view paintings so immensely popular in the eighteenth century, such as Canaletto's *Perspective*, Francesco Guardi's *Island from San Giorgio*, and Bernardo Bellotto's *Scuola Grande di San Marco*. Vignettes of eighteenth-century life and society are preserved in a series of paintings by Pietro Longhi, and a group of pastel portraits by Rosalba Carriera displays the skill that singled her out as one of the most sought-after portraitists of the period. Other eighteenth-century artists of note represented in the collection are Alessandro Longhi, Giuseppe Nogari, Sebastiano Ricci, Antonio Diziani, Giambattista Pittoni, and Jacopo Amigoni.

The Academy's drawing collection is an outgrowth of the initial purchase by the Gallery of the private collection of Giuseppe Bossi in 1822. Its catholic content is of the finest quality and includes priceless drawings by Leonardo, as well as a wide range of sketches by Venetian masters.

There is a modest library that is available to scholars who are engaged in research on the Prints and Drawings collection. Photographs of objects in the collections may be purchased for 1,500 lire each, plus postage. Requests should be sent to the Office of the Director.

The Academy is an active institution that maintains affiliations with the Amici dei Musei, Università, and the Università Internazionale dell'Arte.

There are no museum publications issued on a regular basis. Exhibition catalogues may be purchased from the Soprintendenza ai Beni Artistici e Storici di Venezia, Piazza San Marco 63, 30100 Venice, or from the Casa Editrice Electa, Via Goldoni, Milan. The chief catalogue of the museum collection is that by Sandra Moschini Marconi. It may be obtained from the Istituto Poligrafico dello Stato, Rome. A current guidebook, *The Galleries of the Academy of Venice* by Francesco Valcanover, is available in English, French, Italian, German, and Spanish.

Selected Bibliography

Selected publications: Bossi, Elena, *La Regia Accademia di Belle Arti di Venezia* (Florence 1941); Folgolari, Gino, ''L'Accademia Veneziana di Pittura e Scoltura del

Settecento," *L'Arte* (1913), pp. 364–94; Lorenzetti, Giulio, *Venice and Its Lagoon* (Trieste 1975); Marconi, Sandra Moschini, *Galleria dell'Accademia di Venezia. Opere d'arte dei secoli XIV, XV, XVI, XVII, XVIII e XIX*, 3 vols. (Rome 1955–1970); Moschini, G. A., *Dell'Incisione in Venezia* (Venice 1924); Pignatti, Terisio, *Il Quaderno di disegni del Canaletto alle Gallerie di Venezia* (Milan 1958); Shaw-Kennedy, Ronald, *Venice Rediscovered* (Philadelphia 1978); Valcanover, Francesco, *Museums and Galleries of Venice* (Milan 1955); idem, *The Accademia Picture Galleries* (Novara 1959); idem, *The Galleries of the Accademia* (Venice, 1981).

                                                                                                  FELICIA LEWANDOWSKI

CORRER MUSEUM AND PICTURE GALLERY (officially IL MUSEO CORRER E QUADRERIA; alternately THE CORRER; also IL MUSEO CIVICO CORRER, IL MUSEO DEL RISORGIMENTO E QUADRERIA), Procuratie Nuove, Piazza San Marco, 30100 Venice.

Il Museo Correr e Quadreria, a collection of art objects and documents from the rich Venetian past, is, ultimately, the expression of one man's taste. Teodoro Correr, member of a prestigious Venetian family, was determined that his personal collection of paintings, sculpture, glass, prints and drawings, books, and decorative art objects be given to the municipality of Venice upon his death. This occurred on February 20, 1830.

When the museum opened to the public in 1836, it was housed in Correr's palazzo at San Zan Degolà, which, along with the estate, was a part of the legacy. The collection so rapidly expanded through private bequests and acquisitions from suppressed religious buildings that it quickly outgrew the space of the palazzo. In 1880 the museum was moved to the newly restored Fondaco dei Turchi, a thirteenth-century market on the Grand Canal. It reopened in 1899 to a public that saw the artifacts organized thematically. Continual purchases, endowments, and legacies augmented the collection to such an extent that, once again, new facilities had to be acquired to accommodate it. Therefore, the Correr Museum moved to the Procuratie Nuove in the Piazza San Marco. The sixteenth-century building was designed by Vincenzo Scamozzi and completed by Baldassare Longhena in 1640 to house the nine Procurators of the Venetian Republic. With the fall of the Republic in 1797, the Procuratie Nuove became Napoleon's Royal Palace. After his downfall, it passed to the Royal House of Savoy, which returned its ownership to the municipality of Venice following World War I. By 1922 the transferral of the museum to the Procuratie Nuove was complete, and the Museo Correr was accessible once more. Initially, only twelve rooms were opened, and those remaining on the first and second floors were gradually readied for installation.

Not more than ten years had passed before it became apparent that the ever-expanding collection would have to be dispersed among several buildings. As the Town Council of the island of Murano was absorbed by that of Venice in 1932, so were joined under one roof at Murano the glass collection of the Correr and that of the Murano Glass Museum, thus creating a display of glass that dates from antiquity to the present. The reorganization of the Museo Vetrario has been completed.

The museum's eighteenth-century holdings were gathered into the Ca' Rezzonico at San Barnaba, a seventeenth-century palazzo acquired by the Town Council for Venice in 1935 and opened in the following year. The Ca' Rezzonico, or Civico Museo de Settecento Veneziano, is administered by the Correr Museum (q.v. Rezzonico Palace).

Due to a generous gift, the Correr obtained the Casa Goldoni at San Tomà and established there in 1953 its collection of documents and manuscripts focusing on the history of Venetian theater. In addition, the building houses the Theater Arts Center, a focal point for Goldoni studies. Together, these collections constitute the Civic Museums of Venetian Art and History.

The core of the collection remained, as it does today, in the Procuratie Nuove. During World War II, the art objects were removed for safekeeping. In 1953 the Museo del Risorgimento was reorganized, as was the second-floor Quadreria in 1959. In addition to the historical collections on the *piano nobile*, it is to this body of art objects in the Procuratie Nuove that the reference "Correr Museum" generally alludes.

The municipality of Venice holds proprietorship over the museum, and is its sole source of fixed financial support. A director administers the Museo Correr, including all subsidiary collections. This executive at present has a staff of seven assistants, a secretary, and three conservators. In response to the needs of researchers and scholars, the museum established the specialized departments of Prints and Drawings, Library, and Photographic Archive. The collection itself was divided so as to articulate its vast diversity and to facilitate its study. There are no departments that are administered independently of the Correr. Nor does the museum maintain any affiliation with other art organizations.

The museum at St. Mark's Square houses the historical collections that are approached from the atrium in Ascension Hall. The impressive staircase by Giuseppe Soli (1810–14) follows the direction of the state entrance to what was then Napoleon's Royal Palace. The decor of the interior halls is neoclassical and original. Objects in this collection convey the history of the Correr, as well as that of the Venetian Republic. Noteworthy are the early maps of Venice that chart the development of the lagoon. The chief extant perspective map of Venice by Jacopo de' Barbari (c. 1444-50–c. 1515) was completed in 1500 and not only reveals architectural delights but demonstrates, along with the original woodblocks, the contemporary approach to the medium. Indispensable to a history of Venice are the marble representations of the Lion of St. Mark, dating from the Romanesque eleventh century. Ducal history is presented through a collection of official documents and objects used by the doges. It was customary that the doge pay an annual visit on Easter Monday to the nuns of San Zaccaria nearby. Preserved here is the basket with which the nuns offered to the doge his ducal cap. Along with it is a *corno*, or ducal cap, dating from the fifteenth century. Complementing these objects is a series of ducal portraits and a group of official robes and costumes of state, some of them rare. Among them are the red silk togas of the procurators and senators, the blue ones of the sages, and a red ceremonial robe worn by the doge on Good Friday. Period paintings further document the processional dress of Venetian officials.

The numismatic collection is outstanding in its breadth and comprehensiveness. With only a few exceptions, every coin struck during the Republic is represented. Uncommonly rare is the *osella* (a medal also serving as currency) struck in 1581 under Doge Nicolò da Ponte. The excellence of this array is a result of the contributions of several collectors, among them Teodoro Correr, Gerolamo Ascanio Molin, Domenico Zoppetti, Federico Garofoli, and, in this century, Nicolò Papadopoli. Seals of the doges and public officials are preserved as well. Among the flags and standards is the red silk galley standard of Doge Domenico Contarini (1659–75), unparalleled in size and with a shape made interesting by the addition of six ribbon-like tails. It epitomizes the glories of the Republic.

For centuries, Venice was a pre-eminent naval power, and her victories, especially the one at Lepanto, are recalled by much memorabilia in the collection. The *Bucintoro*, Venice's great ceremonial vessel, was destroyed in 1824, but fragments of its splendor have been preserved here. Records of the Arsenal, or Naval Shipyard, abound. They include the statute of the Ships' Caulkers Guild, maps, navigation charts, maritime treaties, atlases, passports, and globes.

Various types of weapons and armor, most dating from the sixteenth to eighteenth century, have been gathered here. Augmenting these relics are innumerable souvenirs of Doge Francesco Morosini (1688–94), who is remembered even today by the Venetians for his military victory over the Turks at Peloponnesus. Spoils of war, coats-of-arms, the lamp from his flagship, weapons, and so on are among the items in the Morosini Collection.

The Museum of the Risorgimento documents the fall of the Venetian Republic in 1797, the French and Austrian occupations, and the annexation of Venice to the Italian kingdom in 1866. This section of the Correr was inaugurated in 1866 with the gift by Piero Marisch of a quantity of records and documents that focus on the provisional government (1797–98) and the defense of the city in 1848–49. The donation of Marisch, who was the general commander of the Third Defense Sector, was implemented over the years by the generous gifts of many others who were interested in preserving the written accounts of this period in Venetian history.

Originally, the collection was housed in a building owned by Teodoro Correr at San Stae, but in 1898 it was transferred to the Fondaco dei Turchi and finally to the second floor of the Correr in the Procuratie Nuove. The museum closed during World War II; upon reopening in 1948, records of the recent German occupation comprised a new exhibit.

The brief provisional government (1797–98) is represented by Giacomo Guardi's painting *The Festival of the Tree of Liberty in the Piazza San Marco* hailing the fall of the Republic. Objects reflecting the Napoleonic period and the kingdom of Italy (1806–14) include a memorable series of prints that depict the ravages heaped on the city by order of the French emperor. Among the scenes is the destruction of the churches of San Domenico, Sant'Antonio di Castello, and, in order to have space for the *Ala Napoleonica*, San Geminiano. Poignantly recorded is the removal to Paris of the four horses of St. Mark's and the Lion from the Piazzetta. Also preserved here is Antonio Canova's (1757–1822) model for the figure of Pope Pius VI, which is in St. Peter's Basilica in Rome.

Several royal portraits dating from the Austrian occupations (1789–1809; 1814–49) are among many paintings that illustrate political events of the period. Artists represented are Pompeo Marino Molmenti, Odorico Politi, Ippolito Caffi, Luigi Querena, and Giacomelli. A fine series of engravings depicting the major incidents that culminated in the liberation of Venice is worthy of special note.

In addition to these items, there are numerous documents and proclamations relating to Daniele Manin's attempt to lead Venice to freedom in face of the Austrian troops, as well as papers pertaining to the Austrian occupation of 1849–66 and the Garibaldi years. Later additions to the Museum of the Risorgimento recall events of World War I and II.

The Correr's Quadreria boasts a magnificent hall, designed by Vincenzo Scamozzi, and retains its original format. The Picture Gallery is a storehouse of masterpieces. Among the earliest treasures is a chest decorated in the thirteenth-century Byzantine style that belonged to Blessed Juliana (d. 1262). The richness of the Gothic period is conveyed by a fourteenth-century Venetian crucifixion in marble relief, a bas-relief of figures of saints in the Istrian stone so widely used in Venice, and bits of figural sculpture from a Venetian house. Paintings of the same period include two side panels of a lost altarpiece by Paolo Veneziano and the central panel of an otherwise untraced polyptych, signed by Lorenzo Veneziano and dated 1389, *Christ Giving the Keys of the Kingdom to St. Peter*. Exceptional pieces are the *Virgin* by Michele Giambono and the *Virgin and Child* signed by Jacobello del Fiore. A premier piece of the collection is Cosimo Tura's *Pietà* (c. 1468).

Doge Tommaso Mocenigo (1414–23) is an exquisite small-scale portrait in marble by Jacobello delle Masegne. A Gothic altarpiece, signed by the sculptors Bartolomeo di Paolo and Catarino d'Andrea, is the *Presentation of Christ in the Temple* and *Stories from the Old and New Testaments*. There are a number of fine paintings dating from this period, but their authorship is conjectural. Among the fifteenth-century panel paintings are works by Bartolommeo Vivarini and Leonardo Boldrini. A chef d'oeuvre by Antonello da Messina, the stirring *Pietà*, dates from his Venetian sojourn in 1476. Netherlands painters are represented in the collection with *Virgin and Child* by Dirk Bouts, a *Crucifixion* by Hugo van der Goes, an altarpiece *Madonna and Child* by Hans Fries, and a group of anonymous works of the sixteenth and seventeenth centuries.

Two families that dominate any thorough study of Venetian art are the Vivarini and the Bellini. Jacopo Bellini's *Crucifixion* is a significant work, but certainly the paramount series in the collection consists of the four paintings from Giovanni

Bellini's early career, when he was working under the influence of Mantegna. They are the *Transformation, Madonna and Child* (ex-Frizzoni Collection, Bergamo), a *Crucifixion*, and a *Pietà*. There are also several paintings from his workshop.

A chief work by Alvise Vivarini is the *St. Anthony of Padua*. Other noteworthy paintings are the *Madonna* by Marco Basaiti, the *Madonna with Saints Lawrence and Peter* by Benedetto Diana, and the *Madonna with Saints* by Giovanni Martini da Udine.

Rivaling the Bellini series in significance are works by Vittore Carpaccio. Companion paintings to one of them, the *Visitation*, are dispersed among the Ca' d'Oro, the Brera (q.v.) in Milan, and the Accademia Carrara in Bergamo. The second Carpaccio is the *Portrait of a Boy with a Red Cap*. Of note also is a *Madonna and Child* by Lorenzo Lotto. Numerous paintings and sculpture by lesser-known Venetian artists and some sixteenth-century pottery fill out the Quadreria collection.

The Museo del Risorgimento currently is undergoing a general refurbishment that will soon be completed. Plans are under way to remodel and reorganize the first floor of the Correr. At present, there is no policy regarding a regular change of exhibits within the permanent collection. However, the director has expressed his intention to establish a limited rotation of the art objects on display once the restorative work in the museum is complete.

The Department of Prints and Drawings is a valuable repository that is available for study to historians. There are two libraries under the directorship of the Correr Museum. The Biblioteca teatrale di Casa Goldoni has holdings of approximately twenty-five thousand volumes that deal with the history of the theater, especially that of Venice. The chief library, and a major research facility for anyone studying the history of Venice and Venetian art, is the Biblioteca d'arte e di storia veneziana. Its estimated holdings of a hundred thousand volumes include rare editions, manuscripts, and archival materials. Several collections in the library were once portions of the private libraries of the oldest Venetian families. Either of these facilities welcomes scholars. Students can gain access to the library collections upon the recommendation of their professors.

The Photographic Archive maintains a visual record of the objects in the museum collection and is an invaluable resource to scholars. Photographs may be purchased by written request to the Office of the Director.

A collection of scholarly articles and essays appears in the museum's quarterly publication *Bollettino dei Musei Civici Veneziani*. The Correr's exhibition catalogs, guidebooks, and so on are not available for purchase at the museum following the close of the exhibition. They may be obtained by writing directly to the publisher. The supply of successive editions of guidebooks to the museum collections has been exhausted. Generally, popular guides such as *Michelin* and *Touring Club Italiano* are not current. The compilation of a new guidebook is under consideration by the administration of the Correr.

Selected Bibliography

Museum guides: Brunetti, Mario, *Guida del Museo Civico Correr* (Venice); Ferrari, Carlo, *Guide to the Museum of the Risorgimento*, 2nd ed. (Venice 1952); Lorenzetti, Giulio, *Venice and Its Lagoon* (Trieste 1975); Mariacher, Giovanni, *Il Museo Correr di Venezia: dipinti del XIV al XVI secolo* (Venice 1957); Pignatti, Terisio, *Museo Correr* (Bergamo 1958); idem, *Il Museo Correr di Venezia: dipinti del XVII e XVIII secolo* (Venice 1960); Shaw-Kennedy, Ronald, *Venice Rediscovered* (Philadelphia 1978); Valcanover, Francesco, *Museums and Galleries of Venice* (Milan 1955).

Other publications: Lorenzetti, Giulio, *Il Quaderno dei Tiepolo al Museo Correr di Venezia* (Venice 1946); Pallucchini, Rudolfo, *I Disegni del Guardi al Museo Correr di Venezia* (Venice 1943); *Eighteenth-Century Venetian Drawings from the Correr Museum*, circulated by Smithsonian Institution, 1963–64 (Washington, D.C. 1963); *Venetian Bronzes from the Collections of the Correr Museum, Venice*, ed. Giovanni Mariacher, circulated by Smithsonian Institution, 1968–69 (Washington, D.C. 1968); Pignatti, Terisio, "Disegni inediti di Zuccarelli e Zais al Museo Correr," *Arte Veneta* (1956), 177–82; idem, "Un disegno di Antonio Guardi donato al Museo Correr," *Bollettino dei Musei Civici Veneziani* (1957), 1–2, 21–32; White, D. M., and A. C. Sewter, "Appunti su due disegni del Piazzetta al Museo Correr," *Bollettino dei Musei Civici Veneziani* (1962), 2, 24–28.

FELICIA LEWANDOWSKI

REZZONICO PALACE (officially CIVICO MUSEO DE SETTECENTO VENEZIANO; alternately MUSEUM OF EIGHTEENTH CENTURY VENICE; also MUSEO DEL'700 VENEZIANO, CA' REZZONICO, REZZONICO), Ca' Rezzonico, Venice.

The Ca' Rezzonico, or Civico Museo del Settecento Veneziano, was established as an eighteenth-century museum in 1936 after its purchase by the Town Council of Venice. The history of the palace dates from 1660, when Filippo Bon, procurator of San Marco, commissioned Baldassare Longhena, the greatest architect then working in Venice, to build it. As a complete architectural work externally and internally, Palazzo Rezzonico is an eighteenth-century aristocratic Venetian house. The architect died in 1682, and work ceased with the facade only at the first *piano nobile*. Ca' Rezzonico remained unfinished well into the first half of the eighteenth century, and the last heirs of the Bon family were not only unable to continue the work of the building but were unable even to keep the palace, which they were obliged to sell.

In 1746 the Rezzonico family (a wealthy nouveau riche family who bought their way into the Venetian aristocracy) acquired the palace, giving it their name. An important family in eighteenth-century Venice, they also produced a pope, Clement XIII. They completed the construction of the palace and furnished it luxuriously, remaining the owners until about 1810, when the family died out. Subsequent owners have included the Widmann family, Giovanelli family, Zselinski family, the family of Robert Browning, and, finally, Count Herschel de Minerbi, who sold it in 1935 to the Town Council of Venice. The palace has been furnished by the Correr Museum (q.v.) to authentically represent an eighteenth-century aristocratic residence, and it is filled today with fine examples of the best eighteenth-century Venetian furniture, paintings, sculpture, porcelain, and other minor arts. It is administered by the Correr Museum.

In 1756 the Rezzonico family had finished the huge and costly approach on the Grand Canal. Two architects worked on the facade—Gian Antonio Gaspari, who took over the work left unfinished by Longhena, and Giorgio Massari, whose work is more substantial. Massari completed the facade, interpreting more or less faithfully Longhena's design, but also remodeled the back, at the same time adding the sumptuous ballroom with the grand staircase. As with all of the palaces in Venice standing on canals, particularly the Grand Canal, the Ca' Rezzonico has its principal facade on the water. The facade represents externally the characteristic triple plan of Venetian architecture, and the palace is divided inside into three longitudinal sections—a central hall and two rows of rooms down the sides.

The palace today possesses almost nothing of what was in it originally, except for some frescoes, a couple of chandeliers, and a few minor objects. The collections themselves belong entirely to the Correr Museum (q.v.). The oldest part of the collection is that of Teodoro Correr, bequeathed to the city in 1830. The rest was added by successive bequests and purchases, the most recent being the Falier, Gatti Casazza, and Savorgnan-Brazza. The collection was arranged in 1936 by Nino Barbantini and Giulio Lorenzetti, the curators of the Venetian civic museums at the time. The names of many of the rooms do not necessarily reflect eighteenth-century names, and most were named when the collection was assembled in 1936, originating usually from particular works in a room, such as the Longhi Room for the collection of Longhi paintings and the Room of the Pastels.

The original frescoes in the palace are themselves important examples of eighteenth-century Venetian painting. The most splendid example is in the ballroom, a well-proportioned room of great size and height, brightly lit from three walls composed entirely of windows. On the ceiling is *The Chariot of the Sun with Allegories* of about 1753, by Giovanni Battista Crosato. The scenery is by the *quadraturista* Piero Visconti (active 1750–78), who had previously worked for the court of Savoy in the Royal Palace of Stupinigi near Turin.

The Room of the Pastels contains another important ceiling fresco. The Rezzonico family used this room as an audience chamber in which the newly elected pope of the family (Carlo—Clement XIII) officially received the papal nuncio and representative of the doge in 1758. The ceiling was frescoed during the time when the eighteenth-century alterations were in progress and is attributed to Gaspare Diziani. The work is *Poetry Triumphant over the Liberal Arts*, and allegorical figures and architectural motifs in chiaroscuro form the frame.

Two important frescoes are by the greatest master of eighteenth-century Venetian painting, Giovanni Battista Tiepolo. The first is the ceiling in the Salon of the Nuptial Allegory. The subject of this fresco, done in 1758, gives its name to the salon. This was executed to commemorate one of the most important events in the history of the family, the marriage between Ludovico Rezzonico and Faustina Savorgnan on January 16, 1758.

One of Tiepolo's masterpieces, not only in the palace but of all of his Venetian works, is the *Allegory of Merit* (1756), a ceiling fresco in the Throne Room. This room, on the corner overlooking the Grand Canal, was designed as the wedding bed-chamber for the Rezzonico-Savorgnan bridal couple.

There are two other works by Tiepolo in the Ca' Rezzonico but they were added from other collections. A canvas, set into the ceiling of the Tiepolo Room, *Nobility and the Virtues*, was done about 1744–45 for the palace of the Barbarigo family at Santa Maria del Giglio, from where it passed to the Dona delle Rose Collection and finally to Ca' Rezzonico. The second work is a large oval canvas set in the ceiling of the Longhi Room, *Zephyr and Flora* (c. 1730). It was brought here from Ca' Pesaro when the Correr Museum installed its collection in the Ca' Rezzonico.

Another recomposed work is a ceiling of five ovals in the library, the work of the Vicenza painter Francesco Maffei (1625–60), done during his Venetian period. Together with the ten allegorical panels in the Brustolon Room, next door, these Maffeis formed part of a huge seventeenth-century ceiling at the Palazzo Nani in Cannaregio.

The Venetian painter Gian Antonio Guardi also has a room named for him. In it are three frescoes by him—*Minerva, Apollo,* and *Venus*—framed by curved panels of stucco work. They once formed a part, with the oval in the ceiling of the Lacquer Room next door, of the decoration in a room in the Palazzo Barbarigo Dabala. The ceiling is the fresco *The Triumph of Diana* in an oval stucco frame. They are the only fresco works known by the master and the subtle range of Rococo colors is still visible in spite of the damage caused when they were detached from the walls by the so-called *strappo* method during the nineteenth century.

There is another room that houses two famous paintings by Guardi, *Il Ridotto* and *Il Parlatorio*. The first shows the gaming house at San Moise crowded with ladies and gentlemen in masks. The second depicts the nuns of San Zaccaria, a very wealthy Venetian convent, receiving relations and friends and watching a puppet theater for the children.

Another notable feature of the Ca' Rezzonico is the approximate reconstruction of the Villa Tiepolo at Zianigo (a village near Nurano). The frescoes were taken from the walls in 1906, and the reconstruction was done under the supervision of Barbentini and Lorenzetti in 1936. This reconstruction does not pretend to follow the exact layout of the villa, which still exists, only to recreate the original environment. The frescoes are now mounted in canvas frames on the walls. The Villa Tiepolo was bought by Giovanni Battista Tiepolo in 1753 and decorated by his son Giovanni Domenico at various stages in his life. The subjects include scenes from Tasso's *Gerusalemme Liberata* and allegorical subjects and scenes of life among the lower classes in the eighteenth century, such as the *Mondo Novo*. One of the most amusing rooms is that of the Pulcinellas, carnival variations inspired by the well-known Neapolitan maskers. The three most important scenes are: *Pulcinella in Love*, the *Tumblers' Show*, and the *Clowns Resting*. Also by Giovanni Domenico are the Chapel, the Room of the Satyrs, and the Room of the Centaurs.

The largest collection of genre paintings by Pietro Longhi (twenty-nine) is in the Ca' Rezzonico. They have been brought together from various collections, including the Morosini Collection, the Querini Stampalia Gallery, the Accademia, and the Correr Museum. The subjects, always taken from life, afford an unusual and immediate record of the life and customs of the times, from the privacy of drawing rooms to amusing lower-class incidents and open-air amusement, as well as important people going about their daily lives. The most notable are: *The Rhinoceros* (1751), *The Stroll on the Liston* (1760), and *The Morning Chocolate* (c. 1780). There are also eight portraits by Longhi.

Also representative of the Venetian Rococo are the pastel portraits of Rosalba Carriera in the Pastel Room. This was a medium much favored by the Venetians in the eighteenth century. By Rosalba are four portraits of members of the Balbi family, a portrait of a nun, and a portrait of the celebrated contralto Faustina Bordoni (c. 1738), as well as a self-portrait and two very early portraits done on ivory.

Other major Venetian painters of the late seventeenth and eighteenth centuries are represented in the collection. There is a portrait of Pietro Barbarigo by Bernardino Castelli. The monumental frame is a rare masterpiece of carving with an unusual wealth of motifs and allegorical figures. By Gregorio Lazzarini (teacher of G. B. Tiepolo) there is the portrait *Esther and Ahasuerus*. Among other notable works are Jacopo Amigoni's *Portrait of a Lady*, Giovanni Battista Piazzetta's *Death of Darius*, Giovanni Antonio Pellegrini's *Muzius Scevola*, Luca Carlevaris' *River Port*, Marco Ricci's *Winter Landscape*, Bernardo Strozzi's *Portrait of a Cardinal*, and landscapes by both Giuseppe Zais and Francesco Zuccarelli.

Ca' Rezzonico is renowned for its collection of eighteenth-century furniture and objects. There are excellent examples of furniture by Andrea Brustolon, one of the master craftsmen of the period. Much of the furniture was done for the Venier family of San Vio. There are also chairs from the Correr family, as well as furniture from the Falier bequest and the Savorgnan-Brazza bequest. There are fine examples of carved and gilded pieces—tables, divans, armchairs, consoles. The throne that gives its name to the Throne Room is a luxurious Baroque fantasy of mythical figures, putti, and sea horses, all done in carved and gilded wood, a souvenir of the brief stay in Venice of Pope Pius VI in 1782. There are also outstanding examples of furniture by Antonio Corradini and his workshop. There is an unusual set of chairs upholstered in painted gilt leather, a typical example of the famous *cuoridoro* much used by Venetians in upholstery work. There is also a great writing desk, called by the Venetians *bureau-trumeau*, which was a multiple piece of furniture much in vogue in the eighteenth century.

There is a reconstruction of an eighteenth-century bedroom, with rare examples of eighteenth-century wallpaper, a bed with a carved-wood headboard, and an eighteenth-century silk damask coverlet. In this bedroom also is a marriage chest with the family crests of the Correr and Michiel families, a reference to a marriage of these two families in 1758. There is also a very elaborate toilet set, from the Pisani family, which consists of fifty-eight pieces in silver-gilt, with engraving and repoussé work and onyx inlays. Considered a masterpiece of the goldsmith's art, it was created in Augsburg during the late seventeenth century. There are examples of lacquered furniture, most notably a collection that came from the Palazzo Calbo Crotta. There is also furniture from the Balbi-Venier Palace and the Gradenigo and Contarini families, all aristocratic eighteenth-century Venetian families.

There are magnificent examples of eighteenth-century chandeliers, many of which are also outstanding examples from the Murano glassworks. There are two enormous chandeliers, both originals, in the ballroom. They are rare examples of wood and gilt-copper, dating from the middle of the eighteenth century. In the Room of the Pastels, there is a great sixteen-armed Murano chandelier and, in the library, a white blown-glass chandelier, a very rare example of the "chalice" type made in the Giuseppe Briati factory in Murano. Another example from the Briati factory (c. 1730) is an immense chandelier in colored glass, with twenty branches in two rows.

The Palazzo Rezzonico has a huge attic, the plan of which corresponds to the floor below. As was usual in the houses of the period, these rooms were used for domestic purposes. Today they are used to display the minor arts and the costumes of eighteenth-century Venice.

There is a room dedicated to Veneto majolica from the end of the seventeenth to the beginning of the nineteenth century from the factories at Bassano, Nove, Angarano, Ente, Treviso, and Venice. There are fine examples of ornamental vases, complete dinner services, baskets, fireplace tiles, engraved mirrors, a rare example of a washstand with its ewer and bowl, and decorative figures. There are extremely rare pieces from the first Venetian porcelain factory (Francesco Vezzi, active 1719–40), as well as excellent examples from foreign factories (Meissen, Saxony, Delft, Sèvres, and Chantilly, among others). There are also good examples of terracotta and clay models by various eighteenth-century Venetian sculptors, such as G. Maria Morlaiter, A. Brustolon, and Jacopo Piazzetta (father of G. B. Piazzetta).

There is a fine collection of toilet and clothing accessories, mostly lacquered, an art in which the Venetians were very skilled and celebrated in the eighteenth century. There are traveling toilet sets, some in chinoiserie style, table mirrors, card cases, trays, boxes, candlesticks, small boxes for gambling, snuff boxes, and so on.

The interior of a small room has been designed as a marionette theater, as was sometimes done in aristocratic palaces for home amusement. This one comes from the Palazzo Grimani. The stage is completely fitted out with its curtain, scenes, wings, and footlights, all original eighteenth-century work. There are complete sets of the well-known eighteenth-century commedia dell'arte characters, and a number of prints showing theater subjects hang on the walls.

A complete eighteenth-century pharmacy was brought here and reconstructed in all of its details. This one was called *Due San Marchi* (*Two St. Marks*) in Campo San Stin. In itself, it constitutes a collection of the greatest interest both for the variety of the large and small vases, the little modeled cylindrical vases called *alberelli*, and the pretty shapes. All of the pieces are in majolica and decorated with flowers with the words denoting their contents. There is also a costume room with a few examples of eighteenth-century dress that completes the collection.

Photographs and slides of selected works in the collection as well as of the palace itself are available. An illustrated guide to Ca' Rezzonico is also available.

Selected Bibliography

Bassi, E., *Architettura dei Sei e Settecento a Venezia* (Naples 1962); idem, *Palazzi di Venezia* (Venice 1976); Cristinelli, G., *Baldassare Longhena* (Padua 1972); Lorenzetti, G., *Ca' Rezzonico* (Venice 1936); Mariacher, G., *Ca' Rezzonico* (Venice 1967); idem, "Il restauro della facciata di Ca' Rezzonico," *Boll. dei Musei Civici Veneziani*, 1964; Pignatti, T., *Tesori di Ca' Rezzonico* (Milan 1965); Precerutti-Garberi, M., *Affreschi settecenteschi delle Ville Venete* (Milan 1968); Semenzato, C., *L'architettura di Baldassare Longhena* (Padua 1954).

GREGORY OLSON

Japan

—— Atami ——

M.O.A. MUSEUM OF ART (officially MOKICHI OKADA ASSOCIATION MUSEUM OF ART), 26–2, Momoyama-chō, Atami, Shizuoka Prefecture 413.

The Hakone Museum of Art was nearing completion when its founder, Mokichi Okada, decided in January 1952 to build another museum in nearby Atami, a popular hot springs resort on the eastern shore of the Izu Peninsula, about seventy miles southeast of Tokyo. It was to be an integral part of a religious center that this charismatic leader of a new religion, the Church of World Messianity, envisioned creating on a 236,400-square-meter plot of land acquired there in 1944. Since Okada died in 1955, before realizing his plans, his adherents decided to found in 1957 a small interim museum, the Atami Museum of Art, that held monthly exhibitions to display, on a rotating basis, the painting, calligraphy, sculpture, and decorative arts acquired by Okada. His collection of Oriental ceramics continued to be exhibited at the Hakone Museum of Art. A committee was formed in 1971 to plan and construct a monumental museum that was completed in 1982, the centennial of his birth. The property and funds for the construction of the M.O.A. Museum of Art, adjacent teahouses, and extensive gardens were donated by the Church of World Messianity. The museum derives its revenue from entrance fees, contributions from Friends of the Museum, and supplemental funds provided by the Mokichi Okada Association, a foundation that promotes cultural, educational, and charitable programs in Japan and abroad.

Okada had established a separate organization named the Tomei Art Conservation Foundation to manage the Hakone and the projected Atami museums of art. It was superceded in 1980 by the Mokichi Okada Association, which now oversees both the Hakone and the M.O.A. museums. This foundation is governed by a board of trustees, whose seven members are chosen by church officials and serve for a period of two years. The Board of Trustees, in turn, elects its chairman and the eleven-member Board of Councilors, whose members likewise serve for a period of two years. It also appoints a director and a manager who jointly operate the museum. The director, in consultation with the Board of Trustees and an advisory panel of five noted art historians, determines policy, programs, and acquisitions. The manager, aided by an assistant manager, is responsible for administration and a staff of fifteen, who are employed in three departments: Research and Curatorial, Public Relations, and General Affairs.

The museum was officially opened on January 11, 1982. Extensive research on new developments in museum design, conducted in Japan and abroad, went into the planning of this impressive structure, built of reinforced concrete and faced with honey-colored sandstone especially quarried in the Deccan Plateau of India. The museum is visible from afar, superbly situated on a bluff over-looking Sagami Bay. The entrance is at the foot of the bluff, adjacent to the church's colonnaded Hall of Worship. The granite portico, bordered by a wall of continuously flowing water, is linked to the museum by five underground escalators equipped with complex lighting and sound systems. The first three rise steeply to a large circular hall with elaborately inlaid walls and floor of imported marble and a domed ceiling containing special equipment for projecting slides, changing light patterns, and sound effects. Veering to the left is a fourth escalator that opens onto a spacious granite terrace facing the sea and dominated by a large bronze sculpture, *King and Queen*, by Henry Moore. A monumental sandstone staircase ascends to the portico that subdivides the main facade of the rectangular, three-story building into two wings differing in size and fenestration. The central staircase leads to the first floor lobby and to the main lobby on the second floor, which can also be reached directly or in inclement weather by means of a fifth escalator. The handicapped can be driven directly to an entry on the third floor of the museum. The joint outer wall of the two lobbies contains four two-story windows that provide a panoramic view of Sagami Bay, its surrounding shores, and the sea beyond. The Takanaka Construction Company designed and built the museum and installed the most innovative display cases, storage facilities, lighting, projection, audio systems, air conditioning, temper-ature and humidity controls, special fire-prevention equipment, and a foundation designed to withstand the strongest earthquake forecast for this area. The tunnel-escalator system and surrounding gardens were constructed by the Kajima Cor-poration. It is technologically one of the most advanced museum buildings in Japan.

The M.O.A. Museum of Art is a relatively recent collection that, despite its limited size, provides a comprehensive coverage of Oriental art ranging from early Chinese bronzes to modern Japanese painting and decorative arts. Its su-perior quality is attested to by three National Treasures, fifty-three Important Cultural Properties, and forty-seven Important Art Objects, so designated by the Japanese government. Its principal areas of strength are a remarkably inclusive collection of Chinese, Japanese, and Korean ceramics, some excellent genre paintings of the Momoyama and early Edo periods, an impressive array of *ukiyo-e* paintings and prints, and a number of notable works by distinguished masters of the Rimpa School such as Kōetsu, Sōtatsu, Kōrin, Kenzan, and Hōitsu. Since Okada's death, the trustees have judiciously added to the Oriental collections and have enlarged their scope of interest to include Near Eastern ceramics and the acquisition of some major works of Western art. In addition to acquiring the monumental sculpture of Henry Moore, they have purchased a large bronze figure of *Spring*, dating from about 1910–11, by Aristide Maillol; two paintings of Giverny by Claude Monet, *The Poplars* (1891) and *Lotus Pond* (1918); as well as a still life, *Roses in a Vase* (1910), by Auguste Renoir. The only major lacunae is arms and armor, which is in keeping with Okada's pacifist views.

The earliest examples of Chinese art are a group of bronze vessels belonging to the Shang and Chou dynasties, a series of excellent mirrors that range from late Chou to T'ang, and some Chinese Buddhist sculptures, the finest of which is a Sui Dynasty bronze statuette of Kuan-yin. There is a rare example of painting on paper dating from the T'ang Dynasty (618–907), *Beauty under a Tree*, which forms a pair with the *Man under a Tree* that is now in the Tokyo National Museum (q.v.). It was found in a tomb at Kara-Khoji, near Turfan in Central Asia, by a team of Japanese archaeologists from a leading Kyoto temple, Nishi Honganji. The figure is similar to those in the famous eighth-century screen *Ladies under Trees*, preserved in the Shōsōin in Nara, and marks the broad diffusion of T'ang culture. A lively painting of two Ch'an eccentrics of the T'ang Dynasty, *Han-shan and Shih-te*, by the thirteenth-century painter Liang K'ai, once belonged to the shogun Ashikaga Yoshinori. There also are numerous landscape and bird-and-flower paintings attributed to Liang K'ai, Mu Ch'i, Ma Yuan, Ma Lin, Fan An-jen, Ch'ien Hsüan, and other noted masters of the Southern Sung (1127–1279) and Yüan (1260–1368) dynasties. From this same period are several fine examples of calligraphy by noted Ch'an masters such as Ch'u-shih Fan-ch'i, Ku-lin Ching-mou, Ch'ing-cho Cheng-ch'eng, Wu-shüeh Tzu-yüan, and, most notably, Wu-chun Shih-fan, all who directly or through their Japanese disciples influenced Zen studies and institutions.

Okada's interest in the tea ceremony was undoubtedly the impetus for acquiring so extensive a collection of Oriental ceramics. The Chinese wares date from the Neolithic period through the Ch'ing Dynasty (1616–1912). Okada secured some fine examples of Yueh ware, pre-Sung celadons produced in Chekiang province, such as the ewer with rooster-shaped spout and dragon handle that dates from the Six Dynasties Period (third-sixth century) and a covered box with flying phoenix that stems from the ninth century. Two remarkable Sui (581–618), or early T'ang, pieces are an eight-eared jar with a light brown glaze and lotus petals in relief and an ewer with dragon handle that has a vessel shape derived from Persia and a black feldspathic glaze that is distinctively Chinese.

The finest of the Northern Sung (960–1126) pieces are two contrasting examples of Ting ware—one a cream-white bowl with incised lotus and floral scrolls and the other a black glazed bowl with traces of floral design rendered in gold, a lustrous celadon plate from Ching-te-chen decorated with a carved lotus design, a rare long-necked vase of Yao-chou, and an enchanting Tz'u-chou bottle decorated with peonies and butterflies. The collection also contains several superb Southern Sung celadons from Lung-ch'üan. Dating from this same period is a tortoise-shell *temmoku* tea bowl of the type that was so prized by Japanese tea masters, as were several of the tea caddies with dark brown glaze. One of these caddies is known to have belonged to the first Tokugawa shogun, Ieyasu (1542–1616).

The most remarkable of the Yüan to early Ming (1368–1644) porcelains is a large *mei p'ing* with phoenix and flowers in underglaze red and a large plate with flowers and plants in underglaze blue. Other fine Ming porcelains from Ching-te-chen are a polychrome covered jar decorated with fish and plants and a gourd-shaped vase and square ewer decorated with gold leaf over enamel, a technique known in Japan as *kinrande*. Of particular appeal is a late Ming blue-and-white covered water jar with floral patterns and playful children that appears to have been made specifically for the Japanese market. The Korean ceramics are limited in number and scope but include a fine selection of celadons from the Koryō Dynasty (918–1392) and a diverse sampling of wares of the Yi Dynasty (1392–1910), particularly some of the simple bowls so avidly sought after by devotees of the tea ceremony.

Japanese ceramics dating from the Jōmon age (c. 7000 B.C. to 200 B.C.) to the Muromachi era (A.D. 1392–1573) are exhibited at the Hakone Museum of Art. It provides in-depth coverage of all of the intervening periods and includes many uncommon specimens. Of particular interest is a *haniwa* figure of a man dating from the Tumulus period (A.D. 250–552) and a remarkably representative selection of jars from ancient kiln sites such as Seto, Bizen, Shigaraki, and Tamba. The ceramics of the Momoyama (A.D. 1573–1615) to modern times are shown at the M.O.A. Museum of Art, and, being of a more durable nature, the best of them are regularly on display. Okada went to great lengths to acquire some choice tea wares dating from the Momoyama and early Edo (A.D. 1615–1868) periods, such as the simple tea caddy of Seto ware named after the color of its glaze, "Wild Cherry," which had once belonged to the Mitsui and Fujita families, and another caddy of Bizen ware named "Daybreak," which seems to embody the rustic charm implicit in the term *wabi*, so essential to the aesthetics of the tea ceremony. A highly prized example of raku ware is a tea bowl named "Iris" by Chōjirō, which is known to have been used by the great tea master Sen no Rikyū at a ceremony held in 1587.

There are beguiling examples of other fine wares developed in connection with the tea ceremony in Mino Province, notably a square bowl of Shino ware with the design of a plum tree and a covered fan-shaped container of Oribe ware named for a leading tea master, Furuta Oribe, as well as the wares modeled on Yi Dynasty prototypes produced at Karatsu in Kyūshū. An unusual pair of tea bowls with gold and silver decor by the originator of Kyoto ware, Nonomura Ninsei, were made as a present for Tōfukumon-in (1607–78), the daughter of the shogun Tokugawa Hidetada and wife of Emperor Go-Mizunoo. The museum has superlative examples of Imari, Kakiemon, Nabeshima, and Kutani porcelains, as well as a modern porcelain vase with phoenix and floral designs based on these Edo wares by Itaya Hazan (1872–1963).

Apart from pottery, other early examples of Japanese art include a bronze bell, or *dōtoku*, from the Yayoi period (c. 400 BC-A.D. 200), various implements from the Tumulus period, and numerous Buddhist sculptures and religious objects dating principally from the Heian (794–1185) and Kamakura (1185–1333) periods. A wood sculpture of the Shō Kannon that may have come from Enryakuji on Mt. Hiei and an Amida Triad have both been designated Important Cultural Properties. Three other Heian objects of that category are a wooden chest with secular figure paintings, a circular wooden container decorated with bird-and-flower painting that originally belonged to Tōji, and a black lacquered priest's seat with finely incised floral scrolls and mother-of-pearl inlay, as well as lacquered boxes dating from the Kamakura, Muromachi, Momoyama, and Edo periods that feature a wide range of techniques.

The earliest Japanese painting in the collection is a fragment of the *Ingakyō, Illustrated Sutra of Cause and Effect*, a Tempyō period work based on a Chinese riginal of the Six Dynasties Period. The museum also possesses a fine pair of Buddhist paintings that were once in the possession of Tōji in Kyoto. Other paintings classified as "Important Cultural Properties" that merit attention are a handscroll of esoteric Buddhist iconographic drawings; an unusual depiction of the Bodhisattva that personifies wisdom known as the *Eight Letter Monju (Sanskrit Manjusri)*; an awesome representation of the esoteric Buddhist deity that symbolizes the identity of human passions with enlightenment; *Aizen Myō-ō (Sanskrit Ragaraja)*; a set of 4 hanging scrolls that portray eight stages of the Buddha's life in a landscape setting; and deftly rendered portraits of two of the Thirty-Six Immortal Poets, *Taira no Kanemori* and *Minamoto no Shigeyuki*, all dating from the Kamakura period. The best example of Muromachi ink painting is the *White-Robed Kannon*, dated 1424, by Kichizan Minchō, the renowned Zen priest-painter of Tōfukuji in Kyoto. There are many superb pieces of calligraphy secured by the museum, most notably an album containing 311 fragments of calligraphy by emperors, court nobles, poets, priests, and other famous calligraphers, dating from the Nara (710–94) through the Muromachi period, that have been deemed a National Treasure.

A series of splendid screens enable the visitor to view the different aspects of Momoyama painting. *Landscape with Pavilions* executed by Kaihō Yūshō for the daimyō of Inaba is based upon his study of Sung Dynasty painting. Representative of another original talent who was similarly influenced, Hasegawa Tōhaku's *Chinese Historical Figures* depicts in a landscape setting two brothers famed for their rejection of worldly power. *Cherry Blossom Viewing and Falconry* is a richly colored genre painting by Unkoku Tōgan, a reputed successor of Sesshū, active chiefly in the field of monochrome ink painting. A brilliant *namban* screen, *Westerners Playing Music*, also depicts a grape harvest, figures in Renaissance garb, and Western ships executed in Japanese pigments mixed with a binding agent to render the chiaroscuro effects of oil painting. Okada particularly favored another distinctive school of Japanese painting that originated during the Momoyama era. The seminal figure was Hon'ami Kōetsu, a sword expert whose achievements as a calligrapher, potter, and lacquer artist can all be viewed here. *Poem Scrolls with Printed Flowers* displays his elegant calligraphic style based upon mid-Heian models. The gold and silver woodblock prints of flowers are thought to be the work of the founder of the Rimpa School, Sōtatsu. Their collaboration is more certain in the *Deer Scroll*, where the simplified drawing of the animals in gold and silver attributed to Sōtatsu is perfectly attuned to the somewhat mannered and decorative quality of Kōetsu's calligraphy. The latter half of this scroll is in the Seattle Art Museum (q.v.).

The *Zeze Tea Bowl* is one of a famous set that Kōetsu made in 1636 for a tea ceremony in honor of the shogun. A black and gold lacquer writing box with the bold design of a woodcutter depicted in lead and mother-of-pearl is attributed to him. An ink painting, *Fighting Rooster*, attributed to Sōtatsu shows the effective use of *tarashikomi* (literally, "dripping ink") developed by this school. There are numerous paintings by other leading members such as Ogata Kōrin and Sakai Hōitsu, as well as a set of plates with birds and flowers of the twelve months and a covered container with plum blossoms by Kōrin's younger brother Ogata Kenzan.

The museum has a variety of works by an early Edo painter, Iwasa Matabei, who was once thought to be the father of *ukiyo-e*. His deft, whimsical portrayal of two noted poets, *Kakinomoto no Hitomaro and Ki no Tsurayuki*, reveals that Matabei was familiar with Sung ink painting and the work of Liang K'ai. More characteristic is his delicately executed *Scene from the Tales of Ise*, which is thought to date from the Kan'ei period (1624–44). A handscroll with an animated account of *The Tale of Lady Jōruri* is attributed to him but was probably produced by his studio. The museum's distinction in the field of genre painting rests upon masterpieces such as *Bathhouse Girls*, painted in the Kan'ei era by a local *machi-eshi* (town painter), who depicted the vigorous energy of these lowly women who served as bath attendants by day and prostitutes by night. Representations of various trades was a popular genre theme beguilingly illustrated in the painting *Weavers and Dyers* by an anonymous Kano master of the early seventeenth century. Their most outstanding *ukiyo-e* painting is undoubtedly *Manners and Customs of Women during Twelve Months* by the highly esteemed Katsukawa Shunshō, but only ten of the original set of twelve hanging scrolls survive. A similarly fascinating set of three scrolls by Shunshō, *Three Women Symbolizing Snow, Moon, and Flowers*, ostensibly represents their activities during Winter, Autumn, and Spring, but their pose recalls the famous literary figures Sei Shonogan, Murasaki Shikibu, and Ono no Komachi, all garbed in the latest fashions. There is, in addition, a fine selection of prints by all of the leading *ukiyo-e* artists.

Okada also had the discernment, confidence, and commitment to collect the art of the recent past. Thus the museum possesses a remarkable cross-section of Japanese-style painting of the Meiji, Taishō, and Shōwa periods (1868-present). He was particularly fond of one of the ablest of the modern artists, Takeuchi Seihō (1864–1942), and acquired many fine paintings by him such as *Deer in Summer*, a pair of six-fold screens painted in 1936.

Off the main lobby is a documented replica of the Golden Tea Room that Toyotomi Hideyoshi erected in 1586, when he restored the Imperial Palace for Emperor Ogimachi. One of the three great unifiers of Japan during the Momoyama era, Hideyoshi was an ardent patron of the tea ceremony, noted for his lavish and ostentatious ceremonies. Yet it was his chief tea master Sen no Rikyu who established the austere principles of tea ceremony, based upon the use of natural, humble materials such as reeds and plaster and vessels of wood, bamboo, and clay. Since it is these principles that still prevail, the glittering surfaces of the Golden Tea Room are apt to seem garish to the modern viewer.

At the opposite end of the main lobby is a full-scale Nō theater that seats five hundred. It is equipped with simultaneous translation facilities that enable the foreign visitor to hear an immediate English translation of a Nō play. The cables supporting the roof of the stage permit the removal of the pillars and railing requisite for Nō, thus making it suitable for other forms of dramatic and musical performances that are held there as part of the cultural program of the museum. On the floor below is a lecture hall equipped with simultaneous translation facilities, where public lectures are given each month by specialists in various fields of art. As a further extension of its educational program, there are audiovisual booths in the lobby nearby, where visitors can familiarize themselves with various aspects of the collection on an individual basis.

To further expand the visitor's awareness of the aesthetic values of Japan, there is a large teahouse in the section of the garden near the Nō theater. It has rooms of various sizes designed to meet the needs of the different schools of tea ceremony. In these rustic rooms sheltered by pine trees, tea is served to the solitary visitor or to large groups. On the first floor of the museum is a restaurant, which accommodates two hundred, that looks out on the garden and the teahouses.

The M.O.A. Museum of Art has a library capable of holding twenty thousand volumes but at present has less than five thousand volumes on art, which are reserved for the use of the staff.

Photographs of objects in the collection are available for research and publication in art journals and books. Slides, picture postcards, and calendars illustrating objects in the collection are on sale in the museum shop. Objects in the collection have been featured in many publications, but few of the special studies are available in English. The museum is now issuing a new catalogue comprising six volumes to be divided as follows: General Catalogue; Painting, Ukiyo-e Painting and Woodblock Prints; Chinese Ceramics, Japanese Ceramics; Calligraphy; Sculpture; and Lacquerware and Metalwork. The museum has generously loaned objects for exhibition both in Japan and abroad and has sent exhibitions of *ukiyo-e* paintings and prints to Los Angeles, Honolulu, and Buenos Aires.

Selected Bibliography

Museum publications: *M.O.A. Museum of Art*, 1982; *Selected Catalogue: MOA Museum of Art*; *Hakone Museum of Art*, 1982; *Selected Catalogue: Vol. 1, Painting and Decorative Arts*, 1968; *Vol. 2, Ceramics*, 1968; *Vol. 3, Ukiyo-e Painting and Woodblock Prints*, 1973; *Selected Treasures: Vol. 1*, 1963; *Vol. 2*, 1972.

Other publications: *L'Oeil*, no. 318 (January 1982), Special issue devoted to the M.O.A. Museum of Art.

ELLEN P. CONANT

—— Kobe ——

KOBE MUNICIPAL MUSEUM OF NAMBAN ART (officially KOBE SHIR-ITSU NAMBAN BIJUTSUKAN), 1–8–21 Kumochi-cho, Fukiai-ku, Kobe-shi, Hyogo-ken.

The Kobe Municipal Museum of Namban Art was originally a private museum named the Ikenaga Art Museum, established in 1940 by Ikenaga Hajime (1891–1955). In 1951 Ikenaga gave to the city of Kobe most of his collection and the building that contained it. The remaining objects were purchased by the city, which now completely owns and funds the museum. The Friends of the Museum was founded in 1951. Members receive informational mailings from the museum and have an active travel program.

The museum is entirely governed by the Kobe city government. It is administered by a director and chief curator. A small, three-story, Western-style building designed by Ikenaga houses the collection in the upper part of the city. Plans are being formulated to move the collection to a larger, climate-controlled building in the downtown area. This future home is a pre–World War II edifice, now the Bank of Tokyo's Kobe branch office. In these more spacious quarters will be three display focuses: Namban Art, Kobe City History, and Japanese Archaeology. The latter items will come from merging with the Sumakokokan Archaeological Museum. A three- or four-story annex will be built to house several international loan shows each year. The curatorial staff will be enlarged accordingly. This new museum may be named the Kobe Hakubutsukan.

In its present location the exhibition galleries are changed about ten times a year, including one special loan show. The most famous paintings are on view in April, May, October, and November. Due to the limited size of the display area, the objects are selected with a specific theme in mind. Labels are in Japanese and usually also in English.

The collection was formed by the late Ikenaga, who showed remarkable insight and forethought by choosing to concentrate on acquiring items within a specialized area, showing the impact of imported art upon Japan in the seventeenth through the nineteenth century. This area included Namban art influenced by the Portuguese, Komo art influenced by the Dutch, perspective prints, Obaku portraits of Zen priests who had emigrated from China, Nagasaki school Chinese bird-and-flower painting, *ukiyo-e*, and purely Japanese-style paintings of exotic subjects. The original collection comprised about forty-five hundred pieces to which about one hundred have been added through purchase over the years. Although these artworks were not produced in the Kobe area, their cosmopolitan flavor is totally in keeping with the international atmosphere of this thriving port city.

In the middle of the sixteenth century Japan was exposed for the first time to European culture through the accidental arrival of two Portuguese ships in 1541 and 1543. Then in 1549 Spanish Jesuit Father Francis Xavier went to Japan to spread the Christian faith. These contacts with Europe based upon trade and missionary activities resulted in the creation of so-called Namban art from the last decade of the sixteenth century to the first half of the seventeenth century.

The word *Namban* literally means "southern barbarians," referring to the Europeans who visited Japan at that time. Namban art encompasses Japanese paintings modeled on European paintings, engravings, and book illustrations, as well as paintings and objects in purely Japanese style depicting foreign themes. The missionaries brought with them devotional objects and secular pictures. The schools they established to train Japanese priests also gave lessons in painting religious subjects. As the number of Christians grew, the demand for religious paintings increased. Not able to import enough originals from Europe, the Japanese turned to painting their own Christian pictures.

The success of missionary activity varied with the tolerance of the ruling political forces. Christians were persecuted with varying degrees of severity until finally in 1639 all foreigners were expelled from Japan. During the persecutions, much Namban art was destroyed. The Kobe Museum is fortunate to possess a variety of high-quality examples, several of which are registered by the Japanese government.

The screen paintings are the most splendid items in the collection. A four-fold screen, *Western Princes on Horseback*, shows two Christian monarchs dueling with two who are Moslems. In this work the theme is European, and the painting technique also reveals Western influence in the spatial perspective, the definition of cast shadows, and the illusionistic modeling to communicate three dimensionality in the forms. However, purely Japanese taste is evident in the effective juxtaposition of colors, with the splendid gold background and the placement of the figures dramatically close to the surface of the picture plane. A pair of six-fold screens by Kano Naizen depicts a popular subject: the arrival of Portuguese ships. Again, colorful figures are placed against a dazzling gold background. Within the screens one can search out details of everyday life in Japan, as well as amusing caricatures of the tall, bizarre-looking foreigners and their dark-skinned Javanese servants. Another pair of six-fold screens, *European Genre Scenes*, illustrates foreign social customs in the European manner. The Japanese zeal for things European is further documented by a pair of eight-fold screens: the right one with a map of the world; the left one with bird's-eye views of Constantinople, Rome, Seville, and Lisbon. These scenes were probably based upon maps in books brought to Japan from Europe.

More specifically Christian paintings include the *Christian Father with Two Children* and the *Portrait of St. Francis Xavier*. Namban objects consist of tea bowls with a cross as decoration, sculptures of the Holy Mother, and swordguards with a cross design for foreigners. In addition, lacquer ware was embellished with exotica. A drum displays matchlock guns. Figures of foreigners decorate writing boxes, medicine cases (*inro*), and a saddle inscribed with the date 1604.

The severe persecution of Christians and closing of Japan to foreigners in 1639 resulted in the decline of Namban art. However, despite the official policy of national isolation, Japanese interest in foreign art and ideas persisted. Trade was permitted only with China and Holland and limited to the port city of Nagasaki, where the Dutch were confined to the man-made island of Deshima. The year 1720 was a turning point, after which foreign books and goods were permitted to be imported if they had no relationship to Christianity. The influences that entered Japan through this narrow opening bore fruit in a variety of artistic creations. *Komo*, literally meaning "red hair," refers to the Dutch people, whom the Japanese observed and depicted with endless fascination. The Kobe Museum's collection includes paintings in the European style of generalized Dutch subjects by Hiraga Gennai, Shiba Kokan, Kitayama Kangan, Ishikawa Tairo, Tashiro Tadakuni, Araki Jogen, and Sakaki Yurin. The Dutch who lived in Nagasaki provided more specific subjects. The family of the Captain Blomhoff, including its Javanese servant, was portrayed by Ishizaki Yushi and by Kawahara Keiga, who also did a portrait of another Dutch captain, Doeff. Scenes of a Dutch factory at Deshima were depicted in purely Japanese style.

During the period of seclusion that lasted until the Meiji restoration of 1868, Nagasaki became a popular sightseeing area for Japanese travelers. In response to the need for portable and inexpensive souvenirs of their visits, woodblock prints were produced illustrating exotic scenes such as Dutch ships and figures, elephants, camels, Chinese figures, and Russians and their ships, which came in the early nineteenth century. The Kobe Museum owns a large variety of these Nagasaki prints.

The museum also possesses a fine selection of *uki-e* and *megane-e*, which demonstrate the influence of European methods. *Uki-e* are *ukiyo-e* prints using one-point perspective. Okumura Masanobu was the first *ukiyo-e* master to explore this area, and his success is clear in his *Nakamura Theatre, Edo* and *Riverside Restaurant*. He was followed by Furuyama Moromasa, who is represented by the *Poetess*. The Japanese were intrigued by the Dutch glasses (*Oranda megane*), which enhanced the three dimensionality of perspective pictures. *Megane-e* refers to the pictures created to be seen through that gadget. Maruyama Okyo did numerous paintings and prints of that type and was the first artist to apply the one-point perspective technique to landscape scenes. The museum owns several works by Okyo that depict sights in Kyoto as well as China.

The intellectual zeal of the Japanese is reflected in the term *Rangaku*, "Dutch learning," which focused on the study of Western sciences. Shiba Kokan was a pioneer and proselytizer in this field. Not only did he paint in the European style (*Hollander on a Pier* and *Dutch Woman Beneath a Tree*), but he constructed his own *Nozoki Karakuri* ("Optique") to be used when viewing his illusionistic prints. They were the first copper-plate prints produced in Japan and show scenic spots in Tokyo and England. All of them are owned by the Kobe Museum.

Finally, the collection includes paintings that document the Chinese influence entering Japan in the seventeenth and eighteenth centuries: portraits of Obaku monks and Shen Nan-p'in school bird-and-flower paintings. The Obaku monks were a group of Zen masters who, unhappy over the fall of the Ming Dynasty in 1644, immigrated to Japan. After obtaining special permission, they established a temple named Mampuku-ji on Mount Obaku near Uji. Obaku monks brought with them elements of Chinese culture to which the Japanese responded with enthusiasm. They included Chinese painting, calligraphy, architecture, poetry, tea ceremony, religion, and philosophy.

The tradition of realistic portraiture is particularly strong in Zen Buddhism because of its emphasis on direct doctrinal transmission from master to pupil. Itsunen went to Nagasaki in 1644, bringing late Ming figure-painting styles. In Kobe he is represented by paintings of Buddhist images Daruma, Hotei, Kannon, Kanzan, and Rakans. The museum also has a marvelous handscroll illustrating the arrival of Sokuhi in 1657, when he was welcomed by Ingen. Kita Soun and Kita Genki were the most skillful Obaku portraitists. The museum owns paintings by them of Daruma, Ingen, Mokuan, and Sokuhi. The effectiveness of these portraits is augmented by the calligraphic inscriptions above them by Obaku monks.

The tradition of decorative bird-and-flower painting in Japan was revitalized by the 1731 arrival of Shen Nan-p'in in Nagasaki. His refined, colorful depictions of birds or animals in a reduced garden setting created a sensation. The museum has one of his most famous paintings, *A Lion's Family*. Shen Nan-p'in's most prominent pupil was Kumashiro Yuhi, whose works in Kobe include *Moon, Crabs, and Reeds*, *A Heron*, and *Ducks under a Willow Tree*. So Shiseki was the Nagasaki school's most accomplished painter. Of his numerous paintings in Kobe, *Mandarin Duck*, *Long-Tailed Birds on a Plum Tree*, and *Gallinules and Pickerelweed* are noteworthy. Obaku Kakutei studied Nagasaki bird-and-flower painting and carried the style to the Kyoto region when he moved to Mampuku-ji. Several fine examples of his work may be seen in Kobe: *White Hawk*, *Long-Tailed Bird on a Peony*, and *Small Bird and Flowers*.

As a whole, the collection is remarkable for its quality, depth, and diversity within a deliberately narrow area of artistic specialization. This selected segment is important, since it reveals the Japanese responses to foreign influences from Europe and China.

At present the Kobe Municipal Museum of Namban Art has no art library. However, one is planned for the new building. The library will concentrate on Japanese history and art and will be open to the public.

Although slides and photographs of the collection are not available for purchase, it is possible to take photographs for study purposes. The museum has published a handsome five volume *Pictorial Record of Kobe City Museum of Nanban Art*. They anticipate reprinting the now unavailable catalogue of Ikenaga's original collection. A small pamphlet describing the museum is available in Japanese.

Selected Bibliography

Museum publications: *Pictorial Record of Kobe City Museum of Nanban Art*: Vol. 1: *Nanban Art*, 1968; Vol. 2: *Komo Art*, 1969; Vol. 3: *Nagasaki Prints*, 1970; Vol. 4: *Uki-e and Megane-e*, 1971; Vol. 5: *Portraits of the Obaku School and Flower and Bird Paintings of the Shen Nan-p'in School*, 1972.

Other publications: French, Calvin, *Through Closed Doors: Western Influence on Japanese Art, 1639–1853* (Ann Arbor 1977); Tani, Shin'ichi, and Tadashi Sugase, *Namban Art* (New York 1973).

ALICE R. M. HYLAND

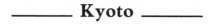

——— Kyoto ———

KYOTO NATIONAL MUSEUM (officially KYOTO KOKURITSU HAKU-BUTSUKAN), 527 Chayamachi, Higashiyama-ku, Kyoto.

The origins of the Kyoto National Museum date from 1875, when a collection of treasures owned by Shinto shrines and Buddhist temples in the Kyoto area was exhibited in the Kyoto Imperial Palace. This exhibition was organized by the Kyoto prefectural government to protect and preserve objects of art that were in danger of being scattered or lost during the nationwide trend toward westernization. In 1888 an organization called the Temporary National Treasure Research Bureau made a survey of valuable works of art owned by shrines and temples. As a result of this study, the government found it necessary to establish national museums in both Kyoto and Nara. The Imperial Estate at Shichijo (the present museum site) was chosen as the location for the museum in Kyoto.

The construction of what is now called the "Old Exhibition Hall" was begun in 1892, completed in 1895, and officially opened in May 1897 as the Imperial Kyoto Museum. It was renamed the Kyoto Imperial Household Museum in 1900. Designed by the court architect Toyu Katayama, the red brick Old Exhibition Hall is an excellent example of the Western-style architecture of the Meiji period (1868–1912) and has now been designated as an Important Cultural Property. It was renovated in 1977 and is now used only for concerts and special exhibitions.

In 1924 the museum was given to the Kyoto city government by the imperial family in commemoration of the wedding of Crown Prince Hirohito. At that time, the name of the museum was changed to the Kyoto City Museum. However, after World War II, according to the law of Protection of Cultural Properties, the museum was reorganized as the Kyoto National Museum under the administration of the Ministry of Education (present Cultural Affairs Agency). The construction of the present New Exhibition Hall was begun in 1963, and it was opened to the public in October 1966. It is a modest, two-storied structure made of reinforced concrete; unique is the use of temple roof tiles for paving some of the interior halls.

Although originally built to preserve and display art objects owned by temples in the region, the Kyoto National Museum has acquired a sizable collection of its own, which now comprises about three thousand objects. The total extent of the museum's collection, including entrusted works, numbers more than eight thousand items, more than six hundred of which are registered as National Treasures and Important Cultural Properties. Holdings consist mainly of both Japanese and Chinese art, including archaeological materials, ceramics, Buddhist sculpture, painting, calligraphy, textiles, lacquer ware, and metalwork.

The archaeological finds from the Jōmon (c. 8,000–300 B.C.), Yayoi (300 B.C.-A.D. 300), and Kōfun (A.D. 300–552) periods are arranged so that one can study the chronological development of early Japanese art. Photographs of the excavation sites often accompany the works, offering valuable supplementary information. The collection includes many stone artifacts from the Japanese Neolithic age such as axes and arrowheads. The cord-marked pottery of the Early Jōmon period is represented by only one piece on permanent display, but eight vessels dating from the Middle Jōmon period exhibit a wide variety of form and design, testifying to the remarkable individuality and inventiveness of the potters of that age. Four small jars dating from the Late Jōmon period are also on display, as well as two small clay figurines.

Particularly noteworthy is the large quantity of pottery from the Yayoi period (300 B.C.-A.D. 300), which is distinguished by a warm red or buff-colored clay. Only three specimens from the Early Yayoi period are on display, but the Middle Yayoi period is especially well represented by more than twenty pieces that display a wide range of vessel shapes and modest surface decoration. Of special interest are three very large jars that are believed to have been used as coffins. One can also study the development of bronze culture during this early age, a technique that was introduced to Japan from continental Asia. In the collection are several bronze mirrors, daggers, and five *dotaku* (large, bronze, bell-shaped objects), some of which are decorated with flowing wave patterns or other designs in relief. The museum's selection of early Japanese art also includes fine examples of *haniwa*, hollow clay figurines of humans, animals, houses, and other artifacts that were originally set into the soil surrounding the great imperial tomb mounds of the Kōfun period (A.D. 300–552). Contemporary with the production of *haniwa* was the manufacture of *sueki* ware, represented by five pieces among which the high-footed vessels with the characteristic sculptural decoration can be seen. The three-color glazed pottery of the Nara period

(A.D. 645–794) is well exemplified by a cinerary urn that resembles in form a medicine jar of the Imperial Repository Shōso-in.

During the Kamakura (1185–1336) and Muromachi (1336–1573) periods there developed a high-fired stoneware tradition dominated by the Six Old Kilns, and the museum has vessels representing each of these pottery centers (Tokonome, Seto, Echizen, Tamba, Shigaraki, Bizen). The taste for teawares during the succeeding Momoyama period (1573–1615) is represented by two Shino bowls and several examples of Oribe ware, distinguished by irregular and asymmetrical shapes: bold, abstract designs; and copper-green glaze. Raku ware was also specifically designed for use in the tea ceremony and was developed in Kyoto by the potter Chojiro. Greatly influenced by the great tea master Sen no Rikyu, the special flavor of Raku can be studied in a tea bowl by Chojiro, owned by the museum, and also in a bowl by his son Nonko. Contemporary with these wares was a glazed, high-fired stoneware called Karatsu, represented by seven examples. Porcelain was introduced into Japan during the early seventeenth century, and in the museum's collection are several fine examples of the more popular wares, Kakiemon, Nabeshima, and Imari. Kyoto emerged as a great center of ceramic production in the late Edo period and one of its most outstanding potters was Nomomura Ninsei, represented by a lotus-shaped incense burner and tea caddy. The tradition of Ninsei was carried on in the work of Ogata Kenzan, whose personal interpretation can be seen in three square dishes, one of which is decorated with a landscape.

Toward the end of the eighteenth century, Kyoto also became a center of porcelain manufacture. The man responsible for the introduction of fine porcelain wares to the Kyo-yaki tradition was Okuda Eisen, represented by a fine incense burner. The museum also owns several examples done by his students Aoki Mokubei and Ninnami Dohachi.

The museum owns a sizable collection of Chinese ceramics. The earliest examples are five small Chou Dynasty (1030–221 B.C.) ash-glazed bowls. The Han Dynasty (206 B.C.-A.D. 220) is represented by a large jar, and the Six Dynasties Period (A.D. 220–581), by three earthenware grave figurines. The ceramic art of the T'ang Dynasty (A.D. 618–906) is well exemplified by the selection of twenty earthenware tomb figurines, many exhibiting the three-color glaze so characteristic of the pottery of this period.

The development of ceramics, especially porcelain, reached a high point in the Sung Dynasty (960–1279) and is reflected in the museum's small collection of Sung porcelains and stonewares, among which are five examples of *lung-chuan* celadon ware. The museum also owns a superb example of *Tzu-chou* ware in the form of a *mei-p'ing* vase. The famous *temmoku* glazed ware is well represented by a tea bowl decorated with a stenciled design of a phoenix. A small selection of blue-and-white porcelain vessels and several examples of colorful overglazed enamel wares exemplifies well the decorative tastes of the Ming period (1368–1644).

Ceramic art also flourished in Korea, and examples dating from the Yi and

Koryŏ periods are on display. The Chinese custom of placing stone figures of humans and animals along the roads to the imperial tombs was adopted by the Koreans and can be studied in the museum's two stone statues of the Yi period in the east corner of the garden outside.

Because of the strong influence that Buddhism had on the arts of both China and Japan, a major part of the museum's collection is Buddhist sculpture. Among the Chinese holdings are several pieces dating from the Six Dynasties Period (220–534). Buddhism came to China from India, and the museum owns a particularly fine fourth-century, small, bronze, standing Buddha that reflects the Chinese assimilation of Gandharan Buddhist art styles. Also outstanding is the fragment of a standing Bodhisattva taken from the walls of a Chinese cave temple at Kung-hsien. From the same cave temple complex there is a section of a relief depicting a group of devotees. Other works from the same period include several stone stelae with carved inscriptions accompanied by incised drawings of Buddhist deities. Chinese Buddhist art of the later periods is not well represented here, with the exception of a large wooden statue of the Buddhist deity Kuan-yin dating from the Sung Dynasty (960–1279).

As would be expected, the Kyoto National Museum has exceptionally strong holdings in Japanese Buddhist art. Although there is no free-standing sculpture from the Asuka period (538–645), there are several roof tiles with incised pictures of Buddhist deities. The Buddhist art of the succeeding Nara period (645–794) is exemplified in two handsome eighth-century statues of the Buddha Yakushi, both of which were executed in dry lacquer. The high point in the development of Esoteric Buddhism during the ninth century is represented by an impressive group of five wooden statues, with the Buddha Dainichi in the center. The art of another kind of Buddhism called Pure Land, whose followers believed that complete faith in the Buddha of the Western Paradise, Amida, would lead them to enlightenment, can be seen in a large eleventh-century wooden sculpture of Amida. A 1258 version of the same Buddha done in dry lacquer is also on exhibit. The museum owns sculptural works of many other Buddhist deities, and among the most interesting are the guardian figures originally found standing at temple gates. Guardian figures from several different periods are on exhibit, but particularly notable are a pair of thirteenth century *ni-o* carved out of wood displaying characteristically ferocious expressions and contorted poses.

The museum has exceptionally rich holdings in Japanese paintings of all periods, and items on display are generally rotated on a monthly basis. One of the most important works owned by the museum is an eleventh-century *senzui byobu* (landscape screen) that, although painted in a manner following Chinese traditions, contains stylistic elements that make it one of the earliest and most important examples showing the Japanization of Chinese painting styles. The narrative handscroll (*emakimono*) reached its peak of development in Japan during the twelfth and thirteenth centuries, and in the museum's collection are several examples including the twelfth-century scroll *Gaki Zoshi* (*Scroll of Hungry Ghosts*) and the thirteenth-century *Kuge Retsuei Zukan* (*Portraits of Cour-*

tiers). There is also a picture scroll by En'i, the *Life of Ippen*, dated 1299. The museum owns many fine early Japanese Buddhist paintings as well, among the most spectacular of which is the set of the group of Buddhist deities called *Juniten*, dated 1127 (once in the To-ji), and the thirteenth-century *Yamahara mandara*, which depicts the Buddha Amida rising over the top of a mountain.

All forms of Japanese painting from the Muromachi (1336–1573) through Edo (1615–1868) periods are all represented. During the Muromachi period ink painting was in vogue, and among the most important works in the museum's collection are Sesshu's famous landscape *Amano-hashidate*, a bird-and-flower painting by Shokei, and *Wild Geese Flying to a Sandbar* by Shikan, which includes an inscription by the Chinese monk I-Shan I-ning. The splendor of the succeeding Momoyama period (1573–1615) is well represented by a seventeenth-century anonymous gold screen of willows and a bridge and by a series of *fusuma* depicting crows that is attributed to Unkoku Togan. Various schools active in the Edo period (1615–1868) are also represented, and among the most interesting paintings are Tawaraya Sotatsu's *Waterfowl in the Lotus Pond* and a set of four hanging scrolls by Ikeno Taiga depicting landscapes of the four seasons. Other artists such as Maruyama Okyo, Yosa Buson, Yamamoto Baiitsu, Tsubaki Chinzan, Tani Buncho, and Watanabe Kazan are also represented. In the corner of one of the exhibition rooms is a *tokonoma* (alcove) with painted walls and *fusuma* panels depicting genre scenes that were taken from the Amman-in Temple in Shiga Prefecture and completely restored. They are believed to have been executed by an artist of the Kano school during the seventeenth century.

The museum's collection of calligraphy is considered to be one of the best in the world in terms of quality as well as quantity. Although the majority of the Chinese examples date from the Sung through Ch'ing periods, the museum owns a fine Han Dynasty (206 B.C.-A.D. 220) stone stele fragment on which is engraved an inscription using an ancient form of script called clerical. There is also a twelfth-century album of rubbings from stelae that were engraved with the calligraphy of the famous Wang Hsi-chih. The museum has exceptionally strong holdings in Ming Dynasty (1368–1644) calligraphy, and important artists such as Ch'en Chi-ju, Chang Jui-t'u, Want To, Ni Yuan Lu, Chu Yun-ming, and Wen Cheng-ming are all represented. The museum also owns a considerable group of later Chinese paintings as well, including works by Ch'en Tao-fu, T'ang Yin, Wen Cheng-ming, and Ch'iu Ying of the Ming Dynasty and by the Four Wangs, Wu Li, and Yun Shou-p'ing of the Ch'ing Dynasty (1644–1912).

Among the Japanese holdings is a twelfth-century album of calligraphy containing fragments of poems by several of the renowned Thirty-six Poets and excerpts from the *Kokin Wakashu* and the *Man'yoshu*. Written in beautiful, flowing Japanese phonetic script called *kana*, these examples from the Heian period (794–1185) are important for studying the development of Japanese calligraphy. The museum also owns many Buddhist texts of the Nara through the Muromachi period, writing by the great priests of the Heian period, and examples of calligraphy by Zen monks in the Kamakura and Muromachi periods.

The museum has a notable collection of Japanese textile items of various types from different periods. Particularly fine are the Edo period Nō robes and kimono. Exhibits are changed seasonally and feature different themes related to the time of year. The museum also has a representative collection of the various kinds of lacquer ware from the Heian to Edo periods, as well as from China and Korea.

1
Selected Bibliography

Kyoto Kokuritsu Hakubutsukan zōhin zuroku (Catalog of the Art Treasures, of the Kyoto National Museum), 1966; *Zen no bijutsu* (Arts of Zen Buddhism), 1981; *Kachō no bi: kaiga to ishō* (The Art of Birds and Flowers: Painting and Design), 1982; *Shohekiga no Hōko: Kyo-Ōmi no meisaku* (Exhibition of Japanese Screen Paintings: Masterpieces from Kyoto and Shiga Prefectures), 1979; *Kozan-ji ten* (Exhibition of Treasures of Kozan-ji Temple), 1981; *Sansui: shisō to bijutsu* (The Ideas and Art of Landscape), 1983; *Heike nokyō* (Illustrated Sutras Dedicated to Itsukushima Shrine by the Heike Family), 1973; *Kodai-ji maki-e* (Kodai-ji Maki-e Lacquerware), 1971.

PATRICIA FISTER

Nara

MUSEUM YAMATO BUNKAKAN (officially YAMATO BUKAKẠN), 1–11–6 Gakuen-minami, Nara.

The Museum Yamato Bunkakan was conceived in 1937, when the late Oita Torao, president of the Kinki Nippon Railway Company, asked the late Yashiro Yukio to advise him in creating a public institution that would make a significant cultural contribution to the region served by the railway. This area includes Osaka, Nara, Kyoto, and Mie Prefecture and, appropriately, is the repository for much of Japan's ancient culture and art.

For several years Yashiro contemplated and studied how best to carry out the wishes of Oita. Finally, he suggested the establishment of a museum whose purpose was to collect beautiful objects that would enrich the lives of those who visited the museum. Oita enthusiastically supported the realization of this goal until his death in 1948 at the age of sixty-four. Yashiro was primarily responsible for the formation of the collection, much of which was purchased after World War II, when objects from many old Japanese collections came onto the market. Yashiro became the first director of the museum and continued to guide it until his retirement.

The museum is entirely owned and funded by the Kinki Nippon Railway Company. Members are entitled to free admission and receive the *Museum Quarterly News* (in Japanese). The original conception of the museum as the collaboration between a successful businessman and an erudite scholar continues in its present organizational structure. The museum is governed by a board of trustees, which consists of the director of the museum, the chairman of the board of the Kinki Nippon Railway Company, the president of the Railway Company, its former president, and its vice-president. The president of the Railway Company serves as the chairman of the Board of Trustees. These men remain on the board as long as they hold those executive positions within the railway company. In addition, there are two financial comptrollers. The administration of the museum is carried out by the director, five full-time curatorial staff members, and one part-time curator. One of the curators serves as assistant director. The curatorial responsibilities are not strictly divided. Their collective areas of expertise include sculpture, ceramics, and painting of India, China, Korea, and Japan. Japanese painting is covered in the greatest depth, with concentration on Buddhist painting, Muromachi ink painting, Yamato-e, Rimpa School, Namban, Komo, and Nanga.

The museum was opened on October 31, 1960, to commemorate the fiftieth anniversary of the Kinki Nippon Railway Company. It is located in the suburbs of the ancient capital city of Nara in a setting of extraordinary beauty. To reach the museum, one walks through a pine forest planted with unusual trees and flowers. Behind the building is a large lake. The present director is deeply involved with the continued development of the natural surroundings. The building was designed by the late architect Yoshida Isoya, member of the Japan Art Academy. It is a modern structure incorporating distinctively Japanese features. The exhibition gallery is a large square room, with a central interior court planted with bamboo. From the far end of the room one looks out through large windows toward the lake. The display is modern, with labels in Japanese and English. Photography is allowed in the gallery, but the use of both tripod and flash requires permission. The museum changes its exhibition about eight times a year, including a special loan show either in the spring or autumn.

The collection itself consists of approximately two thousand items of Far Eastern art of exceptionally high quality. All media are included: painting, calligraphy, ceramics, lacquer, metalwork, sculpture, prints, and textiles. Many of the objects are registered by the Japanese government as National Treasures or Important Cultural Properties.

The strongest holdings are in the Japanese area. Important handscrolls from the twelfth century include an illuminated scroll, the *Lotus Sutra*, with each character supported by a lotus pedestal; an illustration of the *Tale of Nezame*; and an album of Buddhist iconographical drawings. Early calligraphy is represented by a fragment of the eleventh-century *Manyo-shu* (Japan's earliest poems) and twelfth-century sections of the *Wakan-roei-shu* and the *Tale of Ise*, the latter written on elegant decorated paper. The colorful thirteenth-century *Portrait of the Poetess Kodai-no-kimi* is considered one of the "Three Beauties of the Yamato Bunkakan." From this era the museum also possesses a fine series of two ink illustrations to the "Ukifune" chapter of the *Tale of Genji*, and a series of three ink illustrations to the *Tales of Ise*, over which is printed a sutra in sanskrit. Of special interest is the *Kasagi Mandala*, which depicts the now nonexistent colossal stone image of Maitreya at the Kasagi Temple.

From the fourteenth through sixteenth century Zen Buddhism imported from China profoundly influenced the Japanese. The museum has calligraphies by Zen priests such as Seisesu Seicho, Kokan Shiren, and Jakushitsu Genko and a portrait of Bakugan Toshin. Ink paintings of this time include the *White-Robed Kannon* by Ue Gukei, *Bamboo and Sparrow* by Kao, and two *Landscape* screens attributed to Shubun. The range of Sesson's painting is documented by two bird-and-flower screens and three hanging scrolls: *Lu Tung-pin Sporting with Dragons, Moonlight Reflecting on the Water*, and *Self Portrait*. The second of the "Three Beauties" is a *Portrait of a Lady* from the late sixteenth to early seventeenth century. The design of her kimono is executed in tie dye, embroidery, and painting. Gorgeous women are shown to full advantage in a pair of screens from the seventeenth century: the *Matsuura Byobu*. Painted in brilliant colors on a gold-leaf background, eighteen women of fashion are involved in various amusing leisure pastimes. This is an important precursor of *ukiyo-e* painting.

The seventeenth- and eighteenth-century decorative Rimpa School is another area of the collection that shows great depth of development. The early master Sotatsu is represented by an album leaf illustrating the eloping scene from the *Tales of Ise*, a *Portrait of a Priest, Cherry Blossoms*, and the Zen hermit *Kanzan*. Koetsu calligraphy includes a letter and a Waka poem on a piece of paper decorated with bell-flowers and pampas grass in gold and silver dust. Ogata Korin's fan paintings embellish a gold-leafed wooden box. His famous wave design is found on a square wooden tray. There is a rare portrait by him of Nakamura Kuranosuke. Korin also painted a landscape on a square pottery incense burner fashioned by Ogata Kenzan. Other noteworthy ceramics by Kenzan include a tea bowl named *Yugao (Evening Glory)* and a set of five plates with designs of maple leaves on a stream. The museum also owns Kenzan calligraphy: a series of six Waka poems and a recipe for pottery making.

Notable from the eighteenth and nineteenth centuries are two pairs of screens, *Landscapes of the Four Seasons*, by Maruyama Okyo and an amusing pair of screens by his pupil Watanabe Nangaku, *March of Frogs Pretending to Be a Feudal Lord and His Attendants*. The museum has excellent holdings in the field of Nagasaki painters working in European style. The painting *Enoshima* by Shiba Kokan is particularly impressive. The collection includes a number of paintings and calligraphies by Tomioka Tessai (1837–1924). Themes consist of landscape, figures, fish, flowers, and birds.

The Japanese ceramics collection is broad in scope. Early pieces include a large Jōmon jar, several Yayoi pots, and two handsome Haniwa figures. A Sue ware vase from the seventh to eighth century is distinguished by its elegant silhouette. An eighth-century bowl has splashes of green glaze. From the twelfth through sixteenth century, the so-called Six Old Kilns are represented by wares made at Tokoname, Tamba, Shigaraki, Echizen, and Bizen. Edo period (1615–1867) wares comprise Seto, Mino, Oribe, and Karatsu. Porcelain types are numerous and include Arita, Kakiemon, Nabeshima, Satsuma, and Kutani. The museum also possesses an incense case by Ninsei and a bowl and cup by Mokubei.

There are a limited number of Japanese sculptures, the most notable being a wooden Shinto goddess from the eighth to tenth century. The lacquer collection is extensive and high quality.

The Chinese art collection is small and selective. The best early paintings are album leaves from the Sung Dynasty (960–1279): *Autumnal Scenery by the Lake*, attributed to Chao Ling-jang; two album leaves by Li Ti, both titled *Leading a Buffalo Homewards in the Snow*; and two album leaves attributed to Mao I. Two Ch'ing Dynasty (1644–1912) paintings are noteworthy: *Viewing Autumnal Leaves* by Chang Feng, dated 1660, and *Landscape* by Ch'eng Sui, dated 1648.

In the ceramics field there are pieces from all eras. From the prehistoric period are several Yang-shao pots. A black pottery bell shape with *t'ao-t'ieh* mask in relief dates from the Shang Dynasty (c. 1600–1027 B.C.). The Chou Dynasty (1027–221 B.C.) is represented by a white earthenware jar and dancing figurines in black pottery. There are a number of Han Dynasty (206 B.C.-A.D. 221) burial objects. From the Six Dynasties Period (A.D. 265–588) are more tomb items and several Yüeh ware pieces. An extraordinary white pottery hill censor dates from the Sui Dynasty (A.D. 581–618). T'ang Dynasty (A.D. 618–906) wares include monochrome pots as well as three-color glazed objects and figures. A standing court lady is considered the third "Beauty of the Yamato Bunkakan." Products of Northern Sung Dynasty (A.D. 960–1127) kilns consist of celadons, both white and red Ting ware and a wide variety of Tz'u-chou pieces. From the Southern Sung (A.D. 1127–1279) Dynasty the museum has several superb Lung-ch'üan wares, Ch'ing-pai and Chün. The most important Yüan Dynasty (A.D. 1279–1368) piece is a porcelain Mei-p'ing vase with a phoenix design in underglaze red. Most of the Ming Dynasty (A.D. 1368–1644) porcelains are decorated in underglaze blue or overglaze enamels. The Ch'ing Dynasty porcelains are less numerous. Notable are a K'ang-hsi period (A.D. 1662–1722) peach-bloom-glazed seal-ink box and a bowl with an overglaze enamel design of birds and flowers.

The Chinese sculpture selection is small but contains some fine stone Buddhist pieces from the fifth through eighth century. There are some attractive T'ang bronze mirrors and several beautifully worked silver objects: cups, covered boxes, and a bowl.

The library holdings of the Museum Yamato Bunkakan number approximately fifteen thousand books and manuscripts. Most of them are in Japanese, although some books in European languages on Oriental and European art have been received as gifts. The collection is extensive, especially for a private museum. Its particular strength is in the Japanese area that covers diverse topics such as history, literature, anthropology, Buddhism, Shintoism, architecture, painting, calligraphy, paper, tea ceremony, Ikebana, textiles, ceramics, metalwork, glass, lacquer, folk art, and crafts. Books on China deal with its history, archaeology, metalwork, jade, ceramics, sculpture, painting, and calligraphy. There is a more limited selection of books on the arts of Korea, Central Asia, and India. The library also possesses a large number of old exhibition catalogues, museum periodicals from abroad, and foreign and Japanese journals. It owns catalogues of Treasure Houses, temples, and private collections. Its reference materials include a number of encyclopedias and catalogues of other library holdings in Japan. The library is not open to the public but is available to scholars with specific research projects and a proper introduction. Its collection does not circulate.

Slides and photographs are available for purchase. The museum has negatives of everything in its collection, as well as objects that have been borrowed for special exhibitions. The museum's publications include the *Selected Catalogue* of its masterpieces, a seven-volume catalogue of the collection, and the catalogues for special exhibitions. *The Journal of Eastern Art Yamato Bunka* was founded in 1951. Edited by the director of the museum, Ishizawa Masao, it is published biannually in Japanese with a brief English summary. It is available by subscription with some back issues still in print.

Selected Bibliography

Museum publications: *Illustrated Catalogue Series*, No. 1, *Japanese Ceramics from the Museum Yamato Bunkakan Collection*, 1978; No. 2, *Paintings and Handwritings from the Museum Yamato Bunkakan Collection*, 1974; No. 3, *Lacquer Wares from the Museum Yamato Bankakan Collection*, 1975; No. 4, *Ceramics: Korea and Miscellaneous Countries excepting Japan and China from the Museum Yamato Bunkakan Collection*, 1975; No. 5, *Sculpture, Metalwork, Gem and Stone, Glass, Textile, and Miscellaneous Pieces from the Museum Yamato Bunkakan Collection*, 1976; No. 6, *Works of Tomioka Tessai from the Museum Yamato Bunkakan Collection*, 1976; No. 7, *Chinese Ceramics from the Museum Yamato Bunkakan*, 1977; *Special Exhibition: Chinese Literati Paintings from the Jōrakuan Collection*, 1979; *Special Exhibition: Korean Buddhist Paintings of Koryŏ Dynasty*, 1978.

ALICE R. M. HYLAND

NARA NATIONAL MUSEUM (officially NARA KOKURITSU HAKUBUT-SUKAN), 50 Noborioji-cho, Nara.

The Nara National Museum was constructed at the same time as the Tokyo and Kyoto museums. Although it was completed in December 1894, it was not opened to the public until April 1902. At this time the museum was placed under the direction of the Imperial Household Department and was named the Nara Imperial Museum. In May 1947 it was put under state control and renamed the National Museum, Nara Annex. In August 1952 the museum was reorganized and put under the direction of the Committee of Cultural Properties. Since that time it has been called the Nara National Museum.

Because the Nara National Museum is a government institution, its director is appointed by the minister of education, who officially governs the museum. The director is assisted by the Hyogiin-kai, which is composed of fourteen members appointed by the Commission of the Agency for Cultural Affairs. The Hyogiin-kai meets once or twice a year, and its members are appointed every two years.

The museum is divided into two major sections. The General Affairs Department deals with the budget, appointments of museum staff, correspondence, and security. The Curatorial Department consists of five divisions: Fine Arts, Applied Arts, Archaeology, Reference Materials, and Education. Each division has its own curator, and the chief curator presides over the Curatorial Department. An organization called the Society of Museum Friends was created in 1952. Upon payment of annual dues, members are entitled to participate in lecture courses and programs organized by the museum and receive museum news bulletins and are provided with passes to visit the other two national museums in Japan (Tokyo and Kyoto).

The Nara National Museum is located in the central part of Nara Park and consists of an Exhibition Hall and Office. The Exhibition Hall is made of brick and finished with a plaster coating and includes twelve exhibition rooms. In the surrounding garden is a shop and dining room for the public and a teahouse named the Hasso-an. Now considered one of the best teahouses in Nara, it was originally installed in the garden of the Imperial monastery named Daijoin at the Kofuku-ji.

The Nara National Museum was originally intended to house and display works of art belonging to temples and shrines in the Nara area. Nara became the capital of Japan in 710 and remained so until it was moved to Kyoto in 794. Because Buddhism flourished in Japan at this time, the Nara area is abundant with Buddhist temples and art. Accordingly, the holdings of the Nara National Museum are extremely rich in Buddhist art, especially from the Asuka (538–645) through the Muromachi period (1185–1336). In addition to having works on long-term loan, the museum has also been improving its own collection during the past few years, and it now contains several hundred paintings and many fine examples of sculpture and calligraphy. Objects on view are generally changed once a month. The percentage of objects on view at any time depends on the type of exhibition. There is a special show each autumn, when objects from the eighth-century Imperial repository, the Shoso-in, are exhibited. Another show in the spring is usually devoted to some aspect of Buddhist art. These special exhibitions are usually accompanied by illustrated catalogues. An illustrated guidebook to the museum is also available that contains a general discussion on Buddhist art.

Among the holdings of early Buddhist art on deposit is a small bronze sculpture from Todai-ji of Shaka at his birth, dating from the Nara period (710–794). Other Buddhist sculpture from this time includes a wooden statue of the priest Gien, which is on loan from the Okadera, and a wooden image of Bonten. During the eighth century contacts with the Chinese mainland were very strong, and due to the interest in Buddhism, many scriptures were brought to Japan for study. Japanese monks began to copy sutras as well, and there are several fine examples in the collection. Painting was another art form put to the service of Buddhism, and the Nara National Museum owns a section from the *Inga-kyo*, dating from the eighth century, that illustrates the past and present world lives of the historical

Buddha. The museum also owns an extraordinary Nara embroidery showing the Buddha preaching. Other early artifacts include a large bronze bell from Kofuku-ji, dated 727.

Although during the Nara period, bronze, lacquer, and clay were the most common mediums for Buddhist sculpture, in the succeeding Heian period (794–1185) the use of wood became paramount. The holdings of the Nara National Museum are particularly rich in wooden sculpture from temples dating from the Heian period. Among the most outstanding works is the often-published seated sculpture *Miroku* from Todai-ji, dating from the ninth century. Carved out of a single block of cypress wood, the figure conveys a feeling of great monumentality and spiritual intensity. Another important sculpture is the standing image *Buddha Yakushi* from the Gango-ji, also carved from a single block of wood. Typical of the early Heian style are the heavy, broad proportions and the austere facial expression. Highly stylized drapery folds of this and many other early Heian works produce a fluent linear pattern often referred to as the "rolling-wave" style. In addition, the Nara National Museum owns an impressive seated wooden statue of Yakushi that dates from the ninth century.

Other sculptures showing this preference for and love of wood are two Shinto deities, Nakatsu-hime and Sogyo Hachiman, from the Yukushi-ji. Thought to date from the ninth century, they are some of the oldest extant examples of Shinto sculpture. Their solemn facial expressions and handling of the folds of the drapery reflect the sculptural tradition of the early Heian period, but unlike Buddhist sculpture, these Shinto figures appear very compact, even squat.

Later Heian period sculptures include a painted wooden statue of Tobatsu Bishamon-ten, who was a special manifestation of the Guardian God of the North. From the Kofuku-ji are several flat wooden representations of the *Juni-shinsho* (twelve divine generals) that exhibit characteristically ferocious facial expressions and dramatic poses. The patterns in the grain of the wood are exceptionally beautiful in these pieces. Also from the Kofuku-ji is a wooden portrait of the priest Gyoga. The museum has many other important Heian sculptures, and among them are wooden statues of Shaka (Horyu-ji), Sho Kannon (Hosomi Collection), Kannon (Yunen-ji), Juntei Kannon (Shinyaku-ji), Juichi-men Kannon, Amida, Jizo, Fudo Myo-o (Bujo-ji), Godai-Myo-o, Dainichi (Gango-ji-cho), and Kokuzo Bosatsu (Hokuso-bo Temple).

Paintings dating from the Heian period are always rare, but the museum's collection includes several fine examples. From the Saidai-ji is a set of hanging scrolls of the Twelve Devas, which, although in poor condition, still serves as an example of the high quality of Buddhist painting of the period. The narrative handscroll (*emakimono*) reached its peak of development in Japan during the twelfth and thirteenth centuries, and the museum houses the *Pilgrimage of Sudhana* from the Todai-ji and the *Life of Ippen* from the Kankiko-ji. The *Jigoku Zoshi* (*Scrolls of Hell*), which are owned by the museum, date from the thirteenth century. Holdings also include several Shinto mandalas. Sutras continued to be produced throughout the Heian period but began to exhibit the elegant and decorative tastes of the aristocracy, here represented in the sutra from the Kongobu-ji, written in gold and silver on blue silk.

The museum's holdings also include several fine examples of Kamakura period (1185–1336) painting; especially notable is a triptych with Shaka flanked by Monju and Fugen (Soji-ji) and a Raigo painting (Saikyo-ji) showing Amida descending to earth to receive the souls of the dying. The Kamakura period is also represented by an impressive amount of Buddhist sculpture. Among the most outstanding is a Shaka carved of wood owned by the Nara National Museum, a seated Shaka also of wood from the Todai-ji, and a wooden sculpture of Prince Shotoku from the Jofuku-ji. Numerous wooden sculptures of other Buddhas and Buddhist deities such as Bishamonten (Saifuku-ji), Daitokuten (Kofuku-ji), Amida, Fudo Myo-o, and Jizo are also in the collection.

By the Muromachi period (1336–1573), Zen had taken over as the dominant sect of Buddhism in Japan. The character and function of Buddhist painting changed considerably. A major form of art of the Zen sect was *chinso*, or portraits of Buddhist monks. It was the tradition for a Zen master to give his portrait to a departing student as a certificate of graduation and of the teacher's approval. Portraits would also be kept in temples where a great monk had lived to be displayed at yearly memorial services. A fine example of such a painting in the museum's collection is a portrait of Ikkyu, who although known for his unconventional behavior was the greatest leader of Zen Buddhism in the mid-Muromachi period.

In addition to sculpture and painting, Buddhist materials in the collection include miniature shrines and reliquaries, sutra boxes, and other objects used in Buddhist rites. An excellent series of roof tiles in the collection shows their development from the Asuka to the end of the Heian period.

Given the special nature of this museum, it is not possible to give a detailed account of what the museum may be showing at any time. One can only emphasize that the exhibitions include examples of the best of Japanese art.

The museum's library contains roughly twenty-three thousand volumes on Japanese and other Asian art. The museum is planning to establish the Information Center for Research of Buddhist Art, which will be equipped with publications, descriptions of major Buddhist art works, and x-ray or infrared photographs, and will be available to the public.

Selected Bibliography

Museum publications: *Nara Kokuritsu Hakubutsukan meihin zuroku* (Catalog of Masterpieces in the Nara National Museum), 1980; *Hokke kyō no bijutsu* (Arts of the Lotus Sutra), 1979; *Todai-ji ten* (Exhibition of Todai-ji Treasures), 1980; *Jōdo mandara* (The Pure Land Mandala), 1983; *Nihon bukkyō bijutsu no genryū* (Sources of Japanese Buddhist Art), 1978; *Nihon no bukkyō o kizuita hitobito* (Special Exhibition of Buddhist Portraiture), 1981.

PATRICIA FISTER

———— Osaka ————

OSAKA MUNICIPAL MUSEUM OF FINE ART (officially OSAKA SHIR-ITSU BIJUTSUKAN), 121 Chausuyama-cho, Tennoji-ku, Osaka 543.

Open to the public since 1936, the Osaka Municipal Museum of Fine Art is beautifully situated in Tennoji Park, which is southwest of the famous Shitennoji Temple, founded by Prince Shotoku in 593. It is housed in a large, imposing Western-style building, which had been the main residence of the Sumitomo family, who donated it to the city of Osaka in 1921 for use as a museum. The museum was closed during World War II. It reopened in 1947 and has remained open since then, except for a brief period in 1979, when it was undergoing renovation. The museum was designated as the Facility for the Exhibition of Important Cultural Property by the Agency for Cultural Affairs.

The Osaka Municipal Museum of Fine Art has an excellent collection of Japanese, Chinese, and Korean art, which is displayed on two floors of the museum's left wing with sculpture, bronzes, ceramics, and lacquer on the ground floor and paintings and calligraphy on the second floor. Temporary exhibitions are usually shown in the museum's right wing. As of 1980 the museum listed holdings of 1,554 objects dating from prehistoric to modern times, 3,000 objects on loan, and a collection of 7,000 books. The museum has been the fortunate recipient of two donors' gifts, which constitute the strengths of the collection.

The centerpiece of the Osaka Municipal Museum of Fine Art is the group of 160 Chinese paintings from the Abe Collection, which was given to the museum in 1943 by Kojiro Abe, son of Fujasiro Abe, who compiled this amazing selection of Chinese paintings, regarded as one of the best collections of Chinese painting in the world.

Formerly the president of the Toyoboseki Company, Fujasiro Abe collected Chinese paintings during the first three decades of this century. The collapse of the Ch'ing Dynasty in the early twentieth century provided the fortuitous circumstances for Abe's collection. With the fall of the Ch'ing Dynasty, prominent Chinese families, whose fortunes were tied to the imperial family, found themselves in financial straits and were forced to sell their collections of paintings. In contrast to other Japanese collectors of Chinese paintings, who generally bought works that had been in Japan for a long time, Abe made it a practice of buying directly from China and sent agents there to look for works to add to his collection. Consequently, although most Japanese collections of Chinese paintings are restricted to those works reflecting a distinctly Japanese taste, the Abe Collection displays a broader, more comprehensive view of the rich spectrum of Chinese painting; it includes works from all schools of Chinese painting dating from the T'ang to the Ch'ing dynasties.

By the mid–1930s Abe had collected about two thousand paintings that he then published in a two-volume catalogue, the *Soraikin Kinsho*, copies of which he generously donated to universities, research institutes, and art museum libraries throughout the world. In 1943, 160 paintings from the collection were given to the Osaka Municipal Museum of Fine Art.

Included in the Abe Collection at the museum are masterpieces that were once in the collection of the Sung Dynasty ruler Emperor Hui-tsung, who himself was an accomplished artist and under whom Chinese art and culture flourished. His Imperial Gallery was legendary and regarded as the finest collection of paintings ever assembled. Other paintings in the collection were cited in ancient texts on history and painting theory.

Perhaps the most famous work of the Abe Collection is a small scroll with a portrait of the Han Dynasty scholar Fu Sheng attributed to the T'ang master Wang Wei (699–750). Designated a Registered Important Cultural Property, this painting has an awesome pedigree, bearing the seals of the emperors Hui-tsung and Kao-tsung.

Sung works from the Abe Collection include the painting *Reading the Memorial Stele* ascribed to Li Ch'eng and Wang Hsiao, who were active during the second half of the tenth century. As the portrait of Fu Sheng, this painting was acquired from the Wan-yen family. A particularly charming work is *The Hundred Gibbons* attributed to I Yuan-chi (d. 1064), who was regarded as the supreme master in the depiction of monkeys.

Another work designated as a Registered Important Cultural Property is the painting *Consort Ming Crossing the Frontier*, ascribed to the enigmatic artist Kung Su-jan of Chen-yang of whom we know only that she was a Taoist nun active in the first part of the twelfth century.

Among the important dated works of the collection is an exquisite painting of orchids of 1306 by Chen Ssu-hsiao. It is a subtle pictorial statement of the artist's strong political views. When the Sung Dynasty fell to the Mongols, Chen Ssu-hsiao, known for his expertise in painting orchids, stopped depicting the ground in his paintings of them to signify that Chinese soil had been lost to the Yüan barbarians from the north.

The Abe Collection also has examples of work attributed to the so-called Four Great Masters of the Yüan Dynasty: Huang Kung-wang, Wu Chen, Ni Tsan, and Wang Meng. Among the Yüan paintings is the *Pavilion in an Autumn Landscape*, dated 1348 and ascribed to Ni Tsan, and *A River Meandering between Ridges*, dated 1349 and ascribed to Wang Meng.

The Abe Collection is especially strong in paintings from the Ming and Ch'ing dynasties. Outstanding examples of Ming Dynasty painting include the famous scroll painting *Seven Famous Ancient Cypresses*, dated 1484 by Shen Chou; the *Landscape* by Wen Po-jen, dated 1535; the *Illustration to the P'i-P'a Song* by Wen Chia, dated 1569; and a superb handscroll, designated a Registered Important Cultural Property, the *River Landscape*, illustrating a famous poem by Han yu, the T'ang poet, "Preface to Sending Off Li Yuan as He Returns Home to P'an ku" by Tung Ch'i-chang (1555–1636). The leading Ch'ing Dynasty painters, Shih-t'ao, Pa-ta shan-jen, Fu Shan, and Kung Hsien, are all represented in the Abe Collection.

After receiving the Abe Collection, the museum added 59 examples of Chinese painting and calligraphy to this core group, bringing the total number of its holdings in this area to 219. Among these later additions are four leaves of calligraphy, honored as Registered Important Cultural Properties, by Mi Fei, who was considered one of the four great Sung calligraphers.

The museum is also known for its collection of thirty-three works by Korin, which was donated by Muto Kinta. This group is especially significant since it is part of a larger collection of materials that include Korin's notes, letters, order books, receipts, and sketches, handed down through generations of Korin's descendants, the Konishi family.

Of the general Japanese collection, there is a good sampling of prehistoric objects. The Jōmon period is represented by stone implements and a fine clay figurine wearing a mask that was excavated at Takeishi, Chiba Prefecture. There are pottery vessels, *dotaku*, and spearheads from the Yayoi period and Sue-ware vessels, a *haniwa* horse, bracelets, beads, and gilt-bronze horse trappings from the Kofun period. Much of the Japanese sculpture on display is on loan from local temples. The Japanese collection also includes Nara tiles; Negoro lacquer from the Muromachi period; a good selection of Imari, Iga, Karatsu, Kutani, Nabeshima, and Oribe ceramics; and a brush pot by Kenzan, a contemporary of Korin.

In addition to housing the fine collection of Chinese paintings and calligraphy, the museum also has a good collection of Chinese bronzes, porcelain, sculpture, and decorative arts. The museum owns several Yin bronzes, a fine set of mirrors dating from the Han to the T'ang Dynasty, Sung celadon, a Yüan blue-and-white dish, and a group of Ming blue-and-white porcelain. Figure ceramics are represented by a beautiful brown-glazed horse dating from the Han Dynasty and a figure of a camel from the Northern Wei Dynasty. Of the Chinese sculpture, the museum owns a Chin Dynasty stone relief, delicately carved with figures of elegant court ladies and their attendants; the head of a celestial flutist of the Northern Wei Dynasty, excavated at the Kung-hsien caves; and a white marble stele depicting a pair of seated Buddhas, who are thought to be representations of Shakyamuni and Prabhataratna, dating from the sixth-seventh century.

The Korean section contains fine examples of Korean ceramics, with pottery vessels of the Silla period, Koryŏ inlaid celadons, and blue-and-white porcelain of the Yi period. Besides these Far Eastern collections, the Osaka Municipal Museum of Fine Art's holdings also include a group of Coptic sculpture and textiles. A collection of Etruscan works was also given to the museum from an Italian museum in exchange for Japanese archaeological and folkloristic materials.

The museum sponsors lectures and art courses, as well as a support organization called the Museum Friends Association. A workshop for the study of Western-style sketching, painting, and sculpture is affiliated with it.

Selected Bibliography

Museum publications: *Miotsukushi* (Museum bulletin); *Kaikan kinen meiho tenkan zuroku* (Illustrated catalog of famous treasures, Japanese, Chinese, and European paintings and ceramics, celebrating the opening of the new museum), 1936; *Daisankai meiho tenrankai zuroku* (Illustrated catalog of the third famous treasures exhibition held at the museum October 9–25, 1938), 1938; *Jōmon Shuei* (Collection of Jōmon culture); *Suibokuga* (Water ink painting); *Osaka Exchange Exhibition: Paintings from the Abe Collection and Other Masterpieces of Chinese Art*, 1970.

Other publications: *Chinese Paintings in the Osaka Municipal Museum of Fine Art* (Tokyo 1975).

MARSHA C. TAJIMA

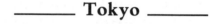

——— **Tokyo** ———

IDEMITSU MUSEUM OF ARTS (officially IDEMITSU BIJUTSUKAN), 3–1–1 Marunouchi, Chiyoda-ku, Tokyo.

The Idemitsu Museum of Arts was established in 1966 by Idemitsu Sazo, founder and chairman of the Idemitsu Kosan Company, Ltd., one of the largest oil companies in Japan. The museum operates as an independent foundation financed by money from both the oil company and Idemitsu. Members of the museum are admitted free once a month and may attend lectures, which are held every two months. They also receive the quarterly *Bulletin* of museum activities.

The museum is governed by a seven-member board of directors who serve three-year renewable terms. Idemitsu is the chairman of the board; the other members either are art specialists or are connected with the oil company. In addition to the director, the museum administrative staff includes a deputy director, three managers, and four curators. The curatorial areas of specialization cover archaeology, Chinese and Japanese ceramics, Near Eastern ceramics, Japanese painting and calligraphy, and painting by Zen monks.

On October 29, 1966, the Idemitsu Museum of Arts opened on the ninth floor of an office building across from the moat that surrounds the Imperial Palace. The galleries in Japanese style were designed by the architect Yoshiro Taniguchi. The exhibition is changed three to four times each year.

There is a branch of the museum in Fukuoka, the Idemitsu Gallery, 8–26–2 Daimyo, Chuo-ku, Fukuoka-shi, located on the fourth floor of the Idemitsu Kosan Building. Opened in 1964, its exhibition space is small, and the material is changed three to four times a year. These displays focus on a theme and come exclusively from the collection housed in Tokyo.

The majority of the collection was assembled by Idemitsu, who started collecting in the early twentieth century. The only other source of objects was a few purchases made to fill gaps in the collection or take advantage of outstanding purchase opportunities. For example, the museum bought a series of fifty-four

Rouault paintings that were going to be sold separately and possibly leave Japan. The twenty thousand items that constitute the total collection not only cover a broad range but are impressively high quality. Reflecting Idemitsu's personal interest, areas of greatest strength are painting and calligraphy by the Zen monk Sengai (1750–1837) and Karatsu ceramics produced from the late sixteenth century on in northern Kyushu. The museum has a representative selection of other Japanese ceramic wares as well as one of the largest Chinese ceramics collections in Japan. It also has ceramics from Korea, Vietnam, Thailand, Iraq, Iran, Egypt, Turkey, England, France, Germany, and the Netherlands. Other sections of significance are Japanese calligraphy and painting, Chinese bronzes and jades, and Chinese and Japanese lacquer ware.

One of the Gallery's unique features is its pioneering ceramics study room. This offers a veritable paradise for potters and students of ceramics, where they may study potsherds first hand. These sherds are from kiln sites in China, Korea, Japan, and the Near East and are permanently on exhibition.

The Chinese ceramics are comprehensive and outstanding in quality. The group of neolithic pieces includes a handsome painted jar of the Pan-shan type. There are also a number of earthenware pots from the Warring States period (480–222 B.C.) and green-glazed pottery of the Han Dynasty (202 B.C.-A.D. 220). The large Han watchtower is especially fine. Six Dynasties (A.D. 265–581) pieces include a rare chicken-headed ewer. T'ang Dynasty (A.D. 618–906) products are the most impressive group. Two white porcelainous wares are a vase with lion handles and a jar with a phoenix head. There is also a white porcelain dish from Chi-chou with a fluidly carved design of peonies. The three-color glazed wares form the largest group in Japan. Among them, a white camel and a seated lady are notable. Northern Sung Dynasty (A.D. 960–1127) wares include two Ching-te-chen pieces with ch'ing-pai glazes, a pitcher and a pair of vases with floral scroll designs, and two Tz'u-chou ware vases, one with a painted peony design in black, the other with sgraffito design of peony scrolls. The collection includes Ting and Chun wares.

From the Southern Sung (1127–1279) period there are Temmoku wares, Lun Lung-ch'uan celadons, a lovely *kuan* ware celadon vase, and a bowl with a fish painted in red enamel. A jar with a design of equestrian figures and a pilgrim bottle with a design of dragons, both in blue and white, are the cream of the Yüan Dynasty (1279–1368) ceramics. The late fourteenth-century pitcher with a design of a banana tree in underglaze red is remarkable for the quality of the red color. Masterpieces from the Ming Dynasty (1368–1644) begin with a Yung-lo period (1403–24) dish with underglaze blue flowers. A Chia-ching period (1522–66) ewer decorated with overglaze enamels and gold is registered as an Important Art Object. A rectangular covered box with a pattern of figures in a landscape painted in underglaze blue has a Lung-ch'ing reign mark (1567–72). A Wan-li period (1573–1620) covered, compartmented vessel has a design of fish and shells in overglaze enamels. Two pieces from the Ch'ung-chen period (1628–44) are a ewer and a dish. Dating from the Ch'ing Dynasty (1644–1912),

Yung-cheng period (1723–35), the jar with a spectacular floral scroll design in underglaze blue and red is a registered Important Art Object. From the Ch'ien-lung period (1736–96) there is a brush-holder with an exquisitely painted design of figures.

The Japanese ceramics in the collection begin with the Yayoi period (B.C. 200-A.D. 300) and continue through the Edo period (A.D. 1615–1867). The late Yayoi period painted pottery vase is registered as an Important Cultural Property. The Momoyama period (A.D. 1568–1614) is represented by several significant pieces. An Old Seto ware covered jar has an incised design of peonies and lovely pale green glaze. Karatsu wares include a tea bowl, a dish with a pine tree design, and a jar with a reed pattern. A Shino ware bowl is painted with carp and waterfall. There is also an Oribe flat bowl with a loop handle. Edo period works present a wide variety of wares. Two Old Kutani dishes are particularly fine. A jar with enameled poppies is an Important Cultural Property. There are a covered octagonal Kakiemon jar, some Nabeshima dishes, a Kenzan jar embellished with maple leaves, an old Imari covered jar, and a Takatori ware mallet-shaped flower vase. Other wares found in the collection are Hagi, Izumo, Bizen, Tamba, Raku, Iga, and Shigaraki. There are also pieces by the Kyoto potters Mokubei, Hozen, and Dobachi.

The Near Eastern collection focuses on Iran, including prehistoric earthen-wares. A fourth-century Sassanian silver dish shows a king hunting lions. Thir-teenth-century objects consist of a luster-painted, bird-headed pitcher; a dish decorated with polychrome horsemen; and a pair of jars painted in gilt on tur-quoise blue glaze. There are also Egyptian, Roman, and Islamic glass and Turkish and Islamic ceramics.

The Chinese antiquities are mainly bronzes dating from the Shang (c. 1600–1027 B.C.) through the T'ang Dynasty. The group of Shang ritual vessels are distinguished by a pair of *chia*, which are Important Art Objects. The collection includes a handsome *kuei* from the Western Chou Dynasty (770–404 B.C.) and a T'ang gilt-bronze mirror decorated with winged horses and grapes. Archaic jades include several Shang Dynasty ritual knife blades.

Japanese calligraphies of superb quality date from the Nara (646–793) to the Edo period. There are sutra fragments and other Buddhist writings from the Nara and Heian periods (794–1184). Heian secular writings include sections of the *Kokinshu* (a collection of classical Japanese *waka* poems) and the *Iseshu*. The album of calligraphy known as *Minuyo-mo Tomo*, compiled in the Edo period, dates from the Nara to the Muromachi (1392–1567) period and is a National Treasure. A calligraphy by the founder of Daitokuji, the largest Zen monastery in Japan, Daito Kokushi (1282–1337), is an Important Cultural Property. Writ-ings of other Zen monks include works by Muso Kokushi, Myoe, Zekkai Chūsin, Kokan Shiren, and Ikkyu.

Japanese paintings represent a variety of styles from different eras. Two Ka-makura period (1185–1333) works, *Portrait of the Poet Henjo* (816–90) attributed to Fujiwara Nobuzane (1176–c. 1265) and the anonymous handscroll *Tachibana*

Naomoto Moshibumi Ekotoba (*Tales of the Petition Presented by Tachibana Naomoto*), are registered as Important Cultural Properties. A pair of Muromachi period (1334–1567) hanging scrolls by Gakuo Zokyu (active 1470–1515) illustrating two Chinese themes—*Li Po Viewing a Waterfall* and *The Peach-Blossom Spring*—are Important Art Objects. The Edo period painting collection is particularly rich. Three pairs of six-fold screens are noteworthy: the late sixteenth-century *Gion Festival* in Kyoto; the early seventeenth-century *Namban Byobu*, showing the arrival of Portuguese ships; and the late eighteenth-century *Genre Scenes of Spring and Autumn* by Hishikawa Morohira. *Ukiyo-e* paintings are numerous and of high quality. The museum owns fine portrayals of courtesans by masters such as Kaigetsudo Ando, Nishikawa Sukenobu, Ippitsusai Buncho, Kitagawa Utamaro, Hosoda Eishi, Utagawa Toyokuni, Utagawa Toyohiro, and Teisai Hokuba. There are also *uki-e* landscapes painted by Katshushika Hokusai (1760–1849) and Ando Hiroshige (1797–1858).

Nanga painters were inspired by the Chinese scholar-painter tradition. The Idemitsu has excellent examples of landscapes by Yosa Buson, Ike Taiga, Uragami Gyokudo, Aoki Mokubei, Tanomura Chikuden, and Takahashi Sohei.

The Idemitsu has the largest collection in the world of painting and calligraphy by the Zen master Sengai, abbot of the Shofuku-ji, the oldest Zen temple in Japan. He depicts the universe as a circle, a triangle, and a square. A frog sitting in meditation is on the way to enlightenment. More traditional Buddhist themes concern images of Hotei, Jurojin, Fudo Myo-o, Bodhidharma, Fukurokuju, Kanzan, Jittoku, and Kensu. He also painted Plum Blossoms, Bamboo, Lotus, Eggplants, Orchids, and famous spots such as Mount Fuji, the Bay of Futami, the Kiso Gorge, and the Evening View of Hakoura Beach, to name but a sampling of the works owned by the museum.

The Idemitsu does not have an official library, but with an introduction, it is possible to consult the books it owns. Photographs and slides of objects in the collection are available with special permission.

Selected Bibliography

Museum publications: *One Hundred Masterpieces of the Idemitsu Collection*, 1975; *Masterpieces of the Idemitsu Collection: Painting and Calligraphy*, 1968; *Ancient Chinese Arts and Crafts*, 1978; *Ceramics and Other Crafts*, 1969; *Ceramics of the Yuan and Ming Dynasties*, 1977; *Tanomura Chikuden*, 1978; *Treasures of the Orient*, 1979; *Idemitsu Gallery Series* (in Japanese): Vol. 1, *Sengai*, Shokin Furuta, 1966; Vol. 2, *Chinese Ceramics*, Fujio Koyama, 1971; Vol. 3, *Chinese Bronzes*, Yuzo Sugimura, 1966; Vol. 4, *Persian Pottery*, Tsugio Mikami, 1966; Vol. 5, *Itaya Hazan: A Japanese Modern Potter*, Sensaku Nakagawa, 1969; Vol. 6, *Ko-Karatsu Ware 1*, Wasaburo Mizumachi, 1973; Vol. 7, *Ko-Karatsu Ware II*, Wasaburo Mizumachi; Vol. 8, *Minuyo-no Tomo*, Kyozo Koresawa, 1973; Vol. 9, *Hand-Painted Ukiyo-e*, Sadao Kikuchi (English list of plates), 1976.

Other publications: Suzuki, Daisetz T., *Sengai, the Zen Master* (New York 1971).

ALICE R. M. HYLAND

NEZU ART MUSEUM (officially NEZU BIJUTSUKAN), 6–5–36 Minami-aoyama, Minato-ku, Tokyo.

The Nezu Art Museum was established in October 1940 through the generosity of Nezu Kaichiro, Sr. (1860–1940), a successful businessman and collector, whose special interest lay in tea-ceremony objects. His large and varied bequest provided the core of the collection; one-half of the remainder was purchased, the other consists of gifts to the museum. As a private museum, the Nezu receives half of its operating funds from the Nezu Foundation; the rest it derives from the sale of books and rental of its various tea-ceremony rooms. It was the first Japanese museum to rent out its tea-ceremony rooms; others have followed suit. Although there are no members of the museum, in 1955 there began the Friends of Tea Ceremony, for whom a tea ceremony is performed each month with the exception of August and December. There is also a lecture series that takes place once a month.

The museum is governed by a six-member board of directors, who each serve five-year renewable terms. In addition, there are thirteen trustees. It is administered by a director and an associate director. There are three curators, whose areas of expertise include archaeology, tea ceremony, Japanese history, calligraphy, and ink painting. The main museum building is located in a spacious garden. The display area consists of a large rectangular room, with balconies along two sides and one end. Also within the garden are situated six teahouses, which are in great demand for tea ceremonies. Due to the large size of the collection and the relatively small viewing space, the exhibition changes once a month and always focuses on a single theme. Loan shows are scheduled in the spring and autumn. The large sculpture and Chinese bronzes are kept continuously on display.

The collection is extraordinary in its diversity, size, and quality. At present the museum owns about 5,000 items, if sets of objects are counted as one regardless of their size, or more than 10,000 if each article is counted individually. Of them, 209 are registered by the government. Tea-ceremony objects comprise the most important section. Other significant areas are Buddhist art and ancient Chinese bronzes. The museum has fine examples of Japanese painting and calligraphy; Chinese painting; ceramics of Japan, China, and Korea; sculpture; lacquer ware; metalwork; bamboo; and textiles.

The Nezu's Japanese painting collection excels in Buddhist works. Dating from the Heian period (794–1184) are an exquisite *Dainichi Nyorai* and six framed panels, *Sudhana's Pilgrimage to Fifty-three Saints*. Kamakura period (1185–1333) hanging scrolls include *Samantabhadra and Ten Raksasi, Mahatejas, Vajrasattva, Raga, Illustration of Buddha's Life, Nirvana, Vajradhatu Mandala*, and *Hosso-shu Mandara*. Kamakura handscrolls are represented by the *Illustrated Ingakyo*, dated 1254, with the painting by Keinin and Shojumaru and text written out by Ryosei; the *Tengu Soshi Picture Scroll*; and the *Juni Innen Picture Scroll*. The most renowned early Japanese painting is the Kamakura period *Nachi Waterfall*, which shows the popular Shinto pilgrimage spot and exemplifies the beginnings of a pure landscape painting tradition in Japan. Other Shinto paintings are the *Kumano Mandara* and the *Kasuga Miya Mandara*.

The Muromachi period (1334–1567) paintings are also high in quality. The museum owns two paintings by Kichizan Mincho from an original set of fifty paintings, each portraying ten of the *Five Hundred Rakan*. Ink paintings include an anonymous landscape, *Koten En-i*, with inscriptions by twelve Buddhist priests, one of whom was Shuko. The collection includes *Priest Viewing a Waterfall* by Shingei; *Landscape* by Kenko Shokei; and *Landscape* by Shosen, with an inscription by Gesshu Jukei, dated 1523. One Muromachi figure painting by Chuan Shinko is a Chinese priest, *Pu-tai*.

Several pairs of six-panel screens are noteworthy. An anonymous Muromachi pair shows a ball-kicking game called *Kemari*. A Momoyama period (1568–1614) pair attributed to Kano Sanraku or Yamaguchi Sekkei is the *Cherries at Yoshino and Maples at Tatsuta* in brilliant color against a gold background. A variety of Edo period (1615–1867) styles are represented. An anonymous pair, *Ladies Kimonos on Racks*, reflects the obsession with fashion at that time. Kusumi Morikage chose a more traditional theme for his screens *Bugaku Dancers*. The most famous screens in the collection are *Irises* done by the Rimpa School master Ogata Korin. Maruyama Okyo's *Wisterias* is lyrical. Nagasawa Rosetsu's well-composed *Landscape with Figures* demonstrates his skillful modulation of ink tones.

The calligraphy divides into three categories: Buddhist scriptures, writings of Zen priests, and writings in the old Japanese style *wa-yo*. Of the Buddhist scriptures, four date from the Nara period (646–793) and two from the Heian period, and one by Joben (Myo-e) is dated 1192. There are Zen calligraphies from the Kamakura period by Shigen Sogen, dated 1280; Issan Ichinei, dated 1316; and Minki Soshun, dated 1330. Yüan Dynasty (1279–1368) calligraphies were done by Chu-ching, T'ieh-pi-yen, Lung-yen Te-chen (dated 1331), and Yüeh-chiang Cheng-yin (dated 1343). Registered early Japanese style writings dating from the Heian period consist of a fragment of the poetic anthology *Wakan Roei-shu* and the *Record of a Poetry Contest*, held at Naidaijin's house, dated 1119. There are two Kamakura pieces, *Poem on Autumnal Foliage at Dawn* by Asukai Masatsune and the poetic anthology *Kokin Waka-shu* by Fujiwara Tameuji, with a colophon by Fujiwara Tameie, dated 1260.

The collection of Chinese painting is small but selective, with special strength in the Southern Sung period (1127–1279). Ma Lin's *Landscape at Sunset* bears an inscription by Emperor Li Tsung, dated 1254. An oval fan painting, *Quail*, is attributed to Li An-chung. Two paintings are attributed to Mu Ch'i: *Evening Glow over the Fishing Village* and *Bamboos and Sparrows*. Yüan Dynasty works consist of the anonymous *Lohan, Bamboos by the Rock*, with an inscription by Ch'ing-cho Cheng-ch'eng (1274–1339); and Yin T'o-lo's mid-fourteenth-century *Pu-tai and Chiang Mo-ho Discussing Buddhism*. The Ming Dynasty (1368–

1644) is represented by the fine painting *Melon and Insects* by Lu Ching-fu. The only Korean painting is the refined Koryŏ period (918–1391) *Amitabha Buddha*, dated 1306.

The Chinese ceramics date from the T'ang (618–906) through the Ming Dynasty. Registered pieces include two Southern Sung Lung-ch'üan celadon *kinuta*-type objects, a flower vase and an incense burner, and a Ming Dynasty underglaze blue-and-white dish, with a design of flowering plants and a Chia-ching period (1522–66) flower vase decorated with overglaze enamels and gold. Many of the registered tea-ceremony objects were also given names and classified as "things of fame" during the Momoyama, Muromachi, or Edo period. This group is composed of a Sung Dynasty tea caddy and flower vase and a Ming Dynasty tea caddy.

Ceramics from Korea are also significant for their classified tea-ceremony objects. The Nezu owns an important Koryŏ period (918–1391) celadon ewer with a carved lotus design under the glaze. Dating from the Yi period (1392–1910), there are five named and registered tea bowls and one incense burner.

Almost all of the Japanese ceramics are tea-ceremony utensils: tea caddies, tea bowls, flower vases, incense containers and burners, water jars, dishes, and bowls. Registered pieces are a Muromachi period Seto ware tea caddy with a black-brown glaze, a Momoyama period Grey Shino ware tea bowl, an enameled tea bowl by Nonomura Ninsei, and a *chatsubo* (jar for storing tea leaves). The Nezu also owns two Seto ware lion-shaped incense burners: one from the Muromachi period, the other Momoyama. Another registered tea-ceremony object is a kettle of Ashiya ironware, dated 1517, with a design of pine and plum trees and raised dots.

The Nezu's collection of lacquer covers China and Japan. There is a rare Chinese table with an inscription stating that it was made in 109 in the province of Shu. The registered Japanese lacquer wares consist of a Heian period box for a priest's vestment, a Kamakura period *maki-e* (gold lacquer) cosmetic box, three Muromachi period *maki-e* writing boxes, and an Edo period cabinet for volumes of the *Tale of Genji*.

The sculpture selection is small and entirely Buddhist. From India there is a Gandharan standing Bodhisattva of the fourth to fifth century. The Chinese group is distinguished by an impressive marble standing Buddha dating from the Northern Ch'i Dynasty (550–77). Gilt-bronze objects include a Northern Wei (386–535) shrine with Sakyamuni and Prabhutaratna, dated 489; seven Buddhas from the Sui Dynasty (581–618); and the repoussé T'ang *Triad with Two Monks and Two Devas*. In addition, there are several Northern Wei stone stelae and fragments from T'ien-lung-shan of the Northern Ch'i and T'ang. The Japanese sculpture is limited, but there is an important Early Nara period (646–709) bronze standing Avalokitesvara.

The Nezu is justifiably proud of its Chinese ritual bronze vessels of the Shang (c. 1600–1027 B.C.) and Chou (1027–221 B.C.) dynasties. They are extraordinary in their large size and exuberant decoration; many of them are registered.

The museum owns a set of three quadrangular wine ewers (*ho*), decorated with *t'ao-t'ieh* and imaginary beasts. Other Shang wine vessels consist of a *p'ou*, *ts'un*, *chia*, *lei*, *yu*, and *fang-i*. An early Chou Dynasty *tsun* in the shape of paired rams presents an unusual form.

The Nezu has an art library of about one hundred thousand volumes in both Oriental and Western languages. It is open to scholars who present an appropriate introduction. Slides and photographs are available through the Otsuka Kongeisha publishing company, which acts as an agent for the museum. Permission must be obtained from the museum before the company will issue any material. The museum plans to publish a new edition of its *Illustrated Catalogue* in collaboration with Kodansha. It will be in Japanese and English and contain two volumes of plates and one of text.

Selected Bibliography

Museum publications: *Seizanso seisho* (*Illustrated Catalogue of the Nezu Collection*): Vol. 1, *Paintings of the Sung, Yüan, Ming, and Ch'ing Dynasties*, 1939; Vol. 2, *Calligraphs: Chinese and Nipponese*, 1942; Vol. 3, *Tea Utensils: Part 1. Cha-ire, cha-shaka, and natsume*, 1942; Vol. 4, *Tea Utensils: Part 2. Censers, Incense Cases, and Tea Bowls*, 1942; Vol. 5, *Tea Utensils: Part 3. Flower-holders, Water Jars, Kettles, Lacquered Boxes, . . .*, 1942; Vol. 6, *Chinese Bronzes*, 1942; Vol. 7, *Japanese Painting: Part 1. Kakemonos and Byōbu*, 1943; Vol. 8, *Japanese Painting: Part 2. Illustrated Scrolls*, 1943; Vol. 9, *Buddhist Scriptures*, 1943; Vol. 10, *Buddhist Paintings*, 1943; *An Illustrated Catalogue of Selected Masterpieces from the Collection of the Nezu Art Museum*, 1955, 1968, and 1978; *Illustrated Catalogue of the Twentieth Exhibition of the Nezu Art Museum*, 1960; *Exhibition of Chinese Paintings from the Museum's Collection*, 1971; *Exhibition of Paintings of the Hsiao-hsiang Eight Views*, 1962; *Aoki Mokubei* (1767–1833), 1960.

ALICE R. M. HYLAND

TOKYO NATIONAL MUSEUM (officially TOKYO KOKURITSU HAKU-BUTSUKAN), Ueno Kōen, Taito-kū, Tokyo 110.

The Tokyo National Museum is the first and foremost museum founded in Japan. The concept of a museum was one of a host of new ideas that reached this hitherto secluded empire following its resumption of relations with the Western world in 1854. The Bansho Shirabesho, Institute for the Study of Barbarian (i.e., Foreign) Books, established in 1856 to facilitate the conduct of foreign affairs, created the Bussankyoku (Products' Bureau) to supervise the importation and study of foreign products and machinery, mostly of a scientific nature. This bureau was responsible for the first exhibition that the Japanese sent abroad to the international exposition in Paris in 1867 and the subsequent display of the artifacts that the mission brought back. This formed the nucleus of what was to become the Tokyo National Museum, much as the Crystal Palace Exposition of 1851 gave rise to the Victoria and Albert Museum in London.

The measures taken by the Meiji government (1868–1912) to formulate new national policies and to create the ministries to implement them had a direct bearing on the museum's early activities and acquisitions. Soon after the restoration, the Bussankyoku became part of the Seido Gakumonsho, the leading academic institution of the Shogunal government, and acquired its extensive collection of books, scrolls, and other artifacts. It was renamed Daigaku Nanko and later became part of Tokyo University, which was founded in 1877. This new entity was headed, during its critical initial phase, by Machida Hisanari, a cultured upper samurai and educator from Satsuma who had studied in England from 1865 to 1868. He was in charge of selecting Japanese products suitable for export and exhibiting the machinery and reference material purchased abroad. Machida was, more importantly, the first to recognize the need and to secure official authorization, early in 1871, to investigate and safeguard religious and artistic treasures threatened by the Meiji government's edicts disestablishing Buddhism and abolishing feudal ranks and domains. The Bussankyoku next became part of the Ministry of Education soon after it was established in July 1871. It was renamed the Hakubutsukyoku (Museum Bureau) and moved to the main hall of the Yushima Seido, the former center of Confucian studies in Edo, present-day Tokyo. There it established a museum that opened formally in March 1872 with an exhibition of the objects about to be sent to the international exposition held later that year in Vienna. In May 1872 the Museum Bureau also established a separate library, the Shōsekikan, and was placed in charge of the Botanical Gardens in Kōishikawa.

In December 1871 the Council of State set up another organization known as the Hakurankai Jimukyoku (Exposition Secretariat) to manage the extensive preparations for the Vienna Exposition and related research projects. After its reorganization in March 1873, this organization acquired control of the museum, library, and botanical gardens and moved into a group of vacant buildings near the present site of the Imperial Hotel. Its opening exhibition in this new location consisted of material brought back by the delegates to the Vienna Exposition. In March 1875 it in turn was absorbed by the Kangyōryō (the Industrial Development Division) of the Home Ministry, headed by Kawase Shuji, which was in charge of Japanese exhibits at the Centennial Exposition in Philadelphia in 1876 and the two subsequent national expositions. While planning the first National Industrial Exposition in Ueno Park in 1877, the authorities decided to erect on the site of the present museum a large Western-style museum building that was designed and built by Josiah Conder, a British architect then in the employ of the Ministry of Technology. By the time the new building was formally dedicated by the Meiji emperor in March 1882, both the museum and the zoo that had been built nearby in Ueno Park had come under the jurisdiction, in April 1881, of the newly formed Ministry of Agriculture and Commerce. The differing policies of this succession of new ministries, which managed the museum and were responsible for its fortuitous association with national and international expositions, foreign trade, Western technology, preservation of national treasures, a library, and botanical and zoological gardens, had a decisive influence on the early development of the Tokyo National Museum and, in a larger sense, on the development of Japanese art and art history.

A decisive change occurred in March 1886, when the museum was transferred to the newly established Ministry of Imperial Household, where it remained until 1947. Accordingly, in 1889 it was renamed the Tokyo Imperial Museum. Dating from this period, the art department began to assume a dominant role under the leadership of Kuki Ryūichi, who was director of the museum from 1888 to 1900 and served concurrently as vice-president and chief juror of national and international expositions and head of the committee for the investigation and protection of national treasures. The museum was gradually divested of its educational, scientific, and industrial development divisions and in 1900 became in name and fact the Imperial Household Museum. This in turn led to the decision to limit the scope of the museum to the art of Japan and the related arts of Asia, a policy to which it still adheres.

By then the collections had so increased that the museum had expanded to several nearby buildings remaining from the second National Industrial Exposition of 1881. Therefore, to commemorate the marriage of the crown prince, the governor of the prefecture and the mayor of the city of Tokyo in 1909 built, adjacent to the museum, a splendid new gallery known as the Hyōkeikan. It was the only museum building to survive the earthquake of 1923 and served as the locus of activities until a new building was erected in 1938 on the former site. The museum continued to function during most of World War II, but most of its treasures were returned to their former owners—private individuals, temples, and shrines—or sent to branch museums and storehouses located in remote areas for safekeeping. In February 1945 the museum closed because of air raids and did not reopen officially until 1947. On May 3, 1947, the same day that the new constitution was promulgated, the museum was renamed the Tokyo National Museum and placed, as at the outset, under the direction of the Ministry of Education. From 1950 to 1968 it was governed by an agency of that ministry, the Cultural Properties Protection Committee.

Since June 1968 the Tokyo National Museum has been operated and funded by the Bunka-cho, an external organ of the Ministry of Education. The museum derives additional revenue from admission fees, the publication of books and catalogues, and the sale of photographs, slides, and films, as well as contributions from a volunteer organization known as Friends of the Museum. Ueno Park and the museum buildings have belonged, since 1924, to the Tokyo municipal government.

The Ministry of Education Enabling Law No. 37, issued at the time of its transfer to the Bunka-cho, reaffirmed the museum's responsibility for protecting national treasures and expanded its role to include the investigation and study of cultural properties, here defined as "buildings, paintings, sculpture, crafts, calligraphy, ancient books, archival records and archaeological material which are of cultural or historical value to the nation." Administrative rules were modified, the role of the Board of Trustees was simplified and the number of trustees reduced, and additional regulations were issued in 1970 regarding the Oriental division and its management of the new building for Oriental art. With but minor modifications, the museum still conforms to this administrative structure. It calls for the appointment of a director and vice-director to operate the museum, in consultation with a board of trustees consisting of a chairman and fourteen members. Responsibility is delegated to two general managers, one of whom is in charge of administration and the other of arts and sciences. The former is divided into four sections: maintenance, budget, facilities, and publications and publicity; the latter into five sections: the records and research section is in charge of general affairs, records, the library, the photographic collection, and Hōryūji treasures; the art section is responsible for painting, sculpture, calligraphy, architecture, and research; the craft section deals with metalware, swords, pottery, lacquer, and dyeing; the archaeology section covers material dating from prehistory through the Tumulus period (250–552); and the Oriental art section includes the art and archaeology of all areas of Asia other than Japan.

The museum was opened officially on March 10, 1872. It was housed temporarily in the Daiseiden of the Yushima Shrine, which is near the Tokyo University Medical School. From 1873 to 1882 the museum occupied a group of Japanese-style buildings at Yamashita-chō in the vicinity of the Imperial Hotel. In 1882 the museum moved to its present site in Ueno Park, where Josiah Conder had erected a spacious, two-story, brick building embellished with Oriental decorative motifs that was considered one of the major Western-style buildings of the period and is featured in contemporary prints and lithographs. It was the main museum building until leveled by the earthquake of 1923. The committee formed in 1928 to raise funds for a new museum also held a national architectural competition that was won by Watanabe Hitoshi. His Neo-Oriental, two-story, stone structure, built on the same site between 1932 and 1937, was dedicated by Emperor Hirohito on November 10, 1938. The building typifies the arid eclecticism fostered by the strident nationalism of the 1930s and is significant chiefly as a major example of pre-war architecture to have survived the World War II bombing of Tokyo. It is flanked on the left by one of the finest extant examples of late Meiji architecture, the Hyōkeikan, which houses the archaeological material. Designed by one of Conder's pupils, Katayama Tōkuma (1853–1917), this handsome French Renaissance structure was completed in 1909, the same year as his masterpiece, the Akasaka Detached Palace, which is now reserved for visiting foreign dignitaries. Opposite the Hyōkeikan, to the right of the museum, is a reinforced concrete building of comparable size that has creatively adapted traditional architectural elements to a modern idiom. Completed in 1968, this building, which was designed by Taniguchi Yoshirō and associates, is reserved for Oriental art and archaeology and in addition maintains a series of galleries set aside for special exhibitions.

Some sense of the size and scope of the Tokyo National Museum can be gleaned from available inventory figures for 1980. Museum records listed a total of 86,189 objects, subdivided into the following categories: painting—10,635; sculpture—1,065; calligraphy—1,472; architectural models—21; metalware—15,535; swords—3,167; pottery—2,828; lacquer—3,723; dyeing and weaving—3,421; prehistorical objects—11,861; ethnographical material—1,107; protohistorical objects—12,121; historical materials—2,726; Hōryūji treasures—318; Oriental archaeology—8,453; and Oriental art—6,736. In the field of Japanese art, this record cannot be matched by any other museum in Japan or abroad.

The archaeological collection is unsurpassed, both quantitatively and qualitatively. Considering the constraints imposed upon Japanese archaeology, it is surprising to note that more than a third of the Japanese material is archaeological, and if one were to include other Asian archaeological remains, it would constitute more than a third of the entire holdings of the museum. This reflects a persistent preoccupation with this politically sensitive field of scholarly endeavor that, only since World War II, has been partly liberated from subservience to cosmological legends concerning the origins of the imperial line. Because of belief in these legends, early archaeological finds were invariably ascribed to the gods, and it was only toward the end of the seventeenth century that scholars such as Arai Hakuseki recognized finds such as the work of earlier cultures and noted their relation to the Chinese mainland. There was a mounting interest in archaeological finds throughout the Edo period (1615–1868), but it was not until after the Meiji restoration and the discovery and excavation in 1877 of a shell-mound at Ōmori by an American scholar, Edward S. Morse, that the Japanese began to conduct excavations.

The preponderance of prehistorical and protohistorical material reflects post–World War II concerns of Japanese archaeologists with the preliterate period, and their findings have revolutionized the whole sequence of Japanese history and its relations to the cultural centers of the Asian mainland. The museum possesses examples of the crude stone implements of Early Paleolithic, now believed to date from about fifty thousand to thirty thousand years ago, as well as knives and a variety of small tools from Late Paleolithic of about 30,000 to 11,000 B.C. Aesthetically more rewarding are the many fine examples of the distinctive and dynamic pottery with cord patterns of an abstract nature known as Jōmon that lent its name to the Neolithic period of Japanese prehistory. Although the extremely early dates for the origins of this pottery, based on Carbon–14 tests, are disputed, scholars have discerned five phases of evolution that are tentatively ascribed to the period of 7,500 to 200 B.C. Among the other important works of the Jōmon period in the museum collection are an intriguing variety of anthropomorphic clay figurines (dōgu), possibly associated with cult practices, whose abstract distorted features have a haunting quality.

A sharp change in pottery style occurs with the advent of the third prehistoric period, the Yayoi (c. 200 B.C. to A.D. 250), which is marked by the importation of advanced rice-growing methods from the mainland and the introduction of bronze and, a century later, iron. The museum owns a wide variety of vessel types, all of which are marked by a simplicity of shape and an economy of design, consisting principally of rows of incisions or wavy lines. An unusual example is a pottery vase with the representation of a human face from Ozakata, Ibaraki Prefecture. There are also numerous examples of bronze swords, spears, mirrors, and objects of glass and jade, some possibly of Chinese origin, that were recovered from cist and jar burials of this period, as well as Japanese adaptations of Chinese spearheads, mirrors, and bells (*dōtoku*) for ceremonial needs associated with fertility rites.

The latter half of the Bronze–Iron Age, which constitutes the final phase of Japanese prehistory, has been termed protohistoric because this period is referred to in ancient records. A new culture arose following the arrival from the Korean peninsula of a warrior class of horseriders who centralized the existing clan structure and unified the country under a sovereign. The museum has an exceedingly large number of objects from this Tumulus period (250–552) named after a new type of burial mound, usually round, but more typically keyhole shaped in the Kansai area (which includes the ancient cities of Kyoto, Nara, and Osaka), such as the fifth-century tomb of Emperor Nintoku at Mozu, Sakai city, near Osaka Bay, which is of a staggering scale. The perimeter and upper slope of the major tombs were surrounded by *haniwa* (circles of clay) originally in the form of vessels and then of weapons, followed by animals, and, by the end of the fifth century, human figures whose abstract form yet expressive character are enormously appealing to contemporary audiences. The museum has excellent examples of early jars and cylinders; of weapons such as sheathed sword, quiver, armor, and helmet; of various artifacts such as a boat, numerous houses, and storehouses; of a large horse, a dog, and a strikingly alert-looking monkey; and some of the finest representations of human figures.

ELLEN P. CONANT

The paintings department, which also includes prints, drawings, and monumental reliefs, is the finest collection of Japanese paintings anywhere. The Heian period (794–1185) is represented by a remarkable group of paintings that depict images associated with the Tendai and Shingon sects that flourished during this period. Closely connected to the Heian nobility, these sects based their teachings on the *Hokke-kyo* (*Lotus Sutra*). Painting from this period is characterized by elaborate detailed ornamentation, brilliant palette, and delicately precise draftsmanship. Outstanding among the incredible riches of the collection from this period, which include several National Treasures, are the *Fugen Bosatsu* and the *Juroku Rakans* or *Sixteen Arhats*.

The painting of the Bodhisattva Fugen (Sanskrit name, Samantabhadra) is one of the masterpieces of Heian painting. This meticulously executed image features the Bodhisattva Fugen, who is the protector of the *Lotus Sutra*, seated on a white, six-tusked elephant.

According to Buddhist doctrine, the Arhats were spiritual beings who remained on earth to protect the Buddhist law. Established in Chinese Buddhist iconography during the T'ang period, these figures are thought to have been introduced in Japan in 987 by the monk Chonen. The National Museum series, which has been classified as a National Treasure, dates from the second half of the eleventh century and is one of the earliest-known Japanese representations of this subject. Stylistically, this group reflects some influence of the emerging *yamato-e* style of the Heian period.

Other fine examples of Heian Buddhist painting in the collection include the magnificent twelfth-century *Kujaku Myoo (Peacock King)*, designated as a National Treasure; the mid-twelfth-century *Kokuzo Bosatsu*, also a National Treasure; and the late-twelfth-century *Butsu Nehan (The Death of the Buddha)*.

Another valuable painting is *Senju Kannon (Thousand-armed Kannon)*, dated from the twelfth century, which is considered one of the finest and oldest depictions of the Senju Kannon. In this version, the Kannon is depicted with two attendants, Kodoku Ten and Basu Sen.

Stylistically related to the *Fugen Bosatsu* are detached segments from a late-twelfth-century scroll that depicts stories from the Buddhist sutra *Kegon-kyo* titled the *Kegon Gojugo-sho*. Other segments of this scroll, which is classified as an Important Cultural Property, are housed in the Todaiji Temple in Nara.

An important set of illustrations in the early *yamato-e* style of the Heian period is a series of fifty-eight scenes depicting the life of Prince Shotoku, the *Shotoku Taishi Eden*, dated 1069. Historical sources record that these paintings were executed by the painter Hata no Chitei. Originally used to decorate a pavilion of the Hōryūji, these paintings were removed and remounted on a five-panel screen in 1788.

During the late Heian period and Kamakura period, the Japanese illustrated narrative handscroll tradition known as *emaki*, or *emakimono*, achieved its richest expression. These scrolls, which are considered by the Japanese to embody the purest manifestation of the native aesthetic, known as *yamato-e*, encompass a wide range of subject matter: biographies of priests, ghostly tales, historical accounts, legends of shrines and temples, records of poetry contests, and romances.

The depth of the National Museum's collection of *emakimono* is breathtaking. Several scrolls are classified as National Treasures: the *Gaki Zoshi*, the *Jigoku Zoshi*, the *Heiji Monogatari*, and the *Ippen Hijiri-e*. The *Gaki Zoshi (Hungry Ghosts Scroll)* and the *Jigoku Zoshi (Hell Scroll)* are examples of the type of didactic Buddhist painting known as *rokudo-e (Painting of the Six Paths)*. Dating from about 1180, the *Gaki Zoshi* depicts the fate of those souls with too strong an attachment to worldly things with graphic intensity. The museum possesses the scroll *Jigoku Zoshi*, a work of horrific imagination, depicting the different realms of the Eight Hells of Buddhism. The other extant scroll from this set is in the Nara National Museum (q.v.).

Considered one of the high points of Kamakura period narrative painting, one of the most famous historical scrolls is the *Heiji Monogatari (The Story of the Heiji Rebellion)*. Besides the scroll in the National Museum, two other scrolls from this work survive—one in the Boston Museum of Fine Arts (q.v.) and the other in the Seikado Collection. The Tokyo scroll illustrates the escape of Emperor Nijo to the mansion of Taira Kiyomori at Rokuhara. This work has been attributed to Sumiyoshi Keion, a painter, who influenced the Tosa school.

The National Museum has a major portion of scroll VII of the *Ippen Hijiri-e* (*Life of Ippen*) dated 1299. Originally a set of twelve scrolls once housed in the Kankijo-ji, this masterpiece of the *emaki* tradition recounts the life and trials of Ippen, a religious leader who founded an offshoot of the Jodo (Pure Land) sect known as Jishu. In addition to being recognized for the exquisite quality of the painting, this work is also notable for the sumptuousness of the materials and the existence of a very informative colophon. Only one other Kamakura period scroll executed on silk is known. The colophon located at the end of the last scroll gives the date of the work, its patron the priest Shoku, and the painter's name, En'i.

The National Museum also has one painting from the celebrated early-twelfth-century *emakimono* of the *Genji Monogatari* (*The Tale of the Genji*), which is the earliest extant *Genji emaki*. The Goto Museum (q.v.) and the Tokugawa Reimeikai Foundation own the largest portions of this dispersed National Treasure. Unfortunately, the National Museum's page is heavily overpainted.

Besides the National Treasures discussed above, other important *emakimono* include the *Kitano Tenjin Engi* (*Story of the Sanctuary of Kitano Tenjin*); the *Bai Zoshi*, a treatise on veterinary medicine; the *Tengu Zoshi* (*Stories of Conceited Priests*); the *Tohoku-in Shokunin Utaawase* (*Tohoku-in Poetry Contest among the Members of Various Professions*); the *Sumiyoshi Monogatari* (*Tale of Sumiyoshi*); and the *Obusuma Saburo* (*The Tale of Obusuma Saburo*).

During the Muromachi period (1337–1573), the monochrome-ink-painting tradition, known as *suibokuga*, flourished. Introduced at the end of the Kamakura period from China, where this style flourished during the Sung Dynasty, this technique was closely tied to the Zen Buddhist sect, which was favored by the military rulers of the time.

Many of the early masters were Zen priests or monks. One of the first to practice this style was Kao. His imaginary portrait of the monk Hsien-tzu (Kensu) is in the National Museum's collection.

The painter monk Shubun is regarded as the first great master of *suibokuga*. The National Museum's *Chikusai Dokusho* (*Reading in the Bamboo Study*) is perhaps the best-known work associated with him. There are inscriptions by six Zen priests on this scroll, and the preface, written by Jiku'un Toren, is dated 1446. Other works attributed to him in the collection include a hanging scroll of the Zen hermits Han-shan and Shih-te and a pair of six-fold screens depicting the four seasons.

Other early Muromachi works worthy of mention include a rainy landscape attributed to the early-fourteenth-century master Gukei; a landscape ascribed to Gakuo Zokyu; a landscape by Kantei; a white-robed Kannon by Mincho; and a portrait of Shoichi Kokushi, the founder of the Tofuku-ji, by Mincho.

One of the most important examples of Muromachi portraiture is the fifteenth-century portrait of the priest Ikkyu by the artist Bokusei, who was also his pupil.

Ikkyu was one of the most important figures of Japanese Zen Buddhism. The sketchiness of the rendition has an immediacy that suggests it was painted from life, a notion that is supported by the inscription on the painting.

Several masterpieces by the greatest proponent of the *suibokuga* tradition, Sesshu, are housed in the National Museum. Considered the successor to Shubun in the Japanese ink-painting tradition, Sesshu was also a priest, as was his predecessor, at the Shokokuji in Kyoto. He traveled in 1467 to China, where he was able to experience at first hand the landscape that had inspired the great Chinese painters.

A vigorous, dynamic line, deeply indebted to Hsia Kuei, characterizes his work. His mastery of *suibokuga* was such that it was said that his blacks could suggest five colors. His virtuosity is clearly evident in the museum's famous *Landscape* dated 1496. This work contains inscriptions by Sesshu and six priests. In his inscription, Sesshu stated that he learned the *haboku* ("broken ink") technique he employed here from Chang Yu-sheng and Li Tsai.

A series of hanging scrolls depicting the four seasons, which like the 1496 *Landscape* is designated a National Treasure, clearly shows an indebtedness to Li Tsai. This series, in fact, dates from the period of Sesshu's sojourn in China, 1467 to 1469. Also in the collection are two famous hanging scrolls depicting autumn and winter from what must have originally been a set of the four seasons. These scrolls represent Sesshu in his maturity. Another outstanding work of the *suibokuga* tradition is a magnificent pair of hanging scrolls of hawks in a pine tree by the painter Sesson Shukei, who claimed descent from Sesshu.

Although the monochrome-ink-painting tradition dominated painting during the Muromachi period, the *yamato-e* tradition survived through the work of the Tosa school, founded by Tosa Mitsunobu (1434–1525). The museum houses a 1487 dated handscroll, registered as an Important Cultural Property, by Tosa Mitsunobu titled the *Chronicle of the Seiko-ji*, a temple constructed in Kyoto in 1230 by Taira Sukechika in memory of his mother. Other important works from this school in the museum's collection are a pair of six-fold screens depicting pine trees on a beach and a six-panel screen of moonlight landscape that has been tentatively attributed to Tosa Mitsuyoshi.

The museum also has a rare portrait of Momonoi Naonori attributed to Tosa Mitsunobu. Although portraits survive of priests and statesmen from this time, few portraits depicting men of the arts have survived. Momonoi Naonori is credited with the introduction of *Sachawaka-mai*, a form of dramatic presentation of war stories and literary romances.

A period of flamboyant historical personalities, the Momoyama period (1573–1603), is noted for the sumptuous extravagance of its arts. The painting of this period is dominated by the artists of the Kano school. The Kano school was founded during the Muromachi period by Kano Masanobu. Under his son Kano Motonobu, the ink-monochrome style became mixed with elements borrowed from the *yamato-e* tradition, thus establishing the visual personality of the school.

The Kano school is well represented in the museum's collection beginning with a painting dated 1509 by Kano Motonobu of *Zen Master Hsiang-yen Attaining Enlightenment*. Originally painted on the *fusuma* in the abbot's quarters of the Daisen-in, a subtemple of the Daitokuji in Kyoto, the painting was later remounted as a hanging scroll.

The greatest Kano school artist of the Momoyama period was Kano Eitoku, who enjoyed the patronage of the great feudal lords Oda Nobunaga and Toyotomi Hideyoshi. The flamboyance and sweep of his style perfectly suited these dynamic individuals.

The National Museum's collection includes several works associated with Kano Eitoku: a magnificent pair of eight-fold screens depicting Japanese cypress trees; a preliminary drawing of a design for a lacquer saddle; and a pair of hanging scrolls depicting Chao fu and Hsu-yu, the legendary Chinese hermit-sages.

The pair of screens, depicting the cypress trees, exemplifies the so-called *kimpeki* style of painting, a highly decorative style calling for the use of vibrant colors and gold leaf. The boldness of the composition and sumptuousness of the colors on the gold leaf epitomize the ostentation favored during the Momoyama period.

Noteworthy paintings by other Kano school artists include the mid-sixteenth-century *Maple Viewers at Takao* by Kano Hideyori; an early-seventeenth-century pair of four-fold screens, the *Battle of the Carriages*, by Kano Sanraku; a pair of six-fold screens, *Merrymaking under the Cherry Blossoms*, by Kano Naganobu, a National Treasure; a pair of hanging scrolls, one depicting mynah birds and gardenias, and the other, small birds and a plum tree, by Kano Shoei; and a pair of six-fold screens, the *Eight Scenes of the Xiao and Xiang*, by Kano Naonobu.

Maple Viewers at Takao by Kano Hideyori depicts a celebrated scenic spot on the outskirts of Kyoto known for its maple trees. It stands as a landmark work in the development of Japanese genre painting. The pair of screens, *Merrymaking under the Cherry Blossoms*, is the only surviving work by Kano Naganobu, a younger brother of Kano Eitoku.

The design of a sumptuously decorated pair of six-fold screens dating from the late sixteenth century had been attributed to Kano Eitoku. Depicted on these screens is a moonlight scene of a waterwheel and bridge with willow trees—a popular subject traditionally associated with the famous bridge at Uji. A number of versions of this subject exist, but only a version in the Kyoto National Museum (q.v.) rivals the Tokyo screens.

One of the greatest paintings of the period is a pair of six-fold screens of a pine forest by Hasegawa Tohaku, a Kano school rival, who traced his artistic lineage to Sesshu. The ink-monochrome-painting tradition that began with the painters of the Sung and Yüan dynasties is reworked here in the Momoyama vernacular of bold compositional accents. There is also a pair of six-fold screens attributed to Tohaku that pictures samurai endeavoring to capture wild horses, which recalls the *yamato-e* style.

The museum also has one of the most important paintings attributed to the Momoyama master Kaiho Yusho. A six-fold screen dated 1602 of a landscape was originally executed for the Katsura Palace in Kyoto.

The strongly decorative tendencies of the Edo period were exemplified in the work of the four leading masters of this age: Koetsu, Sotatsu, Korin, and Kenzan. These artists did not confine themselves to one medium, and the museum has examples of work by this quartet that display their remarkable virtuosity in different media.

The painting collection includes a *kakemono*, or hanging scroll, depicting the lotus cycle in gold and silver on paper, executed jointly by Tawaraya Sotatsu, who painted the lotuses, and Honami Koetsu, who did the calligraphy. Works attributed to Korin include a pair of two-paneled screens, *The Gods of Wind and Thunder*, a subject popularized by Sotatsu, and a hanging scroll, the *Yatsuhashi* scene from the *Ise Monogatari*.

The Sotatsu-Korin school survived until the nineteenth century. The last great practitioner was Sakai Hoitsu, whose pair of screens *Autumn Wind and Summer Rain* in the National Museum represent the last masterpiece of this tradition of decorative painting.

Other outstanding examples of Edo period painting in the collection include a pair of sumptuously decorated six-fold screens of about 1650, *Flowering Plants of Autumn* by Tawaraya Sosetsu, the immediate successor of Sotatsu; a pair of hanging scrolls, *Apes, Deer, and Pines*, by Mori Sosen, a painter celebrated for his depictions of the Japanese monkey; a pair of six-fold screens, *Scholars Riding and Walking in the Country*, ascribed to Yosa Buson; a pair of six-fold screens depicting a landscape by Ike no Taiga, which is classified as a National Treasure.

Japanese painting was not immune to the influence of the European art that filtered into Japan from the time of the first European visitors in the mid-sixteenth century. An example of Japanese painting executed in the "European manner" is a six-fold screen, *A True View of Mt. Asama*, of about 1790 by Aodo Denzen, whose adopted name Aodo means "Hall of Asia and Europe." This work is considered one of the greatest Japanese paintings in the Western style executed before the Meiji period. Another fine example of the European style is the portrait of Takami Senseki by Watanabe Kazan (1793–1841). Classified as a National Treasure, this hanging scroll is a sensitively observed portrait that strongly evokes the sitter's personality.

The revival of the Tosa school during the Edo period is credited to Tosa Mitsuoki. He is represented in the museum's collection by a pair of hanging scrolls illustrating poems of the twelve months and the painting *Quails and Chrysanthemums*.

The Edo period is noted for the rise and development of the *ukiyo-e* style. An early masterpiece of this school is a handscroll of about 1720 with scenes of popular entertainment, ascribed to Miyagawa Choshun. Here the "floating world" of entertainers and courtesans is exuberantly celebrated in unabashed detail in reaction to the "Chinese" qualities of the Kano school.

730   Japan

Two *ukiyo-e* paintings, one of a woman and the other *Preparations for the Kabuki*, are associated with Hishikawa Moronobu, considered the originator of the *ukiyo-e* print. The latter work is a pair of screens, which has been attributed to the artist on stylistic grounds.

The museum also has a large collection of prints, which contains representative examples by the most important printmakers of the period, including Suzuki Harunobu, credited with the technique of full-color printing known as *nishiki-e*, and Torii Kiyonaga, Toshusai Sharaku, Kitagawa Utamaro, Katsushika Hokusai, and Ando Hiroshige. Among its series of prints are the famous series *Ten Physiognomic Types of Women* by Utamaro, *Fifty-three Stages on the Tokaido Highway* by Ando Hiroshige, and *Thirty-six Views of Mt. Fuji* by Hokusai, completed between 1829 and 1831.

Of the museum's collection of modern painting, one of the finest is a series of eight hanging scrolls, the *Eight Sights of Omi*, by Imamura Shiko (1880–1916), modeled after the popular subject of classical Chinese painting, *Eight Sights of the Xiao and Xiang*. Another important modern work is a 1915 dated pair of six-fold screens by Shimomura Kanzan titled *Yoroboshi* after a popular Nō play.

The National Museum has an outstanding collection of calligraphy, which is regarded as an important art form by the Japanese. Outstanding among the examples of Nara period calligraphy is a fragment of the *Kengu-kyo Sutra*, which is traditionally attributed to Emperor Shomu (701–756). Because of its association with Shomu and its style of execution, this famous work is popularly known as *Ojomu*. Designated a National Treasure, *Ojomu* is on a special paper called *dabi-shi*, which is a mixture of pulp and incense wood powder that is used to prevent worm damage.

The National Museum is particularly rich in examples from the Heian period, a golden age of Japanese art and culture, when a purely Japanese style of calligraphy was attained and a distinctly indigenous style of painting was also developing. One outstanding example of Heian calligraphy is the chapter of *Hoben-bon* from the *Hoke-kyo Sutra* known as *Chikubushima-gyo*, written on paper decorated with patterns of birds, butterflies, and flowering plants. Other portions of this National Treasure are preserved in the Hogon-ji Temple at Chikubushima.

Another National Treasure is a document titled *Enchin Shingu Chokuksha* by Ono Michikaze, who with Fujiwara No Sukemasa and Fujiwara No Yukinari comprises the *Sanseki*, or Triumvirate, of Heian calligraphy. Dated 927, this manuscript has both historic and artistic value. Also attributed to Ono Michikaze is a work known as *Akihagi Jo*, which is designated a National Treasure. The *Tsugi Shikishi* is traditionally attributed to Ono Michikaze, but it is most likely a later work of the second half of the eleventh century.

A manuscript of poems by the T'ang poet Pai Lo-t'ien by Fujiwara Yukinari is dated 1018 and classified as a National Treasure. An example of calligraphy known as *Masu Shikishi* has also been attributed to Fujiwara Yukinari, but it is probably slightly later.

Yet another National Treasure from the Heian period is the eleventh-century *Gunsho Chujo*. This manuscript represents the earliest surviving transcription of an anthology that was originally edited by the scholar-courtier Wei Cheng and other scholars at the order of the Emperor T'ai Tsung (reigned 626–649). Included in this work are excerpts from Confucian scriptures, historical works, and philosophical treatises by, among others, Lao Tzu and Chuang Tzu. The original work is lost and is preserved only in later transcriptions found in Japan, where they were used as a basis for lectures in the Imperial Palace. This particular set, which is incomplete, was handed down in the Kujo family, one of the five families, collectively known as the Go Sekke, who served as advisors to the emperor.

An interesting development of the Heian period was the writing of sutras, particularly the *Lotus Sutra*, on fans over paintings. The National Museum has a celebrated example of this type of representation of the *Lotus Sutra*, which is designated a National Treasure.

A noteworthy example of later calligraphy in the collection is a manuscript of the Heian text *Sanjurokkasen* (*Poems of the Thirty-six Poets*) by Shokado Shojo, one of the "Three Great Brushes" of the early seventeenth century along with Koetsu and Konoe Nobutada. The museum also has a version of the same work by Konoe Nobutada, which is also on sumptuous paper decorated with gold and silver. Besides being renowned for his calligraphy, Konoe Nobutada also rose to prominence as an advisor to the emperor. Another example of his calligraphy is a book consisting of extracts from the *Genji Monogatari*.

Most of the museum's collection of Japanese sculpture consists of examples from the Asuka, Nara, Kamakura, and Muromachi periods. Also on display in the museum are many pieces on long-term loan from temples.

The introduction of Buddhism from the mainland to Japan in 552 inspired a new era of artistic expression in Japan centered in the Kyoto-Nara region. The heart of the museum's holdings from the Asuka (552–645) and Nara periods (710–794) is a group of works that were once housed in the Hōryūji, one of the oldest and most important Buddhist temple complexes in Japan.

One of the finest and perhaps most important early sculptures is a bronze gold-plated *Miroku Bosatsu* that bears an inscription that dates the work, depending on the reading, from either 606 or 666. Elegant and slender, the figure is seated in a characteristic meditative pose with the head resting pensively on an upraised hand and the right leg bent across the left knee.

Also dating from this period is an unusual bronze of a seated Bodhisattva executed in the style of the Tori school, the official style of the Suiko reign. Unlike the typical pensive pose seen in the Miroku Bosatsu, the right arm is raised here with an open palm in the *abhaya mudra*, or "fear not," gesture.

Now in the National Museum is a group of thirty-one Gigaku masks dating from the late Asuka period that was presented by the Hōryūji to the Imperial Household in 1876. Carved of camphor wood with remnants of original color still found on them, these masks were used for sacred and profane dances in monasteries and courts. Copied from Chinese models, these masks portray a range of characters including men, women, birds, and divinities with exaggerated and grotesque features.

Also once a possession of the Hōryūji is a famous group of forty-eight gilt-bronze figures. It has been asserted that some of the images of this group are of Korean origin although several reflect the Tori school style. Of these figures, most noteworthy is a charming group of the Buddha's mother and her attendants. These figures are caught in graceful dancelike poses in the depiction of the birth of the Buddha. The tiny figure of the infant Buddha seen emerging from his mother's sleeve suggests the moment of his birth in the Lumbini Grove on the outskirts of Kapilavastu.

An exquisite gold-plated copper plate repoussé of an Amida triad was also originally in the Hōryūji. Many examples of this technique from the second half of the seventh century and eighth century survive, but the National Museum's Amida triad represents the finest extant example of this type of relief.

Another important early work is a gilt-bronze image of Juichimen Kannon (Eleven-headed Kannon), which was excavated at Nachi. With the introduction of Buddhism, the worship of the Bodhisattva Kannon began to grow in popularity and influence. One of the most important early forms of the depiction of the Kannon was the Eleven-headed or Juichimen type, and this image represents one of the earliest surviving examples.

Classified as an Important Cultural Property is an eighth-century dry-lacquer Nikko Bosatsu, which was originally one of two attendant figures to a seated Shaka Nyorai of the Kozanji in Kyoto.

From the Heian period is an eleventh-century wood sculpture of a Fudo Myoo, one of the major deities of the Shingon (True Word) sect of Esoteric Buddhism. This popular divinity was widely depicted in the painting and sculpture of this period. Designated an Important Cultural Property, this sculpture was probably originally painted blue and has the standard ferocious features of the Fudo Myoo meant to intimidate all earthly evils.

Outstanding among the Kamakura works is the magnificent portrait of the formidable Minamoto no Yoritomo, the founder of the Kamakura period. Classified as a National Treasure, this work is made by what is known as the *yosigi* technique in which blocks of wood are joined together. This technique enabled the Kamakura sculptor to convey the heightened realism that characterizes the work of this period. With the quest for realism, crystal eyeballs were used to enhance the naturalistic effect.

An example of a type of figure popular during the Kamakura period is a Divine Guardian carved of cypress wood instead of the usual sandalwood. As is characteristic of this type of figure, the visual emphasis is to express an image of power and dynamism. The musculature of the torso is prominently and sugges-

tively defined, if not anatomically accurately, and the guardian is posed un-
sheathing his sword ready to strike into action.

Also included in the museum's sculpture collection is a fine collection of Nō
and Kyogen masks. A Muromachi period Ko-omote, a mask representing an
innocent young girl, is one of the finest examples of this type.

The museum's collection of metalwork includes coins, utensils, temple ornaments, furniture, ritual objects, and bronze mirrors dating from the Yayoi
period (c. 300 B.C.-A.D. 300). Several outstanding items of early metalwork
from the Kofun period (A.D. 300–600) survive: a gold-plated bronze helmet, a
bronze mirror decorated with a hunting scene from Gumma-ken, and a gold-
plated bronze pair of bit ornaments from Shizuoka-ken.

Not only did the fine arts flourish during the Asuka period, crafts also reflected
the new aesthetic awakening inspired by the introduction of Buddhism to Japan.
Two of the finest examples of metalwork surviving from the Asuka period in
the collection are a gilt-bronze standard, or *ban*, decorated with apsaras, or
celestial nymphs, designated a National Treasure, and a slightly later gilt-bronze
banner, which was included in a 737 dated inventory of the Hōryūji treasury.
Other examples of metalware from the Asuka and Nara periods in the collection
include a group of Buddhist ritual implements. Of them, perhaps most noteworthy
is a brass censer dated in the Asuka period. Once in the Hōryūji, this censer
has a long handle in the shape of a bird's tail and is the oldest-known example
of this type.

Several Heian period objects are worth citing. Classified as an Important
Cultural Property is a gilt-bronze *nyoi* (priest's baton), which was allegedly used
by the priest Gyoshin. It is dated from the first half of the tenth century. An
outstanding example of furniture is a gilt-bronze *kongo-ban*, a small table used
for Buddhist ritual implements. Ritual objects from this period are also found
in the collection, including a gilt-bronze *goko-rei*, or Buddhist ritual bell, with
a five-pronged handle.

One of the effects of the growing popularity of the tea ceremony during the
Muromachi period was the production of implements for use during the ceremony. The museum owns one of the most famous tea kettles of the period, an
iron tea kettle of the *shinnai-gana* type that features ring-shaped handles in the
form of monster heads. The surface is decorated in relief with five small horses
set against a hilly landscape. An important later tea ceremony kettle of the
Momoyama period is a kettle that is attributed to the famous kettle maker Yojiro.
Decorated by a chrysanthemum and kiri crest in relief, this kettle is thought to
have been owned by Hideyoshi.

Designated an Important Cultural Property is a Muromachi period bronze
lantern with an open-work design of plum trees and bamboo. This type of lantern
was usually hung in the eaves of Shinto shrines or Buddhist halls to offer light
to the deities. The octagonal-shaped roof bears an inscription, which states that
it was donated to the Aizen-do of the Chiba-dera in Chiba in 1550.

The museum has an extensive collection of mirrors. One of the finest mirrors in the collection is a superb Momoyama period mirror said to have been used by Emperor Goyozei. An incised inscription gives the artist's name Ao Ietsugu and the date 1588. The mirror is decorated with a tortoise, symbolic of longevity, in the center and a circular pattern of paulownia leaves, flowers, and bamboo around the perimeter. Dated slightly later is a fine bronze *ekagami*, a mirror with a handle that is decorated with a picture of a raft under a barren willow. This seventeenth-century mirror is attributed to Itani Hoju.

The museum has an outstanding collection of lacquer that contains a wide variety of objects: musical instruments, furniture, games, ritual objects, burners, architectural models, ship models, carriages, cosmetic boxes, and writing utensils. With the heightened aesthetic sensibilities and demand for luxurious items during the Heian period, the craft of lacquer attained a remarkable degree of technical and aesthetic sophistication toward the latter part of the period. It was during this time that the *maki-e* technique in which powdered gold and silver are applied onto still tacky lacquer to form designs became popular.

Considered one of the greatest examples of Japanese lacquer ware is a late Heian cosmetic box, which is the earliest-known cosmetic box. Designated a National Treasure, this exquisite box features a design of wheels in water. The wheels are encrusted with mother-of-pearl and inlaid with thin gold leaf on lacquer dusted with gold. The interior of the box features designs of flowers, birds, and butterflies executed in *maki-e* with gold and silver dust.

Other fine examples of Heian lacquer include a box for a priest's robe ornamented with a design of Horai, the island of the Taoist immortals; a *kara-bitsu* (box on legs), classified as a National Treasure, with a design of rounded phoenixes and mother-of-pearl inlay from the Hōryūji treasury; and a saddle with mother-of-pearl inlay.

Lacquer technique also made great advances during the Muromachi period. The museum owns a *suzuribako* (writing box) that once belonged to Shogun Ashikaga Yoshimasa. Considered one of the finest examples of Muromachi lacquer ware, the box is decorated with a depiction of a moonlit landscape executed in a style similar to contemporary painting.

The lavish taste prevailing during the Momoyama period is reflected in contemporary lacquer. An elegant example of Momoyama lacquer is a magnificent saddle of black lacquer with stylized gilt leaves, said to have been designed by Kano Eitoku. This saddle belonged to Hideyoshi.

One of the masterpieces of the early seventeenth century is a writing box by Honami Koetsu, who sought to equal the standards set by Heian period lacquer ware. The decoration of the box was inspired by a poem about the Suro boat bridge. The bridge, depicted by a fine lead plate, is placed diagonally over a row of boats represented in dull gold.

Another fine lacquer piece is an Edo period inkstone box by Ogata Korin. The design of the box is based on a section of the *Tales of Ise* that deals with the *Yatsuhashi*, a famous bridge in Mikawa (Aichi) Prefecture. The bridge is depicted in lead with the supporting posts in silver. The irises, associated with the bridge, are in inlaid shell with the stalks of iris in *maki-e*. There are also examples of work by some of the most famous lacquer craftsmen of the Edo period including the Kajikawa family, a family of lacquerers retained by the Edo shoguns, and the Shibayama family.

The museum houses a large and comprehensive collection of Japanese ceramics, featuring work representing the major types. An important Nara period work is a vase with a type of glaze called *sansai* (three colors) that originated in the west and traveled east across Asia by way of Iran. This vase, which contained cremated ashes, was excavated in 1907 from a tomb in Ibaraki. There are examples of raku ware by Koetsu, whose raku ware represents the culmination of this type of ceramic.

The museum has a group of work, representing the collaborative efforts of the brothers Ogata Kenzan and Ogata Korin. There is a square dish of Kyoto ware fashioned by Kenzan with a depiction by Korin in a loose brushwork style of the poet Huang Shan-ku viewing sea gulls in flight. Other joint productions by this illustrious team include two raku ware cake dishes by Kenzan with, respectively, a painting by Korin of Jurojin and a painting by Korin of a breaking wave and seabirds.

An outstanding Edo period example of Kyoto ware is a vase with an overglaze of enamels of the so-called *ommoyaki* type, precious porcelain pottery enameled in white or ivory, by Nonomura Ninsei, one of the most admired ceramic artists of the Edo period. The vase is exquisitely decorated with prunus flowers and branches among golden clouds.

The textile department has an extensive collection of Japanese private and ceremonial clothes, accessories, decorative materials, and dolls. Two early works, dating from the Asuka and Nara periods, are among the most valuable works of art in the museum's entire collection. Regarded as a National Treasure, a seventh-century silk banner woven in the *tatagasuri* or *ikat* method is one of the oldest preserved examples of Japanese textiles. This banner was included in a group of gifts presented to the imperial household from the Hōryūji during the early part of the Meiji era. Dated from the Nara period is a beautiful brocade once preserved in the Shosoin repository of the Todaiji monastery. This famous brocade of nine shades of thread woven in a floral pattern on a sapphire blue base has traditionally been identified as the cover of a lute since a large fragment is cut in that shape.

Especially noteworthy is the collection of Momoyama and Edo period Nō robes. Outstanding items are a sixteenth-century robe of the *nui-haku* type with an embroidered design and gold-leaf imprint of birds and chrysanthemums within bands of different colors, a sixteenth-century robe of the *suri-haku* type with a design of grapes in gold-leaf imprint, and a white silk robe of the *kata-suso* style with the design of flowering plants depicted on the shoulders and lower edge of the skirt alone.

One of the museum's most prized textiles is a silk kimono of the *nui-haku* type, a kimono that was used by actors playing women's parts in Nō theater.

Embroidered with silk and gold threads, the kimono is decorated with large red and white rectangles within which are depicted foliage, flowers, and little bridges. The museum also has a fine *kosode* designed by Korin. The design is of autumn flowers and grasses.

A significant addition to the textile department was the purchase of the collection of Nomura Shojiro in 1972. The collection includes some one hundred screens of rare textile fragments, including *kosode* once owned by Lady Tokugawa Iyetsuna and the princess of Emperor Gomijuno.

The museum houses an impressive collection of swords, armor, and sword guards, or *tsuba*. One of the most valued items, classified as a National Treasure, is a rare sword mounting of the *hyogo-gugari* type with a blade of the school of Ichimonji. This type of mounting, featuring chains hanging from a girdle, was particularly fashionable during the late Heian period.

The Kamakura period was noted for the great strides made in swordmaking and armor-manufacturing techniques. During this period, the *maki-e* technique was often applied to adorn sword sheaths as in the famous sword of the museum's collection known as "Uesugi-no-tachi." Two other valued swords in the collection are a thirteenth-century sword of the *tachi* type known as "Daihannya Nagamitsu" and a thirteenth-century sword of the *tanto* (short sword) type known as "Atsushi Toshiro" by Yoshimitsu.

Tsuba or sword guards were used as a balance between the blade and the handle and as a protection for the hand. Now they are appreciated for their aesthetic qualities as well. Of the museum's extensive collection of sword guards, perhaps one of the most famous is a mid-sixteenth-century sword guard made of iron with a design of three commas, which has been registered as an Important Cultural Property. The sword guard is inscribed with the maker's name, Nobuie, from the province of Owari, where a renowned tradition of open-work sword guards was established from the middle of the Muromachi period. This *tsuba* was handed down through generations of the daimyo household of Kuroda.

One of the most unusual examples is a sixteenth-century *tsuba* with a *kirishitan* (Christian) design by the noted sword-guard maker Nobuie. The perforated design of the sword guard features stylized symbols, one of which has been identified as a cross. Another noteworthy *tsuba* is attributed to the craftsman Hoan. Dated from the early sixteenth century, this *tsuba* features an open-work design of a wheel.

The National Museum also has an outstanding collection of Chinese art, which encompasses paintings, sculpture, bronzes, calligraphy, and ceramic ware. Among the earliest Chinese works in the museum's collection are some fine jade pendants and ritual objects from the Shang-Chou period in the shapes of beasts, insects, birds, and fish, a good luck symbol of fertility.

Noteworthy examples of the sculpture holdings are a Northern Ch'i Dynasty standing Bodhisattva, a limestone standing Bodhisattva of the Sui Dynasty, and a T'ang seated Bodhisattva from T'ien-lung Shan. Special mention should be made of an Eastern Han Dynasty limestone relief from about the second century.

This relief is from the famous Wu family funerary chambers, built 147–168 near Shantung. Tomb reliefs from this period typically depict historical scenes, myths, legends, hunting scenes, and scenes of daily life. The museum's relief features a kitchen scene.

Also outstanding is a Northern Wei Buddha head found in the cave temples of Yun-kang. The To-pa nomads of Central Asia, who founded the Wei Dynasty, constructed the Yun-kang temples near Loyang. Consequently, early sculpture from this site reveals a close stylistic and iconographic affinity to Indian and Central Asian sculpture. Later work, however, like this Buddha head, shows a greater assimilation of Chinese stylistic features.

Dated from the T'ang Dynasty is a lacquer-covered wood reliquary found in Kusha, a caravan center of the Silk Route. In the shape of a stupa, the reliquary is decorated in Central Asian style with geometric designs, figurative scenes, and fantastic creatures. The reliquary was excavated in the early twentieth century by the Otani expedition to Central Asia.

There are several fine early examples of Chinese metalware, although the collection of bronzes is generally weak. An exceptional bronze, however, is a magnificent *yu* from the Shang Yin period (1300–1027 B.C.). Other fine examples of bronzes include a *chung* (bell) dated from the fifth century B.C., decorated with fantastic animal forms, and a Han Dynasty bronze *lien*, a circular receptacle that was probably used to hold toilet articles, whose lid is in the form of the sacred Taoist mountain Po-sha.

Probably a Chinese work is a superb mirror that was presented to the Hōryūji in 736 by Empress Komai in commemoration of Prince Shotoku's death. Made with the *cire perdue*, or lost-wax, technique, the mirror is decorated with the Taoist subject of the Islands of the Blessed, where one is able to find the elixir of immortality.

Another magnificent example of what is probably a Chinese production is a gilt-silver pitcher dated from the seventh century. Registered as a National Treasure, the pitcher is incised with a depiction of a winged horse, an image rarely portrayed in the pictorial arts of East Asia. The mouth and lid of this splendid object is in the form of the head of a Chinese dragon. An inscription reveals that the work was first donated to the Hisoji, one of the oldest Buddhist temples in Japan. Eventually, the pitcher was deposited in the Hōryūji Collection.

The painting collection largely reflects the Japanese taste for Southern Sung academic painting, which was a major influence on the development of Japanese painting during the late Kamakura period and Muromachi period. There are two rare examples of eighth-century painting, which reflect the prodigious multi-cultural blending of Central Asia. A painting on paper from Turfan depicts two figures standing under a tree. Slightly later in date is a depiction of the Bodhisattva Ksitigarbha on a silk banner, which was found by Paul Pelliot at Tun-huang in 1908. Assigned a slightly later date is a series of Lohans arguably attributed to Kuan-hsiu (832–912).

The strength of the collection is the Sung and Yüan Dynasty paintings. Dated from the Northern Sung or Five Dynasties period, a pair of *kakemonos*, or hanging scrolls, of Zen patriarchs is associated with the untrammeled, or *p'o mo*, style of Shih-K'o. This pair of scrolls is registered as an Important Cultural Property.

One of the Sung artists most admired by the Japanese was the thirteenth-century master Liang K'ai, whose spare, spontaneous style was especially influential in the development of the Japanese monochrome-ink-paintng tradition. Although an honored member of the Academy in Hangchow, Liang K'ai disdained official honors and is said to have left the Academy to settle in a Ch'an monastery. The works attributed to him in the museum's collection include an idealized portrait of the poet Li Po, a snowy landscape, a hanging scroll titled *Shakyamuni Descending from a Mountain Retreat*, and a painting of the Sixth Ch'an patriarch Hui-neng cutting bamboo.

Another important artist of the Sung period was Ma Yuan, who was instrumental in the establishment of the Ma-Hsia school of landscape painting. Classified as a National Treasure is the National Museum's famous *Solitary Angler on a Lake*.

The Sung Dynasty is also noted for the highly refined bird-and-flower paintings espoused by the Academy of Emperor Hui-tsung. An important work in the collection by a later follower of the school Li Ti is an album leaf dated 1197 depicting two hibiscus flowers.

Two paintings in the collection have been associated with Li Kung-lin or, as he is better known, Li Lung-mien (1046–1106). A major painter, Li Lung-mien was noted for his fine line style known as *pai miao*, which is seen in the National Museum's *Vimalakirti*. The second painting attributed to him is the scroll *Imaginary Voyage into the Hsiao Hsiang Region*, which has been designated a National Treasure.

A Chinese artist primarily known through his work in Japanese collections, Yen Hui was a specialist of religious figures such as monks, ascetics, and demons. A pair of hanging scrolls, depicting the Taoist genii Han-shan and Shih-te, in the collection demonstrates the dramatic characterizations and forceful line that appealed to the Japanese taste. This famous pair is registered as a National Treasure.

An important work in the development of Zen Buddhist iconography is a hanging scroll depicting a seated Daruma. This painting, classified as an Important Cultural Property, is ascribed to the priest-painter I-shan I-ning (1247–1317), who went to Japan in 1299 and was a major influence in the literary culture of Zen.

The museum houses several outstanding works, some of them registered National Treasures, by the Ming masters Li Tsai, Chu Tuan, Lu Chi, Wen Po-jen, and Tung Ch'i-chang. Registered as a National Treasure, a mountain landscape scene by Li Tsai from an album of landscapes dated from the mid-fifteenth century is closely related to the *Four Seasons* scrolls by Sesshu also in the National Museum's collection. A member of the court of Hsuan-te (1426–1455),

Li Tsai was a follower of the Che school, which carried on the tradition of landscape painting established in the Southern Sung Academy by Ma Yuan and Hsia Kuei.

A winter landscape by Chu Tuan dated from the first half of the sixteenth century also recalls the work of Ma Yuan, evoking memories of the National Museum's *Solitary Angler on a Lake*. Like the Ma Yuan work, this hanging scroll is registered as a National Treasure.

The sixteenth-century painter Lu Chi was renowned for his bird-and-flower paintings. The museum owns a series of four paintings depicting the birds and flowers of the four seasons that are attributed to him. Classified as a National Treasure, these paintings recall the work of the Hui-tsung Academy with their delicate execution and use of lightly contrasting pigments.

Dated 1551 is a famous series of four hanging scrolls of the four seasons by Wen Po-jen, a nephew and pupil of Wen Cheng-ming. All four paintings have inscriptions by Tung Ch'i-chang, the noted critic and artist, as well as the artist's signature. Tung Ch'i-chang's inscription on the painting depicting autumn suggests that it was based on a work by Chao Meng-fu.

A true "Renaissance man," Tung Ch'i-chang was one of the most imposing intellectual figures of his day whose writings on Chinese painting continue to influence scholarship long after his death. The National Museum owns an important album ascribed to him that contains six landscapes and ten examples of calligraphy.

Among later Chinese paintng in the collection, noteworthy is *Autumn Journey*, a handscroll dated 1657 by Hsiao Yun-ts'ung, the founder of the school of Anhui, and a fine late example of bamboo painting by Cheng Hsieh dated 1753.

The museum also has a collection of Chinese calligraphy. Foremost of its collection is a work by Feng Tzu-chen, one of the four great calligraphers of the Sung Dynasty. Dated from the first half of the fourteenth century, this National Treasure is an example of the free, varied movements of *ts'ao shu*, or the "grass-writing" style.

The museum has a fine collection of Chinese ceramics ranging in date from Neolithic times to the Ch'ing Dynasty. Dating from the Neolithic era is an earthenware vase with a painted decoration of spirals. The vase was excavated in the Yang-Shao region of Kansu province.

Of the collection of T'ang ceramics, outstanding examples include several works in the popular three-color glaze of that period: a large dish with a lotus leaf design; a *ming-ch'i*, or funerary figure, of a civil official; and a vase with dragon handles that was once in the Yokogawa Collection.

The museum has two outstanding examples of the Persian and Central Asian-influenced blue-and-white style of ceramic ware that first took hold in China toward the end of the Yüan Dynasty. Classified as National Treasures are a Yüan Dynasty vase, depicting a fish wiggling through algae, and a Ming Dynasty dish. Considered one of the finest examples of Ming ceramic ware, the dish is decorated with a lotus plant, symbolizing purity and prosperity, in the center of the plate. The central image is surrounded with a lotus frieze, and the outer edge of the dish is decorated with wavelike acanthus leaves.

The museum's holdings of ceramics were greatly enhanced by the acquisition of the Yokogawa Collection and the Hirota Collection. Noteworthy of the Yokogawa Collection is a *tzu-chou* ewer with a clear-cut floral pattern covered with a transparent glaze and the aforementioned T'ang Dynasty vase with dragon handles. Besides having Chinese ceramics, the Hirota Collection of 496 pieces includes Chinese lacquer, stationery, and calligraphy, as well as Japanese calligraphy and Korean tea bowls. The Chinese ceramics, which comprise most of the collection, has pieces dating from the Han to the Ch'ing Dynasty and is particularly rich in Ming enamel ware. One of the most outstanding pieces is an early Ming jar with a lid that is one of the finest and most well-preserved pieces of this type anywhere.

The collection of textiles includes two rare early samples: a sixth–seventh-century fragment of figured silk with beasts, birds, and a floral design that was excavated in Turfan and a seventh-century fragment of figured silk with a "biting lion" design.

Of the collection of Chinese lacquer, special mention should be made of a sixteenth-century lacquer-covered cinnabar tray carved with a design of lotuses and a Ming Dynasty covered box ornamented with a depiction of a pavilion in a landscape in gold lacquer and mother-of-pearl inlay.

The museum's collection of Korean art includes some outstanding works. One early work is an exquisite bronze scroll holder that was excavated by Japanese archaeologists in 1913 from a Lo-lang period tomb in South P'yongnan Province in Korea. The scroll is decorated with an intricately detailed mountainous landscape that features bears, peacocks, deer, birds, and tigers. Registered as a National Treasure, a gilt-bronze head ornament dated from the fourth-sixth century is thought to be a Korean production.

Korean celadon was greatly admired throughout East Asia and some of the most beautiful examples of this technique are in Japanese collections. The museum has an outstandng Koryŏ period (935–1392) box with an open-work design of peony scrolls. Also noteworthy is a beautiful twelfth–thirteenth-century vase decorated with a landscape of water birds, insects, bamboo trees, and plum trees. An outstanding example of Korean lacquer is a fourteenth-century Koryŏ period sutra box with mother-of-pearl inlay.

The library of the Tokyo National Museum is for staff use only. However a photo archive and research center may be used by visiting scholars with appointments. Photographs and slides may be purchased from this center. Museum catalogs and postcards are available in the bookstore.

Selected Bibliography

Tokyo Kokuritsu Hakubutsukan Shuzohin Mokuroku (*Catalogue of the Tokyo National Museum Collections*), 3 vols. (Tokyo 1957); *Tokyo Kokuritsu Hakubutsukan Meihin*

Hyakusen (*One Hundred Masterpieces of the Tokyo National Museum*) (Tokyo 1959); *Tokyo Kokuritsu Hakubutsukan* (*The Tokyo National Museum*), 3 vols. (Tokyo 1966); *Tokyo Kokuritsu Hakubutsukan Kiyo* (*Proceedings of the Tokyo National Museum*), vol. 1 (Tokyo 1965); *Museum, Art Magazine*, edited by the Tokyo National Museum.

MARSHA TAJIMA

Korea

―――― **Seoul** ――――

NATIONAL MUSEUM OF KOREA IN SEOUL , 1, Sejongno, Chongnogu, Seoul, Korea.

The National Museum of Korea in Seoul officially opened on December 3, 1945. Its collection at present consists of art objects formerly in the custody of the Yi Royal Household Museum established in 1908 and archaeological relics and works of art selected through nationwide surveys by the Museum of the Government-General of Choson, as well as later donations, acquisitions, objects from excavations, and art objects returned from Japan after the normalization of relations with that country.

The National Museum of Korea in Seoul is the central body of a network of museum branches, composed of Kyongju National Museum, Kwangju National Museum, Puyo National Museum, Kongju National Museum, and the National Folklore Museum in Seoul. The Chinju National Museum was completed and added to the network of the national museums in 1985. The director-general of the National Museum of Korea in Seoul supervises all of the branches as well. Under the director-general are a chief curator, the Department of Fine Art, the Department of Archaeology, Registrar's Office, Conservation Laboratory, Library, International Programme Coordinator's Office, Museum Construction Bureau, and the Administrative Bureau, which includes the Cultural Exchange and Education Division. The five national museums are similarly organized, with the exception of international programs and museum construction.

The national museums in the network exchange personnel and they are funded entirely by the central government. In 1974 the Museum Membership was organized. Its members pay annual dues and may make special contributions toward the support of curatorial research, lectures on Korean culture, and other worthy projects. The museum is one of the few in the world that conducts excavations and displays finds from such field work.

The National Museum of Korea in Seoul is housed in domed Renaissance-type four-story granite structure on the southern end of the historic Kyongbok Palace ground facing one of the main avenues of Seoul. Built in 1926 it originally was the central government building. Extensive renovation work begun in 1983 has turned the building into a museum equipped with modern facilities.

Of the total floor space of 56,100 square meters including underground storage, 9,640 square meters are devoted to twenty-two galleries to exhibit around 7,000 objects. In addition to Korean culture and art, Central Asian murals and artifacts, Lolang objects, ceramics and other items salvaged from a Yüan Chinese trading ship sunk off Sinan coast of Korea, and Chinese and Japanese artifacts are on permanent display.

Paleolithic objects in the museum include Acheulean hand axes, choppers, and chopping tools excavated by the museum archaeologists at Chonkok-ri, disproving the previously accepted contention that no Acheulean hand axe would be discovered in the Chopper and Chopping Tool Culture. Neolithic and Bronze Age objects suggesting ancient Korea's cultural ties with hunting-fishing tribes of southern Siberia and Northeast Asia include comb-pattern pottery with abstract and straight lines, carbon dated at five thousand years old; stone daggers; bronze daggers; black pottery jars; and Shamanist ritual implements and ornaments such as bronze rattles and bronze ornaments decorated with a pair of birds.

The majority of the objects from the Three Kingdoms period (Silla, Paikche, and Kokuryo) (57 B.C.-A.D. 668) in the museum came from tombs. Silla goldsmiths are credited with ornate and delicate works of art that include gold crowns with pendants, gold necklaces, gold finger rings, gold bracelets, gold cups, gold girdles, and filigreed gold earrings. Silla gold crowns have frontal uprights and simulated antlers, believed to symbolize life and supernatural power in the Shamanist beliefs of Northeast Asian culture. Objects from Paikche include the gold diadem retrieved from the tomb of King Muryong and gold hairpins for a king. Glass objects, such as necklaces, bottles, and cups, and comma-shaped jade objects from Old Silla are part of the collection. Reproductions of the tomb murals of Kokuryo, the northernmost of the three Korean states, are on semipermanent display in the museum. Bronze objects from the period include a vessel from the Ho-uch'ong Tomb, a horn-shaped vessel, several chao-tou vessels, and equestrian trappings. The *Ho-uch'ong Vessel* bears sixteen Chinese characters on the bottom, establishing that it was made in A.D. 415, possibly in Kokuryo. Stoneware vessels of the period include a jar incised with figures, a jar with twin deers, a jar with clay figurines, and the inkstone with a cover supported by animal feet.

Pottery vessels in various shapes used as ritual and burial objects during the Three Kingdoms period in the collection include pottery vessels in the shape of a mounted warrior, a chariot, a granary, and a horse. The pottery vessel in the shape of a mounted warrior unearthed from the Gold Bell Tomb in Kyongju, for example, is 21.3 centimeters high and 26.3 centimeters long and faithfully depicts costumes, equestrian customs, and horse trappings of Silla. The seated figure with a conical hat is highly realistic with a touch of humor. The collection of Silla pottery vessels (ritual and burial) shows that Silla developed its own style, retaining Northeast Asian traits, less influenced by Chinese vessels of the time, compared with Paikche or Kokuryo vessels. The floor tile with a lotus flower in relief from Paikche (28.55 centimeters long, 28.55 centimeters wide, and 4.5 centimeters thick) is one of the representative tiles of the Three Kingdoms period in the museum. Ever since the introduction of Buddhism into Korea in 372, the lotus was the dominant tile and roof-end tile design. Other designs of the period included monsters, landscapes, and medallions of a phoenix in relief. There is also a tile with a landscape design unearthed in Puyo, one-time capital of Paikche, which indicates the Taoist influence in the monk's figure and stylized tri-peaked mountains. The lotus designs on Kokuryo tiles were forceful and masculine, while those on Paikche and Silla tiles give a sense of maturity and serenity. Tiles and roof-end tiles from Unified Silla (668–935) in the museum collection include sculptured tile with one of the four Buddhist guardians in relief, tile with floral medallions in relief, and a tile with a monster in relief. Tiles and roof-end tiles were of earthenware, and during the Unified Silla period some of the earthenware tiles were glazed. Also in the collection are urns, bronze sarira cases of various shapes, and gold-tableted Buddhist sutras from Unified Silla and miniature objects such as a gilt-bronze Buddhist niche (28 centimeters high), five-storied bronze pagoda (12.5 centimeters high), and gilt-silver pagoda (13 centimeters high) from the Koryŏ (918–1392) and Choson dynasties.

Korean Buddhist bells in the museum include the gilt-bronze bell from the site of Samch'on-sa Temple, the bronze bell retrieved in Kyonggi-do province near Seoul, and a bronze bell with the date 1058 inscribed on it—all from the Koryŏ period. Bronze objects in the museum also include bronze mirrors with designs such as trees, cloud and cranes, and twin flying fish and clouds. One of the finest examples of *kundikas* in the collection of the museum came from the Kaesong area, where Buddhist Koryŏ had its capital. This 37.5 centimeters high bronze Buddhist ritual bottle has on the surface thin wires of inlaid silver alloy describing drooping willows, ducks peacefully swimming in the reeds, and so on. The inlaying technique on metal objects opened the way for the unique inlaying technique on Koryŏ celadons.

The collection of Buddhist statues of the museum ranges from the Three Kingdoms through the Choson period. Gilt-bronze, clay, steatite, gold, iron, and granite were used to make Buddhist statues in Korea. The standing gilt-bronze Buddha with an inscription is believed to have been made in Kokuryo in 539, according to the inscription on the nimbus. The face was given undue emphasis in sculptural rendition, indicating that it was in the fashion of early Buddhist image making, under North Chinese influence. This object was discovered in southeastern Korea, which had been part of Silla, in 1963. The half-seated gilt-bronze *Maitreya*, one of the ten half-seated Maitreyas in meditation poses in the museum collection, is large for a half-seated image (93.5 centimeters high). Developed in sixth-century China, the half-seated image was introduced to Korea via Kokuryo, and subsequently all of the three kingdoms made half-seated Maitreya statues. In strong contrast with the formalistic and idealistic statues of the Six Dynasties of China, this particular one bears a faint smile on its youthful features. Its body proportions are naturally rendered, and gilding is still partially retained. The statue sits in a relaxed pose, surrounded by an air of serene spirituality.

The standing gilt-bronze *Avalokitesvara* (20.7 centimeters tall), is presumed to have been made in the sixth or seventh century. Although it had not entirely outgrown the rigidity of the standing gilt-bronze Buddha with an inscription, its accent on the neck between hanging hair on either side, the graceful opening formed by the left sleeve hanging down from the arm, and the natural way of holding the *kundika* in the right hand indicate that this statue represents a step ahead sculpturally. Korean Buddhist statues came to bear more Korean-like expressions and grew less remote and forbidding to the Korean populace. The standing granite *Maitreya Bodhisattva* from the Kamsan-sa Temple (183 centimeters tall) has the face of the Silla people, rather than an idealized expression typical of earlier images, characterized by sharp noses and solemn mouths. The inscription on the back of this statue reveals that it was made in 719. The seated gold *Buddha* from Kyongju (12.1 centimeters tall) was retrieved from the second story of the three-storied pagoda at the site of Whangbok-sa Temple in Kyongju along with the standing gold *Buddha* in 1943. From the inscription on the bronze case containing the two gold images, it was determined that they were made in 706. Since it had been protected in the safety of the pagoda, the image is complete with nimbus and pedestal and is regarded as important material for the study of the development of Korean Buddhist statues, especially of the transitional process to the Unified Silla statues.

The seated iron *Buddha* (150 centimeters high) is one of the most representative iron images made from the eighth through the twelfth century in Korea. Despite the difficulty of handling the material, the images were executed with remarkable precision. The seated gilt-bronze *Avalokitesvara* (18.1 centimeters high), presumed to have been made in the thirteenth or fourteenth century, shows possible influence of Yüan China Buddhist statues. The seated *Bodhisattva* from the Hansong-sa Temple (92.4 centimeters high) is the only marble statue in the collection.

One of the world's largest collections of Korean ceramics is found in the National Museum of Korea in Seoul. More than eighteen thousand ceramic objects at the museum include the most representative celadon works of the Koryŏ Dynasty and p'unch'ong and white porcelain and blue-and-white porcelain wares of the Choson Dynasty. As of February 1980, nearly twelve thousand Sung and Yüan Chinese objects were being processed to be added to the collection of the museum. The Chinese pieces began to be retrieved from the sea bottom off the coast of Sinan, southwest Korea, in 1975 after a Korean fisherman accidentally snagged seven ceramic vessels in his net. Ensuing investigation revealed that a Chinese trade ship presumed to be of the fourteenth century had been wrecked in a storm off the Korean coast and had been lying on the dark bed of the sea for the past six centuries. In addition, the museum has a large collection of ceramic sherds from important kiln sites in Korea; Koryŏ celadon sites such as Kangjin and Inch'on, the blue-and-white kiln site at Toma-ri, and the p'unch'ong ware kiln site at Kwangju.

The vase in the form of muskmelon with design (height, 22.8 centimeters; diameter across the mouth, 8.6 centimeters; and diameter across the base, 7.8 centimeters) and the cup and stand with an incised design of flowering plants contained in a group of celadon objects unearthed from the tomb of Koryŏ King Injong (reigned 1123–1146), with a document giving the date 1146, are two examples of the unique green of Koryŏ celadon, known as "kingfisher" color glaze and compared to the pure green of jade, achieved through highly sophisticated reducing firing. Inlaying of patterns on celadon ware was another unique accomplishment of Koryŏ potters. The bowl with an inlaid decoration of flowers unearthed from the tomb of King Mun Mu (?–1159) and the vase and cover with inlaid cloud and crane designs are examples of this technique. The gourd-shaped ewer and supporting bowl with designs of boys among grapevines demonstrate the development of the inlaying technique using copper-red, which had been completed by the latter half of the twelfth century. The bottle-shaped vase with a fish design painted in brown underglaze iron is representative of p'unch'ong ware. A departure from aristocratic Koryŏ, p'unch'ong ware was widely used in the fifteenth- and sixteenth-century Choson Dynasty and was known for rich Korean originality and robust ethnic characteristics. The museum's collection of Choson white porcelain includes ritual vessels from the sixteenth through the eighteenth century and a jar (41.2 centimeters high and 16.2 centimeters diameter of the base, seventeenth century). There are also white porcelain objects with copper-red decorations such as the jar with a bamboo design (eighteenth century) and a writer's water dropper. There is also a collection of white porcelains painted in underglaze brown iron. The blue-and-white porcelain objects include the bottle with an orchid design (seventeenth century), the wine bottle with a plum blossom design and inscription (eighteenth century), the open-work vase with a peony design (eighteenth century), and the jar with a landscape design (nineteenth century). The museum recently received a gift of 362 Choson Dynasty porcelains from the late Park Pyong-rae. The Park Collection is known for superb blue-and-white objects.

The majority of the five thousand-odd paintings in the collection of the museum are works of Choson Dynasty painters. Landscapes, figures, birds and flowers, animals, and grass and insects were the most frequent subjects of paintings both by members of the professional Painting Bureau, a government agency dedicated to portraiture of kings and dignitaries, recording official functions, and painting landscapes ordered by the court, and literati painters who were scholars or officeholders. *Eight Scenes of the Four Seasons* (ink and light colors on silk) attributed to An Kyon (1418-?) is representative of paintings of the early Choson period, showing the influence of the Southern Sung school. *Sage at Rest on a Rock* (ink on paper) by Kang Hui-an (1419–1464), a high government official, also shows obvious influence of the Sung school. Yi Sang-jwa (1465-?), a member of the Painting Bureau, was in the tradition of An Kyon. His *Moon Viewing* (ink and light colors on silk) indicates a strong influence of the Ma Hsia school of Southern Sung. The *Landscape* (ink and light colors on silk) attributed to Yi Kyong-yun (1545-?) is an example of the influence of the Ming Academy school on a highly gifted and strongly individualistic sixteenth-century Korean artist. Kim Myong-kuk (1600-after 1662) gave a Korean interpretation to the Che school as demonstrated by his *Snowscape* (ink and colors on ramie).

The works of literati painters in the museum such as Cho Sok (1595–1668), Yi Am (1499-?), Yi Chong (1541-?), and Madame Shin Saimdang (1504–51) indicate that they freed themselves of the traditional school influence in their artistic works, while Painting Bureau members were still preoccupied with traditional approaches. *Ch'ongp'ung Valley* (ink and light colors on paper) and *Chong-yang-sa Temple of Mt. Kumkang* (light colors on fan) by Chong Son (1676–1759) demonstrate how successfully he assimilated the Southern school, contributing to the development of Korean painting in the late Choson Dynasty. Chong is credited with painting real Korean scenes in earnest, rather than imaginary Chinese landscapes. Kim Hong-do (1745-?) developed his own independent style on the basis of Chong Son's achievement, and Kim's landscapes, in which figures play a significant role, are unusual, as shown by *Figures under the Willow* (ink and color on paper) and *Landscape and Figures* (ink on light colors).

Kim, with his contemporary Shin Yun-bok (active mid-eighteenth century), pioneered genre paintings whose subjects were often life of the common people in the stratified Confucian Choson Dynasty. *Wrestling Match* and *Dancing Boy* (both ink and light colors—album leaves) and *Village School Teacher* (ink on paper—album leaf, 27.8 by 24.7 centimeters) are included in the museum collection of Kim's genre paintings. Shin's genre works include *Playing on Korean Lute* (ink and light colors on silk). Animals were favorite subjects of Choson painters, and *Mother Dog and Puppies* (ink and color on silk) by Yi Am, *Cats and Sparrows* (ink and color on silk) by Pyong Sang-bok (active mid-eighteenth century), and *Tiger* (ink and color on paper) (painter unknown) are included in the collection. There are about two hundred portraits of Choson Dynasty dignitaries in the museum. There are more than thirty-four hundred rubbings of epitaphs and recordings on monuments and other landmarks since the Three Kingdoms period in the museum collection.

The museum has a collection of objects from the Lolang period (108 B.C.-A.D. 313), which includes a gold buckle with dragon ornament, a bronze incense burner, and many lacquered objects. The Lolang objects are valuable for the study of the culture of Han China, for they were brought from China. The majority of the Buddhist wall paintings and other objects that the Ohtani expedition from Japan brought back from Central Asia between 1902 and 1914 are in the museum. Donated by Japanese businessman Fusanosuke Kuhara in 1916, more than two thousand Central Asian objects include wall paintings (fragments included), sculptures, pottery, bone, stone, bronze, and hide items. The sixty-three wall paintings were mostly from the Turfan region.

The library has about fifteen thousand volumes in the fields of archaeology, art history, and history. The Choson Dynasty publications on art are also in the library. Of them, 1,721 volumes are in European languages. In addition, it has a considerable number of reports and papers on Korean archaeology and art. Use of the library is limited to staff members of the national museums, Museum Membership holders, and graduate students and professors. It is run under the closed system.

There are more than 6,800 negatives (including more than 500 in color) of art objects in the museum collection from which reproductions may be made at cost. Those wishing to have reprints made may write to the registrar of the museum. Regular publications of the museum are *Misul Charyo* (The National Museum of Korea Art Magazine), a semiannual in Korean begun in 1960, carrying research papers and reports; *Bakmulkwan Shinmoon* (The Museum Newspaper), a monthly periodical in Korean started in 1970; and *Kukrip Bakmulkwan Kojok Bokoso* (Report of Research on Antiquities of the National Museum of Korea), an annual with English resumé, reporting on Korean archaeological activities.

Selected Bibliography

Museum publications: *The National Museum of Korea*, 1979; *Kukrip Chungang Bakmulkwan* (Guide Book to the National Museum of Korea in Seoul), 1978; *Hankuk Hoewha* (The Korean Painting—A Catalogue), 1977; *Hankuk Ch'osangwha* (The Catalogue of Selected Choson Dynasty Portrait Exhibit), 1979; *Hankuk Misul O Ch'onnyon: Five Thousand Years of Korean Art*, 1976; Kwon, Yong-pil, "Chungang Asia Byokwha Ko: On Central Asian Murals in the Collection of the National Museum of Korea in Seoul," *Misul Charyo* (National Museum of Art Magazine), no. 20 (June 1977), pp. 10–23.

Other publications: Ministry of Culture and Information, *Kukrip Chungang Bakmulkwan Chunkong Bokoso* (The Construction Report of the National Museum of Korea) (Seoul 1972); Choi, Sunu, *5,000 Years of Korean Art* (Seoul 1978); idem, Introduction, Selection, and Notes, *Kankoku Kokuritsu Hakubutsukan, Toyojiki Taikan*, Vol. 2 (The National Museum of Korea, Vol. 2 of Oriental Ceramics) (Tokyo 1976); *Puyo Bakmulkwan Chinyol Pum Tokam* (Selected Treasures of the Puyo National Museum) (Seoul 1977); d'Argencé, René-Yvon L., *5000 Years of Korean Art* (San Francisco 1979); Keith, Donald H. (Introduction), and Kim, Edward H. (Photographs), "A 14th Century Cargo Makes Port at Last," *National Geographic*, vol. 156, no. 2 (August 1979), pp. 231–43.

CHURLMO HAHN

Mexico

———— Mexico City ————

MUSEUM OF MODERN ART (officially MUSEO DE ARTE MODERNO; also M.A.M.), Bosque de Chapultepec, Mexico 5, D. F.

The concept of a national museum of modern art was formulated in 1953 through the joint efforts of Carmen Barreda, the founder of the Commission for the Museum of Modern Art; Francisco Javier Gaxiola, the secretary of the commission; and President Ruíz Cortínez. The permanent collection, then housed in the Museum of Fine Arts, was moved to the Museum of Fauna and Flora until a new structure could be built large enough to provide space for both the collection and temporary exhibitions. Slightly more than a decade later, on September 20, 1964, the present Museum of Modern Art was inaugurated by President Adolfo López Mateos. As part of an extensive government educational program, the museum's fundamental purpose was and is to bring modern art to the people of Mexico.

In keeping with the tradition of national ownership and funding, the museum belongs to Mexico and receives appropriations from the government through the secretary of public education (SEP). It is governed by the director of the museum, the director of plastic arts, and the director of the National Institute of Fine Arts (INBA), all of whom serve under the secretary of education. It is administered by the director and the five coordinators of the departments of Museography, International Expositions, General Coordination, Cultural Events, and General Administration.

The museum was constructed by Edificadora Mexicana, S.A., and was designed by Rafael Mijares and Pedro Ramírez Vásquez, the prominent Mexican architect who also designed the National Museum of Anthropology (q.v.) and the Museum of History. Its buildings and sculpture garden occupy an irregularly shaped lot of some 36,528 square meters, located prominently at the entrance to Chapultepec Park, Mexico City's major recreational area. Although the original design included four buildings, only two have been constructed: the large main building used for both the display of the permanent collection and temporary exhibitions and the small Temporary Exhibition Center. Surrounding these two buildings is a large sculpture garden that permanently displays a selection of large exterior sculpture from the collection of the National Institute of Fine Arts and that serves as the site for the Sculpture Biennial and other temporary exhibitions.

Sensitively integrated with the natural environment of the site, the main building is set back slightly from the street and is placed within the thickly wooded park behind an open-meshed screen. It is a free-form, horizontally disposed, two-storied building constructed of steel, aluminum, and large panels of grey and green solar glass. The transparent glass curtain wall moves around the steel skeleton in one sweeping undulation, swelling at either end to form the large interior gallery spaces and falling at the middle to announce the entrances. The building is a diaphanous organic form that, because of its transparency, allows direct visual communication between exterior and interior space and that, because of its shape, suggests the natural rhythm of the site.

The spaciousness created by the extensive use of glass is further emphasized by a series of translucent fiberglass domes that cover open interior shafts. One large dome, eighteen meters in diameter, crowns the central core of the building, announcing the main entrance and illuminating the monumental interior circular staircase. Three smaller domes, nine meters in diameter, are distributed between the two unequally sized wings—a single dome illuminates the open shaft in the smaller east wing, and two domes illuminate two open shafts in the larger west wing.

The building houses five separate exhibition spaces. On the ground floor in the east wing, Salon I is dedicated to José María Velasco, the famous Mexican landscape painter. With the exception of one month a year, when the salon is used for the art-book fair, it continuously exhibits the museum's Velasco Collection. In the west wing, Salon II is used for temporary exhibitions by both Mexican and foreign artists. In addition, there is the audiovisual center in which exhibition-related conferences, films, and lectures are held; the museum bookstore in which exhibition catalogues, art magazines, and books are sold; and the storage areas. The second floor carries three salons, the administrative offices, and the office of the director. In the west wing, Salon III exhibits a selection of twentieth-century Mexican painting from the permanent collection, and in the east wing, Salon IV exhibits various national and foreign artists. Adjacent to Salon IV is Salon V, a very small gallery space dedicated to José Alvarez Bravo, the outstanding Mexican photographer. It displays the museum's Bravo Collection and works by other important photographers.

Connected to the main building by a wide promenade is the Temporary Exhibition Center to the south. Although much smaller and circular, it echoes the main building in its placement, its use of materials, and its construction. Placed within the wooded park, the center is built with steel, aluminum, and glass and is roofed with a large translucent fiberglass dome that, as in the main building, crowns an open central staircase.

As the name indicates, the center is used exclusively for temporary exhibitions. It houses two salons, one on the ground floor and one on the second floor. The lower salon is divided into two separate but equal parts by the central staircase and provides an intimate space for small-scale exhibitions. In contrast, the upper salon encircles the staircase and forms one continuous open space for large-scale exhibitions.

Connecting these two buildings is a wide promenade that divides the sculpture garden into two equal sections. Leading into the garden are narrow footpaths that weave through the park in an easy rhythm that encourages leisurely movement and invites unhurried pauses in front of the sensitively placed sculpture. The gardens, together with the two museum buildings, form an organic whole in which curve and movement, transparency and spaciousness, nature and architecture, are harmoniously unified.

Although the permanent collection is small—consisting of some five hundred paintings, forty sculptures, fifteen hundred drawings and prints, and four hundred photographs—it is highly selective and contains a representative sampling of works by the most important nineteenth- and twentieth-century Mexican artists, as well as some works by foreign-born artists resident in Mexico. Among the painters represented are the well-known nineteenth-century portraitists José María Estrada and Hermenegildo Bustos; the famous landscape painters José María Velasco, Joaquín Clausell, and Dr. Atl; the muralists Diego Rivera, José Clemente Orozco, David Alfaro Siqueiros, Rufino Tamayo, Juan O'Gorman, and José Chavez Morado; the women Surrealists Frida Kahlo, Leonora Carrington, and Remedios Varo; the younger generation painters Gunther Gerzso, Carlos Mérida, Cordelia Ureuta, and Julio Castellanos; and the avant-garde artists Pedro Coronel and José Luis Cuevas. The sculpture holdings include pieces by prominent artists such as Ignacio Asúnsolo, Oliverio Martínez, German Cueto, Francisco Zúñiga, Waldemar Sjölander, Francisco Marín, and Feliciano Béjar.

The museum's greatest strength is its outstanding José María Velasco Collection. Formerly owned by the Bank of Mexico, it includes many of Velasco's most important works executed between 1875 and 1908. Best known for his landscapes of the Valley of Mexico, the collection is highlighted by three outstanding paintings with this theme: *The Valley of Mexico* (1875), *Mexico* (1877), and *El Citlaltepetl* (1897). Extraordinary in their imposing monumentality, atmospheric purity, and ability to capture the essence and beauty of the landscape, these works are masterpieces of "Mexicanism."

Also worthy of note is the museum's collection of twentieth-century Mexican painting. In addition to being generally comprehensive, it includes particularly important works by the four major muralists: Diego Rivera, José Clemente Orozco, David Alfaro Siqueiros, and Rufino Tamayo. Rivera's classic *The Miller*

(1924) and notable *Portrait of Lupe Marin* (1938); Orozco's highly expressive *Self Portrait* (1946) and *The Tyrant* (1947); Siqueiro's powerful *Proletarian Mother* (1930), *The Devil in the Church* (1947), and *Image of Modern Man* (1947); and Tamayo's masterful *The Sleeping Women Musicians* (1950) deserve special mention.

Furthermore, there are works of singular beauty in the collection. Roberto Montenegro's *Self Portrait* (1942) stands out for its power and simplicity, and Francisco Goita's superb *Tata Jesucristo* (1927) must be considered one of the masterpieces of Mexican painting.

In addition to displaying works from the permanent collection, the museum hosts about twenty-five temporary exhibitions a year. Although their policy of regularly changing exhibitions is flexible, shows are usually on view for six weeks.

At present, the museum does not have a library, a catalogue of the permanent collection, or photographs of its holdings. It does, however, have a small archive of catalogues, posters, and invitations from the temporary exhibitions it has hosted.

The museum publishes *Artes Visuales*, a quarterly journal founded by Fernando Gamboa in 1973. It includes scholarly articles on various aspects of modern art, exhibition reviews, and museum news.

Selected Bibliography

Museum publication: *Artes Visuales* (Mexico 1973).

Other publications: Cooper, Barbara, and Maureen Matheson, editors, *The World Museums Guide* (London 1973); Barreda, Carmen, "The History of the Museum," *Artes de Mexico*, no. 127, vol. 17 (1970), pp. 5-14; Lifchez, Raymond, "Four Museums in a Park," *Architectural Record*, no. 145 (June 1969), p. 180; Moyseén, Xavier, "Mexican Painting in the Museum of Modern Art," *Artes de Mexico*, no. 127, vol. 17, (1970), pp. 15-20.

SUZANNE GARRIGUES

NATIONAL MUSEUM OF ANTHROPOLOGY (officially MUSEO NACIONAL DE ANTHROPOLOGIA), Paseo de la Reforma y la Milla, Mexico 5, D.F.

The National Museum of Anthropology located in Mexico City's famous Chapultepec Park was inaugurated on September 17, 1964, under the auspices of President Adolfo López Mateos. Masterfully conceived and constructed by a team of museum directors, museographers, educational specialists, archaeologists, ethnographers, architects, engineers, artists, and Indians, the museum stands as a monument to Mexican Indian culture and is a veritable treasury of the nation's indigenous history, both past and present. That its singular mission is to educate and that it is a museum of history rather than of art is everywhere evidenced. From the initial planning and selection of the site, to the architectural style and disposition of the building, to the organization and installation of the exhibitions, every aspect of the museum is thoughtfully and sensitively adjusted to the overriding concept of public education.

In keeping with the tradition of national ownership and funding, the museum belongs to the people of Mexico and receives appropriations from the secretary of public education (SEP) through the National Institute of Anthropology and History (INAH). It is governed by its director and the director of the National Institute of Anthropology and History, both of whom serve under the secretary of public education. It is administered by the director and the heads of the sections of Administration, Public Relations, Guides, Promotion, Archaeology, Ethnology, Museography, Educational Services, Physical Plant, and Electronic Machinery.

Although the present museum opened in 1964, its real genesis dates from 1790 with the chance discovery and unprecedented preservation of three Aztec stone monuments—the Sun Stone, the statue of Coatlicue, and the Stone of Tizoc. Although the preservation of these monuments signaled the first consciousness of the importance of Mexico's cultural past, it was not until 1825 that the museum was formally established and housed in a section of the building of the former home of the National University in downtown Mexico City. During these years it was a general museum that included not only anthropological material but momentos of Mexican history and a natural science collection. In 1865, due to the size of the collection, the museum moved to the old Mint Building beside the National Palace on Moneda Street. Finally, in 1940, both the natural science collection and all of the post-Conquest materials were moved to separate locations, and the museum's anthropological character was established.

Initial plans for the building of the present museum began in late 1959 with a detailed report formulated by the old museum's directors, a small group of anthropologists, and museum experts. This report outlined the broad objectives and needs of the new museum and became the basis for the selection of the site, the architectural design and layout of the building, and the museum's entire organization.

To demonstrate properly the correspondences between the past and present indigenous cultures, it was decided that equal attention would be given to Mexican archaeology and ethnography. Chapultepec Park was selected as the most appropriate site, because it is easily accessible to large numbers of people and because it has the historical significance of having been the popular recreational area of the Aztec emperors. This location, together with the nature of the material exhibited in the museum, would ensure its immediate educational impact and thus accomplish its goal.

Once these basic decisions were made, a comprehensive program of researching and planning began. Specialists prepared a series of monographs on all available information on each of the archaeological and ethnographic areas. These studies, with contributions from museographers and educational specialists, were used in the planning of the exhibition rooms. In less than eight months, some seventy ethnographic expeditions gathered materials from all regions of Mexico, resulting in a collection of more than fifteen thousand photographs, hundreds of drawings, tape recordings of Indian music, and languages and films—all of which are now part of the museum's vast ethnographic archives. To add to the extant archaeological collection, thousands of new pieces were acquired. Special excavations were sponsored in the Maya cemetery of Jaina in Campeche, where nearly four hundred burials with offerings were found. The giant monolithic sculpture of Tlaloc, the rain god, the largest archaeological sculpture in the hemisphere, was transported from the village of Coatlinchán, some twenty kilometers from Mexico City, where it had lain for centuries in a dry stream bed. In addition, hundreds of pieces were acquired through donations or by purchases from private collections. The famous Miguel Covarrubias Collection, one of the finest privately assembled collections of pre-Hispanic art in Mexico, was acquired in toto, and some four thousand pieces representing all of the pre-Hispanic cultures were acquired from the Spratling, Navarrete, Field, Pepper, Hedlung, Villanueva, Leof, Kamffer, Juárez, Frias, Corona, and Hecht collections.

The museum was designed by the well-known Mexican architect Pedro Ramínez Vásquez. Highly expressive of its function and the cultural heritage it houses, the museum's design and orientation to the site are based upon an understanding of and adherence to the pre-Hispanic architectural principles of integration with the natural environment, balance of open and closed spaces, and direct expression of materials.

The buildng is a low, two-storied, rectangular structure built with prefabricated steel girders, aluminum, plate glass, and marble. It covers some 44,000 square meters and incorporates an additional 35,700 square meters of the surrounding park for exterior courtyards and exhibition spaces. In spite of its tremendous size, the museum is essentially a quiet, noble structure that, through its horizontality, its transparency, and its integration of exterior with interior space, is fully incorporated into the landscape.

A broad open plaza, articulated only by concrete paving and a border of natural vegetation, serves as the main entrance to the museum and establishes the monumental scale and spaciousness maintained throughout the entire complex. Moving through a glass-walled lobby of the same width, the plaza leads to a huge interior patio: the museum's central space distributor and basic organizing unit. Intensely austere and breathtakingly monumental, the patio is the interior focal point of the museum and provides a resting place convenient to the exhibition halls that surround it. It is divided into two distinct areas. The first section is covered with an umbrellalike structure supported by a single central column and serves as an entranceway to the first exhibition halls. Measuring some eleven meters in height and spanning an area of fifty-four by eighty-two meters, the umbrella stands as a colossal three-dimensional sculpture whose vast proportions reinforce the monumental scale of the patio as well as of the entire museum complex. Falling from a circular hole in its roof, a curtain of water veils the central support and fills the area with the sound and the mist of a cascading waterfall. This enclosed area contrasts with the other section of the patio, which is completely open and light filled. There a reflecting pool, planted with indigenous lake vegetation, creates a peaceful, contemplative environment and recalls the legendary lake origins of the Aztec culture, whose exhibition hall is located directly behind it. This play between open and closed spaces, light and shade, silence and sound, stillness and movement, provides two distinct yet integrated environments that together recreate the special grandeur of pre-Hispanic architecture.

The exterior design of the building is based on Maya Puuc palace architecture and is divided into two clearly articulated stories. The plain bold treatment of the highly polished, marble-walled ground floor is broken by a projecting second story that is enclosed by a decorative aluminum grille. Based on a highly stylized version of the Maya serpent motif, this grille, with its broken rhythmic patterning, contrasts sharply with the lower level, where only the entrances to the exhibition rooms interrupt the smooth continuous wall plane. This bipartite division of the exterior is a hallmark of the Puuc style and, in this case, specifically recalls the Palace of the Governors at Uxmal.

The nearly 217,000 objects housed within the museum represent the largest and most comprehensive collection of Mexican archaeological and ethnographic material in the world. As a result of the national ownership law of 1968, which established that all artifacts found in Mexican soil belong to the government, the collection is constantly growing. When new archaeological sites are excavated, the artifacts unearthed are transported to the museum or to the other national museums throughout the country. Of the 217,000 objects, 27,000 are currently on display—12,000 archaeological pieces and 15,000 ethnographic pieces. The remaining 190,000 objects are housed in museum storerooms and are displayed occasionally in temporary exhibitions.

The careful organization and clarity found in the architectural design and layout of the museum are also seen in the arrangement of the exhibition halls. Twenty-two galleries are distributed between the two floors and surround the central patio, twelve rooms on the ground floor devoted to archaeological material and ten rooms on the second floor devoted to ethnographic material. The archaeological exhibits are arranged in geographical and chronological order, and wherever possible, the ethnographic exhibits on the second floor are located directly above the corresponding archaeological rooms. This arrangement emphasizes the historical continuity between past and present cultures and underscores the museum's educational role.

To offer the broadest integration of each of the groups' cultural aspects, each exhibit, both archaeological and ethnographic, provides basic information about environment, means of subsistence, forms of daily and communal life, historical development, cultural achievements in science and learning, and religious practices and beliefs. Through the generous use of explanatory notes, maps, charts, murals, models, reconstructions, and dioramas, each exhibition presents the cultural context within which the works of art were produced. Hundreds of imaginative installations fill the museum's exhibition halls and aid in the understanding and appreciation of the cultural achievements they represent. Particularly noteworthy are the large outdoor model of Teotihuacán, a full-scale replica of the first three segments of the Temple of Quetzalcoatl from the same site, reproductions of the Danzantes from Monte Albán, a reproduction of a section of the mosaic wall from Mitla, a replica of the burial crypt from the Temple of the Inscriptions from Palenque, a full-scale reproducton of the Maya temple at Hochob in Campeche and the Temple at Bonampak with its murals in Chiapas, and dioramas of the Maya Cha-Chaac religious ceremony and the Aztec market of Tlatelolco.

In addition, murals, sculptures, and wall decorations by twenty-five of Mexico's leading artists supplement and help to integrate the material exhibited in the various rooms. The better known works include: Rufino Tamayo's allegorical mural, located in the lobby, of Quetzalcoatl struggling with Tezcatlipoca; José Chávez Morado's reliefs covering the patio's central column and his mural in the Mesoamerican room; Gonzalez Camarena's mural placed at the entrance to the anthropology exhibit; and Mathias Goeritz's *ixtle* rope screens and wall decorations adorning the Coro-Huichol display.

The first floor of the museum is devoted to introductory rooms and archaeological exhibits of the great ancient Mesoamerican cultures. Beginning in the north wing, the first three exhibition halls provide general information on anthropology and prehistory: Hall 1, Introduction to Anthropology room, presents the general meaning and scope of the discipline itself; Hall 2, the Mesoamerican room, shows those elements that different cultures had in common, their evolution within particular environments, and the cultural elements that were passed down intact, modified, or lost in time; and Hall 3, New World Origins and Mexican Prehistory room, presents the first sedentary cultures whose efforts created the first works and traditions of the subsequent Mesoamerican civilizations. The information presented in these halls serves as a basic introduction to the individual cultural exhibitions that follow.

The remaining rooms along the north wing trace the chronological and developmental sequence of the central Mexican cultures from their most remote origins through the Pre-Classic, Teotihuacán, Toltec, and Aztec stages, and the rooms along the south wing present, regionally, the cultures of Oaxaca, Veracruz, the Maya area, and western and northern Mexico. Within each exhibit the material is arranged chronologically from the most ancient to the most recent.

The Pre-Classic Art and Archaeology of Central Mexico hall displays a fine collection of small terracotta ritual and utilitarian objects from numerous archaeological sites in the region. Dating from the twelfth to the seventh century B.C., there are bottles with stirrup handles, vases with fresco decoration, koalin jars, vessels in the shape of whistles and aquatic animals, and anthropomorphic and zoomorphic vases. Particularly important is a large collection of small clay figurines, mostly female, from the burial site of Tlatilco.

The hall that follows exhibits a representative sampling of ceramic, stone, and inlay work from the famous Classic period site of Teotihuacán (c. 200–

700). Objects include important pieces of Thin Orange ware, tripod vessels decorated with frescoed ceremonial scenes, and stone sculpture in the form of ball-game stelae, human skulls, and anthropomorphic masks. Particularly noteworthy are a beautiful funerary mask inlaid with turquoise, serpentine, and shell mosaic and the monumental statue of Chalchiutlicue, Goddess of Waters, which stands some three and one-half meters high.

The Post-Classic period Toltec hall (c. 1000–1500) contains several outstanding examples of monumental stone sculpture. A giant five-meter caryatid, or atlantean figure, in the form of a warrior; a five-meter temple column from Tula carved in relief; and a reclining Chac Mool, the enigmatic Toltec deity, are among the more impressive pieces on permanent exhibition. In addition, there is an extraordinary plumbate vessel inlaid with mother-of-pearl, representing the face of a warrior emerging from the jaws of the sacred coyote.

Because the Aztecs are the best known of the pre-Hispanic cultures and are the source of some of the most impressive works in the museums, their exhibition hall is the largest and occupies the prominent west end of the court. Hundreds of examples of sculptures, painting, pottery, lapidary work, goldsmiths' art, wood carving, and feather work are displayed in an area of more than two thousand square meters. Although the list of masterpieces is too long to enumerate, special mention must be made of the most renowned pieces in the collection. The so-called *Aztec Calendar*, or *Sun Stone*, a massive monument dedicated to the previous four suns or cosmogenic worlds and measuring twelve feet in diameter, is perhaps the best-known single work in the museum. The *Stone of Tizoc*, the circular relief-carved monolith commemorating the Aztec ruler's victories in battle, is vigorously executed and brilliantly conceived. The statue, *Coatlicue, Goddess of the Earth, of Life and Death*, is the quintessential piece of Aztec sculpture whose originality of concept and form is without rival in the pre-Hispanic world. In addition to these monumental masterpieces, there are many small sculptures of remarkable naturalism. A magnificently carved squash, a simply rendered grasshopper, and a number of gracefully executed serpents are among the more noteworthy examples.

Continuing along the south wing, the first hall is devoted to the Oaxaca region. It is divided into two sections, one displaying Zapotec art and archaeology and the other displaying Mixtec art and archaeology.

The Zapotec section contains a representative sampling of monochrome ceramic vessels, a fine collection of elaborately headdressed anthropomorphic clay funerary urns, and a series of incised and painted boxes with lids all dating from the third to the eighth century. Among the important individual pieces in this collection are a spool potstand in the form of a spinal column, a model of a temple with columns and a macaw in the center symbolizing the sun, and a strikingly powerful bat mask of finely worked jadeite segments, with eyes of shell inlay and pendants of differently colored slate.

The works exhibited in the Mixtec section date from the thirteenth to the fifteenth century and include beautiful polychromed ceramic vessels, tripod jars and vases, incense burners with handles, large terracotta jars for funerary use, and replicas of the famous codices. In addition, an outstanding collection of gold work from Tomb VII at Monte Albán features rings with pendant ornaments, composite pectorals, bracelets, pendants, necklaces, noseplugs, and earrings. Of particular beauty is the famous shield pectoral from Yanhuitlan, which is worked in gold with a mosaic of turquoise.

The Gulf Coast region occupies the next hall and is subdivided into three cultural areas: the southern, or Olmec, area (c. 1500–400 B.C.); the central area, where the Tajín culture flourished (c. A.D. 300–900); and the northern, or Huasteca area (c. A.D. 300–900). Of the many excellent examples of works from each of these regions, certain individual pieces and collections deserve special mention. The Olmec section boasts two of the extraordinary multicolored basalt colossal heads; the well-known *Wrestler*, which is a masterpiece of naturalistic stone sculpture; Stela C from Tres Zapotes, which bears the date 31 B.C., one of the earliest recorded dates in Mesoamerica; and a large and very fine collection of jade pieces in the forms of jaguars, werejaguars, figurines, celts, awls, and breastplates. Featured in the Tajín section are many examples of exquisitely carved stone yokes, axes, and palmate stones, forms believed to have been connected with the ritual ball game and several of the well-known hollow clay "smiling head" figurines. A piece of singular beauty in the Huasteca section is the world-famous *Adolescent* of Tamuín, whose beautifully proportioned body is decorated with delicately incised symbolic and mythological reliefs.

The Maya hall that follows contains a wealth of truly fine pieces in all media. There are relief-carved stone slabs, lintels and stelae, jadeite figurines, pectorals and other delicately carved ornaments, polychrome ceramic vessels, large urns and cylinders, as well as terracotta figurines and stucco relief panels. The lintel with scenes of offering from Yaxchilán, the left segment of the relief panel of the Temple of the Cross from Palenque, and the ball-game marker disk from Cinkultic are first-class examples of Maya relief sculpture. The terracotta figurine collection from Jaina is world famous and includes several hundred pieces that display the physical type, dress, paraphernalia, and customs of the Maya from the sixth to ninth century. In addition, the jadeite mosaic mask from the burial crypt in the Temple of the Inscriptions at Palenque is a masterpiece of lapidary work.

Ceramics from the various regions of northern Mexico occupy the next hall and date from the ninth to the twelfth century. There are fine collections of polychrome vases with schematic decorations from Casas Grandes in Chihuahua, variously decorated bowls from Durango, and many anthropomorphic pot covers from northern Guanajuato.

The last hall on the first floor is devoted to western Mexico and displays ceramic work from the eighth to the tenth century from the states of Jalisco, Colima, and Nayarit. Pieces in the collection include clay figures in the form of warriors or ball players, seated figures, family groups, and hunchbacks; many fine examples of the famous Colima dogs depicted in various positions; and a striking hollow-clay female figurine in the position of giving birth.

The ten halls on the second floor of the museum house the ethnographic material and display more than fifty exhibitions of contemporary Indian groups. Beginning with the Introduction to Ethnography room, which provides the most important aspects of the material culture of the Mexican Indians, the next eight halls, arranged according to geographical or cultural affinities, display the ethnography of the Cora-Huichol, Tarascan, Otomi-Pame, Sierra de Puebla, Oaxaca, Gulf Coast, lowland and highland Maya, and northwestern Mexico. The sequence ends with the Synthesis of Mexico room, which through carefully planned installations demonstrates the continuity between past and present cultures.

Each of the ethnographic exhibitions presents basic information about the environment, language, history, economy, handicrafts, dress, architecture, and religion of the various groups. There are many installations showing various aspects of daily life, as well as means of production and subsistence. For example, there are life-like scenes depicting Indian women sitting together spinning thread, weaving cloth, and making dresses. There are displays of implements and tools used for fishing and hunting, such as hooks, nets, and spears; musical instruments like flutes, drums, and harps; and a variety of handicrafts, including lacquerwork boxes, incised and painted gourds, various types of pottery, woven baskets and mats, bark paintings, tissue paper dolls, and many styles of weaving and embroidery. One of the most important contributions to the ethnographic section is the series of past and present regional dwellings. They were built by the local Indians according to their traditional designs and, in some cases, constitute the only existing examples of regional domestic architecture.

The last hall on the second floor, conceptually and functionally the last hall of the entire museum, is the Synthesis of Mexico room. There carefully conceived and coordinated installations present a panoramic view of those elements that combine to form Mexico's present national and cultural identity. By juxtaposing the old with the new, the integration of the Indian, the colonial, and the modern is clearly demonstrated in architecture, city planning, painting, dance, music, literature, and the folk arts. This hall is truly the culmination of the entire museum and again boldly underscores its educational function.

Over and above the first-class collection, the dignified structure in which it is housed, and the sensitively arranged and installed exhibitions, the museum provides many additional resources to facilitate its decidedly educational mission. They include some two thousand square meters of research offices, workshops, laboratories, and storerooms; the National Institute of Anthropology and History library consisting of some 350,000 volumes, with an historical archive of 30,000 manuscripts and documents, archives of maps, photographs, and music, and the exceptional Alfonso Caso Collection acquired during the Echeverria administration; a temporary exhibition hall of seven thousand square meters; an auditorium seating 350 people, with stage, film, and simultaneous-translation equipment; provisions for schoolchildren, including a projection room, studios for drawing, an outdoor theater, and play area; and a cafeteria and restaurant for 400 people. In addition, the museum has a sizable bookstore that sells many National Institute of Anthropology and History publications, records of ethnographic music, slides of work in the collection, and a large selection of art, history, and anthropology books.

Selected Bibliography

Museum publications: None.

Other publications: Bernal, Ignacio, *Museo nacional de anthropologia* (Mexico City 1965); Bernal, Ignacio et al., *The Mexican National Museum of Anthropology* (Mexico City 1972); Groth-Kimball, Irmgard, *Obras selectas del arte prehispanico: adquisiciones recientes* (Mexico City 1964); Ramírez Vázquez, Pedro, *The National Museum of Anthropology of Mexico* (New York 1968); Aveleyra Arroyo de Anda, Luis, "Pre-Columbian Art in the New National Museum of Anthropology in Mexico City," *The Connoisseur*, vol. 160, no. 644 (October 1965), pp. 91–101; Cervantes, Maria Antonieta, "Olmec Materials in the National Museum of Anthropology, Mexico," *Origins of Religious Art and Iconography in Preclassic Mesoamericas* (Los Angeles 1976), pp. 9–25; Lifchez, Raymond, "A Brilliant Museum Reflects Mexico's Cultural Ambitions," *Architectural Record*, no. 145 (June 1969), pp. 176–81.

SUZANNE GARRIGUES

——— Tepotzotlan ———

NATIONAL MUSEUM OF THE VICEROYALTY, THE (officially EL MUSEO NACIONAL DEL VIRREINATO), Tepotzotlan.

The Museum of the Viceroyalty was established in 1964 to represent all aspects of artistic culture in New Spain. It operates as part of the huge complex of museums, libraries, schools, national monuments, and publications programs governed and funded by the Mexican National Institute of Anthropology and History (Instituto Nacional de Antropología e Historia—INAH).

The museum at Tepotzotlan is administered by a director, who oversees several departments. The Research Department is responsible for obtaining information on all objects in its collections and exhibitions, the photographs in its archives, and books in its two libraries. The Museography Department organizes special projects and exhibitions, and the Curatorial Department handles preservation and restoration of the collections.

The building is a museum itself of architectural styles from most of the three-hundred-year colonial period, and its singular importance as a colonial monument was the reason for the collection's establishment outside of metropolitan Mexico City. The ex-Jesuit seminary complex was the most important religious center in colonial Mexico. First constructed in 1585, it was enlarged in 1690 and refurbished periodically until 1762. After the Jesuits were expelled from the country in 1767, it was abandoned until 1777, when it was made into a Royal College and Seminary for the Education, Voluntary Retreat and House of Correction for the Secular Clergy. It passed back into the hands of the Jesuits, who returned to Mexico in 1809, but was again secularized in 1821. Although the Jesuits regained control for several short periods thereafter, all churches were permanently secularized in 1856, and Tepotzotlan fell into disuse until the INAH declared it a national monument at the turn of the century.

In 1964 its own collection of liturgical furnishings, paintings, and sculptures was expanded by the addition of several other collections of colonial objects that had previously been exhibited in other national museums. The core of the collection was that of the former Museum of Religious Art, which had outgrown its space in the Metropolitan Cathedral in Mexico City. To round out its holdings, a selection of paintings and porcelains was transferred to Tepotzotlan from the National Museum of History, also in Mexico City. An anonymous private patron donated a comprehensive European armor collection, which is unique in Mexico and the only deviation at Tepotzotlan from its otherwise colonial focus.

The domestic areas of the seminary complex house objects that were not part of the original Jesuit holdings. There are seven main permanent exhibition spaces, each devoted to a single subject. The first relates the history of the Jesuit establishment at Tepotzotlan, with maps, documents, portraits, and models of the complex. The second room is dedicated to ''The Image of New Spain,'' illustrating contact between Spaniards and Indians, exploration and discoveries, conquest and evangelization, and aspects of social, economic, and cultural life. Included in this room's items is a collection of scale model ships of the sixteenth century. Areas three, four, and five display important examples of colonial painting, sculpture, graphics, architecture, and decorative arts. The sixth section contains the armor collection, and the last is reserved for temporary exhibitions that seek to illuminate individual facets of life and art in the colonial period. Recent exhibitions have concentrated on ancient weapons and armor, nuns' portraits of the seventeenth through the nineteenth century, terracottas in New Spain, and commerce with Asia.

The fine arts are represented with works by major artists of the Mexican colonial era and European artists whose paintings and sculptures were regularly exported to Mexico, original architectural plans of important Mexican monuments, reproductions of architectural elements typical of the styles of the epoch, and a rotating exhibition of prints from the permanent collection. Paintings include anonymous sixteenth-century religious subjects, as well as attributed works such as St. John Writing the Apocalypse by Maarten de Vos. A large assemblage of seventeenth- and eighteenth-century paintings reflects the increase of artistic patronage in those centuries and includes the Virgin of Bethlehem, attributed to Murillo, as well as characteristic examples of religious subjects by seventeenth-century painters such as Nicolas Rodríguez Juárez and eighteenth-century artists like Luís de Villalpando, Juan Correa, and Andrés López. A portrait gallery contains paintings of important figures in Mexican colonial history and is significant from both visual and historical standpoints.

Sculpture is surveyed with examples of images in ivory, metal, stone, stucco, wood, and cane, all materials characteristic of the period and region. One particularly prized object is the eighteenth-century *Niche of Hueyapan*, which was discovered and rescued from a nearby abandoned church. The carved and brilliantly polychromed *Christ Carrying the Cross*, with expressionistic images of Adam and Eve, the Evangelists, and Death, is a unique example of the elaboration of colonial folk art.

Among the most precious and exquisite articles are those housed in the decorative-arts sections. Predominantly religious, they include liturgical vestments and vessels, oriental ivories, native feather work, ceramics, furniture, and ironwork. Examples of ternaries lavishly embroidered in gold, silver, and silk complement in style and ornamentation the gold and silver vessels used in services that rivaled Europe in material splendor. Intricate sixteenth-century feather mosaics made around the region of Michoacan are rare examples of native Indian craft traditions continued out of a need for church decorations in outlying areas.

The colonial period's religious emphasis is brought into especially sharp focus by the church decorations forming the literal and artistic climax of the museum complex. When the building was restored in 1963, a series of twenty-two paintings by Cristobal de Villalpando depicting scenes from the life of St. Ignatius of Loyola was restored to its original sequence in the cloister of the Cistern. During the same period, renovation of wood altarpieces and their images, executed between 1690 and 1758, and restoration of the stone facade of 1760–62 revived the church's original Baroque splendor, characteristic of eighteenth-century Mexico and defined by an overall ornamental surface carving and repetition of *estipite* pilasters. Only three other stylistically similar and contemporaneous churches are as well preserved, and none displays the iconographic or artistic comprehensiveness of Tepotzotlan.

The museum has two libraries. One is reserved for use by the staff and consists of works relating to colonial Mexico. The second is the Old Library of the Jesuit Priests of Tepotzotlan, which includes not only their collection of religious and philosophical books published in the seventeenth and early eighteenth centuries but also that of the archbishop who first secularized the seminary and bequeathed his own library of three hundred volumes. This library may be consulted, like the photographic archives, by scholars with prior permission from the INAH.

A small selection of books about Tepotzotlan and related subjects is available for purchase in the museum shop, but photographs must be requested from the Department of Colonial Monuments (Departmento de Monumentos Coloniales) within the INAH, which also handles museum publications.

Selected Bibliography

INAH publications: Obregón, Gonzalo, *Official Guide—Tepotzotlan*, 1961; *Colegios de Tepotzotlán: Restauraciones y museología*, 1964; Consuelo Maquívar, Ma. del, *Los*

Retablos de Tepotzotlán, 1976; *El Galeón de Acapulco: memoria de la exposición sobre el Comercio con Asia en el Museo Nacional del Virreinato*, 1977; Toussaint, Antonio, *Escenas de la Vida de San Estanislao de Kostka*, 1978.

Other publications: Muriel, Josefina, *Monjas coronadas*, 1978; "Tepotzotlán," *Artes de México XII*, 62–63 (1965).

BARBARA C. ANDERSON

The Netherlands

—— Amsterdam ——

THE RIJKSMUSEUM (also THE NATIONAL MUSEUM), Stadhouderskade 42, Postbus 50673 (1007 DD), Amsterdam.

The Rijksmuseum in Amsterdam houses the finest collection of Dutch art in the world and includes excellent examples of European and Asian art. Founded as the national museum of The Netherlands, the Rijksmuseum was one of the first museums of its kind established. Today, a director-general administers the museum and its collections. There are five curatorial departments, each with its own director: Paintings; Print Room; Sculpture and Decorative Arts; Asian Art; and Dutch History. A comprehensive library and a department of Education are also part of the Rijksmuseum. A secretary-general is responsible for financial administration, personnel, security, and building maintenance.

There is no strictly formulated acquisitions policy at the Rijksmuseum, but since its founding, the museum has built a representative collection of the arts of The Netherlands ranging from the fifteenth through the nineteenth century: paintings, works on paper, sculpture, and decorative arts. Funds for acquisitions are provided by, among other sources, the state, the Rembrandt Society, the Prince Bernhard Fund, and the Rijksmuseum Foundation (which directs sales of photographs, books, and so on at the museum).

The history of the Rijksmuseum dates from 1795, the year that the French under Napoleon occupied Holland and drove out Stadholder Prince William of Orange. The prince's personal art collections were divided: part went to Paris; another part was sold publicly. Some paintings and sculptures had been left in the residences of the Orange family, and these objects were brought together at the Huis ten Bosch, a summer palace near The Hague. This National Art Gallery, precursor to the Rijksmuseum, opened to the public in about 1800.

In 1806 Louis Napoleon (brother of Napoleon) took the throne of Holland, and it was under him that a royal museum was officially established in Amsterdam. The Grand Musée Royal was founded by decree on April 21, 1808, to be housed in the Palais op de Dam (Palace at the Dam), a former royal residence. A director was appointed: Cornelis Apostool, a consular agent and amateur painter. The original collection was enriched by an important loan from the city of Amsterdam, which included among other treasures Rembrandt's *Night Watch*. In 1816 the collection was moved to larger quarters, a mansion on the Klaviersburgwal called the Trippenhuis.

During its first years the museum expanded rapidly with purchases and gifts to the collection. But from 1830, the year of economic depression following the Belgian Revolt, the museum made fewer acquisitions and for a time became virtually inactive. Quarters at the Trippenhuis were nevertheless extremely crowded, and in 1838 nineteenth-century paintings were moved to the Pavilijian Welpelepen in Haarlem. In the 1860s plans were made for the construction of a new building with more space and better lighting. It was not until 1870 that an architect was appointed, P.J.H. Cuypers, a major Dutch architect of the late nineteenth century. A site was chosen in the southern part of the city, and in 1876 construction began. The new Rijksmuseum opened on July 13, 1885. Paintings, drawings, and prints from the Trippenhuis were installed in the new structure, and nineteenth-century paintings housed for several years at Haarlem were again united with the historical works. The Van de Hoop Collection, an outstanding group of paintings bequeathed to the city of Amsterdam in 1854, was added to the Rijksmuseum bringing Rembrandt's *Jewish Bride* and Vermeer's *Young Woman Reading* to the museum. The Rijksmuseum also became home for the Dutch Museum for History and Art (formerly at The Hague), the core of today's collections of sculpture and decorative arts and of Dutch history.

The Rijksmuseum building, located on Stadhouderskade, was constructed of red brick in a neo-Gothic style. The achitect Cuypers was a follower of Viollet-le-Duc's archaeological approach to design, and Cuypers' eclectic and monumental structure reveals this influence. The Rijksmuseum is an imposing structure with a broad main facade and high towers. The exterior is decorated with sculpted representations of Dutch history and art; bas-reliefs and statues ornament the facades of the building. A series of halls, galleries, and small rooms all elaborately decorated by Cuypers in the neo-Gothic mode are installed with works of art. After its opening the Rijksmuseum building received mixed reactions: the French poet Paul Verlaine described the structure in 1892 as "a big polychrome monument with turrets, the only impressive monument in Amsterdam; it is neither beautiful nor ugly, but it is undeniably big."

Since its completion, the Rijksmuseum has undergone several additions and renovations. In 1906 new rooms were added onto the back of the museum, and in 1909 the Drucker Wing was constructed to house the museum's extensive collections of nineteenth-century art. In 1962 thirty new rooms were opened in the museum's right courtyard, and in 1969–73 rooms in the left courtyard were inaugurated, including the Exhibition Hall.

The Rijksmuseum houses an outstanding collection of Dutch paintings, enriched over the years through major gifts and bequests. Fine early examples include works from the fifteenth century by Geertgen tot Sint Jans, the Haarlem painter. *The Tree of Jesse*, an oil on panel, was acquired in 1956 through the Rembrandt Society. Another panel by the artist represents *The Holy Kinship*. Jan Mostaert, another artist of the early Haarlem school, is included in the collection with his *Adoration of the Magi*. The Master of the Virgo Inter Virgines, active about 1480–1500, takes his name from the Rijksmuseum panel *The Virgin with Saints Catherine, Ursula, Cecilia, and Barbara*. Another painter whose name is from a work in the museum is the Master of the Amsterdam Death of the Virgin. His panel reveals the influence of contemporary Flemish masters (van Eyck, van der Weyden) on Dutch painters. A *Crucifixion* is an excellent example of Late Gothic Mannerism by the Amsterdam painter Jacob Cornelisz van Oostsanen, and a series of seven panels, the *Seven Arts of Charity* (framed together and dated 1504), is by the Master of Alkmaar.

From the sixteenth century are works by Lucas van Leyden: the *Adoration of the Golden Calf* is from about 1530 and was acquired by the museum in 1952. *The Sermon*, an oil on panel attributed to Lucas van Leyden, was acquired in 1897 through the Rembrandt Society. Jan van Scorel is represented in the collection by an elegant half-length figure of *Mary Magdalene* in contemporary Dutch costume. A pair of portraits, *Anna Codde* and *Pieter Bicker Gerritsz*, are by Martin van Heemskerck, a pupil of Jan van Scorel, and date from 1529. Another student of van Scorel, Anthonis Mor, a native of Utrecht who gained acclaim in the courts of Portugal, Spain and England, is represented by his formal portraits *Sir Thomas Gresham* and *Anne Ferneley, Lady Gresham*. Works by Dirck Jacobsz, son of fifteenth-century painter Jacob Cornelisz van Oostsanen, include his portrait *Pompejus Occo*. *The Adoration of the Shepherds* by Pieter Aertsen is a fragment of a larger scene, most likely the *Nativity* painted by Aertsen for the Niewekerk in Amsterdam and destroyed in 1566. Cornelis Cornelisz van Haarlem, an artist responsible for the interest in Mannerism at Haarlem in the late sixteenth century, painted *Bathsheba* in 1594. Another Mannerist artist, Abraham Bloemaert, created the large canvas *The Preaching of St. John the Baptist*. Landscapes from the sixteenth century include Joos de Momper's *Landscape with Boar Hunt* (c. 1600) and the small *Mountain Landscape*, an early work by the artist. The *Landscape with Ruins and Rebecca at the Well* was painted by Willem van Nieuwlandt in oil on copper. Still lifes feature works by Jan Bruegel, among them *Flower Piece*, a depiction of a pot filled with dozens of small blossoms.

The seventeenth century, known as the Golden Age of painting in Holland, is represented at the Rijksmuseum by masterpieces of the period. Rembrandt,

Ruisdael, Vermeer, and others are included with key works. From the early part of the century, Frans Hals is represented by his *Portrait of a Married Couple* (c. 1621); *The Merry Toper* (c. 1635); *The Company of Captain Reynier Reael*; and *Lieutenant Cornelis Michielsz Blaeuw* (dated 1637). A pair of portraits, *Lucas de Clercq* and *Feyntje van Steenkiste*, were executed in 1635 by Hals and presented in 1891 to the city of Amsterdam by the de Clercq family. The expressive portrait *Nicolaes Hasselaer* dates from 1630–35, and a monochromatic, late canvas is *Maritge Voogt Claesdr* (1639). Hendrick Terbrugghen, one of the Utrecht artists who was influenced by the Italian Caravaggio, is represented by his dramatic biblical composition *The Incredulity of St. Thomas*. Italy drew generations of Dutch artists to study and paint the landscapes, among them Bartholomeus Breenburgh, whose *Roman Landscape* abides by the lessons of Dutch painting.

Landscapes from the first part of the seventeenth century include works by Hercules Seghers, known for his fantastic representations, among them the small oil on panel *River in a Valley*. Jan van Goyen's works in the Rijksmuseum include *Landscape with Two Oaks* from 1641 and his atmospheric riverscape *View of the Dordtse Kil before Dordrecht*. Salomon van Ruysdael painted his magnificent *River Scene with Ferry* in 1649. *Winter Scene*, a typical landscape/genre scene by Hendrick Avercamp, is in the collection, as are Aert van de Neer's *River Scene in Winter*, a small oil on canvas, and *River Scene by Moonlight*, one of the artist's earliest works.

Paintings of architecture and architectural interiors are numerous in the Rijksmuseum and mid-seventeenth-century examples include Pieter Jansz Saenredam's *Interior of the St. Odolphuskerk at Assendelft*, dated 1649, and his *Old Town Hall of Amsterdam*, from 1657. Portraits from mid-century feature Johannes Cornelisz Verspronck's charming *Portrait of a Girl*, from 1641, and Thomas de Keyser's *Portrait of Pieter Schout on Horseback*, and oil on copper dated 1660. The *Lady with Two Children at a Harpsichord* by Jan Miense Molenaer is according to tradition a portrait of the painter Judith Leyster, the artist's wife. Judith Leyster is represented in the collection with *Serenade*, a portrait of a musician that demonstrates the influence of her teacher Hals.

Public portraits from the seventeenth century include Bartholomeus van der Helst's *Banquet of the Civic Guard* representing a celebration of the Peace of Westphalia, which took place in the St. Jorisdoelen (Hall of the Crossbow Archers' Guild of St. George) in Amsterdam on June 18, 1648. Ferdinand Bol, a pupil of Rembrandt, painted the *Four Governors of the Amsterdam Leper Asylum* in 1649.

The Rijksmuseum houses the finest collection of paintings by Rembrandt in the world and features the artist's masterpiece *The Night Watch*, a large group portrait commissioned for the Hall of the Civic Guard in Amsterdam (1642). Another public portrait, *The Syndics of the Cloth Guild*, was completed by the artist in 1662 for the Guild Hall in Staalstraat, Amsterdam. A fragment of Rembrandt's *Dr. Deyman's Anatomy Lesson* dates from 1656; it was painted for the dissection room of the Surgeons' Guild in the Sint Anthonierswaag, Amsterdam. The artist's biblical subjects at the museum include an oil on paper from about 1636–37, *Joseph Telling his Dreams*; an oil on panel from 1630, *Jeremiah Lamenting the Destruction of Jerusalem*; and a small panel executed about 1645–46, *Holy Family by Night*. The famous wedding portrait, *The Jewish Bride* from after 1665, shows the Jewish poet Don Miguel de Barrios and his wife, Abigael de Piña. A portrait, *Rembrandt's Mother*, is an early work from 1631, and a depiction of the artist's son, *Titus*, was produced about 1660. Rembrandt's *Self Portrait as St. Paul* is a late work dated 1661. Landscapes by Rembrandt at the Rijksmuseum feature *The Stone Bridge* from about 1638, acquired for the museum in 1900 through the Rembrandt Society and the scholar A. Bredius.

Dutch genre and interior scenes include masterpieces by Vermeer. *The Kitchen Maid* from about 1658, *The Letter*, *A Street in Delft*, and *Young Woman Reading a Letter* are housed at the museum. Adriaen van Ostade's *Interior with Peasants* dated 1650 and his *Fish Vendor* from 1672 are in the collection as is *Night School*, a nighttime scene by Gerard Dou. Works by Jan Steen, well known for his lively representations of Dutch life, include the *Feast of St. Nicholas*. A rare religious subject by Steen is *The Adoration of the Shepherds*, a small-sized, intimate view of the New Testament story. Other works in the collection by Steen are *The Sick Lady*; *The Toilet*; *The Merry Family* from 1668; and *The Sick Child*, a small oil on canvas showing a child on its mother's lap. Gerard Ter Borch's elegant interiors and portraits include *A Company in an Interior* and his full-length portrait *Helena van der Schalke*, a depiction of an elaborately dressed child against a neutral ground. Other portraits of members of the Schalke family by Ter Borch are also housed at the Rijksmuseum. Paintings by Pieter de Hooch include *At the Linen Closet* dated 1663, *A Country Cottage* of about 1665, *Maternal Duty* about 1660, and *The Pantry* of about 1658, all demonstrating the artist's fascination for interior spaces.

Other genre paintings include Cornelisz Bisschop's *Woman Peeling Apples* from 1667 and Nicolaes Maes' *Dreaming*, an image of a young woman at an open window from about 1655. Michael Sweerts, an artist who studied at Rome, painted *A Game of Checkers*; his elabrate *Painter's Studio* is also in the collection.

Architectural interiors and exteriors were favorite subjects for Emanuel de Witte, whose *Interior of a Gothic Church* is a composite view of the Nieuwe Kerk in Amsterdam and the city's Oude Kerk. Jan van der Heyden's *View of the Martelaarsgracht in Amsterdam* and his *View of the Dam at Amsterdam* demonstrate in their exactness the artist's knowledge of engineering and architecture. Gerrit Berckheyde, another artist known for his architectural views, painted *The Spaarne at Haarlem*. Other seventeenth-century masters included in the Rijksmuseum's large collection are Jan Asselyn, Philip Wouwerman, and Paulus Potter.

A fine group of Dutch paintings from the eighteenth and nineteenth centuries is housed at the Rijksmuseum. *Garden of a Town House*, an elegant Rococo-style scene, is by Cornelis Troost as is a *Family Group in an Interior*. Hendrick Keun's *Garden with Stables, Amsterdam* from 1772, also in Rococo style, shows the exterior of a grand palace. The heritage of genre scenes is carried on by Isaak Ouwater with his *Office of the Amsterdam Lottery* from about 1780. Still lifes were popular subjects in the eighteenth century, and examples in the collection include Jan van Huysum's *Still Life with Flowers and Fruit*, Melchior d'Hondecoeter's bird composition *The Floating Feather*, and Abraham van Beyeren's traditional *Still Life*.

Early nineteenth-century painters represented at the Rijksmuseum include Pieter Rudolph Kleyn, whose *Park of St. Cloud, Paris* (1809) demonstrates the influence of French neoclassicism. Wouter Johannes van Troostwijk, an Amsterdam artist, painted *The Raamportje of Amsterdam under Snow* in 1809 as well, but his subject is traditional. *The Horse in Front of the Stable* from 1828 by Anthony Oberman was created for the Van der Hoop Collection and also represents a traditional subject. A group of documentary paintings include Adriaen de Lelie's *The Sculpture Gallery of "Felix Meritis," Amsterdam* and *The Collector Jan Gildemeester in his Gallery*. *The Bookshop*, dated 1820, is by Johannes Jelgerhuis, an actor and painter who lived in Delft and Amsterdam. Johannes Weissenbruch's *The Town Gate of Leerdam* represents the nineteenth-century interest in realism.

French Impressionism influenced a group of late-nineteenth-century Dutch painters, among them Isaac Israel, who is represented in the Rijksmuseum with *Girls on a Donkey*, among other works. George Hendrick Breitner painted *The Bridge over the Singel at the Paleisstraat of Amsterdam* in 1893–98, and Paul Joseph Constantin Gabriel's *In the Month of July*, an oil on canvas, is from 1889. Both Breitner and Gabriel employed the light palette and Impressionist brushwork favored by the French.

The Rijksmuseum houses, in addition to important and representative works of Dutch paintings, major examples from the Flemish, French, Italian, and Spanish schools. Seventeenth-century Flemish painting is highlighted by works by Peter Paul Rubens: the *Portrait of Hélène Fourment*, the artist's first wife from about 1630–35, and *The Procession to Calvary*, a sketch from an altarpiece commissioned in 1634 and now in the Musée Royal des Beaux-Arts (q.v.), Brussels. Anthony van Dyck's portrait *Prince William II and His Young Wife, Princess Mary Stuart* dates from 1641. His early work *The Penitent Magdalene* is from about 1620 and shows the influence of his teacher Rubens.

French paintings include Mathieu Le Nain's oil on canvas, *The Gamblers*, from about 1645–50. Five canvases in grisaille are by Gerard de Lairesse: *Minerva and the Seven Liberal Arts*, *Painting and Poetry*, *World Fame and Honor*, *Charity*, and *Ostentation*, all acquired in 1970. From the nineteenth century Pierre Paul Prud'hon's neoclassical portrait *Rutger Jan Schimmelpenninck and his Family* dates from 1801 or 1802.

The Italian school is well represented with works from the fifteenth through the eighteenth century. From about 1420 is the panel *St. Jerome in his Study* by

Lorenzo Monaco. Carlo Crivelli's *Mary Magdalene* dates from about 1475–80. The diptych *Portrait of Giuliano da Sangallo* and *Portrait of Francesco Giambert* was painted by Piero di Cosimo about 1500–1504. The bust-length *Portrait of a Man* is by Antonio Pollaiuolo. The North Italian painter Vincenzo Foppa is represented by his bust-length *Portrait of a Young Woman* from about 1465–70, and the *Portrait of a Man* by Giovanni Geralamo Savoldo dates from about 1540. Venetian paintings include Jacopo Tintoretto's *Portrait of Ottavio Strada* from 1576. *Portrait of Daniele Barbaro*, the humanist and translator of Vitruvius, is by Paolo Veronese (c. 1565–70) as is the canvas *Venus and Cupid* (c. 1580). The eighteenth century features excellent examples of the Venetian school. Works by Tiepolo include *Telemachus and Mentor* from about 1740, a fragment of a larger composition perhaps a representation of the adventures of Telemachus, son of Ulysses, and Minerva as Mentor. The sketch *The Vision of St. Anne* was produced by Tiepolo about 1759 as a study for the convent altarpiece now in Dresden. Francesco Guardi's *Regatta on the Grand Canal* from about 1765 is an early example of that artist's view paintings. The North Italian artist Alessandro Magnasco is represented at the Rijksmuseum with *Monks in a Landscape* of about 1720–30 and its companion *Capucin Monks at Prayer*. Also by Magnasco is a dramatic composition, *Massacre of the Innocents*, from about 1735–42. From the Spanish school, a small *Crucifixion* by El Greco from about 1600–1611 highlights the collection.

The Print Room at the Rijksmuseum is one of the finest in the world. Its origins date from 1798, when the library of the former Prince William II became state property. Fifty-two portfolios of prints and drawings were moved to the Binnenhof at The Hague. The nucleus of today's magnificent collection was formed in 1807, when the Van Leyden Collection of 250 portfolios of prints and drawings was acquired. Rare works by Rembrandt, Lucas van Leyden, Hendrick Goltzius, Dürer, and Hercules Seghers, and eighty-one sheets by the anonymous Master of the Amsterdam Cabinet were included. The following year the Van Buren Collection was purchased bringing, among other treasures, the early drawing ascribed to Jan van Eyck and a group of Indian miniatures. In 1816 the collection was moved from The Hague to the National Museum at Amsterdam, then housed in the Trippenhuis. There a room was set aside for the viewing and study of works on paper. Under the direction of Cornelis Apostool, the Print Room made only modest acquisitions, but after 1847 the collection was enriched through numerous purchases and gifts. After 1875 the aims of the Print Room were established: to form a distinguished collection of prints and drawings and to acquire documents of Dutch history and art. It was not until after World War II that the collection of foreign drawings was significantly enriched; sheets by Michelangelo and Raphael and other works were acquired for the Italian collection. French drawings from the eighteenth century were actively sought, and in prints, early German sheets and works of the Japanese school were acquired.

The print collection comprises single sheets, albums of prints, illustrated books, and woodcuts. An overview of Dutch and Netherlandish works from the fifteenth through the nineteenth century highlights the collection. Early works by Alart du Hameel and Erhard Reuwich (fifteenth century) are in the museum. From the sixteenth century an outstanding group of prints by Lucas van Leyden includes an engraving from about 1510, *Return of the Prodigal Son*. Works by Goltzius, Roeland Savery, and Abraham Bloemaert are also in the collection. The seventeenth-century print collection is highlighted by works of Rembrandt. *Christ Healing the Sick* (The Hundred Guilder Print) dates from 1649, and the landscape etching *Jan Six's Bridge* is from 1645. More than eighty prints by Hercules Seghers are at the Rijksmuseum including examples from the eighteenth-century Hinlooper Collection. Examples by van Ostade, Ruisdael, and Adriaen van de Velde are at the museum. Peter Paul Rubens is well represented as is Anthony van Dyck (a complete collection of this artist's paintings is at the Rijksmuseum). Eighteenth- and nineteenth-century Dutch and Flemish works by hundreds of artists are included; among them are prints by Vincent van Gogh.

Fine examples of early German printmaking are at the museum with sheets by the Master of the Hausbuch, Master E.S., and others. A fine group of prints by Dürer is at the Rijksmuseum as are landscape prints by Albrecht and Erhard Altdorfer. German prints from the seventeenth through the nineteenth century are well represented. An overview of French printmaking is presented with examples from the sixteenth through the nineteenth century. Early works by Jean Duvet and Étienne Delaune are in the collection. An exceptional group of works by Claude Lorraine includes many rare proof sheets. The eighteenth century is represented by Watteau, Boucher, and Greuze, and extensive collections of prints by Delacroix and Millet highlight the nineteenth-century collection. Fine examples by Degas, Manet, and Toulouse-Lautrec are housed in the Print Room. The Italian school is well represented at the Rijksmuseum with works from the fifteenth through the nineteenth century. Of special interest are prints by Mantegna and Tiepolo. English, East European, Scandinavian, Spanish, Portuguese, and American prints are also housed in the collection. The Japanese collection includes excellent examples by the eighteenth-century master Masanobu, and from the nineteenth century are woodcuts by Hiroshige and Hokusai.

Drawings in the Print Room include single sheets, sketchbooks, cartoons, architectural drawings, and miniatures. The Dutch school is exceptionally well represented. The Italian, French, and English schools are also represented by important examples. Early Dutch and Netherlandish drawings include a rare silverpoint sheet attributed to Hugo van der Goes, *A Head of a Woman*. From the sixteenth century, the pen drawing *The Farm* is by Jacques de Gheyn II (1603). *The Monkey*, a chalk and brush drawing, is by Roeland Savery (c. 1604–15) and was probably executed while the artist was in Prague and Vienna as court painter to Emperor Rudolph II. A brilliant collection of seventeenth-century drawings includes many sheets by Rembrandt, among them a pen study, *Woman at the Door*; a pen and brush work, *Portrait of Shah Jahan* (one of a series of drawings done from Indian miniatures); and a late work, *Reclining Nude*. Jan van Goyen's black chalk and brush drawing *The Dunes near Scheveningen*, dated 1649, is a classic landscape study by the artist. Flemish artists such as Rubens are well represented in the collection. More than four hundred other Dutch and Flemish artists active in the seventeenth century are included in the museum's collection with major and minor works. Drawings from the eighteenth and nineteenth centuries comprise a large part of the collection. Special collections of interest include more than 681 sheets by the two Gerards and Mozes Ter Borch.

The German school is represented by two early drawings, one by the Master of the Drapery Studies and the other by the Monogrammist AS. Sheets by Urs Graf, Wolf Huber, and Adam Elsheimer date from the sixteenth century. Fine German drawings from the seventeenth and eighteenth century are housed at the Rijksmuseum as are nineteenth-century sheets by Rudolf von Alt, Max Liebermann, and Adolf Menzel. A collection of English drawings from the seventeenth through the nineteenth century includes an early sheet by Jonathan Richardson I as well as drawings by Thomas Gainsborough and George Romney.

The French collection is highlighted by eighteenth- and nineteenth-century drawings by Watteau, Boucher, Fragonard, Delacroix, Millet, Degas, Renoir, and Gauguin. Early drawings include a small group of sixteenth- and seventeenth-century works, among them studies by Simon Vouet, Claude Lorraine, and Poussin. A study by Vouet in the collection is a preparatory work for the artist's *Aurora and Cephalus* at the Hôtel de Sully in Paris.

A very fine collection of Italian drawings includes fifteenth-century works by Filippino Lippi, Domenico Ghirlandiao, and Lorenzo di Credi. Renaissance masterpieces in the collection are a study sheet by Michelangelo and a drawing attributed to Raphael. Other works by Fra Bartolommeo, Baccio Bandinelli, and Giorgio Vasari are in the Print Room as are works by Giovanni Bellini and Domenico Campagnolo. A series of studies for the decoration in the Sala del Concistero at the Palazzo Pubblico in Siena are by Domenico Beccafumi. Other artists represented include Veronese, Tintoretto, Pellegrino Tibaldi, and Bartolommeo Passarotti. From the seventeenth century, all three Carracci are represented: Annibale with a landscape, Agostino with a figure study, and Lodovico with a portrait of a young man. The Venetian school dominates holdings from the eighteenth century with exquisite drawings by Tiepolo, Francesco and Antonio Guardi, Sebastiano Ricci, and Giuseppe Galli Bibbiena. The nineteenth-century Italian school is represented by Mancini and Luigi Sabatelli, among others.

Drawings from Eastern Europe, Scandinavia, Spain (including works by Murillo and Ribera), and Japan are in the collection. The Print Room houses many documentary sheets including portraits, historical works, and folk and children's prints. A large and excellent group of topographical works, among them a series on Rome, is of interest. The Print Room organizes special exhibitions on selected topics and publishes catalogues of these exhibitions, along with catalogues of works in the collection.

The Department of Sculpture and Decorative Arts comprises examples of

Dutch and European sculpture, ceramics and glass, silver and jewelry, tapestries and other fabrics, and furniture. A survey of Dutch sculpture from the fifteenth through the nineteenth century is presented at the Rijksmuseum and although sculpture did not have as rich a development in Holland as painting, the museum houses some magnificent examples. A group of Italian and French pieces by major masters is also at the museum. The core of today's sculpture and decorative arts collection came to the Rijksmuseum in 1883, when works from The Hague Museum were moved to Amsterdam. Acquisitions made in the late nineteenth and twentieth centuries have enriched the collection. A highlight is a group of North-Netherlandish works from the sixteenth century.

From the fifteenth century a rare oak sculpture, *Joachim and Anna at the Golden Gate*, is by the Master of Joachim and Anna and dates from about 1460–80. An anonymous North-Netherlandish sculpture created the polychromed oak work *The Flight into Egypt* (c. 1500), and a Late Gothic group, *Music-Making Angels and St. Joseph*, is by Adriaen van Wesel. A group of small sculptures is by Pieter Zavy of Antwerp and dates from the late sixteenth century. From 1606 is a polychromed terracotta, *Bust of a Man*, by Hendrick de Keyser, a major Dutch sculptor of the seventeenth century. Also attributed to de Keyser is the sculpture *Mad Woman*, formerly in the garden of the old Lunatic Asylum of Amsterdam. The terracotta sketch *Prudence* is one of several works in the museum produced by Artus Quellinus in preparation for the large bronze figures on the roof of the Amsterdam Town Hall. Rombout Verhulst's terracotta *Bust of a Woman* is believed to portray Maria van Reygersbergh, wife of Willem Baron van Liere, lord of Oosterwijk and the two Katwijks. A sketch by the same artist was executed for the tomb of Admiral Tromp in Delft. A *Virgin and Child* from about 1700 by an anonymous Antwerp sculptor exemplifies the rise of the Antwerp school in the last quarter of the seventeenth century; the work in ivory is an unusually large piece in that precious material standing about twenty-three inches high. Other pieces from the seventeenth century include a fireplace by Philip Vingboons from 1639, a wood sculpture of *Erasmus* by Aelbert Vinckenbrink, and a Baroque altar from the church in Rijsbergen in North Brabant. A magnificent bronze horse is by Adriaen de Vries.

German sculptures in the collection feature rare examples of wood carving from the fifteenth and sixteenth centuries, among them a sculpture group of the *Last Supper*. From Italy is a bronze candelabrum by Andrea Verrocchio, and by Francesco of Valdambruno is a polychrome group, the *Annunication*. Other Italian Renaissance works are in the collection as well. French pieces feature a fifteenth-century *Madonna and Child*. A highlight of the collection is Étienne-Maurice Falconet's marble *Seated Figure of Cupid* (1757) carved for Madame de Pompadour for her Château de Bellevue.

The ceramics collection is dominated by magnificent examples of delftware, the Dutch blue-and-white porcelain produced during the seventeenth and eighteenth centuries. Works include plates, vases, statues, and the famous pictorial tiles with landscape, portrait, and decorative motifs. Highlights of the collection include a large tile picture (66 1/2 by 35 3/8 inches) representing an eighteenth-century garden. A tulip vase in the form of a Near Eastern ziggurat is composed of ten water compartments, each a separate vase with four spouts. Polychromed delftware includes a ewer and basin by Pieter Adriaensz Kocx produced like much of delftware in imitation of Oriental porcelain. Another Delft potter Rochus Jacobsz Hoppesteyn produced a fine pitcher in the collection between 1680 and 1692; the piece is signed R.I.H.S. and marked with a moor's head, the sign of the best of the Delft potteries. A factory near Amsterdam, the Loodsdrecht Pottery, produced the porcelain chocolate jug decorated with shells, a lizard, and a scene of a spider and wasp in combat.

A large and excellent collection of Meissen porcelain from Germany is housed at the Rijksmuseum. Among the many pieces is a vase in the shape of a Chinese ginger jar from about 1725. Figural groups include Johann Joachim Kändler's harlequin group (c. 1740–45) with characters from the Italian commedia dell'arte and also by Kändler a brilliantly colored cockatoo dated 1734. Other works in the ceramics collection are from France and Italy, among them a terracotta altar from 1502. The work was executed by Benedetto and Santi Bulgioni in the tradition of the della Robbia.

An exquisite collection of glass is at the Rijksmuseum with outstanding examples of various techniques (turned, engraved, and blown glass) from eighteenth-century Holland and abroad. From the seventeenth century, a glass marriage dish with diamond engraving was created by Willem van Heemskerk and is dated 1685. An elaborate rummer or ceremonial cup with diamond engraving is decorated with the Siege of Damietta, a historical battle between the Frisian and Dutch crusaders and the Saracen-held Egyptian city Damietta. From Italy (which introduced glassblowing to Holland in the seventeenth century) are fine examples of glassware from Murano and Venice. A dragon-shaped vase made of rock crystal and enamel is by an anonymous Italian craftsman; the vase, in the form of a fabulous beast, was intended as a festive ornament.

The collection of silver and jewelry features Dutch works from the sixteenth century, among them a rare drinking horn made for the Arquebusiers Guild. The piece, a buffalo horn mounted in silver, is dated 1547. The seventeenth century was for silver, as for painting, a golden period, and examples from this rich time include Paulus van Vianen's oval dish, the *Story of Diana and Actaen*, an elaborate work with reliefs on both sides (1613). A pedimented drinking bowl by Adam van Vianen epitomizes Baroque ornamental style as does the craftsman's fine gilt-silver vase or ewer made at Utrecht in 1614. Johannes Lutma the Elder, chief silversmith of Amsterdam in the seventeenth century, designed the ceremonial pitcher and basin for the inauguration banquet of the Amsterdam Town Hall in 1655. Lutma also created two decorative salt dishes ornamented with cupids. The works are among the earliest examples of gold-plated silver made in Holland. An anonymous Amsterdam silversmith made the silver scalloped plate with chased decoration (a pastoral scene and floral designs) in 1661.

A coffee urn in the French style dates from 1729 and is by Andele Andeles; its unusual shape is derived from that of a classical garden urn.

German metalwork is well represented at the Rijksmuseum with examples from the famous Jamnitzer workshop at Nuremberg (active in the sixteenth and seventeenth centuries) and from the renowned Lencher shop in Augusta. A series of Italian crystal and silver vases dates from the sixteenth century and includes notable works from the Saracchi workshop at Milan.

The jewelry collection features exquisite examples by German craftsmen such as the pendant with a depiction of Cimon and Pera fashioned in gold, enamel, pearls, rubies, and other precious stones (c. 1600). A toothpick, also from about 1600, is made of gold, enamel, turquoise, and other stones, and a fanciful brooch in the shape of a cockerel is set with decorative Baroque pearls (late sixteenth or early seventeenth century).

The Rijksmuseum's group of Dutch and Flemish tapestries features outstanding examples of the art. A tapestry fragment woven at Tournai in the second half of the fourteenth century is decorated with heraldic designs. Also from Tournai is a fifteenth-century weaving with a complex representation of the *Crucifixion*. A tapestry fragment, *Tales of Hercules*, is from the fifteenth century, and a rare verdure-type tapestry dates from 1520–30. Weavings from Brussels, an important center in the sixteenth century, include *Diana and her Companions*. From 1510–15 the composition *Triumph of Fame* is also from Brussels. A weaver from Delft, Frans Spierling, created the silk and wool tapestry *Niobe's Pride and Punishment*. This work was part of a cycle with the Story of Diana and is dated 1610. The Gobelin Factory in Paris is represented by, among other works, a tapestry from the cycle *Amours des Dieux*. The museum's example was presented by Louis XVI to Prince Henry of Prussia in 1784.

A group of embroideries and lace from Holland, Italy, and France offers a survey in style and taste from the sixteenth through the nineteenth century, from exquisite Flemish collars to fanciful Rococo textiles and nineteenth-century veils. A rare man's collar in reticella needlepoint lace, made in 1600–1620 by an anonymous Italian lacemaker, is one of the highlights of the collection. Costumes at the Rijksmuseum feature a group of elaborate Dutch eighteenth-century fashions. The Rijksmuseum furthermore owns the largest collection of white linen damask in the world.

The department's collection of art from the Near East and related regions comprises works from Persia, Asia Minor, Turkey, Turkestan, and Central Asia as well as from Egypt and Spain. Aside from significant holdings in the area of tiles and ceramics dating from the thirteenth through the nineteenth century, the department possesses an imposing collection of Oriental rugs, the most important of which date from the sixteenth and seventeenth centuries.

Strengths of the Rijksmuseum's furniture collection include Dutch and Italian pieces of the sixteenth century and Dutch, French, and German works from the seventeenth and eighteenth centuries. Furniture by anonymous Dutch cabinetmakers features an oak credence or "treasure chest" from about 1525 made probably for the Guild of the Civic Archers at Alkmaar. The chest, carved in four sides, was intended as a freestanding piece to hold the Guild's plate and other ceremonial ware. A two-door cupboard of Brazilian rosewood (palisander) on oak is decorated with arms of the Alberda Family of Groningen. An armless chair from the first half of the seventeenth century is also made of palisander. From the late seventeenth century is a pine bedstead formerly at the Castle Rozendaal in Gelderland. The piece is draped with Italian plain and cut velvet, and its style shows the influence of the French architect who worked in Holland, Daniel Marot.

French furniture of the eighteenth century is well represented and includes two dressing tables signed J. Oeben. Works by Riesener include a "bonheur-du-jour," a small writing table surmounted by a bookcase. A group of chairs was designed by George Jacob. German pieces include an elaborate writing table by Abraham and David Roentgen made of oak, maple, and walnut veneers. The work was created about 1765 for Johann Philipp von Walderdorf, elector of Trier, and is decorated with marquetry scenes taken from prints by, among other artists, the Dutch painter Nicolaes Bercham.

The Rijksmuseum has a number of period rooms including one from the house of Willem Ph. Kops in Haarlem (c. 1790). This salon with its silk wall covering from France, its crystal chandelier on the mantelpiece, and its furniture covered in silk damask is completely original. The woodwork ornamented with sculpted figures, garlands, and acanthus tendrils was most likely designed by the Amsterdam architect Abraham van der Hart. Other rooms recreate various periods such as mid-seventeenth-century Holland (a room furnished with cupboards, turned chairs, and so on) or early eighteenth-century France (with a *lit-de-repos*, armchairs, and a carved console table).

An unusual collection of two dolls' houses from the seventeenth century and one from the eighteenth century is at the Rijksmuseum. These minutely worked dwellings, created for collectors, document daily life in Holland. Architectural details, furnishings, utensils, and decorations all reflect the taste and style of the historical periods. Dolls dressed in contemporary costumes inhabit these miniature houses.

The Department of Asian Art was established at the Rijksmuseum in 1965. At that time the Museum of Asian Art, administered by the Society of Friends of Asian Art and housed in the Rijksmuseum's Drucker Wing, was incorporated into the Rijksmuseum. The history of the collection dates from 1918, the year the Society of Friends of Asian Art was founded. In 1919 the society organized its first exhibition, and throughout the years, fine examples of Asian art were acquired. From 1928 small exhibitions were held in the National Academy of Art in Amsterdam. The society began publishing bulletins on a regular basis, first in collaboration with Dutch art periodicals and then independently. The first Museum of Asian Art opened in the city's Stedelijk Museum, where it was housed for twenty years. In 1952 the collection was moved to the Rijksmuseum, which already possessed a considerable collection of Eastern art. Major bequests to the collection from that point included in 1968 the Westendorp Collection, a group of more than six hundred objects including an outstanding collection of Japanese tea-ceremony ware and, in 1970, the Verburgt bequest, a group of thirty-eight rare objects.

The collection today comprises Chinese, Japanese, Korean, and Indian art as well as objects from Ceylon, Nepal, Burma, Thailand, Cambodia, Tibet, and Central Asia. Indonesian art is exceptionally well represented. In July 1982 galleries were renovated, and examples are now arranged by cultural region.

The collection of Chinese art is comprehensive, with examples of metalwork, ceramics, painting, and sculpture. Bronze Age food and wine vessels as well as knives, mirrors, daggers, buckles, and jewelry (Shang-Yin through T'ang dynasties) offer a survey of metalwork in China. A *chung* (bronze bell) from about 482 B.C. is decorated with bands of *t'ao-t'ieh* (mask) motifs; it was purchased for the Museum of Asian Art by the Society of Friends with the aid of the Rembrandt Society. A group of gilded bronze figures range in date from the Han through the Sung Dynasty. The earliest ceramics in the museum are Predynastic earthenware vessels on long-term loan from the Bourdez family. Vases, pots, and figures are from the Han through the Ming period. Of special note is a series of six tomb figures (four horses and two camels) from the T'ang period fashioned in unglazed terracotta. These rare pieces were acquired through the Rembrandt Society in 1965. Fine examples of blue-and-white porcelain from the Ming Dynasty are housed at the Rijksmuseum as are examples of polychromed and monochrome porcelain from the Ch'ing Dynasty. A group of mid- to late-seventeenth-century "roll-wagon" vases is exhibited. The department's holdings in monochrome porcelain feature two sets of five vases together with other objects, all with a *bleu poudré* ground. A magnificent collection of famille verte porcelain, much of which was bequeathed by Mr. and Mrs. J.C.J. Drucker-Fraser in 1944, is in the Rijksmuseum. Among these objects are two rare Fo dogs. Two famous K'ang Hsi vases are among the department's group of famille noire ware. A range of famille rose pieces dates from the Yung-Cheng and Ch'ien-Lung periods. Blanc-de-chine, sang-de-boeuf, and turquoise crackle-glaze porcelain are represented among the Rijksmuseum's monochrome pieces from the Ch'ing Dynasty.

A fine collection of jade from the Late Chou period is at the museum as are works of cloisonné enamel. A sacrificial table from the Ming period is fashioned with enamels and is decorated with five-clawed imperial dragons.

The Chinese sculpture collection is highlighted by several masterworks, among them, a seated Bodhisattva Avalokiteshvara of Guanyin. This twelfth-century (Late Sung) work is of polychromed wood, and it was acquired by the Society of Friends in 1939. A special feature of this statue is the use of *kirikane*, unique among known examples of Chinese sculpture.

A modest collection of Chinese painting also graces the department. A pair of paintings on silk with representations of herons, kingfishers, and pheasants date from the Ming period. The works were donated after World War II by Mrs. J. E. Westendorp-Osieck in honor of the reopening of the Museum of Asian Art. An album of twelve landscapes from the seventeenth and eighteenth centuries bears on each leaf an inscription by the artist Keo Ch'i-p'ei together with his seal. A fourteenth-century painting on silk from the Verburgt bequest depicts Avalokiteshvara in the "royal pose" with the boy Sudhana.

The collection of Japanese art at the Rijksmuseum encompasses both religious and secular objects. The secular works include examples of lacquer ware from the seventeenth and eighteenth centuries: segmented boxes for medicines or incense (inrô), boxes for tobacco, writing implements and/or paper, and interior furnishings such as a writing table and a bird cage. One seventeenth-century lacquered fan of the uchiwa (rigid) type is also in the collection. A group of tsuba (sword guards) are in the museum as are kozuka (scabbard knives) and netsuke (girdle ornaments) of various materials. A number of riding accoutrements and implements of war are also in the collection: a pair of stirrups, a helmet, and a pistol, all dating from the Edo period.

One of the highlights of the collection is the tea-ceremony ware acquired through the Westendorp bequest. Westendorp had developed a singular appreciation for the Japanese, Zen-Buddhist-influenced ideals of beauty embodied in these simple, non-decorative forms, often irregular in shape. Among the most famous of these pieces is a Raku teabowl called kengyô, supposedly made by Chôjirô for the tea-master Sen-no-Rikyû at the end of the sixteenth century. The dark brown body is covered with red-brown and greenish-yellowish glazes that overlap. Also of note is a seventeenth-century, ribbed sake bottle with a cream-colored glaze applied on the gray body.

Porcelain was not produced until the seventeenth century in Japan, long after its introduction in China. Several good examples of the Chinese-influenced early blue-and white pieces manufactured at Arita on Kyûshû are present at the Rijksmuseum. Such works were imported into Holland at an early date by the Dutch East India Company. After 1650 more decorative Imari porcelain reached Europe as did the more simple Kakiemon porcelain, both of which are represented in the collection. From the nineteenth century, porcelain from Hirado on Kyûshû and from Kyoto is represented.

Of the secular Japanese paintings in the Rijksmuseum several deserve special mention. A seventeenth-century silk scroll depicting two quails and flowers is signed by and exhibits the seal of Tosa Mitsuoki. A six-paneled screen from the Verburgt Collection (late eighteenth or early nineteenth century) represents a battle from the Heiji War (1159–60). The fierce-looking figures of the winning clan are typical of the so-called Matabei style, a warrior type invented by the scroll painter Iwasa Matabei in the seventeenth century. A pair of seventeenth-century Namban screens depict Portuguese sailors landing at a Japanese harbor (probably Nagasaki) and are considered masterpieces of the Kano school. The screens were the first important acquisition made by the department after its establishment.

Japanese religious art includes examples of painting and sculpture. A Buddhist painting dating from the latter half of the thirteenth century portrays the Bodhisattva Jizô (guardian deity of children) standing on two lotus flowers. A painting on silk probably from the fifteenth century depicts a dying Buddha surrounded by deities and animals. Executed in ink, colors, and gold, the work also employed the *kirikane* technique. Sculptures include a number of rare early wood pieces. One of the most striking is an Amida Buddha dating from the mid-twelfth century (late Heian or Fujiwara period). The Buddha is represented in a cross-legged sitting position while his hands form a variant of the *vitarka-mudrâ*, the gesture of augmentation. Another notable work is an early-fifteenth-century lacquered and polychromed wooden statue of the Bodhisattva Seishi, which was probably the right-hand figure of a trinity group with Amida at the center. The concept of the Descent of Amida (Raigo) upon the occasion of the death of a pious person is generally reduced to this triad of the Amida Buddha and the two Bodhisattvas Kwannon and Seishi. Seishi is represented with his palms together in the position of *anjali-mudrâ*, the gesture of salutation.

One of the most important Asian works of art at the Rijksmuseum is the South Indian bronze Shiva Nataraja (Lord of the Dance) from the Chola period in India (twelfth century). The god Shiva is represented as dancer of the cosmic dance, surrounded by a circle of flames. His right foot rests on the dwarf-demon Apasmara-purusha. The work is considered the most beautiful of its type in Western European collections.

From South India or Sri Lanka is a bronze Buddha Gautama of the Amaravati (c. eighth century) found in East Java, Indonesia. North Indian art is also represented in the collection including a Bodhisattva Maitreya from Ghandara (Kushana period, second or third century). A group of architectural reliefs and fragments as well as figurines and freestanding pieces is also in the Indian collection.

Art from Thailand includes bronze and ceramic works of the third and second millennia B.C. as well as figurines and sculptures from later periods. Of note is a grey limestone Buddha head from the eighth century A.D., which was bequeathed to the collection by C. S. Lechner. A bronze Buddha head is from the early Ayudha period (fifteenth century).

The department's collection features art from Korea including a number of lacquer-ware boxes from the thirteenth to the fifteenth century. Works from Cambodia, Burma, Tibet, and Nepal are also in the collection.

Indonesian art is particularly well represented at the Rijksmuseum as a result of the close relationship of Holland to the region from the early seventeenth century. Indonesia was a colony of Holland, and the first governor-general of Dutch East India was appointed in 1610. Indonesia achieved independence only after World War II. Indonesian art began with the immigration of eastern and southern Indians to the island of Java, and its first great flourishing took place in Central Java during the seventh and eighth centuries with the establishment of important pilgrimage centers. The museum's collection is concentrated in the

Central Javanese period, and among its holdings are small figurines of Buddhist and Hindu gods (eighth-tenth century). An andesite statue of Manjushi from the Chandi Plaosan (probably tenth century) is among the sculptures in the collection as are two andesite *Makara* (mythical aquatic animals). These two sculptures were originally placed at entrance ways to Central Javanese temples and represent a horned monster with a human figure in its mouth (from Chandi Bubrah) and a creature with an elephant's trunk (from a temple in the Prambasan region). From the stupa of Barabudur is a head of a Buddha also made of andesite.

The Eastern Java period (begun in the tenth century) is represented in the collection. Examples of minor arts include mirrors, vessels, ceremonial lamps, ornaments, and gold jewelry, as well as a number of terracotta figures. Especially worthy of mention are three *krises*, the Javanese national weapon. Such daggers were made both for practical and ceremonial use and were thought to be imbued with magic power. Most distinctive of the pieces is a woman's *kris* dating from the sixteenth or seventeenth century with a blade fashioned in the *pamor* technique. Sculptures from the Eastern Java period include a seated Nandi made of andesite; the bull Nandi was the favorite mount of the god Shiva.

The Department of Dutch History has its origins in the Dutch Museum of History and Art founded at The Hague in 1875 by Victor de Suters. The museum was transferred to Amsterdam in 1883, where it remained an independent entity beside the State Museum of Paintings (the Rijksmuseum) until 1927. In that year the museum was divided into two sections, one of which became the Dutch Museum of History. The objects in the collection were considered more important for their historical than their art historical value. In 1967, during a thorough reorganization, the Dutch Museum of History received its present status as one of the curatorial departments of the Rijksmuseum. The Department of Dutch History opened on the ground floor of the renovated east wing in 1971.

The department provides an overview of Dutch military and political history from the Late Middle Ages through the first half of the twentieth century, with particular emphasis on the seventeenth and early eighteenth centuries, a period when the Dutch navies dominated the seas. The arrangement of the collection is not entirely systematic but is roughly chronological with a number of special themes interspersed.

Artifacts from the fifteenth and sixteenth centuries document religion, war, and politics. From the period of The Netherlands' revolt are portraits of Spanish leaders and prominent Dutch military and political figures. Also in the collection is the restored clockwork of the southern tower of St. Nicholas' Church at Utrecht; the frame dates from the fifteenth century, and the pendulum is from the sixteenth century.

Celebrated events of the Eighty Years' War are represented in a series of paintings, such as Hendrik Corneliszoon Vroom's *Battle of Gibraltar* of 1607. Adriaen van der Venne's *Zielenvisserij* (*Soul-fishing*) of 1614 is an allegory of the religion of Catholic Spain and the Protestant Republic during the Twelve-Year Truce (1609–21). Special themes of the seventeenth century are treated, all of them related to Holland's position as a maritime power and seat of vast colonial holdings. Among them is the cargo of the East Indiaman *Witte Leeuw*, which sank near St. Helena in 1613. The wreck was salvaged in 1916, and its cargo included pepper, Chinese porcelain, stoneware and earthenware pottery and personal possessions of the crew. A large group of ship models document the various types of Dutch ships constructed in the seventeenth and eighteenth centuries.

A collection of gold, silver, porcelain, and other objects reflects the Dutch presence abroad during the colonial period. Paintings of harbors and settlements in Southeast Asia are in the collection as are representations of Brazil and North Africa. A large map documents the Dutch colonization of Surinam by the West India Company with the locations of plantations marked. Objects related to Holland's naval heroes and the second Anglo-Dutch War (1665–67) include the escutcheon of the *Royal Charles*, an English flagship captured in 1667.

The French invasion of The Netherlands in 1672 is documented in paintings and other objects, and Holland's role in Ceylon (Sri Lanka) is illustrated with jewelry, weaponry, and documents. Objects related to the artificial island of Deshima, an important Dutch trading post in the bay of Nagasaki, Japan, include a laquered panel, ceramics, drawings, woodcuts, and paintings from Japan, some of which reveal the Japanese view of their European visitors.

The late eighteenth and early nineteenth centuries are documented with objects from the stadtholderly era in Holland. Relics, portraits, and so on are presented. Also from this time are works illustrating the Batavian Republic followed by objects related to the French domination of Holland. The huge painting *Battle of Waterloo* by P. W. Pienemen is exhibited. From the late nineteenth and twentieth centuries are portraits of the royal family, furniture belonging to the court, and other documents. A collection of Dutch newspapers is in the museum as is a cast-iron pulpit from the Dutch Reformed Church at Woorschoten. Documents, pamphlets, and newspapers issued during World War II are collected by the department. Photographs also illustrate historical events, social phenomena, religious institutions, and living conditions in modern Holland. An annual photographic exhibition focuses on a theme from modern history.

The Rijksmuseum also includes a study collection, open to the public on weekdays. On display here are mainly paintings which for lack of space cannot be displayed in the main galleries but which are valuable as objects of study. A small area of the study collection is devoted to the decorative arts, especially ceramics and tiles.

The library at the Rijksmuseum is the largest art history library in The Netherlands. It contains some eighty-five thousand volumes, subscribes to about five hundred art periodicals, and houses a collection of more than twenty-five thousand auction catalogues, the oldest of which dates from the sixteenth century. The library is open to the public but is noncirculating and is intended primarily for the research purposes of the museum staff.

Opened in 1888 the library incorporated the combined libraries of the former

Rijksmuseum housed at the Trippenhuis. One of the nuclei of the collection is formed by 139 books on the arts of printing and drawing, which originated from the library of the last of the Dutch stadtholders Willem V. Since 1885, the library has followed an acquisitions policy that encompasses all of the areas of art collection by the museum: general art history, painting, sculpture, decorative arts, architecture, topography, and museum and exhibition catalogues from the Middle Ages to about 1930. The library has benefited from a number of major bequests: in 1897 the A. N. Godefroy Collection (architecture and associated arts), in 1923–25 the libraries of the State Normal School for Applied Arts and the State Normal School for Teachers of Drawing, and in 1933–35 the F. G. Waller Collection of auction catalogues dating from 1722 to 1932.

The Rijksmuseum organizes and hosts special exhibitions on particular themes. Catalogues of these exhibitions are published under the direction of the museum, as are catalogues of the collection. Most recently a reference volume on paintings at the Rijksmuseum, *All the Paintings of the Rijksmuseum* (Amsterdam 1976), was produced. *The Bulletin of the Rijksmuseum*, with information on the collections, activities at the museum, and so on, is published quarterly.

Other facilities at the Rijksmuseum include a restaurant located on the ground floor. A shop for books, catalogues, postcards, slides, and so on is run by the Rijksmuseum Foundation and is also on the museum's ground floor.

Selected Bibliography

Museum publications: *Het Rijksmuseum, 1808–1958*, 1958; *All the paintings of the Rijksmuseum in Amsterdam*, 1976; *Honderd Jaar Rijksmuseum, 1885–1985*, 1985; Blankert, Albert, et al., *Gods, Saints and Heroes: Dutch Painting in the Age of Rembrandt*, 1980 (English edition); Boon, K. G., *Netherlandish Drawings of the Fifteenth and Sixteenth Centuries*, 2 vols., 1978; *Catalogue of the Collection of Japanese Prints*, 3 vol., 1977–84; *Catalogus van de nederlandsche teekeningen in het Rijksmuseum te Amsterdam*, 1943; *Catalogus van goud en zilverwerken benevens zilveren, loden en bronzen plaquetten*, 1952; *Catalogus der Kunsthistorische Bibliothek in het Rijksmuseum te Amsterdam*, 3 vols. and index, 1934–36; *Catalogus van meubelen en betimmeringen*, 1952; Lim, K. W., *Aziatische kunst uit het bezit van leden*, 1978; *Museum van Aziatische Kunst in het Rijksmuseum*, 1952 (Supplement 1962); *Prentenkabinet: Gids voor het Rijksprentenkabinet, een overzicht van de versamelingen met naamlijsten van graveur en tekenaars*, 1964; Van Schendel, A.F.E., *Nederlandse Geschiedenis in het Rijksmuseum te Amsterdam*, 1971; *Bulletin van het Rijksmuseum*, vol. 1 (1953)– vol. 33 (1985); *Facetten der verzameling* vol. 1 (1955)–13 (1973).

Other publications: Bredius, A., *Les chef-d'oeuvres du Musée royal d'Amsterdam* (Paris 1891); Fagin, Giorgio T., Ugo Ruggieri, and Raffaele Monti, *Rijksmuseum Amsterdam* (Milan 1969); Haak, B., *Art Treasures of the Rijksmuseum* (New York 1966); Meijer, E. R., *Rijksmuseum di Amsterdam* (Novara 1914); *Het Trippenhaus te Amsterdam* (Amsterdam 1983).

LORRAINE KARAFEL and ANDREA GASTEN

The Hague

ROYAL CABINET OF PAINTINGS, "MAURITSHUIS" (officially KON-INKLIJK KABINET VAN SCHILDERIJEN, "MAURITSHIUS"; alternately MAURITSHUIS), Korte Vijverberg 8, 2513 The Hague.

Built in the seventeenth century by a member of the Stadholders' family, the Mauritshuis today contains a state-owned collection of more than five hundred paintings, miniatures, and sculptures based on the collections of the House of Orange. This splendid example of Dutch classical Baroque architecture was built for Count (later Prince) Johan Maurits of Nassau-Siegen, a grandson of Willem the Silent's brother Jan the Elder, by Pieter Post between 1633 and 1644 from the plans of Jacob van Campen, who later designed the Stadhuis, now the Royal Palace, in Amsterdam. Located in the center of The Hague, just off the Binnenhof, or inner courtyard, the exterior still maintains the character of a seventeenth-century Dutch residence.

Johan Maurits, from whom the Mauritshuis takes its name, lived in his house for only three years before becoming stadholder of Cleve in 1647; on his death in 1679, it was sold. The building was leased to the States-General in 1685 for use as a temporary residence for ambassadors and distinguished guests. After the departure of the duke of Marlborough in 1704, the interior was destroyed by fire. Restoration unifying the hall, landing, and staircase into a single space began in 1718, at which time were added the present open staircase and the ground-floor reception room decorated in the style of Louis XIV. The Venetian artist Giovanni Antonio Pelligrini's panels *Apollo*, *Aurora*, and *Night*, with the *Four Elements* and the *Four Temperaments* (1718), in the Great Hall date from this restoration; the Dutch painter Jacob de Wit's five ceiling panels of which *Apollo* and the *Nine Muses* (1793), now in the Reception Hall, were originally designed for a house on the Rapenburg in Leiden. During the eighteenth century, the Mauritshuis was used for many purposes, from the leasing of its cellar to a wine merchant to serving as the seat of the Military High Court. The building was plastered between 1855 and 1879, but it was returned to its original sandstone and brick exterior in 1885. Parquet floors were added in 1890, along with dark red wall coverings. They were replaced in 1950 with the current lighter coverings, and central heating and a new lighting system were installed. In spite of these later alterations, the Mauritshuis still projects the intimacy of its original design, an ambiance that complements a collection that is generally contemporary with the building.

Johan Maurits had originally built his house to contain the collection of art and natural history artifacts he had obtained during his tenure as captain-governor and admiral-general of the Dutch colony in Brazil. Many of the works completed by the six artists he employed there between 1637 and 1644 were dispersed by Johan Maurits himself during his lifetime; however, two works, Albert Eeckhout's *Two Brazilians* and *Tortoises* (c. 1642), are in the current collection. During the nineteenth century, the Mauritshuis was returned to its original purpose when it was first designated as the site of the National Library by Louis Napoleon in 1807, and later, after King Willem I presented his personal art collection to the nation in 1816, it was purchased by the state and declared the Royal Cabinet of Paintings and Curiosities in 1820.

The early museum was divided into two collections, the Cabinet of Paintings on the upper floor and the Cabinet of Curiosities on the ground floor. The collections were formally opened on January 1, 1822. Admittance was granted on Wednesdays and Saturdays, between ten and one o'clock, to anyone who was well dressed and not accompanied by a child. The first catalogue listed 274 items, including more than 100 works that had previously formed the collection of stadholders (Willem I through Willem V) and King Willem I. In 1875 the Cabinet of Curiosities was transferred to another building, and since that time, the Mauritshuis has been devoted to painting and sculpture.

The historical core of the collection is those works originally belonging to members of the House of Orange. Among them are four works by Rembrandt and Holbein, as well as paintings by Rubens, van Dyck, Jan Steen, Ostade, and other notable Dutch and Flemish artists. Willem I's notable collection, which had included Hieronymus Bosch's *Garden of Earthly Delights*, fell to the Spanish during the sixteenth century, and his successor, Prince Maurits, was not an avid collector. However, his second son, Prince Frederik Hendrik, and his wife, Amalia van Solms, were enthusiastic patrons who established an art gallery in the Stadholder's Quarters, not far from the Mauritshuis, that contained more than fifty works, emphasizing contemporary Dutch artists such as Honthorst, Roeland Savery, Cornelis van Haarlem, and Paulus Bril. By the end of Frederik Hendrik's reign in 1647, the royal collection had expanded to include paintings by Bloemaert, Goltzius, Rembrandt, and Terbrugghen. On the death of Amalia van Solms in 1675, her personal collection, containing some of the works referred to above, but by now greatly expanded, was divided among her four daughters, and consequently, a large part of the Orange Collection again left The Netherlands.

What remained was the inheritance of the king-stadholder Willem III from his grandfather Willem I and his father Willem II, and it was soon considerably enlarged with numerous additions of Dutch and Italian masters, some from the English Royal Collection. Consequently, Willem III's collection had a more international flavor than those of his predecessors. It was also more extensive, being housed not only in the Oude Hof in The Hague but also in the Orange country houses of Soestdijk, Het Loo, Huis ten Bosch, Honselaarsdijk, and Rijswijk. However, it seems that this collection, too, had been formed only to be later dispersed. Queen Anne of England, Willem III's successor, laid claim after her accession to those works originating from the English Royal Collection, and the widow of Johan Willem Friso, heir to the properties of the House of Orange on the death of Willem III in 1702, proceeded to sell the remainder of the collection at auction.

This pattern of acquisition and dispersal was halted with the accession of Willem IV in 1732. He had inherited not only parts of the collection of the stadholder of Friesland (which contained a quarter of the Solms bequest) but also part of the collection of Willem III and, through his grandmothers, still other works from the collection of Frederik Hendrik and Amalia van Solms. Willem IV increased the collection beyond those works he had inherited, acquiring a Rembrandt in 1734 and showing a preference for artists such as Schalcken, van der Werff, Dou, Poelenburgh, and Lingelbach. Although Willem IV died prematurely in 1751, his wife, Anne of Hanover, not only maintained the collection but increased it with works such as Jan Steen's *As the Old Sing, so Twitter the Young*. Her son Willem V appears to have inherited her zest for collecting, making his first purchase at the age of twelve and thereafter significantly increasing the collection. In 1768 he acquired forty-one major works from the collector Govert van Slingelandt, which included examples of Rubens, van Dyck, Rembrandt, Holbein, Ter Borch, Potter, Mor, Metsu, Ostade, Steen, and Teniers.

It was Willem V's collection, numbering more than two hundred works, that was confiscated by the invading French troops in 1795, moved to France, and only partially returned in 1815, with sixty-eight paintings still in French collections today. Those works that were returned were presented to the nation by King Willem I in 1816, and throughout his reign, this monarch acquired additional masterpieces that were subsequently presented to the Mauritshuis. They included Rogier van der Weyden's *Lamentation*, Rembrandt's *Anatomy Lesson of Dr. Nicolas Tulp*, and Vermeer's *View of Delft*. The immense private collection of King Willem II was auctioned in 1850–51, and therefore it is not included in the present collection; however, members of the House of Orange have generously donated works to the collection during the past century. The directors of the Mauritshuis have augmented and shaped the collection as did their royal predecessors, from J. W. Mazel (1841–75) to H. R. Hoetink (1972–).

The museum staff consists of a director, an assistant curator, and a part-time assistant curator, all of whom are art historians; other staff include a registrar, a secretary, and a part-time assistant.

The Mauritshuis collection contains Netherlandish and German art of the fifteenth and sixteenth centuries and Flemish and Dutch art of the seventeenth and eighteenth centuries. To consolidate the collection, all Italian and Spanish works originally a part of the collection were loaned to the Rijksmuseum (q.v) in Amsterdam in 1950, and in exchange, the Mauritshuis received a number of works from the fifteenth and sixteenth centuries, Flemish paintings from the seventeenth century, and forty-six miniatures. For the sake of historical continuity, the Italian and Spanish paintings have been included here along with the loaned miniatures that reinforce the collection's ties to the House of Orange.

The Mauritshuis exhibits an outstanding collection of seventeen works by Rembrandt that were acquired primarily from the Cabinet of Willem V and from the bequest (1946) of A. Bredius. The heart of this group consists of three self-portraits dating from 1629, 1633–34, and 1669, the latter purchased in 1947 with funds provided by the Vereniging Rembrandt and friends of the museum. Related to these works are portraits of Rembrandt's mother (c. 1628), his father (c. 1629), and his brother Adrian (1650, purchased in 1891). Among the earlier works are *Simeon's Song of Praise* (1631), *Andromeda Chained to a Rock* (c. 1631), and the *Anatomy Lesson of Dr. Nicolas Tulp* (1632). Works from Rembrandt's middle period include *Bathsheba* (1637) and an unusual *Forest Scene with Ruins* (c. 1638, on private loan to the collection). Later paintings on display are the *Two Negroes* (1661) and *Homer* (1663). The museum also owns three works by the Delft painter Johannes Vermeer: they include *Diana and Her Companions* (1654), *View of Delft from the South* (1658), and *Head of a Girl* (1660, from the bequest of A. A. des Tombes, 1903).

All of the traditional subject categories of seventeenth-century Dutch painting are represented in the collection. The vast number of portraits on exhibit indicates the strong tradition of portraiture in the Low Countries. Depicting members of the House of Orange, famous men and their wives of the United Provinces, local dignitaries, and prosperous couples, the Mauritshuis collection is virtually a mirror of contemporary Dutch society.

Prince Willem of Orange (Willem I) is shown in two works from the late sixteenth century by Adriaen Key (c. 1579) and Michiel Mierevelt (one of eleven works by the artist in the collection). Other notable examples from this period include two male portraits by Anthonius Mor from the 1650s; the anonymous portrait *François de Virieu* and *Françoise de Witte* (1574); and Pieter Pieterzoon's *Cornelis Cornelisz Schellinger* (1584). The Hague artist Johannes van Ravesteyn is represented in the collection by a series of twenty-five portraits of officers (c. 1611–21), originally from Honselaersdijk Castle. Other works from the first half of the seventeenth century are Fans Hals' portrait *Jacob Pietersz Olycan and Aletta Hanemans* (1625); Gerard van Honthorst's portraits *Willem II, Frederik Hendrik*, and *Amalia van Solms*; Jan Lieven's study, an *Old Man* (c. 1630, from the Cabinet of Willem V); Govaert Flinck's *Manasse Ben Israel* (1637); Thomas de Keyser's historicizing portrait the *Burgomeesters of Amsterdam Learning of the Arrival of Marie de Medici* (1638); and Adriaen Hanneman's unusual portrait *Constantine Huygens with His Five Children* (1640), an interesting contrast with Cornelis Janson's *Jan Beck, Elector of Middleburg, and His Five Children* (1650).

The collection contains many works from the second half of the century as well, with a particular concentration in works from the 1660s. They include Nicolas Maes' portrait of the Dordrecht merchant *Jacob Trip*; Ferdinand Bol's portraits *Admiral Michiel de Ruyter* (1667), *Maerten van Juchen*, and *Vice-Admiral Engel de Ruyter* (1669); and Gerard Ter Borch's *Self Portrait* (1668–70) and the portrait *Cornelis de Graeff* (1674). Later seventeenth-century works include Caspar Netscher's *Michiel Ten Hove* and his wife *Elizabeth van Bebber* (c. 1675), and Godfried Schalcken's *Stadholder-King Willem III* (1699). Other Dutch portraitists included in the Mauritshuis collection are Backer, de Baen, van Dyck, van der Helst, Moreelse, van Musscher, van der Mijn, Mijtens, van den Temple, Verspronck, and Westerbaen.

The Mauritshuis' extensive collection of landscape paintings is second in size only to its holdings in portraiture. Like the portraits, these landscapes present a particularly fine survey of the evolution of this subject in the United Provinces during the seventeenth century. Perhaps the earliest work on exhibit is Hendrik Avercamp's *Winter Scene* (1610, on loan from the Rijksmuseum), followed by Esaias van de Velde's *Repast in the Dark* (1614, purchased in 1873). There is a small group of works from the 1630s, such as Pieter Post's *Landscape with Cavalry Engagement* (1631), Jan Porcellis' *Shipwreck off the Coast* (1631), and several works by Salomon van Ruysdael, including *Bridge* (1628–29) and *Waterside with Old Trees* (1633); however, the majority of the holdings are from the second half of the century.

The collection includes an interesting group of works by Dutch artists who traveled and worked in Italy during this period. They include Jan Asselijn's *Italian Coast with the Tomb of Cecelia Metella* (purchased by the Stichting Johan Maurits van Nassau), Nicolas Berchem's *Fording a Brook*, Joannes Both's *Italian Landscape*, Karel du Jardin's *Young Shepherd Playing with a Dog* (among five similar panels), Frederick Moucheron's *Italian Landscape* (c. 1670), and three rare Italianate panels by Jan Willemsz. Lapp. These European scenes are complemented by Frans Post's *View of Itamaraca Island, Brazil* (1637), and *Brazilian Landscape* (1667, donated 1906).

The majority of the Mauritshuis landscapes reflect the familiar Dutch countryside, as seen in works such as Joris van der Haagen's *Panorama Near Arnhem* (1649), Guillam de Bois' *Road through the Dunes* (1649) and *Hilly Landscape by a Stream* (1652), Egbert Poel's *Landscape with a Fish Market* (1650), Jan van de Capelle's *Water Scene* (1653), and Aert de Neer's *Ice Sport* (1655, purchased by the Vereniging Rembrandt). Notable works of the 1660s include Jan Wijnant's *Forest Edge* (1659) and *Road in the Dunes* (1675), Cornelis Saftleven's *Landscape with Sheep* (1660), and Adrian van de Velde's *Landscape with Cattle* (1663) and *Beachview* (1665), both from the Cabinet of Willem V.

The Mauritshuis also contains several works by each of the major seventeenth-century Dutch landscape painters. The Dordrecht artist Albert Cuyp is represented by four works, including his *Salmon Fishing, Cattle in a River, Ruins of Rijnsberg Abbey*, and *Migrating Peasants in a Southern Countryside* (1655–60). Meindert Hobbema, who lived and worked in Amsterdam, appears with his *Watermill*, and *Landscape with a View of Deventer* (1660–65). The third artist emphasized in the collection is Hobbema's teacher, Jacob van Ruisdael. Among his seven works on display are the *View of Haarlem from the Dunes at Overveen* (1660), *Beachview*, and *Waterfall* (1665).

The collection has important holdings in two related areas, the seascape and the cityscape. Outstanding are the five water scenes by Jan van Goyen, including his *View of Dordrecht from Papendrecht* (1633), *River View* (1640–45), *Fishermen by a Lake* (1651), *View on the Rhine near Hoogelten* (1653), and *Estuary*

(1655). Other significant seascapes are Willem van de Velde's *Conquest of the Ship "Royal Princess"* (purchased in 1822), and *Sunset at Sea* (from the Bredius bequest, 1946), Simon de Vlieger's *Beach View* (1643), and Jan van de Capelle's *Ships off the Coast* (1660).

Just as he admired the land he had created and the sea he had turned to his profit, so did the seventeenth-century Dutch patron take pleasure in the views of the cities he had built. The extent to which the real was seen as derived from the ideal can be seen in Hendrik van Steenwijk the Younger's *Imaginary City Square* (1614, from the Cabinet of Willem V). Most of the cityscapes are from the second half of the century, and although numerous, they represent fewer artists than is the case with the landscapes. Important works are Jacob van Ruisdael's *View of the Vijverburg, The Hague*, and *View of the Damrak, Amsterdam*, Jan van der Heyden's *Townscape with the Jesuit Church, Dusselforf* (1667), *Church of Veere*, and *Oudzijdsvoorburgwall, Amsterdam*; and Gerrit Berckheyde's *View of the Hofvijver and the Buitenhof, The Hague, The Hunting Party Leaving from the Hofvijver, The Hague*, and the *Oude Gracht, Haarlem*.

Complementing the collection's cityscapes are a number of works showing the interiors of major Dutch churches. Although some of them are anonymous or idealized, such as Bartholomeus van Bassen's *Interior of a Catholic Church* (1626), the majority depict specific churches, such as Hendrik van Vliet's *Interior of the Oude Kerk at Delft*, Gerard Houckgeist's two variations of the *Ambulatory of the Nieuwe Kerk in Delft with the Tomb of Willem the Silent* (both dated 1651); and Antonie de Lorme's *Interior of Sint Laurenskerk, Rotterdam*. The Mauritshuis also includes works by the two acknowledged masters of this subject. They are Emanuel de Witte's *Oudekerk in Amsterdam during a Service* (1654, purchased by the Vereniging Rembrandt) and Pieter Saenredam's *Interior of St. Cunera, Rhenen* (1655, also purchased by the Vereniging Rembrandt) and *Exterior of the Church of Our Lady, Utrecht* (1659).

Dutch genre painting from the seventeenth century, with several later examples from the eighteenth and nineteenth centuries, is well represented in the collection. Of special interest are the thirteen works by Jan Steen, including his *Dancing Peasants* and *Village Fair* (both c. 1648), the *Toothpuller* (c. 1651), *Girl Eating Oysters* (1658–60), the *Doctor's Visit* and *The Sick Girl* (both from 1660), and two works on the theme *As the Old Sing, So Twitter the Young (The Way You Hear It Is the Way You Say It)* (both from 1665).

Important works from the first half of the century are Pieter Codde's *Backgammon Players* (1628), Jan Molenaer's panels of the *Five Senses* (1637), Adriaen Brouwer's *Inn with Drunken Peasants* and the *Smoker*, Judith Leyster's *Man Offering Money to a Young Woman*, and Issack Ostade's *Travellers Outside an Inn* (1646). From this period as well are nine works by the Haarlem artist, Philip Wouwermans, many of which were originally in the Cabinet of Willem V.

The majority of the Mauritshuis' holdings in genre painting date from the second half of the seventeenth century, particularly in the decades of the 1650s and 1660s. From the 1650s, one finds the Zwolle artist Gerard Ter Borch's *Mother Fine-Combing the Hair of Her Child* (1650), *Unwelcome News* (1653), and *Woman Writing a Letter* (1655); the Leiden painter Gerard Dou's *Young Mother with Child* and *Young Woman Holding Keys* (both dated 1658 and purchased in 1690 by the States General as part of a gift to Charles II of England); and the Delft master Pieter de Hoogh's *Courtyard in Delft* (1656). The following decade produced a group of outstanding works such as Frans van Mieris' *Teasing* (1661) and *Boy Blowing Bubbles* (1663), Gabriel Metsu's *Young Woman Composing Music*, Adriaen Ostade's *Peasants in an Inn* (1662), and Jacob Ochterveldt's *Fishmonger* (1665–70). Dou's follower Godfried Schalcken appears in two works from the end of the century, *The Wasted Lesson in Morals* and *The Medical Examination*. These works, like many of the genre scenes noted here, were originally in the Cabinet of Willem V.

The collection includes a number of works by The Hague painter Cornelis Troost, such as his *Nine Moralizing Theater Scenes*, *Garland Alongside Biberius* (five pastels from 1740), *Organgrinder*, and *The Guard Room* (1747). Also from this period are two works by Philip van Dyk that were originally in the Cabinet of Willem V, the *Woman Playing a Lute* and *Lady Attending to Her Toilet*, and the Hague painter H. W. Schweicknardt's *Vegetable Seller*. Another Hague native, A. H. Bakker-Korff, is represented by *The Warrior* (1876).

As might be expected from its representative holdings from the Golden Age of Dutch painting, the Mauritshuis includes examples of works devoted to birds (Carel Fabritus' *Goldfinch* from 1654, and Melchior d'Hondecoeter's many scenes of hens, ducks, and geese from the 1670s), animals (Paulus Potter's *Bull* and *Cow Reflected in Water*, from the late 1640s); and hunts (Adriaen Beeldemaker's *Fox Hunt*, and Nicolas Berchem's *Wild Boar Hunt*, from 1659).

The collection of still-life paintings contains early seventeenth-century works by Ambrosius Bosschaert and his brother-in-law Balthasar van der Ast. Also from the first half of the century are Pieter Claeszoon's *Vanitas Still Life* (1630) and *Still Life with a Lighted Candle* and Gerrit Heda's *Still Life (Breakfast Piece)* from 1629 and *Still Life with a Nautilus Cup* from 1640. As in other areas, the greatest concentration and often the best examples come from the second half of the century. Jan Davidsz. de Heem's several works can be compared with those by artists he influenced such as Cornelis de Heem and Maria Oosterwyck. The collection also presents a number of works by The Hague painter Abraham van Beyeren, including his *Still Life with Seafood* and *Still Life with Game and Fowl*, and by the Amsterdam artist Willem Kalf, including his *Still Life with Shells and Coral*. Significant examples from the latter part of the century are Rachel Ruysch's *Flowers* and Jan Weenix's *Dead Hare* (1689), *Still Life with Game and Fruit* (1704), and *Hunting Still Life* (1708).

Although allegorical painting did not enjoy the popularity in the United Provinces that it did elsewhere in Europe during the seventeenth century, the Mauritshuis presents several such works dating primarily from the first half of the century. The Haarlem landscape painter Hendrik Goltzius appears in three works

(*Minerva, Hercules and Cacus*, and *Hercules*), all from the beginning of the century, and works of Joachim Wittewael (*Mars and Venus Surprised by Vulcan*) and Abraham Bloemart (*Theagens and Charicleia* of 1626 and the *Marriage of Peleus and Thetis* of 1638) suggest the evolution in this area to mid-century. The collection also contains an unusual series of rondels, the *Five Senses* (1636), by Dirk Hals, as well as an interesting historical allegory, *Putti with a Cartouche Bearing the Birth Date of Frederik Hendrik* (1651), by Salomon de Bray. Other artists represented in this category include Nicolas Berchem, Willem van Haecht, Nicolaes Moyaert, and Pieter Quast.

Although few in comparison to its holdings in other areas, the Mauritshuis' collection of history paintings includes several important works that relate to the House of Orange and to Dutch history. Among the earliest of them is a work by The Hague painter Hendrik Pacx, *The Princes of Orange and Their Families Riding Out from the Buitenhof, The Hague* (1625–30), followed closely by Adriaen van Nieulandt's *Maurits, Prince of Orange, on the Beach at Scheveningen* (1640), and a related work by Johannes Lingelbach, *Charles II Leaving Scheveningen* (1660). Of particular interest as well are two panels by L. Backhuysen, the *Arrival of Prince Willem III at Orange Polder in January 1691* (1692) and the *Dock of the Dutch East India Company in Amsterdam* (1696). Also noteworthy is Dirck van Delen's *The Knights' Hall during the 1651 Assembly of the States-General*, since it shows that meeting place adjacent to the Mauritshuis.

Examples of Dutch religious painting from the fifteenth through the seventeenth century are also on display. Among the earliest works are a triptych by the Master of Alkmaar and *Joseph Interpreting Dreams* (1495) by the Haarlem artist Jan Mostaert. Representing Haarlem painting in the sixteenth century are the *Adoration of the Shepherds* and the *Adoration of the Magi*, both by Maerten van Heemskerck, and the *Massacre of the Innocents* (1591) and *Before the Flood* (1593), both by Cornelis Cornelisz. van Haarlem. The Amsterdam artist Pieter Aertsen, who also worked in Antwerp before returning to his native city, is responsible for a *Crucifixion* (1550). The collection contains seventeenth-century examples of religious art by Rembrandt's teacher (Pieter Lastman's *Raising of Lazarus*, 1622) and two of his followers (Aert de Gelder's *Judah and Tamar*, *The Temple Entrance*, and the *Presentation in the Temple* and Barent Fabritius' *Departure of Benjamin*). Also included is Hendrik Terbrugghen's *Deliverance of St. Peter* (1624), an interesting example of Utrecht Caravaggism.

The Mauritshuis owns an outstanding collection of western European Renaissance and Baroque paintings from outside of Holland. These Flemish, French, German, Italian, and Spanish works reflect the taste of the members of the House of Orange who originally owned them, as well as that of the museum directors who arranged for their purchase. As noted earlier, most of the Italian and Spanish works have been loaned to the Rijksmuseum (Amsterdam) in exchange for Netherlandish, Dutch, and Flemish works complementing those works comprising the majority of the Mauritshuis' holdings.

The historical and cultural ties between The Netherlands and Belgium account for the unusually large number of Flemish works on display. Perhaps the earliest of them is Rogier van der Weyden's *Lamentation*; other fifteenth-century paintings include three anonymous works from the Bruges school, *Resurrection* (1450) by Dirk Bouts, a portrait by Hans Memling, and two *Forest Scenes* by Gerard David. Many anonymous masters from this period are also on display. They include the Master of the Legend of St. Barbara, the Master of the Brandon Portraits, the Master of the Solomon Triptych, and the Master of Frankfort.

Sixteenth-century Flemish holdings span that century. Works from the first quarter, showing the Italian tendencies especially strong in works from Antwerp, include Jan Gossaert's portrait *Floris Van Egmond* (1517) and *Madonna and Child* (1520), Quentin Metsys' *Christ Carrying the Cross* (1510), Joachim Patenier's *Landscape with St. Anthony* (1520), and Jan Provost the Younger's *Triptych with Madonna and Saints* (1525). Important works from early in the second quarter of the century are Adrien Isenbrandt's *Enthroned Madonna and Child* (1525), Henri Met de Bles' *Paradise* (1525–30), and Joos van Cleve's *St. John the Baptist and Christ as Children* (c. 1530). The diverse subject matter so prevalent in the latter part of the century is suggested in panels such as Joachim Beuckelaer's *Kitchen Table with Christ at Emmaus* (C. 1566), Martin de Vos' *Moses Showing the Tables of the Law to the Israelites* (1575), four works by Jan Bruegel, including the *Depiction of Cybele*, *Paradise*, *Rest on the Flight into Egypt*, and *Christ Releasing Souls from Limbo* (1597); and David Vinckboons' *County Fair*.

The seventeenth-century Flemish holdings are dominated by the presence of Peter Paul Rubens and his followers. The Antwerp master is represented by eight works, including *Adam and Eve in Paradise* (c. 1615, from the Cabinet of Willem V); *Assumption of the Virgin* (c. 1619); portraits of his wives, *Isabella Brandt* (c. 1620) and *Helena Fourment* (c. 1638–44), both from the Cabinet of Willem V; the *Faun and Nymph*; and the *Triumph of Rome* (1622–23, donated in 1947). Rubens' one-time assistant Anthony van Dyck is responsible for a number of portraits, including those of the Antwerp painter and connoisseur *Pieter Stevens* and his wife *Anna Wahl* (1627); the sculptor *Andreas Colijns de Nole*; and *Jan III of Nassau-Siegen*. Other artists associated with Rubens who are included in the Mauritshuis collection are Hendrik van Balen, Frans Snyders, and Frans Francken the Younger.

Other important Antwerp works from the first part of the century include Jacob Jordaens' *Adoration of the Shepherds* (1618) and *Marsyas Punished by Midas* (1635) and Pieter II Neeffs' *Interior of Antwerp Cathedral*. The Liège artist Gerard de Lairesse and the Brussels painter David Teniers the Younger are also present, the latter in two works originally in the Cabinet of Willem V, the *Alchemist* and *Kitchen Interior* (1644).

The Mauritshuis holdings also include a large group of works by German artists that date primarily from the sixteenth century. Although some religious subjects are present, such as in Hans Kulmbach's *Mary Cleophus and Her Family* and *Mary Salome and Her Family* (both from 1513), the emphasis in this period is on portraiture. Important examples include Jacob Susenegger's three portraits of the children of Ferdinand of Austria (c. 1530); Hans Holbein the Younger's five portraits, including *Jane Seymour* (1536–37) and *Desiderus Erasmus*; Bartholomeus Bruyn the Elder's *Double Portrait* (1529) and *Portrait of a Young Woman* (1540); and Lucas Cranach the Elder's depiction of the Reformation leader *Philip Melanchton* (1545). Also on display is Anton Tischbein's portrait *Carolina Wilhelmina, Princess of Orange* (1778).

With the exception of Piero di Cosimo's portraits *Francesco Ciamberti* and *Guillano da San Gallo* (c. 1490), works in the Italian collection are primarily from the sixteenth and seventeenth centuries. Most prominent in the earlier group are the Venetians, including Jacopo de Barbari's portrait *Hendrik, Duke of Mecklenburg* (1507), Paris Bordone's *Christ Blessing*, Titian's *Venus and the Organist*, Veronese's portrait *Charles V*, and two portraits by Tintoretto. Painters from Parma include Parmagianino, represented by his *Circumcision*, and Antonio Correggio, represented by his *Madonna and Child* and *Christ on the Mount of Olives*. High Renaissance painting from Rome includes Raphael's *Holy Family with St. John the Baptist*.

Although limited, the Italian holdings present a good survey of Baroque painting. The earliest work in this sequence is Annibale Carracci's *Holy Family*, followed by Domenico Feti's *Ecce Homo*. The Roman interest in landscape, perhaps influenced by the Northern painters who were working there in the middle of the century, is seen in panels by Luca Carlevarijs, Gaspard Dughet, and Alessandro Magnasco. Works from the second half of the seventeenth century include Sassoferrato's *Praying Madonna*, Francesco Solimena's *Annunciation*, and Luca Giordano's *Four Women Making Music*. Giovanni Antonio Pelligrini's decorations for the Great Hall of the Mauritshuis (c. 1718) extend this survey into the eighteenth century.

In contrast to holdings in the areas decribed above, the collections of French and Spanish painting are very small. Among the most important are Philippe de Champaigne's portrait *Jacobus Govaerts* (1665), Jean Baptiste Siméon Chardin's *Still Life*, Juan Mazo's portrait *Infante Balthasar Carlos* (c. 1635), Mateo Cerezo the Younger's *Penitent Mary Magdalene* (1661), and Bartolomé Murillo's *Madonna and Child*.

The Mauritshuis exhibits a notable collection of forty-six portrait miniatures depicting members of the House of Orange and the English Houses of Tudor and Stuart. Among the earliest of the Dutch sovereigns portrayed is the *Stadholder Frederik Hendrik* and his wife, *Amalia Solms*. Other family portraits of particular interest include *Stadholder Willem III* (by Benjamin Arland); *Willem Frederik, Stadholder of Friesland* (c. 1665); and the portraits *Stadholder Willem V* and his sister *Wilhelmina Carolina* (by Robert Musoard, 1751). Also portrayed are *Henrietta Maria Stuart*, wife of Stadholder Willem II, and *Frederika Sophia of Prussia*, wife of Stadholder Willem V (by Loch Phaff, c. 1790).

Edward VI of England, son of Henry VIII, is shown at the age of three in a miniature by John Bettes, and his older sister, *Elizabeth I*, is portrayed in a work by Nicolas Hilliard, as is their cousin *Mary Stuart, Queen of Scots* (c. 1565). Mary's husband, *Henry Stuart, Lord Darnley*, is also depicted (c. 1565), as is their son, the future *James I* of England, shown in portraits of him as an infant (by Arnould van Brounckhurst), at the age of ten (c. 1565), and as a young man (by Nicolas Hilliard). *Charles I* appears frequently in the collection in works by Peter Oliver (1621), John Hoskins (as a pendant to a portrait of the queen, *Henrietta Maria*, 1632), and Henri Toutin (1636). Works by Samuel Cooper (1665) and Nathaniel Thach are titled *Charles II*. The collection also includes a rare portrait of the Flemish sculptor *François Duquesnoy* by Peter Oliver (1613).

The museum houses a small but select collection of sculpture by Dutch and French artists from the seventeenth and eighteenth centuries. Perhaps the earliest of these works is an unusual gilded earthenware bust *Willem I, Prince of Orange*, by Hendrik de Keyser. Other members of the House of Orange are portrayed in a series of marble busts by Rombout Verhulst from 1683. They include the *Stadholder Frederik Hendrik*; the *Stadholder Willem II* and his wife *Mary Stuart*; and the *Stadholder Willem III*. Verhulst is also represented by two terracotta studies for the monuments of the navel heroes *Michiel Adriaensz. De Ruyter* (1676) and *Willem Joseph, Baron Van Gent* (1677). Jan Blommendale, a student of Verhulst, is responsible for two figures, each titled *Stadholder Willem III* (1676 and 1699). The collection contains a bronze bust (by Theo van Reijn, 1933), *Dr. Abraham Bredius*, the art historian who was director of the Mauritshuis from 1889 to 1909 and whose bequest (1946) significantly enriched its holdings.

The French sculptor Jean Antoine Houdon's marble bust *Vice-Admiral Pierre André de Sufferen de Saint-Tropez* (1781) can be compared with the nearly contemporary busts *Stadholder Willem V* and his wife, *Frederika Sophia Wilhelmina* of Prussia, by Marie-Anne Falconet (1782). The sculptress' father-in-law, Étienne Falconet, is represented by the small marble *Amour Mechant* (1757).

The library of the Mauritshuis and the archives are open to the public upon prior application. Annual reports on the museum's holdings are included in ''Jaarverslagen van het Koninklijk Kabinet van Schilderijen, Mauritshuis te 's-Gravenhage'' in *Verslagen Van's Rijks Verzamelingen Van Geshiedenis en Kunst*, which is available from 1878.

Selected Bibliography

Museum publications: *Mauritshuis, The Royal Cabinet of Paintings: Illustrated General Catalogue*, 1977; Van den Bogaert, E., P.P.J. Whitehead, and H. R. Hoetink, eds., *Johan Maurits van Nassau-Siegen (1604–1679), a Humanist Prince in Europe and Brazil*, 1979; Vries, A.S. de, M. Toth-Ubbens, and W. Froentjes, with a foreword by H. R. Hoetink, *Rembrandt in the Mauritshuis*, 1978.

Other publications: Drossaers, S.W.A., and Th. Lunsingh Scheurleer, *Inventarissen van de Inboedels in de Verblijven van de Oranjes I, II, Em III*, 1974–76; Hudig, F., *Frederik Hendrik en de Kunst van Zijn Tijd*, 1928; Terwen, J. J., *Opnieuw Kennismaken*

Met de Mauritshuis, Rede Uitgesproken Bij de Aanvarding van Het Ambt van Gewoon Hoogleraar in de Geschiedenis van de Bouwkunst Aan de Universiteit van Leiden, 1972; Vonk, A. W., *De Kunstverzamelingen van Stadhouder Willem V en Hare Lotgevallen Sedert 1795*, 1933; Brenninkmeyer-DeRooy, B., "De Schilderijengalerij van Prins Willem V op het Buitenhof te Den Haag," *Antiek* (1976), pp. 138–76; Willemijn Fock, C., "De Schilderijengalerij van Prins Willem V op het Buitenhof te Den Haag," *Antiek* (1976), pp. 113–17.

CYNTHIA LAWRENCE

——— Rotterdam ———

BOYMANS MUSEUM-VAN BEUNINGEN MUSEUM (officially MUSEUM BOYMANS-VAN BEUNINGEN; alternately BOYMANS-VAN BEUNINGEN), 18–20 Mathenesserlaan, Rotterdam.

In 1949, at the one-hundredth anniversary of the founding of the Frans Jacob Otto Boymans Museum, Daniel George van Beuningen permitted a selection from his extensive private collection to be displayed in the museum in celebration of the event. Van Beuningen's collection as the choice for the centennial celebration of the museum was aptly appropriate. Within ten years some 180 objects from van Beuningen's collection would be purchased by the city of Rotterdam, and in 1961 his name would be added to the title of the Boymans Museum in recognition of the significance of his legacy and his support of the museum over the years.

As collectors, Boymans and van Beuningen were very dissimilar individuals. Boymans' collecting tastes were eclectic and eccentric. During his lifetime (1767–1847), Boymans accumulated hundreds of paintings and almost countless drawings in his home (and eventually even in his stable) in Utrecht. Reports of Boymans' avid collecting and rumors about his own amateur attempts at restoration, coupled with a lack of knowledge by anyone except Boymans himself of exactly what his collection contained (although part of it was catalogued in 1811), created an atmosphere in Utrecht that was completely unreceptive to Boymans' wish that the city accept his collection and provide a museum for its display. Meanwhile, M. C. Bichon van IJsselmonde, the burgomaster of Rotterdam, who had been a childhood schoolmate of Boymans, moved to obtain the collection for Rotterdam. IJsselmonde was keenly aware that in recent years his own city had allowed the important art collection of Verstolk van Soelen to leave Rotterdam; before Boymans' gift, there were only eleven paintings in the city's collection.

Just eight days before his death, Frans Boymans bequeathed his entire collection to the city of Rotterdam with the understanding that it would be displayed in a museum bearing his name. The museum building obtained by IJsselmonde was the old Schielandshuis, the administrative building for the drainage project of the Schieland, built in 1662–65 by Pieter Post (architect of the Mauritshuis).

In 1852 Arie Johannes Lamme was appointed director of the museum, which opened on July 3, 1849. When Arie Lamme and his father, Arnoldus, inventoried Boymans' possessions in 1847, they found 1,193 paintings, thousands of drawings, and a large number of European and Asiatic porcelains. Those works that the Lammes believed were not of museum quality were auctioned off in 1853 to create an acquisition fund for future purchases. In 1864 a disastrous fire in the Schielandshuis destroyed a substantial portion of the remaining Boymans Collection (including works by Rembrandt, Aelbert Cuyp, Steen, Ruysdael, and Koninck and a signed and dated domestic interior of 1648 by Carel Fabritius).

In contrast to Boymans' apparently unrestrained tastes, van Beuningen's collection reflected his careful selection of studied acquisitions made over decades of discerning connoisseurship. In addition to including old furniture, Delft faience, and Italian majolica, his collection in 1949 contained no fewer than thirty-six fifteenth- and sixteenth-century Netherlandish panels, forty-one Dutch and Flemish Baroque paintings, more than two dozen Italian Renaissance pictures, sixteen Rococo works from Italy and France, thirty-one modern paintings, and seventeen Renaissance and Baroque drawings. By the time his collection was acquired by the city, these numbers had increased. In the area of fifteenth-century Northern art alone, van Beuningen added panels to his collection by the Master of the Life of the Virgin, Gerard David, and Geertgen tot Sint Jans. Van Beuningen was also instrumental in obtaining several works directly for the Rotterdam museum by supporting their purchases as early as 1916. Most important was his gift to the Foundation Museum Boymans in 1940 of the largest part of the Franz Koenigs' collection. Taken in its entirety, van Beuningen's collection brought to Rotterdam artworks from some of the finest dispersed private collections of England and Europe, including objects obtained originally by the duke of Norfolk, Cook, and von Auspitz.

After the 1864 fire, the Schielandshuis was rebuilt and the remainder of the Boymans Collection was reinstalled in 1867. It was not until April 12, 1928, that the Municipal Council of Rotterdam decided to establish a new museum building; the size of the collection had grown considerably since 1921. Funds left to the city from the estate of G. W. Burger were directed to the project in combination with public donations. Specific designs for the new building were begun in 1931 by the city architect Adrianus van der Steur in collaboration with the museum director D. Hannema. The new facility was opened on July 6, 1935. Built with two open courts in red brick on three levels, with some 3,270 square meters of exhibition space, the museum was designed to maximize the effect of its collections by its open design and well-lit galleries. As early as 1942–43, van der Steur advanced an idea of expanding the museum, which has since been called the "Westersingel project." His thought was to extend the museum toward the Westersingel on the east through one of the courts. After the acquisition of the van Beuningen Collection in 1958, the museum was seriously overcrowded, and plans for the "Westersingel project" were drawn up by A. Boden of the firm of J. P. van Bruggen, G. Drexhage, J. J. Sterkenburg, and A. Bodon. On

February 28, 1964, the City Council considered preliminary plans for the project, and the first stage of construction was authorized on March 12, 1964. Funds were allocated for the building on May 30, 1968, and construction began in April 1969. The new wing opened in 1972. Its design reflected the museum's new interest in modern and contemporary art; galleries of the upper floor were designed to be subdivided to increase exhibition space by mobile partitions. Also built on three levels and in red brick, the new wing added 2,325 square meters of exhibition space to the museum.

The museum's holdings exhibit particular strengths in paintings, drawings, and prints by Netherlandish artists from the fifteenth century through van Gogh, with exceptional examples of art by the Flemish Primitives and by Dutch and Flemish Baroque artists. There are substantial numbers of sculptures, pieces of furniture, glass, ceramic, silver objects, and, recently, a large collection of modern art. These acquisitions were the result of numerous gifts from private collectors and benefactors (such as E. van der Ryckevorsel, J. P. van der Schilden, A. J. Domela Nieuwenhuis, J.C.J. Bierens de Haan, A. van Hoboken van Cortgene, J. N. Bastert, Philips-van der Willigen, and W. van der Vorm, in addition to van Beuningen and Koenigs), as well as a selective acquisition program to complement these gifts, especially in the years before the war, by F. Schmidt-Degener (director between 1908 and 1921) and D. Hannema succeeding him. Purchase support for new acquisitions is provided by the Boymans Museum Foundation (founded in 1939), the Erasmus Foundation, and the Rembrandt Society.

There were few examples of Northern fifteenth- and sixteenth-century paintings in Boymans' original bequest. Acquisitions of works by South Netherlandish, Dutch, and German artists from this period were due mainly to van Beuningen's legacy, F. Koenigs' collection, and separate purchases made during the last half century. Works by Northern Renaissance artists from Boymans' collection that survived the 1864 fire included the panel *St. John on Patmos*, usually attributed to a follower of Dieric Bouts (but recently reattributed to the Master of the St. Lucy Legend); a fragment of two priests attributed to Bosch; and the *Entombment* by Maerten van Heemskerck. Jan van Scorel's *Portrait of a Young Scholar*, dated 1531, was purchased after the Schielandshuis fire; Bernard van Orley's *Christ on the Cross between the Virgin and St. John* was donated to the museum three years later in 1867 by Mrs. M. Viruly-van Vuren van Dalem, and in the same year Pieter Pourbus' *Portrait of Joris van den Heede* (d. 1569) was purchased. Before Schmidt-Degener left the Boymans Museum for the Rijksmuseum (q.v.), he established a Flemish Primitives room in the museum and was responsible for the purchase of Jan Provost's *Disputation of St. Catherine* in 1918. Other works acquired singly over the years include a fragment of an Old Testament illustration of Nebuchadnezzar by Pieter Aertsen (given by A. van Veen in 1926), Bosch's well-known *Prodigal Son* (purchased in 1931), Jan Mostaert's portrayal of the prophets *Isaiah and Jeremiah* (given to the museum in 1940 by the Hennema-de Steurs family), and the problematic panel *Three Marys at the Tomb* attributed to Petrus Christus (acquired in 1968).

Although drawings were always F. Koenigs' major interest, he also acquired paintings. In his collection were Bosch's *Marriage at Cana* and two other works attributed to him (*St. Christopher* and two wings of a hell scene), an early work by Patenier, *Landscape with the Burning of Sodom*, and the *Last Supper* by the German artist Jörg Ratgeb (or his shop). Of the forty or so works from this period that were part of van Beuningen's bequest, a number of them are frequently mentioned in the literature. The anonymous triptych, the *Redemption*, once in the duke of Norfolk's collection made for the Bishopric of Liège (probably in Maastricht) about 1410, is a particularly important work from The Netherlands before the van Eycks. The large panel, *Three Marys at the Open Sepulchre*, which van Beuningen purchased from the Cook estate, has been heatedly debated by art historians as a work by Hubert van Eyck or his brother Jan.

The Master of the Aix Annunciation's panel, the *Prophet Isaiah*, from the dispersed *Annunciation* triptych in the Church of Mary Magdalene in Aix-en-Provence is one of two panels for the altar in the Low Countries; a companion panel *Jeremiah* is in the Musées Royaux des Beaux-Arts de Belgique (q.v.), Brussels. Other important fifteenth-century van Beuningen panels are two paintings by the anonymous French artist the Master of St. Gilles; two panels, *St. John the Evangelist and Mary Magdalene*, by Stefan Lochner; and *Visitation* by the unidentified Cologne painter the Master of the Virgin. The masterwork of the van Beuningen Collection of sixteenth-century painting is Pieter Bruegel's *Tower of Babel*. It is generally thought that this picture is the smaller of two versions of the theme that Carel van Mander (*Schilderboeck*, 1604) recorded as owned by Emperor Rudolf II; van Mander also mentioned "a large piece" of the same subject, which is probably the picture now in the Kunsthistorisches ([q.v.] Vienna Art Museum). Important works from the same period include Gossaert's *Metamorphosis of Hermaphrodite and Salmacis*, Quentin Massys' *Madonna in a Landscape*, Lucas van Leyden's *Potiphar's Wife*, and Albrecht Dürer's *Holy Family*. Dürer's picture was purchased by Ruy Fernandez de Almadas from the artist when Almadas visited Antwerp in 1521.

Flemish painting of the seventeenth century in the museum includes an important number of sketches by Peter Paul Rubens from the Koenigs Collection. Franz Koenigs, a German naturalized as a Dutch citizen in 1939, acquired the core of his extensive collection of paintings and drawings in the 1920s and the early 1930s. Financial setbacks forced him to place his art holdings in the Boymans museum in 1935 as collateral for a large bank loan. In 1940 van Beuningen took over the collection and donated the majority of it to the Boymans Museum. Of the twenty-five paintings by Rubens presently in the museum, thirteen came from the Koenigs Collection, eight from van Beuningen, and the remaining four from separate gifts and purchases; no works by Rubens were in Boymans' 1847 bequest. The most complete of the series of oil sketches by

Rubens are seven of the eight panels, the *Life of Achilles*, painted designs for tapestries, dating about 1630–32 (the eighth panel is in the Detroit Institute of Arts [q.v.]). Other sketches include mythological scenes painted about 1636–37 for the Torre de la Parada of Philip IV and the panel *Union of the Crowns of England and Scotland*, a study for the Whitehall Banqueting House ceiling. Other examples of Baroque painting from the South Netherlands include several works by Anthony van Dyck, genre scenes by Adriaen Brouwer and David Teniers, and still-life pictures by Joannes Fyt.

The museum's significant holdings of Dutch seventeenth-century paintings present a cross-section of the major artists, stylistic modes, and subject types typical of the century. Some of the more important examples of Dutch portraiture include works by Rembrandt (the 1655 *Portrait of Titus at a Reading Desk* and the *Portrait of a Man in a Red Cap* from the early 1660s), Frans Hals, Carel Fabritius (*Self Portrait*, c. 1647–50), Bartholomeus van der Helst, and Gerard Ter Borch. Still-life painting is well represented with pictures by Pieter Claesz, Willem de Poorter, Jan Jansz. van de Velde, Abraham van Beyeren, and Willem Kalf. The pristine clarity of Dutch church interiors is evident in works by Pieter Jansz Saenredam, Antonie de Lorme, Hendrick van Vliet, and Emanuel de Witte. Dramatic landscapes of the Dutch countryside include works by Hercules Seghers, Salomon van Ruysdael, Aert van der Neer, Jacob van Ruisdael, Meindert Hobbema, Philips Koninck, Aelbert Cuyp, and Jan Wouwermans. Numerous seascapes are represented in the collection by painters such as Willem van de Velde, Reinier Nooms, and Julius Porcellis. There is a variety of Dutch domestic scenes by Pieter de Hooch, Adriaen van Ostade, Jan Steen (*Easy Come, Easy Go*, 1661), and Gerard Dou. Mythological scenes (by Abraham Hondius and Emanuel de Witte), biblical themes (by Pieter Lastman, Aert de Gelder, and Gerbrandt van den Eeckhout), and animal subjects (by Aelbert Cuyp, Adriaen van de Velde, and Paulus Potter) are also present in a number of examples. Finally, the Dutch Baroque collection represents the range of Rembrandt's influence upon his many students throughout his life, including paintings by Samuel van Hoogstraeten, Willem de Poorter, Jacob Backer, Govaert Flinck, Ferdinand Bol, Barent Fabritius, Nicolaes Maes, and Christoph Paudiss, in addition to Dou, van den Eeckhout, and de Gelder.

As early as 1908, Adolphe Schloss' gift of the canvas *Two Girls* by the Le Nain brothers indicated a resolve on the part of Schmidt-Degener, and expanded upon by subsequent directors, to extend the Boymans Collection beyond Dutch art. Only a few examples of art produced outside of The Netherlands had been a part of Boymans' original legacy; the panel *A Faun and Nymph*, variously attributed to Titian or to Dosso Dossi, and the *Fortunate Mother* by Jean-Baptiste Greuze were owned by Boymans. Shortly after the museum opened to the public, a Florentine *Pietà* was donated to the collection in 1851 by J.L.C. van den Berch van Heemstede. In 1870 Jean-Baptiste de Champaigne's and Nicolas de Platte-Montagne's unique *Double Portrait* of 1665 was given to the museum by the heirs of D. Vis Blokhuijzen. After Schloss' gift of the Le Nain picture, gifts and purchases of non-Netherlandish art increased. They included a work by Boudin in 1911; a still life, formerly attributed to Chardin but now ascribed to Henri-Horace Roland de la Porte in 1916 (van Beuningen's first gift to the museum); a Pissarro in 1917; a Bonington in 1920; a Redon in 1922; a Monet in 1928; a portrait by the sixteenth-century German artist Hans Maler zu Schwaz in 1929; and in the 1930s, until the outbreak of the war, various other gifts of works by Domenichino (1935), Domenico Feti (1935), and Paul Signac (1936), and a seventeenth-century Russian icon (1938).

Clearly, the key element in making the museum's collection of art produced outside of The Netherlands more representative was the purchase of the van Beuningen Collection in 1958. His holdings of Italian Renaissance paintings and sculptures were due in the main to his acquisition of twenty paintings and a dozen small sculptures from the Viennese collector Stefan von Auspitz. Other objects acquired by van Beuningen in combination with the von Auspitz works provide a particularly good sampling of Northern Italian art, including pictures by Ercole de' Roberti, Titian, Veronese, and Tintoretto. Van Beuningen's interest in Venetian art is also reflected in his purchase of eighteenth-century works by Guardi and Tiepolo.

French Rococo art in the museum includes only a few paintings, among them two canvases attributed to Chardin, a chinoiserie study by Boucher, two pendant fêtes by Jean Baptiste Pater, a self-portrait of Hubert Robert in his studio (all from the van Beuningen purchase), *Fortunate Mother* by Greuze (from the Boymans bequest), and the *Portrait of the Prince de Rohan* by Hyacinthe Rigaud (acquired in 1948).

Acquisitions of paintings in the museum dating after 1800 at first emphasized works by nineteenth-century Dutch artists. Generally, these pictures are patterned after seventeenth-century Dutch master still lifes, domestic interiors, and landscape views of the Dutch countryside. Some of the best objects within this category are paintings from the Boymans Collection by Jan Hendrik Verheijen and Georgius Jacob Johannes van Os and works acquired between 1864 and 1875 by Wouter Johannes van Troostwijk, Barend Cornelis Koebboek, Wijnandus Johannes Nuijen, and Cornelis Springer. Although acquisitions of Dutch modern artists naturally continued into the twentieth century, French Impressionist and Post-Impressionist paintings were also added to the collection; an early acquisition in 1903 of a painting by van Gogh (*Landscape of Poplars near Nuenen*) perhaps aided in the expansion of the collection from Dutch to French nineteenth-century artists. Again, the van Beuningen purchase complemented early acquisitions in this area by the museum. Paintings by Daumier, Boudin, Daubigny, Monet, van Gogh, Gauguin, Renoir, Sisley, and Redon, among others from the van Beuningen Collection, were added to earlier accessions of paintings by many of these same artists in addition to those by Pissarro, Théodore Rousseau, and Signac.

Under J. C. Ebbinge Wubben, who retired as director of the museum in 1978, and the curator of modern art, J. C. Heyligers, between 1952 and 1960, a conscious decision was made to expand the museum's holdings to include more examples of modern art and, in fact, to make this area a new emphasis of the museum. Of the hundreds of paintings, drawings, and sculptures by modern and contemporary artists acquired by the museum, more than six hundred of them were added between 1945 and 1978. Artists from the Dutch CoBrA movement (1948–51) are well represented: especially Appel, Constant, Corneille, and Jorn. Also paintings from the post-World War II École de Paris by artists such as Vieira da Silva, Soulages, Riopelle, Poliakoff, Bazaine, Bissière, and Manessier are predominant in the contemporary collection.

The museum's vast holdings of prints and drawings are due greatly to F. Koenigs' collection of drawings acquired in 1940, to A. J. Domela Nieuwenhuis' 1923 gift, and to the print bequest of J.C.J. Bierens de Haan in 1951–52. The particular strengths of the Koenigs Collection are German, Italian, French, Early Netherlandish, and Dutch and Flemish Baroque drawings (especially Rubens and Rembrandt); his collection also contained nineteenth-century French drawings, including twenty-three by Cézanne.

Finally, mention should be made of the decorative arts department of the museum. Acquisitions of old glass, porcelain, majolica, silver, pewter, pottery, and lace are especially representative of Dutch art from the sixteenth century through contemporary ceramics.

There is a museum library of more than ninety thousand volumes. Opened in 1936, the library is for reference only. The museum began a bulletin with scholarly articles in 1937, but in 1972 the format changed to a bimonthly publication emphasizing current exhibition news.

Selected Bibliography

Museum publications: Hannema, D., and A. van Steur, *Het Museum Boymans te Rotterdam*, 1935; *Catalogus Tentoonstelling van Oud-Aardewerk uit de Verzameling Bastert-van Schaardenburg*, 1940; *Meesterwerken uit de Verzameling D. G. van Beuningen*, July 9–October 9, 1949; *Catalogus: Schilderijen tot 1800*, 1962; Hoetink, Hendrik R., *Franse Tekeningen uit de 19e Eeuw*, 1969; idem, *Tekeningen van Rembrandt en zijn School*, 1969; Hammacher-van den Brande, Renilde, *Kunst van de 20e Eeuw: Catalogus*, 1972; *Old Paintings, 1400–1900*, 1972; *Boymans-Bijdragen: Opstellen van Medewerkers en Oud-Medewerkers het Museum Boymans-van Beuningen voor J. C. Ebbinge Wubben*, 1978; *De Collectie Moderne Kunst van Museum Boymans-van Beuningen, Rotterdam: Inventarisatie van Schilderijen, Sculpturen, en Oorwerpen, Verworven van 1945 tot 1978*, July 1–September 10, 1978.

Other publications: Special issue of *Apollo*, vol. 86 (July 1967): Sutton D., "The Boymans-van Beuningen Museum," pp. 2–4; Boon, K. G., "Cross-Currents in Early Northern Painting," trans. Angus Malcolm, pp. 5–15; de Jongh, E., "Austerity and Extravagance in the Golden Age," trans. Angus Malcolm, pp. 16–25; de Neeve, Bernardine R. M., "Decorative Arts Department at the Boymans-van Beuningen Museum," pp. 26–37; Haverkamp-Begeman, E., "Rubens in Rotterdam," pp. 38–43; Shaw, James Byam, "Notes on some Venetian Drawings," pp. 44–49; Hoetink, H. R., "Three Centuries of French Art," trans. Angus Malcolm, pp. 50–55; and Hammacher-van den

Brande, R., "A Cross-Section of Modern Art," pp. 56–60; also Decoen, Jean, "The New Museum at Rotterdam," *Burlington Magazine*, vol. 67 (September 1935), pp. 131–33; Hannema, D., *Catalogue of the Daniel George van Beuningen Collection*, foreword by Max J. Friedländer (Rotterdam 1949); Luttervelt, R. van, *Masterpieces from the Great Dutch Museums* (New York 1961); Wubben, J. C. Ebbinge, "A New Wing of the Boymans-van Beuningen Museum, Rotterdam," *Museum*, vol. 28, no. 1 (1976), pp. 42–129.

BURTON L. DUNBAR III

Nigeria

——— Onikan-Lagos ———

NATIONAL COMMISSION FOR MUSEUMS AND MONUMENTS (Includes Lagos National Museum, Jos National Museum, Esie National Museum [Esie House of Images], Ife National Museum at Ile-Ife, Benin National Museum, Kaduna National Museum, Oron National Museum, Owo National Museum, Gidan Makama National Museum at Kano, Kanta Museum at Argungu), PMB 12556, Onikan-Lagos.

Nigeria may be said to have one of the best organized and coordinated museum systems in Africa. Under the able leadership of Dr. Ekpo Eyo, Director-General of the National Commission for Museums and Monuments, himself a distinguished archaeologist and administrator, the Commission has responsibility for establishing and administering all national museums, antiquities, and monuments throughout Nigeria. It is responsible as well for arts and crafts, architecture, natural history, and education services. The National Commission for Museums and Monuments was established by decree of the federal government in 1979, replacing the former Antiquities Commission and the Federal Department of Antiquities. The decree broadened the area of responsibility to include arts and crafts, architecture, natural history, and educational services as well as antiquities; it empowered the Commission to make recommendations to any state government, persons, or authority concerning the establishment and management of museums and the preservation of antiquities and monuments. The 1979 Nigerian Constitution granted powers to state and local governments to set up museums. The National Commission, however, has to approve all privately run museums and controls all archaeological excavation in Nigeria. It oversees all university museums in the country.

There will eventually be a National Museum in each of the nineteen states of the Federal Republic of Nigeria and one in each state formed thereafter. Presently, the Commission runs thirteen museums in the country: the Lagos National Museum, which was established in 1956–57 and is the headquarters of the National Commission for Museums and Monuments; the Jos National Museum, established in 1952 and the first public museum in the country; the Esie National Museum (Esie House of Images), established in 1948; the Ife National Museum at Ile-Ife, established in 1954; the Benin National Museum, opened in 1973; the Kaduna National Museum opened in 1975; the Oron National Museum opened in 1957–58 and to be reopened in 1985; the Gidan Makama National Museum in Kano, opened in 1985; and a local museum run by the Commission, Kantas Museum, in Argungu.

The following museums were opened to the public in 1985: the National War Museum at Umuahia, Emo State; The Colonial History Museum at Aba, and the National Museums at Calabar, Kano, and Owo. Others still in process of construction are at Enugu, Ibadan, Maiduguri, and Sokoto. The former office and storage at Port Harcourt were closed in 1982; and an old building, converted to a new museum, will be opened as the new Port Harcourt National Museum, in 1987. Additions to the Lagos National Museum are under construction and will house the antiquities while these premises will become a Museum of Natural History. No date is set for these openings now.

The earliest museums of local and national importance in the years following World War II were Owo Museum in Ondo State, Esie Museum in Kwara State, Ife Museum in Oyo State, and the Jos Museum in Plateau State.

The Director-General is the chief executive officer of the National Commission for Museums and Monuments. Within the Commission are three major departments, each headed by a director, who is aided by an assistant director. The Department of Administration and Finance handles all financial, budgetary, and daily administrative and staff matters. The Department of Museums and Monuments is responsible for the care and administration of all museums and monuments under its jurisdiction. It identifies antiquities and historic sites and buildings to be declared National Monuments. It collects relevant materials, and it is responsible for the educational activities of the Commission. The Department of Research and Training coordinates all research and projects and collates and publishes the related materials. It sees to the training of the technical and professional staff of the Commission as well as those who come from other countries for that purpose. The department also maintains the Commission's library.

The staff of the Commission includes the chief executive, the Director-General, who has overall charge of the effective performance of all departments and staff. In addition to the directors and assistant directors, there is a professional and technical staff. The professional staff consists of curators, ethnographers, archaeologists, and education officers. The technical staff includes architects, superintendents of monuments, audiovisual officers, technical officers, photographers, conservators, and exhibition officers. Many attendants and maintenance people are employed for the museums and grounds, as are workers on various sites. Some five thousand people are employed in all.

The funding for the museums, monuments, and sites administered by the National Commission for Museums and Monuments is provided by the federal government of Nigeria, which approves a yearly budget. The Commission allocates these funds according to its needs; it may acquire objects by purchase and retrieve others from museums and private collections abroad. The Commission registers and documents all national antiquities, including those privately held. From 1974 to 1977 more that 1 million such objects were photographed and registered. In the last decade, with the increased scope and staff of the Commission, its expenditures have been substantially increased. These reflect its efforts in the areas of research and preservation, interpretation, and expansion of the museum system. It is evident that the Federal Republic of Nigeria has made a serious commitment to collect, preserve, and present its cultural heritage within the country and abroad.

The present National Commission for Museums and Monuments was established by a federal decree in 1979, replacing the former Antiquities Commission and the Department of Antiquities. The British Colonial Administration was first persuaded to set up the Antiquities Service in 1943 through the efforts of Kenneth Murray, an Englishman, who had come to Nigeria in 1920 as an education officer. The Antiquities Service with Kenneth Murray (who died in 1972) as its head was concerned to preserve indigenous cultural artifacts and to stop the increasing flow out of the country. In 1953 the Federal Department of Antiquities was established by the British via the Antiquities Act No. 17. The department was to report directly to the Antiquities Commission; it was attached to the Federal Ministry of Information later for purely administrative purposes. Act No. 17 made it mandatory to obtain an export permit for any Nigerian work of art. Many steps have been taken to control the illegal export of Nigerian antiquities and works of art.

Epko Eyo, Director-General of the National Commission for Museums and Monuments, has been a strong advocate of international cooperation and the prevention of traffic in illegal artworks. He was educated at Cambridge University and the University of Ibadan and also holds a post-graduate diploma in prehistoric archaeology from the University of London, as well as diplomas in museum administration and in chemical conservation of museum objects. He first joined the Department of Antiquities in 1951 as antiquities assistant. Since 1966 Eyo has taught African Studies at the University of Lagos and lectures widely on the art and archaeology of Nigeria. He was named director of antiquities in 1968 and became Director-General of the National Commission for Museums and Monuments with its establishment by federal decree in 1979.

The first museums established by the former Department of Antiquities were regional museums containing specific groups of objects that had been gathered to save them from dispersal and destruction and to conserve the traditions they represented, for example, the museums at Esie (House of Images) and at Oron. In 1946 a museum in Benin housed objects returned from abroad and found locally. The first museum to have proper study, storage, and display areas was completed in 1948, at Ife, but was not opened until 1954 due to construction problems. The Jos museum, built between 1949 and 1952 by Bernard Fagg (the second director of the Antiquities Commission, 1957–66), with "direct labor," however, was the first national rather than regional museum in Nigeria.

The Esie National Museum (Esie House of Images) is southeast of Ilorin, Kwara State. It contains more than a thousand soapstone sculptures that were found on the farmlands near Esie. These soapstone figures represent the largest collection of stone carvings still in Africa. They range in size from eight inches, or fourteen centimeters, to nearly four feet, or one meter, high. A "king" presides over the other figures, which number more than eight hundred men and women who are shown with musical instruments and some with weapons. There is a yearly festival for the images that has been held throughout the reigns of fifteen chiefs of Esie. Other ceremonies and rituals are held throughout the year accompanied by sacrifices that are presented to the images through the *Aworo* or chief priest. The soapstone sculptures have been housed at Esie since 1945, when a House of Images was built. A new museum with an altar for use by the Esie people was opened in 1970.

The soapstone figures from Esie have been known for some time; Leo Frobenius collected three heads in Esie style by 1912, although H. G. Ramsey, schools inspector for the Church Missionary Society, is said to have "discovered" the figures in 1933. It is thought that the present Esie people arrived in the area in the late eighteenth or early nineteenth century and found the soapstone figures already there. According to local legend, the figures are said to represent foreign visitors to Esie who were turned to stone by Olorun, the supreme deity, because of their quarrels and malicious acts against the king or Elesie of Esie. Their origins remain a mystery.

The figures are usually represented sitting on stools with their hands on their knees. Sometimes they are shown kneeling, sometimes playing an instrument or holding a weapon. Two figures in the exhibition wear triple-strand necklaces and elaborate hairdos as do many of the others.

The Oron National Museum was first opened to the public in 1959, when it housed mainly most of the eight hundred known *Ekpu*, or ancestral figures, of the Oron people. These works were placed there in trust, on loan from their owners, who still worshipped them. There were also Igbo houseposts and drums and a Cross River monolith among the original collections. This museum was damaged during the Nigerian Civil War, and it was reopened in 1977. Presently, it contains between two thousand and four thousand ethnographic pieces.

The original ancestral carvings were two hundred to three hundred years old. They were made of special hard woods (*Coula edulis* and *Pterocarpus soyauxii*), which are resistant to termites and the weather. As early as 1938 these *Ekpu* carvings were recognized as important by Kenneth C. Murray. When he became

head of the Nigerian Antiquities Service in 1943, he took steps to preserve them
and to repair some of the shrines where the *Ekpu* figures were housed; others
were removed for safekeeping. The shrines had become neglected as the cult
had declined. By 1948 the Oron Clan Council and the District Officer had helped
to collect some three hundred examples while a museum was being built. Before
the museum was completed in 1958, while the figures were stored in the Rest
House at Oron, twenty figures were stolen by an African art dealer and have
never been recovered.

During the Nigerian Civil War, 1966–70, the *Ekpu* figures and collections
were removed from the Oron Museum. Many of them were destroyed afterwards,
scattered, and stolen and sold abroad. After the Civil War ended, the Department
of Antiquities was able to retrieve some hundred of them. A new Oron museum
includes objects now from all over Nigeria, as well as the surviving *Ekpu* figures;
this includes artifacts from the Civil War and a Craft Village. The museum
reopened in 1977.

There is an excellent *Guide to the National Museum, Oron*, 1977, by Keith
Nicklin, formerly with the Federal Department of Antiquities. It details some
of the many artistic traditions east of the Niger River, of which most remain
little known to archaeologists, art historians, and anthropologists. The *Guide*
benefited from four years of field work by Nicklin, then an ethnographer with
the Federal Department of Antiquities. The seventy-three-page *Guide* contains
thirty-five illustrations and recommended readings, which include published and
unpublished articles that are available through the Curator's Office to scholars
and students.

Nicklin, now director of the Horniman Museum, in London, acknowledged
the important contributions of the staff of the Federal Department of Antiquities.
He called attention to the museum's display of cement sculptures, by S. J. Skpan
of Ikot Obio Offong, Uyo, and to the hand-woven cloth used in the cases, made
by the Government Textile Centre, Uyo. A mural painting, *Girl from Fattening
Room* by the Annang-Ibibio artist Imeh Fabian of Ikot Esse, Ikot Ekpene, from
the museum restaurant is illustrated in the *Guide*. Also illustrated is a tree stump
carved in the form of a Cross River monolith, made for the museum grounds
by Alpant Chukwu of Utu Etim Ekpo, Abak. Good examples of Cross River
stone monoliths may be seen on the grounds of the National Museum, Lagos.

Of interest to art historians and anthropologists are the photographs in the
Guide illustrating masquerades: Annang-Ibibio, at Utu Etim *Ekpo*, Abak; Annang-Ibibio *Ikem* masquerade with two skin-covered cap masks, made by Nwa
Nkwa, Urua Inyang, Abak; Bokyi *Bikarum* skin-covered cap masks made from
an antelope skull, worn with a modern insecticide spraying mask on the dancer's
face, Ntemante, Ikom; and a Bokyi *Obassi-Njom* masquerader at Abontakon,
Ikom. Other illustrations of interest are: Yoruba *Egungun* masqueraders, Ilorin,
Kwara State; Ogoni *Karikpo* masquerader, N. Kana, Rivers State; Chamba hunters' disguises made from the skull of the ground hornbill covered with leather,
Donga Wukari, Benue State; and Qua *Ekpe* masquerader paying homage to the

Ntoe of Akim Qua, Ntoe Usang Iso, during his installation ceremony in 1976, Calabar.

Although there have been relatively little archaeology and systematic excavation of sites in Cross River State, some of the finds indicate the potential and importance of the area for future investigation. Tools and objects from the Late Stone Age have been found; polished stone tools occur throughout the area and are used in contemporary shrines as part of the thunder cult, similar to those in western Nigeria. A burial, Iwo Eleru Man and other artifacts found in what is now Ondo State, show the site was occupied from about 9000 B.C. to 1500 B.C. Pottery, considered to date from about five thousand years ago, has been excavated in eastern Nigeria at sites near Afikpo on the Cross River and at Nsukka. It is believed the pottery was traded by water transport. There is evidence of ceramics and bronze elsewhere in the area.

Among the well-known finds from Cross River are the stone monoliths that are phallic in form. The conical torsos have a protruding navel, arms carved in low relief, and distinct human facial features that include tribal marks and beards. These works are large sculptures, ranging in height from one-third meter to two meters or from one to six feet high. More than three hundred of these carved stones called *akwanshi* or *atal*, locally, have been found from Middle Cross River. They may have been memorials for deceased chiefs or *ntoons*, among the Nta group. Dating is uncertain, but the monoliths were probably made as early as the sixteenth century and continued to be made until the nineteenth century. They have been found primarily among small groups of Ejagham peoples (Ekajuk, Abanyom, Nnam, Nselle, Nta, Nkum, and others). The monoliths, left largely in place and unprotected, have suffered damage from looters and from construction work. There is a good example of a Cross River monolith from Nlul on the grounds of the Oron Museum. Also on the grounds is a tree stump carved in the form of a Cross River monument by Alphant Chukwu, a sculptor, from Utu Etim Ekpo, Abak.

The most striking and perhaps best known of the artistic traditions of Cross River is the skin-covered mask, having a restricted distribution in Nigeria and Cameroon. There are two main types: the cap mask and the helmet mask. They are most often human heads with single, double, or Janus faces, and multifaces. Sometimes an animal, like a leopard or antelope, or a mask combining human and animal features is produced. Skin-covered masks are both naturalistic and grotesque. They are carved from wood and are usually covered with antelope or deer skin; an animal or human skull is sometimes used, and it is believed that human skin was used to cover masks in the past. Metal is set to form the pupils of the eyes, and boars' teeth as well as strips of cane, bone, ivory, metal, and wood may be set into the sockets of the incisors in the open mouths. They give a sense of realism and stark expression to the masks. Masks are worn at funeral ceremonies, at initiation ceremonies, and when other public rituals are performed. Skin-covered masks are frequently used by age sets, dance groups, and associations of hunters and warriors. In the past, some associations like the

Etung *mbwa-mbak* and Bokyi *nkang*, that used masks, practiced human sacrifice and head hunting.

The cap mask, often with a basketry base, is worn on top of the head with a string holding it under the chin. The helmet mask covers the head and rests on the shoulders. A common form of the cap mask is a female head with spiral hairdo that can become very elaborate. The helmet mask may have two-faced and four-faced versions carved, covered, and painted. The "male," or dark side, of the mask has pierced eyes for the wearer to see through, and the "female," or light side, faces backwards and is worn blind, the eyes not being pierced for the wearer. Skin-covered masks are believed to have originated among the Ejagham forest people.

Other artistic traditions represented in the Oron Museum include the Ibibio *Ekpo*, which uses two types of masks, those portraying ghosts and those portraying souls; and the Bokyi *Obassi-Njom*, a complex ritual performance used to detect witches. The latter includes a carving by Bessong Ojua of Abontakon, made and used before being installed at the museum. Members of the *Obassi-Njom* cult installed it, led by Chief Edmund Bakui-Asu, the village head. The Calabar *Ekpe*, or Leopard cult, is also represented in the museum, as are Ibibio wood carvings. Some modern metalworkings and outside influences are also noted. But the area not distinguished for its metalworking lacks use of the lost wax method, a technique widely known in Nigeria and West Africa. Currency in the traditional form of manillas, copper, brass, and bronze U-shaped and sometimes twisted rods is still used as a design motif on masks and even commercial signboards today, as symbols of security and wealth in Cross River State. Some examples may be seen in the Oron Museum.

The National Museum, Oron, is mostly ethnographic and has a strong local flavor. Its carved entrance doors were commissioned from Igbo carvers of Amawbia in 1976 and are decorated with ichi designs used by titled men of Onitsha and Awka. The museum cafeteria, *Sirenia*, alongside the Cross River, is decorated with murals showing myths, masquerades, and species of animals from various parts of the state and its peoples. The muralist is Imeh Fabian, the Annang-Ibibio artist. Three large Ibgo *Obu* houseposts, from a group collected by K. C. Murray and displayed in the original Oron Museum (1959), may be found on the grounds and in the new museum.

The museum is divided into two main exhibition areas. One gallery contains a display of "The Oron Ancestors (*Ekpu*) in Wood," Ibibio ritual objects, Cross River skin-covered masks, and examples of the Bokyi *Obassi-Njom* cult. The other gallery includes displays of the *Ekpe* Leopard cult, masks, music and dance, and crafts of the region; at the far end of the building is a major display of Annang clay funerary art. The museum installation emphasizes the methods of production and the functions of the pieces shown. Black and white photographs taken in traditional villages, showing objects being made and in use, provide cultural context; cement action figures and sound recordings increase enjoyment of the displays. Wherever possible local artists, craftsmen, and ritual specialists were engaged to create and to install the galleries and museum facilities.

The Owo National Museum is located on the grounds of the palace of the Olowo of Owo and was originally built to house antiquities that were formerly in the palace. The collections, made in 1957–58, before Nigerian independence, include archaeological and ethnographic objects. In the last decade or so they have been augmented through excavations of the National Commission for Museums and Monuments. The collections now include more than ten thousand objects.

Owo is an important center for traditional art of the Eastern Yoruba. The town itself is approximately eighty miles southeast of Ife. Oral tradition has it that Owo was founded by the youngest son of Oduduwa, called Ojugbelu. Oduduwa is the deity who founded the Yoruba city of Ile-Ife. In 1969 excavations were carried out by Ekpo Eyo, director-general of the National Commission for Museums and Monuments, at the site of Igbo'Laja, in Owo. The site, which is near the palace of Olowo of Owo, is about a quarter mile from the center of the city; it is located at the foot of the hill called Okitisegbo, where the founder Ojugbelu and his chiefs settled sometime in the fifteenth century. The works of art uncovered in the excavations show strong affinities between Owo and the art of Ife and Benin. They include terracotta heads, animals, parts of figures, and a leopard gnawing on a human leg. The context of the finds suggests an arrangement similar to shrines at Ife and Oshogbo today. In intervening centuries and today, occasional finds of terracotta heads and fragments of sculpture have been made. They have sometimes been reused. The present *Alaja*, or priest of the Igbo'Laja sacred grove, has one such ancient head, which he wears as a pendant. Although it has not been established with certainty that the Owo people migrated from Ife, the finds made by Eyo and features of architecture, royal regalia, titles, and so on show their connections with Ife and Benin.

The Ife National Museum has a long history, beginning in the dry season of 1938–39, when eighteen exceptional brass, zinc, and copper heads and sculpture were uncovered about two hundred yards from the palace of the Oni or king, of Ife by a man digging a house foundation in Wunmonije Compound. The Oni kept most of the finds, and of the three sold then, two have since been returned to Nigeria and one remains in the British Museum (q.v.). From 1938 on, the Oni took an active role in collecting Ife metal and terracotta works of art that were being discovered around the city when houses were built and lands cleared and planted; he brought many works kept in local shrines and sacred groves into the palace for safekeeping. The Ife Museum was first completed in 1948 on the grounds of the palace. The land was given by the Oni of Ife for this purpose, along with the collections he had made. But the museum was not opened to the public until 1954 because of construction problems. Around the courtyard, before the entrance to the main building at Ife, are window cases showing objects from other parts of Oyo State and Nigeria.

The high art of Ife is, perhaps, best seen in the heads found in the Wunmonije Compound, which are unique in Africa for their naturalism. The mostly life-size heads are believed to represent a dead king or Oni, in the prime of life. The delicate modeling and finely cast features give each head the distinct appearance of a portrait. Many of the heads have small rows of holes around the mouth and along the hairline into which, it is thought, real hair might have been inserted. These heads and other terracotta finds are kept in the Ife National Museum. An additional mask said to represent the Oni Obalufon is a rare and exquisite copper casting, and a terracotta head said to represent the usurper Lajuwa resembles the Wunmonije heads in style and execution. These outstanding pieces were kept in the Oni's palace, Ife.

Following the accidental finds in the dry season of 1938–39, scientific excavations were begun in 1949 at Ife by Bernard Fagg, William Fagg, and John Godwin, at the site of Abiri. The three returned to the same site in 1953 and also worked at the sacred groves of Osangangan, Obamakin, Olokun Walode, and elsewhere. Frank Willett excavated a shrine at Ita Yemoo, 1957–58, after promising initial finds at the site. A second shrine was discovered at Ita Yemoo during the second season, 1962–63; it was here that the first radio-carbon and thermoluminescence dates for Ife were obtained. Other excavated Ife sites include Igbo Obameri and Oduduwa College, 1964, by Oliver Meyers, and Odo Ogbe Street, in the city, 1969, by Ekpo Eyo, who also excavated the site of Lafogido in the same year. The Lafogido site revealed a rectangular pottery pavement, with a series of some fourteen globular pots inserted around the edge over what was probably a royal burial. There were five animal heads as lids on the pots, including an elephant, a mythical beast (possibly, a hippopotamus), and a ram. Peter Garlake carried out later excavations in Ife in 1971–72 at the sites of Obalara's Land and Woye Asiri. The finds from paved courtyards and other clay sculptures are now at the University of Ife, which sponsored the investigation.

The Ife National Museum, which is home to the world-famous "bronze" (zinc, brass, and copper) and terracotta life-size heads, contains other rare and little-known sculptures and pottery. The Classical period, from about the eleventh to the fifteenth century, is well represented in the museum, although earlier Ife finds, dating from about 600, and those as late as the seventeenth century are also shown.

Rare pieces on display in the Ife Museum include a large stone sculpture of a male figure, from Ore Grove. Ore is a mythical figure, who got a wife by shooting the son of Oduduwa. It will be remembered that Oduduwa is the god who founded Ife and became the first Oni. Also from Ore Grove is a large stone sculpture of a fish with its nose and eyes inlaid with iron. The largest fired clay terracotta sculpture yet found in Africa may be seen in the Ife Museum. This is a sculpture of a male figure seated on a stool. A smaller figure seated on a stool, similar to the large sculpture, may be found in the British Museum. In a nearby case is the lower half of another complex clay sculpture, a seated figure on a stool, placed over a large pot. The lower legs and feet, pot and stool remain of what had been a very large seated figure which would have measured three feet or more.

In wall cases surrounding the large terracotta sculptures are outstanding examples of Ife art such as the double sculpture of a king and queen, *The Oni and Wife*, from Ita Yemoo. The couple is shown standing side by side with their legs intertwined. Seven small clay heads with fine facial striations and some torsos from Iwinrin Grove are on exhibit. There is an elephant's head from Lafogido and assorted clay sculptural fragments of feet, arms, hands, legs, and torsos from the Classical period, found at Laguwa and Ita Yemoo. Much pottery is shown, some of it anthropomorphic, others with figures, weapons, leopards, staffs, swords, skulls, and bound men modeled in relief on the shoulders and bodies of the pots. The pottery from Abiri and Aiyetoro is a gift of Chief Obaluru. Also of interest are some glass crucibles used to make the blue and black beads displayed.

The Benin National Museum is situated in the main commercial area of Benin City, the capital of Bendel State. It was opened to the public at official ceremonies held on June 15, 1973. The beginnings of the museum may be traced to 1944. At that time there were few Benin antiquities remaining in the city. Most of the more than two thousand pieces looted in the 1897 British Punitive Expedition against the Benin Empire were, and many remain, in public and private collections in Europe and North America. During the earliest period of the formation of the Benin Museum, traditional art was preserved and assembled by His Royal Highness the Oba of Benin, Akenzua II, within the palace in the Royal House of Iwebo, where it was under the care of Chief Jacob Egharevba. Soon, however, public interest and desire for greater access led to the museum being moved to one of the rooms of the Benin Tax Office and later to another building.

About 1958 the government began to assemble existing pieces in Nigeria and to buy back Benin art from abroad for display in a museum. A Benin museum opened in 1960, with collections formed by excavations of the Federal Department of Antiquities and by accidental discoveries. The Benin Divisional Council assumed care of the collections. While the museum awaited construction of a permanent home, the collections were housed in a specially prepared wing of the Benin Post Office. Later, through the support of the military governor, Colonel S. Osaigbovo Ogbemudia, a circular building of modern design was created, and the funds made available for the purchase of Benin works of art. A library and schools service were also planned for the new museum, which opened in 1973.

The new Benin Museum focuses on the history and traditions of the Benin Empire, which flourished from the fourteenth to nineteenth century, to the present. The first, or Ogiso, dynasty and its rulers reigned at an early period; the present dynasty was established to end previous problems of succession among the Ogiso. The present Oba, His Royal Highness Oba Erediauwa I, is the thirty-ninth ruler of the second dynasty, in a continuous line of succession.

Through works of art, labels, graphics, and reconstruction on the ground floor of the museum, the visitor is guided through the history of Benin and the empire and the growth and organization of the city and the palace of the Oba. At the entrance to the galleries is a cast of the bronze head of Queen Mother Idia that is still in the British Museum, London; there is a photograph of the Queen Mother head in the Lagos National Museum. A section of the Oba's palace displays architectural elements, for example, a large bronze python head, probably mounted on the roof of the gatehouse or in the Palace Conference Hall. Bronze plaques of people and events (for example, *Ofoe*, the Messenger of Death, and *Stilt Dancers*, who perform at festivals) that were mounted on supporting roof posts are also shown in this section. Some outstanding examples included are: a rare Oduduwa bronze head; a pendant mask with serpents coming out of its nostrils; a bronze hornblower, shown with an ''erere'' that is blown at the sacrifice to the Oba's coral bead regalia; three bronze horsemen, each in a different style; and fine examples of ivory and wood equestrian staffs seen in the ground-floor galleries. Brass aquamaniles or ewers used by the Oba for ritual hand washing were made in the form of leopards. An ancestral shrine, similar to those in use at the Royal Court of Benin, is reconstructed on the ground floor, on the altar. Bronze heads of preceding Obas, bells, celts, and other paraphernalia used in connection with these rituals are displayed.

Above the mostly archaeological and historical works shown on the ground floor are cultural and enthnographic displays from different parts of Bendel State. Objects from Benin and Owo chiefs are shown. Wood altars of the hand, divination objects, and heads are included. There is Olokun pottery used by women when asking to be blessed with children. Masks used in the yearly cycle *Ehofekpo* and the *Ekpo* cult are displayed. Objects are documented where possible. They include an Ishan costume with the head made by Okeleke, an artist, and the costume made by Lawrence of Oginga. This costume represents Odogu, the Mother, and is part of a dance-play called *Okakagbe*, in which one child dancer and four or five adults perform.

Headdresses from the Delta region are shown: the *emedjo*, or headdress with human figure; the fish headdress used by those who had inherited rights to do so; and the crocodile headdress having its forefeet stretched out at either side. Musical instruments are on display in the galleries: *akpara*, or Benin harp; *asologun*, or linguaphone; and many examples of flutes, drums, and rattles. There are also utilitarian objects: combs, containers, wooden food platters, palm wine servers, and other items. Motifs like serpents, mudfish, and human figures with mudfish legs are found often in Benin, Ife, and modern Yoruba art. Six pedestal cases contain casts of Ife and Benin bronze heads for comparison and study.

The second floor of the Benin National Museum is not yet opened to the public. When completed it will contain displays from different parts of the federation. The main ethnic groups in Bendel State are the Edo (Bini), Urhobo, Ibo, Itsekiri, and Ijaw peoples. Like all Nigerian museums, it will have national as well as state and local representation, creating a sense of national unity and identity.

Some of the smaller museums in Nigeria include the university museums at

Ibadan, Ife, Lagos, Nsukka, and Zaria. They are under the National Commission's overall supervision but are not run by it.

The Kano National Museum is a small museum housed in the Gidan Makama, an architectural jewel of the Old City of Kano. It was the residence of the Makama, a traditional title holder who was responsible for administering smaller provincial districts of the Kano Emirate. The Gidan Makama was built by the same master builder who did the famed Zaria Mosque and the City Walls of Kano. At MOTNA, Museum of Traditional Nigerian Architecture in Jos, the Zaria Mosque and the City Walls of Kano have been rebuilt as part of the exhibition of indigenous buildings of distinction from northern Nigeria. At Kano, the Gidan Makama was completely restored by the former Department of Antiquities, and it is run by the National Commission for Museums and Monuments. The museum building has been expanded to show other examples of traditional architecture from the Kano Emirate; on display also are local crafts and the Emir's regalia.

The Kanta Museum is the only local museum among the first ones run by the Department of Antiquities and still under commission jurisdiction. The museum building is the former residence of the Emir of Argungu, used by him until 1935, when a new palace was constructed for him. Located at Argungu, Sokoto State, the collections focus on artifacts and tools used by local peoples in pursuit of their occupations, mostly hunting and fishing, and in warfare. The most important fishing festival in Nigeria is held at Argungu each year. The local authority and the National Commission run the museum.

The Kaduna National Museum was opened to the public in 1975. It is divided into sections of archaeological, ethnographic, and craft collections. The innovation at Kaduna was the introduction of a craft village in the museum compound, where visitors could observe and acquire the work of potters, weavers, smiths, and wood carvers and the services of hairdressers all in traditional styles. This idea has spread and has been adopted at other national museums where craft villages have been established.

The archaeology gallery presents the evidence of human beings in prehistory, beginning with the finds made in East Africa more than 2 million years ago. Some early pebble (Oldowan type) tools are shown, including three examples found at Pingell, thirty kilometers northeast of Jos, Plateau State, believed to be more recent. These Early Stone Age tools are followed by Middle Stone Age tools of similar type found in West Africa; those found in Nigeria come from the southwest and northwest of Jos Plateau. Examples from the sites in the Jebba, Keffi-Nassarawa-Abuja areas, dated about sixty thousand to forty thousand years ago, are shown. Most of the examples, however, come from the site of Zenebi, where the radiocarbon date obtained, about fifty-five hundred years old, is considered by many archaeologists to be too recent. A display of Late Stone Age tools shows both the microlith and ground tools usually associated with this period; in Nigeria abundant finds have been made at excavations carried out at

Rop, Dutsen Kongba, in the Plateau area, and at Mejiro and Iwo Eleru, in the forest zone. The earliest find of a human skeleton, about eleven thousand years old, in Nigeria was made at Iwo Eleru. The Late Stone Age lasted from about twelve thousand to two thousand years ago in West Africa, and finds from this period are common in Nigeria.

Other archaeological displays in the Kaduna National Museum trace the history of iron smelting in West Africa to the Nok culture about twenty-five hundred years ago. The display shows Birom smelters at work in Jos, in a 1911 photograph. The absence of copper in West Africa meant that the Iron Age followed the Stone Age, without going through a Bronze Age, as was the case in many parts of the world. A case in the Kaduna Museum shows five stages of the *cire-perdue*, or lost wax method, which was widely used in West Africa from about the ninth century. Trade in brass rods from North Africa to West Africa in the thirteenth century and coastal trade with Europe from the fifteenth century on made increasing quantities of copper alloy available for casting. The rods often took the form of manillas that served as currency in many forest states. As a result of this trade the kingdoms of Benin, Ashanti, and Dahomey produced many works of art by the lost wax method, in increasing size and quantity.

The archaeology gallery displays sculptures from the ancient Nok culture about twenty-five hundred years ago, as well as other artistic traditions from northern Nigeria, from Zaria and Yelwa, of later date. Examples of classical Ife terracotta heads and copper-alloy pieces are shown, some copies and some originals; works from the Benin Royal Court include a replica of a bronze plaque, bells, an ivory sideblown horn, wood and bronze heads, and a free-standing sculpture of a soldier with a gun, cast in bronze. The bronze casters of Benin are ranked with those of the European Renaissance in skill and execution. Ornate copper-alloy pieces from Igbo-Ukwu, east of the Niger River, in the Awka area, about ninth to eleventh century, are displayed. A fine example is a large bowl, measuring nine inches in diamater, with a single handle; it is decorated with four rows of three sets of interlocking loops making up each row, in a geometric pattern in relief; the whole is cast by the lost wax process.

The ethnography gallery depicts masquerades that involve rituals devoted to ancestral cults and to various deities. Some are performed at death, puberty, marriage, and other critical points in the life cycle and in the agricultural cycle. Masks of the Mmo society, probably from Onitsha, may represent water or maiden spirits; some masks from the Ekpo society portray disease-ravaged faces. Many ethnic groups are represented.

Ethnographic exhibits at the Kaduna National Museum include cases devoted to figures in wood, which serve many religious purposes. There are *Orisha* figures of the Yoruba; *Ikega*, or *Ikenga*, sculptures associated with the hand or arm, found throughout southern Nigeria, that celebrate the success of their owners; and ancestral figures from Mumuye and Ibo peoples. A large Epa helmet-shaped mask of the Yoruba is on display; it was carved by Akinyode and is known as *Epa Alaba*. The superstructure of the mask is complex: a seated figure is beneath a carved canopy with a bird on top. Surrounding the figure are two rows of twenty-five smaller figures that include hunters, flute players, and motherswith their babies. The whole of this large structure is worn by young men at a dance celebrating the Epa festival. Wearing the mask and dancing, they perform feats of strength and skill.

Other ethnographic exhibits comprise textiles that show a variety of weaving techniques and looms, used by men and by women to make head cloths and wrappers and used for bride wealth. Both the horizontal (men) and vertical (women) looms are shown. The warfare section includes a large collection of weapons and armor, many of which may have come from manufacturing centers in the Islamic world. Some of them are from Europe; for example, there is a coat of chain mail in iron with charms and amulets attached for protection that is probably of German origin. A case in the museum is allotted for Koran writing. It shows the copy boards used by Nigerian Muslin Mallams, or teachers, to teach their students. Several books of the Koran, boards of wood, and one of bone are displayed. A large display of musical instruments from Nigeria and from other parts of the country is used to show the many uses: to accompany singing, dancing, communal labor, story telling, and so on. They are made of diverse materials, many in combination with each other: wood, bronze, brass, ivory, glass, clay, skin, leather, bone, horn, and iron. Rattles, pot drums, zithers, horns, double-gongs, clappers, xylophone, harps, banjos, and violins are shown.

The tobacco pipes exhibit shows that tobacco has been known and smoked in Nigeria for a very long time. The earliest Europeans who visited West Africa in the fifteenth century saw pipes being smoked. Clay- or brass-bowled pipes are used in the middle of Nigeria to smoke tobacco and hemp. They are "knee-shaped," or bent, bowls, different from the tubular pipes used in East and South Africa. Only knee-shaped pipes are displayed at Kaduna. European pipes were introduced into West Africa about mid-seventeenth century.

Currency had its beginnings in the fifteenth century, with extensive outside contacts. The Portuguese and Dutch sought trade in pepper, ivory, and slaves. The currencies that developed in response to trade were: manillas, cowrie shells, currency hoes, rods and bars of copper and brass, tobacco, gin, palm oil, cloths and shirts, animals, beads, salt, tin, silver, rings, and ornaments. In Nigeria manillas and copper and brass bracelets and anklets were used not only for trading but for bride wealth and burial ceremonies. Manillas were most used in southeastern Nigeria and cowrie shells in the western and northern parts. Iron bars and currency hoes were widely used in the North, and copper and brass rods found extensive use in the Southeast.

Cases display leather products (footwear, bags of various kinds, sheaths, and ornaments) made of hides of buffalo, horses, and cattle and skins of calves, pigs, goats, and sheep. They come from Kano, Zaria, Maiduguri, Sokoto, and Oyo in the North. Exhibits of calabash carving and decoration, of pottery, and of wood utensils are presented. Examples of brass casting and hammering may be seen in collections made in Katsina and from the smiths working at the craft village at Kaduna. A wide variety of ornaments typical of northern Nigeria are also displayed in the ethnographic gallery.

The craft village at the Kaduna National Museum is housed in traditional buildings of Hausa type, called Habe I and II. *Habe* is the name the Fulani gave to the Hausa people of northern Nigeria at the end of the thirteenth century when they arrived there. The crafts contained in Habe I are weaving, pottery making, leatherworking, and blacksmithing. In Habe II matting, calabash decoration, and brass work are practiced. There is hair plaiting for women, done at a reasonable price. A restaurant has also been constructed in traditional Hausa architecture. The Kaduna National Museum also has a botanical garden, where species of African plant life can be seen.

The Jos National Museum complex is located in Jos, the capital of the Plateau State, northern Nigeria. It was the second public national museum, opened in 1952. The complex consists of the main museum building, which houses archaeological and ethnographic works; the Pottery Museum, the Tin Museum, the Bauchi Light Railway Museum, the Zoological Park, the Craft Center, the MOTNA (Museum of Traditional Nigerian Architecture); the Training Center of the Commission; and the Bilingual Training Center for the Preservation of Natural and Cultural Heritage, jointly sponsored by the federal government of Nigeria and UNESCO, organized in 1963 at Jos for Africa south of the Sahara. Courses are given in French and English and offered in museology and conservation. The Jos National Museum serves as the center for archaeological research of the commission. It houses one of the two research libraries of the commission, the other being in Lagos. Eventually, it is planned for each museum to have its own library in each state. As the second oldest museum in Nigeria, Jos was for a long time the headquarters of the Federal Department of Antiquities and its main research station.

The Jos Museum covered eleven acres in 1952; today it covers some eighty acres, exclusive of the 120 acres allotted to MOTNA. Additions were made to the museum in 1957 and in 1975. At present, a new auditorium and library are being built at Jos. The museum is noted for one of the finest collections of Arabic manuscripts in Nigeria.

The National Museum at Jos owes its beginnings to tin-mining operations in the area. (The city is located in the center of Nigerian alluvial mine fields, which form a large part of the Jos Plateau, and its neighboring lowlands.) In 1903 tin was discovered by European prospectors on the plateau. They introduced new technology and heavy equipment to extract and use lode deposits. The Tin Museum at Jos shows European methods of extraction; indigenous methods, using traditional techniques of obtaining alluvial deposits and refining the tin in ground and cylindrical furnaces, are also shown. Tin mining predated the Europeans in the North; like Kano-dyed cloth and Sokoto leather, first tin ore and later straw tin were traded across the desert with the Arabs, as an important part of the economy, as early as the sixteenth century. Tin was a vital ingredient for brass manufacture at Biba and at Benin and Ile-Ife. The Tin Museum building was set up in 1977.

Objects that were being uncovered during mining operations in the 1920s and 1930s led to the recognition of Jos as a major archaeological center and home of some of the earliest cultures in Nigeria. For example, in 1928 the well-fired head of a monkey was washed out of tin-bearing gravels in the Nok Valley; it was taken to Jos where a museum was beginning to form. In 1943 the famed *Jema'a Head* was found twenty-five feet below alluvial deposits at Tsauni, in the hills above Jema'a; it, too, was taken to Jos. The importance of these and like finds was recognized by Bernard Fagg and Kenneth C. Murray; using "direct labor," Fagg and museum workers built a museum at Jos. The foundation stone was laid on September 23, 1949, and the museum was officially opened by the British governor on April 26, 1952, at a cost of 10,000 pounds. The characteristic dressed stone, now used on museums all over Nigeria, was first used at Jos on the front wall. In the first year, nearly sixty-five thousand visitors went to the museum.

The Pottery Museum at Jos displays some three hundred specimens collected between 1957 and 1962 by Sylvia Leith-Ross, who was a former education officer in southern Nigeria. The compound where the pottery is shown was designed by Z. R. Dmochowski, chief architect, Department of Antiquities; and the museum was laid out and developed by Mr. and Mrs. Wimbush. Species of shrubs and trees from all over Africa are contained in the Pottery Museum courtyard; three fish ponds are stocked with tropical fish varieties. It was opened to the public in 1963.

The Pottery Workshop was initiated by an American, Mrs. Spruyt, who donated fifteen hundred pounds in 1959 to build a museum workshop. Kilns were built in 1963, and Michael Cardew, who founded the workshop at Abuja, did the same here and trained the potter, Kofi Athey, who has achieved international recognition. Pottery has been produced here since 1964 and is for sale to visitors. Wheel-made glazed pottery is produced in a variety of shapes and sizes, for use and for display. UNESCO donated the machinery for making pottery.

Craft workshops are found on the grounds at the Jos National Museum. They include weavers, leatherworkers, and brass workers. Two Buji blacksmiths are at work in another part of the craft compound; a woman potter, from Jarawa village of Fobur, southeast of Jos, has worked there. Visitors can purchase the crafts made by the museum craftsmen.

MOTNA (Museum of Traditional Nigerian Achitecture) is an open-air museum, located on 120 acres, in the city of Jos. It is divided into regions: the Northern section opened in November 1983; the Eastern section has some five units completed, but is not yet open; and only one foundation has been laid for the Western section. When complete, it will comprise outstanding examples of indigenous architecture from the north, south, east, and west of Nigeria. These buildings will be replicas of the actual constructions, done according to local techniques. (Some modifications to meet the change in climate in the North were made.) The basic materials used are earth, loam, timber, and grass. These materials are susceptible to weather and insects. MOTNA represents, therefore, an important center for preserving and experiencing the achievements of the past. MOTNA will represent a kind of miniature architectural map of the country, linked by a network of footpaths.

The Jos National Museum is particularly rich in Nok archaeological materials that come from sites of the region and that extend widely in distribution from Kagoro to Katsina Ala and elsewhere. Human heads and figures, parts of figures, and less stylized animal heads are represented. The famed *Jema'a Head*, now in the "Treasures of Ancient Nigeria" exhibition, usually resides at this museum. The earliest evidence of iron smelting south of the Sahara comes from the Nok culture some twenty-five hundred years ago. Separate storerooms are devoted to archaeological specimens and contain work space and study areas.

Ethnographic galleries at the Jos National Museum represent local, state, and national collections. Some worth mentioning are Mumuye ritual carvings, a Kanembu papyrus boat, and Ibo and Yoruba carvings that include doors, house-posts, and sculptures. Most of the latter are not more that seventy to a hundred years old, due to handling, exposure, and insects. There are Daka Kari funerary pottery sculptures, frequently of horsemen, elephants, and other animals. Yoruba *Gelede* masks, Ibibio *Ekpo* masks, and Ijo men's society masks are among those on display. Stained, scorched, engraved, and decorated gourds and calabashes from the North are well represented in the collections. Brass work is concentrated in the Nupe capital of Bida; examples may be seen in the galleries. The ethnographic storerooms have many examples of costumes worn with masks, colonial wood carvings, Epa masks, musical instruments, agricultural tools, and hunting gear. There is a large collection of metal weapons and horse trappings in a separate storeroom; there is also a separate pottery storeroom.

The Nigerian National Museum Society was founded July 1969 in Lagos. Its purpose was "to promote and encourage community participation in expanding activities of the National Museum." It provides a forum for the study of antiquities and prepares and distributes information on the work and discoveries of the National Commission for Museums and Monuments. As a voluntary organization, it aims to assist the goals of education, research, and cultural services for children and adults and to participate in the preservation, conservation, and display of Nigerian antiquities and cultural resources.

The Lagos National Museum is the main museum of the country, located in the capital city of Lagos. It serves as the headquarters of the National Commission for Museums and Monuments, which maintains its offices there. This museum was built in 1956–57 and houses extensive collections from all over Nigeria, including some of the finest examples collected among the 250 ethnic groups who make up the country. Only about 1 percent of the more than five hundred thousand objects, valued collectively at more than $1 billion, are on view. Most are contained in the archaeological and ethnographic storerooms of the museum.

The Lagos National Museum (P.M.B. 12556, Onikan-Lagos, Nigeria) consists of several buildings: the main building that comprises three galleries, the Benin Gallery, Ethnography Gallery, and Technology Gallery, as well as a temporary exhibition space; a circular building of political character, "Nigerian Governments Yesterday and Today"; the Crafts Village compound; and the Museum Kitchen. There is a group of administrative buildings where the offices of the director, a library and meeting rooms, and various offices for staff are located.

Presently under construction is a new wing of the National Museum, Lagos. It will house the one hundred objects of the exhibition "Treasures of Ancient Nigeria," spanning some two thousand years. Organized and curated by Ekpo Eyo, Director-General of the Commission, in cooperation with Michael Kan, deputy director of The Detroit Institute of Arts, the exhibition has been seen in cities across the United States, in various countries of Europe, and in Great Britain and Canada, from 1980 to 1984. When the wing is completed, the returning exhibition will go on permanent view in Lagos. A Museum of Modern Art and Museum of Natural History are also planned.

The policy of the National Commission for Museums and Monuments, set by its Director-General Ekpo Eyo, is evident at the Lagos National Museum. It aims to educate, to unify, and to bring pleasure to the varied peoples of Nigeria, the most populous country in Black Africa, numbering an estimated 80 million to one hundred million people.

The Benin Gallery has a group of five carved ivory tusks; they were used on palace altars set into the memorial bronze heads of Obas of Benin. Some of the fine ivories on display consist of a female attendant figure, a carved and footed bowl, a shield-shaped pectoral, and two ivory staffs with horse and rider. Three Oba's bronze heads (one eighteenth century, the two others nineteenth century) of good quality are exhibited; an early bronze head of an Oba, sixteenth century, is badly crushed; there is another nineteenth-century bronze Oba's ancestral head. Bronze sculptures of worth include a European soldier with gun, sometimes called an "Arquebusier," and two horses with riders, two equestrian figures dating to the eighteenth century and to the nineteenth century, respectively. A fine shield-shaped pendant shows the Oba with two figures supporting him at either side. A noteworthy seven-figured plaque shows the Oba surrounded by two male attendants carrying offerings, two holding shields over his head, and smaller Portuguese figures at each side.

Among the bronze masterpieces of Benin art that traveled in the exhibition "Treasures of Ancient Nigeria," and that will be permanently located in the Lagos National Museum, are the early period *Queen Mother* head, the sixteenth-century *Standing Figure of a Messenger*; the magnificent *Pair of Leopards*, mid-sixteenth century; and an elegant stool with a seat in the form of intertwined mudfish, sixteenth century; also worthy of note is an ivory lidded bowl from the sixteenth century.

Benin art represents the largest corpus of Nigerian art and is probably the best known of the many traditions outside of Nigeria. This is largely the result of the British Punitive Expedition of 1897, which ended in some two thousand pieces being taken from the Oba's palace to Europe and the Oba being sent into exile at Calabar. The bronzes that reached Europe caused general astonishment because of their sophistication and skilled casting; they were, at first, thought to be of European or other foreign origin. It is now clear that they were products of Black African artists. From about the fourteenth to the nineteenth century there was political continuity and an elaborate court that flourished at Benin City, the capital of Bendel State, in modern Nigeria. With the restoration of Oba Eweka II, in 1914, by the British, the same dynasty has continued in direct succession to the present, with the ascension of Oba Erediauwa in 1979.

The Ethnography Gallery of the Lagos National Museum has on display objects connected with the Cult of Twins, Ibeji figures, Sango Cult objects, masquerade costumes, Epa headmasks, Ifa divination objects, and musical instruments. Noteworthy is a beaded ceremonial clothing worn by a late Yoruba Oba. It is completely beaded, made of about 1 million beads into a long robe or gown, a pair of boots, and a crown. The crown is made in traditional Yoruba style, surmounted by sixteen birds. It was made for Oba Abimbolu Afonlade II, of Ode Remo, near Shagmu in Ogun State, Nigeria.

The Technology Gallery of the museum shows the evolution and development of tools and metalworking in Nigeria, from the Stone Age on, from gathering and hunting to farming. There is a full-scale model of an iron-smelting foundry, dating from the fifth century. Bronze casting in Benin is also shown, and the lost wax method is illustrated and explained. Examples of metalwork from Nok, Igbo-Ukwu, Benin, and other cultures are included.

The Temporary Exhibition Gallery has had a long-running show, "2000 Years of Nigerian Art." It attracted more than ninety thousand people in the first year it opened and has remained popular. It recaps the sequence of ancient Nigerian cultures shown in the country's traveling exhibition "Treasures of Ancient Nigeria"—Nok, Igbo-Ukwu, Ife, Owo, Benin—and the problematic Tsoede bronzes and Esie soapstone sculptures. There is a series of cases set into the walls of the covered walks around the interior courtyard of the Lagos National Museum. In the cases are contemporary beadwork, traditional games, pottery, wood doorposts, doors, and panels. Some Akwanshi stone carvings from Cross River State are set on the grassy interior courtyard, and some are placed on the front lawns of the museum's main entrance.

Storerooms of archaeological materials, Benin works, and more than forty thousand ethnographic items are located on the museum grounds. The latter include musical instruments, costumes, face and helmet masks, weapons, ornaments, money, horse trappings and ornaments, armor, pipes, and one entire storeroom devoted to Yoruba Ibejis, or twin figures, that are to be preserved for study, loan, and exhibition.

The Craft Village on the grounds of the Lagos National Museum has a series of traditional African houses, each devoted to a different craft: bead workers make hats and ornaments for sale; hairdressers do braiding in a variety of styles for women; goldsmiths create ornaments; women specialists show examples of their weaving and of tie-dying batik and ikat cloths; and Yoruba woodcarvers offer sculptures, combs, and carvings for sale and also carve-to-order items such as a screen or pair of wood doors and houseposts, made to specifications of the client.

The Museum Kitchen has become very popular at Lagos National Museum, where special luncheons are often planned with traditional music in the background. During the week a different regional dish is featured each day, and the cooks use only traditional methods of preparing the meats for the many varieties of "soups" (stews) that are eaten. Fish and vegetable "soups" are also popular, and mortars and pestles are used to pound yams. Palm wine and other drinks are served.

The whole complex at Lagos is intended to educate and to serve the many communities of the city and the country.

Selected Bibliography

Museum publications: *Guide to National Museum, Lagos*; *Guide to National Museum, Oron*; Boston, John, *Ikenga*; Eyo, Ekpo, *Nigeria and the Evolution of Money*; idem, *2000 Years of Nigerian Art*; Fagg, Bernard, *Nok Sculptures*; Horton, Robin, *Kalabari Sculptures*; Nkanta and E. N. Arinze, *Lost Treasures of Ancient Benin*; Stevens, Phillips, Jr., *The Stone Images of Esie, Nigeria*.

Other publications: Ben-Amos, Paul, *The Art of Benin* (New York 1980); idem, *Bibliography of Benin* (New York 1968); Bradbury, R. E., *Benin Studies* (London 1973); Connah, Graham, *The Archaeology of Benin* (Oxford 1975); Dark, Philip J. C., *An Introduction to Benin Art and Technology* (Oxford 1973); idem, *The Art of Benin: A Catalogue of an Exhibition of the A.W.F. Fuller and Chicago Natural History Museum Collections of Antiquities from Benin, Nigeria* (Chicago 1962); Dark, Philip J. C., and B. Forman and W. Forman, *Benin Art* (London 1960); Egharevba, Jacob U., *A Short History of Benin*, 3d ed. (Ibadan 1960); Eyo, Epko, and Frank Willett, *Treasures of Ancient Nigeria* (New York 1980); Fagg, William, *Divine Kingship in Africa* (London 1970); Fagg, William, B. Forman, and W. Forman, *Afro-Portuguese Ivories* (London 1959); Kaplan, Flora S., ed., *Images of Power: Art of the Royal Court of Benin* (New York 1981); Mabogunje, Akin L., *Urbanization in Nigeria* (New York 1968); Pitt-Rivers, A., *Antique Works of Art from Benin* (1900; Reprint New York 1976); Read, Charles H. and Ormonde M. Dalton, *Antiquities from the City of Benin and from other parts of West Africa in the British Museum* (1899; Reprint New York 1968); Roth, Ling H., *Great Benin: Its Customs, Arts, and Horrors* (1903; Reprint London 1968); Ryder, Alan, *Benin and the Europeans, 1485–1897* (New York 1969); Shaw, Thurston, *Nigeria: Its Archaeology and Early History* (London 1978); Willett, Frank, *Treasures of Ancient Nigeria* (New York 1980); idem, *African Art* (New York 1971); Williams, Denis, *Icon and Image: A Study of Sacred and Secular Forms of African Classical Art* (New York 1974); Ben-Amos, Paul, "Owine N'Ido: Royal Weavers in Benin," *African Arts*, vol. 11, no. 4 (1978); Fraser, Douglas, "Tsoede Bronzes and Owo Yoruba Art," *African Arts*, vol. 7, no. 3 (1975); Neaher, Nancy C., "Nigerian Bronze Bells," *African Arts*, vol. 7, no. 3 (1975); Peek, Philip M., "Isoko Bronzes and the Lower Niger Bronze Industries," *African Arts*, vol. 13, no. 4 (1980); Posansky, Merrick, "Brass Casting and Its Antecedents in

West Africa," *Journal of African History*, vol. 18, no. 2 (1977); idem, "A Reconsideration of the Ife Benin Relationship," *Journal of African History*, vol. 6, no. 1 (1965); Tunis, Irwin L., "The Benin Chronologies" (book review), *African Arts*, vol. 14, no 2. (1981); Willett, Frank, "The Benin Museum Collection," *African Arts*, vol. 6, no. 4 (1973).

FLORA S. KAPLAN, NNENNAYA SAMUEL UKWU,
and EMMANUEL N. ARINZE